AGONY IN THE PULPIT

Agony in the Pulpit

Jewish Preaching in Response to Nazi Persecution and Mass Murder 1933–1945

Marc Saperstein

Hebrew Union College Press

HEBREW UNION COLLEGE PRESS

Typeset in Legacy Serif by Raphaël Freeman, Renana Typesetting
Cover art by Paul Neff Design, Cincinnati, Ohio

Cover photograph: Hollem, Howard R, Maclaugharie, and Edward Meyer, photographer. New York, New York. June 6, 1944. Rabbi Stephen S. Wise at the D-Day rally in Madison Square. New York, 1944. June 6. Photograph.

Library of Congress, https://www.loc.gov/item/owi2001040507/PP.

Printed in the United States of America

Library of Congress Cataloging-in-Publication Data

Names: Saperstein, Marc.
Title: Agony in the pulpit : Jewish preaching in response to Nazi persecution and mass murder : 1933-1945 / [edited and introduced by] Marc Saperstein.
Description: Cincinnati, Ohio : Hebrew Union College Press, {2018] | Includes bibliographical references and index.
Identifiers: LCCN 2017058895 | ISBN 978-0-87820-160-0
Subjects: LCSH: Holocaust, Jewish (1939-1945)--Sermons. | Jewish sermons, English.
Classification: LCC D804.3 .A385 2018 | DDC 940.53/18--dc23
LC record available at https://lccn.loc.gov/2017058895v/2017058895

To my brother, David

and to

Ellen, Danny, and Ari

Contents

Preface and Acknowledgments xi
Abbreviations, and a Note on Style xxvii
Introduction 1

CHRONOLOGICAL SELECTIONS

Sermons from 1932 87
Sermons from 1933 91
Sermons from 1934 173
Sermons from 1935 211
Sermons from 1936 243
Sermons from 1937 279
Sermons from 1938 299
Sermons from 1939 375
Sermons from 1940 461
Sermons from 1941 533
Sermons from 1942 603
Sermons from 1943 677
Sermons from 1944 739
Sermons from 1945 797

COMPLETE SERMONS

1932 (Prelude)

Jacob Xenab Cohen, "The Menace of Hitlerism to American Jewry," Free Synagogue, New York 835

1933

Harry Joshua Stern, "Hitlerism, Germany and Civilization," Temple Emanu-El, Montreal, Mass Rally 845

Israel Levinthal, “Old Pharaoh in Modern Garb,” Brooklyn Jewish Center, NY 851

Jacob P. Rudin, “Dark Horizons – 1933,” Temple Beth-El, Great Neck, NY 859

1934

Harold I. Saperstein, “The Call to Battle,” Temple Emanu-El of Lynbrook, NY 867

1935

Ferdinand Isserman, “My Second Visit to Nazi Germany,” Temple Israel, St. Louis, MO 877

1936

Abba Hillel Silver, “‘But Mordecai Bowed Not Down,’” The Temple, Cleveland, OH 893

1937

Israel Mattuck, “The Church Conflict in Germany,” Liberal Jewish Synagogue, London 901

1938

Abraham Mayer Heller, “A People’s Voice is Silenced,” Flatbush Jewish Center, Brooklyn, NY 907

Tobias (Tuviah) Geffen, “Sermon on Ḥayyei Sarah 5699, at the Time of the Great Destruction of the Jews in Germany at the Hands of the Evil Oppressor, Hitler, May his name and his Memory be Blotted Out,” Congregation Shearith Yisrael, Atlanta, GA 919

1939

Julius Cohn, “Farewell Sermon” (Abschiedspredigt), Ulm Congregation 929

Ignaz Maybaum, “The Anniversary of November 10,” Brondesbury Synagogue, London 937

1940

Leo Franklin, “Is This the End?” Temple Beth-El, Detroit, MI 945

1941

Eliezer Berkovits, "Because of Our Sins?" United Hebrew Congregation, Leeds, England 959

1942

Yitzhak Katz, "Things I Intended to Say…", Conference of Jewish Social Self-Help (Zy-dowska Samapomoc Spolczna, ZSS), Warsaw Ghetto 969

Michael Elton (formerly Emil Ehrnthal), "The Death Camps," Intercession Service, Day of Fast and Mourning, Bedford, England 975

1943

Bertram Korn, "The Prayer for Life," Shaarei Shomayim, Mobile, AL 983

Akiba Predmesky, "The Ark of G-D Has Been Taken," Jewish Center of Williamsbridge, Bronx, NY 991

1944

Joseph Hertz, "The 'Battle of Warsaw'," Bevis Marks Synagogue, London 1003

Louis I. Newman, "The Cup of Fury," Congregation Rodeph Sholom, New York 1013

1945

Abraham Cohen, "Peace Celebration," Birmingham Hebrew Congregation, England 1023

Sources and Bibliography 1033

Rabbis Cited 1066

Index to Rabbis and Dates of Included Sermons 1073

General Index 1087

PREFACE

"Silence"?

"I am obsessed with silence because of the silence of the world. I do not understand why the world was silent when we needed its outcry.... Where were the humanists, the leaders, the liberals, the spokesmen for mankind? The victims needed them. If they had spoken up, the killers would not have killed, or would have killed less. If they had spoken up, the slaughterer would not have succeeded in his task."[1]

"Why did American Jews not act like Mordecai, who, when he heard the evil decree, 'went into the city and raised a great and bitter alarm' (Esth. 4:1)? Why weren't there public demonstrations, with mass tearing of garments, as Mordecai did, to awaken Jewish leadership and to arouse the conscience of Christian America? Had we responded like Mordecai, would President Roosevelt have acted as callously as he did? Perhaps we should add another *al ḥet* to our Yom Kippur confessional: 'for the sins which we have committed in being unresponsive to the cries of our brethren in Europe who were being brutally slaughtered.'"[2]

"During the terrible Holocaust when European Jewry was being systematically exterminated in the ovens and crematoria, the Amer-

---

1 Elie Wiesel, lecture at California Lutheran College, April 27, 1977, in *Against Silence: The Voice and Vision of Elie Wiesel*, 3 vols., 1:110.

2 Joseph Dov Soloveitchik, "The Profundity of Jewish Folk Wisdom," in Abraham Besdin, *Reflections of the Rav*, p. 68. Cf. also the different translation quoted by Yoel Schwartz and Yitzhak Goldstein in *Shoah: A Jewish Perspective on Tragedy in the Context of the Holocaust*, p. 247, and Chanan Tomlin, *Protest and Prayer*, p. 191 n.14.

ican Jewish community did not rise to the challenge, did not act as Jews possessing a properly developed consciousness of our shared fate and shared suffering as well as the obligation of shared action that follows therefrom, ought to have acted. We did not sufficiently empathize with the anguish of the people and did very little to save our afflicted brethren."[3]

The passages above were written by intellectual and spiritual giants whom I admired beyond measure while they were alive, and whose memory I treasure after their deaths. In both cases, the impact was not merely from what they wrote, but from hearing them speak. During my rabbinical studies, I frequently heard Elie Wiesel lecture at the 92nd Street Y in New York, speaking on biblical, rabbinic, Hasidic, and modern themes. Soon after he began to talk, I would become totally absorbed in the voice and the content, losing all conception of time until he stopped speaking and – glancing at my watch – I realized that an hour and a half had elapsed. I heard Rabbi Soloveitchik deliver a eulogy for the mother of his son-in-law, my teacher Isadore Twersky, near the beginning of my PhD studies at Harvard, and here, too, it was as if time was suspended, and one wanted the message to continue indefinitely. In very different ways, I felt that they were among the outstanding Jews of my lifetime.

And yet my book is a rebuttal to the accusation that American Jews in general, and their rabbinic leaders in particular, remained silent; that they failed to speak out on behalf of the suffering Jews of Europe and were unresponsive to their pleas. It is also a rebuttal to the further accusation that if they had only spoken out, "the slaughterer would not have succeeded in his task."

It is difficult to correlate these assertions with the historical reality. From the very beginning of the Nazi regime, Jewish leaders were speaking out from the pulpit in condemnation of the new persecution of Jews (see below the texts from sermons delivered on February 12, 26 and 28, and March 11, 12, 19, 24 and 26, 1933). *The New York Times* of Monday, March 27, 1933 headlined an article on page 4, "ATTACKS

3 Joseph Dov Soloveitchik, *Kol Dodi Dofek*, translated in *Fate and Destiny: From the Holocaust to the State of Israel*, pp. 63–64.

ON JEWS SCORED IN PULPITS," with the sub-headline, "Rabbis Denounce Hitler and Express Conviction German People Will Not Back Acts." The article began: "Condemnation of the persecution of the Jews in Germany by the Hitler government and the Nazi legions was voiced yesterday [Sunday, March 26] in many pulpits throughout the city in churches and synagogues alike."

In addition to the sermons delivered in the preachers' congregations, there were massive public protest rallies (below, March 27, 1933). These rallies received considerable coverage in the general press. *The New York Times* of that date featured a three-column article on page 4 with the headline "250,000 JEWS HERE TO PROTEST TODAY," and sub-headlines "More than 1,000,000 in All Parts of Nation Also Will Assail Hitler Policies," and "Four Demands to Be Presented to German Envoy Urging End of Anti-Semitism." An important passage from Rabbi Stephen S. Wise's sermon the previous day at Carnegie Hall was included (below, March 26, 1933). The article also reported that the rally was being held despite communication from the leadership of a large organization of German Jews urging that the rally be cancelled, out of fear that it might be used by the Nazi leadership for greater persecution.

The following day, March 28, 1933, *The Times* ran a three-column first-page headline, stating "55,000 HERE STAGE PROTEST ON HITLER ATTACKS ON JEWS; NAZIS ORDER A NEW BOYCOTT." Sub-headlines were: "Other Faiths Join In," "Crowd Overflowing the Garden Hears Leaders Assail Persecution," and "Manning, Wise, McConnell and Green Denounce Bigotry – 1,000,000 Meet in Nation." The article, continued on page 12, stated that 35,000 Jews for whom there were no seats in Madison Square Garden jammed the streets outside and heard the addresses over microphones. *The Times* also reported that public protest was accompanied by private anguish for the Jews in Germany: "Responding to the call of their rabbinical leaders, Jews here and in other cities spent the day in fasting and prayer for the cessation of the persecutions." On the same date and shortly thereafter, the Jewish Telegraphic Agency reported similar mass Protests or Days of Fasting in Poland, Palestine, Bulgaria, Argentina, England, France, and Canada.

This one event, together with the sermons that preceded it or were delivered on the actual day, dramatically illustrates the problems with the accusation of "silence" on the part of American Jewish leaders in response to Nazi persecution. It is clear that they were not silent in their pulpits, and that they were not silent in public – not merely in New York but in some eighty other cities where public protests were organized. It is also clear that newspapers, including *The New York Times*, which has been severely criticized for its reticence in featuring the realities of later persecution and mass murder, presented these protests as sympathetically as any of the participants could have desired.

But there is also the assertion that "If they had spoken up, the slaughterer would not have succeeded in his task." The efficacy of such protest – the extent to which it led German leaders and the German people to consider abandoning persecution and later mass murder, as opposed to strengthening the determination to push ahead with their policy – remains unclear. To return to March 27 in New York, alongside its coverage of the spectacular protest event, *The Times* ran a page 1 column with sub-headlines: "Hitler's Party Prepares Boycott in Revenge for 'Atrocity Tales' – Vast Propaganda Opens." This refers to the boycott of Jewish businesses throughout Germany held on April 1, 1933, which also received wide publicity – *The New York Times* provided first-page coverage of this event on both April 1 and April 2. Despite the absence of violence, the boycott, with its clear identification of all stores owned by Jews, was a cause for deep dismay among German Jews, and it raises at least the theoretical question whether – as some leaders of German Jewry contended – the public protests, or the proposed boycott of German goods, might be counterproductive and, rather than pressuring the German government or people to greater leniency, might actually make things worse.

The protest of March 27, 1933 was of course not the only such event. A meeting of protest was held at Queens Hall, London on June 27, with leading Christian speakers condemning German persecution of Jews; this was followed by a Service of Prayer and Intercession at the Royal Albert Hall on July 9, at which Chief Rabbi Joseph Hertz gave the major address.[4] To jump ahead, massive protest rallies were held in England following *Kristallnacht* (November 20 and December 1, 1938), and in Palestine (January 1, 1939). The end of 1942 was another such period of protest, following the public disclosure of information about the Nazi policy of systematic mass murder; days of Mourning, Fasting and Prayer as well as public protests were declared in Palestine and the United States and England. More politically oriented events occurred in the spring of 1943, with a massive "Stop Hitler Now" demonstration at Madison Square Garden held on March 1, almost ten years after the first such event, and forty demonstrations in twenty different states were held throughout the spring.[5]

Throughout this period rabbis continued to address the issues of Nazi persecution and mass murder of Jews from their pulpits, though often without much practical content beyond continuing to raise funds for refugees and provide havens for those who might still escape, support for the war effort (in the US, after December 7, 1941), and insisting on an opening of the largely shut gates to Palestine (see below March 1, 1943).[6]

Could even greater outspokenness by Jewish leaders have made a real difference, to the point of preventing (or at least significantly diminishing) the number of Jewish victims? This is the kind of hypothetical question that can never be convincingly answered. In retrospect, it appears that the only possible way a change in American policy might have prevented the murder of six million Jews was if the United States had entered the war on September 3, 1939 as an ally of Britain and France. That would conceivably have altered everything,

4 *Jewish Chronicle*, June 30, p. 7 on the Queens Hall Protest rally; Joseph Hertz, *Sermons, Addresses and Studies*, vol. 1: *Sermons*, pp. 145–52, on Royal Albert Hall; see below, July 9, 1933.

5 Wyman, *The Abandonment of the Jews*, pp. 87–89, 93–94; Wyman and Medoff, *A Race Against Death*, p. 32.

6 The rather controversial movement led by Peter Bergson endorsed open criticism of American policy regarding efforts to save Jewish civilians, and sponsored major announcements in leading newspapers and additional public events featuring popular Jewish figures, such as Ben Hecht's dramatic pageant, "We Will Never Die," which opened at Madison Square Garden on March 9, starring Paul Muni and Edward G. Robinson.

including the German decision to invade Soviet-occupied territory in June 1941 and to begin a policy of systematic mass murder in newly conquered regions. Was it indeed an unforgiveable failure on the part of American Jewish leadership, which should have been calling on the government to enter the war from the moment it began?

Putting ourselves back in that historical moment, and imagining the future as opaque as the future is for us today, with knowledge only of the past and a portion of the present, it becomes clear that this was simply a totally unrealistic option. The President of the United States, the Congress, and the overwhelming majority of the American population were all opposed to American entry into the war in September 1939. And despite their hatred of Nazi Germany, the majority of American Jews with their rabbinic leaders of all denominations were strongly opposed to an American declaration of war, for reasons that seemed compelling. "Let's learn the lesson of history," they said. "In April 1917, we entered a European war based on idealistic goals: it was a 'war to end war,' 'to make the world safe for democracy'; it would provide freedom and self-determination for minority peoples. For these goals we compromised on important values, including freedom of speech and fair working conditions in factories. But none of these goals were achieved.

"Let's learn the lessons from the past, by recognizing that modern war with its inevitably devastating loss of life is the greatest of all evils; let us maintain the purity of American democracy, while giving our moral but not our military support to the Free Nations."[7] Many of the rabbis had become pacifists in the 1930s. I have not found a single rabbinic sermon text delivered on the High Holy Days of 1939 arguing that America should enter the war on the side of Great Britain (see September 1939 below). The historical reality at the time – when there was as yet no indication of a systematic German policy of mass murder for Jews – suggests that even *if* rabbis

---

7 The passages in quotation marks are not direct quotations from any specific sermon, but represent a broad consensus of passages in the texts of American rabbis preaching in 1939 and 1940. In addition to the texts below from this period, see Marc Saperstein, *Jewish Preaching in Times of War, 1800–2001*, pp. 390–92, 396–98.

and their congregations had made this demand, it would have been devastatingly counterproductive, generating or intensifying the view that "the Jews dragged us into a 'Jewish war'" against the interests and the desires of the American people.

There was indeed anguish and agony in the pulpits of the United States, England, and the other countries represented in the source material during these years. But there was also powerful communication that helped to inform, inspire, and reassure large numbers of listeners. I am confident that the material presented below will demonstrate clearly that Jewish religious leaders – the rabbis representing the full spectrum of religious movements – were certainly *not* guilty of the sin of silence.

ACKNOWLEDGMENTS

The majority of the sources are taken from books published by the preachers in the late 1930s or 1940s. Many of these show copyright by the authors; copyrights for many others were held by publishers of Jewish texts, especially Bloch Publishing Co., or small companies that have long since disappeared. All of these publishers are noted in the Bibliography, but in some cases contact was no longer possible, and in many others the copyright has expired. The other major source was archival collections; by far the most important was The Jacob Rader Marcus Center of the American Jewish Archives (see p. xxi).

In general, the right to republish this material is retained by surviving members of the authors' families. For all texts beyond brief passages that would be considered "Fair Use," I have made a concerted effort to find and contact surviving members of the preacher's family (children or grandchildren), in order to seek formal permission to use the passages that will be found in this book. Not a single person whom I contacted has denied such permission; to the contrary, the overwhelming majority expressed pride and enthusiasm for the realization that material delivered as sermons by their father or grandfather more than seventy years ago was being made available to a new generation of readers in a readily accessible format. I have expressed my gratitude individually and am proud to list all of the names of the descendants who have granted permission.

In the following list, I have avoided using titles for the heirs such as Prof., Dr., M.D., etc., except for the title "Rabbi," which I have included simply to indicate how many of the children or grandchildren of the rabbinical preachers whose sermons are used are themselves rabbis.

Fay Amias and Eve Yardeni (Alexander Altmann); Yohoyada Amir (Hermann Neumark/Yehoshua Amir); (Rabbi) Marc D. Angel (David de Sola Pool); Deborah Band (Harris Swift); Lionel Barash (Jacob Bosniak); (Rabbi) Barnett J. Brickner (Barnett Brickner); Randall C. Belinfante (David da Sola Pool); Avraham Berkovits (Eliezer Berkovits); Joshua Burack (Aaron David Burack); Jenni Calder (Salis Daiches); Leon Chameides (Kalman Chameides); David Cohen (Abraham Cohen, including provision of unpublished MSS); Shulamith Predmesky Cohn (Akiba Predmesky); David Dworkin (Louis Hammer); Lisa Newman Eckstein, Debbie Newman Fine and Martha Gay Newman (Louis I. Newman); Susan Hershman Ellis (Abraham M. Hershman); Howard Elton (Emil Ehrnthal/ Michael Elton); Esther Farbstein (Moshe Kahlenberg); Julian Feibelman (Julian B. Feibelman); Debbie Fertel (Harry H. Epstein); Trudy Festinger (Stephen S. Wise); (Rabbi) Joyce Galaski, Joshua Goldstein and Ken Olum (Israel Goldstein); (Rabbi) David Geffen (Tuviah Geffen); Mordecai Gerstein (Israel Gerstein); Stephanie Glaymon (Harry Joshua Stern); Chuck Greene (Maurice N. Eisendrath); (Rabbi) Joshua Heller and Miriam Stern (Abraham Heller); (Rabbi) Walter Jacob (Ernest I. Jacob); (Rabbi) Deborah Kahn-Harris and (Rabbi) Alexandra Wright (Israel Mattuck); Eve Raskas Kafitz (Abraham Halpern); Francis Kaplan (Jacob Kaplan); Menachem Kellner (Abraham A. Kellner); Frances Kiradjian (Louis Wolsey); (Rabbi) Haskel Lookstein (Joseph H. Lookstein); Judith Lyons (Israel Levinthal); Jeffrey B. Magnes (Judah L. Magnes); Lee Mandel (Roland Gittelsohn); Chanan Morrison (Abraham Isaac Kook); Deborah Nord and (Rabbi) Daniel Zemel (Solomon Goldman); Bentzion Kalmen Nurok (Ephraim Sokolover); Gabriel Nussbaum, Lily Nussbaum, Margaret Sinai, Danny Marsh and Sy Devore (Max Nussbaum); Ken Olum (Israel Goldstein); Nehemia Polen (translations of Kalonymus Kalmish Shapira; (Rabbi) Jonathan Prinz (Joachim Prinz); Jimmy Rabinowitz (Louis Rabinowitz); Joshua Reichert (Irving F. Reichert); (Rabbi) Arnold E. Resnicoff and Steven Resnicoff (Mnachem Risikoff); Rosalind Romem (Israel Abrahams); Marcella Rosen (Leo Jung); (Rabbi) Jonathan Rosenblatt (Samuel Rosenblatt); Stephen I. Rudin (Jacob P. Rudin); Lenore J. Sayers (J.X. Cohen); Jonathan Seres (Samuel Daiches); Walter Shapero (Leo Franklin); Jeremy Schonfeld (Joseph H. Hertz); Adele Silver and Sean Martin (Abba Hillel Silver); Chenya Spungin (Israel Shachter); Avraham Steinberg (Isaac Herzog); Jonathan Steinberg and David J. Steinberg (Milton Steinberg); Peggy Wolf (Morris Lazaron); Mark Zaid (David Max Eichhorn)

Among the printed texts for which the copyright is held neither by the author or his descendants, I would like to express gratitude for permission to Carol Czelezny, Jonathan David Co., Inc. (Felix Levy), Nathan Ganesan, Souvenir Press (Leslie Edgar), Ben Kennedy, Oxford University Press (Shlomo Zalman Ehrenreich, Shlomo Zalman Unsdorfer), Andrea Laws, University Press of Kansas (David Max Eichhorn), Ayala Peretz, Yad Vashem Publications (Yitzhak Katz), Patricia Zline, Rowman, Lexington Books (Harold I. Saperstein)

Despite concerted efforts to find the copyright holders for these texts and to obtain their permission for their use, in some cases this has not been fully successful. I would be grateful to be notified of any additions or corrections to the above list that might be incorporated in future reprints of or additions to this book.

As noted above, in addition to the printed texts, a second major source of materials was unpublished typescripts preserved in archival collections. Of these, by far the most important collection is that of the American Jewish Archives in Cincinnati. Indeed, an invitation to visit the AJA as a visiting scholar in March and April of 2016 was crucial in launching my systematic research for the current book. The sermons in this massive collection discussing Nazi persecution and later mass murder are more numerous than any single researcher could master; I consider the most important the unpublished texts of sermons delivered by Ferdinand M. Isserman of St. Louis and by Stephen S. Wise of New York (the Wise texts are microfilms of the original typescripts held in the Robert D. Farber University Archives of Brandeis University). At least a dozen other rabbis are represented in sermons taken from the AJA collection. I am deeply grateful to Gary Zola, Director of the AJA, Kevin Proffitt, Dana Herman, and other members of the Staff, for arranging for my month-long visit and for their consistent helpfulness during the month I spent on the site and their continued help in response to specific questions raised later. The AJA has granted permission for the use of the material by Samuel S. Cohon, Abraham H. Feinberg, Ferdinand M. Isserman, and Bertram Korn.

Many unpublished texts by Leo M. Franklin of Detroit were originally accessed at the Franklin Archives of Temple Beth-El in Bloomfield Hills, Michigan, by Alan Dodkowitz, then my student at George Washington University. These are now at the American Jewish Archives. I have also used material from the Archives of the Jewish Theological Seminary of America (Israel Levinthal), Yeshiva University Archives and Special Collections (David Burack), the Western Reserve Historical Society (Abba Hillel Silver), and the Leo Baeck Institute (Julius Cohn). Shulamith Berger, Chaim Bronstein, Sean Martin, Michael Simonson, and Anne Woodrum have been graciously helpful in finding material and granting permission. The Fortunoff Video Archive for Holocaust Testimonies at Yale University does not contain the texts of sermons, but I discovered that it does indeed contain survivors' memories of sermons that they heard during the war which, although they are not always inspiring or appealing, are also part of the historical record of Jewish preaching.

In the United Kingdom, I have made extensive use of three extremely important collections of unpublished sermon texts. Those written and delivered by the Liberal Rabbi Israel Mattuck of London were made available to me in his own office by Rabbi Danny Rich; these texts are now catalogued in the Leo Baeck College Library. A second major archival collection, though still in the process of systematic organization, is the hand-written sermon texts by the Edinburgh Rabbi Salis Daiches, held by the Archives of the National Library of Scotland in Glasgow. I am grateful to Hannah Holtschneider for calling these to my attention and to Mia Spiro for facilitating my access to the material, which deserves more comprehensive and systematic study.

The third significant collection of unpublished material is the hand-written sermon texts delivered by Abraham Cohen of Birmingham, England. These are not held in any formal archive, but have most graciously been made available to me for inclusion by Cohen's grandson, David Cohen of London. Unlike the Daiches manuscripts, which are often challenging to decipher, these texts were written in beautifully clear handwriting; they provide – together with Mattuck and the printed texts of Chief Rabbi Hertz – the most comprehensive sermon responses to current events.[1]

As noted above, reference to contemporary sermons frequently appears in the Jewish press; especially noteworthy in this respect is *The Jewish Chronicle* of England, which often published long passages of sermons delivered on special occasions by Chief Rabbi Hertz. *The New York Times* frequently included passages from sermons delivered by New York rabbis on Jewish holidays and at massive protest gatherings. The Jewish Telegraphic Agency, appearing daily, was not especially interested in sermons, but was often especially important in identifying events that are less well known today but to which rabbis referred in a manner that assumes knowledge on the part of their congregants. The articles of these three institutions have been extremely important in annotating passages in this book.

The many books and articles that I have used to annotate the rabbinical sermons and to guide interested readers to further background for what was being said from the pulpit are listed in the Bibliography.

Special thanks goes to a handful of individuals. My brother-in-law Prof. David De Vries, of Tel Aviv University, has been of immeasurable help in the process of tracing the surviving relatives – children or grandchildren of the rabbis who were preaching between 1933 and 1945 – so that I could seek their permission to publish the texts I

---

1 Unfortunately disappointing were the Alexander Altmann Archives held by University College London. Altmann came to England from Germany in late 1938, and was appointed Community Rabbi of Manchester, a position he held until 1959, when he accepted a university position at Brandeis University. Frequent references to his sermons appear in *The Jewish Chronicle,* but the archives – abundant in other texts – contain no collection of sermons. It is possible that Altmann did not write out the texts of his sermons, or that he decided that this was not material he wanted to retain in permanent form when he left England for the United States.

had chosen. In most cases, I was able to find the relatives myself, but where my efforts came to a dead end – especially for relatives living in Israel – Dr. De Vries has surprisingly discovered what I could not find.

More than any other American scholar, Gershon Greenberg has devoted himself to a probing academic analysis of the sermons delivered by European Orthodox and ultra-Orthodox rabbis during and after the Holocaust. His work has led me to many texts of which I was unaware, and he has been consistently supportive of my research. Our approaches differ to some extent: he is more interested in the theological content of the sermon texts, where I focus more on the historical content. Gershon has remained extremely helpful both through his abundant essays and his personal guidance.

Another American scholar who has helped pave the pathways of the present book is Nehemia Polen. My review of his book, *The Holy Fire*, based on the texts of sermons delivered in the Warsaw Ghetto by Kalonymus Kalman Shapira (Shapiro/Szapiro), published in *Modern Judaism* in 1996, was an initial recognition of the importance of this genre for the articulation of rabbinic responses to ever-worsening persecution. He has graciously permitted me to use many passages of his translations of Hebrew passages from Shapira's work.

Several Israeli scholars have also provided extremely helpful guidance. Throughout my academic career I have followed and learned from the work of Mendel Piekarz, especially related to Hasidism; his Hebrew book on Polish Hasidism between the two world wars and during the Holocaust contains extremely important sermonic material. Esther Farbstein has published extensively and powerfully on rabbinic texts, especially sermons, in response to the growing catastrophe. The writings of Chief Rabbi Isaac Herzog have been illuminated through studies by Shulamit Eliash in a manner that has been extremely helpful. Finally, Kimmy Caplan is one of the very few Israeli scholars who has investigated and analysed the sermons of Orthodox Rabbis in America, as well as of the leading Conservative Rabbi Israel Levinthal.

Pierre Birnbaum and Jay M. Winter have been supportive with with answers to questions on the French material.

I believe that my book has been enriched by the work of all of these scholars. But they all focus on Orthodox and ultra-Orthodox rabbis, with little if any interest in non-Orthodox sermons. And – except for Caplan – they all focus on east European rabbis or rabbis in Palestine, overlooking the abundant material in sermons produced by rabbis in the United States, England, France, South Africa, and many other countries. I hope that the present collection of sermon texts – all clearly dated, presented chronologically, and explicated where necessary – will build on the work of these colleagues.

During my academic career, I have written books published by Harvard University Press (1980), Yale University Press (1989), SCM – Trinity Press International (1989), and Littman Library of Jewish Civilization (2008, 2014). But no Press has been as supportive of and accommodating to my work as has the Hebrew Union College Press, which has previously published *"Your Voice Like a Ram's Horn": Themes and Texts in Traditional Jewish Preaching* (522 pages, 1996), *Exile in Amsterdam: Saul Levi Morteira's Sermons to a Congregation of "New Jews"* (585 pages, 2005), and – together with the University of Pittsburgh Press – the book co-authored with Jacob Rader Marcus, *The Jews in Christian Europe: A Source Book, 315–1791* (723 pages, 2014).

I am grateful to David Aaron and Jason Kalman, Directors of HUC Press, for their encouragement and guidance regarding permissions for the many hundreds of sermon passages incorporated into this book, and to Carl Pace, the Acquisitions Editor, for his guidance in selecting an appropriate cover for the book. Most of all, I am deeply indebted to Sonja Rethy, Editorial Director of the Press, who has spent an untold number of hours and days reviewing the components of the book with unending patience and stunning attention to detail, helping me to find the proper balance between respect for the distinctive literary styles of some 135 rabbis from fifteen countries, and the overarching stylistic consistency of the book as a whole.

The person who was undoubtedly most important in making this book possible was my father, Rabbi Harold I. Saperstein, who served one congregation in Lynbrook, New York for forty-seven years. He was a chaplain with the American Army from 1943–1945, and entered Dachau a few days after its liberation by American forces. A few months later he discovered a Belgian priest in Namur who had sheltered and saved the lives of more than a dozen young Jews. Listening to his sermons week after week gave me a sense of the potential power of the pulpit to teach and the inspire.

Opening the drawers of his filing cabinet when he and my mother were no longer living in Lynbrook, I found folders containing the typed texts of sermons he had delivered going back to 1933. This discovery was one of the most powerful influences in convincing me that I could write about sermons as historical sources not only from the medieval and early modern periods, but from the twentieth century as well. Recognizing this material as an important and often neglected resource, I edited a collection of his texts with one from each year of his rabbinate in Lynbrook, including sermons from the years covered in the present book. No less significant was the collection on his bookshelves of sermons published by other rabbis, which I eventually brought with me to England, and supplemented with my own additional acquisitions. Having these books and pamphlets readily accessible for reference has been at least as important as the Archival Collections and Libraries that I have used.

During the past forty-three years, my brother David has emerged as one of America's most powerful and compelling spokesmen for social justice and religious liberty, both as the Director of the Religious Action Center of Reform Judaism (1974–2015), and as the Ambassador at Large for International Religious Liberty, 2015–2017. Although not a congregational rabbi, his voice has been consistently heard – like the voices of the rabbis in the present book, who tirelessly and poignantly reviled persecution and mass murder – condemning injustice both in the United States and abroad. Through his work in the "real world," he has remained an inspiration to me throughout my academic career, and I dedicate this book to him and his family.

ABBREVIATIONS

AJA The Jacob Rader Marcus Center of the American Jewish Archives

AJHS American Jewish Historical Society

BUASC Brandeis University Archives and Special Collections

CCAR Central Conference of American Rabbis

HUC-JIR Hebrew Union College-Jewish Institute of Religion

JC *The Jewish Chronicle*

JPS Jewish Publication Society

JTA Jewish Telegraphic Agency

JTSA Jewish Theological Seminary of America

NYT *New York Times*

UAHC Union of American Hebrew Congregations

A NOTE ON STYLE

DATING: Most of dates provided for the sermons are taken either from published collections and pamphlets, or from the unpublished texts in archival collections. Occasionally the date, though not provided by the preacher, can be determined by references in the documents (e.g., a statement about "this new year of 5700"). In a very few instances I have considered a text important enough to include even though the dating provided is only for a specific month and year. Where more than one sermon was delivered on the same date (e.g., "September 14, 1939, Rosh Hashanah Morning"; "April 2, 1942, first day of Pesach"), the date is provided only for the first sermon used on that date; following sermons without a listed date were delivered on the same occasion as the previous dated text.

For ordinary Shabbat sermons (Friday night or Saturday morning), I have included the Torah *parashah* following the date only if the selection refers to a passage from that *parashah*.

BIBLICAL QUOTATIONS: In the English-language sermons, I have followed the wording that appears in the published or archival texts, mostly taken from the Jewish Publication Society 1917 translation, but in some cases the preacher's own translation. These verses are identified in parentheses: (Gen. 1:1). Where there is a general reference to a biblical passage without a specific quotation, I have identified the reference with square brackets, e.g., "fifty or even ten righteous individuals therein" [Gen. 18:23–32].

Quotations of or references to passages from rabbinic literature (Talmud, Midrash) are identified in the footnotes.

I have used square brackets in the texts of the sermons to explain a reference or allusion that the preacher has made in a passage that is not included in the selection presented, e.g., "They [the Nazi leaders] indeed arouse envy . . . "; "My creatures [the Egyptians] are drowning in the sea." Square brackets are also used when translating a word used by the preacher from a foreign language: "the word Milchamah ["war"] is derived from the same root."

TRANSLITERATION: For my own transliterations of Hebrew words in the Introduction, notes to the texts, and titles of Hebrew books, I have used a system that is closer to modern Israeli speech than to technical academic linguistics. The purpose is not to enable a reader to reconstruct each Hebrew letter, but to recognize the word by its sound. The distinction between *ḥet* and *khaf* has been retained (e.g., *Shulḥan Arukh*); a sub-dot produces *al ḥet* rather than *al chet*. There is no distinction in transliteration between *alef* and *ayin*, *tet* and *taf*, *samekh* and *sin*, *kaf* and *kuf*.

Sheva na (an unvocalized consonant) is indicated by the letter "e" rather than an apostrophe (*reshut* not *r'shut*, *shekhinah* not *sh'khinah*, *teshuvah* not *t'shuvah*). Apostrophes are used following a vowel when absence would lead an English reader to mistake two syllables for one: *ha'ir* rather than hair, *Ne'ilah* not Neilah or N'ilah.

Hyphens are not used between a prefix and the main word (Shabbat haGadol, not ha-Gadol, *BeArtsenu haKedoshah* not *Be-Artsenu ha-Kedoshah*).

An exception to the general rules is made for Hebrew words that are commonly known: Pesach rather than Pesaḥ, Rosh Hashanah rather than Rosh haShanah.

FOOTNOTES: The footnotes are almost entirely my own; where a few printed editions of the sermons include the author's footnotes or endnotes, I have identified these as "author's note." My own footnotes are intended to clarify references that would have been familiar to most listeners when the sermon was delivered, but require explanation for most readers today.

GENDERED LANGUAGE: The texts written during this period (1932–1945) commonly use gender specific language (including in translations of biblical verses) that would be unacceptable today, but was standard at the time: e.g., "in the mind of every man is deposited the memories of the experiences of his forefathers." Despite the unease that reading such discourse arouses, I have reproduced the English language texts as they appeared in print and typescripts or manuscripts. (In referring to general statements about the preachers, I have occasionally used the pronoun "he" - "the sound of the preacher's voice, the pace of his speaking" - as this reflected the reality of the time.)

INTRODUCTION

I begin with a confession: I am *not* a Holocaust scholar. In the spring of 1986, after having taught Hebrew and Judaica courses for nine years at Harvard, I was invited to serve in the newly endowed Gloria M. Goldstein Chair in the History Department and Jewish Studies Program of Washington University in St. Louis. There was one condition: that in addition to my other topics, I would teach a course each year on the Holocaust. Although I had taught broad surveys of post-biblical Judaism for seven years at Harvard Divinity School, I thought of myself primarily as a medievalist. Not only had I never written anything or taught anything on the Holocaust before, I had never even taken a university course on the subject. When I was an undergraduate (1962–1966), there simply were no such courses offered at American universities. I accepted the offer, but insisted that my course would be offered in the spring semester of 1987, not in the autumn. That summer and autumn were an intensive learning experience for me. I have been teaching this material ever since, but except for one substantial article on the question of continuity or discontinuity between medieval and early-modern anti-Judaism and Nazi mass murder, I have not substantially previously published on this topic.[1]

Needless to say, there is an abundance, perhaps a superabundance, of literature pertaining to virtually all aspects of the Holocaust.

1 Marc Saperstein, "Christian Doctrine and the 'Final Solution': The State of the Question," in *Remembering for the Future: The Holocaust in an Age of Genocide*, vol. 2, pp. 814–41.

While it took some time before the first comprehensive treatments appeared, starting with Gerald Reitlinger's *The Final Solution: The Attempt to Exterminate the Jews of Europe, 1939–1945* (1953) and Raul Hilberg's *The Destruction of the European Jews* (1961), subsequent books, based not only on German sources as were the first extensive studies but on Jewish sources as well, continue to appear. Among the classic texts are Nora Levin, *The Holocaust: The Destruction of European Jewry: 1933–1945* (1968); Lucy Dawidowicz, *The War Against the Jews, 1933–1945* (1975); Yehuda Bauer, *A History of the Holocaust* (1982); Leni Yahil, *The Holocaust: The Fate of European Jewry, 1932–1945* (1990); Abraham J. Edelheit, *History of the Holocaust: A Handbook and Dictionary*, 2 vols. (1994); Saul Friedlander, *Nazi Germany and the Jews*, 2 vols. (1997 and 2007), and two written by colleagues who have tragically died within the past few years: Martin Gilbert's *The Holocaust: A History of the Jews of Europe During the Second World War* (1985), and David Cesarani's massive *Final Solution: The Fate of the Jews 1933–1945*, published in late January 2016.[2]

These are only some of the best-known general surveys in English. When we turn to more specific academic investigations: on the fate of Jews in specific countries; the psychology of perpetrators, victims, and bystanders; the role of and the implications for religion and the literature produced in so many different languages, it seems as if it must be an act of hubris or chutzpah for anyone – especially one who is not an expert – to attempt to write another book and claim that it will contain something new. This is true even for an author whose entire academic career has been devoted to various aspects of the Holocaust. All the more so for myself, whose doctoral work and first book was based on thirteenth-century Jewish history and thought.

Yet my claim is that I have something significant to add to the enormous scholarly literature: the texts of rabbinic sermons delivered during the period 1933–1945 responding to contemporary

2 See now also Lawrence Rees, *The Holocaust: A New History* (2017). In all such bibliographical references to secondary works, I have, with few exceptions, limited the listing to books published in English; inclusion of material written in Hebrew or in German would have added extensively to the length without being of use to most readers.

events. With all that has been written, this is a topic that is virtually untouched.[3] A generation ago, a leading scholar wrote that "In spite of the vast amount of research literature on the Holocaust, the aspect of Jewish religious life during that period has, until recently, almost entirely been neglected."[4] But in order to proceed, I need to make a second case: for the relevance and importance of these texts. For this, several important distinctions are necessary.

The surveys I have cited were written by historians who look back to events in the past, review and analyse these events as fully as possible using both the relevant primary sources and the writings of earlier colleagues, and then compose an encompassing narrative adding their own perspective to the questions of what happened, and why. I make no pretensions of belonging to this esteemed cadre. But there is a different category of historical research and publication, and that is to discover, analyse, and present relevant primary sources in a manner that will allow readers to judge the material for themselves. In my teaching undergraduate courses on the Holocaust from 1987 through 2006, and again at Yale in the spring of 2013, I have always used Lucy Dawidowicz's *A Holocaust Reader* (1976) as one of the basic texts because of its presentation of translated sources produced by both perpetrators and victims.[5]

---

3 Important exceptions are Gershon Greenberg, who has written extensively about the religious responses to the Holocaust by ultra-Orthodox rabbis, including sermons, although he is interested primarily in their theological significance, not in their historical value, Nehemia Polen, whose book *The Holy Fire* is based almost entirely on sermons delivered in the Warsaw Ghetto, and Esther Farbstein, "Sermons Speak History," as well as her other major studies discussed below.

4 Dan Michman, "Jewish Religious Life under Nazi Domination," p. 148. Yet, in this article on religious life, there is no reference to a single sermon.

5 Other fine examples are *Sources of the Holocaust*, edited by Steve Hochstadt (2004), although this is much more heavily weighted toward the perpetrators, and is not as committed as is Dawidowicz to the avoidance of later memoirs. Also *Documents on the Holocaust: Selected Sources on the Destruction of the Jews of Germany and Austria, Poland, and the Soviet Union*, ed. Yitzhak Arad, Yisrael Gutman, and Abraham Margaliot (1981), and *Witness to the Holocaust*, ed. Michael Berenbaum (1997); for the period before the outbreak of war, Monty Noam Penkower's recent *The Swastika's Darkening Shadow: Voices before the Holocaust* (2013).

There are also more focused collections of primary sources. For example, Randolph L. Braham's *The Destruction of Hungarian Jewry: A Documentary Account*,

There is, of course, an important distinction between sources produced later, presenting the events in retrospect, and sources more or less contemporary with the actual events. The clearest example of this first category would be the memoir – written after its subject matter is already in the past, mainly by victims, in a few cases by perpetrators or bystanders. A notable example of a perpetrator is Rudolf Hoess, commandant of Auschwitz, whose autobiography, including detailed information about many aspects of the camp, was written while he was in prison; he was ultimately hanged within the camp in April 1947.[6]

Kurt Gerstein was an SS officer who visited the death camps of Treblinka, Sobibor, and Belzec in the summer of 1942 and tried to communicate what he had seen to the outside world. His deposition, written soon after the end of the war while in prison, is the only non-contemporary source included by Dawidowicz in her source book (pp. 104–9; extensive conversations are included which he certainly did not transcribe in shorthand as they were occurring).

The best-known memoirs are of course by surviving victims of Nazi persecution – Elie Wiesel, Primo Levi, Alexander Donat, Eugene Heimler, Leon W. Wells, and dozens of others. In addition, there are recorded statements solicited at a later time from individuals who lived through the events. A fine example is Ruth Levitt, ed., *Pogrom, November 1938: Testimonies from "Kristallnacht,"* containing 356 eyewitness reports of the event with names of the individuals reporting (some only "Herr X"), most of them dated (some from November and December, 1938, others significantly later).

---

containing 969 pages of documents in their original form; all these sources were produced by perpetrators or are official reactions by governments, none produced by Jews. Treating exclusively Jewish sources, *To Live with Honor and Die with Honor! Selected Documents from the Warsaw Ghetto Underground*, ed. Joseph Kermish, is based largely on the *Oneg Shabbes* collection of primary source material. A different kind of focus is in the documents presented by Monty Noam Penkower in *The Swastika's Darkening Shadow: Voices before the Holocaust*, pp. 119–255, covering the period from 1933 until the beginning of the war, including texts from the Jewish Telegraphic Agency and many non-Jewish writers.

6 *Commandant of Auschwitz* was published in Polish, English, and German between 1956 and 1958.

Then there are of course the unpublished survivor testimonies in archival collections, especially Steven Spielberg's USC Shoah Foundation Institute for Visual History and Education with some 52,000 testimonies from survivors and other witnesses, and the Spielberg Film and Video Archive at the US Holocaust Memorial Museum, along with the smaller Fortunoff Video Archive for Holocaust Testimonies at Yale. Well known and more accessible is Claude Lanzmann's film "Shoah," and his book *Shoah: An Oral History of the Holocaust: The Complete Text of the Film*.

Another important published collection is Isaiah Trunk, *Jewish Responses to Nazi Persecution*, composed of "Eyewitness Testimonies," mainly survivor memories recorded in the late 1940s and 1950s. Striking for our purposes is the Testimony of Noach Denenberg, dated June 24, 1948, about the rabbi from Tluszcz, then in Jadowa, a district of Warsaw, who "preached to the Jews of Jadowa that the moral obligation of our people was to resist with courage and commitment." As a result the Gestapo demanded that the rabbi immediately be surrendered, or they would take ten hostages. The *Judenrat* decided to turn over ten hostages, but the rabbi protested to the *Judenrat*, then turned himself over to Gestapo, which had him executed as he was condemning them.[7]

Certainly our knowledge and understanding of the Holocaust would be severely impoverished if we were to eliminate this genre from significant historical consideration.[8] This is indeed the most significant weakness of Dawidowicz's source book, *A Holocaust Reader*. As a matter of principle, she has used only contemporary sources (with the exception of Gerstein and the 1944 deposition of two Jewish escapees, who reported events beginning in 1942) and the result is that her book contains very little about the realities of life and death in Auschwitz. But it should be recognized that this category of source – written considerably after the events described, usually

7 Trunk, *Jewish Responses to Nazi Persecution*, p. 78.

8 For a recent discussion of the academic dispute over the value of Testimonies and Memoirs as a basis for research on the Holocaust, see Esther Farbstein, *Hidden in the Heights*, vol. 2, pp. 525–33. See also her book, *The Forgotten Memoirs*.

without any sources other than the author's memory – contains challenges for the historian.[9]

In contrast with this category are the sources produced more or less contemporarily with the events. Perhaps the clearest example of this is the diary, with dated entries day after day.[10] The best-known example is probably the *Diary of Anne Frank*; but of course this tells us only of the experience of a teen-aged girl who knew nothing of the mass murder that was occurring while she wrote her entries.[11] One of the finest sources for the experience of a highly educated Jew (though not an active part of the Jewish community because of his Aryan wife) during the Nazi regime is the massive two-volume Diary of Victor Klemperer, published in German (*Ich will Zeugnis ablegen bis zum letzten*) in 1995, and in English (*I Will Bear Witness: A Diary of the Nazi Years, 1933–1941 and 1942–1945*) in 1998. This reveals what a sensitive German Jewish civilian was able to learn about mass murder at various points in its progression. For example, the entry for April 19, 1942: Klemperer's wife Eva had been to a pub with a carpenter they knew, now serving as a corporal. "He had been in Russia for several months during the winter (until Christmas) as a driver for the military police. Ghastly mass murders of Jews in Kiev. The heads of small children smashed against walls, thousands of men, women, adolescents shot down in a great heap, a hillock blown up, and the mass of bodies buried under the exploding earth...."[12]

Crucial for our understanding of life in the ghettos of Nazi-

---

9 Consider, for example, the Trunk passage cited above, in which the reported memory of the event includes no name for the rabbi, no date for the sermon, and no indication of the topic of the sermon that created the problem – only an ambiguous message without specifics: did "to resist with courage and commitment" refer to physical or to spiritual resistance?

10 For a fine discussion with examples, see Esther Farbstein, *Hidden in Thunder*, vol. 1, pp. 617–44: "Diaries Versus Memoirs as Historical Sources."

11 One of the most frequently quoted lines from this work is "It's a wonder I haven't abandoned all my ideals, they seem so absurd and impractical. Yet I cling to them because I still believe, in spite of everything, that people are truly good at heart." This was written in hiding on July 14, 1944. One wonders if she would have written the same after being discovered and deported to Auschwitz.

12 Victor Klemperer, *I Will Bear Witness: A Diary of the Nazi Years, 1942–1945*, p. 41; cf. also

occupied Poland are the Diaries of the Hebrew teacher and author Chaim Kaplan, the historian Emanuel Ringelblum, and the Chairman of the *Judenrat* Adam Czerniakow, written respectively in Hebrew, Yiddish, and Polish, but now available in excellent English translations, as well as Michael Zylberberg, *A Warsaw Diary*, Janusz Korczak, *Ghetto Diary*, Hillel Seidman, *The Warsaw Ghetto Diaries*, and Abraham Lewin, *A Cup of Tears.*[13]

A fine collection of articles demonstrating the importance of the Diary as a historical source is *Holocaust Chronicles: Individualizing the Holocaust through Diaries and Other Contemporaneous Personal Accounts*, ed. Robert Moses Shapiro.[14]

But the Diary as a genre is limited in that it reflects the outlook of a single individual. Sometimes the writer will report events that affect the community as a whole, but other times it may be difficult to be certain to what extent a unique outlook is being recorded. Therefore, the more diaries that are preserved from the same environment – e.g., the Warsaw Ghetto – the more reliable is the picture that emerges.[15]

Another genre of contemporary sources is the large number of dated letters that have been preserved in various archives. Many of

---

pp. 162, 180, 203–4, 392, 397 (the last reporting a speech by Thomas Mann that stated that Germans had murdered a million-and-a-half Jews in Auschwitz).

13 Also Zelig Kalmanovich's *Diary of the Vilna Ghetto* (for a passage, see below, October 11, 1942). Accessible only in a new German translation from the Yiddish is Josef Zelkowicz, *In diesen albtraumhaften Tagen: Tagebuchaufzeichnungen aus dem Getto Lodz/Litzmanstadt, September 1942* (2015). Dawidowicz has published excerpts from both of these in *A Holocaust Reader*, pp. 225–33 (Kalmanovich) and 298–316 (Zelkowicz). For a general treatment of the diaries as history and literature, see Antony Polonsky, *The Jews in Poland and Russia*, vol. 3, pp. 539–49.

14 This collection ends with a brief six-page article on "Rabbinic Works," which should not have been included, as it is personal and not academic.

15 Especially powerful are the diary notes produced and preserved by Jewish members of the *Sonderkommandos* in Auschwitz, who were eye witnesses to the hundreds of thousands of Jews undressing and entering the gas chambers, and were then responsible for liquidating the corpses. See Nathan Cohen, "Diaries of the *Sonderkommando*," and, for a fuller picture of contemporary sources in various genres produced by these unique witnesses to the mechanism of Nazi mass murder, see now Nicholas Chare and Dominic Williams, *Matters of Testimony: Interpreting the Scrolls of Auschwitz*, especially the broad survey in the Introduction.

these are of a personal nature, providing insight into the experience of at least one person at a specific point in time. But other such texts have much broader repercussions. Some of the most poignant and exasperating letters sent during the war were written by Rabbi Michael Dov Weissmandel of Bratislava in Slovakia, desperately trying to inform outsiders of the danger and rally support for rescue efforts.[16]

Representative of a broader community are Minute Books that have been preserved from the Lublin, Bialystok, and Lodz Ghettos with their dated entries and other archival records of the various *Judenräte*; these became the basis of Isaiah Trunk's magnum opus *Judenrat: The Jewish Councils in Eastern Europe Under Nazi Occupation.*[17] More public contemporary records are statements published in *ad hoc* underground ghetto newspapers and broadside proclamations of particular political groups such as the Bund and the Communists within the ghettos. In the Warsaw Ghetto the Bund also published a clandestine weekly, *Der Veker,* "The Alarm Clock," copies of which are accessible in archival collections.[18]

Occasionally such documents were published by Polish Christians outside the ghetto. An extraordinary example is the leaflet entitled "Protest," written and circulated in the summer of 1942 by Zofia Kosak-Szczucka, a member of the Polish underground affiliated with a Catholic organization (Front Odrodzenia Polski), showing detailed knowledge of life inside the ghetto and the mechanism of deportation in sealed freight railroad cars.[19]

Perhaps most important for their ability to move beyond the world of the victims to the wider population were contemporary communications to the Polish government-in-exile, located in England. Public statements issued from the Polish Government

16 The letters were published in the original Hebrew in 1960; Dawidowicz included texts of letters dated May 11, 1943 and May 31, 1944 in *A Holocaust Reader,* pp. 318–27.

17 Dawidowicz published passages from these Minute Books in *A Holocaust Reader,* pp. 259–87.

18 See, for example, Daniel Blatman, "Poland and the Polish Nation as Reflected in the Jewish Underground Press," pp. 126–32, and Blatman, ed., *Geto Varsha: Sippur Itona'i.*

19 Nehama Tec, *When Light Pierced the Darkness,* pp. 107–12, including a reproduction of the complete text in Polish with English translation, pp. 86, 110–11.

beginning in June 1942 were given broad coverage in the general media. Jews who escaped from Nazi labor or death camps were also sometimes able to issue their own reports, the most famous being the report of Rudolf Vrba and Alfred Weczler, following their escape from Auschwitz in the spring of 1944, and return to their native Slovakia.[20]

A different type of contemporary source within the community of victims were rabbinic responsa providing decisions in Jewish law to the novel circumstances that arose. The advantage of this type of literature is that it is produced not by theoretical questions, such as the piercing problem of how God allows this persecution, humiliation, and massacre of His people to occur, but rather by specific situations that arise within the community. And because it is a legal question and response that is needed, the facts presented need to be accurate for the decision to be fully valid. Many of the rabbis providing these decisions were also delivering sermons to their congregations.[21]

Contemporary sources produced by the perpetrators are also extremely important. Aspects of the Final Solution were kept secret, but certainly until the beginning of the war and to some extent afterward many of the public statements made by Hitler were publicized. A massive resource was collected beginning in 1932 by the German journalist and scholar Max Domarus, later published (1965) in his multi-volume *Hitler: Reden und Proklamationen 1932–1945: Kommentiert von einem deutschen Zeitgenossen*, in which complete texts of every public address made by Hitler are recorded in chronological order, together with commentary. The texts amount to 2323 pages. (There is

20 http://www.holocaustresearchproject.org/othercamps/auschproto.html.

21 See Robert Kirschner, *Rabbinic Responsa of the Holocaust Era*. This includes a responsum by Tzvi Hirsch Meisels taken from *Mekaddeshei HaShem* (1955), which also contains many texts of sermons, including one directly pertaining to the same situation that evoked the responsum (pp. 112–23). See below the sermon by Meisels delivered on Rosh Hashanah, 1944, with reference to the article by Daniel Landes. There is no mention of the sermon in the discussion of the responsum in the same text, but together they present a haunting reflection of life on the edge of the abyss. Other studies in English include H.J. Zimmels, *The Echo of the Nazi Holocaust in Rabbinic Literature* (1975), and Irving Rosenbaum, *The Holocaust and Halakhah* (1976).

an English translation of the entire work: *Speeches and Proclamations: The Chronicle of a Dictatorship, 1932–1945.*) These contemporary texts are crucial to an understanding of Nazi Germany. They reveal what various groups within Germany heard the Führer say, and they indeed provide corroboration for Domarus's assertion that by listening to Hitler speak and interviewing public figures who had direct contact with him, he was himself able to witness "Hitler's astonishing power and influence as an orator."[22]

Moving from ideology and theory to implementation, one of the most important contemporary sources for the history of Nazi mass murder is the *Einsatzgruppen* reports, which were sent by courier from the Eastern Front to various offices in Berlin. These provide a detailed record, day after day, community after community, of citizens in the newly conquered territories of eastern Europe, primarily Jews, being rounded up by special forces, ordered to march out of their communities, often compelled to dig long, broad ditches, and then to strip naked and stand at the edge of the ditch as the *Einsatzgruppen* fired and the bodies of the victims fell into the ravine below. The extraordinary aspect of these texts is the details of accounting: in addition to a general narrative, there are listings of the numbers of Jews killed day after day in town after town, sometimes specifying the number of men and the far lower number of women, together with the much smaller categories of Russian Communists or Lithuanian Communists. These reports were of course considered top secret and were not discovered until after the war had ended, but they are a crucially important contemporary record of the devastating events.[23]

One obvious source for contemporary information about Nazi persecution are books or booklets presenting the realities of persecution in prose narrative. These could be based on the personal experience of visitors. Ferdinand M. Isserman of St. Louis spent June 1933 in Nazi Germany studying the situation of German Jews; upon returning to his congregation in St. Louis he not only delivered sermons reporting his experience, but published a pamphlet accessible

---

22 Domarus, *Hitler: Speeches and Proclamations*, vol. 1, Preface, p. 9.

23 See on these texts Arad, Krakowski, and Spector, *The Einsatzgruppen Reports.*

to a wider audience.[24] Julius Gordon, like Isserman also the rabbi of a large Reform Congregation in St. Louis, published in 1938 a book of 194 pages with the ironic title, *Pity the Persecutor.*

Other booklets presenting the realities of persecution in prose narrative, sometimes together with documents, and appearing while the events were occurring, include *The Yellow Spot: The Outlawing of Half a Million Human Beings.* This was published in London in 1936, with no author identified but with an Introduction by Herbert Dunelm, the Bishop of Durham. The paper cover of the book gives a subtitle different from that on the title page (cited above) and more radical: "The Extermination of the Jews in Germany." The documents provided are primarily from National Socialist sources. While the term "extermination" may seem radical at a time before there was any systematic mass murder in place, it was used frequently in periodicals and speeches even in 1933.

Once the war begins and reports of deportation, ghettoization, and mass murder are circulated, the number of books contemporary with the events increases. Vladimir (Ze'ev) Jabotinsky is well known as the Russian Zionist who established the Revisionist Movement, and was instrumental in establishing several militant Jewish Zionist self-defense organizations in Palestine. He favored mass emigration of Polish Jews in the late 1930s, and – following the issuance of the White Paper – called for a Jewish revolt in Palestine against British rule. His book, *The War and the Jew*, which was published in New York in 1942, two years after his death in August 1940, was actually written in January–February 1940 (p. 42). In it he included material about the Nazi persecution of Jews – including the "wholesale execution of Jews by Nazis in many towns in the province of Lodz" – that was published by the Jewish Telegraphic Agency (JTA), but that he "did not see reproduced in any of the leading British newspapers" (pp. 32–34). "Despite the deliberate policy of Jewish extermination pur-

24 Ferdinand M. Isserman, "Sentenced to Death: The Jews in Nazi Germany, an Opinion Based on One Month's Study in the Third Reich." Isserman also published a pamphlet two years later reporting on a second visit: "I Revisit Nazi Germany" (St. Louis, 1935). For the sermons based on these visits, see October 20 and 27, 1933, and October 25, 1935, below.

sued by the Germans in the occupied territories, the Jewish angle has been almost completely suppressed in the Allied press and radio reports" (p. 103). One chapter, including the sentence just cited, was described as "condensed from a memorandum submitted to the British Government early in 1940" (p. 102).

Israel Cohen, the Anglo-Jewish Zionist journalist who was for a time the Berlin correspondent for *The Times of London* and *The Manchester Guardian*, published *The Jews in the War* in 1942, describing it as, although necessarily incomplete, "the first attempt to give an account of what the Jews are suffering and of what they are doing in the war." The third section, entitled "The Destruction of European Jewry," is "based upon reports obtained by the various governments-in-exile, upon those published by neutral correspondents, upon those of eye witnesses who have escaped from the Nazi terror, and also upon those that the German Government itself has shamelessly issued as proof of its ruthlessness." No less impressive is Cohen's five-hundred-page book on the history of the Jews of Vilna, published by the Jewish Publication Society of Philadelphia in 1943. The last major component is "Under the Polish Republic, 1933–1939." But the book includes a brief Epilogue, including the statement that:

> By the end of January 1942, it was reported in Polish circles of London that, since the German occupation [in the summer of 1941], over 30,000 Jews had disappeared from Vilna – half of them transported to the labor camps on the East European front and the remainder either interned or executed. Appalling as this report was it was entirely overshadowed by another far more horrible a few months later. A fugitive from Vilna, who had escaped on May 25... related that he had been the witness of a wholesale slaughter of Jews.... Night after night, for fourteen days, these mass butcheries continued, until a total estimated at about 60,000 had been exterminated.... The silence that the German government has consistently preserved concerning the many reports published in the western world of mass murders of Jews by the Nazi soldiery can be regarded only as a tacit confirmation of their substantial truth. (pp. 477–79)

The book was dedicated "to the memory of the tens of thousands of Jews of Vilna who were martyred by Nazi barbarity, 1941–1943."

A fine collection of documents appearing during the war is the ninety-five-page pamphlet entitled "Jewish Emancipation Under Attack" by a leading scholar on Polish Jewry, Bernard Dov Weinryb, published by the American Jewish Committee in 1942. It contains translated texts issued by the Nazi regime beginning in April, 1933, and continues with the Nuremberg Laws of 1935 and a series of documents from January 1938 to March 1939 revealing oppressive exclusion of Jews in Germany, Austria, Bohemia-Moravia, Rumania, Slovakia, Hungary, and Italy.

Another similar work is *Starvation Over Europe (Made in Germany): A Documented Record, 1943*, written by Boris Shub on the basis of research by Z. Warhaftig, and published by the American Jewish Congress and the World Jewish Congress. The three components of the book are, 1: "Germany Eats," 2: "Europe is Hungry," and 3: "The Jews Starve," the first subsection of which is entitled "The Strategy of Extermination." This still reflects data primarily from 1940 to early 1942, a period when the dominant image was "skeleton-like corpses lying unclaimed in the gutter, a commonplace sight in the ghettos" (83). But the detailed factual material is remarkably impressive. A review of this booklet published in December 1943, written by William Zukerman, a Bundist anti-Zionist journalist and editor of the *Jewish Newsletter*, presented the following conclusion: "While the horrors of this national murder cannot be described in words, the results of the nearly two years of operation have now been published in an exhaustive book by the American Jewish Congress and substantiated by numerous official documents, reports of eye witnesses and admissions of Nazi newspapers. . . . The sum total of this terrible chapter of horrors is two to three million Jews deliberately murdered by the Nazis in what is certainly the greatest massacre of innocent and unarmed people in history."

Regarding the important question of what was known about Nazi persecution and mass murder outside the Nazi regime, an important distinction is to be made between what was known at the highest levels of the various governments, including the intelligence services, and what was made accessible to the general public. A dramatic example applies to the systematic massacres of whole communities of Jews by the *Einsatzgruppen* in the wake of the German invasion of Soviet-controlled territory and then of the Soviet Union itself. As mentioned above, these massacres are now well known from the detailed reports to Berlin submitted by the officers in charge, detailing community by community the number of Jewish men, women, and children killed each day, in addition to other individuals killed for specific reasons. Copies of these reports were captured by the Americans in 1945 and used in the Nuremberg trials.

What was not public knowledge until 1996 is that the first reports over the summer of 1941 were sent back to Berlin by radio in code, and that British Intelligence had deciphered the code and was aware of this new chapter of Nazi persecution – the beginning of mass murder. A decision was made by the Government that it could not go public with this knowledge, as that would inform the Germans that their code was no longer secure.[25] Obviously, this kind of knowledge that was intentionally kept secret (for whatever reason) has no relevance to our present topic, which is what was known to many in the general population.

Another example of tension between levels of knowledge pertains to the "Riegner Cable" from the summer of 1942. One of the best-known texts of the Holocaust period, it was sent by Dr. Gerhart Riegner, representative of the World Jewish Congress in Switzerland, to the New York and London offices of the WJC. Based on a disclosure from a sympathetic German industrialist, the cable warned of an encompassing plan by the Nazis to annihilate all Jews in occupied Europe in one coordinated effort. Stephen S. Wise, who received the message in New York, was instructed by the State Department not to announce it publicly until its content could be confirmed, and it was not until November 24 that he was permitted to disclose the shocking news to the media.[26] Up until that point, the tension was

25 Robert J. Hanyok, *Eavesdropping on Hell*, p. 73.

26 See Walter Laqueur, *The Terrible Secret: Suppression of the Truth about Hitler's "Final Solution."*

between what was known to a select group of individuals and what was accessible to the broad population. From the disclosures of late November on, a different question arises: the relationship between what was publicized in the media and what significant numbers of the Jewish or general population actually knew.

The most obvious medium through which to determine what was known in broader circles is the newspaper. Over the past two generations, a significant number of academic studies have been devoted to the reports of persecution and mass murder, which have been published in various types of newspapers, popular magazines, and journals – both general and specifically Jewish – recording exactly what information was accessible to various groups of readers who were interested in the subject.

Some of the most important such works, in chronological order, are Andrew Sharf, *The British Press and Jews Under Nazi Rule* (1964); Franklin Gannon, *The British Press and Germany, 1936–1939* (1971); Alex Grobman, "What Did They Know? The American Jewish Press and the Holocaust, 1 September 1939–17 December 1942," (1979); Robert Ross, *So It Was True: The American Protestant Press and Nazi Persecution of the Jews* (1980); Deborah Lipstadt, *Beyond Belief: The American Press and the Coming of the Holocaust, 1933–1945* (1986); Herbert Freeden, *The Jewish Press in the Third Reich* (1993; German original 1987); Robert Shapiro, ed., *Why Didn't the Press Shout? American and International Journalism During the Holocaust* (2003); Laurel Leff, *Buried by The Times: The Holocaust and America's Most Important Newspaper* (2005); and Yosef Gorny, *The Jewish Press and the Holocaust, 1939–1945: Palestine, Britain, the United States, and the Soviet Union* (2012).

An example of a recent work specifically focused on a critical event is Ruth Levitt, ed., *Pogrom, November 1938: Testimonies from 'Kristallnacht'* (2015). While the major part of the book is composed of testimonials from eye witnesses of *Kristallnacht* who reported their experiences soon after the events (see above, current pp. 4–5), a substantial section (some seventy pages) is devoted to contemporary newspapers, including some fascinating passages (pp. 685–93) from German newspapers defending the attack and blaming German Jewry as a whole for the assassination that precipitated it. Most of the newspaper accounts, from beyond Germany, are of course sympathetic to the victims, though mostly without direct condemnation of the perpetrators.

The presence of articles in newspapers and journals is certainly evidence of what information was available to concerned readers. But as Deborah Lipstadt herself noted, most of the reports of mass murder were often not featured on the front pages, but were consigned to internal pages where they were published in part of a single column without banner headlines.[27] The fact that information appeared in newspapers or magazines is therefore not compelling evidence of what was widely *known*. Needless to say, there are many intelligent individuals who do not read newspapers cover to cover every day.

In addition to the general media, there were of course the specifically Jewish media. The Jewish Telegraphic Agency published daily reports that included abundant information about the persecution of German and eventually European Jews; many of these reports were later used by local weekly Jewish newspapers throughout the country. An example of contemporary influence at a relatively early stage can be seen in Vladimir Jabotinsky's citation of a long article from the JTA of December 29, 1939, on the persecution of Polish Jews, including random execution and burning of synagogues.[28]

In England, the most important medium of communication was *The Jewish Chronicle* (*JC*), which remains a major repository for evidence about what was known and publicized on specific dates by committed Jewish leaders, and what could be known by Jews who read the *JC* regularly. The lead articles and opinion pieces published by the *JC* retain their impressive power even seven to eight decades after they were written. As one recent scholar has written, "After the outbreak of war, although the free flow of news from Nazi Europe was impeded, it did not dry up. *The Jewish Chronicle*, indeed, published

27 E.g., Lipstadt, *Beyond Belief*, pp. 164–65, 211.

28 Jabotinsky, *The War and the Jew*, pp. 33–34. In the same chapter he refers to "a sort of shamefaced conspiracy, almost entirely dominating Parliament, the Press, and the public platform, to obliterate the Jewish war-issue by silence" (pp. 31–32). The JTA is a major source for Monty Penkower's recent book, *The Swastika's Darkening Shadow: Voices Before the Holocaust.*

remarkably early and accurate accounts of the stages of Nazi mass murder."[29]

The Sermon as Historical Source

This brings us to the sermon as an example of the contemporary source. It may seem somewhat absurd to place the texts of sermons alongside the texts of newspapers as an important source of contemporary information. This is at least partly because the significance and status of the sermon today is so much lower than it was three generations and more ago. For much of medieval and early modern history, the sermon was one of the most important modes of education and the dissemination of ideas for broad circles of a society that did not have books or pamphlets or even broadsides readily accessible. Even after newspapers, radio broadcasts, and newsreels introducing motion pictures in local cinemas became prevalent, it may well be that, in the 1930s and 1940s, a higher percentage of the general population attended worship services at least once a week, and were exposed at least that often to a sermon delivered by the religious leader of their congregation, than the percentage of those who read daily newspapers. For at least some – and perhaps for many – worshippers, the sermon was the most important part of the weekly service.

One distinguished preacher lamented from his pulpit the practice of congregants to come late to the service so that they will miss most of the fixed liturgy, as their interest was primarily, and in some cases exclusively, in the sermon.[30] Newspapers often featured announce-

---

29 Bernard Wasserstein, in *Jewish Leadership During the Nazi Era*, p. 32. See also David Cesarani, *The Jewish Chronicle and Anglo-Jewry, 1841–1991*, esp. pp. 145–83, and Cesarani, *Final Solution: The Fate of the Jews 1933–1945*, p. 574: "The London *Jewish Chronicle* was the only newspaper that regularly published reports of the massacres of Jews in Poland and on the territory of the USSR."

30 "Today, however, save for the rigidly Orthodox synagogue of the Jew and the Catholic churches among the Christian, the liturgy has been relegated so far into the background that many are the so-called worshippers who rush into the house supposedly of prayer, at the precise, split-second that the sermon is scheduled to begin. Whether we preachers approve or disapprove of this practice, whether we

ments of the titles of sermons to be delivered by leading rabbis, and on the occasion of Jewish holidays, *The New York Times* would regularly devote a column to quotations from sermons delivered the previous day by leading New York rabbis – who had provided an excerpt (often delivered by messenger) to the editor.[31] Sometimes newspaper reporters would actually come to the synagogue for a newsworthy extract from the sermon.[32] My argument is that the content of a sermon delivered at critical historical moments, especially on Rosh Hashanah, Yom Kippur, Purim, or Pesach, to large congregations eager to hear the message from the pulpit, is an important source of evidence for what was known and how this knowledge was communicated that deserves to be carefully studied.

Yet scholars who have recognized the importance of such texts are the rare exception.[33] These texts of sermons delivered to Jews living through the events have been virtually ignored in the academic literature, even in works focusing on the leaders of various Jewish communities. A book edited by the distinguished scholar Randolph L. Braham, entitled *Jewish Leadership During the Nazi Era*, contains

are flattered or disquieted by this undue importance which our words have today assumed, there is no escaping the conclusion that this is the state of affairs." Maurice N. Eisendrath, "Preachers in War Time," December 8, 1940, *Holy Blossom Pulpit*, 10, 2.

31 On Thursday, September 14, 1939, the first day of Rosh Hashanah, the *Newark Evening News* devoted a full page (p. 29) to long quotations from the sermons delivered by three Newark rabbis – Solomon Foster, Leon S. Lang, and Joachim Prinz – all of whom addressed the situation of German Jewry.

32 Abraham Cohen, *Jewish Homiletics*, p. 26: "It is an established practice in Birmingham [England], and I believe it obtains elsewhere, for a local newspaper to send a reporter to the synagogue on Rosh Hashanah or Yom Kippur and print an extract of the sermon" (written in 1936).

33 A recent study has recognized that, "Rabbinic sermons, aside from their educational and moral value, are unique historical documents because they preserve certain facets of life in real time" (Farbstein, "Sermons Speak History," p. 146). And an expert on Polish Hasidism has noted that especially in times of trouble, "Things that could not be said in the Parliaments, or in public gatherings, or in defense pamphlets, or even on the pages of Jewish newspapers, were said by rabbinic preachers in their synagogues" (Piekarz, *Ḥasidut Polin*, p. 303). This, of course, applies to sermons by Polish rabbis delivered in Yiddish, not to sermons by German rabbis delivered in German, when a member of the Gestapo was seated in the synagogue guarding against any explicit criticism of Government policy.

articles by David Wyman (on the United States), Bernard Wasserstein (Great Britain), Bela Vago (on the *Yishuv* in Palestine, Switzerland, and Latin America); but rabbis are rarely cited as leaders in these essays, and there is not a single citation of their sermons. This is true even of works focusing on religious leadership. There is no reference to "sermon" or "*derashah*" in the Index to Shimon Huberband's *Kiddush Hashem: Jewish Religious and Cultural Life in Poland During the Holocaust*, or in the Index to Pesach Schindler's *Hasidic Responses to the Holocaust in the Light of Hasidic Thought*.

Rafael Medoff has written extensively about various aspects of American Jewish responses to the Holocaust and Zionism, including his *The Deafening Silence*, published in 1987. While public statements made by some organizations are occasionally cited (e.g., about the fate of the ship *St. Louis*, pp. 60–62), no sermons are used as evidence. Medoff has also recently (2015) published *The Anguish of a Jewish Leader: Stephen S. Wise and the Holocaust*. This is a sound academic study of the role played by Wise as one of the most important leaders of American Jewry during this crucial period, based on extensive use of unpublished archival material both in the United States and in Israel. Especially important are the vast collections of correspondence between Wise and other figures, supplemented by interviews with some of Wise's students at the Jewish Institute of Religion. Direct quotations are furnished for conversations between Wise and President Roosevelt, with whom he met privately on many occasions. Medoff presents effectively "the anguish of a Jewish leader" in responding both publically and privately to unimaginably catastrophic events.

What is totally missing, however, is any reference to Wise as a rabbinical leader who – in addition to his other significant leadership responsibilities – regularly delivered sermons in New York to members of the Free Synagogue, and to the broader community (Jewish and non-Jewish) gathered at Carnegie Hall on Sunday mornings and on Jewish holidays. The texts of these sermons, along with addresses at public meetings held at venues such as Madison Square Garden, are readily available in the archival collections used by Medoff. Some of the sermons and addresses were published by Wise in 1944 in his book entitled *As I See It.* Quotations from some of these texts were often published in *The New York Times* and other newspapers. One would think that this material, addressed to thousands of listeners, would be relevant, showing the role played by a leading American rabbi in informing American Jews about the reality and the meaning of events occurring in Europe, and asserting what could be done to help the Jewish victims. But Medoff's book has only a passing reference in a note to a sermon delivered by Wise in 1925 (p. 23, n. 41), and a quotation of a joke he made in a sermon from 1938 about congregants threatening to resign (p. 8). The other sermons and addresses he delivered week after week from 1933 to 1945 are totally ignored as evidence of Wise's role as leader. I hope it will be obvious from the material below that what Wise chose to say between 1933 and 1945 about the realities of German persecution and mass murder certainly belongs in a study of the anguish and the vision of this Jewish leader.

Especially surprising are books on this theme written by rabbis who overlook the rabbinic sermon as a historical text. Haskell Lookstein is an eminent New York Orthodox rabbi whose father, Joseph H. Lookstein, preceded him as senior rabbi of Congregation Kehilath Jeshurun from 1936 until his death in 1957. Yet Haskell Lookstein's 1985 book, *Were We Our Brothers' Keepers? The Public Response of American Jews to the Holocaust, 1938–1944*, includes no sermons in the Primary Sources section of the Bibliography. New York rabbinic colleagues of the elder Lookstein such as Israel Levinthal and Louis I. Newman are not listed in the Index; Abba Hillel Silver is cited for one statement on Palestine. I trust that the material to follow will demonstrate how important the sermons delivered by these three figures, and by so many others in America and elsewhere, were for evaluating the "Public Response of American Jews to the Holocaust."

I turn now to a discussion of the nature of the neglected source material, beginning with the occasions for Jewish preaching, which are rather more complicated than the Sunday morning sermons of Christian preachers. The most common occurrence of the sermon throughout Jewish history was at the Saturday morning service.[34]

34 This is true even in eastern Europe, where the rabbi of the congregation would

The advantage of this is that it would generally come immediately after the readings from the Torah and the Prophets, which provided a natural basis for discussion of the ancient texts and – in many cases – application to contemporary issues. The disadvantage is that the Shabbat morning service was rather lengthy even without a sermon, and since in traditional Jewish practice nothing would be eaten on Saturday until the worshippers returned home following the service, there were often reports of impatience within the congregation if the sermon was perceived to be too long.

An alternative was to deliver the sermon later in the day, preceding the afternoon worship (*Minḥah*). This kept the morning service from excessive length, and allowed the preacher to speak more extensively. The disadvantage was that it made the sermon no longer an integral part of a worship service that was attended by most members of the traditional congregation, but rather an optional, supplementary experience that members might or might not attend. In modern times, this was the option most widely used for Hasidic preaching. But the standard in Orthodox and many Conservative congregations was that the main sermon would be delivered as part of the Shabbat morning service, virtually always with a connection to the scriptural readings for the week.[35]

Following the emergence of Reform Judaism, a change, which began in Germany and soon shifted to the United States and Canada, developed in many large congregations as the Sunday morning week-day service became a major event. The underlying problem that fostered this innovation was that employment in the nineteenth and early twentieth centuries often required that one work six days a week, including on Saturday. This left Sunday as the one day when Jews would be certain to have free time, as did their Christian neighbors. A few of the reformers actually abandoned the Saturday

---

often deliver sermons only on two fixed days a year, Shabbat Shuvah, between Rosh Hashanah and Yom Kippur, and Shabbat haGadol, before Pesach (as well as on other special occasions). In these congregations, the sermon would often be delivered on Saturday morning by a preacher who specialized in this art.

35 See on this Saperstein, *Jewish Preaching, 1200–1800*, pp. 28–31. The many sermons cited below by Israel Levinthal and Abraham Cohen, as well as others, were mostly delivered on Saturday mornings.

morning service in favor of Sunday morning, when they used a weekday liturgy, but most continued with sparsely attended Shabbat morning worship alongside the much larger congregation the following day.[36] Because there were no prescribed biblical readings on Sundays, the preacher had both ample time for an extensive sermon and flexibility in choosing readings relevant to the preaching topic. In many large congregations, there was a huge regular attendance, and many of those present – including a considerable number of non-Jews – came primarily to hear the address by the preacher. The most famous was Stephen S. Wise, who regularly spoke on Sunday mornings at Carnegie Hall to more than a thousand listeners. But there were others as well, including Abba Hillel Silver in Cleveland, Solomon Freehof in Pittsburgh, Leo Franklin in Detroit, Maurice Eisendrath in Toronto, and Israel Mattuck in London.[37]

It may be questioned whether these Sunday morning speeches deserve to be called "sermons" and therefore belong in the category of "Jewish Preaching." I am using these terms somewhat loosely, recognizing that some of the rabbis referred to their speaking on Sunday mornings not as a sermon but, with more encompassing terms, as a "discourse" or "lecture" or "address." I have included passages from the texts delivered on these Sunday morning gatherings because they were important occasions for the rabbi to convey what he knew about the fate of European Jewry to consistently large and diverse audiences.

A different innovation pertained to Friday evening. Traditional Shabbat evening worship was fairly short, even when it followed directly on the afternoon service. Its timing depended upon sunset, and the pattern was that at the conclusion of the service, worship-

36 See on this W. Gunther Plaut, *The Growth of Reform Judaism*, pp. 64–65, 269–76, 281–83; Michael Meyer, *Response to Modernity*, pp. 290–92.

37 On the impact of the Sunday morning sermons delivered by Mattuck, his associate wrote: "The sermons which he gave at the Sunday services, held in addition to the Sabbath Services, very frequently dealt with acute present social problems and were quoted widely in the press.... Many people of prominence in national life attended the Sunday Services, which were also unique in that written questions from the congregation were sent up for Dr. Mattuck to answer and comment upon from the pulpit"(Leslie I. Edgar. *Some Memories of My Ministry*, p. 11).

pers would return home for a leisurely Friday evening meal with singing of traditional songs. Reform Judaism created the institution of the fixed-time Friday evening service, held throughout the year beginning at 7:00 or 8:00 or 8:30 p.m., *after* the Shabbat meal (which in the summer months would occur before the Sabbath had technically begun).[38] This change was instituted to motivate congregants to devote most of the evening to the Sabbath in the synagogue, rather than going out to socialize or watch a movie or a play. The worship service, including the sermon, would be between an hour and a quarter and an hour and a half long, followed by a leisurely social gathering with refreshments. The short evening service left time for a sermon of twenty minutes to half an hour, which did not evoke the problems that a sermon of similar length on Saturday morning would raise. In such congregations, Saturday morning worship was largely focused on the Bar Mitzvah, and there would usually be no sermon other than an address to the child, which included reference to but not lengthy discussion of the biblical readings for the week. The Friday evening sermon was free from Saturday's need to focus on biblical readings: it could be devoted to any significant issue of the day, including a controversial new book, drama, or motion picture, or contemporary events of political significance.[39]

Beyond sermons connected with the Sabbath are the sermons delivered in connection with the holidays and festivals of the year. Rosh Hashanah, celebrating the beginning of the Hebrew year, and Yom Kippur, the Day of Atonement coming nine days later, were times of peak attendance in synagogues throughout the world, and the sermon was an integral component of the worship experience. A minimum of four major sermons would be delivered in association with these "Days of Awe": for Reform rabbis, Rosh Hashanah evening and morning and Yom Kippur evening (Kol Nidre) and morning; for many Orthodox rabbis, the mornings of the first and second

38 See on this James G. Heller, *Isaac M. Wise*, pp. 383–84; W. Gunther Plaut, *The Growth of Reform Judaism*, pp. 277–79; Michael Meyer, *Response to Modernity*, p. 291.

39 The many sermons cited by Ferdinand Isserman of St. Louis were almost all delivered at Friday evening services.

day of Rosh Hashanah plus Yom Kippur evening and morning; for some Conservative rabbis the first evening of Rosh Hashanah plus two mornings plus twice on Yom Kippur. In addition, this period included the important preaching occasion of the intermediate Sabbath, known as Shabbat Shuvah, the Sabbath of Repentance. During the entire period of September 1933 through September 1945, it is difficult to imagine any Reform, Conservative, or Modern Orthodox congregation where the congregants would *not* hear at least one sermon devoted to what was happening to the Jews in Europe and the implications for their own lives.

The other most important preaching occasions were connected with holidays that provided major opportunities for addressing not only the distant past but also events in the present. Purim, based on the Book of Esther, is not a major festival, as it has no roots in the Torah, but the figure of Haman – an enemy seeking to destroy the entire Jewish population of the Persian Empire – and the ultimate triumph of the Jews had obvious resonance for preachers who sought both a historical precursor for Hitler and a happy ending. The Sabbath immediately preceding Purim (Shabbat Zakhor) contained an additional reading (Deut. 25:17–19) that evoked the memory of Amalek as the archetypal enemy of the Jewish people.

Pesach, coming a month later, eventually seemed even more relevant, for the policy of killing new-born Hebrew males was actually proclaimed by Pharaoh long before Moses could liberate his people, who eventually would witness the destruction of the Egyptian army in the sea. Hanukkah provided another preaching occasion (usually on the intermediate Sabbath), evoking the memory of an enemy, Antiochus Epiphanes, who attempted to prevent the Jews from observing their own traditions and then went to war against them. Pharaoh, Haman, Amalek, Antiochus – these were all familiar figures whose stories could be connected with the agonies of the present and furnish hope for the future.[40]

40 German rabbis in the 1930s had very limited freedom, as a member of the Gestapo was assigned to each synagogue service in order to ensure that would be no criticism of the regime, but sermons about Haman, Amalek, Pharaoh, and Antiochus, despite their obvious resonance, were generally permitted. Max Nussbaum later reported,

In addition to preaching occasions integrally connected with the Jewish religious calendar, there were also unique public events that brought together Jews of the various denominations, and often, also sympathetic Christians. These were gatherings of mass protest, and eventually days of mourning (sometimes including fasts). The public protests began in New York on March 27, 1933, less than three months after the Nazi Party came to power; on this occasion Madison Square Garden was filled to capacity and tens of thousands more stood in the streets, listening to speeches through amplification systems. These speeches were not technically sermons or examples of "Jewish Preaching," but I have included passages from the addresses because they are such important pieces of evidence for what was known and what was widely communicated, through speech, to a public audience.

Of a somewhat different nature were addresses made to rabbinic gatherings of the Central Conference of American Rabbis and the Rabbinical Assembly, or to various Zionist organizations, which got fairly wide publicity in the Jewish press and sometimes also in the general press. These too have been included.

Finally, there are the texts of addresses delivered by leading rabbis in Jewish radio broadcasts such as "The Message of Israel," and occasionally carried by regional networks such as WOR in New York and even national networks such as NBC. These messages eliminate the visual quality of the sermon or conference address, but I include them because they share with the sermon and address the dimension of verbal communication between speaker and listener, and likely may have reached a wider listening public than many of the sermons delivered in synagogues.

In general, the preachers included are rabbis addressing their congregations or broader groups of listeners. I have not included sermons or addresses by secular leaders, even if delivered in a syna-

---

"Preaching in those days required a technique all its own.... The sermons of those years might not have been remarkable in normal times but – full of innuendoes and rendered in a kind of spiritual code language – they were highly meaningful to the Jewish audiences in Berlin..." (from *Gegenwart im Rückblick: Festgabe für die Jüdische Gemeinde zu Berlin*, p. 243).

gogue. The one modification of this rabbinic criterion pertains to British preachers who received their credentials from Jews' College in London, a category that applies to the religious leaders of the overwhelming majority of Modern Orthodox synagogues in England during the period under investigation. Jews' College did not offer rabbinic ordination in the traditional sense; their graduates serving as religious leaders in synagogues throughout the UK did not use the title "Rabbi," but rather "Rev." Delivering effective sermons was central to their role, and the teaching of homiletics – by renowned figures such as Samuel Daiches and Abraham Cohen – was a major component of their education and training. With this exception, all of the other preachers used the title "Rabbi" (sometimes with the additional title "Dr."), and I have not included the title in identifying the authors of sermons within the collection.[41]

Most of the sermons delivered during our period were of course not directly relevant to our topic. No congregation will tolerate sermons on the same subject week after week; there will always be other themes, both religious and societal, that a preacher will want to address. One may distinguish between what might be called the "timeless" and the "topical" sermon. The "timeless" sermon treats central themes of a religious tradition – biblical narratives, theological doctrines, traditional moral values, requirements for proper Jewish living including the observance of the Sabbath, holidays, and dietary laws – without application or even reference to contemporary events. This kind of sermon could have been delivered ten years earlier or ten years later, in some cases fifty years earlier or fifty years later, than the actual date of delivery.

The "topical" sermon may also discuss ancient traditions, but its focus is upon contemporary reality. It therefore could not have

41 Something of a stretch is to include several addresses delivered by Judah L. Magnes, a Reform rabbi from New York who moved to Palestine and became Chancellor and then President of the newly established Hebrew University of Jerusalem. His addresses were delivered to the student body and faculty at the beginning of the academic year, and I consider them in the same broad category as the Sunday morning addresses delivered to large American congregations.

been delivered even five years earlier or later. Think of the sermons delivered on the first preaching occasion after the Pearl Harbor attack,[42] or at the Friday evening or Saturday morning worship service immediately following the assassination of President John F. Kennedy, or sermons delivered on the first preaching occasion after the 9/11/2001 or 7/7/2005 attacks.[43] These capture a unique moment in time and – if preserved in a written text – provide evidence for the perceptions and values of the preacher, and to some extent of the listening congregation, that may not be readily accessible decades later. Reading the texts of sermons responding to Nazi persecution and mass murder more than seventy years after the end of the war, we can only attempt to put ourselves back in the position of Jews who were actually responding to unprecedented events reported in the media, or who were learning some of the horrifying details as they were listening.

One simple way to distinguish between these two categories, even without a thorough reading, is that in collections of published sermon texts, the "timeless" sermons are generally presented without an indication of the date of delivery. The major purpose of providing a more permanent record of these sermons was to make them useful to other preachers and inspirational to other Jews. The occasion will sometimes be made clear, whether in a Table of Contents or by internal reference – a specific holiday, or the weekly Torah lection (*parashah*) – but the year is generally not relevant, and therefore not noted. Although some collections include topical sermons but do not record the date,[44] in most cases the date of delivery for the topical

42 See, e.g., Ferdinand M. Isserman, "The United States is at War," December 12, 1941, in Saperstein, *Jewish Preaching in Times of War*, pp. 450–61.

43 See Harold Saperstein, "Martyr for the American Dream," November 22, 1963, in *Witness from the Pulpit*, pp. 226–29, and the three sermons delivered on September 14, 15, and 18, 2001 in *Jewish Preaching in Times of War*, pp. 529–48. Whatever power the surviving texts of those sermons may have retained, the original impact cannot be reproduced.

44 For example, a generation earlier, Morris Joseph of the West London Synagogue published three volumes of his sermons, in 1893, 1907, and 1930: none of the sermons included have dates, although some can be determined by the content (cf. Saperstein, *Jewish Preaching in Times of War*, p. 310, n. 1).

sermon will be given. Because of the nature of the current book as a collection of historical documents responding to historical events, I have used only texts where the date of delivery is explicitly provided, or in some cases clear because it can be deduced by internal content.

For the period covered by the current book, Harry Joshua Stern, the distinguished rabbi of Temple Emanu-El in Montreal, published three volumes, in 1937, 1944, and 1950 (see Bibliography). But no dates are included, which precludes my incorporating more than a few passages from sermons that can be dated from the content.[45] Turning to unpublished sermons in archival collections, The American Jewish Archives has a large collection of fully written sermons texts by Abraham H. Feinberg of Rockford, Illinois, and later (starting in 1942) of Youngstown, Ohio, but not a single one of them has a date, and – with a few exceptions where a date can be determined by internal content – most of his sermons could not be considered for inclusion in accordance with my criteria.[46]

Israel Levinthal, one of the great American preachers of the era, notes the importance of context in the Preface to an extremely important collection, published in 1943: "The reader is urged to take note of the date and the occasion when each of these messages was uttered. It will help him to relive the period in which they were spoken, and thus to see how utterly mankind failed to read the handwriting on the wall which gave clear warning of the disasters that were approaching."[47]

---

45 E.g., the sermon beginning with the words "This New Year 5700 marks the turn of a century and what a tragic hour it is in the turn of world events!" – clearly delivered on Rosh Hashanah, 1939 (in *The Jewish Spirit Triumphant*, p. 11). Similarly, Leo Jung, with volumes of his sermons published in 1942 and 1956, and Louis Rabinowitz, an important rabbi and scholar in London and then in South Africa, who published volumes of his sermons in 1951, 1955, 1958, and 1965: in both cases, no dates are provided, but there are occasional datable references to current events.

46 In the vast collection of sermon texts at the AJA, there are two modes of organization. Those with dates are organized in accordance with the date of delivery, so a folder will have sermons for a given year or two, arranged chronologically. In cases where the dates are missing, they are organized in a far less useful manner for the historian, usually by alphabetical order of the title.

47 Levinthal, *A New World Is Born: Sermons and Addresses*, p. ix. (I will later comment on the problems in the part of the second sentence invoking "the handwriting on the

Here we must linger on the very nature of the sermon as historical source. Despite the comparison I have suggested between newspaper article and sermon as contemporary historical sources, there is of course a fundamental difference. The article – or the dated Diary or letter – is indeed the source itself, and it can often be accessed in its original form in archival collections and even frequently on the Internet. But the texts of the sermons that I use in this book are *not* the actual sermons. They bear a relation to the sermon analogous to the relationship between the symbols on sheets of music paper and the sound of the first performance of a fugue based on these symbols played on the organ by Bach, or the first performance of a sonata played on the piano by Beethoven.[48] Or, to provide another example – which, with all its abhorrence is still within the memory of people living today – it is analogous to the relationship between the written text of a speech of Hitler's from the 1930s or early 1940s (as printed by Max Domarus, whether in the original German or in translation) and watching and hearing the speech when it was originally delivered (or – a step removed but still better than reading a written text – watching and listening to a video-tape).

Totally missing from the written text of the sermon is everything that we would include in the category of "delivery": the sound of the preacher's voice, the pace of his speaking,[49] the emphasis on certain words and phrases,[50] the occasional pauses, gestures and facial expressions, and the extent to which it is apparent that the

---

wall" [Daniel 5] as an assertion about what *should* have been known by "mankind" about the future.)

48 Cf. Abraham Cohen, *Jewish Homiletics*, p. 182: "The written text of the sermon is comparable to a musical score, words taking the place of notes. The score is a dead thing until it is brought to life by the performer." The difference, of course, is that the sermon is delivered by its creator, not by a different "performer."

49 I have used masculine pronouns when referring to rabbis of this period because it reflects the reality of the 1930s and 1940s.

50 In 1994, the *St. Louis Post-Dispatch* published an article recounting an experience the author had reciting Lincoln's Gettysburg Address the previous year in a nursing home. When he had finished, a woman in her 90s came over and told him that she had recited the Address at an Independence Day event in 1911, when a "grizzled Union army veteran" came over and corrected her emphasis on "*of* the people, *by* the people, and *for* the people," saying, "Young lady, I heard those very words from

preacher is reading a text or actually is talking to people. All of this is lost in the written text on which we must depend.[51]

The preachers themselves were clearly aware of this distinction. As a leading New York rabbi, Louis I. Newman put it, "But it is one thing to preach a good discourse, and another to make it rousing and inspiring. No preacher knows how effective his sermon will be until he is in the midst of it, for there must always be a quality of vivid creativity, almost extempore style, in addition to the carefully prepared and written material he brings to the rostrum."[52] Or Abraham A. Kellner of Albany: "The speeches as printed in this collection were preached essentially as they appear in cold print varying only in those essentials needed in transmuting the living word into black-face type. But it is common knowledge that the effect of the spoken word depends for its success not only on the material preached, but equally so upon the inspirational value which emanates from the enthusiasm and eloquence of the speaker."[53]

There are other ways in which the written text fails to communicate much of the impact of the sermons delivered between 1933 and 1945. I have mentioned above the importance that many congregants

President Lincoln's lips, and he emphasized each time '*the people.*'" Bert Minkin, "Emphasis on the People," in *St. Louis Post-Dispatch*, July 3, 1964, p. 122.

51 For a fine general treatment of the importance of delivery for a preacher see Abraham Cohen, *Jewish Homiletics*, pp. 183–200. Cf. on this theme Menahem Blondheim, "Divine Comedy: The Jewish Orthodox Sermon in America, 1881–1939," pp. 193–94 on the "methodological nightmare" of studying the sermon in the context of its time and space: "The sermon, after all, is a one-time public, oral experience; it is evanescent. The text of the sermon is at best only a reflection, a written echo of the verbal role of one participant in a public event, or as anthropologists would call it, a cultural performance. The full meaning of such performances emerges only in the process of playing them out, in the present case, through the social context of preaching and the cultural significance of the occasion." The distinction is often ignored, even by people working on the material. In an extensive review of a book on Cicero published in the *London Review of Books* (February 4, 2016), James Davidson wrote, "It is amazing enough that Cicero's great speeches survive, giving us a ringside seat at these momentous trials and pivotal votes" (p. 14, column 2). But of course the "speeches" did not survive, only the texts of the speeches, and this is rather different from providing a "ringside seat."

52 Louis I. Newman, "The Modern Clergyman and His Duties," Radio Address on WMCA, November 21, 1935, in *Sermons and Addresses*, vol. 3, p. 113 (113–17).

53 Abraham A. Kellner, *A Rabbi's Faith: Sermons of Hope and Courage*, p. vii.

attributed to the sermon two to three generations ago, sometimes more than to the liturgy. In looking for a new rabbi, it was standard practice that leading candidates would visit the prospective new congregation and be asked to deliver a sermon (sometimes after members of the search committee had heard the rabbi in his own congregation); the effectiveness of the sermon was always a critical component of the hiring decision. Preaching ability is far less central today; even the term "sermon" is sometimes avoided in favor of "*d'var torah*," which suggests a message considerably less formal and more focused on the scriptural reading.

There is also a significant difference in length. Sunday morning sermons as part of a weekday service would often be an hour long. A common length for sermons on Shabbat at the beginning of the twentieth century was forty minutes. By mid-century, the common length was twenty minutes.[54] Now it may be ten to twelve minutes, and occasionally a rabbi will speak even more briefly and open up an opportunity for discussion. This of course reflects a general diminution in attention span in society over the past 150 years. During the Lincoln-Douglas Debates, the first speaker was allowed sixty minutes, the rebuttal was allowed ninety minutes, and then the first speaker given thirty minutes for a rejoinder. A century later, the format in the 1960 Kennedy-Nixon debates was an eight-minute opening statement for each, two-and-a-half-minute responses to questions, optional rebuttals of the same length, and three-minute closing statements. The basic unit of time in the 2016 debates was two minutes for each candidate in direct response to each question, plus brief opportunities for reactions.

A final theme that makes these sermons from 1933–1945 so contrary to contemporary taste was the high value placed on oratory.[55] Today the emphasis seems to be on "plain speaking." It is all right

54 Cf. Abraham Cohen, *Jewish Homiletics*, p. 178: "I might prescribe this timetable as one practised by myself: the Sabbath sermon should last from fifteen to twenty minutes. On a Festival another five minutes may be added; and on Yom Kippur, when a long day has to be filled in, the discourse may extend to half an hour."

55 For a recent discussion of the importance of rhetoric in the past and its contemporary antithesis through the "debasement of political language" in "the age of the

for a preacher to come up with a memorable phrase at some point in a sermon, but a style of communication that is suffused with long and complicated sentences, literary allusions, or words or phrases that would not be used in ordinary conversation, will often evoke a negative reaction in listeners. In short, much of the material below was written and delivered in a style that is no longer fashionable, but for our purposes, it is the substance, rather than the rhetoric, that is of paramount importance.

The reaction of the listeners is obviously lost in the written text, though it could indeed be argued that what the listeners heard and remembered may be as important a source for the effectiveness of communication as the analysis of a surviving text. We know this from the impact that Hitler had on those who were present at his speeches. As has been noted, the German historian Max Domarus published, in 1965, a massive four-volume work presenting the texts of speeches delivered by Hitler between 1932 and 1935. In the Introduction, he wrote (using the English translation):

> During my university studies and as a journalist, I had the opportunity to travel widely in Germany from 1932 to 1939 and to gain a close view of many significant aspects of the Third Reich. I personally heard Hitler speak and was able to interview public figures who had direct contact with him. In this way I was able to witness for myself Hitler's astonishing power and influence as an orator. The enthusiasm his speeches prompted was not confined only to easily-aroused mass audiences, but also infected – perhaps even more strongly – individuals belonging to Germany's leading circles.

It was the speeches delivered and heard, not the written texts published in the *Völkischer Beobachter* or the German News Agency, and not *Mein Kampf*, that had the major impact.[56] More surprising is a

---

tweet," see Simon Schama, "War of the Words," in *Financial Times*, September 3, 2016, "Life & Arts," pp. 1–2.

56 Max Domarus, *Hitler: Speeches and Proclamations, 1932–1945*, p. 9, and 60–71 on "The Methodology of Hitler's Oratory."

similar evaluation of the impact of Mussolini's addresses. Before hearing him speak, a twenty-four-year-old Italian woman from Padua had written critically in her diary about his "campaign against the Jews." Two weeks later, she heard him speak, and on September 24, 1938, wrote:

> I did not miss a word of the speech or an expression of his face, and came away with a marvellous impression. He is an exceptional man who emanates an immense force, capable of shackling endless multitudes. His face is unique and inimitable, full of strength and sweetness, hard and human. You should have seen how he smiled at the cheering crowd and with what perfect style he made the Roman salute! To behold that face is to feel ready for anything, for any sacrifice, for any struggle.[57]

Apparently, it was not that Mussolini convinced her that his policy concerning the Jews was correct; rather, it was that the charismatic speaker made other things seem far less important.

Needless to say, the substance of Jewish preaching could not be more antithetical to the messages of the German and Italian dictators, but the impact of the gifted speaker was in some ways similar. Although today the role of the sermon in Jewish worship is far less dramatic than it was in the past, the principle that the impact of a sermon is usually more evident in the delivery than in a written text remains.

Many reports on the impact of hearing a powerful preacher have been written by the listeners. Jacob P. Rudin first encountered Stephen S. Wise when Wise spoke at Harvard in 1923, where Rudin was an undergraduate. Thirty years later, he recalled his reaction in an address to rabbinical students: "I heard a man speak as I had never heard a man speak before.... I knew then and there that I would go to the Jewish Institute of Religion if Dr. Wise would have me."[58]

---

57 Maria Teresa Rossetti, cited in Agnes Grunwald-Spier, *Who Betrayed the Jews?*, p. 185.

58 Rudin, "Concerning a King: Founder's Day Address," 1954, pp. 3–4. Apparently the same decision was made by John J. Tepfer in the 1920s upon hearing Wise preach: *American Jewish Archives*, MS 586, "Biographical Sketch." The obituary for Albert Gottschalk published by the *NYT*, Sept. 16, 2009, p. B16, states that "he decided to

My father, Harold Saperstein, then an undergraduate at Cornell, similarly described, years later, the impact of hearing Wise deliver a sermon in the spring of 1931: "I shall always remember the sense of pride I had that morning in Sage Chapel as I looked around and saw the faces of thousands of university faculty and students, practically all non-Jewish, listening with rapt attention and profound respect to this Rabbi."[59]

Other preachers with considerably less national reputation than Wise also had an impact upon their listeners. Here is how a congregant described Louis Wolsey, rabbi of Congregation Rodeph Shalom in Philadelphia from 1935–1947:

> As a preacher and public speaker, Dr. Wolsey has few peers. He has occupied pulpits in churches of almost all denominations and has addressed groups from every walk of life. His deep, resonant voice coupled with his impeccable diction and knowledge of semantics have created a great demand for his services as a pulpiteer and also a speaker before civic, communal and other organizational groups throughout the country."[60]

Or here is the description of the young Abba Hillel Silver, recently ordained and rabbi of a small congregation in Wheeling, West Virginia, written by Abraham L. Feinberg, who – like Rudin and Saperstein – himself became a rabbi. Eventually he succeeded Maurice N. Eisendrath at Holy Blossom Temple in Toronto, and was once

become a rabbi at [age] 15, partly because he was inspired by the anti-Hitler orations of Rabbi Stephen Wise." Gottschalk eventually became President of the Hebrew Union College-Jewish Institute of Religion.

59 Saperstein, *Witness from the Pulpit*, p. 149. In this sermon delivered at the time of Wise's death in 1949, Saperstein continued, "It was only when he was expressing something that he felt very deeply, when the great fire of his spirit smouldered and burst into flame, that his voice became infused with passion. His whole body became transformed; he rose to oratorical heights, and lifted his audiences to levels that he alone could do. He was a dramatic speaker, but dramatic quality was not something that he achieved artificially. It was something that flowed out of the fervor and sincerity of his message" (p. 150).

60 Gustav C. Tassman, Introduction to Wolsey, *Sermons and Addresses*, p. v. Tassman was a distinguished academic in dentistry.

designated in a national poll as one of Canada's "Seven Greatest Preachers":

> The choir finished. [Rabbi Silver] uncrossed his legs, placed his hands on the two arms of the chair and pushed himself up with elaborate slowness – a Lincolnesque giant bestirring himself from repose. Then the voice began, like a soft syllable prying loose an avalanche, its music packed with enormous power and gaining force with each word, until the air quivered with pathos, rumbled with wrath, and glowed with sheer grace of phrase and thought. When he closed his eyes, mine were opened on a realm of harmony and rapture. When he stepped back and lifted his mighty arms, intellectualized thunder rolled up and out from him, and shook the clustered lights and swept from pew to pew into the choir loft and out through the windows into the night.[61]

About twenty-seven years later, on September 1, 1943, Abba Hillel Silver delivered an address to a meeting of the "American Zionist Emergency Council" at the Waldorf Astoria hotel, New York. Emanuel Neumann, an American lawyer with strong Zionist commitments, described the effect of this speech:

> Silver rose to speak, and he was superb. It was not only an emotional speech, but also an extremely well-constructed and closely-reasoned appeal to the intelligence of the delegates.... It is impossible to describe the electrifying effect of Silver's speech, which swept the Conference like a hurricane. There was repeated and stormy applause, the delegates rising to their feet in a remarkable ovation. The battle for our "extreme" position was won hands down and the decision was put into parliamentary form in committee.... The overwhelming majority were carried along to a ringing affirmation of a "Jewish commonwealth" in Palestine.[62]

61 Abraham L. Feinberg, *Storm the Gates of Jericho*, p. 191. In the book, he identifies the preacher whom he heard while growing up as "Solomon Goldner," for reasons unclear to me (he also masks the true names of other rabbis to whom he refers). His substitution of "Goldner" for "Silver" seems like something of a game.

62 Emanuel Neumann, *In the Arena*, pp. 189–92.

In a very different context but with similar evidence, Nathan Netter heard Jacob Kaplan (many of whose texts are presented in translation in this book) deliver a sermon in Vichy on Rosh Hashanah, September 21, 1941. Netter wrote, "The congregation, visibly moved, followed as if entranced the dynamic orator who, seeing us in effect abandoned by the powerful of the land, without help, without protection from those in positions of authority, found the perfect way of communicating the immense distress of this Jewish community, so distraught by fate."[63]

And again in a different context, just nine days later, Yosef Yehuda Levy, a young man from Hungary who had been conscripted into the Labor Service, described hearing a sermon delivered by Rabbi Baruch Rabinovich, the young Rebbe of Munkácz, who had been deported to Kamanets-Podolski: "On the night of Kol Nidre [1941], I went to hear his sermon. I will never forget the moving sermon that he delivered. The *beit midrash was* packed full and he recounted everything that had happened to him, their Rebbe, near Kamanets-Podolski.... The tears flowed from all of our eyes like water; we couldn't restrain ourselves."[64]

The environment for Rabbi Shlomo Unsdorfer – placed under strict German military police guard in an old castle near Bratislava with his family and about 180 other Jews in September 1944 – was dramatically different. According to the memoir written by his son, Simha Bunem Unsdorfer, the rabbi conducted services throughout the day, and asked especially that all Jews, "even those who have forsaken our religion and no longer believe in prayer," should gather together for the *Yizkor* (Memorial) service. His son wrote, "They all came, and never shall I forget the short parable with which my father illustrated his sermon. Everyone was in tears: that was what he wanted to achieve. 'The gates of tears are never closed,' say our rabbis. If nothing reaches the ears of God, the tears of the innocent will always find Him."[65]

63 Netter, *La Patrie égarée et la patrie renaissante*, p. 113.
64 Esther Farbstein, *Hidden in the Heights*, vol. 1, p. 136.
65 S.B. Unsdorfer, *The Yellow Star*, pp. 20–21; the quotation is from b. Bava Metzi'a 59a.

Not all the listeners preserved positive memories of the sermons they heard. The Fortunoff Archive of Survivors' Testimonies at Yale University contains many references to sermons heard by the survivors. Some of these memories are negative. A survivor reports having gone to hear the Munkaczer Rebbe (Chaim Elazar Spira) preach on a Friday evening (T509, no date provided; the Rebbe died in 1937). During the sermon, the Rebbe "cursed and condemned" the Jews in Palestine; as a result, the listener states that he never went back to hear another Friday evening sermon. A survivor from Salonika (T 535) said that the rabbi of the community, who came from Germany, was openly opposed to cooperation with the Germans. According to the survivor's report, the rabbi was taken away and came back an entirely different man, who gave sermons "telling us to follow the orders of the Germans." As there was no-one to contradict him, ninety-five percent of the Jews were deported without resistance. Sermons did apparently have an impact, though not necessarily what the preacher intended.

Sometimes memories can be used for polemical purposes. Arthur Hertzberg, in the documentary film "America and the Holocaust," reported:

> I remember a sermon, a bitter sermon of my father [R. Zvi Elimelech Hertzberg, of Congregation *Shomrei Mishmeres* in Baltimore]. The year was 1940. It was Yom Kippur, 1940. He got up in the synagogue and said, "Our brothers are being killed in Europe by the Nazis." (The murders had already started on a small scale). He said, "If we had any Jewish dignity we would, at the end of this fast, get into our cars and go from Baltimore" – where we lived – "to Washington; we would picket the White House and we would demand of the President that he use his influence on the Nazis, as the great neutral power, to stop the killings." And then he added, "The reason why you hesitate to do this is that sons and daughters of yours have jobs in the 'New Deal' agencies, which are now open to Jews, and you are afraid that you are going to rock the boat." That night, within an hour after the end of the fast, my father got a note from the board of this little synagogue,

> firing him for his disrespect of the President. I ask the Jews of America, has anything changed?[66]

I would have loved to use quotations from this sermon in the present book. But Hertzberg does not mention the existence of a written record where the text of this sermon is recorded; although the passages are presented as direct quotations, it seems as if they depend – as the passage is introduced – on the memory of one listener (the preacher's son).

Three years after the sermon was delivered, Hertzberg, at age twenty-two, accompanied his father on a march to the gates of the White House (held three days before Yom Kippur) with some four hundred Orthodox rabbis. Organized by the Emergency Committee to Save the Jewish People of Europe and the Union of Orthodox Rabbis, it was intended to dramatize the plight of European Jewry and pressure the US government to act more decisively on their behalf. Nothing directly came of the event. There appears to be no evidence of any call for such a demonstration three years earlier; and it would be extremely surprising had his father issued one. There is of course no evidence that the sermon quoted by Hertzberg did *not* contain the statements Hertzberg cites, but memories articulated decades later, especially if they are used to make a political point, do not justify inclusion. Note that despite the letter "firing him" that came a few hours after the end of Yom Kippur, Rabbi Zvi Elimelech Hertzberg actually remained as the spiritual leader of Congregation *Shomrei Mishmeres* throughout the war, after which he was invited to serve as rabbi of a new Orthodox congregation in a different part of Baltimore: Beth Abraham, also known as "Hertzberg's."[67]

Nonetheless, memories can also supply important insights, not only about the content of a sermon, but about the dynamic process that produced this content. It is well known that German rabbis were

66 http://to.pbs.org/2yW1n9D.

67 In an article published at the time of Hertzberg's death, *Haaretz* writer Shlomo Shamir wrote that "In his room at Columbia University he kept cartons full of notebooks and writings that contained his father's sermons and Torah commentaries," but there is no indication of where these texts may be now, http://www.haaretz.com/the-eternal-rebel-1.186436.

permitted to lead religious worship, including a sermon, after the Nazi regime came to power, but with clear restrictions. A member of the Gestapo, as has been noted, was present at every worship service to ensure that the sermon, delivered of course in German, would contain no criticism of the regime. Here is how the Martha Appel, wife of Rabbi Ernst Appel of Dortmund, later described the process of preparation for the sermons to be delivered:

> He had to find words to describe our current situation not directly, but would unambiguously transmit to his audience what he wanted to tell them.... My husband and I attentively checked his sermons. Word for word we read them out loud and pondered if this or that sentence would rouse the disapproval of the Gestapo officer present in all services. There was so much my husband would have liked to say to his community on these Holy Days, that he could not.... My husband subjected himself [to this difficult task] in particular because he did not want to give the Nazis with his sermons the smallest pretext for banning his services and to arrest the community board.[68]

These severe limits to freedom of the pulpit, the challenge to communicate a meaningful message to a congregation without falling victim to the restraints of a totalitarian regime, has severely limited the extent to which the texts of German sermons during this period seem appropriate for the present book.

Preachers who published texts of their sermons were of course very much aware of the distinction between a sermon delivered and a written transcript. Maurice N. Eisendrath, of Toronto, wrote in his Introduction to *The Never Failing Stream*, a collection of his sermon texts published in 1939: "Whatever efficacy such spoken words may possess is derived essentially from the circumstances surrounding their delivery, the manner of the presentation, the mood of the hear-

68 Martha Appel, cited by Astrid Zajdband, *German Rabbis in British Exile*, pp. 55–56. On this dynamic, cf. Alfred Jospe, "A Profession in Transition: The German Rabbinate 1910–1939," pp. 59–61, and Joachim Prinz, *Joachim Prinz: Rebellious Rabbi*, pp. 105–6, 118–19, 166–67.

ers, the fervour of the speaker – all of which are far too evanescent and elude too dishearteningly the vain endeavour to reproduce them on the cold, white printed page" (p xi). And yet he published these cold, white printed pages, first – like a number of his colleagues – in pamphlet form not long after delivery, and later in a collection going back almost a decade.

In his Preface to *Between Yesterday and Tomorrow*, a collection of twenty-six sermon texts delivered in Leeds between June 1940 and October 1943 by Eliezer Berkovits, a German rabbi who came to England as an immigrant in the spring of 1939, the preacher wrote, "It is with some hesitation that I submit these sermons to a wider public. The spoken word is essentially different from the written one. Committed to print, it must lose some of the force and emphasis derived by it from both the original situation in which it has been spoken and the oratory of the speaker. To my mind the justification for this volume lies in the persistence of the 'original situation,' which will most probably not pass for many years yet." Here Berkovits explains that his decision to publish is based not on the sermons' historical value as a source for future understanding of the past, but rather on the extremely pessimistic view that the realities addressed in his sermons from earlier years in the war are still relevant in December 1944, when he wrote the Preface.

Because of these considerations, the reality of any delivered speech or sermon would be conveyed much more closely by a videotape than by a typed or hand-written text. But the largest number of such preserved audio-visual texts from this period are probably by Nazi speakers, predominantly by Hitler.[69] There is indeed an extremely large number of audio recordings made of sermons and

69 Pertaining to the rhetoric of Nazi speeches, Randall L. Bytwerk refers to an "oral version" of an important speech, delivered by Goebbels at the Sports Palace in Berlin on February 18, 1943, that is available in his book, *Landmark Speeches of National Socialism*, stating that there are "significant differences between the written text and the oral recording: The most striking is that in the oral version, Goebbels begins to mention the extermination of the Jews, then catches himself in the middle of the word. It's also interesting to note that the audience reactions reported in the text below are sometimes stronger than the recording justifies," http://research.calvin.edu/german-propaganda-archive/goeb36.htm.

addresses delivered by Stephen S. Wise.[70] But the disadvantage of the recording for scholars using the sermon as a historical source is, of course, that one does not have the ability to skim through pages of hundreds of printed texts to determine what is relevant to the subject at hand, and then slow down to analyse in depth. A recording is heard in real time. Though clearly a step removed from the actual sermon, written texts are both far more prevalent and considerably more useful for research than the relatively few recordings that have been preserved.[71]

There were more than a few distinguished and effective preachers who never wrote complete texts of their sermons. Occasionally, there were no texts at all, and no direct records of the sermons exist. Joachim Prinz, one of the most influential young Jewish preachers in Nazi Germany before he left for the United States in 1937, wrote, "I have no manuscripts of any of my sermons as I am not in the habit of writing them. Had I collected them, they would convey to us today the method I used to approach our people." He provides a good description of the nature and impact of his preaching, but unfortunately not the kind of material that fits the criteria of the

---

70 For Wise: American Jewish Archives, MS-49, Series 3: Audio Recordings, 1931–1942 (20 Phonograph Boxes). According to Walter Jacob, Solomon Freehof's sermons and addresses at Rodef Shalom Congregation of Pittsburgh were also regularly recorded (*Pursuing Peace Across the Alleghenies*, p. 47). Cf. also the statement written by the daughters of Rabbi Abraham M. Hershman of Detroit about their father: "During his ministry, his father-in-law, Eliahu Ze'ev Lewin-Epstein, had urged him to record his sermons on a Dictaphone. Unfortunately, being uncomfortable with any kind of mechanical device, he had resisted the suggestion. As a result, he was obliged to reconstruct most of his sermons and addresses [for publication] from notes." Ruth and Eiga Hershman, "Rabbi Abraham M. Hershman," p. 36.

71 In a fascinating study of sermons in the ultra-Orthodox communities of Israel, Kimmy Caplan has shown how recordings of sermons have recently become extremely popular, to the point where women will listen to recordings of sermons as they are preparing meals in the kitchen, thus making the preacher's voice now *more* accessible than a written text. Some halakhic authorities have permitted recordings to be made of sermons delivered on Friday evening through the use of the Sabbath clock. Caplan reports that some seven thousand sermon titles were available for purchase in 2006 (when his book was completed), with more being added week after week. Caplan, *Internal Popular Discourse in Israeli Haredi Society* [Hebrew], chap. 1, pp. 49–93.

present collection.[72] Alexander Altmann, himself the son of a distinguished German rabbi, left a record of at least one of his sermons delivered in Berlin (see below, Rosh Hashanah, 1934).[73] He moved to England shortly before *Kristallnacht*, and was appointed by Chief Rabbi Hertz to the prestigious position of Community Rabbi of Manchester. *The Jewish Chronicle* frequently reported that Altmann would be delivering the sermon on such-and-such an occasion, and later occasionally included quotations from what he said; the *JC* published his review of Chief Rabbi Hertz's three volumes *Early and Late: Addresses, Messages, and Papers*, under the title "Battling for Humanity: Chief Rabbi, Guide and Champion."[74] His Memorial Address for Hertz, delivered at the Great Synagogue in Manchester on February 3, 1946, was printed.[75] But a thorough investigation of the massive Altmann Archives held by University College London reveals no texts of sermons delivered during his twenty years in Manchester. Either he preached from notes that were eventually discarded, or extemporaneously in a language that was not his native tongue.

A striking American example of a preacher who used only outline notes is Milton Steinberg, Conservative rabbi of the Park Avenue Synagogue in New York, who died in 1950 at age forty-six. A collection of his articles was gathered and published by his wife in 1953; a few of the essays appear to have been sermons, very few of which are dated or clearly from our period, or directly address our theme.[76]

72 Joachim Prinz, "A Rabbi Under the Hitler Regime," in *Gegenwart im Rückblick*, pp. 231–38, with a full description of the service held on Friday evening, March 31, 1933, immediately before the Nazi-imposed boycott of all Jewish stores, describes the service, the nature of the congregation, and a bit of the content of the sermon (232–34). A passage from Prinz's sermon delivered on the first day of Rosh Hashanah, September 14, 1939, was published in the *Newark News* on that day and is included below.

73 The Fortunoff Archives at Yale (T-261) contain an interview in which he discussed the challenges of preaching in the presence of a Gestapo agent at every worship service, using biblical and rabbinic texts as coded references to contemporary circumstances. He mentioned especially a Rosh Hashanah sermon in which he spoke of "Rachel weeping for her children" (Jer. 31:15), when he heard a "terrible sobbing from the balcony."

74 *JC*, May 26, 1944, p. 6.

75 In *Essays and Addresses in Memory of Dr. Joseph Herman Hertz*, pp. 3–6.

76 *A Believing Jew: The Selected Writings of Milton Steinberg*, chap. 12: Rosh Hashanah 1948;

Two subsequent collections provide sermon texts linked with the holidays and with weekly Torah readings respectively.[77] Both books contain material not in paragraphs or even in full sentences, but in outline form. The editor, Bernard Mandelbaum, wrote in his Preface to the first book, "The outlines indicate that Rabbi Steinberg spent a great deal of time in organizing his message to insure the logical and orderly flow of his ideas. He did not preach from a finished manuscript lest it impede the dynamic inter-communication between his listener, his theme and himself" (pp. vii–viii). Unfortunately, even in those relatively rare places where he refers explicitly to Nazism and persecution, with one notable exception (see below, February 14, 1945), the incompleteness of the formulation and the absence of dates make it impossible to include more than this one selection in the book.[78]

In the British context, one of the most important non-Orthodox rabbis during our period was Harold Reinhart, who followed Morris Joseph as the spiritual leader of the large Reform West London Syn-

---

chap. 13: Kol Nidre (no date); chap. 16: Rosh Hashanah morning (no date); chap. 17: Rosh Hashanah (no date); chap. 19: Yom Kippur (no date); chap. 20: High Holiday season (no date); chap. 21: Rosh Hashanah (no date); chap. 23: a brilliant, beautiful sermon based on his personal experience of illness (no date).

77 *From the Sermons of Rabbi Milton Steinberg: High Holydays and Major Festivals*, ed. Bernard Mandelbaum (1954); *Only Human – The Eternal Alibi: From the Sermons of Rabbi Milton Steinberg: The Weekly Sidrah and General Themes*, ed. Bernard Mandelbaum (New York: Bloch, 1963).

78 E.g., *From the Sermons of Rabbi Milton Steinberg*, p. 56:

"Would we not seek a scapegoat too?

even Hitler –

starving housepainter – cafes in Vienna – obsessed

one confines a lunatic – does not hate him

The saints would forgive, but fight Nazism – so must we."

A few quotations from Steinberg's *High Holydays* sermons are cited in *NYT* articles reviewing the preaching of New York rabbis on the day following the delivery, but there is nothing that justifies inclusion here. Other examples would be Jerome Malino of Danbury, Connecticut: the AJA has a complete collection of sermons delivered throughout his career, but all of the hundreds of texts are typed in the form of detailed notes. Similarly Julian B. Feibelman, Assistant Rabbi at Keneseth Israel, Philadelphia, 1926–1936, then at Temple Sinai, New Orleans, 1936–1967: the AJA has six boxes of sermons, the great majority of which are hand-written detailed notes.

agogue of British Jews from 1928 until 1957. Reinhart wrote monthly messages for *The Synagogue Review*, and some of these – written with considerable eloquence – do indeed include material relevant to Nazi persecution of Jews.[79] But except for one essay entitled "A Sermon to Confirmands," identified as "A sermon preached in the West London Synagogue on 1st June 1941," nothing is given a specific date beyond the month when the essay appeared. My investigation of the "sermons" contained in the Parkes Institute Archives Harold Reinhart collection was rather disappointing. Almost all of the material was in the form of notes, most of them far less extensive than those of Milton Steinberg.[80] Reinhart may indeed have been a powerful preacher, but although it was reported in his *Memorial Volume* that "it was in the pulpit that he exerted his most telling influence," the extant record of his sermons leaves hardly anything usable for our purpose.[81]

Sometimes the same preacher reveals a mixture of approaches to the preparation of sermons. It might be that a person started with fully written texts, and then – as he became more accustomed to public speaking – shifted to outlines. Or used complete texts for holidays and important occasions, but outlines for ordinary Sabbath sermons. An interesting shift is revealed by the French Protestant

79 "Passover," April 1933; "German Jews," May 1933; "Joyous Jews," March 1934; "The Terror Abroad," June 1936; "The Terror at Home," November 1936; "Defence," May 1938; "Refugees," October 1939; "Worship in the Fortress," July 1940; "A Sermon to Confirmands," August 1941; "Judaism and War Aims," September 1941; "Baruch Haba: Rabbi Leo Baeck," August 1945. All of these appear in *Harold Reinhart, 1891–1969: A Memorial Volume*, compiled by Lewis and Jacqueline Golden.

80 E.g., his sermon for Rosh Hashanah, September 21, 1933:
" the Jewish tragedy: physical torture
worse: morale, pride, hope
worst: bankruptcy of Jew spirit
reproach, mockery"
One of the preachers widely used in this book is Israel Levinthal, a contemporary colleague of Steinberg. He published collections of complete sermon texts in several books, but the texts preserved in the JTSA Archives are largely in outline form.

81 The tribute continues, "His exposition of Judaism was vividly imaginative in its statement of ethical principles, and boldly direct in the application of those principles both to individual conduct and to the wider affairs of the community and the world at large." *Harold Reinhart, 1891–1969*, p. 7.

pastor André Trocmé, who would become renowned for his leadership in providing refuge in Le Chambon-sur-Lignon for Jews trying to escape deportation by the Germans. In the summer of 1944 a camp for German prisoners of war was established near his village, and Trocmé decided that he would deliver sermons to the prisoners on Sunday afternoons after addressing his own congregation on Sunday morning. But this required something of an adjustment in his routine:

> The preparation of my sermons for the Germans required a considerable amount of work. My usual routine was to deliver my sermons based on rather complete notes. Now I had to write out my text in full and request that Mlle. Hoefurt translate it into German. As my visits to the Germans were unpopular among the French, especially to the *maquisards,* I decided to preach in French on Sunday morning precisely the same sermon as the one I would deliver in the afternoon to the Germans.[82]

The challenge of addressing the same content to German POWs and French villagers who had suffered under German occupation must have required considerable thought and preparation; no Jewish preacher that I am aware of had a similar experience.

What can be said about texts of sermons that have indeed been preserved, and that form the core of the current book? Other than tape-recordings, probably the most reliable record of sermons comes from those that were delivered without a written text but recorded stenographically during delivery, then typed up, reviewed by the preacher, and printed soon afterward in pamphlet form.[83] Obviously

---

82 Magda Trocmé, *Magda et André Trocmé: Figures de résistances. Textes choisis et présentés par Pierre Boismorand*, pp. 187–88. Mlle. Hoefurt was a professor of German at the Collège Cévenol, founded in 1938 by French pacifists in Le Chambon-sur-Lignon, where the Trocmés also taught. Maquisards were French resistance fighters during the Occupation.

83 Stenographic transcription during delivery was used for Patristic sermons (especially Augustine, Chrysostom, and others), providing texts that were apparently not subsequently edited by the preacher (see Johannes van Oort, "Augustine, His Sermons and Their Significance," *Harvard Theological Studies*, 65:1 (2009): Article 300, p. 364.

this was impossible in traditional Jewish practice, and it was apparently used only by Reform rabbis in Germany and the United States.[84] Occasionally, where stenographic transcriptions are preserved in archives, we find small blank gaps in the text, where the preacher used a Hebrew or Yiddish word unfamiliar to the stenographer.

This was the pattern used by J. Leonard Levy of Rodef Shalom Congregation, Pittsburgh (no longer living during our period). An eminent successor in that congregation, Solomon Freehof, had a similar technique; according to Walter Jacob, who eventually succeeded him: "Freehof occasionally discussed his sermons casually with me as a young colleague but nothing was written down before delivery, and printed texts came from stenographic or tape recording."[85] Max Nussbaum, describing his experience as a rabbi in Nazi Berlin, wrote, "Leafing through my sermons of those years – which a faithful secretary of mine took down in shorthand while I spoke – I find one from November 4, 1938."[86] This certainly promises a close relationship between the text and what the listeners heard. But the text published in part in his 1970 essay – later included in full in *From Berlin to Hollywood* – is in English, while the sermon was delivered in German. Without a careful comparison between the English text and original German transcription, we cannot be certain exactly how close the words on the printed page are to what was heard. Lewis M. Barth, who grew up in Nussbaum's Los Angeles congregation and helped edit his collection of sermons, wrote, "Nussbaum's greatest talent was in oral presentation. He employed

84 In a collection of his "Sermons, Addresses, Studies" delivered after our period, the American Orthodox rabbi Leo Jung wrote, "Many of them I dictated to Sylvia Haber, my loyal secretary, at the insistence of friends who wanted to see them in print" (Jung, *Harvest: Sermons, Addresses, Studies,* Preface)." This occurred after the delivery, possibly based on outline notes used by the preacher during the delivery and later in the dictation.

85 Jacob, *Pursuing Peace*, p. 54. He continued, "His published sermons were taken from tape-recordings with only the most minor corrections.... Freehof's manner of speaking was free of notes or a text. The sermon had been very carefully thought out, sometimes with notes for us at home, but no sentences were fixed, with the exception of a few opening and closing phrases (p. 55).

86 Nussbaum, "Ministry Under Stress: A Rabbi's Recollection of Nazi Berlin, 1935–1940," in *Gegenwart im Rückblick*, p. 244.

a stenographer to take down his sermons from the tapes on which they were recorded. These 'first drafts' were edited, often by Ruth Nussbaum [the preacher's wife], and then typed in final form by Thelma Cohen, Nussbaum's devoted secretary of many years."[87] Here the stenographic transcriptions were indeed "first drafts" in relation to the published text, but they were the most authentic version of what the congregants actually heard. What was eventually published was several steps removed.

Stenographic transcription, however, was a rare exception to the general pattern, applying only to very large and wealthy congregations with distinguished rabbis who wanted a permanent record of the sermons. Of the many important (and even more of the unimportant) preachers who spoke without written text, the great majority did not have their words stenographically transcribed during delivery. Far more common as evidence for the sermon is the written text, typed or occasionally hand-written by the preacher before delivery.

In many cases, the sermons used in this book were never published, and the texts preserved are in archival collections of institutions or synagogues, or in some cases of family members. The most important examples were sermons by Reform rabbis Leo M. Franklin of Detroit, MI, Ferdinand Isserman of St. Louis, MO, Orthodox Rev. Abraham Cohen of Birmingham (England),[88] Liberal rabbi Israel Mattuck of London, and Orthodox rabbi Salis Daiches of Edinburgh. In the cases of Franklin, Cohen, and Mattuck, as well as Stephen S. Wise of New York and Chief Rabbi Joseph Hertz of London, a large number of sermon texts from the entire period beginning before the First World War and continuing through the end of the Second World War have been preserved. These were obviously texts written by the preacher before delivery, some by hand (Cohen, Daiches), and some on typewriters (Wise, Isserman, Franklin, and Mattuck), although the relationship between the text and the sermon heard

---

87 Lewis M. Barth, "Introduction," in *Max Nussbaum: From Berlin to Hollywood*, p. 2.

88 A collection of Cohen's *Sabbath Sermons* was published by the Soncino Press in 1960, three years after his death, but they are more of the "timeless" nature.

by the listeners is still never absolutely clear. Some preachers may have simply provided a dramatic reading of the text they brought to the pulpit. Others would memorize the written text and speak more freely, occasionally departing from it in matters of style and the formulation of ideas, or sometimes even of content, whether because a new idea occurred to the preacher in the midst of delivery, or because the observed response from the congregation suggested or required modification of what was written, or because the written text was simply taking too long.[89] On the whole, however, the texts preserved in archival collections may be assumed to provide fairly reliable evidence for what was said.

With regard to texts published by the preacher, the relationship is more problematic. In some cases, the differences are not insignificant. One issue pertains to language. In medieval and early modern Jewish homiletical work, a change in language was universal: preaching was almost always in the vernacular, but preachers who wrote up their texts for circulation and later for publication wanted them to be intelligible to educated Jews throughout the world, and they therefore wrote in Hebrew.[90] The published text is therefore in one sense fundamentally different from the sermon that was heard. Moshe Idel, speaking about the Hasidic sermon, has written: "The Hasidic sermon is pre-eminently an oral event taking place between the leader and his disciples, and it is the main tool of creating and communicating his ideas. This is why the vernacular is crucial. The Hebrew versions of the sermons are important for modern scholarship, but they reflect the events in the field to a smaller degree. Com-

89 Describing Abba Hillel Silver, Rabbi Herbert Weiner, who edited the first collection of his sermons, wrote that "It was not unusual for [Silver] to spend two or three days researching and writing down every word of a sermon then memorizing the whole" (*Therefore Choose Life*, p. viii). On the memorizing of fully written texts, cf. Avi M. Schulman, *Like a Raging Fire: A Biography of Maurice N. Eisendrath*, p. 19: "He memorized every speech, amazing his listeners with his vivid prose," and Harold Saperstein, *Witness from the Pulpit*, p. 4.

90 See Marc Saperstein, *Jewish Preaching, 1200–1800*, pp. 39–43, and *Exile in Amsterdam*, pp. 49–51.

munication to the sympathetically predisposed audience therefore invites creativity in a new medium...."[91]

This pattern of preaching in a vernacular language (usually Yiddish) and publishing in Hebrew remained in our period. Shlomo Zalman Ehrenreich in Transylvania preached in Yiddish; the texts of his sermons were translated into Hebrew by his grandson and published posthumously.[92] Shlomo Zalman Unsdorfer in Bratislava preached in Yiddish; the texts of his sermons were found by his son, translated into Hebrew and published in Brooklyn. Unsdorfer actually wrote a full Yiddish text of his sermon on the day before delivery (usually Friday), then made a brief outline which he used during delivery.[93] Kalonymus Kalmish Shapira delivered his Warsaw Ghetto sermons in Yiddish, but they were written - either before or immediately after the holiday or Sabbath - in rabbinic Hebrew.

Tobias (Tuviah) Geffen, preaching in Atlanta in the United States, apparently delivered his sermons in Yiddish, but published them himself in Hebrew.[94] Moses Kahlenberg of Metz served in a congregation of Polish refugees and must have preached in Yiddish, but he himself prepared the texts for publication in Hebrew. His sermons appear in a highly literary style, filled with allusions to biblical and rabbinic texts that seem to be intended more for rabbinic colleagues than for ordinary Jewish listeners. Although the basic content would be the same, there may indeed have been a very different style in the Yiddish delivery.

These are all sermons delivered in Yiddish but originally pub-

---

91 Moshe Idel, *Hasidism Between Ecstasy and Magic*, p. 242.

92 Gershon Greenberg, "Shlomo Zalman Ehrenreich's (1863–1944) Religious Response to the Holocaust," p. 66.

93 Gershon Greenberg, "Shlomo Zalman Unsdorfer: With God through the Holocaust," pp. 62–63, n. 2; also p. 64, reporting that "Before and after giving the sermon he added marginal notes about current events."

94 See the discussion of language in the Introduction to the Geffen sermon in the "Complete Sermons" section. Cf. Menahem Blondheim, "Divine Comedy: The Jewish Orthodox Sermon in America, 1881–1939," p. 194: "A substantial majority of Orthodox American sermons were delivered in Yiddish but published in Hebrew. Built into the study of these texts, therefore, is a very significant distancing between the oral performance and the written record."

lished in Hebrew – and appearing in this book in an English translation. Whenever there is a discrepancy between the language of delivery and the language of the printed text, some of the nuances of style are likely to be lost, but these nuances usually will not undercut the text's importance as a historical source.[95]

In several other cases, the sermons delivered in a vernacular language were originally translated into English for publication. Kalman Chameides, preaching in Katowice, Poland, spoke in Polish (or occasionally in German); his texts were later translated into English for publication by his son.

Although not strictly a sermon or even an address to a Jewish audience, I have included a passage from a speech delivered by Isaac Herzog, then Chief Rabbi of Palestine, on February 15, 1939, at the Roundtable Conference, in St. James's Palace, London. This was an extremely important meeting, in which Jewish leaders sympathetic to Zionism tried to convince the representatives of the British Government to keep the gates of immigration to Palestine open, while Palestinian Arabs, who refused to be in the same room as the Jews, argued the opposite. Herzog, who had been Chief Rabbi in Ireland until 1936, was now Chief Ashkenazi Rabbi of the Yishuv. He must have delivered the address in English, but I have been unable to find the original English text, and have therefore had to translate back into English a selection from a Hebrew translation of his speech.[96]

Ignaz Maybaum, a Liberal rabbi in Germany, was among an impressive number of rabbis permitted to immigrate to England in the spring of 1939; soon after his arrival in London, he began to

95 Saul Levi Morteira, the leading preacher of the Portuguese community of Amsterdam in the first half of the 17th century, preached in Portuguese, the only language his listeners understood; yet he prepared the texts in advance in Hebrew (*Exile in Amsterdam*, pp. 50–51). As a parallel, it is reported by Leo Baeck's granddaughter that when he went on a speaking tour of the United States in 1948, he wrote out his text in his native German, and then prepared to deliver it in English, using a dictionary as reference for the precise meaning of specific words: Marianne C. Dreyfus, "Remembering My Grandfather, Leo Baeck," *CCAR Journal* (Winter 1999), p. 52.

96 In Herzog, *Masu'ah leYitzḥaq*, pp. 118–20; the Hebrew text was originally published in *Haaretz*, April 18, 1939. See the full note at the text.

preach in German to congregations composed of other German-speaking refugees, many of whom did not know English well enough to be able to follow an English-language sermon. In 1941, Maybaum published a collection of sixteen such sermons, "Preached at the Refugees' Services of the United Synagogue London," dated between May 12, 1939 and February 8, 1941, and presented chronologically. In his Preface, he wrote,

> Till the war the sermons were preached in German. Then it was gradually replaced by English, until only English was used. . . . One cannot, even when most of the listeners are German-speaking, preach in the German language while German bombers, as on the Day of Atonement, 1940, roar overhead during the service. (p. viii)

Seven of the sermons were delivered before the outbreak of the war, and were therefore clearly delivered in German. His statement indicates that the 13th sermon, delivered on Yom Kippur 1940, must have been delivered in English, as were the following three sermons. But there is no obvious distinction in the style of the published texts between the first seven (definitely delivered in German and translated by the literary figure Joseph Leftwich) and the last four (definitely delivered in English), and it is unclear to what extent Leftwich might have helped in editing English language texts. The sermons are indeed extremely important because of their content, but conclusions relating to homiletical style must remain tentative.

Turning to the texts published in the language of delivery, occasionally we find an author explaining the relationship between the published text and what was actually said. Abraham M. Hershman, a leading Conservative rabbi in Detroit, wrote in his Foreword, "As for the sermons and addresses which the volume now offered to the public comprises, some have appeared in the press; others have been reproduced from type-written pages; most of them have been written out from notes. Those belonging to the first and second categories are presented just as they were originally written and delivered. I have not added thereto, nor diminished therefrom. The sermons and addresses of the third category have, as a general rule, been abridged, which accounts for their brevity."[97] Very few of the collections, however, contain such clear explanations from the author.

It would not be surprising to learn that a preacher preparing the texts of sermons for publication would review the text, perhaps add references to biblical or rabbinic quotations not mentioned in delivery, and polish the style. This might also be done by a widow, or son or daughter of the preacher following the rabbi's death. But the possibility of more substantial changes remains. The preacher might indeed have determined that the fully written text was simply too long for delivery, and eliminated one or more paragraphs from the text before him – often indicating this by putting the material in [ ]. Thus the published text (or archival text) may contain more than what the congregation actually heard, with the deleted material serving as evidence for what the preacher knew but not for what he transmitted.[98]

Alternatively, the preacher preparing a text for publication might have added a sentence or a paragraph or a page to complete a thought, or to introduce a new theme, that could not be adequately addressed in delivery for reasons of time. This may especially be true with regard to the more "timeless" sermons, the publication of which might be intended as help for future preachers. It is certainly the case that a preacher can often get away with an assertion or theme that is not fully developed in addressing his own congregation, but in a book intended for a wide readership decides that further development is necessary.

In sermons published not for a potential reader's future use but as a record of what was said in crucial moments of the past, such tinkering with the original text is more problematic. Occasionally we encounter in published texts terminology or formulation that simply does not appear to fit the date of delivery. For example, a sermon delivered in Bedford by Emil Ehrnthal (later Michael Elton)

97 Hershman, *Israel's Fate and Faith*, p. xiii.

98 See, for example, *Jewish Preaching in Times of War*, p. 439, on two-and-a-half paragraphs placed in parenthesis by Maurice Eisendrath in a sermon delivered on Rosh Hashanah evening, 1941.

on December 13, 1942 (in his book published in Johannesburg in 1961) bears the title "The Death Camps." There is, however, a serious question as to whether this could have been the original title of his sermon, as the term "death camps" was simply not used at this time.[99] Nevertheless, adding a title to a text at some point after delivery does not does not necessarily invalidate the reliability of the text itself, as the title may never even have been announced to the listeners. More surprising is a detail in the body of this same sermon: "As we have not forgotten the Inquisitions of Spain, so we shall not forget Warsaw, Lublin, Auschwitz, Kieff and countless other cities." While information about Warsaw, Lublin, and Kiev had indeed circulated by this time, "Auschwitz" - not at all a city in the same category - was hardly known even as a concentration camp. Oswiecim was identified as a "Death Camp" in the *JC* two months later on February 12, 1943, p. 1; the first appearance of the word in its German form in the *JC* was not until July 7, 1944. This appears to indicate minor editing of details in the body of the sermon for the purpose of publication. More significant is a passage from a sermon delivered by Abraham M. Hershman on February 19, 1944, Shabbat Shekalim: "In 1938 there were, according to the figures given by Doctor Ruppin, 16,717,000 Jews all over the world. But the plague that had been stayed for a fairly considerable time broke out anew in all its ferocity and worked havoc in Israel. About 6,000,000 Jews perished

99 "Extermination Camps" (*Vernichtungslager*) was used in a publication by the Polish government-in-exile entitled "The Mass Extermination of Jews in German Occupied Poland," reporting publicly on the Note given by the Government to the United Nations on December 10, 1942. It was published in New York, and it contains a text of a Broadcast dated December 17, 1942, so the publication had to be some time after the Ehrnthal sermon, probably in 1943. The earliest use of "death camp" in the JTA was on June 6, 1943, referring to a report of deportation from Bulgaria to Treblinka; on June 29 the JTA again used "death camps" regarding a deportation of Dutch Jews from Theresienstadt. The first use of the term in the *JC* came in August 29, 1942, p. 7, referring to Mauthausen in Austria, where Jews were "murdered by poison gas" (cf. also Sept. 18, 1942, p. 6), but in both cases the term is placed in quotation marks as a reference to a single institution, not to the systematic mass murder being perpetrated in the Polish *Vernichtungslager*. The *JC* began to refer to Oswiecim as a "death camp" on February 12, 1943, p. 1, without any reference to the Polish "death camps" that had been established solely for the murder of Jews.

in the second World War."[100] The number of Jews at the end of 1938 appears in Arthur Ruppin, *The Jewish Fate and Future*, published in 1940. But it is inconceivable that a preacher in February 1944 – some fifteen months before the war ended and before the mass murder of the Hungarian Jewish population – would have announced that "about 6,000,000 Jews perished in the second World War." Indeed, in the Foreword to his book (published in 1952, cited above), Hershman writes that in this one case he has "deemed it necessary, in the interest of correctness, to revise the figures given in two paragraphs" of this sermon (p. xiii), and this is clearly what he has done.

Occasionally we receive a different kind of editorial change admitted by the author. In the Introduction to his *Jewish Survival* (p. xiii), Abraham Mayer Heller, of the Flatbush Jewish Center in Brooklyn, wrote, "The reader must realize the difficulty of recapturing in print the spirit of the spoken word. The success of the sermon is often much the result of the inspiration received from the audience. Recognizing that it is well-nigh impossible to capture in cold print the warmth inherent in the spoken word, I have deleted from these published discourses, where feasible, such methods of approach and phraseology which characterize the oral sermon." This is a clear statement of stylistic change intended to make the text more appropriate for those who would be reading it, but also making clear that in some or perhaps many cases, the text before the reader is not exactly what the listeners actually heard.

Something else that is lost as we read these texts is the situation of the moment. The preacher may assume that the listeners come with some knowledge of what has recently happened, and refer to "the events of the past week" without needing to explain exactly what events he has in mind. Even more important than what listeners might know are their feelings: do they come to the sermon with a sense of sadness, or discouragement, or confusion, or fear, or indifference? And how does the congregation of listeners respond to what is being said as they hear the words, and as they process the message immediately after?

100 Hershman, *Israel's Fate and Faith*, p. 205.

In order to be able to appreciate the significance of a sermon or part of a sermon as a historical source, we need to try to imagine ourselves back in the position of the listeners, hearing the text being delivered by a good public speaker who is (usually) highly respected. In order to understand these texts, we need to try to remove from our minds everything we know about what happened in the months and years after the sermon was delivered, to imagine that as the sermon was being prepared and then delivered, the future was as obscure and opaque as the future is for us today. After the fact, subsequent events may seem obvious – like the "handwriting on the wall" improperly invoked by Israel Levinthal in the Introduction to his collection of sermons. Before the fact, we are simply blind.[101]

As noted above, in some cases passages from a sermon or speech were printed within a few days by daily or weekly newspapers (based on texts submitted to the newspaper either in advance of delivery or afterward, and occasionally based on a reporter who was present). A rather stunning example occurred on Thursday, September 14, 1939, the first day of Rosh Hashanah: the *Newark Evening News* devoted a full page (p. 29) to long quotations from the sermons delivered by three Newark rabbis – Solomon Foster, Leon S. Lang, and Joachim Prinz – all of whom addressed the situation of German Jewry. In the absence of archival texts written by the preachers themselves, these quotations published within a day of delivery are clearly justified as accurate evidence of what was said, probably more so than texts published in collections years later.

An example of greater complexity would be Ephraim Levine's

---

101 For a fine articulation of this principle with regard to the Holocaust by a leading historian, see Jacob Katz, "Was the Holocaust Predictable?," in *The Nazi Holocaust, Part 1: Perspectives on the Holocaust*, ed. Michael R. Manus, pp. 118–37, http://bit.ly/2fNaxRb.

See also Michael André Bernstein, *Foregone Conclusions: Against Apocalyptic History*, p. 16 on "'backshadowing'...in which the shared knowledge of the outcome of a series of events by narrator and listener is used to judge the participants in those events *as though they should have known what was to come*" (Levinthal's statement about the "handwriting on the wall" is a fine example of this), and quoting Michael Ignatieff: "In no field of historical study does one wish more fervently that historians could write history blind to the future."

Shavu'ot sermon, delivered at the West End Synagogue in London on May 31, 1933. A lengthy summary of the sermon, including both direct quotations and paraphrase, was published two and a half weeks later beginning on the first substantial page of *The Jewish Chronicle*, followed later in the same issue by the complete text of the sermon, obviously based on a text submitted by the preacher.[102] The identical complete text of the sermon was then published two years later in Levine's book, *The Faith of a Jewish Preacher: Sermons Spoken and Written*. In using the sermon as evidence not only for what was written but for the message that was communicated, which would be the most important source? The editor's selection of direct quotes and paraphrase, or the complete text as published two weeks after delivery (but on p. 24, which some readers would never get to)? This pattern of publishing lengthy passages of sermons by Chief Rabbi Hertz in the issue of the *JC* soon after delivery, the complete text of which would later be published in collections of the Hertz's addresses, was not at all uncommon during this period.

I turn now to the categories of material *not* included in this collection. Perhaps the most important category to be excluded is the sermon texts for which the preacher provides no clear evidence for the date and place of delivery.

Texts of sermons written by medieval preachers never included the date of delivery. The main purpose of such texts was not so much to provide a record of what an individual had said on a specific occasion, but rather to provide homiletical material for other religious leaders to incorporate into their own sermons. Only on rare circumstances when a sermon was responding to a specific event is the date provided.[103]

Starting in the sixteenth century, when printed collections of sermons became commonplace, a few preachers – e.g., Moses Almos-

102 *JC*, June 16, 1933, pp. 6–7, 24, 27.

103 See, for example, Joseph ibn Shem Tov, in Saperstein, *Jewish Preaching 1200–1800*, pp. 168–69, and in general on the shift in the fifteenth century from texts intended for other preachers to adapt for their own use, to texts intended to record what the preacher had said on a specific occasion, pp. 18–19.

nino in *Ma'amatz Ko'ah* (published in 1588), and Solomon ben Isaac Levi in *Divrei Shelomoh* (published in 1596) – provided full dates for each sermon along with the place of delivery. This practice by no means became standard, however. Saul Levi Morteira, author of the largest number of extant sermon texts, did not regularly provide dates, although many such dates can be determined by his practice of systematically moving from verse to verse through each *parashah*, and occasionally providing dates when he repeated a sermon.[104] In any case, listing dates remained the exception, though in the eighteenth century it was done by Jonathan Eybeschuetz in *Ya'arot Derash* (first published in 1779), and in the nineteenth by Moses Sofer in *Sefer Ḥatam Sofer: Derashot* (first published in 1829).

In the twentieth century, many collections of unpublished sermons have no dates, as can be seen in the American Jewish Archives in Cincinnati. Where the preacher assigned dates to the sermon texts, they are listed in chronological order. But in the more frequent case of dates not provided, they are listed in the archive in alphabetical order by title. With rare exceptions when the date can be determined by internal content, such texts are unusable for the present collection. The same is true for published collections, including, as noted above, much of the material in the three volumes published by Harry Joshua Stern of Temple Emanu-El in Montreal.

An interesting collection of sermon texts was published by Chaplain Aryeh Lev, under the title *What Chaplains Preach*, "a thesis submitted in partial fulfillment of the requirements for obtaining a Certificate of Capacity for promotion to the rank of Captain," completed in September 1941, when the United States was not yet at war. The 128 pages include thirty-four complete (though comparatively short) sermon texts, and thirty-three detailed outlines of sermons, all intended for both Jewish and Christian audiences. Some of these may actually have been delivered by the author, but there is no indication of this, no dates of delivery, no addressing of any clear historical situation.

---

104 At the end of the sermon text, he would write, ("I preached this a second time in the year x"): see Saperstein, *Exile in Amsterdam*, pp. 68–69; since the *parashah* is always clear, the precise date of such sermons can be determined.

Another category of material that will not be included is the "Holiday Messages" written by various religious leaders. A fine example is Joseph H. Hertz, Chief Rabbi of the United Hebrew Congregations of the British Empire. Many of his New Year Messages were published in *The Jewish Chronicle*; at least six of them were later published in books of his writings (1933, 1935, 1937 in *Sermons and Addresses: II Addresses;* 1938, 1941 and 1942 in *Early and Late*). They are powerful, moving statements. But because they do not have the aural dimension, and because there is abundant material from the texts of sermons and addresses delivered to audiences, I have not used this material.

On a more local level, Israel Mattuck of Liberal Jewish Synagogue also wrote New Year Messages, some of which were published in *The Jewish Chronicle*, all published in the synagogue monthly newsletter. Again there is abundant material from his sermons, making the material in the written Messages easy to omit. As noted above, the same applies to the material published by Harold Reinhart each month in "The Synagogue Review" of the West London Synagogue. I have used only one such passage from "The Synagogue Review," where the date of delivery is clear.

I have not used newspaper articles or editorials from Jewish or general newspapers, except where they provide direct quotations from sermons and the date of delivery is clear. (An example would be the text of the sermon delivered on September 9, 1939 by the leading rabbi of Scotland, Salis Daiches, which is quoted extensively in *The Jewish Chronicle*, apparently based on a text submitted to it.) During this period *The Jewish Chronicle* included a weekly column entitled "Sermon of the Week," a feature introduced in 1912; occasionally these texts touch upon topics relevant to Nazi persecution, but I have not used them because there is no clear connection with oral delivery to a congregation of listeners.[105] In general, the newspaper articles

105 Since these sermons appear in the Friday edition of the paper and apply to the scriptural readings for the following day, it is extremely unlikely that the author of the column would use the same text for his own congregation, when many of them would have read it already. (One Scottish preacher, Rev. M. Simmons, was subjected to complaints by congregants in 1931 because of "the modern subjects of his sermons, which Simmons allegedly published in a daily newspaper on the

and editorials have already been studied in a number of important academic works, and I have therefore decided to focus on the texts bearing direct reference to oral communication.

At one point in the preparation of this book I had considered including a limited number of Christian sermons alongside the Jewish texts, for purposes of comparison. At virtually every public protest gathering, leading representatives of Protestant and Catholic Christian communities were included among the speakers, and I have gathered some very powerful examples of Christians condemning the treatment of their Jewish neighbors. I have decided to omit this material for reasons of space, but with the conviction that a similar study of the Christian pulpit is desirable.[106]

Links with Biblical Themes

There was a natural tendency in sermons, especially those delivered by Orthodox or Conservative rabbis, to connect their message with a biblical theme, especially a theme related to either the holiday on which the sermon was delivered, or the biblical passage being read on Shabbat. These connections generally assert a theme of continuity between the startling events of the present and the familiar events of the past, implying that there will be some comfort in realizing that our ancestors have survived similar forms of persecutions, that there is a pattern in history, that all is part of a divine plan. As a bridge to the actual texts, I will provide a few examples of such connections as a conclusion to this Introduction.[107]

---

day proceeding the Sabbath service when he was supposed to deliver them"; Ben Braber, *Jews in Glasgow, 1879–1939*, p. 151.) The archival papers of Salis Daiches of Edinburgh include typed texts of at least twenty-one sermons that he sent between 1940 and 1944 to be used as the Sermon of the Week to the *JC*; these were of course published without his name. The same is true for the weekly column written by Rabbi Abraham J. Feldman as Editor of *Connecticut Jewish Ledger*, the local Jewish newspaper of Hartford Connecticut.

106 A model would be Dean C. Stroud, ed., *Preaching in Hitler's Shadow: Sermons of Resistance in the Third Reich.*

107 The fuller passages in which these brief quotations appear can be found below through the date of delivery and the preacher's name.

Pesach of 1933, coming a few weeks after the first mass protest rally in the United States, presented a fine opportunity for making connections with the past. On April 11, 1933, the first day of Pesach, Israel Levinthal of Brooklyn, New York, preached on the topic, "The Old Pharaoh in Modern Garb," a theme that continues throughout the sermon:

> Not for many years has the story we read in the Passover Haggadah, as we sit at our Seder table, had the reality for us that it has in our day. What new meaning do we find in the words, "For not one alone arose to destroy us, but in every generation some rise up against us to destroy us!"
>
> We thought that now, at least, in this glorious twentieth century, we had passed this stage of history – that Pharaohs were a thing of the past – when, lo and behold, another Pharaoh rises before our very eyes. "In every generation it is incumbent on every Israelite to look upon himself as if he had actually gone forth from Egypt," the Haggadah says. Alas, in this generation, it has become necessary for every Israelite in certain lands of Europe to look upon himself as if he were actually living in Egypt once again."

On the same day across the ocean, Chief Rabbi Joseph Hertz turned to a rather unfamiliar rabbinic tradition in making the connection between "Ancient Egypt and Present-Day Germany":

> Rabbinic legend tells us that Pharaoh did not share the fate of his horsemen at the Red Sea. He alone escaped drowning; nay more, he escaped death. He stands forever at the gates of Hell; and as, in the course of the centuries, oppressor after oppressor enters, he greets them with the words, "Why have ye not profited by my example?"...
>
> I shall not labour the Egyptian analogy. But one need be neither Rabbi nor even religionist to see that the world is built somehow on moral foundations, and that no nation which chooses anti-Semitism, i.e., the will to hate, as the basis of its national life, can have a future.

And here is Marcus Ehrenpreis on the same day in Stockholm, Sweden: "A comparison between the memory of Egypt and the events of today inevitably obtrudes, at once disheartening and consoling. It proves that despite several thousand years of civilization, we have failed to gain any appreciable ground in terms of our humanity."

A year later, Israel Goldstein in New York would also emphasize in his Pesach sermon the similarities between antiquity and the present: "The four-fold condition suffered by our ancestors in Egypt is duplicated in the tragic story of the Jew in Nazified Europe since 1933. Physical atrocities have been perpetrated upon thousands of Jews with a brutality reminiscent of the Egyptian Pharaoh." But nine years later, in the spring of 1942, Hertz would emphasize the differences: "The tidal wave of ghastly carnage passing over Russian and Polish Jewry is infinitely worse than anything that Pharaoh of old ever was guilty of. The murderers will have the same end. . . . " There were indeed some traditionalist preachers who delivered Pesach sermons in the ghettos without any reference to the present, as if the insistence on refusal to recognize the Nazis and the world they had created was a kind of internal triumph.[108] But for most, the connection with antiquity was too natural to ignore.

If Pharaoh and the enslavement of the Hebrew was a natural theme, another, though somewhat less familiar, was Amalek, who also became an archetypal enemy of the Jews.[109] Sometimes he was presented as a source of hope. Here is Harris Swift at the St. John's Wood Synagogue in London, 1936:

> To-day, we stand at Rephidim (Exod. 17:8). Amalek assails our people in many countries of the world, yes, even in this citadel of freedom in which we are proud to claim ourselves as loyal subjects. At Rephidim Amalek was overcome by the uplifted

108 See, for example, the Pesach sermons of Ephraim Oshry delivered in the Kovno Ghetto: Saperstein, "*Your Voice Like a Ram's Horn*," pp. 21–22.

109 This theme could of course be used in different ways. Compare the sermon "War With Amalek!" delivered by David Einhorn in Philadelphia on Shabbat Zakhor, March 19, 1864, in the middle of the American Civil War, in Saperstein, *Jewish Preaching in Times of War*, pp. 197–98, 210–21.

> hands of Moses, by the faith in God which those uplifted hands symbolized (Exod. 17:11–13). At Rephidim to-day, our answer to Amalek must continue to be the same message that Moses taught the children of Israel, the same lessons that have been the bulwark of Israel's spiritual life throughout the ages, the same Torah, the same ideals, the same faith. Our answer to our enemies to-day must be hands uplifted and eyes upraised to the God of our fathers.

Here it is a victory through the spirit that is emphasized, not a physical confrontation.

In the spring of 1939, almost three years later, Israel Levinthal in New York, though also emphasizing the continuity, had a different emphasis:

> In describing and in analyzing the battle which the Amalekites, the first anti-Semites in history, waged against the Jews in the wilderness, the Bible significantly says, *Milchama la-Adonoy Ba-Amalek*, "the war which Amalek wages is against God; *Midor dor*, in every generation when Amalek appears, *Ki Yad al Kes Yah*, for the hand of Amalek is against the throne of God!" (Exod. 17:16). That is the meaning of the attacks of the modern successors to the ancient Amaleks. It is a war to destroy God, to eradicate God from the hearts and minds of men. In this struggle the Jew is not only defending himself, he is battling in defense of God, in defense of civilization.

And here, a year later, is a strikingly different use, in a sermon delivered by Kalonymus Kalmish Shapira in the Warsaw Ghetto:

> Before Amalek came to fight with you, there were among you some lowly individuals to whom secular wisdom, of which Amalek boasted, was attractive. For this reason your enthusiasm for the Torah and the Torah's wisdom was cooled. You said in effect, "Secular wisdom too, is admirable; it too presents [guidelines for] ethical behavior; it contributes to the improvement of this physical world." God arranged matters so that Amalek would engage you with all his vaunted wisdom, exposing for you all his

> wickedness, the foulness of his heart, his murderous character, and the decadence of his wisdom..... Therefore, "It shall be that when the Lord your God gives you rest,... you shall blot out [the memory of Amalek]" (Exod. 17:14) – at least from now on, when, with God's help you will be delivered from him and he will be obliterated, you must at least come to recognize that in all the world's wisdom there is not even a shred of goodness. They are able to preach beautifully, but their insides are of mire.

For this ultra-Orthodox preacher, the present Amalek represents the seductions of secular wisdom, and is now exposed in all his wickedness to convince the Jews that everything related to the secular world must be rejected.

Amalek appears again in a sermon for Purim entitled "The Wandering Amalek," delivered on March 8, 1941, by Eliezer Berkovits, who had moved from Germany to Leeds in England:

> The wandering Jew does not travel alone; he is accompanied by the wandering Amalek. We have known him since first we made our appearance on the stage of the world's history. Amalek has driven us from country to country, he has followed us from nation to nation. It has always been the same story: Jews fleeing from oppression, wandering on deserted tracks, hoping for rest, longing for safety, and when they thought that they found it at last – "Then came Amalek" (Exod. 17:8). Jews run from Amalek, but Amalek is everywhere. They say the Jew is ubiquitous, much more so is Amalek. They call us international, much more so is Amalek.
>
> Once more Amalek has come; but this time he has laid aside his mask and revealed himself in his true shape. This time he has come not only to us Jews, but, like a lightning scourge, he has swooped down on the nations and the whole of mankind. For the first time in history he has revealed himself in his true colours. Amalek! The enemy of the Jews, the enemy of the world.

Purim was a holiday that did not have nearly the level of significance or high seriousness that Pesach brought, but its story provided another powerful connection between persecution in the past and contemporary realities. Here is Abba Hillel Silver of Cleveland, preaching on Purim, 1936:

> Haman prepared the gallows for Mordecai, and on those gallows not Mordecai but Haman was hanged. The Nazis prepare destruction for the Jewish people, but there is a law of history which operates not only in Shushan but in Berlin. And that law of history says that in the long last, bigotry, intolerance, and hate do not win the day. Haman, the symbol of hate, is led by Mordecai, the symbol of faith, in triumph through the capital. In the long last, it is the ideals of freedom, good will, and tolerance that will win in these days.
>
> So Purim comes to us with a reassuring message.... [H]owever dark the world around them may be – on the festival of Purim, on this festival of reassurance, on this day which reminds them of recurrent threats and of the deliverance of their people, the brothers of Mordecai laugh joyously and confidently and, laughing, they face the future.

Two sermons delivered by New York rabbis on Purim 1938, a few days after the *Anschluss* that ended Austrian independence, reveal strikingly different uses of the Purim story and the homiletical difficulties in applying biblical texts to contemporary events. Here once again is Israel Levinthal, preaching on "The Story of Purim: A Challenge to the Hamans of All Ages," arguing that the holiday has a deeper meaning than is usually assumed:

> We should make more of this festival, because it is a challenge to all the Hamans – past, present, and those to come!...
>
> But though the world was crushed beneath his [Haman's] heel, he met his end, nevertheless. He was eventually destroyed by the very force that he tried to annihilate: the spirit of the Jew! It happened in the past, and it shall happen again in our days. The race is not to the swift, nor the battle to the strong (Ecclesiastes 9:11). One nation after another may be conquered and crushed, one hundred and twenty-seven peoples may be forced

> into bondage for the modern *Herrenvolk*, but *bigness* alone will not avail the tyrant. The end is already foretold. What happened to the Haman of Persia will happen to the Haman *hamolekh*, who [currently] holds sway.

Haman, the villain of the story, is clearly a reference to Hitler. But in the Purim story, Haman was not the person who had ultimate authority in the Persian realm. This realization apparently led Levinthal's colleague Abraham Heller, to provide a novel reading of the biblical narrative:

> Ahasuerus, according to the rabbis, personified autocratic dictatorship in the ancient world, with power of life and death over all. The salient facts in the book of Esther corroborate this rabbinic version. Haman was only the anti-Semitic German Streicher of the Persian era.[110] With all his influence and power, his life was forfeit at the first displeasure of Ahasuerus, the real dictator.
>
> As I listened in the synagogue to the reading of the tale of woe, recounted in the Purim Scroll, my very being rebelled against dictators of all times, including those of our day… Noble voices in the days of Persia were silenced because of the dictatorship of Ahasuerus who, as the self-appointed ruler, made foreign conquest and internal oppression the policy of his reign; the policy is no less pursued by the dictators of our day. It therefore becomes our stupendous task to bring democracy back to a stricken world….

Here Haman plays a secondary role, while the true villain of the story is the man of highest political authority, Ahasuerus, who represents Hitler in Nazi Germany. The underlying theme is the danger of dictatorship and the need for democracy. But it twists the biblical narrative (and most of the rabbinic expansions as well) to make the Persian king the ultimate villain, and to suggest that the idea of

---

110 Founder and editor of the viciously antisemitic periodical *Der Stürmer*, Julius Streicher was a friend and associate of Hitler, from 1934 through the rest of the 1930s. See the full text of Heller's sermon below in, "Complete Sermons."

persecution and ultimately murder of the Jews came not from Hitler himself but from Streicher, a lower figure in the regime.

The following year, in a sermon probably delivered on Purim 1939, Orthodox rabbi Mnachem Risikoff of Brooklyn, preaching in Yiddish, drew upon aggadic passages from the Talmud to emphasize the connection between Haman and Hitler (though the published version of the sermon in Hebrew never spells out the name "Hitler"). While severely criticizing the silence of the free nations in response to the persecution of Jews and the recent Nazi seizure of control over Austria and the Sudetenland, Risikoff insists that God is ultimately responsible for Hitler, as a means of inspiring the Jewish people to repentance for their sins:

> There is also a statement in the Gemara [b. Sanhedrin 97b] that the Holy One, praised be He, will in the future raise a king as cruel as Haman, who will cause the Jews to repent; see the passage there. When we see the wicked H-r . . . and all that he has done, it becomes clear that he is indeed the primal, wicked Haman, about whom the Sages wrote that He "will raise a king . . . in order to punish the Jews and bring them to repent," for the function of both [Haman and Hitler] is the same. . . .

Risikoff concluded his sermon with the assertion that this punishment administered by God was the prelude to the messianic redemption, which he believed would occur in the current year 5699, before September of 1939.

Three years later on Purim 1942, when the situation had become significantly worse as systematic mass murder on the Eastern Front had begun, Israel Gerstein of Chattanooga, Tennessee, recognized the homiletical difficulties of a simple matching of characters and proposes his own solution:

> Does the *Megillah* give us any hope that the story will repeat itself in modern times? This is a vital question, not only for our people in Europe. It is a question that all are asking, and not only Jews. Can we derive any comfort from the *Purim* story? Is Hitler another Haman? The conditions today are so unlike those in

> far-off Persia. For one thing, Haman was not a dictator. Before he could do anything, he had to consult the king. Hitler is Haman and *Ahashvayrosh* rolled into one. Is there any hope that a modern Esther will turn his head? Hitler is supposed to be immune to women. The German propaganda machine pictures him as a sort of *Tsaddik* who cannot even bear to look at a woman. That rules out the Esther angle. But does that mean there is no hope?...

Here is a preacher struggling to make a connection between the current realities, the biblical past, and the opaqueness of the future.

The final holiday that provided a natural occasion for linking the present reality with an oppressor from the past was Hanukkah. Not surprisingly, the sermons delivered on the Sabbath or Sunday during Hanukkah week frequently used the Maccabees as models of resistance to an external oppressor, though usually overlooking the extent of divisiveness within the Jewish population during the second century BCE. In December 1936, Solomon Freehof of Pittsburgh preached on the topic "When Religion Goes to War: A Call to Jews and Christians." His theme here was not persecution of the Jews, but rather the intrusion of the state into the realm of religious freedom: "As in ancient Judaea against Antiochus, as in Germany against the Nazi state, so it will be everywhere against all forces which seek to dominate the prophetic function of mankind's sanctuaries. Religion may be at times ignored, it may be often attacked, but it will never permanently be controlled." Two years later, a month after *Kristallnacht*, the situation of the Jews was Freehof's focus:

> We Jews are on the defensive. Why should we not be? We are being attacked on all sides. Slanders are disseminated against us and we have the wearisome task of answering them. Great Jewish communities are being disintegrated under the hammer blows of tyranny. We must find means of "picking up the pieces." We are in a position in the modern world where we must use up all our energies in self-protection.

Pointing to the active, dynamic response of the Maccabees as a model for contemporary Jews, he continues, "Whenever Hanukkah comes and we think of the Maccabean valor we feel a little bit ashamed of the fact that we have gotten to be so timorous, that life has made us so meek and apologetic."

A year later, the war had begun, though Americans had no part in it. Abba Hillel Silver of Cleveland, preaching on "The Weak in the Hands of the Strong," set up the role of the Maccabees in a rather compelling manner:

> It was a resistance against an attempt to establish totalitarianism in that part of the world, an attempt to coordinate Judea and the Jewish people into the vast fabric of a uniform paganism. The Jews resisted this attempt at *Gleichschaltung*.... [Today] many see nothing but doom. The Jewish people are being liquidated with fire and sword. Yet, by all records of history, we are not weak at all but strong, so strong as to frighten the Antiochus's of our day, the modern exponents of neo-paganism. We Jews are today, even as we were then, the principal adversaries of all who would be dictators of mankind. Judah the Maccabee has shown us the road, the road of sacrifice and suffering, perhaps the road of martyrdom, but the road of conviction, the road for the whole of mankind, and the road for us Jews particularly. We have been attacked. Our answer should be a counterattack - determined, powerful - upon all kinds of wickedness and shameful unjustness....

The counterattack endorsed by the preacher, unlike the role of the Maccabees, was not of a military nature.

In addition to the themes raised by holidays, there are other biblical narratives arising from the weekly readings that often were used in sermons addressing Nazi persecution and mass murder. The binding of Isaac is read both during the cycle of weekly readings and on Rosh Hashanah. Its relevance to Nazi persecution is not nearly as apparent as the narratives about Pharaoh, Amalek, and Haman, but it was occasionally invoked. Here is Israel Goldstein, preaching on Kol Nidre evening, 1938, linking current events with the experience of Jews in the past, but then moving on to present the *Akedah* as a model of sacrifice for spiritual values that goes beyond previous experience:

> What Polish Jewry suffers one year, German Jewry another year, and what nearly all of European Jewry suffers today, are the latest links in a chain of tragedy which stretches from the barbarity of the Roman legions in the first century, to the ferocity of the Christian Crusades in the eleventh century, to the sadistic bigotry of the Inquisition in the fifteenth and sixteenth centuries.... Never before has the ethical basis of our existence been so convincing. It makes the "Akedah," the sacrifice, worthwhile. Jews in many lands stand not only on the physical war front. They are in the front-line trenches of the spiritual war front. The story of Isaac's sacrifice at Moriah becomes a lesson in current events.

Here the role of Abraham seems to be ignored, while the emphasis is purely on the theme of sacrifice, understood largely in a spiritual sense, as it preceded the realities of mass murder.

More compelling homiletically is the use by Kalonymus Kalmish Shapira in the Warsaw Ghetto in October 1940, which was on the first *yahrzeit* of the death of Shapira's son Elimelekh during the German bombing of Warsaw.

> [T]he test of Abraham and Isaac involved their will and intention [to martyrdom], but was not completely consummated in actuality, since the angel said, "Lay not your hand upon the lad" (Gen. 22:12). Therefore, every occurrence of Jews being killed by Gentiles with circumstances reversed – that is, with the actuality of death but without the intentional choosing of martyrdom – is a fulfillment of Isaac's *Akedah*. The *Akedah* was the beginning, characterized by intention and desire [for martyrdom]; the conclusion and actualization is now. That is to say, the *Akedah* together with all subsequent cases of Jews being murdered [on account of their Jewishness] constitute one event.

Here the preacher appears to identify directly with Abraham, as he himself and other Jews go beyond the biblical narrative in actually experiencing the death of their children, though without being given a choice.

Another biblical theme used in the sermons was the relationship between Jacob and Esau. On November 11, 1939, the first anniversary of *Kristallnacht*, Ignaz Maybaum, preaching in German to a congregation of German refugees in London, began his sermon by quoting the verse from the weekly *parashah*, "And Esau hated Jacob because of the blessing that Isaac had given to Jacob" (Gen. 27:41). "This explains Jewish history as far as it is a history of suffering," he continued. "'Because of the blessing!'" "Such hatred" – referring of course to the hatred exhibited by the Nazis – "is devilish. And Jacob-Israel must for a part of his life's road be accompanied by this devilish hate." There are certainly other components of the story that could be emphasized, including the deceitful behaviour of Jacob and the later reconciliation with his brother. Here – following a theme in rabbinic and medieval exegesis – Esau is used to represent the most oppressive, "devilish" force at the time: Nazi Germany.

A somewhat surprising example of applying enemies in the weekly readings to contemporary events is revealed in a sermon delivered by Israel Levinthal of Brooklyn in June 1941 entitled, "The Rebellion of Korah: A Parallel to Events of Today." In the biblical narrative, Korah heads a challenge to the leadership of Moses, but is by no means an arch-enemy of the Israelites; in at least one passage of the rabbinic literature, he is presented rather sympathetically as trying to protect an impoverished widow from the oppressive financial demands imposed upon her by biblical law.[111] But this is not how Levinthal presents him:

> Korah still lives, and has risen out of the darkness of hell to do his devilish work again. Change the name of Korah to Hitler, and all the Biblical and Rabbinic descriptions take on a living significance for our day. *Va-yikach Hitler, Lokach Et Atzmo.*[112] Hitler took himself for this task of destruction. People ridiculed him and laughed at him for his attempt to win world leadership.... But

111 Midrash on Psalms, 1:15.

112 Literally, "Hitler took" (based on the first two Hebrew words of Num. 16:1), followed by Rashi's interpretation of these words ("he took himself"), cited earlier in the sermon.

> ignorant though he undoubtedly was, *Pi-ke-ach Hayah*,[113] he, like Korah, was shrewd, and intuitively he knew how to make the most of other people's weaknesses. And through the drawing power of words, he won to himself the leaders of hate and evil.

Levinthal apparently felt compelled to make these kinds of connections, emphasizing the continuities between the biblical past and the present, but occasionally congregants – though undoubtedly impressed by a degree of homiletical ingenuity – might have felt that he was pushing too hard.

A final example of biblical connections, here not from the Torah but from the Early Prophets, is found in a powerful Rosh Hashanah sermon delivered by the young Orthodox rabbi Akiba Predmesky on Kol Nidre, 1943. Here Predmesky focuses on a surprising figure, Eli, High Priest of the temple at Shilo, who allowed the ark of the Law to be taken out of its shrine and brought with the Israelite soldiers into battle with the Philistines. The narrative builds when a messenger comes back from the battlefront and reports to Eli (1 Sam. 4:17). It was one of the great disasters of biblical history, and each of the phrases in the report is applied to the present. I cite just the key phrases from the biblical verse and the beginnings of their application:

> *Israel has fled before its enemies and there has been a great slaughter among the people.* Aye, from the English Channel to the Mediterranean, from the Baltic to the Black Sea, from the marsh-lands of Russia to the yellow earth of China, Israel has been defeated. In the past year, two million Jews have been murdered in cold blood, in Hitler's Europe alone....
>
> To many of you I bring still another message, *and thy two sons Chophni and Pinchos are dead*, a message not only of national tragedy but also of personal grief. How many of us who are here tonight had fathers and mothers in Poland, brothers and sisters in Germany, relatives and friends in Russia, of whom we have

113 Based on Rashi's comment on Num. 16:7, cited earlier in the sermon with regard to Korah.

> not heard since the beginning of the war; relatives by blood and marriage whose whereabouts are unknown, whose very life and death is in the balance!…
>
> But there is still a third and more tragic message that I must bring to you on this holy eve – a message which even the heroic High Priest Eli felt to be the most heart-rending and the most threatening of all: *The Ark of G-d has been taken* by the enemy! In every land that has been conquered, in every country that has been vanquished, in every city where the hordes of barbarians have passed, our synagogues have been burned to the ground, the Holy Arks desecrated and the Scrolls of the Law trodden and spat upon. Our great schools of learning in Lithuania and Poland are closed; our famous Yeshivoth of Slabodka, Telz, Mir, destroyed; and countless numbers of their scholars, rabbis, and leaders, tortured and executed.…

Powerful as these words seem in a printed text, how much more they must have been when spoken by their rabbi at a time when the battle was not yet completed.

Continuity versus Uniqueness

All of these passages raise a central issue for the preachers. They seem to reflect the keen desire to present a message of continuity between the past and the present. As noted above, the reason is apparent: despite the calamities of the past, starting from Pharaoh and Amalek and Haman and Antiochus, and continuing through the destruction of the Temple by the Romans, the Crusades, the Spanish Inquisition and the pogroms, the Jewish people has survived and often continued to thrive, while the enemies are preserved only in the ancient records. That pattern appears to reveal a plan on the part of the Almighty: the suffering of Jews exists for a purpose, and it is only temporary.

We find many examples of this message in the sermons. In his Address to British Preachers given in 1935, Chief Rabbi Hertz appealed to more recent history, asserting that the tragedy of German Jewry "reproduces many of the horrid details in the measures taken by the Inquisition against the New Christians 500 years ago, and is a resurrection of the spirit of Czarist Russia in its attitude towards the Jewish people." Similarly, though with a longer span of precedents, Israel Goldstein of New York on Kol Nidre, 1938: "What Polish Jewry suffers one year, German Jewry another year, and what nearly all of European Jewry suffers today, are the latest links in a chain of tragedy which stretches from the barbarity of the Roman legions in the first century, to the ferocity of the Christian Crusades in the eleventh century, to the sadistic bigotry of the Inquisition in the fifteenth and sixteenth centuries."[114]

A more general statement was made by Charles E. Shulman, of Glencoe, Illinois, in a sermon delivered on Rosh Hashanah, 1940: "How much of the present-day suffering is a repetition of past cruelties inflicted upon innocent peoples only the Jew of the world can tell. How much of the wanton destructiveness of European culture by the Nazis is a memento of other depredations and injuries only he who bears memories of similar events can know. He has seen it happen before. His life has protested against it while he has continued the dream and the labors for a better day. In the thirteenth century many Jewish graves were desecrated and plundered in Spain, Italy, and Germany, lands which are under Fascist rule today...."[115]

Emil Ehrnthal in London, presenting the events of the past in reverse chronological order, insisted in the spring of 1941 that the contemporary oppression actually could help Jews understand their previous history: "Events and personalities of our days have revitalised the dead figures of the dusty pages of history. Incredulous as we were of the tortures and cruelties inflicted upon our people in the

114 In both passages, the connection between Nazi Germany and the Spanish Inquisition – a judicial institution of the Church that had no jurisdiction over Jews per se but investigated the heresy of "Judaizing" by Jews who had been baptized and their descendants, and executed only those who were deemed guilty and refused to repent – seems extremely problematic.

115 Note that the preacher portrays the present as a recursion of medieval persecution, which is a sign of hope! There is no sense of a radical difference, as systematic mass murder has not yet begun.

Middle Ages, now we see them all re-enacted on a more thorough and gigantic scale. It is not bygone days anymore, it is not yesterday, it is *today*. The first ghetto in Rome, the sailing of our brethren from the shores of Spain, the long siege and fall of Jerusalem, the battles of the Maccabees, the frustration of Haman, yes, even the oppression of the Pharaohs, we all understand them, we feel them, *now*."

There were, however, also many who emphasized the element of discontinuity, the difference between the contemporary persecution and that of the past. At a Day of Intercession and Prayer held in July 1938, Rev. D. Bueno de Mesquita of the Spanish and Portuguese Synagogue in London said that "it has been left for these days of twentieth-century civilization to contribute the saddest, the cruellest, the most inhuman chapter in all the long and chequered history of the Jews. There is a coldly calculated campaign of ultimate annihilation, being pressed home with every weapon known to brute violence and to warped intellect." On Rosh Hashanah 1939, Israel Levinthal said that "As far as the Jew is concerned, there is no period in his sorrowful past that offers a parallel to the tragedy that has come upon him today."

A year later, on Rosh Hashanah 1940, Leo Franklin of Detroit ratcheted up the rhetoric of uniqueness further: "Before the fate which Nazism has decreed for us, all the tragedies of the centuries, if they could be counted and combined, would be insignificant. Rivers of tears the Jew has shed through centuries of time, but all of them emptied into a common sea would not compare in magnitude and depth with the oceans of bitterness which his weeping has formed in the single year which comes to a climax tonight." And here is Orthodox Rev. Abraham Cohen of Birmingham, England, in his sermon entitled "A New Universe," extending the uniqueness beyond the historical experience of the Jews to all of human history, "I doubt whether in the whole career of the human race so much cruelty, havoc, and wretchedness have been witnessed within the space of a single year. The worst atrocities committed by savages in the darkest periods of the past were far less cruel than what has been perpetrated during the year which has gone, because the modern barbarians acted in the coldest deliberation and with calculated ferocity, consciously planned with the aid of the vastly increased scope of devastation which scientific invention made possible for them."

Six months later, Mesquita condemned the German nation for crimes against the Jews "which, for sheer colossal weight, for fiendish cunning, for savage cruelty, for callous contempt of all that is sacred and humanly decent, has known no equal in the long history of mankind." And on Hanukkah 1942, in response to the public confirmation of the German policy of mass murder, Israel Mattuck said that "Several million Jews are suffering from a persecution more vile, cruel, and far-reaching than any which our forefathers ever had to endure." Rather than using previous historical examples of persecution and trauma as a way of reassuring listeners that the Jewish people will survive the current oppression as well, these preachers, and others, articulated a recognition of aspects of the Nazi program that were unprecedented. The irony is that except for the last quotation from Mattuck, these formulations were made before the true uniqueness of systematic mass murder applied to all the Jews in German-occupied Europe began to be implemented.

Where Is God?

The purpose of this collection is to present sermon texts chronologically as historical sources for what rabbinical leaders in various countries knew about the events and how they responded in presenting this knowledge to their congregants and others. It is not intended to focus on the theological dimensions of the material, as theology is not my field of expertise. Nevertheless, there is some historical significance in the extent to which rabbinic sermons raise powerful questions about the role of God in the events being discussed, as these questions undoubtedly – and in many cases explicitly – reflect the profound dismay not only of the preacher but also apparently of congregants. It is important to recognize which external events made rabbis begin to acknowledge explicitly a problem that they could not ignore.

Very few examples of this theological question can be found in the sermons delivered during the first six years of the Nazi era. An apparent exception to this is found in a sermon delivered by Abraham Halpern, a Conservative rabbi of St. Louis, Missouri, on the seventh day of Pesach, 1934, entitled "Is God to Blame?" The problem he raises, however, is not directly linked with persecution of the Jews, but rather with the growing militarism of European countries:

> Armies are being increased at a more staggering rate. Navies are being built, and nations are hating one another more than before. They are jealous of one another. And war is said to be nearer to us, as if we had forgotten the horror of the last war.... And if this new war comes upon the world, are we going to ask, "Why does God allow the war?" Will God be to blame?

The rhetorical questions indicate a recognition that this was not a new problem, but one that had already been raised during the Great War.[116]

After *Kristallnacht*, the focus on Jews becomes critical. A fine early example is a sermon by Ignaz Maybaum delivered in German to a London congregation of refugees in May 1939, not long after his own arrival in England as a refugee from Germany.

> Is the faith of our fathers our faith? Is it our unshakeable possession? Or are we like a man I know – and each one of us nowadays knows such a man himself – who said to me when he came out of the concentration camp, "Well, Rabbi, after what I've gone through, can you still tell me that this is God's world, that this is a world that was created by a merciful and compassionate God?"
>
> Every refugee is a Job. And Job's question is on the lips of us all: Why do the just suffer?...

Here the rhetorical questions, which continue for four more sentences, reflect the experience of those who had faced persecution directly.

It was during the High Holy Days of 1940, following the German

116 For a clear example of this, see the sermon delivered by J. Leonard Levy of Pittsburgh on the first preaching occasion after America entered the war: Saperstein, *Jewish Preaching in Times of War*, pp. 327–28, 332–35.

conquests of Belgium, the Netherlands, and France, and the humiliating British retreat from Dunkirk the previous spring, that the theological problem becomes a central concern of the preachers. I have published elsewhere the complete text of a sermon entitled "God in the Blackout," delivered by Reform rabbi Jacob Rudin on Rosh Hashanah evening, which expresses his own agony in reconciling his beliefs with the realities of the contemporary world: "Where is God in this blackout of humanity? How can He permit this savagery to come to pass? How can He allow the destruction of little children, of cities and of homes, to go on unchecked?" These questions were of course posed before America had entered the war, and before Jews were being systematically murdered.[117]

The same theme was addressed by a number of other leading rabbis. Irving Reichert of San Francisco spoke similarly on the evening of Kol Nidre of the same year: "Bewildered by the triumphs of the forces of evil, confounded by the tragedy that has overwhelmed peace-loving peoples, baffled by the success of an inverted morality, people are asking in tones of bitterness and sorrow, of meditation and challenge: How can God permit such things to happen? 'Where is thy God?'... Today this question is one which no honest preacher will attempt to evade."

And here is Abba Hillel Silver of Cleveland on Rosh Hashanah, 1940: "Frequently during the past few years, and more especially during the past few months, I have heard men ask: 'Where is God?'" Silver, however, appears to be significantly less sympathetic to the question than Rudin and Reichert:.... "It is when men are hurt, bereaved, or helpless that many people become rebellious and caviling and demand, 'Where is God? Why does He allow this? Why does He not intervene?' The power which they did not invoke gratefully in times of prosperity they cavil at fretfully in their adversity."[118]

Nor was this kind of questioning restricted to Reform rabbis. On

117 For the complete text, see *Jewish Preaching in Times of War*, pp. 399–418.

118 The original title for this sermon is "Our Responsibility for Evil." Silver published the same sermon text in the second volume of his sermons under the title, "Where is God?," vol. 2: 16–22.

Shabbat immediately preceding Rosh Hashanah, 1940, Orthodox rabbi Leo Jung of New York preached on the topic "God in the Crisis." "'Where is God?' People query.... 'What is the use of our faith in the Lord and of all our hopes? What can we do against ten thousand death-dealing airplanes? What is the value of the still small voice of conscience against the roaring fury of totalitarian propaganda?'" And in France, which had directly suffered the devastating humiliation of a German conquest and partial occupation, Orthodox rabbi Jacob Kaplan, who had left Paris for Vichy, spoke in December 1940 on the topic "Not By Might, Nor by Power." He too recognized the questions that were being raised in response:

> At present, because once again we have found ourselves under trial, it is our fellow Jews who are asking whether God may have abandoned us. I am well aware that they speak this way because of their extreme suffering, and because despair elicits cries of doubt along with cries of pain. I would like to say simply the following: others in the past have had doubts like yours....[119] Each era has thus brought its cluster of sufferings that have evoked crises of doubt and despair among our ancestors.

Apparently Kaplan thought it would be reassuring to his congregants to validate their questions by reminding them that Jews in earlier periods had asked them as well.

By Rosh Hashanah 1941, preachers had processed the surprising German invasion of the Soviet Union and its own occupied territories, which drove the Russian forces back to the east. It was of course not yet known that *Einsatzgruppen* had that summer undertaken a campaign of systematic mass murder of Jews in communities in the newly conquered territories, but it was obvious that millions of additional Jews were now under German control and therefore potential victims of a new persecution. Here is Reform rabbi Louis L. Mann of Chicago on Rosh Hashanah evening; the title of his sermon was "Where Now Is Thy God?"

---

119 Here Kaplan cites Exod. 6:9; Ezek. 37:11; the destruction of the First Temple; Haman; the Maccabees, and the destruction of Second Temple, as examples.

> I doubt whether Jews have ever faced a Rosh Hashono with hearts more contrite and spirits more humble.... It is the first time that persecution, expulsion, and crucifixion have become well-nigh universal.... Some of my friends...have said plainly, "I pity you having to preach this year. Haven't the events of the last years shaken your faith?"...Since Germany is clearly in the wrong, why should she conquer a dozen or more countries with a population of one hundred and fifty million and add six hundred thousand square miles of territory? Why should millions be haunted, hounded, and harried, forced from one country to another until the thought of death seems sweet? Why should the innocent be robbed, pillaged, plundered and dispossessed?...

Reform rabbi Harry Joshua Stern of Montreal had a similar title for his Rosh Hashanah sermon: "Where is Thy God?" – reflecting the questions being widely asked. "But, on Rosh Hashanah 5702, amidst a world in convulsion, a world reeking and shrieking with appalling horror, men everywhere do ask, 'Where is God?' Only the feeble-minded can truly refrain from such questioning when now twenty-five lands are engaged in the most savage and cruel war of all time, that is characterized by its scientific methods of human slaughter and destruction."

Even the ultra-Orthodox rabbi Kalonymus Kalmish Shapira, preaching in the Warsaw ghetto, acknowledged this questioning in a sermon delivered in mid-December, 1941: "To our sorrow, we see now that even among those people who had been firm believers, certain individuals have had their faith weakened. They pose questions, saying in effect, 'Why have You forsaken us? If the suffering is being inflicted upon us in order to bring us closer to Torah and divine service, we see the opposite happening. The Torah and everything sacred is being destroyed.'" And sixteen months later, on the Sabbath preceding Pesach in 1943, Shlomo Zalman Ehrenreich, an ultra-Orthodox rabbi in Transylvania, which had not yet come under German control, reported similar questions from his own community:

> Many thousands and tens of thousands of Jews are exiled from their country and land. How many tens of thousands have been

> killed by the evildoers for no reason? How many have been buried alive: they, their wives, their sons, and their daughters? The reckless among us will open their mouths, asking questions and doubting G-d: 'Why did G-d do this to pious and good Jews?' They will actually ask, 'Where is our G-d?' But we remain silent and closed. For we are unable to answer these people at all until G-d has mercy on His people and sends us our redeemer and takes us out of this dark and long exile.

Soon afterward, on the seventh day of Pesach, Orthodox Rev. Abraham Cohen of Birmingham, England, for whom the realities of mass murder had been established more clearly than for his colleague to the east, delivered a sermon entitled "God and Evil," including the following passage:

> What are we to think of God in these dreadful days? For years evil has been triumphant; innocent human beings, whose colossal number He alone knows, have been tortured, robbed, and murdered by fiendish monsters; right is stamped under foot; whole nations have been overrun and their lands devastated. Is God powerless to save? Or, worse thought still, is He indifferent? How can He be so callous as to allow them to continue? These questions are inescapable; and because no convincing reply is forthcoming, the faith of many has been shattered. The bitterness of their experience has forced them to the conclusion that there is no God and the world is at the mercy of blind forces without any directive Mind. Is that conclusion justified?

Here Cohen has presented the questions not as quotations coming from outsiders, but as his own articulation of a painful confusion that is understandable and legitimate under the frightful circumstances.

By the High Holy Days of 1944, the spirit of American and British rabbinic preachers was significantly different. The Allies had successfully landed in France and much of the country was liberated from German control. On the Eastern Front, the Soviet forces were dramatically advancing, pushing the German army out of territories they had occupied, while the catastrophe of Hungarian Jews deported to Auschwitz was not yet fully known. It is not surprising, therefore, that wrenching questions about the role of God were no longer a major theme in the sermons. Indeed, a leading American Reform rabbi, Louis I. Newman of New York, in his radio message on the eve of Rosh Hashanah, expressed a certain disdain for those who had earlier articulated confusion and doubts about God.

> Looking back upon the anxious days and years that have passed, we, the survivors, can truly count our benedictions. It was only yesterday that we were at Dunkerque and the Nazi conqueror was dancing his jig at Compiègne. Do you remember those men and women who, at the advent and during the course of the War announced that they had lost their faith in God, and that religion was a sham? How, they asked, with sophomoric simplification, could a gracious and clement Deity permit such sufferings and tragedies to befall mankind? It is always easy to be negative in judgment, and to indicate the shortcomings, both of our fellowmen and of our Heavenly Father. I wonder whether the doubters are so vehement in their denunciations today, now that God seems to be smiling upon our fortunes.[120]

In retrospect, the assertion that in September 1944 "God seems to be smiling upon our fortunes" may appear to be just as much "sophomoric simplification" as the questions raised earlier about God's role in the devastating contemporary events of 1940–1943.

Of course it is needless to emphasize that in all of these cases, the preachers who articulated the questions being asked about God's role in the catastrophe for the Jewish people and for progressive democratic values went on in their sermons to provide a response. Such responses take us into the realm of the theological dimensions of the Holocaust as it was occurring, a topic on which the work of Gershon Greenberg is especially illuminating. I will therefore sum-

120 An apparent reference to the victories of Allied armies on the Western and Eastern Fronts, though God "smiling on our fortunes" seems to overlook entirely the tragedy of Hungarian Jewry during the previous months.

marize these responses very briefly by noting that while the questions raised by Progressive and Orthodox rabbis are fairly similar, the answers are not. Among Reform and Conservative rabbis, the most common response was to remove God from active involvement in contemporary historical events. God created human beings with freedom of choice, a quality that differentiates them from animals and angels. Therefore, God does not intervene in the decisions made by human beings – evil as their behavior may be – except by inspiring other human beings to resist such decisions. God may indeed feel intensely the pain of the victims, but He relies on human efforts to bring about the eventual defeat of the forces of evil in the world. This theme shifts the blame from God to human beings, highlighting the failure of leaders of the democratic nations to act decisively in opposition to the Nazis, the Japanese, or the Italians in the 1930s, before the war began.

Orthodox rabbis (especially the ultra-Orthodox) often had a different kind of response to questions about God. They tended to insist that God is in full control of all historical events, and therefore that what was happening must be consistent with the divine will. It might well be a punishment of the Jewish people for the failures of liberal and secular Jews to observe all of the commandments, and for their desire to assimilate to the values of the surrounding culture, especially in Germany. Some even asserted that Hitler was an instrument of God, sent into the world to oppress the Jews in a manner that would lead to their sincere repentance. This response became increasingly difficult with the realization that fully observant Jewish communities in central and eastern Europe were being wiped out, including the most devout and learned rabbis, while secular Jews who had moved to Palestine in the 1920s and 1930s appeared to be safe from Nazi attack.

An alternative was the traditional rabbinic motif of *ḥevlei Mashiaḥ*, "the birth pangs of the Messiah," taking as a model the experience of women suffering pain as an integral component of the ultimate goal of bringing new life into the world. Applied to history, this enabled Jewish thinkers throughout the ages to deal with periods of persecution through the hope that they were a necessary part of the events that would directly lead to the messianic age, with its ultimate vindication and triumph of the Jews. As the number of Jewish victims continued to increase, this became more difficult to maintain: who would be left to welcome the Messiah when he arrived?

Eventually, some ultra-Orthodox rabbis insisted that we simply could not understand why God was permitting the atrocities to continue, that human beings should simply cling to their faith that the suffering was consistent with the divine will, and that the only appropriate response was the willingness to die as martyrs. Others appeared to sacrifice belief in the omnipotence of God, asserting that God was also suffering because of the agonies of His people.[121]

To summarize, the texts of sermons preserved from the Holocaust period provide important information not only about what was known and communicated to congregants, and when, but also information about the tensions faced by preachers when confronted with their congregants' questions about fundamental theological issues as the events were occurring. It is now time to turn to the actual texts in context.

121 Gershon Greenberg, the leading expert on ultra-Orthodox theological responses to the Holocaust, has published extensively on this topic. See Bibliography.

CHRONOLOGICAL SELECTIONS

Prelude: 1932

February 14, 1932 (Sunday)

Jacob X. Cohen, "The Menace of Hitlerism to American Jewry," Free Synagogue, NY. AJA MS-146, Box 2, Folder 3; see Complete Sermons

Maurice N. Eisendrath, "Now What About Versailles?," Holy Blossom Synagogue, Toronto. *Holy Blossom Pulpit*, II, 9

(3:) **1. Revision or Revolt?**

Confronted by a world crisis far more precarious and grave than that which we witnessed in 1914; with country after country hastening toward the brink of economic collapse; with the first rumblings of cataclysmic revolutions threatening the domestic security of many lands; with the bitter and bloody battle actually joined in the Far East, and with acrid notes being exchanged between the great world powers...with an entire world in turmoil, what point is there in wasting this precious Sunday morning in discussing a problem so remote and theoretical as the Treaty of Versailles...?

But anyone who has even the most superficial acquaintance with the European scene to-day knows full well that far from settling anything, the Versailles Treaty unsettled everything and left the peoples of Europe in utter chaos; in a chaos which once more threatens to disrupt the entire world....

(14:) **8. Versailles Must Go**

All of which means that if we would bring peace to Europe that Treaty, libelous and ungodly, must be swiftly revised, not *after* Disarmament, but *before*, for there can be neither security nor peace in the world as long as one people is branded as a super-criminal and all the others vaingloriously exalt themselves in their lying innocence.

The admission of Germany as an equal in the society of nations must precede any decisions of the delegates at Geneva. France's rather ingenious and clever device (15:) to have all her former allies pledged to guard, with an international police force, her ill-gotten gain to the very end of days, must be recognized for what it is: a selfish and vindictive endeavor to keep Germany forever in her place – in a place of humiliation, ignominy and shame, which she deserved in no wise more than France herself. It means further that reparations must go – not merely, as the materialists argue – because of economic necessity, true and inescapable as that may be, not merely because Germany is unable to pay – but because it is *unjust* and *unfair* to exact this requital from her for a crime which not she alone committed.

October 1, 1932 (first day of Rosh Hashanah)

Abraham J. Feldman, "Singing the Lord's Song," Temple Beth El, Hartford, CT. *Sources of Jewish Inspiration*, pp. 67–87

(71:) The lot of the Jew during the past year was not a happy one. Evil tidings came to us from different parts of the world, often with startling frequency and in dispiriting succession. In Russia the process of spiritual sterilization of the Jew is continuing apace. In Poland the old policy of repressive discrimination against Jews and occasional riots continues without halt or cessation. In Romania torture and abuse are the lot of the Jew without much opposition from the government. In Germany our people have experienced a year of dread and anxiety and humiliation such as German Jewry has not known for generations. And in our own country discriminations against Jews in employment and against Jewish students seeking admission into colleges and universities and more particularly into some professional (72:) schools have been a steady source of annoyance and irritation.

November 20, 1932 (Sunday evening)

Rev. M.L. Perlzweig, "The Challenge of Anti-Semitism," Presidential Address to B'nai B'rith, Adolph Tuck Hall, London. *JC*, November 25, 1932, p. 14

The speaker regarded it as constituting one of the most serious problems in the Jewish world to-day. He believes that the Jewish people was in graver peril to-day than they had ever been in their whole history. He believes this to be true not because anti-Semitism was so strong and powerful a movement, but because the inner resistance of the Jewish people was everywhere breaking down. This anti-Semitism, which was so rampant all over Eastern and Central Europe, was more bitter and relentless in its pursuit of the Jews than any other anti-Semitism that they had known before. They would have read in last Friday's issue of *The Jewish Chronicle* word for word what it was that the Hitlerists proposed to do about the Jews in Germany.... It was only the beginning, because these people had captured the youth of Germany, who in years to come would be the judges, the lawyers, the doctors and the teachers of Germany....

1933

February 12, 1933 (Sunday)

Stephen S. Wise, "Germany Chooses Hitler - America Chose Lincoln," Lincoln's Birthday Address, Free Synagogue, New York. JTA, February 14, 1933

Insofar as Hitlerism includes a definitely formulated and activated anti-Jewish policy, we are deeply concerned, and we believe that Americans, irrespective of faith and racial origin, will come to share our concern touching the danger to the German republic of forswearing its enlightened and basic policy of equal and inviolate rights for all its citizens.

Nor will Americans of faith and race other than our own view with tolerance or equanimity the threatened invasion of Jewish rights and the continuance of assaults upon Jewish life and property by the followers of Hitler. Jews are not strangers or aliens in Germany. They have lived in Germany for a thousand years; they have been among Germany's builders and creators....

Israel Mattuck, "Hitler and the Jews," Liberal Jewish Synagogue, London. Unpublished

(1:) Hitler and his followers have made hostility to the Jews an important part of their party's political policy.... The most vehement anathemas are hurled at the Communists. But the Socialists, the Jews, and Roman Catholics have all been denounced by Hitlerists as enemies of the Fatherland. In the case of the Jews, however, the hatred has gone, and threatens to go, further than mere insulting names. Their defenseless position makes them an easy object for hostile action. Anyone in power can hurt them. They are so few in number that they cannot by themselves prevail, or fight, with any reasonable prospect of success, against the hostile plans, or policies formulated or launched against them by those wielding political power. The arrival to power of Hitler and his party holds a grave threat for the Jews in Germany....

(4:) It is difficult for us in England to comprehend the gravity of the Jewish position in Germany. Our experience here is such as to make us doubt the reality of the menace because it is so great. The thought naturally occurs: Surely at this stage in human civilization, and in a civilised country, a group of people will not be deprived of their human rights!...

(5:) The pathos in the situation is transfigured by [the hope of the German Jews] that the better Germany will assert itself in defense of the country's inheritance, honour, and humanity against those who threaten it. Is their hope justified? Hitler, who does the threatening, has come to power. The hope seems vanished. Yet Germany has a strong national tradition for liberty and humanity. It has been among the most civilised countries in the world. It is hard to believe that it can, or will, sink to the position of Russia in the middle of the 19th century or Spain in the 15th. The country of Schiller, Lessing, Goethe and Kant like the country of Rasputin or Torquemada! The belief in humankind rejects such a plausibility.

February 26, 1933 (Sunday)

Stephen S. Wise, "Hitlerism and Its Meaning," Free Synagogue (Under Auspices of American Jewish Congress) at Carnegie Hall, New York. AJA, Box 20: SSW Microfilms of AJHS and BUASC papers[1]

(1:) Today, the American Jewish Congress, true to that tradition from which I pray it will never depart, invites representatives of two of the great Christian churches in America to lift up their voices in

1 See Bibliography on Stephen S. Wise. This shorthand way of identifying Stephen S. Wise's unpublished sermon texts indicates that I have accessed the microfilms of these texts at the AJA, that another accessible collection of the microfilms is held by the AJHS, and that the originals are at the Robert D. Farber University Archives & Special Collections Department of the Brandeis University Library, which has granted me permission to cite these passages.

order that Germany may know that it is not a handful of Jews – for four million are as a handful compared with a hundred and thirty millions of Americans – but it is Americans, it is public opinion, the American spirit, and the American conscience that cries to the spirit of Hitlerism, "Thou ailest here, and here."[2]

(3:) We Jews are not the only victims of Hitlerist terror and oppression. We are merely the earliest and the chiefest victims of Hitlerite hatred and rage.... Hitlerism means the rule of hatred. A nation that is served by hatred is tragically dis-served. A leader who sets out to divide his national home against itself may have electoral triumphs for an hour but he is bound to go down in the end in moral defeat and in spiritual disaster.

(6:) We turn to Germany today – Catholics, Protestants, Jews. Gathered under the aegis of the American Jewish Congress – and we utter the hope that Germany will not stoop from the high level of justice and equality for all its people. Germany is greater than Hitlerism. Germany means freedom. Germany means justice. God give it that Germany choose the way of peace, the way of honor, the way of justice. May Germany be greatly and abidingly blessed!

Feb 28, 1933 (Tuesday evening)

Ferdinand M. Isserman, "Taking the Old Testament out of the New," Address delivered at Fellowship Dinner of St. John's Methodist-Episcopal Church, Second Baptist Church, and Temple Israel at Temple Israel, St. Louis, MO. AJA, MS-6, Box 13, Folder 4

(1:) The avowed purpose of Hitler in recasting the Bible of the church so as to eliminate the Old Testament, which is Jewish, and to preserve the New Testament, which is Christian, was discussed in a sermon at Christ Church Cathedral last Sunday morning by my very good friend, Dean [Sidney] Sweet....

---

2 A quotation from Matthew Arnold's poem "Memorial Verses: April, 1850," written in response to the death of Wordsworth. In this passage, however, he is speaking of Goethe: "He took the suffering human race, / He read each wound, each weakness clear; / And struck his finger on the place, / And said: *Thou ailest here, and here!*" It is unclear to me whether Wise expected his audience to recognize the quotation.

(2:) The religion of Hitler and the religion of the prophets are in sharp and hostile contradiction. Between Hitlerism and Prophetism there must be eternal warfare. Between Hitlerism and the ideals of the Old Testament there can be no truce. Hitlerism stands for the welfare of one people. Prophetism stands for the welfare of humanity. Hitlerism speaks of the beauty of one race, Prophetism speaks of the beauty of all races. Hitlerism speaks the language of autocracy. Prophetism speaks the language of democracy. Hitler is right in seeking to exclude the religion of the Old Testament from the religion on which he vindicates his policies. Between Jesus and Hitler there can be no fellowship because Jesus is rooted in the soil of the Old Testament, and Hitler is not merely a foe of the Old Testament people but also a foe of the Old Testament humanitarianism.

March 11, 1933 (Shabbat haGadol)

Moses Kahlenberg, "The Great Sabbath [Shabbat haGadol]: at a Time of Sorrow, Oppression and Persecution for the Jews in the land of Germany," *Kehal Yere'im* ("The Polish Congregation"), Metz, France. *Darash Moshe*, 2, pp. 51–59, translated by MS

(52:) Something very similar is happening now to our brothers in Germany.[3] They risked their lives and died in the World War on behalf of their native land, they loved their national identity, their judicial status as citizens, they expanded their productivity, they made their commerce international, they energetically raised their cultural achievements to a world-class level. After all this, "there arose over them a man – not a king – who knew not Joseph" (cf. Exod. 1:8); "the citizen was left on the ground while the visitor rose to the heavens"; the one who [recently] came to live there[4] is now

3 "Similar" to what was discussed at the beginning of the sermon: David, having fought against the Philistines, aroused the envy of Saul and was severely persecuted; he also mentions that the Hasidic Rebbe Israel of Roszhin was arrested and imprisoned by the Czar.

4 The reference here and in the previous phrase is to Hitler's coming as an outsider from Austria and now determining the fate of Jews who could trace their lineage in Germany for centuries in the past. The phrase about the citizen on the ground and the visitor in the heavens is in Aramaic, taken from b. Eruvin 9a. This entire

making judgments (cf. Gen. 19:9), and reaching out for booty and spoil (cf. Esth. 9:16). He has banished our brothers, our fellow Jews, from commercial acquisitions; they are subjected to vilification and abuse, to death and destruction. Every heart melts when hearing the acts of cruelty that are inflicted upon them both openly and in secret.

But this is not a unique phenomenon with us. Whoever reads the Torah and accounts of Jewish history will see that from beginning to end... the envy of peoples and their nobles have always pursued us for no reason. The nations of the world have always marvelled at the tremendous strength of Israel, the strength that fortifies them among the encircling wolves who would prey upon them. It is also wondrous in our own eyes, to the point that the Men of the Great Assembly already said, "These are His mighty deeds, these are His awesome powers: that this tiny nation is able to persist among the nations" (see b. Yoma 69b). Also the words of King David, "I rejoice over your promise" (Ps. 119:162),[5] have always inspired the living spirit within the soul of Jacob, and fresh blood into the arteries of his heart, enabling him to stand up before the weak and the poor. With the Torah at his chest and the Psalms in his arm, he has passed through the paths of the seas and the borders of the land, and never trembled or diverged one bit despite all the world's winds. "And that which has sustained our ancestors and us in every generation, etc."[6]

March 12, 1933 (Sunday, Purim)

David Philipson, "The Roosevelt Inaugural and the Hitler Triumph," Rockdale Avenue Temple, Cincinnati, OH. Typescript in AJA, MS-35, Box 5, Folder 5

(1:) [Following great praise for FDR's Inaugural Address] I felt that

---

passage is highly rhetorical, filled with allusions to biblical and rabbinic texts, but the sermon was delivered in French, and we cannot know how much was enriched in the Hebrew version.

5 This was the second of two verses cited together at the very beginning of the sermon; the previous verse begins, "Princes have persecuted me without reason."

6 The "etc." is in the text, but in delivery the preacher would undoubtedly have continued the familiar passage from the Pesach Haggadah: "in every generation, some rise up against us to destroy us, but the Holy One saves us from their hands."

the dawn was breaking after a very dark night. But my heart was still heavy, for I was looking forward with apprehension to what would occur across the sea in the land of Germany the next day when the elections to the Reichstag were to take place. A violent and virulent campaign accompanied by brutality and bloodshed had been proceeding for weeks. Repression and ruthless measures had been taken by the Hitler Party against their opponents. It was apparent that they were stopping (2:) at nothing to insure their triumph at the polls. Naturally I was particularly interested in the bitter anti-Jewish outbursts of Nazi leaders. The offices of the leading and most representative organization of German Jews had been entered by Hitlerite minions, and men of the highest probity had been grilled for hours on the specious plea that they had communistic sympathies.[7] Wild reports had been printed in a London paper that there was to be a general massacre of German Jews on the eve of the election. Little wonder that last Sunday [March 5], the day of the election, was looked forward to with fear and trembling.

Thank God that the fears were not realized. Hitler, it is true, has triumphed and seems to be safely anchored in the Chancellor's seat for some time. The week however has passed without there having taken place any of the dread occurrences which were feared, although there are still disquieting rumors. Will the responsibility of office, as is frequently the case, sober this demagogue? Germany under his guidance will doubtless move towards fascism. His National Socialist party have the Communists on the hip. Violence may be looked for in the clashes between these extremists on governmental procedure. Constitutional democracy is for the present fading out of the German picture.

But what of the blood and thunder ravings of the Nazis against the Jews? I have the firm faith that sober second thought will bring even Hitler and his henchmen to their senses in this matter. Germany is not Czaristic Russia of evil autocratic memory. True, anti-

---

7 The JTA on March 7 reported that there had been raids by Nazi Auxiliary Police in the Dortmund, Erfuhrt, and Essen local offices of the *Zentral-Verein deutscher Staatsbürger jüdischen Glaubens*, and that "In these three cities a great deal of alarm was aroused among Jews by these raids, though nothing incriminating was found."

Semitism is still very strong in Germany but there is also a large element of the German people that is sane and sound in this matter. Possibly now that Hitler is ensconced in power he will see a new light. There is an old hymn to the effect that God works in strange ways his wonders to perform.[8] Who knows but that this Hitler triumph may be one of those strange ways, and that out of it may come the wonder of a change of attitude?

March 19, 1933 (Sunday)

Stephen S. Wise, "Father Forgive Them," Free Synagogue at Carnegie Hall, New York. AJA, Box 20: SSW Microfilms of AJHS and BUASC papers

(6:) I deal for a moment with a world savagely, Christlessly, Godlessly bent upon hurt and wrong and contumely and crucifixion for the Jew. I say today, "Father forgive them, for they KNOW what they do".... (7:) They know in Russia, which with all its vaunted virtue of impartiality as between Jew and non-Jew is merely robbing three million Jews as far as it can of God, of faith, of people.

In Poland, which is merely robbing another three quarter million Jews of a livelihood through the diabolical instrumentality of the economic boycott and all that the economic boycott means; in Romania, which is shattering the political and economic conditions of its nine hundred thousand Jewish dwellers; in Austria and Hungary, where there is nothing left to take from us Jews excepting our shame and our chains – everything else they have taken from us; in German-speaking Austria and in neighboring Hungary –... honor, dignity. They have left us rags.... They know what they do – Austria, Hungary, Romania, Poland, and in another sense and with, thank God, some saving reservations, in the Soviet Republic....

(9:) 95% of the [Jewish] physicians in the hospitals of Germany are driven out. The lawyers are to be debarred from practice unless they can prove that they are Nazis. This is a boycott. This is outlawry. This is degradation because of all the concealment, the evasions, the dis-

8 Reference is apparently to the hymn written by William Cowper, beginning "God moves in mysterious ways, / His wonders to perform."

honesties, the lies of which Jews will be guilty in order to live, in order to protect wife and children from these ruffians and hooligans....

We Jews must speak out; we Jews must protest despite every warning on the part of some of our fellow-Jews in America and Germany who say to us that we Jews must (10:) be silent, we must let non-Jews speak for us. I say, unless we wish to be lost to shame and degradation we Jews must speak out in the terms of horror and of shame.

What of non-Jews?...I turn to the Christian world, to the Christian churches of America, Catholic and Protestant alike, to Cardinals, Bishops, Priests, Ministers, and I say, "Gain for them forgiveness by moving them to a change of heart, to a consciousness of the sin they are committing."

Israel Mattuck, "The Present Position of the Jews in Germany," Liberal Jewish Synagogue, London. Unpublished

(1:) Before the recent election in Germany I spoke from this pulpit on the antagonistic attitude of Hitler, who had then just been appointed Chancellor, and his party, to the Jews, and of the grave menace with which the Jews of Germany were confronted.[9] Their position is so serious, and even terrible, that I do not feel it necessary to apologise for returning so soon to a discussion of it. It would be a sufficient explanation that I want to express our sympathy with them in their sufferings and black anxieties, a sympathy which the Jews the world over must feel with aching hearts and which the whole civilized world must share.

It does not call for any imagination to appreciate the seriousness and sadness of the Jewish position in Germany. The facts reported in the daily press reveal clearly its horror. Jewish homes have been visited by bands of armed men and plundered; shops belonging to Jews have been ruined; Jews have been beaten, shut in unauthorized prisons, maltreated in a hundred different ways, and some have been killed....

(2:) Not because of approval of the political ideas of those in Germany who are now suffering for their political views[10] must the

9 Reference is to the sermon delivered on February 12, 1933, above.
10 Referring primarily to German Communists.

persecution of them be condemned, but because it violates the spirit of humanity....

In the case of the Jews, that violation, if possible, is still greater. They are being made to suffer simply because they are Jews. It does not matter what political opinions a Jew holds, what position he occupies, or what his trade (3:) or work may be; he is threatened with a real physical danger. An Orthodox Rabbi in Berlin, who was probably as far removed from politics as a hermit, was attacked in the street by a few Nazis and almost beaten to death.[11] The only reason was that he was a Jew. The flood of hatred against the Jews caused by anti-Semitic victory is now producing its terrible harvest of wreckage. Without cause or purpose. Merely hatred delighting in cruelty!

(4:) The physical sufferings of some Jews in Germany, and the anxiety of all [German] Jews, does not exhaust the measure of their misery. There is also the pain of spiritual humiliation. They love Germany, they have trusted it, they have made sacrifices for it.... But they have not lost their faith. Either in their Judaism or in Germany. Herr Hitler has given them some comfort. He has bidden his followers to stop their private persecutions, and he has given the Jews some vague assurances of protection. We shall be able to judge in a short while the effectiveness of the command, and the practical value of the assurances to deliver the Jews from the immediate sufferings and dangers. Only Hitler can save them.... (5:) Will Hitler and his lieutenants combine the spirit of humanity, the standards of civilization, with their power? All depends on the answer to that question.

(6:) The almost universal agreement outside Germany in the comments on the recent events have been impressive and stimulating. The newspapers of London, ranging from the *Daily Herald* on the left to the *Morning Post* on the extreme right have, with no exception, agreed in protesting against the acts of violence of which Nazis have been guilty. This unanimity reflects the public opinion of the civilized world.

---

11 The *JC* of March 17, 1933 (two days before the sermon was delivered) reported (p. 22) that Rabbi Dr. Jonas Fraenkel, a citizen of Poland, "was set upon in his house in Berlin and so mercilessly beaten that he had to be taken to the hospital, where his condition is causing grave anxiety." Fraenkel was able to escape from Berlin to Prague, where he reported publicly about his experience (JTA, April 30, 1933).

It is one of the sad features of their position that the Jews of the rest of the world can do nothing to help their fellow-Jews in Germany. Their sympathy cannot be translated into any action or even into any useful protest against the treatment which [the Jews] are receiving....[12] But Christians and Christianity have a special responsibility in this crisis in Germany's life....

March 24, 1933 (Friday evening)

Ferdinand M. Isserman, "Adolf Hitler: Germany's False Messiah," Temple Israel, St. Louis, MO. AJA, MS-6, Box 13, Folder 4

(1:) Adolf Hitler is the Shabbatai Zevi, the false messiah, of modern Germany....

(2:) Like Shabbatai Zevi, he is possessed of personal magnetism. Like Shabbatai Zevi, he is gifted with the powers of mystic eloquence. Like Shabbatai Zevi, he has come to a people, crushed and defeated. Like Shabbatai Zevi, he has spun for that people apocalyptic dreams and messianic visions. Like Shabatai Zevi, he has abandoned the cause of the masses, which he originally espoused. Like Shabbatai Zevi, his appeal has been to the passions and not to the intellect, to emotions and not to logic, to sentimentality and not to sanity. Only a fool, he says, seeks to convince the philosopher and the teacher. The masses must be reached through sentiment.

What tragedy has happened to the masses of sober, intelligent, artistic Germans that they have succumbed to the mystic pleadings of an apocalyptic visionary? If any people in modern history have suffered, the German people suffered.... (3:) The Treaty of Versailles, by placing the war guilt upon the German nation, by thus branding it as an outlaw and as a pariah, made a beaten, suffering people desperate, especially because the charge was unfair and unjust....

(4:) Why had it not won the war? Why had it not conquered the obstacles which confronted it after the war? If it is such a super-race, it should have done all that. Hitler discovered the reason. Hitler dis-

---

12 It is unclear whether Mattuck was aware of the New York Protest rally scheduled for March 27, or if he was speaking exclusively about British Jews.

covered the disease which had prevented the German people from realizing their greatness. That disease was an internal cancer, a foreign, parasitic body which had attached itself to the vital parts of the German nation, which had sapped its strength, decreased its vitality, and thus destroyed this great world mission. That foreign body had rendered impotent the great Aryan super-race. If this super-race was to regain its virility, its health, its vigour, its power, it must rid itself through radical surgery of that diseased element responsible for its deterioration. Who was that foreign element? But the Jews....

(5:) Of what did he accuse the Jews? Of everything that haters of Jews have always accused them. He accused them of being the capitalists and bankers who seek to exploit the masses, and the brains of the communists who seek to destroy the capitalist system....

March 24 and 25 (Friday, Saturday)

"Rabbis Denounce Hitler in Sermons." *NYT*, March 26, 1933

RABBIS DENOUNCE HITLER IN SERMONS; Newman Warns "Mailed Fist" Threatens World Conflict - Denials Not Believed. PROTEST TO JAM GARDEN. Two Overflow Meetings Planned for Tomorrow Night - Non-Jews Join in Condemnation.

[article:] Protests against anti-Semitism in Germany, as manifested since the rise to power of Adolph [*sic*] Hitler, found expression here yesterday in sermons at Jewish services, in further plans for the protest meeting to be held tomorrow night in Madison Square Garden and in resolutions and statements by various organizations.

March 26, 1933 (Sunday)

Stephen S. Wise, Address to Free Synagogue at Carnegie Hall, New York. *NYT*, March 27, 1933, p. 4[13]

13 Shortly before leaving home for this Carnegie Hall service, Wise received a phone call from the German Embassy in DC, urging Wise to call off the rally scheduled for Tuesday evening, in return for an "amelioration" of anti-Jewish acts. After consulting with Justice Brandeis, Wise decided that the rally would not be cancelled (Rudin, *Pillar of Fire*, p. 306).

[Following meetings to be held today, the American Jewish Congress would present the German ambassador with "four vital demands":] There must be an immediate cessation of all anti-Semitic activities and propaganda in Germany; the abandonment of the policy of racial discrimination against and economic exclusion of Jews from the life of Germany; the protection of Jewish life and property; there shall be no expulsion of "Ost-Juden who have come into Germany since 1914." . . .

I wish again to record my conviction that the Versailles peace treaties should have been revised long before this; that the Allies in the last years have been guilty of deep wrongs against Germany, the German people, the German State, and that Germany has the right to demand that either the allied nations shall disarm as they promised and covenanted that they would, or that Germany shall have the right to arm.

Germany has the right and has had the right to demand certain things of the Allies which should have been granted long before this, and had they been granted, we might never have seen these days come upon Germany.

March 27, 1933 (Monday evening)

Stephen S. Wise, "To the Conscience of the World," Address at Protest Rally, Madison Square Garden, New York. *NYT*, March 28, 1933, p. 12; *As I See It* (1944), pp. 85–89[14]

(85:) Not out of the bitterness of anger but out of the deeps of sorrow and the spirit of compassion do we speak tonight. . . . We who would secure justice from the nations for Germany and justice to Jews from Germany affirm tonight that Germany cannot hope to secure justice through injustice to its Jewish people.

This protest of tonight is not against the German people, whom we honor and revere and cherish. . . .

---

14 See, on this rally, Gottlieb, "The First of April Boycott"; Waite, "'Raise My Voice Against Intolerance'"; Medoff, *The Anguish of a Jewish Leader*, pp. 14–19. For a powerful description of the impact of this rally on a young rabbinical student, see Saperstein, *Witness from the Pulpit*, pp. 19–28 and 151.

(86:) This protest of tonight is not against the political program of Germany, for Germany is master within her own household, but it is against the present anti-Jewish policy of the Nazi Government. There is no need for our German-born neighbors in America nor for our fellow Jews in Germany to appeal to us to avoid an anti-German demonstration. We are not against Germany, and it is an unforgivable calumny to declare that we are *"Deutschfeindlich"*....

We know that it is not easy to cancel the Nazi program of thirteen years and still we know that it can be done....[15]

We understand the plea and the plaint of our brother Jews in Germany. There are German patriots who love their Fatherland and have had reason to love it. Some of their leaders are under the impact of panic and terror, others under some form of compulsion, in any event the compulsion of a great fear if not actual coercion. Do they (87:) appeal to the Nazi Government to bring about a cessation of its anti-Jewish campaign, as they have appealed to us to end our protest? We have no quarrel with our Jewish brothers in Germany and their leaders, but their policy of uncomplaining assent and of super-cautious silence has borne evil fruit. They who have virtually been silent through the years of anti-Jewish propaganda cannot be followed by us as the wisest of counsellors.

What are these elementary maxims of civilization as we call them? The immediate cessation of anti-Semitic activities and propaganda in Germany, including an end to the policy of racial discrimination against Jews and of economic exclusion of Jews from the life of Germany. That is, (88:) Jewish life and the human rights of Jews must be safeguarded. One other absolutely reasonable and just axiom rather than demand: The revocation of all special measures already taken against Jewish non-nationals, and their equal treatment with all other non-nationals in Germany....

Every economic discrimination is a form of violence. Every racial exclusion is violence. To say that there will be no pogroms is not

15 Reference is to the "Program of the National Socialist German Workers' Party," adopted in 1920, which restricted citizenship (and its privileges) to "racial comrades," therefore excluding Jews.

enough. A dry and bloodless economic pogrom remains violence and force.[16]

Ferdinand M. Isserman, Address at German Protest Meeting at Christ Church Cathedral, St. Louis, MO. AJA, MS-6, Box 13, Folder 4

(1:) In this sacred shrine consecrated to the worship of a Jew whose name it bears and dedicated to the dissemination of his ideals and principles, we have met in a precedent-breaking meeting.... What better answer is there to the propaganda of hatred of the Nazi party in Germany than that in the city of St. Louis Catholic and Protestant leaders are joining their Jewish fellow citizens in a condemnation of anti-semitism. A sense of sacred satisfaction fills me that I am privileged to stand in Christ Church Cathedral, in this religious season, to present the cause of my suffering brethren.... That throughout the world Christian preachers and laymen have raised their voices in protest against the barbarity to which some Jews in Germany have been subjected is a harbinger of a new age and of a new spirit of enlightenment which cheers even in these dark moments....

Raphael Yehezkel Hochberg, "'Wounds [...] from the Enemy'[17] (Concerning the Events in Germany: The Oppression of Our Brothers Suffering the Blows of the Tyrant Hitler, when a Public Fast was Decreed Throughout the World" (Monday, Erev Rosh Ḥodesh Nisan, 5693 [March 28], *VaYiqra*),[18] Gliniany/Galina (Eastern Galicia). *Mareh Yeḥezkel*, vol. 2, pp. 10–12,[19] translated by MS

---

16 Cf. Suzanne McIntire and William E. Burns, *Speeches in World History* (2009), pp. 325–27; Myles Martel, "A Rhetorical Analysis of the Anti-Nazi Protest Speech of Rabbi Stephen S. Wise, March 27, 1933, Madison Square Garden" (MA thesis, Temple University, 1967); *NYT*, March 28, 1933, with texts of many of the speakers.

17 Cf. Prov. 27:6.

18 The "Day of Fasting and Prayer" was declared by Agudas Yisrael in Poland; see Piekarz, *Ḥasidut Polin*, p. 292 and, more recently, Dovid Kamenetsky, "Is It Permissible to Establish a Fast Day Nowadays" [in Hebrew], *Tevunot*, 2 (2016): 897–900, which focuses on the suffering of the Jews in Soviet Russia rather than in Germany. The choice of this date seems to be independent of the protest events in the United States held on the same day.

19 Cf. the use of this text, with a few direct quotations, by Piekarz, *Ḥasidut Polin*, pp. 301–2.

(10:) Rabbotai, I bring no good tidings today. Our gathering is not for the purpose of offering praise for something miraculous; I have not come to deliver a sermon about the... forthcoming month [of Nisan], which is filled with redemption. To our great consternation, it is the opposite.... To our dismay, it is a time for weeping. We have gathered to weep and to express what is in our hearts, by recounting the painful policies that have been applied to our brothers in Germany. Our hearts dissolve upon learning the media reports of the suffering imposed upon them there. From the time when Hitler came to power, all Jews have been expelled from their responsible positions, so that their lives hang in the balance.[20] We have not heard of anything like this in the past century: that the Minister of the Interior would publicly announce that he has no military force to protect the Jews, so that they are exposed to trampling whenever they enter the public domain.[21]

During the Middle Ages, it was decreed to sprinkle the wicked waters over Jews,[22] but these remained Jews who had been victims of compulsion, accepting the behavior of the majority only externally, while inwardly remaining observant of the Torah and the commandments. Many of them eventually fled in boats to other lands in order to save their souls. But now, even Jews who had years ago converted voluntarily are said by Hitler to be legally considered as

---

20 The assertion that "all Jews have been expelled from their responsible positions" is a bit exaggerated at this date, but the *NYT* of March 21, 1933, p. 10, reported that "the dismissal of Jews from responsible positions goes on," specifying the removal of Jewish physicians from hospitals, and Jewish lawyers from criminal (though not yet civil) courts.

21 The first Minister of the Interior under the Nazi regime was Wilhelm Frick, an important member of Hitler's Cabinet with an established background of antisemitic views, but I have found no evidence for the statement attributed to him. Indeed, the *NYT* of March 24, 1934 (p. 13) reported that Frick had instructed the State Governments to prevent any interference with private business, and continued, "His order appears to have been effective, as no cases of anti-Semitic outbreaks or attacks on department or chain stores were reported from Berlin or elsewhere in Germany." Most of the violent attacks during the first two months of the Nazi regime were against Communists and Social Democrats.

22 Referring to the waters of baptism; sometimes Jews had to choose between baptism or death, although from the time of Pope Gregory I (ca. 600) this was always deemed by Church leaders to be improper.

Jews, for "Even though he has sinned, he remains a Jew,"[23] so that the vengeance of the Gentiles may be enacted against them. All the borders are closed with a hundred locks, and not a single nation will grant permission for Jewish refugees to save themselves there....

What then can we do? We have no power except through what we say...to make our protest heard throughout the world, our voice bursting forth to all the nations, so that they will help us to stop the evil that is imminent for them as well. For the Party of these murderers begins only with us, just as with every kind of oppression, it is the Jews upon whom it imposed first, just as it is the heart that first feels the pain of an illness threatening the body of an individual.... (11:) All the nations will eventually feel the coming of this disaster, for the goal of the Hitlerites is to spread suffering by expanding their territory by breaking through their borders....

Every nation must now participate in the suffering of the Jewish populace and help the Jews, whose number now reaches a total of fifteen million, and, if counting just our brothers in Russia and in Germany, there are about five million who are suffering persecution; we should all feel that the pain reaches every Jewish heart. Thus it is also the duty of the Gentiles to identify with this large number [of contemporary Jewish victims], lest they say, "What does this have to do with us?"...For all the Gentiles, who are like the limbs of the [sick] body – they too will feel the pressures and the stresses resulting from this Hitler, for the illness spreads from the heart to the other parts of the body....

But Rabbotai, we have not fulfilled by this Protest our duty to the Creator. These events also have a hidden and clandestine content.... If only we would observe the two fundamental principles of our faith – "Hear, O Israel..." (Deut. 6:4), and "Love your neighbour as yourself" (Lev. 19:18), and if we would remove the groundless hatred that is prevalent and entrenched within us, in our many sins – this hatred that is the "root sprouting poison weed and wormwood"

---

23 Hochberg is quoting a talmudic statement used by Rashi to affirm the legal principle that a Jew cannot lose his status as a Jew even after voluntary conversion to another faith, therefore suggesting – somewhat ironically – that the Nazi definition of Jewish identity is similar to that of Jewish law.

(Deut. 29:17), which was the cause of the destruction of our city [Jerusalem]; and Satan is still dancing among us to this moment. But if we bring our hearts together in love and friendship, then we need not fear any sudden terror, or catastrophe that will come from the wicked....

Now we are abandoned, without protection, without a staff to lean on...; we have become impoverished, our life-support diminishing because of the burdensome taxes and the evil decrees that turbulently descend upon us time after time. We have no advice other than to observe the two fundamental principles of the Torah....

They gave us freedom to rise to high levels, joined shoulder to shoulder, so that we might be like all of the Gentiles, especially in Germany – for the Jewish people was in their hands like a golden scepter, and the Jews rose on the wings of eagles to the heavenly heights of success. But their intention was not for the welfare of the Jewish people....

The distinctive virtue of our people is to be secluded, "A people that dwells apart, not reckoned among the nations" (Num. 23:9).

March 30, 1933 (Thursday)

Israel Mattuck, "Jews and Christians: Their Agreements and Differences," Address to Cardiff Business Club. Unpublished, extensive newspaper coverage

(3:) [T]he civilized opinion of the world has risen in horror against the outrages (4:) which have been perpetrated recently in Germany against the Jews. For several years the propagandists of the Nazi party have preached hatred against the Jews, supporting their preaching by the assertion that the Jews were responsible for all Germany's misfortunes. They were responsible for Germany's collapse in 1918; they were responsible for Germany's economic and financial difficulties that followed the peace; they were responsible for the revolution that made Germany a republic; and they were responsible for Communism and its spread....

(5:) Jews have been maltreated, plundered, beaten, and imprisoned, simply (6:) because they are Jews! It all sounds like medieval barbarism. It is hard to believe that such things could occur in the country that has given the world Goethe, Wagner, and Einstein![24] And we must hope that the spirit of the better Germany is not dead, and that it will triumph to restore the rule of civilized humanity in that country.

(8:) Far from being disruptive, Jews in Germany have been among the builders, while Herr Hitler and his party have been the destroyers. The German Jews ask no credit for what they have done for Germany. It is their country; they love it; what they have given they have given in the spirit of true national love.

March 31, 1933 (Friday evening, immediately before one-day boycott)

Ferdinand M. Isserman, "The Anti-Semitism of Hitler: Is the Jew a Menace to German Culture?," Temple Israel, St. Louis, MO. AJA, MS-6, Box 13, Folder 4

(1:) The smoke is clearing upon the German-Jewish scene. The reports of physical violence have been substantiated by the American embassy and the Hitler government's protestations of innocence have had the effect of curbing it. But though the violence has been curbed, the Machiavellian purpose of the present government toward the Jews stands revealed in its brutal nudity. Massacring 600,000 Jews is inconceivable in a modern civilized state, and would produce a shock upon the countries of the world from which no nation could recover. Physical violence against the Jews has therefore been ordered to cease. In its place is to come a form of torture more insidious. The Nazi party has announced its intention of boycotting Jews, of circumscribing their activities or ousting them from their professions, of denying their children educational privileges. In short, of reducing a group of patriotic and distinguished citizens to the rank of the untouchables of India. If the conscience of humanity is shocked by some violence done to a few hundred individuals, what should it

24 It seems rather surprising that Wagner, who is widely associated with antisemitism and was a favorite of the Nazis, is mentioned in this context rather than Bach or Beethoven.

say in the face of this satanic plan of reducing an intelligent, idealist people to the level of helotry?... Far worse than physical violence is the proposed stripping of every vestige of civilization from the Jews of Germany.

April 2, 1933 (Sunday)

Leo M. Franklin, "Germany and Her Jews," Temple Beth-El, Detroit, MI. Unpublished, Rabbi Leo Morris Franklin Archives, now at AJA, MS-246

(1:) At a time when the whole civilized world stands indignant and outraged by the forces that confront Germany in relation to her treatment of the Jews, it behooves us to remember the rabbinic maxim, "Ye wise men, be cautious of your words" (Avot 1:11). Let us beware lest no rash words or ill-considered act on our part shall make their burden heavier when we intend to make it lighter. Let us be sure that we deal with facts objectively and be not roused to unholy passion by rumors that are not well-grounded.... Fervent oratory and unrestrained passion may be an outlet for our own overcharged emotions but they may cause harm to our brethren whom we seek to help....[25]

I say these things neither in derogation nor in criticism of those who have sought other methods of approaching one of the most serious problems that has ever confronted the Jews of the world. That the plight the Jew in Germany at this moment is a most precarious one, that his whole future there is threatened, that by their own pronouncements the leaders of the party in power will take vengeance upon their Jewish subjects for any utterance here or elsewhere that may be made to impugn their (2:) integrity... no one can possibly doubt. The program now being carried out in Germany, if reports in the public press are to be credited, was actually a part of the pre-election program of the Nazi leader.... All these things have

25 The warning would appear to be aimed at the approach taken by Stephen S. Wise and others in the American Jewish Congress, based on statements by some leaders of German Jewry asserting that harsh criticism of Germany makes things worse for them.

been occurring for a long time and all of them before a single protest voice was raised from this side of the waters....[26]

(14:) That there have been atrocities during and preceding this latest revolution, reliable witnesses have testified, and the announcement on the part of the Hitler government that not a single Jew has been killed is in itself a confession which the world can understand. Even if it were true that no Jews have been killed, who shall be so stupid as to give Hitler a clean bill of health in the light of other happenings. One can die but once, but mental torture, spiritual agony, can go on and on through untold time. That in some states Jews have been exiled, and in others herded together in concentration camps – who can deny that it is the purpose in part of Hitler, in part already fulfilled, to drive Jews out of the professions which they had honored by their skill, their integrity, and to make it impossible for Jewish merchants, even in a small way, to carry on is attested by the Germans themselves.... That Jewish stores have been looted, and Jewish homes raided and robbed, that pillage and plunder have been ruthlessly carried on by the storm groups without interference even from the police, is authenticated not merely from Jewish sources, but from non-Jewish sources that are reliable....

(17:) The one consolation is that these things that are occurring do not and cannot represent the heart and the spirit of the German people. Surely sanity will some day return, and though the price for the mad orgies through which we are passing today will have been very bitterly high, it will seem at last that it has been but an ugly nightmare from which there shall come an awakening....

(18:) He [Hitler] may destroy Jews, he may drive them from his borders, he may close his schools and his universities to them, he may put Jewish judges off the benches and deprive his people of the services of Jewish physicians, he may destroy the manuscripts of Jewish writers and dismantle the laboratories of Jewish scientists – but every such act is a stab at the heart of Germany, and a nail in the coffin of German culture and usefulness and respect in the eyes of the world, and of service in the economy of nations.

26 This is followed by a long review of Jewish history in Germany, pp. 3–11 of the typescript.

April 6, 1933

Harry Joshua Stern, "Hitlerism, Germany and Civilization," Mass Protest Meeting, Montreal (10,000 people).[27] *Judaism in the War of Ideas*, pp. 83–85. See Complete Sermons

April 7, 1933 (Friday evening)

Abraham H. Feinberg, "Passover and Easter: What Message Do They Have for Contemporary Germany?," Temple Beth-El, Rockford, IL. AJA, MS-85, Box 2, Folder 9[28]

(1:) The position of the German Jew is, indeed, pitiful. They are on an island jungle. They can turn neither to the right nor to the left. They must wander about in an underbrush of bigotry, prey to the ravenous anti-semitic appetite of brown-shirted beasts.

In a plea couched in sycophantic language reminiscent of documents which used to be sent to Russian Tzars, German Jewry is appealing to Hindenburg. Terror-stricken, the Jewish population of Germany ask the Jews of the outside world to cease their protests and boycotts against Hitlerism, for Jewish boycotts and protests outside of Germany, they plead, make matters worse, giving Hitler a chance to shout self-defense and to retaliate with further discrimination.

(2:) A spectacle unprecedented in modern history is being enacted in Germany. Jewish judges are being removed from the bench, Jewish lawyers are being disbarred, Jewish doctors are being boycotted, Jewish film and stage-actors are compelled to resign, and Jewish musicians are forbidden to participate in musical productions.

Germany is repaying her debts of gratitude to Einstein, her greatest scientist, by confiscating his modest fortune and threatening to hang him if he appears on German soil. Einstein, in revulsion has renounced his Prussian citizenship....

---

27 James Walker, "Claiming Equality for Canadian Jewry," in *Nazi Germany, Canadian Responses*, ed. Ruth Klein, p. 224 (and n.12).

28 As with all of Feinberg's sermons, no date is provided; I have dated this, which clearly applies to 1933 (Einstein's renunciation of German citizenship, mentioned in the sermon, is dated March 28, 1933), by the opening statement that "Israel will observe Passover [which would begin the following week]. Christianity will observe Easter."

Ferdinand M. Isserman, "The Conflict between God and Country, between Religion and Nationalism, in Germany, in the United States," Temple Israel, St. Louis, MO. AJA, MS-6, Box 13, Folder 5

(5:) In Germany there seems to be little religious opposition to the mad nationalism of the Nazis. According to Reinhold Niebuhr, 80% of the protestant ministers of Germany are Hitlerites and from them has emanated no protest against the philosophy of persecution, of hate, of oppression, which is the platform of the Nazi party.... It is to the glory of the Roman Catholic Church and it is an evidence of its true internationalism (6:) that it had forbidden its devotees from becoming members of the Nazi party....

(7:) Nationalism has thus become religion's foremost rival. To say that loyalty to God comes before loyalty to country is nationalistic blasphemy....

April 9, 1933 (Sunday)

Leo M. Franklin, "Germany and Her Jews: Part 2," Temple Beth-El, Detroit, MI. Unpublished, Rabbi Leo Morris Franklin Archives, now at AJA, MS-246

(1:) The remarkable self-control that has been manifest by the Jew during these terrible times which his brethren in Germany have had to face betokens a strength of character which the mere vituperation of his enemies would have denied.... We are tremendously grateful, however, that the most stirring words of protest have come from Christians rather than from Jews.

(8:) [W]hen the excesses of anti-Semitism are spread in flaming headlines in every newspaper in Germany, and indulgence is given to the expression of sadistic tendencies, wherever they exist, when to the blare of trumpets and military marches is given its boycott holiday, the minds of the people are so filled, not to say inflamed, with the joy of vengeance that for a little while they forget that millions of their own people are hungry and unemployed, and that the republican form of government for which the best minds of Germany had been fighting has been ruthlessly wrested from them. That essentially is the reason why Hitler's (9:) madness has turned itself against the Jews.

(9:) It must have been plain to the Nazi party from the start that there is a limit to which such excesses can be carried. They realize that the boycott of the Jews in Germany would be a boomerang, and literally stifle the business life of Germany itself. Why, the Jew is the economic genius of Germany.... No wonder they have put up the barriers now against Jews leaving Germany....

(15:) Hitler...has gone forward another step in his mad career during the last few days and has taken a stand that must alienate from him not only the sympathy and the respect of the Jews the world over, but of every Christian group within the circle of civilization by his pronouncement that the Old Testament must be eliminated from the churches of Germany, and that the stories of the Prophets must be replaced by Teuton heroes of philosophy.... In this instance, Hitler has carried his campaign a bit too far, and with the blood and the tears of outraged German Jews will be mingled the tears of Christian Germany (17:) because this man and his hordes have dared to lay their unclean hands upon their most sacred institution and tradition....

[O]n many unrepeated occasions [Hitler] has said that no violence would be done to the Jew. Well, history shall tell whether what he has been saying is true or not. But the fact is that he has driven unnumbered Jews to self-destruction, because he has deprived them of a livelihood within their native land and put barriers against their leaving for other shores. And now spiritually he would kill them by taking away from them the source of their inspiration – their sacred books. But in this he will not succeed.

I said last week, and I repeat it now: He may kill Jews, he may banish them from his borders, but Judaism will live on and its banner will proudly wave to the breezes of the world when Hitlerism and his hating hordes shall be forgotten, or, if remembered, be remembered only as a nightmare is remembered, as a distorted vision of a mind diseased.

April 11, 1933 (first day of Pesach)

Israel H. Levinthal, "The Old Pharaoh in Modern Garb," Brooklyn Jewish Center, Brooklyn, NY. *A New World Is Born*, pp. 148–55; see Complete Sermons

Ferdinand M. Isserman, "Will the Messiah Ever Come?," Temple Israel, St. Louis, MO. AJA, MS-6, Box 13, Folder 5

(6:) Hitler will pass as have the Pharaohs, and the song of freedom will again resound from the lips of Israel. Germany will be as ashamed of the chapter in its history now being written as Spain is ashamed of the records of the Inquisition. The perspective of history shatters for us the despair of the defeatism of the moment....

Joseph H. Hertz, "In Ancient Egypt and Present-Day Germany," St. John's Wood Synagogue, London. *Sermons, Addresses, and Studies* 1: 137–44 (also *JC*, April 21, 1933, pp. 18–19)

(139:) Rabbinic legend tells us that Pharaoh did not share the fate of his horsemen at the Red Sea. He alone escaped drowning; nay, more, he escaped death. He stands forever at the gates of Hell; and as, in the course of the centuries, oppressor after oppressor enters, he greets them with the words, "Why have ye not profited by my example?"[29]

(140:) When, six weeks ago, the Nazi party came (141:) into power,[30] it immediately set in motion a ruthless elimination of the Jew from the schools and universities, from all Government employ and the higher professions. Neither achievement, nor position, nor lifetime of service is a safeguard against brutal and summary dismissal.

(142:) "Not a hair on a single Jew's head has been touched," is the Chancellor's proud boast.[31] Alas, the representatives of the British Press have proved, beyond the shadow of a doubt, this boast to be both hypocritical and false. But even if it were true, there are things worse than physical violence; and among these things is the unbelievable trampling under foot of the human dignity of the Jewish population. Jews as a body are constantly branded in the Nazi Press,

---

29 Hertz repeated this in his *Pentateuch and Haftarahs* on Exod. 14:28 (pp. 269–70), and later in "The Meaning of Passover," broadcast 10 April 1941, *Early and Late*, p. 2. For the rabbinic source of this legend, see Rachel S. Mikva, *Midrash vaYosha: A Medieval Midrash on the Song at the Sea*, pp. 182–83, and discussion by Bezalel Narkiss, "Pharaoh is Dead and Living at the Gates of Hell," *Journal of Jewish Art* 10 (1984): 6–13.

30 Referring to the Reichstag election of March 5, 1933.

31 Hertz may have based this on a statement in an article written by Goebbels published in the *Sunday Express* and taken from there by the *JC* of March 31, 1933, p. 18, but the statement is also attributed to Hitler himself.

and by means of every form of Government propaganda, as "traitors" and "criminals," and are spoken of as "vermin" and "monsters" who forever plot the ruin of their fellowmen. In various German towns, public placards have been posted broadcasting the foul and satanic lie of Jewish ritual murder....

(143:) The sons and daughters of Israel in Germany are meeting their bitter ordeal in a spirit of inner freedom and unconquerable faith. It is for us, fortunate children of British Jewry, to be worthy of our brethren.

(143–44:) May the moral indignation of the civilized peoples lead to at least a partial resurrection of the forces of justice and liberty in Germany. Otherwise, the outlook is dark for our brethren, and darker still for their persecutors. I shall not labour the Egyptian analogy. But one need be neither Rabbi nor even religionist to see that the world is built somehow on moral foundations, and that no nation which chooses anti-Semitism, i.e., the will to hate, as the basis of its national life, can have a future.

(144:) It is the fervent prayer of all good men and true that, both for the sake of Jewry and of Germany, the eyes of its blind rulers be opened, racial hysteria and oppression vanish like so much smoke from that land, and righteousness and peace and freedom again become mighty on earth.

Marcus Ehrenpreis, "Malachi's Cry to the Ages" (*Malakis rop till tiden*), Great Synagogue, Stockholm, Sweden. Translation and citation from Stephen Fruitman, *Creating a New Heart: Marcus Ehrenpreis on Jewry and Judaism*, pp. 49–50, 116[32]

(49:) A comparison between the memory of Egypt and the events of today inevitably obtrudes, at once disheartening and consoling. It proves that despite several thousand years of civilization, we have failed to gain any appreciable ground in terms of our humanity. We

32 The sermon was originally published in 1933 as a pamphlet in Stockholm by Albert Bonnier; it is also mentioned in *JC*, June 30, 1933, p. 41. And cf. the citation by Göran Rosenberg, "Philo of Stockholm: The Unrequited Love of Rabbi Marcus Ehrenpreis," *European Judaism* 17:1 (Spring, 2017): 16.

have not become better, nobler, more humane. All cultural progress, all the victories of technology (50:) and the gains of science have but scratched the surface of life. They have not been capable of turning hearts of stone into hearts of flesh. We turn our gaze to religion – at this moment, religion apparently does not possess the power to tame the animal within man. The spiritual authorities stand helplessly before unbridled bestiality. Art and science, culture and education yield to the wild shouts of the street, retreat before the blind masses inflamed by demagogues. In the end, we stand in the same place: that which happened fifteen hundred years before our common era in Egypt can also happen and is happening before our eyes in the year 1933, in almost the same form, with the same purpose, for the same reason. Our humanity has not progressed at the same pace as our technology.

Jacob Kaplan, "The Seder of the Persecuted" ("*Le Seder des persécutés*"), Synagogue de la rue N.-D de Nazareth. *Les Temps d'épreuve*, pp. 17–23, translated by MS

(19:) Let us say in honor of humanity that it has not remained passive in the face of the events that have unfolded in Germany. The universal conscience has been outraged.... The world's hue and cry has had the effect of temporarily disturbing the persecutors; unfortunately, it has not been able to prevent the continuation of their criminal plans. Instead of violence committed openly, violence that percolates in the shadows has been substituted. While the Party in power floods the whole world with postcards, letters, circulars, even telegrams, announcing that there has never been anything seriously bad and that all is now in order, it systematically deprives the Jewish population of all possibilities for earning a livelihood; even worse, by a refinement of cruelty, it refuses to allow Jews to leave the country, as if to enjoy observing their ultimate suffering....

(20:) As Jews, reunited in the synagogue on this day commemorating the anniversary of the Exodus from Egypt, we call out to God the crimes committed by the Hitlerians. We denounce the vile murders, the cowardly killings, of which a large number of our brothers have been victims. We denounce before God the heinous treatment, the shameful abuse, to which an even greater number of our brothers have been subjected. We denounce before God the daily insults they have been forced to swallow, the regime of terror that weighs upon them, the withdrawal - against all standards of justice - of their rights as citizens, the impoverishment, the plundering. We denounce before God the more or less acknowledged religious persecution, which is expressed today in the prohibition of ritual slaughter, and tomorrow perhaps by the closing of the synagogues.[33]

For the moment, drunk with pride, with power and cruelty, the new persecutor of the Jews, like the biblical Pharaoh, pressing his yoke upon the Hebrew slaves, cries out ironically, "Who is the Lord?... I do not know the Lord" (Exod. 5:2)....

(21:) Do not believe, dear brothers, that the silence of God is proof of weakness, an admission of impotence. (22:) Leave that heretical assumption to Pharaoh when he redoubled the violent oppression of the Hebrews (cf. Exod. 5:6–9), or to Haman taking control of the fate of the Jews in the ancient Persian empire (cf. Esth. 3:8–11). Those of you who have studied our history, who know how Pharaoh and his army were drowned in the sea, how Haman and his sons were hanged on the gallows, will recall that sooner or later, God punishes the impudence of the fools who dare to compete with Him.

April 16, 1933 (Sunday, sixth day of Pesach/Easter Sunday)

Stephen S. Wise, "A Man Crucified, A People Crucified: A Passover-Easter Sermon," Free Synagogue at Carnegie Hall, New York. AJA, Box 20: SSW Microfilms of AJHS and BUASC papers

(1:) As you know, on the tenth day of May there is going to be a great (3:) conflagration by order of the German Government, and all Jewish books are to be burned!...

(7:) I shall not live to see it, but you younger people will live to

33 On German legislation in April 1933 prohibiting traditional Jewish ritual slaughter, which was proposed during the Weimar Republic before the Nazis came to power, see Robin Judd, *Contested Rituals: Circumcision*, pp. 190–241, and Trude Maurer, "From Everyday Life to a State of Emergency," in Marion A. Kaplan, ed., *Jewish Daily Life in Germany, 1618–1945*, pp. 277–82.

see the day – remember my prophecy – the day will come when you will speak of the dark foul days of Hitlerism as I speak of Haman, Pharaoh, Torquemada, Pobdonostieff[34] – Hitler will be just another name added to the roles of shame and dishonor. His immortality will be that of infamy in the story of an unforgetting and imperishable people.

(9:) I know of two men who have spoken nobly and in covert and cryptic fashion: Dr. [Otto] Dibelius, [Bishop of Kurmark] and [Karl Josef Schulte] the [Arch]Bishop of Cologne, in a beautiful pastoral sermon....[35]

One Judas – eleven faithful apostles under death. I want eleven Christians to arise in all of the sixty-five millions of Germans and speak as men, as Christians, to Hitler, to Goering, to Goebbels.[36]

Leo M. Franklin, "Germany and Her Jews: Part 3," Temple Beth-El, Detroit, MI. Unpublished, Rabbi Leo Morris Franklin Archives, now at AJA, MS-246

(2:) Germany since the war has been living in an environment of suspicion, fear, and hatred. Unjustly accused of full responsibility for the World War, badly dealt with by the framers of the Versailles

34 Constantin Pobie'donostzeff or Pobedonostsev was the Ober-procurator of the Greek Orthodox Church in Russia, to whom was attributed the statement that one-third of the Russian Jews should emigrate, one-third should become Christians, and one-third should perish.

35 The mention of Dibelius is surprising as he was known (and described himself) as an antisemite, and he actually made a radio broadcast to the United States defending the moderation and restraint of the April 1 Boycott (Richard Gutteridge, *The German Evangelical Church and the Jews*, p. 78; Wolfgang Gerlach, *And the Witnesses Were Silent*, pp. 14–15; Robert P. Ericksen, *Complicity in the Holocaust*, p. 30). I have found no reference to the "beautiful pastoral sermon" by the Archbishop of Cologne, who was considered to be "a resolute opponent of National Socialism" (Klaus Scholder, *The Churches and the Third Reich*, 1: 392).

36 The day the sermon was delivered was also Easter Sunday. Cf. the passage cited in Rudin, *Pillar of Fire*, p. 305, from the *Free Synagogue Weekly Bulletin*, April 25, 1933: "They [the German Jews] are a people crucified, and crucifixion is not too strong and terrible a term.... Where are they who are faithful to Christianity? The spectacle of nineteen hundred years ago is in a very real sense less tragic than the spectacle of this Easter/Passover. For these who crucify a people still invoke his [Jesus's] name while they betray him, while they despise him, while they crucify him and his people 'anew'."

Treaty, the chosen scapegoat for the ills of the post-war world, her pride humbled, her banners dragged in the dust, her rulers disenthroned and exiled, her people impoverished, her culture derided, her very language despised and in many instances cast out of the schools of other countries, once-proud Germany felt within her soul a rising resentment against the peoples whom she held responsible for her downfall.

(7:) Germany represents a proud people in the depths of humiliation at its defeat.... Moreover, it is a hungry people, and there is nothing that leads to social anarchy like hunger. Then comes upon the stage the romantic figure who now controls its destinies, at least for the moment.... (8:) Germany must be purged of every alien element and restored to its native sons. But because the conscience of the world may stand against us if we try to exterminate Jews, so argues Hitler, directly and indirectly, perhaps we could get around our problems by exterminating Judaism.

(11:) Suppose that Mr. Hitler would personally accept the invitation that has been proffered him, together with other European statesmen and diplomats, to come to this country to participate in the Economic Conference that President Roosevelt is calling. What would he find here?...(12:) He might say, "What right have you to criticize me for my attitude toward the Jews of my country? Are your own hands so clean?.... Are not your negroes of the south practically disenfranchised, and have they almost anywhere in your country the same protection of the law as is accorded to the white citizen?"...[37]

April 17 (seventh day of Pesach)

Rev. Gatchell Isaacs, Emeritus Minister of South Hackney Synagogue, London. *JC*, April 21, 1933, pp. 10, 16[38]

(10:) "Art Thou for us or for our enemies?" (Josh. 1:13).

---

37 It is a rather challenging exercise to determine at precisely what point in the 1930s the status of German Jews became *worse* than the status of African Americans in the segregated American South.

38 According to the *JC* article, Rev. Isaacs delivered the sermon, then fell ill during *Musaf* and died on the same day.

We have enemies enough without seeking them within the pale of our own brethren. On this Passover day, Israel still writhes in bondage, a people that belongs to all peoples, yet stands alone, the feeder of the world's teachers, scientists, judges, philosophers, and statesmen, yet starved of its need for recognition, the advocate and preacher of peace and love and brotherhood, and compelled by the cruel irony of history and the vicissitudes of a wandering people to see her sons as we see them today in Germany, persecuted and humiliated.

It is not my purpose this morning to take advantage of my occupancy of the pulpit to give utterance to hysterical denunciations, or the advocacy of a boycott, or any retaliatory measures. My purpose, rather, standing as I am in this holy place, is to advise quiet and peaceful methods of procedure. It is only by unity and co-operation with the responsible leaders in our Community and by their guidance that we can hope to achieve justice for our unfortunate co-religionists. We must be prepared to be led by them and ready to make any sacrifices which may be demanded of us.... Unless we act in unison - let us remember that unity is strength - we shall not succeed in our aim, which is never to rest satisfied until our people throughout the length and breadth of Germany are placed on an equality with their fellow citizens, and all who have been humiliated shall be re-instated to their former positions of dignity, honour and livelihood.

I ask for your prayers to God, to join with mine, that wiser counsels may prevail in the hearts and minds of those who turn day into night and sweet into bitter, and that Israel may once again chant a song of triumph as in the day when she went forth from Egypt. Let us look on Passover as a "sign forever" that all wrongs which men inflict on men shall end; that persecution, no matter how disguised, is antagonistic to Divine Laws and must therefore cease; that oppression is always wrong and, though it be countenanced by a dictator, cannot endure; that even as the phantom (16:) of ignorance vanishes before the illuminating rays of education, so the barbarous barriers raised by reaction and intolerance shall disappear before the commonsense of enlightenment and education.[39]

39 The column continues describing the funeral conducted by Louis I. Rabinowitz and Chief Rabbi Hertz.

April 23, 1933 (Sunday)

Leo M. Franklin, "Germany and Her Jews: Part IV: Bonfire of the Books," Temple Beth-El, Detroit, MI. Unpublished, Rabbi Leo Morris Franklin Archives, now at AJA, MS-246

(5–6:) [Hitler's order for May 10th burning of non-Germanic books at sixty-five German universities] (6:) It will be another chapter in the sad story that has to do with the closing of University doors to Jewish students and professors, of the banishment of Einstein and of Reinhardt,[40] and the casting out of Jewish scientists, physicians, artists, chemists, pharmacists, teachers, and in general of those who have made cultural Germany respectable in the eyes of the world! It follows close upon the heels of the anathema that has been pronounced upon the Old Testament and the replacement of Jehovah by legendary heroes of Germany.... It is all a part of what has become known as the "cold" boycott of the Jews in contra-distinction to a boycott that would have carried with it physical violence. It is an attempt to kill the soul of the Jew or permitting his body to stalk among men the ghost of what it once was....

(13:) Funny, isn't it, that this man who by a legal trick became a German within a couple of years reads out of the circle of German citizens those who helped to lay the foundations of his country's greatness fourteen centuries ago.[41]

(14:) Already you have seen the first results of his banishment of the Old Testament....

(19:) What has happened to Judaism and the synagogue may also happen to Christianity and the Church. Madness, fanaticism, bigotry

---

40 Max Reinhardt was well known as director (and owner) of the *Deutsches Theater*; he was out of the country when the Nazis came to power and never returned to Germany.

41 This would imply that Jews helped lay the foundations of German greatness in the sixth century. I cannot reconstruct the basis for this dating. Marvin Levinthal's book, *The Jews of Germany: A Story of Sixteen Centuries*, first published in 1938, provides evidence of a Jewish presence in Cologne in the early fourth century, based on a 321 edict of Constantine the Great (p. 4), but then states that "four centuries of silence fell upon the Jews of Germany" (p. 4) until new evidence appears in the eighth century. But none of this quite justifies the assertion that Jews "helped lay the foundations" of the country's greatness.

cannot run riot in one quarter of a land and leave the others scot-free. When Judaism is attacked, all religion is attacked, and when the Bible of the Jew is burned, the Bible of the Christian Church cannot be saved.... (20:) Now the time has come when Christianity, the Daughter Faith, for her own sake must speak, not merely in protest meetings called by Jews and attended by Jews, but in the pulpits of Christian Churches and to professing Christians. Will the Church speak the word that needs to be spoken, or will she, satisfied in her own security, lie placidly down and let the bloody work go on?...

April 28, 1933 (Friday evening)

Ferdinand M. Isserman, "Are the Jews the Chosen People and is Persecution Good for Them?," Temple Israel, St. Louis. AJA, MS-6, Box 13, Folder 5

(3:) The Germans, or rather the Nazis, are loyal to their country, and such loyalty is desirable if it does not exclude loyalty to humanity, loyalty to principles, loyalty to ideals. It does exclude that in Germany. Therefore, that loyalty which might be a virtue becomes a sin because it is purchased at the expense of the highest loyalty. Upon the Jews of Germany persecution, too, has had the effect of drawing sharply the lines of class and of tribe. The Jewish youth denied admission to the Nazi party, shut out from participation in the national life of Germany, have developed a nationalism of their own, a Jewish nationalism, and have become Zionistic.... Just as (4:) the German youth desired to go back to the mythology of the ancient Germans, so the Jewish youth, desiring to emphasize their Jewishness, began to observe customs and ceremonies long discarded by their parents.

The whole Zionist movement in Jewish life is a reaction to persecution.... (6:) [P]ersecution, while it develops group loyalty, crushes the creative capacities of a people.... (7:) Knowing from our history what persecution means to a people, we ought to become the champions of the oppressed and the dispossessed.

Harold I. Saperstein, "Nazi Nationalism." Complete text in *Witness from the Pulpit*, pp. 20–28

(21:) But merely to protest is not enough. Now that the heat of emotional fervor that permeated all discussion on this subject a month ago has cooled – although, Heaven knows, our vital concern has not abated – it is time that we, to whom the welfare of Jews and Judaism is precious, take inventory....

(24:) If it were not for the consistent reports from reliable sources, it would be difficult to realize the extent of combined cruelty and idiocy to which the zeal of the Nazis has brought them. My friends, do not be of those who maintain that because we no longer read of Jews being murdered and beaten, robbed and kidnapped, things are on the road to recovery.[42] Though the Executive Committee in charge of the boycott in Berlin declared that the battle against the Jew will be completed in perfect quiet and with greatest discipline, the last words of the Nazi regulations maintain, "We shall finish with the Jews through the relentless power of our regulations."[43]

Economic strangulation may be worse than physical torture. He who takes away a man's livelihood takes away his life. What greater brutality could there be than to compel the Jews to remain in Germany while making it absolutely impossible for them to earn a living? The condemnation of children to ignorance (25:) through limitations on the number of children admitted into schools, the barring of the doors of opportunity to talented youth through exclusion from professional schools, the reduction of Jewish merchants and professional men to despair through starvation, through the picketing and boycotting of shops, and the dismissal of Jewish lawyers, doctors, professors, and public employees[44] – this is cruelty of the most hateful kind!

But even this is not enough. The Hitlerites are not satisfied with making the participation of Jews in the public life of Germany impossible. Having cleansed themselves of the influence of living Jews, they still fear the pernicious influence of Jewish ideals, which

---

42 *Witness from the Pulpit*, p. 24, note 9.

43 Ibid., n. 10.

44 By means of the "Law for the Restoration of the Professional Civil Service" and the "Law Regarding Admission to the Bar," both dated April 7, 1933; see Dawidowicz, *A Holocaust Reader*, 38–40.

are expressed in literature. And so they are extending their warfare to inanimate books. First came the notice of the attempt to eliminate the Hebrew Old Testament from the German Bible and to substitute for it the ancient Germanic saga.... And not content with this, a great demonstration has been planned for May 10, at which all books of Jewish authorship are to be publicly burned.[45] Ladies and gentlemen, if that demonstration is carried through on May 10, it will be the final proof of the return of the German leaders to the barbarism of the dark days of the Middle Ages. Such a thing might have been conceivable in 1242, when by order of Louis IX of France, twenty-four wagonloads of talmudic literature (26:) were burnt in the public square of Paris.[46] But to think that we are witnessing a repetition of this atrocious act after almost seven centuries!

When, on May 10, those flames arise, they will mean more than the destruction of certain books of Jewish authorship and the finest expression of German culture. These flames will mean the negation of all the progress man has made toward the goal of peace and liberty; they will mean that all the blood that has been spilt, all the lives that have been sacrificed for such fundamental rights as freedom of speech and of religion and of conscience, have been for naught. These flames on May 10 will light up the utmost depth of degradation to which it is possible for a nation to descend. And against it we will protest and continue to protest, not only for our sake but for their own.

May 18, 1933 (Thursday)

Isaac Herzog, Address at Reception for Nahum Sokolow, Mansion House, Dublin. *Irish Press*, May 19, 1933, p. 2

While the Jewish national home was rising out of the ruins of centuries, tens of thousands of Jewish homes were being torn up by the very roots in Western Europe in a land deemed to be the centre of the highest form of culture and truth. Jews had been established

45 On the May 10 book burning, cf. Franklin, above.
46 See Saperstein, *Jewish Preaching in Times of War*, p. 26, note 16.

in Germany much longer, indeed, even than Englishmen had been established in Britain. Jews had contributed to German progress and culture, science, art, music, philosophy, medicine, everything that had made the name of Germany great.

May 31, 1933 (Wednesday, Shavu'ot)

Ephraim Levine, "Revelation and the Present Day Problems," New West End Synagogue, London. *The Faith of a Jewish Preacher*, 140–47; *JC*, June 16, 1933, p. 24

(144:) On this festival of Shevuoth when we of the House of Israel celebrate the giving of the Torah we think, alas, of the prevalent chaos and darkness of the world, which strives to live in defiance of the Word of God. The terrible evils which beset our people and which mar the progress of the world are the direct outcome of disobedience and defiance of the laws which should govern men and nations. Murder, theft, jealousy, false witness are the ruling powers which seek to dethrone God. The return to the age of barbarity, which modern Germany has proclaimed, is another evidence of the dire need in the world today for a return of a recognition of Divine Revelation.

Of the persecution heaped upon our brethren in the land of darkness we need not speak. We are, unhappily, too familiar with the details of the systematic and relentless campaign of murder, robbery and starvation which aims at the annihilation of a whole people.[47] No one can tell what the outcome will be; whether the conscience of humanity will awaken some day in the hearts of German leaders; whether the persecution may prove to have been a dark episode; or whether it inaugurates a permanent system of anti-Semitism in Germany.

But the duty of us here is plain: it has been shown by what means

---

47 This is the earliest use of the term "annihilation" pertaining to German policy toward the Jewish people in our sermons. Hitler himself apparently did not use the term until an address delivered on January 30, 1939 ("*die Vernichtung der jüdischen Rasse in Europe*"): Domarus, *Hitler, Speeches and Proclamations, 1943–1945*, vol. 3, p. 1449, and there is no evidence that any policy of systematic mass murder of European Jews was being considered even in January 1939. Cf. also below, July 9, 1933.

our Community can prove its sympathy and its brotherhood. (145:) The call has gone forth from the responsible voices of Jewry to rally to the needs of our brethren; to supply a large sum of money to enable the work of reconstruction to proceed in Palestine and other countries whither the refugees may go, and in this country which has already shown its hatred of persecution and its desire to shelter within limits those who seek an asylum within its shores. Already there has been a great response. But it will require the united effort of the whole community to satisfy the want which has been created. We doubt not that, as far as financial assistance can help to alleviate the situation, our Community will rise to its responsibilities and provide the committee charged with the task with the aid they require.

Isaac Herzog, Address at Morning Service including appeal for funds for the relief of German Jews, Adelaide Road Synagogue, Dublin. *Irish Press*, June 1, 1933, p. 7

Before Germany can speak of wrongs inflicted upon her, before she can speak of justice, she must first and foremost cease to trample under foot 600,000 of her most faithful and creditable citizens.

A veritable hurricane of criminal madness, of savage race-hatred, of internal anti-semitism or rather anti-humanism unparalleled in any modern State is sweeping over Germany and is working the destruction of German Jewry, of the intellect, the flower and pride of world-Jewry, of that part of the German citizen-body which, although forming barely one percent of the population, has actually contributed more than forty percent of Germany's cultural wealth in medicine, science, mathematics, philosophy, literature, art, music, etc.

The position is going from bad to worse. Numerous measures of anti-Jewish persecution are springing up daily and are being put vigorously into force by the German Government. The Jew is being brand-marked by the ruling powers, and is thus made a ready target for cruel hatred and savage brutality.

The Irish race, whose record even in the Middle Ages is free from anti-Jewish persecution – that ancient historically venerable race whose soul seems specifically attuned, by racial temperament, by historic trial and tribulation, to respond to the cry of a helpless, down-trodden people – will assuredly join the mighty chorus of protest in the name of the most sacred cause of religion, of justice, of humanity!

June 4, 1933 (Sunday)

Stephen S. Wise, "Ordination Address," Jewish Institute of Religion, New York. AJA, Box 20: SSW Microfilms of AJHS and BUASC papers

(2:) The second difficulty which these young men face lies today in the tragedy that has befallen our people in that a nation of intellectual light, though never quite of cultural sweetness, has come under the spell of darkness and the dominance of death. It is a tragedy of tragedies, this annexation of the German Reich within the still mightier Empire of unreason and hate. This tragedy overshadows, almost excludes, everything else.

We will not deal at this time with the woe and the misery which the new Reich regime entails, flinging, as it has flung, six hundred thousand Jews in a sea of sorrow without shore.

(5:) In my last word as President of the school I have founded, and of which you have been earnest and faithful students during four years, I say to you be not deceived, be not caught in the snarl of compromise. . . .

June 22, 1933 (Thursday)

Morris Newfield, President's Message to Central Conference of American Rabbis, Milwaukee, WI. *CCAR Forty-Fourth Annual Convention*, pp. 127–38

(127:) We meet this year with saddened hearts. The deplorable events in Germany cast a pall of gloom and sorrow over our deliberations, as they do over American and World Israel. It is not my purpose in this message to discuss in detail the unhappy developments that (128:) threaten German Jewry with physical and spiritual annihilation. Alas, the sad story is well known to you. What is transpiring in the boasted land of *Kultur* has shocked the moral sense of the civilized world. It is difficult to believe that such a nightmare of recrudescent barbarism and of ruthless disregard of humanity can occur in Western Europe of the Twentieth Century.

The whole truth concerning the terrible incidents of last spring in the Nazi-controlled Germany has yet not been made known to the world. It may never be known how many inoffensive Jews and non-Jews have been victims of raging and rabid mobs. Strict government censorship of the press and other channels of information has prevented a full report of the atrocities and indignities from reaching the world. However, much as the German authorities may deny the perpetration of excessive atrocities, they do admit the existence of a cold or bloodless pogrom whose avowed purpose is not only the degradation but the destruction of German Jewry. This the Nazi leaders have shamelessly acknowledged and flauntingly proclaimed.

In face of these manifestations of terror and persecution, it is comforting to know that the civilized peoples of Europe and America have spontaneously expressed their sympathies with the Jews of Germany in their sad plight and have fearlessly condemned these outrages and brutalities....

June 24, 1933 (Saturday, Rosh Ḥodesh Tammuz)

D. A. Jessurun Cardozo, "The Moses Montefiore Centenary," Ramsgate Cemetery, Ramsgate, England, 110th Anniversary of its Dedication. *Ye Are My Witnesses*, ed. Israelstam and Weiwow (Samuel Daiches Festschrift), pp. 166–71

(171:) Alas a cloud rests upon our festivities, as we think of our brethren in other countries who are again being refused justice and peace, and who are again suffering from malicious libel and cruel oppression. Our task is difficult. We have still to pray and work for the peace of our brethren.

Let us not be discouraged. Let the example of the founder inspire us this day. Let us show to the world that the love for the House of God has kept before us those ideals for which it stands: Brotherhood, Justice, and Peace. Strengthened, then, by our prayers, let us devote ourselves unselfishly to the promotion of those ideals, so that justice may speedily be restored to Israel and peace to mankind.

June 25, 1933 (Sunday)

James Waterman Wise, Address at Town Hall Meeting, New York. *NYT*, June 26, 1933, p. 7[48]

It is difficult for Americans – Jews and Gentiles alike – to understand the silence of President Roosevelt in the face of one of the great human disasters of our time. The tragic and needless sufferings of the Jews in Germany are such that it should have been impossible for the President of the United States not to have spoken a word of warning and condemnation to the German government. I am aware of the niceties of diplomatic procedure and the amenities of international life. But in a crisis such as exists in Germany today diplomatic discretion must yield to moral indignation.

July 9, 1933 (Sunday)

Joseph H. Hertz, "Out of Depths I Cry Unto Thee," Royal Albert Hall, London, Service of Prayer and Intercession. *JC*, July 14, 1933, 24–25, and *Sermons*, pp. 145–52

(145:) Only four months ago, German Jewry was on the heights – illustrious through its achievements in every walk of life, strong in religious endeavour, and rich in worldly blessings. To-day, it is hurled down from its eminence; facing misery, insult, and degradation, and sinking in deep waters of intolerance and hate. It is battling for very life against a tidal wave of mass hysteria and racial persecution that threatens it with annihilation.

(146:) [H]ow much easier is the Nazi way of fastening all these sins, blunders, and unforeseen misfortunes upon the Jew, and giving the German mob not one scapegoat but 600,000 scapegoats. "There can be no salvation for Germany" – is the Nazi cry – "unless there is a complete elimination of the Jews from its political, cultural, and economic system."

48 This article was quoted by Arthur D. Morse, *While Six Million Died*, p. 121, but attributed erroneously to Jonah B. Wise. James W. Wise, son of Stephen S. Wise, was the author of *Swastika: The Nazi Terror*, published in 1933; see especially chap. 5, "World Reaction."

The first-fruits of that monstrous doctrine were the expulsions of the Jewish intellectuals from the Universities, professions, and every form of State service. This is followed by a campaign of such relentless ruin against (147:) the Jew in commerce and industry that it is tantamount to denying him the elementary right to work and live. In addition, the Jew is subjected to veritable lava-torrents of defamation. . . .

Nothing less than the extermination of the Jew would, it seems, satisfy the wilder spirits among the Nazis. They repeatedly state that if, from any quarter, an attempt is made on the life of the Chancellor, even if the attempt is an unsuccessful one, they "would follow the hard rule of heathen days and send a whole people after him to the Beyond. All Jews in Germany would immediately be put against a wall, and a bloodshed would result which in its ghastliness would exceed anything the world has ever seen."[49]

"We are anti-Semites, but we are not barbarians," the Reich Minister of Justice recently declared.[50] There is bound to be considerable doubt as to the truth of the second half of the declaration, so long as his Government permits the Satanic idea of mass massacre to be disseminated in regard to a helpless minority.

(148:) When the noonday of our German brethren was turned into the darkness of some deep well, they, too, beheld their firmament studded with stars. I refer to *ḥasidei umot haolam* [Hebrew letters], the men of light and leading who in Parliament, in the Press, and on the Platform, have given expression to the world's indignation at the attempt to humiliate and degrade a whole section of the human family.

(151:) In the light of this Service of Prayer and Intercession, at which all sections and organizations of the community are united as

---

49 The second sentence of this quotation and the general idea was apparently taken from the *Leipziger Tageszeitung*, March 21, 1933; it is quoted in translation in *The Jews in Nazi Germany* (New York: American Jewish Committee, 1933), p. 45, http://www.ajcarchives.org/AJC_DATA/Files/THR-18.PDF

50 The quotation attributed to Dr. Hans Frank, who would later become the General Governor of Occupied Poland, was apparently taken from a *JC* article entitled "The Nazi Barbarism," May, 26, 1933, 14a–b, referring to a speech made on May 22.

one religious brotherhood, our duty is clear. Anglo-Jewry will surely do its share to rescue the Jabnehs in this new *Churban* [destruction], and salvage the religious life of those hundreds of thousands who must remain under the Swastika. In that religious life alone is their safeguard against despair and suicide; therein alone lies the invincibility of soul which no tyranny will be able to crush.

July 29, 1933 (Saturday)

Salis Daiches, Edinburgh Hebrew Congregation, Scotland. *The Scotsman*, Monday, July 31, 1933, p. 7, "NAZIS AND JEWS: Edinburgh Rabbi's Protest" [51]

[The desecration of the Mannheim synagogue] was one of the worst cases of vandalism and sacrilege ever recorded in modern times.

Nothing has been spared by those uniformed barbarians – the Holy Ark, the scrolls of the law, the silver ornaments, the ritual appurtenances, the rare books, the candlesticks, the Bible and prayer-books – they all had been ill-used, damaged, or stolen, and the house of worship had been turned into a scene of ruin and desolation.

What excuse could the Nazi leaders give for such savagery? Was this also one of the methods by which the superiority of the "Aryan" race was to be demonstrated? Was this to help to turn Germany into a great world Power? Were such outrages to be justified by the plea that there were too many Jews in the learned professions, or that the Jews were "Marxists"? What would the civilized world think of it?...

It is high time, that the Governments of all civilized nations made a real effort to stop the cruel persecution of Jews and Judaism in Nazi Germany.

September 14, 1933 (Thursday)

Stephen S. Wise, Temple Emanu-El, Montreal. JTA, September 17, 1933.

---

51 The newspaper report states that the protest in Daiches' sermon was primarily about the reported desecration of the synagogue in Mannheim by Nazi "storm troops," which the preacher characterized as "one of the worst cases of vandalism and sacrilege ever recorded in modern times." The description was apparently taken from a JTA report; the *JC* includes a brief paragraph on the event in its August 4 issue, p. 17.

A plea that Canada "make a grand gesture for humanity" by opening her doors to persecuted German Jews.[52]

September 20 (Erev Rosh Hashanah, 1933)

Jacob P. Rudin, "Dark Horizons – 1933," Temple Beth-El, Great Neck, NY. See Complete Sermons

Irving F. Reichert, "The New Year and the Nazi Terror," Temple Emanu-El, San Francisco, CA. *Judaism and the American Jew*, pp. 116–21

(117:) The appalling tragedy that is taking place in Germany has bowed all Israel low in sackcloth and ashes....

It may be that there are among you some who object to this macabre theme [tonight].... who would fain close their eyes to all that is sordid and ugly in the world and flee before the presence of tragedy.... I know that the story of Jewish suffering in Germany is not new to any of you. A thousand times it has been dinned into your ears.[53] Each new dispatch from that affrighted land repeats the gruesome tale with dolorous reiteration. And yet I would be recreant to the prophetic tradition of my calling, and faithless to every pledge of assurance and assistance I gave our persecuted brethren a few short weeks ago, did I not make their cause the dominating theme of my Rosh Hashanah message.

(118:) To one who has but recently returned from Germany, who has been an eye-witness to the terror which engulfs our stricken people, the comparative complacency and inaction of our American Jewish communities is hopelessly incomprehensible. Here is

---

52 On Wise's address in retrospect, see Harry J. Stern (rabbi of Temple Emanu-El), "Stephen S. Wise – in Memoriam," in *Canadian Jewish Review,* April 29, 1949, p. 16; *Martyrdom and Miracle,* pp. 184–85: "When we brought Stephen Wise to our own city of Montreal, as he was returning from the shores of Europe in 1933, he dared, from the very pulpit of Temple Emanu-El, to denounce the Third Reich and designate it for what it really was. There were those even within the Jewish community who regarded his courageous utterance as not in keeping, to say the least, with good taste and diplomacy. For then Canada was doing business with Nazi Germany. No wonder that, for the Jews in the European underground, the name of 'Stephen' became the symbol of resistance and the rallying word for the brave and the courageous."

53 A rather surprising hyperbole for September 1933.

a population of 600,000 of our fellow-Jews, bound to us by every sacred claim of tradition and fellowship and humanity, that has been stripped of civic rights hard-earned and dearly-purchased, expropriated from all trades, professions, and opportunities for earning a livelihood, condemned as a cancerous growth to be excised and destroyed, humiliated and degraded to such ignominy that self-destruction is accepted as an honorable escape.... [T]he situation daily grows more ominous. The steady and determined advance of the anti-Semitic juggernaut continues on its path of destruction and *schrecklichkeit*, unchecked by a single restraining influence....

As far as German Jewry is concerned, its lot is hopeless. The Nazi government ... has effectively executed every sadistic item in its program of anti-Semitism. When some day the whole frightful tale is told, the story will constitute one of the most lurid chapters in the history of man's inhumanity to man.[54]

(119:) What are the implications of this tragedy for us as American Jews?... (120:) Up to the present time, the niggardliness of American Jewry in this crisis has been appalling... The very least we can do is to protect this proud and heroic element in Jewry from the ravages of famine, disease, and destitution, and to make it possible for some of them to escape from the living hell of Germany into the free atmosphere of other lands... [N]o Jews should have to be admonished against lending aid and comfort to Germany by the purchase of German-manufactured products, or the patronage of German-owned industries and services. For any Jew to contribute a single dollar, even a single penny to the prosperity of a government and a nation that not only reviles and persecutes its own Jewish citizens but carries on a well-organized campaign of hatred and vilification against all Jews in every land is to subsidize one's own degradation.[55]

Leo M. Franklin, "In a Time Like This!" Temple Beth-El, Detroit, MI. Unpublished, Rabbi Leo Morris Franklin Archives, now at AJA, MS-246

---

54 A painfully astute assertion in light of what was to come.

55 On the boycott movement, which Reichert strongly endorses here, see Moshe Gottlieb, "The Anti-Nazi Boycott Movement in the United States," and Gottlieb, *American Anti-Nazi Resistance, 1933–1941*, chaps. 6–15.

(3:) And so in times like these it behooves the Jew, accustomed as he is to suffer sword-thrusts when others are afflicted only with pin-pricks, to realize that while the attacks dictated by the malice of madmen that have as their purpose the extermination of the Jew and Judaism are to him dominant and supreme in importance over every other malign symptom in the modern world, they cannot engage to the exclusion of everything else the sympathies or the attention of all the nations. If this situation were clearer to us...we would be less spectacularly insistent in our demands upon the world's attention.... It's easy for certain of our leaders to call "craven coward" to those who will not join them in protest parades and in organized boycotts,[56] but (4:) whether their methods or ours represent the higher ethics and the sounder statesmanship the not distant future will inevitably tell....

The second result...has to do with the building of a defense program on the part of the Jew that shall avail him not merely in his momentary crucial need, but shall be to him as well a fortress of strength in the coming days.... [B]e warned that hysteria may work more mischief than inaction. If ever there were a time in Israel's history when the utmost wisdom and the sanest council was needed, it is in this very hour. The mistakes we make today in dealing with the German situation may be paid for in blood and in (5:) bitterness through a very long tomorrow. The time calls for statesmanship and for the utter sinking of personal interests on the part of individual leaders and of the groups that follow them. And, alas, one and the other of these have been wanting among us.

I am charitable enough to believe that it has been the zeal of service and not the urge of self-aggrandizement that has betrayed some of our people into doing the things that to us seemed more spectacular than wisdom would dictate. But the grim fact stands out that in a time when the Jews of the world, and in particular the Jews of America, should have presented a solid front to the world – when

56 This would certainly apply to the sermon by Reichert immediately above, but it was delivered on the same occasion. Franklin may be referring to Stephen S. Wise. Wise did not initiate the boycott, but he came to strongly support it at the World Jewish Conference in August 1934. For a condemnation of Jewish opponents of the boycott, see Harold Saperstein, "The Call to Battle," Rosh Hashanah morning, 1934, in "Complete Sermons," below; *Witness from the Pulpit*, p. 41.

like a Macedonian phalanx they should have faced their foe – there has been a division of our forces. Instead of unity there has been dissension. Whereas with one voice we should have addressed ourselves to the conscience of mankind, a dozen self-appointed spokesmen have appeared each speaking his own language and offering his own solution and making his own demands. Where the methods of the enemy should have been cried down as mediaeval, some have sought to imitate them by way of reprisal. We have shouted when we should have prayed, and we have cried for vengeance at the hands of men when we should have sought guidance from the God whose hand has never been too short to save....

(6:) I do not know, and neither does anyone else, what the ultimate fate of the German Jew is likely to be. We do know that in his undoing Germany herself will be undone. History has made that quite clear.... Six hundred thousand Jews in the Reich, degraded, pauperized, imprisoned, exiled, driven to suicide, may not survive it. Beyond aiding them to exist through our generous gifts of funds, beyond buoying them up and sustaining their morale with the assurance that in their pain we suffer, beyond appealing to the conscience of mankind against the continued brutality of a regime that has turned back the hand of civilization by two thousand years, it may as well (7:) be confessed that we are pretty powerless to change the present situation very much....

(9:)We stand today in a precariously perilous position, we Jews. Racked with pain for our brethren against whom a nation gone mad has thrust itself, we find ourselves well-nigh powerless to help them. The least and the most that we seem able to do is to send them funds to get out of their hell-hole and to start them anew in Palestine and other lands whose gates are not yet closed to them. So far as may be done by diplomatic means, we must arouse the conscience of the nations in their behalf.

Abraham J. Feldman, "The Forgotten," Temple Beth El, Hartford, CT. *Sources of Jewish Inspiration*, pp. 131–51[57]

57 This sermon was first brought to my attention by Chana Rosenblatt Mayefsky, a student of mine at Harvard Divinity School in the early 1980s.

(133:) [W]ith very few exceptions – and, alas, there are exceptions! – we have all been shaken to the very depths of our beings by the calamity that overwhelmed that portion of our people who live in Germany. We have been shaken and shocked not alone because of the inconceivable beastliness of Hitlerism and narcotic fiendishness of Hitler's lieutenants and amazing revival of sadism among the German people. These are not the sole elements of the tragedy. What is even more distressing is the fact that (134:) this could have happened at all, and of all places in the land of modern "*Kultur*," in the citadel of modern scientific theory, in the land of music, art and the much acclaimed "Enlightenment." What is so alarming is that it happened in the full view of the world, shamelessly and brazenly flaunted and boasted about, and that the beastly propaganda is tolerated in other lands, even here in America, and that there are those who sympathize with Hitler and are eager to emulate that wicked example.

For if Germany has her Brown Shirts, in America there is a movement (however small, but present) of the Khaki Shirts and the Silver Shirts stimulated by the Nazi example and literature and money.[58] What will the morrow bring – for us? Who knows? Our German brethren did not believe a year ago that they would be where they are today. Without any desire, believe me, of being a prophet of doom, it seems reckless not to ask the question as to Israel's security anywhere and everywhere. And the very suggestion of the question is (135:) painful, horrifying, like a bad dream that is not forgotten; it is haunting, torturing, dreadful....

(145:) In this time of distress for our people in Germany, their spirit is not broken. From a cable that came yesterday, I quote the following:

> A pathetic appeal was issued to the Jews of Germany by the Berlin Jewish Community:

58 "Khaki Shirts" was founded by Major L.I. Powell in 1932. "Silver Shirts" was a popular term for the "Silver Legion" founded by William Dudley Pelley in February 1933; he was eventually sentenced in August, 1942 to fifteen years in prison for sedition and undermining the war effort. See McMillan, "Pro-Nazi Sentiment in the United States: March, 1933–March, 1934," pp. 248–53; Dinnerstein, *Antisemitism in America*, p. 126.

> "All we pray for the new year," says the appeal, "is that we should remain alive, despite life being full of worries and despair for us. Many are unable to withstand life's storms, parting with life. Our nation (146:) was faced with thousands of dangers in the past but we are still alive, because God wishes us to live. In the most difficult times our forefathers prayed, *Zochrenu Lachayim* (Remember us, that we may live). So we pray now."[59]

This is loyalty! This is faithfulness!

Ferdinand M. Isserman, "The Century of Progress," Temple Israel, St. Louis, MO. AJA, MS-6, Box 13, Folder 5

(1:) Never before since I entered the ministry did I find it so hard to speak to my people as I do tonight, and yet never before since I have entered the ministry have I had so much to say, or did I feel more profoundly the eternal truths of religion and the effective way in which Judaism has given voice to them.

I find it hard to speak because I hesitate to convey to you the sense of tragedy which tortures my spirit, when I shake off the concern over petty routine and reflect upon the catastrophe for which mankind seems headed.... (2:) Civilization is in danger. Nations are arming. Fears abound. Suspicions are rife. Men have lost faith in each other.... Germany is militant once more. Its youth, maddened by the oppression of the Versailles Treaty, thirst for vengeance and clamor for victims upon whom they vent their spleen. The German army numerically may be small, but the German war spirit is gigantic and threatening. The war cry of Hitler's hordes has sent a frenzy of terror over Europe. In mad haste the neighbors of Germany are strengthening their fortifications, improving their armies.

(3:) Even as the national and international scene furnished us with shattering and devastating conclusions, so too the Jewish scene. This has been the most tragic year in all of Jewish history.[60] Nothing

---

59 JTA, September 19, 1933 (dated Berlin, September 18).

60 Sentences like this, which seem ironically hyperbolic (as well as historically inaccurate) in light of what was to come, would be repeated by this and other preachers as conditions continued to worsen.

in our annals can equal the tragedy (4:) of the triumph of Nazism in Germany.... (4:)...Much more tragic, however, than the hopeless situation of a half million Jews in Germany is the undermining of the Jewish dream of peace and of amity and fellowship with neighbors of other peoples and of other religions.... Al Smith was right when he said, "The Jews may be able to stand what the Nazis are doing to them but civilization cannot." For the tragedy to the Jew is indeed a tragedy of civilization.

September 21, 1933 (first day of Rosh Hashanah)

Harry H. Epstein, "The Jewish Conception of Progress," Ahavath Achim Synagogue, Atlanta, GA. *Judaism and Progress*, pp. 3–18

(4:) When we look without, we are appalled by the tempest of hatred, persecution, and inhumanity which has been loosed against the House of Israel. Sorrow, disaster, and suffering are again our lot. Another chapter has been added to our long *Tochechah* [chastisement]. In at least one foreign country new names are inscribed on the tragic scroll of Jewish martyrs. Germany replaces medieval Spain, Hitler, Torquemada, as the most horrible monster to arise and torture the Jew.... Our suffering today is without bounds, our grief is beyond expression.[61] When a civilized nation turns against us we sadly ask ourselves: here in all the world – where amidst all its culture and sense of human justice – where can we find security? In anguish we cry out: "Wherefore dost Thou forget us forever, and forsake us so long a time?...." (5:) Palestine, amidst the encircling gloom, is proving itself to be our sole encouragement and only assurance.

(14:) Tragic has been the fate of the assimilationists. Not only have they diluted Jewish consciousness and weakened Jewish solidarity, leaving Jewish hearts bleak and cold, but they even failed in self-preservation. The Hitler terror has proved conclusively the absurdity of the doctrine of assimilation. Bitter has been the fate of the *Deutscher Staatsbürger des Mosaischen Glaubens*!![62] Discarding their

61 A formulation that appears ironic and even hyperbolic today in light of the far greater persecution to come.

62 "German citizens of the Mosaic faith" (actually *jüdischen Glaubens* was the common

past they aped the ways of their country, only to be cruelly disinherited by the Nazis. They remain *kereach mikaan v'kereach mikaan*, neither here nor there, "naked souls, wandering between heaven and earth."[63] Assimilation will go down in history as a stark failure. Your bulwark of strength, O Israel, is your past; separate from it and you are ruined spiritually!

Leo M. Franklin, "Facing the Future," Temple Beth-El, Detroit, MI. Unpublished, Rabbi Leo Morris Franklin Archives, now at AJA, MS-246, Text 1165

(6:) [T]oday it would be the height of folly not to acknowledge that our position is a bit more precarious than it has ever been before. I am not now thinking only of the German situation, though God knows no Jew can escape the thought of it on a day like this. Rather I am thinking of the grim possibility that the conditions which now obtain in Germany may spread through a far wider area.... I call your attention to the fact that though at one time or another the monster of anti-Semitism had reared its ugly head in Germany, but five years ago, yes, three years ago, anyone (7:) who would have predicted that in this year 1933 of Christian civilization organized hatred against the Jew could have assumed its present proportions would have been deemed a madman – nothing less. You would have been told that the German people is too sane and too sensible to tolerate such a vile and vicious manifestation of inhumanity within its borders. Why, less than a year ago a very eminent Jew and a

---

term). This definition of Jewishness as a purely religious category was forced upon Jews by requirements imposed by the French Assembly that granted them full citizenship, insisting that the new France could accommodate different religions but not different nationalities.

63 The Hebrew phrase, meaning "bald from one and from the other," alludes to a folk tale about a man who had an elderly wife and a young wife. The young wife picked out from his head all hairs that were white; the elderly wife picked out all that were black, leaving him completely bald. The quotation appears to be taken from Nahman of Bratslav, *Likkutei MoHaRaN*, 65; cf. Arthur Green, *Tormented Master*, p. 213. "Naked souls" are souls without the clothing of good deeds, having no proper home, like the German Jews who are no longer accepted as Germans, but who do not feel comfortable as Jews.

leader in one of the great Jewish organizations in this country said in a public gathering that the finest thing that could happen to the Jews of Germany would be that Hitler should be chosen for the Chancellorship because then, this gentleman said, he would show his weakness and within a month he would pass out of the picture and be utterly forgotten.[64] And that sentiment was voiced by many another thinking Jew in America.

For my own part, I realized all too well that such a diagnosis of the situation was utterly mistaken. And now if we tell people that there is danger that the virus of German anti-Semitism shall spread to this country, again they say that such a thing is unthinkable.... I see what is happening around us. I read the American press, and while now and then there appears some editorial utterance condemnatory of Hitler and his tribe, on the whole there is a strange silence so far as the Hitler regime affects the Jew.[65] I follow what is being said from the pulpits of the great churches in the land, and their almost uniform silence upon this subject distresses my soul. I have yet (8:) to hear from a single Christian pulpit or have it reported to me that there has been anywhere anything like such a passionate protest as would have rung from the soul of a Prophet of ancient Israel in the face of such injustice and inhumanity.[66]

And, too, I see very positive evidences that the seeds of hatred against the Jew are being sown in this country in a way that is not

---

64 It seems as if the preacher assumes that many in the congregation would know to whom he was referring, but the reference is not clear to me. It certainly does not seem to apply to Stephen S. Wise.

65 For coverage in the American Press up to September 1933, see Deborah Lipstadt, *Beyond Belief*, pp. 13–37. A "strange silence" is not fully justified by the material cited by Lipstadt.

66 This statement also fails to recognize Christians who did speak out, such as John Haynes Holmes in his address at the Protest Rally in Madison Square Garden the previous March 27: "What shall we do in such an hour? 'Cry aloud and spare not' (Isa. 58:1). Yea, protest till the very stars shout back the echo of our cry. Such a cry will be heard, as it has already been heard.... And let us do what we should have done long since, reach out our hands to our stricken brethren in the Reich, and, understanding them, trusting them, loving them, join with them in ridding Germany and the world of this monster born of the terror of the night" (James Waterman Wise, *Swastika, The Nazi Terror*, pp. 83–84).

dissimilar to what took place in Germany before the rise of Hitler to his present power....

Stephen S. Wise, Free Synagogue at Carnegie Hall, New York. AJA, Box 21: SSW Microfilms of AJHS and BUASC papers

(1:) [report received on September 14:] Christian firms all over Germany have been advised by the Department of Commerce that they must obtain special Nazi trade signs which will make it clear to their customers that they are neither Jewish nor foreign.

(2:) Jewish communities in the Provinces of Germany have decided to abstain from all synagogue services celebrating the Jewish New Year in order to avoid anything that might be considered as provocation to the Nazis.

(3:) I shall not deal any longer with the tragedy of unworthiness, of lack of vision, of undaring Jewish leadership of German Jewry, which will be upon us too if we assent to these basely comprising terms in our own country...

(4:) I wonder whether Germany would have been denied to them if German Jews had not blatantly, super-clamorously insisted "*Wir sind nicht Juden*" ["We are not Jews, we don't belong to the Jewish Rasse or race"], "*Deutsch, Deutsch, Deutsch sind wir*' ["We are Germans, only Germans"]. One wonders whether Hitlerism and whether Naziism is not the inevitable answer of history to them that chose to misread, to misunderstand and to misinterpret the terms of their own tradition in order that smirkingly and contemptibly they might eliminate, minimize, and banish every difference between themselves and those among whom they lived.

(5:) One-third of the Jewish funerals in Frankfurt in the last six months have been the funerals of Jews who have committed suicide – one-third. The tragedy for me lies in those Jews who took their lives, or who go on living as ghosts, saying: If we cannot be Germans, if we cannot be Aryans, we are nothing, then we have no place, then we are homeless and anchorless.

(9:) The tragedy [of German Jewry] lies in this. There is no union of Jews. I did not come upon, I did not find any large planning, I did not find any statesmanlike leadership. I found Jews attacking Jews, Jews accusing Jews and Jews quarrelling with Jews. I found no abatement of the vulgarities and the mendacities that obtain in so-called Jewish leadership. *That* is the Jewish tragedy. That we who are supposed to be one cannot even find ourselves united in the presence of the seismic catastrophe which has shaken the very foundations from under our feet.

And there is another tragedy... the gravest tragedy of all: the tragedy of Jews prepared to yield to the enemy; Jews who, in the sight of a great and powerful foe, consider flight, escape, self-effacement as the only way out. The tragedy of the Jew lies in the heart and spirit of Jews such as the writer of this epistle to me...

The real tragedy is that we Jews may come to think there is only one thing: To guard against Hitlerism, whether in Germany or in Italy, or in Switzerland, Belgium, England, France, or in the United States – and that is, of foreswearing ourselves. By foreswearing our basic and, as I believe, uncancellable ideals, we can save ourselves....

(11:) Why is Hitlerism, why is Naziism needed in order to give us back our own again?

(12:) I would infinitely prefer extermination or self-extermination, for that were no tragedy, to something infinitely more tragic: that be we faithless to ourselves.

Aaron David Burack, "For Rosh Hashanah, 5694 [1933]," Congregation Ohel Moshe Chevra T'hilim, Brooklyn, NY. Unpublished notebook in Yeshivah University Archives, Burack, Box 4, Folder 4

(200:) Never before in the long history of mankind was an age more concerned about the questions of life and death than ours....

(202:) Why are we suffering from persecution all over the globe? Why are we driven from Germany? Haven't we participated in all scientific, economic and philanthropic endeavors of the German empire? We have given them an Einstein, who is now the man without a country, not being sure of his life. The murderers are threatening to destroy him....[67]

67 Einstein was visiting in the United States when Hitler came to power. He returned

Israel Mattuck, "The Jew and His Religion," Liberal Jewish Synagogue, London. Unpublished

(1:) The year since last we met together for the observance of this solemn day has been completely darkened by the terrible calamity which has befallen the Jew in Germany. It may without the slightest exaggeration be described as one of the greatest catastrophes in our history[68] – a history so often broken by calamities as to take on throughout a catastrophic character. There has been so much suffering in Jewish history that it may be said of the Jews of the past that they have lived by suffering. But we thought that the time of suffering was the past.... That confidence has been weakened, if not broken, by the Nazis. Their mediaeval treatment of the Jews affects all Jews the world over. The blow which has fallen directly on German Jewry must be felt also by Jews in all other lands. It must be felt because of the feeling of sympathy which unites universal Jewry, so that what affects one section must be felt by others, as the pain in one limb of a body affects all its parts. It must also be felt by all Jews because it is a challenge to their position, a denial of their equal humanity.

The thought of this calamity will be present with all (2:) Jews in the worship and prayers of this day, forcing out of them the question "Why?" and the cry "How long, O Lord?"... The Jews' suffering is the price we pay for our faith in God and humanity, and with the triumph of that faith over the whole world, and the hearts of all men, will come the time of the Jews', as of the world's, peace.

(3:) The Germany that is persecuting the Jews has become a grave menace to the peace of Europe. And there is one reason for both the persecution and the menace: the present rulers of Germany have reverted to the worst ways of mediaeval Europe. It is a revolution indeed, but a revolution not forward but backward.... (5:) The

---

to Belgium, turned in his German passport, and renounced his citizenship; his bank account was soon confiscated by the German authorities. During the summer of 1933, while he was in England, there were reports that his name was on a list of assassination targets. In October, he returned to the United States and settled at Princeton.

68 Here too a rather ironic formulation in light of the far greater persecution to come.

Jews are suffering in Germany to-day as they suffered in mediaeval Europe, and as they suffered in Greek Alexandria or in Syria under a Greek ruler, Antiochus: for their religion. In this fact lies the deeper significance of the terrible catastrophe.[69]

(6:) [I]t has made us proud to be a Jew to see the response of the German Jews to their persecutors. It is as if they said, "You persecute us for being Jews; we will, therefore, be Jews all the more!" Their courage will live when their persecutors are only a black page in history. Justification will come as surely as God lives."

Jacob Kaplan, "Return, O Israel, to the Lord Your God" (*Reviens, ô Israël, à l'Éternel ton Dieu*)," Synagogue de la rue N.-D de Nazareth. *Les Temps d'épreuve*, pp. 25–35, published also in *L'Univers israélite*, September 22, 1933,[70] translated by MS

(25:) The religious year that has just begun will remain sadly distinctive in the annals of Judaism. It will perpetuate the memory of a tragic catastrophe that will be counted among the great catastrophes of our history. Tragic because of the scope of the disaster, for six hundred thousand of our fellow Jews are suffering in honor and dignity. Tragic also because of the certainty that there is never true security for Israel, and that neither rights that have been granted, nor services that have been rendered, nor blood spilt in common, nor the progress of civilization will assure (26:) an effective safeguard for a considerable component of Judaism.

Abraham Isaac Kook, "The Call of the Great Shofar," Old City, Jerusalem. *Silver From the Land of Israel: A New Light on the Sabbath and Holidays*, pp. 49–51.[71]

---

69 Note the theme of continuity with the past in this presentation. It would take some time before new German policies of mass murder would bring a realization that the present persecution was fundamentally different from the medieval past.

70 The sermon was also revised for a radio transmission preceding Yom Kippur: David Shapira, *Jacob Kaplan, 1895–1955*, pp. 72–73 and 343 nn. 26–28.

71 This is adapted from *Mo'adei haRe'iyah*, pp. 67–70, http://ravkooktorah.org/ROSH_65.htm (Feb. 21, 2017). I am grateful to Chanan Morrison and to Tzvi Mauer of Urim Publications for permission to use this text.

There are three types of shofars that may be blown on Rosh Hashanah. The optimal shofar is the horn of a ram. If a ram's horn is not available, then the horn of any kosher animal other than a cow may be used. And if a kosher shofar is not available, then one may blow on the horn of any animal, even one which is not kosher. When using a horn from a non-kosher animal, however, no blessing is recited.

These three shofars of Rosh Hashanah correspond to three "Shofars of Redemption," three Divine calls summoning the Jewish people to be redeemed and to redeem their land.

The preferred Shofar of Redemption is the Divine call that awakens and inspires the people with holy motivations, through faith in God and the unique mission of the people of Israel....

There exists a second Shofar of Redemption, a less optimal form of awakening. This shofar calls out to the Jewish people to return to their homeland, to the land where our ancestors, our prophets and our kings, once lived. It beckons us to live as a free people, to raise our families in a Jewish country and a Jewish culture....

There is, however, a third type of shofar. [At this point in the sermon, Rav Kook burst out in tears.] The least desirable shofar comes from the horn of an unclean animal. This shofar corresponds to the wake-up call that comes from the persecutions of anti-Semitic nations, warning the Jews to escape while they still can and flee to their own land. Enemies force the Jewish people to be redeemed, blasting the trumpets of war, bombarding them with deafening threats of harassment and torment, giving them no respite. The shofar of unclean beasts is thus transformed into a Shofar of Redemption.

Whoever failed to hear the calls of the first two shofars will be forced to listen to the call of this last shofar. Over this shofar, however, no blessing is recited. "One does not recite a blessing over a cup of affliction" (b. Berakhot 51b).

We pray that we will be redeemed by the "great shofar." We do not wish to be awakened by the calamitous call of the shofar of persecution, nor by the mediocre shofar of ordinary national aspirations. We yearn for the shofar that is suitable for a holy nation, the shofar of spiritual greatness and true freedom.

September 22, 1933 (second day of Rosh Hashanah)

Harry H. Epstein, "The Jewish Way to Progress," Ahavath Achim Synagogue, Atlanta, GA. *Judaism and Progress*, pp. 19–33

(30:) Tragic has been the disillusionment of the German assimilationists. Breaking with their past not only availed them nothing, but left them broken in spirit and bereft of hope.... What bitter irony! In the very city of the "*Protestrabbiner*" of 1897 was established the odious "brown house" of the Nazis, the headquarters from which hatred and terror were spread over the land; it has become the "inquisition chamber" for 600,000 Jews.[72]

Who can foresee what the future holds? The sad plight of German Jewry of today may, God forbid, be ours tomorrow. The events of the past year (31:) impress upon us the imperative necessity that we build our defense. Who knows but that our children, in the not distant future, may yet need the Maccabean courage and the Akiba-martyr-spirit with which to face life. If in civilized, cultured Germany of 1933 Jewry has been so brutally crushed, well may we shudder when we contemplate our insecurity in all parts of the world.

Israel H. Levinthal, "The Demands of the New Jewish World," Brooklyn Jewish Center, Brooklyn, NY. *A New World Is Born*, pp. 173–79

(173:) [on the *Akedah*]: Strange, that this story should jar the minds of the Nazis in Germany. Only yesterday the press reported a story cabled from Schleswig, that the biblical account (174:) of Abraham's sacrifice of Isaac was stricken from the schedule of religious instruction on the ground that it was *un-German*, contrary to the spirit of the new Germany.[73] We can well understand how uncomfortable the Nazis must feel as they read of such devotion to a Higher Being, to whom not only the individual but the State and all the world owe allegiance.

---

72 For documents produced by the *Protestrabbiner* in 1897, see Mendes-Flohr and Reinharz, *The Jew in the Modern World*, 2nd ed., pp. 538–40. The "Brown House" was the national headquarters of the Nazi Party (NSDAP) in Munich. Herzl originally planned that the first meeting of the Zionist Congress would be held in Munich, but opposition in Munich led to him to shift the location to Basel, Switzerland.

73 Author's note: *NYT*, September 21, 1933.

(177:) I take it as a high compliment that the German tyrants, the representatives of the new barbarism of our age, have singled out the Jew as the leader of all the liberal and humanitarian causes (178:) that they seek to crush. That is the Jew's function: to sound the trumpet-call of the Messiah – to further the Messianic ideals of world peace, economic justice, and political righteousness.

(179:) We are living in too critical a time to carry on merely through the inertia of the Jewish past. Something more vital is essential today....

September 23, 1933 (Shabbat Shuvah)

Leo Jung, "The Choice," The Jewish Center, New York. *Crumbs and Character*, pp. 68–75[74]

(68 :) The slow economic and social strangulation of 600,000 of our brethren in the Hitlerite prison transcends in cruelty the wiles of Pharaoh and the ruthlessness of the Czar. It is our sacred duty to defend Germany's benefactors in this war declared on them by Germany's destroyers. The world boycott may cause Hitler to change his tactics. The sympathy for our people of increasing numbers of enlightened non-Jews is a source of comfort and strength. But the poison of Hitlerism is spreading.

(70:)They [the German Reform Jews] eliminated every reference to Zion from their prayer book. Hebrew became almost the forbidden language to them....

(71): There were no assimilationists like German assimilationists. There were no Jewish Jew-haters like the German Jews.... Hitler drove Jews to Jewry.... We cannot escape Judaism. We cannot escape Jewishness.

(74:) Stimulating Jewish consciousness is not enough. Nation-

---

74 The sermon text is not dated, other than "Tishri 1933." The preacher says, "As we enter upon the New Year," and recounts a story of the Baal Shem Tov "on a Rosh ha-Shanah" (p. 73), so it might have been delivered on Rosh Hashanah. But earlier in the sermon he quotes and applies a verse from *Nitzavim* (p. 68) and discusses the last words of Moses (p. 69), so I believe it is more probable that he delivered it on Shabbat Shuvah, for which the Torah reading is *Nitzavim*, in 1933, the day following Rosh Hashanah.

alistic self-aggrandizement has a way of changing into depression-mania.... Mass-meetings to arouse the public conscience are impressive, but they will not bring us salvation.... We must go back for ultimate salvation to the Rock of the Ages...

Moses Kahlenberg, "Sermon for Shabbat Shuvah," *Kehal Yere'im* ("The Polish Congregation"), Metz, France. *Darash Moshe* 1, pp. 92–108, translated by MS

(103:) The question asked by the prophet Isaiah, "Who was it that gave Jacob over to despoliation, and Israel to plunderers?" (Isa. 42:24),... has to our great sorrow turned into a question that confronts us today in the land of Germany across the border. "Who was it that gave Jacob over to despoliation?" including men of learning, philosophers, physicians, lawyers, military officers, nobles who own great factories. The great men of our people have indeed been given over to actual despoliation...

"And Israel to plunderers": they changed their honor into shame, their wealth and possessions have been lost,... day by day there pass before our eyes the terrible pictures of those who had assembled at the gate during the World War at the head of the German Army to serve their Fatherland, the country of their birth, and now they rush to find refuge in a land where they will be able to save themselves from the enemy, to seek food for their little children who are asking for bread. The sound of our brothers' blood is crying out to us from that cursed land (cf. Gen. 4:10); it is breaking through and rising to the heaven and engaging the attention of the enlightened world.

Indeed "a baffling matter has come to judgment *involving legal decisions*" (cf. Deut. 17:8). What is the difference between a Jewish lawyer and a nationalist Nazi lawyer, who has the legal right and permission to argue a legal case, while the Jewish lawyer, who studied together with him in Law School and served together with him on the same legal team, has no right to walk across the threshold of the gate of the Law in order to present his case and to make a legal argument....

[A baffling matter] "involving homicide, *Rassenblut*" ["foreign/racial blood"], something that has never before existed, that our ancestors could not have imagined, a kind of new compassion that is only temporary, showing pity for the suffering of animals: they think of their blood and oppose slaughtering an ox and spilling its blood,[75] but the blood of the Jew is open game, and one human being may spill the blood of another through tortures more bitter than death. This is what Hosea denounced (13:2): they say that sacrificing a human being is permitted, while they kiss the calves, showing more pity for them than for human beings.

[A baffling matter] "involving physical injury": Only the non-Jewish doctor may examine injuries and illnesses, not the Jewish doctor.

"Matters of dispute within your gates" (Deut. 17:8): They [the Nazi leaders] indeed arouse envy among the people and make quarrels within the gates, poisoning their spirits with foolish deceptions, arousing hatred of the Jews so that no nationalist will set foot on the threshold of a Jewish store for any manner of trade or purchase. Indeed, every opportunity for earning a livelihood is blocked for the Jews. Indeed, "a baffling matter has come to judgment" (Deut. 17:8): why are we different from the others, what shall the oppressed and the persecuted do? "You shall arise and go up to the place that the Lord your God has chosen" (Deut. 17:8). This is the one piece of advice provided from divine providence at this time for the house of Israel: to immigrate to our Holy Land. Perhaps that is where these exhausted Jews will find rest.

However, the door may once again swing closed on its hinges.... There in the land of Israel (104:) they will demand money for entrance, and the enemy will not permit money to leave the country. Even when it was earned by their own hard work, they have spread distress over the Jews by prohibiting them to remove money from German borders, and thus "the wilderness has shut them in" (Exod. 14:3). It is forbidden for them even to make a formal request for this right, a capital crime. Indeed, we shall see a vision of the Almighty eye-to-eye, for even those who have fully assimilated and learned the Gentile ways: they too have been devastated and forced to accept the conse-

75 This same argument would be used regarding the efforts to prohibit ritual slaughter in Poland, early 1936; see sermons below from February and March 1936.

quences of their behavior; they have been trampled down as if they were a well-trodden door mat. The Nazis take the wealth and the possessions and the livelihood of everyone they consider to be a Jew.

Thus the question "Who was it that gave Jacob over to despoliation, and Israel to plunderers?" (Isa. 42:24) returns in all its subtleties, returns and perturbs throughout the world, from one end to the other....[76]

September 29, 1933 (Friday evening, Kol Nidre)

Ferdinand M. Isserman, "The Scapegoat of History," Temple Israel, St. Louis, MO. AJA, MS-6, Box 13, Folder 5

(4:) Today in Germany history is merely repeating itself. The German people, defeated in the war, crushed by the economic depression, victimized by their leaders, who promised them grandeur and glory and instead gave them hunger and suffering, lacking the moral courage and the spiritual stamina to face themselves, to recognize their (5:) own initiatives, are offering a human sacrifice. From innumerable Christian leaders in Germany, I was told that the German people wanted a *Sündenbock*, a scapegoat, and that the Jew is being sacrificed in order that the German might believe that he lost no war. That his sufferings are due to malevolent forces, and that he himself is pure, innocent and guiltless....

(6:) Thus we have become the scapegoats of western civilization.... When I heard from government officials and from Nazi leaders in Germany what a great menace to their security these half a million Jews were, among whom there may not have been one hundred thousand breadwinners; when I heard that these hundred thousand were responsible for the war, for the defeat of the German army...; when I heard again that these same hundred thousand adults are

76 The preacher does indeed go on to present an answer, based on a rabbinic story discussed in the first part of the sermon, in which R. Joshua ben Hananiah, travelling to Rome, finds a Jewish child in prison and asks the question with which our selection begins and ends. The child responds with the continuation of the verse, "Surely, the Lord, against whom we sinned, in whose ways they would not walk, and whose teaching they would not obey" (Isa. 42:24).

the cause of the entire calamity which now afflicts Germany, I, who had always had great respect for the talents and abilities of Germans, began to lose my respect for them. I began to increase my respect for the ability of Jews. (7:) In every walk of life, in law, in medicine, in journalism, in commerce, in industry, in government, in literature, in music, the arts and in the sciences, in education, the great German people feared that the abilities of a hundred thousand Jews would master them and dominate their vast empire.

HAROLD REINHART, "Day of Peace," West London Synagogue, London. Harold Reinhard Archives, Parkes Institute, University of Southampton

It seems to us that this question cannot be confined to Jewry. It is an international question in which every civilized Government must take an active interest. The protection of Jewish refugees is not a political problem but an elementary duty, and plans should at once be made for the reception of exiles.[77]

September 30, 1933 (Yom Kippur)

MAURICE N. EISENDRATH, "Jews: By Chance or By Choice?," Holy Blossom Temple, Toronto. *Holy Blossom Pulpit*, VI, 1

(1:) Not for many centuries have such multitudes of white-robed worshippers assembled in their synagogues as the reports from all over the earth give testimony to today. Not only in these sun-kissed lands of freedom, but even under the leaden skies of vilest serfdom and persecution have our fellow Jews in unprecedented numbers repaired to the house of their God. Thus for example, we have read that never in the history of Germany did such vast and uncounted multitudes seek the synagogues as they did this year.[78] Halls and theatres, homes and public institutions all were transformed into

---

77 Almost all of the documents providing evidence for Reinhart's preaching are in the form of outlines, consisting of brief phrases, not full sentences. This is one of the very few passages that is written out, possibly because he thought that the content – Governmental responsibility for foreign refugees – was especially important.

78 A headline in the JTA of September 24, 1933 reads "Jam Reich Synagogues on Rosh Hashonah."

temporary synagogues, services were scheduled in two shifts, lay preachers were called upon to assist for there were not sufficient rabbis to take care of such swarming hordes of Jews, some of whom mayhap for the first time in their lives sought the Temple during this Holy season....

And yet I wonder. I wonder just what measure of strength will flow into our veins by virtue of these vast numbers of Jews who return to the house of Israel by grace of the enemy alone. I wonder just how meaningful is the surge of Jewish emotionalism which flows forth as a result of the fulmination of our Hitlerite foes.... (2:) Yea, verily this is the challenge of this distressing hour...whether in this critical moment for the destinies of Israel, we shall be Jews by chance or by choice.

(7:) I was in the office of a Jewish leader there [in Germany] who expected momentarily to be put under arrest and perhaps dispatched to some concentration camp, but who refused steadfastly to desert the ship, refused to flee while his brethren required his help. Those Jews may have been *externally and superficially* assimilated, they may have *sloughed off some of the more superstitious accretions of the medieval pale*,...they may have talked and dressed and eaten and even worshipped very much in the fashion of their neighbours, but their hearts were as strong as any kaftaned Jew who surreptitiously fled the moment the danger signal was sounded....

(8:) In such a time as this, we must all be Zionists, in the sense that Achad HaAm was a Zionist, in the sense that Einstein is a Zionist..., in the sense that Judah Leon Magnes is a Zionist, envisaging a center of culture and spiritual idealism which will flood the earth with beauty, truth and peace..... Such (9:) Zionists we must be; but raucous self-seeking politicians craving vaingloriously to satisfy our vanity and conceit by casting to the persecuted masses the same dry bone of flags and boundaries and sovereignty such as have just bathed the world in blood and threats imminently to annihilate the human race – such a nationalism, *such an assimilation to the idols of the mob is not the answer to our present plight....*

(10:) Do not for a moment think that Hitlerism is bent on any mere destruction of the Jew. Ah no, even that, even the massacre of a half million Jews is not the most terrifying feature of this contemporary Teutonic madness. Not the *Jew* is at stake, but *Judaism!*

Israel Mattuck, "The Jews and the World," Liberal Jewish Synagogue, London. Unpublished

(7:) There is nothing of permanent significance, I suggest, to be inferred from the accession to power by the Nazis in Germany. They represent a relapse from civilisation to barbarism. They call their work a revolution; but it is a revolution backward. The new names which they use cannot conceal the essentially retrogressive character of their thoughts and deeds. Such retrogressions occur occasionally in humanity's development in civilisation. The struggle upward is not without slips and backslidings. We cannot accept Nazi philosophy, nor Nazi policy, as a final, or even lasting, element in human civilisation even in Germany. The rest of the world has shown its abhorrence. For the position of the Jews in the world there is more to be inferred from the unequivocal condemnation of anti-Semitism that has come from every civilised country in the world than from the unequivocal barbarism of Nazi anti-Semitism.

Jacob Kaplan, "Nazism and Judaism" (*Nazisme et judaïsme*), Synagogue de la rue N.-D de Nazareth, Paris. *Les Temps d'épreuve*, pp. 37–44, translated by MS

(40:) The struggle in which Judaism finds itself presents itself in effect as a chapter in the conflict of barbarism and civilization. On one side, the persecutors have only words of hatred in their mouths; on the other, those who are persecuted invoke the Torah, where it is written, "You shall love your neighbor as yourself" (Lev. 19:18). On one side, the persecutors who pretend to be the people chosen to dominate and enslave the world; on the other, the persecuted, whose election is by God, recounted in the Bible, made with the purpose of serving and improving all of humanity. On one side, the persecutors boast of having as their ideal the life of animals in the jungle; on the other, the persecuted who believe that the only future worthy of humanity is the dawn of an era of universal brotherhood. Finally, on one side, the persecutors, who have emblazoned on their armbands and on their flags an emblem that represents the whirling of a hammer, that of Thor,[79] the warrior god of the ancient Germanic peoples; on the other, the persecuted, we who have our own equivalent insignia: the mezuzah, affixed (41:) to the doorposts of our house, reminding us constantly of the law of goodness and of love which God has bestowed upon us.

And this was not the first time in history when Judaism became the target of the enemies of civilization. In every era, in every country, Israel – persecuted, martyred – embodied the principles that were to triumph with the progress of the human spirit....[80] (42:) If in world history no people has faced martyrdom as much as the people of God, if whenever the progress of civilization is interrupted and barbarism raises its head the members of the Jewish community are the first victims of reaction, this is because Judaism is to be found at the vanguard of civilization. It owes this place of honor to its religious teachings, which have already bestowed upon humanity gifts that are infinitely precious.

October 8, 1933 (Sunday)

Israel Mattuck, "The Future of the Jews," Liberal Jewish Synagogue, London. Unpublished

(4:) The Nazi persecution of the Jews aims in so far as possible to exterminate them from Germany, and to give (5:) to those who from necessity or policy are allowed to live on an inferior position. The present rulers of Germany have made it clear that they want to kill and drive away as many Jews as possible, and to push the rest into a spiritual, political, and economic ghetto. It is obvious what the future of the Jews is if Nazi ideas prevail; it would be a return to their position in Mediaeval Europe...."

The German Jews refuse to accept as final their exclusion from

79 In Scandinavian lands the swastika was apparently called "Thor's hammer" (Mjölnir).
80 Here he continues with a brief discussion of Nimrod confronting Abraham, of Antiochus and Judah Maccabee, and of the intolerance of the Middle Ages.

German life which the Nazis have decreed, or the inferior position in a German nation to which they have been degraded. Their dignity and courage in the face of such violence will be one of the proud pages in Jewish history.

October 20, 1933 (Friday evening)

Ferdinand M. Isserman, "The Fate of My Brethren in Germany," Temple Israel, St. Louis, MO. AJA, MS-6, Box 13, Folder 5[81]

(1:) For weeks and weeks, I feel as if I have spoken to hundreds of men, women, and children who are condemned to death; condemned to death as inevitably – if the present Nazis remain in power – as is the criminal who has been refused a stay of execution by the chief executive. The massacre of all the Jews of Germany which seems to have been part of the Nazi plan has not taken place. It has not taken place because the conscience of the world has protested. When the conscience of humanity shall seem to be indifferent to the fate of Jews in Germany, or else the Nazis become indifferent to public opinion, then their doom will be sealed.

(2:) I find it hard to speak because I do not want to be interpreted as being a foe or an enemy of the German people. I know that many Germans are as pained over the situation as am I. I have spoken to such Germans....

I must speak. I bring a mandate, an unspoken mandate from Germany to tell the world and to inform you, my brethren, what has transpired to our peoples in the land some of them call their Palestine, whose capital city their Jerusalem.

I shall not now discuss the truth about atrocities. These are not to be ignored, but they are insignificant in comparison with the economic death-sentence which the Nazi leaders have passed upon the Jews of Germany. If the atrocities account for a hundred or a

81 This is the first of two Friday evening sermons in which Isserman reported about his visit to Germany in the summer of 1933. Other rabbis from America (e.g., Julius Gordon, also of St. Louis) and Canada (Maurice N. Eisendrath) also spent time in Germany during that summer and reported their experience and insight from the pulpit.

thousand Jewish deaths, the economic regulations may ultimately account for half a million. And if we include the human beings of one-fourth Jewish ancestry, then we may count two million deaths....

(9:) With all these stupendous difficulties, my brethren in Germany do not know when the laws against them will be made more rigorous, when their status will be changed. They live with the sword of Damocles hanging over their head....

October 27, 1933 (Friday evening)

Ferdinand M. Isserman, "Personal Experiences with Victims of the Brown Terror: Nazi Atrocities: Anti-German Propaganda or Shocking Truth?," Temple Israel, St. Louis, MO. AJA, MS-6, Box 13, Folder 5

(1:) You will understand the necessary restraints under which I must speak. I hesitate to mention names and places lest reprisals be visited on individuals who furnished me with the information. Not everyone I spoke to was willing to say anything about atrocities. Some were exceedingly hesitant and some refused altogether....[82]

(8:) Every foreign embassy, every foreign consulate, every foreign newspaper correspondent, reported atrocities and atrocities and atrocities. These diplomatic officials are not deceivers.... (10:) It is important for the American people to know this in order that they might know that the present rulers of Germany cannot be trusted and their gestures of friendship and humanitarianism are belied by their actions.

Why these atrocities? They are the fruit of victory that Hitler and his associates have promised to their followers. They have promised them work and bread. By ruining Germany's economic system, they are giving them neither. In order to keep their followers satisfied and content, they are allowing them to take vengeance against their personal enemies. In the streets you see no atrocities. Men are taken from their homes in the night. They are tortured in the halls and cellars of Brown Houses where a bloody story has been enacted.

---

82 He continues to describe his experience with eight different victims of Nazi persecution.

Alongside of that story inquisitorial dungeons will seem like Eden and Paradise. Nor are these atrocities over. From all sides I heard that this so-called bloodless revolution has been one of the bloodiest in history. That is why the sentiment of Europe, which had been for the revision of the Treaty of Versailles, and had become sympathetic with Germany's plight, has changed overnight. Americans might believe Hitler's professions of peace and good will, but the people of Czecho-Slovakia, Poland, Holland, Belgium, England, and of France, who have seen the victims of Hitler's brown soldiers, who have seen the welts on their backs, the bruises on their faces, who have seen them maimed for life, know that Nazism is not the rebirth of a great nation. They know that Nazism is the degradation of a noble people. They know that Hitler is neither a prophet nor a messiah, but a fanatical maniac, who is leading a revolt against civilization, against the humanities, against God.

October 29, 1933 (Sunday evening)

Alexander Lyons, Congregation Beth Elohim (Eighth Avenue Temple), Brooklyn, NY. Symposium on "Hitlerism and Christianity." *Brooklyn Daily Eagle*. Monday, October 30, 1933, p. 5

Hitlerism is a contortion and caricature of everything associated with the cross. It is in essence the attempt of a jungle brute principle to reassert its ravening power and sate its appetite with blood and booty.

From the standpoint of Hitler, the Jew possesses no cultural value, no idealism, and is only a ferment of decomposition trying to conquer the world. This is the basis of Hitler's agitation, and in pursuance of his purpose he is applying the principle that might makes right....

Hitlerism insists upon the racial purity of the Germans, and this is a presumption permitted only by ignorance. Racial purity has disappeared everywhere. Against this claim Christianity says there must be no Greek or Jew, bondsman or freeman, but only man.... Christianity asserts that spiritual reclamation through righteousness is the determiner of human duty and compels self-sacrifice in the interest of spiritual and moral realization. Hitlerism says physical strength determines what is right and approves material appropriation by a process of highway brigandage.

November 5, 1933 (Sunday)

Judah L. Magnes, "The Opening of the University Term, 1933–34," Jerusalem. *Addresses by the Chancellor of the Hebrew University*, pp. 207–26

These are days when we must look into our very souls. The Jews of Germany are being driven out or ground down because they are held to be of an inferior race. There is no hope, they are told, for any Jew's salvation – political, economic, religious – because no matter how much a Jew tries as an individual to perfect himself he is doomed to failure because of his low birth. When Abraham our Father saw the impending doom of Sodom and Gomorrah he prayed that the city be saved for the possible fifty or even ten righteous individuals therein [Gen. 18:23–32]. No matter how degenerate and corrupt these cities of violence, there was always the possibility that the individual might rise above his surroundings. But in the dominant German theory of race and salvation a Jew is condemned before his birth. There is no chance for him of achieving goodness, usefulness; there is no hope of his salvation even though he become a worshipper of the German God. There is no virtue even in his baptism as a Christian; he is congenitally incapable of "rebirth" in the spiritual sense because one grandparent was born a Jew....

(223:) A high official of the Prussian Ministry of Education is said in the newspapers to have ordered the elimination of Chapter 22 of Genesis – the "Binding of Isaac" – in German schools as not in harmony with the German spirit.... (224:) It is no wonder that the official... is put out with this chapter. The highest ideal of the present German state is brute force, the bearing of arms, which means eventually the spilling of human blood. Moloch is the great god, not Jehovah, and the children of the German state are being trained as sacrifices to this all-devouring divinity. The admonition "lay not thine hand upon the lad" (Gen. 22:12) is not for those who are ready to conscript the lives of their young for the next world holocaust....

This is obeying the voice not of the God (225:) of Abraham, Isaac and Jacob, but of the furies and demons of Teutonic forests.

November 6, 1933 (Monday)

Salis Daiches, Address to the Union of Democratic Control, Glasgow Branch, "Hitlerism and the Jews." Salis Daiches Archives, National Library of Scotland[83]

There is scarcely a topic that creates keener interest and commands more general attention today than that of the new spirit that has been created in Germany by the rise of Herr Hitler and the serious consequences that have followed his assumption of power in the Reich.... There are a good many people in this country who are ready to evince sympathy with Hitler on the ground that he was an impressive representative of intense German nationalism and fervent German patriotism and that the sentiments Hitler expresses are due to the bitterness created by the defeat of Germany in the Great War and the Versailles treaty that followed it. This, I venture to submit, is a mistaken view. All that can be said is that that bitterness weakened the resistance of the German people to the infection of the spirit which Hitler began to spread in Germany some ten years ago, i.e., the spirit of race hatred, more especially enmity against the Jews that is embodied in his book and that formed the topic of his countless speeches before millions of Germans until his appointment as Chancellor.

It cannot be maintained that the teaching of this Nazi leader is in itself a true manifestation of the German spirit as embodied in German history and literature and in the cultural achievements of the German people. It must be remembered that before the war Germany was regarded everywhere as one of the most civilized countries of the world....

83 The Union of Democratic Control (UDC) was established in 1912 in order to foster greater public input into government decisions; its period of peak activity was during the Great War and in the 1920s. This was therefore an address to an audience primarily of non-Jews. *The Scotsman* published a report of Daiches' address in its issue of November 8, 1933, p. 15.

(2:) In order to win over the German people to his policy of exterminating the Jews by first of all depriving the Jewish citizens of Germany of their elementary rights,[84] Hitler had to devote ten years of constant agitation and utilize his remarkable oratorical powers to the spreading of the most fantastic tales about the Jews and their influence on German life and on general civilization. No story was too wild, no slander was too base, no accusation too mean or too senseless in order to rouse the hatred of his vast audiences against the Jews of Germany and of other lands. He did not hesitate to use such forged documents as the so-called "Protocols of the Elders of Zion" for his purpose, and to (3:) [f ? ? ? t] the important events of history in a deliberately falsified version, to [misp....] and distort the writings and sayings of great men for his [...] end.[85]

His book *Mein Kampf* contained a rehash of some of the worst medieval legends concerning the nature and activities of Jews, combined with the most senseless allegations regarding a conspiracy of international Jews to destroy Germany, to subjugate the world to Jewish domination, to establish a universal language for his own mean purpose (Esperanto) [*sic*], to destroy civilization by a union with Freemasonry, to turn the world into a heap of ruins so that the Jews unified ultimately establish themselves as the [...] and become the sole rulers of the Universe. The generation of young Germans who had taken no part in the war were made to believe that the German defeat had been due to the treachery of German Jews, and that the Versailles Treaty had been planned by men who were either Jews themselves or had been influenced by Jews. The unemployed workers were told that their misery was due to Jewish capitalism and large business organisations. The conservative elements were made

84 The use of the term "exterminating" here does not imply that Daiches or his contemporaries believed at this point that Hitler's ultimate goal was what he would later (January 30, 1939) call "the annihilation [*Vernichtung*] of the Jewish race in Europe." That "exterminating" is used metaphorically here is shown by the actual policy mentioned: of denying the German Jews of some of the basic rights of citizens.

85 Here and in all passages taken from the hand-written texts in the Daiches Archives, dots in the middle of [ ] indicate that the I have found the writing to be indecipherable.

to believe that Communism was a Jewish movement. The third-rate men in the professions were persuaded that their failure was due to the pushfulness and gusto (?) of their Jewish colleagues; the students at the universities were persuaded that there was no future for them if Jews retained their posts at the universities, in the civil service, and in the established institutions.

In spite of all this it was safe to say that the majority of the German people are against Hitler's "death to the Jews" policy, and that if Anti-Semitism by itself were made the subject of a free plebiscite in Germany it would be defeated even if Nazism as a whole would triumph....

(8:) If one of the ancient prophets of Israel or Judea would arise today and survey the situation would he not address to the present ruler of Germany the words that are recorded in the first chapter of the Book of Isaiah? "Wash yourselves, make yourselves clean, put away the evil of your doings from before mine eyes, cease to do evil, learn to do well, seek judgment, relieve the oppressed, judge the fatherless, plead for the widow" (Isa. 1:16–17). This is how a nation can attain equality in the moral sense and [...] the respect and the good will of the nations. But not in the way Hitler and Göring and Goebbels are trying to achieve it. There is nothing in the Brown Shirt or in the Swastika that can command respect and secure the good will of the outside world. There is a great deal in these symbols and the deeds with which they have been associated that repels and disgusts. Surely clean hands are more important than brown shirts.

So far there is no sign of any change of heart on the part of the Nazis. Indeed we know that the aggressiveness of the Nazis is not even confined to the borders of the German Reich. Nazi agents are at work in almost every country in the world trying to spread their doctrines and to foster race hatred and to create enmity against the Jews. They are at work even in this country, and they are indulging in a campaign of insidious propaganda against Jews which thoughtful people would do well to counteract wherever it is discovered. A victory of Germany in the sphere of diplomacy and international relations would enhance the prestige of the Nazis and give a new impetus and strength to their agitation in other lands.

November 11, 1933 (Saturday)

Harold Reinhart, "Prayer on Armistice Day," West London Synagogue. *Harold Reinhart, 1891–1969*, pp. 69–71

(70:) We remember before Thee, O Lord, the pain of those days of the War, and we think with sympathy of the agony of many whose personal grief is still crushing. Solemnly we recall the far-reaching miseries of the world today, the roots of which stretch back to the dark War days, the physical and psychical, the economic and national wrongs which drag on as a heritage of those four years of hell let loosed. We behold those who cruelty has led to injustice, injustice to despair, despair to madness, madness to cruelty.

Scarcely do we dare, in the midst of the disillusion of this moment, to pray for healing for individuals or balm for nations. And yet, O Lord of love, Thou has bidden us trust in Thee, even though we walk through the Valley of the Shadow, and Thou waitest for us to turn to Thee even when our failings have raised a barrier before our souls.

And so we do lift up our voices and our hearts and cry to Thee now to fulfil the hope that once we voiced: that *that* might be the war to end war.... Keep alive in us that hope, that passionate demand which burst spontaneously from all our hearts fifteen years ago on this blessed day of Armistice: *that it shall not be again*, that the world *must* be saved from a repetition of such unspeakable horror.

Kalman Chameides, "Anniversary of the Resurrection of the Polish State: A Celebratory Service in the Synagogue,"[86] Katowice, Poland. *On the Edge of the Abyss*, pp. 206–11, translated from the Polish by Leon Chameides

(210:)The tragedy that has befallen our brothers in Germany over-

86 November 11 was celebrated in Poland not as the day that brought an official end to the Great War, but as the day when Józef Piłsudski was appointed Commander-in-Chief by the Polish Regency Council and entrusted with creating a national government for the restored Polish State (http://www.truecalendar.com/poland/1933). Five days later he signed a telegram notifying the superpowers and neutral countries of the creation of an independent Polish State. There was a large celebration in the synagogue at Shabbat services, November 11, 1933, the fifteenth anniversary of the restoration of Polish independence, at which the rabbi gave "a moving address suited to the occasion," which was soon published in the monthly journal.

whelms us like a terrible nightmare. Even though months have already passed since the outbreak of this terrible insanity – the sudden mania that overcame that once-great nation of poets and thinkers – we are still dazed, wounded, and mute from the blow that has been delivered to us. We have not yet been able to come to terms with the idea that the enlightened 20th century could give birth to (211:) the Middle Ages, a dark era of pain and suffering.

But are we [Jews] to be the only sacrifice to that dangerous insanity? Doesn't that megalomania contain within itself the spark of a new, bloody world war, a spark of *bellum omnium contra omnes* [a war of all against all]? Indeed, the theory of lower and higher races, their false measure of the value of a human being, is in opposition to a basic principle of the Church, scoffs totally at all religious views about the mission and purpose of a human being. Consequently we have a common enemy who lies in wait for our destruction, and who – at the first opportunity – will not hesitate to lift its sword against the freedom of Poland, the freedom for which the nation has suffered so much and fought so hard....

Let us therefore be aware of our obligations to the future. Let us be unceasingly mindful about the development and growth of the Republic, and let us have hope and confidence that God will deign to give us His blessings for ever and ever.

November 12, 1933 (Sunday)

Louis I. Newman, "Must Jews 'Walk Softly'?," Radio Address, Station WBNX. *Sermons and Addresses*, vol. 3, pp. 168–71

(169:) To those who counsel pianissimo tactics, we declare that we contend for what are not "probably" but "certainly" our human rights.... If these rights are infringed and Jews are made the scapegoat for the offenses of tyrants or fanatics, shall they be silent? If, after being citizens of Germany, loyal patriots of the Fatherland, they are disenfranchised, driven from their callings, ground underfoot like a helot-class, shall they meekly submit without appealing to the conscience and public sentiment of mankind, without asking for the restoration of their rights at the tribunal of the League of Nations?...

We will not clamor for our rightful privileges without dignity, but we will not permit ourselves to be the doormat of barbarians.

November 19, 1933 (Sunday)

Maurice N. Eisendrath, "Why Are Jews Persecuted? Part One," Holy Blossom Temple, Toronto. *Holy Blossom Pulpit* IV, 1

(3:) While the Jew is not by any manner of means the sole sufferer in Nazi Germany; while every dissenter from the present ruthless regime – and there are still millions of them despite the recent farcical opera bouffe election; while every liberal and pacifist, every erstwhile trade unionist and uncompromising Christian, is likewise groaning beneath this crushing and tyrannical dictatorship – still there is a very real sense in which the Jewish question is fundamental, in which it underlies and cuts through whatever is happening in Germany to-day. For whatever is evil in the Reich, Herr Hitler and his obsequious followers are convinced that it is due to the malign influence of the Jew.... So we see that although it is true that in actual numbers there are fewer Jews than non-Jews in concentration camps; although there are other groups who are being mercilessly liquidated in the Reich (4:) to-day, still all of them are hated and despised and persecuted primarily because in the blinded Nazis' sight they have become tainted by anti-Jewish propaganda.

(5:) Now I have read as much of these nauseating publications as I could stomach. While in Germany, particularly, I took great pains to read great tomes of this venomous propaganda which one can procure in any book stall or official Nazi store....

(7:) The Jew must be feared, so the accusation runs, because he is an international conspiracy scheming and plotting to gain possession of the entire world, and by pitting nation against nation and arousing class against class to accomplish their mutual slaughter, thus to gain complete domination over all mankind.

(8:) But surely only a blind man could gaze upon the altogether pathetic attempts of the Jewries throughout the world to aid their downtrodden brethren not merely in Germany but in Romania and Poland and throughout eastern and central Europe, and yet maintain that world power was in our hands. Ever since the war, the Jew has been enduring a death-in-life struggle throughout the continent. There have been pogroms in Hungary, student riots in Poland, atrocities in Romania – why could not this so-called International Empire have prevented such wholesale slaughter of their fellow-Jews?...

November 26, 1933 (Sunday following Thanksgiving Day)

Leo M. Franklin, "Thanksgiving – For What?," Temple Beth-El, Detroit, MI. Unpublished, Rabbi Leo Morris Franklin Archives, now at AJA, MS-246, Text 1177

(9:) The real danger of a great European war, however, naturally centers at this time in [Germany: crossed out] Central Europe. How far the madman of Germany can go before striking the match that shall set all Europe aflame is of course difficult to say. Despite Hitler's assertion that he wants peace above everything else, there seems to be considerable ground for belief that under the guise of productive industry his munition factories are working night and day....

As one looks over the face of modern events (10:) he cannot fail to realize that Germany is today the menace to World Peace, and that until the power of Hitler is curbed and some semblance of sanity is restored in the Reich, any sense of security that the nations may feel will be at best an illusion.

As to the Jewry of the world, for what shall it give thanks today so long as the German situation remains what it is. I am not of those who can persuade myself that out of this present tragedy shall come eventual triumph. I cannot delude myself into believing that the suffering of our German brethren will ultimately serve to add sturdiness to the spirit of the Jew. Even if that were the case, for one I am not willing to pay so high a price, nor am I comforted, as some seem to be, by the fact that the degradation of the Jew in Germany will open to him more widely the gates of Palestine.

(11:) I have a suspicion that there are those who feel that the German persecution was in the hands of God, a means of bringing to fulfillment the Zionistic program. Of course I am glad that even in some small measure the gates of Palestine have been opened to the refugee German Jew.... But we all know that Palestine alone will not solve the problem of the German Jew....

(12:) I do not delude myself into the belief that there is anything in the German situation which warrants any thanksgiving on the part of the Jew, nor am I unmindful of what is happening over here in relation to that German situation. The propaganda that is going forward in this country in behalf of the Nazi philosophy, far from being controlled and lessened, is in my opinion becoming ever more virulent and widespread....

November 27, 1933 (Friday evening)

Harold I. Saperstein, "What Have We Jews To Be Thankful For?," Temple Emanu-El, Lynbrook, NY. AJA, MS-718, Box 1

(10:) I have here a pamphlet called "The Voice of Religion," which contains not only statements from leaders of Christian opinion like Bishop Manning, Dr. Cadman, Dean I. Inge, and the Archbishops of York and Canterbury, but also a number of editorials from the Christian religious press. Among them are included no less than twenty-seven religious periodicals representing seventeen different Christian sects, and all of them are unanimous in their denunciation of the Nazi persecution of Jews. It is noteworthy that the majority of them not only condemn anti-Semitic acts but maintain that it is their Christian duty to cry out against these practices. The words of the Archbishop of Canterbury are typical when he says: "When injustice like this is abroad violating the elementary instincts of humanity, it is impossible for those to whom these things are precious to remain silent. They are bound to speak out if only to relieve their own conscience."

(13:) Shall I tell you of one of the profoundest experiences of my life? It was on March 27 of this year. I was at Madison Square Garden at the great protest meeting sponsored by the American Jewish Congress.... There around me was a sea of faces, more than 20,000 of them, my fellow Jews. As I thought of those 20,000, and more than twice that many more milling around the streets outside, and hundreds of thousands more listening to the radio at home, all our hearts beating in unison, petty differences of parties and beliefs forgotten, all united in a common interest and a common sympathy for other Jews more than 3,000 miles away, my heart filled with emotion.... And when I looked at the rostrum and heard Bishop McConnell and Bishop Manning (14:) and Alfred E. Smith raising their voices, that the world might hear, against a great wrong perpetrated upon our oft-wronged people, a thought came to my head, and it intoxicated me like wine: the thought that I was standing on holy ground, witness to a great event in Jewish history.[87]

December 10, 1933 (Sunday)

Maurice N. Eisendrath, "Who is 'The Chosen People?'" Holy Blossom Temple, Toronto. *Holy Blossom Pulpit*, IV, 3

(12:) (I)f you be not politically naïve as are a host of my friends, who see in Hitlerism only the persecution of eternally troublesome Jews, you will behold in the rise of National Socialism in Germany not a passing storm *but the torrential tempest of an ego-intoxicated regime convinced that it alone hath been given the right to dominate the whole of humankind.*

December 12, 1933 (first night of Hanukkah)[88]

Tobias Geffen, Hanukkah Radio Address, WSB, Atlanta, GA. Translated to English (from Dov Levin's Hebrew translation) by David Geffen, in *The Jewish Georgian*, Jan.–Feb. 2015, p. 31

In these days of spiritual and ethical crises, when many Jews afflict

87 Francis J. McConnell was Bishop of the United Methodist Church, serving a large congregation in Brooklyn, NY. William T. Manning was the Episcopal Bishop of New York. Alfred E. Smith, a Roman Catholic, previously Governor of New York State, had lost the 1928 presidential election to Herbert Hoover, and lost the 1932 Democratic primary to FDR, but remained a powerful and influential figure. For excerpts from Wise's speech at this rally, see March 27, 1933, above.

88 The specific date in December is not provided in the text, but Geffen wrote that he delivered the same message on the first night of Hanukkah in 1950, so I am assuming that this was originally broadcast on the first night in 1933. It could, however, have been on a subsequent evening of the holiday.

themselves with sadness and trepidation as they read in the newspapers what is happening to the Jews in Europe and in our cities here in America,[89] Chanukah arrives to make its impact felt with the burning candles, parallel to the sun's shining rays which enlighten the souls of the depressed. These candles are small, but their impact is very great. These little candles arouse within us the great national pride of yore when we were a monumental light for the entire world....

The Jewish people will triumph over all manner of enemies – the Hitlers and the Goebbels – who reign in the land of our exile, and others who rule in *Eretz Yisrael*. Then we will be privileged to see the fulfilment of the prayer we recite daily: "Cause a new light – *or ḥadash* – to shine over Zion."

December 18, 1933 (Monday)

Irish Press, p. 1

Headline: RABBI ARRESTED

Police have taken Dr. Dienemann, Rabbi of Offenbach, into "protective custody," for comparing the local chief of police to the ancient King Herod, in a sermon before a Jewish congregation. He intimated that the administrators of both were marked by similar violence, such as also occurred under the French occupation. – Reuters.

Also *JC*, December 22, 1933, p. 12

Max Dienemann, who was born in 1873, was Rabbi of Ratibor, in Polish Silesia, from 1908–19, since when he has been Rabbi of Offenbach, near Frankfurt. On Thursday of last week, his flat was searched by police and three books were removed, one of them a novel by Thomas Mann. On Friday he was arrested without reason given and taken to the concentration camp at Osthofen. It is suggested his crime was a sermon which he preached in the synagogue in which, after

89 It is somewhat surprising to find the situation of Jews in American cities in December 1933 placed in the same context as that of German Jewry. Allusion may be to the emergence of organizations such as the "Friends of New Germany" and the "Silver Shirt Legion"; cf. the 1932 sermon by J.X. Cohen.

describing the atrocities under King Herod, he went on to say that as far as the Jews are concerned it is the fact that they are ill-treated that matters, and not whether they are ill-treated under the orders of a French General or under the German police. We learn that police were present at a recent lecture that he gave at the Jewish Historical Society of Offenbach, which suggests that he was a marked man.[90]

December 24, 1933 (Sunday)

Maurice N. Eisendrath, "Swastika or Crucifix?," Holy Blossom Temple, Toronto. *The Never Failing Stream*, pp. 360–81

(369:) Even the Jew, helpless and hated, might have fought back more heroically, might have resisted more valiantly, as he did in the Middle Ages, had *his religion* been attacked. But it was not his religion *per se* that the Nazis persecuted when they imprisoned, starved, and murdered the Jews. It was his *blood*, his racial characteristics which he could not possibly change. Therefore he was not even given the satisfaction, had he struggled and resisted, of being martyred for a cause. But in turning so furiously against the Church, the Nazis found that there were many martyrs ready to be sacrificed for their fealty to principles more precious than the good graces of such pagan violators of their shrines, yes, principles which they loved more than security and life itself

Perhaps the first voice raised against this pollution of the Temples of the Lord was the stirring challenge of one of Germany's greatest theologians and rarest (369:) spirits, Karl Barth, a Swiss by birth but a professor of theology at the University of Bonn.... Now I do not agree with the creedal basis from which Barth's ringing protest sprang, but my heart became filled with admiration and my eyes welled with tears of joy as while I was yet on German soil, I read that monograph from his pen which seemed to me as the one faint glimmer of hope that flashed across the abysmally darkened land.[91]

---

90 Cf. also Astrid Zajdband, *German Rabbis in British Exile*, p. 55. Dienemann died in Tel Aviv in April 1939.

91 It is not clear which of Barth's works Eisendrath read during his visit to Germany

December 29, 1933 (Friday evening)

Ferdinand M. Isserman, "The Five Outstanding Events of 1933," Temple Israel, St. Louis, MO. Typescript in AJA, Box 13, Folder, 6

(5:) [3rd of 5]: While Roosevelt believes that the new society which industrial civilization has made imperative can be achieved through democratic and evolutionary processes, Hitler believes that democracy is an outworn superstition and revolution through the destruction of democracy a medium of progress. Far more important than the anti-Semitism of the Nazis, and far more dangerous, is their contempt and scorn towards democratic processes. What is fundamentally back of democracy but faith in one's fellow-man, belief in his divinity, in his perfectibility, in his eternal worthwhileness? Out of democracy comes the conception of world brotherhood. It implies belief and faith in all men. The franchise is merely the practical expression of that faith in one's fellow-man. This lack of faith in human beings has characterized the Nazis, and is responsible for their arrogant racial doctrine, and for their militant attitude toward other people. Democracy, world peace, world brotherhood are spiritual concepts linked together. When one link is destroyed, all are. In the philosophy of Hitler we note scorn for democracy, scorn for peace, scorn for the mass of men, contempt for other races. The Hitler phenomenon is not merely of significance to Germany. It is not merely a political movement confined to one country. It is a philosophy of life put forth in the modern world to oppose the democratic philosophy which has held sway since the era of the French Revolution.

December 31, 1933 (Sunday)

Maurice N. Eisendrath, "Happy New Year? What Odds?," Holy Blossom Temple, Toronto. *Holy Blossom Pulpit*, IV, 4

(4:) How disappointing and discouraging have been the past twelve

---

the previous summer of 1933, presumably something published after Hitler came to power. A significant number of books by Barth was published in 1933.

months for us all.... [One year ago] [w]e had felt that the Depression had reached the bottom-most depth and that prosperity could not but be around the corner; we had prophesied that the Disarmament and the Economic Conferences simply could not fail; we "knew" that the menacing madman of Europe had reached the height of his popularity and that his followers were falling away at last, that therefore the cockpit of the continent would be safe from radical rebellion, world tension would be eased and war was yet far distant.... Such were the hopes which throbbed within our hearts just one year ago, and while in some directions - particularly as concerns the faith of America in its wisely chosen leader - we have progressed; in nearly every other sphere we have stumbled tragically backward....

(8:) And that we are closer to war to-day than we were those tense and fevered days of 1914, no one but a fool or an ignoramus can deny.... [D]uring the year just gone by, although it was greeted with fond hopes of disarmament and peace, we have drifted so rapidly and seemingly so irrevocably toward war that even as sober scientists meeting at the convention of the American Association for the Advancement of Science assert, peace can be maintained only through a miracle. The horizons of our day are black with the approaching storm of battle....

1934

January 13, 1934 (Saturday)

Ignaz Maybaum, "Predigt am Sabbat Waera," (Sermon for the Sabbath *Va-Eira*), Frankfurt a. d. Oder. *Predigten an das Judentum von Heute*, pp. 58–63; translator unidentified

(59:) In our times we often hear the opinion, based upon statistical data, that prophecies the end of the German Jewry. To be certain, the numbers are unsettling. The reduction of the birthrate is great. The middle-class citizen wants a risk-free life and shies away from having too many children. In addition to Jewry becoming more bourgeois there is the political situation that makes our future existence in Germany unpredictable. All that is correct. But what is to be, we cannot determine based on numbers. The future belongs to God, Who is free to do as He wishes. Whether or not there will be a Jewish people in Germany in 50 years we simply do not know. But we pray for this German Jewry, like we pray for the rebuilding of Palestine....

But just as we pray for the rebuilding of Palestine, (60:) we pray for the preservation of German Jewry. Yes, we pray for the preservation of German Jewry! This prayer is based not only on material considerations, about which we are deeply concerned as creatures with physical needs. It is also about the intellectual possessions of German Jewry that must be preserved for Jewry as a whole, possessions that could be lost to all Jews if German Jewry should perish. German Jewry has in its *kehillot* a dynamic and profound Jewish orderliness for which the Palestinian Jewry will still need to struggle. They have a strongly pulsating political and cultural life, but organized communal life does not exist. The Orthodox have formed their closed groups, not too different from – indeed similar to – the way the free-spirited Jews of North America come together. This is sectarianism. Very different is Jewish communal life, as in Germany – ultimately stronger than Jewish factionalism – that keeps the free-spirited connected with the devout. If we pray for the continued existence of German Jewry, we pray for the preservation of inclusive Jewish Communities.

Furthermore, German Jewry has in its academic Jewish scholarship and theology, and in its more popular Jewish book publications, a high level of literature that makes us conscious of our Jewishness. That one could simply translate this literature into Hebrew is not yet sufficient. There must also be a cluster of people who will sustain such literature. However, Palestinian Jewry is (61:) still too weak to produce on its own such a sustaining echelon, that is necessarily of intellectual character. For all these reasons we can say: We pray for Jewry as a whole when we pray for the preservation of German Jewry.

February 1, 1934 (Thursday)

Woolf Hirsch, "The Jew and Nationality," Address to Rotary Club of Pretoria, South Africa, published in *Pretoria News*, February 2, 1934. *Selected Sermons and Addresses*, pp. 84–91

(91:) The present position of the Jews in the world is a difficult one, more difficult, perhaps than it was in the past. The recrudescence of the old prejudice, with all the repulsiveness of a bygone age, certainly makes it more hurtful in the twentieth century than it was in the seventeenth. But I do not think Dean Inge is right when he says that there is not such a thing as progress, that man is the same fighting beast to-day as he was two thousand years ago.[1] Judaism, unlike Hellenism, assumes a world process, a gradual growth and development, a slow advance towards an ideal end. This belief, at any rate, is a consolation. It enables one to take courage and hope for a better future.

February 16, 1934 (Friday evening)

Ferdinand M. Isserman, "Will Christianity, Protestant and Catholic, Survive in the New Germany? The Courageous Struggle of Ministers and

1 Reference is to William Ralph Inge, then Dean of St. Paul's Cathedral, whose famous statement appeared in his Romanes Lecture of May 27, 1920 entitled "The Idea of Progress" and was published in a thirty-four-page pamphlet by the Clarendon Press of Oxford. In this lecture he thoroughly analyzed what he called "the superstition of progress."

Priests Against the Nazi Juggernaut," Temple Israel, St. Louis, MO. AJA, MS-6, Box 13, Folder 7

(1:) The American people, in thinking of Hitlerism, are not aware that Hitlerism is not merely a temporary phase in German development, but that Hitlerism is a new philosophy of government which repudiates democracy, liberty, free-speech, free-thought, freedom of religion, and which is being hailed by Nazis as the new salvation for all government of the world....

(2:) [Cardinal Faulhaber] continued to point out that alongside of the ancient Jews who produced an Amos, a Hosea, an Isaiah, and a Jesus, the Teutonic tribes were savages and barbarians who were enlightened by Christian missionaries who brought to them the spiritual fruit of the Jewish people. These attacks – vigorous, bold, challenging – of the Munich Cardinal were practically ignored in the censored press of Germany....[2]

(3:) This protest of the Cardinal is a glorious event in the tragic history of Nazi Germany, but even more glorious has been the record of the Protestant clergy.... [Unlike Faulhaber, backed by the Catholic Church, Protestant clergy] are standing alone, backed only by their own congregations, and the protest of six thousand Protestant ministers against the attempt of Hitler's henchmen to emasculate Christianity and to prostitute the church by enforcing the acceptance of a tribal faith is one of the stirring epochs in the story of contemporary religion.

(7:) In the city of Stettin, Pastor [Gerhard] Wilde preached a sermon upholding the universal character of Christianity, and denying the right of the state to interfere with his faith. That afternoon, Pastor Wilde was removed from his post, though his congregation was with him, and a squad of brown shirts was quartered in his parsonage.[3]...

---

2 This refers to Faulhaber's five sermons delivered in the Munich Cathedral in December 1933, defending the moral values of the Old Testament, though not condemning the Nazi treatment of contemporary Jews.

3 This was probably based on a *NYT* article, November 22, 1933, p. 10, under the headline "Reich Clergy Fight Nazi 'Heathendom'," referring to "an incident that occurred in a suburb of Stettin last Sunday [November 19] when Pastor Wilde, an opponent of the Nazi church policies, took his congregation to a schoolhouse near

(8:) [Karl] Barth is the voice of the Protestant revolt against the Nazis.

(9:) At first it seemed that only Jews were going to be the foes of Nazism, and now we see that Catholics, Protestants, and Jews in Germany stand in the way of being crushed by this juggernaut. In Cardinal Faulhaber's appeal, he urged Protestants to unite with Catholics, and stand together to fight for religious freedom, and for the liberty of conscience. I have often felt that in this maze of conflicting religious beliefs, when Catholics, Protestants and Jews can unite, there must be eternal truth, there must be the will of God.

February 18, 1934 (Sunday)

Israel Mattuck, "Jews and Fascism," Liberal Jewish Synagogue, London. Unpublished

(1:) Jews have good and unfortunate reasons for being suspicious of Fascism. In Germany it is combined with anti-Semitism, so that its attainment to political power has had disastrous consequences for our co-religionists there. In other countries it seems similarly associated with a campaign against the Jews. On the other hand, there is a group of Jews in Germany that has supported the Nazi programme outside its anti-Semitism....

(5:) We may now draw our conclusions. Where Fascism has made anti-Semitism an integral part, or even a related part, of its program, the Jews must be opposed to it, even if they approve much else in its general aims. That opposition is not only natural, but it is a duty. Anti-Semitism is more than a danger to the Jews, it is a danger (6:)

---

his church and there attacked [verbally] the Reich Bishop [Ludwig Mueller]...and the German Christians, all of whom he accused of having introduced false teachings and force into the church. The rebellious minister was removed from his pastorate by the provincial Bishop [Karl Thom of Pomerania] the same afternoon, although he had the backing of his congregation, and a detachment of storm troopers was later billeted in his parsonage.... The Stettin episode was only mentioned in one [German] newspaper [the *Frankfurter Zeitung*] and very briefly at that." A brief AP bulletin dated November 21 also mentioned the incident, but I have not been able to find any other reference to the event or what later happened to the courageous pastor.

to some of the last ideas underlying our civilization.... (7:) The other aspect of Fascist teaching about the supremacy of the nation above international obligations and in defiance of international peace and unity is opposed to Judaism and all religion.

March 1, 1934 (Purim)

Max Dienemann, Offenbach, Germany. Two-page handwritten text in Leo Baeck Institute, NY papers, Band 1 of section 2, from *Morgen Heft* 9 (1933–1934), March 1934, translated by MS

It is a unique wonder in the history of Israel: it is forever on the edge of extermination, forever confronting the end. If this people chose to rely upon its own strength, it would certainly be lost; if it depended upon human beings, it would be helpless. That it remains and endures is always the ruling of God, the divine directing of history. From Purim there emerges the recognition that is valid for all contemplation of Jewish history and Jewish experience: it is a wonder not to be comprehended, not to be understood.

Purim is the day on which we should remember that God can remove from our shoulders our anxiety and our fear.

Samuel H. Goldenson, "The True Argument for Service," Temple Emanu-El, New York. JTA, March 5, 1934

Mordecai might have staged a great mass-meeting in Shushan, with great orators to tell the story of the achievements of his people.[4] He might have asked Esther to come to the meeting to listen to the story. Moreover, he might have appealed to her vanity, he might have flattered her, challenged her to show her influence with the king. He might have reminded her of what he, Mordecai had done for her....

We are now at a time when a Haman like that of old is seeking to destroy an entire nation.... In moments of trial, we should look more deeply into ourselves, and present to the world the better part of our natures. We are the children of a spiritual destiny.

---

4 A fairly clear critique of the mass rallies held at Madison Square Garden, led by Goldenson's colleague, Stephen S. Wise.

March 2, 1934 (Friday evening, Shushan Purim)

Ferdinand M. Isserman, "Why Remain Jews: Members of a Chosen or a Cursed People?," Temple Israel, St. Louis, MO. AJA, MS-6, Box 13, Folder 7

(5:) The tragedy of Germany's Jews weighs upon my soul, but its glories are evident. I am happy that Nazis feel compelled to extirpate the Jews from Germany because the Nazis seem to state to the world that their barbarian conception of the state can never endure if there are Jews in Germany. Therefore, the German Jews must be crushed, because they are too civilized, too pacifistic, too internationalistic, too intellectual, too spiritual, for Nazi palates.

Samuel Daiches, "The Lord Will Give Strength unto His People." Great Synagogue, London, printed as an eight-page pamphlet by Williams, Lea & Co., Ltd.[5]

(5:) Israel is weary. And Amalek is pursuing, is pursuing relentlessly. . . .

(7:) How shall Amalek show his face in the world? "And Amalek fought" (Exod. 17:8), fought with the sword and with the tongue. He killed and maimed mercilessly. And he slandered. He fouled the air with his falsehoods. "Israel does not fear God! Israel is only a horde of slaves! They robbed the Egyptians and ran away! They are ungrateful materialists!" . . .

(8:) And the voice of God was heard to say, "Write this for a memorial in a book" (Exod. 17:14). *And the history of Israel is the history of the world.* Amalek will again and again endeavor to fight Israel with the sword, with material force, and with the tongue. But the throne of God is established. . . .

(10:) My friends, Amalek has arisen against Israel in our own days. The last twelve months have been Amalek-months. Amalek has been endeavouring to destroy a portion of Israel and to cause the downfall of the whole of Israel. This has been a hard year. But Israel lives. . . .

(11:) If the Jews were to disappear to-day, or at any time, the Bible would return to God, would disappear from the world. But Israel lives, Israel *will* live. "And in His Temple everything saith, Glory" (Ps.

5 I am grateful to Jonathan Seres, a grandson of Rabbi Samuel Daiches, for calling my attention to this text and providing a copy of the pamphlet in which it was printed.

29:9). And a voice calls from generation to generation – unto eternity: "The Lord will give strength unto His people" (Ps. 29:11).

March 4, 1934 (Sunday)

Stephen S. Wise, "Roosevelt and Hitler," Free Synagogue at Carnegie Hall, New York. JTA, March 5, 1934

A year ago today, no one would have dreamed that one man would have transmuted hopelessness into hope. And a year ago today, no one could have imagined that one man could bring so much evil over mankind.

March 18, 1934 (Sunday)

Abraham J. Feldman, "If I Were a Christian: A Lenten Sermon," preached by invitation at First Church of Christ (Congregational), Hartford, CT. Printed pamphlet

(7:) The recrudescence of medieval barbarism in the land of "*Kultur*," the invocation of paganism in the land of Luther, the projection of fictitious racial doctrines in Germany and elsewhere, the plight of my people in Poland, in Romania, in Hungary, in Austria – these are not signs of daybreak, but of a deepening night.

Nor are things altogether heartening [for Jews] in our own country....

(12:) I want you to know also, that to the Jew, the Cross of Christ represents no such sacrificial love, no such redeeming hope, no such token of inner peace. To the Jew, the Cross is the symbol of persecution, of oppression, of discrimination, of the pyre and the gibbet. It is by the sign of that Cross of Peace that hundreds of Jewish communities were annihilated, thousands were slaughtered, millions robbed of life and happiness, by those who failed to grasp the significance for Christians of that drama of which the Lenten Season is the monitor and Easter Day the culmination.

Israel Mattuck, "What Christianity and Judaism Owe to One Another: (1) Christianity's Debt to Judaism," Liberal Jewish Synagogue, London. Unpublished

(1:) Cardinal Faulhaber gave last December a series of sermons in the Cathedral at Munich on Christianity and Judaism. His purpose was to answer the attacks on the Old Testament and Judaism made by some Nazis who, in their hatred of the Jews, want to separate completely Christianity from Judaism. In reply to them, the Cardinal expounds the permanent religious and moral values of the Old Testament, and describes the debt of Christianity to Judaism. He, as was to be expected, confines the indebtedness to the Judaism of the time before Christ.

April 1, 1934 (Sunday, second day of Pesach, Easter)

Stephen S. Wise, Free Synagogue at Carnegie Hall, New York. JTA, April 2, 1934

Hitlerism stands for what Pharaoh stood for: the enslavement of man, for what Pontius Pilate stood for: despotism and the degradation of a race. Hitlerism means hate, not love, enmity, not brotherhood, subjugation, not freedom.

Against Hitlerism, the Jew has only one weapon: not hate, but the love of an idea. Let us face the truth: Hitlerism means war, and the Jew is the prophet of the end of war. Let them call us cowards! Who can be cowards who stood conqueror against the world?

Let us say we are done with war. Everything which makes for war must go, whether it be nationalism or capitalism.

If I were to die today, the word "Hitlerism" would be found on my heart. Yet I as a Jew would not take a weapon in my hand to end Hitlerism, for Hitlerism was born of war. War breeds Hitlerism as Hitlerism breeds war, War bred Pharaoh, war bred Pontius, and war breeds Hitlerism.[6]

Isaac Herzog, Sermon at Adelaide Road Synagogue, Dublin. *Irish Press*, Monday, April 2, 1934, p. 14

---

6 A strong expression of the pacifist commitment that Wise had held and abandoned when the United States entered the Great War (see *Jewish Preaching in Times of War*, pp. 348–49, n. 10). Although he pledged never to make that mistake again, the new circumstances of the Second World War would cause him once again to abandon his pacifist commitments. See Urofsky, *A Voice That Spoke for Justice*, pp. 308–10.

[In an appeal for the relief of German Jewish refugees, Herzog referred to attempts made to associate Jews with Communism.]

This is one of the most groundless and most outrageous libels ever invented by human wickedness. Its sole object is to discredit the Jewish community and pave the way for anti-Semitism. There are men and women born of Jewish parents who happen to be Communists, or who are sympathetic towards that dangerous atheistic creed, but their Communism or Communistic sympathy has as much to do with the fact of their Jewish birth as the Communism or Communistic sympathy of the members of other races has to do with the fact that they were born into the Christian faith of Russian, English, American, French or Irish parents.

The Jewish religion, in fact, is suffering in Soviet Russia as much persecution as Christianity, and even more, and the future of Judaism in Communist Russia is a matter of the gravest concern to Jews all over the world. Judaism in that part of the globe is, alas! threatened with utter extinction. To associate the Jewish name with Communism or Communist sympathies is the height of falsehood and wickedness!

April 6, 1934 (Friday, seventh day of Pesach)

Abraham E. Halpern, "Is God to Blame?," B'nai Amoona Congregation, St. Louis, MO. *A Son of Faith*, pp. 5–10.

(8:) Because we have not found a way to solve our national and international problems, we are going to set the world afire again and the new war will be worse than the last. If engineers were called upon to devise ways and means for the last war, the scientist with all his genius is being called upon to invent machines of death that will destroy whole towns and cities. . . .

God will permit all this until man himself will find a way to live in peace in the world which God created for his happiness.

Joseph H. Hertz, "A Moral Challenge to British Jewry," Central Synagogue, Great Portland Street, London. Summary in *JC*, April 13, 1934, p. 23; complete text in *Sermons*, pp. 153–59.

(153:) The tragedy of our German brethren is so appalling that it can dispense with exaggeration. Several Jewish spokesmen have referred to it as the greatest calamity that has (154:) befallen Jewry since the Destruction of the Temple, and declare it to be without parallel in the annals of Israel. Neither of these statements is correct, and their repetition can only retard spiritual orientation. Even in our own times there have been far more bestial attempts at annihilating the Jew. In the Ukraine, during the years after the Great War, there took place 891 large and 349 small pogroms, with a toll of 60,000 slain, and over 100,000 wounded. And as for sinister attacks on the Jewish Faith, I need only point to the infamous strangulation of Jewish, as of all religious, teaching in Soviet Russia.

Even Nazi persecution of men and women who are merely of Jewish *descent* is not something novel.[7]...(155:) [W]e are today witnessing a striking instance of history repeating itself.... (156:) When the first political honours were conferred on German Jews, there were those who thought that the millennium had indeed come. No less a man than Professor [Heymann] Steinthal,... says, "Never again will Jews be sold into bondage. Never again shall we be deprived of our human rights." He was surpassed in his millennial assurance by the rabbi of the Berlin Liberal Synagogue who published a sermon under the title, *Kaiser Wilhelm: ein Messias unserer Zeit.*[8] Alas, it was only another false Messiah who was thus hailed fifty years ago. And now it is seen that all the sacrifices that were exacted by assimilation have been in vain....

(158:) [T]he terrible plight of our German brethren is a moral challenge to the Jews of Great and Greater Britain. This is a time neither for denunciation nor lamentation, but for action.... Large funds are required, if we are to save the refugees from hunger and want. Moreover, the religious structure of the German communities – the great fabric of Jewish knowledge and culture built up by a long succession of saints and scholars – is in danger of collapsing.

7 Here he gives as examples the "crusade of holy hate" in 1391 on the Iberian peninsula (which did *not* attack those of Jewish descent), and the Spanish Inquisition.

8 This was indeed the title of a sermon delivered by Moritz Levin on March 18, 1888 at a memorial service following the death of Kaiser Wilhelm.

That would be the crowning disaster. It would go a long way towards fulfilling the Nazi dream of reducing German Jews to the level of gypsies. That must be prevented at all cost.

April 8, 1934 (Sunday)

Abraham H. Feinberg, "Hitler and the German Situation," Temple Beth-El, Rockford, IL. AJA, MS-85, Box 1, Folder 2

(6:) We Jews have suffered many persecutions. There was the bondage of Egypt, the heel of Rome, the torch of the Inquisition, the Cossacks of Russia, but the cruelty which the children of Israel are suffering at the hands of the brown-shirted beasts of Nazidom is greater than any persecution which has ever befallen the Jewish people in the 3000 years of their history.[9]

Listen to these beautiful verses of love and mercy which the Nazis take great delight in singing:

> And when the hand grenade shall burst,
> The heart within the breast shall laugh....
> When Jewish blood spurts from the knife,
> Then all goes well again.[10]

(9:) Just a week ago today the National Conference of Jews and Christians set aside a Sunday and proclaimed it Brotherhood Day.[11] Never was Brotherhood more needed than in this present hour. A world enveloped in the fog of strife, hate, and Hitlerism looks to the sun of religion to shine through – and the sun of religion will indeed shine through.

---

9 A wildly hyperbolic statement for April 1934, in comparison with the number of Jews killed in eastern Europe in the years immediately following the Great War (see Hertz, immediately above, April 6, 1934).

10 The original German of the last two lines is, "*Wenn das Judenblut vom Messer spritzt,/ Dann geht's noch mal so gut.*" The English rendering of the four non-consecutive lines was probably taken from Lion Feuchtwanger, *The Oppermanns*, p. 158

11 It is this sentence that enabled me to date the sermon, as – unlike most other preachers – Feinberg neglected to indicate the date of delivery on any of the hundreds of his sermon texts in the AJA. The first Brotherhood Day, widely observed, was set for Sunday, April 29, 1934. The April 1 date on which the NCJC met is provided by the *American Jewish Year Book 5695*, vol. 36 (1934–1935), pp. 131–32.

Israel Mattuck, "What a Year of Hitlerism Has Taught the Jews and the World," Liberal Jewish Synagogue, London. Unpublished

(1:) While almost everything possible has been done to degrade [the Jews] spiritually, and to oppress them economically, nothing has been done to define their position theoretically in the new Germany. The most serious concrete consequences for the Jews of Hitler's rule are:

(i)The professions are practically closed to Jews. That exclusion falls with greatest weight upon the young men and women who were preparing for a profession, or had just begun the practice of it. And it is not yet certain how far they, and other young Jews, will be admitted to handicrafts and agriculture.

(ii) The Jewish traders in many, perhaps most, of the smaller cities have been completely ruined. There is evidence of this in the large decline of some smaller Jewish communities, and in the practical disappearance of others.

(iii) The State Schools have (2:) been made impossible for Jewish children by the instructions in anti-Semitism, which all the teachers are commanded to give. This is connected with what is in some ways the most serious consequence of all: the poisoned atmosphere in which they live, poisoned by brutal and subtle hatred, and by conscious efforts to shame and degrade them....

The question, therefore, arises: How far can what has happened to the Jews in Germany be taken as a symptom of a disease, or danger of disease, that exists in other lands too, and, therefore, (3:) be taken as a warning signal to Jews all over the world?...

[On "narrow and aggressive nationalism":] Hence the attitude of some of Sir Oswald Mosley's followers in this country who recently plastered their Black House with the inscription: "Shall the Jews drive us into war with Germany?"...[12]

We Jews, therefore, may not, and must not, ignore, or neglect, the danger for us in the spread of this kind of nationalism. It has even infected some of those who call themselves Jewish nationalists....

---

12 Mosley was the founding leader of the "British Union of Fascists"; the "Black House" headquarters was in Chelsea.

(4:) The year of Hitlerism has taught the world the danger of this bastard nationalism sprung from over-weening pride coupled with hatred. It must be opposed by the legitimate nationalism born from loyalty and the spirit of humanity.

(5:) [T]he Zionists in Germany join with the non-Zionists in the claim to the rights of the German Jews in Germany; and that not only because Palestine cannot take them all, but because Germany is their homeland. The fact that Hitlerism denies the right does not destroy it. And the majority of the nations of the world have shown clearly and emphatically that they recognise that right. Hitlerism denies that the Jews belong in Germany, but the Jews have shown that they do.

May, 1934

Samuel S. Cohon (Prof. of Theology, Hebrew Union College), "The German Situation" (Outline-draft). AJA MS-276, Box 18, Folder 6

(2:) At this very time, an organization of about 10,000 Jews in Germany seeks to identify itself with the Nazi ideology and to justify Nazi atrocities against the Jews.[13] Outside of Germany, too, there are numbers of Jews who set up the idol of Jewish nationalism, and worship it in place of the God of truth and justice. In Jewish nationalism they see not the instrument of religion but a substitute for religion. By virtue of the intensity of their agitation and propagandizing, they appear to the unthinking as the most loyal of Jews.

The tragedy in Germany is not limited to that country. The poison which has been at work there is spreading to other lands. Energetic efforts are made to inject it into English and American life as well. Why should be our attitude to the problem? There are those who hold out Jewish nationalism as a solution. Nazification of Judaism would be the greatest of disasters.

---

13 Reference is apparently to the *Verband nationaldeutscher Juden* (League of National German Jews), founded in 1920 by Max Naumann, which supported German nationalism and therefore vehemently opposed the Zionist movement and all links with international Jewish organizations. After Hitler came to power, it attempted to prove its German loyalties by supporting the new regime, until it was finally disbanded by the Nazis. See Steven Aschheim, *Brothers and Strangers*, pp. 220–24.

Others plead in all sincerity that the answer is Palestine. To be sure, for thousands of victims of German persecution, Palestine does offer a haven of refuge. But we are a people of seventeen million souls; and by no utopian scheme can more than a fraction be accommodated there. Furthermore, the heralding of Palestine as the solution to our vexing problem is playing into the hands of our enemies. They might even enter into trade agreements with Palestine, as long as Jews get out of Germany and other lands where they belong by right.

No, my friends, the solution lies in no such short cuts. It is rather in the long, long struggle for justice in the world, for human equality, for good-will, and for peace.

May 16, 1934 (Wednesday)

Ferdinand M. Isserman, Address before the St. Louis Council of American Jewish Congress, at YMHA, St. Louis, MO. AJA, MS-6, Box 13, Folder 7

(1:) Fellow Jews, last year at this time we were crushed, stunned, and bewildered when the news of the terrible calamity which had befallen our brethren in Germany reached us....

(2:) Wherever Jews were gathered over the world, they expressed their sorrow and voiced their protest. Many joined us in our protest. Among them were leaders of all civilized nations, Protestants and Catholics, legislators and statesmen, [Episcopal] Bishop [William T.] Manning and [former Governor of New York] Alfred E. Smith, Senator [Joseph T.] Robinson and Senator [Millard] Tydings,[14] the Archbishop of Canterbury [Cosmo Gordon Lang] and Sir Winston Churchill. In the great parliaments of nations men rose and denounced the persecution of Jews.... (3:) What has been overlooked because of sympathy for Jewish suffering is that Naziism is not solely an attack upon the Jews, but an attack upon the foundations of civilization in which Jewish persecution is an incident, a cruel

14 Robinson, from Arkansas, was Senate Majority Leader at the time; in June 1933 he delivered a powerful address condemning Nazi persecution (see JTA, June 24, 1933). Tydings was Senator from Maryland; he introduced a resolution in January, 1934 "condemning Nazi oppression of Jews in Germany," but it never succeeded in passing the Senate Foreign Relations Committee.

incident.... (8:) Only the synagogue has not been disturbed, because the aim of the Nazi government is the "humane extirpation of the Jews" from Germany.[15]

May 20, 1934 (Sunday, first day of Shavu'ot)

Abraham Mayer Heller, "Satan in Search of Torah," Flatbush Jewish Center, Brooklyn, NY. *Jewish Survival*, pp. 35–47

(44:) Think of present-day Satanic leadership. No agreement, no pledge even of their own making is sacred to them. They in no way resemble any of the noble spirits that helped make their nations great.

We today are aware of the fate of those who dare prophecy in the face of Satanic rule suppressing the will of a nation. The concentration camp, however, for those who differ with Satan's Torah, is no new invention.[16]... (45:) Exile, concentration camp, imprisonment and bloody purges are the ways of Satan's Torah, but God's law as exemplified in the leadership of Moses proclaims to humanity, "Would that all the Lord's people were prophets" (Num. 11:29).

June 9, 1934 (Saturday, *Shelaḥ*)

Ephraim Levine, "Inferiority or Superiority Complex," New West End Synagogue, London. *The Faith of a Jewish Preacher*, 51–59

(58:) So-called Civilisation still toys with the idea that men were born to fight, that women are to rear sons for the slaughterhouse; the means of destroying life rather than of preserving life are primary charges on a nation's budget. Germany still argues about the status

---

15 Isserman cited this phrase in his booklet "Sentenced to Death," published in late 1933 and based on his one-month visit to Germany during the previous summer, attributing it to "one of the most important Nazis in Germany" (p. 25). Independently, the phrase was cited in a JTA report of January 22, 1934 about an address delivered in Montreal by the General Secretary of the International Committee of the YMCA, stating that he heard it from "a very high official" on a recent visit to Germany.

16 "Satan's Torah," expressed in the title of the sermon and recurrent throughout, is based on a rabbinic legend recorded in b. Shabbat 89a. It is clearly applied here to Hitler's rule of Nazi Germany.

and constitution of her religion at a time when the whole policy of that nation is the very negation of the first elements of Religion. Greed and jealousy are the only connecting links between nations, and the whole world is in a worse chaos than when God first called: "Let there be light" (Gen. 1:3). And in the midst of all this muddle the Jew is the scapegoat for all the world's ills. What a travesty of history, what a re-statement of Jewish beliefs! If we are grasshoppers now in our own eyes we deserve to be thought thus in the eyes of others.

No. The Jewish standpoint is not the inferiority complex. If we can triumph and are strong as Joshua and Caleb in the face of the majority, it must be the superiority complex.... (59:) The modern Joshua and Caleb will counsel us: "Let us go up for we can conquer" (Num. 13:30).[17] The cry is back to Judaism, back to Jewish belief, back to Jewish faith. The Promised Land is still there, awaiting the arrival of the children of God.

June 14, 1934 (Thursday)

Samuel H. Goldenson, President's Message to CCAR Convention in Wernersville, PA, 1934. *World Problems and Personal Religion*, pp. 107–19, and *CCAR Yearbook* 66 (1934), pp. 147–62

(107:) We are living, as every one of us knows, in difficult times.... In such times we Jews are, alas, always the first to feel the wrath of the disappointed and enraged men.

At this moment, the seat of the great difficulty and sorrow is in Germany: the land of the philosophers, the poets, and the musicians, strange to say! The present rulers of that land are bringing home to us afresh, with brutal force and with humiliating intent, the meaning of the Jewish problem. The Third Reich is giving us a new insight into the nature of human history and is especially teaching us the significance of the phrase "our times." We now understand more than ever that we are (108:) living in a pluralistic universe, temporally considered....

---

17 This might have led to a Zionist message, but it did not; as the concluding sentences show, it is "back to tradition," with the Promised Land understood metaphorically.

Hitler, chronologically, is a contemporary of Thomas Mann, Albert Einstein, and Franklin Roosevelt, but psychologically, he is centuries apart from them. Yet in Hitlerism we find the most important factor in determining our day. The German dictator, in the year 1934, has his seat of office and power in Berlin, where he has the use of devices for expression that are completely modern – the telephone, the telegraph, and the radio – but the things that he says and the spirit in which he says them are altogether a reproduction of the superstitions and the venom of those who perpetrated the Inquisition in the fifteenth and sixteenth centuries. The major difference between the medieval persecutors and him is that he is able, through the swift agencies of communication, to distil his poison with electrical dispatch.

But we must hasten to remark that deleterious influences, like beneficent ones, must have fertile soil. Men like Hitler unfortunately are always present in the world; at any rate, potentially. It is only when their fellowmen are greatly disturbed, defeated and frustrated, that they become a prey to these demagogues and false messiahs. For it must be noted that behind Hitlerism is a broken and thwarted Germany, surrounded by a world totally demoralized and envenomed by the war and also completely impoverished by the inevitable depressions that followed....

If we were wise and good physicians as we should be, we would not spend all our time and energy in denouncing Hitlerism, but reserve some of our strength for the greater and more useful task of understanding the background and the causes of its power and seek to eradicate them....

(III:) If we should take proper counsel from the nature of the attacks made upon us in Germany and if we study their origin and the way they are justified by our enemies, we would be especially on guard against the development in Jewish circles of narrow and trivial conceptions of culture, of chauvinistic nationalism, and of the advocacy of rigid and regimented solidarity.[18]

---

18 An apparent critique of Zionist sympathies and public appeals to Jewish solidarity as manifest in mass protest rallies.

Such solidarity, I fear, is being urged upon us at this very time....

In Germany today there is the same insistence upon solidarity. Hitler claims to have more solidarity behind him than any former leader has enjoyed. Alas for the world that such is the case, if it is so. If we, as Jews, develop the kind of solidarity that is merely the result of the pressure from the outside and if we herd together at the cry and call of any champion, we may be led to the valley of destruction without having spiritual recourse to the redemptive powers....

(112:) In many cities our people have been called together by self-appointed leaders for the assertion of Jewish rights and for the promotion of special programs and objectives. The appeal has almost invariably been made in the name of Jewish solidarity. Such an appeal, we should be reminded, is not unlike that of the super-patriots who frequently go so far as to insinuate that if one does not heed their call, it is a certain sign of disloyalty to one's people and one's country.

At present, the German Jews are in dire difficulty. The duty should be clear to every one of us and should not be beclouded by any other issues. If Palestine can offer a haven to some of the German Jews, then Palestine and our German brethren should be helped to come together. Should Russia or any other land offer them a place of settlement, the same duty should prompt us to offer like assistance.

July 2, 1934 (Monday)

Joseph H. Hertz, "Theodor Herzl: His 30th Yahrzeit," Great Synagogue, London. Summary in *JC*, July 6, 1934, p. 31; complete text in *Sermons*, in *Sermons, Addresses and Studies*, (henceforth *Sermons*) 1, pp. 119–26

(120:) The Jewish intelligentsia of Vienna and Berlin, Paris and New York, ridiculed his forecasts of Jewish persecution in Western lands, and dubbed him a pessimist and a dreamer. "My happier co-religionists will not believe me, till Jew-baiting teaches them the truth," he bitterly complained. Now that Jewish emancipation has been repealed in Central Europe, and anti-Semitism has (130:) broken all bounds, it is seen that *they* were the dreamers, and he, the one waking man among them.

(124:) I need not remind you what a Providential haven the New Judea is proving in the heart-breaking tragedy that has overwhelmed our brethren in Nazi Germany.

July 3, 1934 (Tuesday)

Elias Margolis, President's Message to the Thirty-Fourth Annual Convention of the Rabbinical Assembly, Tannersville, NY. *Proceedings of the Rabbinical Assembly of America,* vol. 5, pp. 64–68

(64:) No message to any Jewish gathering today can afford to omit an opening statement on the situation of world Jewry.... I am content with the simple observation that although the Jewish situation may appear to be even worse than it was a year ago today, the prospects are a shade brighter. This optimism is not based on the news which comes daily from Germany of the rift between the left and right wings of the Nazi group. Past experience, bitter and costly, bids us to be wary and to place no confidence in rumors and in what may turn out to be a vain hope. Long before Hitler was known, the so-called Nazi conservatives, the militaristic-monarchic party, were working overtime, infecting the German people with the virus of Jew-hatred. The only hope for the German Jews is that the Nazi family quarrel may end in mutual destruction and that the suppressed liberal forces in Germany will once more lead Germany back to civilization and sanity.

August 21, 1934 (Tuesday)

Stephen S. Wise, Address at Third World Jewish Conference, Geneva, Switzerland. AJA, Box 21: SSW Microfilms of AJHS and BUASC papers

(6:) If we say American Jews initiated the boycott, I am prepared to say that that is not inaccurate. The Jewish consciousness began it, the American conscience carried the boycott on. For, after all, the American Federation of Labour is in no wise Jewish. It represents six millions of workers in America, and they, the Federation, declared in mighty terms a boycott against German goods and services, which they have faithfully observed. I would remind you that not merely does the boycott go on, but it *will* go on...

A boycott means peace and not war. It means the self-respect of Jews and non-Jews throughout the world who feel wounded, either by what Nazi Germany has become or has done – a world which cannot do any business with, or have any contact with, or in any sense co-operate with, Nazi Germany. That is what the boycott means.

(11:) In my own country, men like Bishop [William J.] Manning, Bishop [Francis J.] McConnell, John Haynes Holmes, S. Parkes Cadman, Harry Emerson Fosdick, and many more too numerous to name, lifted up their voice to protest against that enemy of civilisation; and that most prophetic voice, the voice of Cardinal Faulhaber, of Munich, gave utterance to the most solemn protest. I give reverent thanks to God and to Cardinal Faulhaber's Church to-night. If against us we have the gangsters of Germany, with us we have the great moral and spiritual leaders of mankind.

Late August, 1934

Harry Joshua Stern, "Cardinal Faulhaber," Temple Emanu-El, Montreal. *Judaism in the War of Ideas*, 89–92 [undated, internal evidence: apparent use of *JC* Aug 17, 1934]

(89:) In the Christian revolt against paganism in the Third Reich there looms largest the personality of a Cardinal Faulhaber, Archbishop of Munich... Wherein lies the greatness of this man? Faulhaber, at the very hour when Nazi mad racialism and paganism reached its height, dared to stand squarely across the path of Hitler's campaign for suppressing truth. In the face of persecution and concentration camps, the Archbishop of Munich during the advent season of 1933 preached a series of vigorous sermons in defense of the Old Testament and indirectly of the Jewish people.[19] Thousands listened to these challenging addresses. And these had a tremendous influence upon people in Germany. The Cardinal saw in German paganism a threat to the very foundation of civilization. (90:) The

19 See Faulhaber, *Judaism, Christianity and Germany*. Faulhaber made it clear (as perhaps he had to do in his public preaching) that he was speaking about ancient Israel, not contemporary Jews.

longing on the part of the Nazi to propagate the worship of Wotan meant turning back the clock of religion.

After the tragic Hitler clean-up of last June 30th,[20] the Cardinal delivered a sermon of protest against the persecution of the Jew by the Nazi. He declared in this passionate appeal to the Catholic community: "History teaches that God always punished the tormentors of His Chosen People, the Jews. On June 30, the God of Israel meted out punishment against their persecutors. Do not you, Catholic brethren, see that this is God's retaliation, and a fully deserved one? We must respect the Jews, who have given to the world the greatest and most precious gift: the Bible. We shall never exterminate this old people, this oldest of all peoples, by persecutions. Enlighten your brethren that racial hatred is a wild growth in our life. Tell your household who the Jews are. Wipe out this terrible inhuman prejudice against the ever-suffering people. Repent, Catholics, if you have ever done wrong to God's people, the Jews."[21]

Brave words these are by a brave religious soul. One would have thought that such quality of courage would have been displayed by some apostle of science. But no! The scientists, editors, and the leaders of Germany's literary world have all abdicated in the face of the Hitler Terror. Not science but religion has throughout history dared to be prophetic.

---

20 Reference is to "the Night of the Long Knives," a purge of the *Sturmabteilung* (SA) and its leader, Ernst Röhm, in which at least eighty-five active members of the Nazi Party were killed. See Paul Maracin, *The Night of the Long Knives: Forty-eight Hours that Changed the History of the World.* It seems rather incredible that a religious leader such as Faulhaber would have publicly interpreted this as divine punishment by the "God of Israel" (see following note).

21 The text cited here appears to have been taken verbatim from the British *Jewish Chronicle*, August 17, 1934, p. 16: a–b. (A citation from the same sermon in JTA, August 21, 1934 provides a different translation of the text.) The final paragraph cited from Stern's sermon is also derived from the *JC* article; cf. also *JC* August 24, 1934, p. 13a–b, and September 7, 1934, p. 37a. Unfortunately, the text of the Faulhaber sermon, first published in a Social Democratic newspaper in Prague, then reprinted in part by the Basel *National-Zeitung*, turned out to be a fabrication, and Faulhaber's secretary was instructed to protest the citation in his name. See Guenter Lewy, *The Catholic Church and Nazi Germany*, p. 276, citing *Amtsblatt Munich*, November 15, 1934, Supplement; Theodore S. Hamerow, *On the Road to the Wolf's Lair*, pp. 142–43.

Friends from Germany have informed us that Faulhaber's (91:) sermons are cherished in every Jewish home. No wonder! The common fate facing Jew and Catholic in Germany is bringing them into close sympathy and is forging a friendship between them never experienced hitherto.

September 8, 1934 (Saturday)

Israel Mattuck, "A Review of the Year," Liberal Jewish Synagogue, London. Unpublished

(1:) As we approached the High Holydays last year our thoughts were dominated by the catastrophe in Germany which was then less than six months old. In the year that has passed the catastrophe has become no less, but we have come to see more clearly its dimensions, and to measure some of its effects. Under the first impact of the blow, we were dazed, deeply and acutely pained, and naturally full of fears about the future. The shock has passed off, the pain has become dulled. Time has exercised its inevitable, and at times merciful, healing effect. In this case, however, the effect is not an unmixed good. The greatness and gravity of the catastrophe call for an intense response, that we should be moved to do our utmost, both in relieving those who suffer materially under it and in fighting against it. But the year has brought an ability to look at the facts and prospects more calmly and to appraise them more judiciously.

(2:) Nothing has occurred during the year to improve the position of the Jews in Germany. All the edicts made by the Nazi Government as soon as it came into power, restricting their participation in the social, cultural, and political life of the country, remain. Their devastating effect in practice has not been so extensive as the anti-Semites wished and as the Jews feared. Some lawyers and doctors among the Jews have been allowed to continue in their professions. The number of them, however, who are doing so with profit, is probably small. In other professions, the position is much worse. The exclusion of Jews from political, academic, and cultural positions and activities is practically complete. So far as is generally known there are no Jews left among the conductors of orchestras, the editors of newspapers, the directors of theatres, the judges of law courts, and State or municipal officials. Among the professors and lecturers of universities, there may be a few non-Aryans left, but I (3:) doubt whether any of them are professing Jews. The number of Jewish students at the universities is severely restricted.

(5:) The number of Jews who left Germany is less than what would have been expected under these circumstances.[22] There are several explanations for this small number. One is that there was no place for them to go to. The countries of the world do not welcome immigrants; they admit only a few very reluctantly. That applies to Palestine as well as to other countries.... (6:) Only about 10,000 German Jews have found a new home there. Another reason for the comparative smallness of the number of German Jews that have left Germany lies in their natural attachment to their country, which holds strong even against the ill-treatment which it inflicts on them....

(7:) [T]hough the Jews of Germany are not free to challenge even the laws against them on the grounds of righteousness, they have made it clear that they do not accept them as right even while they obey them, and that they reject all that they imply for the political status of the Jew....

(10:) In this country Sir Oswald Mosley, modelling himself after Hitler in the hope of achieving a political success like Hitler's, has gone as far as he dare for his ends – in taking over Hitler's anti-Semitism – but he has had a reminder from (11:) an unexpected quarter, his sometime ally the *Daily Mail*, that anti-Semitism is an exotic poisonous plant that will not grow in this country....

(12:) The best opinion of England felt this responsibility in the present case of Germany's treatment of the Jews. Mr. Ormsby Gore expressed it at a meeting of the League of Nations Assembly.[23] The Archbishop of Canterbury [Cosmo Gordon Lang] expressed it at

22 Here he provides estimates: 51,000 by the League of Nations; 65,000 by the German government.

23 Referring to a speech delivered on October 9, 1933 by William Ormsby-Gore, 4th Baron Harlech, at the Fourteenth Assembly of the League of Nations, in which – in the presence of the German delegate – he strongly criticized the Nazi doctrine of

a Protest Meeting in the Queen's Hall. Sir Austen Chamberlain and others expressed it in the House of Commons. There remains, however, the danger that some people may be misled by the general attractiveness of the doctrine of non-interference to apply it in this case, which, because it involves some of the precious moral achievements of the human race, calls for a most emphatic and constant denunciation.

The most disastrous effect of German anti-Semitism outside Germany has occurred in Austria.... (13:) On the other hand, it may be accounted one of the good effects which Hitlerism has produced outside Germany that in Poland the Government has turned more earnestly toward the protection of the rights of the Jews and their position against the attacks of the anti-Semites in that country, who have been stimulated into more virulent activity by the events in Germany.

(14:) [W]hen we look (15:) back on all that has happened during the past year, our general conclusion is one of natural sadness for the evil that anti-Semitism has caused, but of deep gratitude for all the evidences that the best of humanity condemns it, and of gratitude mingled with a justifiable pride in those Jews who, most afflicted by it, have responded to it with a heroic dignity.

September 9, 1934 (Sunday, Erev Rosh Hashanah)

Stephen. S. Wise, "For Better or for Worse," Free Synagogue at Carnegie Hall, New York. AJA SSW Microfilms of AJHS papers, Box 21

(1:) Humankind faces the question today as perhaps never before of a "for better or for worse," for we are entering upon one of the epochal years of history. There will be no short cuts either back to prosperity, such as it was, or to security, as it ought to be....

(2:) As "for better or worse" for Israel, whether it is to be better depends largely upon two decisions of the Jew. One: to live at his best, and for the best, and for life's highest values. Two: not to be

racial intolerance. See *JC*, October 13, 1933, p. 17; *American Jewish Year Book 5695*, vol. 36 (1934–1935), pp. 103–5.

like "dumb driven cattle" led to slaughter.... It is not easy to speak of "better or worse" for the Jewish people in a year which has beheld infinite sorrow and suffering. We have in the past year plumbed depths of woe and anguish. And still things infinitely worse than hurt and suffering might have been, things far more tragic than to have become among the earliest and most brutally crushed victims of Hitlerism. Namely, to have been singled out for *favor* by Hitlerism, or if Hitlerism had been indifferent to us. I count it nothing less than our honor and our distinction that we were first to be singled out for Hitler's disfavor. Apparently and actually, it has not been good for our fellow Jews in Germany, but good it is indeed for us that when civilization from foundations to crown (2b:) attacked, we Jews are the earliest and the chiefest victims of the devastation.

September 10, 1934 (first day of Rosh Hashanah)

Stephen S. Wise, "For the Mountains Shall Depart," Free Synagogue at Carnegie Hall, New York. AJA SSW Microfilms of AJHS papers, Box 21

(2:) "For My mercy shall not depart from thee" (Isa. 54:10). That mercy reveals itself in many ways.... The great among the leaders of public opinion, and the utterance of such a mighty and prophetic spirit as Cardinal Faulhaber of Munich, whose word to his country is, "Racial hatred is a wild and poisonous weed in our life. Root out this awful, inhuman prejudice against the eternally suffering people."[24]

(3:) Barbarism – is that not too strong a term? Rather it is too mild. For even barbarians are loyal to their own, and these neo-barbarians are not. Witness the slaughter of their own comrades and leaders, an orgy of assassination in which each of the chief miscreants was free to slaughter those he deemed dangerous to himself.

For these reasons, because of the fulfillment of this prophecy, the Hitler horror has befallen the Jew, the Jew who is the prophet of justice, the Jew who is the apostle of peace. Hitlerism calls it Marxism and International Pacifism. So be it! The prophecy will be fulfilled;

---

24 Unfortunately, this quotation turned out to be a fabrication. See above, Harry Joshua Stern, Late August, 1934, with note.

the Jew will not be goaded to yield up the substance of his eternal quest, justice, nor become an advocate, defender, glorifier of war. The prophecy must remain valid, and, if it is to be, the Jew takes up the heaviest responsibility in history. For this generation will witness the Armageddon of Armageddons, justice versus injustice, liberty versus enslavement, peace versus war. Jew: be equal to the prophecy of old!

Jacob Shachter, "The Blast of the Shofar," Belfast Synagogue, Northern Ireland. Published in *World Jewry*, September 1934, also in *Ingathering*, pp. 64–66

(64:) The beginning of the year that is about to pass into eternity witnessed the outbreak of an assault on the Jew, unprecedented in its ferocious shamelessness.... [N]ow that we have come to the end of the year we see an invigoration rather than a weakening of that open battle cry against our existence. "Israel has been brought to an extraordinary stage in its history." This slogan, unfortunately, has been so oft repeated of late that it fails in its purpose and is regarded as one of the platitudes employed by platform speakers. In that itself we may trace our tragedy. It is usual to refer to the crisis through which Jewry passes and to point, as a matter of course, to its cause in the phenomenon of that world-wide movement led by Hitler, which gives the world the Jew as the scapegoat for its ills. That is only one aspect of the crisis. There is yet another factor which aggravates the situation. It is the lack of strategy how to meet the enemy which itself is a result of the lack of concerted effort – a weakness that has accompanied us from time immemorial.

The allegation that our enemies usually throw up against us as a crime, that we are internationally united, is a tragical farce. Not only are we divided into so many Jewries, but Jewry in every country is divided within itself. Consequently, there is no mouthpiece through which the Jewish people can speak authoritatively at this, the darkest hour in its history. This bitter truth comes to the fore whenever the question of a World Jewish Congress is discussed. Another notorious feature which constitutes one of the (65:) gravest of problems is the lack of unswerving faith in the truth of our ideals, in our teachings of justice and righteousness, in our glorious heritage, in our God-bestowed mission for all times – spiritual forces which have always shielded us. Consequently, our battlefield has taken on an undisciplined and disorderly aspect. Admittedly, the only bright spot in the darkness is Eretz Israel. But even this is dimmed by clouds which gather at frequent intervals on the horizon. Nor is the policy of the mandatory power to be given as the only cause. The disruption which we ourselves have created within our own camp is perhaps more to blame.... [T]he Yishuv is divided, unfortunately, more than ever....

This tragic disintegration in the ranks of Jewry in the Diaspora as well as in Eretz Israel – these internal conflicts and party clashes which are the order of the day – encourages our enemies in their deadly onslaught. The first and foremost message which we must issue through the blast of the Shofar throughout the camp of Israel is for a consolidation and rallying of forces for our defence.... Secondly, we must arouse the dormant spiritual forces of our youth and afford them the insight and proper frame of mind to understand their fellow Jews and Judaism.... (66:) If Rosh Hashanah can arouse Jewish consciousness to the extent of bringing about the regeneration of our soul within, and the unification of forces without, it will have conveyed its message. We might, therefore, spurn our enemies and say, "Our soul is invincible. No tyrant can crush us."

Harold I. Saperstein, "The Call to Battle," Temple Emanu-El, Lynbrook, NY. *Witness from the Pulpit*, pp. 37–43; see Complete Sermons

Alexander Altmann, Passauer Strasse Synagogue, Berlin. In *Predigten an das Judentum von Heute*, pp. 12–17, translated by Jens Laurson and MS

(12:) Amidst these difficult times, ראש השנה [Rosh Hashanah] has come again. It used to be nothing more than a day of calm contemplation. Life flowed along smoothly. One did not expect a new directive from this day, no signal, no shock. It was no תרועה, no powerful trumpet blast that one heard, no wake-up call, but merely a זכרון תרועה – a "remembrance of the trumpet blast" – a stirring of symbolism removed from reality. Judaism did not penetrate to the innermost core. It was a matter of edification, not of re-structuring our lives, a matter of experienced remembrance, not of the actual present.

For us, however the תרועה is heard and we are startled. When in ancient Israel, at the beginning of the jubilee year the ram's horn of freedom sounded and ushered in a new epoch, when everyone had to release his accumulated possessions and had to give up cherished attachments,[25] it must also have brought about a powerful stirring of hearts. But we have come to the end of more than just a jubilee period; we have come to the end of a historical epoch.

"If a shofar is blown in a city, will the people not be afraid?" (Amos 3:6). Woe to us, if we do not become afraid! The God of history Himself calls to us the words, ושבתם איש אל אחזתו ואיש אל משפחתו, "You shall return, every one of you to your property and every one of you to your family" (Lev. 25:10). Return to Judaism is the sign of our times....

(13:) The Jew of the *Golus*[26] must allow people to say, "You lack creative energy, (14:) your existence is worthless." He sees life around him growing, spreading; he stands like a stranger in the midst of the world. Should he deceive himself to think that he is a people like the others, an equal link set in the chain of the peoples of the world? Surely, he roams through the life of this world with the others; he does not shut himself off, yes, he even renders a contribution to the production of goods on this planet that is not insignificant. But is he not in reality a חטיבה אחת בעולם, a unique entity in the world,[27] a type whose character somehow doesn't fit into the environment – and therefore is subject to misunderstandings? Can anyone deny that ever since the beginning of our passage through the *Golus*, we have ceased to possess the legal basis for our very existence that all other peoples possess?

The era of Emancipation wanted to convince us: see, Jewry fits excellently into this world! But today we know: As long as we are in *Golus*, we do not fit into this world. And yet we bear the weight of

25 See Lev. 25:8–13.

26 *Golus*, used frequently in this passage, is the Ashkenazi pronunciation of the Hebrew word generally rendered "Exile," almost always with negative connotations that do not apply to other Hebrew terms rendered "Diaspora."

27 b. Berakhot 6a.

Golus. That is the greatness of the Jew: to know of his fate and yet – feeling the rift in his soul – not to sink. That is the meaning of bearing the Jewish destiny. Such is Jewish pride. To feel the tragedy of our being and yet stand with dignity. Not to approve of the *Golus* – for in reality one negates it inwardly though spiritual assimilation – but rather as God's servant to be willing to endure the *Golu*s as *Golus*....

(15:) Are we still able to pray? The confident person, the person spoiled by luck, cannot pray. He thinks his hand is at the helm of his destiny. What does he need a God for? He cannot pray – at best he can fear. Until "the bows of the mighty are broken" (1 Sam. 2:4). Our bow is broken. If we have forgotten how to pray, we can now learn again. The Days of Awe are the university for prayer. Suffering is its pre-school. Many of us have preserved the dignity of suffering for themselves, but have not yet discovered the beauty and power of prayerful pain. We must again strengthen this kind of prayer.... (16:) Only from suffering can redemption be born. Even now in our days the glimmer of future redemption already shines. This curse of the *Golus* is beginning to depart from us.

(17:) If the signs do not all deceive, the Jewish people seems not only to be about to put an end to the epoch of the aberrations of blind assimilation, but even more, to overcome, through God's mercy, the millennia of its "Wandering Jew" existence, the long night of *Tokhecha* [rebuke], the great punishment. The land of our ancestors is changing from the desert back to the Promised Land.... The suffering of our times is – already today – overshadowed by the blessing of what is to be.[28]

To be sure, *Golus* is not by any means yet overcome. No one believes that we have already been redeemed.... But we know: *He raises up the poor from the dust, lifts up the needy from the ash heap...; for the pillars of the earth are the Lord's, He has set the world upon them* (1 Sam. 2:8).

---

28 A rather painfully optimistic evaluation of present and future for German Jews. Despite the strong repudiation of Jewish life in *Golus* and the apparent endorsement of Zionism as the authentic solution to Jewish suffering, when he left Germany Altmann went to England, where he served as rabbi for twenty years, and then eventually to the United States, where he had a highly successful career as Professor of Jewish Philosophy at Brandeis University.

September 11, 1934 (second day of Rosh Hashanah)

Israel H. Levinthal, "Fashioning a New World," Brooklyn Jewish Center, Brooklyn, NY. *A New World Is Born*, pp. 15–23

(20:) Again the world is threatened with *Tohu Vo-vohu* [void and nothingness]! One must be blind not to see in the rise of Nazis in Germany the beginning of a new flood of misery that is bound to engulf the world.

You can now understand why these new forces that have come to power in Germany have centered their great hatred upon the Jew. They want a world opposed to the Moral Law.... The Jew to them is the first target, because to them he is the symbol of that Law which he was the first to proclaim. But their hatred goes beyond the Jew, it embraces Christianity as well, because they perceive in Christianity – and rightly – the continuation and the re-emphasis of the Judaic ethic that came from Sinai's heights. This much must be said in the Nazis' favor – they are frank, they are open and above-board, in the declaration of their purpose. "The time has come," says Rosenberg, the philosopher of the Nazi movement, "to take up the fight against Christianity. Germans, liberate yourselves from the cultures of alien priests. Abandon the Jewish conception of sin, pity, and loving the enemy. Be hard. Pity and mercy be damned. Germans must realize their conversion to Christianity was brought about by Rabbi Paul, and was a crime against their race!"[29]...

(22:) You ask how long this struggle will go on. Is there no hope for man? Must worlds continue to be destroyed before man takes this eternal truth to heart? It is difficult to give the answer. Truth, like the budding flower, comes to fruition slowly....

(23:) Eventually – that is our supreme faith – man will hearken to

29 The quoted material does not come from Alfred Rosenberg's *The Myth of the Twentieth Century*, but rather from August Hoppe, Press Representative of the "Hitler Youth," in an Associated Press report dated Berlin, August 21, 1934, and published in many American newspapers on the same day. The report states also that Hoppe praised Rosenberg in the article from which the quotations were taken; Levinthal apparently confused the two in his notes when preparing the sermon text. Cf. also Max Hunterberg, *Tragedy of the Ages*, p. 74.

the Voice of God. Through suffering and misery he will yet learn the great truth that no world can endure unless it rests upon the Law of God. In the meantime we Jews, who were the first to proclaim this message to the world, must not forsake it now....

September 18, 1934 (Kol Nidre)

Ferdinand M. Isserman, "Whither Jewry?," Temple Israel, St. Louis, MO. AJA, MS-6, Box 13, Folder 8

(1:) In many lands, almost in all lands, Israel is engaged in a war which is to decide whether the gains of the era of emancipation are to be retained or lost, whether a dark age again is to swallow it up, whether the ghetto is once more to become a reality, whether to be shut from cultural contacts with one's fellow, to be branded as a pariah and outlaw, is again to be Israel's lot. Israel will not be destroyed. The centuries attest to its imperishability, and the God of history wills that it live. But will it live like a hunted animal or like a free people?

The battle-front of this war for dignity and decency, for right, for liberty, is not merely in Germany. It extends from Cape Town to Iceland, from the Straits of Magellan to the Arctic Circle. Wherever the influence of the Reich penetrates, where the persuasive power of its gold can be felt, wherever its prestige has meaning, these Jews are on the defensive.... (4:) Nor must the events in Germany fill us with too many false hopes.... Even if Hitlerism goes, Jews are not safe, for one of the last acts of the Nazis may be the bloodiest pogrom of all history, and their revenge on the foe, who they claim is responsible for the world's hostility to them and their impending economic collapse.

(5:) The aggressive fight of Jews everywhere against the Nazis has excited the respect and the admiration of the world. One high in European government circles informed me that never before have European ministers shown the respect for the Jew that they do now. They respect him for his public protests. They respect him for his help to the exiled. They respect him for the boycott. No future Hitler will assail Jews within the memory of modern events....

(6:) The boycott initiated by Jews, participated in by others, has been effective.... I hope no man here [*sic*] has purchased goods from Germany. I hope no man here has that on his conscience, for which his children and children's children will revile him....

But we must do more than ambulance work. We must carry on continuous, ceaseless propaganda for Judaism; not for converts, but to have our faith correctly understood.... (7:) Let us answer the lies of Naziism with the truth of Judaism. What we need is a war chest: Jewish liberty loans to finance the war for Jewish rights.... Into the teeth of the foe who attacks we will fling Judaism, Judaism, and more Judaism. Torah, Torah, and more Torah. In days like these we draw courage from the knowledge that there lives a God, and that because he lives justice will triumph as it did in ancient Egypt.

September 19, 1934 (Yom Kippur)

Edward L. Israel, Bolton Street Temple, Baltimore, MD. JTA, September 21, 1934

We must come to the conclusion that the effort to laugh Hitler out of court has not made much progress. He is obviously not a clowning sign-painter. He combines a Messiah complex with shrewdness and cold cruelty...a dangerous person, a fiendishly capable person.

Ferdinand M. Isserman, "Honoring the Dead" (*Yizkor*), Temple Israel, St. Louis, MO. AJA, M-6, Box 13, Folder 8

(2:) Perhaps it were well on this day as we recite the Kaddish that we bear in mind the martyrs of this fresh wave of persecution, the men who lost their lives in concentration camps, in the torture cells of the Nazis, or those who like [Jakob] Wassermann and Fritz Haber perished of grief, broken by the suddenness and unexpectedness of their tragedy....[30]

---

30 Wassermann was one of the leading German Jewish writers, author (among many other books) of *My Life as German and Jew* (published in English in 1933); he died in Austria, at age sixty, on January 1, 1934. Haber was a Nobel Prize-winning German Jew who left Germany in the summer of 1933 and died, on his way to Palestine, on January 29, 1934. The rest of paragraph explains the psychology of suicide in response to Nazi persecution.

(7:) In the world today, the names of those you honor are being defamed. German Jews are persecuted not because of their theological beliefs, but because of the blood that courses in their veins. What is this persecution of race in our age but slander upon our fathers and our mothers, the men and women from whose loins we have sprung. They are attacked sleeping in their graves.... What shall we do? Come here and recite the Kaddish as a formal ceremony? Or rather shall we rise wherever we be to defend our fathers from abuse and to prevent the ghouls of this day from feeding upon their corpses?...

Recently, we heard reports that cemeteries have been desecrated, and that the dead are not even immune from the physical attacks of rowdies.[31] These can only disturb their bodies. But when their children and their children's children fail to rise in their defense, then indeed their memories are outraged and their honor suffers....

November 10, 1934 (Saturday, day before Armistice Day)

Abraham H. Feinberg, "It Shall Not Be Again," Temple Beth-El, Rockford, IL. AJA, MS-85, Box 2, Folder 1[32]

(1:) Just twenty years ago a madman in the obscure village of Sarajevo released the trigger of a gun; and the echo of that shot was heard throughout the world. When night passed and day dawned, we looked upon a scene the like of which no human eye had ever seen and no imagination, however fiendish, had ever conjured up. Appalled with horror, we vowed in the name of the martyred dead that this carnage, this bestiality, this madness, "shall not be again."

That was only yesterday. And today... more suspicion, more hate, more intrigue. 1934 moves in the direction of 1914, this time to a greater holocaust and a more sweeping devastation.

---

31 JTA articles reported desecration of Jewish graves in Paderborn (July 25, 1934) and Flieden (August 3), as well as a general reference to desecration in "hundreds of cemeteries" (August 2).

32 The date of this undated sermon is determined from the opening paragraphs, and from the rhetorical conclusion that begins, "Standing this night on the eve of a great anniversary...."

(2:) Terrifying as all this is, despair is futile. To stave off disaster we must know the factors which are bringing us and our neighbors to the edge of oblivion. Why in the face of a world that does not want war do we drift toward another war?...

(7:) The choice before us in this hour is of peace or war. The choice before us is God or Mars, Humanity or Chauvinism, Civilization or Barbarism. The seeds of peace, despite the glib assertion of our National Defense patriots, are not bullets or cruisers or poison gas. The seeds of peace are justice, tolerance, and sacrifice...and "as you sow so shall you reap."

Wars will cease when we prepare for peace.

Wars will cease when courts which settle international disputes are established.

Wars will cease when men refuse to bear arms.

Wars will cease when men refuse to fight.

In 1914 a world went mad, mad with hate, mad with death. Will madness of yesterday be repeated tomorrow? A question more momentous has never been faced in the history of mankind.

Harris Swift, "Great is Peace," St. John's Wood Synagogue, London. *Because I Believe*, pp. 243–48

243: Four years of bloodshed, of carnage, of wholesale murder – can we allege for one moment that these spelt aught [*sic*] for the human race but the lowest depths of degradation and degeneration...that these four years have left us any legacy but a shameful and tragic remembrance?

(244:) There dare not be another war, for war as it is prognosticated in the future, when the chief victims will be little children or the helpless old, when it will take its toll mainly of the civilian populations whom it will poison by noxious gasses or shatter limb from limb by air-dealt bombs, compared with which the most destructive that were used in the last war were but toys; such a war can come too near to the complete annihilation of the race. There can be no glory in such a war.... (245:) There dare not be another war. There must be peace....

(246:) For is it not the function of the Jew, carrying aloft the banner of the Torah, to spread the ideal of universal brotherhood of man. . . .

(248:) Let us pray that the hatred of one people of another, shall, through the medium of international peace, give place to the universal brotherhood of men.

November 30, 1934 (Friday)

David de Sola Pool, "A Hanukkah Message," radio message, in *Rabbi David de Sola Pool: Selections from Six Decades of Sermons, Addresses and Writings*, pp. 72–76

(75:) The world looks on at the Jew and wonders whence has been born that marvelous inner strength which has enabled him to achieve the miracle of Jewish survival through centuries of accumulated impossibility. The Jew who celebrates Hanukkah knows whence comes this strength, because he recognizes the weakness of self-surrender, of refusing to battle the current, and of floating with the stream that leads out of Jewish life.

The voice of history will acclaim those who have withstood the violent imposition of sameness, and who (76:) have thereby served not only themselves, but the world. The true heroes in Germany today are those church members who have challenged the tyranny which would crush the individuality of the church and destroy freedom of conscience; and the true heroes of the spirit have everywhere and in every age been those who have dared to fight this battle for religious individuality and liberty of conscience.

December 16, 1934 (Sunday)

Stephen S. Wise, "What Christians Should Remember and Jews Forget," Free Synagogue at Carnegie Hall, New York. JTA, Dec. 17, 1934; AJA, Box 21: SSW Microfilms of AJHS and BUASC papers

[JTA: At his sermon delivered yesterday at Carnegie Hall, Dr. Wise attacked Reichsbishop Ludwig Mueller for the Nazi clergyman's recent assertion that "Christ was the first of the anti-Semites":]

Nothing could be further from the truth, nothing could be a grosser travesty of the truth, no fouler libel against Jesus could be devised.... One might just as validly urge that Abraham Lincoln was anti-Anglo-Saxon or George Washington anti-American.

If at times Jesus spoke in grave rebuke to them among his brothers who seemed to be wanting in the vision or the will to obey the word of God, it must be admitted that he was no harsher nor severer than have been the prophets of every age who, without forsaking or deserting their people, have almost uniformly employed terms of bitterest reproach against them. Jesus was no more un-Jewish when he scourged a handful of money-changers out of the Holy of Holies than President Roosevelt was anti-American when in his inaugural address he too spoke in lashing terms against the money-changers of a day nineteen centuries after Jesus....

The Jew would sin if he forgot that in this crisis of the world's history, in the presence of perhaps the mightiest insurrection of paganism and barbarism which the world has witnessed in 1,000 years, the only redeeming hope of the world can be that Israel and Christendom stand together in united resistance to the enslaving forces of that barbaric paganism which would reinstate the godlets of passion and of lust and substitute them for the God of justice and of truth and of love whom Christian and Jew together worship.

December 22, 1934 (Saturday)

Israel H. Levinthal, "The Book Versus the Sword," Address at a Dinner in the presence of Albert Einstein and Heinz Liepmann, marking the Inauguration of the American Library of Nazi-banned Books, Brooklyn Jewish Center, Brooklyn, NY. *Judaism: An Analysis and an Interpretation*, pp. 267–72

(270:) We are privileged, too, in that we greet tonight another great son of our people: Heinz Liepmann. We honor him because of his achievements as writer, as novelist, as a distinguished man of letters. But we honor him for yet another and more cogent reason – because we know what he suffered and the horrors he endured at the hands of those cruel tyrants who now rule the (271:) destinies of the sixty million German people. We see in him a symbol. He is to us the personification of that large group of liberal thinkers, writers, and students who, because they dared to be true to their conscience, suffered untold tortures, and are now exiles from their land as a result of the merciless and relentless attitude of those who have turned back the clock of civilization thousands of years.

And we are privileged, too, in that we are inaugurating in this building tonight a library of all those books that were burned and are banned in Nazi Germany....[33]

December 23, 1934 (Sunday)

Maurice N. Eisendrath, "Was Jesus a Christian?," Holy Blossom Temple, Toronto. *Holy Blossom Pulpit*, v, 4

(4:) "He was a one-hundred per cent Aryan, nothing less blue than the blood of the Indo-European coursed through his veins," wrote Houston Stewart Chamberlain in his "Foundations of the Nineteenth Century," while his Nazi compatriots plagiarize his writings and seek to impress the world with their ostensibly original "discovery," that a good and noble Galilean could not possibly have been otherwise. "Jesus was the first anti-Semite," chimes in Reichsbishopf [Ludwig] Mueller, (5:) star-spangled, bemedalled dictator of the official German church, as his followers, thus self-righteously assured of the Scriptural validity of their hatreds, proceed to annihilate the Jew, people from whom he was descended.[34]

December 28, 1934 (Friday evening)

Ferdinand M. Isserman, "The Silver Lining of 1934 and the Hope for 1935," Temple Israel, St. Louis, MO. AJA, M-6, Box 13, Folder 9

(1:) The thirtieth of June, I would regard as the most important date in 1934. It was the beginning of the historic blood purge of Hitler,

---

33 On this event, at which Einstein and Liepmann also gave speeches with some five hundred people attending, see http://bit.ly/2fOiJAJ. Liepmann (who changed his name to Liepman) had recently published *Murder – Made in Germany: A True Story of Present-Day Germany*.

34 Cf. Stephen S. Wise, above, from the previous week, on Mueller.

when at his orders, and those of his henchmen, one thousand eighty six human beings were executed within one week, without any public trial, without any charge being lodged against them, without them even knowing the reasons for their assassinations. That date is most important for it marked the climax of the strength of the dictatorship movement in Europe.[35]

(2:) As a result of these bloody events,[36] the philosophy of dictatorship was discredited in countries where fascist parties had been making successful propaganda.... (4:) The overwhelming endorsement of the policies of President Roosevelt at the election recently held in this country may be counted as another triumph for the democratic ideal....

(8:) As we stand on the threshold of 1935, we see hope written upon the skies which beckon us, hope that the gains of democracy will be maintained, hope that an order of social justice will be established, hope that our generation, chastened by suffering, and humbled by sorrows, cleansed and purified, may become with the blessing of God the instrument of destiny to lead humanity to a promised land of ease, security, peace, and good-will.

35 Another example of the perils of prognostication about the future from the pulpit. For the events on the "Night of the Long Knives" – a purge of Ernst Röhm and the SA – see Richard Evans, *The Third Reich in Power*, p. 31–41.

36 Including assassination in July, 1934 of the dictatorial fascist Austrian Chancellor Engelbert Dollfuss and "the recent executions in Soviet Russia."

1935

January 12, 1935 (Saturday)

Israel Gerstein, "Those on Trial with Hauptmann,"[1] B'nai Zion Congregation, Chattanooga, TN. *Reveille or Taps?*, pp. 65–70

(65:) The most sensational trial in a century – and some even go further and call it the most astounding one in the history of the American courts – that is the consensus among the molders of public opinion about the trial now in progress at Flemington.... But the news of the trial monopolized the (66:) attention of all.

(68:) There with Hauptmann on the bench of guilt sit a number of invisible and yet real Hauptmanns. Hauptmann is accused of kidnapping one child, and these other Hauptmanns are guilty of kidnapping thousands of little children. And while Hauptmann is supposed to have carried out his plan at night, and thereby showed a little respect for civilization, these numerous Hauptmanns I am speaking about executed their diabolical plans in broad daylight, in full view of all humanity, impudently, shamelessly. For at this very moment, the countrymen of him who is now being tried at Flemington are keeping thousands of innocent men and women in concentration camps, in prisons, subjecting them to horrible and inhuman torture. How many thousands of little children are suffering the physical and spiritual pains of kidnapping even though they (69:) are ostensibly free! Thousands of children are denied the happiness and the possibilities of growth which are the recognized rights of children everywhere. Only one God knows how many of them carry within themselves the seeds of an Einstein, a Liebermann,

1 All listeners would have known the reference to Bruno Hauptmann, whose trial for the kidnapping and murder of the twenty-month-old son of Charles and Anne Morrow Lindbergh began on January 2, 1935.

a Wassermann, or a Feuchtwanger. And these are denied every opportunity of free development because they happen to be of a certain faith and blood.

The world shall never know how many a genius has been robbed from it, how many a scientist and philosopher have been kidnapped from it who would have enriched the world's culture and advanced the welfare of all humanity. The whole government of Germany stands accused of this dastardly crime of wholesale kidnapping. And yet men and women have assumed an attitude of indifference towards the fate of the several hundred thousand people who are the innocent victims of medieval barbarians. On trial with Hauptmann are not only the many Hauptmanns in this home country, but men and women everywhere who look on with indifference and even complacency at the sufferings of people of our faith and other faiths in Germany and do not even utter a word of protest. And so would it not be well that we spare some of our interest from the Lindbergh case and give it to these victims?

January 20, 1935 (Sunday)

Israel Goldstein, Congregation B'nai Jeshurun, New York. JTA, January 21, 1935

A sympathetic interest in the plight of other oppressed minorities would broaden the intellectual and spiritual horizon of the Jew.... The Jew should feel a spiritual kinship with every oppressed minority, be he the Armenian in Turkey, the Negro in America or the Catholic in Mexico.

[There are among the Jews] those who grow egocentric in the envisagement of their problem and who turn a deaf ear to the plight of others.... There are also those who indulge themselves in orgies of self-pity and even derive a pathological satisfaction from contemplating themselves as the special martyrs of humanity.

February 16, 1935 (Saturday, possibly evening)

Salis Daiches, "The Unity of Israel," Edinburgh Hebrew Congregation,

Launching of the Third Appeal for the Central British Fund for German Jewry. Salis Daiches Archives

(3:) It is utterly wrong to say that the Jews in this country who come to the rescue of their brethren in other lands, or who protest against the persecution of the Jewish citizens in Germany in the best way they can, show by their attitude that they place the interests of Jewry above the interests of Britain. The reverse is true...

The Appeal which is now addressed to us by our communal leaders on behalf of the victims of persecution in Germany must be responded to whole-heartedly and generously.... If we make a real effort we shall succeed, with the help of God, in saving from the ruins of the Jewish communities of Central and Eastern Europe a remnant that will be restored to Jewish life, and will grow in freedom and security, to become a source of strength to us, and a mighty factor in the advancement of humanity as a whole.

February 17, 1935 (Sunday)

Israel Mattuck, "Nationalism: Good and Bad," Address before Epsom Brotherhood, London. Unpublished[2]

(1:) Two things happened in Germany that at first appear unrelated, but on examination show a close connection. One is Germany's treatment of the Jews, and the other is her policy indicated by her withdrawal from the League of Nations and her re-armament in spite of the Treaty of Versailles.

(2:) The treatment of the Jews has shocked the world and, I think, puzzled many. It is no exaggeration to describe that treatment as an attempt to destroy the Jews. Many of the Jews... have been stopped by law from practicing their professions. Several thousands of Jewish lawyers, doctors, journalists, teachers and university professors have been ruined, so that, as might have been expected, there have been a number of suicides among them, and with every report of the suicide

2 The Epsom Brotherhood was a Christian group affiliated with the Congregational Church, founded in 1909 for study and charitable activities; it published *Watchtower Magazine*.

of a Jew, Nazi newspapers expressed their joy. Jews in commerce have not suffered so much if they happened to own a store or factory in a large city, but the Jewish shop-owners in the smaller cities, and Jewish workers in shops everywhere, have suffered disaster as a result of the Nazi campaign against them. The inhuman extremes to which the Nazi hostility against the Jews goes is perhaps most sadly shown by the treatment of Jewish children in the schools. They have to listen to the race instruction in which the teachers inform their classes that the Jews are all that is evil, and they, as a natural result, suffer continuous ostracism by their fellows.... (3:) The concentration camps in which Jews and non-Jews alike have suffered most barbaric tortures have given the world some idea of the savagery of these people who persecute the Jews. They have shown it even more in their subtle cruelty to Jewish children.

The cruelty to the Jews which I described, and the cruelties in the concentration camps, are occurring in the land of Goethe, Schiller, Kant and Bach! What has happened to its people?...[3]

February 24, 1935 (Sunday)

Solomon B. Freehof, "Are Jews a Race?," Rodef Shalom Temple, Pittsburgh, PA. *Race, Nation, or Religion*, pp. 3–13

(4:) Among those who insist that Jewry is a separate race are the Hitlerites. It is the basis of Hitlerite philosophy that Jewry constitutes a distinct race, an inferior race. Because Jewry is a distinct and inferior race, Jewish physicians are kept from hospitals, Jewish lawyers from the courts, Jewish businessmen from their customers – and Jewish unemployed are cynically allowed to die of starvation in the alleys of Berlin.

Maurice N. Eisendrath, "Forgotten Men," Holy Blossom Temple, Toronto. *The Never Ending Stream*, pp. 173–97

---

3 This is followed by a discussion of various accusations made against the Jews, including that they were responsible for the World War and the collapse of Germany in 1918, that they profited from the post-War inflation, that they are closely associated with Communism, and have excessive influence on German thought and life.

(181:) "But surely in sheer desperation and destitution there is no people in the contemporary world to compare with Israel?" even our sympathetic non-Jewish friends will be constrained to ask, as they contemplate the harried refugees fleeing from before the Nazi terror; as they behold the many millions of our brethren quite literally starving in those Eastern European hells which are their noisome homes; as they observe the gates of every land tightly barred against them; and perceive this people entrapped, like so many hunted rats in a cage, men without a country – and women and children too, drifting on the seven seas like so much flotsam with no harbor (182:) to call their home, not knowing whither to go nor whence will come their help. A heart-rending and distressing picture indeed, which seems at last to have touched the very nadir of human pathos.

And yet once more methinks we must admit that while Jewish suffering today may be more extensive than that of many other persecuted peoples, it is by no means a burden which Israel bears alone. Our tragedy may differ from that of others in *degree* but not in *kind*, for surely when one is being beaten and broken on the wheel of cruel oppression, numbers do not count....

Even in darkest Germany, as I have so frequently iterated, and even as we have observed throughout the past, the Jew is being destroyed not merely *qua* Jew, but as part of the general barbarity of our time, as part of a tyrannical programme, a totalitarian (183:) principle rapidly gaining headway throughout the whole world.

March 22, 1935 (Friday evening)

Ferdinand M. Isserman, "Germany's Rearmament and the Future of Europe," Temple Israel, St. Louis, MO. AJA, M-6, Box 14, Folder 1

(1:) Nazism has dropped its mask. The peace-beating of Hitler was only the artificially-silenced growling of a wolf. The sheep's clothing has been cast aside. Hitler and Hitlerism stand before the world divested of all camouflage. The Nazis mean war....[4]

4 Isserman continues to discuss the announcement of universal military conscription in Germany.

(3:) The public announcement of tearing up the military clauses of the Treaty of Versailles also marks the continued triumph of the military clique in Germany....

(5:) It is not impossible that the German government is preparing for war not against France, not against England, nor against Poland, but against Russia....

(7:) The only group now satisfied with the rapid march of events in the international scene are the makers of munitions.... The tragedy of the whole situation is that for his immoral international policy, Hitler has moral justification.[5]...

(8:) What another war is going to bring to Europe is no longer uncertain. There was no victor during the World War. There will be no victor in another world war. H.G. Wells has said that modern society is a race between catastrophe and civilization.[6] If a world war breaks, catastrophe wins....

(9:) What shall we do? Shall we resign ourselves to our doom? Or shall we puny mortals cleanse our souls and spirits, and reaching out our hands to human beings everywhere make one desperate effort to arrest the forces of darkness, to rout the legions of evil, and to save Germany and humanity from Naziism, militarism and chaos.

March 25, 1935 (Monday)

Louis Wolsey, "The Future of Judaism in America," Banquet Address at UAHC Biennial in Washington DC. *Sermons and Addresses*, pp. 10–16

(10:) We are disturbed but we are not dismayed by the spiritual confusion and the moral chaos which beset us and the world everywhere. It is an age which is reaping in tears and in madness the logical results of a despiritualized humanity. Everywhere we see moral deterioration, demagoguery, bigotry, the preaching of social justice by fomenters of class hatred, the pious cant of "Father forgive them" by those who

---

5 Referring to the policy of the Allies at the end of the Great War, especially the Treaty of Versailles.

6 The actual wording of the statement by Wells is "Human history becomes more and more a race between education and catastrophe" (*The Outline of History*, p. 504). It is also frequently quoted in the form our preacher uses.

vomit venom upon their deserters, the alienation of religious leaders from religion, religious defeatism by those whose responsibility is to the teaching of religion, a secularization of life by those who are consecrated to give it a hallowed interpretation. It is no wonder that such a confused civilization should defame the one group that has made religious steadfastness a career and a consecration. A brutalized and demagogic leadership always attacks a minority, because that is the safety of its courage. A truculent monster always exploits the non-resistance and spirituality of his victim. If we had been a conquering people who lived by the sword and strength, there never would have been a Haman or a Hitler, for they both tread softly when power raises its hand....

Judaism may live in spite of oppressors who, while they oppress, glibly talk of charity and religion; or who say that alienism must be destroyed in the United States, meanwhile allying themselves with the alienism of the New Friends of Germany.[7]

We have survived not because we are artists, or scientists, or politicians, or statesmen, or civilizationists, or industrialists, or philosophers, or scholars, or humanists, but because of a divine heritage. "Truly in the Lord God is the salvation of Israel" (Jer. 3:23). Neither assimilationists, nor an escape mechanism, nor a retreat, nor a secularistic culture with its stressing of folkways, language, race, and art, can save the Jew.... Truly, we may say that in the future, the only means of salvation for Israel is in our religion, in the Lord our God.

April 7, 1935 (Sunday)

Stephen S. Wise, "Must War Be? What Can We Do?," Free Synagogue at Carnegie Hall, New York. AJA, Box 21: SSW Microfilms of AJHS and BUASC papers

(1:) If war is to be – not *must* be – it will be because of these things:

---

7 An organization supporting Nazi Germany and promoting its propaganda in the United States; it was replaced by the German-American Bund. "Alienism" is a term used to refer to recent immigrants whose primary identity is said to be to their own ethnic group rather than to the country in which they live. "Anti-alienism" was a broad term akin to the more specific "antisemitism."

1) The Hitler program and the Hitler threat, which will bring Europe to the breaking point and precipitate war,
2) the indifference of men everywhere, the unconcern of the masses of the nations, as if the possibility of war were not their problem rather than the problem of politicians, and
3) the failure of America to claim the leadership of humankind in making war impossible.

At this moment it looks as if Hitlerism had brought about the thing which has been dreaded since the day of his advent, namely, the feeling of the European nations that Germany cannot be suffered mightily to re-arm against the world and to be able to strike and strike destructively at any point which her war forces may choose. Hitlerism means something infinitely graver than repression of labor, persecution of Catholic and Protestant churches, or annihilation of the Jew. It means war....

(2:) If it be said that even though war break out in Europe, this time we shall be able to stay out of war, the doubly unpalatable answer is "war that destroys the sons of France or Russia, of England or Germany, of Italy or Romania, is just as tragic as a war which strikes down the sons of our own land." Or are we to be indifferent to war because we imagine it is not to hurt or destroy us? Let us not be deceived. A world conflict will embroil us....

Early- to Mid-April, 1935

Joachim Prinz, "Ghetto 1935: The Jewish Situation Today," selection from a Speech published in *Jüdische Rundschau*, April 17, 1935 (no. 31/32), p. 3, trans. in *The Yellow Spot*, pp. 175–76; translator unidentified

(175:) That we live in a ghetto is now beginning to penetrate our consciousness.... The ghetto of the Middle Ages was closed every night. Cruelly and inevitably the door shut to. Carefully it was bolted, the Jew came out of the "world" and went back into the ghetto. To-day it is the other way round. When our house door shuts behind us we come out of the ghetto and go into our home. This is a fundamental difference. The ghetto is no longer a district with geographical boundaries, at least not in the sense that the Middle Ages knew. The ghetto is the "world." Outside is the ghetto. On the market place, in the street, in the public tavern, everywhere is ghetto. And it has a sign. That sign is "neighbourless."

Perhaps this has never before happened in the world, and no one knows how long it can be borne: life without a neighbour.... The Jews of the big cities do not notice it so keenly, but the Jews of the small towns, those who dwell on the market-place without a neighbour, whose children go to school each morning with no neighbours' children, it is they who feel the isolation that neighbourlessness means, a fate crueler than any other, and perhaps the fiercest that can be suffered in the social life of man....

In culture, too, our roots have been torn up. With one blow (176) we must sever the great literature of old, that we love, from the literature, the painting, the music of to-day, that we must not love. The fact, for example, that we may play no German dramatist of to-day upon our stage, the fact that no great German orchestra may play the melodies that are created by any Jew of to-day, the barriers that confront the creative activity of our painters, all these condemn our cultural life to a pretense, grimly aloof from reality. Nothing can serve to avert this: no studio, no club, no league of culture. I do not know how long such life can be endured....

One needs but travel through the German land, now in springtime, when new life is growing, and the fresh green is spreading over the meadows, the brooks glittering silver in the mountains, the trees in blossom, and the woods ranged young and fresh upon the hillside. One needs but this to feel with deepest certainty and with an elementary force, strong as an axiom: that we are tightly bound to this landscape, bound to all eternity and that the home-sickness of many Jews who leave Germany for bleak Palestine, a home-sickness for the rustling woods and the lush meadows, is right and healthy. We have been born into this landscape.... Yet be this so, the landscape in which we live begins to change its mask. For how in the world could the ties to it remain unshattered, when within this landscape now stand barriers, pales, placards, that forbid me, who dwell in this landscape, access to it?...

April 18, 1935 (first day of Pesach)

Tobias Geffen, Congregation Shearith Yisrael, Atlanta, GA. *Karnei haHod* (*The Rays of Glory*), translated by Joel Geffen in *Lev Tuviah*, pp. 107–11

(109:) Indeed we observe in this age of modern advanced civilization with its new inventions like radio and the airplane, in this enlightened era, we see a regressive trend in the intense hate for Jews in all the emancipated nations. Anti-Semitism spreads in the free nations which exult in their ideals of "Justice" and "Love" of their fellow men. Is this not amazing and strange? Rabban Gamaliel teaches us not to be amazed. This phenomenon has occurred throughout history, even in Egypt. At first, the Egyptians seemed to befriend the Jews – this is *Pesach* and *Matzah* – but *Maror* and hard labor followed the friendship and brotherly love.[8]

April 24, 1935 (seventh day of Pesach)

Harris Swift, "The Answer to Anti-Semitism," St. John's Wood Synagogue, London. *Because I Believe,* pp. 155–60

(159:) On those too frequent occasions when the Jew suffers with greater violence than usual at the hands of his enemies, they are to be seen organizing protest meetings and mass demonstrations.... "Let us protest against them," "Let us make an outcry against them." And so when the terrible massacres of our people occurred in pogrom-ridden Russia, at the close of the last century, when the accession to power in Germany of the most ruthless of Jew-haters in modern history brought in its train the suffering of our stricken brothers there, this group echoed the cry of their ancestors, *nitzave'aḥ ke-negdan.*

Too often, however, does it happen that their Judaism begins and ends there. They are to be seen at the protest meeting but not at the House of Worship; their voices are to be heard at the demon-

8 The preacher is discussing the passage in the Passover Haggadah in which Rabban Gamaliel emphasizes the meaning of *Pesach, Matzah* and *Maror,* the first two symbolizing freedom, and the third symbolizing the bitterness of life. Geffen goes on to explain the meaning of bitterness as pertaining not only to antisemitism but also to divisiveness among Jews.

stration but not at the Bet Hamidrash and the be-all and end-all of their Judaism is this *nitzave'aḥ ke-negdan*, this raising of an outcry....

(60:) Economic weapons, diplomatic weapons, are of questionable value as our history but too tragically emphasizes. The Jew must employ those arms with which he was equipped at Sinai, his glorious ideals of human fellowship, of love for one's neighbor and respect for his property – these are the weapons with which the Jew must fight. That the best answer to anti-semitism is more Semitism has become a by-word, and truly does it summarise in epigrammatic fashion the lesson Moses taught on the shore of the Red Sea.[9]

May 28, 1935 (Tuesday)

Joseph H. Hertz, "Address to Anglo-Jewish Preachers," Woburn House London. Summary in *JC*, May 31, p. 24, complete text in *Addresses*, pp. 105–17

(209:) And now we come to the tragedy of German Jewry. It reproduces many of the horrid details in the measures taken by the Inquisition against the New Christians 500 years ago, and is a resurrection of the spirit of Czarist Russia in its attitude towards the Jewish people.

(210:) Christian amateurs in rabbinics join in the unholy sport of Jew-baiting. Erich Bischoff is outdoing Eisenmenger as, unlike that notorious vilifier of Judaism, *he* spreads the "blood-libel"; while Gerhard Kittel is all enthusiasm over Hitler's crusade. "Israel," he says, "claims to be the Suffering Servant in Isaiah." Well, Hitler is making it possible for Israel to be the Suffering Servant. He is supplying the suffering – for which the Jews should be grateful....[10]

(211:) In the press and pulpit, on platform and in parliaments, they [men of light and leading outside Germany] voiced the indignation of all lovers of mankind against the attempt to crush and degrade a whole people, rob its members of civic equality, and trample on

---

9 Note the repudiation of boycotts and even diplomatic weapons as solutions to the current problem.

10 Erich Bischoff's defense of the blood libel was published in 1929 as *Das Blut in jüdischem Schrifttum und Brauch*. On Gerhard Kittel: Robert P. Ericksen, *Theologians Under Hitler*, pp. 28–78.

their human dignity.... But, alas, protest meetings disperse; speeches, resolutions, editorials are forgotten; and the evil continues.... What is most terrible of all is that mankind has come to accept the outlawing in Central Europe of 500,000 human beings as a legal thing, with which no outside Government has the least right to interfere....

It has been asked why Scripture calls Haman "the enemy of *all* the Jews," seeing that he (212:) planned the destruction of the Jews of the Persian Empire alone. The answer is, because his proposal encouraged the Hamans in all other lands, near and far to preach his doctrine. Even so is it in our day....

(213:) A few special words must be said in regard to Polish Jewry. We are confronted by the stark and terrible situation of one million Jews given over to actual starvation. The economic condition of our brethren in that country makes it impossible for them to help themselves; and, if multitudes of them are not to die of the hideous maladies that follow in the wake of hunger, help must be given by their brethren of other countries, and that help must be given quickly....

This is indeed a time of darkness for Israel. The night would be darker still but for one bright star (214:) heralding the dawn in the Land of our Fathers....

June 17, 1935 (Monday, 20th anniversary of battle of Carency-Souchez)

Jacob Kaplan, "Jewish Patriotism" (*Le patriotisme des Juifs*), Synagogue de la rue de la Victoire, Paris, delivered on third day of first World Conference of Jewish Veterans. Shapira, *Jacob Kaplan*, pp. 86–87, translated by MS

(50:) Israel's destiny is painful enough by itself without human perplexity adding even more cruel persecution. Is it not sufficiently hellish that in time of war Israel is obliged to tear itself apart, with its sons in opposing camps competing in deadly struggles? I know quite well that this is the tragic fate of other men as well; I do not forget that all men are brothers, and that consequently all war is fratricide. But I say that Jews possess the love of humanity affixed in their hearts to such an extent that if it had depended upon them, the world would long ago have renounced warfare....

July 19(?), 1935[11]

Kalman Chameides, "Herzl and Bialik," Katowice, Poland. *On the Edge of the Abyss*, pp. 345–50, translated from the German by Leon Chameides

(350:) It is becoming ever darker in the Jewish street. Previously, we had to deal with individual enemies of the Jews. Today, states and nations have conspired against us. For many, Jew-hating has become a philosophy of life, the essence of life, a creed and yes, even a religion. It is proclaimed and preached like a holy sermon from the highest lecterns. It is fomented, disseminated, and incited by false apostles and prophets. It penetrates like poison into the souls of the deluded masses, and disturbs the harmony of human society. In such a difficult time, we turn our gaze into the past. We remember our holy ones, our heroes and martyrs, and we remember both great heralds of the Jewish renaissance: Herzl and Bialik.

Let their lives be a model for us! May their greatness strengthen us! May their enthusiasm arouse us! May their determination animate us! Today and evermore!

August 8, 1935 (Tisha B'Av)

Kalman Chameides, "Jewish Children as Martyrs" (Sermon delivered in the cemetery of Katowice, Poland). *On the Edge of the Abyss*, pp. 70–76, translated from the German by Leon Chameides

(75:) The portals of the children's cemetery are closing. Deeply moved, we take our leave of the graves of Jewish children – heroes of a bygone day.[12] We find ourselves once again in the heart of Europe in the first half of the 20th century. Today a Jewish child sees a world of enemies confronting him like once little David faced the giant, Goliath. His

11 This is the only information provided in the relevant archival note. Bialik died on July 4, 1934; his Yahrzeit according to the Hebrew calendar (21 Tammuz) would have been on July 22, 1935.

12 This alludes to two highly embellished narratives, the first concerning four hundred captured Jewish children who threw themselves into the sea in order to avoid dishonor and prostitution, the second of seven children, each of whom in turn accepts a martyr's death rather than accept the faith of the Roman Emperor, as their mother looks on (based on b. Gittin 57b).

martyrdom begins in his earliest school days where the first principles of racial prejudice are taught....

Jewish children have hardly become conscious of life and joy, when they realize that they are surrounded by enemies, encircled by hatred and distrust.... Today, the Caesar is no longer trying (76:) to win over Jewish children's hearts. He no longer tries to convert them to his own faith. He wants to annihilate them. He knows no pity. Sympathy is a stranger to him.

And because of this, Jewish children must once again become heroes. Teach your children the affirmation of the one God early.... Teach them to bear humiliation with pride; to accept degradation in peace, and teach them, in suffering, never to deny; in an assault from hostile forces, never to lose hope.

Hope in the enlightenment of humanity. Hope in the deliverance of the Jewish people.

August 26, 1935 (Monday)

Stephen S. Wise, Address at 19th Zionist Congress, Lucerne, Switzerland. AJA, Box 21: SSW Microfilms of AJHS and BUASC papers

(1:) The status of the Jewish people in the Third Reich is not a German, or a German-Jewish question. It is a Jewish question, a world-Jewish question, a world question. World-Jewish, because Nazism has not declared [only] German Jews to be of inferior race, of degraded and empoisoning blood, but *Jews*, all Jews, the Jewish race. Even if Nazi dealing with German Jews were not the shame of civilization and an inexpiable crime, even if Nazi influence and example were not immeasurably evil outside the Third Reich, still the fate of German Jews is our fate, their tragedy is our sorrow, for we are one....

(2:) [T]he wounds are still being inflicted day by day with the gravest wound threatening in the near future: the withdrawal or cancellation of the German citizenship of all Jews.[13] ... Very well, then let us say that they who are in the front-line trenches of the

13 This would indeed occur at the Nuremberg Rally three weeks later: see David Feuchtwang, below.

Third Reich's warfare upon civilization cannot expect to direct the movements of the entire defending army. We dare not and we shall not forsake the [...], but decisions must be taken by all of us, not by some of us.

September 27, 1935 (Erev Rosh Hashanah)

Abraham H. Feinberg, "Light in Darkness," Temple Beth-El, Rockford, IL. AJA, MS-85, Box 2, Folder 4[14]

(9:) In one of the darkest chapters of history, the light of religion is not only shining, but refuses to be extinguished. I am referring, of course, to the gallant stand of 6000 German pastors who resisted and defied the inroads of Nazi paganism.[15] What makes their deed all the more heroic is that they alone, of all the groups in the Empire, had the courage to live their convictions. Where the bar, the medical associations, the teachers and the writing craft capitulated, the religious leaders held their ground, and, in the end, they made Naziism capitulate.

(10:) In America the stand of organized religion has been less spectacular, perhaps, but by no means less noteworthy.... In particular, I call your attention to the reaction of our Christian neighbors to the re-appearance of medieval barbarism. The response revives our faith in man. Twenty-six journals of Christian opinion have put themselves on record with stinging rebukes to Naziism and all that it stands for, and a resolution of protest, prepared by Harry Emerson Fosdick, was signed by 1200 Christian clergymen in the U.S. and Canada.[16]

---

14 Although all of Feinberg's sermon texts are without dates, this one is dated based on the reference to "this eve of Rosh Hashanah" and "six years of effort and study" since the economic crisis (p. 1), and the statement, "In 1916...we shuddered. In 1935 we applaud" (p. 5).

15 This was apparently based on an article published in *Newsweek* of June 9, 1934 under the headline "6000 German Pastors Oppose Hitler."

16 This may be based on a declaration of protest published by the National Conference of Jews and Christians in November 1934 "bearing the signatures of 1800 Christian clergymen and rabbis": *American Jewish Year Book 5696*, vol. 37 (1935–1936), p. 161.

Oberrabbiner David Feuchtwang, "Harsh Decrees (*Geseroth Kaschoth*)," Leopoldstädter Temple, Vienna. *Die Stimme*, September 27, 1935, p. 8, translated by MS[17]

Through the recently adopted [Nuremberg] Jew-Law, our Jewish brothers and sisters in Germany have been mortally wounded.[18] The honor not just of the Jewish community in Germany, but rather of the entire world, is insulted and defiled. This defamation is all-encompassing, and Jews throughout the entire world must defend their honor. We want to do so fearlessly and decisively. No people in the world, no regime, no statesman, no intellectual, no poet acts as a defender of Jewish honor.... Why are you silent? Is not the entire Christian world insulted and offended by the disenfranchisement of Jewishness and Judaism? You too cannot, must not, and will not remain silent!... It is the duty of nations, which claim to be nations of culture, to intervene with a mighty hand, so that they themselves will not be afflicted by this pestilential disease of the soul that has threatened the flock throughout the world.

September 28, 1935 (first day of Rosh Hashanah)

Israel H. Levinthal, "The Mad Laughter of the World," Brooklyn Jewish Center, Brooklyn, NY. *A New World Is Born*, pp. 32–39

(34:) It is in this description of the laughter of Ishmael[19] that we get a true portrayal of the life and character of those barbarous nations which are seeking to establish a new world order in our day. The tragedy that we behold is not that we find there idolatry, murder, butcher, and immorality. The world has always known these wrongs. The tragedy for the world lies in this, that these nations (35:) enjoy

17 The passage from *Die Stimme* is cited in Evelyn Adunka, "Oberrabiner David Feuchtwang (1864–1936)."

18 A clear reference to the anti-Jewish legislation passed by a special meeting of the Reichstag on September 15, 1935 at the end of the annual Nuremberg Rally. For the text, see Lucy Dawidowicz, *A Holocaust Reader*, pp. 44–45; for the context, see Richard Evans, *The Third Reich in Power*, pp. 542–54.

19 This follows a midrashic interpretation of the laughter of Ishmael (Gen. 21:9), taken from Genesis Rabbah 53,15.

these evils. It is to them a great source of delight and glee. It is *Metzachek*, the mad laughter of a mad world that we behold!

It is the laughter of *Avodah Zarah*, of idolatry, that these nations enjoy so much today. It is a new idolatry, a revulsion against the old Good of morality. That is the real meaning of the new paganism which has taken hold of the leaders of Germany and Italy today. It is not only against the Jew and against the Jewish faith that they direct their attacks, but against the ethics of the New Testament as well. And they find delight in their idolatry. Witness the laughter and the shouts of joy that accompanied the attack on the palace of Cardinal Innitzer by those Nazi hooligans. See their delight in the suffering of a Niemöller in the concentration camp.[20] It is *Metzachek*, the laughter of *Avodah Zarah*, in which these peoples indulge!

And it is also the laughter of *Shefikot Damim* [spilling of blood] that we behold today. Mass murder, human butchery have become the new sport, a game to give them delight. The very sight of human blood inspires them to laughter. In Italy and in Germany young children are today trained to carry a gun and to find joy in using it. Notice the glee with which Mussolini's brigands attacked the Ethiopians and brutally slaughtered them. And the irony of it all is that we are told it was all done "to civilize the Ethiopians." ... (36:) Italy and Germany find their greatest joy in the sport of *Shefikot Damim*.

It is not only that they wage wars, but that they take delight in their wars, Bernhardi's notorious aphorism has been seized and adopted by them with joyous glee: "The verdict of war is biologically just!"[21] They see in the sword the greatest badge of human worth

---

20 This sentence is impossible for the date provided for the sermon. The attack on the palace of Cardinal Innitzer occurred on October 8, 1938, after the Anschluss (*NYT*, October 9, 1938, p. 1). Niemöller was arrested by the Nazis because of his preaching on July 1, 1937; the legal case against him resulted in a decision of "Not Guilty" of dishonorable conduct, but he was then confined to the Sachsenhausen concentration camp outside of Berlin in February 1938. One explanation is that Levinthal repeated his 1935 sermon in 1938 and added some sentences pertaining to more recent events, but provided the date of the original sermon when it was being prepared for publication.

21 Cited in Herbert Stewart, *Nietzsche and the Ideals of Modern Germany*, p. 98, where it is presented as "Bernhardi's notorious aphorism."

and dignity. See how the faces of these brutes suddenly become radiant with joy as they brand with hot irons the Swastika upon the flesh of innocent men and women in the Sudetenland. It is the *Metzachek* of Ishmael – the sport of shedding human blood.

"And we see, too, the *Tzechok*, the laughter of *Gilui Arayot* [revealing one's nakedness]...

(37:) If you wish to see the difference between the laughter of Isaac and the laughter of Ishmael – between the *Weltanschauung* (38:) of these two, contrast what you see in Germany, even today, among the Nazis, who have seized the power, and the downtrodden Jews, who have become the modern pariahs. In the last issue of the *Monatsschrift für Geschichte und Wissenschaft des Judentums*, a Jewish scientific periodical which happily still appears,[22] and is now in its seventy-ninth volume, the leading article discusses the theme, "*Um das Gebot der Nächstenliebe*,"[23] and gives us, in the midst of the Nazi savagery, the Jewish conception of love for one's fellow man!

If the world is to be saved, if the garment of true civilization is to conceal and adorn the nakedness of man, we must take heed of the warning of Sarah of old: "Cast them out, they must have naught to do with us or with our children!" We must drive those bestial concepts of life from our mind; there must be no contact between those who find delight in the laughter of Ishmael! This does not necessarily mean that we must proclaim war against them – though I am convinced that eventually, without proclamation, they will force war upon all other peoples of the earth. It does mean, however, that we must proclaim the moral equivalent of war: ostracism from all social, economic, and diplomatic contact. We ought to regard them as moral lepers, as dangerous as those affected with physical leprosy.... The world cannot be half free (39:) and half slave.[24] We

22 Levinthal's note: "The right to publish the *Monatsschrift* was revoked soon after the sermon was preached."

23 The meaning of the German is expressed in the last words of the sentence. This was indeed the first article in *Monatsschrift für die Geschichte und Wissenschaft des Judenthums*, 1935, Heft 3, pp. 209–23; the author, Max Katten, treated the commandment of loving one's neighbor, which appears in the Talmud and in such medieval texts as Bahya ibn Pakuda's *Duties of the Heart* and *Sefer Ḥasidim*.

24 An allusion to the well-known statement by Abraham Lincoln in one of his debates

would say the world cannot be happy, with half finding their joy in the fresh, innocent laughter of Isaac, and half finding their joy in the mad, wild laughter of Ishmael....

The Ishmaels may laugh today; but the future belongs to the Isaacs! History is with the forces of freedom, democracy and human brotherhood.... Let us gird ourselves with the armor of our faith, and we shall yet laugh, not the mad laughter of the brute, but the laughter of the children of God, who find delight in the fulfillment of His word!

October 6–7, 1935 (Yom Kippur)

Leo Baeck, Prayer/Sermon/Exhortation, from the *Reichsvertretung* to be read in all synagogues of Germany[25]

At this hour, all Israel stands before the Lord, the merciful Judge. Before Him we shall have to confess our ways, confess what we have done and what we have omitted to do, confess where we have gone and where we have failed to go. Where we have transgressed, we shall openly confess, "We have sinned," and, firmly resolved to return to God, we shall pray, "Lord, forgive us."

We stand before our Lord. With the same strength with which we have confessed our sins, the sins committed by individuals and the sins committed by the whole Community, we repudiate root and

---

with Senator Douglas: "'A house divided against itself cannot stand.' I believe this *Union* cannot endure permanently half free and half slave" (my emphasis). Lincoln himself was echoing Mark 3:24–25.

25 The translation is taken from *JC*, October 18, 1935, p. 16. A different translation appears in the Eichmann Trial Record, 1961, http://linkis.com/PRkDa. Cf. Baker, *Days of Sorrow and Pain*, 205–7, (with important omissions); German text in *Leo Baeck Werke*, vol. 6: *Briefe, Reden, Aufsätze*, ed. Michael A. Meyer, pp. 312–13. Baker wrote (somewhat hyperbolically) that "The German Jews who heard the prayer that day or who read it later were moved emotionally by it, never forgot it, and spoke of it years later. It was a prayer, a sermon, an exhortation, a challenge to the oppressors, a statement of religious strength" (p. 205). He continues to describe how the reading of this text was banned by order of the Gestapo, and that Baeck was consequently arrested for some twenty-four hours by a high Gestapo figure (p. 206–7). The *NYT* (Oct. 10, 1935, p. 13) reported that Baeck had been arrested because of this prayer, then released after twenty-four hours.

branch, with a feeling of abhorrence, the lie which is being directed against us and the calumnies which are being spread about our religion and its eternal truths. We declare our faith in our religion and in our future.

Who has proclaimed to the world the mystery of the eternal and the one God? Who has revealed to the world the conception of purity in individual life and purity in family life? Who has given to the world the conception of respect towards man, the image of God? Who has given to the world the law of justice and social righteousness? The spirit of the prophets of Israel, God's revelation to the Jewish people, has left its mark on all of this. In the Jew, the seeds have taken root and have grown. Every insult hurled at us rebounds from these facts.

We stand before the Lord; we put our trust in Him. In Him, our history, our endurance during the years of our wanderings, our steadfastness in face of all persecution, has found its truth and its honour. Our history is a history of spiritual greatness and spiritual dignity. It is to our history that we turn whenever we are humiliated, whenever misery and sufferings encompass us. From generation to generation, the Lord has led our fathers. He will also lead us and our children in these days of tribulation.

We stand before our Lord. The fulfillment of His commandments gives us strength. Before Him we bow down, but we remain upright before man. It is Him that we serve, but we remain firm in all the changes of the present day. Humbly we put our trust in Him, and our path lies clearly before us; we face our future with confidence.

The whole of Israel stands at this hour before its God. Our prayer, our trust, our confession is the prayer, trust, and confession of all the Jews on earth. We look at ourselves and we know what is; we look up to our Lord and we know what will remain.

"He that guardeth Israel neither slumbers nor sleeps" (Ps. 121:4). "He that maketh peace on high places will also make peace for us and for all Israel."[26]

Sorrow and pain fill us. In silence before our Lord we express what our souls desire. Let the silent prayer, which is more eloquent than any words, speak.

---

26 Taken from the conclusion to *Sim Shalom* in the Amidah liturgy.

October 6, 1935 (Sunday evening, Kol Nidre)

Stephen S. Wise, (no title on separate title page), Free Synagogue at Carnegie Hall, New York. AJA, Box 21: SSW Microfilms of AJHS and BUASC papers

(3:) I ask tonight the question, not "What next *for* Israel?" but "What next *from* Israel?"... Today, I confess to you, I read a German paper that brought me to tears: the latest number of the *Rundschau*, the *Jüdische Rundschau*, which, in calm measured words, every word of which must have been weighed lest it (4:) bring upon the writer and the publisher tragic penalties and consequences, in measured words the *Jüdische Rundschau* tells the story of the new *Diffamierung*, or defamation as it may be imperfectly translated, of the new defamation.

There seems to be no shore or boundary to the sea of disaster, to paraphrase the Greeks, that is overwhelming us today out of the land which I shall not again name. I know what may happen: new hurts, new wails, new wounds, new disasters, new tragedies; but tonight I turn to you, my fellow Jews, and I ask you not what will befall us, but how shall we act and react to the world independently of hurt and wound and blow and smiting and burning?

(10:) Shall we be silent? Shall we say as some Jews would have us say, "Our business is to construct and not to destroy?" I urge war – moral, spiritual, social, economic – upon the Nazi madness, not alone, nor even solely, believe me, because of what it does to Jews, but because if *they* triumph, all that we stand for is gone, all that we have dreamt of is lost, all that we have suffered is cancelled, all that prayed for is obliterated. And I might tell you much more tonight of the business, the inescapable business of us Jews to destroy, to destroy, to destroy, in order that a new, fairer, juster world may be rebuilt....

Israel H. Levinthal, "Taking the Name of God in Vain," Brooklyn Jewish Center, Brooklyn, NY. *A New World Is Born*, pp. 155–161

(159:) The Jew throughout the ages has rejoiced in this spiritual partnership. "This is my God and I shall glorify Him!" (Exod. 15:2) – were the words that animated all his thoughts and all his deeds. It was the thought of this spiritual union that gave meaning to his life and purpose even to his death. It enabled him to hold his head high in the midst of all the shame and degradation that a cruel world heaped upon him. We have seen its effect even in our day. In the midst of Nazi Germany, where our brethren are still able to publish their own periodicals,[27] there recently appeared emblazoned on the front page of *Das Yiddische Rundshau* [*sic*[28]] these words: *Jude – Eine Ehrenahmen!* – Jew, a name of honor!

Ferdinand M. Isserman, "Tragedy or Pathos" (*Yizkor*), Temple Israel, St. Louis, MO. AJA, MS-6, Box 14, Folder 2

(2:) As a result of the catastrophic events that have overtaken the Jews of Germany, there are evident among them two types of persons. Both are agreed that the calamity before them is complete.... (3:) One group is meeting its fate with heroism and dignity, and interprets into it a divine significance, an opportunity to testify to the moral values of civilization, a duty to maintain one's morale in face of the barbarian terror. The other group is completely whipped. From its ranks come daily suicides.... Why is it that one group of Jews are living tragically, and another group of Jews pathetically? The answer is easy. The Jews with faith are prepared to face this calamity. The Jews without faith are crushed spiritually as well as physically.

(5:) I do believe in God who is giving the crushed German Jews the power to live heroically midst misfortune.

October 20, 1935 (Sunday)

Israel Mattuck, "Germany's Return to the Ghetto," Liberal Jewish Synagogue, London. Unpublished, but text sent to Press Association and *Daily Telegraph*, and partly published in "Liberal Jewish Monthly," November 1935

(1:) Germany has gone back to the Ghetto! The latest development in her persecution of the Jews is a series of laws aiming to segregate the Jews. On the pretext of protecting the purity of the Aryan race, the Nazi Government have prohibited, in so far as laws can prohibit,

27 Author's note: "This was in 1935. The right was soon after withdrawn."
28 The correct name of the periodical was, of course, *Jüdische Rundschau*.

social relations between Jews and Christians. These prohibitions are not very serious; they are childish ways of trying to impress on the Jews the Nazi judgment of their inferiority. Much more serious, however, are the political and economic aspects of Germany's return to the Ghetto.

The chief law passed at the session of the Reichstag held in September at Nuremberg in connection with the annual rally of the Nazi Party deprived the Jews of Germany of the rights of citizenship.... (2:) The principle which the Nazi Government has practiced that the Jews have no rights has now become the law of Germany. She has thus written into her constitution her return to the discarded and condemned ideas of the mediaeval ages. Over a century ago they were discarded, and Germany has now dug them out from the rubbish heap of European thought, feeding herself intellectually, like a certain animal does physically, on refuse.

(3:) At the recent Zionist Congress, Dr. Stephen Wise of New York informed the Jews of Germany that they would have been better off if they had not insisted on being "Germans of the Jewish faith."[29] Therein he agrees with Dr. Goebbels and the other Nazis who also objected to the German Jews calling themselves Germans. But except those who agree with Dr. Goebbels, all must feel a deep sympathy with the Jewish Germans whom oppressive rulers exclude from the life of Germany.[30]...

(4:) When Goebbels likens the Jews to fleas, or Streicher pours out his unspeakable vilifications, I confess myself completely undisturbed in my Jewish sensibilities.[31] It means to me no more than the barking

29 The Nineteenth World Zionist Congress met in Lucerne, August 1935. This terminology (*Zentral-Verein deutscher Staatsbürger jüdischen Glaubens*) has a long tradition, perhaps emanating from the decision of the French Assembly that it would tolerate religious differences but not national differences (cf. Harry Epstein, September 21, 1933, above). Wise, as a Zionist rabbi who was chairman of the Congress, asserted in his sermon delivered on the same day [below, pp. 228–29] that the proper terminology should have been "German Jews," which did not reduce Jewish identity to one of religion.

30 This sentence appears to contain a rather shocking attack on Wise as being in the category of those who, supposedly agreeing with Dr. Goebbels, lack "deep sympathy with the German Jews."

31 Mattuck is probably referring to a speech given by Goebbels in June 1935. Streicher's

of a dog, except that in this case unfortunately the barking dog has also a vicious bite. The Jews have the consciousness of a more reliable judgment – that of history – which puts them among the peoples that have made great contributions to the world's civilization.

That possession of the Jews – their spiritual self-respect – saved them from the degradation in the ghettoes of the past, which have become in history a symptom of the (5:) degradation of those that imposed them. The Ghetto laws which Germany's Nazi rulers have enacted will hurt the Jews, but will not degrade them. They show, however, Germany's degradation. The Jews have the pain of being forced back into a Ghetto; the rulers of Germany have the moral stigma.[32]...

These laws, however, have a greater significance than their effect on the position and fortunes of the German Jews. They constitute a challenge to European civilization.... (6:) Such a flagrant attack on a fundamental principle of our civilization calls for protest. But who shall do the (7:) protesting? There are two organized forces upon whom that duty devolves. One is the League of Nations....

The churches also have a special responsibility in this matter.... (8:) A year ago last July, the International Conference of Baptists, meeting in Berlin, protested against the persecution of the Jews.[33] Germany's return to the Ghetto calls for official condemnation by religion, not only because of the inhumanity it means toward the Jews, but because it violates our civilisation.

Germany must be left in no doubt about what the world thinks of her policy....

October 21, 1935 (Monday)

Abba Hillel Silver, Address at Brooklyn Jewish Center, Brooklyn, NY. *Brooklyn Daily Eagle*, October 22, 1935, p. 5

Der Stürmer was a notorious source of antisemitism, especially the May 1934 issue with a headline "Jewish Murder Plan Against Gentile Humanity Exposed," based on the blood libel; see *The Yellow Spot*, pp. 78–88, 102–4.

32 Note that language about being "forced back into a Ghetto" is purely rhetorical. Actual "ghettos" were never enforced on German Jews while in Germany, even during the war; they were imposed only in Poland.

33 Reference is to the Barmen Declaration of the Confessing Church passed at the Conference of May 1934. Cf. https://bit.ly/2IANeCK

[On recent statements by Brig. Gen. Charles H. Sherrill that Jewish opposition to American participation in the 1936 Olympics would result in a wave of antisemitism in the US]:[34]

It was the most thoughtless language to come from the lips of an American officer. The General forgets that the greatest champion of this cause [i.e., boycott of the German Olympics] is Judge [Jeremiah] Mahoney [president of the American Amateur Athletic Union] – a Catholic. General Sherrill has been too long in Germany. He has gotten the Hitler slant....

We cannot be scared. We will not be intimidated. We are going to fight to the last bitter end for the rights of any Jewish group in any part of the world who are oppressed or deprived of their rights....

In this unprecedented new world order, we ought to be able to discover some few causes that will act as a common denominator for all of us. We must learn to organize not merely among ourselves but with other minorities likewise handicapped by oppression. There are great groups of liberals who see the rising tide of dictatorship. They are our natural allies.

October 25, 1935 (Friday evening)

Ferdinand M. Isserman, "My Second Visit to Nazi Germany," Temple Israel, St. Louis, MO. Typescript in AJA, MS-6, Box 14, Folder 2; see Complete Sermons

October 27, 1935 (Sunday)

Stephen S. Wise, Preaching before the Community Church at Town Hall on Sunday Morning, in exchange with Dr. John Haynes Holmes, who occupied the pulpit of Dr. Wise at the Free Synagogue in Carnegie Hall. AJHS MS-49, 5,8; AJA, Box 21: SSW Microfilms of AJHS and BUASC papers

(1:) I shall deal with the truth and above all, with fictions about the

---

34 For more detail on Sherrill, cf. the sermons by Stephen S. Wise on October 27, and Harold I. Saperstein on November 1, below. The full statement of Sherrill includes the sentence, "The Jews constitute only a small percentage of our population, 5,000,000 out of 130,000,000, and this agitation for a boycott will start an anti-Semitic wave in this country" (*Cincinnati Enqirer*, October 24, 1935, p. 14).

German Olympics in my own pulpit next Sunday. Suffice it for today to say that, even though General [Charles H.] Sherrill succeeded in inducing the management of the Olympics to invite two German Jews to have a part in them, it remains true that in the town of Parthen-Kirchen, where the wonderful Olympic trials were held last winter, huge placards were seen forbidding entrance to the town to Jews....

As for the charge that politics is being dragged into a pure question of sports and games, it is the Nazi government which by its deeds and decrees compels civilized nations such as our own to ask themselves, how can the Olympics – which are to be the supreme illustration of sportsmanship and the very incarnation of fair play – be held under a regime from which every semblance of sportsmanship has been eliminated?

As for the Sherrill threat that the insistence of Jews upon America staying out of the Olympics will bring about a great anti-semitic movement in America, this Hitler-like threat will intimidate only the basest of cowards, whether Jews or non-Jews. Self-respecting Jews and Catholics will not be deterred from doing that which is right because of the spectre of the Sherrill threat!

November 1, 1935 (Friday evening)

Harold I. Saperstein, "The Great Olympic Idea," Temple Emanu-El, Lynbrook, NY. *Witness from the Pulpit*, pp. 44–49

(47:) [T]he fact remains that the Jews of Germany have, after a thousand years of residence, been robbed of their citizenship, their businesses, their properties. Thousands of them have been forced to flee the country, penniless and friendless. No self-respecting Jew, whether from Germany or anywhere else, could go to the Olympics if staged in Berlin.

To me the argument is simple. Germany has denied, opposed, and repudiated the Great Olympic Idea. The Nazi regime in Germany is the negation of all those concepts of international friendship that the Olympics represent. Under these circumstances, the Olympics in Germany will be but a farce, a gigantic act of international hypocrisy. America must not so demean itself as to participate in such hypocrisy.

[Continues to quote General Charles H. Sherrill]: "There is a grave danger of an anti-Semitic wave here because of agitation of Jews for German brethren. I would not be surprised if it reached such proportions as it did in Spain in 1492, when the Jews were expelled from there. It is all due to the Jews over-playing their cards. The whole problem started when the Jews, who held a disproportionate number of high positions, over-played their cards."[35]

(49:) Participation in the Olympics would not only bring Germany millions of dollars. It would also enhance the prestige of Hitler's rule within the country, and give tacit consent of the outside world to Nazi terrorism. The boycott of the Olympics would be an effective means of expressing the moral indignation of the civilized world at Germany's return to barbarism, and hasten the day when the people of Germany will come back to their senses.

November 10, 1935 (Sunday)

Maurice N. Eisendrath, "Rome or Jerusalem: An Armistice Message," Holy Blossom Temple, Toronto. *Holy Blossom Pulpit*, VI, 2

(9:) For, is it not as plain as day that the policy we are pursuing, that the campaign upon which Britain herself is now embarking, in answer to Mussolini and Hitler and possibly Stalin, will lead to sheer suicide for the entire human race? For what is it that we all of us crave and need most? Is it not security? And because we fear that we are not secure we are madly arming to the teeth.

November 12, 1935 (Tuesday)

Judah L. Magnes, "The Opening of the University Term, 1935–36," Jerusalem. *Addresses by the Chancellor of the Hebrew University*, pp. 278–89

(289:) What is it that has most stirred the hearts and conscience of mankind? The plight of Jewish industrialists, the Jewish politicians? No. The Jewish university teacher, the Jewish scientist, the Jewish author and artist – it is in large measure through their merit and

35 *Witness from the Pulpit*, p. 47, n.5: an imprecise paraphrase from the *NYT.*

suffering that the eyes of the world watch with indignation and pity the tragedy that is Germany.

November 17, 1935 (Sunday)

Maurice N. Eisendrath, "Hitler Invites the Youth of the World - Shall Canada Accept? Facts and Fictions About the Olympics," Holy Blossom Temple, Toronto. Holy Blossom Archives, Series ZA 1935, Box 2, File 16; quotation taken from Menkis and Troper, *More Than Just Games*, pp. 103–5 and 235 n. 83

[T]he Nazi regime has not so much insulted and offended and humiliated a few Jews or Catholics or Protestants as it has derided and scorned and violated everything Canadians and Britishers are supposed to hold dear.... [Instead] of waiting ignominiously for the counsel of the motherland, spontaneously and of her own accord [Canada should] stand upon her own feet and courageously declare that she will not compete in games of sport with those who have given all the abundant evidence that they recognize not the first principles of fair play and sportsmanship.... Of course, our cause may be lost. Apathy and ignorance are against us. The moral lassitude of the majority may conquer our utmost zeal. But is that any cause for capitulation? Should we who love peace surrender to the warmongers because it seems certain that the dogs of war will be let loose again? Should we ourselves favor the trafficking with moral lepers merely because the official action of some sports organizations is predicated on "practical" rather than ethical grounds?[36]

By similar and incessant action we can place every moral obstacle possible in the path of those who would raise funds to send our athletes into this inferno of burning hatreds which would reduce all Europe in a shambles.

November 23, 1935 (Saturday)

Harris Swift, "Constancy and Conviction in All Vicissitudes," Great Synagogue, London. *Because I Believe*, pp. 55–60

36 The answer to these rhetorical questions was, of course, "No," although the preacher realized that the odds were against the success of the boycott campaign.

(59:) In the dire troubles with which Jewry is now, alas, confronted, with maniacal hatred, brutal persecution and inhuman barbarity wedded to the callous destructive forces of a great state machine in one country, and hunger and terrible want in another...we must never cease to trust in the power of God to relieve suffering, to redeem the oppressed and to bring (60:) to the needy the satisfaction of all their manifold wants....

Let not lethargy and despair, *ye'ush* [despondency] and indifference, become our worst enemies.

November 24, 1935 (Sunday)

Maurice N. Eisendrath, "I Re-Visit Nazi Germany," Holy Blossom Temple, Toronto. *Holy Blossom Pulpit*, VI, 3[37]

(11:) Thus whereas in 1933 there was yet some spark of hope in the breasts of the few, today even the most stalwart know full well that the day can no longer be delayed when the half-million Jews of Germany, as well as millions of their fellow-sufferers among the trade, the liberals, the pacifists, the demurring Protestants and the faithful Catholics, will become like unto the pariahs of India, tramping the roads, begging for a dry crust of bread, or lying prostrate and starving upon the soil they once loved as well.

(12:) Scarcely had I left these doom-ridden folk behind than the Nazi party met in its favorite haunt, the picturesque and historic town of Nuremberg, once famous as the scene of the *Meistersingers*, now infamous and forever desecrated as the spot where were recently enacted those unprecedented Nuremberg Laws, where there was committed that most heinous crime ever perpetrated upon an entire people whose only common and universal fault was that they loved their fatherland too well, spilled for it the blood of generations and watered its soil with the sweat of creative toil and enriched its life with the sublimest achievements in science, culture, and art. Yet by this single edict they were plunged back one thousand years, back into a sequestered, secluded ghetto once again; into a ghetto far more

37 In the summer of 1935, Eisendrath first visited Palestine, and then decided to revisit Europe after hearing reports of "new atrocities...barbarism and brutality."

terrible and torturous than any ghetto of the Middle Ages.[38] Then at least they had the protection of those high towering walls and those carefully guarded gates to shield them from the marauding and oft drunken mob. But there is a ghetto bereft of gates and walls where, forsaken and alone, the Jew is at the mercy of any supercilious and arrogant Nazi who *by law* has been given *carte blanche* to arrest anyone who does anything whatsoever that may seem displeasing in his supreme and unquestioned sight.

(13:) Such is Nazi Germany today, and unless something happens soon, unless in every land as in Great Britain, the other day, such men as the Archbishop of Canterbury[39] arise in their wrath and righteous indignation to excoriate this monstrous, maddened regime and to excommunicate it morally, socially, athletically, politically, and economically as the moral leper that it is, the Olympic Games will come and go, and the Nazis, relieved of the restraint which this year is imposing on them in order not to jeopardize their chance to hold these contests, may break forth in the Fall of 1936 into a wholesale massacre even more bloody and brutal than Kishinev or St. Bartholomew's Eve.

December 6, 1935 (Friday evening)

Ferdinand M. Isserman, "Which is Worse: Berlin or Warsaw?: Impressions of a Week with Polish Jewry," Temple Israel, St. Louis, MO. AJA, MS-6, Box 14, Folder 2

(1:) I spent one week this summer with the Jews of Poland. The poverty that I witnessed amongst them I did not believe existed anywhere. There are three million Polish Jews, one million, or one-third

38 The word "ghetto" as applied to the Jews of Nazi Germany immediately following the Nuremberg Laws is of course used metaphorically, as the actual ghettos were never established in Germany.

39 Cf. *JC*, November 29, 1955, p. 10: "…the men in Berlin…had better remember the words spoken by the Archbishop of Canterbury last week: 'I am sure that the continuance of the present persecutions must seriously affect the goodwill with which the people of this country desire to regard the German nation.'" If this is indeed the speech mentioned by Eisendrath as having occurred "the other day," it would date the sermon as Sunday, November 24.

of whom are starving. The others lead a hand-to-mouth existence. They lack the necessities of life. They have insufficient food, insufficient clothing, insufficient medical care. If not for the German-Jewish tragedy, their shocking plight would long have aroused us.

(10:) From Berlin I had flown to Warsaw. Berlin shocked me; Warsaw stunned me. Who are worse off, I ask myself, the Jews of Germany or those of Poland? Months have passed. I have not yet decided. A change in politics can help the Jews of Germany. They still have enough to eat. But what can help three million Jews in Poland, for whom there is no economic future? A lowering of tariff barriers? Peace and security in Europe? But when? How long? And how?

December 20, 1935 (Friday evening, first night of Hanukkah)

Ferdinand M. Isserman, "The Olympic Victory and the Maccabean Victory: A Hanukkah Sermon," Temple Israel, St. Louis, MO. AJA, Box 14, Folder 2

(1:) Antiochus, the fourth, the villain of the Hanukkah festival . . . was the model dictator whom the moderns are imitating. . . .

(5:) Today, we are witnessing another assault upon civilization saved for humanity by the Maccabeans. Hitler occupies in modern civilization the place that Antiochus Epiphanes occupied in the old. . . . The issue in Germany today is not what happens to a handful of Jews, but what will happen to civilization if Naziism triumphs. . . . Like Antiochus, Hitler has sought to establish a totalitarian state and has sought to make the paganism of the Nazis the worship of the state, the only philosophy of Germany. As Antiochus ruled with a reign of terror, so Hitler rules with a reign of terror. . . .

(6:) The decision of our Amateur Athletic Union to participate in the Olympic Games in Berlin, to send our youth to be the guests of the murderers and gangsters who rule Germany, who seek to bring on the dark ages, who plan for wars of conquest, who have destroyed liberty and freedom of thought, will be branded by history as an inexcusable moral crime. . . .

1936

January 10, 1936 (Friday evening)

Ferdinand M. Isserman, "The Resignation of High Commissioner [James G.] McDonald and the Fate of Germany's Jews," Temple Israel, St. Louis, MO. AJA, MS-6, Box 14, Folder 3

(1:) After twenty-six months of self-sacrifice and devotion, [McDonald] finds that he cannot carry on; the situation of the Jewish refugees is hopeless. It must be solved through political, not philanthropic measures.[1]

(3:) He too points out that for the Jews of Germany there is no hope as long as present policies continue. Not only does he find the Nazis not abating their persecution of the Jews, but intensifying it day by day. (4:) [Quoting from the McDonald report:] "Of the 80,000 refugees who have left Germany since Hitler assumed power; all but 15,000 have been placed. There still remain 450,000 Jews in Germany."

(5:) [Quoting McDonald:] "The League must take political action and intercede with the Hitler Government to change its policies towards the Jews...." In the light of this statement of McDonald, the result of study and observation, buttressed by facts and by documents, how puerile seem the reports brought to this country by... college professors who were the guests of the Nazi government, and casual tourists who beheld the beauties [of the German landscape] and who reported that all was well in Naziland.

---

1 In the fall of 1933, James McDonald was appointed by the League of Nations as High Commissioner responsible for German refugees. According to Isserman, his first report, made several months later, was criticized by some as anti-German propaganda. His letter of resignation, first published in the *NYT* on December 30, 1935, was described as "an incisive critique of the League's refugee activities and an open attack on Nazi racial policies." See Sheldon Spear, "The United States and the Persecution of the Jews in Germany, 1933–1939," in *Jewish Social Studies*, vol. 30, no. 4 (Oct., 1968): p. 224.

(6:) The McDonald resignation not only exposes the propaganda which the Nazis have assiduously spread in America, but it brings the tragedy of the non-Aryan in Germany, and the brutality and cruelty of the Hitler regime, officially and squarely before all the nations who are members of the League.... There is no satisfaction in my soul over the fact that McDonald has vindicated my reports about the status of the German Jew. I wish he had proved me wrong. I wish he had convinced me that my visit was a horrible nightmare. But such is the colossal tragedy. What is to happen to the Jews of Germany?

January 12, 1936 (Sunday)

Solomon Goldman, Report of the Conference of Jews and Christians, Congregation Anshe Emet, Chicago, IL. AJA MS-203, Box 22, Folder 12

(19:) Our experience in Germany, Poland, or Romania is nothing new. In Alexandria, in Toledo, in Rome, we faced situations more or less similar. We faced the problem in old Memphis. According to some Egyptologists, there were some forty-two oppressed and suppressed peoples in Egypt when the Jews lived there. Those people were divested of their form and gradually levelled to Egyptian uniformity by the tyranny of Pharaohs and the pressure of majorities.[2] Those people disappeared. If they made any contributions to religion, civilization, ethics, or art, the historian and archaeologist are not aware of them.

In that Egyptian Empire was born a child named Moses. He quickened the memory of the Jewish slaves, reminded them of their ancestry and urged upon them to retain their distinctiveness.

Is the Jew, because he insists on the preservation of his identity, a "foreign element?"...(20:) The Jew, everywhere he lived, contributed to the welfare and progress of the country.

February 2, 1936 (Sunday)

Stephen S. Wise, "Three Years of Hitlerism," Free Synagogue at Carnegie Hall, New York. AJA, Box 22: SSW Microfilms of AJHS and BUASC papers

2 The subjugation of forty-two peoples is generally associated with the Assyyrian Tiglath-Pileser rather than the Egyptian Pharaoh.

(1:) The three years of Hitlerism that ended on the twenty-ninth day of January have confuted optimists and pessimists alike. The pessimists held from the beginning that the regime would come but that it could not last, and that a year or two of its horror would suffice to destroy it. These three years have no less confuted the optimists who believed that the Nazi triumph would be no more than nominal, and that after Nazism had brought itself into power it would forget its program, ignore its threats, and proceed along the way of political parties which promise everything and perform little or nothing. What these three years of Hitlerism have done to Germany, how they have dishonored its great name, how they have brought it to the low estate of world-wide scorn, is illustrated, though it is not adequately told, by the reluctance of civilized nations to have part in the Olympic games at Berlin....

(2:) But my special problem is with the Jewish aspect of the three years of Hitlerism.... The truth is that not the most fearful and cowed of Jews could have imagined in 1933 on the eve of the regime's advent that Hitlerism would pursue its anti-Jewish purpose with unrelenting fiendishness – that it would execute every threat that once sounded as if mere idle [talk with the] *Gruendlichkeit* [thoroughness] of the German character. Not only has every threat, however ominous and infernal, been fulfilled, but the Nazi regime, little challenged save by Jewish lamentations and feeble-hearted Christian protest, has moved from strength to strength in executing the program of oppression, destruction, defamation, degradation, for all that is Jewish in Germany....

(4:) Today sees a great anti-Christian movement in full progress within the Nazi Reich and only the fear of offending Rome and England prevents the utter dominance of the pagan leaders such as Alfred Rosenberg and General Goering. In a word, the Jew does not stand alone!...

(5:) So utter is become the destruction of the Jewish people, the expulsion of their best, beginning with Einstein, the terrorization of men and women and particularly children, that it becomes no exaggeration to maintain that no comparable disaster has been visited upon the Jewish people in all the Christian centuries.

And still there are Jews who believe... that whatever be the horrors and the tortures that Hitler Germany visits upon its Jewish victims, we may not even seem to assent to the spirit of surrender.

(6:) If it be asked... whether Jews have abandoned all hope of release from the torture chamber that Nazi Germany has become, the only answer is that the solution will come either from the revolution of the German people against their masters and despots, though such revolution means a Germany bathed in blood, or it will come through the world-war which Hitlerism is bound within a measurable period to provoke and make inevitable.

(7:) The Jewish status in Germany is hopeless; but world Jewry is not hopeless. For the first time in a millennium it becomes conscious of and begins to gather that strength divided, dissipated by the all-but-devastating ways of assimilation. World Jewry has learned that assimilation is not even a way out, let alone the pathway of individual or collective redemption.

(8:) Three years of Hitlerism. For the sake of the Germany that was, for the sake of every high interest of human life imperiled, invaded, violated, in Nazi Germany, for the sake of all humanity inclusive of my ancient people, may there by no fourth anniversary of the Hitler regime!

February 16, 1936 (Sunday)

Stephen S. Wise, "The Swiss Assassination: 'Made in Germany,'" Free Synagogue at Carnegie Hall, New York. AJA, Box 22: SSW Microfilms of AJHS and BUASC papers[3]

(7:) Hitler [in his funeral address] spoke of the deed as if the Jewish people had organized and instigated that act of assassination as if it were unthinkable that among fifteen or sixteen million Jews on earth, one poor youth should be moved all by himself to commit this irresponsible act. Hitler threatens the whole Jewish people

3 The "Swiss Assassination" in the title refers to the murder on February 4, 1936 of Wilhelm Gustloff, head of the Foreign Section of the Nazi Party in Switzerland, by David Frankfurter, son of a Croation rabbi, who had studied in Germany and Switzerland. The event was widely reported on the following and subsequent days; Hitler delivered the eulogy at the funeral service on February 12. See Martin Gilbert, *The Holocaust*, p. 51; David Cesarani, *Final Solution*, p. 117.

with punishment.... Finally Hitler utters the most monstrous lie in history, a lie that Nazis have committed no act of violence. Hitler's word is, "the Jew is an enemy whom we have never harmed." I quote his funeral address: "The Jew is responsible for all the misfortunes of November 1918 and the succeeding bad luck visited on Germany."...

(9:) I who am a believer in non-violence, I cannot find it in my heart to condemn Frankfurter. I understand, I pity, I regret, I deplore, but my protest is against *you*. My protest is against the Christian world which has failed to follow the lead of the Lord Bishop of Durham [Hensley Henson].[4] (10:) If Christendom felt and spoke as does the Lord Bishop of Durham, when he says, "It is not to be wondered at if Jews everywhere felt deep and justified wrath against their enemy," there would not have been a David Frankfurter.

February 23, 1936 (Sunday, Erev Rosh Ḥodesh Adar).

Shabbetai Rapoport, "Go, Assemble" (Esth. 4:16), Pinczów, Poland. *Siftei Kohanim*, pp. 71c–74b; cf. Piekarz, *Ḥasidut Polin,* pp. 302–10, translated by MS

(71c:) Because of our many sins, we stand today under a depressing sign, for new enemies constantly rise up against us to seize the food from our mouths, and to deprive us of our livelihood through various deceptive plots. But more than this: they now are planning to prohibit us from fulfilling the commandment of the ritual slaughtering of meat, and thereby to nullify a positive commandment of the Torah. Our opponents are of various categories: some are representatives in the Parliament, who have proposed this plan for ratification as a law, with various justifications, both "humanitarian" and administrative....[5]

(72a:) Now our oppressors have risen to plunder and to rob from

4 Wise is referring here to a sermon delivered by the Bishop of Durham at the West London Synagogue on February 6, 1936, two days after the assassination. The address was covered extensively by the *JC*, February 14, 1936, p. 18, including the statement that "the ultimately responsible authors of this criminal act are the present rulers of Germany." This may have been the source of Wise's information.

5 On this political movement in Poland, see Emanuel Melzer, *No Way Out: The Politics of Polish Jewry, 1935–1939*, pp. 81–87. Compare also the reaction by another Polish preacher to the further development below, March 23, 1936.

us the sanctity of sacrificial meat. Alas, what has happened to us; alas, what has occurred in our age! There is not a single day when one curse does not seem worse than its predecessor. Sorrows come upon us one after another. And "because of our sins we were exiled from our land, and distanced from our soil,"[6] while every other nation dwells upon its own soil. While every other city is standing proudly in its place, the City of God is sunk to the nethermost depths. There is no High Priest, there is no sacred sacrifice upon the altar, our soul is dried out, empty; we are cut off from all branches of agriculture and sustenance. And so all parts of the soul become desiccated, dried out, with nothing to turn to except the evil Haman and his black faction for our sustenance.[7] "For Your sake we are being killed all day long" (Ps. 44:22). Yet despite it all, we turn to God, and we lift up our eyes to the heights. (72a)... "Pour out Your wrath upon the nations that do not know You" (Ps. 79:6)....

(73a:) That is why the Gentiles have come to profane what is holy for us – the holiness of religious sacrifice – and decree that we may not eat meat. Perhaps, God forbid!, it is because we deprive them of their livelihood, and this results in a lessening of gifts to the poor and gifts to their priests.[8] Let us look at our behavior and try to determine the reasons why this painful event has come upon us, assailing, assaulting us, by taking from us our ritual slaughter, and then let us return to God, for we can only rely on our heavenly Father to accept our entreaty, to listen and respond to our tribulation and deliver us from our suffering.... (73b:) After all this, we must not despair, God forbid; to the contrary, we must encourage ourselves and hope for God's multiple beneficent acts....

(74b:) Think of the Jews of Germany: they imagined that they were protected by a wall, and that antisemitism would not reach

6 From the High Holy Day *Musaf* service.

7 It is not clear to me who was the Haman figure that listeners undoubtedly would have known. The "black faction" was probably a reference to the National Democratic Party ("Endeks").

8 If I understand this correctly, it is a rather stunning recognition that insensitive Jewish behavior in economic and commercial activities may be connected with the hostility reflected in the proposed legislation.

them, whereas it was actually upon them that the fury of antisemitism landed first, breaching their protective wall, so that they would confess that they had repudiated the God of Israel and the surety of their brothers, while relying on the protection of their wall. Similarly, we must remember our brothers, subjects of Soviet Russia, to pray on their behalf, that all evil will be nullified from your people, the House of Israel, and the heart of the kingdom, its ministers and advisors, will be turned toward us for the good. Not only this, but perhaps God will have mercy upon us and say "Enough!" to all our sorrows, and – as in the days of Mordecai and Esther – He will work marvelous miracles on our behalf and redeem us, so that Israel will be delivered by God in a universal deliverance and total redemption.

March 8, 1936 (Sunday, Purim)

Abba Hillel Silver, "'But Mordecai Bowed Not Down,'" The Temple, Cleveland, OH. *Therefore Choose Life*, pp. 277–81; see Complete Sermons

March 15, 1936 (Sunday)

Israel Mattuck, "Germany's Outlawry and Its Effect on International Morality," Liberal Jewish Synagogue, London. Unpublished

(1:) Germany has shocked the conscience of the world, and very gravely intensified the feeling of crisis in Europe, by her action last week in sending troops into the Rhineland, denouncing, at the same time, the Treaty of Locarno.[9]

(3:) By a series of actions – and the movement of the troops into the Rhineland is only the latest of them – Germany has turned (4:) Europe into an armed camp.... One step after another, aiming to destroy what there was of a peace foundation in Europe, and the result has been that every country in Europe is spending immeasurably more money to-day on navies, armies, and air fleets than

9 Negotiated in September 1935 and formally accepted by Germany, France, Belgium, the United Kingdom, and Italy soon afterward, this Treaty fixed the western borders of Germany. In June 1930, Allied troops completed their withdrawal from the Rhineland, which was to remain demilitarized. These details are provided in the continuation of the sermon.

they were spending four years ago, before Hitler came into power. And not only in Europe; the military budget of the United States of America is this year the largest budget that country has ever passed for military purposes in peace time.

It is entirely a mystery. German militarism was beaten on the fields of France and Flanders between the years of 1914 and 1918, and to-day German militarism is winning a victory in forcing its philosophy on every country in Europe, and almost every country in the world. . . .

(10:) The responsibility of this country is tremendous. They who speak in the name of Great Britain to-day hold in their power the future peace of Europe, and they in turn depend upon public opinion. Public opinion is right when it says we must have no war, not even because Germany has violated many a treaty. We must have no war. Public opinion must also say, at the same time, that to avoid war in the future we must have confidence and faith, and only they shall be admitted to the society of nations who show that they have faith, and that they can be trusted. The spirit of humanity depends upon the judgment we make now.

March 20, 1936 (Friday evening)

Ferdinand M. Isserman, "Can a European War be Avoided," Temple Israel, St. Louis, MO. AJA MS-6, Box 14, Folder 3

(1:) The crisis caused by the German reoccupation of the Rhineland is directly due to the Franco-Russian alliance. It upset the apple-cart of Nazi foreign policies. . . . It is my opinion that the conferences being held in London between the powers of Europe will succeed in avoiding an immediate European war. If the aggrieved party had (2:) been a dictatorship and not a republic like France, I should not be so comforted. . . . No European war will take place immediately. It will only be postponed.

(5:) Anything, therefore, that the present conference may do is but a temporary make-shift which will postpone and not avert a European war. A European war can be avoided by the development of a sense of internationalism, and of the inter-dependence of all nations. . . .

(8:) A press dispatch this week, emanating from the anti-semitic leader in France, intimated that Jews are seeking to foment a European war in order that Hitlerism might be destroyed and that Nazi anti-semitism will disappear. This anti-semitic leader intimated that should there come a war, a great wave of anti-semitism will spread through France and throughout the world, and those Jews who are left will be crushed everywhere. For the Jew who knows Jewish history, the warning of Colonel de la Roche [*sic*] is unnecessary.[10] He knows that wars bring only calamity and destruction for Jews....

March 23, 1936 (Erev Rosh Ḥodesh Nisan)

Moses Kahlenberg, "Eulogy Delivered Between *Minḥah* and *Ma'ariv* for Rabbi Joseph Rozen of Dvinsk, and for the Horrors Occurring to Our Brothers in Various Lands," *Shomrei Shabbat, Kehal Yere'im* ("The Polish Congregation"), Metz, France. *Shalosh Dema'ot*, pp. 78–104, translated by MS

(79:) To our dismay, on the 11th of Adar [March 5] the sorrows were multiplied, and the Fast of Esther came early.... The rabbinic leaders declared a public fast over the sorrows of the Jews, and the painful edicts that had been passed in Poland, prohibiting ritual slaughter[11]...So to our dismay a flood of evil decrees have come to sweep away our brothers, and the suffering of the Jews in the East makes us forget the suffering of the Jews of Germany.[12]...

---

10 Here "the anti-semitic leader in France" mentioned at the beginning of the paragraph is named: François de la Rocque, leader of the right-wing *Croix de Feu* league. The Associated Press on March 17 stated: "Paris Government sends 2,000 troops to frontier. Nationalist leader De La Rocque charges 'three or four Jews for financial reasons are attempting to start war'" – although Isserman's source seems to have been somewhat different.

11 This was the second such fast proclaimed by the Polish rabbinate. The proposed prohibition of Jewish ritual slaughtering was first brought before the Polish Sejm on February 9 (see above, February 23, 1936); for the next month and a half, major protests were made both in Poland and from outside, including the United States (JTA has reports on the topic almost every day in the second half of February). The adoption of the new legislation, with an amendment that permitted ritual slaughter only for Jews, was described in a *JC* article on March 27, p. 26, next to an article on anti-Jewish riots following the March 9, 1936 pogrom in Przytyk (on which see Melzer, *No Way Out*, pp. 55–56).

12 A statement that seems rather extraordinary in retrospect, but reminds us that

They eliminated oxen and all kinds of cattle from the original total prohibition of Jewish ritual slaughter. That radical legislation would – Heaven forbid! – have uprooted Judaism completely, leading Jews to defile their souls with forbidden meats that also contaminate the entire body. If there were to be no kosher meat – Heaven forbid! – there would be no need for Jewish congregations, and no need for rabbis, or judges, or ritual supervisors, or yeshivah scholars, or community supporters, or Jewish butchers. Approximately a quarter of a million people would be deprived of their livelihoods....

(80:) Rabbotai, this is nothing new for us. For the past thousand years, indeed since we went into exile from our land, we have learned about bearing up under blows and afflictions. Hatred of religion and race is an ancient hatred, and it will not come to an end until the promises of God's prophet are fulfilled, "And the earth shall be filled with the knowledge of the Lord" (Isa. 11:14), meaning precisely, not filled with other doctrines. But look and see the difference between the horrors of earlier times and the horrors of today. In the past, those who revealed their hatred were ignorant, uneducated,... who did not know of or appreciate our value, while the upper classes, those with education, had total disdain for them, as if they were wild animals foraging through the woods....

But (81:) now, to our distress, it has become reversed; the hatred comes in great anger from the upper classes, from educated people who take pride in their knowledge of how to do evil; they appear to disguise themselves by claiming that they oppose causing pain to animals, that they have pity for beasts and other living creatures, but for human beings born in their image and likeness they show no mercy. For the lives of three-and-a-half million human beings they show no pity; they trample them underfoot, without compassion. They pay no attention to all the statements made by expert doctors, who have come to testify that ritual slaughter with a sharp, smooth knife in accordance with Torah law is the most humane way of death for the animals....

---

in the spring of 1936, while Germany was letting up on anti-Jewish persecution in preparation for the Olympic Games, it was not unreasonable to conclude that Polish Jewry was suffering more than were their German neighbors.

(82:) May our standing up in honor of the holy deceased serve as a sign and a beacon for us, that all the waves of the sea that are breaking against us will pass over us, and we, the people of Israel, will endure forever. We organize ourselves in a Protest that will be sent to that country, and we raise our voices in total disapproval of the injustice that has been done there to our fellow Jews in these scandals, while others look upon them with equanimity and fail to stop the acts of oppression. And similarly about the harsh legislation imposed upon the Jews, taking from them their free expression and the living freedom of religion and the spirit.

April 7, 1936 (first day of Pesach)

Israel Mattuck, "The Sufferings of the Jews," Liberal Jewish Synagogue, London. Unpublished

(1:) The sufferings of the Jews in the present, no less than their sufferings in the past, are connected with their religion. It has made them, and still makes them, a distinctive group among the peoples of the world. Those who persecute them give all sorts of reasons for the persecution, but at bottom it issues from a psychological quality in little minds which makes them suspicious of differences and hostile to those who are different....

2:) The religious distinctiveness of the Jews has not interfered with their contributions to the diverse nations to which they belong. They have shared fully in the lives of these nations. And they have established their right to do so by centuries of residence, by their services and sacrifices, by their sentiments of loyalty. It is a right which oppression denies them in Germany, but which the German Jews cannot, and will not, relinquish. Some are forced to leave the country, and the Jews in other lands must help them to find homes elsewhere. But neither their decision to leave, nor the efforts of others to help them, mean any diminution in their claim that the German Jews have an inalienable right to their citizenship in Germany. And that claim will be maintained silently though eloquently by the Jews who will remain in Germany. All but a fraction of the German Jews must remain in their country, rebuilding there in relation to the circumstances their individual lives and the life of the Jewish community, and hoping for a time when the better spirit of Germany will re-assert itself.

They cannot resist their oppressors, but by their silent suffering they can perform a service to humanity. Though they can only stand and wait, they serve those ideals of tolerance and respect for human personality upon which our civilization depends. Their suffering evokes the sympathy (3:) of the civilized world. They are entitled, too, to all the help which the civilized world can give them, because their suffering is due to a violation of the principles of civilization, and because by their silent endurance they are contending for the firmer establishment of those principles in the life of humanity.

April 11, 1936 (Sunday, *Ḥol haMo'ed* Pesach, Easter)

Abba Hillel Silver, "The Mystery of Our Survival," The Temple, Cleveland, OH. *Therefore Choose Life,* pp. 219–22

(222:) I am not a pessimist, though so much is happening to make men depressed and dejected. We shall outlive Hitler as we outlived Pharaoh. The story of Pharaoh is exactly the same as the story of Hitler.

They know – the Hitlerites do – that they are doomed. Hence the cruelty and desperation. They know that the spirit of Israel which they fear will ultimately triumph. That love of justice which speaks from every page of the Bible they must read today in every church in Germany. They cannot help themselves. What they would like to do is to revise that Bible. They would like to forget that every page is written by Jews. They would like to obliterate every reference to freedom, tolerance, and fair play, and substitute for it war, hatred, intolerance, and racial bigotry.

You cannot forge a religion. You can be pickpockets, as the Nazis have been, and take the wealth which the Jews achieved through their labor in Germany and rob them of it. You can cheat. You can lie. You can break treaties. But you cannot undo history. Every time the Bible is read on Easter morning in a church in Germany, the thought will sink into the minds of the listeners that the Bible is the book of the

Jews, whose descendants are today being degraded and humiliated and persecuted in their very midst, that the founder of the religion they follow that morning was a Jew,[13] was of the race of Israel, of a race which Hitler tells them to regard as an inferior race – a race which teaches not of hatred nor war but of freedom and peace and justice and love of thy neighbor.

Ultimately these things will undermine this regime of wickedness...."

May 1, 1936 (Friday evening)

Ferdinand M. Isserman, "Collective Security, Neutrality or War? Which Will America Choose?," Temple Israel, St. Louis, MO. Typescript in AJA, MS-6, Box 14, Folder 4

1: [Context: Germany's "remilitarization of the Rhineland":] [The American people must] "work out a policy that will stand us in good stead in critical times, and will prevent the hysteria of the moment from sweeping us into another Armageddon [as in WWI]. That another clash between mighty nations is imminent, no student of the international scene doubts. Europe is a powder keg. The fuse is laid. No one can predict when the match will be struck and the explosion take place. Another war is inevitable, not merely because nations are rearming, but because there are three great powers [Germany, Italy, Japan] wedded to the philosophy of fascism, and the very nature of the fascist states is such that wars (2:) are part of their natural existence.

(9:) [Urges] enacting stringent neutrality laws. These laws will only be passed by Congress when the American people demand it. A world war is imminent. This world war would involve us unless action is taken now.... It therefore seems that the cause of humanity and of America can best be served by having our country notify the world of its resolution to have nothing to do with the scourge of war, and of expressing that resolution of neutrality through laws

13 This of course overlooks the movement among German Christians to deny the Jewishness of Jesus, on which see Susannah Heschel, *The Aryan Jesus.*

now so that neither propaganda nor hysteria will be able to deter our people from this inflexible purpose clearly seen in these days when sanity still reigns, and reason can triumph over passion, and noble emotion over beclouded prejudice.[14]

May 23, 1936 (Saturday)

Abba Hillel Silver, "The Ancient Paths," Address at Graduation Exercises, Hebrew Union College, Cincinnati, OH. *Therefore Choose Life*, pp. 418–26

(420:) Think with what desperate problems of survival – sheer political and economic survival – our present generation of Jews is being confronted in many parts of the world. There are powerful governments today which are bent upon our systematic destruction, or, as they would have it, elimination of their Jewish – not citizens any longer, but unwelcome aliens. They have a full-blown program of anti-Semitism, an anti-Semitic metaphysics, an apologetics and an elaborate technique. And Nazism, be it remembered, is not confined to Germany, though in Germany it has had its freest play and its most shameful victories. It is a plague of lethal ideas, sweeping over the world today, victimizing the Jew wherever it reaches, comparable to the centuries-lasting madness which was let loose upon Europe by the Crusades,[15] and equally menacing to the peace and security of our people.... The times are desperately critical for all mankind, but most of all for that most sensitive seismograph of all mankind's earthquakes and disturbances – Israel.

(423:) [T]he fearful heresy of our day proclaims not the supremacy of the moral law but the supremacy of the state or the nation. The state or nation can do no wrong. The party in control of the state can do no wrong. The party boss, the *duce*, the *Fuehrer*, the commissar, can do no wrong. The eternal cry of the Jew through the ages

---

14 It is worth noting that the sermon ignores the possibility of America being attacked (as would occur in December 1941).

15 Even at this relatively early stage of Nazi persecution, it is difficult to imagine how it was truly "comparable" (in the sense of "similar") to the centuries of European history beginning with the Crusades, in which royal governments were committed to the protection of Jews, and the worst fate was an orderly expulsion.

has been not "There is no king but Caesar" but "There is no King but Thee!"[16] The new paganism recognizes only one mortal sin for which a nation should do penance, the sin of having been defeated in battle, and recognizes only one impartial judge above the nations, as one of the military experts of the Nazis declared – *success!*

June 24, 1936 (Wednesday)

Felix A. Levy, Presidential Message to CCAR Convention in Cape May, NJ. *His Own Torah*, pp. 111–31;[17] *CCAR Yearbook* 46 (1936), pp. 139–64; cf. JTA, June 24, 1936

(123:) The heroism of our co-religionists in Germany continues to command our high admiration. While their desire to escape from this chamber of horrors is natural, one wonders whether even a general exodus of Jews is the solution for our brethren there, provided all could leave the Rhineland. Some will, throughout their life, and others, until such time as they can get away, have to meet as best they can their manifold problems. As a whole, German Jewry has borne itself with honor, has worn the Jewish badge of shame with pride, and has really by its demeanor "sanctified the name."[18] It is astounding and gratifying to find that, despite their disabilities, poverty, and persecution, their work in Jewish fields of study and organization

16 The first phrase is from John 19:15; the second is from "*Nishmat Kol Ḥai*" of the Sabbath and Holiday liturgy and *Avinu Malkenu* of the High Holy Day liturgy.

17 Reproduced by arrangement with Jonathan David Publishers, Inc., www.jdbooks.com.

18 The traditional phrase used for acts of martyrdom. The phrase "has worn the Jewish badge of shame with pride" is apparently an allusion to an editorial entitled "After the Boycott" published in the Zionist periodical *Jüdische Rundschau* on April 4, 1933 by its editor Robert Weltsch. The article makes no mention of *wearing* a "Jewish badge of shame"; it refers to the requirement that for the Boycott of April 1, a "yellow badge on a black background" be painted on Jewish stores to identify them, and responds, "We accept it and propose to turn it into a badge of honor" (*Wir nehmen sie auf, und wollen daraus ein Ehrenzeichen machen*). The article ends, "We are being reminded that we are Jews. We affirm this, and bear it with pride" (*Man erinnert uns, dass wir Juden sind. Wir sagen Ja, und tragen es mit Stolz*). The erroneous title was perhaps first introduced with a front-page headline in the *Jewish Daily Bulletin* of April 24, 1933: "Let Us Wear Our Jewish Badge With Pride – Jüdische Rundshau." (Jews in the Reich were not required to *wear* a yellow badge until September 1941.)

still maintains its former high quality.[19] The present generation of German Israel is not lacking in Jewish loyalty or in singleness of Jewish purpose. In this we find the assurance that when the regime of wicked Haman will have vanished, Jews and Jewish ideals will still remain, as testimony to the indestructibility of spiritual values and to the ultimate victory of truth and righteousness. We suffer with our brethren and trust that relief may come to them speedily.

(125:) There are other manifestations of anti-Semitism in this country and we view with regret the increase of feeling and the spread of propaganda against the Jew. We cannot, however, share the alarm expressed in some quarters which would have us believe that the United States is becoming another Germany....

June 25, 1936 (Thursday)

Morris S. Lazaron, "War and Peace: A Non-Pacifist Point of View," Address at CCAR Convention in Cape May, NJ. *CCAR Yearbook* 46 (1936), pp. 222–32

(224:) Many things have entered into the situation, and *all* nations share the blame. But don't forget that Europe is in terror. With a silent (225:) grim insistence, the program laid down in *Mein Kampf* is the goal of the Nazi leaders today. One by one the items have been achieved. Like the rising waters of the recent floods before which people stood in dazed fascination.... One authoritative spokesman told me – it is an open secret in every chancellery in the world: "Nazi Germany is out for the hegemony of Europe, nothing less and perhaps a great deal more."...

(230:) The real peace-lover, then, will not strip his country bare of the power to defend itself in a world which still knows only the final resort to arms.... (231:) The real lover of peace will be on his guard lest our foreign policy as a nation be determined in the interests of selfish groups or individuals and thus throw us into war. The real lover of peace will seek to stem the rising tide of arrogant nationalism which feeds upon prejudice and hate.... The real lover of peace

---

19 Perhaps alluding, among other examples, to the significant number of publications by German Jewish authors on various aspects of Jewish culture by Schocken Verlag.

will know that in all the countries of the world there are millions who see these things as he sees them, millions of haters of war and lovers of peace, and he will join with them to remove the stumbling blocks out of the way and to prepare a way in the wilderness for the Kingdom of God.

July 18, 1936 (Saturday)

Harris Swift, "The Journeys of Israel," St. John's Wood Synagogue, London. *Because I Believe*, pp. 251–55

(254:) To-day, we stand at Rephidim [cf. Exod. 17:8]. Amalek assails our people in many countries of the world, yes, even in this citadel of freedom in which we are proud to claim ourselves as loyal subjects. At Rephidim Amalek was overcome by the uplifted hands of Moses, by the faith in God which those uplifted hands symbolized. At Rephidim to-day, our answer to Amalek must continue to be the same message that Moses taught the children of Israel, the same lessons that have been the bulwark of Israel's spiritual life throughout the ages, the same Torah, the same ideals, the same faith. Our answer to our enemies to-day must be hands uplifted and eyes upraised to the God of our fathers.

August 8, 1936 (Saturday)

Stephen S. Wise, Address at First World Jewish Congress, Geneva. *Protocole du Premier Congrès Juif Mondial, Genève, 8–15 Août 1936*, pp. 7–17; cf. AJA, Box 22: SSW Microfilms of AJHS and BUASC papers; Moshe Gottlieb, *American Anti-Nazi Resistance*, pp. 144–47

(8:) We regret today the absence of the representatives of two great Jewries, that of Germany and of the Soviet Union. To the Jews of Germany we offer our deep and brotherly sympathy understanding that they, alas! are not free to meet with fellow-Jews who speak the language of free men. Their absence is intelligible. But unforgiveable is the attempt of their now leading journal, the *Jüdische Rundschau*, to erect their involuntary absence into a Jewish philosophy. . . .[20]

20 This strong criticism was apparently based on an article published by the German

As for the Jews of the Soviet Union, we Jews of other lands refuse to believe that these are forever to be lost out of the fellowship of World Jewry. We venture to predict that by the time of the next World Jewish Congress session, representatives of the Jewish millions of the Soviet Union will have part in our assembly....

(9:) We welcome with rejoicing and with pride the participation in this Congress of a group of distinguished representatives of the Yishub, the Jewish population of Palestine. The last months have not been easy for the Yishub. It has been tried anew, indeed, as never before, and it has met the trial with unlimited courage and with noblest heroism... We know not of a more gleaming page in Jewish history than that which will tell the story of Jews who, set upon by their neighbours, lives taken, houses destroyed, children attacked, trees uprooted, harvests burned, yet in the midst of the most bestial and perhaps deliberate provocation refrained from counter-attack, and revealed a self-restraint which is the despair of our enemies....

(10:) The heartening value of meeting together with one's people I have lately come to see for myself in Poland....

August 9, 1936 (Sunday)

Ferdinand M. Isserman, "Judaism and World Events," Sermon delivered at Meeting of the National Council of Christians and Jews at Estes Park, CO. AJA MS-6, Box 14, Folio 4[21]

(1:) Judaism and world events is my theme this evening. Does it imply that I ought to discuss with you the tragic story of European Jewry, the sentence of death passed upon and slowly being executed against German Jewry, the utter hopelessness of three million Polish Jews caught between the Scylla of a hatred made in Germany and the

Zionist periodical on July 21, 1936. The following day, the JTA headline was, "Reich Zionist Organ Sees World Congress Futile"; the article began: "Strong opposition to the World Jewish Congress, scheduled to hold its first session at Geneva next month, is expressed in an editorial today in the *Juedische Rundschau*, official organ of the Zionist Federation of Germany."

21 This sermon was used again by Isserman on Rosh Hashanah morning, Sept 17, 1936, in his own congregation, Temple Israel of St. Louis, MO, with stylistic corrections, using the title "The Message of Judaism to the Modern World."

Charybdis of a nation economically bankrupt, or shall I speak of the persecution of Romania, the difficulties in Palestine, the shadow over Austrian Jewry, the Mosley attacks on the Jews of England, or the whispering campaign in our own country?

But the suffering of religionists is not a new phenomenon in history, certainly not the suffering of Jews. Greater than the danger inherent in persecution of a religious group is that its devotees concentrate their energies in dodging it rather than in making their message or mission effective. For Jews today, I fear less the havoc that anti-semitism may cause to individuals, and more that anti-semitism instead of Judaism become the urge behind Jewish conduct, that the fear of man instead of the fear of God become the basis of Jewish life. It is the message of Judaism to the modern world which is to be the basis of my discussion....

(3:) King David, too, was a despotic dictator who by force of arms extended the territories of his country, began a program of building to enhance the glory of the royal family, encouraged his son, Solomon, so that the Hebrew kingdom was split into two and the result of that Hebrew totalitarian state was chaos, confusion and suffering.[22]

September 5, 1936 (Saturday)

Jacob Bosniak, "A Month of Spiritual Preparedness," Ocean Parkway Jewish Center, Brooklyn, NY. *Interpreting Jewish Life,* pp. 63–68

(63:) In these days of grave crisis in the life of humanity, when the world is preparing for war,[23] and the human heart is gripped by fear of the impending catastrophe, when the Jewish heart is burdened by sorrow because of the wicked tyrant who has declared his avowed purpose to destroy our people, there is nothing more consoling and more encouraging than the words of the "Sweet Singer of Israel":

---

22 This is a rather striking characterization of one of the best-known and most popular Jewish leaders of the biblical period. The point is apparently to assert that Judaism is strongly opposed to totalitarianism, racism, and perverted nationalism in a manner that applies even to the political behavior of the traditional author of Psalms.

23 A striking formulation for September 1936.

"The Lord is my light and my salvation, whom shall I fear?..." (Ps. 27:1,3,9)....

(65:) We too live in a time when the Tables of the Law lie shattered before us. The moral law of religion has been challenged by the Nazis of Germany. Their leaders and followers speak openly and defiantly against the fundamental conceptions of religion:

> Thou shalt not kill.
> Thou shalt not steal.
> Thou shalt not bear false witness against thy neighbor (Exod. 20:13).
> Love thy neighbor as thyself (Lev. 19:18).

These commandments of God have been substituted by rules of conduct promulgated by Hitler and his cohorts: (66:)

> We must proceed according to the motto: And if you will not be my brother, then I will smash your skull.[24]
> I see in power strength, and in strength the eternal mother of right.[25]
> Truth is relative. Repeat a lie a thousand times and the world will believe it.
> The very enormity of a lie contributes to its success.[26]

Who can deny that these new commandments have been accepted by millions of people in every part of the world? There is now a definite tendency in old Europe to throw off "the yoke of the Kingdom of Heaven," and to revert to the pre-Christian days when the Teutons worshipped Wotan, the god of might and brutal force, when the stronger destroyed the weaker without mercy or compunction, when war and bloodshed were the most honorable activities of humanity.

Every open-minded person must admit that a vulgar cynicism and

---

24 Bosniak's note provides the German text and attributes it to Alexander Stein, *Adolf Hitler*, p. 46; it is attributed to Bernhard von Bülow in a Reichstag speech of 1903, https://de.wikiquote.org/wiki/Bernhard_von_B%C3%Bclow.

25 Bosniak's note states "*Volkische Beobachter*, March 13, 1933, from Hitler's speech," apparently reporting Hitler's speech in Munich on the previous day.

26 Bosniak's note states: "well-known quotation from Hitler's *Mein Kampf*."

a brazen indifference to truth is prevalent in our midst. Lies, falsehoods and slanders, trickery and deception, forgery and fabrication are the daily bread and meat of certain governments. They commit atrocities upon innocent human beings and then shamelessly deny them, hiding behind strict censorship. He who converted (67:) Europe into an armed camp dares to cry that his purpose is peace.

The world is full of violence. The tables of the Law lie shattered on the ground. But those who cling to their faith in God and the moral teachings of the Bible are confident that the Law will be restored to us. It therefore behooves us to utilize the present period of waiting for the Master who will restore the Tables of the Law, in prayer, in charity and in loving-kindness....

September 16, 1936 (Wednesday, Erev Rosh Hashanah)

Stephen S. Wise, "As a Watch in the Night," Free Synagogue at Carnegie Hall, New York (media excerpt). AJA, Box 22: SSW Microfilms of AJHS and BUASC papers

(1:) What a watch-night Israel has lived through in the year that now ends!

Palestine has witnessed one of the epic hours of Jewish history marked by savage slaughter on the part of Arabs, the savagery of the desert, to which Israel has replied with the perfect restraint of a self-disciplined people under a leadership which moved its followers to scorn reprisal and retaliation....

Poland, seat of one-fifth of the Jews of earth, has witnessed and made itself guilty of economic strangulation and an almost Nazist political attitude towards its three million Jews who, among a population of thirty millions and more, are singled out as "superfluous ones."

In Nazi Germany the world has beheld in these days at Nuremberg a veritable orgy of primitive and bestial hatred, the aim of which was to confound the Jews of the world with, and to make them seem responsible for, Communism. The accusers have forgotten that anything is infinitely to be preferred to the Hitler brand of Dictatorship, which will yet result in world massacre and the suicide of civilization.

If the Jew, even as the watchman of Isaiah, answers the query,

"Watchman, what of the night?" in the words, "The morning cometh" (Isa. 21:11–12), it is because of the Jew's faith that he has been watchman throughout the night, watchman of humanity not for himself alone. For he has suffered and endured for all mankind, and despite all that he has suffered and endured, he has, for the most part, kept his spirit pure, "the fortress and abode of holy things."

(2:) As a watch in the night! Never was the threat of night so engulfing, never was the danger of darkness so overwhelming, and still the unfaltering faith of the Jew remains! "The morning cometh!" The morning will come! If the Jew be equal to himself, if the world conscience awaken to the threat of the darkness which assails the highest and the holiest treasures of mankind, freedom, truth, justice!

September 17, 1936 (first day of Rosh Hashanah)

Abraham Mayer Heller, "Five Sins of Man," Flatbush Jewish Center, Brooklyn, NY. *Jewish Survival*, pp. 203–14

(209:) There was no good purpose served when some years ago the Japanese snatched Manchuria away from China for no other reason than because the land looked attractive to the eyes of the military potentates at Tokyo. All the nations of the world stood by without a sincere word of protest. And later, when without even a formal declaration of war, all of Ethiopia was annexed by the dictatorship of Rome, could anyone take seriously the pretext of bringing civilization to a backward country? What was involved was: the land looked good for food. All phases of human relations – economics, politics, international affairs – all are ruled by greed. . . .

And the sin of Cain and Abel – brother against brother – also envelops our modern world. . . . In Spain alone the civil war cost countless lives; in Portugal a revolution is brewing; in Bolivia men of the same faith and blood are slain; in Russia, wholesale executions are in vogue; in Hitlerland, quiet purges à la guillotine are daily occurrences.[27] In all instances, "The voice of the blood of brothers

27 Note that Nazi Germany is not presented here as a unique challenge to Jews and to the democratic world, but placed alongside other threats to world peace as an equivalent evil.

cries unto God from the ground" (cf. Gen. 4:11). And there is neither rhyme nor reason for all these acts of madness....

(212:) Eighteen years ago the world witnessed the infancy of modern dictatorship. To gain control of the proletariat, millions perished through violence and starvation and even bosom comrades associated in philosophy and program were purged to establish the despotic rule of one of their number.... Of equal abomination is the autocratic power of life and death in the hands of the Teutonic madman who would be God.

Louis I. Newman, "Doing Judaism a Favor," Congregation Rodeph Sholom, New York. *Sermons and Addresses*, vol. 3, pp. 94–101

(100:) Whenever a radio-priest, or a propaganda minister, or a *Reichsfuehrer*, or his insane henchmen make violent attacks upon the Jewish people, each one of you waits until your leaders come to the defense of the stricken and misrepresented people and faith that you share. I know there are some Jews who say, "We should answer nothing: we should keep quiet; perhaps they won't notice us, let us (101:) slink away from the limelight." My friends, Judaism and Jews are too significant in Western civilization to be ignored; we are the carriers and transmitters of Jewish influence, and we must take our chances and suffer the consequences, for weal or woe.... We lie helpless and exposed to the Endeks, the Nazis, the Black-Shirts, the Silver Shirts of the various nations. And those who are most responsible for our infirmity are Jews themselves. We strangle our own hard-won and painfully-born organizations; we starve them if they attain infancy; we criticize and destroy them if they reach adulthood.... My friends, this must not be!

Stephen S. Wise, "Not Without Hope," Free Synagogue at Carnegie Hall, New York (media Excerpt). AJA, Box 22: SSW Microfilms of AJHS and BUASC papers

(1:) I have seen with mine own eyes something of what a great section of Jewry is enduring in these days; Polish Jewry, three and a quarter millions, where pogroms have not only been condoned but the penalties have been visited not upon the doers of the crime but upon the victims thereof. In all my life I have shared no more mournful and yet heroic experience than meeting with a little group of Polish Jews from the town of Zitik,[28] who came to me in Warsaw not to complain, not to declare that they would surrender, not even primarily to protest against the immeasurable wrong which had been done them in that they were sentenced to prison while the culprits and the murderers and pogrom makers were set free, but merely to beseech me, as one associated with the leadership of the Zionist movement, to secure a handful of certificates...which for them meant Palestine. And these certificates...will be granted them. I have seen to that as their reward and their consolation. This they implored at a time when Palestine seemed to be the seat of bitter, cruel, and bloody warfare....

(2:) Not without hope we suffer and we mourn....

(3:) It is not an accident; it is a part of the design of destiny that in the last days Hitlerism has declared that we Jews must be uprooted, destroyed from the earth. I know why, Hitler knows why, and for once we are in complete accord. Hitlerism knows it cannot universalize the era of tyranny, of injustice, of darkness, as long as Jews survive, as long as Jews are permitted to live and labour and to sacrifice for the ideals of justice, of freedom, of democracy, and of religion. We stand in Hitler's way; we are the historic enemy of Hitlerism, and I repeat for the last time, not without hope we suffer and we mourn, for the Nazis' enmity against the Jew is a part of the Jewish destiny....

Louis Wolsey, "The Price of a Jew's Death," Congregation Rodeph Shalom, Philadelphia, PA. *A Set of Holiday Sermons* 5697/1936, pp. 13–19

(15:) A gloomy year! Who could exclaim in this fashion more justifiably than the Jew? For the Jew – conscious, unconscious, and subconscious – the period has been replete with fear and a sense of insecurity. Rumors of impending prejudices, news of planned

28 This is what appears to be written in the text, but I cannot identify it with a Jewish community in any Polish town.

attacks and reprisals, persecution within Germany and exile out of it, anti-Semitic parties and programs in Austria, Romania, Poland, Bulgaria, and France, Arab threats in Palestine, anti-Jewish outbursts in Algiers, Fascist movements in England, and proletarian shirt-and-know-nothing uprisings in America, together with rumors of plots among industrialists and financiers to scapegoat their dishonesty and the financial depression upon the long-suffering head of the Jew. There has hardly come a single calamity or misfortune to mankind but that someone believed the Jews were responsible…

Isaac Herzog, Adelaide Road Synagogue, Dublin. *Irish Press,* Friday September 18, 1936, p. 2

Think of Germany, think of Poland, and think of a country nearer home. Could it have ever entered into our minds that in free, democratic England there would arise a tide of anti-Semitism, which threatens to widen and deepen and which gives our brethren over there cause for very grave anxiety?

And what is the position in the land of Israel – in that little land of ours, thousands of miles away, for which we have been praying and hoping and shedding torrents of tears for nearly two thousand years?

The Israelite has lived by his faith for thousands of years, and he will continue to live in that faith to the end of his days.

September 18, 1936 (second day of Rosh Hashanah)

Israel H. Levinthal, "Three Words Tell the Tragedy," Brooklyn Jewish Center, Brooklyn, NY. *A New World Is Born*, pp. 60–66

(62:) Little wonder that the reactionary forces everywhere point to the Jew as the arch enemy of the world. They would prefer a concept of sin that would turn men's minds to the Other World alone. This world is to the strong, the mighty, the powerful, to those who have and those who wish for more!…

(64:) Here, again, we learn the reason for much of the hatred leveled at the Jew by the forces of darkness and cruelty. These forces love war and bloodshed, because war helps them to maintain their grip upon the *Lechem* – the sustenance that God has created for the needs of all men.[29] Until mankind learns the evil of its ways, it will oppose the spirit of Israel, which proclaims peace – but a peace that can only come through a new ideal, the result of an economic justice that shall enter the lives of all men.

...A new gospel – nay the revival of an old devilish gospel – has recently taken hold of men – the State can do no wrong; the State is infallible; the State is to rule God, not God the State.

(65:) Against this barbaric doctrine Judaism is a living protest.... Here, again, you note the conflict between the new savagery enthroned today and the spirit of Judaism. And here, again, is revealed for us the great tragedy that has come upon the world in our age....

Bruno Italiener, "On the Second Day of the New Year," (*Am zweiten Tage des Neujahrsfestes*). Hamburger Israelitische Tempel, Hamburg, Germany. Andreas Brämer, *Judentum und religiöse Reform: Der Hamburger Israelitische Temple 1817–1938*, Document 35, pp. 262–66; taken from original publication, *Einziger Gott–einziges Volk*, pp. 1–4; translator unidentified

(262:) Moses repeats the very phrase "Who is like You" towards the end of the Torah (Deut. 33:29), but this time referring not to God but to the people of Israel, whose remarkable history he now views as his death is approaching. (263:) These are the last words of the dying Moses to his people – his testament, his blessing. Then is Israel blessed, only then can we say "Fortunate are you, Israel" (Deut. 33:29), when we do not forget that we are unique in this world, just as our God is unique.

"Fortunate are you, O Israel" – *really*? There is no page in our history that does not tell of suffering, no page that is not soaked in blood and tears. "Fortunate are you, Israel, who is like you" – *today*? Not a day goes by that does not inflict a wound on us, where the tragedy of Judaism touches not only a part of the community, as was the case in earlier times, but rather where now all over the world Jews are no longer safe. Thoughtless people we would be were we not to ask such a question.

29 Earlier he has said that "the word *Milchamah* ["war"] is derived from the same root from which comes the word *Lechem* – bread."

And yet, the verse "Fortunate are you, O Israel" is apt, so much so that our Sages believe that it was not the word of humans but rather that God Himself, who proclaimed this phrase to the people as a response when, in gratitude for their being saved at the Red Sea, they sang מי כמכה, "Who is like You" (Exod. 15:11).

Yes, the phrase applies especially today, as we have become aware that Jewish history is not, as was formerly believed, something that belongs to the past. To the contrary, Jewish history is vibrant, a flowing stream, in which all of us are encompassed and from which we cannot extirpate ourselves, just because we are Jews, because we are Israel, always made vile and condemned, having been summoned and favored, like the fathers, to experience that which is contained in the words "Fortunate are you, O Israel; who is like you, a people saved by the Eternal" (Deut. 33:29)....

(265:) Our children look at us and ask: "Why all of this?" Let us respond to them, but not as before with the same hollow, insipid answer, with mere words, with mere speeches which today sound so unbearable. Let us respond to them that the only possible answer today is action, which means that in spite of everything we must live a proud upright Jewish life. A Jewish life has at all times presented its own face. Jewish life today means emerging from our superficial secular being, driven and torn apart by narrow partisanship and regarding once again the one thing that unites us, that affords us a sense of connectedness, comfort and strength, (266:) that will not forsake us in our suffering, but rather speaks to us through our suffering, and recalls the words that have resounded for millennia; "Fortunate are you, O Israel; who is like you forever saved by the Eternal."

September 25, 1936 (Friday evening, Kol Nidre)

Ferdinand M. Isserman, "Hope, Honor and Heroism," Temple Israel, St. Louis, MO. AJA, MS-6, Box 14, Folio 4

(8:) No greater compliment could have been paid to the Jews of Germany than that a party which endeavored to bring about a reversal of modern civilized values knew (9:) that between it and its Machiavellian goals there stood a stiff-necked people. Before Naziism could succeed, Judaism had to be crushed and Jews fettered. Before

Nazis could wreak their will upon Germany, they had to shackle, to paralyze, and annihilate a small handful of men and women in their midst. No more glorious epitaph will ever be written about the Jews of Germany, no nobler eulogy will ever be spoken about them than in the orations of their foes, who as the first item in their policy of restoring and resurrecting the jungle ideal in Europe, found it necessary to seek out and crush the Jew. What a tribute to half a million people that their moral qualities, their intellectual capacities stood in the way and blocked the road to another dark age in Europe.... (10:) Their martyrdom is their glory. Their persecution is their badge of honor.

September 25 and 26, 1936 (Kol Nidre and Yom Kippur)

Isaac Herzog, Sermon at Adelaide Road Synagogue, Dublin (Kol Nidre) and New Synagogue, Dolphin's Barn, Dublin (Yom Kippur morning). *Irish Press*, Sept. 28, 1936, p. 3

In Poland, the plight of three and a half millions of Jews is appalling in the extreme, from the economic standpoint, and in addition to their dire poverty, they were made to suffer from the poisonous darts of Jew-hatred and Jew-baiting.

In Germany, the Jewish position is going from bad to worse, and systematic efforts are increasingly being made to make existence impossible for the 500,000 Jews still remaining there. About 70,000 have already emigrated, and the greater part of them are in a distressful condition. Whither should they flee? Alas! the plague of Jew-hatred, the most wicked, and at the same time, the most senseless, phenomenon in this age of enlightenment, is spreading.

Thank God, this country, geographically small, but morally, culturally, and historically very great, has been proof against that wicked craze. Unfortunately, in a country so near home as England, anti-Semitism is beginning to become a source of disquietude to Anglo-Jewry.

The position in Palestine is far from satisfactory. The prophetic cradle-land of the Jewish race, for which Israel has been shedding torrents of tears during two thousand years of exile, is still in the claws of savage terror. The fate of Zion, and with that the fate of Jewish history, is hanging in the balance.

And yet, despite all that, Yom Kippur brings a message of light and hope.

September 26, 1936 (Yom Kippur)

Maurice N. Eisendrath, "The Only Gate," Holy Blossom Temple, Toronto. Unpublished, AJA, MS-167, Box 2, Folder 4

(1:) It is with a grim sense of reality that in every corner of the earth, the children of Israel will pray in words of atonement during the *Ne'ilah* service this afternoon, *P'sach lonu sha'ar, be'es ne'eelas sha'ar, ki phono yom*: "Open unto us, O God, Thy gates of mercy, before the closing of the gates, ere the night descends." *Hayom yiphneh, hashemesh yoveh veyiphneh, b'es n'eelas sha'ar*: "The day vanishes, sun is setting, at the time of the closing of the gates."

Could more appropriate words be found anywhere to describe the unspeakably tragic plight of the House of Israel the wide world over? One by one the shadows of night have descended; one by one the gates of hope have closed. Rarely before, in our long and poignant past, have we felt so helpless, so forlorn and hopeless. Through all the blood-spattered centuries, even amid Crusade and Inquisition, ghetto and pogrom, there were always some avenues of escape for our ceaselessly harassed forebears. Not yet were the frontiers of every land tightly sealed, and so, from country to country these hapless thousands were free to wander with their packs upon their shoulders, their staffs within their hands and their God within their hearts. But today, even the wandering Jew is halted with scarcely any place whereon to rest his weary head....

(2:) Lost we are, in very truth; like whimpering rats in a trap; like piteously bleating sheep led to the slaughter; like a terrorized beast in his iron-bound cage we seem knowing not whither to turn or where to seek refuge, as the face of all mankind seems turned implacably against us....[30]

30 Because the current collection focuses on sermons actually delivered to a group of

(3:) Desperate as our present plight indubitably is, if there is even a scintilla of Jewish faith within our hearts we need not despair completely, nor altogether abandon hope. Forever in the past, our fathers found at least one gate of hope open to Israel, a gate that was never shut in the face of him who earnestly sought to enter it. *P'sach lanu sha'ar*, our fathers further entreated in that selfsame *N'eilah* prayer which I have taken as this morning's theme: "Open unto us, O Lord, Thy gate of mercy," *no-voh-oh sh'orecho*: "let us enter *Thy* gates."

Shut out by the world of MAN, Israel must seek refuge once again at the Gate of God, where alone through all the torturous centuries, he has found succor and salvation. Routed from every land, barred from every frontier, hounded from pillar to post, cruelly catapulted from country to country – it is time that Israel came HOME, to that HOME which alone has been the haven of our people through all the relentless ages;...to that HOME...which is to be found not upon any soil from which brutal men may at any fitful moment rout us, but within the SOUL which God has given us to nurture, and in which our fathers found an eternal resting place and a certain promise of their ultimate redemption.... One gate is open to us still. The gate of Judaism, our historic faith, the one gate from which we have wandered so aimlessly and thoughtlessly away....

Israel Mattuck, "The Spirit of the Jews," Liberal Jewish Synagogue, London. Unpublished typescript

(1:) There is no Jew in the world among those observing the Day of Atonement who does not, in his prayers and meditations on this day, feel the presence of the sufferings of the Jews in the lands where they are oppressed. The nature of that feeling is varied. It includes sympathy for the oppressed, abhorrence for the ways of the oppressors,

---

listeners, I have omitted four powerful paragraphs on the first two pages of this long text (11½ pages single-spaced) specifying the persecution in Germany, Poland, and Palestine, as Eisendrath has crossed them out and written the word "out" in the margin, apparently recognizing that the text was too long, and not wanting to *over*-emphasize the negative theme. One of these paragraphs can be found in Menkis and Troper, *More Than Just Games*, pp. 213–14, without any indication that the passage was never heard by the congregants listening to the Yom Kippur sermon.

and a prayer for the deliverance of the oppressed from their suffering, and of the oppressors from their cruelty. There must also, however, be present the question about the meaning, and the possible value, of the suffering.

It would be contrary to all theistic belief to suppose the possibility that the suffering might be meaningless....

(4:) Those who oppress the Jews, or want to oppress them, are actuated by ideas and aims that are in irreconcilable conflict with the principles upon which our western civilization has been based, and with the higher goals which it has envisaged for humanity. Where the Jew is suffering, it is because the rules of a nation, or a powerful section of the nation which seeks to rule, deny the rights of man. That denial, however, does not mean only suffering for the Jews; it means evil for humanity....

(5:) The suffering of the Jews, when borne with dignity and courage and indomitable loyalty, as the Jews bore their sufferings in the past, shows the might and the greatness of the Jewish spirit. But also, when its meaning is realized in connection with the life of humanity, it brings enrichment to that spirit. There is a grandeur in suffering bravely borne when it reveals an evil in humanity against which humanity must contend. There is a grandeur in a resistance to oppression, though silent, which aims not only for the right of a group, but for rightness in humanity. The Jews in Germany who face Nazi oppression with (6:) a calm strength, demanding by silent opposition their human rights, are serving the righteousness of humanity. That is why they deserve our utmost support to maintain themselves, to maintain their institutions, to maintain their resistance against unrighteousness, to maintain their struggle, though in silence, for a better humanity.

(7:) The Jews stand for faith in God and the value of the human spirit, the Nazis stand for faith in might and the value of national conquests. That is why the Nazis also persecute those Christians who have remained faithful to the spiritual heritage they have received from Judaism rather than accept for their religion a crude materialism decked out in the garb of a barbaric mythology. There can be no harmony between those who worship power and those whose life and spirit are rooted in the message spoken long ago: "Not by might, nor by power, but by My spirit, saith the Lord" (Zech. 4:6)....

(9:) The Jewish Community, like many Jewish individuals, has not escaped contamination by materialistic standards. The subject is an unpleasant one, especially as it implies a criticism of some who are among the leaders of the Community, who face Jewish problems in a material way, and appreciate only physical needs. It is hard to say it, but it must be said on a day like this, that some of the leaders of the Community, and as a result [leaders of] the life of the Community in some aspects, do not show the spirit of the Jews, which is the spirit of faith, and the attitude that values above all else the things that belong to the spirit. The sufferings of the Jews in Germany have a large spiritual significance, yet they have been for the most part faced only by considerations for their material and physical aspects. The Jews live for a spiritual purpose, and only by serving it can they live.[31]

Bruno Italiener, "*Neïlah*" (Closing Service for Yom Kippur). Hamburger Israelitische Tempel, Hamburg, Germany. *Einziger Gott–einziges Volk* (One God – One People) , pp. 9–13; translator unidentified

(11:) To be responsible one for the other: how the meaning of that word has changed in the course of our lives! When we were children, what did responsibility mean? Not much more than money – material helpfulness, like the annual contribution we would make to this or that organization, often without receiving any thanks. And what has "responsibility for each other" become today? The meaning has changed completely. It has become sinister, fateful, inescapable, something that has befallen us beyond our control, that has seized us, and, no matter how much we might struggle, we are unable to extract ourselves. Let us look at life. Somewhere in the world an injustice occurs and one hears at once the word "Jew," sent out by telegraph, telephone, radio, screaming from one country to the other; the whole world listens while Jewish hearts beat in great fear, beating more and more quickly, because of the consequences which

31 This apparently alludes to an internal Jewish polemic, with Mattuck criticizing leaders of the Jewish community for what he considered to be their over-emphasis on the material needs of German Jews.

the alleged deed of one individual can bring to the community.[32] My friends: Responsibility, that is the ערבות as our fathers called it, of which we did not want to know, that is now seizing us and that has invaded our consciousness in all its gravity.

Fortunately this is only one side of the question. It would be unfortunate, no, intolerable, if we Jews would traverse this world joined by only external circumstances, by a fate that has invaded us, linked together by fear of this fate alone. No, we are Jews.

October 8, 1936 (Shemini Atzeret)

Israel H. Levinthal. "Economic and Political Freedom," Brooklyn Jewish Center, Brooklyn, NY. *A New World Is Born*, pp. 72–78

(74:) [T]he Jew realized that political freedom, unless (75:) bound by law, can become not a blessing but a curse to man... Freedom without Law is as useless and dangerous as Law without Freedom. This, in reality, touches one of the sore spots in the political struggle of our age. What is Fascism and what is Communism, in their political aspects? Simply this: Law without Freedom. Laws not only to define freedom but to abolish all freedom of political life and expression....

(76:) [E]conomic freedom must likewise have this restrictive force of law.... And here again we are face-to-face with one of the plagues that afflict the world in our economic life: the failure to recognize the truth that freedom without law is as dangerous in the realm of economics as is law with freedom. What is the economic gospel of Communism and of Fascism? Law without Freedom! Both have proclaimed laws which restrict the individual in his economic life to such an extent that he is deprived of all individual freedom...[33]

November 28, 1936 (Saturday)

Harris Swift, "Jewish Defence," St. Johns Wood Synagogue, London. *Because I Believe*, pp. 145–52

---

32 This sentence apparently alludes to the assassination of Wilhelm Gustloff (see Stephen S. Wise, above, February 16, 1936).

33 In this and in several other passages of Levinthal's sermons (until 1939), Nazi Germany is not presented as a unique challenge to Jews and to the democratic world, but placed alongside Stalinist Communism in the USSR as an equivalent evil.

(150:) And as we see the forces that are at work in the world to-day, forces that seek to crush everything that is noble and fine; forces that have ranged themselves against every accepted principle of tolerance, of truth, of justice – of faith; forces that seek to wipe out our people, as never before in their chequered history have they been threatened; we must realize that it is because the spiritual in the world is being ousted, and the material reigns in men's hearts. It is because all those lofty thoughts that are inseparable from faith in God do not animate men as they should, but that in their place, callousness, and cruelty, and greed have crept in to threaten mankind with such a convulsion as moves us to shudders of horror as we envisage it; so that racial hatred and discrimination have become doctrines that, alas, find a willing ear in too many places, so that our people to-day are encircled by antagonism in too many of the countries of their sojourn, so that even (151:) here, in fair England, there are those who strive by falsehood and calumny to stir up hatred against us.

December 6, 1936 (Sunday)

Louis Wolsey, "Progressive Religion," Sermon delivered at Chapel of University of Chicago, IL. *Sermons and Addresses*, pp. 41–47

(45:) Our utter incapacity to realize the truth of both science and religion that there is no pure race, and that all human beings are human and that the individual has indefeasible rights, is responsible for those curious group loyalties that have been the madness and the tragedy of our modern civilization.

Dr. Goebbels has said, "Beyond the State, nothing,"[34] when he should have said that beyond the State, nothing but human beings – sensitive, passionate, earnest, ambitious, sentient, loving, striving human beings – and that they may be ignored or oppressed, neglected or enslaved only at the cost of civilization's equilibrium. The arraying of nation against nation, class against class, group against group, can but have one end.

---

34 The statement is ordinarily associated with the Italian Fascist philosopher Giovanni Gentile, who wrote "Nothing beyond the state; nothing against the state; nothing outside the state."

(46:) A civilization marked by tyranny and despotism, by the revival of the sword as the savior of the State,... by conquest as a holy purpose, by the shaming of liberty, by the fomenting of national hatreds, by the disintegration of moral standards, by the repudiation of solemn treaties, by the multiplication of armament, by the ravishing of other people's territories – is a civilization that can be saved only by a religious revival, and a religious readjustment....

December 11, 1936 (Friday during Hanukkah)

Ferdinand M. Isserman, "Jews Have the Jitters: A Chanukah Sermon," Temple Israel, St. Louis, MO. AJA MS-6, Box 14, Folder 5

(3:) Jews all over the world have the jitters. They tremble. They are afraid. They huddle together in their tents. Fear fills their souls and terror seizes their spirits. Nor is this to be wondered at. The antisemitic policies of the Nazis in Germany have been a rude shock and a blow to Jewry everywhere....

December 13, 1936 (Sunday during Hanukkah)

Solomon B. Freehof, "When Religion Goes to War: A Call to Jews and Christians," Rodef Shalom Temple, Pittsburgh, PA. *Rodef Shalom Pulpit*, New Series, vol. 2, no. 2

(8:) There is a mood in the modern soul which disturbs the peace of religion and will drive it sooner or later to open resistance. It is not the mood of despair so prevalent today, although religion deplores the hopelessness of modern man.... Nor is it the mood of doubt which religion finds intolerable.... Nor is it the mood of rebellion which should awaken the indignation of synagogue and church.... It is the mean sneer, the cynical snarl which desecrates the sanctities of life.... We are living in the most cynical, irreverent age in the recorded history of man....

(12:) No self-respecting religion will long permit itself to be dominated by the state or any other power....

(13:) Thus grows clear the most heroic episode in modern history. In the German state, where scientific leaders have shamefully allowed themselves to twist the truths of science at the behest of tyrannical government, where a free press has permitted itself to be the docile voice of a dictator, where literature has permitted itself to become the sycophant of tyranny, only the church found the courage to resist. In spite of storm troops and concentration camps, in spite of repression and violence, the church in Germany has built a spiritual edifice of heroism which mankind will for centuries respect and revere.

As in ancient Judaea against Antiochus, as in Germany against the Nazi state, so it will be everywhere against all forces which seek to dominate the prophetic function of mankind's sanctuaries. Religion may be at times ignored, it may be often attacked, but it will never permanently be controlled.

(14:) A war against evil, by the instruments of peace; a war against darkness, by the eternal light; that is the common mission, the eternal task for Christian and Jew.

1937

January 1, 1937 (Friday evening)

Ferdinand M. Isserman, "The Christmas Message of the Pope," Temple Israel, St. Louis, MO. AJA MS-6, Box 14, Folder 6

(6:) I cannot fully agree with the *Christian Century* in its assertion that the Vatican is allied with fascism.... The Pope, in his Christmas message, not only attacks Adolf Hitler and Nazis, but says that although Hitler claims to be opposing communism, nevertheless, he actually is promoting it.[1]

(9:) [In a recent National Preaching Mission held in St. Louis,] these great Protestant-Christian leaders championed the cause of peace, voiced their opposition against fascism and against communism alike, and stated that the alternative to humanity is not to choose between communism and (10:) fascism, but to choose the pathway of religion and to walk the kingdom of God. Thus we see the ideal of Catholicism as voiced by a great Roman Catholic Pope, the ideals of Protestantism as phrased by its able and most eloquent spokesmen, harmonize with the ideals of the synagogue as articulated by its rabbis....

January 3, 1937 (Sunday)

Abraham Cohen, "Reflections on the Present Situation of Jewry," Literary and Arts Society, Communal Hall, Birmingham, England. *JC*, January 8, 1937, p. 34

[*JC* summary:] Cohen, in the course of his address, said that there was a time when the English Jew looked upon the oppression of his

1 This is followed by a long quotation from the Pope's Christmas message, followed by a discussion of what was happening in Spain, especially in Madrid.

brothers abroad in a spirit of self-complacency. But now the problem impinged on him personally. The spectre of anti-Jewish animus had come to England, the final home of freedom for the Jews. There was now an anti-Semitic Party in England, striving for power, employing Continental methods of Jew-baiting as a pathway to power. Anti-Semitism was no new phenomenon in Jewish history, but to-day the situation was different. They were being attacked on all fronts. No Community was immune. The lecturer asked whether modern anti-Semitism was a spontaneous growth or whether it was artificially aroused and cultivated. In the anti-Semitism of all countries there was a striking similarity of technique, accusations, even of verbal form. The speeches of Sir Oswald Mosley resembled the effusions of Dr. Goebbels' lie-factory in Berlin.[2] Germany was spending huge sums of money on propaganda to create anti-Jewish feeling in all parts of the world. History showed that when people were happy and contented they paid no attention to anti-Jewish calumnies, but when people were discontented, hungry, and lacked employment, the dormant anti-Semitism became active. The world had rarely been so disturbed as it was at the present time.

After exposing Hitler's lie that Bolshevism was 90 per cent Jewish, and referring to the anti-Semitic tendencies of the British administration in Palestine, Dr. Cohen said: [direct quotation] "Every Jew to-day must live under a sense of tremendous responsibility. Every Jew is sitting on a gunpowder barrel asking for trouble if he throws lighted matches about. We are living to-day under a microscope. Every act of ours is carefully scrutinized. Our conduct must be irreproachable." Dr. Cohen added that Anglo-Jewry was not doing enough in self-defence. The problem was not being tackled with sufficient energy by their leaders. There should be a widespread dissemination of well-written brochures giving the lie to the charges made against them, not by argument, but by irrefutable facts. The

2 Sir Oswald Mosley, founder of the British Union of Fascists in 1932. He had the reputation of being one of the best orators in England. The notorious "Battle of Cable Street," in which anti-Fascist groups (including many Jews) blocked a march by the BUF led by Mosley in the East End of London, was just three months earlier than this address.

men with expert knowledge to fight the campaign of calumny were there, but their services were not being utilized.

January 17, 1937 (Sunday)

Israel H. Levinthal, "The Jew Looks at Tomorrow," Address at Special Conference, 50th Anniversary of the Jewish Theological Seminary of America. *A New World Is Born*, pp. 111–21

(114:) Look at Russia, that then [fifty years ago] was the reservoir of Jewish life and strength, and view the religious life of the three million Jews who are there today. Look at Germany, where fifty years ago the belief was cherished that with Jewish assimilation would come joy and blessedness for our people, and behold her Jews today, forced to wear a new yellow badge of shame.[3] On the other hand, look at Palestine fifty years ago, when the idea and ideal of Jewish rebirth in the land was but a dream – alas, an empty, a vain dream to many Jews – and behold Palestine today, when the dream has suddenly and miraculously turned into a reality....

February 7, 1937 (Sunday)

Samuel H. Goldenson, "When Propaganda is Substituted for Education," Temple Emanu-El, New York. AJA, MS-81, Box 2, Folder 4

(4:) In Germany they have developed propaganda to the nth degree. They have instituted a new office in their government, the Ministry of Propaganda, as part of the business of government – the Ministry of Propaganda, whose purpose it is to use every instrumentality of publicity. There the daily publications, the weekly publications, the magazines, the books, the history written today, and even the Scriptures of the German people, are being used for the dissemination of ideas, ideals, and purposes in order to bring about the acceptance of the ideology underlying the new state: the doctrine of racial superiority.... And because of their racial superiority, there is found in their way of thinking the idea that their people must have

3 This was a metaphorical statement; see above, June 24, 1936, with the accompanying note. German Jews were not compelled to wear a yellow badge until September 1941.

supremacy.... (5:) And because of these doctrines – the doctrines of superiority and supremacy, the whole community, the whole nation must exhibit superiority too.... And every child in Germany...is taught to accept unquestionably this terrible doctrine of racialism of the new Nazi regime.

February 14, 1937 (Sunday)

Maurice N Eisendrath, "Should Canada Remain British?," Holy Blossom Temple, Toronto. *Holy Blossom Pulpit*, VII, 8[4]

(2:) [Quotes Haman's speech (Esth. 3:8–9), then continues:] So spoke Haman thousands of years ago. And so – it is platitudinous and commonplace to add – speak his lineal descendants in Nazi Germany today. But it is not commonplace or platitudinous to assert that similar sentiments are voiced not merely in Hitler's barbaric Reich, nor in medieval Poland or darkest Romania, but that this hate-filled plaint is heard well-nigh in every corner of our so-called modern world. As a matter of fact, on many a doorstep right here in our own city of Toronto, one can find this edifying pamphlet entitled "The Canadian Nationalist," which in the precise spirit as well as even in the virtual language of Haman of old, proclaims...[referring to the "Protocols of the Elders of Zion"].[5]

(3:) Neither Haman of old nor Hitler of today could improve upon the language or the sentiment of this canard which week after week is finding its way into thousands and perhaps hundreds of thousands of Canadian homes, to turn the wrath of the population against a particular people, and to root them out as ruthlessly as Haman sought to do in Persia so many thousands of years ago.

February 28, 1937 (Sunday)

Israel Mattuck, "The Church Conflict in Germany: Its Significance for

---

4 No date is given for the sermon, but the preacher refers to Purim coming "on Wednesday next," which suggests that the sermon was delivered on the Sunday ten days earlier.

5 *The Canadian Nationalist* was the monthly paper of the Canadian Nationalist Party, established in September, 1933. A portion of the paper's material came from the German news agency "World Service" (*Welt-Dienst*).

the Jews," Liberal Jewish Synagogue, London. Unpublished; see Complete Sermons

March, 1937 (exact date unspecified)

Woolf Hirsch, "An Appeal to the Dutch Reformed Church," Meeting of Dutch Reformed Church Ministers, Pretoria, South Africa. *Selected Sermons and Addresses*, pp. 92–106

(93:) I think we have a right as men, as Jews, and as citizens of South Africa, to ask the Church, which stands for truth, for right and moral rectitude, to exert a restraining influence on the vile passions that are being stirred up now in the country, and which, if persisted in, must have disastrous consequences, disastrous for the Jews and disastrous for the country as a whole....

(94:) In Germany the Nazis made their way to power by offering their followers the loot of the Jews. This method is now being tried also here. [Notes Dr. D.F. Malan as example]...But what was done in Germany will not be so easy in South Africa. Here the non-Jewish population is not sixty-five million but hardly two million, deeply divided, surrounded by a sea of natives, and threatened by potential enemies against whom the Government is trying hard to organize a defensive force....

(95:) If anything will save religion in Germany, it will be the inspired voice of Christian priests who in the face of danger and persecution now and then cry out against injustice, whether the victims are Jews or Gentiles. In the present time of anxiety and uncertainty I appeal to the Christian Church to range itself resolutely on the side of right and truth.

March 7, 1937 (Sunday evening)

Abba Hillel Silver, Address at Mass Rally, Temple Emanu-El B'ne Jeshurun, Milwaukee, WI. *Wisconsin Jewish Chronicle*, March 12, 1937, p. 1

The ancient Jewish principle that all Jews are responsible for their brethren is more applicable today than at any other time....

A movement has set in against the rights of man, against the forces of democracy, against all those forces which have contributed toward the advancement of mankind during the past 150 years. In its place has come a progressive disenfranchisement of not only Jews but all those opposed to the totalitarian state.

Since Jews are everywhere a ready scapegoat, it is easy to saddle upon them all the ills of mankind, and in a world caught between the opposing forces of Fascism and Communism, the Jews are trapped in the no-man's land in between....

The result of these factors is that the Jew is being pushed back into the position he occupied during the Middle Ages, and the favorite pastime of that period – expulsion – is being invoked against him. By a series of edicts, the German government has driven out 100,000 Jews, and the new Polish government, taking cue, has avowed that it favors a mass exodus of its 3,000,000 Jews....

We insist that the Jews who have lived in their countries for as long as a thousand years have every right to remain where they were born, and we in America will mobilize to assist our brothers abroad in fighting for that right....

Hitler has not written the last chapter. Let us keep our historical perspective and remember that Hitler is only 4 years old, while the history of the Jewish people can be traced back 4,000 years.

March 13, 1937 (Saturday evening)

Barnett Brickner, "Which Way for the Jew?," Radio Address on NBC, "Message of Israel." Printed text in AJA, MS-98, Box 1, Folder 11

(1b:) Mankind has a bad habit, especially in times of crisis, to revert to chromosome- hunting. Witness the tragic lot of a million and a quarter Germans, who are being denied the right to call themselves either Christians or Aryan because, forsooth, they were so careless as to choose a great-grandparent who was Jewish. Now, that surviving speck is casting its shadow on their lives and has made them Pariahs, outcasts....

(2a:) In the face of what is happening to our people in Germany, Poland, and Romania, the Jews of America must charge themselves with relieving the distress of their brethren in these lands of persecution. I saw it with my own eyes last summer. Its horror is indescribable. Intimately linked up with this cause is the task of building Palestine as the Jewish homeland. It is typical of Jewish history that when darkness covers one part of our world, the light of hope dawns in another....

(2b:) The present moment is dark, but not hopeless. Our history has brought us many trials, but it has also taught us to be patient, to judge our present tragic situation not in the light of the moment but in the light of historical experiences.... We have seen regimes more brutal than National Socialism rise and fall, and we have lived through them. We have seen more formidable dictatorships than the present ones take birth and disintegrate. We have seen worse fanaticism than those which demoralize the world today break up. And the balance sheet of our tragic past proves to us that we and not they have survived.... Malevolent forces are never more brutal than in periods which immediately precede their collapse....

Today we are witnessing the insane exaggeration of nationalism with its false racialism, militarism, paganism, and intolerance. It is the last gasp before the end.[6] In such a world in which the majority is deranged by passion and prejudice, our only salvation as a minority is adherence to the Jewish way of life.... Only as we fortify our spirit will we be able to endure the treacheries of the age, without breaking under its burdens. And if we are internally healthy, we can wait patiently for the day to dawn when truth, justice, and peace will again fill the hearts of all men.

March 14, 1937 (Sunday)

Abraham J. Feldman, "Judaism in a Changing World: A Lenten Sermon," preached by invitation at First Church of Christ (Congregational), Hartford, CT. Printed pamphlet

(2:) I find it difficult to speak of the Jews because my heart is heavy, and because fears concerning the immediate future are tugging at the heart strings. You see, we are not merely Jews in America, or Jews in Poland, or Jews in Romania, Austria, Germany, Palestine. We are

6 A rather painfully ironic expression of optimism.

an organic body, and the pain and suffering of one part reaches every other part.... I say to you with complete and precise accuracy, that the blow aimed at, and the suffering caused even to the least of my brethren is a blow aimed at every one of us everywhere, and woe betide the Jews who fail to realize this historic truth! The Jewish situation in the world today is difficult beyond words. We are a people entrapped and surrounded. The siege is laid against us and is continually intensified....

April 2, 1937 (seventh day of Pesach)

Jacob Kaplan, "Zionism" (*Le sionisme*), Synagogue de la rue de la Victoire, Paris. *Les Temps d'épreuve*, pp. 53–63, translated by MS

(55:) In many countries, millions of people continue to suffer because they are Jews and they continue to see in the ancestral homeland the harbor of safety, today as in the past, and perhaps more than in the past, because in the interim the dream of almost two thousand years has become a reality.[7]

April 2, 1937 (Friday evening, beginning of the eighth day of Pesach)[8]

Ferdinand M. Isserman, "The Ten Plagues of Ancient Egypt and of Modern Germany," Temple Israel, St. Louis, MO. AJA, MS-6, Box 14, Folder 6

(1:) When it became evident to the world that Germany was going the way of Egypt, that Hitler was walking in the footsteps of the Pharaohs, Jews everywhere asked, "Where is the god of Israel? Where is the god of justice? Where is his power? Where his love for his fellowman? [*sic*] Why does he stand idly by and permit this tragedy of

---

7 According to Kaplan's biographer, David Shapira, this was "one of his most celebrated sermons" (*Jacob Kaplan, 1895–1994*, p. 100), but this is the only sentence that is even indirectly relevant to the subject of this book. He goes on to argue that Zionism is not incompatible with loyalty to France.

8 An ordinary Sabbath service, as the eighth day is not observed as a holiday in Reform Judaism. Isserman had also delivered a sermon that morning at the service for the seventh day of Pesach, entitled, "Let Freedom Ring."

tragedies? Why does he not punish the tyrant and rescue his victims? Why does he not hurl his (2:) thunderbolts?" Again, it is possible that we modern Jews, like the Jews of Egypt, concentrated our energies on our own suffering, and failed to observe the inner decay of the German nation, and the plagues with which the god of history has already afflicted them. In reading the biblical account of Israel's emancipation from bondage, I could not help but be struck by the remarkable parallelism of the ten plagues which afflicted ancient Egypt with those which already afflict modern Germany....[9]

(8:) The last plague in Egypt was the death of the first-born in every household. That plague has not yet come upon Germany, but it will come when the fruit of Nazi policies is realized, when the next European war breaks forth. Even as in the previous European war, Germany will not be victorious. Her militarism will again be crushed. Her armies will again be defeated. Already, France is armed to the teeth and her defenses seem well-nigh impregnable. England is rearming and becoming bolder. Czecho-Slovakia, Poland, Russia are feverishly drilling and preparing their armies. When the war comes, a plague graver than the destruction of the first-born will envelop the Third Reich and will end in devastating catastrophe for the present regime. Even as Egyptian civilization was destroyed, who knows whether after that final day of reckoning European civilization will not be destroyed as well?

April 3, 1937 (Saturday)

Samuel H. Goldenson, "The Enemies Within," Temple Emanu-El, New York. *World Problems and Personal Religion*, pp. 256–64

(258:) That we Jews are living in difficult times, I believe is known even to the youngest child among us. That we are beset by enemies in almost every land is a fact that is filling the consciousness of every

9 What follows is something of a homiletical tour-de-force, applying each of the plagues in turn to aspects of modern Nazi Germany. The emphasis is on continuities with the biblical past, together with prognostications of the future that are sometimes spot-on, and sometimes wildly overly optimistic, especially pertaining to the escape from bondage of the Israelites without harm.

Jew of our day. "Verily, these enemies compass us about; yea, they compass us about" (cf. Ps. 118:11) with ever greater hostility. And yet I believe that it is time for us to turn our attention away from them and study instead our internal conditions. There is a greater menace that can develop for a people than the antagonism of men on the outside, and that is the paranoiac conviction that outsiders alone are responsible for all our difficulties, failures, trials, and troubles....

April 4, 1937 (Sunday, immediately after the end of Pesach)

Solomon B. Freehof, "What Chances Have I? – The Complaint of Youth," Rodef Shalom Temple, Pittsburgh, PA. "Getting Old or Growing Up: A Series of Three Addresses." *Rodef Shalom Pulpit*, New Series, vol. 2.

(3:) When the German Republic still stood, Hitler, the Nazi, came to the youth of Germany. He called and they assembled. He spoke and they listened. He found a message that went directly to their hearts. He described to them their beloved country. He spoke of its tragic defeat in the World War, of how it lost campaign after campaign not because of its own weakness but because of "trickery"; how since the War was lost new enemies surround it and grind it down: how poverty is increasing. Then he turned to the young people and he said, "You are going to (4:) school. You are being educated; you are being prepared for a profession. What opportunity will you have to earn a living in the tragic Germany of today? Young people of Germany, what chance have you?" And they nodded and said, "He is right. He understands us. What chance have we in the modern world?" In this way the demagogue capitalized their despair and he pointed out a road for them and they marched. Thus on the bowed back of despondent youth Hitler rode to power.

What happened in Germany has happened in other lands. In many countries in the post-war, demagogues took advantage of the broken heart of youth. In many lands youth in despair was an explosive force threatening the foundation of society. It is therefore not a theoretical question when we ask, "What is the mood of the youth of America?"...

(12:) It is not only a question of prejudice which has increased so tragically in the modern world. We are faced with a brutal militaristic belligerence which has been on the verge of plunging the world into widespread war almost every day for the last two years. Whose war will it be? We are a little too old for the battlefield. The trenches, the welter of blood are the inheritance of youth.

I am convinced that those forces in our world which have intensified prejudice and which increased the militaristic spirit are doomed to fail, perhaps even sooner than we know, because although dictatorships look powerful they are puffed up by prestige.... (13:) The dictatorial countries only seem strong. Sudden and calamitous may be their collapse. I am convinced that we will see the end of those powers which embittered the human relationship of the world. But the generation after us will discover that the prejudice and the bitterness thus engendered will still linger on like a poisonous cloud.

Our job is to outlive, to outlast, the Fascism of the modern world. Our successor's job will be to clean up the debris of prejudice and hatred which remains....

It is true that Hitler exerted his greatest influence with the youth of Germany. It is true therefore that despairing youth is a dangerous and an explosive force in every civilization. But the obverse of the medal is at least equally clear: If youth in despair is generous to the stability (14:) of the world, youth courageous and youth hopeful is the world's only salvation....

MAURICE N. EISENDRATH, "Communism: Its Challenge to Religion," Holy Blossom Temple, Toronto. *Holy Blossom Pulpit*, VII, 9[10]

(5:)[We note with satisfaction] the clarion call which the Pope at Rome has recently sounded for all Christendom to gird its loins and to set out upon a holy war against Communism in its every form and manifestation.[11] ...So successful has Herr Hitler, and innumerable

10 No date is given for the service but the reference to the "recently" issued papal encyclical (following note), and the intervening holiday of Pesach (March 26–April 3), suggests the date of April 4 or April 11.

11 This was undoubtedly a reference to the Encyclical *Divini redemptoris*, issued by Pope Pius XI on March 19, 1937. Unlike his better-known critique of Nazism, *Mit brennenden Sorge*, issued five days earlier, this was a condemnation of Communism.

others of his ilk, been in spreading through the world this myth to the effect that Judaism and Communism are identical that vast numbers of men everywhere share in this gross delusion....

(10:) But the recent history of events in Germany demonstrates beyond peradventure of a doubt the fulfilment of that prophecy which I made several years ago, to the effect that Hitler would not persecute the Church and thus make martyrs out of whose blood the seeds of faith would spring, but that he would profane and pervert it instead. And so precisely has he done, seeking to bore from within and to exploit the Church for his own malign purposes. Both Fascism and Communism, therefore, are anti-religious and anti-God, for both preach a totalitarianism of their own – the brown shirts a totalitarianism of the State, and the red shirts a totalitarianism of the Class....

May 8, 1937 (Saturday)

Harris Swift, "King George vi: Coronation Sermon," St. John's Wood Synagogue, London. *Because I Believe*, pp. 223–29[12]

(224:) Let your minds roam for a brief space over the countries of the world – see how the rule of force governs in one country, and the rule of hate in another; see how in one land, men are mercilessly slaying their countrymen in a meaningless and barbaric war, and in another the dread disease of discrimination and bigotry is spreading. See how Europe is an armed camp, with nations distrustful of each other, with the ideals of (225:) brotherhood relegated, if retained at all, to a place of no importance in men's minds; see how men are propelled by an orgy of greed and barbarism, and exult in the technique of murder; see the injustice that rules in some countries; see the perversion of truth; see the degradation to which loyal sections of the public are subjected; see how on all sides hymns of vengeance and hate and ruin take the place of the gentle songs of human sympathy; and see England's calm dignity in the face of these influences.[13]

---

12 The Coronation ceremony was to take place "next week" (p. 225).

13 In this formulation, at least, the preacher seems not to recognize any distinctive problem in Germany.

Here in England there is no injustice and no falsehood; there is no tyranny in the rulership of this country; there is no bigotry in the administration of her affairs.... (228:) Here, the country's statesmen do not point to us as our brethren are singled out elsewhere for unwarrantable discrimination....

May 25, 1937 (Tuesday)

Felix A. Levy, Presidential Message to CCAR Convention, Columbus, OH. *His Own Torah*, pp. 132–45;[14] *CCAR Yearbook* 48 (1937), pp. 177–93

(132:) The present situation of the Jew in the world is no exception to the general thesis that Israel's history is the chronicle of the passion of a people, for today's scene repeats the main features of the old drama of suffering and misfortune with occasional interludes of tranquility temporal and local. I do not wish to open old sores, perhaps it would be better said, to pour salt on fresh wounds, by a detailed reminder of our people's plight. Yet I must make mention of the rising tide of resentment against us, traces of which are discoverable even in the free western democracies. If Palestine, Poland, and Germany be the three focal points of Jewish danger, it does not mean that there is no peril elsewhere, but only that it is less, or not quite so obvious. The picture of world Jewry in May 1937 is no brighter than it was a year ago; the outlook, though not without its gleams of hope, just as dark.

May 29, 1937 (Saturday)

Maurice N. Eisendrath, "Retreat or Advance?," Sermon delivered at CCAR Convention, Columbus, OH. *CCAR Yearbook* 47 (1937), pp. 202–24

(207:) Far more tragic, it sometimes seems than the macerated bodies and the physical affliction of our brother Jews – horrifying as that is – is the distorted thinking which would predicate our entire Jewish *Weltanschauung* on the particular political and economic, social and religious reaction which admittedly darkens our day. If the fathers of Reform Judaism were egregiously mistaken in

14 Reproduced by arrangement with Jonathan David Publishers, Inc.

their nineteenth-century optimism, then surely those black-robed pessimists of today are equally in error in believing that the sun of freedom and emancipation and brotherhood will never again break through the low-hanging clouds of the present, and in positing their (208:) whole philosophy of Judaism upon the eternal persistence of Hitlerism as though we had not seen more formidable dictatorships and totalitarianisms come to birth and disintegrate, rise and fall; as though the profounder of political analysts were not convinced that this terrifying contemporary reaction were but the final death-throes of an outmoded, corrupt, and thoroughly leprous society, presaging, they hope, a new and better day.

How disturbing then is this mood of utter defeatism that is creeping so insidiously over the entire Household of Israel today. . . .

July 3, 1937 (Saturday)

Israel Abrahams, Farewell Sermon at Great Synagogue, Manchester, England.[15] *JC*, July 9, 1937, p. 35

[*JC* summary:] In the course of his remarks, he said that only a flaming religious revival, preaching God and righteousness, would restore to the world justice and peace, brotherhood and happiness. Loyalty to his ancestral faith had never made a Jew a worse citizen. On the contrary, the better the Jew, the better the man. "We must give our children Jewish knowledge and a Jewish heart; we must give them Jewish education, a Jewish environment, home, and upbringing. Girls must take their place side by side with boys in our education system. Jewish fathers and heathen [*sic*!] mothers you cannot have, you dare not have."

September 5, 1937 (Sunday, Erev Rosh Hashanah)

Ferdinand M. Isserman, "The Day Cometh," Temple Israel, St. Louis, MO. AJA MS-6, Box 14, Folder 7

(1:) In our own day, we have witnessed unexpected cruel tragedy mar

---

15 After four years of service in Manchester, Abrahams was preparing to move to Cape Town, South Africa.

the destiny of individuals because they were linked with the Jewish people. Men who were successful as physicians and as scientists, as administrators and as lawyers, as business men and as workers, as musicians and as artists, men who had achieved in their domestic lives bliss and happiness, suddenly found their success dissipated, their joys embittered, their security blasted by the inescapable web in which Jewry was enmeshed. Such was the lot of the Jews of Germany.... They are in the process of liquidation. Their youth are migrating to the far corners of the earth, wherever hospitable shores can be found, wherever doors are thrown open to receive them.... German Jewish communities are rapidly becoming like homes for the aged, whose members resignedly wait for death.

The plague has spread. Polish Jewry stands paralyzed, baffled (2:) and well-nigh helpless before the fury blessed by a bestial government, and executed by human dregs, which has been released against them.[16] In Romania, too, the pall of gloom envelopes the tents of Israel, as a government drunk with mad nationalism, uncertain of its power over its new subjects, influenced by German propaganda, proceeds to tighten the shackles that strangle the efforts of its Jews to earn the pittance of a livelihood. Hungarian Jewry stands with its back against the wall. Heroically, gloriously it struggles to maintain the Jewish name, and to serve as a dyke to stem the barbarian tide in Germany. Austrian Jewry, helpless and timorous, wonders when the verdict of death will be pronounced upon it.

Even here in this country, we have heard false prophets of doom and of fear feeding the flames of our insecurity, proclaiming the spread of the anti-semitic virus, paralyzing Jewish life, freezing its normal laudable activities, filling it with a fear psychosis. "Watchman, what of the night?" (Isa. 21:11). Watchman, what of Israel?...The prophetic voice answered, "The morning cometh." This, too, is my answer to you, who are troubled by the night. "The dawn cometh" (Isa. 21:12). A new day is being heralded, a better day for Israel and for humanity.

I bring to you this answer, not in a desire merely to buoy your

---

16 The lead headline in the JTA of September 3, 1937 reads, "Jews Desperate as Riot Wave Sweeps Poland: Many Flee Villages."

spirits, to lift from your brows the clouds of gloom, to ease your minds, to soothe your hearts. I bring you this answer, the fruit of study and observation, of readings and reflection, of weary travel and conversations with men of many nations in positions to understand the currents of the modern world and to evaluate them. I therefore bring you a message of hope and of cheer, and bid you enter the New Year with confidence and with courage that a new sun is rising.

(3:) In the past year, decisive have been the victories along the democratic front in Europe.... (4:) The German dictatorship is four years old. The longer it survives the more does it fortify the positions of democracy in western European countries.... Today democracy is solidly entrenched in France. That Leon Blum, a Jew, presided for a period over the French government, a Jew whose ancestors had been emancipated by the French Revolution, was concrete evidence of the cementing of the mortar of democracy in the French Republic. Discredited and ridiculed is the fascist party in England.... But a few days ago, from Poland, being put through the paces by a malevolent dictatorship, came reports of revolt among the peasants who demanded more freedom and more liberty and more democracy. In Spain, democracy has not been discredited....

(4:) Not only can we rejoice in this evidence of democracy entrenched, but the practice of anti-semitism by a strange paradox has brought its blessing to world Jewry, so that in a way those who cursed us have blessed us. You will wonder what blessing there may be in the desolation of German Jewry, in the suffering of Polish and Romanian Jews, in the worry and concern of American Jews. But something amazing is happening. Anti-semitism is being discredited in the eyes of the masses of the world.... (6:) What is even more important to us is the fact that the oppressed people of Germany are beginning to realize that anti-semitism was a bait which enticed them to the Nazi party, that they were deceived by it, that it was the medium whereby they lost their liberties. The God of history is punishing the German people for having succumbed to the wiles of the anti-Semite.... God's ways are mysterious. He has performed this modern miracle. The institution of anti-semitism in Germany has awakened the masses of the world to the menace to them of hatred and (7:) persecution of Jews, and has revealed to Christian teachers, peasants, workers, democrats, intellectuals, that anti-semitism is a ruse and not a solution.

(11:) Therefore, I say to you, my people, face the future not with fear but with faith, not with cowardice but with courage, not with cringing but with confidence.... A new sun is arising. It is the sun of human re-emancipation. It is the sun of human liberty. It is the sun created by the God of the universe. It is the sun in the beneficence of whose rays the children of men will find peace, and the children of Israel among them.

September 6, 1937 (first day of Rosh Hashanah)

Stephen S. Wise, "Our Friends, Our Foes, Ourselves," Free Synagogue at Carnegie Hall, New York. AJA, Box 22: SSW Microfilms of AJHS and BUASC papers

(1:) My dear people, my text of this morning was written under circumstances which if they were clearly understood and known, would bring tears from stone. The central organization of German Jewry, now alas for the fifth time, beginning at the High Holy Day season of 1933, addresses an appeal to the Jews of Germany, stricken, shattered, and crushed after four and a half years of pitiless persecution and never-ending hurt and oppression. We live in times of rush and change... "Wait, I say, on the Lord" (Ps. 27:14).[17]

(4:) And yet with all that, I make the startling statement today that even though our eyes are constantly fixed upon the Hitlers and Becks and Cuzas and Francos, still the real enemies, the endangering foes of the Jewish people, dwell within and not outside of our camp.

---

17 This is a direct quotation from the translation of the message published by the JTA on September 3. The complete text, which was undoubtedly read by Wise, is: "We live in times of rush and change. Every year appears to us to be a separate chapter in our history. What will befall us is in the hands of the Almighty, but our behavior, whatever is in store for us, depends upon ourselves. Man must show his worth in his every trial and must strive to make God's will a reality. Our wish to all and sundry is summed up in the verse of the psalm with which the Jews usher in their New Year: 'Wait on the Lord and be of good courage and He shall strengthen thine heart. Wait, I say, on the Lord.'"

We shall survive the Hitlers, we always have survived the Hitlers and the Hamans, etc. But can we survive, shall we survive, I ask the question *ought* we to survive them who poison the wells of Jewish life from within?...

September 7, 1937 (second day of Rosh Hashanah)

Hermann Neumark (later Yehoshua Amir), "Väter und Söhne" ("Fathers and Sons"), Elberfeld Synagogue, Wuppertal, Germany. *Deraschot: Jüdische Predigten*, pp. 30–34, translated by MS[18]

(31:) Father and son walk together? (cf. Gen. 22:6, 8). Today, it is different among us. The father is here, the son is in a foreign country. Parents take their children overseas; one son lives in Palestine. The father must give in to his son – that applies even today. And the son goes. But the father? Greetings, letters, pictures – can there be any complete replacement for the everyday life, for the genuine walking togetherness of question and answer, the silence of mutual understanding, in which the older shares something from his maturity and the youth from their ambitions. It has become one of the tragic questions of our everyday life: parents and children want to "walk together," yet they cannot.

But in the background there remains a source of distress that is not so visible from the outside, but is no less profound: parents and children simply do not understand each other. Even where they are still living together, they go their separate ways....

September 15, 1937 (Wednesday, Yom Kippur)

Israel H. Levinthal, "The Foundations of an Enduring World," Brooklyn Jewish Center, Brooklyn, NY. *A New World Is Born*, pp. 54–59

(56:) Learning is a beautiful thing, a most essential accomplishment for the benefit of man and the world. But learning can be a curse as well as a blessing. The world today has learning, more than it ever

---

18 The preacher's son, Dr. Yehoyada Amir, has informed me that his father was on this date a rabbinical student at the *Hochschule für die Wissenschaft des Judentums*; his ordination would be in 1939. As often occurs today, rabbinical students were sent to serve part-time in small congregations that could not afford a full-time rabbi.

had in days gone by. Look at Germany with its ancient seats of learning – Heidelberg, that now celebrates its five-hundredth anniversary, Göttingen, founded two hundred and fifty years ago. We have learning in abundance, but it is not the learning that brings blessedness to man. It is a learning that is divorced from all moral values, so that while the mind is trained to conquer the physical forces, the heart is not taught to master its own nature. And so you have the strange phenomenon of learned men whose hearts are filled with hate, with cruelty, with sadism....

September 20, 1937 (Monday, first day of Sukkot)

Israel H. Levinthal, "The Role of the Messiah." Brooklyn Jewish Center, Brooklyn, NY. *A New World Is Born*, pp. 67–71

(71:) The Jew believes in nationalism, but not in chauvinism. Every people is entitled to its own national life, its own home. Every people has a right to develop its own life, to strengthen its national foundations. But every people must, at the same time, have this broader vision: it must be able to see the universe beyond its own borders and to develop an interest for the welfare of the peoples in that universe as well as for itself.

Alas, this is the great sin for which the world seeks atonement today: "his shall be the punishment of Egypt, and the punishment of all the nations, *asher lo ya'alu*, because they do not go up" – or, as I would translate these words: "because they have not risen to that conception of life – *lachog et chag haSukkot*, to keep the Feast of Tabernacles" (Zech. 14:19).

When the nations of the earth will rise to the heights of this interpretation of national life, when all the peoples will accept this truth proclaimed by the Festival of Tabernacles, then, indeed, shall we behold the dawn of the Messianic era, when peace and justice and happiness will mark the lives of all men and all nations!

October 9, 1937 (Saturday, *Noaḥ*)

Israel H. Levinthal, "One Language and One Speech," Brooklyn Jewish Center, Brooklyn, NY. *A New World Is Born*, pp. 79–81

(81:) There we have the true purpose of these builders [of the Tower of Babel]. *Na'aseh Imo Milchamah*, "We shall make war with God."[19] It was to dethrone God and all the ideals of peace and justice for which He stands, and to enthrone, in His stead, the new god with a sword in his hand – a threat against every advance of real civilization.

No wonder the Jewish genius pictures God in anger at this danger to all humanity. It is the spirit of Democracy protesting, through the Jewish soul, against any attempt to bind the conscience of man, to force him to have the thoughts and to speak the words prepared and ordered by others who are in control of his destiny. And that protest is needed today even more than it was in ancient times. The inherent evil of Fascism is not what it does to the bodies of its victims, but what it does to their spirit, to the essence of their manhood. When peoples are forced to speak only *devarim achudim* ["chosen words"],[20] to surrender their own minds, their own personalities, then you have the breakdown of all true culture, of all civilization.

October 29, 1937 (Friday evening)

Ferdinand M. Isserman, "I Visit the Jews of Germany, Romania and Poland," Temple Israel, St. Louis, MO. AJA, MS-6, Box 14, Folder 7[21]

(3:) Four years ago, the rabbis of Germany measured up to the occasion and stood by their posts like captains, remaining on the bridges of sinking ships. Today, the rabbis know that the German Jews are lost. There is little left but to recite the Kaddish for them. More than a score of them would leave for other countries if they could minister elsewhere. Some of them are planting the germs of the Reform movement in lands to which they have migrated.... The Jews of Germany veritably are sentenced to death, and any individual or family taken out are like human beings saved from destruction.

19 Levinthal note: Genesis Rabbah 38,6.

20 The modification of the biblical phrase is based, as Levinthal shows in a footnote, on Genesis Rabbah 38,6.

21 This was Isserman's third summer visit to Nazi Germany (previously in 1933 and 1935), after each of which he reported in autumn sermons.

1938

January 22, 1938 (Saturday)

Jacob Kaplan, "Polish and Romanian Antisemitism" (*L'antisémitisme Polonais et Roumain*), Address at a meeting organized by *Comité français de rassemblement mondial contre le racism et l'antisémitisme*, Gymnase Japy (Sports Center), Paris. *Les Temps d'épreuve*, pp. 65–68, translated by MS

Once again the gangrene of Hitlerist antisemitism spreads its havoc. Yesterday, Poland, with its separate banks for Jewish students in the universities; today, Romania, with the exclusion of Jews from its national life.[1] That Germany, which – during the war – symbolized force and not right, violates the rights of its Jewish citizens, that is unfortunate, indeed, that is certainly criminal, but in this way Germany is only cynically revealing its own character. But as for Poland, which had lost everything, which had been dismembered, wiped off the map of Europe when force was triumphant, and which owed its national resurrection entirely to the victory of the Allies – how could it not see that in trampling justice underfoot, it is betraying its own interests....

The same is true for Romania, the territorial expansion of which was the work of the Allies. When it annexed Bessarabia, Bucovina, and Transylvania,[2] with their populations of Jews who for the most part enjoyed the rights of citizens in their respective countries, (67:) it pledged to consider "how as Romanian citizens, with full rights

---

1 This was the notorious "Revision of Citizenship" decree, passed on January 21, 1938, which removed all citizenship rights granted to Jews who entered Romania (e.g., from Galicia and Russia) after the Great War, thereby affecting about one-third of the Romanian Jewish population. See Ezra Mendelsohn, *The Jews of East Central Europe Between the Two Wars*, pp. 206–7.

2 The annexation was of the result of Treaties agreed at the conclusion of the First World War.

and without any formalities, the Jews may inhabit all the Romanian lands and need not avail themselves of any other nationality"; it promised, further, that "all Romanian citizens will be equal before the law and will enjoy the same civil and political rights regardless of race, mother-tongue, or religion." How then can it not see that by breaking its word, it too is betraying its own interests?...

The anti-Semites always misconstrue the higher interests of their country....

January 23, 1938 (Sunday)

Samuel H. Goldenson, "Shall We Pursue 'Racial Interest' or 'Democratic Ideals and Policies'?," Temple Emanu-El, New York. AJA, MS-81, Box 2, Folder 4

(2:) Just two days ago a reporter, reporting in *The New York Times*, was given a special interview by some leaders of the Romanian government, at present in the hands of racialists and anti-Semites. In the course of the interview, one of them very clearly, with brutal clarity, told the reporter, and asked him to report to the American newspaper, just what they meant by their racial policy. The writer interviewed the leader of the greater anti-Semitic movement.... Corneliu Zelei Codreanu, the chief of the Iron Guard, said this:

> Our program? Its essence is the greatest imaginable ideal: the creation of a new race of Romanians, a new type of human, a man of high ideals, fundamentally moral and entirely uncorrupt, patriotic and self-sacrificing.
>
> We have studied the Jewish problem scientifically. Essentially it is an abnormal situation that the Jews should live among other races, whereby they violate the great natural law that every race shall live in its own country.... We must all find for the Jews territory where they can live and thus return to obedience to nature's law.[3]

3 *NYT*, January 22, 1938, p. 2, columns 2–3. The headline of the article reads: [Professor Alexander] "Cuza Insists Jews Must Quit Romania." Cuza – joint leader, with the Romanian Premier, of the National Christian Party – was known as a vicious antisemite.

Now that is racial policy....

Solomon Fisch, "Jewish Internationalism: Sermon Delivered on Hospital Sunday," Central Synagogue, Sheffield, England. Published as a Pamphlet by Norton Printers, Liverpool, 1938

(5:) The Anti-Semites of late who have invented the fictitious theory of blood and race accuse us of being international in character. Yes! We are international; we gladly admit the charge. But not only is there no inconsistency between the internationalism and the nationalism of the Jew, but it is because of his international idealism that the Jew has been able to contribute so large a share toward the cultural advancement of the land of his birth or adoption.

February 4, 1938 (Friday evening)

Ferdinand M. Isserman, "As I Saw Romania and Her Jews," Temple Israel, St. Louis, MO. AJA MS-6, Box 15, Folder 1

(7:) The Jews of Romania largely engaged in commerce. The economic status of the masses of Jews is pitifully low.... In the slum areas of Kishinev, Jews live in hovels that are worse than dog kennels, hovels without windows, without floors, where five and six live in one room, where the atmosphere is foul and disease reigns. In these sections, I saw the most grotesque human beings I have ever seen, hunch-backs, distorted bodies, plagued by famine, by poverty, by hopelessness. In large cities, I found tuberculosis spreading amongst Jews, tubercular sanitariums which had no funds for x-ray machinery or for surgical (8:) treatment. I saw the leaders of the community living pitifully, men and women of forty, looking older than men of eighty in the United States.... They have no place to which to migrate. They must insist on their rights to live in Romania....

(9:) Why is there this terrific anti-semitic wave in Romania if the level of living of the Jew is so low and the difficulties of the Jewish community, under normal conditions, are so staggering? It is merely artificial and not popular. It is made by the government and does not exist among the masses....

America likewise should voice its protest through diplomatic channels.

February 17, 1938 (Thursday, Service Commemorating Jewish soldiers who had died in the Great War)

Werner van der Zyl, Neue Synagoge, Oranienburger Strasse, Berlin. In Anneliese van der Zyl, *Werner van der Zyl: Master Builder*, pp. 23–24[4]

At that time we were celebrated for our heroism in the service of this country. Now we are criminals.

February 25, 1938 (Friday evening)

Ferdinand M. Isserman, "Hitler's Reichstag Address and Eden's Resignation," Temple Israel, St. Louis, MO. AJA MS-6, Box 15, Folder 1[5]

(6:) As usual, he [Hitler] becomes venomous when he speaks of bolshevism, and to him bolshevism and Judaism are synonymous.[6] It is Jewish bolshevism which afflicts Russia. It is a curse brought by a handful of intellectual Jews upon the masses of the Russian people. Hitler is endeavoring again to give the Jew the historical role of being the villain in civilization. In medieval Germany, when the cholera broke out, which decimated its population, the Jews were blamed for the cholera. They were said to have poisoned the wells of Germany.... Communism has become the cholera of our age, and Hitler seeks to identify his pet hate with the (7:) pet aversion of the modern man. Bolshevism and Judaism to him are synonymous....

(8:) But perhaps Hitler is shrewder than is apparent. He is very

4 The statement from this sermon is based not on a surviving written text but on the memory of this dramatic moment by the preacher's wife, Anneliese. She went on to write, "I stood trembling in the gallery. He could at any moment have been arrested" [by the member of the Gestapo who was stationed in the synagogue to ensure that there would be no criticism of the Nazi regime]. This was van der Zyl's last sermon delivered in Germany, attended by Jewish veterans, many of whom had been awarded the Iron Cross.

5 The Reichstag address was delivered on February 20, 1938. For the text in translation see Domarus, *Hitler: Speeches and Addresses*, vol. 2, pp. 1019–1034.

6 This follows a rather complete review and critique of the substance of Hitler's speech.

cleverly using the communist bogey as a mask for his Machiavellian desire and as a smokescreen behind which he hopes to conceal from the simple masses of the world his own plans for empire....

(11:) In the closing paragraph of his address, Mr. Hitler appeals to god, the god of the German race.[7]... Hitler's god is not concerned with Jews, Hitler's god is not concerned with democrats, Hitler's god is not concerned with liberals. Hitler's god is only concerned with German national socialists. Thus do we see in the hands of this political upstart the crucifixion of the Hebrew-Christian god being re-enacted....

(12:) We must form a united religious front in order that Judaism and Christianity together may challenge with all their powers this new paganism, that in the future the Edens will triumph over the Hitlers, and that the greatest spiritual legacy of humanity will not perish from the earth.

February 27, 1938

Abraham Joshua Heschel, "Search for a Meaning" (*Versuch einer Deutung*), Speech to Quaker Leaders, Frankfurt-am-Main, Germany. In Edward Kaplan and Samuel Dresner, *Abraham Joshua Heschel: Prophetic Witness*, pp. 260–61, translated by Kaplan and Dresner[8]

(260:) Carved over the gates of the world in which we live is the escutcheon of the demons. It happens in our times that the peoples are forging their sickles into swords, and their scythes into spears. And by completely inverting the prophetic words, the peoples turn away from the words that come from Zion. Our lot is that we must face that world. We know that the prophets' vision is fulfilled by our distorting the two characteristics of the human face: the likeness to

7 Cf. Domarus, p. 1034, where Hitler asks "the Lord God, to bestow his blessing upon our work and our actions, our insight and our resolve."

8 Copyright Rabbi Abraham Joshua Heschel, reprinted with permission of Prof. Susannah Heschel. The original German text of this address is in the Rare Book and Manuscript Library at Duke University, Box 271, Folder 5, and in *Begegnung mit dem Judentum: Ein Gedenkbuch*, ed. Margarithe Lachmund and Albert Steen, pp. 11–13. I am grateful to Michael Marmur and Brooke Guthrie for providing the precise date of this address.

the Creator and the mark of Cain, of which the latter shows more and more clearly and threatens to wipe out the former more and more thoroughly....

(261:) Through the millennia, His voice has wandered throughout the world. How it was trapped and imprisoned in the temples! How it was misunderstood and distorted, cheated and disfigured! And now we behold how this voice gradually withdraws, grows faint and is muted.

If a person sees something evil, he should know that it is shown to him so that he may realize his own guilt – repent for what he has seen....

Perhaps we are all (262:) now going into exile. It is our fate to live in exile, but HE has said to those who suffer, "I am with them in their oppression." The Jewish teachers tell us: "Wherever Israel had to go into exile, the Eternal went with them."[9] The divine consequence of human fate is for us a warning and a hope.

March 10, 1938 (Thursday)

Woolf Hirsch, "An Appeal to the Christian Conscience," "Spoken at a meeting of the Ministers Fraternal of Pretoria [South Africa], and published by the Johannesburg Society of Jews and Christians." *Selected Sermons and Addresses*, pp. 107–19.

(108:) Evil passions once aroused overflow their original channel. The hatred of the Nazis that was at first directed against the Jews is now assailing Christianity itself. So the evil passions that are now roused against the Jews in South Africa will later vent themselves on others....[10]

(115:) The Nazis persecute also the Catholics and Protestants, if they dare to live up to their convictions. How many liberal-minded Christians are languishing in the concentration camps of Germany, and how many Christians will suffer now in Austria, if they have the courage to live by their faith?

---

9 See y. Ta'anit 1,1, 11:5, where the statement is attributed to Yohanan ben Zakkai.
10 This is followed by a lengthy discussion of South African antisemitism.

(118:) Hitler set out to destroy the half-million Jews of Germany. But before he could accomplish his purpose, there arose in Palestine a Jewish community of about the same size, overflowing with energy, busily engaged in rebuilding the broken fabric of their national life and creating values that astonish the world. This continual process of renewal which can be traced in Jewish (119:) history for three thousand years is quite unparalleled in the life of other peoples....

March 11, 1938 (Friday evening)

Ferdinand M. Isserman, "The Crime and Creed of Martin Niemoeller, Christian Martyr," Temple Israel, St. Louis, MO. AJA MS-6, Box 15, Folder 1[11]

(2:) It is said that Martin Niemoeller refused to pledge to cease his attacks upon the Nazi leaders, and, therefore, for religious reasons, sits in a felon's cell, a Christian martyr of the twentieth century, a religious martyr.

Martin Niemoeller is not concerned with politics.... (3:) Nor was Martin Niemoeller unduly alarmed over Jewish persecutions. He expects Jews to suffer. That is part of the Christian worldview. The Jews must suffer because they rejected Jesus. "I cannot help saying quite harshly and bluntly that the Jewish people came to grief and disgrace because of its Positive Christianity! It bears a curse throughout the history of the world...."[12]

(4:) It has long been known that the Nazi philosophy, seeking to build the state on a racial basis with its special emphasis upon Jews, must of necessity become anti-Christian.... The whole thesis of racial Naziism collapses on the Jewish origin of Christianity....

(6:) An immediate cause of conflict between the religion of Niemoeller and the philosophy of Naziism centers about converted

11 Isserman informs his listeners that Niemoeller had been arrested on July 1, 1937 after speaking to a group of Americans; he had recently been tried, fined, released, and was now placed in "protective custody."

12 "Positive Christianity" was actually a movement within Nazi Germany that was initially favored by Hitler; here it is used by Niemoeller both to repudiate the Nazi movement and and to repudiate an aspect of Judaism. This is followed by a long quotation from Niemoeller's *Here Stand I!*; there is no condemnation or critique by Isserman of this traditional Christian anti-Jewish teaching.

Jews and the conversion of Jews. Thus does anti-Semitism crop up again. And thus does the racialism of Naziism prove to be a wedge between it and Christianity.... (7:) Niemoeller has faced and recognized this conflict between Christianity and Naziism. He has chosen Christianity. He has preached it vigorously from his pulpit.... (8:)... There is a greatness of soul in Niemoeller that Jews who know the history of their martyred past can appreciate. (9:) Niemoeller too has lightened the Jewish burden.... Jews all over the world today know when they hear of Christian martyrs that in Naziism there is an attack upon the Christian values of civilization, and in their suffering Jews have good company.

(10:) The martyrdom of Martin Niemoeller is a symbol of the spiritual power within Judaism and within Christianity. He is a symbol of the moral courage religion engenders. He is a reminder that men who fear God fear no mortal power....

Max Nussbaum, "Schopenhauer and Us," Lützowstrasse Synagogue, Berlin. AJA, MS-705, Box 3, Folder 4; translator unidentified, possibly the preacher

(4:) Schopenhauer once said, "The Jews are a people whose homeland [*Heimat*] is always the other Jews."

How the world has changed in the last century. Jewry at that time was so well settled that reading these words it felt disgraced because it saw in them the unjustified reproach that the borders of its homeland were not identical with those of the country where it lived, and as part of which it considered itself to be. Through what tragedy these words have come true today. And into what a blessing their alleged "offense " has turned! How could we live if other Jews in the world were not our homeland? How could we send our children out into the world if we did not know that there is someone to smooth their paths in the beginning? How could we effect an emigration on this large scale if it were not for the great Jewish organizations, encompassing the globe and making it homeland for us?....

Jews indeed are living through the fact that other parts of our people have understood the challenge of Jewish life, that they are building a homeland, that they *are* indeed a homeland. Each Jew who emigrates today is a homeland for the one who will go tomorrow. Therefore we have the strength – in spite of all the sorrow the world has brought over us, in spite of all the sacrifices that are being asked from us today and tomorrow, in spite of the disappointments and the misery of our situation – to stand upright and to believe in life. We, a small and beaten people, are standing on guard for Jewish life, and from the silence of the night our song goes out to all those who can hear it: "*Ve'af al pi ken, ge'ulah,*" and despite it all: redemption!

March 17, 1938 (Thursday, Purim)

Abraham Mayer Heller, "A People's Voice is Silenced," Flatbush Jewish Center, Brooklyn. See Complete Sermons

March 18 (Friday evening, Shushan Purim)

Samuel Daiches, "The Book of Esther: The Rule of Moral Law," Great Synagogue, London. Daiches: *Essays and Addresses*, pp. 127–32

(129:) "And the king and Haman sat down to drink, and the city of Shushan was perplexed" (Esth. 3:15). Haman was celebrating the coming destruction. And the city of Shushan was in consternation. Not only the Jews, but all decent citizens were troubled. When the wicked men prevail and brute force reigns, not only the Jews, but all enlightened and liberty-loving people suffer untold misery. Life, freedom, fortune, everything that civilized men and women hold dear, loses its value. Banditry and brigandage make the land desolate. (130:) When the Jew suffers, civilized humanity suffers. When the Jew suffers, moral law is crushed....

Haman...gathered his friends round him and he made a speech (cf. Esth. 5:11–13). Haman was always making speeches; to the king, to his household, to his followers. He boasted of his successes and of his greatness, of his exalted position. He was the first man in the land. But his venomous nature would not let him rest....[13]

(131:) "The Jews had light and gladness, and joy and honour" (Esth.

13 In this passage, the implied resonance with Hitler (though not explicit) seems clear; it is the kind of discourse that German rabbis could use on Purim without fear of trouble from the Gestapo figure sitting in on every worship service.

8:16). When the Jews cry out against persecution, against barbarity, they do it not only for their own sake. They do it for the sake of humanity, for the sake of civilized human life, for the sake of the rule of moral law. When the Jew suffers, freedom is crushed and men become slaves. It happened, or nearly happened in the days of Haman. And the same is happening in our own days....

We should remember this. However strong wicked (132:) people may seem to be, and however much they may seem to prevail, relief and deliverance will come (cf. Esth. 4:14)....

Israel H. Levinthal, "The Story of Purim: A Challenge to the Hamans of All Ages," Brooklyn Jewish Center, Brooklyn, NY. *A New World Is Born*, pp. 135–40

(135:) We should make more of this festival, because it is a challenge to all the Hamans – past, present, and those to come!

(137:) But though the world was crushed beneath his [Haman's] heel, he met his end, nevertheless. He was eventually destroyed by the very force that he tried to annihilate: the spirit of (138:) the Jew! *Vayehi* and *Vehayah*, it happened in the past, and it shall happen again in our days. The race is not to the swift, nor the battle to the strong (Eccl. 9:11). One nation after another may be conquered and crushed, one hundred and twenty-seven peoples may be forced into bondage for the modern *Herrenvolk*, but *bigness* alone will not avail the tyrant. The end is already foretold. What happened to the Haman of Persia will happen to the Haman *hamolekh*, who [currently] holds sway....

(139:) In this eve of darkness that is setting upon the world, the Jew must strive to be the light to illumine the (140:) path that all peoples must tread. There dare be no surrender! Nazism may spread to one hundred and twenty-seven lands [cf. Esth. 1:1] – but we know that that is not the end of the tale. What happened to Haman of old will – nay, must – happen to every Haman today. With that faith firmly imbedded in our hearts, we shall proclaim not only that "to the Jews there was light and gladness, and joy and honor" (Esth. 8:16), but also *Ken tihyeh lanu*, "So shall it be with us of today."

Ferdinand M. Isserman, "The Nazi Invasion of Austria," Temple Israel, St. Louis, MO. AJA, MS-6, Box 15, Folder 1

(9:) I cannot help tonight but think of the effect of the Nazi invasion of Austria upon the Jews. Austria had 250,000 Jews, 220,000 of them lived in Vienna. I visited with them three times in the past five years. Each time I found them more hopeless.... Their fate is too horrible to contemplate. The cities of refuge to which some German Jews fled are closed.... Is the civilized world going to say nothing about them? Are they not human beings? (10:)... A great president of our country, Theodore Roosevelt, spoke out against the government of Russia for its atrocities against Jews. Is it too much to ask that [Franklin D.] Roosevelt follow in the footsteps of his predecessor, and speak a direct word on behalf of the Jews of Austria?... Must the democratic nations of the world hold their peace in the face of such a sacrifice?

The Nazi invasion of Austria proclaims again to the world the imperative need of an international society... through which the conscience of mankind can find expression in laws of justice and morality.... Today it is Austria. Tomorrow it will be Lithuania. The next day, Spain. The following day it will be Belgium and Holland. What is going to happen to civilization?

(11:) As in the world war the Jews were found in no man's land, and were the first to fall beneath the rush of armies, so today we find the Jew to be the first to bear the brunt of the attack.... (12:) A generation ago, we may have questioned the value of our mission. Today, it is clear. Everywhere we must become the voices for the message of the one God and the one humanity.... My fellow Jews, I appeal to you in this crisis to herald forth to (13:) humanity the platform on which our fathers have stood, to proclaim afresh the principles for which they lived and died. We shall not be the ones to blow the trumpet of doom, but instead we shall send forth the flares of hope....

March 22, 1938 (Tuesday)

Stephen S. Wise, Excerpts of Radio Address Delivered on Station WABC, 10:45 P.M. AJA, Box 22: SSW Microfilms of AJHS and BUASC papers

(1:) The Jewish world had naturally imagined that January, 1938, would long be memorable not only because of the suddenness with which Romania went Fascist but [...][14] throughout some lamentable weeks under the domination of that ignoble pair of brothers, Goga-Cuza.[15] But that month has yielded in mournful interest to a week in March which, culminating on the blackest of Fridays, March 11th, witnessed a *coup d'état* unprecedented in the annals of history.

While the Nazi Ambassador and his lady were taking their leave of England at Buckingham as the guests of England's King and Queen and after the most shameful blackmailing threats at Berchtesgaden to Chancellor Schuschnigg, Hitler issued a series of ultimata to the proud old Austrian Reich, which for a time in any event has ceased to be....

The moment the Nazis fell upon Vienna they set the seal upon Austrian Nazification by issuing special Aryan decrees against Austrian Jews and, it is reported, performing typical Nazi acts against Jewish notables of Vienna. Within the last week 60 eminent Austrian Jews have committed suicide.[16] The President and Secretary of the Jewish Community, the President and Secretary of the Zionist Organization, Professor Frankfurter: all have been imprisoned.[17] The institutions of the Jewish community, including the Zionist office, have been closed; all Jewish newspapers prohibited; Zionist funds confiscated; prominent and venerable Jews have been forced to clean the streets. Jews are being dealt with in Vienna more brutally than in the worst days of Nazi Germany.

(2:) France and England protested against a deed such as has not hitherto been known, and Ribbentrop's predecessor, von Neurath, replied scornfully, as did Hitler. Thus has a deed been consummated which would stagger people in a world that had not grown accustomed to Hitler ferocities and Nazi brutalities....

(3:) And yet it is for Jews to bethink themselves touching problems

---

14 Several words are illegible in the typescript.

15 See above, Goldenson, January 23, 1938, with reference to the *NYT* article of January 22.

16 Suicides by Austrian Jews were noted in the JTA of March 17, 18, 20, and 21.

17 The arrest of leading Austrian Jewish figures was reported by the JTA, March 20.

that cannot remain unanswered. The manner of Austria's rape and the accompanying method of Jewish destruction in Austria should prove anew that Fascism in its assault upon democracy is bound early or late to make use of anti-Semitism as one of its most beguiling and for its supporters rewarding instruments.... Insofar as democracy and its program are threatened by the forces that would destroy us we may take heart. For human freedom and the love of human justice will not perish in battle with enemies whose only right is might.

March 25, 1938 (Friday evening)

Ferdinand M. Isserman, "Why Does a Just God Permit a Cruel Hitler to Triumph?," Temple Israel, St. Louis, MO. AJA MS-6, Box, Box 15, Folder 1

(1:) For a large part of the western world, Hitler has become a symbol of evil.... Why does a just God permit this satanic individual to go from strength to strength? Why does a just God seemingly remain indifferent to the hundreds of thousands or millions of human beings who are crushed by his tyrannies and who are frightened by the fears for the future that he has aroused?

(2:) First, it must be observed that the triumph of Hitler is not an act of God. A cyclone, a volcano, a shipwreck, an earthquake, we designate rightly as acts of God in the sense that they are beyond human control. But the disease of Hitlerism is man-made....

(4:) Should God have prevented man from permitting this evil to flourish? All great religions would answer this in the negative. Man is a free agent....

(5:) Nor is it good religion to discard one's faith in the face of adverse circumstances. It is during adverse circumstances that religion can fulfill its greatest function in maintaining morale and jest [*sic*] for living, in maintaining courage and confidence and hope....

March 27, 1938 (Sunday)

Stephen S. Wise, Sunday Address (no title), Free Synagogue at Carnegie Hall, New York. AJA, Box 22: SSW Microfilms of AJHS and BUASC papers

(4:) You ask me whether I advocate at this time warring upon Hitler.[18] No. No. No. But I ask you a question: is it fair to let Hitler and Hitlerism go on as if all were well,... as if we were not wounded in our very souls, as if we were not shocked by the most brutalizing act of centuries, which Napoleon never matched and Attila never surpassed?

Why should Hitler be led to imagine that he can go on when one decisive word by England which has not yet been spoken, one strong word by the mightiest of the military and naval powers of earth, might send that degenerate maniac reeling to his lair in cowardice and shame?... (5:) Does England believe that it can satisfy Germany by passing over in virtual silence whatever Hitler does? And so Nazism has been encouraged for five years.

(6:) I haven't said anything about the Jewish problem in Vienna – this is not a Jewish question. I repeat once more what I have been saying for the last five years: Jews are in the front line trenches because Hitler has dragged them there, that he might despoil and evict them.

(8:) Will civilization, will democratic powers forever permit one madman to create hundreds of thousands of refugees year after year at our expense as a burden upon us? The place of those refugees is in their own lands. If they choose to remain in Germany, they must remain. You could have wept, as I did, if you had seen these German refugees as I saw them in the third or steerage class of the *Queen Mary*: broken, crushed creatures, who yesterday walked with pride and self-respect. How long, how long, O Lord? Until civilization bethink itself, until democracies together say, "Thus far shalt thou go, and no further" (Job 38:11).

April 9, 1938 (Saturday)

Shlomo Zalman Ehrenreich, "What I Preached on *Shabbat haGadol*, 5698," Simleul-Silvaniei, Transylvania. *Derashot Leḥem Shelomoh*, pp. 202–7, translated by MS

(204b:) This is what I wanted to explain in this sermon: to show how wrong are those who currently are accusing us in every land of being

18 I.e., war as a response to the *Anschluss*, the invasion and annexation of Austria two weeks earlier. Wise was still maintaining his commitment to pacifism at this point.

rebels and Communists. Look and you will see that we have never been rebels. We are pledged to pray [each Sabbath and holiday] for the well-being of the kingdom [in which we live]. It is impressed in our blood from antiquity that we are not to rebel against the state or its ministers where we are living. I have explained that this was the case in Egypt, even though the Egyptians persecuted us and caused us great sorrow, both physical and spiritual.

Now I have no doubt that the Jews who have indeed rebelled against the state are not true Jews from the seed of Israel; they are of illegitimate lineage. And even if, G-d forbid, they are not illegitimate, then they are total heretics and unbelievers who have abandoned the faith of Israel. Concerning such people and the like, I claim no responsibility. But whoever has a heart that beats on behalf of G-d and His Torah will never rebel against the king and the state.

If this is true, then why has G-d acted in this manner, causing people to rise up against us, harming and scorning us, when we are consistently as well-behaved as our opponents are? It is our sins against G-d that have caused this. And just as in Egypt, the Israelites were compelled to remain for 400 or 430 years, when initially it was to be 210 years, for the suffering to be completed, so now we are suffering various kinds of afflictions until the completion of the time that is known to the Creator.

April 16, 1938 (first day of Pesach)

Abraham Mayer Heller, "*Pe-Rakh* and *Perikho:* False Approaches to Jewish Freedom,"[19] Flatbush Jewish Center, Brooklyn, NY. *Jewish Survival*, pp. 49–61

(60:) "In every generation each individual is obligated to regard himself as if he had personally gone forth from Egypt."[20] Continually we must strive to regain the blessing of freedom for ourselves

---

19 Near the beginning of the sermon, the preacher explains that these two Hebrew words are rabbinic interpretations of the word *beforekh*, the last Hebrew word in Exod. 1:13: "One sage interprets the word *perekh* to mean *perikho* – "hard labor"; another derives its meaning from *peh-rakh* – "persuasion."

20 From the Passover Haggadah.

and posterity, God will it, that we in our day may face our problem Moses-like, with courage and wisdom. The pains of our people, by reason of their taskmasters, make them cry out in anguish. We must help lighten their burdens. We must gather funds for relief, carry on diplomatic negotiations and make alliances with all liberal elements to help rid the world of the plague of darkness. All these and more we must do for the amelioration of the lot of our people in present-day Egyptian countries of affliction. (61:) But of equal concern should be the saving of the Jewish spirit – the Exodus leading to our ancestral land where the Jewish soul reborn will re-create a normal national life....

April 24, 1938 (Sunday)

Solomon Goldman, "Galut," Address delivered at United Palestine Appeal Conference, Chicago, IL. AJA MS-203, Box 22, Folder 11

(1:) Mr. Lipsky is appalled and terrified by the seriousness of the European situation.[21] It is a dark and dismal picture that the fair mistress Europe presents. The suppression of free speech and religious liberty are accepted without protest. Espionage, tyranny, terror, death, suicide, stalk unhampered and unrestrained the capitals of Europe....

(2:) Mr. Lipsky measured European civilization and found it wanting.[22] But he found something even more tragic: the measuring rod of the ages preserved through all of these centuries has contracted.... The Jewish people is morally wanting. It is not conscious in the present moment of its prophetic heritage, it is not consumed with indignation and wrath, it is not seized with anguish over its own hurt. Whenever it can retire to a nook or crevice it is content to

---

21 Louis Lipsky of New York was one of the leaders of American Zionism in the 1920s and 1930s. At this time Chairman of the Administrative Committee of the United Palestine Appeal, he also spoke on April 24 at its Chicago Conference, apparently before Goldman delivered his address; see the following note.

22 A quotation from Lipsky's address was carried by the Associated Press and published in newspapers on April 25: "The Jews relied upon the liberal forces of the world, but they are too preoccupied with preparing their own defense to come to the aid of the Jewish people" (*St. Louis Post-Dispatch*, April 25, 1938, p. 8C).

suck the bone it finds.... Whence comes this cowardice and apathy? What is it that impedes the Jewish will and tightens the Jewish purse strings? Why do we give meager alms where we should bring abundant offerings? Why do we stint where we should sacrifice? Why are we philanthropists when we should be statesmen?

May 1, 1938 (Sunday)

Stephen S. Wise, "Suffering," Free Synagogue at Carnegie Hall, New York. AJA, Box 22: SSW Microfilms of AJHS and BUASC papers

(2:) Perhaps I should be ashamed to admit it but I find it infinitely difficult to be strong and to endure the things that are happening in Central Europe. I find it beyond my strength to be unmoved, to be unshaken by the news of another disaster, another holocaust, another deed of shame day after day, hour after hour. Within 24 hours this week, three or four days ago, came the heart-breaking tidings from the Nazi regime not only that within four years Jews must be out of Austria, but that all Jews must report their possessions, real and personal, to the Nazi government, which is a polite and preliminary way of saying Jews are to be expatriated, all possessions to be taken away.[23] ... The same day brings tidings of something which has grieved me almost as much: that Italy, under the Nazi compulsion, has resorted to the despicable act of incarcerating and imprisoning – for the days of the state visit of the Nazi chancellor – all the German and Austrian refugees....[24]

(7:) Let me put it once again. Suffering which I bravely, decently, gallantly endure is my sublime prerogative, but suffering which I permit others to endure is my fatal curse.... Can I find it possible to live and see millions of my fellow Jews, one-third of all the Jews of

---

23 A JTA headline for March 28 was "Goering Promising 'Systematic Expulsion' in Four Years." The article, however, made it clear that the expulsion announced by Goering applied to Vienna, not all of Austria: "It is our will that in four years Vienna again become German Vienna and that the Jews should be expelled."

24 A JTA headline for March 25 was "Gestapo Sought 'Judenrein' Rome and Florence for Hitler's Visit." This was presented as a security measure for Hitler; the Italian Government agreed to the temporary arrest of Jews who had arrived in Italy during the previous five years.

earth, suffering without lifting both my hands, without doing what one poor man can do through appeal and protest and imploring? But all of us should feel the same way.

May 9, 1938 (Monday)

Israel H. Levinthal, "A Glimpse into the Future," Address at United Synagogue of America Convention, Chicago, IL. *A New World Is Born*, pp. 203–9

(205:) Many of us are overwhelmed today because of the new tyranny that is threatening the Jew and all the world. We stand dismayed and in despair. It is a sad and tragic picture that we behold, but if we know our history, we will understand that it is nothing new. It is the old battle between the brute, bloody hands of Esau and the voice of Jacob. Only the technique differs; the method and purpose are the same....

Alas, the great threat that faces us is not the resurgence of anti-Semitism, but the weakening influence in our midst of the call of the Synagogue....

May 26, 1938 (Thursday)

Ferdinand M. Isserman, "Has God Forsaken Humanity?," Temple Israel, St. Louis, MO, Special Service of Mourning and Intercession for the Victims of Twentieth-Century Tyranny. AJA, MS-6, Box 15, Folder 2[25]

(1:) Reports of a fresh wave of persecution of Jews and liberals in Austria are so harrowing that it seems almost impossible that this is the twentieth century and not the first. If I had not been in Nazi Germany myself, if I had not seen the welts on the victims' backs, the bruises on their cheeks, if I had not heard stories from their own lips, it would be difficult for me to believe the news that is coming from Austria....[26] Insolent, unashamed and unafraid, [the Nazis] parade

---

25 This was a special service organized by Orthodox, Conservative, and Reform St. Louis rabbis together.

26 Here the preacher refers to a three-column article by a *NYT* foreign correspondent, published Monday, May 22, p. 60.

their madness and their savagery before the world. Undeterred by rebukes from ecclesiastics and reprimands from statesmen, unawed by the accusing conscience of humanity, seemingly desiring to prove with fiendishness that there might have been a germ of truth in the war propaganda circulated against the Germans in the [world] war, the Nazis pushed their juggernaut on and on.

(2:) Immediately, the thought may occur to some, why pray to God? Why does he not interfere?...

(3:) At this service, our prayers should be directed towards the goal that we, whose kinsmen are being tortured, kinsmen of the flesh as well as kinsmen of the spirit, do not succumb to the level of the persecutor, that we too do not forsake God....

(4:) At the same time, we must pray for our persecutors. We must not forget that they are human beings, that they are made in the image of God.... (5:) We pray that we may never abandon our faith in mankind, that we may never forsake God, for those are truly forsaken who have forsaken Him.

(5:) And finally, let us remember that there are worse fates for man than suffering: to besmirch his soul, to turn his back upon his destiny, to lower his moral level.... To suffer, to die for justice, for peace, for God, is the greatest human achievement – is *Kiddush Hashem* [the sanctification of God's name]. And that glory in a night of darkness hovers like an inspiring halo over those in our times who perish voicing their faith in the eternal verities, and who die for the glory of God.

May 28, 1938 (Saturday)

Samuel H. Goldenson, "Can We Achieve Jewish Unity by a Referendum?," Temple Emanu-El, New York. Pamphlet, AJA MS-81, Box 2, Folder 4

(3:) [T]he present German leaders find it in their interest to regard the Jewish people not only as different from them racially, but as inferior besides. Moreover, they look upon all Jews as suffering incurably from a taint which they claim inevitably defiles and disintegrates the body politic of the nations among whom they live. Accordingly, the present German government feels wholly justified in causing our people all manner of suffering in order to remove this poisonous element, and where this cannot be done completely, at least to isolate it. This is the direct attack upon the Jews.

Then there is an indirect onslaught. This springs from the growing opposition of the totalitarian ideal to all democratic forms of government.... The Jew, therefore, has a stake in democracy, a stake that he shares with everyone else. Indeed, his concern for the preservation of the democratic tradition should be greater than that of others, for it has been his unfortunate lot to be made the scapegoat whenever men turn away from the ideals of democracy, humanity, and justice.

How strange it is that in the present circumstances when civilization is so threatened and troubled by the totalitarian states, the Jewish people should now be asked by certain of their leaders to establish an agency which, in its "single and all-inclusive" character, appears very much like a totalitarian organization....[27] (8:) Some of our leaders, though they are earnestly setting out to champion the rights of the Jew are, alas, adopting a racial philosophy which is now threatening the life of Europe and which will be certain to give aid and comfort to our enemies. They appeal for unity and yet propose measures and programs which cannot but produce a deep cleavage in the household of Israel and keep all of us in the turmoil of perpetual conflict and strife....

June 5, 1938 (first day of Shavu'ot)

Joseph H. Hertz, "The Tragedy of Vienna," Golders Green Synagogue, London. *Early and Late*, pp. 51–57

(51:) I deem it my solemn duty to devote the great portion of my words to-day to what may at first appear to you as unsuitable for a Festival sermon: the *Churban* [destruction] of Austrian Jewry, the staggering tragedy of Vienna. And yet I unhesitatingly dwell on

27 This was a proposal initiated by the American Jewish Congress in May, 1938 to form an inclusive agency including the Congress, the American Jewish Committee, the Anti-Defamation League of B'nai B'rith, and the Jewish War Veterans. Goldenson was not alone in his strong opposition. See "Review of the Year, (1938–1939)," in *American Jewish Year Book 5699*, vol. 40 (1938–1939), pp. 138–39.

this tragedy to-day, because tragedy – as the ancients rightly held – purifies.[28]...

(54:) To-day, seven hundred years after 1244, not a shred is left of the privileges enumerated in the Great Charter. One word, "rightlessness," (55:) and that in its most naked and brutal form, sums up the whole position of Austrian Jewry. Jews are outlaws. There is for them no safety of life or limb. For weeks, Jews have been cruelly beaten in public and dragged away, even from Seder, to perform degrading labour in the streets. One of the principal synagogues was turned into a citadel of Jew-baiting, and Nazi gangsters devised orgies of sacrilege in connection with everything that Jews deem holy....

And yet, all these inhumanities notwithstanding, a portion of the Jews of Austria, at any rate of its Jewish Jews, will survive the terror.... And the reason why no barbarism can break the spirit of those free men lies in their Judaism. The *Shema Yisroel* clothes the Jewish Jew with the unconquerable will to endure all things for his Faith and People in dignity and resignation; and, at the same time, it fills the heart of his co-religionists the world over with pity and unquenchable charity to help him to some haven of rest in a land of freedom....

(56:) Say not, "We are overwhelmed by appeals in aid of the hundreds of thousands of victims in Germany, Austria, Poland, and Romania." Let me read to you the telling words of a communal leader: "The calls on our Community are many, but we cannot (57:) allow the destruction of German and Austrian Jewries to overwhelm English Jewry, and thus constitute a permanent triumph to the anti-Semite."

June 5, 1938[29]

LEO JUNG, "Of Murder," The Jewish Center, New York. *Crumbs and Character*, pp. 143–46.

---

28 At this point, Hertz reviewed some of the history of Austrian Jewry, including the Charter of 1244, the *Gezerah* of 1420, the Expulsion of 1670, the reign of the anti-Jewish Maria Theresa, and the Emancipation of 1876 (pp. 51–54).

29 No specific date is provided for this sermon, but the first sentence is "Shavuoth is called the moral birthday of Israel...," indicating that it was delivered on Shavu'ot,

(143:) In the *Gleichschaltung*[30] of Germany and now of poor Austria a refined way of murder has been developed. As against the swift blows of the merciful savage, these champions of the culture of force have achieved uncanny efficiency in a type of bloodless liquidation which is a hundred times more cruel. They deny the Jew the right to live, to earn a living, to walk unassaulted in the streets, to enjoy the basic privileges of a human being. They not only take away from him every hope of social or economic or political promotion, but they deliberately drive him into a cul-de-sac of social ostracism, financial despair, and political pariahship so that he be driven to suicide. Here deliberate murder is committed no matter how drawn out....

(144:) There are some relatives of ours – first, second, and third cousins, fourth cousins, fifth cousins – under the whip of Teutonic barbarism, in the abyss of undeserved shame, facing reproach and starvation and destruction, who send frantic appeals to their kindred in the United States for an affidavit – modern miracle word – which would deliver them from Hitler's hell to the freedom of hospitable America. I do hope that there may not be many who one day will be unable to summon the courage to pray for their own, for wife and children, for brother or sister, because they will remember that they were too lazy, too unconcerned, too wickedly indifferent to hearken to the message of their own who begged them, who stretched out their hands in an agony of pain and despair, to implore their help: "Send us the affidavit!"[31]...

(145:) All the world feels profoundly menaced by Adolph [*sic*] Hitler. Few are willing to trace him back to the source of all the evil he has come to mean in the life of the contemporary man. It is the cruel indifference of the victors in the World War that made Hitler possible. Back of his murderous career was another "murder due to

---

and the reference to the Anschluss (March 1938) "now of poor Austria" suggests that it was delivered in June of 1938, not the following year after *Kristallnacht*.

30 The term was used to mean an imposition of uniformity within a totalitarian society.

31 The "affidavit" in question was generally a commitment to ensure that the person coming to the US as a refugee would not become a public charge, and that the signer would provide for the needs of the refugee if necessary. See Jung, December 17, 1938, below.

indifference." The victorious allies paid (146:) no attention to the hundreds of thousands of German children who for more than a year were kept in a state of semi-starvation.

Lloyd George came back from the Peace Conference saying, "The conditions of peace are terrible but just."[32] But they afflicted not the war-mongers, the Junkers, the professional militarists. They robbed innocent children of food, and denied a chance to democratic Germany to rebuild the country on a new basis of decency and equality. It was because of the despair engendered by indifference to the sufferings of sixty-five million Germans that Hitler could build his Empire of Blood. If freedom is murdered today, humanity had been murdered earlier. This murder stemmed from the callousness of some of the Allies responsible for the chain of tyranny which today enslaves all Europeans who believe in God and human dignity. I fear lest, God forbid, Jewish indifference to Jewish misery abroad bring about a similar despair and degradation. We see, with a sinking of heart, how England's attitude of calm forbearance to the murderous assault of the Arabs on the Jewish population in the Holy Land has brought about a reign of terror in Palestine. This is the inescapable law of historic justice....

Victims of our insufficient identification with our brethren's life, they are all potential fodder for a movement of despair from Hitler to Stalin. Their peace, courage, sanity have been murdered by our peaceful but devastating uninterestedness.

June 6, 1938 (second day of Shavu'ot)

Israel H. Levinthal, "United, Even the Weak Become Powerful,"[33] Brooklyn Jewish Center, Brooklyn, NY. *A New World Is Born*, pp. 162–65

(164:) It is strange that this simple lesson which, according to our

---

32 Reference is to the speech made by Lloyd George to the House of Commons on July 3, 1919 upon presenting the terms of the Treaty of Versailles. This included the sentences, "The terms are terrible," and "There is no doubt that they are severe. Are they just? Let us take those which have been challenged, separately...."

33 The title is attributed to Goethe near the end of the sermon: *Vereint sind auch die Schwachen mächtig* (p. 165). But the statement was apparently made by Schiller.

sages, was realized by these erstwhile slaves from Egypt, has not yet been learned by us Jews today. The mount of *Sin'ah*, of hatred to the Jew, has risen to heights hardly equaled in all the bitter and tragic story of these three thousand years. And the mountain is still rising ever higher, ever more threatening, ever more dangerous. And yet, the observer of world Jewry in particular must say, not "*Va-yichan*" [Exod. 19:2, singular], but "*Va-yachanu*" [plural]. Israel stands divided, torn apart, rent by the spirit of *tarumot* and (165:) *machlokot* – strife and bitterness and dissension. A bewildered world, viewing our sufferings and sorrow, beholds now our inner tragedy, which Israel Zangwill has so poignantly described, when he wrote,

> "Hear, O Israel, the Lord our God, the Lord is One.
> But we Thy people are twain, and therefore undone!"[34]

This is the real danger that faces us Jews today, and it is this that ought to give grave concern both to Jewish laymen and Rabbis alike....

Let the word *Va-yachanu* give way to *Va-yichan*; let Israel take his stand *Neged Hahar*, against the mountain of hate as he stood at Sinai...and then new hope, new faith, new strength can, and we hope will, come to our stricken people, so sorely tried today.

June 27, 1938 (Monday)

Simon Greenberg, "President's Message to the Thirty-Eighth Annual Convention of the Rabbinical Assembly," Tannersville, NY. *Proceedings of the Rabbinical Assembly of America*, vol. 5, pp. 422–31

(430:) Finally, I would say a word about the plight of our sorely pressed brethren abroad. We all recognize that words are powerless to describe the indignities to which they have been subjected, and the physical cruelties visited upon them. Not since the days of the destruction of the Temple and the expulsion from Spain have so many Jews been the prey of men from whom the image of God has

---

34 This does not appear among the eighty-four quotations from Zangwill listed in Joseph L. Baron, *A Treasury of Jewish Quotations*.

been completely erased. The amount of financial assistance we have been able to offer to the suffering hardly sufficed to bandage their wounds, much less to cure them, and the amount of healing our efforts might have effected was more than counterbalanced by the new wounds daily inflicted upon them by a soulless clique of sadists temporarily exercising authority. Peoples with powerful governments to speak in their behalf have been helpless in their attempts to check the beastly mob. What could we hope to achieve? It is heartening, however, for us and for our brethren abroad, to hear the powerful voice of our government raised in unequivocal denunciation of the barbarities practiced upon the defenseless bodies of our people abroad....

July 3, 1938 (Sunday)

Morris S. Lazaron, "Unless the Lord Build the House," Address at Vesper Service Opening the Institute of Public Affairs, Charlottesville, VA. AJA MS-71, Box 25

(8:) I believe that religious freedom for Protestants and Catholics is inevitably bound up with the freedom of the Jew. Without any special pleading, the facts confirm this statement.

The population of Germany was 65 million, 550,000 of whom were Jews. Why should the destruction of Jewish rights involve inevitably the destruction of the rights of Protestants and Catholics?...

German Protestants and Catholics received subsidies from the state. German Protestantism felt itself allied with and dependent on the state. There was a tradition of anti-Semitism in Germany. When the present regime went in on an anti-Semitic platform, its anti-Semitism became a state law. Loyalty to the state as well as anti-Jewish feeling in Protestant and Catholic circles for the most part silenced protests, though a number of brave voices were raised in both groups. But German Protestants and Catholics misunderstood the nature of a dictatorial regime. It claimed all loyalties, body, mind and soul. Sooner or later it had to come into conflict with Protestants and Catholics. It could not brook a division of loyalties.... (9:) Dr. Meyer, erstwhile counsellor to the German Legation who resigned his position, pointed this out recently in an address in New York. He called Naziism "anti-Christ." But an objective appraisal of the situation reveals that, believing as they do, the Nazis *had* to persecute Protestants and Catholics as well as Jews. And Protestants and Catholics, believing as they do *had* to resist.

The Jews were only the first victims. A dictatorship makes no distinction between Christian faith in human brotherhood and Jewish faith in human brotherhood. The things for which Jews, Catholics, and Protestants stand – the dignity of human life, the sense of compassion, the ideas of social justice – these are anathema to dictatorships, whether of right or left. Yet they are the pillars on which both Judaism and Christianity are built. Deny them to one and you deny them to all. Guarantee them to one and you guarantee them to all.

July 17, 1938 (Sunday, 17 Tammuz, Intercession Day)

Joseph H. Hertz, Great Synagogue, London. *JC*, July 22, 1938, p. 28

[On 17 Tammuz the tablets of law were broken; later the Romans placed an idol in the Holy of Holies.] Those events in the life of ancient Israel were a very real counterpart to similar moral calamities that darken the life of large and powerful nations today. The shattering of the Law entered into the heart of the nation in totalitarian countries. There the rights and privileges which are the birthright of free citizens were abolished. As to a helpless minority group like the Jews – from them elementary human rights are openly, brazenly, and successfully withheld.

The Brown Bolshevism of Berlin, like the Red variety of Moscow, has launched a determined offensive against every form of traditional religion, whether in worship, education, or social endeavour. At no time has there been such an unbridled attack on the Scriptures. And, most pitiable of all, the souls of the German children are poisoned by a new paganism, hardening the heart and petrifying the feelings....

"Sanctify ye a fast, call a solemn assembly, gather the elders and all the inhabitants of the Land" (Joel 1:14). It is common knowledge that as soon as it was announced that a Service of Intercession and Prayer would be held that day in the Synagogues of the Empire, the religious heads of the Anglicans and of the Free Churches resolved to make the Jewish sorrow their own. Thus these words of Scripture just quoted are being fulfilled, and "all the inhabitants of the land" are that day sending up their prayers simultaneously with their own to the God of the spirits of all flesh.

Rev. D.[avid] Bueno de Mesquita, Spanish & Portuguese Synagogue, London. *JC*, July 22, 1938, p. 28

It has been left for these days of twentieth-century civilization to contribute the saddest, the cruelest, the most inhuman chapter in all the long and chequered history of the Jews. There is a coldly calculated campaign of ultimate annihilation, being pressed home with every weapon known to brute violence and to warped intellect. In very truth, it is a time of trouble unto Jacob. Once again, as in the distant past, may he cry, "Behold and see if there be any pain like unto my pain" (Lam. 1:12).

Beyond their duty to help their harassed brethren to the fullest extent of their power, nothing remains but to pray to Him in whose name the Prophet said, "It is a time of trouble unto Jacob, but out of it shall he be saved" (Jer. 30:7). And to the God of their Fathers they prayed that day; prayed that even as He had saved Jacob in the past from his troubles, so might He take compassion on his sorely-tried people that day, and set a term to their terrible suffering and suspense.

Israel Mattuck, "A Crisis in Civilisation," Liberal Jewish Synagogue, London. Printed pamphlet

(1:) In our Service to-day our first thoughts are of those who are suffering persecution. There are among them Jews and non-Jews. The heaviest measure of affliction has been laid on the Jews. Those who persecute them have proclaimed the desire to destroy them; and to that end they use all the means which unlimited power gives them, unrestrained by a sense of justice. They know neither justice nor mercy.

The tortures inflicted on Jews in Germany are so barbaric as to tax the credulity of civilised peoples. I want to use measured words in describing them, but they are such that even superlatives are measured in relation to the extreme cruelty of the acts.[35] There is, unfortunately, no doubt about their actuality. It is the most emphatic expression of the civilized world's condemnation that men ask in pained astonishment: "How can such things be?"...And the persecuted can do nothing to resist their persecutors; they are impotent and defenceless. But they have the spiritual power to bear their suffering with dignity.

(2:) The discriminatory and oppressive laws against Jews and Christians descended from Jews have a larger significance than the sufferings they inflict, terrible as these are. To deprive men of their right to earn a living, to take their possessions from them, to degrade them by every means possible (3:) to the status of social and political outcasts, to treat human beings with all the mental and physical tortures that bestiality could conceive, for no reason other than that they are Jews, or have Jewish blood in them, would have constituted a terrible evil in any age because of its inhumanity. It is an even graver and more terrible evil in our time because it comes after a development in human thought and moral feeling which should have made it impossible....

(4:) In this Intercession service, we think not only of the Jews who are suffering because they are Jews, but also of the Christians, Catholics and Protestants, who are suffering because they put their religion above a false nationalism, and God above the State.

We are confronted by a crisis in our civilisation.... If it is right to kill and oppress the (5:) Jews because they are weak, then all who are weak have lost all ground for security. And the test of a civilisation is the protection it gives, and the rights it guarantees, to the weak. The strong need law to restrain them, the weak need law to protect them. But those who persecute the Jews recognize no law.

(6:) It is surprising, painfully surprising, to find [a friendly atti-

---

35 Note that this powerful language, used before there was any systematic mass murder, before mass deportation, before even *Kristallnacht*, reveals the challenge of conceptualizing and articulating the far greater oppression of the near future.

tude toward Nazi policy] in a Bishop of the Church, who goes so far even as to defend the imprisonment of a Christian clergyman who has refused to accept State-idolatry.[36] When he writes that the Christian clergy in Germany, "provided they confine themselves to preaching the Gospel," can carry on their work "without any interruption by the State," I cannot help but wonder whether he means the whole Gospel and all (7:) that it contains![37]... There are some fundamental ideas which belong both to Judaism and to Christianity, which religious teachers must insist on at all times. The chief of them is the supremacy of God. Obviously, to preach it in a country where the State claims supremacy for itself has a political implication. But by those who believe in it, it must be preached none the less. And the adherents of religion throughout the world owe a debt of gratitude to those Christians in Germany who have chosen to suffer, rather than be silent, in the face of the political attack on religious fundamentals.

September 10, 1938 (Saturday)

Salis Daiches, "Persecution of the Jews," Edinburgh Hebrew Congregation, Scotland. *The Scotsman*, Monday, September 12, 1938, p. 9

Of all the manifestations of human cruelty recorded in history, none can compare, as regards its effect, with the campaign of slander and vituperation organised by the Nazi and Fascist forces in Europe against the Jews....

Fascist Italy has decided to copy the ways of Nazi Germany. No matter how few the number of Jews in Italy, how honourable their record, how ancient their association with the country – the order had gone forth to malign and revile the Jew and his race, and to crush

---

36 Apparently an allusion to the arrest of Martin Niemöller on July 1, 1937, and his subsequent confinement in a concentration camp despite his acquittal in the legal case against him in February 1938.

37 Reference is to a letter published by Bishop A.C. Headlam, Chairman of the Church Council on Foreign Relations, in *The Times of London* on July 14, 1938, responding to an earlier letter by H. Hensley Henson, Bishop of Durham, condemning the Nazi regime for Niemöller's incarceration. See Owen Chadwick, *Hensley Henson*, pp. 266–67; Tom Lawson, *The Church of England and the Holocaust*, pp. 40–43.

the Jewish citizen out of existence. Fascist Rome wants to seek glory in the destruction of a handful of Jews, and to achieve it by the use of poisoned arrows borrowed from their Nazi friends. The Romans in the days of Caesar and Cicero would have regarded the wholesale condemnation of a community that had rendered unique services to humanity as utter barbarism, unworthy of anyone anxious to style himself Roman. But we live in a strange world. Principles of humanity, of equity, of justice, of fairness are trampled underfoot, while the rest of the world looks on helplessly, and the weak perish by the hands of the strong.

September 25, 1938 (Sunday, Erev Rosh Hashanah)

Leo M. Franklin, "Light at the Eventide: A New Year's Sermon," Temple Beth-El, Detroit, MI. "Printed and distributed by a group of friends."

"At the Eventide, There shall be Light" (Zech. 14:7)....

[W]hile the Jew may be the pariah of the nations – scorned, maligned, hated, persecuted, declassed, exiled, driven from post to pillar and from pillar to post, victim of every malign force that barbarism can muster to its aid, target for the poisoned barbs of infidels and madmen, the truth which he has preached, the justice which he has sought to establish in the earth, the spirit of brotherhood of which he has been teacher and exemplar; the religion which embodies these principles of humanity – these neither the destructive forces or time nor the vicious attacks of undisciplined men and nations have been able to destroy without ultimately destroying themselves. **With the death of the Jew civilization dies.** That is the unique and challenging fact which (2:) above all others this night voices for the encouragement of the Jew and for a warning to his enemies.

Particularly significant is all this when we realize that this New Year 5699, according to our calendar, takes its place in the chain of the centuries at a time when the world is desperately sick. An epidemic of hate has attacked the nations of the earth.... Wherever self-appointed autocrats have sought to turn the thoughts of their own victimized and degraded subjects from their wrongs, a new onslaught on the Jew has been the most convenient means of doing so. It was true in Czarist Russia, it was true in Germany. It was true in Italy and it is true in every Fascistic state in Europe today.

And this is true, mind you, not merely, or chiefly, as some suppose, because the Jew is a minority group everywhere. Minorities as such generally count for little in the setting up of Empires. The last week's tragic history proves this.[38] They can be swept aside by the onrushing hordes of a majority or they can be ignored altogether....

How stupid it is, by way of example, for Germany to preach the doctrine of Aryan supremacy, (3:) while admitting that the Jews, who at best represented one tenth of one per cent of her normal population, were mighty enough to change the character of German personality to such an extent as to make them a menace to the culture and the civilization of the Reich....

(5:) The Christian world, unfortunately too long complacent in its own supposed security, is gradually awakening to the fact that the fate of Jew and Christian are inevitably and indissolubly and irretrievably intertwined and that the synagogue and what it stands for cannot be destroyed and the church survive.... What has happened to the Jew in Germany has happened to the Catholic, and is destined to happen to the Protestant, and to every other group of God-aspiring men and women. And because this is so, the Jew will no longer be compelled to carry on his battle alone. The religious forces of the civilized world will form in phalanx formation, for their own protection, against his assailants. Let one but follow much of the literature that is appearing in opposition to Jewish oppression under the auspices of the various Christian denominations, and he will be readily convinced that our battle is their battle because our defeat is death for them.

(7:) No more notable event in recent history is to be recorded than the Conference on the Refugee problem called early in July at Evian, France, by the President of the United States and to which the representatives of more than thirty nations responded. The setting

---

38 An example of allusion recognizable to the congregation but not to modern readers: The reference is apparently to Neville Chamberlain's apparent acceptance of German claims to the Sudetenland.

up of a permanent bureau with a great American at its head for the resettlement of the victims of religious and political oppression is warning to all the world that the Jew and every other minority group must be protected in their human rights.[39]...

The future of the Jew depends as much upon himself as upon others. He cannot lie supine with the expectation that others shall save him.... Moreover, it is neither good policy, nor to my mind wholly ethical, for the Jew to seek his own survival merely by crying out against the infamy of his betrayers. Boycotts, resolutions of protest, Congresses, and whatnot, will in the end avail him little if they do not actually harm him. What is needed by the Jew is a resuscitation of the moral heroism of his fathers, of the rebirth of the courage, of the faith, of the spiritual aspirations of those heroes of the spirit whose blood flows in his veins.... There are signs on the horizon that such a change is actually taking place among our people.... (8:) Triumph shall yet replace our tragedy and a new and better day shall be born for Israel and for humanity. Grant it, our Father, we pray Thee!

Ferdinand M. Isserman, "How Safe Are We?," Temple Israel, St. Louis, MO. AJA, MS-6, Box 15, Folder 2

(1:) How safe are we Jews? This is perhaps the question which more than any other troubles us assembled here, and which, perhaps, most of us had in our mind when, to the father in heaven we winged the words, "Inscribe us in the book of life." For it has been a trying and a difficult year for all mankind but especially for us, the children of Israel.... The collapse of international morality in the Nazi-Czech crisis has shaken our faith in the pledges of nations. The capture of Austria, the attempt at the sudden ruthless extirpation of its two hundred thousand to half a million Jews and half-Jews, the outbreak of anti-semitism in Romania, stemmed only by the interference of democratic nations in Europe, the lengthening shadow over Hungarian Jewry, the exile of tens of thousands of Italian Jews, and the

39 Another painfully ironic conclusion in light of the subsequent failure of the Conference to accomplish anything significant on behalf of Jewish refugees.

acceptance by the Italian ruling clique of the racial poison concocted by Nazi pharmacists, have made many of us wonder what the fate of the universal Jew is to be. Which Jewish community is next to be doomed?...Brute force has been exalted. The moral gains of centuries have been trampled underfoot, and we wonder tonight whether in the darkening skies we are witnessing the twilight of a great civilization, and whether the barbarian clouds which conceal the sun of humanitarianism are to be followed by a night of untold savagery.

(4:) My answer is: the Jew is safe. And it is not an answer based upon wishful thinking, but an answer based upon a careful, first-hand study of seven years of the impact of German anti-semitism upon the minds of the people of Europe and of America.

It is evident that whenever democracy maintains itself, there the Jew is safe. That is true of Europe. Not a single democracy has succumbed to anti-semitic propaganda.... (5:) Hear the roll call of anti-semitic nations or nations threatened with anti-semitism, and you hear the roster of autocracies. Germany, Italy, Romania, Poland....

(5:) If the Jew is safe in democratic Europe, how much safer is he in the United States of America, where the democratic tradition is older and stronger....

(9:) Though I grieve over my brethren crushed by the cruelty of European tyrants, my inner soul rejoices that the foes of liberty are the foes of Israel, that the tyrants who persecute would have no fellowship with the Jew. I would rather see the Jews wanderers on the face of the earth with their souls unpolluted with tyranny and their hands unstained with oppression, than the trusted lieutenants of dictators and despots....

September 27, 1938 (second day of Rosh Hashanah)

Israel H. Levinthal, "A Program for the Jew," Brooklyn Jewish Center, Brooklyn, NY. *A New World Is Born*, pp. 122–28

(122:) These two prophets, looking upon the world before them – the world that Elijah was leaving (203:) and that Elisha was to face and to mold anew – saw what we behold in our day: a world of cruelty, of barbarism, of hate, and of bloodshed. They saw the intrigues and unbounded lusts of the Egyptians, Assyrians and Philistines – vying with each other in their evil machinations. They saw the rule of force gripping the lives not only of their own people, but of the peoples of every land. But they also saw clearly that no life for the Jew could be safe, even in their own Palestine, with a world about them that was bent upon destruction. . . .

(125:) The idealists do not realize that the Jewish problem is interlinked with the world problem, that we can never have a better world so long as the Jewish problem remains unsolved. As long as the Jew is homeless, the football of all nations, you are giving the reactionaries in all lands the opportunity they seek: to make the Jew the scapegoat for all their devilish plans and deadly schemes. Here is where a Jewish Palestine goes to the heart of the world's problem as well as to the problem of the Jew.

Samuel Rosenblatt, "The Rewards of Sacrifice," Congregation Beth Tfiloh, Baltimore, MD. *Our Heritage*, pp. 22–27[40]

(22:) It is hard, when one considers the setbacks that the cause of the Jewish people has suffered the last few months, to keep from giving way to despondency and despair. Of what avail has been all our work and toil to establish a haven of refuge for our harassed and persecuted race in our ancestral home, of what use the attempts to protect Jewish rights elsewhere? Behold we have but "exerted ourselves in vain and borne for terror" (cf. Isa. 65:13). Our unprecedented accomplishments in the land of our fathers served only to heighten the envy and intensify the destructive fury of our adversaries there. The more we did, the stronger became their determination to demolish and undo. And as for our position outside the land of Israel, instead of being improved as a result of the measures adopted to combat our foes, it has grown steadily worse. The number of Israel's enemies has increased, "and God's people has not been delivered" (cf. Exod. 5:23). Were not our sceptics right? Would it not have been far better for us

40 The dating of this Rosh Hashanah sermon is indicated by the first sentence, "More than a year has elapsed since the report of the Peel Commission was published" (it was published in June 1937).

had we left well enough alone,... had we refrained from identifying ourselves with the forces hostile to the trouble-makers of the world and resigned ourselves to our fate?...

(27:) Never mind, then, the hindrances, the obstacles and impediments placed in our way. If we but possess the spiritual strength to go on fighting, we will, with God's help, reach our goal and live to hear the shofar blast of the Messiah proclaiming that at long last Israel is free.

October 1, 1938 (Saturday, Shabbat Shuvah)

Israel Goldstein, "A Word of Comfort to Czechoslovakians," Address to United Czech Societies, Carnegie Hall, New York. *Toward a Solution*, pp. 49–51

(49:) It is a privilege, though a sad one, to add my voice as an American and as a Jew to this symposium of sympathy with victims of physical force.

As a Jew, I feel a sense of gratitude to Czechoslovakia because of its treatment of its Jewish citizens....[41]

(50:) Perhaps the Golem would be an appropriate token of the state of Europe this first day of October, when soulless robots are on the march. October first will be remembered as a day when a valiant little republic fell victim to a Golem civilization.

In the capitals of Europe, there is jubilation that the day which threatened to be the beginning of a world war witnesses peace instead of war. It is not difficult to understand the jubilation of wives who can have their husbands again, or parents and sons who can have each other again.

What is difficult to understand is the effort to make it appear as a great moral victory. No amount of sophistry or ratiocination can obscure the sad fact that this is not "peace with honor," as Chamberlain and Daladier termed it.... The title "honor" belongs only to one people in Europe today, to the Czechoslovakian people,

41 He goes on to mention 350,000 Jews, involved in every important activity in the life of the republic; then Franz Werfel, old synagogues and cemeteries, and the story of the Golem.

whose steadfast courage, quiet heroism, and magnificent poise are without parallel. It is a sad commentary that such virtues should be thus rewarded....

(51:) We refuse to believe that this kind of terrible world will long endure. We believe that dictatorships, like the Golem, bear the seed of their own destruction....

A people that has been seared by sorrow, lashed by waves of misfortune, lacerated by nineteen centuries of affliction, but undefeated, speaks on this dire October 1st to the spiritually undefeated Czechoslovakian nation in the words of an ancient Hebrew prophet, "Comfort ye, Comfort ye my people" (Isa. 40:1).

October 4, 1938 (Kol Nidre)

Israel Goldstein, "Kol Nidre Summons," Congregation B'nai Jeshurun, New York. *Toward a Solution*, pp. 153–61

(153:) What Polish Jewry suffers one year, German Jewry another year, and what nearly all of European Jewry suffers today, are the latest links in a chain of tragedy which stretches from the barbarity of the Roman legions in the first century, to the ferocity of the Christian Crusades in the eleventh century, to the sadistic bigotry of the Inquisition in the fifteenth and sixteenth centuries.

(157:) Today, living in a world of force, the Jew is excoriated by the high priests of force because his Bible has imposed a conscience of righteousness and justice upon the world. The "prophets" of might want neither the New Testament nor the Old Testament. Both Testaments are condemned as a menace to the "*Kraftanschauung*" of the Aryan "*Uebermensch*."[42]

(158:) In 1933, upon assuming power, Hitler and Nazism served notice on the world that they repudiate democracy, excoriate liberalism, scoff at the principles of human equality and brotherhood, revile the religious traditions of Judaism and of Christianity, exalt nationalist chauvinism, (159:) glorify race hatreds, defy international decencies, and extol war as the highest and noblest way of life. At the same time, they proclaimed a special tenderness toward animals....

42 Literally, the "power outlook" of the Aryan "superman."

Anyone who maintains that this is a war between two equally undesirable imperialisms [Germany and the British Empire] is either a fool or a villain....

In this challenge to civilization it was no accident that the Jew became the first victim. No greater compliment has been paid the Jew than to have singled him out as the special target of Nazi sadism. Alas, it was a tragic compliment which devastated hundreds of thousands of our people. But it put upon the Jew once more the noble yoke of the suffering "Servant of the Lord."

Some Jews are heard venturing the prediction that Hitler's downfall is inevitable because it is an inexorable law of history that whoever persecutes the Jew comes to grief. To put it that (160:) way, as if the Jew were invested with some magic immunity, is to over-simplify and therefore to understate the truth. To believe that would be unworthy and unwarranted chauvinism of which the Jew, least of all, should be guilty....

Never before in the history of our trials and tribulations has the issue been drawn so clearly. We are proud in the knowledge that Hitler is allergic to Judaism, which means also to Christianity. Never before has the ethical basis of our existence been so convincing. It makes the "Akedah," the sacrifice, worthwhile. Jews in many lands stand not only on the physical war front. They are in the front-line trenches of the spiritual war front. The story of Isaac's sacrifice at Moriah becomes a lesson in current events.

(161:) The future will decide between the proponents of the book and the proponents of the sword. It is the modern phase of the irreconcilable conflict between Jacob and Esau. And the Jew knows how to wait. Hitler talks about a thousand years. He is merely talking. The Jew, when he speaks of a thousand years, has the warrant of four thousand years of history to which to point....

Abraham H. Feinberg, "Militant Morality," Temple Beth-El, Rockford, IL. AJA, MS-85, Box 2, Folder 5

(1:) To-night non-Jew as well as Jew stands before the bar of judgment. The mad events of the past half-decade, being allowed to run their course without check, have finally caught up with us. Link after link, forged on hell's anvil of cunning and hatred, is being added daily to an already long chain of black slavery and death. A crisis in history will soon be reached. In this crisis it is no longer a question of Jew or Christian, but of both Jew and Christian, for the survival of a free humanity is at stake.

The first World War ended last Thursday.[43] It was won by Germany; what the Kaiser couldn't do, Hitler did. Germany is now the undisputed master of Central Europe, perhaps also the master of the entire continent. And not one shot was fired.

Today the peoples of Europe are rejoicing; the Nazis, naturally, because they have won a victory; Italy because the diplomacy of black-mail has been vindicated. England and France because, so they think, peace was made....

FERDINAND M. ISSERMAN, "The Salvation of Humanity," Temple Israel, St. Louis, MO. AJA, MS-6, Box 15, Folder 3

(1:) As I step into this pulpit on this most sacred occasion, my first word is one of welcome to the new Americans in our midst, who have come to us in the past year, to flee from the common enemy of democracy and of justice, of peace and of good-will.... You have come as a protest to tyranny and to despotism.... You were good citizens of Germany. You gave it the best there was in you. You helped make its greatness. Some of you fought for it during the world war. Others of you lost parents, brothers, or other cherished kin upon Germany's battlefields. But Germany's rulers were ungrateful. They have been unjust to you. America will try to help you find justice.... You will be an asset to our nation, an advantage to our community, and I know pillars of this and of other congregations. Be assured of the sympathy, the generosity, the affection of all the members of this congregation who, I can pledge, will stand by you and help you to make necessary adjustments. May God bless you and keep you.

(3:) In the past week, we have seen another nation imbued with the spirit of service to all mankind, allowing itself to be dismembered,

---

43 September 29, 1938, the date of the signing of the "Munich Agreement" allowing German annexation of the portion of Czechoslovakia known as the "Sudetenland."

its arteries to be severed, its limbs to be paralyzed that the fierce beast of the modern jungle might be fed, and the calamity of war averted in Europe. I know that there would have been many who would have been thrilled if little Czecho-Slovakia had single-handedly defied the legions that faced it....

(4:) In my estimation what the Czechs have done indicates their true greatness and vindicates the democracy which they cherished. They loved their liberty much, but they did not care to try to purchase it with the civilization of Europe. They might have plunged a continent into blood and have been responsible for the destruction of its cities, and indirectly have brought about the death of millions of human beings, and gone down to defeat midst the applause of the world and the cheers of all free men. What they did was not spectacular. It was not dramatic. It was more difficult. But they did it for the sake of the general welfare of mankind. They have given us example not of cowardice, but of courage, of heroism and of humanitarianism, which must in these trying days renew our faith in humanity, and in the blessings of liberty.

For us of the household of Israel, the martyrdom of Czecho-Slovakia for the sake of peace, its submission to crucifixion for the welfare of Europe, strikes a sympathetic chord....[44]

(10:) Whatever the motives were of negotiators in Munich, this is certain. War would have saved neither democracy nor civilization nor the Jews of Europe. Wars cannot attain moral ends....

As for the Jews, while propagandists say we plot wars, we know that we are the first to suffer from them. If war had been declared, the lot of German Jews, trying now, would have become even worse. They might have been pogromed.

(11:) What then shall we do at this time? If we obey the teaching of the Book of Jonah, to be emphasized on this day, we would not seek the destruction of modern Nineveh and its people. It is God's will that we seek their regeneration and their restoration to sanity, and we have faith that that is possible....

---

44 Here he continues to discuss the Book of Jonah, which he describes as opposed to "the narrow nationalism which has made an armed camp of humanity."

Maurice N. Eisendrath, "This Is the Light Eternal," Holy Blossom Temple, Toronto. AJA Eisendrath Papers, MS-167, Box 4

(5:) Indeed, my friends, we are witnessing no new phenomenon today, even though terrified, hysterical Jews, ignorant of their past, and unaware of history's verdict against our adversaries, believe that in this latter hour we are being confronted by something altogether unique and novel. On the contrary, however, the self-same forces are arrayed against us today as have been so continuously through the past – and for the self-same reasons. Racialist Jews and willfully blinded Christians may give tacit or vocal assent to the allegations of the Hitlerites that we are despised and persecuted today because through our veins there flows a stream of blood repellent to the noble Nordic and the sublimely virtuous Aryan; that we are hated and oppressed because our business ethics are somewhat less laudable than, let us say, the bullying of weaker peoples and the treaty-breaking code of morals observed by the "righteous" Anglo-Saxons; but these are all subterfuges for the real and basic cause of our afflictions yesterday as well as today, and that is our insistence upon holding high the flame of freedom, of truth, of humanity, amid ever succeeding generations who seek but tyranny, falsehood, and barbaric plunder. The words of Friederich Nietzsche are being fulfilled, not alone in the Fatherland but throughout the entire earth in this . . . hour. . . .

How swiftly has Nietzsche's prophecy been fulfilled. . . . And Nietzsche's most fervid disciple, Adolph [*sic*] Hitler, will succeed in extinguishing one after another of those lights which Lord Grey, as early as 1914, saw going out in Europe "'to be rekindled no more in our day," as he dolefully but all too truly put it; he [Hitler] will (6:) succeed as he overruns country after country and causes nation after nation to bend in cowardly retreat before his blustering wrath; he will succeed in putting out the lights of an entire civilization, to flame no more mayhap for a thousand years unless, unless – how foolish it sounds, and yet history offers ample evidence of the truth of the seemingly extravagant boast I am about to make – unless, my friends, in the House of Israel, as in the Land of Goshen in distant Egyptian days, the *Ner Tomid* continues still to burn.

And that, Herr Hitler himself knows full well. Hitler and his ilk, and I fear he will now win increasing cohorts to his cause. Hitler, and the peoples who follow him in all his vainglorious madness, hate the Jew because ever since that flaming word of God's revelation entered the soul of Israel, the Jew has been the conscience of the world, the visible symbol - and at no time more so than in its Atonement Day, in *this* Atonement Day especially - of how far astray the sons of man had wandered. The Jew is maltreated, he is hated, he is rent asunder because he has believed in democracy, freedom, justice, peace, in age after age when brutish men have sought to efface these ideals from the earth. What a bitter irony of fate. Of all the children of men, we are the most inhumanely treated because we believe most passionately in humanity....

Israel Mattuck, "God and Men's Lives," Liberal Jewish Synagogue, London. Unpublished

(1:) It may seem at first that the Day of Atonement does not fit with immediate circumstances. Its somber, almost gloomy, tone does not express the jubilation caused by the escape from the danger of war.[45] Yet there is an aspect of the recent crisis and its outcome which the atmosphere of the Day of Atonement suits and to which its message is appropriate. We are all deeply thankful for the preservation of the world's peace. (A high price was paid for it, and it was justified in view of the terrible destruction that a war would have wrought. But it is saddening that it should have been necessary to pay so high a price for peace, it is saddening that those who love peace had to surrender to force. Not because it riles, but because of the moral degeneration.) But all that has happened shows the need for the re-assertion, perhaps it would be nearer to say recovery, of spiritual and moral standards and guides for human life. This day and the period it concludes are dedicated to that purpose.

---

45 The context of this paragraph is of course the Munich Conference of September 29, five days before the sermon was delivered, in which British Prime Minister Neville Chamberlain agreed to German occupation of the Sudetenland in return for "peace in our time."

(6:) We feel deep gratitude for religion, but we are aware that it is combined with a kind of sadness. We are sorry for the gallant little country that has suffered. But saddened most of all by the knowledge that there are in the world forces working for war with an unscrupulous disregard for all divine etc. [*sic*]. There are no words of condemnation strong enough for a man who will say that he was prepared to risk a world war which, according to President Roosevelt, would have meant the death of millions and the destruction of civilization. But his attitude may be the most hideous manifestation of a sin which prevails among others.

October 10, 1938 (Monday, first day of Sukkot)

Stephen S. Wise, "Dishonor Without Peace," Free Synagogue at Carnegie Hall, New York. AJA, Box 22: SSW Microfilms of AJHS and BUASC papers

(2:) Oh, it would be so much easier today and these days to remain silent in the midst of one of the great sins in all of history, but there are times when despite every counsel of compromise and expediency, silence would be a sin.

I tell you today that history will say – and I am merely anticipating the verdict of history – that Chamberlain brought back not peace with honor, as did Disraeli [from the Berlin Peace Conference in 1878], but dishonour without peace.... (3:) I do not believe that he believes that he averted war. He postponed war at best, as he knows.

(5:) I wish to speak of the moral wrongs for which the prime ministers of England and France, Chamberlain and Daladier, will be forever inculpated before history, in addition to the utter betrayal and desertion of Czechoslovakia, to the support of which France's honor was pledged. (6:) As if the triumph of force were not awful enough, the dictatorships are today much, much, much more powerful than they were before the Munich Conference.... (7:) Hitler today is looked upon by his people as a mighty conqueror and prince of peace, and Hitler, thanks to Chamberlain and Daladier, faces his people with enormous prestige and power. And when Hitler chooses to go to war – and he will choose when war is easiest for him – he will go with a larger population and ample resources taken from

Bohemia's plains and Romania's oil wells, so as to make blockade and perhaps defeat of Nazism on any terms impossible....

October 21, 1938 (Friday evening)

Ferdinand M. Isserman, "Will Palestine Be Another Czecho-Slovakia?," Temple Israel, St. Louis, MO. AJA, MS-6, Box 15, Folder 3

(7:) Rumor has it that Hitler and Mussolini have demanded of Chamberlain that Jewish Palestine be sacrificed even as Czecho-Slovakia was sacrificed before they would consent to any peace in Europe. What Hitler and Mussolini want the Jews to do, no one knows. Apparently, they want to destroy and annihilate them from the face of the earth. Not satisfied with not allowing them to live in their own countries, and having heaped upon them torture and execution, the like of which has never been known in the whole tragic and bloody history of the Jew, they are pursuing the Jew with a vengeance in all parts of the world.... For Great Britain to yield to the pressure of Hitler and Mussolini in Palestine would be for Great Britain to permit the crucifixion of the Jewish community in Palestine, would be for Great Britain to strengthen the force of tyranny and dictatorship, would be as tragic for the British Empire as for the Jew.

(8:) Palestine must not become merely a Jewish state. Palestine can become a Switzerland of Asia, with Jew and Arab and Christian living together in peace side by side....

(9:) The forces seeking to destroy Jewish Palestine are the forces which crushed Czecho-Slovakia, are the forces which fear the word of the law from Jerusalem. It will be a sad day for the British empire, a sad day for the Jews of the world, and a sad day for all humanity if these forces are permitted to triumph, and if Palestine becomes another Czecho-Slovakia, the symbol of broken pledges, of man's divorce from God.

Roland Gittelsohn, "Peace with Honor, or Dishonor without Peace: Which is It?," Central Synagogue, Rockville Center, NY. Lee Mandel, *Unlikely Warrior*, pp. 153–54, based on AJA MS-704, Box 53, Folder 5

(153:) Over ten years ago, in his self-written Bible, *Mein Kampf*, Hitler announced to the whole world that he would use any kind of chicanery or deceit to achieve his ends. He said so openly and publicly. So far that's the only promise he *has* kept.... [Quoting from *Mein Kampf*] "The very enormity of a lie contributes to its success. The masses of the people easily succumb to it, as they cannot believe it is possible that anyone should have the shameless audacity to invent such things. Even if the clearest proof of its falsehood be forthcoming, something of the lie will nevertheless stick."...And this is the man Chamberlain would believe. That's the philosophy he would trust! That's the basis of his hope for peace!...

(154:) Hitler couldn't stop with Czechoslovakia even if he wanted to. Hitler's trouble to begin with is the fact that he has too many mouths to feed and not enough food to fill them. Austria and Czechoslovakia gave him more mouths to feed. He took them for one reason only. Because they weren't an end. Because after them come the oil fields of Romania. And after that come the rich grain fields of the Ukraine. And after that comes an about-face and the absolute, resolute crushing of France. This isn't idle prediction or prophecy. This is a plain, honest, literal reading of *Mein Kampf*, by which Hitler has been guided in the past and from which he hasn't any intention of departing in the future.

October 28, 1938 (Friday evening)

FERDINAND M. ISSERMAN, "What Can the American Jews Do Now?," Temple Israel, St. Louis, MO. AJA, MS-6, Box 15, Folder 3[46]

(2:) The first point in the program is to bind up wounds, to relieve the afflicted and render first-aid service. Judaism and the Jews are at the present time engaged in a gargantuan conflict for the preservation of the Jew and the perpetuation of the message for which he has been spokesman. Like every war, this war has its locale and its battlefield in Germany and in central Europe. There, the poisonous gasses of propaganda, the bombs of hatred and of malice, have broken the bodies and shattered the homes and the careers of one to five mil-

46 The preacher notes that this extremely long sermon text was originally intended for Kol Nidre but was postponed because of the Czech disaster.

lion Jews. Many of them literally and figuratively lie groaning on battlefields, waiting for the ambulances to cart them away, for the surgeons to dress their injuries, for kind hands and kinder hearts.

These victims are our brethren, and they suffer not because of any crime they have committed, not because any sin taints them which does not taint the general run of men, but because their fathers and their mothers, and our fathers and our mothers, were descendants of the prophetic and moral geniuses who gave to western civilization its sense of the moral law, its knowledge of right and wrong, and its belief of one God and of one humanity. These war-wounded are our obligation, and we, who live in the secure places of the world, in the promised lands of mankind, in the peaceful areas of democracy, must send agents to succor our warriors in the front line trenches.

The figures of American Jewish generosity (3:) since 1933 do not bespeak the decency and the goodness and the divinity which inheres in American Jews. The per capita gifts for our country in these years have not averaged one dollar per person. We have not realized that we are not confronting an ordinary case of philanthropy, but an unparalleled situation involving masses of men and women....

October 30, 1938 (Sunday)

Israel Mattuck, "The Jews' Present and Future: (i) In the World," Liberal Jewish Synagogue, London. Unpublished

(1:) If anyone had in 1932, before the Hitler rule in Germany, predicted that the position of the Jews in 1938 would be what it actually now is, no one would have believed him and many would have laughed at him as at a madman and at his prediction as the lurid imaginings of one deranged by pessimism. Before the persecution of the Jews began it was unthinkable that it should occur in our civilized world. We did not realise that those who said they would persecute them scorned civilization. After the persecution began, none could believe that it would go to the extremes which it has now reached. Its incredibility shows the measure of its horror.[47]

47 Another example of the strongest language mobilized even before *Kristallnacht* or any hint of mass murder.

The Jews in Germany have been practically destroyed. Of 600,000, 200,000 have managed to remain there [apparently should read: "to leave the country"]. The remaining 400,000 are like shipwrecked men struggling in a hostile sea. Bad as their position was, it has during the past year become terribly worse. The world knows something of the cruel treatment of Jews in the streets and concentration camps. But more cruel still is the progressive and (2:) unrelenting exclusion of the Jews from all opportunities to earn even a humble living. They have only two possibilities of escape: death or emigration.

The number of Jews in this unspeakably sad plight has increased during the year through the annexation by Germany of Austria and Sudetenland. That means another 300,000 or 400,000 Jews under the Nazi rule subject to the Nazi torture. Nazi influence, too, has spread and increased. That must be, in part a least, the explanation for Italy's adoption of antisemitism, euphemistically called "a racial policy." The gravity of the change becomes fully evident when we recall that the position of the Italian Jews was like that of the Jews in England, and is now nearer to the position of the Jews in Germany. A similar change, though not so wide, has occurred in Hungary. The Jews there possessed the full rights of citizens and respect for their rights as human beings. Now those rights have been partly abolished and partly diminished.[48]

(4:) The search for places of immigration for persecuted Jews is a necessary, a most urgent task. It means the saving of lives. It is a task that calls for a vast effort. The Jews and Jewish charity cannot cope with it. Palestine offers no escape or adequate escape. Only the governments and the peoples that are dominated by humanitarian ideals can together accomplish it....

(6:) This general thesis supplies the answer to the particular question about the effect on the Jews of the Munich agreement. It depends on the answer to another question: What will be the effect

48 This refers to a law passed by the Hungarian Parliament on May 24, 1938, limiting employment of Jews in public business firms to twenty percent (Dawidowicz, *The War Against the Jews, 1933–1945*, p. 381; David Cesarani, *Final Solution*, pp. 170–71; Moshe Herczl, *Christianity and the Holocaust of Hungarian Jewry*, pp. 82–90.

of the agreement on the moral life of Europe? If, as a result of the agreement and the consequent enlargement of Germany and its power, there should be a spread to other countries of the ideas and methods of Germany's present rulers, then the outlook for the Jews is frightfully black. The crisis must, however, have another effect. It shows the brutal character of totalitarianism. If, as a result of that lesson, the forces of democracy, freedom and humanity are strengthened, then the prospect for the Jews is full of hope.

November 4, 1938 (Friday evening)

Max Nussbaum, "Slaves of Space" (last sermon delivered in Berlin's Friedenstempel before it was destroyed on *Kristallnacht*). *Gegenwart im Rückblick*, pp. 244–45; complete text of sermon in translation in *From Berlin to Hollywood*, pp. 220–22

(220:) How else is it possible that this great world of ours does not seem to be able to cope with such a tiny problem, comparatively speaking, of a few hundred thousand people [German Jews] in need of a little space where they could live in peace and security? The (221:) world has become the slave of space, the slave of border-lines, of frontiers, and human beings are shipped back and forth between these sacred borders as if the humans were lifeless objects. It is as if this magnificent and advanced world of ours has never been told not to shed human blood, has never heard of families torn asunder, has forgotten how a father loves his child – in short, it acts, this world of ours, as if all elements of humanity, of humaneness, do not exist any longer.

Having to live in this world, we Jews, a timeless as well as a spaceless people, take out our old book, the Bible, lift it up like a mirror to the world, and say, "Look, world, this is the image in which you were made! What have you done with it? Are you still the descendants of Abraham, of Isaac and Jacob, of Moses, Isaiah and Amos, or even of Jesus?" They were just. They loved Mankind. They loved peace. And they have compassion. We Jews have not always lived up to their image, but whenever we strayed, the prophets came and reproached us and reminded us of our responsibility toward humanity and toward the ideals of our heritage. Who preaches this responsibility to the world of to-day? Kant and Nietzsche? Rousseau and Voltaire? Do they impose any ethical commitment on the world?

We modern men are able to sit at a radio and listen to Beethoven and Brahms, to Chopin and Wagner, serenely being broadcast through the space of the (245:) universe and totally unaware of tens of thousands of homeless people down below. Art, music, even the great thinkers and philosophers of the world, have no longer any influence on its morals and ethics. The cord is cut, and no radio, however precise and sensitive, is able to receive or to transmit the cries of children, the souls without compass, the moaning of men between frontiers....

November 10, 1938 (Thursday)

Judah L. Magnes, "Italy and Her Jews," Presidential Address at Opening of a New Term at the Hebrew University, Jerusalem. *In the Perplexity of the Times*, pp. 9–15

(9:) Several days ago, one of our Library workers handed me the leaflet which I hold in my hand. It is an announcement of the University of Bologna in Italy concerning the registration of foreign students there. Across the face of this leaflet the following words are printed in red: "*Gli studenti Ebrei stranieri non possono ottenere l'ammissione alla Università Italiana.*"[49]

(15:) In these days I often feel, and it is doubtless thus with most of us, that I have seen with my own eyes the rise of powerful nations and kingdoms and their downfall – Egypt, Assyria, Babylon, Persia, Greece, Rome – empires as mighty as those of to-day. If Israel is called an historical People it means but this: that the whole history of Israel is alive for us to-day, that our sense of history is made keen and deep by unceasing tragedy, and that we share the life and the sufferings and the hopes of our People through all its generations. We seem to see even now with our own eyes – and our children or

49 "Foreign Jewish students are not permitted to obtain admission to an Italian University."

our children's children will look back upon – the downfall of these empires of to-day, built as they are upon greed, upon the beast in man, upon the hypocrisy of their holy men, these empires that are built upon slavery and the spilling of blood, and upon the torture and torment of human beings.

November 11, 1938 (Friday)

Jacob Shachter, "Remembrance Day," Belfast Synagogue, Northern Ireland. *Ingathering*, pp. 78–83

(79:) The doctrine of brute force is proclaimed as the only rule of national conduct, leading to a creed which denies the nobility of the individual and his over-riding claim to brotherly treatment as a fellow child of God. In this state of moral drift and confusion a great nation has taken advantage of a defenceless minority which had lived among it for many centuries – citizens of the Jewish faith who loved their country and served it with unparalleled loyalty and devotion – and is persecuting it in a manner that to use the word "mediaeval" to describe what is going on would be an insult to the past....

(80:) [T]he theory by which the Germans cover their vicious motives is such which spares neither creed nor age, neither rank nor sex. Its key-note is the blood-cult, in the name of which one of the most loyal, patriotic, and intelligent communities that any country might be proud of is deliberately ruined politically, socially, and economically. Innocence is no protection; weakness is no armour; wisdom affords no escape; old age does not stay the hand that strikes. Nor are professing Jews the subjects of this campaign; the fact that one of the four grandparents was Jewish is sufficient to brand a man as an outcast, to rob him of his possessions, and drive him to penury and despair.

There are many red-letter days engraved in the history of the barbaric Nazi anti-Jew campaign, such as Boycott Saturday of April 1933; the introduction of the Nuremberg Laws in 1935; the mass hooliganism in Vienna. The present savageries, however, dwarf all of them. Sadistic cruelty is being exercised against a whole community which still numbers over half-a-million. Small (81:) wonder that suicides have taken on such proportions. Many who see their whole world shattered at one fell blow, deprived of their means of livelihood, insulted and degraded in every possible way, without hope of a future, put an end to their own lives. It would be superhuman to speak with restraint of the savagery perpetrated by human beings against human beings. On top of it all, the shadows of these events grow darker day by day, owing to the utter helplessness of the sufferers, and the apparent inability of the peoples of the world to intervene. There can be no grimmer record of a damning indictment of civilization . . . [50]

November 16, 1938 (Wednesday, *Busstag* [Day of Repentance] in Germany.)[51]

A.S. Super, Rabbi, Moortown Synagogue, Leeds, England. Address at Protest Meeting at Queens Hotel, Leeds. *JC* November 25, 1938, p. 39; cf. *The Manchester Guardian*, November 17, 1938, p. 14 (headline: "The Protest to Germany")

I would ask everyone here to see to it, in the days ahead, that the lessons of to-day are not forgotten, and that the Jewish people will respond to acts of violence with dignity, a deepening of Jewish spirituality and a determination that civilization will ultimately conquer.

November 18, 1938 (Friday evening)

Julius Gordon, Temple Shaare Emeth, St. Louis, MO. *St. Louis Post-Dispatch*, November 19, 1938, p. 3A

It is apparent that the economic motive rather than spontaneous indignation is the cause of this new barbarism. The penalty of $400,000,000 imposed upon German Jewry has no parallel even in

50 The sermon, delivered on November 11, also contains many anguished comments about the Great War and the total failure of the ideals for which it was fought.

51 For two powerful sermons delivered by German preachers on this day, see Dean G. Stroud, ed., *Preaching in Hitler's Shadow*, pp. 106–14 (Julius von Jon) and 115–26 (Helmut Gollitzer).

the history of indemnities in time of war. The Nazi procedure recalls the actions of pirates in the Middle Ages who used to capture distinguished Jews and hold them as hostages for ransom. But despite all the threats of Nazi kidnappers, they have not succeeded in silencing an outraged world. In the name of thousands of Germans, both inside and outside Germany, who resent this violence and are deeply conscious of the disgrace of their Fatherland, we pray that this once great nation may be restored from savagery to sanity.[52]

Julian Miller, B'nai El Temple, St. Louis, MO. *St. Louis Post-Dispatch*, November 19, 1938, p. 3A

Hitler is a beast who resembles more a vulture than a buzzard. There is no beast created by Almighty God that has ever sunk so low, that has ever been so vicious, that has ever gloried in the slow agonizing death of a group of innocent, harmless, defenseless people as has this thing dwelling temporarily in luxury and security on the mountain top in Germany. The blackest page in history is now being written, and the world stands aghast and dumbfounded that such bestiality, such insanity, such blood-sucking, such body breaking and such a mind-dethroning program can be carried out by anything in human form.

Ferdinand M. Isserman, "Assassination: Not the Way of Judaism," Special Service of Prayer for the Persecuted Peoples of All Groups, Temple Israel, St. Louis, MO. AJA, MS-6, Box 15, Folder 3

(1:) This sacred Sabbath is dedicated and consecrated to the victims of persecution, Christian and Jewish, Catholic and Protestant, who this eve lie physically crushed beneath the boot of tyrants, yet are morally strong because of their faith in God, and their realization that on their side are the decent peoples of the world. I feel that my first words must be of deep gratitude and thanksgiving to the political, intellectual, and religious leaders of America, of all parties, of all

52 Gordon, full-time rabbi of a large St. Louis Reform congregation, published in 1938 an important book on Nazi persecution before *Kristallnacht* with the ironic title, *Pity the Persecutor.*

creeds, of all walks of life, who, in the past week, with one voice, have prophetically denounced the injustice and cruelty, whose aroused indignation became articulate in the statement of the President, and in his recall of the American Ambassador to Germany.... This solidarity of free American citizens in this greatest crisis of Jewish history is like a rainbow of hope arching its way across the darkened skies.[53]

(2:) The catastrophic events in Germany in the past ten days were set off by the desperate act of a desperate youth, who, in assassinating a diplomatic official of the Nazi regime, believed that in this fashion he was taking vengeance upon all Nazis for his own and for his parents' outrageous suffering. This marks the second Nazi to be assassinated by a Jewish youth. The other, William Gustloff, was assassinated by a Yugo-Slavian youth in Switzerland.[54]

That thousands of German Jews and half-Jews and quarter-Jews, Catholics and Protestants, have realized since the Nazi triumph that their lives were worthless, and yet, of all these victims only two have resorted to violence, one of them not even a resident of Germany, is a notable tribute to the heroic caliber and sterling quality of the victims of Nazi tyranny. (3:) [This] indicates also what the German Jews have known: that assassination is not the way of Judaism. Assassination is a resort to violence, to brute force. It ignores the laws of justice.... (4:) For Jews to resort to violence to secure justice would be to deny Judaism, to deny justice, and to deny God....

(6:) That government [Germany] takes cognizance of the mad act of a desperate victim of its injustice, deliberately coolly, indifferent to world opinion, oblivious of the conscience of man, orders vengeance upon hundreds of thousands of human beings in what has been one of the bloodiest massacres in all the annals of man. Nothing has demonstrated before the bar of public opinion, the total lack

---

53 The designation of *Kristallnacht* as "the greatest crisis of Jewish history" is of course hyperbolic with regard to events of the past, and seems poignantly ironic with regard to events of the future. See also the formulation below on p. 6 of the typescript.

54 Gustloff, head of the Foreign Service of the Nazi Party in Switzerland, was assassinated on February 4, 1936 by David Frankfurter, son of a Croatian rabbi (see above, February 16, 1936). Frankfurter was pardoned and released from his Swiss prison sentence in June, 1945.

of decency, of respect, the total unawareness of the values of civilization, the complete abrogation (7:) of the principles of morality and of religion, of the ideals of Christianity of these powerful rulers of eighty-eight million people, as when they visited upon innocent men and women their wrath over the desperate act of a lonely lad. Nothing that the Nazis have done has so clearly proved to the world their incapacity to govern the great German people than the events of the past few days.

Nor must it be said that these riots and mobs arose out of the air and were expressions of popular wrath. The Nazis are all-powerful in Germany.... When, in Switzerland, Gustloff was assassinated, the Nazis held their people in check. Why then and not now?... (8:) What the Germans have been doing retail for five years, they have done wholesale in one week. The suffering is unchanged. It has only multiplied ten thousand times fold....

November 19, 1938 (Saturday)

Tobias (Tuviah) Geffen, "*Derush leFarashat Ḥayyei Sarah 5699*, at the Time of the Great Destruction of the Jews in Germany at the Hands of the Evil Oppressor, Hitler, May his name and his Memory be Blotted Out," Congregation Shearith Yisrael, Atlanta, GA. *Naḥalat Yosef*, pp. 60–64; see Complete Sermons

November 20, 1938 (Sunday): Special Services of Prayer and Intercession on behalf of Jews of Germany throughout UK. *JC*, "Prayer and Intercession," November 25, p. 27

Joseph H. Hertz (*JC* summary):

The destruction of the Synagogues, the defilement of the sacred Scrolls of the Law, should make every Jewish heart bleed. They must ask with the prophet, "Is there no balm in Gilead? Is there no physician there?" (Jer. 8:22). It was some comfort to feel that good men and true were everywhere asking this question and were seriously grappling with the problem. In England, America, Holland, and all free countries, they had evidence that the human conscience was not dead. English public opinion had never been more unanimous or more sincere than had that shown during the past ten days.

Alexander Altmann, Manchester, England. Address delivered Sunday evening, following a Day of Fasting and Prayer, in articles from *The Manchester Guardian*, November 21, 1938, p. 13, and *Daily Express*, November 21. University College London Altmann Archives

A time of sorrow incomparable in its tragedy has come upon us. German Jewry, the most cultured, the most wealthy, the best organized, the proudest Jewry in the world, has perished; its synagogues are burned down, its homes destroyed, even the orphanages and the homes of rest for the aged and the infirm have been wrecked. For them there was yesterday no Sabbath. A new Jeremiah must needs arise to deplore the immensity of the tragedy.

The world will only help us if we do our duty. Every Jew must make sacrifices for our people. We must unite every resource and use all our strength to create Jewish homes in Palestine and overseas. We must regard it as a sacred duty to give help to the individual sufferers. Every one of you can do something on behalf of these tormented people. In Holland 2,000 children have been invited into Jewish families. It is an example we in Manchester must follow - to throw open our homes to these poor children. There must be no Jewish home which has not helped in some way.

Leslie Edgar, at Special Service, Liberal Jewish Synagogue, London. *The Manchester Guardian*, November 21, 1938, quoted in Ruth Levitt, ed., *Pogrom, November 1938: Testimonies from "Kristallnacht,"* pp. 705–6[55]

No words can adequately express the gratitude of us Jews for the sympathy shown us during the present German persecution.... In all this we have seen once again the power of the Christian spirit in England, the love of humanity, of justice and tolerance so characteristic of our country. There is a widespread realization that not only the fate of half a million Germans is at stake but the whole future of civilized standards in the western world. England has already

55 Cited with permission of the publisher, Souvenir Press, Ltd.

shown to the Jews her traditional and generous hospitality. But if the onslaught against human rights is to be effectively answered, some even greater gesture to the world is needed. Our hopes are pinned to England, and our fervent appeal is addressed to her as a nation of vast resources and great influence who could give the lead to others and find in one of the wide spaces of the British Empire a home for our persecuted brothers.

Abraham Cohen, Birmingham Hebrew Congregation, Birmingham, England. *JC*, November 25, 1938, p. 27

One feature of the pogrom was significant. Hitherto, the attack had been racial. But the outstanding incident of the reprisals had been the burning and demolition of Synagogues, which indicated that the aim of the Nazis was the extirpation of Jewry root and branch. There could be no other solution than the evacuation of all the refugees from Germany.

Rev. A.S. Super of Leeds, England, preaching at Princes Row Synagogue in Liverpool. *JC*, November 25, 1938, p. 27

To-day men realise that they must stand up for righteousness or perish. Even though the price for this stand be unparalleled suffering for the Jews, if the reawakening be a real one, we shall say that the price will not have been too high.

Salis Daiches, Edinburgh Hebrew Congregation, Scotland. *The Scotsman*, Monday, September 21, 1938, p. 9, entitled JEWS IN GERMANY: Edinburgh Rabbi's Sermon: MANY CHRISTIANS PRESENT[56]

A new record has been created in the heart of Europe in the display of barbarism and savagery by those who constituted the Government of the land towards the citizens of their own country. There is no parallel in modern history for the cruel and cowardly attack of the

56 The newspaper account reports that "The congregation, which numbered about 900 people, included many Christian sympathisers, including several ministers of Edinburgh churches."

rulers of present-day Germany on its Jewish citizens, in defiance of all laws and principles and of the outraged sentiments of the civilized world. . . .

Those rulers concealed neither their motives nor their aim. Their motives were hatred and greed, and their aim was the infliction of endless pain and misery on helpless and defenceless people. But why have they now begun to add acts of sacrilege to deeds of cruelty? Why have they burnt the synagogues and destroyed the Scrolls of the Law, with everything appertaining to them? Do they think that by burning the manuscripts of the Holy Writ they have destroyed the words of the divine law which said, "Thou shalt not murder" (Exod. 20:13), "Thou shalt not hate thy brother in thy heart" (Lev. 10:17), or "Thou shalt love thy neighbour as thyself" (Lev. 19:18)? Do they think that they might rob peaceful citizens of their possessions, their livelihood, their human dignity, and at the same time compel all who believe in God and His law to keep silence and condone the outrage?

[Regarding the current discussions of rescuing the German Jews and finding them havens of refuge:] Lives are being lost and precious human material is being wasted. If a ship is wrecked at our shores, do the men in charge of the lifeboats spend their time deliberating and discussing as to who should go first to the rescue of the drowning, or as to how shelter and food could be found for those to be saved?[57]

Day of Mourning Declared by Canadian Jewish Congress[58]

Harry Joshua Stern, "Lamentations," Temple Emanu-El, Montreal. *Jewish Spirit Triumphant*, 63–66

---

57 The newspaper article reported that Daiches concluded with a strong appeal to the members of his own community to offer hospitality to refugees, especially to children, and to contribute generously to the various funds that have been created to render help to those who escape from the German furnace.

58 In Montreal, a mass meeting was held in a venue far from the Jewish area, in order to accentuate its universal character. "The *Chronicle*, with a front-page photograph of the meeting, illustrated the Christian character of the rally, as non-Jews dominated the platform." "Montreal Voices Horror at Plight of German Jews," *JC* November 25, 1938, headlines, in Max Beer, "The Montreal Jewish Community and the Holocaust," *Current Psychology*, 2007.

(63:) Never have I felt more deeply the grief of heart and mind which inspired these Jeremiads [in *Eicha*] as I have during these past few days of Nazi plunder and sheer barbarism. Were Jeremiah with us today, I am certain that, despite his fiery tongue and gift of oratory, he would be unable to find words adequately to express the present-day martyrdom of the Jew.[59]

This indeed is not a meeting of protest against Germany. It is rather a meeting of lamentations. Five years ago when Hitler assumed power we protested. Then at a vast meeting at the Mount Royal Arena I uttered a warning as to the spread of the Nazi (64:) pestilence and its threat to civilization. There were those among us then who charged me with a lack of diplomacy in having spoken thus in condemnation of the Caesarism of the Third Reich.... But five years have now come and gone and so much of the world has tragically become Nazified. We verily behold, as Jeremiah of old, the destruction of the Temple, the temple of civilization. Gradually our civilization is slipping back into barbarism; gradually but surely the lamps of civilization are being extinguished.

(65–66:) [Mentions Cardinal Faulhaber, Cardinal Innitzer, Pastor Niemöller in prison] and hundreds of pastors and priests are in concentration camps. Verily, Nazism wages war against Christianity as well as Judaism.

Would that what some of us foresaw five years ago had not come to pass! But there it is. And I do not wish to play the role of prophet. However, I foresee darker, still darker days ahead for us. Jews and Christians are destined to suffer together for faith and truth, for democracy and freedom. Together they will be forced to walk the "via dolorosa".... But through our trials and tribulations we shall await the new dawn and work for that day when all men shall come to recognize and live by the ancient injunction: "Thou shalt love thy neighbor as thyself" (Lev. 19:18).

---

59 Once again the irony in retrospect: the preacher using the strongest possible language for events that would seem relatively moderate in light of the future realities.

Maurice N. Eisendrath, "World Without Jews," Holy Blossom Temple, Toronto. *Holy Blossom Pulpit*, VIII, 1 (1938–1939); cf. *The Never Failing Stream*, pp. 306–37[60]

(2:) For five years now the world, with a few notable exceptions here and there, has stood silently by while the Nazis have driven steadily and determinedly toward this [the "humane extirpation of the Jew"], the foremost goal of the national policy; while they have striven to make life so utterly intolerable for the Jewish population that the day will not be long delayed when they will drive their last Jew across their frontier. Already certain German towns have achieved this purpose and riotous celebrations have been held at the limits of many a Nazi village when, with cheers of derision and contumely, their last Jew has been sent, homeless and helpless, upon his way. But the process of liquidation has taken too long to glut the bloodthirsty appetites of the more radical of the Nazis who have risen (3:) steadily to the leadership of the party and who today, aided and abetted no little by the events of the past few weeks, are now in complete control of the government of the land.

And in the sight of these "gangsters" of the Nazi party, the "*humane*" extirpation of the Jews was taking too long; humane, let us remember, being defined in the newly coined lingo of the Nazis, as that process which enabled them slowly to starve an entire people to death rather than to end their misery more quickly by driving them to suicide, booting them over the frontier, or actually bashing out their brains. But now these radicals in the party – Goebbels, Rosenberg, Ribbentrop, Himmler, Streicher and the rest – for expediency's sake have previously been kept somewhat in leash, due to the fear on the part of the more cautious and conservative Nazis of the outside world, have recently been completely vindicated by the fulfilment of their prophecy that Hitler could out-bluff the world at Munich, and it is they who are now exclusively in the Nazi saddle. Away, therefore, with such weak and cowardly and decadent phrases as the "*humane*

60 The text in *The Never Failing Stream* appears to have been edited, with occasionally significant differences; I have used the earlier publication as closer to the sermon that was actually delivered.

extirpation of the Jew."[61] Let murder and madness and massacres be unconfined, that these noble Aryan lords and masters of creation may no longer be compelled to stomach the sight of even a single Jew within the borders of the Reich.

Morris S. Lazaron, Address at "Service of Intercession," Baltimore Hebrew Congregation, Baltimore, MD. AJA MS-71, Box 26, Folder 1

(1:) The Nazi regime began by burning the Reichstag. The burning of the synagogues is the beginning of its end.[62] And it is not by chance that the Reichstag was burned first, nor by chance that houses dedicated to the worship of God should be the latest victims. The Reichstag building symbolized man's acknowledgment of law.... It now denies the law of God.... It is not by chance that Innitzer and Faulhaber, kneeling in their cathedrals, were assailed by the mob. It is not by chance that consecrated men of God have been ridiculed and vilified and held up to scorn. It is not by chance that Niemöller, Protestant leader, still languishes in prison together with several hundred of the pastors of the Confessional Church.... These things are basic elements of a deliberate planned effort to destroy the spiritual foundation of Western civilization....

(3:) I saw a picture of the gutted ruins of the Fasanenstrasse Synagogue in Berlin, just off the fashionable Kurfürstendamm, on whose pulpit I have stood, a magnificent structure as beautiful as the most beautiful synagogue here, filled with the warmth of Jewish symbolism in inlaid mosaics. There it stands, its silent, blackened walls. What do they say to you and me? They say to us, those upthrusted walls of mighty stone: "We are the living testimony of that which cannot be killed in the Jew. Enemies may deprive us of our right to work, may take from under our feet any opportunity for livelihood, may drive us from one end of the world to the other, but

61 On this phrase, see Isserman, May 16, 1934 above, with footnote.

62 Needless to say, a rather ironically overly optimistic assertion. The idea apparently expressed here that the burning of the Reichstag was actually perpetrated by the Nazis in order to justify the suspension of civil liberties is not generally accepted. See Richard Evans, *The Coming of the Third Reich*, pp. 328–37.

here we stand lifting our proud strength to high heaven, symbol of our deathless faith in the Living God." Aye, that and that alone gives Jewish life strength and dignity. That is why you are here today – not because you fear, not only because you have sympathy with our stricken fellow Jews and fellow Christians, but because something deep within your mind and heart, something you could not put into words, drove you here to the place consecrated to the highest you know and the noblest you can conceive, which you felt challenged and endangered by the evil and malignant forces that in the world. That is why you are here.

November 21, 1938 (Monday)

JACOB KAPLAN, "The Burning of Synagogues in Germany" (*L'incendie des synagogues en Allemagne*), Speech at meeting organized by Ligue international contre le racisme et l'antisémitisme (LICRA), Salle de la Mutualité, Paris. *Les Temps d'épreuve*, pp. 69–72, translated by MS

(70:) Nazism has not however, changed its true countenance. If it presents itself in all its horror at the end of the year 1938, no longer pretending with the game it has played up to now out of fear of striking the universal conscience too violently, it is because today it imagines that it can prevail. It believes only in force. It boasts that through violence it can establish an empire to which, in its foolish arrogance, it assigns a period of a thousand years.... (71:) What we can concede to the master of the Third Reich is that, setting aside his empire, his own memory may indeed remain for a thousand years and more, but it will be an abhorrent memory, like that of Nero for Christians, and like that of Haman for Jews.

These are dark days, even darker than in the past, that arise over Germany. With the burning of synagogues, racism enters a new phase in its development. Just as the first attacks against Jews were the prelude to persecution that eventually befell all religious believers, so does the burning of synagogues herald an era of anxiety not only for us, but for all human beings.

Actually, the fate of the Jews is the most appalling. Stripped of their rights, of their belongings, set outside the law, at the mercy of whoever comes by, there is only a single step to hurdle, only one, for the program of racism to be actualized in full: extermination by violence or by death through starvation. It is impossible that the world, which knows this, will not intervene in time [to prevent it].

That is why, in the name of God, Creator and (72:) Father of all human beings, I implore the nations of the world to open their gates to allow the wretched, who have committed no crime other than not belonging to the Aryan race, to escape this cruel fate that awaits them....

November 24, 1938 (Thanksgiving Day)

Edward N. Calisch, "The Conscience of America," Address delivered at the First Baptist Church, Richmond, VA, at the Union Thanksgiving Service of the First Baptist Church and Beth Ahabah Synagogue. Edith Calish, *Three Score and Twenty*, pp. 149–54

(152:) Just because of our relative isolation from the scenes of tyrannical persecution, the voice of America's protest is clearer and the more potent. It is not clouded by the shadow of selfishness, nor weakened by the threat of fear. It is the conscience of America, speaking through the voice and action of its humanitarian president, and overwhelmingly through the words of its great leaders in all walks of life and its untrammeled press. It is the conscience of America that will not permit to go unrebuked conduct that shames humanity itself, that will not be silent when the very principles of democracy are challenged by the madness of totalitarian governments. It is the conscience of America that protests in no uncertain tones against the brutal persecution of defenseless minorities, against the savage butchery of the concentration camps, and the searing of the souls of little children by heartless (153:) humiliation. We thank God to-day for the conscience of America that speaks out in behalf of tortured humanity and in defense of human brotherhood....

November 25, 1938 (Friday evening)

Leo M. Franklin, "After Germany: What?," Temple Beth-El, Detroit,

MI. Unpublished, Rabbi Leo Morris Franklin Archives, now at AJA, MS-246, Text 1405

(1:) The conscience of civilized peoples that seemed to have been dormant suddenly awakened, and from every quarter came indignant protests against the unrestrained activities of a madman.... Perhaps it was natural in the hour when cruelty and inhumanity seemed to have reached its apex, so that all the horrible butchery and barbarism of five years paled into insignificance before the new onslaught of terror, that the indignation of decent people should have burst its bounds and have found expression in emotional utterances the wisdom of which was not uniformly well considered. As a result, during these past weeks and days many things, wise and unwise, have been done and many words, both sagacious and foolish, have been spoken. This is only natural and we can well forgive those who in their desire to express their sympathy with a suffering people have allowed their sentiment to run away with their reason. On the other hand, there have been certain utterances which cannot be so easily condoned.[63]

(2:) Some of the most pernicious things in literature that have been written against the Jew have cloaked themselves in the cloak of friendliness and have contained just enough truth to hide their fundamental falsity.[64]

(7:) If you have followed the press reports, even of the last few days, you will realize that the terror, instead of abating, has become intensified and that there is no device which the distorted minds of perverts can conceive which is not being considered by the "beast of Berlin."[65] The latest report, as you know, has to do with the vengeance that is being directed against Britain for its proposal to settle

63 Alluding apparently to something that listeners would probably have recognized: possibly remarks of Father Coughlin?

64 Franklin proceeds to mention Chamberlain's *Foundations of the Nineteenth Century* and Sombart's *The Jews in Modern Capitalism*; (3:) criticizing those who take statements out of context, or cite incomplete phrases, to make them say "what they know the writers never meant to have them say" (including from Jewish newspapers of eighteen–twenty years ago). He describes these attacks as an effort to counteract "the magnificent outpouring of sympathy and understanding on the part of Christians in our time of trouble."

65 It is of course extremely unlikely that the Nazi leadership was at this time considering

large numbers of Jews in [Tanganyika] formerly a German province, but which was ceded to England in the post-war settlement.[66] Rather than have that occur, the Jews still remaining in Germany will be horded into ghettos that in filth and degradation will outrival (8:) those of the Middle Ages. Thousands of Jews, huddled together in them will be literally starved out and, according to the Germans who show their utter lack of ability to understand the character of the Jew, they will be compelled to resort to criminal methods in order to maintain themselves alive and then, they will be dealt with – so runs the report – as criminals in Germany are dealt with – by fire and sword. The very threat issuing this week from authorized spokesmen in Germany indicates, as well as anything else, the depth of degradation to which this blood-thirsty people has sunken.

(10:) Britain, I believe I dare say it – repentant for her weakness which made the Munich Pact a possibility – and France, realizing the error of her ways, will, to the extent of their powers, see to it that the Jew will not be (11:) utterly crushed under the heavy heel of European dictatorship....

Thus, my people, in these days when the heart of every Jew bleeds for his people – in these days when the conscience of every decent man and woman of whatsoever faith or creed is stirred to its depths by the turn-back of civilization under the dictatorships that have betrayed humanity, we dare still look forward to a day of cultural creativity on the part of the Jew and to believe that neither pogrom nor robbery, nor murder, nor expatriation, nor fire, nor sword, which are the weapons with which Nazism fights its battle, will prevail against the constructive tools of civilization which shall be wielded, even with more determination than before by the democracies of

---

the deportation of German and Polish Jews to death camps where they would be sent upon arrival to gas chambers.

66 See JTA, November 21, 1938, under headline, "Report Britain to Open Tanganyika to Refugees." A review of the Parliamentary debate, including the Prime Minister's suggestion of Tanganyika as a potential haven for refugees, can be found in *JC*, November 25, 1938, p. 7. The typescript has a blank space where I have added [Tanganyika], suggesting that it may have been produced from a stenographic transcription of the sermon, not typed by the preacher himself. Other such blanks may have resulted from the preacher's use of a Hebrew term.

the world. There will still be Hitlers but they shall fulminate in vain against the forces of righteousness.

Ferdinand M. Isserman, "My Three Visits to Nazi Germany," Temple Israel, St. Louis, MO. AJA, MS-6, Box 15, Folder 3

(10:) What has been done to the Jews of Germany need not be restated here. They are being destroyed... It is the only plank in the Nazi platform which the government has kept... But this week, the magazine *Der Schwarzer Korps* stated that the Jews of Germany will be destroyed by fire and sword unless they migrate.[67] ... Today, the Nazis are using the Jews as a means of silencing domestic opposition, and are confiscating their property as one way of meeting their impossible armament bills.

(14:) As I think of Nazi Germany, I think of a fierce giant which has risen like a prehistoric man, is sharpening its dagger and pressing it to the heart of civilization, unconcerned about moral principles. As I think of the US of A, I think of the Statue of Liberty, a beautiful woman, kindly, hospitable, and generous, holding in her hand the torch of liberty and enlightenment, not for one people, but for all people. Thank God for our democracy!

November 27, 1938 (Sunday)

Samuel H. Goldenson, "What Have the Jews to be Thankful For?," Temple Emanu-El, New York. AJA, MS-81, Box 2, Folder 4

(2:) We are living in one of the darkest periods of human history. The persecution of men is nothing new. The persecution of the Jewish people is certainly nothing new. But there is something new about the persecution of our day and the new quality is most unsettling and threatening. The persecution of our day has a double quality. One is its extreme intensity. It is a persecution that does not seem to let up. It is a persecution completely deliberate and cold-blooded, as cold-blooded as genuine hatred can be.... It is not the persecution of spontaneity, as one of the leaders of the German regime wanted

67 Cf. the passages from this newspaper cited by Martin Gilbert, *Kristallnacht*, p. 171.

to (3:) make out.[68] It is the persecution of downright, complete deliberateness coming out of the intensity of a passion of hatred that knows no satisfaction. It is unlimited.... It pursues Jews to the end of the earth by all those hateful methods.

But there is another reality in the persecution of this day, and that is that it moves with scientific organization and precision....

Samuel Daiches, "The Present Jewish Tragedy: A Message of Hope," Presidential Address for B'nai B'rith, First Lodge of England, London. Pamphlet published 1939

(4:) The great, cultured, and prosperous Jewish Community in Germany has been laid in the dust... Freedom and righteousness have hidden their heads. The sky is dark, hopes are vanishing, and the heart is heavy.

Where can one find the words, with which to say what one feels, with which to describe the present human distress? "Human distress" might be a general description of the state of things in the world at the present time. The greatest human distress is to be found in Germany. Under Nazi rule forces of hatred and violence have been let loose in that land as they have never been known before in the recorded history of the human race – not in war, but in peace; not against (5:) enemies, but against parts of its own population. Human beings have become wild beasts in the undisguised meaning of these two words. Ordinary wild beasts can only kill their prey, and the Nazi wild beasts think out and devise devilish plans how to persecute and torture their victims, apart from killing many of them. And their victims are, in the first instance, hundreds of thousands of Jewish men and women, who have enriched the life of the German people.

Who could read the reports of the terrible happenings in the German concentration camps during the last fortnight without a shudder, without feeling that man has been degraded, that human

68 This emphasis on spontaneous righteous anger within the German people was the Nazi propaganda explanation of *Kristallnacht*; see Richard Evans, *The Third Reich in Power*, pp. 591–92.

beings have sunk to the lowest depths of depravity and cruelty?[69] And to their cruelties the Nazi rulers add lies, perverse falsifications of facts, and brutal absurdities. What has happened in Germany during the last two or three weeks has staggered the world, has staggered the conscience of humanity. And when you read the speeches of the Minister for Propaganda, Joseph Goebbels, in which he pretends to try to justify the devilish acts of the Nazi government you feel that never before has hell sent forth such a miscreant to plague the world. Every one of the Nazi leaders is a cruel, brutal gangster. And these cruel, brutal gangsters are inflicting a terrible punishment upon the Jews and upon humanity. They have substituted violence for right. They are turning their country into a jungle, and they would like to turn the whole world into a jungle. The deeds of their wickedness cry to heaven.

What can we do?... The Governments of the West European countries should allow the German Jews to come to their countries and to stay there for six or twelve months, until room can be found for them in lands overseas. Half-a-million (6:) are drowning and call frantically for help, and the captains of the seaworthy ships on the ocean of life, of the life of the nations, must cast anchor and take the drowning men, women, and children on board. Release from the concentration camp, often from torture and death, may depend now upon a *visa* to another country....

We must also help to preserve the moral basis of the world. We must not tire to call out "Violence, violence!", and we must not weaken in our protestations against the wicked deeds of the evildoers. We must help to keep the conscience of humanity alive. Great Britain and the United States have spoken out like the great moral nations, and we are grateful, grateful in seeing the moral strength of these nations. The debate in the House of Commons last Monday was also an event with which to be gratified.[70]

---

69 See, for example, the *JC* article published on November 25, 1938 under the subheadline, "Inhuman Torture of the Aged, the Sick and the Children."

70 The debate occurred on Monday November 21, 1938, following a large delegation of Jewish and non-Jewish groups working on behalf of refugees; one of the results of

(8:) The sky is dark, hopes are vanishing, the heart is heavy. But new light must come, new hope, and a new, a comforted heart. As of old, Israel must bring it about. We must stand in our watch-tower, undismayed and full of faith. And when out of the wilderness a voice calls, "Watchman, what of the night? Watchman what of the night?," the watchman answers, "The morning cometh, and also the light" (Isa. 21:11–12)....[71]

December 1, 1938 (Thursday)

Joseph H. Hertz, "National Protest against Nazi Persecution," Albert Hall, London. *Early and Late*, pp. 58–60.

(58:) As to the cause that has brought us together to-night, it is indeed a saddening one to every believer in moral progress. We are appalled at the ferocity displayed in the Nazi drive against a helpless minority, at the studied atrocity of this harrying of an entire population, at the cowardly delight in its frenzied derision and merciless spoliation. The resultant mass misery of 500,000 men and women, unceasingly being subjected to a state-directed torture, constitutes at once a crime against humanity and an international perplexity.

And this orgy of sadism is accompanied by an orgy of sacrilege; three weeks ago, 581 synagogues were wholly or partially destroyed, 181 of them bombed, in the course of one day. Nazism is a persecuting paganism, and the determined enemy of every form of traditional Religion. The souls of German children are poisoned by a new heathenism, hardening the heart and petrifying the feelings. They are bidden blindly to bow down to a fetish – the State deified, with its blood-cult, war-cult, hate-cult. Nazism is now more and more (59:) seen in its true light, as "the negation of God erected into a system."[72]

Now as to murder, every Jew repudiates with abhorrence the stupid and abominable crime of the distracted youth in Paris; but

---

the debate would be the development of the *Kindertransport* program. For details, see http://hansard.millbanksystems.com/sittings/1938/nov/21.

71 The correct quotation for the watchman's reply is "Morning cometh, and also the *night*"; Daiches substituted the more optimistic word for his conclusion.

72 Hertz cites here what was then a fairly well-known statement by William Gladstone.

have not the Nazi leaders for years been extolling the assassins of Rathenau to the skies, and are they not themselves responsible for the loathsome murder of Dr. Dollfuss?[73]

But there is something that is even more appalling in this tragedy than Nazi hypocrisy, sacrilege, and sadism: and that is, *our* helplessness to provide a comprehensive remedy for the injustice and inhumanity; the consciousness of our impotence effectively to deal with the immeasurable suffering consequent upon that injustice and inhumanity.

(60:) If the recent German pogrom is for all time a memorial of burning human shame, may our reactions towards that outburst of savagery remain a luminous milestone in the annals of this age, of what has been done by British men and women to wipe out the memory of that burning human shame.

December 2, 1938 (Friday evening)

Ferdinand M. Isserman, "Should Anti-Semitism Lead Jews to Avoid Parenthood?," Temple Israel, St. Louis, MO. AJA, MS-6, Box 15, Folio 3

(1:) The terribleness of the tragedy to the Jews of Germany, which cannot be fully imagined, the extent of which it is difficult to ascertain because of rigid censorship, has, of course, cast a pall of gloom over Jewish life in America and throughout the world.... Physically, Germany is stronger than ever. Its attitude to the Jews which concealed a camouflage at first is now revealed to the world in all its brutal nudity. Exile as paupers, starvation, or death are the choices for the Jews of Germany. But not satisfied with destroying the Jews of Germany, the Nazi government with all its power and its influence is determined to mitigate its own sins by inducing other states to adopt its anti-semitic policies.

(3:) For Jews to refuse to bear children would be to plead guilty

---

73 These two events would have been widely known by listeners. Walther Rathenau, a German-Jewish statesman serving in the Weimar Republic as Foreign Minister, was assassinated on June 24, 1922. Engelbert Dollfuss, an Austrian statesman serving as Chancellor who banned the Austrian Nazi Party, was assassinated by Austrian Nazis on July 25, 1934.

to the accusations hurled against them, would be to affirm the falsehoods and the lies and misrepresentations of anti-semitism.... (5:) If Jews would determine to end the Jewish group, they would be betraying these decent men and women in all nations who sympathize with Jewish suffering. They would be pronouncing a doom upon all mankind in the future. They would also be denying hope of freedom to the millions of human beings oppressed by dictators and tyrants in all parts of the world who suffer almost as much as the Jews of Germany.

December 4, 1938 (Sunday)

Alexander Altmann, Address given at Induction Ceremony, led by Chief Rabbi Hertz, as Communal Rabbi of Manchester, England. *The Manchester Guardian*, December 5, 1938, p. 13. University College London Altmann Archives

Our history proves that something very great will arise from our sorrows. With our German brethren the whole of Israel suffers and the whole civilized world suffers – perhaps God Himself suffers.

December 16, 1938 (Friday evening)

Solomon Goldman, "From Warsaw to Vienna," Congregation Anshe Emet, Chicago, IL. AJA MS-203, Box 22, Folder 11

(4:) In Germany, it is a fight to the finish. Here it is a people that means our end; they want to destroy us – not only in Germany but wherever we are to be found the world over. They are spending millions of marks in the United States, in the Near-East, in Hungary, in Romania, in Poland, in England, all over the world. It is a fight to the finish, and that is why, friends, as hard as it is going to be, I personally – not knowing what other Jewish leaders will resolve to do – will oppose the giving of one cent of our money to Germany.... (5:) And so, because of this fight to the finish, the war of Germany on the Jews of the world, we have forgotten what is going on in Poland....[74]

74 Goldman had recently returned from a visit to Poland in November.

(6:) In the city of Warsaw I saw the worst. In the Jewish streets, in the Jewish ghettos of Warsaw, I saw hundreds.[75] Not just a handful of people but nearly a thousand, not that, about a million and a half people [...].[76] I stood before those Jews and I asked myself, "Are we of the same people? Of the same human race? How can we bear their misery?"

They don't live in homes. They live like rats in holes. I didn't go into a basement on stairs, I jumped. There were no stairs. I jumped into a cellar and when I came into the cellar, I saw an opening. Dark on each side of the opening, just like a cave, there were holes. In those holes, my brothers and sisters lived. The "rich" Jews. The "communists" who are planning the overthrow of mankind. Those rats are planning the overthrow of mankind....

(7:) If the Jew has a home, a house of his own, which is hardly anything that we would consider here to be a house, the Polish commissioner of the town or village may decide that he wanted the Jew's home to be torn down.... Another Jewish family equally poor will take them in and they will suffer that misery together.

Now the economic poverty of the Jews in Poland is aggravated by political anti-Semites. The Poles have forced the Jew out.... Industry after industry developed in Poland within the last two or three hundred years by Jews have been taken over by the government, and the Poles are now in control of these industries. It is not done as brutally as in Germany, but you have the same result....

In the high schools and the colleges of the country the Jew's lot is the worst. I have told you one time about the young men and (8:) young women standing at the lectures. Just imagine what that involves....

There are many cafes in Poland where a Jew dare not enter; benches the Jew dare not sit on. Of course the headline is Germany. Nothing ever happens in Poland.... The idea is to force the Jews

75 "Ghettos" here is used metaphorically, as the official ghetto of Warsaw was still several years in the future, under German occupation.

76 The text of this sermon does not appear to be a text written in advance by the preacher, but is more likely a stenographic transcription, in which errors either in the speaking or in the stenography were included without change.

out, to get what they created, to retain their possession. That is the difference between the civilized 20th century and the so-called dark middle ages! . . .

(10:) But friends, in that Poland I found Jewish life organized. The Jew is firm in his conviction that he is . . . to remain. I found schools, yeshivas, a literature created by Polish Jews in Polish, in Yiddish, in Hebrew. I found venerable rabbis and distinguished poets and countless journalists. Skillful chemists, physics instructors going about their work, and I attended some of their meetings. I heard their singing, saw the dances of the younger generation of the HIAS with so much vim, with such intensity. . . . I think that the boys and girls of Poland, in the intensity of their dances and songs were forgetting their misery, and they went about maintaining an organized life in Poland. . . .

Ferdinand M. Isserman, "How Shall Jews Defend Themselves? A Chanukah Sermon," Temple Israel, St. Louis, MO. AJA, MS-6, Box 15, Folder 3

(1:) History repeats itself. . . . Never was I so keenly aware of the truth of this proverb than when reading in the past week, in the first Book of the Maccabees, the story of the political maneuvers of Antiochus Epiphanes which led him first to incorporate Palestine into his realm, and second to establish within it a totalitarian rule, which meant the end of the Jewish religion, the destruction of biblical literature, and the slogging up of one of the great streams of human inspiration which had just begun to flow over the soil of Palestine and upon the soul of humanity. . . . (2:) Again we see history repeating itself in modern Germany. . . . (3:) There are many in Germany out of sympathy with the totalitarian philosophy of the Nazi regime. There are Catholics and Protestants who still recognize that they must take their orders not from the state but from God. . . .

December 17, 1938 (Saturday, *VaYeishev*)

Leo Jung, "The Dream of a German-Jewish Child," The Jewish Center, New York. *Crumbs and Character*, pp. 173–79

(176:) A few weeks ago at midnight, the agents of the Gestapo, the

German equivalent of the Russian Ogpu, of the henchmen of the Inquisition, knocked barbarously at the gate of the home, took the father away, and not a word has been heard from him since. His wife, his children live in frightful terror. Perchance, God forbid, his may be the fate of the neighbor or the Jewish doctor in the next street who was seized by Hitler's fiendish brutes on Monday to be returned on Friday in a leaden coffin with a note attached, "*Oeffnen Verboten*" [Opening is Forbidden]. During the day, young Joseph or Heinz or Alfred lives in a perpetual state of paralyzing fear, before the sadist refinement of Nazi cruelty. The park, the swimming pool, play in the street, are forbidden to him. Children of his age taunt him obscenely. His steps are dogged by wicked men in uniform.... It is the valley of the shadow of death in which these victims of the Greater Germany are walking every day.

But at night...a merciful dream, as if by magic power, banishes all the ghastly scene from his soul.... The word is America, and the (177:) magic formula is "Affidavit, adoption, or being received for one, two, or three years in the home of his people in the land of liberty...."

These dreams you may make true.... Our selfishness, our indifference to human woe, the evil unconcern of the unconcerned, stand like (178:) a wall between ourselves and our Father in Heaven.... I beg you for more affidavits.[77] They mean the difference between Concentration Camps and a chance for peaceful labor, between soul-destroying poverty and the working out of one's economic salvation. I appeal to you to open wide your arms, and to make your hands ready to welcome to your homes those children of our own across the sea. (179:) "Affidavit," "Adoption," or "fostering of children" are words of salvation to our own beyond the pale of civilization.... I

77 On the importance of affidavits, see Jung, above, June 5, 1938, and footnote. In an interview conducted in July 1984, Jung cited as the major success in his rescue efforts during the Holocaust the securing of a total of 1,176 affidavits certifying that immigrants would not become "a public charge"; it was estimated that these documents enabled 9,000 European (mainly German) Jews to find refuge in the United States. Monty Penkower, "Jewish Cataclysm and Jewish Restoration," pp. 238 and 261 n.1; Penkower makes no mention of the sermons.

appeal to you, my family, the men and women of the Jewish Center, who have never failed in any great cause....

December 18, 1938 (Sunday during Hanukkah)

Solomon B. Freehof, "What to Fight For," Rodef Shalom Congregation, Pittsburgh, PA. "To the American Jews: A Series of Three Addresses." *Rodef Shalom Pulpit*, New Series, vol. 4, no. 5, pp. 3–15

(3:) We Jews are on the defensive. Why should we not be? We are being attacked on all sides. Slanders are disseminated against us and we have the wearisome task of answering them. Great Jewish communities are being disintegrated under the hammer blows of tyranny. We must find means of "picking up the pieces." We are in a position in the modern world where we must use up all our energies in self-protection.

(4:) [Points to active, dynamic response of Maccabees as model:] Whenever Hanukkah comes and we think of the Maccabean valor we feel a little bit ashamed of the fact that we have gotten to be so timorous, that life has made us so meek and apologetic. [Also Catholic Church in America: target of slanders.]

(5:) But in recent years the Catholic Church, conscious of its growing strength, has wisely abandoned the mood of the defensive and begun actively to attack certain evils in American life.

(8:) I for one am suspicious of any attack on the evil of Communism which is singularly blind to the evil of Fascism. I am suspicious of those denouncers of Communism who do not seem to be aware of the German American Bund in every city. A campaign against the Reds which slurs over with quick and easy words the evil of the Browns and the Blacks is the Nazi type of propaganda and we will have nothing to do with it.

(10:) The Fascist method is not class war but race war. Fascism has used that method now with great success in many European countries. It divides the country, makes one group hate another, creates exasperating bitterness between one race and another, and when the country is thus broken up, when the country is fragmentized by these hates, then the power of unified Nazi Germany rises supreme....

(12:) Even in Germany, a cultured country, as Nazi power tightens its hold on the people, it is the cultured, the scientific, the great literary minds which are driven into exile. Bitterness and hate thrive most in an atmosphere of ignorance.

Stephen S. Wise, "Which Light Failed: Maccabean Lamp or Christian?," Free Synagogue at Carnegie Hall, New York. AJA, Box 22: SSW Microfilms of AJHS and BUASC papers

(1:) Is there anyone who will say today that the light of the Christmas candle has failed? I do not.... I am prepared to speak of the Christmas candle as token and symbol of Christianity as a great civilizing illuminating power for many, many centuries throughout the western world.... (2:) When that civilizing influence has been withdrawn or overcome, as it is today in Nazi Germany, there results chaos: the worst chaos that can be, namely, the chaos of paganism... I think that the supreme failure of the Christmas candle has lain in the failure of Christendom, or shall we say Christianity, to bring about the greatest of all human desiderata, namely the avoidance, the abolition, the end of war.

(3:) I consider...the paganism which has beat Christians in Germany, who mourn as I do over the failure of Christianity, who weep over the extinction of the Christmas candle in our part of the western world's treatment of the Jew through the ages, its supremely mournful and tragic failure.... (4:) And it is not merely the Archbishop of Canterbury [Cosmo Gordon Lang], Bishop [William T.] Manning and Bishop [Stephen J.] Donahue, who on this platform a week ago Friday uttered a noble protest against the sin and shame of unchristian treatment of the Jews in Germany. It is not they alone; there are tens and hundreds of thousands of simple honourable Godly men and women, Christians, who are ashamed of the paganism which has beat Christendom in Germany....

Alexander Altmann, Address to a Gathering of three hundred German-Jewish refugees in Higher Broughton. *The Manchester Guardian*, December 19, 1938, p. 13, headline: "Refugee Jews in Manchester." University College London Altmann Archives

We cannot but think with deepest sorrow of all this suffering. But those who have found a home in this happy land, among friendly and homely people, can no longer feel themselves abandoned and depressed. We must meet the challenge of this great change in our lives, acclimatise ourselves, and play our part in the social and religious life of this great community.

December 23, 1938 (Friday evening during Hanukkah)

Israel H. Levinthal, "The Hanukkah Lights," Brooklyn Jewish Center, Brooklyn, NY. *A New World Is Born*, pp. 129–34

(130:) And yet, while we follow the injunction of the Hillelites (131:) many Jews of our day have adopted the attitude of the School of Shammai. A fierce despondency, a dark pessimism has taken hold of many a Jew of our generation. "Our glory and grandeur were all in the past. Now they are dwindling and the future holds little prospect for us. . . ." The recent havoc wrought among the Jews has tended to spread this spirit of depression and gloom still more. Undoubtedly, there were such Jews also in the days of the Maccabees; but had their attitude prevailed, there would have been no Israel and no Judaism today.

(133:) The Jews in the Purim story are symbolized by the anvil. The Jews in the Hanukkah tale are symbolized by the hammer – the Maccabees. As we view Jewish life across the sea today, the same symbolism appears (134:) once again. Under the Nazis, the Jew is the anvil, beaten and hammered at will. In the new Palestine we see the resurrection of the Maccabean spirit – we see the Jew hammering away, building, fashioning, molding Jewish destiny.

It is this Maccabean spirit that must take hold of the Jew here and everywhere.

December 30, 1938 (Friday evening)

Ferdinand M. Isserman, "The Five Outstanding Events of 1938," Temple Israel, St. Louis, MO. JTA, MS-6, Box 15, Folder 3

(10:) From the Jewish point of view, however horrible the suffering of the Jews in Germany, the protests against Jewish persecution, the gestures of friendship coming from all religious groups, from all political parties, from all walks of life, mark a new epoch and a new era....

(11:) 1938 was a black year, but it has its silver lining. It seems as if the worst is over. Perhaps the best omen is to be read in the news of this week when Mussolini backed down (12:) from his threats against France.[78] Perhaps this may mean that dictators have been checked and that in the future the will, the courage, the readiness for sacrifice of the democratic people will check them even more....

78 This alludes to Italian territorial aspirations toward control of French territory, including Tunisia, Corsica, Nice, and Savoy, which created considerable tension in late 1938 and early 1939. The passage seems in retrospect to reveal how even those who care profoundly about contemporary events have limited insight into the future.

1939

January 1, 1939 (Sunday, Day of Prayer and Intercession throughout Palestine for Victims of Nazi Brutality)

Isaac Herzog, Jeshurun Synagogue, Jerusalem. *Palestine Post*, January 2, 1939, p. 1

The Chief Rabbi, Dr. Isaac Herzog, preached the sermon, taking as his text Joel 1:14. He said that they had assembled to invoke divine mercy on their stricken brethren and to signalise the great spiritual movement of Repentance, the return to God and Divine Law and the return to the age-long hope of Israel which centres in Zion. Dr. Herzog voiced the feeling of gratitude of Jewry towards the friends of Israel in Europe and America, who had raised their voices in protest against the inhuman atrocities and against destruction of the synagogues and the Scrolls of the Law. The Chief Rabbi called on the congregation to pray to Him in whose hands are the hearts of Kings and Rulers, to incline the hearts of the Democratic countries, particularly Great Britain, in whose hands providence had placed the keeping of the Holy Land, to throw the Gates of Zion open to their German and Austrian brothers and sisters and to the young children who had no alternative left to them but migration.[1]

January 8, 1939 (Sunday)

Stephen S. Wise, "Hitler's *Mein Kampf* and Van Loon's *Our Battle*," Free Synagogue at Carnegie Hall, New York. AJA, Box 22: SSW Microfilms of AJHS and BUASC papers

(1:) And mark you: nothing, nothing has been done, not even the

1 The article reported that sermons were also delivered by Chief Rabbi Amiel, at the Great Synagogue, Tel Aviv, and Chief Rabbi Uziel, at the Ohel Mo'ed, Tel Aviv.

unspeakable horrors of the days beginning November 10th, nothing that is not promised and forecast and threatened in this book. If every Jew in Germany, for example, were to die at the hand of some assassin, that horror would not be greater than the moral horrors pre-figured and frankly outlined in this volume [*Mein Kampf*].[2]

(3:) [Citing Romain Rolland:] "But you, my friends, the Jews, whom I see cast down, do not resign yourselves to despair.... In the course of the ages, your people have seen empires crumble and pass away and will see the rule of your persecutors vanish."

(4:) There is yet much more to be said about the so-called six warless years [of Hitler's reign]. He has waged war: six years of bitterest, brutalist, bloodiest warfare, liberating, in quotation marks, Germans only, to enslave Europe, and in the end invading, conquering Austria and Czecho-Slovakia and in spirit Hungary, and perhaps on the morrow, if he be not resisted, Poland, Romania, Yugoslavia, and that by terrorization....

(9:) [T]they who preach intolerance are the enemies of democracy. That is what makes the priest in Detroit [Father Coughlin] the most dangerous enemy of democracy in America today. He may deny that he has associations with Hitler and Hitlerism, although you will have noted that a speech of his a few Sundays ago was nothing more than a duplicate of a speech of that devil Goebbels, voiced again in Detroit, Goebbels the enemy of Catholicism, of religion, of civilization, of humaneness, repeated almost word-for-word by the priest of Royal Oak.

(10:) There are many methods short of war; all I say to you today is: try those methods short of war, magnify them, multiply them, remember: either weaponless in defense of democracy, or war against dictators outside of our own country. Choose wisely.

---

2 Here Wise warns against relying on the English version published by Houghton & Mifflin, which he describes as "attenuated, deleted, moderated and amended in order to be unoffending to that particular people in whose languages it is translated. I am therefore glad to know that shortly two firms are to publish a translation literally and without abridgement or curtailment or modification." He recommends that congregants read and "study the volume."

January 14, 1939 (Saturday)

Abba Hillel Silver, Address at the opening session of the National Conference on Palestine, Washington, DC. *Pittsburgh Press*, January 15, 1939, p. 14

Jewish leadership should make it unmistakably clear to all the governments of Europe that it is impossible to evacuate six million Jews; there are no countries prepared to receive them, no colonies available for their settlement, and no financial means at hand for effectuating such a program even if it were feasible.

January 17, 1939 (Tuesday)

Abba Hillel Silver, "Religion in Present Day Life," Address at 36th Biennial Convention of UAHC, Cincinnati, OH. *Therefore Choose Life*, pp. 288–98

(291:) For the Jewish people, the World War and its aftermath spelled Golgotha! A quarter of a century of mounting disasters and calamities culminating in the unprecedented horrors of recent months. Great Jewish communities, rich in history, culture, and achievement, among whom the dream of a free, enlightened, and tolerant humanity was most ardently cherished, have been plunged into Hell. Gone for them are enlightenment and emancipation. Gone are the dreams of human brotherhood and equality. Gone are the beckoning horizons of great careers and great service. Gone are all shelter and all security. Gone, even, the scant and tenuous security of the ghetto! Into exile, broken, stripped, and impoverished, they must go, even as their forefathers before them, who knew neither enlightenment nor emancipation. From countries and homes where they had known dignity, honor, power, and wealth, Jews, in their mounting legions, must now wander forth, bewildered and disillusioned, into a bewildered and disillusioned world.

For the world, generally, stands today bewildered and disillusioned. The strong and sure foundations upon which it had builded its life have been rudely shaken. That high optimism which fed upon truly remarkable achievements in every scientific field has vanished.... (292:) For twenty-five years now, men have lived in a world of mounting hate, intolerance, and bigotry, of revolutions, invasions, wars, of the rise and fall of empires amidst the slaughter of millions of their kind. Great peoples have destroyed their liberties and enslaved themselves. Millions of men cower today in terrorized submissiveness....

(296:) The present-day expulsions of the Jews from Germany and Austria, the dismal plight of Jews throughout eastern Europe, the stress under which Israel finds itself everywhere, coupled with the distressed mood of mankind generally, may give rise to a strong mystic movement which will express itself in religion, literature, and art and in personal habits of thought and conduct.... The choice today is not between survival and extinction, but between doom and destiny, between burden and mission. Shall we live our Jewish lives greatly or meanly?...

January 19, 1939 (Thursday)

Israel Goldstein, "A Rabbi's Score," Address celebrating his twenty-year anniversary as Rabbi of Congregation B'nai Jeshurun, New York. *Toward a Solution*, pp. 115–27

(115:) If we are going to survive merely on a socio-biological basis, it may be enough reason to justify condemning those who would annihilate us, but it is hardly enough reason for us to justify to ourselves the price we must pay for our survival....

(116:) In the demonstration and fulfillment of the identity of the Jewish people, Zionism is an indispensable ideal....

(122:) In view of the world-shaking events of our time, an extraordinary responsibility devolves upon us.... The catastrophe which has befallen European Jewry summons us to strengthen our sinews. It is more than a temporary emergency which challenges us. Whatever developments in the international situation may be in store, it is certain, so far as the Jewish situation is concerned, that American Jewry will become, more and more, the mainstay of Jewish life in the Diaspora....

(124:) 1939 finds disillusionment in the place of hope. The most terrible of wars is in the offing. The whittling down of the Balfour Declaration is in keeping with the "let-down" in all the great promises of 1919. If the Jewish settlement of Palestine has grown substantially in spite of all obstacles, it is an amazing tribute to the indomitable will of a "stiff-necked people."

The Joint Distribution Committee is still "in business," alleviating distress on a greater scale than ever before. On many fronts a relentless war is being waged against the Jewish people. Even American Jewry, the Joseph among the brethren, favored by benign Providence, even this prince in the house of Jacob, does not feel too secure and is not untroubled....

Whether the new sense of Jewish awareness will take the form (125:) of creative, positive Jewish thinking and Jewish living, or will be limited to apologetics and "damn Hitler" meetings, remains to be seen....

(127:) Since 1933, the Jew has borne the brunt of the attack against Democracy. He should accept the commitment with pride and passion. His struggle is thus lifted to a plane far beyond the struggle for self-preservation....

This blessed land, cynosure of the eyes of the harassed world, is still young, fresh and relatively unspoiled. The decadence which has corroded Europe has as yet not infected us. Sporadically depressed by pessimism, we have a youthful resiliency which comes to our aid in a crisis. Diverted, now and then, here and there, by seductive voices appealing to our basest instincts of fear and provincialism, we recover our sanity and our soundness, when the authentic voice of American tradition exhorts us. In this congenial atmosphere, Jewish life has a chance to flourish, and by flourishing, to add valuable qualities to the whole of American life and civilization.

January 22, 1939 (Sunday)

Solomon B. Freehof, "How To Behave," Rodef Shalom Congregation, Pittsburgh, PA. "To the American Jews: A Series of Three Addresses." *Rodef Shalom Pulpit,* New Series, vol. 4, no. 6, pp. 17–31

(19:) If you think of the situation of the Jew of Germany you know the details of behavior played no role at all. In the first place, no one was as German as the German Jew. More than that, in the North of Germany, the German Jew had the discipline and demeanor of the German. In South Germany he had the hearty good-nature of the Bavarian. He fitted his environment perfectly. His behavior was as well-adjusted to modern life as it could possibly be adjusted. Yet in spite of his careful attention to the little courtesies of life, the little details, his fate is as horrible as human imagination could have conceived.[3] In other words, if the Jews of Germany had been complete saints they nevertheless would have been treated as the most corrupt of sinners.

Certainly Jewish behavior, whether a Jew wore a beard or did not wear a beard, whether he read a paper with Hebrew letters or with German letters, whether there was a Hebrew word on his butcher shop or not, did not make any difference to the Nazi Party. They disliked Jews, the noble and the ignoble, the great and the small, the rich and the poor alike. So Jewish behavior in Germany was a complete irrelevance. You could not possibly have (20:) behaved in such a way as to please Streicher and Goebbels.... Germany was a land which for its own purposes consciously developed a public policy of anti-Semitism, an official technique of Jew-hatred; and it is perfectly clear that in a country where there is a public official policy of anti-Semitism no Jewish behavior can make a difference....

(21:) Did you ever wonder at the reason for the great success of Nazi anti-Semitic propaganda? This is not an idle question. That propaganda is manifestly silly. It makes accusations that no sensible person can possibly believe. Normally, one would think such propaganda would be laughed at as soon as it is heard, and yet that silly, baseless propaganda spreads and spreads and has an astounding success. Why? The reason is this: This propaganda, although it is foolish in itself, roots itself in certain vague notions which are already widespread among millions of people. There are certain moods, certain series of moods in the average non-Jew, which are not in themselves particularly harmful but are the natural soil for the rooting of the weed of the absurd anti-Semitism of Nazi propaganda.

3 A formulation that – like so many others in this sermon literature – seems painfully ironic in light of what was to come.

In other words, when you estimate Nazi anti-Semitic propaganda, you can sum it up as follows: Factually it is foolish, psychologically it is brilliant.

Consider, for example, one of the main tenets of the absurd Nazi propaganda, namely, that the Jew dominates the world. It is nonsense on the face of it and yet it is constantly reiterated: "the conquering Jew." The whole text of "The Protocols of the Elders of Zion" reiterates that manifest (22:) absurdity.[4] Why do people begin to believe, even in non-German countries, that the Jews can really be the master of the world? Because already in the hearts of the average non-Jew, while there is not yet that absurd notion that the Jew is the **conqueror**, there is already the feeling that the Jew is **conspicuous**. He is noticeable....

(24:) The classic Nazi propaganda began with the charge that the Jew is the conqueror and continues with the horrible charge that the Jew is incurably corrupt. This charge also is spread on all the pages of the "Protocols of the Elders of Zion." The Jew is corrupt. In literature he destroys standards; in art he defaces beauty; in music he is responsible for jazz and all the wild origins of modern sounds. The Jew befouls whatever he touches; he is a corrupting cancer in modern life....

(27:) Fortunately the German propaganda has not yet been successful in persuading the world that the Jews are the world's "*Unglueck*," the world's misfortune.[5] But they will find it a comparatively easy job to persuade Poland and Romania of that fact [*sic*!],

---

4 The "Protocols of the Elders of Zion" was the notorious forgery that purported to be a record of a secret conspiracy by Jewish leaders to take over the world. Although its spurious nature had been clearly established by *Times of London* reporter Philip Graves in 1921, it influenced Hitler at the beginning of his career, and he continued to refer to it as authentic. See the work of the German scholar Benjamin W. Segel, *Die Protokolle der Weisen von Zion, kritisch beleuchtet* and *Welt-Krieg, Welt-Revolution, Welt-Verschwörung, Welt-Oberregierung*, translated as *The Protocols of the Elders of Zion: The Greatest Lie in History*; Norman Cohn, *Warrant for Genocide*; Stephen Eric Bronner, *A Rumor About the Jews.*

5 The sentence, "*Die Juden sind unser Unglueck*," (The Jews are our misfortune), used in an important essay by the nineteenth-century German historian Heinrich von Treitschke, was taken up as a motto by the Nazi periodical *Der Stürmer.*

because Poland and Romania already believe that the Jews are superfluous. Those nations are convinced that the Jews are surplus population and if the Jews could be removed, Poland and Romania would be happier. Beginning with the notion that the Jews are a burden it will be very easy to leap to the horrible conclusion that the Jews are a misfortune.

January 29, 1939 (Sunday)

Solomon B. Freehof, "How to Defeat Propaganda," Rodef Shalom Congregation, Pittsburgh, PA. "To the American Jews: A Series of Three Addresses." *Rodef Shalom Pulpit*, New Series, vol. 4, no. 7, pp. 33–47

(33:) Propaganda, specifically German propaganda, had exasperated the relationship between the Sudeten Germans and the rest of the Czecho-Slovak Republic, and so weakened that outpost of democracy and liberty that it fell an easy prey to Nazi rapacity.

(34:) Consider Germany itself. Here is a country in constant excitement, its people are getting hungrier every day. They are getting more and more afraid of war to which their leaders are inexorably dragging them. You would think the German people would be ripe for propaganda persuasion, and indeed propaganda has been directed against Nazi Germany from all sorts of sources by all sorts (35:) of methods for six years and the Nazis are still strong and firmly in the saddle.... Of course propaganda can be defeated. All you need to do is to turn your own nation into an armed camp, clamp down on every free expression of public speech and of the press, and no propaganda from outside can easily hurt you.

(38:) Nazi propaganda is an avowed treason and an avowed invasion with the intention of destroying the United States and putting "Unser Amerika," "our German America," in its place.... (45:) There is a great worldwide net of Nazi propaganda organized in Germany, centralized now chiefly in Stuttgart. Its head is von Bohle.... (46:) Hitler has had to recall four successive leaders of the Nazi propaganda from the United States because they had failed; and, notice, they had failed in recent years when the American people as a whole was more or less indifferent to what was happening in Germany.

February 3, 1939 (Friday evening)

Ferdinand M. Isserman, "Hitler's La[te]st Address," Temple Israel, St. Louis, MO. AJA, MS-6, Box 15, Folder 4[6]

(1:) One of the secrets of the Nazis' rise to power has been their mastery of the art of propaganda. They have contended that repeat a lie often enough and people begin to believe it. This is unquestionably true especially if that lie goes unanswered, or if that lie is answered once but not repeatedly. That is one of the grave errors that Jewish leadership in America is committing at the present time. It is answering anti-semitic lies once. The lies are repeated. Jewish leadership has failed to recognize that these lies must be answered as often if not more often than they are repeated.

The last address of Hitler again is replete with the usual Nazi distortion and misrepresentation. They must not go unanswered. I know of no more sacred use to which this pulpit could be put at this time than to endeavor to answer for our community the misrepresentations of Naziism and Nazi leaders, not merely for the sake of the Jewish record, but for the sake of American democracy and civilization. . . .

(10:) Mr. Hitler again misrepresented when he accuses the Jews of a world conspiracy to bolshevize Europe and to bolshevize civilization. He is merely carrying out the scheme of painting the Jews red, a scheme that finds echoes in America among his lieutenants, clerical and lay. He threatens to destroy the Jews in Europe in the event of the next war. He threatens also to carry on a campaign against the Jews all over the world. His minions will bring the science of anti-semitism to people in every corner of the world. They are doing it already.

6 Unlike most of the texts of Isserman sermons in the AJA, this is clearly not a final version but triple-spaced, filled with corrections in black ink handwriting (which have been incorporated into the above text). This version probably would have been retyped by a secretary for use in the pulpit. It may well be that all of his sermon texts went through a similar process, but only the finished versions were kept in files to be submitted later to the AJA. In addition, there is a separate section of 2¼ pages entitled "Excerpts," apparently intended to be sent to the media. For a fairly complete text in translation of Hitler's January 30 address delivered to the Reichstag in the Kroll Opera House, see Domarus, *Hitler: Speeches and Addresses*, vol. 3, pp. 1436–59, with discussion of the Jews on pp. 1447–49 and 1456.

His agents are carrying on anti-semitic propaganda, repeating the lies and the distortions about Jews, printing books that have been declared to be forgeries, that have been denounced by great ecclesiastics, that have been proved to be false in the courts. Day after day, week after week, these agents of Hitler are at work defaming the Jew.

This challenge the Jew must accept. He must accept it not merely for his own sake but for the sake of the democracies of which he is a part. For where anti-semitism gains a foothold, there democracy disappears....

February 15, 1939 (Wednesday)

Isaac Herzog, Address Delivered at the Round Table Conference, St. James's Palace, London, 26 Shevat, 1939. *Masu'ah leYitzḥaq*, pp. 118–20,[7] translated by MS

(119:) Filled with enthusiasm, almost a messianic enthusiasm, which you inspired within our hearts, we have brought great, massive sacrificial offerings, including actual risking of life, and made heroic efforts in facing obstacles and difficulties, part of them to be charged to the account of the British government in the land of Israel. Over a period of twenty years, praise be to G-d, we have done great things, and after hundreds of years of terrible neglect, resulting from laziness and boredom and idleness [of the native population], we have restored the land of our forefathers and the prophets to humane culture. And now, precisely in this tragic moment of our tragic history, when the national home should and must serve as a life-giving refuge and shelter from death for tens of thousands of Jews, men and women, old and young, infants and babies, you have invited us to

7 This is the Hebrew text of the address, which was published in *Haaretz*, April 18, 1939. But while some of the participants (e.g., Isaac Ben-Zvi, Menachem Ussishkin, and Rabbi M. Blau) spoke in Hebrew, Herzog would certainly have spoken in English. I have come across a reference to the "Stenographic Protocol of the Meeting at St. James's Palace," ([Central Zionist Archives, S25/630] in Abraham Edelheit, *The Yishuv in the Shadow of the Holocaust*, p. 312, n. 105), but I have not been able to identify this text from the CZA website. The following passage is therefore my translation of the Hebrew text of an address originally made in English. Cf. the one-paragraph summary of Herzog's address in David Ben-Gurion, *My Talks with Arab Leaders*, p. 240, although he quotes extensively from Weizmann's address on Feb. 8 (pp. 202–13).

appear before you – and why? To apologize because we are vigorously insisting upon the fundamental claim – the justice of which is so obvious – that it is a criminal offense, an unforgivable sin, to annul the solemn commitment you have given to the Jewish people, the only nation in the world that has no home of its own....

Your great leaders and intellectuals have not infrequently articulated an echo of the outcry of my people; from time to time your robust, powerful voice has been raised on behalf of my oppressed and downtrodden people, plundered and pillaged. But now comes the great test, the great touchstone: everything depends upon your actions at this moment, at this moment of monumental decision in this wondrous drama, this awesome spectacle in Jewish history.

February 19, 1939 (Sunday)

Abba Hillel Silver, "Pope Pius XI" [died February 10, 1939], The Temple, Cleveland, OH. *A Word in Its Season*, pp. 359–65

(361:) "And anti-Semitism," he declared, "is a movement which Christians cannot share. It is not possible for Christians to take part in anti-Semitism."

In an editorial headed, "The Tragedy of Israel," he said, "The foes of the Jewish people are waging war not only against the Jews but also against God, and against religious values. This ought to be taken into consideration when watching the present tragedy of the people of Israel."

Pope Pius, when he read of the frightful happenings to the Jews, ordered prayers in all the churches of Christendom to be said for the persecuted Jews. Last March, when the frightful scenes in Vienna shocked the world, as a gesture of good will and a slap in the face to the Nazis, and as an appeal to the world to imitate his act, Pope Pius sent a money grant to Jewish refugees....

February 25, 1939 (Saturday)

Louis I. Newman, "'We Are All Semites Spiritually': The Message of Pope Pius XI," Congregation Rodeph Sholom, New York. *Sermons and Addresses*, vol. 2, pp. 124–29

(125:) This utterance by the late Pope Pius XI is of extraordinary importance today.[8] It is destined to take its place among the historic pronouncements of the Roman Catholic Church.... In addition to condemning Anti-Semitism as un-Christian, he goes further and affirms the Semitic origins of Christendom and Christian believers.... It is good that this reminder be advanced and emphasized in these days of incitement and hatred against Jewry.... (126:) The service which Pope Pius has rendered in the struggle against "racism" in Italy and Germany has won for him the gratitude of freemen everywhere.

(128:) Last November, at a time when the Jewish people were in the deepest anguish as a consequence of the November 10th pogrom against German Jewry when hundreds of synagogues were burned, tens of thousands of Jews were imprisoned in concentration camps, and the most dreadful indignities were visited upon their families, Charles Coughlin, a priest of the Catholic Church, saw fit on the radio and in his publications to defend Nazism as a "defense mechanism against Communism," for which, he asserted, Jews are responsible.... We believe that the task of answering Coughlinism is the responsibility not of Jews, but of Catholics.[9]

February 26, 1939 (Sunday)

Samuel H. Goldenson, "The Propaganda of Hatred and Its Tragic Consequences," Temple Emanu-El, New York. AJA, MS-81, Box 2, Folder 4

(8:) This morning I picked up a paper and I saw a headline. The Third Reich, the Hitler regime, has decided overnight that they must drive 100 Jews out of Germany every day. That is contrary to the agreement made just a few weeks ago with the Evian Conference.[10] Only a few

8 Reference is to the text of a Statement by Pius XI, taken from the London *Tablet*, September 1938, which Newman has just cited.

9 Six years later, Newman wrote that this sermon was delivered "at the height of Coughlin's diatribes against the Jews": *A "Chief Rabbi" Becomes a Catholic*, p. 167 n. 59.

10 Reference is to a front-page article in the *NYT* of February 26 under the headline, "100 JEWS EACH DAY MUST LEAVE REICH," with the sub-headline "Violates the Recent Refugee Compact." The extensive article was continued for several columns on p. 23. Goldenson apparently assumed that many of his congregants did not read the *NYT*.

weeks ago they entered into an agreement. They made a pledge. They accepted an arrangement. And now it is broken because at bottom there is no feeling, because at bottom there is no sympathy, because at bottom there is no regard, because at bottom there is no responsibility for the words uttered and the pledge undertaken....

[W]e are living in one of the most disturbing and uncertain periods of human life, uncertain because we have removed the foundations that lead to mutual co-operativeness, that lead to stability, that lead us to have confidence in one another. And when that happens, we might as well live in a hurricane blowing in every direction. We might as well live upon a (9:) volcano. We might as well live in a society in which there is nothing but evil forces in motion. And that is what is happening after all. Friends, may I remind you that you and I are not the only victims. We are the latest and in one way the earliest. We suffer most. But what lies in this doctrine is something deeper than anti-Semitism itself. There is a revulsion against the moral and spiritual laws in accordance with which the human family has tried to live for generations and centuries.

Shlomo Zalman Ehrenreich, "What I Preached on the Day Established as a Public Fast Because of the Troubles for Israel," Simleul-Silvaniei, Transylvania. *Derashot Leḥem Shelomoh*, pp. 283–85, translated by Gershon Greenberg, with slight modifications by MS[11]

(284a:) At this time the words of the prophet Jeremiah are being fulfilled, "Weep not for the dead, neither bemoan him; but weep sore for him that goes away, for he shall return no more, nor see his native country" (Jer. 22:10). So it is at this time. Thousands of Jews have been expelled from Germany and Austria. Everything has been taken from them and they suffer immeasurable troubles. They have nowhere to turn. They are not allowed to enter the land of Israel or America. They are neither in heaven nor upon the earth. This is a greater reason for weeping than is the loss of the [Hasidic] *tsadikkim*,

11 For a full translation of this sermon, see Gershon Greenberg in *Wrestling With God*, pp. 62–65; for a general discussion, see Greenberg, "Shlomo Zalman Ehrenreich's (1863–1944) Religious Response to the Holocaust: February 1939–October 1943."

for they have gone to their reward, but these are reduced to weeping.[12] Expelled from their native country and from their houses, they have become "fugitives and wanderers" (cf. Gen. 4:12)....

(284b:) At this time there are unheard-of troubles for Israel. The people who passed in a transport through Grosswardein [Oradea in Transylvania, Romania] had swastikas [on] their faces and their flesh. Some had no fingers; the evil ones bit them off. There were those whose fingernails were torn out and other such things.[13] Things that wild animals do. Some think this is an accident. In Germany the people are educated. How could such cruelty be found among people? Expelling people and taking their wealth to the last penny? With such great troubles?

But it is the hand of G-d, because of the gravity of the sins that were committed [by the Jews] there through their assimilation among the Gentiles. For several generations they would take Gentile wives. One rabbi who was expelled from Germany maintained that he justified the punishment; he said that he had arranged hundreds of divorce documents for Jews who had come from Russia and Poland to live in Germany, and they sent these divorce documents to their wives back home, and all of them married Gentile women. The same is true of Vienna: it is hard to imagine the sins committed by the daughters of Polish Jews who came there, including the daughters and granddaughters of rabbis and Hasidic rebbes, who lived in their homes on the third floor, while their wives and daughters and granddaughters went to the theater!"

March 4, 1939 (Saturday, Shabbat Zakhor)

Salis Daiches, Edinburgh Hebrew Congregation, Scotland. Salis Daiches Archive

(1:) "Therefore it shall be, when the Lord thy God hath given thee

---

12 The Hebrew is a play on words: the *tsaddikim* have gone *li-menuḥot,* but the others are reduced to *anaḥot.*

13 I find it extremely difficult to connect with documented historical events this description of a transport of Jews, apparently organized by sadistic Nazis, moving through Grosswardein before the date when this sermon was delivered.

rest from all thine enemies round about, in the land which the Lord thy God giveth thee for an inheritance to possess it, that thou shalt blot out the remembrance of Amalek from under heaven; thou shalt not forget" (Deut. 25:19).

To many of us it may seem that the spirit of Amalek has grown in the last few years in such a way that nothing and no one can stand in its way. The spirit of aggression, (2:) of inhumanity, that prompts the incessant attacks on the weak and the helpless, on the unprotected and the defenseless. There is scarcely a period in the world's history when Amalek had greater power, and his spirit was more rampant, more oppressive, more destructive. This can be said not only of the attitude of our enemies in the heart of Europe, but also of the method of attack adopted by our adversaries in the very land of which our Torah speaks as the land given to our people to possess it forever and to become the centre of the campaign against cruelty and tyranny and every manifestation of inhumanity.... And yet today, this Sabbath, the Torah reading beginning "*Zakhor*" (Deut. 25:17) and the eve of the festival of Purim, we are bidden to remember our duty to be ready for the fight against Amalek and to be sure of our ultimate victory....

But you might ask, "How are we to undertake this fight against Amalek at the present time?" So far as remembering what Amalek has done – and is still doing – to us, is concerned, that is easy. In fact we could not do otherwise, for if we wanted to forget, this evening [Purim] would not let us. And the similarity of our position today with that described in the special portion of the Law we have read today is also obvious: a large section of our people is faint and weary and unable to defend itself (cf. Deut. 25:18).... (3:) There is therefore no prospect of our people enjoying rest from its enemies round about us in the near future, whether in the land of Israel or in the lands of tyranny situated in Europe. But our duty to defend ourselves against attack is equally clear, as long as we do not copy Amalek's methods and do not perpetuate his spirit of hatred and terrorism. Our defense must consist in exposing and condemning the spirit of Amalek, the spirit of hatred and cruelty, and manifesting our faith in ourselves and in our future.

March 5, 1939 (Sunday, Purim)[14]

Mnachem Risikoff, "Comfort for Israel," Congregation Dibre Mnachem, Brooklyn, NY. *Palgei Shemen*, Text 110, pp. 105–9 (Hebrew numbering), 210–17 (English numbering), translated by MS

(105b/210:) We find in Tractate Sanhedrin (98b): "The son of David will not come until the evil kingdom – namely Edom – will spread itself over Israel for nine months."...(106a/211:)There is apparently a problem here, for in Tractate Yoma (10a), it says pretty much the same, but there it says "the kingdom of Rome," and it uses the term "kingdom," not "the rule of Rome," and there it adds, "and over the entire world." See the passage there.

We may explain this as follows: the Sages, inspired by the holy spirit, envisioned the future events occurring right now in our own time, with the rise of the wicked H-r, ruler of the **sizaN**,[15] may his name be blotted out. The **sizaN** State is the wicked Edom.[16] This H-r has established an alliance with **inilossuM**, his friend, the ruler of Rome, and they have bonded together for a single purpose: to conquer the entire world, and to spill innocent blood, and to create terrible suffering and destruction for all the nations, but especially to do evil by eradicating the Jewish people.[17] Now how do we know that the wicked H-r, may his name be blotted out, is the one who

---

14 Risikoff did not provide specific dates for the sermons he published in *Palgei Shemen*. However, the frequent references in this text to the present year as 5699 (Sept. 1938–Sept. 1939), and the references to the German treatment of Austria and Czechoslovakia limit the possibilities. Because the central theme of the sermon is the connection between Hitler and Haman, I have assumed that it was delivered at the service on the morning of Purim.

15 Risikoff had decided that – at least in the printed text of his sermon – he would not write the name "Hitler" or "Nazis" or Mussolini" or "swastika" in the usual form. The H-r (ה"ר) for Hitler is obvious, but the spelling backwards of the other three terms took some time to decipher. I have followed the pattern of writing the names backward, although what the preacher actually said in delivering the sermon is unclear.

16 Mentioned in tractate Sanhedrin.

17 The Hebrew text, beginning with the sermon title, consistently uses "Israel" when referring to the Jewish people. Without knowing what he would have said in the original Yiddish delivery, I have generally (but not always) used "the Jewish people" or "the Jews" for these references as most natural for English readers.

rules over Edom? From the statement in Tractate Megillah (6a–b), "Germamia (or Germania) is Edom." And in the same passage it states that if Germania should go forth to war, it would destroy the whole world; see the passage there.

And so we have seen in our own time that "Edom" has destroyed several countries, and it has inflamed almost the entire world with the murderous polluted spirit of **msizaN**.... There is also a statement in the Gemara [b. Sanhedrin 97b] that the Holy One, praised be He, will in the future raise a king as cruel as Haman, who will cause the Jews to repent; see the passage there. When we see the wicked H–r, the ruler of the **sizaN**, and all that he has done, it becomes clear that he is indeed the primal, wicked Haman, about whom the Sages wrote that He "will raise a king...in order to punish the Jews and bring them to repent," for the function of both [Haman and Hitler] is the same....

(106b/212:) Ahasuerus hated the Jews as Haman did, but there is an important difference in their hatred.... Ahasuerus hated them only because of their religion, the faith of Israel.... But the policy of Haman and his hatred of the Jews was of a different nature, for even if all the Jews had converted and accepted the Persian faith, that would not have helped them, as Haman's hatred was entirely bound up with the Jewish *race*, and his intent was nothing less than to destroy the Jewish people completely, even if they had converted (heaven forbid!) – that would not have helped them at all....

(107a/213:) And so the wicked man of our own time, H–r, ruler of the **sizaN**, has done evil that no wicked person has done until this time: he committed every kind of murder, but while doing so, he proudly displays on his body this **akitsaws**, as if to demonstrate to all that he is an honest man who wants the entire world to behave peacefully and honestly, pretending to the world...(107b/214) that he does not want war, while in truth he himself speaks war, while all the world is afraid that he will go to war....

(108a/215:) This is what we have seen with our own eyes: that the great nations of the world first promised to the governments of Austria and Czechoslovakia they would go to their aid if the **sizaN** State and Rome should go to war against them, but later they backed out of their unambiguous promises, to the amazement of the entire world, and therefore these governments fell, and the nations and their lands were lost, even though they were ready to fight against their enemies.... (108b/216:) Thus what holds sway in the world is the lie. What people have said, even what they have written, means nothing. And the suffering of the Jews has increased and grown stronger. Regarding this suffering of the Jews, the nations react in almost the same way, hiding themselves as if they are blind and deaf and dumb, seeing nothing, hearing but without understanding that the suffering of the Jews has increased until it has as reached the vault of the heavens and the depths of the deep, without end.

Yet this is indeed the time for the end of the misery of Israel. All of its sufferings are signs of the coming of the Messiah, in accordance with the words of the Sages. They have reached their completion, for the lie has entirely prevailed. That is why we may hope, with G-d's help, in accordance with the words of the Sages, that the time for the redemption of Israel has arrived, in this very year, the year 5699!...[18]

Samuel H. Goldenson, "How Can We Celebrate Purim this Year?," Temple Emanu-El, New York. AJA, MS-81, Box 2, Folder 4

(7:) [Mordecai said to Esther,] "If you do not do this you will lose an opportunity for service." And then he reminded her in terms of the universal: "And who knows whether it may not be for a time such as this that thou hast been exalted unto a throne" (Esth. 4:14). There was a higher purpose in your selection than merely to gratify the king on the one hand and your feminine ambitions on the other. There was a higher purpose. It has something to do with the economy of the spiritual world.

18 The passage continues with a discussion of the Hebrew letters representing the previous year (5698), which spell the word that means "you shall murder," but if their order is reversed means "you shall be washed" clean of all suffering, so that the suffering will end in the current year, 5699; see Gershon Greenberg, "American Religious Responses to Kristallnacht," p. 162. Greenberg notes that a few months later, Risikoff apparently repudiated the idea that Hitler was an instrument of God sent to punish the Jews (p. 163). Obviously the expression of faith and hope is painfully ironic in light of what would occur in the years following the date of the sermon.

You see, friends, here is another element. Who knows whether it is not for a time such as this that you and I in America, you and I have been saved, so that we might extend help to our German friends and Romanian friends and Polish friends. Who knows why we have been scattered? Who knows why at this time of the world's history the bulk of us are in America, and the richest of us are in America. May it not be that we may have the opportunity, the glorious opportunity, of extending our hand of helpfulness to the persecuted of our people, and to others the world over?

JULIAN B. FEIBELMAN, "Has Religion Failed?," Temple Sinai, New Orleans, LA. Radio Address, WSMB. AJA MS-94, Box 15, Folder 5

(1:) There are other signs which keep us awake. Poland and Hungary are now greedy, Japan is insatiable. The puppet Dictator of Spain seeks further physic victories. The refugees are still wandering. And there are millions of Jews who this week witnessed the curtain of the finale rung down on their year of hope in the homeland in Palestine. Now the Jew, who has built it up, made it flourish, saw it bloom, raised it as a sign of hopeful haven to thousands of oppressed who have been cruelly exiled, sees it this week given over to the Arab, and finds himself reduced to minority status.[19]

(6:) Even this week, the Palestinian compromise virtually concluded in London is another Munich in the Holy Land. Like Czecho-Slovakia, the hopes of millions, the faith in the solemn pledge of Britain in the Balfour Declaration, are crushed, another scrap of paper. Dr. Weizmann said before the conference that the hostility of the Arabs to Britain would be rewarded, while the unwavering loyalty of the Jews would be punished. This is so bitterly true.

There are hundreds of thousands of refugees, of all faiths, families

19 An allusion to the London Round Table Conference, held at St. James's Palace beginning February 7, 1939, to determine the future of Palestine with the end of the British Mandate (see above, February 15, 1939). By the beginning of March it had become clear to the Jewish delegation, led by Chaim Weizmann, that – with the failure of the conference – there was a British plan to establish a bi-national state that would consign Jews to minority status in Palestine (see JTA articles from February 27–March 3, 1939).

split, minorities crushed, little children cast out, unwanted, friendless. Why ask if Religion has failed? Where is humanity, where is civilization, where is the spiritual in man, when we countenance the madness of fiendish acts, whether in Ethiopia, in China, in Geneva, in London or in Berlin? No, my friends, religion has not failed. It is not being tried. God has not failed, He is being forgotten and His word ignored. But man is being tried, and he is failing, failing miserably. Of old they cried, "How long, O Lord, how long?" (Ps. 13:1–2). Today we cry, "How long, O man, how long?"

March 12, 1939 (Sunday)

Stephen S. Wise, "The London-Palestine Conference and Arab Appeasement," Free Synagogue at Carnegie Hall, New York. AJA, Box 22: SSW Microfilms of AJHS and BUASC papers

(1:) My dear people, instead of speaking fully and perhaps even exhaustively, if not exhaustingly, on the Palestine Conference which is not quite ended in London and which I left a week and two days ago after four weeks of ceaseless participation therein, I might read to you from two documents....[20]

(7:) I suppose, dear friends, if there were no Hitler and no Mussolini, and there were no Hungary, no Poland, no Romania, and if there were no Czechoslovakia, which tomorrow is to become a German province – I dare say we might have been led [to decide that] – for the sake of compromise – for a few years we will be prepared to limit and lessen and even to forego immigration. When the Lord Bishop of Jerusalem, the Rt. Rev. Brown, asked me, "Cannot you get your people to suspend immigration to Palestine for ten years?" I looked at him with scorn and horror and said to him, "My Lord Bishop, Christendom has taught us for 1900 years the lesson of self-sacrifice; how can you ask us to give up Jewish immigration to Palestine for ten years when millions of Jews wander homeless

---

20 On Wise's role at the St. James Conference, including his pro-British sympathy and his reluctance to antagonize Great Britain as the strongest potential military opponent to Nazi Germany at the time, see Medoff, *The Anguish of a Jewish Leader*, pp. 127–29.

upon the face of the earth?" I might have told him of those Jews who were wandering through the snowdrifts of the Alps (8:) getting out of Italy before the law forced them out, wounded and foot-sore, finding possible hospitable lands of Switzerland and Holland, who fear the heavy hand of the dictators which already threatens to fall upon them....

(11:) War may come, it may come this month, next month, in September.

March 17, 1939 (Friday evening)

Ferdinand M. Isserman, "Czechoslovakia Disappears," Temple Israel, St. Louis, MO. AJA, MS-6, Box 15, Folder 4

(1:) The pact of Munich, it is evident now, was merely the overture of the tragic opera that the Nazis are staging in Europe. The curtain has now been raised on the first scene. Czechoslovakia is no more. Actually it had ceased to exist immediately after Munich.... By the *coup d'état* of the past few days, Hitler gained no raw materials which have not been at his command since last fall. Czechoslovakia had been drawn into a custom's union with Nazi Germany and all of its resources had been at Hitler's disposal. Its rulers could not have made a move without permission from Berlin. In fact, Czechoslovakia was a colony of Germany. Now all pretense of independence has been withdrawn.... It seems as if the theoretical independence of Czechoslovakia had to go because it lay in the path of the Nazi Juggernaut. It is headed eastward, to Russia perhaps; to Baghdad perhaps; to India perhaps. In the meantime, Romania and Poland and Hungary lie in its way. Will the juggernaut roll over them and crush them? Will England and France be safe from victorious Nazi (2:) armies successful in Central and Eastern Europe?...

(4:) The Chamberlain appeasement policy is exposed. He gave a hungry tiger a bone, which merely whetted the tiger's appetite for more. Already he has taken more. He is licking his chops and is eyeing his next morsel... (6:) The disappearance of Czechoslovakia into the maw of the Nazi tiger reveals to us again the technique of Nazi propaganda. Twenty million people have been added to the domain of Hitler, who may well be called the Propaganda Napoleon. For to achieve this huge addition to his territory, no open warfare had to be waged. Mr. Hitler and his associates know that propaganda is more effective than bullets....

(8:) [Refers to] the demonstration held by the German Bund in Madison Square Garden on the eve of Washington's birthday. There the Bund sought to link Americans of Irish descent, Americans of German descent, Americans of Italian descent, Americans of Father Coughlin [*sic*] on their side with their hate for democracy and their malice towards Jews. Even though the press of America unanimously condemned the Bund rally, Nazis believe it does create some discontent. If it does that they have achieved their goal....

(11:) What is the Jew in the European scene? The symbol of a weak minority. If it is just to maltreat the Jew, to take advantage of his weakness, to butcher and to degrade him, then it is just to destroy Czechoslovakia and to conquer every small nation in Europe. What protection is there for the Jew and the other weak peoples in the modern world?...This is a dark hour for humanity, but it is no time for despair and hopelessness. For to yield to these is to court defeat. In the gloom I discern a light, the light of the reality of God's existence. That light will expel the darkness....

March 18, 1939 (Saturday)

Abba Hillel Silver, "Seeing Our Problem Against the Larger Background," Radio Address, UJA, for Refugees and Overseas Needs. *Therefore Choose Life*, pp. 282–87

Czechoslovakia has ceased to exist as an independent country, and the situation has again changed for the worse. Hitler destroyed it. The Czech nation has been absorbed and politically obliterated within the Third Reich. Slovakia, too, is now a German protectorate. Thus the Nazi Government, which in six short years has made stateless and homeless two million people, Jews and non-Jews, is now shattering the lives and fortunes of hundreds of thousands of new victims in a conquered land which is non-German by race, and which until recently was a free and tolerant democracy. Another half-million potential refugees, Jewish and non-Jewish, have been created overnight. All who had loved their country too dearly, and had resisted too loyally Nazi propaganda and penetration, all who belonged to a different political faith, all who had fled from Germany to Czechoslovakia for refuge, and all Jews, and those who are declared to be Jews by the infamous Nuremberg race laws, are tonight marked and doomed men – they and their wives and their children. Many are already in concentration camps. Many more are on their way there to taste the savage brand of Nazi sadism and *Schrecklichkeit*....

(288:) Close upon the heels of this disaster comes the news of further anti-Jewish legislation in Hungary. Hungary has now absorbed one of the dismembered parts of Czechoslovakia – Ruthenia – which has a substantial Jewish population. Many Jews of Hungary will be forced to emigrate as a result of the new legislation which sharply restricts and, in many instances, completely destroys their opportunities to earn a living.

Likewise during this week, Great Britain, following the breakdown of the London Round Table Conference, announced its own tentative plan for Palestine....

Thus, at a time when a strategic and overwhelming catastrophe has overtaken the Jewries of Europe, forcing myriads of them to wander forth in search of new homes, the doors to their own homeland are to be steadily closed to them....

The prospect for millions of our people in Europe today seems hopeless indeed. But our history knows no hopelessness....

(285:) Some of the smaller nations and minority groups of Europe beguiled themselves into believing that it was only the Jewish minority which would be singled out for persecution and destruction. They were immune. Some of them even introduced within their own borders some of the anti-Semitic tactics and practices of Berlin, and consented to act as Nazi marionettes. They erred grievously. They should have taken warning from the Nazi persecution of the Jews.... Hitler, the arch anti-Semite, has now finally revealed himself in his true colors as the archenemy of all minority groups and small nations in Europe. The rape of Czechoslovakia is part of the same outrageous scheme of power politics and empire-building as the robbing and looting of the Jewish group in Germany, and the shameless exploitation of anti-Semitism....

But though our hearts are heavy and our minds perplexed, we should not despair. We should try to understand our age against the background of the ages...

(286:) What seems like Armageddon at first is in reality but another bitter skirmish in the age-old and irrepressible conflict between the religious and moral traditions of mankind, as represented in Judaism and Christianity, symbolized in the concepts of law, freedom, peace, brotherhood, and the inviolable rights of man – and the indurate traditions of paganism symbolized in the concepts of power, state idolatry, autocracy, militarism, conquest, and war.

The outcome of this conflict cannot be in doubt.... (287:) We Jews, especially, should learn to see our problem against the background of the entire world's problem and also against the background not of the last few years, but of generations, nay centuries.... For us Jews, too, this age of surge and thunder, of suffering and menace, should be a compelling and undeniable challenge, not a disillusionment or a despair.

March 19, 1939 (Sunday)

Stephen S. Wise, "Is War Inevitable?: What Can America Do?," Free Synagogue at Carnegie Hall, New York. AJA, Box 22: SSW Microfilms of AJHS and BUASC papers

(1:) Just a week ago, when I first resumed service at your side, we thought we could still ask the question, "Is War Inevitable?" In the last four days we have come to see...that my query "Is War Inevitable?" has become academic and even obsolete. It seems as if the world asks questions, and Hitler answers those questions even before they are really asked....

The pulverization – it isn't division but pulverization – of Czechoslovakia re-established and guaranteed by Germany, England, France, and Italy, that pulverization (2:) is only the last of the acts which prove one thing: not that war is inevitable but that a state of war exists in the world today....

I want you to face the truth today while still you are under the impact of shock and disgust and loathing and shame for humanity. But this is only another culmination of a series of international crimes which it would take the eloquence of a Cicero to describe and the mighty strength of a Demosthenes adequately to condemn. Very briefly, for it is all sickening, let me list the greater – not the lesser – tragedies that went before and of which the culmination of this week was nothing more than an inevitable sequel....

(6:) The democracies turn to Germany and Italy. They must say to the peoples of those countries – and the peoples can be reached in certain ways by publications which ultimately will reach the people – "You face the bitterest, cruelest awards if Hitler and Mussolini be suffered to go on."...(9:) The democracies of earth can have no further contact with Germany and Italy until another day and other leaders come.... No contact, no sale to, no purchase from Italy, Germany, and Japan, until the three leaders go and go forever, and then once again we can deal with peoples whom we respect and whom we (10:) honor and with whom we can deal in self-respect.

March 30, 1939 (Thursday)

Israel H. Levinthal, "The Spiritual Leader in a Time of Crisis," delivered at the Spanish and Portuguese Synagogue, New York, at a Special Convocation and Prayer Service of the Greater NY Rabbinate, inaugurating the UJA. *A New World Is Born*, pp. 245–53

(246:) Our people's lives are broken and shattered. They stand in so many lands persecuted and tormented, the pariahs of the twentieth century. Thousands of them find themselves in No-Man's Land, sleeping like Father Jacob of old upon beds of rock. Like Jacob, too, they find *Naaseh Haolam Kulo K'min Kotel L'fanav*, that the whole world has suddenly become like an iron wall before them.[21] *Wohin? Wohin?* [Whither?] That is the tragic and agonizing question which keeps coming from their trembling lips.

And not only over there in the European lands, but also here,

21 Author's note: Genesis Rabbah 68, 12.

in this blessed land of America, thousands of our brethren stand spiritually depressed. A harsh *Ye'ush*, a feeling of despair, has come over them. They see only the blackness of the night, and there they stand hopeless, many of them without faith.

In these days, we, the spiritual leaders, must first of all bring them the message of hope and courage; we must instill within them new strength and new faith....

(248:) It is not the Jew primarily as an individual who is hated; it is the *Book*, symbol of all that is noble and sacred in life, which he gave to the world and for which he stands today. That is why Christianity, as well as Judaism, is reviled by those pagans who would dethrone all the ideals that make life worthwhile.

Our Bible makes the same analysis in even more striking words. In describing and in analyzing the battle which the Amalekites, the first anti-Semites in history, waged against the Jews in the wilderness, the Bible significantly (249:) says, *Milchama la-Adonoy ba'Amalek*, "the war which Amalek wages is against God; *Midor dor*, in every generation when Amalek appears, *Ki Yad al Kes Yah*, for the hand of Amalek is against the throne of God!" (Exod. 17:16). That is the meaning of the attacks of the modern successors to the ancient Amaleks. It is a war to destroy God, to eradicate God from the hearts and minds of men. In this struggle the Jew is not only defending himself, he is battling in defense of God, in defense of civilization.

April 2, 1939 (Sunday)

Julian B. Feibelman, "Opposites and Extremes," Temple Sinai, New Orleans, LA. Radio Address, WSMB. AJA MS-94, Box 17, Folder 1

(1:) As I speak to you to-day, I am mindful of great extremes in the picture of human affairs. Nothing could be more startlingly opposite than the contrasts which I shall try to describe....

(2:) Now let us look upon the other extreme as it appears in the world of harsh reality.... Suppose you were at this moment a refugee from political oppression in Europe. Suppose you were wandering between the well-guarded boundaries of any country, in that no-man's land of frontier division, where you could neither turn backward nor go forward. Suppose you had been required to leave your possessions, your resources, everything save the bare necessities of life behind you and venture forth, a despised pariah, without hope, without haven, without friend, without home. Suppose you were this day caught in the trap of your own conviction, or the victim of your conscience. Suppose the future held no glimmer of hope for you.

This is the situation in which thousands and thousands of men, women, and children find themselves at this moment. It is not exclusively a Jewish plight; it embraces the faithful among Christians as well. Men and women from high places in society have been reduced (3:) to beggarly wanderers. Professionals and artisans, workers and teachers, students and scientists. From security they have been reduced to insecurity, and from self-sustaining livelihoods to dependence.

But then, suppose you were still enabled to live as one of the favored in any of the lands which have reverted to barbarous militarism, which have changed from the free habitation of social intercourse to an all-encompassing system of spies, secret police, informers and denouncers. Suppose that instead of listening idly to radio programs, you would be constantly subject to the din of propaganda, indoctrinating you along artificial lines of racial nonsense. Suppose the zest for life were totally absent, the freedom of living transformed into a deadened apprehension. You would then realize what brotherhood means; you would pray for it, yearn for it. You would recall the Golden Rule – and beg for the treatment you would show to others.

These reflections of a realistic condition abroad are not exaggerated. They are quite as true as they are realistic. Humanity is on trial, and it divides itself into two hostile camps....

April 4, 1939 (Tuesday, first day of Pesach)

Julius Cohn, *Bezirksrabbiner* [District Rabbi], "Farewell Sermon" (*Abschiedspredigt*), Ulm Congregation, Germany. See Complete Sermons

Samuel Rosenblatt, "The Philosophy of Non-Violence," Beth Tfiloh Congregation, Baltimore, MD. *Our Heritage*, pp. 136–39[22]

---

22 This collection of sermons by Rosenblatt provides no dates of delivery, and most could therefore not be used. However, the reference to Van Paassen's book, published

(138:) Jewish Palestine represents today the severest indictment and the greatest challenge to that philosophy of brute force that is personified by the totalitarian states. That is why neither Hitler nor Mussolini can bear to see it flourish. It might be well to cite apropos this point the testimony of a non-Jew, for commendation is more genuine when it comes from others than when it emanates from ourselves.... (139:) "Totalitarianism," declares Pierre Van Paassen in *Days of Our Years*, "recognizes in the Jew, as the bearer of Judaism – that is to say the bearer of a philosophy of life which makes justice the cardinal principle in man's relationship with his fellow – a natural enemy, and rightly so. The Jew must, therefore, be eliminated because there can be no room for Judaism in a society based on violence and brute force. He must go. He must be exterminated. For not before the Jew is crushed can the forces of darkness attain the other citadels of humanity – humanism, democracy, and Christianity, the three daughters of Judaism."

April 5, 1939 (Wednesday, second day of Pesach)

Max Nussbaum, "Nation and God," Levetzowstrasse Synagogue, Berlin. *From Berlin to Hollywood*, pp. 222–23; translator unidentified

(223:) The Bible demands the utmost, almost the impossible, from the nations of the earth, and all through history people have opposed it. But against their will God forces them from time to time to be confronted with his precepts, and usually it is we, the Jews, as authors of this uncomfortable book, who remind them of its challenge. Maybe this is where the roots of anti-Semitism can be found. Yet our obligation remains unchanged, and as long as we believe in the righteousness of this our mission there is hope for our deliverance....

April 7, 1939 (Friday evening, *Ḥol haMo'ed* Pesach)

Solomon Goldman, Congregation Anshe Emet, Chicago, IL. AJA MS-203, Box 23

---

in 1939, and the publication date of 1940 for Rosenblatt's book (including a Preface dated May 1, 1940) shows that the sermon must have been delivered on Passover 1939.

(1:) It is a dark and critical hour for Jewry. It is an hour that tries the hearts of Zionists. But we have deep faith that the fate of the Jew and the destiny of Eretz Yisrael will not be decided by a Colonial Secretary or a terrorist Mufti.[23] Terrorists may shed blood and secretaries may scrap agreements, but it is not given to living diplomats and terrorists, even as it was not given to those of the past, to mould and shape the destiny of the Jewish people....

(2:) It is one thing to be overtaken by misfortune but another to be overwhelmed by it. To be overwhelmed by misfortune is to yield to violence and injustice. The Jew refuses to accept injustice as the final basis of civilization.

April 11, 1939 (Tuesday)

JUDAH L. MAGNES, "Servant," Hebrew University Graduation Ceremony, Jerusalem. *In the Perplexity of the Times*, pp. 93–96

(93:) You are leaving the University at a time when the world, as we know it, seems to be on the verge of its doom. The smell of death is in the air – death and mutilation, for both body and soul. All about us we hear the old slogans for which you will be asked to lay down your lives. Do not be deceived by them. The slogans are in themselves exalted, but they can never be achieved by war. The good cannot be achieved by war. When you are led as a lamb to the slaughter, know that it is not for the good you are fighting, but against the greater evil, against this paganism that is poisoning the life of the world.

It will not be a *righteous* war, but perhaps – Heaven forgive us! – a *necessary* war...because this iniquity, which is called by the name Hitler, is a far deeper evil than the many iniquities within the imperialisms and the militarisms of the so-called democracies. Close your eyes and your ears when the flags of the armies are blessed by the priests and mullahs and rabbis. What has the life of our faith to do with these sacrifices to Moloch?

23 The British Colonial Secretary was Malcolm MacDonald, who was largely responsible for the "White Paper." The Grand Mufti of Jerusalem was Amin al-Husseini, later notorious for his interaction with Hitler.

April 20, 1939 (Thursday)

Solomon Goldman, Address at United Jewish Relief: Washington Chapter, Woodmont Country Club, Rockville, MD. AJA MS-203, Box 22

(2:) This is not a moment, friends, in which to appeal to Jews as we appealed ten years ago, or eighteen years ago, during the days of the Ukrainian massacres. You will remember when we had a $14,000,000 campaign some years ago. There is a difference, and what the Jew is today depends upon whether he understands the difference in the situation.... (4:) Remember that in 1918 or 1919, the first year after the war and in 1920 and 1921, a quarter of a million Jews were slaughtered in the Ukraine and in northeastern Europe. They were slaughtered by the armies of Petliura, Wrangel, and Denikin, generals who had their reasons for exposing the Jewish communities to their marching armies.[24] They were not fighting against world Jewry. They were not concerned with what was happening to you and to me in the city of Washington, or in the city of Chicago. They were not concerned with the Jews of Paris, or with the Jews of England, or with the Jews of Palestine. Not at all.

It is a different story today. There is today an (5:) organized war on the Jewish people such as we have never known in our history. It is a war to the finish. It is a war of extermination. A group of men have resolved that within ten, fifteen, or twenty years, or a quarter of a century, the Jews – not the German Jew, not the Austrian Jew, but the Jew wherever he is – must disappear from the face of the earth, and these governments, despite the fact that they are poor in cash money are pouring millions of dollars into the United States, into England, into the whole Near East, with one purpose in mind: a war upon us, a war to exterminate us, to bring an end to the Jew.

April 28, 1939 (Friday evening, *Kedoshim*)

Ferdinand M. Isserman, "Judaism's Answer to Tyranny," Special Service

---

24 Petr Wrangel and Anton Deniken were generals in the White Russian forces. Symon Petlyura, head of the Ukrainian government, was considered to have major responsibility for a wave of pogroms against Jews, and was assassinated by a Jew, Shalom Schwarzbard, in 1926. See Antony Polonsky, *The Jews in Russia and Poland*, vol. 3, pp. 33–41.

of Prayer for the Victims of Tyranny, Temple Israel, St. Louis, MO. AJA, M-6, Box 15, Folder 4

(4:) How better can we put [our values] into practice than by meeting the challenge of our afflicted brethren with a generosity that shall by far outstrip the generosity of other generations, with a spirit of self-sacrifice, of enthusiasm and of devotion. We can demonstrate to the world that we ourselves have taken the medicine which we believe holds healing for them.

I need not again assail your ears with all the horrors and tragedies of from two hundred [thousand] to one million Jewish families. From this pulpit, you heard it from my own lips as, broken-hearted and dejected and downcast, I returned year after year from my visits abroad to pour out a tale of tragedy which was so dark that it was unbelievable. I have often hoped that I had been a false prophet and my experiences abroad had been like a bad dream, a nightmare which would be shaken off in the dawn of a new morning. Alas, the swift march of events has sustained every word I uttered to you. But…in the past few years, I have undergone great spiritual experiences. I have risen from the depths and I have found myself again. As a result, I am better qualified today for leadership than ever. I know today not merely from reading our holy books, but from the struggles in my own soul and the revelation they have brought to me, that there is a God to whom we can turn in sorrow, on whom we can rely for strength.

(5:) My people, I say to you, with all the conviction and earnestness of my soul, that more important than material gifts is that you retain your vision, that you yield not to fear, that you maintain your faith.… Not only must we recognize how safe we are in America, but if we would be holy as God is holy [cf. Lev. 19:2], from the weekly Torah reading] we must not allow any bitterness to fill our souls or any desire for vengeance to corrode our spirits. Cherish no grudges and hold no hates, comes the mandate of the ancient prophet.

(7:) My people, I do not ask you to raise funds alone. I ask you to raise your spirits. I do not ask you to help others alone. I ask you to help yourselves. Become children of God. I ask you to be holy as God is holy.…

May 12, 1939 (Friday evening)

Ignaz Maybaum, "Man and Catastrophe," Hampstead Synagogue. *Man and Catastrophe*, pp. 15–23, delivered in German, translated by Joseph Leftwich[25]

(16:) We know that Job does not let his sufferings make him doubt God.

But when we look round to-day and consider the mood that has taken hold of so many of us, we must admit that it is pessimism, often finding expression in the thought that God is losing the wager and that Satan wins.

This is the lowest depth, to which only the complete abandonment of the entire Jewish attitude can descend....

Face to face with what has happened and is happening in Germany to our fellow-Jews we may indeed say that the just suffer. Innocent blood is being shed, and Thou, O Father in Heaven, whom we declare to be merciful and long-suffering, just in all Thy ways, why are such things possible?...

(20:) We must never for one moment forget the great mass of those who suffer in Germany. People must react to it here in the same way as when they are told that the house is on fire and that people are trapped inside. Will you hesitate to save? Run, hasten. Shout, help! Do all you can, risk everything, or the flames will consume these human lives!

How does man behave in a catastrophe?...

(21:) The Jew who is persecuted by Hitler has much to suffer. But it does not affect his dignity. It has made our dignity only more apparent in the eyes of the world. Hitler hates the Jews, the world says. Paganism hates those who have faith. H's attack on the Jews has given us an opportunity to prove to the world the significance of our faith. Judaism is not to be co-ordinated in a world that has become pagan.

---

25 As Maybaum explained in the Preface to his book, the organization of special Shabbat services at the Hampstead Synagogue for German Jewish refugees, with sermons delivered by refugee rabbis in German, was established by Chief Rabbi Joseph Hertz. The first such service was led by Dr. Alfred Jospe on April 7, 1939; see *JC*, April 14, 1939, p. 18 (though no text of Jospe's sermon is provided). Jospe immigrated to the United States in June 1939.

Man can display in suffering a dignity such as no joy can give him....

(22:) If emigration must always at first mean poverty and limitation, it is the great advantage of good breeding that it enables us to endure poverty....

So we wish to say to all to whom we come: We have passed through suffering, but suffering has not broken us....

(23:) We will say to those of our own faith to whom we have come, to all who will not let their faith in the good and the true be torn out of their breasts: Yes, we have come out of catastrophe.... But we come to you as Jews, and that means that we come with faith in our hearts. It is true that we come from a lost battle. But it is not the decisive battle. We come to you as brave and courageous warriors....

April 23, 1939 (Sunday)

Solomon B. Freehof, "A Man and His Friendships," Rodef Shalom Congregation, Pittsburgh. *Rodef Shalom Pulpit*, vol. 4, no. 4, pp. 3–10

(8:) The lowest depth of the psychic depression of the Jewish community occurred in November when on orders from headquarters in Germany every synagogue in Germany was burned and every store destroyed. The November pogroms made the Jews in America feel absolutely defenseless in a mad modern world. Then the voice of Christian America began to be heard, and it gathered in volume spreading from class to class and from coast to coast until all America expressed its horror and its indignation at Nazi brutality. I believe that this arousing of America was the first turn in the course of history, which is now rapidly changing for the better before our eyes. But whatever international change it achieved, I would like you to see that the indignation of the American people achieved also this: It suddenly showed the Jews of America that they are not alone, that they have comrades, that they have friends.

May 12, 1939 (Friday evening)

Ferdinand M. Isserman, "Is 'Confessions of a Nazi Spy' [a film shown in St. Louis] War Propaganda?," Excerpts [for the Media], Temple Israel, St. Louis, MO. AJA MS-6, Box 15, Folder 4

Nothing worse could happen to the Jewries of Europe than war. The Jews of Germany will be immediately destroyed. Streicher, the leading anti-Semite, states that in case of war, he would take a furlough of one week from the army. During that week, he would kill every Jew in Germany, and then Germany would certainly be victorious. He forgets that in the world war 112,000 German Jews were in the German army, that 12,000 were killed on the field of battle, that thousands were decorated by the government, that in the last war German-Jewish soldiers helped the German nation. Whatever there is left of the Jewry of Germany would be annihilated at the outbreak of war. So the Jews of Germany would not be helped by war. If you study the map of Europe, you see that the rest of European Jewry lives in the war zone. If there is war between Germany and Poland, all Poles will suffer, and the three and a half million Jews of Poland will suffer the worst of all. If there is war between Germany and Russia over the Ukraine, the hundreds of thousands of Jews living in the Polish and Russian Ukraine will be immediate victims. If there is war between Russia and Romania, the million Jews of Romania will be crushed.... The Jewries of Europe live in the most vulnerable areas. And any war would prove devastating to them....

Not only do Jews live in the war areas, but Jews know that in the aftermath of war, they are the chief sufferers....

As far as America is concerned, the film "Confessions of a Nazi Spy" must teach Americans that in a modern world there are forces, determined forces, unscrupulous forces, intelligent forces, able forces, seeking to undermine the temple of democracy and to destroy every vestige of government.[26] America must meet these forces in the American way, not with force, not with violence. It must meet false propaganda with truth, the truth of the superiority of democracy....

May 14, 1939 (Sunday)

Israel Goldstein, "Modern Jewish Questions," Address to Conference on "The Jew and the World Crisis," Jewish Theological Seminary of America, New York. *Toward a Solution*, pp. 99–110

26 The film, starring Edward G. Robinson as an FBI Agent who discovers a Nazi spy ring, was released on May 6, 1939, six days before the sermon was delivered.

(101:) Even if all Jews, however, were paragons of virtue, they would still be vilified, condemned, and hounded, because it would suit the purposes of the misleaders of society who need a villain for the melodrama which they are concocting. In the Jew they have someone whom they consider to be a ready-made candidate for the role. There is more psychological truth than fiction in the story concerning an official in high authority in Fascist Japan, who is reported to have cabled to his ally, Germany's Minister of Propaganda, "We are starting an anti-Semitic movement in Japan. Please send us some Jews."

May 19, 1939 (Friday evening, *BeMidbar*)

Ignaz Maybaum, "Priestly Bearing," Hampstead Synagogue. *Man and Catastrophe*, pp. 24–31 (delivered in German, translated by Joseph Leftwich)

(24:) Our Portion of the Law to-day speaks of the priestly status of the Tribe of Levi, that priestly status and mission which ultimately passed to all Israel....

I should like to illustrate this idea, brought up by to-day's reading of the Law, by quoting a man whom I and others consider the greatest German Jew. I mean the late Franz Rosenzweig... The words I have in mind are found in his magnum opus: "The Jew strides through world history without a sideward glance." [27]

(26:) Our duty in these hard times is to preserve a priestly calm that will not give way to panic....

(27:) I had another experience of this not-looking aside that belongs to the priestly bearing. It was in October 1938, when the German Government deported the Polish Jews living in Germany back into Poland. I observed these people. I saw them and their suffering, but I also saw them stand up against the railway lines and say their afternoon prayers. They had said their morning prayers that day in their dark prison cells, encompassed by raw, cruel reality. But they had the strength not to look aside, to maintain their priestly bearing....

---

27 In the original, "*Seitenblicklos geht der Jude durch die Weltgeshichte.*" The "magnum opus" was Rosenzweig's *Star of Redemption* (*Der Stern der Erlösung*), first published in 1921. Maybaum was a disciple of Rosenzweig, and quotes him frequently in his sermons; he also quoted this statement in several of his later works..

I was reminded for the third time a few days ago of this quality that Franz Rosenzweig calls not looking aside, what the Bible means when it requires of us to have the strength of a priestly bearing. I was talking with some Palestinian workers about the situation that the Government White Paper created for Palestine and the Jews.[28] The White Paper was a heavy blow. And these people knew it. But they also knew that there had been White Papers before, other such documents, and they knew that though these could help or hinder the Jewish people in (28:) their claim to Palestine, that claim itself could never be destroyed by any political announcement.... Britain has done more in recent years for the Jewish refugees than any other nation. We rescued ones are the last to criticize our rescuers. Besides, who can say what may still happen? Without a side-glance we go on speaking of Palestine, the Holy Land....

(29:) It [German Jewish refugees speaking German in public] is a serious problem. And I agree with those who have asked me to deal with it from the pulpit.[29] People who speak German in the bus or in the underground must be told that they are behaving tactlessly. They should speak English, even if it is not very good English. We have no right to make English people ask themselves in some parts of London whether they are in a foreign country....

(31:) We must take the Jew-hatred we experience in Germany very seriously. True enough, it was aimed at the Jew who was economically established. But this Jew-hatred was something more. It was aimed at the priest in the Jew, at the Jew who stands for the idea that without possessing political power, it is still possible to give effect to the good and the true. Jew-hatred in Germany struck at the Jew because he represented the idea that politics and justice go together, that the purpose of political activity is to realize justice. By virtue of this faith the Jew is a Jew, and it is this that surrounds the Jew with dignity....

28 The "White Paper" was the document issued by the British Government on May 17, 1939, two days before this sermon was delivered. It limited Jewish immigration to Palestine to 1500 per year for the following five years, thereby further restricting opportunities for Jews who were able to escape from Nazi-occupied Germany.

29 Maybaum was, of course, preaching in German. The problem he was addressing is apparently applied to refugees speaking German in public.

May 25, 1939 (Thursday, second day of Shavu'ot)

Salis Daiches, Edinburgh Hebrew Congregation, Scotland. *The Scotsman*, Friday May 26, 1939, p. 6, with headline: "PERSECUTION OF THE JEWS: Edinburgh Rabbi's Tribute to General Assembly"[30]

The sentiments expressed by the speakers in the General Assembly are such as will find an echo in the hearts of Jews everywhere, and will be received with gratitude by the Jewish people as a whole. The Jewish citizens of Scotland will feel particularly glad and grateful that it has been left to the spokesmen of the Church of Scotland to utter such an emphatic and impressive condemnation of anti-Semitism and race hatred and such profound sympathy for the suffering Jews of Europe, as well as for the remnant of Israel that is seeking shelter and security, freedom and equality, in its ancestral home. The attitude of the Scottish people towards these sufferers is the silver lining to the cloud which has descended upon Jews, and they can only pray that the example set by the religious leaders of this country might soon be followed by the spiritual heads of other countries in Europe, and that the spirit of arrogance and aggression prevailing abroad might soon be changed into that of true humanity and brotherhood as expressed in the teaching of the Hebrew prophets of old.

June 14, 1939

Abba Hillel Silver, "The World Crisis and Jewish Survival." Pamphlet reprinted from *CCAR Yearbook*, 49

(4:) Such is the world crisis to-day, a vast and prolonged convulsion whose end is nowhere in sight. Such a crisis was bound to affect Jewish life most adversely....

---

30 Reference is to the General Assembly of the Church of Scotland. Among the statements issued by the assembly was the following: "The Nazi persecution of Jews has blackened the repute of Christendom and has debased the whole morale of Christian peoples and betrayed its highest tradition" (*The Jewish Echo*, May 19, 1939, p. 13); there was also a strong condemnation of the British White Paper (*The Jewish Echo*, June 2, 1939, p. 3, both references cited by Elizabeth E. Imber, "Saving Jews: The History of Jewish-Christian Relations in Scotland, 1880–1948" (MA thesis, Brandeis University, 2010), p. 82.

(6:) The Third Reich – and as a result of the pressure of the Axis, also Italy – has carried this process to its logical conclusion: complete political disfranchisement and economic outlawry. It has determined not to curb the Jew, but to exterminate him, through economic strangulation.[31] *Juda Verrecke!* In Hungary, an economic *numerus clausus* has been imposed upon the Jew. In Poland, sporadic restrictive measures have been enacted, and only the uncertain international status of Poland, hovering between the two worlds of the Axis and the so-called democratic front, has restrained the government from enacting a drastic code of anti-Jewish legislation in order to force a majority of Polish Jewry to emigrate. In other countries of Central and Eastern Europe, the programs of politico-economic action against the Jew have varied according to the political orientation within each country and the international sphere of influence in which each country moves.

Anti-Semitism has become in our day a matter of political action not only for economic reasons – to appease the job-and-career hunger of the majority population – but also for diplomatic reasons – to realize certain imperial ambitions, and to extend political hegemony. The race theory served the Nazis well as a political weapon by means of which millions of people, Germans by race but not by nationality, were brought within the confines of the Third Reich.... Anti-Semitism today is the Reich's Fifth (7:) Column – a cunning and effective weapon of imperial conquest and domination. This explains the amazing *missionary* character of Nazi anti-Semitism and the sustained drive behind it....

(8:) [L]earning, logic, and statistics notwithstanding, the Nuremberg (9:) laws were enacted, in the year of grace 1935, in one of the most civilized countries of the world, and the reactions which took place in Spain in 1492, and the manifold tragedies of the Spanish expulsion, pale into insignificance alongside the horrible streamlined reaction in modern Germany, and the brutal expulsion of Jews from Germany now going on. Here, in the twentieth century, one can witness reaction, cold pogroms, terror and tragedy at full tide....

31 Note the characteristic use of the term "exterminate" in a metaphorical sense, before there was any program of systematic mass murder.

(11:) Only one fact can we postulate with confidence about the history of our people. As a people, we have survived! ... It should be borne in mind, too, that our survival transpired not in some secluded Shangri-La, sheltered from danger and attack by ramparts of impassable mountains. We did not vegetate in passivity in some quiet, sequestered land away from the world's stern stresses and struggles. We achieve our survival in the very midst of the world's mad and murderous arenas. We were invaded. We were attacked. We were exiled. We were driven over the face of the earth. We were scattered and broken, hounded and harassed, through long and weary centuries. We clashed with great empires. We resisted mighty civilizations. We were surrounded by militant faiths which sought to absorb us or to destroy us. We are today again upon the rack in the torture chambers of the earth. Nevertheless, we survived! And, for our size, we are today the most alive and creative people in the world.

(13:) [U]nless the entire world plunges back into barbarism, and the pathological obsessions of the Teutonic dervishes seize hold of the whole of mankind – a condition conceivable but hardly probable – the exterminationist policies of the Nazis are destined (14:) to be localized. Perhaps even in the Reich itself time will neutralize them....

June 16, 1939 (Friday evening)

Ignaz Maybaum, "Barbarism or Faith?," Hampstead Synagogue, London. *Man and Catastrophe*, pp. 32–41 (delivered in German, translated by Joseph Leftwich)

(33:) The world is back to-day at this period of barbaric segregation of tribes and nations, has sunk back to that stage of raw life out of which Israel found the way as Israel....

(34:) Because the civilized and cultural unity of mankind is again in peril, if it has not actually broken down, because nations that we thought civilized have returned to their original barbaric tribal form, so that civilized people stand aghast, because Edom and Cain are not merely symbolic figures to-day, but are living contemporaries, men and women of our own time, living among us, whom we all know, it becomes necessary now to ask ourselves again the question, how was it that Israel under such conditions was able to remain Israel?...

(40:) The world knows what Jews whose mother-tongue was German have done by way of contribution to German culture. But Homer's sun no longer shines in Germany. Weimar has ceased to exist. That is another reason why there can be no going back for us. What has been destroyed was beautiful, but it was not holy. We may lament it, as all civilized mankind laments this great cultural catastrophe brought about in Germany by barbaric rule. But this lament must not become a complaint against God. God teaches us to be happy and of good spirit at all times...."

June 30, 1939 (Friday evening)

Ignaz Maybaum, "Jewish Defence: The British Cyrus," St. John's Wood Synagogue, London. *Man and Catastrophe*, pp. 42–50 (delivered in German, translated by Joseph Leftwich)

(43:) Erfurt is now the centre of a German anti-Jewish propaganda organization which issues a publication proclaiming itself a "World Service." This modern Balak sends out messengers into every part of the world, with the message, "Come now, curse me this people" (Num. 22:6). Books, pamphlets, and placards are printed in Erfurt in all the languages of the earth and are distributed in the most distant places. Everything to-day is done on a world-wide scale. The lie too is on a world-wide scale....[32]

(48:) Now too a Jewish Science is at work in Germany, but it is born of hatred of Israel. There is an Institute in Munich that professes to be scientific and publishes books and pamphlets about Jews and Judaism, in which hate and lies guide the pen of the writers. This Munich Institute provides the Erfurt World Service with the material for its propaganda.[33]

---

32 Erfurt was indeed the center of the Nazi *Welt-Dienst* (World Service), an agency of Goebbels' Propaganda Ministry that supplemented the local Nazi radio service, which focused more on news relating to the war (see Ernst Kris and Hans Speier, *German Radio Propaganda*).

33 On the Munich Institute, see Weinreich, *Hitler's Professors*, pp. 45–54, describing the *Forschungsabteilung Judenfrage* (Research Department for the Jewish Question), with "academic" conferences held in 1936, 1937, and 1938. In 1939, this was overshadowed by a larger *Institut zur Erforschung der Judenfrage* (Institute for Research into the Jewish Question) in Frankfurt-am-Main, headed by Alfred Rosenberg.

July 4, 1939 (Tuesday, 17 Tammuz)

Abraham Mayer Heller, "Birthday or Yahrzeit?," Rabbinical Assembly Convention, Asbury Park, NJ. *Jewish Survival*, pp. 253–61

(255:) We are met on a day of dual significance, *Fourth of July* and *Shiboh Osor Betammuz* [17 Tammuz] – the celebration of a birthday and the marking of a Yahrzeit....

(256:) While the national American Birthday celebration happily spells for us in this country safety and security, when we think of the *Shiboh Osor Betammuz*, the world over, our hearts cry out: *Ekh noshir* [Ps. 137:4] – "How can we rejoice" in these catastrophic days when our people and faith are threatened with extinction?...

(257:) What more bitter tragedy! Six hundred thousand, rooted for centuries in the soil and culture of their native country stripped of their possessions, of citizenship and all human rights, are made *holkhe midboriyot*,[34] wanderers in a social wilderness, with no port to receive them and no hope of return....

How strikingly similar are our experience of yesterday and today! An Amalek by a different name but he, too, with neither fear of God nor love of man in his heart, brutally assaults us when our people are faint and weary. Nor are the methods of calumny abandoned. Instead of Balak and (258:) Balaam, new military chieftains, false prophets and priests, raise their harsh voices against us. In this crucial hour of our greatest need, the one nation we had the right to call brother – England – though nurtured on the noble teachings of the Bible, nevertheless, like Edom of old, rejected our pleas for sympathy and cooperation with the familiar tantalizing words: *Lo taabor* (Num. 20:18, 20) – "Thou shalt not pass!"[35]

July 8, 1939 (Saturday)

Ignaz Maybaum, "Zeal," Hampstead Synagogue, London. *Man and Catastrophe*, pp. 51–60 (delivered in German, translated by Joseph Leftwich)

(59:) To turn away God's wrath from this world must surely be man-

34 Author's note: b. Berakhot 54b.

35 Reference of course is to the restricted entrance for Jews into Palestine following the "White Paper."

kind's supreme task to-day, when we realize, horror-struck, how low we have sunk in our cultural life, how the descent to barbarism has become the characteristic feature of our epoch. Israel's suffering in this period shows us clearly what has come upon mankind as a whole. Mankind has suffered a terrible reverse. The barometer of our suffering proclaims it to all. If we are to surmount these bitter times we must have genuine zeal, the (60:) zeal of love, faith and good deeds....

July 14, 1939 (Friday evening)

Ignaz Maybaum, "Jewish Migration," Golders Green Synagogue, London. *Man and Catastrophe*, pp. 61–71 (delivered in German, translated by Joseph Leftwich)

(64:) We must and can see in our present fate what is holy. For what has happened? We have been persecuted and robbed. Then we were able to get a permit or an affidavit, and through a narrow door we came out of our inferno of persecution into a free land, but we are aliens there. We encounter new difficulties when we try to adjust ourselves to the life and culture of this country that has saved us. All these are brutal facts....

We were happy where we were, in Germany, Austria, Czechoslovakia. We were happy there, we had been there for generations, and it is a hard and cruel fate to be driven from one's home. Yet here is our patent that there is no room for us in a world returning to paganism, here is our patent like a patent of nobility. That we are aliens is our priestly destiny....

(66:) Zionism goes to show how important Jewish wandering is as a civilizing factor....[36]

(69:) It is completely and entirely in accord with Jewish destiny that Jewish professors are being hounded out of German, Austrian and Czech universities, that Jewish writers, doctors, and intellectuals are driven from their homes and must look all over the world for new places in which to settle and continue their activity and earn their

36 This is followed by a very positive description of achievements in Palestine, and the ideology of the *Halutz*, or Jewish pioneer (pp. 66–68).

living. It is the Jewish destiny. But the full depth and sacredness of Jewish destiny will be understood only if we realize that every little businessman and every petty official from Germany, Austria, and Czechoslovakia who has been deprived of his livelihood is not merely a disposed citizen, but a man who is suffering for the sake of God....

(70:) I have been saying all along in these sermons which I have been delivering in London, as a refugee to Jewish refugees: Take the consolation that our religion offers us. We are, indeed, sufferers in need of consolation. I have urged you to trust and hope.... But to-day I call upon you also to be proud.... (71:) The Jew too is always at the front. The Jew shows his road through the world and God sees the station of his journeys of suffering. Our suffering is endured for the sake of God. That is our pride, our consolation, and our hope.

July 21, 1939 (Friday evening)

Ignaz Maybaum, "Happy and Unhappy Jews," St. John's Wood Synagogue, London. *Man and Catastrophe*, pp. 72–83 (delivered in German, translated by Joseph Leftwich)

(72:) "Comfort ye, comfort ye my people, saith your God" (Isa. 40:1). Jewish refugees stand facing the Sabbath of Consolation, and ask: "What consolation can avail us?"...

Indeed, the people are grass. There was a short story published after 1933 in one of the German Jewish papers which went something like this: An American Jew was standing in a Jewish cemetery. I can't remember now whether it was in Frankfurt-on-the-Main or in Berlin. But I know it was in a city which was one of the larger Jewish communities of former Germany. And this American Jew was saying Kaddish, the prayer for the dead. He was saying Kaddish for German Jewry. This short (73:) story made a deep impression on us in 1933. But we did not know then what we know now, in 1939. German Jewry no longer exists. German Jewry and Russian Jewry have ceased to exist as free and independent branches of the Jewish people. German Jewry is to-day dispersed. Russian Jewry has not even that much. Russian Communism has not allowed it to escape. And its fate is the fate of the lost ten tribes.

(74:) What is characteristic about German Jewry is precisely the fact that lying between the two, it was neither an East European Jewry living entirely according to tradition, nor completely Western Jewry like that of America, living according to its own judgment.... (76:) German Jewry, especially its Zionist section, had its enthusiastic admirers of East European Jewry....

(80:) The Jew is by his very existence a mute, powerful sermon. Jewish suffering is the loudest possible admonition calling to all people to take heed, to look and see that the world is not yet saved, that we are still in the pre-Messianic stage of history. Thus suffering has a purpose, and this purpose is also bound up with the Jewish mission.

(81:) In Germany antisemitism manifested itself in alliance with the persecution of Christianity. Jewish persecution in Germany is the bankruptcy of humanity, and it therefore affects the whole of mankind. What has happened in Germany affects not only Jews. It affects Christianity and civilization.

(82:) Not only through the active form of good deeds, but also through the passive form of enduring suffering do the Jews serve God. This is the service rendered to-day by the Jews from Germany, Austria, and Czechoslovakia. Let no one withhold reverence from them, for suffering, as Job shows us, need not be punishment, but may mean election....

German Jewry has ceased to exist as a separate people of Israel. But there are still German Jews. They live in England, America, or wherever (83:) their Diaspora road has taken them. And through the conscience of both Jews and non-Jews to whom German Jews are now coming along their world Diaspora, it is God who calls to them in the words of His Prophet, "Comfort ye, comfort ye my people" (Isa. 40:1)....

August 26, 1939 (Saturday, *Ki Teitzei*)

Abraham Cohen, "The Crisis," Birmingham Hebrew Congregation, Birmingham, England. Unpublished, David Cohen Private Collection

(1:) Our minds are so pre-occupied with the critical state of affairs which confronts Europe that it is difficult to think of anything else. The feeling of strain and foreboding accompanies us even into the synagogue.... The history of a year ago is repeating itself to-day with an all-important difference. Last year the peoples of Europe were driven to the edge of the precipice, but at the (2:) last moment the deadly peril was averted by a surrender to the threat of war. To-day no such solution can or will be applied. A big price was then paid for the maintenance of peace, largely on the assurance given by the head of the German State that he had no more territorial claims to make in Europe. The democratic powers accepted that assurance in the hope that it would be honoured. Within six months it was broken by the annexation of what was left of Czecho-Slovakia. Soon after that demands were made of Poland which, if accepted, would involve her dismemberment and loss of independence. It is generally recognized that even this would not be the end of German claims in Europe, and that what is really sought is complete domination.... We are consequently faced with these alternatives – submission to German domination or resistance....

[3:] We must continue to hope to the last moment that the rulers of Germany, who now realize that the series of bloodless victories has come to an end, will withdraw the challenge. They have tried to break the nerve of the democratic nations with their display of power, but they failed. They must indeed be devoid of all humanity if, in the fulfillment of their ambitions, they are ready to drench Europe in blood. But we Jews know only too well from their treatment of our co-religionists that such humane considerations have no weight with them. Human lives count for nothing with them; that is why, hoping for the best, we must be prepared for the worst.

WARTIME

September 9, 1939 (Saturday)

Salis Daiches, "The Fight for Justice," Edinburgh Synagogue, Scotland. *JC*, September 15, 1939, pp. 23–24

(23:) No sacrifice can be too great to remove the Nazi terror from Europe. For if this dreadful evil, which has been allowed to grow and expand for more than a decade, is not destroyed now it will affect the whole human race and will put an end to civilised life.... It behooves all who believe in God and His Law and have faith (24:) in God and His Law to unite for the purpose of defeating the tyrannical rulers of Germany, of frustrating their designs, and of undoing the evil they had already accomplished by the use of violence and unparalleled lawlessness. Humanity must be delivered from the scourge of Hitlerism so that peace, based on law and justice, might prevail....

For more than six years, the evil power of Nazism has been fighting Judaism with poisoned weapons, with false and vile accusations, and has been inflicting unspeakable torture upon the body and soul of the Jew, while the outside world could only look on, and the spokesmen of the God-fearing peoples had to be content with verbal protests and expressions of indignation, which were received with derisive laughter and scorn. But the Nazi rulers were not content with crushing a helpless community within the borders of their own country. Having deprived their Jewish citizens of all their possessions and turned them into outcasts, Hitler and his henchmen began to plan the invasion and oppression of the neighbouring peoples who they thought would be unable to offer effective resistance. They succeeded in annexing the territories of two small nations,[37] and with increasing greed and arrogance they began to threaten the existence of Poland. Reluctantly, the statesmen of the Western democracies came to the conclusion that if this evil power were allowed to continue its work every European nation would in time be faced with the danger of having the yoke of servitude placed upon it and of being compelled to bow to the pagan rule of Nazism.

Hence the resolve of the two great freedom-loving nations of Western Europe to rally their forces, in order to stem the tide of aggression and to destroy forever the power of the men who have wrought so much evil in the world. The great struggle has now begun, and it would not end before a complete victory had been won for the cause of human liberty.

---

37 Referring, of course, to Austria and Czechoslovakia.

September 13, 1939 (Erev Rosh Hashanah)

Ferdinand M. Isserman, "After Fifty-Seven Hundred Years," Temple Israel, St. Louis, MO. AJA, MS-6, Box 15, Folder 5

(1:) While the world united in fearful suspense whether war or peace was to be the lot of our age, while cables buzzed with the reports of chancelleries, while men and women in all countries were glued to the radio hungrily awaiting the word which would spell life or death, while millions of men were leaving their homes, sighing their farewells, seeing wife, children, or parent for the last time, while children were practicing the art of donning a gas mask, while statesmen were burning midnight oil, and a whole continent paused from its normal activities to prepare to assault or to withstand assault, I tried to prepare my Rosh Hashono message for you.

Too well did I know the terrain [that] was to be the theatre of conflict.... With millions of lives at stake, with the future of Europe hanging in the balance, (2:) with the destiny of America shrouded in mystery, with rage and hatred, propaganda and malice, dreadnoughts and battleships occupying the center of attention, focusing the interests of men, what mattered Rosh Hashono? Here were life and death issues alongside of its observance. What matters the ritual of an old faith? What was a holy day among a persecuted people?... Rosh Hashono was nigh, but what could it mean? What vitality could it have before these momentous problems?

As a Jew and rabbi, both in a personal and professional capacity, I could not allow this mood to dominate me. This eve was coming. I had to stand here before you. I must give you a word. Custom, convention required it, even though it be trivial alongside of the graver concerns. I must speak and I must prepare....

(3:) With what relief do we leave this old year, what trials it brought, what painful memories we leave behind.... All of us of the household of Israel have drunk from the bitter cup this past year.

The echoes of Munich were hardly over when came the seizure of Prague, the end of Czecho-Slovakia, and over four hundred thousand more Jews were paupered, beggared, brow-beaten, bullied, annihilated overnight. The monster which crushed them seemed to grow stronger with every bit of cruelty and bestiality, boasting that the fate of Germany's Jews would become the fate of universal Jewry. Then came the November pogrom, an insolent flouting of the conscience of humanity, and as brazen (4:) a defiance of the moral law as the twentieth century has witnessed. Do I have to remind you of the cry of terror which came from overseas when sixty thousand or more decent men were torn from their homes like vile scoundrels, when every Jewish home was demolished, every Jewish enterprise destroyed, every synagogue burned by incendiaries, and the highways of the world were filled with the agonized wailing of sufferers? Followed by the Steamship *St. Louis* cruising around with its cargo of human freight, not permitted to land as if it contained the bubonic plague. And here the tentacles of the destroyer reached out, awaking echoes in 800 periodicals seeking to undermine our position, challenging our patriotism, assailing our decency, minimizing our value to our country and our worth as human beings. . . .

How then can I summon you to judgment? How can I challenge you for your sins and myself for mine? Haven't we borne enough? . . .

(5:) [Story of a child with an infected finger told at length: the parent is afraid the child will die, the stranger reassures parent that the child is essentially healthy and sound.] It seems to me that we in America, we Jews in America, are like that child. We have sustained an injury, but the injury is merely like a sore finger on a well body.[38] . . .

(6:) [On US response to *Kristallnacht*, summoning US ambassador back, leading figures speaking out:] I believe that history was being made and a new high watermark in the ancient history of Israel had been attained. Never before had a great nation so unanimously arisen to express its sympathy for suffering Jews. Immediately the reaction had profound effects, and whatever hold Hitler may have had upon some Americans, he lost. It seems to me to be that the tragedy of German Jews turned out to be a blessing to the Jews of America, towards whom there was released a flood of sympathy, of

38 Cf. the very different version of this story told by Kahlenberg on Yom Kippur, October 1, 1941, below: there the child (representing the Jewish people) has an infection from a thorn in his finger that is so dangerous that the father (representing God) has to inflict severe pain in order to save the child's life, despite the child's screams of agony.

good-will, of appreciation unparalleled in all American history.... (8:) What is true of America is true of other countries. [mentions France, England]...(9:) So on this night when we can forget the pain in one finger, we can see that this year, the year which has just closed, brought much blessing....

Jacob Bosniak, "The Approach of Dawn," Ocean Parkway Jewish Center, Brooklyn, NY. *Interpreting Jewish Life*, pp. 114–20

(114:) "One calleth unto me out of Seir, 'Watchman, what of the night?' The watchman said, 'morning cometh, and also the night'" (Isa. 21:11).... How well these words express our feelings and emotions today! We confess that in the face of the present catastrophe in Europe we are somewhat discouraged. A sense of futility and faith in God is struggling within us....

(116:) The captain of the German steamer *St. Louis*, with a cargo of nine hundred and seven men, women, and children, posted guards among his passengers to prevent them from committing a collective suicide. Another captain of a Greek vessel forsook the ship in the midst of the sea, leaving the passengers to their fate.... Thus pained and tortured by the tragedies of our people abroad, we are strongly disquieted by the intensified activities of our enemies in this country. We have watched the spread of prejudice and even hatred against us with bated breath. Open and secret organizations against the Jew have begun to flourish in every part of our land. The poison of anti-Semitism has penetrated every avenue of human endeavor....

(118:) One disappointment after another has been our share during the last years.

But we will never despair of salvation.... We have had many periods of darkness which were always followed by sunshine. Let there be no discouragement or frustration in our midst. Let us redouble our efforts in the struggle against the enemy....

Stephen S. Wise, (no title), Free Synagogue at Carnegie Hall, New York. AJA, Box 22: SSW Microfilms of AJHS and BUASC papers

(1:) Tomorrow, as has been my wont for many years, I shall undertake to tell the story of the year and to have such prophecy as I can touching the days and the years that lie before. Tonight, I would do something simpler, something, I must add, less mournful, less melancholy....

(3:) I would tonight point out with infinite sorrow in my heart that we Jews might have saved the world from the overwhelming disaster that may yet all but destroy the things worthwhile. If that world had only listened, not with (4:) its ears, but with its heart; if the world had put aside its unconcern touching hurt and wrong and evil to the Jew, and come to realize that a regime of which ninety-nine per cent of the population must brutally impoverish, humiliate, torture, destroy one per cent, who have lived within that land for more than a thousand years, then the democracies that today face the bitterest and bloodiest of tests might have bethought themselves that a new evil, a new danger, has arisen for all mankind. We cannot allow this evil to wax strong and create a weapon itself with all the armor of destructiveness. What the democracies found it inevitable to do in August 1939 they could have done, they *ought* to have done, in 1933, not for our sake, but for their own, for the sake of millions of English, French and Polish youth, who will be massacred on the battlefield.

Yet you and I must listen day by day, and upon street corners you read it in the papers that insult our eyes, week after week, that Jews are the war-mongers, we are seeking to drag the United States into war. We who lose most and suffer most terribly under war; we who hate war, we who know there is no help, no healing in war....

(5:) Brothers and sisters of the three million and more Polish Jews who today are being ground down together with their fellow-Poles – and if Poland should be completely occupied will become the tragic victims of that regime of force and terror and shame....

May I as my last word read to you some lines which I have written in *Opinion* (of which I happen to be editor): "By a lightning thrust, Hitler has hurled himself at Poland and on the day this is written, the first day of what may prove to be years of war, the world that is not bound up with the Reich dares to hope that the democracies may save themselves at last by defending the latest victim of the dictatorships...."

Abraham H. Feinberg, "America's Hour of Decision," Temple Beth-El, Rockford, IL. AJA, MS 85, Box 2, Folder 5; Saperstein, *Jewish Preaching in Times of War*, pp. 392–98

(393:) Neither sudden nor unexpected has been the explosion now resounding the four corners of the earth.... Writers and observers of repute, likewise, present incontrovertible evidence of the diabolical intentions of the new Nazi regime.

Even more convincing had been the many lying tantrums of the German Fuehrer himself....

(394:) Storm signals, therefore, had been hoisted again and again. Reveilles of warning were being sounded hourly. Why, then, did the world of decent men slumber until the strength of morning had passed?...

(395:) Condemned before the bar of human decency, repudiated and excoriated even by fellow-countrymen, Adolf Hitler stands convicted as the world's most dangerous criminal... a murderer who has shattered the lives of innocent Jews, killed the Republic of Germany, death-purged opponents and associates, bombed Polish women and children, and upon whose head lies the guilt for the blood now being shed – German and Allied – in the present European catastrophe.

(396:) Faced by the crisis of war abroad and the involvement of Canada here, America's hour of decision is now at hand. Abhorring as all do the Nihilistic terror of Nazism, does it become then our moral duty to make common cause with the forces of democracy against the legions of a snarling autocracy?

Even assuming that Poland, a land of oppressive bigotry, isn't worth saving, that the sincerity of the Chamberlain–Daladier regimes has not yet been proved, the preview of a civilization scarred with the swastika of Nazism affords a spectacle too horrible for contemplation.

Between the banner of democracy and the rag of piracy, the moral decision of America will never be in doubt. Yet impossible as it is to maintain neutrality of opinion, sanity still prescribes neutrality of action. There is a heavy burden of pain in our hearts over the tragedy which has befallen Europe.... Shall we add the bones of our continent, too? The hatred of war in America has become far too deep-rooted. The American distrust for international (397:) intrigue remains still unabated. We Jews, too, know what the meaning of this or any war can be. Even when peace is declared at the end of war, there is for us still no peace; the hysteria in the aftermath of war would gouge out our eyes with its bayonets of prejudice and sear our lungs with its poison gasses of hate.

But there is still another consideration, one grounded in morality, which renders the call of neutrality imperative....

Leon S. Lang, "Peace: the Mirage of Civilization," Oheb Shalom Synagogue, Newark, NJ. *Newark News*, September 14, 1939, p. 29

On this very day there arises from every corner of the earth where Jews live, like the encircling bands of ether waves, one single declaration. It may come from crushed and terrorized Jews of Warsaw, Lublin, and Lodz. It may come from Jews harrowed and beaten in body in concentration camps or behind the lines of German troops. It will come from millions of broken Jewish hearts. All alike will proclaim: "And Thou art ever our living God and King."

Chamberlain labels Hitler a man of senseless ambitions. Hitler parades the pious demand before his own people and before the world: justice and justice alone is the sole aim of *Mein Kampf.* And out of such honest zeal, such reasonableness, are born empires that choke to death all human freedom and truth, and legions of the finest of human fiber to be torn to shreds in a frenzy of self-destruction. Thus men profane the name of Peace.

Justice for the Aryan but death for the Jews. Justice for a German Empire, but death for Polish self-determination. Justice for the Allied victors of the pseudo-peace of 1918, but humiliation and inhuman punishment of innocent generations of the German people. Justice for Arabs who have become useful and necessary for the safety of British imperial ambitions, but outrageous betrayal and cruel abandonment of harassed and homeless millions of Israel. Justice for those who have arrogated to themselves the possession and control of untold resources of the rich bounty of the earth, but misery and slow death for millions of men and women in every land who gasp for a chance to live and let live....

Can you and I make ourselves believe that bloody combat will bring salvation to the 6,000,000 of horror-stricken and hounded Jews beneath the fire-belching skies of Europe today? Can you and I living in this blessed land of freedom make ourselves believe, while the memory of the last World War is still bitterly emblazoned in the minds of living men today, that men maddened with a passion to kill one another can become after such a modern war meek as lambs around the peace table and come to terms that mean an All-embracing justice and a lasting peace among all nations?...

This land of ours is still blessed with peace. Let us know wisely how to treasure this all too rare gift in our day. Let us bend every energy, every fiber of our united strength to the one unerring goal: the preservation of peace for our people, for *all* our peoples upon this Western Hemisphere....

Let us as Jews and as Americans... here on American soil take up the new slogan: "Keep America Safe for World Peace"....

Ephraim Frisch, "How Lovely Are Thy Tabernacles," Temple Beth-El, San Antonio, TX. AJA, MS-187, Box 2, Folder 1

Well may we rejoice that we can withdraw our hurt spirits to a lovelier place. Away from the terrible atmosphere in which we find ourselves, together with the rest of the world. What an awful year we have just passed through. What a terrifying strain on our minds and hearts! As if the left-over misery of the depression years – of want and despair and fear – were not enough, we have been subjected to one tortuous tension after another, caused by the lust of men for power, dominion, and prestige in the pursuit of which helpless peoples were crucified, solemnly undertaken covenants between nations repudiated, flagrant lies passed off before the whole world as the truth. We have witnessed innocent, unoffending people, of all creeds, thrust into prisons or spirited away and killed because of their honest religious or political beliefs, or forced into exile away from their beloved, or stripped of their possessions. We Jews have seen our co-religionists, innocent of any wrong-doing, insulted, tortured, ejected from communities where their ancestors lived for centuries, and which they and their fore-fathers had made prosperous, cultured, and famous, cast out as impoverished wanderers with no place whereon to lay their heads.

And now the radios blare forth and the newspapers proclaim in flaming headlines the dread activities of belching cannon and murderous tanks, roaring airplanes and prowling submarines. The air is full of distorted speech, of violence, cruelty and bloodshed.

(2:) Our historic New Year comes to us this season therefore with a new glory, more appealing than ever. It invites us to shake off the filth and the meanness, the hatreds and the hypocrisies which engulf us and to cleanse ourselves and become uplifted in contact with it. It announces once more, for the thousandth time, the good tidings that every human being is a child of God. . . .

Leo M. Franklin, "Signs of the Times," Temple Beth El, Detroit, MI. Unpublished, Rabbi Leo Morris Franklin Archives, now at AJA, MS-246, Text 1429

(1:) The demons of deviltry thus appear triumphant as we look back upon the events of the year now closing. Who could have conceived by any stretch of the imagination that in the year [5700] which marks the beginning of the 58th century of recorded Jewish history, the clock of civilization should have been turned so far backward and that mankind should have fallen as it has into such depths of degradation as the world has never reached before.

(9:) Never before have refugee ships, laden with Jewish men and women and children, wandered over the lands and the seas with no harbor ready to receive them, their passengers victims of plague and pestilence and courting death by suicide as well as by disease. Never before have Jews in a dozen lands been pillaged of all their possessions and deprived of the right to make a livelihood, however meager. Never before have so many synagogues been burned while firemen have stood by refusing to put out the flames. Never before have so many rabbis and teachers been driven from their posts to concentration camps and worse. Never before has the martyrdom of the Jew extended over so wide an area, and never before in so many lands has the threat of a rising anti-Semitism been so ominous and so brazen as it is today.

(10:) Somehow, by the strange workings of the providence of God, savagery, paganism, cruelty, inhumanity, might...were overcome and the Jew rose triumphant to live on while one after the other of his detractors went down to disgrace, if not to unmarked graves. What has happened before will happen again. By the very nature of things, evil cannot survive while the good and the true and the humane shall perish.

What we need to see clearly is that the Jew, as the missionary of righteousness, must remain true to his task....

Raphael H. Levine, "Facing the Future," Liberal Jewish Synagogue, London. *A Set of Holiday Sermons*, 5700/1939, pp. 4–8

(7:) Now I realize that what I say may be poor enough comfort to those who themselves have been wounded by the slings and arrows of outrageous fortune; to those among you and your friends who at this moment are being buffeted by the floods of persecution and scorched by the fires of hate.[39] I understand how you can feel that the light of God, the spiritual values of which I am speaking, has completely disappeared from the heavens and from the earth and that Hitler is the apotheosis of the world that is now in the making; I know that I speak not as one who himself has suffered and seen all his hopes crumble upon him by an (8:) avalanche of hate. Perhaps if I were a German Jew I might feel differently, but, if I did, I know that I would be wrong. I know that it would be despair that was clouding my vision. Whatever other men may think, as a Jew I know that Hitler is not the final answer to the hope of the world. I...know that not what Hitler stands for, but what we Jews stand for holds the promise of mankind's future.

Harry Joshua Stern, "The Jewish Spirit Triumphant," Temple Emanu-El, Montreal. *The Jewish Spirit Triumphant*, pp. 11–14

(11:) This New Year 5700 marks the turn of a century and what a tragic hour it is in the turn of world events! Never in our experience

39 Levine was undoubtedly addressing a congregation that included recent refugees from Nazi Germany, some of whose loved ones were still there.

was the sacred day of Rosh Hashanah so dark. The sun of civilization has set. We are bewildered. We can hardly think.... We are like children afraid of the night, the night that has overtaken humankind. How fitting for this dark hour the words of the immortal bard: "What are we,/ An infant crying in the night,/ An infant crying for the light,/ And with no language but a cry."[40]

The hour is a fateful one for all mankind. As we write, another great war is now in progress. For the immediate present this war is confined to Europe. But will this catastrophe be localized? Can it be? As we look at Europe, and we know it fairly well, we can only see Europe dying in the duel between two ideologies, above all in the duel of power politics.

But what a pathetic victim of his own fate is man!.... (12:) [O]n all sides there is the universal and accepted recognition of the futility of war. In a war there is no victor. Everybody loses. Is not this the lesson derived from the last world war?

This fateful hour finds the Jew in a most tragic position. Since the curse of Hitlerism came upon the world, the Jew has been singled out for persecution and derision by the Nazis. For over a half-dozen years we Jews were a people practically alone in the strife. We knew and proclaimed it to the world that the attack upon us by the Nazis was in turn the assault upon civilization. But mankind, with some exceptions, was slow to grasp it. We knew that the Nazis feared the Jewish spirit; that prophetic spirit which throughout (13:) history fought autocracy, that Jewish spirit made manifest to greatest fruition in the teachings of an Isaiah and Jesus, which spoke of love for all mankind.

(14:) In the dark grave year, and perhaps years ahead, we Jews pledge our might and substance and manpower in the support of Britain and her Allies.... |

September 14, 1939 (first day of Rosh Hashanah):

Israel H. Levinthal, "Wherefore is the Earth Destroyed?" (Jer. 9:11), Brooklyn Jewish Center, Brooklyn, NY. *A New World Is Born*, pp. 40–47

---

40 The quotation (which apparently the preacher assumed most listeners would have recognized), is from Tennyson, "In Memoriam A.H.H.," section 54, with the actual text reading "What am I?"

(40:) We find ourselves today in one of the saddest moments in world history, and certainly in Jewish history. The impossible has come to pass.... "The world is hanging on nothingness" (Job 26:7) ... It is hanging on a thread; any moment it may fall in ruins. All civilization is threatened with annihilation!

As far as the Jew is concerned, there is no period in his sorrowful past that offers a parallel to the tragedy that has come upon him today. (41:) He escaped from the lion of Nazism. He thought he found safety in Austria, in Czechoslovakia, in Italy, when lo, the bear now faces him there. He runs somewhere else, but the serpent of treachery bites him there too. He cannot escape, there is nowhere to flee.

And the worst of all is our helplessness! It seems that there is no ray of comfort for us.... We stand bewildered. We cannot believe our eyes. After all, this is the twentieth century. How, then, is it possible for the world to once more be an arena of bloodshed?...

(42:) We are baffled and we ask: Wherefore has this destruction come? Our horizon is now not limited to the Jewish world alone.

(44:) We have the confidence that out of this war the *Memshelet Zadon*, the reign of violence, will pass from the earth for all time – that Hitlerism and all that it implies will disappear like a horrible nightmare, and a new day of peace and joy will come for all mankind. There can be no rest and no surrender till (45:) Nazism is utterly annihilated.... There can be no two sides to the present conflict. No Jew worthy of the name – aye, no man of honor or dignity – can hope and pray for aught else but the utter defeat of the Nazi forces in the present conflict....

"Britain, France, their allies also bear a (46:) share of responsibility.... If they had [fulfilled their moral responsibility], they would have had no dealing with the Nazi rulers from the very moment they appeared. If they had, they would not have tolerated the rape of Czechoslovakia. If they had, they would have protested against the barbarism of the Nazis all these years!

And toward the Jew – how these countries failed in their primary duty!... Had [Britain] observed her full obligation to the Jew, there would now be a million or more Jews in Palestine, upon whose strength and self-sacrifice she could today put full reliance....

Jacob Bosniak, "The Distinction of the Jew," Ocean Parkway Jewish Center, Brooklyn, NY. *Interpreting Jewish Life,* pp 48–55

(48:) "We live in a moment of historical significance when the fate of our people, nay, the fate of (49:) the entire world is in the balance. We cannot forget that six years ago, a great and mighty nation, speaking through its Fuehrer, declared war against Israel and adopted a program which called for the destruction and annihilation of the Jews all over the world.[41] With fear in our hearts and prayer on our lips, we have watched the widespread propaganda of hate and slander against us. In helpless despair, we witnessed the wicked tyrant spreading his dominion of arrogance over new provinces and new countries where our people have resided for centuries. Now the civilized world challenged his wickedness and declared war against him. Personally, I believe in perfect faith that this war will bring the retribution of God upon the enemy for the innocent blood that he shed, for the suffering and anguish that he caused, for the deliberate destruction of religion, for all the iniquities and brutalities that he has perpetrated against men and women during the last six years. I am confident that our God, the Father of all humanity, the Divine Judge of the Universe, will cause the end of the evil regime and the disappearance of the Nazi party with the close of the present war.

This is my firm belief. But who can penetrate the curtain which divides the present from the future? Who can enter into the council of God to know His will and His purpose? Our hearts are torn between fear and hope, fear for the outcome of this struggle and

41 This statement is extremely problematic, as there was certainly no such statement made by Hitler in 1933. The preacher may have intended to say (and write) "six months ago" (actually seven and a half months previously), referring to the infamous statement in his January 30, 1939 address to the Reichstag: "Once again I will be a prophet: should the international Jewry of finance succeed, both within and beyond Europe, in plunging mankind into yet another world war, then the result will not be a Bolvshevization of the earth and the victory of the Jewry, but the annihilation (*Vernichtung*) of the Jewish race in Europe" (Domarus, *Hitler: Speeches and Proclamations,* 3: 1449; Mendes-Flohr and Reinharz, *The Jew in the Modern World,* 2nd ed., p. 658). Even this does not speak of Jews "all over the world" as the preacher claims; Hitler stated clearly that he had no interest in the United States or the Western Hemisphere as a whole.

hope for the final redemption from our sufferings. We are filled with compassion (50:) for the unfortunate Poles, Czechs, Austrians, and others who have fallen victims to his brutal power, and we cry unto God for our brethren in these countries, who are singled out to carry the brunt of [Hitler's] savage hatred and sadistic passions....

(53:) We have all recently read in the press that the German Government published a list of distinctly Jewish names for men and women, accompanied by strict orders that they must be used in the naming of children born to Jewish parents.... Yet this law was an absolute necessity from the standpoint of the Nazi sadistic tormentors of our people. In most cases it was impossible for them to distinguish between Jews and non-Jews....

(55:) Should we not concentrate on the cultivation of our traditional characteristics as a moral force for our survival today?

David de Sola Pool, Spanish and Portuguese Synagogue, New York. *NYT*, Sept. 15, 1939, p. 20

As the war goes on, more and more are we likely to see its appeal to the base and the ignoble wrapped up in the glorious flag of patriotism. More and more are we likely to see war's cruelty and barbarism presented to us as noble heroism. More and more is a cancerous nationalism likely to masquerade as loyalty. More and more will the quest of markets and financial profits of war be disguised and paraded before us as love of country.

Stephen S. Wise, (no title), Free Synagogue at Carnegie Hall, New York. AJA, Box 22: SSW Microfilms of AJHS and BUASC papers

(3:) [Cites Philip Nolan in Everett Hale, "The Man Without a Country"] But our tale today is of a hundred thousand men, women, and children who are without a country because they have been lawlessly evicted from their own lands in which they have lived for generations and even centuries. ... . Their fate is due to the murderous spirit of a man who has decreed that Jews of the earth be uprooted and obliterated. In the tale that is old, there is something else, alas, that is new: the fate of the wanderers ... who have gone down to the seas in ships and who come at last not to welcoming havens but who must face the most humiliating of all human tortures: to find themselves not welcome but unwanted, and most tragic of all unwanted because the nations have accepted that madman's evaluation of his victims.

Charles J. Abeles, "Do Jews Want America Neutral?," Park South Synagogue, New York. *NYT*, September 15, p. 20

American Jews would hold their "outraged emotions" in check and realize that "while Europe burns and smolders and though his co-religionists are involved, on this blessed American soil he [the Jew] must help fortify democracy, strengthen the devotion to freedom, and plant tenderly the seeds of hateless faith, and erect to God the government for posterity."

Harold I. Saperstein, "Unconquered," Temple Emanu-El of Lynbrook, NY. *Witness from the Pulpit*, pp. 68–74

(69:) As one who has long been concerned with Jewish history, it seems to me that the present crisis is unique in several respects. For one thing, the tragedy of the Jew has become universal. There was a time when disaster struck the Jew in one country at a time. While Jews were crushed in one land, they were rising in another.... Today, the forces at work in one nation spread like wildfire to its neighbors....

(70:) Secondly, the doors of the world have been closed to the Jew.... Today the Jew knocks at the doors of the world in vain. The few who succeed in finding new homes only touch the surface of the problem. In essence, the world is shut to the Jew....

(74:) My heart bled the other day as I saw the picture of the city of Cracow, the most beautiful and richly historic city in Poland, in flames....

Israel is shattered. But its spirit must remain firm. While at any one moment other things may prevail, in the final analysis it is the spirit that triumphs in history. The spirit of Israel is eternal. With God's help it will march on, as it has through the centuries, unconquered.

Solomon Foster "There Is a Brighter Side," Temple B'nai Jeshurun, Newark, NJ. *Newark News*, September 14, 1939, p. 29

Ghastly and grievous a figure as he is, talking like a madman in his thirst for world power, raving like a fanatic in his arrogance, the German Fuehrer is arousing the whole human family, outside the immediate circle of his influence, to take a stand against his barbaric methods and his arbitrary pretensions. Up till now many people were unconcerned about his mutterings, unaffected by his ambitions, as though they could sit on the sidelines as mere spectators while a tricky, inconsistent, and irresponsible leader was accepted by a once great people as a magician who was as holy as God and just as powerful.

Hitler's present aggressiveness will prove to be a benefit to society in so far as lovers of liberty everywhere, even in Germany itself in increasing measure, now want to be counted on the side of democracy and stand like adamant against the wicked and intolerable system which he embodies.

The world's growing protest against Hitlerism is not a blanket endorsement of British and French diplomacy, not a sweeping approval of all that Germany's enemies do, but is the calm and confident judgment that the political abyss into which Germany is trying to plunge society, the very depths of cruelty and violence, must be covered and barricaded so that the mounting movement toward a nobler and finer democracy than we have ever known may march toward its goal unimpeded. Now that the raw and vicious illustration of imperialism under the guise of a benevolent State Socialism is so crystal clear that the dullest can understand it, civilization is girding itself to defeat it. Let us have no doubt of the ultimate outcome. The world could not go on any longer with such a danger to the peace and security of nations uncontested. . . .

The continual harping on the fiction that a small Jewish minority had the power to crush Germany and to harm the rest of the world, as claimed by Hitler, is now recognized as the mouthings of a coward and a bigot. The marvelous reaction which has set in to such a self-evident falsification is a tribute to the generosity and kindness of the thinking portion of society that is highly advantageous to Israel and a benefit to mankind.

One of the most convincing signs of Israel's sound and constructive spirit is the spontaneous and hearty assurance just given to Great Britain and the cause of democracy by the Jews of Palestine, whose opposition to England on the basis of her radical and cruel change in administering the pledge of the Balfour Declaration and the Palestine mandate could not be condemned.[42] But the Jews of Palestine and of the whole world are unreservedly and enthusiastically on the side of democracy against every form of dictatorship, and most of all against that type of it embodied in Hitler....

This challenge hurled at mankind by a mechanized Germany and an illiterate Russia under the thumbs of vain and ruthless dictators is accepted and is now being answered by the revival of spiritual interests, by the co-mingling of religious groups and by the reaffirmation of the truths of religion as the only foundation on which to build a safe and durable civilization.

Joachim Prinz, B'nai Abraham, Livingston, NJ. *Newark News*, September 14, 1939, p. 29[43]

The Jewish people have always passionately praised peace and fought for peace, and it is the great philosophy of eternal peace that has its foundation in the religious thoughts of the prophets of Israel. With other peace loving peoples we are yearning for the days when peaceful citizens will be laboring peacefully for the welfare of mankind.

---

42 There is of course here a clear reference to the "White Paper" issued in the spring of 1939 that severely limited Jewish immigration to Palestine. The preacher may not have been aware of the statement made by Ben-Gurion two days earlier, that the Jews of the Yishuv would support the war effort as if there were no White Paper, and fight the White Paper as if there were no war.

43 In first encountering this passage by Prinz in a text published later (www.joachimprinz.com/quotes.htm) I was somewhat uneasy about it, as the passages where Prinz speaks about the future – the war "will in all probability plunge the entire world into blood and flames," and it "will undoubtedly be long and cruel enough to destroy not only the European civilization and vast stretches of land, but it will wipe out millions of Jews" – struck me as a bit too prophetic, as if some of the content might have been modified at a later date. However, the publication in the *Newark News* on the evening of delivery confirms its accuracy.

The war on the verge of which we live and which will in all probability plunge the entire world into blood and flames is of a different character. The issues at stake are not only that of democracy and dictatorship but of two philosophies underlying these two forms of government: the philosophy of materialism and the belief in justice and equality. The Jewish people were the first to be attacked by the aggressor nation. It was significant to us because we know of the close relationship between anti-Semitism and national chauvinism.

It is the great tragedy of our time that the other nations did not understand and recognize the danger of the new German regime. On account of the fact that it was only the Jews who were persecuted, they took it for granted that we exaggerated the facts. Had they known the facts, they would have easily noticed the strength, power and cruelty behind the persecution. Had [British Prime Minister Neville] Chamberlain, a representative of the oldest school of democracy, understood the implications of this new spirit, he would have acted differently.

This war will undoubtedly be long and cruel enough to destroy not only the European civilization and vast stretches of land, but it will wipe out millions of Jews. For the battlefields of today are inhabited by 3,500,000 Jews. This is not our war because we are going to benefit from it, but because we believe that were the principle of ruthlessness and persecution to be victorious in the coming war, it will mean the destruction of culture, civilization, Christianity, Judaism and any form of religion.

Abraham Cohen, "War," United Hebrew Congregation, Birmingham, England. Unpublished, David Cohen Private Collection

However highly we may prize our lives and fortunes, there are conditions (2:) [that] would strip these of all worth; and such are the conditions which the leaders of Germany aim at imposing upon the whole of Europe. As Jews we may feel this even more keenly than our fellow-citizens because we know from the experience of German Jewry what fate would be in store for us if this despot achieved his purpose. While we scornfully repudiate the charge of Anti-Semites that Jews wished for an outbreak of war with Germany as the solution of this deadly peril to their race, and we hoped that the ambitions of this megalomaniac would be sated with his bloodless conquests, we join in the feeling which is so widespread that the challenge has now come in a form which cannot be evaded without the sacrifice of the principal features of civilisation.[44]…

(3:) [T]he real enemy is Hitlerism and not the German people. For that unhappy nation nothing but sympathy is felt. For six and a half years they have been dragooned, fed with lies, shut out from the truth and subjected to relentless propaganda all directed to the one end of filling their heads with dread of their neighbours whose alleged aim was to attack them. We must all trust that this sympathy will be sustained throughout the contest and particularly in the ultimate settlement. The hope for lasting peace is that the German people should come to understand that the struggle was fought to release them as well as ourselves from the curse of their pernicious leadership.…

(4:) On the last page of her book "I Married a German," Madeleine Kent has this striking passage:

> It may indeed be that the martyrdom of the thousands of Jews who have been driven to suicide since I began this book will prove the saving of our present civilization. For in that martyrdom the world has seen the effects of race-hatred in its starkest form, and has drawn back appalled. This, if anything, may yet save it from following the Nazi hordes along the barren road that leads straight back to mankind's savage beginnings, to the time when blood-feuds were so ruthless that each tribe lived an isolated life of its own.[45]

There is deeper truth in these words than even the (5:) authoress herself was aware of when she wrote them. The martyred Jewry of Germany could have been the means of preventing this war, if the world had only read the lesson which their treatment so plainly

44 The preacher went on to cite a passage from the Prime Minister's address to Parliament announcing a state of hostilities, and his broadcast to the nation.

45 The book was published in London by Allen and Unwin in 1938, and reviewed in the *JC*, December 30, 1938, pp. 7–8.

taught. Hitlerism, which has now to be extirpated by the fiercest strife, first revealed its true character in a savage onslaught upon a helpless Jewish minority. The world read the ghastly story with horror; but what did it do? There were expressions of protest from sympathetic individuals; but no Government in the world thought it their duty to declare that such brutality ruled out its perpetrators from the category of civilized human beings. Nations which regard themselves as civilized should have refused recognition to leaders who behaved like savages. They adopted a different attitude. As Governments they could not take official cognizance of what was being done elsewhere to men and women who were not their own nationals. It was not their concern – so they imagined.

Jewish speakers persistently urged that it was not a Jewish question at all, but one which profoundly affected all mankind. Time and again they uttered the warning that Jews were only the first victims of this merciless brutality and other victims would follow in due course. Their warnings were unheeded, but they have come true. More than that. Even in this country there were many – including persons of influence – who were ready to shut their eyes to these atrocities and (6:) took every opportunity of praising the new Germany created by Hitlerism. The German leader had many admirers in England. A London newspaper,[46] in its editorial on the day after the declaration of war, had these sentences: "This war became inevitable from the day Hitler seized power in Germany and began his criminal career by enslaving his own people. For his one aim since then has been to enslave all others by the methods of brute force." Had the circumstances not been so tragic I should have felt like laughing aloud at this pronouncement.

If the proprietor of this journal will look up the files, he will discover that for six years he did everything possible to praise the German leader and his achievements for his country. Exclusive interviews with him were published in this paper, which were nothing less than a channel for pro-Nazi propaganda. Furthermore, thousands upon thousands of persons here and elsewhere were prepared to

46 Cohen's typescript contains a note indicating that it was *The Daily Mail.*

overlook and excuse Nazi villainies because, taken in by the pose of the leader as the savior of Western Europe from the spread of Bolshevism – stigmatised as Jewish Bolshevism – they regarded Nazism as a bulwark against Communism. What fools they must be feeling to-day! Well-meaning individuals banded themselves into societies ostensibly for the promotion of good relations between the German and British peoples but really, as the former Home Secretary said, as the medium of anti-Semitic and pro-Nazi propaganda. Still another British organization, (7:) which is nothing more nor less than a Nazi agency, preached the vilest anti-Semitism for the purpose of helping the German leader to have a free hand in Europe. Only last week, when the true issue was so plain, the poster of its weekly journal read "No War for Jewish Finance"![47]

I am not attempting to draw the moral that war has come as a judgment because the peoples of Europe allowed Germany to persecute and continue persecuting her Jews with impunity and without drastic protest. The moral I do wish to draw – and I am absolutely convinced of its truth – is that the Nazi maltreatment of Jews showed the red light, the danger signal, showed the inhuman spirit of the regime which was a menace to all Europe, but they refused to see it. Hitlerism has now to be destroyed at the cost of an incalculable sacrifice of life and treasure. In its earlier stage it could have been easily destroyed without a war. So who is responsible for this war, God or man?

Israel Mattuck, "Faith and Life," Liberal Jewish Synagogue, London. Unpublished

(1:): For six years our observance of Rosh Hashanah has been dominated by a tragic note induced by the persecution of the Jews under Nazism, which grew every year in Germany, spread with the extension of Nazi rule to Austria and Czecho-Slovakia, and with the increase of the Nazis' baneful power, was taken up, in various degrees, by other countries in Europe. Now the Jews' tragedy has been widened out into a larger tragedy. And we have to observe Rosh Hashanah this

47 Oswald Mosley, "For Britain Peace and People – No War for Jewish Finance," *Action*, Sept. 2, 1939, in Richard Thurlow, *Fascism in Britain*, p. 127, n. 38.

year in circumstances of great and extended sadness. The catastrophe which Nazism brought on the Jews embodied a threat to humanity which it has now carried out. The evil power that afflicted the Jews has now openly attacked humanity, revealing the magnitude of its evil nature so clearly that the war against it is truly a fight to subdue evil. Above the sadness, however, of the war that has been forced on Europe rises the confident hope that through it the evil will be completely destroyed, that when peace returns, it will be a peace freed from the oppressions with which the Nazis have degraded the life of their own country and of the fears with which they have darkened the lives of other countries.

H. Jerevitch, Cathedral Road Synagogue, Cardiff, Wales. *JC*, Sept. 22, 1939, p. 14

No country showed so much kindness to the Jewish people as did England in opening her doors to those who, after being robbed of all they possessed and tortured, had to flee from persecution. These people, the refugees from Nazi Germany, were anxious to help England in her hour of need. They were not enemy aliens; they were friends of England, friends who had reason to be grateful to the country which offered them asylum, protection, and safety.

Ephraim Sokolover, Great Synagogue, Ra'anana, Palestine. *Penei Efrayim*, pp. 7–10, translated by MS

(7:) "What we feared has come upon us" (cf. Job 3:25). We are already at the beginning of a difficult and terrifying war, in which the enemy has extended his reach over the entire world.[48] All tremble in this war of modernity.

If the fate of the Jewish people were in every respect like that of the other nations in the war zone, where the cruelty of the enemy is felt already at the outset, perhaps there might be in this something of the category of "suffering shared by many."[49]

---

48 Obviously a hyperbolic formulation for September 1939, or even for any other time during the war.

49 Hebrew: *tsarot rabbim*; the phrase seems to allude to a passage in Midrash

(8:) If the war had come upon us during an ordinary period, following years of tranquility and prosperity, then we might have accepted it in a condition of health, our limbs still intact. But alas, "disaster overtakes disaster" (Jer. 4:20), this war has come upon us, the Jewish people, when we are broken and shattered as a result of all the brutal decrees that have come upon us in recent years. More than once it has seemed to us as if all the nations of the world have united and set for themselves a "single goal": to divest themselves of "the Jewish question" in the simple manner of the wicked Haman, may his named be blotted out! . . .

"Disaster overtakes disaster": it was not long ago that the Jews of Poland were praying on behalf of our welfare here in our land in response to the events that occurred here in recent years, when hundreds of our Jewish brethren fell victim through no fault of their own.[50] The vibrant Polish Jewry declared a day of public fasting and prayer in order to arouse God's mercy upon the inhabitants of the Land.

And now, we are profoundly shocked to have heard that the vicious invader has entered through the borders of Poland, the center of all Jewish life, and is ruling the entire country,[51] and is doing there what they have done in their own country, with even greater cruelty than we had imagined. We have already heard how this glorious Jewish community has come under the power of the vicious beast led by Hitler, may his name be blotted out! Day after day our Polish brethren have fallen as victims, day after day a holy Jewish community is destroyed. . . .

September 15, 1939 (second day of Rosh Hashanah)

Israel H. Levinthal, "As In the Days of Noah," Brooklyn Jewish Center, Brooklyn, NY. Unpublished, JTSA Archives

---

Deuteronomy Rabbah *VaEthanan* 2,4 indicating that suffering or oppression shared by many is less painful than the suffering of an individual.

50 Referring to the uprising by Palestinian Arabs against both British and Jews in the years 1936–1939, leading to the death of some 300 Jews, 260 Britons, and about 5000 Arabs.

51 This is of course not accurate, as the Russian army had invaded and was occupying the eastern one-third of Polish territory.

A flood has come upon the world – a flood not just of rain but of fire, of bombs and guns and poison gas – a flood which, alas, I am afraid, will last not 40 days and nights but much longer....

We all hope that America will be spared from entering this struggle.... The old centers are being destroyed. A new center must be built here.... We can make America now another Golden Era once enjoyed in Spain.

Ira Eisenstein, Society for the Advancement of Judaism, New York. *NYT*, September 16, 1939, p. 7

The time is here for those who seek peace to proclaim courageously that our beloved United States must keep itself clear of the intrigues, perfidies, ambitions and plots of the European nations. Why should we involve ourselves in the mess of a continent in which Spain, Austria, Czecho-Slovakia have been betrayed; in which violently anti-Fascist Russia embraces violently anti-Communist Germany; in which ancient wrongs and established feuds are sugar-coated by lofty ideals of freedom and democracy?

Jacob Kraft, (no title), Congregation Beth Shalom, Wilmington, DE[52]

The *Akeda*, the trial of Abraham and Isaac, is one that we all face on this New Year.... How aware we are of some of the intentions of Hitler in conquering Poland and then perhaps the whole world. God wants us to know that we are being tested as was our patriarch of old [Abraham]. How far will we go in maintaining neutrality and isolation as a great nation when we, its citizens, are terribly afraid

52 This passage has been taken not from a text of the complete sermon but from an article written by Rabbi David Geffen, who succeeded Kraft as rabbi of the same Baltimore congregation, published in the *Jerusalem Post*, Yom Kippur supplement, Sept. 27, 2009, p. 8 (http://bit.ly/2wv8Smg). Rabbi Kraft, whom I consulted, has not been able to recover his source for the passage. My own search in the Kraft Papers at the Baltimore Jewish Archives did not succeed in finding the text of his Rosh Hashanah 1939 sermon; most of the sermons in that collection are from the post-war period. Because the substance of the passage is so fundamentally different from the rabbinical consensus at this time that America should stay out of the war, without a valid contemporary source for the text it should be cited perhaps with a certain degree of skepticism.

of the plight of our European brothers and sisters. Abraham went to the top of Mount Moriah with Isaac – only God saved him. Will we permit our president and our governmental leaders to permit the destruction of Poland and its Jews and then other nations and their Jews? Right now I am not prepared to lead a battle against FDR, but the time will come – America will go to war. Let us not be too late – let the Isaac of our people in Europe survive.

Ephraim Sokolover, Great Synagogue, Ra'anana, Palestine. *Penei Efrayim*, pp. 11–12, translated by MS

(12:) Our task today is to arouse the mercies of Heaven through the abundance of our prayer. Each one of us must consider himself to be the leader of our worship. For, to our sorrow and heart-felt dismay, our brethren in Poland have been deprived of their synagogues, deprived of the ability to pray on these Days of Awe. Who knows whether they even have the capacity to weep in public in accordance with their custom. That is why it is incumbent upon us to fulfill their role in every way. Each one of us may represent a Polish community, mourn for their distress, pour out our words before our Heavenly Father in place of that holy community.

September 22, 1939 (Kol Nidre)

Jacob Bosniak, "Israel and the Synagogue," Ocean Parkway Jewish Center, Brooklyn, NY. *Interpreting Jewish Life*, pp. 16–24

(18:) Oceans of tears were shed within the walls of the Synagogue during the centuries, and even more at the present time. For this period of Nazi ascendancy will be forever identified in our history as years of murder and plunder, starvation and hunger, death and torture, misery and terror for millions of our people.

(20:) There was reason for the beastly German act of burning the Synagogues, with their sacred contents, in the Reich. They knew that the Synagogue was the source of strength and the spiritual fortification of the Jew, and they wanted to strike a blow at the source. In spite of the natural German aversion to waste, and the characteristic inclination for saving and utilizing every scrap of material, the Government ordered the burning of more than four hundred edifices which were worth millions of dollars.

On that fateful day, November 10, 1938, the Nazi (21:) government took special precautions that no reports should reach the outside world in connection with the burning of our Houses of God. Yet the fact did reach us that at least one Jew succeeded in evading the vigilance of the stormtroopers and jumped into one of the burning sanctuaries and probably perished in its flames.[53]

Out of the fiery furnace of such martyrdom came forth the indestructible spirit of the Jew.... This process of refining and purifying resulted in the long life of the Jew, which has enabled him to stand at the graves of a hundred tyrants and conquerors in the past.

September 23, 1939 (Yom Kippur)

Samuel Rosenblatt, "Man," Beth Tfiloh Congregation, Baltimore, MD. *Our Heritage*, pp. 52–60[54]

(54:) The connection between Judaism's conception of the nature of man and the present European war may appear at first blush to be rather far-fetched. Notwithstanding the high professions of their statesmen, very few of us are naïve enough to believe that England and France have entered the contest out of ideal considerations. If the British and French were really so much disturbed by the growth of Hitlerism, why did they wait for so long? Why didn't they nip the movement in the bud? Why did they find it necessary to sacrifice the Czechoslovakian republic in so cowardly a fashion? Why did they allow Poland to perish without as much as lifting a finger to prevent her dismemberment? No, it is not for the safeguarding of any particular ideology that the so-called democracies of Europe are fighting today, but – as Vincent Sheean so aptly expressed it in his recent volume, *Not Peace But a Sword* – "for their dear money

---

53 Author's note: *NYT*, November 12, 1938.

54 None of the sermons in Rosenblatt's collection are given dates, but here the reference to "the present European war" and the pact with the USSR, together with the publication date for the book of 1940 with a Preface dated May 1, 1940, shows that this Yom Kippur sermon must have been delivered in 1939.

bags."[55] Nevertheless, whatever the motives of the British Empire or the French Republic in the present clash of arms may be, whether they be selfish or free from self-interest, a victory of their opponents would be a defeat of the belief that man has a soul and that he is intrinsically superior to the brute....

Events have happened that upset the calculations of the most astute political observers, threw diplomats into confusion, and gave the lie to theories once considered as gospel truth. Not the last of these is the sensational pact concluded between Red Russia and Nazi Germany. It came as a shock to the entire world, this seemingly unnatural alliance, and rightly so. For years the prophet of Nationalism had been preaching hatred of Red Russia. The National Socialist state was literally built up on the carcass of communism. The capitalist world had been led to believe that Nazi-socialism was the strongest and most effective bulwark against the spread of that dangerous doctrine that would put an end to private property and deprive all men of wealth and the substance of their possessions. It was on this account that Hitler was given free rein in building his military machine and that no one interfered with his persecution of the Jews, who were indiscriminately branded by him as Communists....

September 28, 1939 (first day of Sukkot)

Israel Mattuck, "The Belief in God's Goodness," Liberal Jewish Synagogue, London. Unpublished

(1:) Tabernacles this year raises the question in an acute form: how to reconcile the belief in the goodness of God with the existence of evil. This was inevitably present in our thoughts on Rosh Hashanah and Yom Kippur, but it was not directly raised by them. Tabernacles is a joyous festival. The question inevitably occurs: How can we observe it in the unspeakable sadness spread over the world by the war?...

55 The book is the journalist's personal account of events in Prague, Madrid, London, Paris, and Berlin during the twelve fateful months between March 1938 and March 1939.

Hitler, because of the evil thing he is, the evil things he does, and the evil aims he seeks, has brought incalculable sufferings upon millions who are guiltless. The consequences of his evil fall upon many who have no share in it. I am thinking especially of the people of England and France. They, however, by their ready determination to resist Hitler and to destroy Hitlerism, have given an example of the goodness in human life, the deep devotion (2:) to righteousness....

In our judgment of the present state of the world we have to consider not only the iniquity of Hitlerism but the nobility in those who are fighting to destroy it and to free the world of the evil....

Moreover, the evil is temporary, the good is enduring. We do not feel any doubt about the outcome of the war.... (3:) But whatever may happen in the immediate struggle, there can be no doubt about which set of ideas will ultimately triumph, Nazism or the ideals of democracy....

It may at first seem to give but little comfort to say the victory of the right is certain, but it may take long....

The question remains, however, why should evil possess power even for short periods, why is it allowed to exist at all? So far as human life is concerned, the question is answered by human freedom.

October 5, 1939 (Shemini Atzeret)

Abraham A. Kellner, "Man, the Unknowing" (*Yizkor*), Miami Jewish Orthodox Congregation, Miami, FL. *A Rabbi's Faith*, pp. 55–59.

(55:) The moody spirit of Koheleth which is reflected in the heavy hearts at *Yizkor* is particularly pregnant with meaning now, when a new world war has had its beginning with Germany's march on Poland. The lights of the world, which were far from being aglow yesterday, flicker even lower today, and mankind once again is in the grasp of a terrifying nightmare come true.

(58:) When the deepest ingenuity of science is employed to construct the means whereby man plots his own destruction and plans his own suicide, then it is difficult to conclude that the human being is the highest in the scale of species.

October 8, 1939 (Sunday morning after Sukkot week)

Stephen S. Wise, "Who Now Can Believe in God?," Free Synagogue at Carnegie Hall, New York. AJA, Box 22: SSW Microfilms of AJHS and BUASC papers

(2:) Why now? Because of great wrongs which have been done day after day and hour after hour. Wrongs that are so vast and so oceanic that they engulf not individuals, groups and cities but whole nations. Because a republic of Eastern Europe, not without faults, divided among two great religious groups, Jewish and Catholics, lies prostrate between the feet of one so vile that he cannot even respect the fallen.... A whole people is uprooted, a nation is homeless, they have no place to go; their land is divided between two of the mightiest tyrants that earth has seen.

(7:) Surely it is not blasphemy to say that God cannot reverse the order of the universe every hour, every moment, in order to suit the needs, in order to meet the emergencies, of the human spirit, for then God would be the sole author of life and we would be impotent children, babies, infants, crying in the night, but not crying for the light, for the coming of light or darkness would have no relation to us, for our will-less purpose or our purposeless will.

October 10, 1939 (Tuesday)

Stephen S. Wise, "What My Answer to Hitler Would Be," Address Delivered before Student Body, Jewish Institute of Religion, New York. AJA, Box 22: SSW Microfilms of AJHS and BUASC papers

(1:) What a hideous thing it is that Hitler speaks of the "Jewish problem" of Europe. If Chamberlain would only say, "But we accept no such generosity. There is no Jewish problem. Whatever Jewish problem there is, problems of refugees, problems of homelessness, problems of desperation, Hitler has called into being." ... The world faces one problem and only one, and that is the problem of Hitler and Hitlerism.... I should be ashamed to dwell upon the so-called proposal of Hitler, the proposal to establish a Jewish State or Settlement in Poland.... This is to be the Biro-Bidjan of Eastern Europe![56]

56 Biro-Bidjan was the Jewish autonomous region, some 6000 miles east of Ukraine,

(2:) If the democracies are in earnest, if they are to be better than the spirit of Hitlerism, then they must not only demand that Czecho-Slovakia shall be set free and Poland be restored, but that the Jews shall be free to live again as they lived up to the day of Hitler, in all lands in Europe, and in all the lands and commonwealths of civilization.

(4:) Lo and behold, Hitler has struck hands with Stalin, perhaps rendering the world the service of unmasking Stalin and to make the Soviet Union appear the same militaristic regime that the powers of Europe are. He has committed the unspeakable crime of handing over Eastern Poland to the Soviet Union, with utter disregard of the wishes and plans and dreams of the population. He has committed a still greater crime, for whether he has willed it or not, he has given the Soviet Union the power day after day to summon before it representatives of the Baltic states, Estonia, Latvia, Lithuania – and now begin to come the larger states, Finland and Sweden – and to terrorize them one after another into submission to his malign will.... The civilized world will answer Hitler: there is no peace proposal that Hitler can make that civilization can consider. The words "peace proposal" from Hitler is mockery....

October 15, 1939 (Sunday)

Stephen S. Wise, "The War: What Shall Americans Think and Say and Do?," Free Synagogue at Carnegie Hall, New York. AJA, Box 22: SSW Microfilms of AJHS and BUASC papers

(1:) I said there must be no war partisans save of course for those muddle-headed peace advocates, as they call themselves, who would rather that Hitlerism won the war than that war should continue for another hour. As Americans we must not be ready, we must be wholly unready and unwilling to take America into war even for the sake of England and France.[57]

---

established in 1928 by the Soviet Government for colonization by Jews. See Polonsky, *The Jews of Russia and Poland*, pp. 295–96. Wise was asserting sardonically that the Nazi proposal for a "Jewish State or Settlement in Poland" is no more realistic than the Soviet proposal had turned out to be.

57 An extremely strong formulation of the position shared by the overwhelming majority of American rabbis, clearly articulated in the sermons above and the October 20

(3:) As for what we Americans ought to say at this time of war, as Americans who are not at war we must of course be as restrained as we can be in speech, and we must be mindful that our country as a political government is neutral between the two conflicting groups of nations. But covert extenuation of Nazi Germany is at least as un-neutral in my own judgment, infinitely more un-neutral, than the frankest support of the democracies.

(4:) As for saying only that which does not violate the fact of neutrality, I am going to say something to my fellow-Jews. We cannot imprison our minds, we cannot handcuff our spirits, we cannot put chains upon the deepest feelings of our souls, but we must be doubly on our guard in all that we say about the war for two reasons. First, because loose speaking with regard to the duty of America to enter into the war does not in the slightest degree represent the basic changeless Jewish hatred of war, and all of the evil and wrong that war means. And there is a second reason, which perhaps it is impolitic to speak of, but my virtue lies not in being politic but in being honest, because every word uttered by a Jew is liable to find some sort of misunderstanding and mis-construction and mis-interpretation at certain hands. We are not war-mongers – it is the last thing in the world that we Jews are – and we must not sound as if we were war-mongers.

(6:) Neutrality is right; neutrality is the only course of action for us as a nation, but I can't speak to you today without telling you from my heart of hearts, I do not believe that it was enough or that it is enough to keep America out of war. We should have done, we could have done much more to keep war out of the world....

(7:) As Americans, men and women, I say to you, and I speak as a religionist, we must oppose anything and everything that might take our country into war. I am against America's going into war not

---

sermon by Isserman: that despite their convictions about the unmitigated evil of the Nazi regime, Americans should learn the lesson of the Great War and maintain an anti-interventionist position that would preserve the highest ideals of American democracy. Many of these rabbis, including Wise, had made commitments to pacifism that would have to be modified or abandoned in the following years. See also Wise on February 25, 1940, below.

because I am morally or politically or spiritually a neutral as between Hitler's Reich and the British Commonwealth or as between Stalin's empire and France. I am against America going into the war because we ought to keep the Western world, our Western continent or half of the world, out of war and out of every European embroilment....

Alexander Altmann, "Opening Address" to Manchester and Salfeld Jewish Youth Council, England. *JC*, October 20, 1939, p. 16

If it is true that a new world will emerge after this war from the sea of blood and tears, surely a new Jewish world, too, must emerge. What is to happen to the destitute Jewish masses in Central and Eastern Europe and to the thousands of refugees scattered over the face of the globe? What, then, are to be the ultimate aims of Jewish youth? We must discuss in our societies and at our firesides during the coming months what spiritual contribution we Jews, as such, can make towards the reconstruction of the world. We must realise the great part which Palestine has to play in the future for the development of the Jewish people as a whole. The reconstruction of Eretz Yisrael will not only enable refugees to be given sanctuary but will help to weld our people there into a healthy and united nation, making its own specific contribution to world progress.[58]

October 20, 1939 (Friday evening)

Ferdinand M. Isserman, "We Americans and the War in Europe," Temple Israel, St. Louis, MO. Typescript in AJA, MS-6, Box 15, Folder 5

(1:) On the part of the American people there is practically the unanimous desire that the United States keep out of this European war, that no American youth be sent to die on European battlefields in the present struggle. There is no war party in America.... There is no doubt that the overwhelming majority of the American people

---

58 According to the *JC* article, after completing his own message, Altmann introduced "Dr. Abraham Heschel," who was said to have recently escaped from Warsaw, to speak to the group. We cannot be certain about Heschel's command of English at this point, but it is fair to say that rarely has a meeting of Jewish youth been exposed to two such extraordinarily high-level speakers.

would welcome the downfall of Hitlerism. This does not mean that they would desire a destruction of Germany....

(2:) Europe today is threatened by a darker foe than some wild and savage conqueror from another continent. It is threatened by a tyrant as ruthless as any that history has ever known who has at his disposal the mechanisms and the technological inventions of modern civilization.... There is abroad in America a strong propaganda that there is no moral difference between the cause of England and France and the cause of Nazism....

(3:) Although Americans may have sympathies and recognize the greater justice of one cause over and against another, nevertheless, Americans should stay out of the war.... America would be engaged in perpetual warfare if in every international issue it threw its armed forces on the side of justice.... (7:) Out of the last war there came no literature glorifying it; the disillusionment of modern youth with war is a moral advance.... At last, after many centuries war stands revealed in all its savagery, in all its brutality, in all its devastation, in all its hopelessness.

(8:) We know today that we cannot crush tyranny with war, that you only intensify it. Already, war has brought England and France closer to tyranny and weakened their democracy.... (9:) As for us Americans, we must recognize that we can be neutral and can stay out of this war.... Not merely for our own sake but for the sake of mankind we must not become involved in the European conflict. At the end of this struggle, the world will need one people of sanity, one people whose hands are clean, one people whose energies have not been concentrated on hate and murder and destruction. One people free and self-respecting, which will be in a position to give council, to bind up wounds, to assuage pain, to bring relief. From civilization, Americans receive a challenge. That challenge is to use these days to protect American democracy, to end American unemployment, to establish social justice, so that at the end of the strife and the conflict, European peoples will gaze to the west and will be cheered and encouraged by the noble example of a free people made up of all the children of Europe which has maintained a just and good civilization.

October 21, 1939 (Saturday, *Lekh Lekha*)

Max Nussbaum, "To Travel and to Flee," Joachimsthalerstrasse Synagogue, Berlin. AJA, MS-705, Box 3, Folder 5; translator unidentified

(1:) The story of Abraham's life may be expressed in a single word, which dominates his life: "Wandering"! No wonder, therefore, that his life has become the symbolic model of ours throughout the centuries, and it need no longer be disputed why Abraham's years of wandering are the very centre of our current attention....

(4:) If mankind should once succeed in reconstructing the world in such a way that on each spot of the soil only one people would live, and indeed it would be the nation that truly belongs to that spot, so that Land and People would coincide with each other, then we would have solved one of the most difficult problems of human history. No wonder, therefore, that people tried to actualize this theory after the Great War. I remind you of the exchange of populations between Greece and Turkey shortly after the Great War, and of a similar act a few months ago pertaining to the ceding of Hatay to Turkey [July 7, 1939].[59] Similar proceedings are taking place at present, namely, that a certain country takes back many of her minorities out of the adjoining countries into the boundaries of her own territory.

Many people will be struck by the idea that the time has now come when nations other than our own also feel what is called "Galut." Of course, it cannot be denied that all these above-mentioned cases were not lacking in personal grief. Country, homeland, and father's house are also important conceptions for them. But nevertheless, this parallel is not quite right; this problem reminds us of ours and it attracts our attention, but it does not at all mean "Galut." Only we Jews can truly feel what it means when ships of their own nation enter a harbor. It is true that their passengers may have been torn away from their homes, but on the other hand they are welcomed, cared for, and led to that place that had previously been established

59 Hatay was a semi-independent province (for less than a year an independent Republic) on the Mediterranean coast, its capital Antioch/Antakya. It was annexed by Turkey on July 7, 1939 under French supervision.

and that would become their future home. They know where they come from and where they are going. In spite of all the personal grief, this is an exchange of population, a re-organization or whatever else it may be called, but by no means "Galut." We alone – who no longer think it to be peculiar when ships are leaving for an uncertain destination, or to a specified destination but not arriving there, being forbidden to go on shore[60] – we alone can judge and feel this fine yet deep difference between those events occurring among the other nations and our own historical fate.

October 29, 1939 (Sunday)

Judah L. Magnes, "War and the Remnant of Israel," Presidential Address at Opening of New Term at the Hebrew University, Jerusalem. *In the Perplexity of the Times*, pp. 16–26; cf. also *Dissenter in Zion*, document 111

(21:) Satan is abroad. The incarnation of the devil sits on the German throne. It is the principle of evil made flesh. The devil has unleashed his war, and who can sit back and not take sides, with the devil or against him? I shrink from the blasphemy that ours is the side of God, and that we are His chosen. But what I say is: There the devil is for all men to see, his voice for all men to hear, his deeds for all men to abhor, his plans for all men to frustrate. It is the idol in the Temple, the abomination of desolation, and it is ours to bring it down. Perhaps we may be brought down in the effort, for who knows the ways of God's wrath and punishments? But we must make the effort....

(25:) Before our eyes the great centre of Judaism is being destroyed, the Judaism of Poland. Some historians assert that Polish Judaism had been given a Bill of Religious and (26:) National Rights in the

---

60 As with Hatay, this is obviously a contemporary reference to the SS *St. Louis* – mentioned in several previous sermons – which departed from Hamburg in May 1939 with some 937 refugees, bound for Havana, only to be informed that the Cuban government had altered its immigration policy and would not allow the passengers to disembark. The United States Coast Guard patrolled the area near the Florida coast to ensure there would be no attempt to land in US territory. Nor would the Canadian government accept the refugees. The ship returned to Europe, and its passengers were disbursed in England, France, Belgium, and the Netherlands. See Gordon Thomas and Max Morgan Witts, *The Voyage of the Damned*.

year 905.[61] For more than a thousand years the Judaism of Poland has been creative, now in times of great trials and sufferings, now in times of freedom. From it have come some of those deep spiritual values which sustain us to this day. It is beyond our power of imagination to picture our Judaism without this creative original force. All that we can do at this moment is to repeat the Prophet's words, "And they shall weep for thee with bitterness of heart and bitter mourning" (Ezek. 27:31).

In a few days it will be November 10. On that day a year ago 600 synagogues were burnt down in Germany. Let us rise, and remain silent for a moment in memory of the killed, the wounded, the imprisoned, and for the torn and bespattered scrolls of our imperishable Torah.

"Guardian of Israel, guard the Remnant of Israel."[62]

November 11, 1939 (Saturday, Armistice Day)

Ignaz Maybaum, "The Anniversary of November 10," Brondesbury Synagogue, London. *Man and Catastrophe*, pp. 84–91 (delivered in German, translated by Joseph Leftwich); see Complete Sermons

Kalonymus Kalmish Shapira, Warsaw. *Esh Kodesh*, p. 10; *Derashot meShenot haZa'am*, pp. 92–93; Polen, *Holy Fire*, p. 39, translated by Nehemia Polen[63]

"Those who were lost in the land of Assyria and those who were cast away in the land of Egypt shall come..." (Isa. 27:13). Some people are in a state called "lost," while others are in a state referred to as "cast away." "Cast away" connotes an individual who is merely

61 For this legend of a charter bestowed to Jews by Prince Leshek in 905, see Simon M. Dubnow, *History of the Jews in Russia and Poland*, vol. 1, p. 40; this may have been Magnes's source.

62 Citing a well-known line from a liturgical prayer incorporated into the daily Morning Service (see *The Authorised Daily Prayer Book of the United Hebrew Congregations of the British Empire*, p. 64).

63 For this important rabbi and preacher of the Warsaw Ghetto, I am using the second name and the family name (Kalmish Shapira) as they appear in Hebrew on the title page of the author's Hebrew book, although he himself wrote his family name as Szapiro in Roman letters on his stationery. See Polen, *The Holy Fire*, p. xiii, with a reproduction of his stationery.

banished from his place to another far away; he remains, however, recognizable and discernible. The individual called "lost," however, has been destroyed; he is neither discernible nor recognizable. For now the troubles are increasing so greatly; indeed, they are shearing the beards of Jews, so that they cannot be recognized by their external appearance. Furthermore, due to the many persecutions and unbearable, unimaginable torments, people even lost their inner identities. This process can go so far that the individual loses himself (*er farlirt zich*), and does not recognize himself. He cannot recall his self-image as it was a year ago on the Sabbath, or even on a weekday before prayer, during prayer, and other such times. Now he is crushed and trampled, so much so that he cannot discern if he is a Jew, a human being, or rather an animal who does not have the capacity for feeling. He is then "lost" in the scriptural sense....

God will search for us and find us. He will give us everything good, return us to Him, blessed be He, redeem us, rescue our bodies and our souls with great mercy and beneficent acts.

Max Nussbaum, "Jacob's Reconciliation with Esau," Berlin, synagogue not identified. AJA, MS-705, Box 3, Folder 5; translator unidentified

(2:) In the second commentary, it says that Jacob was weak and fled. And this biblical interpretation also can easily be applied to a number of Jews. These Jews see a danger, the frightening danger of having to assert themselves, to persevere and strive, and that, they imagine, is impossible for them (3:)... Cowardly, they turn their backs to the danger and flee. For these weaklings there exists no God who might restrain them from this act of desperation, no God who says to them, "Remain, fight and persevere, and I, the Lord thy God will help you to victory." No, they who wish to try their luck in foreign lands, those who from Europe wander to Africa, Australia, and for the most part to South America, they shall always stand alone, forever remain without a home, never experience the consolation of God's word; for them there shall never exist the God of Zion, for they do not know Zion, and do not wish to know of it.

They thought that in Europe they were firmly rooted and anchored, yet when the very first storm broke over their bowed heads, robbing them of some of their earthly possessions, they turned and fled in wildest haste. For now they had regained consciousness and realized that their souls were not in communion with Europe, had in fact never been.

And now they hoped to acclimatize themselves in South America, to become very soon indistinguishable from the natives. But this could never succeed.... These Jews sense all this, and feel abandoned.... But for them there is no way back anymore, for they do not know the right road any longer....[64]

November 19, 1939 (Sunday)

Israel Mattuck, "The Present Position of Jews in Other Lands." Unpublished; possibly delivered at a church, as he refers to "speaking from this place some time ago."

(1:)In speaking of the Jews in Germany, I shall have little to say which is not known already. From reports that we have received, it would seem that Germany has become for the Jews one large concentration camp. I think that if anything the suffering is worse than before. In Hitler's concern for the Jews, he has taken a bit of Poland on which to settle the Jewish refugees. This piece of land is said to be 40 square miles[65] (2:) and obviously it would be quite impossible to put all

64 This is indeed a surprising sermon, and not only because it does not fit the *parashah* (*Toledot*), or even allude to the significance of November 11. While Nussbaum was one of the last rabbis to leave Germany (in the summer of 1940), this fierce attack against Jews who have emigrated as refugees to distant countries that would accept them, delivered after the Nazi invasion of Poland, seems stunningly misguided. It is unclear whether he is so critical because the refugees did not go to Palestine (which had severe limits under the White Paper), because they went to South America rather than England or the United States, or because they left their European homes rather than remaining, resisting the enemy, and trusting in God.

65 This apparently refers to the "Lublin Reservation," developed in the autumn of 1939 in the eastern part of Nazi-occupied Poland, to which Jews were deported from territories closer to the German border. The size, however, was not forty but approximately four hundred square miles. In the text, it may have been simply a typographical error. An article on this topic appeared in the *JC* on the Friday following this sermon (November 24, 1939, p. 11), citing *The Times of London* as a source; on October 24, 1939, the *Times* had written, "To thrust 3,000,000 Jews, relatively few of whom are agriculturalists, into the Lublin region and to force them to settle there

German and Polish Jews in that place, even if from other points of view it were desirable. However, already Jews have been torn from Vienna and Vilna and carried away to this place. No description of mine is necessary to show you the horror and tragedy of their fate.

I am concerned this morning with trying to explain fairly clearly my view about the Jews in Poland, and I may say at once that the community is completely broken up. Out of 3½ million Jews, 1 million have gone under the Soviet regime.[66] The remainder are under German domination....

I do not want to harrow you by describing the fate of the Jews under German domination. You know enough about Nazi mentality to know what they are capable of when inspired only by the hatred of Jews as Jews. Their venom is now increased because they are motivated by hatred for the Jews as Jews and as Poles. This double hatred has marked the treatment so that we are not surprised when the Archbishop of Canterbury said that the treatment was definitely satanic.[67]

The destiny of Polish Jewry does not only concern the social and political life of the unfortunate people themselves, but it has an effect on all other branches of the community. Polish Jews are the largest section of our brotherhood. From this section have been drawn the largest influences upon the Jewry of New York, England, and Sydney, Australia. Not all these influences have been good.... There has been a strong current of mysticism in the people which has fostered the worst form of superstition, but even when we allow for bad influences, we must remember that Polish Jewry has been to a large extent

---

would doom them to famine" (Andrew Sharf, *The British Press and Jews Under Nazi Rule*, p. 90).

66 As a result of the secret protocol of the treaty between Germany and the USSR signed a week before the outbreak of war, which enabled the Soviets to invade and occupy the territory of eastern Poland while the Germans were occupying its western and central territories.

67 This alludes to an address by the Archbishop Cosmo Gordon Lang, delivered to the diocesan conference on October 30, 1939 and reported in the *Spectator* on November 3, http://bit.ly/2fHLpaV; Robert Beaken and Rowan Williams, *Cosmo Lang: Archbishop in War and Crisis*, p. 189.

the home of Jewish learning, and has produced a large number of Jewish saints and countless examples of Jewish loyalty....

December 1, 1939 (Friday evening)

Ferdinand M. Isserman, "The Causes of Anti-Semitism," Temple Israel, St. Louis, MO. AJA, M-6, Box 15, Folder 5

(9:) What Jews gained from wars can best be seen by the tragic Jewish scene in Europe at the present time. Who knows what the fate of Poland's 3½ million Jews is? As a result of this war, which Nazis ascribe to Jews, 2½ million Jews find themselves exposed to the tender mercies of Hitler's legions trained to hate them. Half of Warsaw was said to be destroyed by Nazi bombers. Two-thirds of the Jewish quarter was destroyed. 60,000 Jewish Polish soldiers died in the Polish army. All Polish soldiers were sent home except Jewish soldiers. How many Jews were executed by firing squads no one knows. Think of 2½ million people exposed to the fury of Nazi soldiers. Jews from Bohemia, Moravia, and Vienna have been taken from their homes, placed in chain gangs and forced to repair the destruction caused in Poland by Nazi fury and savagery. Poland was a great intellectual and spiritual center of Jewry. It had rabbinical schools, libraries, synagogues, rabbis. Where are they now? All gone with the wind. That is what Jews gain from war. How ridiculous and absurd to mislead simple people and tell them that Jews plot the wars of the world.

December 10, 1939 (Sunday during Hanukkah)

Abba Hillel Silver, "The Weak in the Hands of the Strong," The Temple, Cleveland, OH. *A Word in Its Season,* pp. 77–82

(77:) In our own darkening days the warm glow of these little Hanukkah lights is especially welcome. They are the gleam of hope and faith in a nigh universal blackout. They are the little stars which shine and keep their faithful vigil in our dark and storm-swept skies.

(78:) Maccabees: It was a resistance against an attempt to establish totalitarianism in that part of the world, an attempt to coordinate

Judea and the Jewish people into the vast fabric of a uniform paganism. The Jews resisted this attempt at *Gleichschaltung*....

(81:) Whom do the powerful aggressor nations attack as their adversaries? They harass Czechoslovakia.... Think of a mighty German nation of eighty million people bearing down on a defenseless minority of six hundred thousand Jews.

Many see nothing but doom. The Jewish people is being liquidated with fire and sword. Yet, by all records of history, we are not weak at all but strong, so strong as to frighten the Antiochuses of our day, the modern exponents of Neopaganism. We Jews are today, even as we were then, the principal adversaries of all who would be dictators of mankind.

(82:) Judah the Maccabee has shown us the road, the road of sacrifice and suffering, perhaps the road of martyrdom, but the road of conviction, the road of the whole of mankind, and the road for us Jews particularly.

We have been attacked. Our answer should be a counterattack – determined, powerful – upon all kinds of wickedness and shameful unjustness....

1940

January 5, 1940 (Friday evening)

Ferdinand M. Isserman, "The Five Outstanding Events of 1939," Temple Israel, St. Louis, MO. AJA, MS-6, Box 15, Folder 6

(4:) With the crushing of Poland has come one of the greatest tragedies in the history of Jewry. In Germany before the Hitler regime, there lived half a million Jews. In Poland there lived three and one-half million Jews. One out of every ten Poles was a son of the synagogue. Two and one-half million Polish Jews are now in German territory. God have mercy on them! What their fate has been, perhaps the world will never know. Because there were no Jewish eye-witnesses, and others are afraid to speak the truth. An observer who was with the German army in Poland stated that Jews are being herded into a narrow territory, an area less than a hundred square miles. There they are being placed with no equipment, no tools, no animals, with no medicines, no food, with no media for earning a livelihood.... Being placed in that reservation means that these Jews are condemned to a slow death by disease, by starvation... Oswald Villard, writing from The Hague, states that to have murdered all Jews would have been kinder than to abandon them to such a fate. He urges that Christians of America voice their protest because the only thing that Hitler respects today is American public opinion.[1] These are the Jewish gains of war.

January 12, 1940 (Friday evening)

Harry Joshua Stern, "This Hour of Rededication," Dedication of Emanu-El Community Center, Montreal. *The Jewish Spirit Triumphant*, pp. 52–56

1 This apparently refers to an article entitled "The Latest Anti-Jewish Horrors," mailed from The Hague by that respected journalist and published in *The Nation* on December 28 (JTA, Dec. 29). Cf. his earlier *Spectator* article at http://bit.ly/2wcQwIZ.

(53:) We are dedicating our synagogue-edifice in fateful and frightful days of war. That is challenging indeed.... War dehumanizes. In all wars, man becomes coarsened and brutalized. The process of brutalization will be severer still in the present conflict because of mechanized warfare....

(54:) We are dedicating our edifice not only in stormy days of war between nations but in a war of paganism that has struck with special fury the Jew.... How tragic to contemplate that fifty percent of the Jewish people in the world find themselves at the moment under extraordinary (55:) circumstances distributed between two mighty totalitarian states. More than eight million Jews are now under German and Soviet domination.

In the Third Reich it is the Jews that are being destroyed, while in Russia it is Judaism that is being destroyed. And what shall we say of the latest catastrophe that has fallen upon Polish Jewry, one of the richest reservoirs of Jewish life, with a Jewish population of three and a half million – the richest since the golden period of Spanish Jewry. Hundreds of Jewish communities have been liquidated and destroyed. Hundreds of synagogues and their seats of learning have been burned by Nazi beasts. Thousands of our brethren are in flight, in flight seeking havens of refuge....

How dramatic that on this night of dedication, a refugee should have kindled the perpetual light.... How touching, too, that we should have read from a Scroll of the Law rescued from Nazi vandalism....

(56:) Here we have Christian and Jewish clergy, a Christian church choir and fellow-Canadians of all faiths who have come to participate in this joyous sacred service of dedicating a synagogue house.... Verily, out of the appalling misery of Nazi paganism there has come a new sense of fellowship between Jew and Christian. Today as never before, Jews and Christians stand united in defense of the spiritual values of Western civilization.

January 20, 1940 (Saturday, *BeShallaḥ*)

Kalonymus Kalmish Shapira, Warsaw. *Esh Kodesh*, pp. 19–20; *Derashot meShenot haZa'am*, pp. 102–3; Polen, *Holy Fire*, p. 43, translated by Nehemia Polen

When Rabbi Yose prayed in one of the ruins of Jerusalem, he heard a divine voice [*bat kol*].[2] Now why did he not hear it when he prayed in a synagogue?... We have no idea who Rabbi Yose really was, but this much we can say: the story suggests to us that it was because he prayed in one of the *ruins* of Jerusalem – so that his heart was even more broken [over the destruction] – that he heard the divine voice. This insight has a direct application to our own situation. When businesses are folding, heaven forbid, it is a dire calamity, for our people need a livelihood. No matter what happens, however, we must not waste time. If there is nothing for us to do, let us study, let us recite Psalms, and so on. Then the compassionate God will have compassion and will transform the trials to our benefit.

January 21, 1940 (Sunday)

Abba Hillel Silver, "What Are You Afraid Of?," The Temple, Cleveland, OH. *Therefore Choose Life*, pp. 140–46

(146:) I hear of men and women saying, "Oh, this is the end for us. The world is set to destroy us. We are not going to have children. There is nothing to look forward to." Our long past, the longest continuous experience of any people that has come down from antiquity – our past recalls many similar tribulations and ultimate victory for Israel....

If you are afraid, then you simply have not exchanged your fears – all of them – for the one reverential fear which should be yours: the fear of God, who sleepeth not, who has not forsaken His people.

February 4, 1940 (Sunday)

Samuel H. Goldenson, "Human Animosities: The Supreme Indictment of Religion," Temple Emanu-El, New York. AJA, MS-81, Box 2, Folder 5

(3:) Only a few days ago there was published the tales of the hatefulnesses practiced in Poland. I am not talking of Jews only, I am

2 b. Berakhot 3a; the talmudic text says that he heard the divine voice saying, "Alas for My children for whose iniquities I destroyed My house, burnt My Temple, and exiled them among the nations."

talking of what has happened in Poland as described in an official report – names given, places given, incidents given – and when one reads these terms one could not have been but profoundly disturbed.[3] Disturbed that human beings can become so bestial, that human beings can be so cruel, so deliberately, so coldly cruel, that human beings could plan in such coldness the suffering and the pain of others, that human beings were not quite satisfied to see their fellowmen hurt in body, but [wanted them to be] hurt in person, trying to undo them as persons, as persons belonging to the human family, and to degrade them, to undo their very souls.... I say this is the most unpleasant expression of human life certainly in modern history.

February 25, 1940 (Sunday)

Stephen S. Wise, "Nazi Victory: What Would It Mean?," Free Synagogue at Carnegie Hall, New York. AJA, Box 22: SSW Microfilms of AJHS and BUASC papers

(2:) I speak particularly to those who hate war, who seek peace,... yet are in doubt, in confusion,... who do not seem to understand this one truth: that the triumph of Hitlerism or Nazism would be victory for the principle of might and terror throughout the earth.

(3:) This pulpit today addresses itself primarily to one group or class of Americans commonly known as isolationists.... (4:) I address myself even to the pacifists, addressing myself to them in a very humble and reverent spirit, to warn them, that in the event of Nazi victory we shall have a generation of wars and wars and wars. A Nazi victory would... bring about an attempt of Nazis and communists together to conquer the whole world.

(8:) I am opposed to my country going into this second world war. We are not to enter the war against the Nazi regime, nor are we

3 See, for example, the article published by JTA on January 30, 1940, under the headline "Nazis Seek Extermination of the Jews, Polish Survey Holds." *NYT*, January 30, 1940, p. 1, article about a report to the Vatican by Cardinal Hlond, continuing on p. 9 with description of humiliation of priests by placing them next to Jews in prisons and concentration camps; full report on all of p. 8 and part of p. 9, including prohibition of any sermons except if delivered in German (p. 8). The article speaks of extermination of Poles, not of Jews (p. 9).

to fight side by side with the allied democracies. The democracies have not asked us to and I have reason to believe they do not wish it. We will not enter as belligerents into the world war, though we may prove to be militant during the war and after the war on behalf of world peace.

(9:) I shall summarize my own thought as to what a Nazi victory would mean;... not only war and war and war, but such post-war horror as the world has not known.

Friday there was in my office the Rabbi of one of the great synagogues at Nuremberg. He told me the tale of November 10th in Nuremberg, the day of terror, of his own imprisonment in Dachau.[4] Eighty rabbis – one nearly eighty [years old] – were prisoners there in that hell known as a concentration camp.... I know, he said, that you know something, that you know much of what is happening in Germany; but sometimes we wonder at your acquaintance with the facts. This you will never know: you will never know what happened to us. He told me the story of a saintly old rabbi – no murder, no physical assault, but just the degradation visited upon him by foully diseased men who would strip him naked – and then taunt him, "Now go if you can to some (10:) Aryan girl and commit r----- and we will show you what we will do to you...." This to a serene, old saint who after some weeks of that moral torture fell dead.... The world will never know, the curtain will never be lifted upon that unnamable brutality.

As for Poland, Poland and Germany present exactly the same picture....

March 1, 1940 (Friday evening)

Ignaz Maybaum, "Can We Ever Be Happy Again?," Brondesbury Synagogue, London. *Man and Catastrophe*, pp. 92–101 (delivered in German, translated by Joseph Leftwich)

---

4 The most likely figure who fits this description is Rabbi Dr. Isaak (Ernst) Heilbronn (b. 1880) of the Liberal *Haupt Synagogue* in Nuremberg (which was demolished by the Nazis in the summer of 1938, before *Kristallnacht*); he left Germany with his family in February 1939 and settled in New York, where, beginning in 1940, he served as rabbi of Congregation Beth Hillel in Washington Heights, New York, composed largely of German Jewish refugees.

(92:) It is refugees to whom I put this question. We think of the suffering we have had to bear and the suffering that as refugees we shall have to continue to bear. But when we hear this question – "Can we ever be happy again?" – we think of one thing above all: that we must each moment think of those left behind in the Nazi hell. Can we forget them for an instant, those who are still there? May we for a single minute forget? So long as there is one man in need, who would rest?

Our conscience says, "No! Never! Not for a moment, not for as long as to draw breath may we forget those who have not been able to escape. When we think of them we cannot be happy. . . . "

(93:) I know that I speak here to people who have been cruelly uprooted from their secure, comfortable lives and are now faced with the uncertainty which is the fate of the refugee. I speak here to people who, if they belong to a younger generation, see a future before them that is entirely different from that to which the (94:) preceding generation could so hopefully look forward. I see men and women here in front of me who must face a destiny that is to-day once more, with all its hardships, Jewish destiny. And to these men and women I say, as a confession that I make to you here, as a fundamental principle of faith to which I am bound: to be a Jew and to be happy do go together. Judaism teaches the hopeful overcoming of suffering. There are two things to which we must hold fast. We will neither repress suffering nor seek to romanticise it.

March 23, 1940 (Saturday, Shabbat Zakhor)

Kalonymus Kalmish Shapira, Warsaw. *Esh Kodesh*, pp. 29–30; *Derashot meShenot haZa'am*, pp. 114–15; Polen, *Holy Fire*, pp. 109, 126–27, translated by Nehemia Polen

(109, 126:) Before Amalek came to fight with you, there were among you some lowly individuals to whom secular wisdom, of which Amalek boasted, was attractive. For this reason your enthusiasm for the Torah and the Torah's wisdom were cooled. You said in effect, "Secular wisdom too, is admirable; it too presents [guidelines for] ethical behavior; it contributes to the improvement of this physical world."

God arranged matters so that Amalek would engage you with all his vaunted wisdom, exposing for you all his wickedness, the foulness of his heart, his murderous character, and the decadence of his wisdom.

(126:) Therefore, "It shall be that when the Lord your God gives you rest,...you shall blot out [the memory of Amalek]" (Deut. 25:19) – at least from now on, when, with God's help you will be delivered from him and he will be obliterated, you must at least come to recognize that in all the world's wisdom there is not even a shred of goodness. They are able to preach beautifully, but their insides are of mire. When they need to, or when they just want to, then [instead of] all the intellectual disciplines which they devised to argue (127:) for excellence of character, they now produce intellectual disciplines and analyses to argue that theft, robbery, murder, and other corrupt actions are good.

Not so is our sacred Torah and its sacred wisdom. It is not a human fabrication to be distorted in accord with the individual's desires and thinking....

April 5, 1940 (Friday evening)

Ferdinand M. Isserman, "Ambassadors Bullitt, Kennedy: Nazis and War Guilt: On the Eve of the Anniversary of America's Entry into the World War [1917]," Temple Israel, St. Louis, MO. AJA, MS-6, Box 15, Folder 6

(8:) Just recently it was announced that all American consular officials have been asked [by Germany] to leave Poland for no obvious reasons whatsoever.... [The true reason is that] the Nazi government does not want the American State Department to know what it has done to Poland and to its inhabitants.... Someday the awful tragedy of innocent men and women in Poland will be revealed. It will be the blackest page in all history.[5] No conqueror of the past whose memory is execrated, whose name has become a hissing, a reproach, has been one-tenth as cruel and has caused the death of one-tenth as many civilian lives as Hitler has already caused in Poland.... Gallows have

5 Note that this is well before any deportation to death camps, or even the establishment of a walled ghetto, had begun.

been erected in the streets of Warsaw. Weekly quotas are executed to empty the prisons. Typhoid and typhus spread, also hunger and starvation. Men are frozen on cattle trains. Those who survive are shot as the trains arrive at their destination. These are some of the cruelties that the (9:) Nazi government wishes to hide from the world. Perhaps some of our officials are ready with their reports and the Nazi government wishes to discredit our diplomats so that we shall place no credence in what they state. That it seems to me is the purpose of the white papers. To discredit American diplomats....

We Americans have learned from the last war that if we go to war we shall help neither the cause of democracy nor the cause of peace. We shall only become as brutalized as the rest of Europe is being brutalized....

April 6, 1940 (Saturday)

Irving F. Reichert, "When a Man Takes Religion Seriously," Radio Address on "The Message of Israel," coast-to-coast NBC. *Judaism and the American Jew*, pp. 208–12

(209:) This is a bad time for people to be apathetic to religion.... Take a good long thoughtful look at the methods employed by contemporary barbarians to enslave whole populations and unleash upon the world a fury greater than hell! For the authority of the moral law (210:) they substitute the arbitrary expediency of the Duce, Commissar, and Fuehrer, and in place of the dignity and worth of the human spirit they proclaim the absolute and total domination of the state. No wonder that they are compelled to use every weapon in the arsenal of persecution against religion and its classic institutions in order to achieve their purpose....

April 12, 1940 (Friday evening)

Ignaz Maybaum "The Way of the Remnant," Brondesbury Synagogue, London. *Man and Catastrophe*, pp. 102–12, (delivered in German, translated by Joseph Leftwich)

"Lord, how long?" (Isa. 6:11) is also our cry to-day. We have seen one Jewish centre after the other overwhelmed by the catastrophe. The fate of German Jews was but the first act in the tragedy of European Jewry. The Barbarians have also brought down the fist of destruction upon Austrian, Czech, and Polish Jewry. European Jewry is to-day one vast martyr community.

But we are not the only ones who ask, "Lord, how long?" Hitler's war on Christianity is the most formidable it has faced since the time of Mahomet. It is a war no longer only against Jews and Judaism. The question is now how (103:) the spirit of man can be saved from this brute aggression, how justice, truth, and liberty can save themselves from this onslaught of the barbarians.

(105:) We Jews of to-day must also relate our history, preserve it, and reflect upon it. Each one of us has a duty to act as one of the chroniclers. The term "atrocity propaganda" can acquire a very profound meaning if it is understood as the duty to relate what atrocities occur wherever paganism rules. Paganism and atrocity go together like cause and effect. Such atrocity (106:) propaganda is a duty for both Jews and Christians. Only fate has imposed this duty on us Jews more forcibly than on others.... We are refugees. We have escaped. What does it mean? It means that we were in the power of the heathen, but we are alive. So we speak of a miracle.

We German Jews, unlike the Jews of Poland, who were handed over at one blow to the barbarism of the Nazi regime, had a long controversy, a long struggle with paganism.... We experienced a history of suffering, while Polish Jewry succumbed at one blow. We German Jews owe it to the power of humanity that we did not experience on April 1st, 1933 what we experienced on November 10th, 1938.[6] The Nazi regime did not feel strong enough then; that is why it had to submit to the pressure from the rest of the world, which held fast to Christianity and to humanity....

(107:) April 1st, 1933, was followed by a Back to Judaism movement.... The period from April 1st, 1933 till November 10th, 1938 is not only a chapter of suffering in the history of German Jewry, but a chapter of rebirth....

---

6 April 1, 1933 was the day of the national boycott proclaimed by the Reich of stores marked as owned by Jews. November 10, 1938 was, of course, *Kristallnacht* and its immediate aftermath.

But then came the pogroms of November 10th, 1938, and we had to retreat. Once again it was the humanity of the rest of the world, though it had failed us in the Evian Conference, that saved us now. Britain, loyal to her ancient tradition, opened her gates to us refugees.

When we now look back to the history of what we have experienced since 1933, we ask ourselves, "How did we live through it?"...

April 13, 1940 (Saturday)

Irving F. Reichert, "How Much Do We Want Liberty?," Radio Address on "The Message of Israel." *Judaism and the American Jew*, pp. 213–18

(214:) We are living in one of those crucial periods in which the principle of human freedom must face anew the challenge of a cruel and truculent illiberalism. All the values of the human spirit which civilized men hold dear and honorable are threatened with extinction by a force more sinister and ruthless, more powerful and determined, than any which our world has ever known. In one country after another the brutal fist of tyranny has crushed the heritage of humane and cultured living which is the finest flower of the spirit of man. Every marvelous device which science has made available for the extension of human happiness and freedom is turned with savagery and staggering might into an instrument for the annihilation of those precious possessions. Mile by mile the frontiers of liberty are shrinking as the victorious hosts of destruction press their evil gains....

(218:) Do we cherish liberty enough to refuse to risk its destruction in a war overseas? Make no mistake about it, my friends, the moment our nation enters a foreign war, you can bid adieu to the Goddess of Liberty.... War demands dictatorship for its efficient waging. It demands the total resources, spiritual as well as material, of a nation. And in return it gives back corpses, blind and crippled sons and husbands, starvation, bankruptcy, unemployment and dictatorship.[7]

---

7 Note here another rhetorically powerful stance against American participation in the current war based on the experience in the Great War and the Depression.

Kalonymus Kalmish Shapira, Warsaw. *Esh Kodesh*, pp. 40–41; *Derashot meShenot haZa'am*, p. 129; Polen, *Holy Fire*, p. 19, translated by Nehemia Polen

We know and believe that whatever God does to us – even when, God forbid, He smites us – it is all for the good. But when we see now that God is smiting us not only with physical torments, but also in ways which, God forbid, distance us from Him – there is no *ḥeder* for school children, no *yeshivah*, no *bet hamidrash* for communal prayer, no *mikveh*, and so on – then God forbid, a doubt, a suspicion enters our hearts: could it be that now too His intention is for good?

[We think:], "If it were for the good, He would have afflicted us in ways which bring us closer to Him, not by calling a halt to Torah study and prayer, indeed the calling a halt to almost the entire way of Torah life, God forbid! Could this be anything other than afflictions expressing divine rejection of us, God forbid?"

April 12, 1940 (Friday evening)

Ferdinand M. Isserman, "Scandinavia is Invaded," Temple Israel, St. Louis, MO. AJA, MS-6, Box 15, Folder 6

(1:) It is with a sense of sorrow and humiliation that I step into the pulpit this evening. Sorrow over the new tragedy that has befallen two great and honorable peoples; humiliation over the seeming impotence of civilization to work out some medium of preventing such catastrophes which have overwhelmed Denmark and Norway in the past few days.

(2:) Reports indicate that a dozen transports bearing Nazi soldiers were torpedoed or blasted by the guns of the British fleet. And that as these Nazi ships were sinking, the seas were dotted for a few moments with bobbing heads of men trying to save themselves, who after a few moments gave up the struggle, realizing that their efforts were in vain. We may read this news item in the press and if our sympathies are with the allied sides, we may cheer the frustration of Nazi plans in our hearts. Yet, what grief and what tears and what anguish that same exploit brought to German mothers, to German fathers, who reared their sons through sacrifice and privation, who remember their first smile, who were buoyed up in their dark days when they thought of the future and career of their children, only to learn now that all their efforts were futile and vain, that the son they loved lies rotting at the bottom of the sea, fallen while sent on an errand of brutality and cruelty by the tyrant whose will and word has become law.

April 20, 1940 (Saturday, Shabbat haGadol)

Irving F. Reichert, "Short-Cuts to Utopia," Radio Address on "The Message of Israel." *Judaism and the American Jew*, pp. 203–7

(203:) There is no short-cut to the Promised Land!…(205:) Moses did not lead the children of Israel through the land of the Philistines (cf. Exod. 13:17) because he knew how dangerously seductive were their methods, how powerfully they appealed to the prejudices and passions of the mob, and he knew, moreover, that if our forefathers tried to imitate those vulgar patterns of conduct, they would never achieve the Promised Land.

You see, do you not, the deadly parallel between that ancient situation and the choice which confronts our world today. The philistines still walk the earth, although to be sure, they bear different names in our time.… The doctrine of brute force is a philistine doctrine; the doctrine of racial superiority is a philistine conceit. The doctrine of militarism is philistine fist-brandishing. The doctrine of state supremacy which annihilates the rights of the individual is a philistine survival in modern civilization.

Ephraim Sokolover, Great Synagogue, Ra'anana, Palestine. *Penei Efrayim*, pp. 233–41, translated by MS

(237:) Our Jewish brethren in Poland are also now preparing for the Seder on the evening of Pesach.… But what will be their condition? In how many households will the father and mother come to arrange their Seder, and check in the cracks for *ḥometz* with their children who will ask the Four Questions? How many orphans will look for their parents whose bodies remain under the ruins?

At this moment as I stand here and deliver my sermon to you,

I hear the voice of the great rabbis throughout Poland, who are deprived even of the joy of expressing the sound of weeping before their congregation. They do not even have the opportunity to use the words of the prophet Jeremiah, the godly elegist, who said, "Would that my head was water, and my eyes a fountain of tears; I would weep day and night for the fallen of my people" (Jer. 8:23).

It is clear that at this moment they are aware that in this great world there are Rabbis – may they live on – who are now preaching sermons as always before Jewish congregations. Are these wretched [Polish Jews] aware that we are simply unable to help at present? Do they know that, if we could, we would share our bread with our brothers and sisters, our flesh and blood? Clearly every one of us would make use of every opportunity, no matter how remote, to help them in one way or another. But to our great sorrow, all the paths of help and assistance have been blocked.... How is it possible now to observe this great and holiday festival without calling to mind the destruction of the Jewish people in our times?

(139:) Yet there remains a profound point; even though we may be unable to sense it, it remains within the depths of the Jewish soul and is implanted in all the 248 bones and the 365 sinews, and that is the Jewish hope for the resplendent future that has been promised by the Holy One, blessed be He, through His prophets and sages....

April 21, 1940 (Sunday)

Stephen S. Wise, (no title), Address for Columbia Broadcasting System (CBS), 2:30 p.m. AJA, Box 22: SSW Microfilms of AJHS and BUASC papers

(1:) The holiday of Passover commemorates the deliverance from bondage of the Jews in ancient Egypt. Its observance this year will have profound significance not only for the Jewish people but for all men and women who have been enslaved, with fading out of the lamps of reason and freedom in many parts of the world. A new and modern Pharaoh has come upon the face of the earth and with lightning strokes he has struck down the small, weak and defenceless peoples, who have been made prisoners in their own lands, strangers in their own homes.

A calamitous war has placed millions of men under arms and millions of women and children in the bread lines.... Men are groping in the dark physically and spiritually. The lights of hope have been dimmed by the mammoth sweep of destruction, and the word "blackout" has, alas, become the symbol of a world struggling to free itself from the threat of doom.

Many small peoples, proud and free only yesterday, are today despoiled and in chains, slaves in body and spirit, helpless in the face of brute force. More than 3,000,000 Jews in Germany, Austria, Czecho-Slovakia, and Poland have been reduced to profound suffering by the lash of the modern Pharaoh. The world has at last realized that the ruthless assault against the Jewish people was the first blow in a concerted attack upon all minority groups and small nations.

(2:) On the Passover eve, Jews throughout the United States will pause in solemn prayer for the men and women whose homes have been destroyed by war, for the innocent thousands who have been herded into concentration camps, for those who have been driven to the verge of extermination on the frontiers of Central and Eastern Europe. In the dark and desolate ghettos of Poland the old and the young will seek consolation together.... But in their deepest despair the Jews of Poland will never account this yellow blot upon civilization as the badge of their tribe....

April 23, 1940 (first day of Pesach)

Israel Goldstein, "Passover Pattern," Congregation B'nai Jeshurun, New York. *Toward a Solution*, pp. 141–48

(143:) The four-fold condition suffered by our ancestors in Egypt is duplicated in the tragic story of the Jew in Nazified Europe since 1933.

Physical atrocities have been perpetrated upon thousands of Jews with a brutality reminiscent of the Egyptian Pharaoh. Economic persecution has been practiced with a relentlessness and thoroughness which are unprecedented. Social degradation, branding the Jew as an inferior race, has reduced him in those countries to the position of "pariah."

While these hardships have been imposed from without, one

inner fault has streaked a large part of the Jewry of Central Europe, long before Hitler came upon the scene. Once more as in Egypt, the Jewish community had elements within it which (144:) had deteriorated spiritually, were ashamed of their birthright, and had turned a deaf ear to the message of Jewish self-emancipation. Now their protective coloration is exposed. Their "camouflage" was to no avail....

Consistent with the Passover pattern, the program for the Jew in an age of oppression has been hinted at by the Rabbis in a series of four possible lines of action....[8]

(145:) Thus the Rabbis have read between the lines of the Passover story. We have something to learn from their analysis.

In the Jewish camp today, there are those who, smitten with fear, can do nothing but pray.... They wrap themselves in their prayer shawls, raise their voices to heaven and imagine that they are thus averting disaster.

There are those who say, "Let us go back to Egypt."...

"There are those who counsel the other extreme, "Let us plunge into the waters of extinction." Some mean suicide literally. Others say, "Let us drown our identity."...

The Jewish camp also has its bellicose contingent, who are ready to take on the adversary in physical battle even if the odds are hopelessly against them.

How evaluate the four points of view as to the best way out of the peril?...

(147:) Today, there are hundreds of thousands of Jews who are fighting in the forces which are ranged against the Nazi-Fascist power. They are fighting as citizens of their respective countries and they are fighting as Jews. Their battle is merged with humanity's battle. Alone, however, Jews would be helpless in any physical combat against the overwhelming numbers of their foes. Only in Palestine, where their proportion is one to three, would they have a fighting chance. Would

---

8 Goldstein provides the source for this rabbinic tradition as *Mekilta BeShallaḥ*, chap. 2, sec. 2, and cites the Polish preacher Isaac Nissenbaum as his source for applying the text to contemporary divisions among the Jewish people. It was used by many other preachers; see Saperstein, *Witness from the Pulpit*, p. 73, n. 7.

any reasonable person have counseled the five hundred thousand Jews of Germany to hurl themselves against the might of the German Reich? It might have been a heroic gesture, more heroic than to have hurled themselves into the sea, but just as futile.

What then is the way out?

"Speak unto the Children of Israel that they shall go forward" (Exod. 14:15).

The difference between rushing to plunge into the sea, in an act of self-extinction, and going forward even though the direction lead straight into the devouring waves, is the difference between despair and faith, between swimming and sinking, between survival and extinction.

Going forward, in these days, means the undismayed continuance of the daily program....

There are Jews in Germany and Poland today who under all the burdens and dangers, are going on, as and when they can, going on with the rearing of their children and the daily problems of Jewish life, and at the same time refusing to renounce the culture of the Western world....

How much more reason have the Jews of America to move forward!

April 26, 1940 (Friday evening, *Ḥol haMo'ed* Pesach)

Ferdinand M. Isserman, "Has God Forsaken Humanity?," Temple Israel, St. Louis, MO. AJA, MS-6, Box 15, Folder 6

(4:) To lose faith in God in the face of a crisis is more calamitous than the crisis itself.

(6:) We Jews have frequently been tried by suffering. Perhaps never on a greater scale than today.... They survived because they retained their faith and that suffering has had a beneficent influence.

(7:) The first victims of this modern revolt against the values of Judaism are the Jews. They are not the only victims. Norwegians suffer. The Danes suffer. Finns suffer. Germans suffer. Czechs suffer. Poles suffer. English suffer. Belgians, Dutch, French, Romanians, Jugo-Slavs suffer. But upon our brethren, the weakest and the most defenseless, the first and most easily exposed, the burden rests the heaviest. Two hundred and fifty thousand to three hundred thousand new Jewish martyrs have been added to the list since the German war against Poland began. Some of them dying a death of an unutterable cruelty. And those who survive deprived of a means of livelihood, torn from their homes, separated from their children, herded into ghettos, where disease is rampant. Their daughters taken from them to satisfy the mad lusts of an invading army. Their plight may be more pitiable than death itself.

(8:) What are we Americans going to do?... The more generous we are, the more lives we save, the more human beings we can snatch from the cauldron of hate and of fury. What we do is important for the victims, but it is also important for America....

April 27, 1940 (Saturday, *Ḥol haMo'ed* Pesach)

Irving F. Reichert, "The Contagion of a Spiritual Pestilence," Radio Address on "The Message of Israel." *Judaism and the American Jew*, pp. 63–67

(64:) "Think not within thy heart that thou shalt escape in the king's house more than all the Jews" (Esth. 4:13). That was the message which Mordecai sent to his niece Esther, queen of Persia. A vicious idea had broken loose in the kingdom, and was infecting the people with its deadly poison. To serve his own dark purposes, the chancellor of the realm was fomenting racial and religious hatred against the Jews, and had fixed the day for their annihilation....

Let no one imagine that this wise warning of an ancient day exhausted its significance when that Persian crisis was past.... (65:) Consider for example the incalculable harm that religious bigotry has done the human family. As has so often happened, you begin by inflaming the prejudices and passions of people against one minority group. You circulate the most incredible and fantastic fabrications about them; you hold them responsible for every community problem you have failed to solve, and you raise a hue and cry for their suppression. For you think that the fury you have unleashed will have run its course when the immediate objects of your persecution have been ruined? The stream of hatred will overflood the narrow channel in which you would confine it, and spread its havoc far and wide. Today it is the Jews who are the victims; yesterday it was the Catholics, the day before it was the Quakers, Puritans, and Huguenots, and tomorrow the cycle may begin anew. Intolerance is a spiritual pestilence whose virus does not select its victims with discrimination or consistency.

April 29, 1940 (Monday, seventh day of Pesach)

Ephraim Sokolover, "Seventh Day of Pesach 5700, before the Commemoration of the Departed (*hazkarat neshamot*)," Great Synagogue, Ra'anana, Palestine. *Penei Efrayim*, pp. 354–58, translated by MS

(354:) How did we sing this pleasant song, "Then [Moses and the Israelites] sang [this song to the Eternal]" (Exod. 15:1) at a time when our Jewish brethren in Poland and Lithuania were drowning in the sea of (355:) indescribable suffering and persecution, and also in other places where the oppressor's cruel hand holds sway, and we feel that his hand is spread over all the lands of Europe where there are centers of Jewish life?... We have committed a great sin up to now, for we have not yet given public expression to our feelings of participation in the suffering of our brothers and sisters in the Diaspora.

Nevertheless, at this moment, when we are preparing to make mention of the tens of thousands of pure and holy souls that have fallen to their death at the hands of the enemy during the wild and bitter winter, "some by the sword, and some by hunger, some by stoning, and some by strangulation,"[9] we should also make mention of those who remain in embittered life, and those who are hovering between life and death. Let us dedicate our hearts and focus our thoughts to the conditions of their lives. Let us imagine for a brief moment their feelings on our final day of Pesach. If we do so, we would not be able to understand how this passage containing the Song at the Sea, which we have just read, is relevant to us. And how we have celebrated this holiday with all its commandments and precise rules, including a well-known component of joy.... "Our brothers are drowning in the sea, and we are singing a song?!"[10]

9 Echoing a passage from the *Unetaneh Tokef* liturgy of the High Holy Days.
10 Alluding to the well-known rabbinic passage in which the heavenly angels, preparing

May 3, 1940 (Friday evening)

Leo M. Franklin, "Retaliation or Non-Resistance?," Temple Beth El, Detroit, MI. Unpublished, Rabbi Leo Morris Franklin Archives, now at AJA, MS-246

(10:) Now these considerations are tremendously important in this crucial hour of human history. To keep out of the war has become the slogan of the American people. To maintain an attitude of neutrality is the warning that is being sounded from the housetops. The wickedness of retaliation and the virtue of forgiveness is being preached from the pulpits of many churches and the Bible is being invoked by the advocates of the sponsors of all these forms of propaganda to uphold their positions. Of course, I know that it has been said that the devil can quote Scripture to his own purpose, and never was that more true than in these days when the forces of evil and the forces of good are meeting in the arena of war. But I sound the warning that it is easy to misinterpret the teachings of religion in a time like this. We are all advocates of peace, but to maintain that the Bible and the teachings of religion, Christian or Jewish, would have us turn the other cheek to those who are striking at the very roots of our (11:) free institutions is to misinterpret the truth and to lead the thoughts of men astray. On the other hand, it is equally a distortion of the biblical teaching to maintain that cruelty should be met with cruelty and force with force even in a day like this. We simply can make no generalizations. We have to face conditions as they exist. If Church and Synagogue – or better, if Christian and Jew – will study their own Scriptures intelligently and honestly, they will surely come to an agreement as to the course to be followed in the light of the situations that may arise.

There may come the day when not in a spirit of vengeance and not with a desire to retaliate wrong for wrong, we may yet have to enter this conflict for the preservation of the human rights that are threatened. And there may come a day when at the conclusion of this

---

to sing God's praises as the Israelites emerged safely from their pursuing foes, were rebuked by God who said, "My creatures [the Egyptians] are drowning in the sea, and you are singing a song?" (b. Sanhedrin 39b).

war, we may have to guide the thoughts of those who shall lay down the terms of peace and then, surely we will not allow ourselves to be guided by the call for vengeance upon the wrong-doer, nor yet shall we be so docile as to offer forgiveness to those who have so bitterly wronged innocent peoples; but, prayerfully, we shall turn to the God Who is the God of Christian and of Jew for guidance and for help....

May 4, 1940 (Saturday)

David de Sola Pool, Spanish and Portuguese Synagogue, New York. *NYT*, May 5, 1940, p. 27

The modern disciples of Nietzsche, who have put into practice what he taught, see in pitiless, ruthless strength the virtue of the world's super man and super race.... In the justice, the love and democratic concern for all humanity that are central in Judaism and Christianity, they rightly see the strongest challenge to their apotheosis of the pitiless strong man. Mankind's ultimate assurance of victory over the new cult of force is still to be found not in armies but in synagogues and churches.

May 10, 1940 (Friday evening)

Jacob Bosniak, "Religion and Democracy," Sermon delivered at United Synagogue Convention, Community Synagogue, Atlantic City, NJ. *Interpreting Jewish Life*, pp. 130–37

(136:) [After the Nazi invasion of Poland, reports of a Hasid from Lodz seeking donations to cover costs of his travel to Leningrad:] "I decided to go to Leningrad to find the burial place of the Czar, and upon his grave I will beg of him forgiveness for the many curses which I invoked against him during his lifetime. In comparison to the Bolsheviks and the Nazis, the Czar was a saint."[11]

The Czar and all the tyrants before him believed in the Supreme Being; they respected no man but were afraid of God, and dared not lift their bloody hands against the Bible. The tyrants of to-day

11 Bosniak's note: "There are several versions of this story."

have no fear of God nor respect for the sacred Book. The Soviet Government banished the volume as unworthy of consideration or study...; (137:) while the Nazis have attempted to rewrite the Bible to suit their philosophy of life.

May 20, 1940 (Monday)

ISRAEL GOLDSTEIN, "Realism Plus Vision," Address to National Convention of Mizrachi Organization of America, Baltimore, MD. *Toward a Solution*, pp. 179–91

(189:) For the Jewish people these fateful, catastrophic days hold much instruction. One lesson above all seems to cry out for emphasis. It is a lesson in what it means for a people to have a land and a home.

When the little Finnish nation of three and a half million was invaded and attacked by a vastly greater power, the world's indignation was aroused, its sympathy flowed out and its generous help went forth to the victim. When, however, three and a half million Jews in Poland were consigned to massacre and spoliation on one side and to material and spiritual dispossession on the other, the world's conscience was not outraged, its sensibilities were not shocked, and its practical sympathies were not aroused. The Jews of conquered Poland were deprived even of the privilege of heroic death. In our contemporary Book of (190:) Lamentations, this is the saddest page, namely, that a people uprooted and divorced from its historic soil can only look for a beggar's crumb at the table of humanity's understanding, consideration, and respect.

Had three and a half million Jews lived on their national soil in Eretz Israel there might be a different story to tell today – witness the story that has been told by the Yishub of less than five hundred thousand souls during the troubles they have had to face since 1936.

(191:) Is it fantastic to believe that the consideration of our just aspirations to Palestine may be on the agenda of the Peace Conference after this war, as it was on the agenda of the Peace Conference following the last war? Is it Utopian to hope that the next Peace Conference may produce a sequel to the Balfour Declaration?

Let us be sure that when the time is opportune, our credentials will be impressive.... It would therefore be an unforgivable sin against the destiny of our people if because of *kotzer ruaḥ*, a shortage not of means but of spirit, vision, and will, we fail to make ours every dunam of land which can be bought, every industrial position which can be gained, and every immigration influx which can be accomplished.[12]

May 26, 1940 (Sunday), National Day of Prayer in Great Britain and Throughout the Empire,[13] (Lag BaOmer).

ALEXANDER ALTMANN, Manchester, England. *The Manchester Guardian*, May 27, 1940, p. 6, headline: "KING AND QUEEN LEAD THE NATION'S PRAYER: Cabinet at the Abbey Service." University College London Altmann Archives

In Jewry's prayers to-day echo the tears and agony, the humiliation and torture of a people who were singled out as the first victims of Nazi bestiality. We above everyone know what issues are at stake and God in His heaven knows that if there is true prayer, ours today are true.

The cry of millions of oppressed peoples goes out to the Allies in whose hands Providence has placed their fate. We cannot fail, for we have the weapon the Nazis have lost – the moral strength that comes of a just cause.

Let the world realise that never again must racial hatred be allowed to raise its ugly head now that mankind had seen the horrors that resulted from it. For the sake of peace let all hatred be abolished and a saner and better world would be built.

EMIL EHRNTHAL (LATER MICHAEL ELTON), "The Threat of Invasion," Bognor Regis Synagogue, Bognor Regis, England. *The Challenge of Destiny*, pp. 17–20

In these fateful days, as we offer our fervent supplications to God for His intervention, let us remember that the efficacy of our prayers

12 This appears to reflect an internal conflict between using funds for communities in Europe or refugees, and purchasing land in Mandate Palestine.

13 On National Days of Prayer during WWII, see http://bit.ly/2fOB9kB.

is measured by the increase of our conviction in the strength and omnipotence of God. Unless God becomes greater and mightier in our innermost hearts, our devotion has been a failure, and our mass-meetings of prayer a spectacular sham for our own delusion....

(18:) This ominous forecast in the Book of Deuteronomy [chap. 28] has become literally fulfilled in the (19:) terrifying phases of the present war.... [Quotes verses] Sensitive people are outraged at this horrific admonition to the Jewish people. But are these not the very same men who turned off the wireless when they heard the stories of the torture-camps of Germany, the men who would stop writers from describing the horrors of war to serve as a warning for all time?...

It was the laziness of heart that could not picture the tortures inflicted upon the Jews of the Continent, it was the laziness of heart that first proclaimed the policy of non-intervention, it was the laziness of heart that allowed the rape of land after land. It is the laziness of heart that (20:) proudly parades in our public life as the policy of realism. Those of us who wish to face facts should face this great fact of history. Whenever man denied God's strength, whenever man forgot to build *in time of peace* the stronghold of pious living, afflictions inevitably followed. This fact also brings us to the inescapable realization and admission that the Lord is our refuge in the day of affliction.

Maurice N. Eisendrath, Radio Address delivered over the Canadian Broadcasting System. Unpublished, AJA Eisendrath Papers, MS-167, Box 2

(2:) It is for *your* Christian Church and my Jewish faith that we are manning the barricades in this hour of decision, yes, for a thousand years; and it is for this reason that we are justified in raising our voices even to God on high to send succour and aid to our side.

Nor is this being maintained by any war-mongering priest or minister or rabbi seeking to turn his pulpit into a recruiting platform as will be cynically urged by subversive fifth columnists now crying "peace, peace" when there is no real peace (cf. Jer. 6:4), but only the lust for domestic chaos and world strife within their hearts. Nay, it is Herr Hitler himself who argues thus. As that prophetic contemporary seer, whom we might well have heeded long ere this, as Dr. Hermann Rauschning tells us, it was the God-denying, Christ-crucifying, Jew-persecuting Fuehrer of the German Reich who long since declared, "The religious are all alike, no matter what they call themselves. They have no future – certainly none for the Germans. Fascism, if it likes," continued Hitler, "may come to terms with the Church. But not I. I shall not be prevented from tearing up Christianity root and branch and annihilating it in the Reich."[14] And since we know now that his ambition is to establish the frontiers of the Reich at the farthermost extremities of the earth we may conclude that nothing would stand in the way of his seeking to tear up Christianity root and branch and destroying its very name and memory from the mind and heart of man.

May 31, 1940 (Friday evening, Memorial Day)

Leo M. Franklin, "What Sort of World Shall We Bequeath to Our Children?," Temple Beth El, Detroit, MI. Unpublished, Rabbi Leo Morris Franklin Archives, now at AJA, MS-246, Text 1472

(1:) There appeared in the public press a few days ago, among other pictures of incidents in war-torn Europe, the picture of a blind Belgian peasant groping his way among the war-torn ruins of his home, his sightless eyes spared the vision of the desolation that surrounded him, but his heart keenly aware of the bitter fact that the foundations of his poor life had been suddenly shattered beneath his feet. In that sightless, decrepit, broken old man, I could not but see a picture of the world in which we are living. How blind the leaders of men have been....

(4:) It is too late in the day to go into detail as to the vital mistakes, not to say the unholy deeds, that followed the War, beginning with the Treaty of Versailles and perhaps reaching their climax in the so-called Munich Pact. From the day that the Armistice was signed to this very day, one stupendous error after the other was committed....

---

14 No source is provided in the sermon text; the direct quotation of Hitler was apparently taken from Rauschning's *The Voice of Destruction*, p. 49 (a translation of *Gespräche mit Hitler*, also published in 1940). Recent scholars have been extremely skeptical about the reliability of Rauschning's extensive direct quotations, for which there was no tape recording or stenographer.

(5:) It is hard to say it and it is hard to think it, but the truth is that if our children and our children's children are to live in a world at peace, we must be ready to pay a tremendous price for it. You can't stop the ravages of a horde of wild beasts by kind words, especially when they have had a taste of their preys' blood. And today, the world is over-run with hordes of untamed savages....

(7:) What, among the dictator nations, has been the first point of attack? Has it not been religion and the church? If the Jew has been the first and the chief victim for a long time of the dictator's wicked assault, surely it has not been just because he is a Jew, but rather because he has been the symbol of religion which is the enemy of all autocracy and of all dictatorship....

(8:) Under the stress of war even Britain has become little short of a dictatorship in that every man's life and every man's property has become subject to the will of the government. How long will it be before France will be driven to the same position?...

(9:) In a day when time and distance have been annihilated and when it is utterly puerile to say "It can't happen here"[15]; when in the mind of a mad dictator of Europe there is the desire not only for dominance in Central Europe, but, in very truth, for world domination, we must build up our defenses, both physical and moral....

June 1, 1940 (Saturday)

Israel Goldstein, Congregation B'nai Jeshurun, New York. *NYT*, June 2, 1940, p. 20

The courage, resolution and faith being displayed by England and France in this, the most trying period in their long history, should shame some of us in American life who become easily upset over relatively minor difficulties. Let us learn from the tragic experiences of European nations the lesson of preparedness, not only physical preparedness but moral preparedness. Our national preparedness should consist of strong physical defenses, national unity, high morale and willingness to make substantial sacrifices for the welfare of the nation.

15 Alluding to the title of the novel by Sinclair Lewis, published in New York and London in 1935.

June 7, 1940 (Friday evening)

Leo M. Franklin, "Is This the End?," Temple Beth El, Detroit, MI; see Complete Sermons

June 9, 1940 (Sunday, National Day of Prayer following Dunkirk)

Emil Ehrnthal (later Michael Elton), "Dunkirk," Bognor Regis Synagogue, Bognor Regis, England. *The Challenge of Destiny*, 21–23

Today, as we are gathered here for prayer, how much more should we remember and mourn the great fall of a *friend and an ally*. A friend of Britain, a friend of culture and liberty, and a friend of the Jewish people. Nothing but the words of Jeremiah (22:) could do justice to the desolation and humiliation of France....

Ready as we are now to defend the soil of our country, the walls of our homes, our own future and that of our children, let us pray for the blessing of God (Ps. 20:17).... A nation's survival cannot be guaranteed. It must be earned by faith, toil and ideals. History attests that the Jewish people have survived overwhelming odds not solely by the grace of God but by their dedication, perseverance, and unceasing efforts "to be a kingdom of priests and a holy nation" (Exod. 19:6)....

(23:) France sought shelter behind the stronghold of the Maginot Line. But what of the life of the people behind the fortified walls? See how they live. We all heard the tragic confession from the trembling lips of Field Marshal Petain, the Grand Old Man of France, of the reasons for this terrible defeat....

On this day of prayer and intercession, we must look into our own selves and ask the question...: Have I taken part in the battles of Israel or have I retired behind the selfish walls of my own home?

June 13, 1940 (Thursday, second day of Shavu'ot)

Max Nussbaum, "Chosen and Called," Berlin. *A Set of Holiday Sermons* 5702/1941, pp. 72–78; *From Berlin to Hollywood*, pp. 67–74; translator unidentified[16]

16 This was one of Nussbaum's last sermons in Berlin, apparently in a congregation that observed two days of the holiday. (The AJA has the German text of the sermon he delivered on July 27.) According to the JTA of August 21, 1940, Nussbaum left

(72:) Shavuos in these days – what a discrepancy between the inner atmosphere of this holiday and the mood of our hearts. The radiance of calm and peace, the ideals and the spirit of this festival seem entirely out of place amid our world, tossed up, war-like, and brutal....

(77:) [T]his is where all the events of these days, unbelievable and cruel as they are, originate: Europe has killed the World-Spirit.

This result, following the efforts, the troubles, and the painful progress of centuries, certainly is alarming, to the world as well as to us Jews. But in spite of that I am not ready to resign and to write Europe off the book of the World-Spirit for all eternity....

(78:) As for us Jews, this time of antithesis may be very sad and may burden our life immensely. But one thing is sure: we Jews will live on in this world, as long as the history of mankind will have sense, or until a voice will sound on Sinai to revoke the mandate once given to us. This mandate is burdened with pains and suffering, but on the other hand it guarantees to our people eternal life. If we only understand this, then we know that all our troubles, strong and agonizing as they may be, cannot lead as far as death and senseless destruction. There is no sorrow so great that it cannot be endured by our people, and no pain so vehement that it will make our people sacrifice its life.

June 15, 1940 (Saturday, Sabbath following the fall of Paris on "Black Friday, June 14")

Eliezer Berkovits, "Not By Might," United Hebrew Congregation, Leeds, England. *Between Yesterday and Tomorrow*, pp. 9–14

(12:) The sin against the spirit committed by our generation becomes clear when we compare ourselves with our opponents in the present struggle. On their side, the side of brute force, the struggle is car-

---

Germany on August 1, 1940, the last German rabbi to leave the country. According to the *JC* of April 14, 1939, he had arrived in England during the previous week and delivered the sermon at the Golders Green Synagogue in London that Sabbath evening. This was apparently a temporary visit for a conference, at which he met for the first time Rabbi Stephen S. Wise; after the conference he returned to Berlin, until Wise was able to provide him with a rabbinic position in the United States.

ried on with a methodical ruthlessness the like of which the world has never seen. There is one thing of which the adversaries of the spirit know nothing to-day: compromise. They could have avoided this struggle, they could have achieved great advantages (13:) for themselves by negotiation and compromise. But "No compromise" has been the watchword of the forces of darkness. And it is precisely compromise which has been the sin of our generation.

Had we been as faithful to the spirit as barbarism has been faithful to its own intentions, the catastrophe would never have occurred. Had the democratic world been as sincere, as uncompromising, as thoroughgoing in what it tried to achieve as the world of darkness was in the pursuance of its own detestable aims, the tragedy would have been avoided....

There was much selfishness in all of us, and out of selfishness we were always prepared to compromise. This was the great sin of our generation against the spirit.

June 21, 1940 (Friday evening)

Ferdinand M. Isserman, "Scared Scapegoat or Suffering Servant?," CCAR Conference Sermon, Charlevoix, MI. AJA M-6, Box 16, Folder 6; *CCAR Yearbook* 50 (1940), pp. 216–35

(216:) As I speak tonight, the republic of France is contemplating surrendering to the barbarian invader....

(220:) To us, it was very apparent that the Nazis were not arrayed against Jews alone.... The British knew what was happening in Germany. So did the French, the Dutch, the Belgians, the Poles, the Czechs, the Norwegians, and the Austrians. Somehow or other peoples conditioned to anti-semitism may have acquiesced in and overlooked the ultimate goal of the Nazis, and thus accelerated the debacle of modern civilization. We Jews know that we are the barometer of civilization.... The persecution of our brethren in Germany was the storm signal for humanity. Whether because of local domestic problems, or because of dormant anti-semitic impulses, little was done about that anti-semitism. The warning was ignored....

(222:) The present war of the Nazis is not aimed at Israel, but at the God of Israel.... With their tanks and planes, they seek first and foremost to destroy the God of Israel, and to wipe out the knowledge of His name from the face of the earth. The chief hurdle in the way of Naziism is the religion of the God of Israel....

As great as is the tragedy of the Jews and of civilization in Europe, so great is the tragedy of the American Jews' failure to understand and to appreciate the significance of the conflict....

Louis Wolsey, "On Being Honest," Sermon given on the "Hour of Peace" of the Federal Council of Churches of Christ in America. *Sermons and Addresses*, pp. 69–71

(70:) When a nation honestly believes in it [peace] and pursues it unflinchingly because it is convinced that peace is a desirable goal, then the robber nation proceeds to exploit its neighbor's honesty and punish it for being virtuously peaceful. No wonder tragedy has come to civilization when honesty is a liability situated in a world of falsehood and unrelenting selfishness.

We may illustrate it with the interview given out last week by the dictator when he says he has no intention to invade the Americas, because he believes in Europe for the Europeans and America for the Americans.[17] Shall we believe these pacific intentions? Let us look to the record to determine the honesty of these peaceful resolutions. In 1934 after the plebiscite in the Saar, he stated that his government was willing and determined in its innermost soul to accept the Pact of Locarno, but in 1936 he violated that pledge by occupying the demilitarized zone of the Rhineland. In 1935 he stated that his nation (71:) had neither the wish nor intention to annex or unite with Austria, but in 1938 he annexed that hapless country. In 1938 he said (and I quote his words) "I repeat here that the problem of the Sudeten is solved and that there will be no further problems

17 The interview occurred on June 15; the report in the *Völkischer Beobachter* quoted Hitler as saying "Germany has pursued no territorial or political interests on the American continent in the past nor does it at present." Domarus, *Hitler: Speeches and Proclamations*, 3:2019.

in Europe for Germany, and that I do not want any Czechs";[18] but on March 14, 1939, German troops marched into Prague. He entered into a treaty with Belgium not to trespass upon its territory, and true to that pledge as to all other pledges, he violated the sanctity of the given word and stole the lands of Poland, Belgium, Denmark, Norway, and the Netherlands – and France. Shall we believe him when he says that he has no intention to invade the Americas?...

Though the dictator says that his regime will endure for a thousand years, we who believe in religion and the right know that lying may not last for a thousand years, but that the opening earth [as with Korah] will vindicate its belief in honesty by swallowing up the apostle of untruth. He fights against God, and the forces of history are inevasible and inexorable.[19]

June 25, 1940 (Tuesday)

Max Arzt, President's Message to the Fortieth Annual Convention of the Rabbinical Assembly, Detroit, MI. *Proceedings of the Rabbinical Assembly of America*, vol. 7, pp. 69–86

(71:) We are assembled in troublous and perilous times. Words are inadequate to express all the conflicting emotions which (72:) race through the mind in contemplation of the terrible spectacle of devastation which is being enacted in Europe. The heart sickens at the thought of the blood which is running and of the priceless treasures of the ages which are being destroyed. One feels a sense of impotent rage at the combination of treachery and brutality which is destroying Western civilization. Ours is the generation which is witnessing the *milḥemet Gog u-Magog* [the war of Gog and Magog]....

All the dark forebodings which we have been voicing from our pulpits ever since that black day when the German people surrendered its soul to the *Satan hamashḥit* [Satan the Destroyer] have come

---

18 The "problem of the Sudeten" refers to Hitler's frequent references to the status of Germans in the Sudetenland, whom he claimed were being persecuted. For "we do not want any Czechs at all" (September 26, 1938), see Domarus, *Hitler: Speeches and Proclamations*, 3:1192.

19 Despite this powerful condemnation of Hitler, it is unclear in this sermon exactly what the preacher's position is about America joining the war.

true in the fullest measure. Our hearts go out in anguish and despair to our unfortunate brethren across the seas. They are drinking the cup of bitterness to its very dregs. They have been tormented and hounded by him whom the world has belatedly come to recognize as the enemy who imperils everything which is decent in the Western world. Even now, when the war has become a total war, when it is a *ḥurbano shel olam* [destruction of the world] and when they find themselves in the distressed company of *aḥim letsarah* [companions in distress], they [the Jews] are the worst sufferers. Their catastrophe is too great for the mind to envision. They are pursued by the fierce and merciless hordes of their vengeful oppressor, who is bent on their annihilation even as he is determined on the enslavement of their companions in distress.... (73:) Our brethren in Europe are literally trapped between the hosts of a modern, crueler Pharaoh and a raging sea. Verily only a miracle can save them from utter destruction.

July 13, 1940 (Saturday)

Louis I. Newman, Congregation Rodeph Sholom, New York. *NYT*, July 14, 1940, p. 28

France's fate is a bitter object lesson and warning to Britain and the United States, and the collapse of French democracy is one of the major tragedies of our time. Bastille Day, which should be a time of national recollection, must now be forgotten, lest the people be tempted to revolt against their present-day oppressors. The farce, hollow and humiliating, which is now being perpetrated in once republican France deceives no one, not even the men who are acting as marionettes, or as mortals with shotguns at their heads.

The same fate will be imposed upon Great Britain, if it is defeated, and will be in store for the United States, if it cannot protect itself adequately. Institutions which have been established for decades and centuries are in a moment overthrown at the command of the conqueror, and alien forms and methods are introduced. Freedom for individuals and nations is at stake in the few outposts where it still remains; let free men act with statesmanship, lest we suffer as do Frenchmen today.

July 20, 1940 (Saturday)

Louis I. Newman, Congregation Rodeph Sholom, New York. *NYT*, July 21, 1940, p. 21

Just as Joshua took up the duties which Moses because of age could no longer perform, so new men of militancy and vigor will in time step forward to liberate the oppressed. Let us pray and hope that it will not require forty years to reach the promised land of liberty, but that in place of a *Blitzkrieg* we will have a "*Blitz-freiheit*," namely, a lightning stroke for freedom in place of a lightning-like war....

The world has confidence in Britain which is more than wishful thinking. Even though Britain has grave responsibilities, flung far over the world, she is ready for action, and grimly determined to confront and repel the invader....

The people of Israel, whose lot is thrown in with the democratic nations, regards with grief the possibility that the guidance of the Jewish National Homeland, created by Balfour and the League of Nations, may pass from beloved Britain to feared and mistrusted fascist rule.

July 27, 1940 (Saturday)

Ignaz Maybaum, "Job's Trust," Brondesbury Synagogue, London. *Man and Catastrophe*, pp. 113–18 (preached in German, translated by Joseph Leftwich)

(115:) There are many to-day who may well say, Mine is the fate of Job. But when we speak of Job's fate we must also speak of Job's hope....

What we need is the faith of Job. We say that we live in a terrible time. Job says so too. Job vehemently demonstrates the fact that there is suffering, that innocent people suffer. To-day, Job would say, "How did this child sin that it should be killed by a bomb in an air-raid?" To-day Job would ask, "Why must the Anti-Messiah for so long go striding on from success to success? God is just. Why must we for so long have to look on and see how justice is violated and the violator goes unpunished?"

(117:) This insistence on a happy ending, in other words, this optimism, is one of the great gifts of the Anglo-Saxon race. In these days of hardships and trials, I, a foreigner, can speak only with admiration of the steady calm with which the British people meet the present difficulties. The bad news from the Continent, that is now subject to Hitler, has come speeding to this country like the messengers bringing evil tidings to Job. Yet on all sides the voice of the (118:) true Englishman speaks to us: "Be strong and of good courage! We shall surely win the war. We always win the last battle."

July 28, 1940 (Sunday)

Louis I. Newman, "Why Is Humanity Suffering Today?," Methodist Church in Providence, RI. *Sermons and Addresses*, vol. 2, pp. 1–7

(5:) Mankind has not yet emerged from the valley of despond, and there are dreadful days before us. The "*Herrenvolk*" still walks unchastened through the earth, and we know not how long they will continue to wreak their will upon the helpless. The notions of the "*Uebermensch*" are being made the Holy Writ of the conquerors, and they may achieve by sheer brutality and by a new "*Schrecklichkeit*" (6:) that which the more humane and gentler peoples of the West decline to seek.... It is not enough, we say, that the Guardian of Israel should watch, but that He should also neither slumber nor sleep (cf. Ps. 121:4). It is imperative that He act, or that He steel the arm of man to act. But our proving and our testing in the fiery furnace of suffering is not yet complete, and we know not the events of the morrow, before the watchman cries out that the dawn has come.

September 3, 1940 (Tuesday), Intercession Services

Joseph H. Hertz, New Synagogue, London. *JC*, September 13, 1940, p. 11

Of all the peoples attacked by Germany, the one which has paid the greatest price in human suffering is the Jewish people. Wherever the Swastika flies, life for the Jew has become a nightmare. Throughout the year there raged in Nazi Poland a continuous anti-Jewish pogrom, with synagogues desecrated and destroyed, and thousands mercilessly massacred. Only with the victory of Britain will there be an end to the agony of Israel and the enslavement of free peoples.

September 8, 1940 (Sunday, "National Day of Prayer 2")

Abraham Cohen, at Service attended by the Lord Mayor and Lady and other representatives of Birmingham Corporation, Birmingham, England. Unpublished, David Cohen Private Collection[20]

(1:) Between May 26th when, at the command of H.M. the King, the peoples of the Empire assembled in their places of worship for national prayer, and this day, there is an interval of three and a half months.... [I]n the course of those few weeks events of tremendous importance have occurred.... All opposition to the German onslaught came to an end on the Continent. Holland, Belgium and, most important of all, France, in rapid succession gave up the struggle, leaving Germany for the time being mastery of their territories.

But in that brief period an event occurred far transcending in importance all these happenings.... A fateful decision had to be taken by the Government and people of this country, viz., shall the fight continue?... [T]he fate of civilization depended upon the answer.... (3:) With open eyes, understanding to the full what was involved, the challenge was accepted. "We fight on" were the dauntless words of the Prime Minister....[21] There was no thought of surrender or compromise. A deadly peril threatened the world, and the only course open for a nation which prized freedom and honour was to stake everything upon the effort to destroy it.

(4:) You remember the words spoken by the President of the United States, who is able to scan the situation from a more detached point of view than we who are in the thick of the smoke of the battle. In the impressive speech he made on July 19th when accepting nomination, he said this:

> It is not an ordinary war. It is a revolution imposed by force of arms which threatens all men everywhere.... It is... the continuance of civilisation as we know it versus the ultimate destruction of all that we have held dear: religion against godlessness, the

---

20 Gratitude for "our invitation to attend this service" is expressed to the Lord Mayor and Lady on p. 7 of the text.

21 For the details of this decision, see John Lukacs, *Five Days in London: May 1940*.

> ideal of justice against the practice of force, moral (5:) decency versus the firing squad, courage to speak out and to act versus the false lullaby of appeasement.

Very true words. But it is rather difficult to understand how, seeing the issues with such clarity, the speaker could continue with a declaration that the United States must keep out of the war!

(7:) [In Nazi Germany,] Jews have been reduced to a caste of untouchables; here we share with our Christian fellowmen the duties of citizenship.

September 27, 1940 (Friday evening)

Max Nussbaum, "What This Country Means to Me," Address at Installation Service, Beth Ahaba Temple, Muskogee, OK. *Southwest Jewish Chronicle*, September 5702/1941, pp. 9–11 (AJA), complete text in *From Berlin to Hollywood*, pp. 114–18

(115:) The tragedy of the Jews in Europe consists in their being deprived of their homes. They became strangers in the very place where they and their parents were born and where God had wanted them to live. On the other hand, hundreds and thousands of Jews have gone to foreign countries, for instance to America, and they have found themselves – at home! . . . Nevertheless, I cannot deny that it was hard to leave family and friends behind.

(116:) [T]he Jewish people, having become homeless in nearly all European countries, have one home which cannot be taken from them, and that is religion; This home, being in our souls, cannot be lost and will always stay with us, wherever we are, even when we are "homeless." . . .

Do you realize what these words – freedom and peace – mean to me? Freedom for us is freedom of speech – without Secret Police; freedom of press – without the control of a nationalist party; freedom of opinion – without concentration camp, and freedom of religion – without government supervision. This is freedom for us, and there is no happiness in the world without it.

And peace: to walk in the streets, meeting people you are sure are not your enemies and who do not hate you. To see the shop windows of the town without the inscription, "No entrance for Jews." To take leave of your friends in the evening knowing that you will see them again the next morning undisturbed by the idea that some of them or you yourself might be transported to some other place during the night and carried away forever. To stay in one's house with one's family or friends, and (117:) not to be frightened when the telephone rings or when somebody knocks at your door. This is peace to us, and there is no happiness in the world without it.

September 28, 1940 (Saturday)

Leo Jung, "God in the Crisis," The Jewish Center, New York. *Crumbs and Character*, pp. 25–31

(25:) Trust in God is no excuse for our failure to do our bit....

Where is God? people query.... What is the use of our faith in the Lord and of all our hopes? What can we do against ten thousand death-dealing airplanes? What is the value of the still small voice of conscience against the roaring fury of totalitarian propaganda?...

(28:) It was not God who started munition factories or poison gas. The mind He gave us could have used machinery for more good, more health, more food. It is our stupid selfishness that produced men and arms to rain death upon our children, and to destroy houses, fields, and gardens. The radio could have brought us words of peace and understanding, the concert (29:) of all nations in healthy competition. Today, owing to our neglect of God's word, we must hear the hellhounds of hatred screaming their gospel of chaos and murder....

It is not He who has failed us. It is we who would not listen to His voice. And thus, since conscience was ignored and divine wisdom considered old-fashioned, the powers of evil have grown strong, supported not by Him but by our own sin of complacency and indifference, and it is they who now show to a disillusioned world how great and deep are the curses which godlessness can produce.

This bitter lesson is now being learned – through Hitler and Stalin, and World Wars, and Strikes, and Lockouts, and Revolutions – and international and interdenominational conflict – the greatest menace this country faces and against which it must defend itself.

October 2, 1940 (Erev Rosh Hashanah)

Stephen S. Wise, "But If Not" [Dan. 3:18], (Abstract for the media), Free Synagogue at Carnegie Hall, New York. AJA, Box 22: SSW Microfilms of AJHS and BUASC papers

(2:) This is the most tragic hour in Jewish history. Not three young men of Jewish birth and upbringing and faith are threatened with the burning fire, but millions of our fellow-Jews who suffer as men never suffered before, not only in the lands of darkness, such as Nazi Germany, but in the lands that yesterday were lands of light and liberation. The black, grim spectre of Nazism over-shadows Europe save for the Soviet Union on the East, the ultimate destiny and fate of which is yet uncertain, and glorious England in the west. Even worse (3:) than in the days of the youth in the Book of Daniel, the Jews in this hour, from the Atlantic to the Russian border, some five millions and more, are not asked whether they will accept the new, false gods or else be thrown into the flames.[22] Whatever their faith or unfaith, whatever their attitude to their destroyers, into the flames they go, and if England should fall – a calamity so unthinkable as to be unmentionable – the Jews of Europe west of Russia would be doomed to infinite suffering and it may be extinction.

It is for us to remember that Jewish history is made up of such scenes and moments as that portrayed in the Book of Daniel.

The glory of England in this hour, unbroken and even unstooping, has been the glory of the Jewish people for not less than thousands of years.

Harold I. Saperstein, "The World We Make," Temple Emanu-El of Lynbrook, NY. *Witness from the Pulpit*, pp. 76–77

(76:) While we are praying here, bombs are falling on the city of London.... Jews in that city, if they can pray at all, must pray in bomb-proof shelters deep under the surface of the earth....

---

22 The reference is to Daniel, chap. 3, in which Shadrach, Meshach, and Abed-nego were cast into a fiery furnace at the order of King Nebuchadnezzar, because they refused to worship the statue of gold that he had erected.

I must admit that in the seven years I have served this Temple, never have I found myself in so difficult a dilemma at the High Holy Days.... What can a religious leader say to his people in times like these, when ideals as well as worlds are being shattered? Even we, who are supposed to preach certainty to others, find ourselves stumbling and groping as if we were blind, for something to which we might cling.

(77:) It is no wonder that as never before, people have begun to lose faith. Where can God be, they ask, when the very heavens are crashing down around us?...

Gavriel Gestetner, Szombathely, Hungary, in Esther Farbstein, *Hidden in the Heights*, vol. 1, p. 75, based on Gestetner, *Siftei Gavriel*, p. 149, translated by Deborah Stern

"I seek my brothers" (Gen. 37:16). When I enter the synagogue and the *beit midrash* I find them almost empty because people have been taken for [forced] labor, due to our many sins.... Tell me, please, Master of the World, where are they "tending the flocks"[23] spiritually, for due to our many sins all the yeshivas have been destroyed, and where are they "tending the flocks" physically, for all livelihoods have been taken from our Jewish brethren. And tell me, please, where are they tending the holy flocks scattered throughout the fields at a crossroads under hard labor?

October 3, 1940 (first day of Rosh Hashanah)

Max C. Currick, "Victory Through Faith," Temple Anshe Chesed, Erie, PA. *A Set of Holiday Sermons*, 5701/1940, pp. 9–13

(9:) [referring to the past year (5700):] May its curses end with it. No one needs to be reminded of the heaped up catastrophes that have befallen Israel, which have taken their toll of hundreds of thousands of lives, which are still destroying the life of many thousands and the hopes of dazed survivors.

A touching and instructive incident of the invasion of Poland was

23 The allusion here and in the other uses of this phrase is to Gen. 37:16.

the proclamation by the rabbis of a day of fasting and repentance. Thus have Jews ever done in times of great trial and sorrow. Sometimes the occasional fast finds a permanent place in the calendar. If Polish Jewry is ever again reconstituted, the fast of last September may take its place with that of the 20th of Sivan, when the atrocities of the Cossacks in Poland are mournfully recalled....

(10:) Only by this faith can we live today. Clearly as it is our opportunity and inescapable duty to express our love for our brethren and our sorrow in their prostration and desolation, to make every sacrifice in our effort to save and support them; humbly, prayerfully, as some may still contemplate the death of the righteous as an atonement for the sins of the people, these thoughts, worthy and helpful though they may be, are not enough....

(12:) Earnestly as we stand on guard against the enemy from without, untiringly, lovingly, and sacrificially as we shall extend our help and comfort to the wretched victims of man's inhumanity, we shall not, if we are wise, neglect the enemy within each of us and the enemy within our people....

Abraham E. Halpern, "The Religion of Little Men," Congregation B'nai Amoona, St. Louis, MO. *A Son of Faith*, pp. 16–22

(16:) After the last war we learned that the munition makers of all lands pooled their interests and betrayed their fellowmen. They deliberately precipitated the last war in order to profit from the sorrow and hunger, the pestilence and famine, the four horsemen that have followed in the wake of every war....

(21:) Today most of us are bewildered by the confusion across the sea, but let not the laymen think that if the trouble should become serious here and after another devastating war we will escape as easily as we did the aftermath of the last war. If England wins, and we pray that she will, then the readjustment will be much easier if the men of industry will awaken in time and make provision for the hungry and unemployed millions. If, God forbid, England loses, then the upheaval will be so great that even America will not be able to withstand a possible dictator who may try to take advantage of the situation to lead the hungry millions and provide them with the religion of Fascism or Nazism. It will become the religion of the little men of America as it did for the little men of Europe. The millions here will be tired of fighting for a crust of bread. They will turn to follow the demagogue and our democracy will have failed.[24]

Leo Jung, "Program for the New Year," The Jewish Center, New York. *Crumbs and Character*, pp. 149–56, (printed first in *Canadian Jewish Chronicle*, Oct 2, 1940, as "A Blue-Print for 5701")

(149:) There is this heartening knowledge above everything else, that whilst the haters of Israel have afflicted us, attacking our defenseless people with a ferocity and a shamelessness that often made us incapable of accounting for such inhumanity, in (150:) the long run we have survived them all... This stagnation under Hitler, this reversion to barbarism under tyranny, this destruction by wicked force, cannot abide! We gather strength from the knowledge that we are not fighting alone....

We must not blame everything on the other side. Honest soul-searching is necessary. It reveals that democracy has failed to light many dark corners and to clean many festering sores. Perhaps the nightmare of Hitlerism on horseback has been necessary for a dynamic appreciation of all nations of the simple truth that whenever we cease being our brother's keeper, whenever we permit persecution and poverty in one corner, we create a focus of social infection. This becomes the happy hunting ground for up-to-date demagogues, who with their marvelous organization of evil will continue to generate oppression, war, and havoc for the generation that allowed them to obtain power.

(154:) 5701 bears dark hues in concentric circles. There is the appalling devastation of one or two continents, of millions of homeless, breadless, hopeless, trampled under the heel and disfigured by the mark of the beast. There is a deeper black in the Universal night, the unimaginable depth of Jewish suffering, the destruction of cultural, religious, human values which generations of matchless devotion had built up. There is the challenging phenomenon of one-

24 The underlying assumption here appears to be that America will continue to remain out of the war.

third of our nation as yet virtually undisturbed, though not utterly serene, in the great oasis of America. The Jewish community is adolescent in this young country, and as a result of the world's chaos (155:) has obligations of maturity suddenly thrust upon it, both as a section of the great American community and as a group with its own cultural and spiritual heritage....

The whole world is shaken to its foundations, the citadels of the past are threatened with constant invasion of the hordes of the godless barbarians. Synagogue as church is denied the right to exist, is denounced as breeding "the noisome doctrines of mercy and truth" as against the efficient method of sadistic prisons, deadly airplanes, and utterly shameless propaganda. The enemy wants to destroy our substance, our hope, our honor, our children, our sense of pride, our significance.... In many cases he has succeeded in turning yesterday's generous friends into today's polite opponents, into tomorrow's snarling dogs of hatred. He accuses us of every crime with incredible impudence, spreading his lies in the name now of Christian, now of Gentile, now of Anglo-Saxon, now of American "culture."...

(156:) When this year with its curses is over, may the New Year commence as herald of peace and blessings.

Louis I. Newman, "My God, My God, Why Hast Thou Forsaken Me?," Congregation Rodeph Sholom, New York. *Sermons and Addresses*, vol. 2, pp. 8–14

(10:) I ask you to note that the martyr recalls the traditional loyalty of his forbears; he finds solace in the experience of those who literally and figuratively established for him a precedent in suffering. Cannot we likewise explore the annals of our people's past, and know that the God of our Fathers, in whom the people trust, and to whom they cried, helped them to bear the pain of the stake, the torments inflicted by the Inquisition, the bloodshed of the pogrom, and the indignity of the discriminatory laws?

(12:) The men who preserved St. Paul's from physical injury were risking their lives for a symbol.[25] Symbols are important, whether

25 Newman is alluding here to the efforts in London to remove a time bomb embedded in the earth near St. Paul's Cathedral, featured in a *NYT* article, September 17, 1940,

they be the Scroll of the Law which Jews rescue from burning synagogues, as they did in Germany, November 1938, or the nation's flag, which men cut their way through opposing foemen to save.

The Germans who hurl down their bombs do not care if churches are demolished. Long ago they took up arms against both Christianity and Judaism as inimical to their program. And the British are fighting not merely to preserve their church edifices, but also to rescue the civilization which they embody. It is for us, if we can, to do the same....

(13:) Whatever the trials of the years that have passed, however bitter our portion, let us believe that the New Year will restore our trust in the Living Word of the Living God.

Irving F. Reichert: "How Can We Find Happiness in the New Year?," Temple Emanu-El, San Francisco, CA. *Judaism and the American Jew*, pp. 225–30

(226:) But however grimly the world tragedy has affected the mood and temper of the generality of mankind, to us of the House of Israel its results and implications are vastly more appalling. For not only has the Jew participated in the common anguish of his countrymen in lands despoiled by tyranny, but he has been deliberately singled out for added indignities that exhaust the repertory of persecution. Jewish life has been destroyed in a thousand communities where once it flourished brilliantly. Not since the Babylonian Exile have the sons and daughters of Israel been so violently uprooted and thrust forth as pariahs upon the friendless highways of the world. Pauperism and degradation, torture and banishment have been meted out to our people in lands whose glory they established with gifts of genius and generosity....

The flood tide of historic destiny is carrying America toward events that will affect the lives and fortunes of every man, woman, and child among us. The future is veiled in deep uncertainty. ... with

p. 5. *The Times of London* of Sunday, September 15, p. 44, reported that St. Paul's had cancelled Sunday worship services "for the first time in memory" because of unexploded and potentially dangerous bombs in the vicinity of the Cathedral.

the thoughts and energies of our nation directed toward military preparedness, with war darkening the horizon every way we look and constantly drawing closer and closer....

(230:) Do you recall that stirring scene on Mount Carmel, when Elijah alone remained of all God's prophets to oppose the champions of paganism? [cites 1 Kings 19:11–12].

Well, the tempests of hate are lashing our planet today. An upthrust of barbarism has convulsed our society to its foundations. The fires of fanaticism are searing the souls of men. But depend upon it, the tumult and the shouting will die away and the "still, small voice" will again be heard.

Jacob P. Rudin, "God in the Blackout" Temple Beth-El, Great Neck, NY. *Very Truly Yours*, pp. 234–40; *Jewish Preaching in Times of War*, pp. 399–405

(403:) Where is God in this blackout of humanity? ... God *is in* the blackout. God is in the blood and misery, in the tumbled homes, in the destroyed cities. He is in the air raid shelters. He is in the heavens that rain destruction....

(404:) Harry Emerson Fosdick is wrong![26] This war *is* about the Jews. It's about those very Polish Jews whose persecution, he says, could have gone on for centuries into the future. This war is about the indifference of the world that let the persecution go on.

This war is about the German Jews who were hounded and torn and crushed into the Nazi mire. This war is about injustice concerning which men kept silent, about unrighteousness that men accepted, about savagery that men said was an internal affair of Germany.

This war is about the repudiation of God's words that men spat upon when they spat upon the Jews and rent to shreds when they tore Jewish flesh. This war is about democracy, about freedom and liberty. It's about all that men hold dear....

(405:) And Israel? What shall Israel say in this dark hour? Do you seek an easy, comfortable answer? There is none. These are evil days, when men must be giants. Out of every abyss of despair and from

---

26 Rudin had just cited a sermon by Fosdick arguing that the war was about the balance of political power in Europe.

every lonely mountain top, Israel's voice of fortitude and of patience, of rock-enduring faith has echoed, "Even though He slay me, yet will I trust in Him" (Job 13:15).[27]

Abba Hillel Silver, "Our Responsibility for Evil," The Temple, Cleveland, OH. *Therefore Choose Life*, pp. 60–66 (cf. "Where is God?," in *A Word in Its Season*, pp. 16–22)

(60:) Frequently during the past few years, and more especially during the past few months, I have heard men ask: "Where is God?"....[28]

(61:) If our days are shot through with agony and despair, if war stalks through the fair cities and lands of the earth, if death rains from the skies and if the four dread, gaunt Horsemen of the Apocalypse again ride through the world, is it not due to the gross and unpardonable sins of our age, to the acts of betrayal, perfidy, and selfishness of governments, leaders, parties, and masses?

(64:) Many trials await our generation and much suffering. We may not be at the end of this world war, but at its beginning. The areas of conflict may widen. The tides of death and destruction are sweeping on and may (65:) engulf other nations before they finally recede. We will do well to regard this universal calamity as God's visitation for the sins of our age....

The remaining free peoples of the earth must rally as one to slay the evil which threatens all mankind, the evil which they tolerated all too long and which they permitted to wax and grow mighty and menacing because they were blind....

Charles E. Shulman, "The Jewish Future," North Shore Congregation Israel, Glencoe, IL. Printed Pamphlet

1:) The world has seen twelve difficult months since Jews assembled last to mark their New Year. The map of Europe has begun to assume

---

27 Note that despite the strong repudiation of pacifism and his strong condemnation of Nazism, Rudin says nothing about America entering the war.

28 Silver proceeds to argue, in sharp contrast with Rudin (above) and most other non-Orthodox preachers, that suffering is indeed divine punishment, retributive justice, divine compensation.

strange and bewildering proportions. Peace-loving individuals have come under the domination of a brutal dictatorship and the Jews, first to suffer on the battlefield of humanity and last to enjoy the fruits of peace, have received more than their share of sorrow and misery.

In this shocking twelve-month period of history Poland died an agonizing death; Finland was maimed and impoverished; Holland and Belgium lost their independence and the flower of their manhood in battle. France surrendered, and now lies prostrate, a shadow of a great nation. England fights with her back to the wall. Romania and other Balkan countries stand helplessly by while the Nazi juggernaut travels over the European continent, clouding the skies with darkness.... Refugees roam over the surface of the earth looking for a haven where they may be free from torture and oppression. Free peoples begin to arm themselves as never before in the realization that the beast is loose in the world and that reason has fled before totalitarian might. For the first time in our history we in America have established conscription of both manhood and wealth to ward off the dangers from abroad.

The Jewish people are soberly concerned with the fate of liberty and democracy on earth. They have become acutely conscious of the fact that anti-Semitism has proved successful in Hitler's Germany. It was established in Austria. It was encouraged in Romania and Hungary. It was instituted in Italy among the pitifully small communities of Jews scattered in a population of forty-five million people. It is even useful in Japan where there are no Jews. Now France announces that special laws to deal with Israelites will be established. Our own America is already familiar with the efforts of Father Coughlin, who betrays his church and his religion in his attacks upon the Jews. It is abundantly clear that wherever liberty and democracy are destroyed Jewish rights are destroyed and Jewish life is made untenable.

(2:) The result of contemporary events has shaken the equilibrium of many Jewish people. They cannot envisage a return to sanity and the ways of peace and progress. Gloomily they scan the horizon and contemplate the forces now at work....

Since 1933 American Jewry has suffered intermittently a feeling of helplessness and hopelessness. The problems of relief have become so staggering that increasing numbers of Jews have questioned the usefulness of endeavors to salvage any portion of humanity lost in the European chaos. Many doubt the wisdom of helping to rebuild Palestine because of the possibility of its being attacked by the Italians or the Germans at a later date. Still others wonder whether any effort toward amelioration is of much consequence in a morally broken world such as this is. It is to these individuals especially that I would address myself.

(7:) How much of the present day suffering is a repetition of past cruelties inflicted upon innocent peoples only the Jew of the world can tell. How much of the wanton destructiveness of European culture by the Nazis is a memento of other depredations (8:) and injuries only he who bears memories of similar events can know. He has seen it happen before. His life has protested against it while he has continued the dream and the labors for a better day. In the thirteenth century many Jewish graves were desecrated and plundered in Spain, Italy, and Germany, lands which are under Fascist rule today....[29]

Harold I. Saperstein, "Sufferance is the Badge," Temple Emanu-El of Lynbrook, NY. *Witness from the Pulpit*, pp. 77–82

(78:) Other peoples at least can die in their homes and mingle the lifeblood pouring out of their wounds in the soil of the land that they have loved. But the Jews of Europe today, with fewest exceptions, have no homes. Poland, once the center of traditional Jewish culture, is now a corpse picked clean by the Nazi and Russian vultures. Its three million Jews are homeless. The freedom-loving lands of Holland and Belgium...no longer proved a safe retreat for the Jewish refugees and residents who had escaped there from the Nazi tempest. Those who managed to find refuge in France had only a temporary breathing spell for their pains and for the risk of their lives.... That

29 Note that the preacher portrays the present as a recursion of medieval persecution, which is a sign of hope! There is no sense of a radical difference, as systematic mass murder has not yet begun.

is the fate of the Jews in the world today; to be harried, uprooted, as driven leaves blown by the wind.

And yet, my friends, at the dawning of this New Year, I dare to speak to you of courage.... (80:) Side by side with us now stand whatever forces of decency there are left in the world. We still cannot see the end of our suffering. But our suffering is not meaningless. Our very existence is the denial of the principles of tyranny. We are still the bearers of an eternal ideal which, though the nations may deny it, the world still needs and will need more than ever when this war is over....

Leo M. Franklin, "Every Man's Problem," Temple Beth-El, Detroit, MI. Unpublished, Rabbi Leo Morris Franklin Archives, now at AJA, MS-246, Text 1416

(1:) Before the fate which Nazism has decreed for us, all the tragedies of the centuries, if they could be counted and combined, would be insignificant. Rivers of tears the Jew has shed through centuries of time, but all of them emptied into a common sea would not compare in magnitude and depth with the oceans of bitterness which his weeping has formed in the single year which comes to a climax tonight....

And yet how happy should we be that we live in this blessed land of ours where for the moment, at least, we enjoy the blessings of peace. Contrast our situation with that of our brethren in Britain where the Chief Rabbi, Dr. Hertz, has issued a circular to all the Rabbis in the United Kingdom. It says, among other things, that "... there will be no sounding of the Shofar at *Ne'ilah*, because prayers must conclude before the blackout, while the fast does not end until 5:54 P.M. in London...."

Abraham Cohen, "A New Universe," Birmingham Hebrew Congregation, Birmingham, England. Unpublished, David Cohen Private Collection

(1:) I doubt whether in the whole career of the human race so much cruelty, havoc, and wretchedness have been witnessed within the space of a single year. The worst atrocities committed by savages in the darkest periods of the past were far less cruel than what has been perpetrated during the year which has gone, because the modern barbarians acted in the coldest deliberation and with calculated ferocity, consciously planned with the aid of the vastly increased scope of devastation (2:) which scientific invention made possible for them.

I have no patience with those who find in the chaos of the present nothing more than a religious problem affecting God. To my mind it is nauseating hypocrisy to try and shift the responsibility in this way. No problem of this kind was created for these critics of God when aggressive Japan bombed innocent people in Manchukuo [Manchuria], or when aggressive Italy slaughtered the practically unarmed Abyssinians. I wonder how many of these critics would have supported the Government if it had proposed direct intervention to stop those abominations and uphold the principle of international righteousness! How often was it said, at the time of acute political crisis, Why should we fight for Austrians, Czechs, or Poles? Apparently, then, we have no complaint against God when bombs rain from the sky upon *other* countries, only when they fall upon the land where *we* dwell.

Moreover, it can hardly be doubted that if, at the occurrence of the earlier outrages I mentioned, the peoples of the world had been moved by moral indignation and demanded that such barbarism must be stopped by concerted action, there would be no war in progress (3:) to-day. So the war is a problem created by, and affecting, man, not God....

(7:) No steps were taken to check the spirit of aggression which was being displayed by strong nations against weak neighbours. When warned of approaching danger, the mass of people preferred to take (8:) refuge in the stupid and wholly false position that what was happening in the totalitarian countries was the internal affair of those States and no concern of theirs. Influential sections of the British public even sympathized with the new regime which had seized control in Germany because they imagined that their personal interests would be well served by it. Not one Government in the entire world uttered a word of protest when innocent men, women, and children in large numbers were mercilessly persecuted for their beliefs or racial origins.... For years past the seeds of this war were being sown before the eyes of all, but they who had the power lacked the will to dig them out before they took deep roots and so produced the inevitable harvest.

Ignaz Maybaum, "Who Shall Live and Who Shall Die – The London Battlefield," Overflow Service, Hampstead Synagogue, London. *Man and Catastrophe*, pp. 119–27

(121:) During these days before our Jewish New Year's festival we here in London have night and day had death, devastation, and homelessness in front of our eyes. Each of us had to ask – when will my turn come? Will the "severe decree," as the New Year's Day service has it, spare me and mine? We asked ourselves that question while the German planes roared overhead. It is human frailty to fear for our lives. But one can also pray for our life to God out of faith....

(122:) We here in London are with our wives and our children in the midst of the battlefield. German barbarism has wiped out all distinction between the military and the civilian population. Totalitarian war recognises no difference between the battlefield and the hinterland. The world views the London battlefield, and the heroism it admires is not only of the men in uniform. There is also the civilian heroism....

(126:) The synagogues in Germany have been burned to the ground. Bombs have crashed down on the churches in England. It is the hand of the barbarian that does this. But we must also see the judgment of God. What we must have is not the proclamation of a faith, but an act of faith, an act that creates history, that makes the Kingdom of God the motive by which to shape life on earth.

Ephraim Sokolover, Great Synagogue, Ra'anana, Palestine. *Penei Efrayim*, pp. 13–16, translated by MS

(13:) Sometimes we find ourselves in a condition like now when not only is it impossible to speak, but we are unable even to moan, and to weep is difficult, or when the sorrow is so intense that moaning and weeping is totally insufficient, and it is better to moan silently (cf. Ezek. 24:17). This is our condition today....

This year, there is massive universal destruction, but even more terrifying is the situation of the Jewish people. If we were to come to calculate and record in detail even part of what we have suffered during the past year, we would not even be able to weep....

(15:) It is possible that the number of those who have been killed now reaches the number mentioned above, if not even more.[30] The difference is that the vicious modern murderer of the (16:) twentieth century, the chief slaughterer of our time, will not become aroused to cease his vicious activities, for he has stated in public more than once that his polluted desire is to solve the "Jewish question" in the manner in which it arose.... Who knows what murderous policies are to come?

(16:) All this has been done while the modern world of culture looks on, a world which reached the pinnacle of technological development and every kind of progress – "the modern world," which excels in courtesy and politeness, which speaks highly of justice and righteousness. This world stands and looks on, and remains silent!...There is no one who will speak out publicly and scream bloody murder at the ferocious massacres that Hitler has announced, may his name be blotted out.

There is nothing for us to do but to rely on our Heavenly Father.

October 4, 1940 (second day of Rosh Hashanah)

Israel H. Levinthal, "The Jew's Primary Duty Today," Brooklyn Jewish Center, Brooklyn, NY. *A New World Is Born*, pp. 141–47

(141:) Were I to designate the present age, I should say that it is the age of the *Tokhechah* [chastisement]. All the maledictions and (142:) the imprecations of that chapter [Deut. 28] seem to have come to pass in our day. Read these verses and you will see how graphically they apply to the scenes of horror that we behold.... [cites Deut.

30 Referring to his discussion of a passage in Yalqut Shim'oni on Ezekiel 24, in which Nebuzaradan is said to have killed 40,000 priests, and many others.

28:23, 24, 34, 67]. This is indeed the age of the *Tokhechah*, when all these curses have been fulfilled, when even the plagues "that are not written in this book of the Law" (Deut. 28:61) have come to pass.

(143:) There is a vast difference between the tragedy that we witness today and the human tragedies that have been enacted before. The world has always known suffering – but it was suffering endured by individuals, be they many thousands or millions. But the world as such was not crippled. Other individuals could offer help and healing and remedy. Today, however, the *Tokhechah* has come not only to individuals, but also… to all the world. Nations have been wiped out. It is not only a question of individual suffering; our tragedy is that whole peoples, nations, a world, are being threatened with annihilation.

And if we scan the Jewish scene, we note the same distinction…. [reviews past persecutions]. Today, the curse is… threatening all Jews throughout the world. The Nazis are not content with annihilating Jewish life in Germany; their aim is worldwide: to annihilate all Jews, everywhere. Their attack is directed against the Jewish people, all of us, without any exception…. There is no break in the horrors inflicted upon us.

(145:) The great centers of our faith in the lands of Europe are now destroyed. Germany, that gave us scholars; Poland, that gave us Rabbis and academies of learning, are gone. We, in America, have the great duty to carry aloft the banner of our faith…. (147:) The Temple of Jewish life is in flames. Let us, like the Levites, remain at our posts of duty….

Israel Gerstein, "Singing in the Sacrifice," B'nai Zion Congregation, Chattanooga, TN. *Reveille or Taps?*, pp. 15–21

(15:) Never, perhaps, in history have Jews assembled in their synagogues in a more critical period for Israel and mankind as a whole. We come into the synagogue, however, not to be haunted, crushed, or terrorized by the stories of death and destruction, of the best sons slain in the fields. No, the purpose of this day is not to impregnate us with fear, the fear of the "angel of death" who is on the loose and has left a path of suffering, moaning, and groaning humanity over half of the world. *Rosh Hashono* was erected by our religion as a guidepost to life, happiness, and well-being.

(16:) We pray God that we shall be spared the ravages of war. We cannot altogether escape the effects of this worldwide conflagration....

(17:) Marshal Petain said that the reason France fell was that "she had become soft. The people were only interested in pleasure and good times." France was doomed because it lacked the spirit of Abraham....

(18:) In short, it is the opinion of the experts quoted that the foundations of civilization are threatened more by our lack of discipline than by Hitler's bombers. Hitler's strength, we must admit, lies in the discipline that he has imposed upon the people.

October 5, 1940 (Saturday, Shabbat Shuvah)

Louis I. Newman, "'Return O Israel' – To What?,"[31] Congregation Rodeph Sholom, New York. *Sermons and Addresses*, vol. 2, pp. 23–28

(27:) Can Jewry today recover from its tribulations? Can the communities of Europe which have been dispersed re-establish themselves when the war will at last have ended? Can Europe redeem itself and return to a good and wise way of life? We speak of the "piping days of peace," but we know that there have been alarums of war in every generation. Can we ever "return" to Wilson's ideal of a League of Nations or [Frank B.] Kellogg's outlawry of war?[32] At this moment no one can say. Mankind has lapsed far from its ideal hopes of a generation ago, and there is no constructive program which the builders of the new order are holding forth. The "new order" of which we hear is described in terms only of raw materials, colonies, redistribution of territory, and the other material things which the war-makers and pillagers seek.

---

31 The title alludes to the beginning of the reading from the Prophets on Shabbat Shuvah (The Sabbath of Return): Hos. 14:2.

32 Alluding to the "Kellogg-Briand Pact of 1928," in which signatory nations pledged never again to resort to war to resolve disputes or conflicts.

Unless, however, we can "return" in repentance to our best self as individuals and as nations, we know not how dark the future will be.

October 10, 1940 (Thursday)

Israel H. Levinthal, "An Agonized World Seeks Atonement," WOR pre-Yom Kippur Radio Address. Unpublished, JTSA Archives

Our beloved America is beginning to sense the danger that faces it – in common with all the world – in the onward march of this brutal force that would destroy the moral foundations of the universe. It is beginning to defend itself against this common danger threatening all humanity.... It is not enough to defend our material and physical resources; we must defend – even more – our spiritual resources, those values and lofty moral ideals.

October 11, 1940 (Kol Nidre)

Louis I. Newman, "Kol Nidre: The Secret of Its Power," Congregation Rodeph Sholom, New York. *Sermons and Addresses*, vol. 2, pp. 29–36

(33:) When we confront the problems of life as Jews, surely we do not wish to share in the process of self-belittlement and self-disparagement which characterizes so many persons of Jewish birth. There are Jews who, when they are among themselves, indulge in a veritable riot of self-hate. They consider themselves accursed for having been born Jews, but they forget that their suffering is only the reflection of the indignities heaped upon the weak and defenseless everywhere by the brigands of our day.... There are some who believe that Jews should bear no more children, so that the race will die out, saying Jewish men should be sterilized and Jewish women prevented from having progeny. Is not this the abyss of self-contempt? The individual guilty of such a statement is degraded, not the people whose blood he carries in his veins....

(35:) To be sure, it is hard to be a Jew today; it may be still harder tomorrow. Thus it has always been, and it may well be that we Jews in America will not be immune to the destiny which has overtaken our brethren elsewhere. But how can we meet our tribulations? By the suicide of individuals, or the self-destruction, granted it were possible, of a whole people?... "*Lo zo haderekh*; this is not the way."[33] "*Lo amut, ki eḥyeh, va-asaper ma'asei Yah*; I shall not die but live and declare the works of the Lord" (Ps. 118:17). Therefore let us put aside the vain and empty vows which spell defeatism and despair, and let us make, in their stead, the resolutions which appertain to God, since they are voiced in terms of courage, fortitude, and high dedication.

Even though we may not wish our feelings harrowed, let me remind you that at this very hour, there are thousands in the pest-hole which is the Lublin Reservation;[34] there are refugees who, once affluent and secure, are now in a most grievous plight, suffering from mental disorders, some having succumbed to insanity. Out of horrors such as these, Kol Nidre was born in days gone by. What great prayer and melody will emerge from the tragedy of our era, if we can prove ourselves of heroic strength!

SIDNEY S. TEDESCHE, "Kol Nidre," Union Temple, Brooklyn, NY. *A Set of Holiday Sermons*, 5701/1940, pp. 18–23.

(20:) For what shall we ask forgiveness? Have we not been more sinned against than sinning? For generations our people have gathered in their sacred edifices, more often in the dark obscurity of ghetto chapels like hunted criminals. They have donned their prayer shawls and covered their bowed heads with awe and respect. "We have sinned, we have transgressed, we have acted perversely." Why this holocaust of remorse? Why these blistering pangs of conscience?...

(21:) Is it 1940 or only 940?... It is so easy to conceal and camouflage one's violence by the smoke screen of propaganda, but let Goebbels and his American imitators beware. The wooden horse with its false labels may have worked in far-off Troy and Norway[35] but "great is truth and it has always and will still prevail." Those who cry

33 A talmudic phrase (b. Bava Metzi'a 37b), known also as the title of an important essay criticizing practical Zionism by Ahad Ha'Am.

34 See above, Israel Mattuck, November 19, 1939, footnote.

35 The link with Norway is rather facetious, as it apparently refers to the carved and painted wooden Norwegian Fjord horse, quite different from that of ancient Troy.

"*Jude Verrecke*" always wend their Satanic refrain with acts that spell: "Down with civilization and all that honor holds dear."...

(22:) A nation can violate treaties, override boundaries, rain death and destruction from the skies, rob and slay and kill, deceive, betray and act in general as though there is no such thing as a moral law, yet they proclaim in utter cynicism that the only unforgivable crime is to be a Jew.... (23:) The Jew may be the scapegoat, but woe to the morals of a people and woe to all conceptions of justice between man and man if nations or individuals be allowed to avoid the consequences of their crimes by blaming a universal whipping-boy.... If there is to be peace, then it cannot, it must not, be a peace of the dead or of those hopelessly enslaved morally, physically, or spiritually.... Against Blood and Iron, Israel still offers its message of peace.

IRVING F. REICHERT, "Where Is Thy God?," Temple Emanu-El, San Francisco, CA. *Judaism and the American Jew*, pp. 85–92

(85:) Bewildered by the triumphs of the forces of evil, confounded by the tragedy that has overwhelmed peace-loving peoples, baffled by the success of an inverted morality, people are asking in tones of bitterness and sorrow, of meditation and challenge: How can God permit such things to happen? "Where is thy God?" Today this question is one which no honest preacher will attempt to evade....

(89:) "It was a sunny day in Paris when Pierre Laval signed the death warrant of the German Republic – and paved the road whereby Hitler entered."[36] I know of no better example in our time to illustrate the operation of God's moral law. Think back through recent years and recall how flagrantly we have trampled upon the elementary principles of decency and justice, the outrages that we have permitted or suffered in silence: the devastation of Spain, the rape of Ethiopia, the conquest of Manchuria, (90:) the spiritual murder of Austria, the dismemberment of Czechoslovakia; and the list might be extended.

---

36 This is a quotation from Pierre van Paassen in *Days of our Years*, describing Herr Bruening (the German Chancellor) unsuccessfully pleading with France's Laval to mitigate the severity of sanctions in the Versailles Treaty ending the Great War.

And now, when the world is convulsed in the therapeutic process of restoring the moral equilibrium, do you still ask, "Where is thy God?"... Why does a just God permit millions, for instance, who were not responsible as individuals for the present world situation, to endure persecution and ruin?...

(91–92:) Hitler's "sensational address to the Reichstag" a few weeks ago, warning England, "don't worry, I'm coming."[37]

Israel Mattuck, "The Jews' Religion and Their Future," Liberal Jewish Synagogue, London. Unpublished

(1:) In these hard times the Jew has a double measure of hardship. He was the first to feel the misery that now engulfs humanity. The Nazis began their attack on humanity with the persecution of the Jews under their rule, and, with the increase of their power, their baneful influence, spreading like a contagious disease, infected other lands, bringing calamity to the Jews in them. In the countries invaded and occupied by the Germans, as in Germany itself, and in lands where rulers wishing to bask in Nazi [blank space] more like satellites under its direction, the lot of the Jews has been reduced to all degrees of degradation down to that of pariahs and slaves. In the countries which lost their freedom, the Jews suffer (2:) with their fellow-citizens the pain of that loss, and in addition they have the further pain of the barbarities inflicted on them by Nazi hatred. The Nazis have made hatred of Jews the weapon with which to undermine the morale of the countries they wish to conquer or dominate. They have everywhere tried to exploit the latent possibilities of antisemitism, and in some countries have succeeded, by saying "Not we but the Jews are your enemies. We are your friends, let us in." And those who have heeded them have seen! They have seen Nazi treachery, arrogance, greed, cruelty and barbarism.

When we turn from the sad actuality to the future, seeking a

37 Reichert is probably referring to Hitler's September 4 address at the Berlin *Sportpalast*; for the complete text in translation, see Domarus, *Hitler: Speeches and Proclamations*, vol. 3, pp. 2081–90, with the passage cited on p. 2084.

prospect of hope for the suffering Jews, we see it in only one direction. England's victory alone offers a hope for them....

October 12, 1940 (Yom Kippur)

Ignaz Maybaum, "London's Dead: The Memorial of Souls," Morning Overflow Service, Hampstead Synagogue, London. *Man and Catastrophe*, pp. 128–34

(129:) The sins to which we confess are sins against God. Those who have persecuted us have not the slightest justification for their persecution. The question has been asked whether Hitler and his henchmen would have attacked us had German Jewry been less prominent in business and in the liberal professions. The question is beside the point. We were loyal citizens in Germany. Had we been angels Hitler's persecution would not have spared us. When we speak to-day of sins – and we do so – we must not be misunderstood. As citizens of the land Hitler now rules we have nothing, nothing at all for which to reproach ourselves....

(130:) Do not believe that it is only a social calamity that has come upon us. Do not believe that what you experience, what you endure, is all politics and worldly affairs. You stand in the midst of sacred history. You are not only a suffering creature, you are God's witness, you are a Jew. Your suffering is not only earthly suffering; it is a witnessing to God. In the Hitlerian era your destiny is to be persecuted. That, Israel, is your glory....

(131:) Jewish history has not ceased to be sacred in the period of persecution by Hitler any more than in the time of Sennacherib, Nebuchadnezzar or Antiochus. ... We are suffering for no other reason than because we are Jews. It is for the sake of our faith, because of our belief in justice, (132:) truth, and love that we suffer.

Ignaz Maybaum, "Messianism," Overflow *Ne'ilah* Service, Hampstead Synagogue, London. *Man and Catastrophe*, pp. 135–41

(141:) The Prophet saw that this King [Cyrus] was in his political aims pursuing Messianic ends, that his political road was the road of justice. This is the sense in which we speak of the British Cyrus, of Britain as Cyrus. Britain's war is a war for the cause of God.

Open the gate for us, even at the closing of the gate.[38] Dusk has fallen upon Europe. It is cold and dark. It is as though the gates of the Temple had closed and the world is left without holiness, without sanctity, an unconsecrated place, ugly, black, gruesome, without light or rest. Is it true that this is the decline of the West? Certainly there are powers of destruction that have emerged with the rise of the Nazi regime. Things look black in this world of ours. But it is the duty of faith to hope. Messianism is belief in the victory of good. We wait with Messianic patience. No matter how strong and powerful evil may appear, its time is set.... Now, in the time when we Jews and the whole world seem to have so little prospect of winning the fight for the sacred values of liberty and justice, we wait and hope. Open the gate for us, before the gate is closed. For the day is nearly past.

Ferdinand M. Isserman, "Memorial (*Yizkor*) Sermon," Temple Israel, St. Louis, MO. AJA MS-6, Box 15, Folder 7

(10:) My friends, I rise at this service to defend the character, the integrity, the name and the memory of our departed now being subjected to a world-wide campaign of slander and calumny, of malicious misrepresentation, which has no parallel in all of our tortured history.

October 18, 1940 (Friday, second day of Sukkot)

Kalonymus Kalmish Shapira, Warsaw. *Esh Kodesh*, pp. 71–74; *Derashot meShenot haZa'am*, p. 162; Polen, *Holy Fire*, p. 64, translated by Nehemia Polen[39]

[T]he test of Abraham and Isaac involved their will and intention [to martyrdom], but was not completely consummated in actuality, since the angel said, "Lay not your hand upon the lad" (Gen. 22:12).

38 Referring to the liturgy of the final service, *Ne'ilah*, at the conclusion of Yom Kippur.

39 This date was the first yahrzeit of the death of Shapira's son Elimelekh in the German bombing of Warsaw.

Therefore, every occurrence of Jews being killed by Gentiles with circumstances reversed – that is, with the actuality of death but without the intentional choosing of martyrdom – is a fulfilment of Isaac's *Akedah*. The *Akedah* was the beginning, characterized by intention and desire [for martyrdom]; the conclusion and actualization is now. That is to say, the *Akedah* together with all subsequent cases of Jews being murdered [on account of their Jewishness] constitute one event.

October 25, 1940 (Friday, 1:30 p.m.)

Max Nussbaum, "The Religious Problem in Germany," Episcopal Church, Muskogee, OK. AJA, MS-705, Box 3, Folder 6

(4:) After the terrible night of November 9th 1938, in which Jewish shops were destroyed, Jewish homes smashed, and the flames of the burning synagogues lightened the sky over Germany, after that night Cardinal Faulhaber of Munich, one of the finest and most courageous Catholics, opened the gates of his palace to hundreds of Jews, thus protecting them from being sent to concentration camps by the Gestapo. That was not only a wonderful trace of humanity, but a symbol of the recently developed religious unity, and it shows us that sometimes the worst projects created involuntarily the best results.

November 3, 1940 (Sunday)

Maurice N. Eisendrath, "Danger Zones – 1940," Holy Blossom Temple, Toronto. *Holy Blossom Pulpit*, x, 1

(14:) Canada today, though it be at war with the symbol par excellence of anti-Semitic fury, is rife with this self-same curse. On every hand I am deluged with reports of a rising tide of animosity against the Jew such as I have not known since I came into this country more than ten years ago: Jews banned from apartments, Jews rebuffed by recruiting officers, Jews officially discriminated against in the immigration policy of the nation, whether seeking entry as evacuee children or as adult refugees who might well enrich our country and aid materially in its war effort.[40] This is dangerous, even subversive business. And it is not primarily out of any hyper-sensitivity to our Jewish hurt but out of profound concern for our patriotic cause that I request an explanation as to how it is possible, in the midst of a war against Nazi hatred and fiendishness, we can countenance not alone these less conspicuous forms of anti-Semitism, but permit the actual publication of such articles as appeared just the other day in an important French Canadian periodical blaming the collapse of France exclusively upon M. Leon Blum and the Jews, condoning, in other words, the treachery of the men of Vichy, apologizing for their unparalleled deeds of treason and, precisely as did the Nazis in the German Reich, ferreting out the Jew as the scapegoat for all the terror and tragedy that have descended upon France.[41]

How long will a united Canada continue to resist without questioning the nobility of its cause, if there should spread throughout our Dominion such insidious innuendos as these, especially when they are coupled with similar suggestions that the Jew in Canada and everywhere else is to be feared even more, so these anti-Semites would have it, than the Nazis themselves?…

(15:) Here is the real danger zone. Let us swiftly man the barricades. Let us dream no longer of distant perils, but awaken to the menace at our very gates, within our very hearts. Only a people bound hand in hand and heart to heart can hope to repel so avaricious a foe, so ambitious and powerful a dreamer of world conquest.…

November 15, 1940 (Friday evening, *VaYera*)

Jacob Kaplan, "The Justice of Abraham and the Jewish Statute" (*La jus-*

---

40 On Canadian immigration policy, see Abella and Troper, *None is Too Many: Canada and the Jews of Europe, 1933–1945* (which fails to mention Eisendrath or Harry Joshua Stern, the leading Reform rabbi of Montreal, both of whom published many sermons responding to Nazi persecution and Canadian immigration policy).

41 There is a large literature of explanations for the quick collapse of France, in dramatic contrast with its resistance during the Great War. Much of it blames alleged decadence in the last years of the Third Republic; see, for example, William L. Shirer, *The Collapse of the Third Republic*. I have not been able to identify the specific "Canadian Journal" that placed the blame "exclusively on M. Leon Blum and the Jews."

tice d'Abraham et le statut des Juifs),[42] Synagogue de Vichy, France. *Les Temps d'épreuve*, pp. 81–85, translated by MS

(83:) As for myself, when I read this biblical narrative [in Gen. 18:22–32, of Abraham challenging God on behalf of the righteous of Sodom and Gomorra], I am ashamed of our own age. In a country as civilized as our own, they have come to adopt a rule of justice diametrically opposed to that of Abraham. The solidarity that exists between human beings, and especially (84:) between members of the same society, this solidarity invoked by Abraham in order to save the guilty, is also invoked in our time, but its purpose is to harm those who are innocent. Abraham said, "If there are some who are just, the entire city should be saved." Today they say, "If there are some worthy of blame, the entire community should perish." And those who use this language are for the most part believers who, like us, revere in their prayers the God of Abraham, of Isaac, and of Jacob. God of Abraham! What irony that these words should be in their mouth. "No," I would respond, "be more honest, face the truth directly, and stop invoking the name of the Patriarch, you who do not hesitate to pervert his teaching and to persecute his descendants."

As for us, we are proud of being the children of Abraham, proud to claim for ourselves his lineage, proud to belong to his religion. We will not renounce our identity as Jews in order to escape the restrictions of a statute which, to the eyes of the vulgar alone, may seem dishonorable.... Like Abraham, in the midst of a corrupt world, despite all the iniquitous measures adopted against us, we will continue to believe in justice....

November 16, 1940 (Saturday, *VaYera*)

Ignaz Maybaum, "The British Cyrus," second anniversary of 1938 pogroms in Germany, Hampstead Synagogue, London. *Man and Catastrophe*, pp. 142–50

42 The "Jewish Statute," passed on October 3, 1940, declared Jews to be in a different category from other French citizens, and made foreign Jews liable to internment. See further details in Kaplan's Pesach sermon on April 18, 1941, below.

(142:) Hitler's hordes dragged us out of our beds, smashed up our homes, inflicting upon innocent people death and destruction, sparing neither old people nor women and children. This brute fist is now lifted against the entire world. It is growing clear that a world in which the Jew, the visible symbol of the man without power, cannot find justice and love that will protect him in God's name, is a world that is on the high road to perdition. There is a definite link between the burning down of synagogues in Germany and the present destruction of churches in England by the German bombers. There is (143:) a connection between the refugee life led by us exiled German Jews and the refugee life of millions of German barbarians.... The refugee, till recently a tragic figure symbolizing our peculiar destiny, has become symbolic of our entire era....

Yet though we remember in our prayers to-day the victims of the pogroms of November 10th, 1938, our intention is rather to look ahead. We can do it better now on the second anniversary (144:) of this evil day than would have been possible on the first anniversary a year ago. For now the world knows that Hitlerist barbarity which first revealed itself by persecuting Jews is actually a danger to the whole world. And all whose hands are still free to fight for civilization have come to see that Britain's war is at bottom a holy war.

November 29, 1940 (Friday evening)

Ferdinand M. Isserman, "'The Fifth Column is Here,' by George Britt," Temple Israel, St. Louis, MO. AJA, MS-6 Box 15, Folder 7

(9:) Two incidents in Europe this week proved this thesis that democracy and the freedom of the Jew are linked, and tyranny with anti-semitism. In the city of Delft in Holland, Christian students struck when a Jewish professor was removed. The Nazi authorities closed the university.[43] This was the Christians' way of stating that opposition to anti-semitism is opposition to Naziism, to fascism, to despotism. In the city of Antwerp, Belgium, the Nazis ordered all

43 The incident was reported by the JTA, November 27, 1940, based on a report from Geneva on November 26.

Jews to appear in public wearing an arm band, with the symbol of Judaism, the six-pointed star. The day this order went into effect, the streets of Antwerp were filled with men and women, Christians and Jews, wearing this arm band.[44] Here they were all Belgians, all foes of the Nazi regime, wearing the symbol of Judaism, thus proclaiming to the Nazi conqueror that anti-semitism is opposed to liberty. (10:) The liberty of Christians as well as the Jews.

Jacob Kaplan, "Israel is My First-Born" (*Israël est mon premier né*, Exod. 4:22), Synagogue de Vichy, France. *Les Temps d'épreuve*, pp. 87–90, translated by MS

(90:) In our days, in Europe, our generation in turn has been confronted with its heroic destiny. A powerful onslaught has been directed against us, an onslaught in which all the forms of past persecution have been brought together: expulsions, massacres, the ghetto, the exclusion from specified positions and from specified professions.

We ourselves will give the same response as did our ancestors. We will proudly declare that we are not Esau, who spurned his birthright (cf. Gen. 25:34). We have for ourselves 3500 years of continuous history, 3500 years of hardship, during which we have triumphed over suffering and prevailed over death. And we have for ourselves in addition the divine word, "Israel is my first-born" (Exod. 4:22). Since that time, no power on earth has been capable of seizing from us this title of inalienable honor.

December 8, 1940 (Sunday)

Maurice N. Eisendrath, "Preachers in War Time: Priests or Prophets?," Holy Blossom Temple, Toronto. *Holy Blossom Pulpit*, x, 2

(2:) In former and more devout generations, when men were drawn to their houses of worship to pour forth their praise unto God in song and prayer, the message of the pulpit was not magnified out

44 This also appears to have been based on a JTA article, dated November 25, 1940, under the headline, "Belgians Signal Sympathy for Jews by Wearing 'Star' Armbands."

of all proportion to the words of the hymnal or the prayer book. Today, however, save for the rigidly Orthodox synagogue of the Jew and the Catholic churches among the Christian, the liturgy has been relegated so far into the background that many are the so-called worshippers who rush into the house supposedly of prayer, at the precise, split-second that the sermon is scheduled to begin. Whether we preachers approve or disapprove of this practice, whether we are flattered or disquieted by this undue importance which our words have today assumed, there is no escaping the conclusion that this is the state of affairs.

All of which places a tremendous and unprecedented responsibility on the shoulders of the contemporary preacher.... [I]t is by no means any ecclesiastical (3:) conceit on my part that compels me, reluctantly, to confess that the majority come to hear – or perhaps to criticize – the word of the preacher.

(9:) It is the unequivocal, uncompromising voice of such prophets rather than the unctuous balm of pandering priests which is the most crying need of this hour, even of this war-time hour....

(11:) And even more clamorous was the prophet of the past in times of war than in times of peace. He arose more frequently in days of national crisis than in days of tranquility and calm.... For if there is one thing that the prophet avoided it was those glittering generalities which newspaper editors have learned glibly to speak of as eternal verities....

(13:) No preacher, especially in wartime, can rest content with the mere task of picking up the pieces strewn about by split-personalities and of salvaging the wreckage wrought by war's brutal ravages. He must not be a mere ambulance-chaser nor companion to the undertaker carrying off the casualties to the burying ground. He must inquire into the causes of all this havoc; yes, and even in the midst of war, he must cry aloud and spare not (cf. Isa. 58:1) concerning the new way of life which man must follow if we are to avoid such tragic pitfalls in the future.

(14:) If the preacher believes that God has forever branded war as wrong, he must join that band of sixty-five ministers who so characterized it at the very outbreak of the conflict, and take the consequences. If however, he believes, as did not a few of our talmudic teachers, that though war be sinful, subservience to evil is more so; that wars in defense of liberty and in defiance of tyranny are justifiable, then he dare not avoid its challenge from the pulpit.

December 13, 1940 (Friday evening)

Ferdinand M. Isserman, "'The Struggle of Two Worlds,' A Reply to Hitler's Last Address," Temple Israel, St. Louis, MO. AJA, MS-6 Box 15, Folder 7

(5:) In this week's address, the Jew was the guiding hand behind the capitalist democracies, the foe and the exploiter of labor and the common man.[45]

(6:) Without compunction, with a ruthlessness that has rarely been equaled in the history of the world, Mr. Hitler has taken peoples from Poland, from Lorraine, virtually uprooted them and thrown them into concentration camps. Their property, their lands, their farms, their churches, their schools, their valleys, their streams, their skies, he has given to others. How can he justify this monstrous cruelty by stating that it is just because it helps his race, even though it destroys the lives of other races?

(8:) I am thrilled to be a member of that people whom Satan seeks to destroy, that his evil conspiracies for me might prevail. . . .

Jacob Kaplan, "Watchman, What of the Night?" (*Sentinelle, qu'en est-il de la nuit*, Isa. 21:11), Synagogue de Vichy, France. *Les Temps d'épreuve*, pp. 81–85, translated by MS

(93:) Our anguish, our suffering, our wounds, the assaults that we have had to endure: all this has been predicted from the beginning

45 In the earlier part of the sermon, Isserman described this as a speech delivered a few days earlier to several thousand workers in a Berlin munition factory; he claims that most of them had supported Socialist or Communist parties, and that therefore there was no criticism of Communism, but rather a vehement denunciation of capitalism. The speech, delivered on Tuesday, December 10, received considerable coverage in the American press, including in the *St. Louis Post – Dispatch*. For a fuller text of the speech in translation, see Domarus, *Hitler: Speeches and Addresses*, vol. 3, pp. 2146–2154.

in our Sacred Scripture.[46] Yes, but it is just as important to know that the struggle will continue only while it is night, and it will end in the morning when the day breaks.... Why are we so dismayed by the attacks against us? It is because we believed that the "night" had ceased on earth when it was actually never so gloomy in the world....

(95:) It is a certainty that never leaves us that the day mentioned in the biblical narrative [of Jacob: Gen. 32:25–32] will eventually shine forth.... Thus, following the example of their great ancestor [Jacob], the descendants of Israel will be blessed even by the very people who have exploited the contemporary night of ignorance in order to slander and to persecute them.

(96:) Today, these prophecies [Isa. 60:3, Zech. 8:23] doubtless seem to be utopian, paradoxical. Nevertheless, there is a logic to them. They are consistent with the philosophy of history. And they justify the optimism of Israel, its assurance that nothing can undermine that better destiny promised for humanity as a whole.... Falsehood, iniquity, hatred, and violence will be replaced by truth, justice, brotherhood, and peace. Yes, one day, light will shine over all human beings.

December 14, 1940 (Saturday)

Eliezer Berkovits, "In the Company of the Lonely Ones," United Hebrew Congregation, Leeds, England. *Between Yesterday and Tomorrow*, pp. 73–78

(75:) One day we too might be in the position of poisoning our youth with the curse of nationalism. The time may even come when we shall be a "proud" and warring nation, driving along victoriously with our own mechanised armies. Naturally, never wanting war, but always prepared to defend the frontiers of our sacred heritage. If so – if the Jewish happiness of the future lies in such or similar conditions – I say "No" to this future and this happiness. If this be the place allotted to us in the world, let us rather have no place at all.

I say this in no pacifist mood toward the present conflict in the

46 Referring to Jacob's struggle during the night recounted in Gen. 32:25–29.

world. After human wickedness on the one hand and human stupidity on the other have pushed mankind into the abyss, there is nothing else left but to fight the struggle out to the bitter end. But Jews should not be blind to the facts. It is enough for us to suffer from human wickedness and stupidity, but what reason can we have for identifying ourselves with them by planning the Jewish future on lines that have led the nations into the present chaos....

We are living in the world, but we do not really belong to it. Wherever we may be, we are strangers.... (76:) We do not belong here.

This has been the Jewish tragedy of the last two millennia, put in a nutshell. We have been pushed about all the time. We have always been in the way of somebody. There has been no place for us. But there has been one great advantage in this. If there has been no place for us, then of course we bear no responsibility for what has been going on in the world....

We are alone. There is no place for us in this world. But great is our compensation that our hands are clean. We have no share in the abominable crimes of human history in the course of the past two thousand years.

We paid a heavy price for the cleanliness of our hands. We have had to live like the relics of some forgotten past; alone in a world that had no use for us. But sometimes I feel that it was worthwhile if only for the sake of our clean hands.

Kalonymus Kalmish Shapira, Warsaw Ghetto. *Esh Kodesh*, p. 83; *Derashot meShenot haZa'am*, pp. 173–74; Polen, *Holy Fire*, 110–11, translated by Nehemia Polen

(110:) There are times that are characterized by the verse, "I am with him in suffering" (Ps. 91:15). At such times, the troubles are, God forbid, (111:) upon Israel, and God simply suffers along with us [empathetically]. But when the troubles are so great that on the basis of Israel's own resources it would be impossible to survive; so great that God alone gives us the strength to survive and remain alive in the face of such bitter and cruel calamities – then the burden has shifted, as it were, to Him.... [T]hen Heaven must rush to our deliverance with mercy, since He is innocent [and the burden is on Him]; why should our Father in Heaven be made to suffer?[47]

December 20, 1940 (Friday evening)

Israel Gerstein, "The Forgotten Man," B'nai Zion Congregation, Chattanooga, TN. *Reveille or Taps?*, pp. 71–77

(76:) Dr. [Carl] Jung, one of the disciples of Freud, insists that in the mind of every man is deposited the memories of the experiences of his forefathers. Every Frenchman carries within him a fragment of the Revolution and no amount of Hitler propaganda can uproot it. Every German carries within him the ancestors who roamed the woods with hatchets.[48] And every Jew carries within him a portion of the spirit of Moses and a spark from Mt. Sinai. In the brain cells of every Jew is written the consciousness of God, the fiery passion of the prophets, and all efforts to make one forget only backfire and cause harm to the individual's peace of mind....

December 21, 1940 (Saturday)

Kalonymus Kalmish Shapira, Warsaw Ghetto. *Esh Kodesh*, pp. 84–85; *Derashot meShenot haZa'am*, p. 175; Polen, *Holy Fire*, p. 81, translated by Nehemia Polen

When we see the devastation in matters of religion and divine service caused by the sufferings; when we see how the calamities have wrought the destruction of the entire heritage of Torah and divine service which our ancestors, as well as we ourselves, impressed upon the coming generations (our children and grandchildren); [when we see the devastation in such areas as] Kosher food, Sabbath observance, *mikveh*, *ḥeder*, education in general, etc., then take care that even under such circumstances your faith is not impaired, God forbid, by even a hair's-breadth.... There are sufferings...whose

47 This appears to represent a theological shift from earlier sermons emphasizing Jewish suffering as a punishment for sin.

48 Ironically, this formulation – together with the following sentence – would appear to support the Nazi doctrine that Jews can never be true Germans.

function and purpose we understand; but there are also sufferings… whose purpose we do not understand, and quite the opposite – we see their counter-productivity. To meet [sufferings in this category], a strengthening of faith is required.

December 22, 1940 (Sunday)

Abba Hillel Silver, "Man and His Loves and Hates," The Temple, Cleveland, OH. *Therefore Choose Life*, pp. 147–51

(148:) Our world suffers today not because it is full of hatred of evil, but because it is full of hate – simple hate. Hate, like fear, is being fostered deliberately, inspired and implanted in the hearts of men as part of the technique of total revolution and total war. The Germans are teaching men to hate Jews. When the Nazis decided to wage war on Poland, they incited their people to hate the Poles. Now they are teaching hatred of the English…

War and revolution always introduce hate. Propaganda is largely a hate device. Anti-Semitism is the hate technique of the twentieth century which is being employed and most exploited by the Nazis today. Hitler is the great hater of our day.[49] … Because these hatreds are not hatreds of evil but devices for perpetrating greater evil, they have proved ruinous to our civilization.

December 27, 1940 (Friday evening during Hanukkah)

Jacob Kaplan, "Not by Might, nor by Power," (*Ni par la force, ni par la puissance*, Zech. 4:6), Synagogue de Vichy, France. *Les Temps d'épreuve*, pp. 97–103, translated by MS

(100:) Never have the persecutions entirely ceased; never have the Jews had significant numbers or held real power. The alleged Jewish power is nothing but a myth that is used like a scarecrow in order to arouse the peoples against us. Would we be where we are if we truly had this omnipotence that is attributed to us? No, it is not from this

49 At this point, Silver cites Hermann Rauschning, *The Voice of Destruction,* and Otto Strasser, *Hitler and I,* on Hitler's capacity for hate.

source that one may discover the secret of Jewish survival; it is rather through the words of Zechariah, "'Not by might, nor by power, but by My spirit,' said the Lord of Hosts" (Zech. 4:6).

(101:) At present, because once again we have found ourselves under trial, it is our fellow Jews who are asking whether God may have abandoned us. I am well aware that they speak this way because of their extreme suffering, and because despair elicits cries of doubt along with cries of pain. I would like to say simply the following: others in the past have had doubts like yours....[50] Each era has thus brought its cluster of sufferings that have evoked crises of doubt and despair among our ancestors....

(103:) Thanks to this divine spirit, Israel is indestructible; it is animated by a spiritual force before which all physical power is ineffectual.... To us today reverts the awesome honor of kindling the lights of the menorah in the midst of tribulation. Let us not allow the flame to diminish....

Samuel Teitelbaum, "No Great and No Small," United Hebrew Congregation, Fort Smith, AR. *A Set of Holiday Sermons*, 5702/1941, pp. 50–56[51]

(53:) Small or weak, nation after nation is being relentlessly assailed invaded and seized, and minority races, peoples and sects, are being ruthlessly crushed and despoiled. That the totalitarian states are guilty of these aggressions goes without saying. But almost equally guilty are the western powers who had remained silent during these assaults, possibly because they or at least their rulers and leaders had entertained similar ambitions, and had even connived with the aggressors and betrayed or deserted the weaker powers, as in the cases of Spain and Czechoslovakia....

(53–54:) At last with the invasion of Poland the western powers were awakened to the dire consequences that might befall them if

50 Here Kaplan cites Exod. 6:9; Ezek. 37:11; the destruction of the First Temple; Haman; the Maccabees, and the destruction of Second Temple, as examples.

51 No specific date is given for the sermon, which is designated as pertaining to Hanukkah; the year 1940 seems more appropriate to the content than the printed date of 1941.

the dynamic, ruthless aggrandizements of Hitler's Germany were permitted to continue.... A keener vision and a more prophetic foresight would have revealed that the anti-Semitic attack upon a feeble minority people was but a smoke-screen, a vanguard assault upon the citadels of civilization. The Nazi and Fascist brutalities and barbarities inflicted upon our people evoked some sympathy but only piddling solutions were proposed for an unbearable human lot. Israel has been one of the major victims of the appeasement politics. And even now, when five million Jews in Central Europe are living in a human hell, Great Britain virtually closes the doors and restricts the sale of land to Jews in Palestine....

December 29, 1940 (Sunday during Hanukkah)

Maurice N. Eisendrath, "The Great Hatred" [by Maurice Samuel], Holy Blossom Temple, Toronto. *Holy Blossom Pulpit*, x, 4

(14:) Like Antiochus, *der Fuehrer* would place a new and pagan idol before the holy of holies of our churches and temples. It is the idol of power and force, of the omnipotent and deified state, the idol of the Great Hatred, a jealous and vengeful god to which would belong all the energies and desires, the very lives of its subjects. The officers of the Reich's armies and the *Luftwaffe* are its high priests, the multitudes in concentration camps and in exile, or brutally assassinated, are the blood sacrifice which they would mercilessly place upon its scarlet-stained altar. To this idol, all that is individual and free, noble and exalted, the Nazis would bring as their offering. That is why these times call for a Mattathias, intrepid and bold, to strike that pagan image from the altar which mankind has so painfully and arduously erected in his tedious struggle against nature without and alleged human nature, his animalistic nature, within. That is why these days demand courageous Maccabees.

1941

January 7, 1941 (Tuesday evening)

Stephen S. Wise, Radio Broadcast, WOR, 10:45 p.m. AJA, Box 23: SSW Microfilms of AJHS and BUASC papers

(1:) In accepting the invitation to give a series of broadcasts over a period of weeks I welcome the opportunity of interpreting world events from the viewpoint of an American, which is only another way of saying interpreting world events in the light of democracy, ancient and modern, from the viewpoint, moreover, of one who is a teacher of the Jewish faith and fellowship.[1]

January 12, 1941 (Sunday)

Maurice N. Eisendrath, "Where Do We Go From Here?,"[2] Holy Blossom Temple. Toronto. *Holy Blossom Pulpit*, x, 5

(1:) [Jeremiah issued, e.g., in 34:17] a solemn and somber warning which, because it went unheeded by his contemporaries, led inevitably to the doom which he had predicted could not but descend upon his blinded and deafened compatriots; a doom which, just as inevitably, will fall upon ourselves should we continue to prove equally as deaf and as blind to our present-day seers who would direct our gaze a bit beyond the headlines of our daily papers or the latest news flash of our radio commentators.

(6:) I for one would look askance at anything that could be

---

1 In addition to his regular preaching and speaking schedule, this commitment required Wise to present two fifteen-minute addresses per week over a period of six weeks. See especially below, January 28, 1941. Unlike the texts of his sermons, which are all double-spaced, these are generally two pages, single-spaced.

2 The title is taken from a then recent book by the British socialist academic and politician Harold Laski.

demonstrated as standing in the way of this supreme undertaking of the present hour: to destroy irrevocably the power of Hitler and his fellow dictators and to bring about as speedily as possible the emancipation of all those whom these fiendish forces of evil have already trampled underfoot or whom they threaten to ravage and despoil. Surely, I have said enough since the outbreak of hostilities in September, 1939 – and even long before most of our contemporaries were awakened to the menace wherewith Nazism threatens the entire world – to render superfluous any further assurances as to my profoundest conviction that all things else must be made subservient to the banishing of every form and manner of brutal dictatorship from the surface of the earth....

January 17, 1941 (Friday evening)

Israel Gerstein, "What Are You Crying About?," B'nai Zion Congregation, Chattanooga, TN. *Reveille or Taps*, pp. 92–97

(96:) And then there are the tears of children in Europe who do not have enough milk, tears of men and women getting their food from the public kitchens supported by the Joint [Distribution Committee] who will now get smaller portions because of lack of funds. And there are tears of shame and humiliation.

A recent arrival from Germany tells how following the "Black Thursday," which will live in infamy, the Nazis set fire to the beautiful synagogue in Dresden.[3] A large crowd of Nazi hooligans turned the occasion into a big festival. Then the chief of the Gestapo ordered that the rabbi and the cantor should be brought to the scene and also the leaders of the community.... When they arrived, haggard and pale from exhaustion and suffering, they were ordered to pick up the Torahs, go up to the roof, and make *hakafos*, just like on *Simhas Torah*. The crowd howled, but when the cantor began chanting '*Ono Hoshio no*' he choked with tears. Indeed, tears are nature's lotion for

3 "Black Thursday" (November 10, 1938) was a term used in American newspapers for what came to be called *Kristallnacht*. The Dresden Synagogue, designed by the architect Gottfried Semper in 1840, was the first to use Moorish architectural patterns, a style followed by many other late nineteenth-century synagogues, including in the United States.

the eyes.... Through the tears, those miserable people beheld a new hope.[4]

January 28, 1941 (Tuesday evening)

Stephen S, Wise, Radio Message, WOR, 10:45 p.m. AJA, SSW Microfilms of AJHS Papers, Box 23

(1:) News comes from Washington today, according to the Chief of the Washington Bureau of the International News Service, which is of such far-reaching importance... that I find myself under the necessity of dealing with it without a moment's delay in this broadcast.[5]

The story as it comes from Washington may be briefly summarized. It purports to be an offer to the American government on the part of the Nazi government to release immediately 450,000 refugees now in Germany and its conquered territories, principally in concentration camps, including Germans, Austrians, Czechs, Poles, Dutch, Belgians and French, most of them Jewish. The proposal, in some detail, is that these 450,000 political and racial refugees shall proceed directly from the places in which they now are to the United States, the Nazi government undertaking to send refugees across Europe in sealed trains to Lisbon for shipment aboard US vessels into American ports. The Nazi government will release only those refugees who have obtained American visas, guaranteeing their admission to the United States and enabling the American government in some degree to control the identity of the refugees.

---

4 Victor Klemperer provides no details in his Diary on the event, though he was living in Dresden: *I Will Bear Witness*, I, p. 274. Martin Gilbert cites the description provided by "a local painter, Otto Griebel": uniformed SA men "hauled a group of totally distraught looking and deathly pale Jewish teachers from the nearby Jewish community house. The force crumpled top hats onto their heads and exhibited them to the baying crowd, to whom the unfortunate victims were forced, on command, to bow deeply and take off their hats" (*Kristallnacht*, p. 117). This may be a description, from a different perspective, of the same acts of humiliation.

5 Based on the same International News Service release, American newspapers would carry the report of the German proposal on the following day. The article in the *San Bernardino County Sun* (California), using the title "Hitler Wants U.S. to Take His Refugees," followed with a brief article under the headline "Rabbi Wise Attacks Hitler Refugee Offer," including direct quotations from his radio address on the previous night (January 29, 1941, p. 11).

The Nazis demand that the US agree to pay in gold for the passage of all the refugees from Germany to Lisbon as well as from Lisbon to the US, the cost of transportation of each refugee being set at approximately $445, of which $245 would go to the German railroad for the fare in trains with doors sealed and windows blackened, and only $200 to the US lines for the trip to America.

It is not easy to speak with any degree of moderation concerning a proposal which is at one and the same time a subtle and yet clumsy attempt not to help refugees, but to do a maximum of hurt to our country is its real purpose. This proposal is made not for acceptance but with the certainty in advance of absolute and ignominious rejection....

[The proposal aimed at] two equally harmful things. 1. To make it appear that our government's rejection of the plan proves its indifference to the fate of the refugees. 2. To divide the American people and to throw into confusion the mind of America with respect to the lend-lease bill by making it appear that the government is even considering a proposal to admit to our shores nearly one-half-million refugees.

February 14, 1941 (Friday evening)

Israel Gerstein, "The Lincoln Legacy,"[6] B'nai Zion Congregation, Chattanooga, TN. *Reveille or Taps?*, pp. 134–41

(140:) [M]editating upon Lincoln, one must be filled with confidence and security as to the future of America. There are people who will prove to you beyond the shadow of a doubt that America is destined to go the way of Nazi Germany, and they have all sorts of evidence to back up their assertions. Such an assertion is an insult to the flag which Lincoln helped preserve. To say it is to prove oneself ignorant of the heart of America. For Lincoln is the heart. He was America in the flesh, and this America fought for justice and for equality; this America in the flesh opposed the Hitler ideas even before Hitler was born.

6 Lincoln's Birthday, February 12, was then a federal holiday, along with Washington's Birthday on February 22. Friday evening would have been the first preaching occasion to follow.

February 23, 1941 (Sunday)

Maurice N. Eisendrath, "Canadians All – Immigrants All," Holy Blossom Temple, Toronto. *Holy Blossom Pulpit*, x, 8

(3:) Instead of living up to the principles upon which the New World was first established, instead of welcoming with open arms the oppressed (4:) and persecuted of foreign lands, instead of sharing with the hungry and homeless multitudes the superabundance which, not our forebears but which God Himself has given unto His myriads of creatures to enjoy upon this heaven-dowered continent, we slammed the doors of our nation in their very faces and bolted our gates more tightly than ever – and it hath not profited us.... Those harassed and hounded peoples were potentially our most formidable allies – far more so than the aristocrats in France and Belgium and elsewhere, upon whom we placed so much reliance.... At least, those hapless refugees had learned, in the cauldron of terror and torture, what this thing is all about.... They had met Naziism face to face, what little they had they would gladly place at the disposal of those forces determined to strike this vilest monster low.

But instead of gathering up these most vehement foes of Fascisms that the world could conceivably contain, we permitted short-sighted, jaundiced immigration officials carefully and cautiously to sort them out; to inquire not whether they were anti-Fascist – which should have been the sole consideration – but whether they were Catholic or Protestant or Jewish...with the consequence that all these staunch allies of democracy and impassioned enemies of dictatorship are now not behind our Canadian borderlines to buttress our own forces, but are rather behind barbed wire barricades of European concentration camps where the Nazis can blissfully starve them to death, thus conveniently ridding the world of just that many additional anti-Fascists, of that many more cursed believers in, and battlers for the "putrescent corpse of democracy."[7]

(6:) Mind you, do not misunderstand me again, as so many of my

7 On Canadian immigration policy, see Abella and Troper, *None is Too Many*, which does not mention Eisendrath or any other Canadian rabbi who delivered sermons regarding the issue of immigration of refugees.

fellow Canadians persisted – sometimes deliberately, I suspect – in misunderstanding me ever since 1933 by believing that whatever I say on this theme is predicated on my exclusive concern for my brother Jews. They were wrong then, as events have too tragically demonstrated. They are just as wrong today, as subsequent occurrences will just as tragically prove. I am not indulging in any special pleading for my fellow-Jews, although, God knows, things have come to a sorry pass, and men and nations have presumption to call themselves Christian, when one must apologize if one does plead especially for these harried and hounded folk. Yet I am not pleading particularly for them or for any other group of refugees – well-warranted though such a petition would be, in the sight of God, if not in the sight of calloused, hardened men and women. At this particular moment however, whether you believe it or not, I am pleading for Canada and its future....

March 8, 1941 (Saturday, Shabbat Zakhor)

Eliezer Berkovits, "The Wandering Amalek," United Hebrew Congregation, Leeds, England. *Between Yesterday and Tomorrow*, pp. 20–25[8]

(20:) The wandering Jew does not travel alone; he is accompanied by the wandering Amalek. We have known him since first we made our appearance on the stage of the world's history. Amalek has driven us from country to country, he has followed us from nation to nation. It has always been the same story: Jews fleeing from oppression, wandering on deserted tracks, hoping for rest, longing for safety, and when they thought that they found it at last – "Then came Amalek" (Exod. 17:8). Jews run (21:) from Amalek, but Amalek is everywhere. They say the Jew is ubiquitous, much more so is Amalek. They call us international, much more so is Amalek.

Once more Amalek has come; but this time he has laid aside his mask and revealed himself in his true shape. This time he has come

8 The sermon is identified (p. 20), following the title, as "Purim, February, 1941." Purim would occur that year on Thursday, March 13. Because of the Amalek theme, the best guess for the date of delivery would appear to be on Shabbat Zakhor, March 8.

not only to us Jews, but, like a lightning scourge, he has swooped down on the nations and the whole of mankind. For the first time in history he has revealed himself in his true colours. Amalek! The enemy of the Jews, the enemy of the world. … This has always been so. Whether people saw it or not, our enemies were always the enemies of progress and happiness.

(23:) Jews are hated because they differ and dare to differ without having a hard fist to defend themselves when the necessity arises. …

And again Amalek has come; not only over us, but as a consuming pestilence over the world. This time he is mightier than he ever was in the past and for this reason he has had the audacity to strip himself of his old disguise. This time he stands before the world in all his naked brutality and hideous ugliness, exposing himself and all the other little Amalekites who were still pretending to hate Jews because of this or that. He has torn the mask from all of them and has taught the world once again that the enemy of the Jew is the enemy of mankind. It is time that the world learned the lesson.

(24:) [W]e have witnessed certain actions on the part of those who are fighting for that better world which are not encouraging at all. Remember the shameful regulations concerning Jewish internees in one of the camps in Canada.[9] Think of the disgusting treatment of refugees who were fortunate enough to escape from enemy-occupied territories and succeeded in reaching the shores of Palestine. After having been rendered homeless (partly also thanks to the stupidity and hypocrisy of "democratic" policy in the years before the war), now they have been deported like criminals in their hundreds, men, women, and children, to some unknown destination.

(25:) Once more Amalek has come; not only over us but over the whole of mankind. Will the nations understand the meaning of this

9 Beginning in the spring of 1940, a number of young male Jewish refugees who had come to England were transported to Canada and consigned to internment camps on suspicion of being "enemy aliens." Berkovits was apparently referring to an article published in the *JC* on January 31, pp. 1 and 7, reporting that the Director of Canadian Internment Camp "B" had ordered Orthodox Jews to work on the Sabbath. It was strongly criticized in the following week's *JC* (February 7, p. 10), and reportedly overturned (*JC* March 7, p.1).

lesson? Will they learn that justice as well as freedom is indivisible: that there can never be one measure of justice and freedom for the use of the Jews and another for the mighty masters of the earth? Will a new period of human history open in which the watchword will be: "Hate the evil and love the good?" (Amos 5:15). Or shall we again be disappointed?

March 14, 1941 (Friday evening)

Ferdinand M. Isserman, "This Is Judaism," Temple Israel, St. Louis, MO. AJA, MS-6, Box 16, Folder 1

(8:) The other day while meditating on this sermon, my mind persisted in reverting to the new ghetto in Warsaw, in which half a million Jews are being imprisoned, with food and labor only for a hundred and seventy-five thousand. A huge concrete wall encircles this ghetto. The streets from other sections of the city that cross its terrain are sealed. Only Jews are seen, so that no Jews can enter and escape, and no Christians can share the lot of the Jews. What is happening to the Jews in that ghetto? They are being shut off from the outside world, shut off from its culture, also shut off from its mad competition, from its injustice, from its brutality. In the Jewish ghetto, Jews will return to their faith. They will once more read and re-read their literature. No matter what the dictators do to Europe, . . the ghetto in Warsaw, now a vast dungeon, will become a spiritual oasis. And there the . . . "children of the (9:) ghetto" will preserve the faith and values of the Bible. . . .[10] The faith of Israel will preserve the Jew of the ghetto of Warsaw. . . .

March 23, 1941 (Sunday)

Joseph H. Hertz, "Intercession Sermon," Great Synagogue, London. *Early and Late*, 61–65 (cf. *JC*, March 28, 1941, p. 5)

---

10 "Children of the ghetto" alludes to the book of this title by Israel Zangwill, first published in 1892, republished by the Jewish Publication Society in 1938. The preacher's presentation of the Warsaw Ghetto as something positive because of its potential renewal of Jewish culture and religious life is understandable at the time, but of course seems rather misguided in light of what was to come.

(62:) Thus the policy of vengeance [leading to the Treaty of Versailles] pursued by a former Ally that has now gone down to defeat and dishonor,[11] is recognized by historians to have undermined the faith of the German people in their newly set-up democratic governments, and to have driven the masses into the arms of any demagogue who would promise them a revival of their martial strength. That demagogue, when he did arise, was a demagogue of genius, and the very incarnation of a spirit inconceivably wicked. The first victim of his vitriolic fury was the Jew. The moment that he seized power eight years ago, medieval Jew-baiting was revived and *surpassed* in methodical torture, frenzied ferocity, and fiendish malice. Among Churchmen and intellectuals all over the world there was genuine, widespread, and continued indignation at this relapse into unbelievable barbarism. Governments, however, maintained a strange correctness and imperturbable passivity. Even the most enlightened of them continued diplomatic relations with a Power that had defied and torn up solemn treaties, revived torture, and was systematically perpetrating unspeakable horrors and obscene bestialities upon tens of thousands of innocent men in its concentration camps.

D. Bueno de Mesquita, Special Service at Spanish and Portuguese Congregation, Lauderdale Road Synagogue, London. *JC*, March 28, 1941, p. 5

During the 18 months of war we have had to face such heart-breaking disappointments as must have reduced any another nation to helpless despair: undreamed of setbacks . . . which led us at one moment to the very brink of disaster. At that time nothing seemed capable of halting the onward march of a nation which, for sheer colossal weight, for fiendish cunning, for savage cruelty, for callous contempt of all that is sacred and humanly decent, has known no equal in the long history of mankind.

Yet that onward victorious march was halted; and that is something for which we can never be sufficiently grateful. With a large part of Europe ravaged and crushed, and the rest quivering with fear

11 Referring, of course, to France.

of a similar fate, this small island of ours, dauntless and unafraid, held up what looked to be an irresistible sweep to final and complete triumph. For this and for much more we have to be thankful....

Alexander Altmann, Great Synagogue, Cheetham Hill Road, Manchester, England. *JC*, March 28, 1941, p. 18

At this important stage of the war, we ought to acknowledge thankfully the gift of leadership which has been our fortunate lot. It has been the claim of the enemy that only they have leaders with boldness, vision, and energy, and that Democracy is senile and incapable of resisting their aggression.

What their "leadership" means has meanwhile become only too obvious. The whole of Europe has been turned into a vast prison camp. The New Order they seek to establish is a new world without God, without a moral code, without a Bible, without Jews and Christians, a world of masters and slaves. A political system like that of the British Commonwealth of Nations, which is a free and voluntary union of nations and Communities, is beyond their powers of imagination. They despise it, they regard it as doomed, but we are sure this British concept alone will endure because it alone safeguards the progress of the human race, and with its dynamic power and irresistible moral force, it will override all obstacles and reach its goal.

Against the concept of dictatorship, we set the democratic form of real leadership as is embodied in the two great leaders which this country and the United States have produced at this decisive moment of history. Great Britain and the USA will lead the world, and prove that the leadership is theirs.

Emil Ehrnthal (later Michael Elton), "Heroes of the Home Front," Hammersmith Synagogue, London, Day of Thanksgiving and Prayer," Sunday following Shabbat Parah. *The Challenge of Destiny*, pp. 24–28

(24:) Events and personalities of our days have revitalised the dead figures of the dusty pages of history. Incredulous as we were of the tortures and cruelties inflicted upon our people in the Middle Ages, now we see them all re-enacted on a more thorough and gigantic scale. It is not bygone days anymore, it is not yesterday, it is *today*. The first ghetto in Rome, the sailing of our brethren from the shores of Spain, the long siege and fall of Jerusalem, the battles of the Maccabees, the frustration of Haman, yes, even the oppression of the Pharaohs, we all understand them, we feel them, *now*.

(26:) You, the civilians are the heroes of this war. The hail of fire cannot blind you, the falling bombs cannot unnerve you, when the walls and roofs totter you stand your ground unshaken, unfaltering and defiant.

But what is our share of tribulation compared to that of our sons and daughters? [in the fighting forces]...

We have more than survived the rigours of winter, we have come out of it stronger and more resolved. The sufferings opened doors hitherto locked to strangers, the common danger made friends of unknown neighbours. Calamities have brought out the best of our hidden faculties of love and heroism....

(27:) Now in Africa they sweep from the South, they sweep from the East, they sweep from the West, and from all corners they march to victory. And to crown it all the greatest democracy has pledged all her heart, all her might, and all her soul to the support of the forces of liberation....

(28:) [Final prayer:] Give us and our sons and daughters a consciousness of a higher purpose that we may forget the meaning of danger and distress, that we all be united in the spirit that we are fighting the Battle of God and be convinced that wickedness shall have no dominion over men. Allow us to see the fulfillment of the words of Thy prophet: [Ezek. 36:27].

March 25, 1941 (Tuesday)

Israel Gerstein, "War and Peace" (Radio Address), B'nai Zion Congregation, Chattanooga, TN. *Reveille or Taps?*, pp. 150–54

(151:) Hitler has charged [the Jews] with this sin of war mongering, of inciting people to war, and on the other hand he has stigmatized them as pacifists, as people who weaken the desire to fight, who have no stomach for war. You don't look for logic or consistency in the pronouncements of the man who has said, "The bigger the lie the easier it is to make people believe it";[12] and it would be useless to ask Hitler or any of his followers to explain how a people can be peace-loving and war-mongering at the same time. However, he was bound to be partly right when he attributed both of these mutually exclusive qualities (152:) to the Jewish people. The long and unbroken tradition of peace has etched upon the Jewish consciousness a longing and an aspiration for the time when "the wolf and the lamb shall lie down together, and nations shall learn war no more" (Isa. 2:4, 11:6).

(153:) The prayer for peace is a perpetual lamp in the soul of every Jew. Yet he realizes that peace with slavery might be worse than death, and the martyrs of the past have instructed him that there are certain things in life that are even more precious than life itself.... These values cannot be maintained under the tyrannies now blanketing Europe. Hence the son of the great prophets must be convinced that this is a time when a righteous and just peace requires even bloodshed.

April 4, 1941 (Friday evening)

Ferdinand M. Isserman, "Lindbergh's Letter to Americans,"[13] Temple Israel, St. Louis, MO. AJA MS-6, Box 16 , Folder 1

(8:) Poland is gone. Her territories are divided. Her people are enslaved. Her priests have been imprisoned. Her prominent men have been hung in the public streets. Her Jews have been annihilated.[14] Her schools have been closed. Her granaries have been robbed. Her daughters have been raped, and the military tyrants and spies infest the land. That is what Lindbergh calls "immoderation."

(9:) In his whole article, not one word of sympathy, not one word of good-will for the enslaved peoples, not one word of condemnation for Hitler, but many words of condemnation for France and

12 Frequently quoted in US newspapers, late June and early July, 1941.

13 This refers to an article by that title published in *Collier's*, pp. 14–15, 76, on March 29, 1941.

14 Note that this assertion was made almost a year before any program of systematic mass murder by gassing in the Polish death camps had begun.

England.... (10:) Because I want to keep America out of war, I say help Britain. Help Britain with everything she needs. Help her with food, help her with weapons, help her with ships, and help her until German morale is broken, until her conquered peoples rise up in revolt. And then let us join with all free peoples in establishing peace in the world.

April 5, 1941 (Saturday, Shabbat haGadol)

Ephraim Sokolover, Great Synagogue, Ra'anana, Palestine. *Penei Efrayim*, pp. 242–57, translated by MS

(253:) In this modern generation, the horrible holocaust [*hashoah ha'ayumah*] has occurred, unique in the history of the Jewish people. The destruction of tens of thousands, perhaps hundreds of thousands of Jews: men, women, and children, in all forms of bizarre deaths, in the most malicious manner, as never before. All this has occurred at the hands of the most highly-cultured state of Nazi Germany, may its name be blotted out, in the sight of the entire world, in the sight of the most erudite scientists, the greatest scholars, men of justice and righteousness, of culture and etiquette. All of them stood by and observed with equanimity and composure; all of them observed and looked on as Jewish blood was being spilled actually like water, with a level of cruelty that only Satan could have invented. All this has happened to us in our generation!...

(256:) This is our Shabbat haGadol. For that was when the foundation was placed in the Jewish heart that enables us to see great and awesome things, surprising and wondrous things, that have preserved us throughout the millennia of our exile, as we fulfilled the prophecy "in your blood you shall live" (Ezek. 16:5), joyously and willingly, with sacred passion, for the sake of the honor of Heaven. And especially in this latest era, in these appalling times when millions of our Jewish brethren have been beset by anguish and distress at the hands of the murderers unprecedented in their cruelty, whose only goal is to destroy the Jewish people, G-d forbid....

Yet on the other side, we are witness to the mighty strength of the Jewish people, who know how to accept the most painful afflictions with supreme spiritual heroism, through the eternal sanctity of their character....

April 6, 1941 (Sunday)

Solomon B. Freehof, "Faith Bewildered," Rodef Shalom Temple, Pittsburgh, PA. "Living in Crisis," pp. 3–15

(4:) The Nazis hope to be world masters. They have said it and their actions prove that they mean it. In the countries which they have overtaken they have destroyed national independence and have established vassal states in which the people are slaves. Even in the countries which they have not yet touched, there is a terror in the air which emanates from the Nazi achievements. Wherever we live nowadays we are uncertain about our political future.

(5:) Our religion has grown vague, uncertain and self-doubting. This fact is all the more unfortunate because nowadays a strong faith is necessary for survival. The Bolsheviks have a powerful faith in the coming world revolution. The Nazis have a tremendous faith in their coming world dominance, and to the extent that democracy lacks faith and is inwardly bewildered, to that extent it is weak. We need a strong faith and it is, therefore, vital for us to understand why our religious faith, for example, has grown uncertain and confused.

(6:) It is not merely that Adolf Hitler shamelessly declares that he will tell lies and that the people will believe him.... It is not merely that the whole Nazi system is an impudent and shameless lie, but it is the *success* of these lies which is almost crushing our spirits.

(9:) What has happened to us is that we are suddenly beginning to believe that human history may be actually heading backwards towards darkness....

(11:) What shocked our belief in liberty was the easy way in which free countries surrendered their freedom.... When we saw the easy way in which people accepted the Nazi yoke, our faith in human dignity disappeared and our confidence in God as the God of freedom weakened. Our old faith in liberty became bewildered.... [W]hat the revolutions have done was to create the kind of world in which it is difficult to believe in the triumph of truth, in the coming of progress and in the strength of the love of liberty in the human heart.

(13:) Since [Hitler] is now no longer believed and is coming to the fate of all liars, this fact will affect his great anti-religious and anti-Semitic propaganda. His anti-Semitism is in danger of collapsing entirely just as his propaganda is collapsing.... Hitler may win more victories but they will have to be military victories, not propaganda victories. Truth is beginning shyly to come back to life and the false propaganda no longer deceives millions of people.

(14:) We have no right to forget that a few million mountaineers, the Yugoslavs, surrounded by the tremendous Nazi machine, have elected to fight and die rather than to live as slaves. There is plenty of love of freedom in the human heart. Indeed we may be confident that even in the countries already conquered, let but the machine of slavery be shaken slightly, and the spirit of liberty will awaken again and the people will "rise like lions after slumber in unvanquishable number."[15]

April 12, 1941 (first day of Pesach)

Eliezer Berkovits, "Tomorrow Will Come," United Hebrew Congregation, Leeds, England. *Between Yesterday and Tomorrow*, pp. 14–20

(16:) The roots and branches of wickedness are very widely spread all over the world. They are here, they are there, and everywhere. In our day, Evil has become a world-power in the shape of Nazidom and Fascism. But it could become such a force in Germany and Italy only because it was mighty and powerful in all countries. When the forces of evil cautiously started to build up their power in Italy and Germany, they found, probably to their own surprise, that they had powerful allies all over the world. Their allies were the "roots and branches" of evil spread among all the nations. Instead of indignation, instead of the wrath of the civilized world, they met with encouragement, understanding, and sympathy, or, at the very least, with timid toleration.

There was one sin of which the whole world became guilty in the

15 The quotation is from Shelley's poem, "The Masque of Anarchy."

last couple of decades: the toleration of evil. In diplomatic language it was called Neutrality. But are we allowed to be neutral towards wrong-doing, brutality, persecution and the suppression of justice, truth and freedom?

(18:) We have all become guilty, every one of us has his own personal share in the terrible crimes of our generation. Humanism died out because it died out in us....

April 12, 1941 (second night of Pesach)

Louis I. Newman, "From Bondage to Freedom," Radio Address on "The Message of Israel." *Sermons and Addresses*, vol. 2, pp. 137–41

(140:) The common danger, which Cardinal Faulhaber of Munich recognized in his historic Advent sermons several years ago [December 1933], continues to menace the safety and security of all freemen, Christian and Jew alike. The world now knows that the persecutions of the European Jews were but a fore-runner of the persecutions of democratic peoples everywhere, and the *Judenschmerz* has become the *Weltschmerz*. The chief conspirator has not suffered a single military setback since his accession to power, and, like a new Pharaoh, is compelling his myriad serfs to make bricks without straw....

Let no one of us, in the midst of the ever-deepening gloom, lose our interest in both the preservation and strengthening of the ideal values of social and economic justice which underlie our democracy.

Passover this year should be a festival not merely for the children of Israel but for all mankind.... We need such assurances in this grim hour, when America's help as the "arsenal of democracy" may come too late unless we continue to act promptly, decisively, and effectively, and unless the President's re-opening of the Red Sea may achieve a new miracle there.

April 13, 1941 (Sunday, second day of Pesach)

Solomon B. Freehof, "Minds Confused," Rodef Shalom Congregation, Pittsburgh, PA. "Living in Crisis – A Series of Three Addresses." *Rodef Shalom Pulpit*, vol. 7, no. 2, pp. 17–29

(22:) Autocracy is not necessarily efficient or heroic, nor is democracy inept or inert. From what has already happened in England it is sufficient for us to be able to say that we need not be ashamed of the doctrine of freedom which has been preached since the first Passover over thirty-five hundred years ago.

(23:) There have been people in recent years who have been obsessed by an urgent desire to be fair-minded to the tyrant of Germany. Some of their fair-mindedness has been published in the newspapers and heard over the radio. That plus the German propaganda itself has blurred our minds and has confused the distinction between right and wrong until some of us have come to believe that in this war, this life and death struggle, there is not a right or wrong side and that both sides are equally guilty. We are told that the poor German people lack *Lebensraum*, living room. England has half the area of the world while the crowded German (24:) people are confined in one little country. Germany must be given the right to expand. Besides that, if Germany is cruel, what of the cruelty of England in India and elsewhere? The British Empire dominates subject races everywhere. There is no choice between one side or the other. We have heard such opinions even in the committee hearings in the Congress of the United States. Thus in many minds the difference between which side is right and which is wrong has grown vague and confused.

(28:) Let us never confuse the difference between an aggressive and a defensive war. They are in different moral worlds from each other.... Common sense will indicate that nothing is gained by any great democratic nation today assuring the German dictator that under no circumstances will it ever resist him. It is, however, possible that peace may be (29:) gained by a democratic nation being forthright and unafraid....

Let us not be deluded by the autocrat's boasts of efficiency and heroism and thus lose our clear faith in democracy. Democracy is vindicating itself today.... If we have a clear mind, we can have a steadfast heart and we can face the future with hope for the day when all the world will celebrate a Passover of freedom.

April 18, 1941 (Friday, seventh day of Pesach)

Ephraim Sokolover, Great Synagogue, Ra'anana, Palestine, before the Commemoration of the Departed (*hazkarat neshamot*). *Penei Efrayim*, pp. 459–62, translated by MS

(359:) After the awful and terrifying winter, it seemed to us that the measure of afflictions had been filled, and even if we had not reached the status of a "generation that is totally worthy," nevertheless we thought and hoped that the difficulties of enslavement, the massive impoverishment, the afflictions – the destruction of Polish Jewry, the demolition of the Lithuanian strongholds of Torah,[16] the cruel slaughter in the kitchens of Bucharest[17] – after the biblical statement "We were considered as sheep led to the slaughter" (Isa. 53:7) had been fulfilled with us, literally!, with all this we thought that these afflictions would soon pass, and we would hurry and expedite our redemption, and the salvation of our souls.

But now, woe to us! "The harvest has passed, and the summer has ended, but we are not saved" (Jer. 8:20). We are now in the last day of the holiday of redemption, but we have not heard the sound of a voice announcing good news, encouraging, and consoling here and there. Instead we have heard once again an ancient voice, well known to us from the proclamation of the traditional beadle [*Shamash*] – though now it seems as if the voice is extremely terrifying and shocking – while announcing: "*hazkarat neshamot*, commemoration of the departed."

(360:) The announcement is different this year, for we are used to commemorating the souls of our parents and friends, names that are familiar to us from our friendships. But this year, we all have a communal commemoration, one that is public and shared. Our

---

16 This is surprising, as it precedes the German invasion of Lithuanian territory. Ephraim Oshry's book, *The Annihilation of Lithuanian Jewry*, begins with events of June 25, 1941.

17 This undoubtedly refers to the vicious massacre by members of the Romanian Iron Guard of some two hundred Jews in a municipal ritual slaughter house, with their bodies made to hang on meat hooks, in Bucharest the previous January. It was reported in *JC*, January 31, 1941, p. 1, based on an account published in the *Daily Telegraph and Morning Post*. Cf. also below, Ferdinand Isserman, Sept. 26, 1944.

obligation is to recall the tens of thousands of our Jewish brethren who have fallen and been killed in various forms of death. And at the same time, not to forget or to overlook those who remain in the lands of inferno, who are in the sullied hands of the wild and crazy beast, victims of scorn and mockery and humiliation.

April 19, 1941 (Saturday, eighth day of Pesach)

Joseph Kaplan, "The School of Suffering" (*L'école de la suffrance*), Synagogue de Vichy, France. *Les Temps d'épreuve*, pp. 105–11, translated by MS

(105:) Despite the tragic situation in which we find ourselves, we have been allowed to eat unleavened bread, to be seated at the Seder table, and to bring forth memories of the Passover in accordance with our sacred traditions.

(106:) Certain phrases from the Haggadah have seemed to have greater relevance for us. When we say, "This year we are slaves, next year may we be free men," we think of our fellow Jews in other countries against whom persecution continues to rage. But war broke out; the defeat that followed has indeed made the unleavened bread into our own "bread of affliction," the bitter herbs represent our own bitterness, and the wording of the Haggadah transmits our own aspiration.

Within a few months, our fate has been transformed. (107:) Measures have been taken that we assumed belonged exclusively to a bygone past. Could we believe it when in July 1940, French Jews in occupied France were forced to wear the yellow badge? Witnesses can attest to it right here.[18] In this synagogue too, are there not many of our refugees [from occupied France] who have been divested of all their belongings? What is there to say of a Statute that excludes Jews from the Army, expels them from the university, and eliminates their public functions?[19] What is there to say, especially, about the slanders of which we are accused, which have no purpose other than

18 A note supplied by the author states that this was in Commercy, in la Meuse. The Vichy government resisted this requirement. Poznanski writes about yellow placards that identified stores owned by Jews (*Jews in France During World War II*, pp. 34–36).

19 Cf. Kaplan's reference in his November 15, 1940 sermon above. On this sermon,

to arouse hatred against us, slanders all the more serious because they are spread publically, officially, and then spread through the French Radio News? (*Radio-Journal de France*).

(108:) It is obvious that God has His own outlook over Israel; it is obvious that God reserves for Israel great glory. And in preparation for this, God has chosen the school of suffering. The Egyptian slavery....

(110:) Jewish history knows of religious heroism, immortalized in the biblical account of the sacrifice of Isaac.... Jewish history knows of the collective heroism of communities undergoing the savage assaults of a population ravenous for massacre and pillage.... Jewish history knows the spectacular heroism of the martyrs, burnt alive in public places.... But Jewish history also knows of heroism without glamour, concealed, the silent, every-day heroism of the Jew who, tirelessly, suffers for God....

Israelites, my brothers, you are made of the same metal as your ancestors....

Louis I. Newman, "The Wrong and Right Uses of Religion," Address on "The Message of Israel." *Sermons and Addresses*, vol. 2, pages unnumbered

Surely religion is needed now, if we are to rescue our crazed society from destruction. It is force, brutal, untamed force, which rules men today and spreads like a pestilence from continent to continent. By the fiendishly skillful use of the gifts of science, a few cruel and bestial leaders have learned how to enslave vast nations; they have captured the chief centers of national life, and transformed freemen into serfs by a strategic concentration of tanks, machine guns, airplanes and other war-implements, abetted by the use of propaganda falsehoods. They have divided the democratic peoples, thereby making them the prey of the invader. Hate and violence are the hallmarks of our times; in many lands they have driven religion and morality into the caves and catacombs. And unless our own beloved America bestir itself even more, unless we hurry, hurry, hurry, in providing with the

---

including Kaplan's role in providing matzah, see also Shapira, *Jacob Kaplan*, pp. 129–30.

sinews of defense those who battle on the frontiers of freedom, we, too, shall go to the tragic and bitter way which other democracies have known. Religion must not make us supine non-resistants in the presence of the evil which rushes on from victory to victory; religion should arouse us all to the resolution, the industrial power, the defensive might, the moral fortitude which freedom asks from those people who are still unconquered.

April 26, 1941 (Saturday)

Louis I. Newman, "Machines and Men," Address on "The Message of Israel." *Sermons and Addresses*, vol. 2, pages unnumbered

If madmen today speak only the language of force, freemen will answer them in their own coin. Surely the people of the United States will not fail to utilize its vast industrial power to defend human liberties. American ingenuity, symbolized by [Thomas] Edison and [Orville and Wilbur] Wright, will again evolve the formulas and techniques whereby our comrades in the front-lines of the battle can check the aggressor. If ever it has been essential for America to rise in its might, to gird itself in strength, to demonstrate its material as well as its moral invincibility, it is now! France, Greece, and other nations, once free, have been despoiled. Surely Americans will not allow Britain ... to be enslaved to Hitler's juggernaut.

April 27, 1941 (Sunday)

Maurice N. Eisendrath, "The Strategy of Faith," Conference Sermon, UAHC, Detroit, MI. *UAHC, 1941, Sixty-Seventh Annual Report*, pp. 179–85

(179:) [T]here is a very real sense in which my address tonight dares be nothing other than a war sermon, in the deeper and more spiritual connotation of that term.

For in the first place, this is an assemblage of *Jews*; and we Jews have been, or *should have been* at war with the Nazi Reich for the past eight long and blood-stained years. There have been those among our brethren who might have willed it otherwise, for honesty demands the humiliating confession that the first appeasers of Nazism were found in our Jewish ranks. They it was who cherished the delusion that if we did not publish it abroad too loudly in Gath or Ashkelon[20] that our brethren were being bestially butchered in the Reich; that if we did not clamor for a world-wide boycott of these most diabolic fiends that man has ever known, somehow it might go well with German Jewry; and as for the rest of the Jews throughout the earth, Hitler would come to recognize our magnanimity and cease his fulminations against us.

Such efforts at appeasement have only served to heighten the hunger of the conqueror, so now we can no longer refuse to face the ugly, naked fact that for nigh unto a decade, a barbaric war of extermination has been waged against us, and that we must either win this war, or our long heroic pilgrimage will soon be ended.

Solomon B. Freehof, "Hearts Bowed Down," Rodef Shalom Congregation, Pittsburgh. "Living in Crisis - A Series of Three Addresses," *Rodef Shalom Pulpit*, vol. 7, no. 3, pp. 31–41

The one hundred and thirty-seventh Psalm is one of the saddest poems in all the world's literature....

We Jews sometimes act as if we are the only people in the world who suffer, that fate has somehow directed all its artillery against us exclusively. This, of course, (32:) is far from being true....

(33:) But now we have come again in our time to a revival of the ancient barbarities. Defeated nations are once again dragged away in chains to exile and made like slaves to labor in the mills of the conquerors. Again mankind has come to weep by the waters of Babylon as captive slaves..... [The] American people are emotionally shaken almost as if it were already an actual victim of the world's tragedy. It is astonishing how much sorrow, how much mental depression exists in this nation today. How do we explain our widespread gloom?

(35:) We Jews have suffered a great deal of the world's scorn and our awareness of that dislike has affected our moods.... What has happened to us in these recent years is that the amount of hate in

20 Echoing 2 Sam. 1:20.

the world has increased a thousand-fold. Instead of one nation or another being the center of infection, the hate has spread all over the world. Wherever the Nazi armies have successfully marched, there a new center of anti-Semitic propaganda is established, infecting a new group of European nationals in the United States. This increasing hatred is directed not only against us but against group after group. The whole world has suddenly become filled with a fog of hate which depresses us all and breaks down our joy in living. We read in the newspapers more and more about anti-Semitism, all quoting statements of the German propaganda machine.... The widespread increase of hatred everywhere (36:) is sufficient explanation in itself of the ever-widening mood of sorrow in the modern world.

The American people has had for three or four generations the gratification of being magnificently helpful to the unfortunate and the miserable.... But unfortunately in the last few years the amount of human suffering has increased so much and has magnified so rapidly that we know there is very little that we can do about it. We might have helped a half-million (37:) refugees, but *all* Europe is refugee today. Starvation and slavery for tens of millions loom up all over the world. Against this tremendous flood of suffering we are helpless. We know that we are helpless. That sense of being useless and helpless adds a heavy burden to our hearts. It is not only the spread of hate which makes us feel inferior. It is the spread of suffering which makes us feel so inadequate and increases the sorrow of decent people everywhere....

There is defeat after defeat for England and victory after victory for the Nazis, and our hope for the achievement of human freedom is deferred and deferred. The unhindered march of Nazi power brings fear and (38:) gloom to our spirits. "Hope deferred maketh the heart sick" (Prov. 13:12).

(40:) We ought to know that our mental depression and the gloomy conviction that it is hopeless now to help England would completely guarantee the Nazi victory. To achieve that (41:) mood of hopelessness is the aim of the whole German propaganda machine. We must resist it valiantly.... As long as Great Britain controls the seas, the ultimate outcome is inevitable. But the resistance must last until the turn of the tide. It will certainly last. The English will resist and victory will come....

May God grant that when we meet again in the autumn to celebrate a new year it may be a new year of blessing and happiness for all mankind.[21]

April 29, 1941 (Tuesday)

Julius Gordon, "I Sell Faith," Address at UAHC Convention, Detroit, MI. *UAHC, 1941, Sixty-Seventh Annual Report*, pp. 202–5

(202:) I have often wondered in the last few years why our people have allowed themselves to be driven into such a state of despair. There are other peoples in the world today who are crushed under the heel of the tyrant. Israel alone is spiritless, hopeless. In our hearts there is no fiery faith in the survival and the revival of our people. Why this gloom and why this morbid melancholy? There is only one answer to this disturbing question. The answer is that we have forgotten the sources of our strength and comfort, the spiritual values of our heritage which alone have sustained our people throughout the ages....

(204:) I must confess that in the last few years I have experienced moods and moments of gloom and despair. There were moments when I asked myself the agonizing question: What can I tell my people in this hour of distress? How can I comfort them? But not for one moment during these years of stress and strain did I experience the vaguest feeling that this was the end of Jew and Judaism. No power and no force can drive us out of the world. The only question is: What have we, an ancient people endowed with a glorious prophetic heritage, to say to a world in travail?

Max Nussbaum, "The Synagogue and the Refugee," Address at UAHC Convention, Detroit, MI. AJA, MS-705, Box 3, Folder 7

(2:) Since 1933 we have known – and the war has justified our predic-

---

21 A rather painful irony, in that the following year (September 1941–September 1942) would be the year in which systematic mass murder of European Jewry began to be implemented. Note that there is no suggestion in this text that America should be entering the war as an ally of Britain.

tion in a horrible way – that German Jewry, persecuted and forced by Hitler's hand to leave their homeland, have had no choice. They have come to the United States because it has been, besides Palestine, the only country in the world the gates of which have been open, and the only true haven of liberty and democracy. (3:) It is in the name of liberty and democracy that the Jews have suffered persecution torture and death since 1933, and that is why we, who daily enjoy the privileges of liberty and democracy, have the natural obligation to face the problem of the Refugee, in order to find constructive ways of help and assistance.

Mid-May, 1941

Eliezer Berkovits, "On a Strategy of Faith: After the British Debacle in Greece," United Hebrew Congregation, Leeds, England. *Between Yesterday and Tomorrow*, pp. 30–34[22]

(30:) In the last few weeks, this country sustained a number of military and political reverses. People went about with gloomy faces. They were disheartened by the long succession of defeats. ... I venture to assert that the reason why their uneasiness was so acute was that they thought in terms of military strategy alone, they thought only of bombers and tanks, of armies and generals, but were unable to judge events by the standard of a moral strategy....

(31:) Bearing in mind this principle of moral strategy, a strategy based on faith, I was not gloomy, I felt no real uneasiness at the disquieting military and political events of the last few weeks. On the contrary, I noted with a thrill of joy the first signs of a future of hope for mankind.

(32:) The world will not forget this.... For the first time, after many years of tragic disappointments (33:) during which Machiavellian heresies were current among men and nations, they have seen that

22 No date is provided for this sermon by Berkovits other than "Spring, 1941," and there is no reference to a Torah reading. The RAF Squadrons left Greece on April 25, and the final evacuation of British forces occurred on April 30, including the capture of some 8,000 imperial forces. Since the preacher refers to "the last few weeks," I would guess that it was delivered on Saturday, May 17.

a great nation was prepared to lose rather than to betray. In the field of moral strategy this is the first success of the cause of justice....

(34:) Let us learn the logic of Faith and the strategy of Faith, and the world will appear in an entirely new light; even disasters and catastrophes will point to a happier future and a new era of hope for all men and all nations.

May 23, 1941 (Friday evening)

Ferdinand M. Isserman, "How to Defeat Hitler: A Confirmation Sermon," Temple Israel, St. Louis, MO. AJA MS-6, Box 16 , Folder 1

(1:) Already Hitler is responsible for the uprooting of five million Jews in Europe, one-third of the world's Jewish population. These five million Jews were most of them respected and useful citizens of the countries in which they lived, supporting every civilized effort, advancing the cause of progress and of learning. Patriotic and upright, toiling and labouring for the flag under whose protection they lived, whose colors they loved and for whose glory they risked and shed their lives. This is true of all the Jewries of Europe now living either in the narrow confines of impossible twentieth-century ghettos, or like degraded criminals in concentration camps where the physical necessities of life are not furnished them, or harassed as free men who above their heads see the sword of Damocles hanging suspended by a slender thread, and who wonder when the darkness is to envelop them and the doom to descend upon them.

One of the most distinguished, Leon Blum, the former premier of France, now sits in a lonely dungeon. His captors fear to try him before the gaze of world public opinion.... (2:) Because of the strength of his spirit, he cannot be touched by the torture of his jailors.

Knowing this fine record of European Jewry, seeing its drab fate, witnessing the injustice which has become its lot because of Hitler's victories, we cannot but ask ourselves the question, "How can Hitler be defeated?"...

(7:) [The answer:] You can defeat him by the spiritual weapons of Israel. You can defeat Hitlerism by strengthening Judaism.... (8:) If you give yourselves to Judaism, you will defeat Hitlerism. You will save humanity from tyranny and war and thus you will save the children of Israel from persecution and hate....

June 1, 1941 (Shavu'ot)

HAROLD F. REINHART, "A Sermon to Confirmands," West London Synagogue. *Harold Reinhart, 1891–1969*, pp. 106–8

(106:) You reach this solemn moment in your personal lives in an hour grave and critical for Britain, for Israel [i.e., the Jewish people], and for the world. The mighty powers of earth are locked in a hideous embrace of total and relentless struggle to determine whether the world shall be given over to humanity or tyranny, justice or villainy, freedom or slavery, light or darkness. Your life's interest is focused on the war. The war is all about you. The war lays waste vast stretches of your mighty city....

(107:) The world war is a gigantic episode in a yet mightier struggle; the continuing human battle of truth and right against cruelty and deceit. The visible weapons of this world war are guns and planes and tanks and ships, munition plants, and all the mighty industrial structure which supports them. But there are other weapons too: the unseen weapons of thought and feeling, longing and indignation, resolve and faith. These spiritual weapons are the mightiest of all, in this war and in all the human struggle. Their manufacture cannot be controlled by decree, even with the aid of the cunningest manoeuvres of propaganda. Their arsenals are buried deep in the life of men and nations. They spring from the labour and the revelation of ages gone, and from the ideals and struggles of our own time....

June 25, 1941 (Wednesday)

JOSHUA LOTH LIEBMAN, "God and the World Crisis: Can We Still Believe in Providence," Address to CCAR Convention in Atlantic City, NJ. *CCAR Yearbook* 51 (1941), pp. 256–74; W. Gunther Plaut, *The Growth of Reform Judaism*, pp. 163–64

(268/163:) To assert that the Jews dying in concentration camps, the liberals standing before the firing squad, the adolescent soldiers perishing upon the blood-stained battlefield; to assert that every tragic loss of life of each individual is directly willed by the personal providence of God, may well be a glowing testimony to a faith which not even the mountains of sorrow can shake. Those who are able to achieve such unshaken confidence are among the blessed of the earth! Yet there is room in the religion of Israel for those who have a different interpretation of Providence.

June 28, 1941 (Saturday, *Koraḥ*)

Israel H. Levinthal, "The Rebellion of Korah: A Parallel to Events of Today," Brooklyn Jewish Center, Brooklyn, NY. *A New World Is Born*, pp. 82–87

(86:) Korah still lives, and has risen out of the darkness of hell to do his devilish work again. Change the name of Korah to Hitler, and all the biblical and rabbinic descriptions take on a living significance for our day. *Va yikach Hitler, Lokach Et Atzmo.*[23] Hitler took *himself* for this task of destruction. People ridiculed him and laughed at him for his attempt to win world leadership.... But ignorant though he undoubtedly was, *Pi-ke-ach Hayah,* he, like Korah, was shrewd, and intuitively he knew how to make the most of other people's weaknesses. And through the drawing power of words, he won to himself the leaders of hate and evil.

But it was the masses that he had to arouse if success was to be his. *Mah Ra'ah,* What did this modern Korah discover to help him turn his rebellion against civilization into a crusade? He discovered the *Parah Adumah*, the Red Heifer of our day![24] He saw in the red flag of Bolshevism the symbol that would turn the minds of men to his cause. Like the Red Heifer. So the red of Bolshevism was the symbol to be seized on by him and utilized to give to his impure heart and

---

23 Picking up a theme from earlier in the sermon, Levinthal writes that Rashi interprets the first words of the *parashah*, "Korah took" (Num. 16:1), which has no direct object, to mean that "he elected himself, pushed himself forward and made himself the leader of a movement to break down and destroy..." (p. 83).

24 Earlier in the sermon, Levinthal cites this rabbinic interpretation of Korah; he provides in a footnote the reference as "Midrash Peliah, ed. by Meier Yoel Vigadar (Jerusalem, 1926), p. 104."

intentions the aspect of purity and at the same time to defile and pollute the minds and hearts of innocent men and women who until then had endeavored to live in purity and wholesomeness.

And the old principle of the Red Heifer worked. The modern Korah appeared to the multitude as a veritable crusader; and even a large part of the Church looked upon (87:) him as a warrior for a holy cause. And when he had achieved his purpose, when he had succeeded in blinding the eyes of vast masses of people, he made the Red Heifer his own ally, and for a while he appeared to be successful in blinding Russia herself to his nefarious purpose.

But now, suddenly, he finds himself losing ground. Victory is too slow in coming. The people are beginning to become disillusioned. Once again, he finds the need of purifying his devilish intent. Once more he must wrap himself in the garb all of purple. And again he sees the Red Heifer. Now the attack against Russia assumes a sacred aspect, and ignorant minds and polluted souls, that glory in their ignorance and pollution, are once more convinced that this modern Korah is a modern Messiah fighting to destroy the red banner of the Bolsheviks.[25]

What will be the end of this struggle? – you ask. I believe that the words of the Sage Resh Lakish, will be verified also today, *Lokach Mekach Ra Le'atzmo*, that this time Hitler "struck a bad bargain for himself," and that this attack upon Russia will be his undoing. The conclusion of the old biblical story will yet come to pass. The jaws of hell will open up to swallow not only this modern Korah, but all his associates – the fascists of all lands – and the words of Rabbi Akiba will be fulfilled: "The cohorts of Korah shall not rise again." All of them, the entire group of Hitler's monsters, shall never again rise to life, and then, we hope, democracy and freedom shall come to bless the lives of all peoples and all men!

Solomon N. Bazell, "American Judaism and the World Crisis," Conference Sermon to CCAR Convention in Atlantic City, NJ. *CCAR Yearbook* 51 (1941), pp. 232–46

---

25 "Operation Barbarosa," the German attack on the Soviet Union, began on June 21, 1941, one week before this sermon was delivered.

(244:) The far-sightedness that sensed forty years ago that the hegemony of Jewish life would reside in America did not however anticipate the horrendous destruction of the Jewish centers which survived even the first World War. The dislocation of entire Jewish populations, the rapine assault on Jewish life, Jewish nativity, and Jewish expression, the almost complete extirpation of Judaism and Jewry on the European continent, can lead few if any to believe that with the end of hostilities – even with an allied victory – European Jewry will be capable of re-establishing the position it held these many centuries.

July 26, 1941 (Saturday)

Eliezer Berkovits, "Because of Our Sins?," United Hebrew Congregation, Leeds, England. *Between Yesterday and Tomorrow*, pp. 78–84; see Complete Sermons

Kalonymus Kalmish Shapira, Warsaw Ghetto. *Esh Kodesh*, pp. 106–7; *Derashot meShenot haZa'am*, p. 175; Polen, *Holy Fire*, pp. 111–12, translated by Nehemia Polen

[Theme is birth pangs of the Messiah] (112:) God states in Scripture, "Shall I labor and not give birth?" (Isa. 66:9). This means that God labors and gives birth by means of Israel. So it is that Israel suffers birth pangs and experiences the annihilation of part of its energies, and thereby gives birth to the light of the Messiah.

August 9(?), 1941 (Saturday)[26]

Harry Joshua Stern, "The Jews, the War and the Future," Temple Emanu-El, Montreal. *The Jewish Spirit Triumphant*, pp. 167–72

Habakkuk (selected verses 1:2–2:3), (168:) One finds these readings from Habakkuk so contemporary! These verses, with little imagination on our part, can well match the daily newspaper accounts

26 Stern's sermons are printed without dates; my choice of this date is based on the preacher's reference to Eden's 5-point program, announced August 6, in newspapers August 7, "but a few days ago" (p. 170).

of the Nazi invasion of European lands. And we, too, like unto the prophet of yore, ask the question, "How long, O Lord, how long?"

(169:) Is not this war the result of the lack of morality among nations? All the nations had a hand in it. As a result of the last world war an instrument was brought into existence by which to establish international order, namely, the League of Nations. But most nations overthrew the responsibility which the League Covenant invoked upon them. The United States, which in main gave birth to the idea of the League from the start, abandoned it soon after....

(170:) Now where does the Jew stand in this conflict? He, the historic scapegoat in this latest catastrophe that has befallen the human race, was the first victim. Hitler began the war against civilization by ruthlessly attacking the Jew. The Jew has long been the bearer of the blueprint of a moral order. When man rebels against morals it is self-evident that the historic bearer of the moral law must suffer. Thus over five million Jews are now enslaved by the Nazis.[27] Theirs is a double suffering as citizens of the responsive conquered lands and as Jews.

(171:) At the moment we are naturally agitated by Nazi invasion Eastward. Will the Nazi barbarians succeed in desecrating Holy Jerusalem even as they have defiled the historic Acropolis? We pray that it may not be! How our hearts do yearn that the Palestinian settlements built up through toil, sweat and tears may be spared from the filthy claws of the Nazi beasts. Will the Jews of Palestine, 555,000 gathered in recent years from the ends of the earth, will these suffer the fate of the Armenians who were massacred in the last war?

The British, perhaps for good reason, have not fully armed the Jews of Palestine. It all has to do with preventing Arab resentment! But there stands Jewish Palestine for the most part defenseless, begging that it be given the tools for self-defense and above (172:) all for the defense of the Empire. We have the hope that the Jews of Palestine will not be left abandoned!

---

27 This follows after the invasion of the USSR. The sermon was delivered after the *Einsatzgruppen* massacres of Jews in territories previously occupied by the USSR had begun, although the first scattered news reports of this mass murder were just beginning to appear in the West in August 1941.

August 16, 1941 (Saturday, the Sabbath after the publication of the Atlantic Charter)

Eliezer Berkovits, "In the Margin of the Atlantic Charter," United Hebrew Congregation, Leeds, England. *Between Yesterday and Tomorrow*, pp. 56–61

(58:) Jews are systematically forgotten. We have suffered most in the present world catastrophe; our lives and our rights were the first to be sold in those shameful years when great nations bought peace by sacrificing the weak and powerless. (59:) European Jewries will probably never recover from the blows which they have sustained. But so far, not a single responsible word has been uttered on the subject of what is to happen after the war to the millions of homeless, uprooted, and broken Jews in Europe.

(60:) No doubt, we shall again be decorated with a festoon of minority treaties. But it may easily happen that the future New World will not want to know that we are Jews, that we are a nation, and that a nation must have a home....

Kalonymos Kalmish Shapira, Warsaw Ghetto. *Esh Kodesh*, pp. 112–13; *Derashot meShenot haZa'am*, pp. 207–12; Henry Abramson, "Metaphysical Nationality in the Warsaw Ghetto," p. 165

Who is unmoved, seeing the extent of Jewish suffering today both physical and spiritual? Who cannot become depressed, seeing that there are no primary schools, and no *yeshivot*, no places of Torah study and no gatherings of Torah study? The destruction of the houses of God not only affects our current situation, but has dire meaning for the future. We will have lost the young men who study Torah. Some of them have been lost to horrific deaths and starvation, may the Merciful One rescue us, and some of them have been compelled to go out and search for food. Where will we find young men to learn Torah if they are not learning now? Some of them could not withstand the test, and went out on the Sabbath to the market, transacting business due to their hunger.... Are these the boys who will one day return to the schools and *yeshivot* as in former times?

August 23, 1941 (Saturday)

Abraham Cohen, "The Worship of Molech," Birmingham Hebrew Congregation, Birmingham, England. Unpublished, David Cohen Private Collection

(3:) There is accordingly a remarkably close parallel to be discerned between the position of Israel which I have just described[28] and the position of the nations of the world to-day.... With the fuller knowledge and clearer understanding which we now have of what (4:) led up to this war, we may compare the Allied Forces to the Israelites, and the enemy to the heathen inhabitants of Canaan. It is no exaggeration to assert that the Nazi tyrants proved themselves to be among the worst Molech-worshippers that ever trod the earth. Mesha, king of Moab, at least sacrificed his own son to gain his ambition (cf. 2 Kings 3:27); these heartless despots were prepared to sacrifice many millions of other persons' lives for the fulfilment of their dream to become the rulers of Europe and beyond. The brutality of the old Roman Empire and Oriental autocrats pales into insignificance in comparison with the blood-lust of these monsters in human form....

As with Israel of old, so with the peoples recently arrayed against Nazism; the purpose of victory must be the utter destruction of pagan worship....

(6:) "A war to end war," "Never again," "the destruction of the military machine" – we heard those phrases then just as frequently as we hear them now. I must have had my doubts whether these purposes would be achieved, because, looking through a sermon I preached in 1917, I came across this passage:

> Not the crushing of Germany and the perpetuation of the evil which brought this war into being should be the aim; for in that case all this precious blood will have been spilt in vain. What must be crushed is the survival of barbaric methods which have brought disaster upon the world. Merely to replace one

28 Based on Deut. 12:29–31.

> self-hypnotized War Lord by another is to prepare for another European war.

What I felt a quarter of a century ago I feel with equal intensity today. If we are to have a real peace this time, the goal of our struggle must not be obscured when the fighting is over, as happened last time....

(7:) A week ago a ray of light illuminated the world which has been plunged into darkness. The proclamation issued by the two greatest statesmen of our time – the Prime Minister of this country and the President of the United States – may indeed prove to be a turning-point in human affairs....[29]

September 7, 1941 (Sunday, Day of Intercession, following *Ki Teitzei*, Amalek)

Joseph H. Hertz, "The Great Synagogue Will Rise Again," Intercession Service held in the ruins of the Great Synagogue, Duke's Place, London. *Early and Late*, pp. 66–70[30]

(67:) Its barbarous destruction is, alas, a symbol of the unparalleled Jewish tragedy that started in 1933. Think of the many hundreds of synagogues that were dynamited and burnt on 10th November, 1938; and of the widespread destruction of Jewish houses of worship throughout Poland and other lands under the swastika, that has been the order of the day since the outbreak of hostilities. They are part of the systematic obliteration of Judaism and the total expulsion of the Jew from Europe that are the aims of Nazi policy, aims and policy preluded by the open harrying of the entire Jewish population with a ruthlessness that has appalled the world.... "

[Amalek] was devoid of the fundamental decency towards (68:) the weak and the helpless that constitutes the humanity of man. The same judgment must be passed on Amalek and its latest spiritual descendant: he fears not God; he closes the gates of mercy on those

---

29 Referring, of course, to the Atlantic Charter, issued on August 14, 1941.

30 See the reference to this by Louis I. Newman of New York in his Rosh Hashanah sermon, below, September 21, 1941.

who cannot resist his heathen might. His resolve is the establishment of a jungle society in which hundreds of millions of robots are to slave for a "master people" with hearts of stone. Lovers of freedom the world over now clearly understand that the moral danger which an Axis victory would bring with it is not confined to the Jew or Judaism, but that it spells death to the sacred heritage of man, and end to all man's hope for the future.[31]

Eliezer Berkovits, "Triumph of the Spirit," United Hebrew Congregation, Leeds, England. *Between Yesterday and Tomorrow*, pp. 51–55[32]

(53:) In the dark winter months [of 1940–1941] that followed, when the bomber was roaming through the skies of Britain, we, let us confess it to-day, often wavered in our faith. We often asked ourselves how long can man endure all this, how long can man of flesh and blood stand up to such incredible trials. One single raid night appeared to last eternities, and this went on night after night, for weeks and months, and still there was no end in sight. A general breakdown of human endurance seemed a very near possibility and with it everything would have been lost.

But a miracle happened.... Steel and iron, high explosive and fire, had been defeated by human hearts of flesh and blood.

One of the greatest miracles in the history of mankind happened before our own eyes. With our own eyes we could see it: the Spirit of God in the hearts of men, conquering, defeating might and power.

(55:) [Prayers for various groups]. Let us remember the heartrending sufferings to which our own Jewish nation is being subjected in all the lands that are now being devastated by the hordes of the barbarians. Not even brotherly greetings, no signs of brotherly love, can reach them from us. They are alone in their sorrow. May God be with them. May He protect them.

---

31 On this use of Amalek by Hertz in the broader context of Jewish discourse on Amalek, see Elliott Horowitz, *Reckless Rites*, chap. 5, esp. p. 143.

32 An extract from this sermon was published in Christiane d'Haussy, ed., *English Sermons: Mirror of Society*, pp. 117–18.

September 13, 1941 (Saturday)

Louis I. Newman, "The Penitential Prayers (Selihot)," Congregation Rodeph Sholom, New York. *Sermons and Addresses*, vol. 4, pp. 74–80

(78:) Perhaps you have seen the recent statement authorized by Pastor Niemoeller, who for four years has been imprisoned by Hitler. The Protestant martyr narrates the story of the diatribes of Hitler, the arch-protagonist of military preparedness, against the Christianity which Niemoeller, though himself a soldier in the First World War, espouses. "You are Jew-infested," shrieked the Fuehrer. "Your Christianity, after all, is nothing but a stepchild of Jewry, grown soft and infested with those stupid humanitarian illusions."

Niemoeller replied: "I have deserted only to Christianity – to my faith – and I am willing to take upon myself all the suffering it involves." And Niemoeller sends forth this message: "During the last four years of my imprisonment, I have never had any cause for regret. As long as I have my cell where I can pray, I am still happier than Hitler, the promise-breaker and incorrigible liar, who hardly dares to go out alone for fear that a bullet might hit him from behind. To the people the world over, I send this message: 'Keep the faith.'"

Niemoeller and others like him, by sheer spiritual authority, are combatting the vast forces of destruction which employ for their diabolical purposes the material of war. Hitler may have prepared for world domination by his air-force, his armies, and his Fifth Column, but Niemoeller and his collaborators are preparing for the triumph of righteousness by solely spiritual weapons. "I am aware," says Pastor Niemoeller, whose story has been so ably portrayed on the screen by the film "Pastor Hall," "that this publication will only make my situation worse, but I consider it my religious duty to tell the world the truth of Hitler's opinion of Christianity, and what he aims to do about it the world over."[33]

---

33 "Pastor Hall," based on a play by the same name by the German emigrant Ernst Toller, was a British film produced in the US by United Artists. A review of the film by the critic Bosley Crowther, published in the *NYT* on September 21, 1940, includes the sentence, "But not until 'Pastor Hall' opened last night at the Globe has any film come so close to the naked spiritual issues involved in the present conflict or

Kalonymus Kalmish Shapira, Warsaw Ghetto. *Esh Kodesh*, p. 117; *Derashot meShenot haZa'am*, p. 215; Polen, *Holy Fire*, p. 40, translated by Nehemia Polen

We see now that we do not feel each pain and sorrow to the extent that we once felt even little irritations. If, indeed, we were now to feel all the pain inherent in the tragic situation with the sensitivity and severity we once felt, it would not be possible to exist for even one day. The straightforward explanation for this is, as the Rabbis say, "The decayed flesh of a living person does not feel the knife."[34] The only thing we feel is that our selfhood is trampled; the world has turned dark for us; there is no day, no night, just turmoil and confusion. It seems as if the whole world lies upon us, pressing down and crushing, to the breaking point…so we do not feel the particularity of each tragedy in accordance with its true dimensions.

September 14, 1941 (Sunday, first day of *Seliḥot*)

Moses Kahlenberg, "That We May Refrain from the Oppression Done with Our Hands,"[35] La Lande Internment Camp, France. *Yedei Moshe*, pp. 151–63, translated by MS

(151:) Experience has taught the meaning of the precious word of God in our own time…as we see (152:) with our own eyes and heartfelt anguish thousands of synagogues with their altars totally demolished, in fulfillment of the biblical statement, "I will destroy your altars" (Lev. 26:30). But the word of G-d will be established forever (Isa. 40:8)….

---

presented them in terms so moving." I have not been able to find a source for the full statement attributed to Niemoeller, or for any significant phrase in it. There is no reference to this statement in the biography by James Bentley, *Martin Niemöller, 1892–1984*. The closest in content, though not in wording, is the article entitled "Niemoeller Speaks," by Leo Stein, published by *The National Jewish Monthly*, May 1941, pp. 284–85, 301–2, http://bit.ly/2vLMc4W. Cf. also below, Sept. 21, 1941, Samuel S. Cohen.

34 b. Shabbat 13b. I am grateful to Nehemia Polen for identifying this quotation.

35 The title of the sermon is taken from the *Ne'ilah* liturgy in the final worship service of Yom Kippur. It is cited near the very end of the sermon with a warning to the listeners to be careful about their behavior (p. 163).

(161:) Now moving on to the matter of the vineyards.[36] I set before you a full biblical verse: "When you enter another man's vineyard, you may eat as many grapes as you want, until you are full, but you must not put any in your receptacle" (Deut. 23:25). The rabbis explained this to apply to a laborer, who urgently requires the food, and is therefore permitted to eat the fruit he has been working on.[37] But it is forbidden for another man, or for a child, to come to a vineyard or to an orchard or a field belonging to someone else, even one's neighbor, and to pick or gather any fruit of the orchard and eat it or place it in a receptacle: that would be a clear case of robbery. More than this, since it is impossible for the owner of the field always to be standing on his property to guard it, whoever takes something from that property is punished more severely by the government than for other kinds of theft. This lesson should be distilled as the dew in the hearts of our children, so that it will make a permanent impression, (162:) in accordance with the verse "Train a child in the way he should go" (Prov. 22:6)....

Our times are not like earlier ages. We are living in a time of war, a time when people are nasty to each other, when a person's sword is turned against his neighbor, when there is no law and no judge to administer it. This is especially true with regard to the Jewish people: without utterance, without words, libels are concocted against our fellow Jews and lives are endangered, heaven help us! Since all Jews are responsible for each other, the entire people are blamed for the sins of an individual. Even if a misdeed is determined to have been committed by a child, who has no legal responsibility, the parents and the entire community is held to be responsible.... Thus it is incumbent upon us to be extremely careful, and to warn our children, lest they (163:) do something vile or evil, heaven forbid, by taking something from the vineyards and orchards that are nearby, not even fruit that has fallen to the ground, for their lives may be endangered.

36 The problem of hungry Jewish interns (including children), before the perimeters of the camp were sealed off, taking fruit from neighboring farms, was considered serious by the leadership of the camp, as it apparently became a source of hostility and anger among the farmers.

37 b. Bava Metzi'a 87b.

In addition to the prohibition of robbery and of theft, it is a matter of endangering the reputation of the entire Jewish community.

Gavriel Gestetner, Szombathely, Hungary, in Esther Farbstein, *Hidden in the Heights*, vol. 1, p. 146, citing Gestetner, *Siftei Gavriel*, p. 146, translated by Deborah Stern

You are present today... you and not our brethren who have been driven out, scattered in the forests and fields without food or sustenance. The words of Jeremiah the prophet in Lamentations, "Better were those slain by the sword than those slain by hunger" (Lam. 4:9), have been fulfilled in us due to our many sins. How many of our brethren have actually died of hunger and thirst, lack of clothing, and so on? There is no end to our troubles.... They are our brethren, driven out into forests and fields and eating the grass of the earth there like beasts due to hunger. We must shout out about this: "Master of the world, is this what the comparison of the Israelites to animals – 'a lion cub is Judah' (Gen. 49:9) – means? That we should really (Heaven forbid) be like animals, 'the eldest of his herd, glory is his' (Deut. 33:17), and so on? That we should really (Heaven forbid) be like animals?"

September 21, 1941 (Erev Rosh Hashanah)

Louis L. Mann, "Where Now Is Thy God?," Sinai Congregation, Chicago, IL. *A Set of Holiday Sermons* 5702/1941, pp. 4–13

4:) I doubt whether Jews have ever faced a Rosh Hashono with hearts more contrite and spirits more humble.... It is the first time that persecution, expulsion, and crucifixion have become well-nigh universal.... Some of my friends... have said plainly, "I pity you having to preach this year. Haven't the events of the last years shaken your faith?"... Since Germany is clearly in the wrong, why should she conquer a dozen or more countries with a population of one hundred and fifty million and add six hundred thousand square miles of territory? Why should millions be haunted, hounded, and harried, forced from one country to another until the thought of death seems sweet? Why should the innocent be robbed, pillaged, plundered and dispossessed?...

(8:) As long as the force of faith is brutally transformed into faith in force, as long as the free spirit of man is ruthlessly regimented for purposes of national conquests, as long as the supreme object of man's devotion is the state and not God, as long as we "sow the wind will we reap the whirlwind" (Hos. 8:7), and the ancient faith will reveal its somber verification and its tragic vindication due not to the abdication of God but to the willful and wanton neglect of man.

Louis I. Newman "Glimpses of the Divine," Congregation Rodeph Sholom, New York. *Sermons and* Addresses, vol. 4, pp. 171–77

(175:) A touching scene has recently been enacted in war-battered London. Standing under the open sky, amid the ruins of what was for 250 years their most venerated place of worship, London Jews heard their Chief Rabbi, Joseph H. Hertz, conduct services marking British Jewry's participation in the National Day of Prayer, on the second anniversary of the outbreak of the war. The demolished walls of the Great Synagogue, destroyed by Nazi bombardment last year, could not hold all the people who responded to the Chief Rabbi's call for victory....[38]

Samuel S. Cohon, "The Battle for the Jewish Mind," Temple Emanu-El, Birmingham, AL. AJA MS-276, Box 16, Folder 4

Isa. 43:1; (2:) What calamities have befallen the nations during the past few years! One proud land after another has been brought down under the booted foot of the savage conquerors. Peace-loving peoples – every one of them concerned with its own affairs, tending its own fields, and cultivating its own commerce and industry – all have been beaten, overrun, and plundered. Each of them hoped to avoid war; each was ready to make concessions; each relied upon the solemn promises and assurances of the aggressor. To avoid giving offence to the Nazis, they refused to band together for mutual defense. (3:) Nonetheless, the Nazi monsters struck them down one by one. Austria, Czechoslovakia, Poland, Norway, Holland, Belgium,

38 See above, September 7, 1941, Joseph H. Hertz.

Jugoslavia, and Greece have been turned into shambles. Ruin, devastation, famine, and disease stalk these lands. Even the allies of the Nazis – Italy, Romania, Hungary, Finland, and Bulgaria – now lie in the grip of terror and mortal dread....

(5:) These lessons must not be lost upon the American people. Insidious attempts are being made to divide our people and to fill them with unfounded fears and suspicions. For reasons best known to themselves, certain men have been endeavoring to paralyze the will of the Americans, to persuade them that the Nazis are invincible and that it is dangerous for us to help Britain in her hour of greatest peril. Ready to turn the world over to Hitler domination, they would have us isolate ourselves from all the democratic elements that are fighting to maintain their right to live as free men. In the name of "America First," they have been sowing dissention among our people and distrust in the government.[39] Some of them have injected racial and religious issues, to promote their short-sighted policy that can benefit only the Nazis. If the battle for America, which Hitler has already initiated, is not to be ignominiously lost by us, we must cleanse ourselves of the poison of division among the different elements of the country and resolve to stand by the government in its efforts to preserve the integrity of the United States.

In their scheme to dominate the globe, the Nazis have made the Jew the first target of their attacks. With diabolical cunning, they singled out the Jew as their "indispensable scapegoat." They represented him as the cause of mankind's ills, who, in league with the Communists, plots to enslave the (6:) world.... With the outbreak of the war, the Jews served the additional purpose of being charged with instigating the slaughter. Hitler himself and his spokesmen in this and in other lands repeatedly point to the Jews as the warmongers. The supposed war aim of the Axis is to destroy the Jewish-Bolshevist-Democratic world-power....

(7:) It is becoming steadily more evident to thinking men and

39 On the anti-interventionist "America First Committee," of which Charles Lindbergh was an active member and leading spokesman, see Wayne S. Cole, *America First: The Battle Against Intervention*.

women that the anti-Jewish measures in Germany and the anti-Jewish agitation in other parts of the world are but the means which the Nazis use to divide the people and to prepare them for destruction.... Jew-hatred operates to break the wall of the inner unity of the nation, and thus to destroy its will to resist Nazi aggression.[40]

While the war in Europe is officially only in its third year, the battle against the Jews has been waged unrelentingly ever since the beginning of the Nazi regime, nine years ago.... The war has been waged for the purpose of destroying the Jews economically and physically; to a still greater degree have the Nazis waged a battle for the Jewish mind, to destroy Jewish creativity, (8:) to eradicate Jewish influence. Their very fight on Christianity, both Catholic and Protestant, purposes to remove the Jewish spirit which underlies much of Christian teaching. The Nazis mean to destroy Jewish morale and to crush the Jewish will to resist. That they have succeeded in achieving much of their purpose is a sad reality. They have created Jewish jitters....

(9:) Our immediate situation is the hardest that we have experienced in centuries. Seventy-five percent of our brethren are either under Nazi power or within its shadow. But taking a larger view of our condition, in the light of history, we gather hope. From his confinement in the concentration camp, the heroic Pastor Niemoeller issued an indictment of the head of the German Reich as the enemy of all religion, and appealed to his fellow Christians to "keep the faith" (*Liberty*, Sept. 20, 1941).[41] For us, too, this is the call of religion.

To the crushed and broken remnants of his people, Isaiah called, "Fear not, O Israel, for I have redeemed thee." We must not permit the paralysis of despair to creep over us. The thousands of years of our history teach us that time and again we have outlived our persecutors. Let us take heart. Though storms rage, the sun will shine again upon a chastened world. The embattled British sing: "There'll always be an England." We are just as certain that there will always be a Jewry!

40 Like many other Jewish contemporaries, Cohon presents Nazi antisemitism as a utilitarian means to an end, not the ultimate goal of the Nazi leadership.

41 Referring to an article entitled, "What Hitler Told Me About Christianity," by Niemoeller, "as told to Dr. Leo Stein." See above, Sept. 13, 1941, Louis I. Newman.

(10:) We must translate our confidence in the ultimate victory of right and truth by giving whole-hearted support to our country and its government in her struggle to maintain our free institutions and our democratic way of life. We must also stretch out a helping hand to our brethren and to other sufferers of Nazi tyranny. Let us do our duty, and wait for the salvation of God.[42]

Leo M. Franklin, "The Day of Opportunity," Temple Beth-El, Detroit, MI. Unpublished, Rabbi Leo Morris Franklin Archives, now at AJA, MS-246

(8:) We [the American people] shall go forward and fulfill our missions as the sponsors and the protectors of ideals of freedom and democracy and peace.

Of course, [as Jews] we have been called upon, as never before, to give without stint to the millions of brethren abroad, who have been plundered and pillaged, robbed and beaten and reduced to the status of beasts. Let me emphasize, however, that whatsoever we have done for these, our brethren, has not been over-much. To give it all to them has been a sanctified privilege. The finger of shame should be pointed at them who have whined at the sacrifices, if any, that they have been called upon to make; let them remember that their homes and ours have not been entered by marauding hosts; their women and children and ours have not been despoiled by moronic demons; their synagogues and ours have not been ruthlessly destroyed; their Torah and ours has not been desecrated; life for us and for them [the complainers] has been a very Paradise, as compared to the hell in which millions of our brethren have been compelled to eke out their miserable existence....

In the holocaust that has consumed Europe, thousands of our people vomited out by the lands that they had helped to make great, have sought a haven here. Their story will go down the centuries as one of the great epics of all time. Such heroism as was theirs, such courage and fortitude (9:) they manifest, no other people and no

42 Note that at this point, two years into the war, and despite the entry of the Soviet Union as an enemy of the Reich, there is still no explicit support for America to join the battle against Nazi Germany.

other age has ever known. In the course of their wanderings many of them perished of starvation, and some found graves in the sea. Some thousands, it is true, were fortunate enough, after untold suffering, to reach the land of their fathers, the so-called Holy Land, and yet others, more blessed than all the rest, have landed on the shores of this, our country.... [J]ust as the United States shall in the line of destiny become the cultural and spiritual center of a new world, so inevitably shall this country become the (10:) center of Jewish life and activity in the years immediately before us.... I am convinced that for the Jew in America a great day is about to dawn....

Ferdinand M. Isserman, "The Wave of the Future," Temple Israel, St. Louis, MO. AJA, MS-6, Box 16, Folder 2[43]

(1:) Our lives are headed for turbulent waters. Tempests and storms loom ahead on the horizon. As we look back on the past year and think of the calamity that has befallen peaceful nations, and the double calamity which has overtaken their Jewish inhabitants, we cannot but pray a bit more fervently and cannot but be a little more concerned. Last year Yugo-Slavia was free. Last year, Greece was free. Last year, the residents of Bessarabia, of Bucovina, of the Ukraine, of Lithuania, Latvia, were comparatively free. Nation after nation, and Jewish community after Jewish community, have been destroyed. Nazi armies seem to have marched first into those areas of Europe where lived our co-religionists and they have felt the double sting of his [*sic*] malicious fury. No one knows how many Jews fell in the armies opposing Naziism, fighting courageously and heroically. No one knows how many Jews died the death of martyrs and felt the glow of "Kiddush Hashem," that by their death they were sanctifying the name of God....

Harry Joshua Stern, "Where is Thy God?," Temple Emanu-El, Montreal. *The Jewish Spirit Triumphant*, pp. 46–51

(46:) But, on Rosh Hashanah 5702, amidst a world in convulsion, a

43 This Rosh Hashanah sermon is largely the same as a sermon delivered on June 8, 1941 by Isserman at the Baccalaureate Services held in the Brewer Field House of the University of Missouri, Columbia, MO. AJA, MS-6, Box 16, Folder 1.

world reeking and shrieking with appalling horror, men everywhere do ask, "Where is God?" Only the feeble-minded can truly refrain from such questioning when now twenty-five lands are engaged in the most savage and cruel war of all time, that is characterized by its scientific methods of human slaughter and destruction....

(47:) It is men, not God, who make wars. Why blame God?...

(48:) For years the best of nations closed their eyes to the evil of Nazism, and evil force, indeed, and permitted it to grow strong. How they pampered it! That evil beast which pounced upon weak Israel first has now turned upon the nations who have nurtured it, and is tearing the world asunder. Violation of God's law leads to disaster. Where is God? God is where he always was, omnipresent and eternal. His laws exist but it is for us to fulfill them.

Maurice N. Eisendrath, "Blackout: How Long, O Lord, How Long?," Holy Blossom Synagogue, Toronto. *Holy Blossom Pulpit*, XI, 4, in *Jewish Preaching in Times of War*, pp. 419–41

(422:) For almost a decade now we have poured forth our vilest curses upon the Nazi regime. When the moment struck, however, to send forth our sons and to pour out our means actually to strike these tyrants low, we continued, on the whole, with business as usual, devoting to the herculean challenge of war only the spare hours left over from our habitual foibles and fripperies.... (423:) Not yet has this continent, nor even the whole of Jewry, awakened to the full realization of the genuine blackout that has descended physically over so many lands and spiritually over the entire earth....

September 22, 1941 (first day of Rosh Hashanah)

Abraham M. Hershman, "Our Allies," Congregation Shaarey Zedek, Detroit, MI. *Israel's Fate and Faith*, pp. 51–54

(51:) These are judgment days for the world at large and for us Jews in particular. Nearly everywhere in Europe, Israel is encircled by mighty hosts bent on his destruction. From our hearts too is wrung the anxious questions, "How shall we do?" "Will Israel survive?" To us too comes the comforting answer, "Fear not."

(52:) Rosh Hashanah bids us take a long-range view of world affairs. All our sympathies are with the democratic nations. Their war is our war; their cause is our cause; their victory is our victory. Yet it would be preposterous to maintain that the leaders of most of those nations come into court with clean hands....[44]

Israel H. Levinthal, "Is It Death or Rebirth of the World That We Behold?," Brooklyn Jewish Center, Brooklyn, NY. *A New World Is Born*, pp. 7–14

(7:) What is the significance of these cataclysmic events which have shaken our world from its foundations? What is the meaning of this war which has been forced upon the world, and which is dragging nation after nation into its bloody net? There is a passage in the Talmud which I wish to interpret for you because I believe that it offers us in concise and clear fashion a striking analysis of what we behold today.... "There are three voices, or sounds, that resound throughout the whole world, from one end to the other: the sound of the revolution of the sun, the sound of the tumultuous hosts of Rome, and the sound of the soul departing from the body..." (b. Yoma 20b).

(9:) It is not only upon the Jew that this darkness has come.... There is darkness everywhere. There is not a spot in all the world where there is undisturbed, undiminished light and sunshine. It is a blackout of civilization which threatens us.

(10:) We, too, hear today the sound of the soul as it departs from the bodies of men. I am not speaking now of the agonizing cry of the millions of souls that have departed on the battle-field or in bomb-stricken lands of Europe – cries that today are heard in every part of the world. It is the Soul of the World that is departing! Herein lies the real danger of the Nazi revolution. Its aim is the destruction of the Soul of Humanity – the breeding of a new kind of world, where hate and torture, cruelty and barbarism, shall be the norms of everyday life, where (11:) deceit and robbery, violence and falsehood, shall be the mark of the new world order!...(11:) [N]o enemy of former days made cruelty the fine art as do the Nazis today....

44 He continues by specifying failures of England and France with regard to Czechoslovakia, Ethiopia, and Manchuria.

(12:) America, too, thank God, is determined that for once these *Reshaim*, these forces of darkness and evil, shall be destroyed forever, so that Democracy's triumph may mark a new *Kol Ledah* [the sound of birth] for all mankind. And for us Jews there is also the sound of birth.... (13:) The remarkable spirit that is today displayed by the half million Jews in *Eretz Israel* is the living proclamation to all the world that the Jew, too, is hearing the *Kol Ledah!*...

I know that it is not an easy task to hold high this light of faith in the midst of the black night that has come upon the world. I know that many are in despair and feel that the end has come, the end to all men's striving for a better day. To all who see only the dark horizon, I would recall a simple but beautiful tale that the Rabbis in the Talmud tell of Adam....[45]

Louis I. Newman, "The Merit of the Fathers," Congregation Rodeph Sholom, New York. *Sermons and Addresses*, 4: 139–46

(145:) We are preparing ourselves for the exigencies of war, in the event that it comes to the shores of our nation. Our sons are being called into uniform, and may be summoned to face immeasurable perils. Perhaps God has it in His intention to deal with us as He did with Abraham.... Let us think of the ram today as being the *materiel*, the supplies, the tanks, guns, planes and other equipment being sent overseas to battle the Satan....

But if we are not to be spared the bloody and the fiery ordeal, let us take courage from the example of our forefathers.... In the long and endless annals of humanity much grief will yet be the portion of the children of men. God will not allow any generation to escape lightly the burdens of life in His universe....

Harold I. Saperstein, "Undying Fires," Temple Emanu-El of Lynbrook, NY. *Witness from the Pulpit*, pp. 83–89

(84:) How much harder it is to know what to say now that two years of bitter struggle have passed. During this period, the war has

45 Levinthal proceeds to recount the story of Adam's despair following the darkness after the first sunset and his joy when the sun arose in the morning; his reference in the accompanying note is to Talmud Yerushalmi, Avodah Zarah 1:3 (39c).

steadily spread over ever vaster areas. One nation after another has been dragged into its vortex. Today, while we listen to the Shofar here, across the sea, people's ears are alert for the sound of air-raid sirens. While we are gathered in synagogues, at the Russian border, millions of men are engaged in desperate conflict on a battlefront spreading over thousands of miles, a titanic struggle which leaves behind only the bodies of the dead and wounded and a scorched earth of utter destruction.

Now our own nation stands on the verge, and the events of any day may hurl us into active participation in this war, from which we have already recognized we cannot consider ourselves as isolated. During these two years, I, like many of my colleagues of all faiths, have had to search my heart, to reconcile conflicting ideals, to revise opinions which could be given up only after soul-searching struggle.

But if all religious leaders find difficulty in knowing what to say, it is doubly difficult for a Jew. As always, our people have suffered in a two-fold capacity: as Jews, and as inhabitants of war ridden countries. Their treatment wherever the Nazis have come - in Germany, Austria, Poland, Czechoslovakia, France, and the invaded portions of Russia - is a story of sheer barbarism for which there is hardly a parallel in all human history. In addition, as in the last war, the great masses of European Jewry are trapped in the no-man's land (85:) between the German and Russian armies, and as the conflict rages, it is over their communities that the great rival war machines sweep back and forth....

(86:) Why have we suffered, why must we suffer? Because humanity has not yet extricated itself from the morass of barbarism....

(87:) Here we find another indication of hope at the dawn of the New Year: the moral awakening of the nations. When the Nazi regime first came to power, the Jew stood alone... We called out desperately to the world.... But there was no one to heed our cry. Aside for a few Christian liberals, the conscience of humanity remained undisturbed....

Today the situation has changed. The democratic nations at last realize what is at stake, and they are facing reality with stubborn determination and unparalleled (88:) heroism. Despite what

American Quislings may say, President Roosevelt spoke the mind of America last week when he took the step which cleared the mist and gave us one clear-cut national purpose: to see that Hitler and his principles are not victorious in the world....[46]

Eliezer Berkovits, "A Way To Judaism," United Hebrew Congregation, Leeds, England. *Yesterday and Tomorrow*, pp. 100–5

(101:) What are these "Sounds" [as might awaken the hearts and minds of men]?: To-day they are the mighty sounding of the voice of History, the voice of God speaking to us through tremendous historic happenings. All the disappointments of men, all the tragedies, the terrible (102:) sufferings of the last few years, they are God's own "Trumpets" calling us; forcibly opening ears that did not want to hear.

Surely, in the last few years History has been a terrible but efficient schoolmaster.... In the last few years, History has taught us that the world never forgets. And whenever Jews or Jewries think they have, at last, safely escaped Jewish destiny, the world ferrets them out from the artificial anonymity, pointing with the finger at them, at the Jew. Think of French Jewry. If there ever was a Jewry without Jewish memories, if ever Jews succeeded in wiping (103:) out their past, it was they. To-day, they are on their tragic way back into the Ghetto again. The whole world is aware of the Jew as never before, because the Jew wanted to forget and make others forget him.

Kalonymus Kalmish Shapira, Warsaw Ghetto. *Esh Kodesh*, pp. 121–24; *Derashot meShenot haZa'am*, pp. 217, 220; Polen, *Holy Fire*, pp. 113–15, translated by Nehemia Polen

(113:) And so we pray: In the past You heard my sounds of prayer and shofar, because the voice of Torah surrounded me as well, so this sound pierced the heavens. Now, too, even though our voices can only be heard faintly, as if from a distance, as one bends to hear the voice of a child, nevertheless, "Do not shut Your ear from my prayer

46 This is followed by several direct quotations from FDR's September 11, 1941 "Fireside Chat on National Defense."

for my relief when I cry out" (Lam. 3:56). It is not we alone who are affected [by our current distress]; it affects, as it were, You as well.... It is not our doing that the entire Torah and divine service are now destroyed....

(114:) Now according to the teachings of Rabbi Isaac Luria, the fate of the Ten Martyrs was precipitated by an increase of *kelipot* at that time, which threatened a catastrophic destruction of the universe, another Breaking of the Vessels. This was averted and rectified by the deaths of the Ten Martyrs.[47]

(115:) But at the present time as well, we see these troubles befall us, with so many Jewish souls taken away, among them scholars, *tzaddikim*, and servants of the Lord, with every Jew suffering so much – the Lord is just; may He have mercy and call a halt to our troubles and the troubles of His people, the House of Israel – we may conclude that now too is a time of Breaking of the Vessels, so we must strengthen ourselves in repentance, finding renewal and new creation.

Ephraim Sokolover, Great Synagogue, Ra'anana, Palestine. *Penei Efrayim*, pp. 17–20, translated by MS

(17:) If we come to describe the condition of the Jewish people at present – our Jewish brethren who dwell in pain and captivity in the lands of inferno, hovering between life and death – we would be unable, nor would there be sufficient time, even to call to mind what has occurred from last Rosh Hashanah to this, based solely on the limited information and rumors that have come to us during the past year....

How difficult it is even to process the current events. But the fact is – to our sorrow and distress – "If I go out to the field, lo, the slain of the sword" (Jer. 14:18): if we make mention of the wide front in

47 On Lurianic Kabbalah and its doctrine of the "Breaking of the Vessels," see the classical presentation by Gershom Scholem, *Major Trends in Jewish Mysticism*, chap. 7, esp. pp. 266–68, and more recently, Lawrence Fine, *Physician of the Soul, Healer of the Cosmos*, pp. 134–38. The "Ten Martyrs" were, in rabbinic tradition, victims of Hadrianic persecution: see Bialik and Ravnitzky, *The Book of Legends/Sefer ha-Aggadah*, pp. 238–42.

greater Russia, where there are millions of Jews, "lo, the slain of the sword," so many corpses that fall every day. "And if I enter the city" (Jer. 14:18): let us recall all the cities and towns that have already been conquered by the obscene murderers, even those that are far from the front, those that during the two year period since the outbreak of war had accommodated themselves to the new situation of life in poverty and sorrow, "they are smitten by illness": here too we have received terrifying reports from there about millions of Jews dying of hunger day by day. In Warsaw, the great center where so many Jews are concentrated, (18:) as well as in other great cities of Poland, large numbers of the dying make it impossible to bring them all to burial.... We now have a more concrete understanding of what is specified in the *Unesaneh Tokef* liturgy: "Who [will die] by water, who by fire, who by starvation."

ELIEZER BERKOVITS, "God's Precious Son," United Hebrew Congregation, Leeds, England, (eve of second day of Rosh HaShanah). *Between Yesterday and Tomorrow*, pp. 84–88

(85:) Yes, we do have our sins, but even the sinners among us are Jews who in the dark hour of testing, in the hour of destiny, are ready to make the greatest sacrifice rather than betray the old weather-beaten flag of Eternity....

We are homeless. We are guests everywhere. Owing to this basic anomaly in our life as a nation, every piece of Judaism that we realise, that we do live, means sacrifice.

(87:) In the course of the last year the Jewish Tragedy has reached a climax which can hardly be surpassed. The Jewish nation is bleeding from a thousand and more wounds. It is bleeding and suffering for God.

This year, we are waiting more than ever before, for we feel our strength failing. Almighty God! There is not much time to lose. Soon there may be nothing left for you to have mercy upon.

(88:) Israel, whom you called your crown to adorn you, is down in the dust. Almighty God, step down from your high throne, bend down to the dust and lift up your crown. In your great mercy wipe the dust from off it....

September 27, 1941 (at the Kiddush for Shabbat Shuvah)

Kalonymus Kalmish Shapira, Warsaw Ghetto. *Esh Kodesh*, pp. 125–128; *Derashot meShenot haZa'am*, p. 226; Polen, *Holy Fire*, pp. 56–57, translated by Nehemia Polen

(56:) [W]hile we no doubt have faith in God that our [Rosh Hashanah] prayers this year had a positive effect, nevertheless our eyes are witness to the fact that before the war, during previous High Holidays, our prayers had greater fervor and enthusiasm, with a greater outpouring of heart, than this year. The obvious reason for this is physical weakness; we have no strength. But even leaving that aside, we see that our Rosh Hashanah... devotions were missing the sense of awe and fervor they had in former years.

There are several reasons for this. The first is that when a Jew prays and his prayers are answered, he then finds strength and enthusiasm for his subsequent prayers. But when people pray and they see that not only are they not answered, but the troubles increase even more, God forbid, then our hearts fall, and we cannot rouse ourselves in prayer.

The second reason is, as we've already indicated [*parashat Shoftim*, 5701], (57:) the attainment of any spiritual state, including faith and joy, requires the existence of a person – someone to do the believing and rejoicing. But when every individual is crushed and trampled, there is no one to rejoice.

And so it is with regard to fervor in prayer. Each of us is now fallen, prostrate, trampled. So there is no inner "I" to arouse us to prayer. But King David said, "From the depths I have called you, O Lord" (Ps. 130:1): not from one depth, but from two. After I fell into the first depth I called You, but not only was I not answered or saved, but I've since fallen into a second depth – a depth within depth. Nevertheless, even in such a circumstance I strengthen myself and I once again call upon You.

Moses Kahlenberg, "Sermon for Shabbat Shuvah, 5702," La Lande Internment Camp, France. *Yedei Moshe*, 3, pp. 171–77, translated by Shira Leibowitz Schmidt in Farbstein, "Sermons Talk History," p. 160

(173:) Regarding all this [referring to those who neglect the obligation of Torah study], I will not refrain from speaking positively about them.... While Israel's heavens are beclouded and befogged, and the sun's light is diminished before us, should they not plead for bread when no one extends it to them? (cf. Lam. 4:4)... (174:) There is not a moment without misfortune.

And so I hope that from the very outset, you will also judge me favorably, for we all have one Father, and I am your brother in distress and am troubled by all your troubles. Understand the difficulty of rendering my ideas in a concise form and preparing myself in these times of anguish, of thinking and creating honeyed phrases with precious words that restore the soul, as befitting this Shabbat, Shabbat Shuvah, and as I have done for many years.... My strength now in exile is not comparable to my strength then... when I would preach on Shabbat Shuvah at considerable length, as you can see in my book *Darash Moshe*, which I published a number of years ago....

September 30, 1941 (Kol Nidre)

Louis I. Newman, "The Vows We Cannot Cancel," Congregation Rodeph Sholom, New York. *Sermons and Addresses*, vol. 4, pp. 158–65

(159:) Still another vow which Judaism has not enjoined is contained in the pledge which a number of clergymen a few years ago publicly declared, never to support any war whatsoever which might come. I was invited to a meeting called at the suggestion of a group of distinguished Christian ministers, who discussed the attitudes we should take if war came again. Dramatically, the minister of one of America's foremost churches proclaimed that he would never give consent to any war, and we were urged to take a similar vow. I declined to do so.... Hitlerism was already rampant and as we foresaw it, it made the renunciation of the anti-war vow necessary; many of the men who signed the ultra-pacifist document have politely forgotten it or reneged. Some of the clergymen who did sign are either silent in the present crisis, or, by their preachment, seem to be giving solace to the Nazi propagandists who would divide our country into warring groups..... A pacifist vow is commendable, but a higher law requires us to view conditions realistically....

Stephen S. Wise, "The Writing on the Wall," Free Synagogue at Carnegie Hall, New York. AJA, Box 23: SSW Microfilms of AJHS and BUASC papers

(2:) We know even in the midst of the horror that now when the Nazis in Holland recently decreed that Jews must wear the Shield of David sewed upon their coat-sleeves, many Christians, Protestant and Catholic alike, insisted, at the risk of grave penalties, upon wearing that badge of honor, not of dishonour. We remember that on the recent New Year's [Rosh Hashanah] Eve, whilst Jews were offering their prayers within the enwalled ghetto of Warsaw, knowing that Jews had been denied the right to purchase fruit or vegetables over a period of months, Polish Christians outside the walls threw flowers and baskets of fruit over these ghetto walls. The secret radio of the democratic Poland broadcasting to their suffering Jewish fellow-Poles: "Every Pole, Catholic as well as Protestant, shares the persecution, torture and degradation which you suffer under the common enemy called Hitler. The walls of the ghetto have not separated you from the Polish people."[48]

These are the things that make the writing on the wall a symbol of hope, not a sign of warning or of terror.

Jacob Bosniak, "Yom Kippur – The Jew Returns to His Spiritual Home," Ocean Parkway Jewish Center, Brooklyn, NY. *Interpreting Jewish Life*, pp. 77–84

(80:) Alas! As a result of the present day catastrophe, many of our brethren are by force of circumstances led to similar mental struggles, to doubt the purpose of Jewish life and to rebel against the God of our fathers.

(82:) I dare say that the Jews in Europe who have survived tragic disasters until now belong to the class of Jews who never discarded their spiritual armor, or those who quickly returned home to the eternal truth of their religion. They have become reconciled with

48 This passage is based on the JTA article of September 26, 1941 under the title "Poles Throw Flowers Over the Ghetto Walls as Rosh Hashanah Gift to Jews."

their fate because of their faith. They feel superiority over the blonde beast and look with contempt upon their sadistic tormentors.

Nathan Netter, "We Are Still Children of God (*Nous sommes encore les enfants de Dieu*)," Avignon. *La Patrie égarée et la patrie renaissante*, pp. 117–20, translated by MS[49]

(117:) What a contrast with what we have been feeling, as despondent victims of the law of the strongest, banished like criminals from the family (118:) of France. Now, transported here to the embrace of divinity, we can align ourselves proudly with our awareness of our individual value.... If divine justice appears to have been obscured, be assured that it will not be too long before it intervenes in a world now totally askew, that will eventually be restored to its proper order.

Actually, afflicted as we are by the excruciating spectacle of liberty overthrown, of all humane sensibility uprooted, we cannot understand any further. Has justice on earth not become totally absent? Has the silence of a somnolent humanity, mute in the face of atrocities committed before its very eyes, not become a sign of our times?

Certainly some may challenge me by citing the marvelous position taken by French clergy, and clergy from other countries. And indeed we would be ungrateful if we did not recognize this with the deepest gratitude. Indeed, Judaism will never forget this. It will always remember how many individuals, especially small children, were hidden in order to allow them to escape deportation. But what we have missed is the initiative of the broader population, the outcry of indignation and protest by the multitude, the agitation of a tormented conscience to end the most abhorrent persecution the world has ever known....

October 1, 1941 (Yom Kippur)

Israel H. Levinthal, "The Jewish V for Victory Campaign," Brooklyn Jewish Center, Brooklyn, NY. *A New World Is Born*, pp. 48–53

---

49 No date is provided for this Yom Kippur sermon, but it is placed in the volume between two chapters dated Rosh Hashanah 1941 and November 1941.

(51:) The tragedy of the world lies in this – that every nation held the closed hand before its eyes; it refused to look through the window, to see the plight of other people. A terrible isolationism took hold of every one of them. Each nation saw only itself and refused to see the light of its neighbors. That was Hitler's good fortune. One by one he overpowered them, because everyone looked to and for himself alone. There was no window before the eyes of any of the nations!

(52:) A new isolationism has taken hold of American Jews. Many have set their closed hands before their eyes, refusing to look at the plight of their brethren across the seas.... We must look beyond ourselves, we must realize that *Chaverim Kol Yisrael*, "all Israel forms one fellowship" – that we are all children of a common destiny, that destruction threatens all of us, and that the hope of victory must embrace all of us. There must not be a reversal of the policy that always guided Israel; the error of isolationism must never overtake us.

Louis I. Newman, "Is Retribution Sure?," Congregation Rodeph Sholom, New York. *Sermons and Addresses*, vol. 4, pp. 150–57

(152:) We have seen disaster overtake France because of her defeatism, her dissension and inner disintegration; a similar fate can overwhelm us if we are not jealous of our national unity, however strong we believe the American democratic system to be.... We must stand to our colors like men, and be prepared for whatever crisis may come....

(155:) Today when we hear Jewish leaders and laymen say, "Let me live at least for one day beyond the downfall of Hitler," we may rest assured that though they may have been called into eternity before the consummation of their wish their paternity will live on to celebrate a new triumph over an oppressor of Israel. I once heard Harry Emerson Fosdick declare at a great Jewish gathering that the Jewish people "has stood at the grave of every persecutor." While this sharp and epigrammatic statement may fall harshly upon our ears, it contains, nevertheless, a profound historical truth.

Israel Gerstein, "*Yizkor* Reunion," B'nai Zion Congregation, Chattanooga, TN. *Reveille or Taps?*, pp. 26–29

(27:) Many will be the tears shed as our people gather for *Yizkor*, and in many places the living will be envious of the dead; because, in their graves, the dead enjoy peace, but the living are driven like cattle to the slaughter, each day heralding new *tsoros*, new persecutions.... [T]oday at this *Yizkor*, parents in the world of the spirit, the saints and martyrs who gave their lives for God, for their faith and their people, say to us: "There will always be an Israel." The clouds will pass, and the sun of enlightenment will again arise, bringing with it healing and balm to the wounded and sorely stricken.

MOSES KAHLENBERG, "Sermon before *Mussaf* on Yom Kippur 5702," La Lande Internment Camp, France. *Yedei Moshe*, pp. 179–86, translated by MS

(181:) In these times, the order of Creation has been changed, all has become chaotic.... "Because their spirits have been crushed by cruel bondage" (Exod. 6:9), not many are prepared to listen to a long sermon, and everyone leaves quickly.

(182:) If it were not for fear of the Holy One, how could one nation survive among the seventy nations? The Rabbi [who authored] *The Fountain of Living Waters*,[50] explained the matter of G-d's greatness and heroism in this matter through a parable of a young boy in whose hand a thorn had become deeply embedded. Seeing this, the compassionate father realizes that if the thorn were to remain in his son's hand, it could develop into a significant and painful wound, eventually becoming dangerous. The father therefore musters all

50 Frequently in traditional rabbinic literature, authors are identified not by their names but by their most prominent book. Here it is Rabbi Chaim ben Solomon Tyrer (or Tiror) of Czernowitz. His massive commentary on the Pentateuch, *Be'er Mayyim Ḥayyim*, was first published in 1810, but it was republished in a single volume of 426 pages, with three columns of small print text on each page, in Poland, 1938, and this must have been the text that Kahlenberg used. The passage cited appears in this edition on p. 168b, column 1, as part of a comment on Lev. 21:4, introduced by "I have no explanation of the simple meaning of this verse." The beginning of the preacher's story is not taken word for word from the text and could have been based on memory, but the application is indeed taken word for word, so that the preacher may have had the text with him in the camp. For another version of the story itself, see Joseph Dan, *The Teachings of the Hasidim*, p. 117; and above, Ferdinand M. Isserman, September 13, 1939.

his valiant strength and acts cruelly toward his beloved son in order to remove the thorn from the place where it had been lodged, even though it was wedged deeply, cutting into the hand and thereby causing considerable immediate pain, and the son was shouting and wailing and crying ever more loudly, furious at his father for causing him so much pain. But the father refuses to listen, digging with a circumcision knife[51] until he reaches the point where he is able to remove the thorn from his son's hand. He does all this because of his love for his beloved son. This suppression of paternal compassion is indeed an act of enormous valor – though not many children are intelligent enough to appreciate this – and only someone who has children can understand and appreciate it.[52]

I make the following comparison. When [the people of] Israel began to commit massive, serious sins, thorns and thistles from the impure shells [*kelipot*] became embedded within them, and if these had been allowed to remain, their painfulness would have spread more and more, so that – heaven forbid! – there would be no cure. The Holy One sent enemies against them to afflict them with many kinds of torture, in order to weaken their power (183:) by means of various kinds of punishment – pestilence and sword and famine and destruction,[53] may the Merciful One protect us! In this way, the thorns that have been internalized may be removed, and in the end the people of Israel may rise up again. Now we cannot express in words the enormity of the anguish that has come to the Creator from the suffering of Israel, and even more from the profanation of His great name, as the nations of the world say, "Where is their God,

51 The sermon text uses the word *izmel* in the Hebrew, which was the word used for scalpel or circumcision knife: the original text simply says *sakin ḥad*, a sharp knife.

52 A more radical use of this analogy was presented by Ephraim Sokolover in a sermon delivered in Ra'anana, Palestine, a year later on Shabbat Shuvah, 1942: there the child is so critically ill that its legs and arms had to be amputated, and even then further surgery was necessary, until it seemed that only the soul was left. See Gershon Greenberg, "Between Holocaust and Redemption," p. 120, and "A Musar Response to the Holocaust," p. 122.

53 The four Hebrew terms are taken from the *Avinu Malkenu* prayer used in the Yom Kippur liturgy, where Jews pray that God will keep these four kinds of suffering far away from them.

the Rock in which they take refuge?" (Deut. 32:37). It is certainly possible for the Holy One to destroy in an instant those who hate Him (cf. Num. 16:21), but His love for Israel is so great that He stifles his compassion with great valor, observing all that they are doing to His people, allowing all the insults and abuses in silence, all this in order for a good result to emerge from this for Israel, His cherished people.

Abraham Cohen, "Why Should the Nations Talk?," Birmingham Hebrew Congregation, Birmingham, England, preached before *Ne'ilah* [cf. Ps. 79:10]. Unpublished, David Cohen Private Collection

(1:) My address before the *Ne'ilah* Service will be shorter than it would have been in peace time, but the plea I have to make has an added urgency because I am speaking in a time of war.…[54]

(5:) I am sure that your experience is the same as my own: I read with dismay case after case where the defendants belong to Jewry.… When the delinquents are Jews, no words can adequately express the horror and detestation in which they should be held. They are allies of Hitler, the arch-enemy and would-be destroyer of their people. Of what use will their money be if the war is lost – and they are helping to lose it? If England goes the way of Poland, France, and Holland, they will suffer as their co-religionists suffered in those (6:) countries; they will be stripped of all they possess. Leaving aside all questions of morality and patriotism, and viewing it only from the practical point of view, I ask what sense is there in their conduct? If our hands are clean, we cannot dissociate ourselves from the behavior of those whose hands are soiled.…[55]

---

54 During the war, Yom Kippur services in the United Kingdom had to be shortened in order to fulfill the blackout requirements, and the Closing Service (*Ne'ilah*) therefore had to be ended significantly before sundown. Much of the sermon is devoted to the issue of Jews profiteering through the black market, avoiding government regulations to enrich themselves, and thereby demeaning the reputation of all Jews. Because of blackout regulations, Kol Nidre services were also not permitted; see Abraham Cohen, September 26, 1944, below.

55 On this problem, cf. also Joseph H. Hertz, sermon delivered on the following Pesach, April 2, 1942, in Saperstein, *Jewish Preaching in Times of War*, pp. 467–69, and Cohen, below, March 29, 1942. A similar theme is reported for a sermon by Cohen delivered on the first day of Rosh Hashanah, 1936, in the *JC*, September 25, 1936, p. 40.

October 4, 1941 (Saturday, Sukkot would begin the following evening)

Louis I. Newman, "Booths in Today's Wilderness," Congregation Rodeph Sholom, New York. *Sermons and Addresses*, vol. 4, pp. 128–33

(132:) It may well be that Hitler will be able, with the resources he is organizing in the occupied countries, to keep up the struggle for many years, before at last he blows out his own brains.... But we are sustained by the confidence that savagery will be crushed; that victory will be granted freedom's armies; that the oppressed peoples will throw off the yoke, and that mankind will be vouchsafed a fresh start once more.

October 17, 1941 (Friday evening, *Bereishit*)

Israel Gerstein, "Beginning of the End or End of the Beginning?," B'nai Zion Congregation, Chattanooga, TN. *Reveille or Taps?*, pp. 47–54

(49:) We are at the end of one era and entering another. But with Hitler knocking at the gates of Moscow, those pessimistically inclined insist that we are at the beginning of *tohu v'vohu*, that chaos, confusion, and void lie ahead, a period when darkness will cover the earth. However, in his soul, the Jew hears a different voice. It says, *Yehi or*, "Let there be light." The Great Director has, aeons ago, issued the order, "Light," and the lights will remain, even if a Hitler should mobilize an entire nation to extinguish them.

November 5, 1941 (Wednesday)

Judah L. Magnes, "It Depends on Us," Opening of the Academic Year 1941/42, Hebrew University, Jerusalem. *In the Perplexity of the Times*, pp. 65–78

(38:) The Nazi Satan threatens us with bondage or extermination. The Nazi Satan is also making this millennial frontal attack upon Judaism and Jewish morality. In this crisis there is no freedom of the will for the Jew, as this is usually understood. Whatever be our philosophy or way of life, our stand in this war has been decreed by the compulsion of our history, by all the generations that have gone before from the Book of Genesis up to this day. Most of the peoples who have been influenced basically and decisively by Judaism, through Christianity, (39:) or in other ways, march, fight, hope, pray, just as we do, for their lives and their ideals.

(40:) I cannot refrain from referring to some recent reports concerning the mass shooting of Jews by Germans in concentration camps in Poland. I abstain from citing figures and other details – they are too revolting. There has been official verification thus far of these latest massacres of innocents, men, women, and children. But one of the most terrible things about such reports is that no matter how appalling they are, the Nazis have taught us to realize that they are possible. The heart cries to heaven. That we might only help! But what helplessness, what futility, (41:) what frustrated pity! We read, too, of the Nazi glee in compelling every Jew in the Nazi clutches to sew a yellow David's Shield on his garment.[56] For want of another way of expressing our feelings, I ask why should not all Jews everywhere sew the same sign on their garments and thus turn this badge of shame into a sign of brotherhood and of honour?[57]

November 8, 1941 (Saturday, *VaYera*: "Day of Remembrance")

Eliezer Berkovits, "The Binding of the Sons," United Hebrew Congregation, Leeds, England. *Between Yesterday and Tomorrow*, pp. 25–30

(27:) In the terrible drama of the Binding of the Sons and their delivering up to the "high causes," which is being acted by the nations all through recorded history, the place of God has often been taken by some bloodthirsty Moloch, and the place of Abraham by so-called great men who have been the mad servants of Moloch. And because of this, unlike the case of Abraham, there is no one to stay the hands of the fathers.

(28:) And yet it seems to me that there is one thing that could

56 The yellow six-pointed Star of David badge was introduced into Poland much earlier (in late 1939); Magnes is probably referring to the decree of September 1941 requiring all German Jews (and Jews in several other countries) age six and older to wear the badge in public. See JTA, September 21, 1941; *JC*, September 26, 1941, p. 10.

57 On this theme, see above, June 24, 1936 and accompanying note.

check the outstretched arm, chase Moloch from his usurped throne, and call back the "great men" to normality: the remembrance of the Mothers.

In these terrible years, I have often wondered whether those who are so well prepared to destroy life and happiness ever think of their own mothers. Whether, thinking of their mothers, they would still be able to destroy and to commit all the acts of brutality with which they are dishonouring human nature?...

(29:) Let us, at least, learn from the mothers how to remember....

To-day, let this be our dedication: to rid the world of every purpose that demands human sacrifice. Let this be our remembrance: to remember the sufferings of the mothers all over this unhappy globe.

November 23, 1941 (Sunday)

Stephen S. Wise, Address Delivered at the Inter-American [Pan-American] Jewish Conference, Baltimore, MD. *As I See It*, pp. 49–53

(51:) We are gathered in part in order to bethink ourselves touching the infinitely mournful fate of our fellow Jews who have dwelt in European lands. Addresses other than my own will deal with the oceanic tragedy which has befallen the peaceable and loyal populations of many European lands, who were the first and will be the last victims of Nazism until the day of liberation from the monstrous calamity of Nazism. And that day is not far off....

But even *though*, not *if*, Hitlerism and Nazism is to be banished from the earth, as it will be, there will still remain a number of most difficult and taxing Jewish problems. The economic basis of Jewish living has been willfully destroyed by Nazism. Jews who, like you and like us, are free must give to the succor of Jews who for nearly a decade have been enslaved and dispossessed. Even though after the war, inter-governmental programs must (52:) have special reference to a people in many lands deprived of the basic possibilities of self-support, the fate of our brother-Jews in European lands cries out to us for immediate succor.... Woe betide us, if amidst the comparative plenty and prosperity of America life, we forget our brother-Jews, whose agonies of suffering have come about largely, if not solely, because they are Jews.

December 7, 1941 (Sunday)

Maurice N. Eisendrath, "Berlin Diaries," Holy Blossom Synagogue, Toronto. *Holy Blossom Pulpit*, XI, 3 (delivered hours before Japanese declaration of war against the United States)

(2:) If these revelations [in recent anti-Nazi films and diaries], however, be not too late for the final destruction of our enemy, then surely none can deny that all this recent preoccupation on stage and screen and in print and press has certainly come too late for hundreds of thousands, nay, even millions upon millions of murdered babes and butchered men and women, (3:)… because you and I and too many of our fellows did not pay sufficient heed to these things which were an open book long before they appeared in print to anyone who would have been a bit more interested in the fate of his fellow men.…

(5:) On the Jewish question – with regard to which, by the way, President Roosevelt, in contra-distinction (6:) to so many others who saw in this merciless persecution nothing to get excited about, had specifically instructed him to seek some manner of amelioration – on this question [William E.] Dodd perceived that absolutely nothing could be done.… One of the most burning indictments of some of our own fellow Jews is contained in a number of paragraphs in Dodd's Diary[58] which reveal how the timorous hush, hush Jews in Germany called upon their co-religionists of similar yellow hue in America to call off the boycott against the Nazis in order, not that the Nazi regime might be weakened, but that they might purchase personal immunity thereby.… To our everlasting shame, the first of the many appeasers whom Ambassador Dodd proceeded to stumble across throughout his career were from among our own number,

58 Reference is to *Ambassador Dodd's Diary*, ed. William E. Dodd Jr. and Martha Dodd, published shortly before the sermon was delivered. Dodd had been appointed US Ambassador to Berlin in June 1933.

were some of our brother Jews who, instead of vowing war to the death against the foe who from its very beginnings had declared a battle of extermination against our people and our faith, naively believed that by stroking the tiger's skin, they could soften its wrath, if not toward their people as a whole, then at least toward their privileged and supposedly protected selves.

December 12, 1941 (Friday evening)

Ferdinand M. Isserman, "The United States Is at War," Temple Israel, St. Louis, MO. AJA, MS-6, Box 16, Folder 2, and *Jewish Preaching in Times of War*, pp. 450–61

(456:) Even as we are not at war with the cultural traditions of Germany and of Italy so we are not at war with the peoples of the Axis countries. We are at war with their governments. We are at war with the gangsters and desperadoes and conscienceless men who by terror and by chicanery, who by fraud and by deceit, who by foul propaganda and unscrupulous demagoguery, by clandestine conspiracy and by cruel conniving, have made themselves the (457:) masters of the governmental machinery of these peoples. After having succeeded in that, they first enslaved, cowed and degraded their own peoples so that they became nothing but appendages to the war machine. Then they robbed them of their sons and trained them for a war against the liberties of men, a war for the conquest of the world.

I am firmly convinced from my own experiences in Germany,[59] from the fact that democracy had to be destroyed before Naziism could triumph, that there are countless thousands, millions among the German people who have not lost their sense of moral values and who groan beneath the lash of their taskmaster, even as do the peoples in conquered lands.

December 13, 1941 (Saturday, *VaYeishev*)

Eliezer Berkovits, "Master of His Dreams," United Hebrew Congregation, Leeds, England. *Between Yesterday and Tomorrow*, pp. 88–93

59 Referring to his visits during the summers of 1933, 1935 (reported above) and 1937.

(89:) The sufferings of Jews in Europe, especially in Poland and the temporarily conquered territories of the Soviet Union, are unutterable. But how deep must the Jewish Tragedy reach if in spite of our faith in the victory of the democracies the Jewish future appears even darker than the present. Every Jew must understand this: in the present circumstances, the future holds no promise for us. Nowhere among the nations is there an adequate understanding for the true plight of the Jewish nation. Nowhere in the world does the sincere wish exist to do justice to the Jewish nation. Let us not fool ourselves, let us open our eyes: the solution which is contemplated, and which will be offered us when the war is over, is assimilation of the Jews in the countries where they live to-day.

(90:) We are caught between two fires. Here – venomous National-Socialist barbarity; there – sympathetic but evasive democracy. Whichever side wins, we shall lose. In the long history of Jewish suffering we have never experienced a period as dark and hopeless as the present one.[60]

However, we have no right to put all the blame on others....

I am much afraid that we may well be left alone, that the future peace conference may try to forget the existence of a Jewish nation, and slowly but surely Judaism and this people may disappear from the surface of the earth.

And what is at the bottom of the present tragedy? This question admits of various answers. To-day, however, I would choose the following: We are losing the battle, because in our generation Jews have stopped dreaming the dreams of Judaism.

(92:) In this manner we have unfortunately wasted the only great achievement of modern Jewry – the dynamic force of Zionism. Lately, even we Zionists have been afraid of the great dreams of Judaism, even we have renounced them....

60 A clear statement of radical discontinuity with the past, rejecting the continuities that are so prevalent in many earlier sermons. The dramatic pessimism is continued in the following sentences. One wonders how the listeners reacted.

December 14, 1941 (Sunday, first night of Hanukkah)

Stephen S. Wise, "Human Rights: The Axis Attacks, America Defends," Free Synagogue at Carnegie Hall, New York (Abstract). AHA, Box 23: SSW Microfilms of AJHS and BUASC papers

(1:) It is not the United States which is under attack; it is democracy, the American democracy as the most significant example of the power of a democracy. The Axis war upon us, beginning with the incredibly treacherous attacks of Sunday, is the prelude of the totalitarian despotisms to the American celebration of the anniversary of the Bill of Rights....

(2:) A week ago we were at peace, today we are embarked upon an adventure, terrible and world-wide, out of which shall come, under God and with His help, a new, just, and free world.

Leo M. Franklin, "The Synagogue and the Way of Democracy: 85th Anniversary of Holy Blossom Synagogue, Toronto." Unpublished, Rabbi Leo Morris Franklin Archives, now at AJA, MS-246

(8:) In every truth, the democratic ideal and the Jewish ideal are one. Stifle one, and you destroy the other... Many a message of men of the type of Roosevelt and Churchill might have been preached from the Jewish pulpit, so close is the identity of Judaism and that Democracy for which they stand. Therefore, since the synagogue is the legitimate mouthpiece of the Jew, it follows that no sentiment uttered from its pulpit and no practice included in its ritual can logically be inconsistent with or in opposition to any basic principle (9:) that is essentially democratic.... Neither fear nor expediency nor self-interest dares still the voice of the Rabbi when great moral and patriotic issues are at stake. Though he be chided and derided for his utterances, though he be threatened with violence if he do not hold his peace, yet in the spirit of an Amos he must take his stand and proclaim, "Though I be neither prophet nor a prophet's son, when the Lord hath commanded, who shall not speak?" (cf. Amos 7:14).

(10:) Civilization stands at the cross-roads. If it is to be saved from utter destruction, the synagogue for the Jew and the church for the Christian must find a way to overcome the subversive forces that are arrayed in phalanx formation against humanity....

December 15, 1941 (Monday, first day of Hanukkah)

Kalonymus Kalmish Shapira, Warsaw Ghetto. *Esh Kodesh*, pp. 140–41; *Derashot meShenot haZa'am*, pp. 241–43; Polen, *Holy Fire*, pp. 82–85, translated by Nehemia Polen

(83:) To our sorrow, we see now that even among those people who had been firm believers, certain individuals have had their faith weakened. They pose questions, saying in effect, "Why have You forsaken us? If the suffering is being inflicted upon us in order to bring us closer to Torah and divine service, we see the opposite happening. The Torah and everything sacred is being destroyed."...

In reality, however, what place is there for arguments and questions, God forbid? It is true that sufferings like these which we are now enduring come only once every several hundred years, but nevertheless, how can we expect to understand these actions of God?... Those people who say that Israel has never experienced sufferings such as these are mistaken. At the time of the destruction of the Temple, and at the fall of Betar, etc., there were [sufferings] such as these.[61]

(85:) At the present time when the evil decrees are directed against all Israel, God forbid, our faith should be strengthened by this very fact.... If everyone were to consider that we are being persecuted not because we have committed robbery or because we have harmed anyone, but rather because we are Jews, attached to our God and His holy Torah, and that our enemies are not merely satisfied with extinguishing the divine spark within us, but wish to destroy both together – the Jew's body and soul – then, on the contrary, our faith and our devotion to Him and His Torah would be strengthened.

---

61 Polen provides a note appended by the preacher to the text of the sermon, written on November 27, 1942, stating that his assertion that the present sufferings had been experienced by previous generations of Jews applied only to what had occurred until the summer of 1942, not to the later persecution (i.e., the liquidation of the ghetto's population through deportation to the death camps). For a study of Shapira's theology, see Avichai Zur, "'The Lord Hides in Inner Chambers': The Doctrine of Suffering in the Theosophy of Rabbi Kalonymus Kalman Shapira of Piaseczno." *Dapim* 25 (2011): 183–237.

December 19, 1941 (Friday evening during Hanukkah)

Abraham M. Hershman, "Our Twofold Task," Congregation Shaarey Zedek, Detroit, MI. *Israel's Fate and Faith*, pp. 130–32

(130:) "Everyone with one of his hands wrought in the work, and with the other held his weapon" (Neh. 4:11).

The Maccabees evinced great valor and won brilliant successes on the military battlefield...But what is even more important is the cause for which they staked their lives, their triumph on the spiritual battlefield.

(131:) It is a mistaken notion that the Jews in the Middle Ages did nothing in self-defense.... The Jews of the Middle Ages knew what they were fighting against, but they also never forgot that they had something "to fight for."...While with one hand he held the weapon, with the other he built.

Here we have a program for the Jew of today. What sort of world will emerge from the global war I do not know. No one (132:) knows.... Now the need for defense work is generally recognized. No one wants to suffer or die because he is a Jew. The question that disturbs many of us is, "How many are determined to live as Jews?" Our main concern seems to be to ward off all attacks from the outside world. We are holding, as it were, the weapon in *both* hands. We have neither the time nor the disposition to engage in positive, constructive work, to build up our inner voices.

December 20, 1941 (Saturday, sixth day of Hanukkah)

Jonah B. Wise, Central Synagogue, New York. *NYT*, Dec. 21, 1941, p. 32

This is a pacifist's war. No man, unless he is bound by an oath not to resist under any circumstances, can stand aloof from the call to meet this brutality. If it prevails there will be peace only for the dead for many generations....

This is the Maccabean struggle par excellence, a cosmic drama of which the epic of 2100 years ago was a miniature preview. The final act of this drama will be a feast of Hanukkah for all mankind, the triumph of light over darkness, the cleansing of the temple of humanity from its pagan pollution, and a rededication of man to the law of God.

December 21, 1941 (Sunday, seventh day of Hanukkah)

Abba Hillel Silver, "Only the Brave Shall be Free: A Maccabean Message to a Nation at War," The Temple, Cleveland, OH. Unpublished, Western Reserve Historical Society Archives

(3:) It has been demonstrated over and over again that powerful weapons in the hands of strong armies frequently fail in their objectives because the mind and spirit back of the army is in critical state of collapse. Those who have the indomitable resolution reinforced by the righteousness of their cause ultimately triumph. The forces of Antiochus came to enslave them [the Jews]. The Maccabees wanted to emancipate themselves and others, and the passion for freedom is a consuming one and a relentless passion; the passion to enslave burns itself out with the first defeat.

(5:) America today is fighting not only for America, but, just as the Maccabees, for the spiritual Americas all over the world, for the islands of free men now enslaved by forces of darkness and neo-paganism....

We have the material, unquestionably greater than the enemies'. The one uncertainty which ought to make us search our hearts is whether the American people possess the spiritual resources. Are the American people spiritually equal to the desperate struggle ahead of them?...

Israel Abrahams, "To Live or Die Nobly," Sermon Broadcast from the Great Synagogue, Cape Town, South Africa. *Living Waters: Collection of Sermons, Addresses and Prayers*, pp. 235–38.

(237:) Where neither freedom nor righteousness is permitted to exist, the religious conscience is, of necessity, completely excluded. Unrestricted faith is even more inimical to Fascist and Nazi ideology than unfettered thought. Hence the Church has been made to suffer as well as the Synagogue, and Christianity is being oppressed side by side with Judaism. The new barbarism is pre-eminently pagan. It has declared war on biblical religion....

(238:) Never has the call to duty been weighted with so many compelling reasons. South Africa needs us. Humanity is appealing to us. The agony of our brothers and sisters living under the shadow of the Swastika is crying aloud to us. Our comrades up North, whose heroism has already made history, are calling us....

In the days of the Maccabees, peace was won for a little corner of the earth and but for a few fleeting years. To-day, it is within our power to banish war forever, to establish peace enduringly, to lay the foundations for a better, braver and nobler world.

1942

January 1, 1942 (National Day of Meditation and Prayer declared by President Roosevelt)

Jacob Hoffman, Congregation Ohab Zedek, New York. *NYT*, Jan. 2, 1942, p. 21

I am sure that millions and millions of people, even in the Nazi-occupied or dominated countries, who have not the possibility of expressing their feelings and wishes openly, join us in silent prayer. For well they know that their salvation and their hope of living in freedom and human dignity depend upon the victory of the allied forces over aggression, tyranny and ruthlessness.

January 2, 1942 (Friday evening)

Jacob Bosniak, "America–Mother of a New Humanity," Ocean Parkway Jewish Center, Brooklyn, NY. *Interpreting Jewish Life,* pp. 121–29

Isa 60:1–5; (126:) [W]hile our gates are no longer open as widely as before the First World War, America is still the hope and prayer of those who cry "unto God by reason of the bondage" (Exod. 2:13) of present-day Pharaohs. Witness the recent influx of refugees, Jews and Gentiles, who were fortunate enough to escape from the hell of Europe. More refugees entered America since the rise of totalitarianism and brutalitarianism than were admitted into all other countries taken together. And all were given an opportunity (127:) to start a new life, a free life.[1] ... The Old World hate-mongers and their

1 It seems rather surprising to note this expression of apparent satisfaction with American immigration policy, despite the scandal of the *St. Louis* having been turned away from American ports, and failures to get Congress to increase the existing quotas in response to the unprecedented emergency. See, for example, *American Jewish History*, ed. Jeffrey Gurock, vol. 7 (*America, American Jews, and the Holocaust*),

dupes in this country point to the heterogeneous elements of the population, to the mixture of many nationalities with their various cultures – as a sign of weakness. But they forget....

(129:) In this hour of national peril, let us all unite in prayer for the continuance of God's blessing upon our country.

January 3, 1942 (Saturday)

Shlomo Zalman Unsdorfer, Weidritz Alley Synagogue, Bratislava, Slovakia, in Katz, Riderman and Greenberg, eds., *Wrestling With God*, pp. 52–56, translated by Gershon Greenberg, slight modifications by MS, based on Unsdorfer, *Siftei Shlomo*, pp. 81–87[2]

(52:) My teachers and masters: To my great sorrow, my head and heart have not been focused to prepare the sermon as is appropriate before this dignified community. This is because of the anguish of servitude. But the mercies of God have not been exhausted. Precisely in a time of troubles such as this, we need to strengthen our study of the Torah in public....

(54:) Woe is me if I speak! Woe is me if I do not speak! The time for words of rebuke is not where there is "trouble for Jacob" (Jer. 30:7), for the afflictions certainly purge the sins of human beings.[3] But it may be that we have an obligation to awaken ourselves about the contemporary events, about the evil decrees that are repeated every day [and to recognize that] "With You, O Lord, is the right, and the shame is upon us" (Dan. 9:7). Many of the decrees which we see with our senses are measure for measure.[4]...

A decree has been issued according to which we are permitted

---

chaps. 2, 6, 7 and 11. The only way in which the sentence would seem to make sense is if the "the rise of totalitarianism and brutalitarianism" were understood to begin with the 1881 pogroms.

2 The preacher's introductory note to the sermon text records that during the previous week a fire had destroyed a home for the elderly in the Patrónka region of Bratislava, and that on the same day, fanatics had come to the synagogues of Bratislava "and beat the Jews who were praying there."

3 b. Berakhot 5a.

4 Many of the decrees mentioned in detail by the preacher were the product of the so-called "Jewish Code" (officially, "On the Legal Position of Jews"), which imposed a Nazi model of discrimination on nominally autonomous Slovakia; it was published

to take no more than one hundred and fifty crowns a week of our money from the bank. This is not enough even for meager bread and water. In our many sins, how miserly we have been in giving charity (heaven forbid!) from the money we had in the bank. We thought of it as our "capital," not to be touched even to fulfil a religious commandment. How miserly we were when it came to paying the wages of those whom we hired to work for us. Their salary was minimal, while the householders had plenty.

On the beginning of the Christian new year, called *Neu Jahr*, they forbade us to leave our homes. In our many sins, during normal, peaceful times we also celebrated and rejoiced according to the calendars of the nations. What did we have to do with their impure holidays? "Rejoice not, O Israel, as the other peoples exult" (Hos. 9:1), "for I the Lord your G-d am holy, and I have set you apart from other peoples to be Mine" (Lev. 20:26). We have, thank G-d, our own holy festival of Rosh Hashanah to distinguish us in thousands of ways. Whatever is good for them should be bad and abominable for us.

They have prohibited us from attending their schools, they have closed the doors of their universities to us. This was punishment measure for measure. How much our written and oral Torah and all of our books of ethical instruction warned us to distance ourselves from their foreign teachings, which are filled with heresy and sacrilege!

They have forbidden us to have a radio in our homes.[5] What business do we have with their entertainment and evil desires, with their instruments of destruction that destroy and confuse the hearts and minds of the holy children of Israel, pure boys and girls, and contaminate their hearts and minds with obscene language and frivolity, God forbid. Our holy Torah has (55:) warned us, "you shall not follow your heart and your eyes [in your lustful urge]" (Num. 15:39).

---

in the Slovak statute book on September 9, 1941. See Ivan Kamanec, *On the Trail of Tragedy: The Holocaust in Slovakia*, pp. 161–65.

5 This was part of a broad series of decrees passed in the autumn of 1941, including "prohibition of possession of radios, telephones, photographic equipment, hunting and fishing equipment, typewriters and calculators, national and state symbols, antiques and so on" (Kamanec, *On the Trail of Tragedy*, p. 182).

They forbade us to visit their theaters. What need do we, the holy seed and the children of the living God have for these houses of prostitution? We need to get beyond shooting range from the stinking animal corpse, from those houses that elicit and arouse all evils....

They have taken away our livelihoods. All Jewish stores have been closed or given over to wicked owners, and we are subservient to them.[6]

They have forbidden us from having gentile servants in our homes. Who knows how much we have sinned against God by having gentile servants who supervised the cooking and the food in the house, with the food cooked by gentiles.

They have ordered us to wear *gele tsechen* [a yellow badge, signifying] that we are Jews.[7] In our many sins, how ashamed we were of our Jewish garments and Jewish names, of the fringes on our garments and the *mezuzah* on our doorposts, despite our religious obligation to have everyone who saw us recognize that we were of a lineage blessed by G-d, our obligation not to commit the significant sin of shaving the beard with a razor. Out of shame before the gentiles, we did not want to be recognized at all by the sidelocks on our heads. Now in response to this the wicked ones have decreed that everyone should recognize that we are Jews. Therefore they have decreed that each of our shops must display a prominent sign so that it will be recognized as a "Jewish shop" (*Yiddische Gescheft*).[8] We have no income, not even enough for a loaf of bread. In our many sins, how much we spent on vile luxuries and worthless pleasures!

They have forbidden ritual slaughter. In our many sins, how much did we transgress with forbidden foods!

In peaceful times we were obsessed with our apartments. We were afraid to bring poor people into our homes, lest they dirty the carpets on the floor.

---

6 "Aryanization" decrees going back to 1939 required that a non-Jewish partner had to own at least fifty-one percent of each formerly Jewish business or company (Kamanec, *On the Trail of Tragedy*, pp. 79–81).

7 On the marking of Jews specifically in Slovakia, see Kamanec, *On the Trail of Tragedy*, pp. 183–84.

8 On this legislation as part of the broad goal of "Aryanization" (going back to early 1940), see Kamanec, *On the Trail of Tragedy*, p. 89.

A decree has gone out that we must give to the authorities all the valuable objects in our homes. Whoever has a garment made of fur must hand it over to the government, because in peaceful times, we imagined that it all belonged to us, and we did not share with the needy who came to ask for our help.[9]

I myself will ask G-d in His goodness to forgive me. It was not my intention, heaven forbid!, to stir up accusations against the holy Jewish people. The worst among us is a thousand times better than the best among them! However, perhaps through the reflections of repentance, G-d may decide to lessen our burdens, and to arouse His mercy and His unconditional lovingkindness for us.

Joseph H. Lookstein, "The Sources of Courage," Saturday evening Radio Address for "The Message of Israel." *The Sources of Courage: War Time Sermons*, pp. 1–5

(4:) A classic example of the triumph of such courage, born of such conviction, is the Jewish people. That courage enabled our ancestors to cross the pathless desert and inhabit the promised land. It gave them the power, in the face of every adversity, to cultivate their divine culture and to transmit it undefiled to succeeding generations of humanity. It enabled them to survive the squalor of the ghetto, the cruelty of the Inquisition, the proscriptions and humiliations of mediaeval Europe. It is making us, their descendants, withstand for more than a decade the relentless fury of the tyrants of our day, who destroyed our houses of worship, wrecked our academies of learning, plundered our communities, and exposed countless thousands of our brethren to starvation, disease, and death.

The courage of the Jew is sustained by an unyielding faith. Our hearts do not tremble because our eyes remain unfailing and our souls unfaltering.

---

9 The commandeering of fur clothing owned by Jews in the winter of 1941–1942 was a general policy in response to the needs of German soldiers on the eastern front. Cf. *The Warsaw Diary of Adam Czerniakow*, entries of December 24, 1941 to January 5, 1942 (pp. 309–12). On the more general confiscation of valuable property owned by Jews, which began in autumn 1941 and included gymnastic and sports equipment and stamp collections, see Kamanec, *On the Trail of Tragedy*, p. 184.

January 5, 1942 (Monday)

Yitzhak Katz, "Things I Intended to Say…", Conference of Jewish Social Self-Help (Zydowska Samapomoc Spolczna, ZSS), Warsaw Ghetto. See Complete Sermons

January 10, 1942 (Saturday)

Moses Kahlenberg, "Sermon for the Dedication of the Synagogue," La Lande Internment Camp, France. *Yedei Moshe*, pp. 189–201, translated by MS

(192:) "I will lay your cities in ruin" (Lev. 26:31): its meaning is clear, for the cities in which we dwelled have been totally ruined for us, "and I will make your sanctuaries desolate" (Lev. 26:31): this refers to our synagogues; "I will scatter you among the nations," (Lev. 26:33), and "as for those of you who survive, I will cast a faintness into their hearts" (Lev. 26:26): our lives are filled with anxiety and fear, day and night, until our captivity will be completed. In addition, all the diseases and tribulations that are not written in the Torah reading *BeḤukkotai*, but appear only in the Torah reading *Ki Tavo*, have come upon us, such as "ten women shall take their bread to a single oven" (Lev. 26:26),[10] about which it is said "Not by bread alone" (Deut. 8:3), for all four hundred people who are here eat from a single oven, and bread is distributed to them according to a specified weight for each.... And so we hope that this punishment with its curses will soon be ended, and that (193:) we will no longer receive such evil.

(194:) After the passage of nine years of the cavernous pit of German Jewry, and four years that they have filled their bellies with the delicacies of Austrian Jewry, more than three years of the exile of Czech Jewry, two and a half years of the destruction of Polish Jewry, and our own departure from our homes and our possessions – exile after exile, more than the ten exiles experienced by the divine presence[11] – fourteen months that we have been here in captivity, and

10 As noted in the commentary by Esther Farbstein, the preacher has made an error here, as the verse that he cites is indeed from *BeḤukkotai,* not from *Ki Tavo.*

11 Cf. b. Rosh Hashanah, 31a.

the last three months the worst of all, when they have fenced us in so that no one can enter or exit: now once again they begin to fix for us a special place for prayer, and apparently (195:) they are thinking that we will be here for a while. But who knows how long?

Joseph H. Lookstein, "The Rewards of Sacrifice," Saturday evening Radio Address for "The Message of Israel."*The Sources of Courage*, pp. 6–9

(8:) By this time every one must have read the releases on the new Bible with brown covers. In this Bible there will be no record of man's creation in the image of God. The Ten Commandments will be replaced by the Nuremberg laws; substitution for God: *der Fuehrer*; substitution for Moses: Alfred Rosenberg; for the temple: the Brown House; for Sinai: the concentration camp.[12] Lives there a man so blind as not to see that whatever we do to destroy such madness cannot be called a sacrifice but a privilege?

(9:) In the days that lie ahead, therefore, let us not dwell upon the duties, the obligations, and the impositions of sacrifice. Let us think rather of the rewards....

January 17, 1942

Joseph H. Lookstein, "The Higher Discipline," Saturday evening Radio Address for "The Message of Israel." *The Sources of Courage*, pp. 10–13

(12:) Take the doctrine of super-indulgence, glorify it into a philosophy, multiply it by eighty million people, and you have the Nazi program in action. Here are some of the catchwords of that program. "*Lebensraum*," "the call of the blood," "blood and soil," the "healthy instincts of the race" – don't you recognize these slogans? The world

12 The "Brown House" was the headquarters of the Nazi Party in Munich. The rest of the paragraph, however, seems to reflect a rhetorical flourish at the cost of historical precision. The extreme of "German Christians," reflected in the "Institute for the Study and Eradication of Jewish Influence on German Church Life," simply withdrew the Old Testament from usage in Church worship, and focused instead on revising the New Testament in a manner that would eliminate any positive references to Jews. See S. Heschel, *The Aryan Jesus*, pp. 106–12.

has been hearing them raucously shouted for almost ten years. They have been the incentives for lust and plunder, for aggression and terror. They have been the music to which an entire civilization has been tom-tommed back to the jungle. Even barbarians do not object to green pastures and still waters, to anointed heads, and to cups that overflow (cf. Ps. 23:2–3). But civilized men understand that to enjoy these gifts, there must be baths of righteousness. There must be a regulating rod in addition to a sustaining staff that can comfort us (cf. Ps. 23:4).

January 23, 1942 (Friday evening, *Bo*)

Israel Gerstein, "Face Lifting," B'nai Zion Congregation, Chattanooga TN. *Reveille or Taps,?* pp. 98–104

(98:) [Pharaoh to Moses and Aaron:] "See there is evil in your faces" (Exod. 10:10).

(103:) Look at the eyes of a Nazi general and you see two balls of blue steel, telling you of a heart from which all mercy or humane sentiment has been banished....

February 14, 1942 (Saturday)

David de Sola Pool, "Discipline," Congregation Shearith Israel, New York. *Rabbi David de Sola Pool: Selections from Six Decades of Sermons, Addresses and Writings*, pp. 83–90

(86:) Such discipline is indeed a profoundly meaningful human need. It is more needful for free human beings than for those living under the fiats of Fascism. This [fascist] discipline,with its arbitrary regimentation in the name of the state, destroys the freedom of the individual. Nazism is inwardly consistent in declaring that Christianity and traditional religion must be swept away and superseded by the Nazi state. The life of the citizen in the Nazi state is so fully determined for him by man-made compulsions in an evil cause that no room is left for the commands of God. The free man, free of such outwardly enforced constraints, needs the more the inward disciplines which religion sets upon him.

February 21, 1942 (Saturday)

Ernest I. Jacob, "Installation in Springfield," Temple Israel, Springfield, MO. *Paths of Faithfulness*, pp. 1–4[13]

(2:) I was released with them after we had promised to leave the land where we had been born, in which we had done our constructive work, and through which we had experienced our most cruel disappointment. Few trials can be harder than to be repudiated by those who are considered fellow-citizens and friends.

I have seen adult men, hardened by the struggles of life, successful in business, cry before me like little children. I have seen the proud facades built by wealth, reputation and influence crash down....

(3:) I am a man who lost everything in life and had to start from the beginning again, but nothing is to be gained by mourning about that.

February 24, 1942 (Tuesday evening)

James G. Heller, "President's Message to CCAR Convention in Cincinnati, OH, February 24–March 3. *CCAR Yearbook* 52 (1942), pp. 213–31

(214:) With the prophetic vision suffering sometimes bestows, we Jews had foreseen this event. We knew that this was a war for the world, that eventually it would divide all men into two camps, that the hateful logic of Nazis could never stop short of an assault upon the greatest citadel of freedom in the world. We knew that anti-Semitism in Germany, and its outbursts of violence and legal suppression against the Jews, was only a premonitory symptom of a profound and pervasive disease, not isolated or irrelevant crimes, but skirmishes before the long-intended battle, first rumblings of the subterranean depths before the earth shook the temples of so many civilizations into tumbled columns and shattered shards.... Many ages of insecurity, of flight, of persecution, have equipped Jews with a sixth sense of calamity. We are the staccato bird-flights that

13 Ernest I. Jacob had served as a rabbi in Germany from 1933–1938; at the beginning of the sermon, he describes *Kristallnacht*, when he was brought to a concentration camp with 150 members of his congregation.

speed over the tranquil heavens before the first faint intimations of the storm.

That mankind gave so little heed to the plight of the Jews of Germany testified to its fatal blindness.... Those within the gates have gone down into darkness. Those without knocked, but too often and in vain, at the grimly barred gates of Palestine, or slept upon the decks of vessels that bore them, past India, to the "open" port of Shanghai. New caravels of suffering (215:) scoured the seven seas, Flying Dutchmen laden with the sons and daughters of Israel, for whom no haven could be discovered. Pestships, loaded to the gunwales with this freight of exiles, preyed upon the agony of a whole people.

February 25, 1942 (Wednesday)

Louis Wolsey, "Trusting in the Lord," Sermon given at Devotional Services of Central Conference of American Rabbis. *Sermons and Addresses*, pp. 52–54

(53:) What a host of evil tidings we hear now. What a lot of tears are shed! What a multitude of broken hearts and homes there are in the world! They are realities... and all the philosophies and debates, all the elocution and pride or oratory of the world, will never cancel their poignancy. They are there... and they must be dealt with. In front of me I see earnest men who have not alone devoted themselves to service to those who suffer, but who themselves are torn and worn by doubt, by lack of appreciation, by ingratitude of those they serve, and by the unkindness of people to whom they speak words of comfort and uplift, by the antagonism of people whose life they have enriched with the consoling words of religion.

(54:) He is not afraid of evil tidings because to him trial is a discipline; sorrow is God's way of giving us an insight into the mysteries; pain and evil may be the means of deepening character, developing fortitude, and meeting difficulty with faith. A world may turn against us... the skies may be darkened and the pathway of life may be crowded with sharp and jagged boulders... but with Job he may say if there be in him a consciousness of the eternal verities, "I know that my Redeemer liveth" (Job 19:25).

February 28, 1942 (Saturday, Shabbat Zakhor)

Kalonymus Kalmish Shapira, Warsaw Ghetto. *Esh Kodesh*, pp. 165–66; *Derashot meShenot haZa'am*, pp. 277–78; Polen, *Holy Fire*, pp. 30, 74–75, translated by Nehemia Polen

(30:) We are now all enduring very acute and bitter troubles; . . . each of our hearts is torn to shreds and life itself is acutely bitter. Every one of us is downcast, broken, bent over to the ground, full of sadness. . . . This is all especially true in view of the fact that the troubles have dragged on for so long. Even someone who had previously strengthened himself and other Jews is now too exhausted to find inner strength; he is tired of attempting to find consolation. Even if he wishes to pull himself together and to say some remarks of consolation and encouragement, he lacks the words, since in the course of the prolonged days of crisis he has already spoken time and again everything he could have possibly said. The words are now stale, they will not have any effect on him or his listeners. . . .

(74:) Experience has made it evident to me that although a person must every moment hope for God's salvation, nevertheless he should not hang all his hopes on an expectation of immediate salvation. This is because if, God forbid, some time passes, and the salvation does not arrive, it can lead to a situation described by the verse "Hope deferred makes the heart sick" (Prov. 13:12). This is particularly so when people rely on some assurance or some expected course of natural events which might result in imminent salvation. . . .

We must pray to God and entreat Him that He bestow upon us beneficent, manifold kindnesses. But if, (75:) God forbid, He wishes us to suffer, then we must accept this too with love, hoping that He will not abandon us, but will save us and bring us close to Him.

In other words, when a person encourages himself merely with the hope of deliverance, then he has not lightened the burden or diminished the acuity of the suffering's pain and anguish; it is difficult for him to endure if, God forbid, the salvation is delayed. However, if together with the hope for salvation he also inclines his head and says, "It is the Lord; let Him do what seems to Him good," then he alleviates and reduces the bitter feeling, the suffering's anguish and pain. He is able to endure more, and his hopes are better able to instill within him a spirit of life, even if, God forbid, the salvation did not come at the anticipated time.

March 2–3, 1942 (Purim)

Israel Gerstein, "Purim 5702," B'nai Zion Congregation, Chattanooga TN. *Reveille or Taps?* pp. 39–43

(40:) In the ghetto of Warsaw, in that town of torture and endless agony, where six hundred thousand Jews are imprisoned behind an eight-foot wall, the Germans granted to a few actors permission to put on a show to bolster the spirit of the crushed and the downtrodden. The production was named, *Dos Redele Dreht Sich* [The Wheel Turns].[14] . . . Jews figure they are miserable today, a Haman is threatening to exterminate them. But the wheel is turning. His turn, too, will come. It has happened before. The *Megillah* is an eternal source of comfort. . . .

Still, does the *Megillah* give us any hope that the story will repeat itself in modern times? This is a vital question, not only for our people in Europe. It is a question that all are asking, and not only Jews. Can we derive any comfort from the Purim story? Is Hitler another Haman? The conditions today are so unlike those in far-off Persia. For one thing, Haman was not a dictator. Before he could do anything, he had to consult the king. Hitler is Haman and *Ahashvayrosh* rolled into one. Is there any hope that a modern Esther will turn his head? Hitler is supposed to be immune to women. The German propaganda machine pictures him as a sort of *Tsaddik* who cannot

---

14 This was actually a comedy, written by Jacob Prns (b. 1901). According to Zalmen Zylbercweig's *Leksikon fun Yidishn Teater,* "In September 1937, during their guest appearances across Poland, Joseph Schoengold and Frances Adler performed in Prns's comedy 'Dos redele dreyt zikh'," http://www.museumoffamilyhistory.com/yt/lex/P/prns-jacob.htm. There were two Yiddish and three Polish theatres in the Ghetto, but I have not found reference to a performance of this play.

even (41:) bear to look at a woman. That rules out the Esther angle. But does that mean there is no hope?

One of the most hopeful developments is that Hitler is now opposed not alone by Jews. Civilized mankind has recognized in him its arch-enemy, and there is an alliance of forces arrayed against Nazi tyranny as will be hard to beat. The last few weeks have been critical to all of us. It was interesting and remarkable that in the week in which we were thinking of Purim, our president made it plain to the people of the world that victory will come in the end in spite of the present setbacks. For me, the words of the President were a kind of tonic, which will enable me to welcome Purim in the usual style.[15]

MILTON L. GRAFMAN, "Will the Old Story Have the Same Ending?," Congregation Adath Israel, Lexington, KY. *A Set of Holiday Sermons*, 5702/1941, pp. 57–61

(59:) When Hitler embarked upon his program of destroying the Jews, we insisted to the world that Hitlerism was a threat to civilization, not merely to Jews. We cried that the Jews were but the first victims, that the world would become his prey unless he was checked. It took years to awaken men to the danger that threatened them. That they were aroused, however, has given significance to our pain, and enables us to continue to bear our burden. It reveals that our persecution has not been in vain....

There will be a joyous conclusion to the crisis through which we are now passing, if we can retain faith in our mission and our destiny....

March 8, 1942 (Sunday)

STEPHEN S. WISE, "The World Crises: What Can Americans Now Do?," Free Synagogue at Carnegie Hall, New York. AJA, Box 23: SSW Microfilms of AJHS and BUASC papers

(5:) The aim of the Axis powers is to enslave mankind, to enslave

15 Reference is to FDR's Fireside Chat, "On the Progress of the War," delivered on Feb. 23, 1942. Text at http://millercenter.org/president/fdroosevelt/speeches/speech-3326.

mankind by ending human freedom, which is the only way in which it can be done – to destroy Democracy.... This is a war between a small portion of mankind which for a decade or more has prepared itself to enslave the vast majority of mankind. The vast majority of mankind, including ourselves, China, the British Empire (with all its faults and delinquencies of which I shall speak later) and the Russian Soviet, the Soviet Union, are resolved, though unprepared for the most part, that the little trio shall not rule the world, shall not enslave mankind, shall not cancel human freedom, shall not obliterate democracy, shall not destroy the religious and moral values that men have cherished and have died for and lived by.

(9:) I cannot withhold from you my sense of heartbreak over what happened a week and four days ago: a little vessel...on which there were about 750 refugees fleeing from Romanian pogroms. For months and months the Jewish Agency, or rather its Executive in Palestine, had been begging that wretched Palestine Governor, that absolutely unworthy and incompetent leader of that Palestine government, Sir Harold MacMichael, to let the 750 men, women, and (10:) children of the *Struma* to leave that ship and enter the ports of Palestine. "No, No, No, they may not, they must not." The ship remained in the [Istanbul Harbor] until two weeks ago today or tomorrow, when the Turkish Government ordered the *Struma*, an utterly unseaworthy ship, fifty feet, I am told, 140 tons, with 750 men, women, and children, to leave the neutral waters – I suppose by command of the Nazis to Turkey – to go out into the open seas. The *Struma* went out, there was an explosion, 749 went down to their death. One survived.[16]

March 12, 1942 (Thursday, Day of Fasting)

Shlomo Zalman Unsdorfer, "[Written on] The Fourth Day of *Parashat Va-Yakhel–Pikkudei*," Weidritz Alley Synagogue, Bratislava, Slovakia, in Gershon Greenberg, "Metahistory, Redemption, and the Shofar of Emil

---

16 The date of the sinking was February 24, 1942, torpedoed by a Soviet submarine (this was not known until many years later). Current figures are that there were 782 refugees (plus ten crew) on board, of which one refugee survived. See, most recently, Douglas Frantz and Catherine Collins, *Death on the Black Sea*.

Fackenheim," p. 111, translated by Greenberg from Unsdorfer, *Siftei Shlomoh*, pp. 128–29)

What will satisfy You? *Teshuvah* and *Vidui* [repentance and confession]? We hereby do *teshuvah*. We confess before you that we have sinned, trespassed, and committed crimes. A broken spirit? All the troubles have broken our spirit. Charity? We hereby give charity. Please do not be excessively furious with us. What is to be achieved by our blood, should You slaughter us? Please consider the piety of Your servants, and those committed to You. All those great in Torah and *Yirah* [awe of the divine] who have sacrificed themselves in sanctification of Your name.[17]

March 13, 1942 (Friday evening)

Israel Gerstein, "Giving Oneself an Account," B'nai Zion Congregation, Chattanooga TN. *Reveille or Taps?* pp. 113–17

(116:) There is something useful for everyone to do. There is the cry of the victims of war, the call of the starved and tortured men, women, and children, our own, who have no one else to turn to but ourselves, who profess the same religion, who call on the same God with the same *Shma Yisroel*. Our Federation is preparing for a drive. Let us do our share.... *Eretz Yisroel* needs our financial support, and our moral help. Even now the homeless risk everything on the treacherous waves of (117:) the mine-infested waters to seek a haven in *Eretz Yisroel*. Answering the urgent call of duty, now particularly the call of our country in peril, we shall with pride be able to point to our record later.[18]

March 14, 1942, (Saturday, Shabbat HaḤodesh)

Kalonymus Kalmish Shapira, Warsaw Ghetto. *Esh Kodesh*, pp. 178–79;

17 The occasion for the day of fasting proclaimed for the Jews of Slovakia was the beginning of deportation of Slovakian Jewry to Poland (mostly to Auschwitz), after the failure of communal leaders to convince Josef Tiso to allow the Jews to remain.

18 This is the final sentence of the sermon, leaving somewhat ambiguous whether "our country" is intended to refer to the United States or to "Eretz Yisroel."

Derashot meShenot haZa'am, p. 293; Polen, *The Holy Fire,* pp. 119–20, translated by Nehemia Polen; also Roskies, *The Literature of Destruction*, p. 508

(119:) God, blessed be He, is to be found in His inner chambers weeping, so that one who pushes in and comes close to Him by means of studying Torah weeps together with God and studies Torah with Him. Just this makes the difference: the weeping, the pain which a person undergoes by himself alone, may have the effect of breaking him, of bringing him down, so that he is incapable of doing anything. But the weeping that the person does together with God – that strengthens him....

Armin (Avraham Ada) Frieder, Nové Mesto, Slovakia, delivered before *Musaf*, in Emanuel Frieder, *To Deliver Their Souls*, pp. 70–72[19]

(71:) This time we have all one thing in common: we are all Jews, with one law and one decree threatening us all. It is this decree which I wish to talk about, this decree of the government to deport the Jews to Poland.[20] Jewish leaders from all circles have tried to avert this evil decree, but to no avail. Since I see no chance of reversing the decision, we must know that we are facing one of the more difficult periods in our history, a new chapter in the annals of expulsions of the Jews. This time, however, we shall be expelled as slaves to a foreign land and who knows if we shall return and see our loved ones again. To begin with we shall lose our daughters, and after them, our sons. As

19 This sermon, described by the preacher as having been delivered with the synagogue "packed tight; more people had come than for the *Kol Nidre* service," was a response to the news that efforts to avert a deportation order had failed and that deportation would soon begin, supported by the Slovakian government. The preacher was a leading young Neologue rabbi, and part of Slovakia's underground "Working Group," a secret rescue organization. The passage is based on his diary, incorporated into the first half of his son Emanuel's book *To Deliver Their Souls*, p. 70. Cf. also the partial citation in Esther Farbstein, *Hidden in Thunder*, vol. 1, p. 52.

20 Less than one month after the sermon was delivered, Reinhard Heydrich signed an agreement with the Slovakian Prime Minister for the deportation of the Jews, which began the following day (David Cesarani, *Final Solution*, p. 526). Lucy Dawidowicz wrote, "in March 1942 five assembly points for deportees were set up, and despite intensive efforts on the part of the Jewish communal leaders to halt them, deportations continued unabated from March through August 1942" (*The War Against the Jews*, p. 378). Cf. also Leni Yahil, *The Holocaust*, pp. 353–54; Martin Gilbert, *The Holocaust*, p. 309.

families are broken apart, the rest – men, women, and children – will be deported as well.

More than once have the nations of the world sought to destroy us, to annihilate us, by expelling us from one exile to a more difficult exile, fraught with danger. What did our forefathers do before they went into exile? I shall read to you from a history book (at which point I opened the prayer book and pretended to read).[21] "They tried to flee to neighboring countries where this danger did not threaten. They hid, they went underground, they disappeared. They did not register in any census, they did not report to any authorities. They hid silver and gold, jewelry, precious stones, and diamonds in their clothes, in their shoes, in their housewares. They tried to find protection and obtain exemption from the decree, or slipped away from those going to the vale of grief...." If we have learned to understand the past, let us make inferences regarding the present. It appears that those who crossed the borders to the nearest country did best.

My dear ones! Perhaps you do not fathom my words; perhaps I have caused you heartbreak; perhaps your illusions have been dashed by the bleak picture which I have presented you. But this is how I perceive the situation and the hopelessness of our position.... Act prudently, and instead of criticizing, take action today and tomorrow!...

(72:) Fathers and sons, my pupils and my teachers: if you be fated to walk along a way full of obstacles, stumbling blocks, and injuries, along the road of harsh exile, may the Omnipresent have mercy on you and guard you against all hardship and suffering, and save you from all pestilence and illness, and may you be blessed with the priestly benediction: May God bless you and keep you...."

March 28, 1942 (Saturday, Shabbat haGadol)

Ephraim Sokolover, Great Synagogue, Ra'anana, Palestine. *Penei Efrayim*, pp. 258–67, translated by MS

21 This deception was apparently because, as the preacher wrote in his introduction, "officially it [the deportation] was still a secret and discussion of the subject was forbidden, since this would arouse panic in time of war" (*To Deliver Their Souls*, p. 70).

(260:) The chastisement of Deuteronomy [chap. 28] entails ninety-eight curses. There is also one blow that is not written in the Torah, making altogether ninety-nine. There will be no more than this: the ninety-nine curses of Deuteronomy. All of these curses and the suffering that has passed over us and continues to pass over us are sufficient to arouse full repentance without additional measures taken by anyone else.

This is our situation at present. We are approaching the holiday of Pesach, the holiday of freedom, the holiday of the spring, all names so pleasant and enjoyable. Throughout the year, when we come to the spring, we feel a kind of internal cheerfulness, an extremely pleasant feeling. After the cold and difficult winter, after the long dark nights, after all of nature seems to have stopped living – something felt especially outside the land of Israel – now the spring comes....

(261:) But how can we now welcome the holiday of freedom? Where is the time of spring for us? It seems for the moment as if someone has been deceiving us (G-d forbid) into believing that this is the day of the beginning of the Pesach season, and that this Sabbath is Shabbat haGadol. How can this be Shabbat haGadol if there is no spring, if the days of spring have been transformed into days of horrible cruelty? For to our deep sorrow, we already know what spring is in this brutal war.... The last two springs have already destroyed entire worlds. The springs of 1940 and 1941 brought death and destruction to hundreds of thousands of men, women, and children. Among them our brethren were first in line, for they suffered uniquely because they were Jews, upon whom the oppressor proclaimed total destruction (G-d forbid). We have already tasted the great bitterness and the pain of the current spring....

We are especially worried about our brethren in the Diaspora, in the lands of inferno: what is happening there? What is their feeling on this Shabbat haGadol? How are they preparing for the spring? When we look a bit into the distance, and sense the pain and suffering which now pervades the lion's share of our Jewish brethren in the Diaspora who are living in hell on earth, in addition to the general fear that encompasses us here in the land of Israel, it is extremely difficult to prepare ourselves for the great holiday....

(262:) Nevertheless, we are commanded even now to observe the holiday of Pesach in accordance with the halakhah, not only the laws concerning unleavened foods and matzah, the cleaning of dishes, and so forth, as is required year after year, but also the laws pertaining to the traditional seder, with all its beauty and regal splendour, with all the sense of liberation, "as if one has himself gone out of Egypt."...The question is simply this: How can we explain to our children the greatness of the holiday at a time when it is so difficult and incomprehensible for ourselves? Even before we have found the eye of the needle, we need to solve this mystery: the holiday of Pesach in these awful times!

March 29, 1942 (Sunday),

Abraham Cohen, "Day of National Prayer, vi," Birmingham Hebrew Congregation, Birmingham, England. Unpublished, David Cohen Private Collection

(p. 5) We have read with chilled hearts what has been done to the Jewish communities in the occupied territories. Everywhere the most inhuman savageries have been perpetrated upon the defeated nations; but special indignities and sufferings have been reserved for their Jewish elements. In a recent speech Hitler avowed his intention to exterminate Jewry. If he had the power to do so, there is not the slightest doubt that he will carry out his intention. Can any Jew be so degraded as to want to help him in his base designs? But are not those Jews doing just that who are involved in dealings which impair the country's morale? I say nothing now of the grave injury they are doing to the Jewish (6:) name – an injury which will long endure after victory has been won – by the association of a comparative few with nefarious practices. One question they should ask themselves, viz., Do I want to be an ally of Hitler and assist him to destroy Jewry? If that question does not pull him up, he is lost to all sense of decency and we can but deplore that he belongs to our community.[22]

22 On this theme of Jewish profiteers, see Cohen's earlier sermon, above, October 1, 1941, and Hertz's sermon delivered four days later on April 6, 1942, immediately below; also Hertz's sermon delivered May 22, 1942, below.

April 2, 1942 (Thursday, first day of Pesach, Day of Prayer for Freedom and Salvation)

Joseph H. Hertz, "Civilian Morale," St. John's Wood Synagogue, London. *Early and Late*, pp. 14–18; *Jewish Preaching in Times of War*, pp. 461–70

(14:) The tidal wave of ghastly carnage passing over Russian and Polish Jewry is infinitely worse than anything that Pharaoh of old ever was guilty of. The murderers will have the same end....

(16:) [It] must be confessed that there has been a certain failure on the civilian front. Think of the hosts of fifth-columnists and quislings, defeatists and strikers in the Allied countries. In our own land, too.... No Jews among the fifth-columnists and quislings, none among the spies and traitors, and only one or two among the looters! Otherwise the reaction might have been quite different, as it is in connection with offenders of another class, of the so-called Black Market. Jews form but a relatively small portion of the 47,000 offenders prosecuted on this head; and yet some enterprising journalists seem to speak of this transgression as an exclusively Jewish crime....

(18:) The drowning cries of the 759 victims of the *Struma*, fleeing for their lives from a butcher-state like Romania, are still ringing in the ears of all those who are not dead to the call of human Brotherhood.[23] Let there be no more "coffin-ships" in connection with Eretz Yisroel, the Jewish National Home promised to the Jewish People by Great Britain, and publicly endorsed as such by fifty-five nations. *LeShanah haBa'ah biYerushalayim.*

Eliezer Berkovits, "A Speedy Victory?," United Hebrew Congregation, Leeds, England. *Between Yesterday and Tomorrow*, pp. 45–50

(49:) We are living in terrible times. Human suffering has reached a pitch which can hardly be surpassed. And, as usual, we Jews are those who suffer most.[24]

23 On the *Struma*, see the news report in *JC*, February 27, 1942, p. 1, the editorial leader in *JC* March 6, 1942, p. 10, and above, the sermon by Stephen S. Wise, March 8, 1942, with note.

24 The statement that the suffering "can hardly be surpassed" was made two months

What would be the good of a victory before its time? Very soon after such premature victory the world would relapse into its old sins and stupidities. It would repeat its old mistakes, and before long it would fall into the madness of a new war....

To-day it has already become a truism to say that the Allies won the last war but lost the peace. They lost the peace because victory came to them as a surprise, before they were morally prepared for peace, before they had learned the lessons of that tragedy.

Abraham M. Hershman, "Passover – Its Scope and Character," Congregation Shaarey Zedek, Detroit, MI. *Israel's Fate and Faith*, pp. 5–8

(8:) The Passover has a special message for us Jews.... We dare not shut our ears to the cry of anguish coming from our hapless people abroad. In the face of the appalling calamity that has overwhelmed European Israel, every one of us must resolve to do all within his power to rescue his kith and kin. He must say והצלתי, "I will make every sacrifice conceivable to snatch Jews from imminent destruction."

It exhorts us, in the second place, to transport our fellow-Jews languishing in the prison-house of Europe to a place or places of safety. Relief, though all-important, is only first aid, a temporary expedient. Displaced Jews must be removed as soon as possible from Europe to countries ready to receive them, where they can make a fresh start and can feel at home.... But whither are they to go? It is a sad commentary on man's inhumanity to man that San Domingo is the only country which has offered an asylum to a very limited number of refugees. Palestine is the one place where Jews are assured of receiving a hearty welcome. At the present juncture, it is unethical for any Jew, regardless of his theory of Judaism and the Jewish people, to oppose Zionism.

Israel H. Levinthal, "Four Freedoms," Brooklyn Jewish Center, Brooklyn, NY. *A New World Is Born*, pp. 88–92

---

before announcements by the Polish Bund claiming that between 700,000 and 1,000,000 Polish Jews had been murdered were widely publicized.

(92:) Yes, it was these four freedoms which gave the promise of the dawn of a new era to the slaves of Egypt. It is these four freedoms proclaimed in the Atlantic Charter, which offer the world today the promise of the dawn of a new day for all humanity. Out of this holocaust there must come for all peoples and for all lands this true liberation, the liberation that shall fully embrace the four freedoms, the only emancipation that can save the world from further bloodshed and further ruin.

April 3, 1942 (second day of Pesach)

Israel H. Levinthal, "The Plague of the Frogs," Brooklyn Jewish Center, Brooklyn, NY. *A New World Is Born*, pp.103–8

(106:) That demon of the new order of barbarism and savagery in Nazi Germany accomplished the two results mentioned by R. Akiba and R. Elazar. "He begat other frogs who soon covered every part of the earth."[25] The mighty frogs in Italy and in Japan and the smaller frogs in other lands, all owe their life and their power to him. He begat them, he nurtured them; he strengthened them.

(107:) Here is the one plague that explains the other plagues that afflict humanity today. It is the one frog that is responsible for the other big and little frogs that have suddenly appeared to curse and afflict all peoples and all (108:) lands. It is the one danger that must be destroyed, if peace is ever to be the hope of the world. Japan may be conquered, Italy may be defeated, but if the one frog – Hitlerized Germany – remains, then all is lost for humanity. Vanquish and annihilate the one poisonous frog – the Nazi regime – and all the other frogs will speedily disappear, and the ideals now sought to be trampled on and crushed will once more appear triumphant in the lives of all mankind.

April 5, 1942 (Sunday, *Ḥol haMo'ed* Pesach)

Solomon B. Freehof, "Chains and Slavery: If We Should Lose," Rodef

25 b. Sanhedrin 67b, referring to one original frog that begat all the others, based on Exod. 8:2, where the word for "frog" is in the singular.

Shalom Congregation, Pittsburgh, PA. "The Course We Take – Three Addresses." *Rodef Shalom Pulpit*, vol. 8, pp. 3–14

(5:) There is no parallel in modern experience to what would happen to us if Hirohito and Hitler should win. The only parallel we could find would be if we went back three or four thousand years to Egypt, to the story of Passover with slaves barebacked in the blazing sun and the crackle of the overseer's whip around their shrinking shoulders. That is not mere oratory. That is happening in countries already conquered.... (7:) It is not a question any more of looking up in *Mein Kampf* or culling the speeches of the Nazi bigwigs to discover what they intend to do if they win. They have shown it to us with monotonous repetition in Holland, in Denmark, in Norway, in France, in Greece, in Yugoslavia.... (8:) Starvation is used as a weapon of war and therefore the Poles – we shall say nothing of the Jews – were led by the thousands into concentration camps improperly and lightly clad, not just because the Germans needed the warm clothing but in order to kill an inferior race wholesale by pneumonia.

(9:) Think of Pharaoh making a broken people build treasure cities for him and you will understand what the Nazis have done and intend to do....

(10:) The Quislings, the Vichy people, all the back-street saloon plotters are the favored ones of the victor and they assume control and immediately start anti-Semitic legislation overnight. The form of the legislation has been previously prepared in Berlin. It begins as usual with the Jews and then spreads to all groups until the conquered country is prevented from attaining unity again.

April 6, 1942 (Monday)

Joseph H. Hertz, "Passover and the Present Crisis," African Service Broadcast. *Early and Late*, pp. 9–13

(10:) Is not all this[26] a parable of the scene that confronts so many free nations to-day, enveloped as they are in darkness, crushed by

26 Referring to the destruction of the First Temple, discussed in the previous paragraph of the sermon.

defeat, doomed to totalitarian destruction? It is only nine years since Nazism came into power, and yet within those few years it has done things so terrible that people will grow grey when they hear the full story. What is most terrible of all, Nazism has made alarming strides towards the establishment of a jungle society, in which – it is planned – hundreds of millions of *robots* are to slave for a *Herrenvolk*, a master-people, with hearts of stone. More than a dozen European nations have been strangulated, or reduced to vassalage and dishonor. And those who have suffered most in this cataclysm of savagery are the Jews. They have been deprived of human rights; tens of thousands of them have endured fiendish tortures in concentration camps; and the harvest of death in the continuous pogrom throughout Nazi-dominated Poland is reminiscent of Armenia a quarter of a century ago.

Now, the suffering which the Nazis are inflicting upon millions to-day is grim warning of the mortal danger that an Axis victory would bring to the whole of civilization....

April 9, 1942 (eighth day of Pesach)

Abraham M. Hershman, "The Passover Hope," Congregation Shaarey Zedek, Detroit, MI. *Israel's Fate and Faith*, pp. 27–29

(17:) We look out upon the world, and what do we see? The spectacle that meets our gaze is one that is calculated to lunge us into despair. Tyranny and oppression are the order of the day; brute force holds sway and reigns supreme. The Angel of Death is abroad, doing his grim work of destruction on a scale unprecedented in the annals of mankind. It would seem as if the prophecy of doom pronounced by Ezekiel were being fulfilled in all its literal sorrow. "I lay all in ruins, ruins, ruins! Everything shall be overturned!" (Ezek. 21:32). The world is in a bad way.

With eternal timeliness comes to us the sustaining and heartening message of this day. It says, "Fear not! The Holy One, blessed be He, will come. Evil often triumphs, but never conquers." The Angel of Death and all the powers of evil will be destroyed. Rectitude will triumph. God's eternal justice will vindicate itself....

(19:) The crying need of mankind at large and of Israel in particular is a rebirth, a regeneration, a consuming passion for the best, the highest, and the noblest in life, and unceasing effort to hasten the advent of the day when [as at end of *Ḥad Gadya*] "the Holy One, blessed be He, will come."

April 11, 1942 (Saturday, after the fall of Bataan)

Israel H. Levinthal, "Bataan and Bethar," Brooklyn Jewish Center, Brooklyn, NY. *A New World Is Born*, pp. 93–98

(93:) It is with heavy hearts that we have come to the synagogue this morning. We are still shocked and overwhelmed by the news that came to us over the radio and through the press that our forces at Bataan had met defeat, that the flag of America on that distant island was forced to give way to the flag of our enemy....

(97:) The plague that visited Bataan is the result of *Lashon Hara*. That was the curse of our American life until the attack on Pearl Harbor. The evil tongue of dissension and disunity held sway. Evil was spoken of our leaders and of all who endeavored to point the way to national defense. There were the disseminators of hate – alas, we still have them – who, through the medium of the evil tongue, did their utmost to disrupt the national unity of our people....

The plague that visited us is due also to the short-sightedness of so many of our citizens who did their utmost to withhold their *Ma'aser*, their tithe that was so essential to enable our government to prepare properly to face our enemies. Many begrudged the government every extra dollar it asked. The government was becoming Socialistic, many charged, because it levied ever-rising taxes; and these same objectors were so blinded as not to see the imminent danger that demanded ever-increasing protection in defense, if our America was to continue in being....

This tragedy came upon us because so many lost their belief in democracy, because so many surrendered their faith in the Divine Law of freedom and liberty. These ideals for which the founders of our Democracy were willing to sacrifice their lives have lost their hold upon the hearts of many in our land today.

April 26, 1942 (Sunday)

Solomon B. Freehof, "Is Life So Sweet?: What Victory Will Bring," Rodef Shalom Congregation, Pittsburgh, PA. "The Course We Take – Three Addresses." *Rodef Shalom Pulpit*, vol. 8, pp. 29–39

(35:) When we think of the war in all its horrors, we think not only of soldiers, sailors, and airmen; we think of the refugees, of the people lining the streets of Europe and being machine-gunned or being hemmed into concentration camps to die. What will happen to these refugees when the war is won?... The refugees of the world will be journeying to a new home at last.

May 9, 1942 (Saturday evening)

Stephen S. Wise, Excerpt from Address to Opening Session of Emergency Zionist Conference, Hotel Biltmore, New York. AJA, Box 23: SSW Microfilms of AJHS and BUASC papers

(2:) The world has come to see that the least it can do by way of reparation to the Jew is to widen (3:) the stakes and to lengthen the borders of Palestine that Palestine may remain not only the home of half a million and more of the Jewish settlers who have remade the land but that it may become home, infinitely more than refuge, for the million or the million and a half of displaced, exiled, broken Jews, who have the right to proclaim in the words of Emerson, "Goodnight proud world, I am going home." [27]

May 17, 1942 (Sunday)

Israel Abrahams, "Goodwill Service" City Hall, Cape Town, South Africa. *War and Peace: Selection of Sermons and Addresses*, pp. 3–6

(4:) Our lads "up North" [in the army] have established the truth of this contention, beyond any doubt of peradventure. Faced with a common danger and spurred by a common patriotism, they have demonstrated to the whole world how men of varied race, creed,

27 The first line in Emerson's poem is actually, "Good-bye, proud world! I'm going home."

and colour can unite in a bond of brotherhood that bears the seal of their life's blood.[28]

May 22, 1942 (Friday, first day of Shavu'ot)

Joseph H. Hertz, "Pentecost and Commercial Honesty,"[29] St. John's Wood Synagogue, London. *Early and Late*, pp. 19–24, partial version in *JC*, May 29, 1942, p. 11

(22:) [H]istory amply proves that wherever Jews have (23:) been guilty of conduct disgracing their Faith, there blind prejudice and causeless hatred become dominant against Israel. And such causeless hatred does not long remain Platonic hatred. Don't say, "It can't happen here"![30] Remember that, after the last War, it was in London that the *Protocols of the Elders of Zion* – "this grotesque myth, founded in malice and hysteria, built up of garbled history, and synthetized by impudent forgery"[31] – was launched. Again, recall the incidents that accompanied the Mosley campaign in the months before the present War, and any illusion as to an impregnable Maginot line round Anglo-Jewry will vanish. Anything is possible, when once a tidal wave of racial hatred sweeps over a population.

Men of wisdom and good faith are striving to prevent such racial hatred.... And no people is suffering or agonizing more in this Battle for Human Freedom than the Jewish people. On the 12th of this month, Mr. Attlee stated in the House of Commons that the total number of killed in the armed forces of the Empire during the first two years of the War was 48,973. Add to this fatal air-raid casualties, and the number does not reach 100,000. Alas, as a direct result of the War, and the mass-executions in tens of thousands by the barbarians

---

28 The resonance in this passage for the "Native problem" in South Africa is unclear, perhaps intentionally. Cf. August 23, 1942, below.

29 The theme is a follow-up on his Pesach sermon of the same year, cited above.

30 Alluding to the title of the novel by Sinclair Lewis, published in New York and London in 1935.

31 Hertz places this long phrase in quotation marks even in the *JC* article; he is apparently citing Lucien Wolf, *The Myth of the Jewish Menace in World Affairs, or The Truth About the Forged Protocols of the Elders of Zion*, p. 18, http://bit.ly/2yVHJdW.

of Berlin and Bucharest, the ghastly total of Jewish deaths is at least double, if not treble that number."[32]

Eliezer Berkovits, "In the Wilderness of the Nations" (Ezek. 20:35), United Hebrew Congregation, Leeds, England. *Between Yesterday and Tomorrow*, pp. 116–21

(117:) To-day, we have reached this stage in our history. The exiles have been exiled anew. Jewries all over the world have been uprooted. Those compact enclosures of Jewish life, each with a history of its own, each with a religious culture of its own suited to its environment, each almost a separate Jewish nation of its own, with distinct traditions and institutions, have been forced open and their contents poured out, spread out all over the world.

Think of Russian Jewry, of Polish Jewry, of German Jewry – they are no more. There are only former Russian, Polish, German Jews uprooted and wandering about in the Wilderness of the Nations.

May 24, 1942 (Sunday)

Max Nussbaum, "We Are At War," Congregation Beth Ahaba, Muskogee, OK. *From Berlin to Hollywood*, pp. 188–89

(188:) Within the United Nations, the British Empire has been at war against the ruthless aggressor for now almost three years, Russia for a year, the United States for about six months; but we Jews – for now nine consecutive years....

All the other nations, even the smaller ones, now Hitler-occupied, will go home [when the war ends]. Where will the European Jews go?... Having been at war with Hitler longer than the other nations, our casualties count higher than the others. Europe today has ten million Jews, and with the exception of those in England and Russia

32 This number of 200,000–300,000 Jews killed is surprisingly understated for late May, 1942. Within two weeks of the sermon, the BBC and British newspapers would carry the report of the Polish government-in-exile that 700,000 Jews had been killed in Poland alone, and earlier media had carried reports of mass murder by the German special forces of Jews in territory conquered during the invasion of the Soviet Union, especially in Kiev (Babi Yar).

and the inconsiderable groups of Switzerland and Sweden, these millions of European Jews live in ghettos, concentration camps and dungeons of the Gestapo. We [Jews], a nation of seventeen million people in the whole, have lost already nearly two million lives – the highest casualty of any nation so far. Those who will survive (189:) in Europe – if there will be any – will not surpass the number of three millions, and even those will be economically broken and psychologically disabled. Where will they go?

It is in this connection that Palestine lends itself to become the only possible solution. We in America... must not cease to proclaim and demand Palestine as a Jewish commonwealth, whose immigration policy be controlled by the Jewish Agency only.[33]

In a threefold way we are at war with the Axis: as Jews against whom Hitler declared a war of extermination nine years ago; as lovers of Palestine, against which the Axis wages a war of annihilation, and finally as Americans and citizens of the United States, whose democratic way of life Hitler seeks to destroy....

June 13, 1942 (Saturday, *Shelaḥ*)

Moses Kahlenberg, "The Jewish People Distinguished," La Lande Internment Camp, France. *Yedei Moshe,* pp. 209–28, translated by MS

(209:) For the past five weeks I have been lying prone because of an ailment in my right foot, in intense pain, unable to come and go. Thank God it has now become a bit better, and I have been able to come to the synagogue....

(210:) During this past week, another contemptible decree has been added: that every Jew age five and older living in Occupied France must securely sew on his outer garment, slightly to the left of the position of his heart, a yellow badge in the shape of the Shield of David, in the center of which is written the word *Juif.*[34] Even to

33 He continues to express support for the establishment of a Jewish army, fighting under its own flag.

34 The Hebrew is טלאי ירוק, a *green* patch or tag. In her note at the bottom of p. 210, Esther Farbstein provides a possible explanation for the surprising use of *yarok* ("green") rather than *tsahov* ("yellow"), citing Tosafot on b. Sukkot 31b: *Etrog yarok*

this humiliation we bow our heads and accept the stain proudly as a sign of honor.[35] It is reported that there are still many decent, good Frenchmen, people of wholesome heart and mind, who show respect for those who wear the yellow badge, and with words of kindness and comfort (cf. Zech. 1:13) try to reassure us by saying that all of this is against their will and that they feel disgraced by these repulsive acts occurring in their country, things that have not been done for centuries. They promise that such acts will not continue indefinitely, and their enduring words testify to their faith.[36]

(211:) The intent of our enemies was to make us appear "the butt of our neighbors, the scorn and derision of those around us" (Ps. 79:4), humiliated before everyone. What they desired, what they truly wished, has been granted. Obviously from now on, the Jew who is identified by the yellow badge will find it difficult to find any employment, even in jobs that are permitted to him. It will be difficult even to walk on the street to which he is restricted. Indeed, walking in the public places of the city will no longer be pleasant, for our enemies will mock us....

(213:) Perhaps this week's Torah reading has been a cause of all this, as it says, "The whole community broke into loud cries, and the people wept that night." (Num. 14:1). Our sages of blessed memory interpreted, "The Holy one, blessed be He said, 'You have wept without any justification; I will therefore bring about a cause for weeping

pasul, in which the word *yarok* clearly refers to the color yellow. The decree in France was signed on May 29 and announced on June 7 (Poznanski, *Jews in France during World War II*, p. 238, stating that it applied to "all Jews over the age of six").

35 As Farbstein notes at the bottom of p. 210, this is clearly an allusion to the well-known article by Robert Weltsch following the Nazi boycott of Jewish stores on March 1, 1933, ending with the statement "*Man erinnert uns, dass wir Juden sind. Wir sagen Ja, und tragen es mit Stolz*"; see note to June 24, 1936, Felix A. Levy.

36 On the reaction of French Christians, see Poznanski, pp. 241–45, including the journal entry written by a French Christian: "People have never been so kind. That is doubtless because there is nothing more disgusting than to force a man to be ashamed of himself at every instant, and the people of Paris know it." This is followed by three additional sources showing that "the public was on the whole indignant over the imposition of the yellow star."

for generations.'"[37] "Our forefathers sinned and are no more, and we must bear the consequences of their sins" (Lam. 5:7).

(216:) For ten years, "God has chastened me exceedingly" (Ps. 118:18), and brought upon us this evil, this disease of Nazism, afflicting us with trials and suffering. "Many are those it has struck dead" (Prov. 7:18) among the people of Israel: countless thousands and tens of thousands are the victims of this adversary and enemy, this evil one (cf. Esth. 7:6) who persecutes us mercilessly to the very end. This plague continues to spread all over Europe.... Its goal is to transform us into the most contemptible of all the nations. In order to make us look disgraceful to all who behold us, they have made us wear the yellow badge....

June 27, 1942 (Saturday)

Kalonymus Kalmish Shapira, Warsaw Ghetto. *Esh Kodesh*, pp. 186–87; *Derashot meShenot haZa'am*, pp. 303–5; Polen, *Holy Fire*, pp. 102–3, translated by Nehemia Polen

(102:) With all the murderous, sadistic cruelty that has swept over us, the house of Israel, the sadistic cruelty and murder directed against young boys and girls has outdone everything else. Woe! What has befallen us?... When we hear the voices of young and old crying out under torture, crying out "*Ratevet! Ratevet!*" [Help! Help! (in Yiddish)], we know that this is their (103:) soul's cry, and the cry of all our souls, to God, the compassionate Father: "Help! Help! While the breath of life is still within us."

It is indeed incredible that the world exists after so many screams. Regarding the Ten Martyrs, we are told that the angels cried, "Is this Torah, and this its reward?" Whereupon a voice answered from heaven, "If I hear another sound I will turn the world back to [primordial] water."[38] But now, innocent children, pure angels, as well as adults, the saintly of Israel, are killed and slaughtered just

37 b. Ta'anit 28a.
38 Polen, note 57: Piyyut *Eleh Ezkerah, Musaf* service of Yom Kippur; cf. Midrash *Eleh Ezkerah*.

because they are Jews, who are greater than angels. They fill the entire space of the universe with these cries and the world does not turn back to water, but remains in place as if, God forbid, He remained untouched! . .

Now surely we are not alone in our prayers; surely our ancestors, the Patriarchs and Matriarchs, all the Prophets and Prophetesses, the righteous men and women are not passive or silent in the face of such troubles; surely they are agitating and storming the heavens with the magnitude of our sufferings. Surely they are not consoling themselves by saying that whatever happens, the Jewish People will remain!...

Isaac Herzog, Jerusalem. *JC*, July 3, 1942, p. 5

Basing himself upon the Bible, Dr. Isaac Herzog, Chief Rabbi of Palestine, declared in his sermon last Sabbath in Jerusalem that there was no danger of the Germans occupying Palestine. The Chief Rabbi referred to the present war situation and emphasized that "there is no hint in any of the Holy Scriptures as to a third destruction of the Holy Land."

July 11, 1942 (Saturday)

Kalonymus Kalmish Shapira, in *Esh Kodesh*, pp. 188–92, 120–21; *Derashot meShenot haZa'am*, pp. 309–11; Polen, *The Holy Fire*, pp. 32, 120–21; cf. also Roskies, *Literature of Destruction*, pp. 508–9, translated by Nehemia Polen

(32:) It is impossible to draw down the Holy Spirit upon oneself at a time of pain and anguish, God spare us.... If prophecy is impossible in a state of sadness, so, the Talmud tells us, is a matter of *halakhah*.[39] Even to preach on the topic of the calamities is impossible at a time when the heart is broken and the spirit is crushed. There are times when it is impossible even to compel oneself to say some words, as a result of one's being broken and fallen, God spare us....

(121:) How can we tell if the sufferings are only on account of our sins, or whether they are to sanctify His name? By [noticing] whether

39 b. Shabbat 30b, b. Pesaḥim 117a.

the enemies torment only us, or whether their hatred is basically for the Torah, and as a consequence they torment us as well.... [In the latter case] it is not appropriate to ask, "For what sin [did the calamity come]," since while they do not expiate sins, they are essentially sufferings of martyrdom [*kiddush haShem*].

July 21, 1942 (Tuesday, day before Erev Tisha B'Av)

Stephen S. Wise, "Deliverance Will Come," Excerpts from Address Presented at the Mass Demonstration against Hitler Atrocities. Madison Square Garden, New York. *As I See It*, 122–25.[40]

(122:) Tonight we meet not only to sorrow over an ancient grief but also over a limitless wrong of our own day, the Nazi threat to destroy the Jewish people.[41]

We would not be worthy of our Jewish fellowship if we did not lift up our voices in solemn lamentation and mournful protest over the oceanic wrongs done to our brother-Jews wherever Nazis live and rule. We would not be equal to our American citizenship if we did not tonight with one voice ask our great-hearted, liberty-loving fellow Americans to join us in solemn condemnation of the infamy of the Axis in dooming unarmed and defenseless men, women, and children by the hundred thousands to suffering, torture and death. Honor is the fate of them who are privileged to fight and die for a cause, (123:) but shame is the portion of such as torture and murder masses who are weaponless and defenseless. Our hearts went out to the people of the heroic little community of Lidice, every member of which in one way or another was slain by Heydrich's avenging monsters.[42] There have been a thousand and more Lidices in the life of the Jews of Central and Eastern Europe in the last year....

---

40 For a critique of this message for its failure to propose "measures to rescue the Jews still alive in Hitler's Europe" and the assertion that "the salvation of our people and all peoples who would be free can only come under God through a victory speedy and complete of the United Nations," see Wyman, *The Abandonment of the Jews*, p. 25.

41 Insisting that the attempts to destroy the eternal people will not succeed, Wise cites President Roosevelt: "The Nazis will not succeed in destroying their victims any more than they will succeed in enslaving mankind."

42 For the details on the Nazi destruction of Lidice in response to the Heydrich

We wish, moreover, in and through this assembly, to say to our fellow-Jews in the lands of Hitler horror: Afflicted of our people, you are not forgotten and under God your day of deliverance will come. We know that one million and more of you, our brothers, have died of Nazi inhumanity to man, that Jewish multitudes have been and are being exposed to spoliation, starvation, disease, enslavement, massacre and execution. These ruthless atrocities are visited by the Hitler rule upon the Jews of whom Dr. Goebbels said in *Das Reich*, that within a few days, "The Jews must be annihilated in order to save Germany."[43] The fact is that neither the Germans nor the Jews will be exterminated, but a civilized world will exterminate the Hitlers and Goebbels and Himmlers who are the scourge of mankind. The salvation of our people and all peoples who would be free can only come under God through a victory speedy and complete of the United Nations.

(124:) [in the spirit of Tisha B'Av]: You stand not alone in your sorrow; let the faith of a whole world of free men sustain you, the faith of men who now understand as never before that you have suffered through the ages because you denied and rejected Hitlers when you might have gained peace by all the pleasant ways of compromise or appeasement or surrender....

[The Jews of Palestine] must not be left unarmed and defenseless. If, heaven forfend, Rommel should reach the outer gates of Palestine, he must be flung back by the heroic prowess and resistless fury of the Jewish defenders of the land. Even today, two or three divisions of young Maccabeans might have helped to turn the tide in British favor on the western border of Egypt. A Jewish Home Guard to safeguard Jewish Palestine is as rightful and fitting and necessary as an English Home Guard to defend England.[44]

---

assassination, see Richard Evans, *The Third Reich at War*, pp. 277–78. The following sentence would be quoted by several rabbis in their subsequent sermons.

43 This quotation was featured in the JTA of July 20 based on a posting from Berne the previous day. *Das Reich* was the official organ of the Nazi Ministry of Propaganda. Goebbels claimed that it was the Jews who were responsible for the fierce resistance to the German armies shown by the Russians on the Eastern Front.

44 This final paragraph was quoted in the *NYT* article on the rally, July 22, 1942, beginning on p. 1 and continuing (where the quotation appears) on p. 4.

August 23, 1942 (Sunday)

Israel Abrahams, "The Holy Camp," Military Service, Broadcast from Great Synagogue, Cape Town, South Africa. *War and Peace: Selection of Sermons and Addresses*, 7–11

(8:) Guns, bombs, torpedoes and all the other infernal instruments of war do not kill. Only thoughts kill. A bullet is an entirely innocent thing; a gun does not make itself, nor does it fire of itself. It is the bullet-thought, the shooting-desire that is truly responsible for the destruction wrought.... It is sinful thoughts, evil ambitions, that have set the world ablaze today, devastating some of the world's fairest cities, murdering innocent women and children, executing hostages, wiping out "Lidices," decimating entire populations by starvation and plague.

(9:) We are fighting what may be termed the *Unbrotherhood of Man* – the pseudo-scientific delusion that Aryans are better than Semites, Japs than Chinese, and German Nordics than all the world. We can conquer this wicked doctrine only with the Truth of Human Brotherhood.

August 29, 1942 (Saturday)

Eliezer Berkovits, "Now!," United Hebrew Congregation, Leeds, England. *Between Yesterday and Tomorrow*, pp. 127–31

(129:) For ends do not justify means. Truth must not be shelved, morality not deferred, and God cannot be postponed until the danger has passed and the emergency is over. Laws and statutes, moral codes and ideals, are no mere luxuries with which one may dispense in times of danger....

Evil cannot be fought with its own methods; evil is contaminating. And the Promised Land cannot be conquered without keeping alive those very ideals to which we intend to dedicate it after we have taken possession.

September 3, 1942 (Thursday),

Abraham Cohen, "Day of National Prayer, 7," Birmingham Hebrew Congregation, Birmingham, England. Unpublished, David Cohen Private Collection

(6:) One thing more remains to be said to a Jewish congregation. We must indeed be mentally blind if we fail to appreciate that individually and collectively our entire future is involved in the outcome of the struggle. Not only is our personal lot as free citizens of the Empire at stake, but the destiny of the Jewish people as a whole. We have read with horror and chilled hearts what has been done to the Jewish communities in the occupied territories. Everywhere the most inhuman savageries have been perpetrated upon the defeated nations; but special indignities and sufferings have been reserved for their Jewish elements. Hitler has avowed his intention to exterminate Jewry. If he has the power to do so, there is not the slightest doubt that he will carry out his intention. Our lives and fortunes hang in the balance. Quite apart, then, from the obligation we have of defending our country and working for its victory, we have the additional sacred duty of throwing in our all for the preservation of our own people. What greater incentive could we have to devote ourselves, body and soul, to the destruction of the foul thing which menaces us?

Alexander Altmann, Great Synagogue, Cheetham Hill Road, Manchester, England. *JC*, September 11, 1942, p. 10

Let us voice our protest against the Government of France which has betrayed the noble tradition of that country, and besmirched her national honour, by allowing the unspeakable tragedy of those 4,000 children who were herded in concentration camps, deprived of their identity proofs and separated from their parents. *Yizkor*! Nazidom has raised man's inhumanity to man to the rank of a principle in its New Order. But this barbarism has drawn closely together all freedom-loving nations.

September 4, 1942 (Friday evening)

Jacob Kaplan, Synagogue de Lyon, France, in Shapira, *Jacob Kaplan*, pp. 146–47, translated by MS[45]

---

45 Reference is to Fonds Kaplan, Box 25. The date is cited in the source, but no title is provided by Shapira.

(146:) We are all equal before God, but we do not all share an identical fate.[46] For some, the fate is to be excruciating, (147:) for others – our own category – it is relatively privileged. For some, the martyrdom that they endure appears to us as a horrible ordeal,... for the others, for the more fortunate, begins a formidable ordeal, which certainly appears to them to be less tragic, but the consequences of which might be totally tragic. God will determine whether they are worthy of the kindness He has shown to them. God wants to see whether they will extend to their wretched fellow Jews all necessary assistance.

September 11, 1942 (Erev Rosh Hashanah)

Stephen S. Wise, "A Year and the Years," Excerpt, Free Synagogue at Carnegie Hall, New York. AJA, Box 23, SSS Microfilms of AJHS and BUASC papers

(1:) The term "tragic" loses its power of characterization of what the world has perforce endured at the hands of Hitlerism, and Jews to an even larger degree than any other people or group. Lands have been overrun. Peoples have been pillaged and enslaved. Every manner of barbarism has been inflicted upon the subjugated. But it is only against Jews that the unashamed threat or edict of extermination has been pronounced. Jews have suffered a thousandfold for wrong and evil and injustices devised by the savage Fascists. But against Jews something unique in its enormity of humiliation and torture has been perpetrated, namely, the re-establishment of the Ghetto, with all that it means of enslavement and torture and exile. No wrong, not even slave labor, equals the horror of the Ghetto, itself a symbol of reversion to an era before men knew pity or even practiced the rudiments of justice.[47]...

46 The preacher is distinguishing here between Jewish refugees from other countries, who were currently being arrested and deported to unknown destinations, and those in the Southern Zone who were until recently French citizens. On these roundups over the summer of 1942, see Renée Poznanski, *Jews in France During World War II*, chap. 8: "The Massive Police Roundups," pp. 251–302.

47 It seems as if Wise was either unaware or unable to announce publicly that deportation from the Warsaw ghetto (and others) to death camps characterized by systematic gassing of the entire population of arrivals had begun in the previous

No volume could encompass the story of the horrors of the Jewish year 5702, coming after "nine iron years of terror and of evil [...] led by the screaming voice that is war and hate."[48]

(2:) Still more foul and brutal deeds have been wrought chiefly by the Gestapo, against men and women whenever found guilty of the crime of mercy to Jews. Thus was the Polish woman executed for providing Jews with bread; thus was a German baker executed as an accomplice of the deed, in addition to the two Jews accused of purchasing the bread. Reading the story of these unmentionable deeds, one must even give credence to the deed of the Nazis in driving hundreds of Jews on to a barge in Yelsk [Belarus] without food and shelter. And when a peasant, hearing their maddened cries, swam at night to the barge to feed them, was discovered, twelve peasants from the collective farm were executed, after which the barge was exploded and all the Jews drowned.[49]...

(2–3:) If such Papal intervention [through the Papal Nuncio to the Vichy Government to end deportations from Vichy] be factual, then Pius XII follows the high example set by his saintly predecessor [Pius XI], whose word in reprobation of anti-Semitism, "Spiritually we are all Semites," will never fade out of the memory of a people which does not forget but forgives.

(4:) Palestine has not fallen into the omnivorous Nazi maw... [A] beginning has been made in organizing a Jewish military force in Palestine.

Ferdinand M. Isserman, "Rosh Hashanah Sermon," Temple Israel, St. Louis, MO. AJA, MS-6, Box 16, Folder 4

---

summer. His public announcement about systematic mass murder of millions of Jews was permitted only in November, 1942. Cf. Saperstein, *Witness from the Pulpit*, p. 94, and note 10.

48 The quotation in the text is from the opening of a radio drama entitled "They Burned the Books," broadcast on May 11, 1942, over the NBC Network, http://gutenberg.net.au/ebooks03/0300841.txt. The author was Stephen Vincent Benet.

49 The report of this incident seems to be based on either an article published in the *JC*, on August 7, 1942, p. 7, or on a pamphlet published in London entitled, "Jews Must Answer: If Not Now When," p. 6. The source for both was a man named Jacob Uzinsky. A similar story, placing the drowning event in Vitebsky on the Dvina River was published by JTA on May 25, 1942.

(1:) During the quiet and peace of my vacation, . . . I chanced to tune in on a broadcast which poignantly brought to my consciousness the agony of the world and the sufferings of millions of human beings. In the course of a news broadcast, I heard the radio announcer state that sixty thousand Jewish men, women, and children had been massacred in Minsk after it had been captured by the Nazi army. The massacre had taken place on four successive days in the outskirts of the city, on each of which fifteen thousand human beings were machine-gunned to death by squad after squad of uniformed German soldiers who carried out their dastardly task between sunrise and sunset.

Tonight, we close unquestionably the most tragic year in Jewish history. All Jewish persecution pale[s] away into insignificance in comparison with what has happened to the Jews of Europe in the past three hundred and sixty-five days, as the German armies invaded and laid low territories where lived a large aggregation of the children of Israel. I could not shake from my consciousness these sixty thousand innocent dead. . . .[50]

(6:) If Hitler succeeds in annihilating the Jews, he will succeed in annihilating the church as well as the synagogue. If he carries out his vow to burn every Jewish book and obliterate every Jewish thought from the memory of man he will have to burn the Bible, the Old and New Testament, and obliterate the name of Jesus as well as the name of Moses from the memory of man, as well as the hope of brotherhood, justice and peace...

(7:) [W]e must and can also be its saviours [of civilization]. . . . I had never expected at any time to stand in this pulpit, or in any

50 JTA, August 14, 1942, presents a somewhat different chronology based on a surviving eye witness, giving the total number as 72,000: approximately 35,000 Jews of Minsk were massacred on November 7, 1941, the anniversary day of the Soviet Revolution, an additional 18,000 on February 23, 1942, 8,000 Jewish women on March 8, and 11,000 more on April 29. Thus the news report cited by Isserman is not evidence of new events, but rather evidence of when the reports of such massacres became available to the American public. The numbers cited above do not reflect the consensus of current historiography, according to which a major massacre of some 30,000 Jews in Minsk occurred between July 28 and July 31, 1942, long after the capture by German forces.

pulpit, and speak to a congregation to urge the support of any war, to commend the strengthening of armed forces, as I do tonight. I do so not because I have changed my basic philosophy. I know that war is just as horrible as I pictured it in many a sermon, but I also know that there can be no peace on earth until this modern tyranny is crushed, and it can be crushed only by superior physical force, by out-bombing and out-shooting and out-daring and out-sacrificing.... If we do not crush Hitlerism, then slavery and serfdom, violence and war will rule over the face of the earth for generations and generations....

Harold I. Saperstein, "The Mount of Sacrifice," Temple Emanu-El of Lynbrook, NY. *Witness from the Pulpit*, pp. 90–95

(91:) [T]his year is different. This year, our beloved nation is at war. In this year, everything we cherish is at stake. Something within tells us that when this year is over, its record will stand as one of the great milestones of human history....

(94:) We Jews, unheralded, have had thousands of Lidices.[51] Community after community has been destroyed; communities I know, where I walked, talked, and worshipped, now have not a single living Jew. The expressed purpose of the Nazis has been the complete elimination of the Jews from Europe. Fortunately, there are limits to the human imagination. For if we really comprehended what the news items reveal of the unending exile and deportation, the pitiless scourges of famine and disease bound up with ghettoization, the ruthless slaughter, we could no longer eat or sleep. We would not be human if we could ever laugh again. And yet the news reports are understatements of the reality....

(95:) But in the last few years, something new has happened. That spiritual brotherhood is no longer confined to Jews. It has expanded until it embraces all the forces of civilization and decency and humanity. ... No longer do Jews march alone to the mount of sacrifice. They are now the battle-scarred veterans in a vast army of those who hate tyranny and love freedom and dream of a better world.

---

51 Echoing the statement made by Stephen S. Wise in his speech at Madison Square Garden, July 21, 1942.

MAX NUSSBAUM, "We Are Not Alone," Temple Israel, Hollywood, CA. *From Berlin to Hollywood*, p. 35

At the beginning of this New Year, 5703, it is fitting to let pass in review not only the horrifying pictures of Jewish life, of which we know, but the advantages and merits of the concluding year, which seldom enter our mind. The characteristic feature of many centuries of Jewish history was not so much persecution as loneliness. In days of tribulation we usually stood completely alone, without friends, and what is more, without neighbors.

The passing year, 5702, changed a very important item in our life among the nations. For the first time in our history, the nations, united in democratic gospel, stand with us and we are a part of them. They and we know that our fate is interdependent. It is this togetherness of a spiritual neighborhood that marks the outstanding symbol of the year 5702 in our Jewish calendar – indeed an unusual result of a war-torn time.

September 12, 1942 (Saturday, first day of Rosh Hashanah)

ELIEZER BERKOVITS, "Common Responsibility," United Hebrew Congregation, Leeds, England. *Between Yesterday and Tomorrow*, pp. 140–45

(140:) Three years of a terrible war have passed over us; for three dark years we have witnessed the collapse of human civilisation. The whole framework of a world which we have already come to call the old has gone to pieces before our eyes.

It is natural that in the midst of such confusion and chaos, under the stress and strain of terrifying events, we should pray on the Holy Days for nothing else but a speedy deliverance from the nightmare of this senseless destruction of values, of life and human happiness.

But this is not enough.... Before we pray, we must think; we must try to understand....

(144:) The terrible tragedy of this war has come upon us because people and nations refused to acknowledge in their actions the principle of common responsibility; because artificial barriers were erected between man and man, between one nation and the other; because individuals, groups, and nations thought of themselves as independent, sovereign, self-contained units....

(145:) "You *are* the keeper of your brother" (cf. Gen. 4:9) is the great message of God that reaches us through the catastrophes of our days. In all the awe-inspiring events around us one truth is illustrated again and again: the interdependence of all life on earth.

Abraham L. Feinberg, "The Spiritual Challenge of This Hour," Temple Emanuel, Denver, CO. *A Set of Holiday Sermons*, 5703/1942, pp. 4–10

(4:) Behind us is 5702, racked with violence, war, slaughter, and increasing sorrow for Israel. Before us is 5703, just born! Fear and hope struggle together in our hearts while we strain our eyes to glimpse its form. What will it bring? Victory or defeat, life or death, joy or pain?

(5:) What are we in the scale of history?... Think of the millions of lives being snuffed out on land, on sea, in the air, and under the sea! Shall then some especial worth be attached to *our* life?...

(7:) The entire history of Israel symbolizes the challenge of suffering. For two thousand years we have endured persecution and exile.... Why didn't we collapse as a people, and vanish as a religion? What preserved us? This! Our forefathers read in the Book of Isaiah that the servant of the Lord must be despised and rejected of men, that to be hated and browbeaten is the training-ground and destiny of him who longs for God! And they were convinced that suffering and affliction are only a prelude to spiritual victory.

The ancient rabbis told of a bowl that God had placed at the foot of His throne. In this the tears of Israel, wrung by persecution, were treasured. On some distant day, when that bowl is full to overflowing, God will at last send His redeemer.[52]

(9:) This generation in which we live today has not been singled out for unique and almost unbearable grief; our period is not the special whipping-boy in Jewish history. In every clime and century, our fathers had even worse things to endure. But they had what we are in danger of losing: namely, faith to overcome their fate.

52 I am unable to identify the source for this passage. The closest I have found is the Book of Revelation, which speaks of golden bowls at the foot of the divine throne that are filled with the prayers of the suffering pious of God's people, resulting in peals of thunder, lightning, and earthquakes upon the earth (Rev. 5:8, 8:3–5).

(10:) Today the light of Israel seems closer to the dark abyss than ever before – yet it shall, it *must* pierce through the gloom that thickens about us, layer upon layer. Like the lamp that burns before the Ark here in our Temple, its tiny ray shall write for all to read, "The Spirit of man conquers."

On these legendary tablets, many historic and somber events of 5702 will be inscribed: global war, blood-letting in all the corners of earth, bereavement and pain and hunger in the camps of Israel? What will 5703 relate?...

Louis I. Newman, "Ye Are My Witnesses," Congregation Rodeph Sholom, New York. *Sermons and Addresses*, vol. 4, 118–26

(119:) A renewed understanding of Israel's historical role as the witness to God's truth and will has come to us recently in the message addressed to us by the eloquent Secretary of the Interior, Harold Ickes, in the following words:

> This is a particularly auspicious year in which to send a message of greetings to the Jews on the occasion of the Jewish New Year. The Jews have been Hitler's first victims, and hence the earliest fighters against Nazism. They have also been the most brutally treated of all of Hitler's victims, and hence his bitterest opponents.
>
> Now the Jews, who were the real shock troops against Hitlerism, are no longer alone in the fight. They are joined by the brave and the free peoples of the world, and they will share in the victory of these peoples. May our common victory bring the fulfillment of the ancient prophet's dream of justice and freedom not only for the Jews, but for all humanity.[53]

What a majestic utterance. Let us dwell for a moment upon the phrase, "Now the Jews, who were the real shock troops against Hitlerism, are no longer alone in the fight...."

(122:) The experience of the past has repeated itself in our own life. We are no different from our fathers, and the greatness which

53 Ickes' New Year's greeting, along with greetings from President Roosevelt and Secretary of the Navy Frank Knox, was published in JTA, September 11, 1942.

perhaps neither they nor certainly we have sought, has been thrust upon us.

(123:) Never has the link between Jewry and free men been displayed more effectively than in the decade through which we have passed. The Satan of our time has promulgated the Nuremberg Laws disenfranchising German citizens of the Jewish faith. He has vowed the destruction of Israel, and he has vowed the death of modern democratic culture.... (124:) The men who stood at the rostrum a decade ago expounding the nature of Hitlerism, and beseeching the world to prepare against its certain and inevitable onslaught upon the liberty of the nations were like Paul Revere and Charles Dawes, crying out in the night: "The enemy are coming! The enemy are at our gates!..."

Louis Hammer, "Dominion of Arrogance," Congregation B'nai Shalom, Brooklyn, NY. *A Word in Season*, pp. 44–51

(44:) As we assemble this Rosh Hashanah in our house of worship, dark clouds cover the horizon. Not only physical but spiritual dim-outs and blackouts prevail. Our hearts are heavy, our minds perturbed, our spirits depressed. The grim spectre of war is in our midst... Now more than ever, we need the comforting word which religion alone can give. We need the courage which our faith can provide....

(45:) As we look about us, we are appalled at the horrible spectacle of devastation. War is raging on three continents and seven seas. The priceless treasures of the ages are being destroyed before our eyes. The wealth of nations is being uselessly wasted. Wickedness, treachery, and brutality have combined to destroy Western civilization. The heart sickens at the bloodshed; the flower of the world's youth is being sacrificed to MARS and MOLECH. The world of moral values is tottering because the forces of evil are undermining its foundations. There is no power to restrain them. They are spreading havoc everywhere. What has caused this upheaval? What is its source?

It is the "*Mamsheles Zadon* – the dominion of arrogance." With the advent of Nazism there appeared a new world outlook... One must go back to the Hebrew original to understand the full implications of this expression....

(46:) It is not uncommon to see one hundred and two hundred hostages killed for the death of one Nazi official or hangman. There is even the case of a whole town (47:) like Lidice completely wiped off the map as a measure of reprisal.... It is a Satanic revolt against the Power above.... Now we can understand why Nazism poured out its wrath against the Jewish people in particular. As soon as it made its appearance, it declared war against the Bible.... Now it is resorting to wholesale butcheries of innocent (47:) victims, employing *firing squads and gas chambers.*

(50:) It is gratifying that two of the great leaders of the United Nations fully realize what is at the basis of this war. In their recent utterances we see almost prophetic insight. Even before we declare war, President Roosevelt and Winston Churchill formulated the Atlantic Charter and its rich implications. Whether these ideals will be fully implemented and the millennium reached at last, is hard to tell. Human nature is changeable and the ideals proclaimed when things are going against us are not always the same as those put into practice when the war is over.

September 13, 1942 (second day of Rosh Hashanah)

Israel Gerstein, "The Shofor Sounds - Reveille or Taps?," B'nai Zion Congregation, Chattanooga TN. *Reveille or Taps?* pp. 1–6

(4:) [I]t would be fooling ourselves to indulge the hope that a victory will be the sulfanilamide that will drive out all the Hitler poison from the American body. Anti-Semitism, in greater or lesser degree, is here to stay. The disillusionment and bitterness that usually follow a war created a fertile field for prejudice....

(6:) The lamps of faith, extinguished on the European continent, must be relighted here.

Mendell Lewittes, "The Call of the Shofar," Congregation Beth El, Dorchester MA. *1943 Manual of Holiday and Occasional Sermons*, pp. 40–50

(42:) A terrible war has been unleashed against the Jew. The whole world reckons the beginning of this war from September 1, 1939. For us this war began on March 1, 1933.[54] From the very day Hitler seized power in Germany, a war was declared and waged against the Jew. For almost ten long years this conflict has been raging between Nazi brutality and the sons of Israel. What words can describe the bottomless pit of horror into which European Jewry has been flung. The *Shevarim Truah* [of the shofar] are but faint echoes of the wailings and tears, the broken bodies and crushed spirits which issue forth from the Ghettoes. The whimperings of innocent children, their bellies swollen from starvation as they ask their stricken parents for a morsel of bread and a few precious drops of milk, as their cries ascend heavenward, piercing the mystery of G-d's habitation, calling to a merciful father. "O father, listen to the *shevarim truah*! How long will you abandon your children to the fury of the beasts? How long will you permit the enemy to decimate your people?"...

(48:) To our intense shame, let it be recorded that there still exist in the United States a few influential men who are but one-quarter for this war and three-quarters against it; who are incessantly continuing their vilification of Roosevelt and the disparagement of the war effort; who still maintain that we can make peace with Hitler and live in a world threatened by dictators....

This is a *Yom Hadin* [Day of Judgment] when we decide once and for all that we cannot return to the selfish imperialism of the twenties and thirties, that America cannot sabotage world peace by an illusory isolationism and refusal to cooperate in a League of Nations. We must make a clear and forthright decision that we can no longer tolerate in our midst the sly propaganda of a Coughlin or a Pelley,[55] that the forces of reaction in our midst must be defeated at the (49:) same time that we defeat the armies of Germany and

---

54 March 1, 1933, was two days after the Reichstag Fire, which Hitler blamed on the Communists and used as an excuse to justify the "Decree of the Reich President for the Protection of People and State" (*Verordnung des Reichspräsidenten zum Schutz von Volk und Staat*), moving toward absolute dictatorship.

55 For Father Charles Coughlin, see the complete sermon (from 1932) by J.X. Cohen, below. William Dudley Pelley, a leader of the Fascist-sympathizing "Silver Shirts,"

Japan. The American people must decide to abandon the smug and selfish aloofness to European tyranny and do its share to guarantee the four freedoms, in the four corners of the earth. And we right here must decide right now that we are for this war one hundred percent, that we are going to lend to its prosecution every ounce of our effort, that we are not going to attempt to avoid our responsibilities and let the other fellow fight our battle.

Ephraim Sokolover, Great Synagogue, Ra'anana, Palestine. *Penei Efrayim*, 25–28, translated by MS

(25:) I would think that all of us in the Jewish community here are obligated to say the blessing, "Who has kept us alive…" with great devotion, for we are indeed "a people saved from the sword" (Jer. 31:1) in the full sense of the words. After having been through such great danger this past summer, with the savage Nazi enemy standing at the gates of the Holy Land, all of us now feel that that the danger is ascending from over our heads.[56]…

We know what Chief Rabbi of Israel, [Isaac] Herzog said when he was in the United States, and everyone tried to influence and convince him to remain there, because the situation [in the land of Israel] seemed so desperate. Blessed by God, we are indeed "a people saved from the sword." What the Chief Rabbi said has been confirmed: "I am certain that no Third Destruction will take place in the Holy Land."[57]… Now we have seen this with our own eyes: how the Rabbi, correct in his decision and his powerful faith, returned in peace to the Land, to the joy of all.…

(26:) But there is a second side, when we are reminded of what

was actually sentenced in August, 1942 to fifteen years in prison for sedition and undermining the war effort (Leonard Dinnerstein, *Antisemitism in America*, p. 134).

56 The Jewish community of Palestine was seriously threatened by the forces of Rommel moving eastward into Egypt, along with hostility of the local Arab population. The appointment of Montgomery in mid-August led to a subsiding of the immediate danger to the Yishuv.

57 There are various versions of this well-known statement by Herzog; see *JC*, July 3, 1942, p. 5, reporting the source as a sermon delivered on June 27, 1942 (see above at that date), and the extensive discussion by Ari Shevat (Chwat) at http://www.yeshiva.co/midrash/shiur.asp?id=10933.

has happened to our Jewish brethren during the past year, and in these very days, in the lands of inferno, given over to be disgracefully downtrodden, subjected to all kinds of terrible, frightening tortures. How many tens of thousands of our relatives and kin have already been killed, based on what we have heard said in an unofficial manner, victims of the sword and of starvation. Knowing all of this, how can we rejoice?…

It is our duty to weep at this time, this time when our parents and children, our brothers and sisters, our flesh and blood, are not only on the war front, but are considered to be as a flock being sent to the slaughter [Zech. 11:4], whose situation is so totally tragic that they do not even have the opportunity on this great and holy day to gather in public and mourn bitterly together over their desperate fate.

September 19, 1942 (Saturday, Shabbat Shuvah)

Abraham M. Hershman, "An All-Out Return," Congregation Shaarey Zedek, Detroit, MI. *Israel's Fate and Faith*, pp. 215–17

(217:) There is no denying that we are witnessing today a part-way return to Judaism. Deeply moved by what has happened to German Jewry and to the Jews of Eastern Europe, many who had hitherto stood aloof from the Jewish people, and had taken no active part in Jewish affairs, have manifested an anxiety "to belong." They have joined organizations composed of Jews, they have even joined organizations that have a specifically Jewish purpose, have connected themselves with Zionism, and even affiliated themselves with the Synagogue. All this is good so far as it goes; but unfortunately it does not go far enough. Affiliation with Jewish organizations, however desirable, will not save Judaism.

David Polish, "Return To the Rock," Temple Israel, Waterbury, CT. *A Set of Holiday Sermons*, 5703/1942

(17:) On this Sabbath of Return we find ourselves in a world which is totally mobilized. Men who are free have rallied to the call for defense and victory. Those who have surrendered their souls to the mad whims of tyrants rally obediently to fulfil the death sentences pronounced upon them by their masters. Millions of slaves are herded together in a ghastly roll-call of dead souls and withered lives. But there is also a mobilization of the spirit. We Jews have practiced it for many centuries.

September 20, 1942 (Sunday, Erev Yom Kippur)

Joseph H. Hertz, "The Day of Atonement," BBC Broadcast September 20, Erev Yom Kippur. *JC*, September 25, 1942, p. 1; *Early and Late*, pp. 32–36

(34:) The story of Job certainly seems to be a parable of present-day humanity. We, too, cannot explain the vast and infinite suffering through which the world is just passing. But once more we see that suffering is a holy thing. It purifies; it educates; and it gives mortals an opportunity for disinterested goodness. The devotion and exalted consecration to high ideals that the War is calling forth are due to the burning conviction, deeper than words, that there are things of absolute and eternal worth, for which we gladly sacrifice all we have and are in life....

(35:) No book [referring to Daniel] could be more appropriate for meditation on the Day of Atonement, which opens for us the portals of eternity in this world, and the gates of immortality in the world to come. And especially so in the present darkness of Nazi persecution. During our solemn Remembrance of the dead to-morrow, we shall be haunted by the thought of hundreds of thousands of fellow-Jews done to death by bombing, machine-gun, and lethal chamber; killed by torture, hunger, and all manner of privation. Many of those who are at this (36:) moment listening to my voice weep for near relatives and friends tortured and murdered by the hell-hounds of Hitler, who spare neither young nor old, and pity neither mothers nor infants.

Louis I. Newman, "Yom Kippur Charity Appeal," Congregation Rodeph Sholom, New York. *Sermons and Addresses*, vol. 4, 147–49

(147:) A veil of secrecy hides from the eyes of Americans the dreadful sufferings of our fellow-Jews in Central and Eastern Europe.... It is not necessary that I speak to you again regarding the destruction of synagogues in the great Jewish communities of Germany, Austria, France, and other Nazi-infested lands. You know too of the compulsory Ghettos, forced labor, and other brutalities to which our helpless co-religionists are being subjected. Stephen Vincent Benet, commenting upon *The Black Book of Poland*,[58] has said:

> Let us imagine, if we can, a ghetto in New York City with an eight-foot wall around it. Let us imagine the forced and sudden deportation of a million and a half of our citizens from the grain lands of the Middle West – shipped out in sealed freight-cars like cattle, but with none of the care that is given to cattle. Let us imagine the closing of every college in the country, the deliberate destruction of Mount Vernon, the Statue of Liberty, and the Lincoln Memorial, the closing of St. Patrick's Cathedral and Trinity Church, and the shooting of boys who whistled "The Star-Spangled Banner." Let us imagine starvation, typhus and death. We shall then get a very faint and feeble idea of what the New Order has meant to Poland and her people.

Such a paragraph can give us, in safe and free America, a graphic picture of our fate under a similar tyranny.

September 21, 1942 (Yom Kippur)

Ferdinand M. Isserman, Sermon at Memorial (*Yizkor*) Service, Temple Israel, St. Louis, MO. AJA, MS-6, Box 16, Folder 2

(4:) At this service, too, we commemorate the Jewish victims of persecution. In Germany, in Poland, in Greece, Jugo-Slavia, Czecho-Slovakia, Russia, Nazi soldiers are in control of the territories where live half the Jewish population of the world. How many died wantonly, murdered in cold blood, not in the course of military action,

58 This 615-page book was published by the Polish Ministry of Information in 1942; its major sections were: 1. Persecutions, Murders, Expulsions (with a subsection on "The Persecution of the Jews and the Ghettos"), 2. Pillage and Economic Exploitation, and 3. The Destruction of Polish Culture. Newman provided the source for this quotation in the printed text: *New Republic*, Sept. 21, 1942, p. 354.

no one knows except that their number is legion. How many died while being transported in cattle cars to the ghettos in Poland, no one knows. How many have died in the ghetto of Warsaw from malnutrition, starvation and sickness, all of which were unnecessary, no one knows. How can we honor them? What can we do for them? On this earth they are beyond our help. That while they were alive that holy relief agency the Joint Distribution Committee, did something for them, is a source of satisfaction....

(5:) Today, there are seven million defenders of Torah who totter on the brink of death. Their synagogues have been destroyed. Their Torahs have been burned. Their rabbis have been murdered. Their teachers have been imprisoned.... We who have been spared their suffering and their martyrdom must fill their vacant places.... The martyred Jewries of Europe expect us to rise to the occasion to maintain that great religious culture for which they have died, which has still a message to give to humanity....

Nathan Netter, "God and Human Suffering (*Dieu et la souffrance humaine*)," Marseille, France. *La Patrie égarée et la patrie renaissante*, pp. 141–47, translated by MS

(142:) Faced with a calamity that is among the greatest that Jewish history has had to record, it can hardly escape us that what is most compatible with our aching souls on this day would be the silence of stoic resignation, or at most of deep meditation....

(144:) How is it possible that the most appalling agony spreads over the entire surface of the earth, and that the One who, through a single phrase, pulled forth the world from nothingness, remains aloof, without intervening to restore order to our terrestrial valley? How is it that the most enormous atrocities are committed here below, without the Master of the Universe allowing His voice to be heard saying, "Thus far shalt thou go, but no further!"? (Job 38:11).

How can divine mercy be reconciled with our incredible suffering? Even if it is satisfying to explain this suffering as a heavenly punishment, imposed because of our repeated unfaithfulness, does a father have no pity?...

(145:) I would consider myself fortunate if I should be able to open for you a way in which you might be able to banish the doubt which must have flourished in a number of disturbed souls, oppressed by so many crimes, so many atrocities, that have overwhelmed our feeble co-religionists. For this purpose, I would like to raise before you the curtain that has fallen upon a biblical drama in which the same problem that troubles us today is treated and artistically resolved. It's about Job that I would like to speak....

September 26, 1942 (Saturday, first day of Sukkot)

Eliezer Berkovits, "On Education," United Hebrew Congregation, Leeds, England. *Between Yesterday and Tomorrow*, pp. 61–66

(64:) In these days, it has already become a truism to say that the Jews are passing through one of the most critical periods of their history. We have suffered defeat at the hand of our enemies as well as at that of our evasive friends. But the Jewish situation is tragic and almost hopeless not because of the nature of our defeats, but because of the nature of the Jews who have been defeated.

Louis I. Newman, "Harvest Festivals for Christians and Jews" (including Thanksgiving), Congregation Rodeph Sholom, New York. *Biting on Granite*, pp. 118–27

(123:) In these days, we speak more and more of the Judaeo-Christian ethic, in view of the peril which both religions face at the hands of the Nazis. For we know that both Christianity and Judaism alike are hated and combated by the tyrants, since the preachment of the Bible and of the religions built upon it is regarded as veritable revolution and counter-propaganda by the promoters of hate....

(126:) The earth is good but some men are evil. This is the message of Sukkoth this year – a festival celebrating abundance, in the midst of a world which imposes starvation. And the ironic corollary of the Nazi barbarism is that the very grain fields they acquire they cannot harness to the harvests for the feeding of their own hungry people. The more Germany appropriates, the less the ration for her own subjects.

October 11, 1942 (Sunday, Rosh Ḥodesh Ḥeshvan)

ZELIG KALMANOVICH, Vilna Ghetto,[59] in Dawidowicz, *A Holocaust Reader*, pp. 225–26; Roskies, *Literature of Destruction*, pp. 509–10, and 620, n. 90, translated by Shlomo Noble

(D: 225:) Our song and dance are a form of worship. Our rejoicing is due to Him who decrees life and death. Here in the midst of this small congregation, in the poor and ruined synagogue, (226:) we are united with the whole house of Israel, not only with those who are here today and with the tens of thousands of the pure and saintly who have passed to life eternal, but with all the generations of Jews who were before us. In our rejoicing today we give thanks for the previous generations, the noble generations in which life was worthwhile. We feel that with our song today we sanctify the name of Heaven just as our ancestors did. And I, a straying Jewish soul, feel that my roots are here. And you, in your rejoicing, atone for the sins of the generation that is perishing. I know that the Jewish people will live, for it is written, "As the days of the heaven upon the earth. . . ." (Deut. 11:21). And even if we were the last generation, we should give thanks and say, "Enough for us that we were privileged to be the children of those! And every day that the Holy One, blessed be He, in His mercy gives us, is a gift which we accept with Joy and give thanks to His holy name."

October 17, 1942 (Saturday)

LOUIS WOLSEY, "Prayer is Not Enough," Sermon Broadcast over NBC. *Sermons and Addresses*, pp. 59–62

(61:) We are today beset by a global catastrophe, largely because we did not tie our ritual with the moral life. Either we did not pray, or we did not yoke our supplications with moral acts. We had (62:) a wealth of masses, litanies, liturgies, hymns and shrines, but we

59 The following passage from Kalmanovich's diary is described by the author as words spoken "on Simḥat Torah, at the invitation of the rabbi, in a house that had been a synagogue and was now a music school." The original source was published in *YIVO Annual of Jewish Social Science*, 8 (1953): 9–81.

must have prayed for the welfare of ourselves or of our family, or our tribe, or our church, or our own nation, and in deed we damned the man of another blood, or another faith, or another nation. There was something wrong with our religion because it did not evoke a spiritual attitude toward life, or a desire to ameliorate the sordid conditions of others' lot. Prayer, instead of binding people together in love, was an exercise designed to exclude, or ostracize, or destroy the folk we did not like. And now the judgment of God is, in logic, upon the world....

Louis Wolsey, "With Faith We Will Win," Blue Network Radio Broadcast. *Sermons and Addresses,*" pp. 63–68, published in *Congressional Record*

(63:) We have read from time to time of the sufferings of the people in ages past: of poverty, famine, pestilence, bloodshed, hatred, war – but we never dreamt that we would ever live to see the world loaded down with an agony that beggars the poor words of the halting tongues and the restricted visions of men.

(64:) Unrighteousness has won. The workers against God and His word are on the soil of the wretched, and they eat up the people of the land. They hold them as hostages and shoot them. They deport them to slave labor among people of strange tongues. They vilify our morals and say that that only is right which ministers to the advantage of the conqueror. They lie and cheat and rob and murder, and they breathe death and destruction everywhere, while the workers for the right and the free give their all, their wealth, their strength, and their precious sons, that they might stem the tide of bestiality and wickedness. How long, O Lord, how long! The three most agonizing years in the history of the world!

It is easy to be discouraged these days. If everything seems to be shipwrecked, why not cry doom to every value we have ascribed to life. Verily it is the end of the world. We are afraid there may be no food. We are afraid of penury in old age. We are afraid of insecurity. We are afraid righteousness will lose the war to unrighteousness....

October 23, 1942 (Friday evening)

Jacob Kaplan, "Abraham and His Descendants in the Crucible" (*Abraham* *et ses descendants dans l'épreuve*),[60] Synagogue of Lyon. *Les Temps d'épreuve*, pp. 113–19, translated by MS

(117:) That [referring to his citation of Ps. 118:22] is the future. For the present, there has been a violation of sanctuary, there have been arrests in the synagogue. In this tragic situation, I take it to heart to express publicly to our fellow Jews who are being hunted down our brotherly compassion, and to emphasize that this compassion will be expressed not only in words, but also in deeds. Since the month of August, the members of the Lyon Consistory, like the delegates, both men and women, have been working with devotion above all praise in order to fulfil their obligation of religious and humane solidarity. To accomplish this noble task, they are on the job from morning until night.

As for the Central Consistory, which already on the (118:) day following the deportations of Jewish aliens had addressed a dignified and moving protest to the Chief of Government [Pierre Laval], it has given to our brothers who have been so sorely tried a new sign of the vigilant concern that it shows for them.... May this act of reparation be the prelude to an improvement of the appalling situation in which so many of our cherished Jewish aliens have found themselves.

Now regarding the violation of the Sanctuary – someone even went so far as to open the doors of the sacred ark order to search among the Torah Scrolls – let us all seek divine forgiveness, let us seek together, as Jews, mercy from on high....[61]

October 25, 1942 (Sunday)

Israel Abrahams, "Winning the Peace," Broadcast from Great Synagogue,

60 Author's note: "On the night of 20–21 October, 1942, French police entered the synagogue of Lyon and arrested some fifty alien Jews who had been given refuge in order to escape deportation. Following a vigorous protest by the President of the Consistoire Central, made the following day against this violation of the principle of Sanctuary, almost all of these who had been arrested were released." Cf. the sentence devoted to this in Poznanski, *Jews in France during World War II*, p. 425, with no mention of Kaplan or his sermon, and the much fuller treatment in Shapira, *Jacob Kaplan*, pp. 147–48.

61 For another selection from this sermon in the original French, see David Shapira, *Jacob Kaplan*, pp. 147–48.

Cape Town, South Africa, at Military Service. *War and Peace: Selection of Sermons and Addresses*, pp. 12–16

(13:) Time and again that ancient tragedy has been re-enacted.[62] And to-day, hard and unpalatable though the truth may be, we must confess that *mutatis mutandis*, the picture that has come down to us of life in the Plain is not unlike our own contemporary times.

Again the old racialist cry goes up to heaven....

The stranger continues to be shut out. The word "alien" has for many become a synonym for undesirable. Boatloads of human beings have perished almost within reach of land and harbor for want of immigration permits. And when at last the stranger is given sanctuary, as often as not the hue and cry of "assimilability" is raised. The ancient "Bed of Procrustes" has its modern counterpart in the insistence on assimilation, soul-uniformity, spiritual and cultural mass-production....

October 30, 1942 (Friday evening)

Stephen S. Wise, "Two English-Speaking Prophets of our Times: Vice President Wallace and Field Marshal Smuts," Media Excerpt, Free Synagogue in Carnegie Hall, New York. AJA, Box 23, SSS Microfilms of AJHS and BUASC papers

(3:) It is not too much to say of [Jan] Smuts that he is the greatest human figure south of the equator, a much greater person than Cecil John Rhodes, even though Rhodes was a builder – for he was a builder through conquest and Smuts is a builder through creation and permeation.... Some of you may have been surprised by the greatness of his recent utterance, when he addressed a unique joint session of the Houses of Parliament. But no one, like myself, who has known him and has followed him for a generation, was surprised. He is one of the world's great figures.... He has been one of the (4:) wisest, truest friends of the Zionist movement, growing

62 The preacher is referring to "unpardonable iniquities of the condemned cities," Sodom and Gomorrah, including the dislike of strangers, gates barred against alien intruders, and a perverted sense of justice.

in part out of his sense of relation to biblical ideals, and in part out of his whole-hearted will to secure reparation for the Bible People.[63]

October 31, 1942 (Saturday)

Louis I. Newman, "My Brother's Keeper," Congregation Rodeph Sholom, New York. *Sermons and Addresses*, vol. 4, pp. 40–44

(41:) In Central and Eastern Europe, the restoration of civil and human rights must be achieved in each country on the spot, when liberation comes at last by the victory of the allied Nations.... Whatever the world's compassion, we know that full economic opportunity will not come to everyone among the Jewish masses abroad, and multitudes will ardently yearn for the boon of migration to a land of promise and hope. Many will gain asylum in lands distant from Europe; many, we hope, will be welcomed at the portals of these United States.

But many thousands... will seek a new life and future at the Eastern end of the Mediterranean, in Palestine.... It is then that the people of Israel, like other minority peoples, must present a unified program, backed by the united public opinion of Jewry and its friends, for the reconstruction (42:) of the battered and shattered communities outside the Western Hemisphere....

November 1, 1942 (Sunday)

Maurice N. Eisendrath, "'We Are United Nations' – How United Are We?," Holy Blossom Temple, Toronto. *Holy Blossom Pulpit*, XII, 1

(8:) Great as is our admiration for China and for Russia as fighting nations, we still distrust them as co-partners with ourselves in charting the destiny of the war and of the peace to follow; we still cherish the fond delusion that somehow we have been summoned by God himself to settle all those things which the lesser breeds without the law cannot possibly understand....

(13:) Notwithstanding the fact that Jewish blood flows as freely

63 On Smuts, see below, Hershman, October 9, 1943, including the relevant note.

as non-Jewish blood in North Africa, in the Solomons, at Dieppe; though bombs make no distinction between Aryan and non-Aryan when they blow their victims to atoms; though Jewish fliers and navigators pilot Sunderland and Catalina bombers nightly over the Reich; strangely enough, Jewish workers ofttimes find it as difficult to enter the industrial plant where such sinews of war are forged as it is for a camel to pass through the needle's eye. Reprehensible as such discrimination is in times of peace, it is subversive of a one hundred percent resistance to the enemy in times of war and should be so designated by the power that be.

November 8, 1942 (Sunday)

Maurice N. Eisendrath, "1917–1922–1942: Twenty-Five Years of Communism, Twenty Years of Communism: Where Stands Democracy Now?," Holy Blossom Temple, Toronto. *Holy Blossom Pulpit*, XII, 2

(7:) In Moscow a Negro can be a hero; in America he must be a servant or a sharecropper, as was the case in [Paul] Robeson's latest picture which prompted his resolution never again to play in any Hollywood production.[64]

And the same attitude has been manifested toward the millions of our brother Jews within the Soviet Union....

(8:) While only today – after a full decade of the most brutish attempt to exterminate the Jews; while only in this latter hour, after ten long years of murder and massacre in Nazi Germany, to say nothing of the two decades of almost ceaseless starvation and slaughter meted out to the Jews in Eastern Europe ever since the Armistice; while only now the heads of the governments of the Western democracies are beginning to speak out in the name of humanity against these unspeakable atrocities perpetrated against our people; while only now even the leaders of the church, supposedly consecrated to brotherhood, have just commenced to voice their protest; as early as the year 1913, Lenin had warned against this scourge of anti-

64 Robeson's decision was based on his experience in the 1942 film "Tales of Manhattan," in which he starred in the fifth story.

Semitism.... And Stalin's attitude likewise was made unequivocal when long before our present belated outburst of sympathy and protest, he too asserted that "Communists, as consistent internationalists, cannot fail to be irreconcilable and sworn enemies of anti-Semitism."[65] And this sentiment was not restricted to the emptiness of speech, for the Soviet Union, alone among the nations of the world, branded by actual legislative edict all such anti-Semitism as subversive of the best interest of their state....

(10:) Such, then, are a few of the challenges that Communism has flung before us of the Western democracies.... (12:) But as a consequence of our encouragement of Fascism throughout the past two decades, revolution and counter-revolution are at each other's throats before the gates of Stalingrad. Where stands democracy now in the midst of this clash of the totalitarians?

November 11, 1942 (Wednesday)

Ben-Zion Meir Ouziel/Uzziel, Address to the Assembly of Representatives (*Asefat haNivḥarim*), Jerusalem, in Shulamit Eliash, "The 'Rescue' Policy of the Chief Rabbinate of Palestine Before and During World War II," p. 293, citing Central Zionist Archives J1/7216

When a person sees his fellow being drowning in the sea, there are no accounts or justifications to be made, and it is his duty to save the other.

November 24, 1942 (Tuesday)

Judah L. Magnes, "Moral Issues in Democracy," Opening of the Academic Year 1942/43, Hebrew University, Jerusalem. *In the Perplexity of the Times*, pp. 44–54

(51:) It is upon the conception of the primacy of the nation, the supreme rights of the German *Herrenvolk*, that the Nazi legal system is based. They have rejected the Hebraic conception of impartial jus-

65 This statement was issued by Stalin on January 12, 1931, in response to an inquiry from the Jewish News Agency in the United States: *Works*, vol. 13, July 1930–January 1934 (Moscow: Foreign Languages Publishing House, 1954), p. 30.

tice to each individual and group regardless of their origin or beliefs. But the Nazi doctrine of the rights of the German nation over every other obligation is not confined to Germany or to the totalitarian Powers alone. There are nationalistic Nazis everywhere.

Let me cite an article in *Le Moniteur* [*du Puy-de-Dôme*], appearing at Clermont-Ferrand and said to have been written by the French Nazi, [Prime Minister Pierre] Laval himself. He warns the church leaders in France not to oppose the deportation of Jews. "Your conscience has allowed you to be led by feelings which though highly honourable are very dangerous, since they excite public emotions and supply our adversaries (52:) with ammunition to be used against the French Government, against the French national revolution, against French national unity."[66]

Such a national unity which is afraid of protests against the deportation and persecution of innocent men and women, is a national unity which has no right to exist....

November 27, 1942 (Friday evening)

Max Nussbaum, "Flames Over Germany: An Eye-Witness Account," Temple Israel, Hollywood, CA. *From Berlin to Hollywood*, pp. 35–37

[Refers to Synagogue Council of America and National Refugee Service request that this Sabbath be devoted to memory of *Kristallnacht*] (35:) "When those three days – of the tenth, eleventh, and twelfth of November, 1938 – were over, we took stock of our tragedy and (36:) counted our curses: more than five hundred synagogues in Germany, Austria, Czechoslovakia and Danzig burnt, scores of charity institutions destroyed, hundreds of homes devastated, thousands of stores pillaged, and one hundred thousand Jews in the concentration camps of Oranienburg, Dachau and Sachsenhausen, beside those who had been ruthlessly slaughtered in their homes during those three nights. The destruction was complete. It surpassed the blackest pages of our tearful history....

---

66 The best-known church leaders to whom the article was referring were Cardinal Saliège and Bishop Théas; see Renée Poznanski, *Jews in France During World War II*, pp. 296–97.

A Jewry which lives in liberty, enjoys the freedom of religion, and does not fill its synagogues and temples to capacity, (37:) destroys them from within as those gangsters have done from without....

Harold I. Saperstein, "What Have We Jews to Be Thankful For?," Temple Emanu-El, Lynbrook, NY. *Witness from the Pulpit*, pp. 96–101

(97:) During the last few days, the papers have given the general public information about what has been happening to the Jews of Nazi-occupied Europe.[67] To me, this information was no shock. As one who is continually in touch with Jewish life, reading reports of various Jewish organizations, the horrible things stated in the papers were long familiar. How many times have I spoken to various groups and said that if I should tell all that I have learned about what is happening to our Jewish brethren across the seas, it would be a story so horrible that you could not believe it. And if we did believe it, we could only thank God that sometimes we are able to forget, because otherwise no Jew knowing these things could eat or sleep or laugh again. I have said that outside of the casualties on the Russian front, the suffering of the Jews of Europe exceeds that of all other people combined. They suffered not only as conquered nations, but doubly, because they were Jews, victims of the diabolic plan of extermination by the Nazis.

Further I did not speak. But the news reports of the last few days have carried the story of what I might have told you, of Jews used as guinea pigs for testing poison gasses, of Jews as victims of mass electrocutions, of countless new and ingeniously contrived methods of killing people, buried by the thousands. And even their dead bodies did not remain inviolate; they (98) were being used, believe it or not, to supply some of the lubricating oils for the Nazi war machine.[68] All history has not known anything so fiendish. As we read these reports, we can well ask, "What have we Jews to be thankful for?"

---

67 A *NYT* article on November 26, p. 16, reported the death of one million Polish Jews, the deportation of Jews to Poland from other European nations, and murder by "mass electrocution" (the last turned out to be inaccurate).

68 This is based on an article paraphrasing S.S. Wise in the *NYT*, Nov. 26, 1942; cf. *Jewish Preaching in Times of War*, p. 98, n. 2.

First, then, let me say that in this situation of unprecedented tragedy, we can be thankful for the faith of the Jews of Eastern Europe who are suffering and dying....

(99:) Secondly, we can thank God for the strength that is America....

(100:) A third thing we can be thankful for as Jews is the promise that is Palestine. It looks now that the danger that that country would be overrun, which loomed so large, is now a thing of the past....

(101:) Finally, we can thank God for the dawn of victory, which already can be seen over the horizon....

November 30, 1942 (Monday)

Isaac Herzog, Address at the Special Session for Mourning of the Assembly of Representatives (*Asefat haNivḥarim*), Jerusalem. *Masu'ah leYitzḥak*, pp. 131–32, translated by MS

(131:) Wolves of the steppe (Zeph. 3:3), wild beasts of the forest, demons of the pit have arisen against us. They have prepared a slaughter for our brothers and sisters in the Diaspora. Almost all of Europe has turned into the valley of Tophet (cf. Isa. 3:33, Jer. 7:31). Our Heavenly Father, Rock of Israel and its Savior in times of woe: are You putting an end to the remnant of Israel? Let the groans of tens of thousands of Jews come before You: Jews who have been killed with cruel modes of death: slaughtered, strangled, burned, buried alive. Let the outcries of infants and babies who have been tossed into the water in sacks come before Your throne of glory; O Father of Mercy, let there come before you the wailing of parents and children, aged and young, young men and maidens; let the scream of the surviving remnant, exposed to the danger of destruction, Heaven forbid!, reach You, so that You may say to the destroyer, Stop!

(132:) O land, land: do not cover up the blood of our brothers in Poland and in the other conquered countries under the control of the wicked of the world who know no compassion. O House of Israel: proclaim a fast, with weeping and mourning; let your voice be heard on high. Rend your hearts and pierce the heavens with the sound of your wailing. All inhabitants of the world: be aroused to respond to this drama of horrors that is truly unprecedented.... Let heaven and earth resound with a terrifying protest against the horrible slaughter of the Jewish people, the people that has given you the principles of justice and mercy, the people that has given you the Book of Books.... Do not be satisfied with protests, important as they are. Do whatever you can quickly to save! Remove our children from the valley of Tophet, and not just the children alone, but whoever can be saved from there!

And you, our brothers, the entire House of Israel: set aside all division and discord. Be united, all of you, as one.... Be aroused to repentance before the G-d of Israel and His sacred Torah!

December 4, 1942 (Hanukkah)

Phineas Smoller, "Martyrdom: The Maccabean Contribution to Judaism," United Hebrew Congregation, Joplin, MO. *A Set of Holiday Sermons,* 5703/1942, pp. 58–64

(63:) We live in a period, comparable to the Maccabean Age for heroism, that produces its martyrs and calls for martyrdom.... The willingness to suffer martyrdom saved them; the resolution to endure martyrdom must be our sure way to salvation. The war against the Axis to-day, like the war of the Maccabees against the Syrians, is a war between two ideologies. In this struggle we cannot waver. With our ancestors, the Maccabees, we must know that the way of dupes and flatterers shall only confound and corrupt them in their breach of the covenant.

December 5, 1942 (Saturday, second day of Hanukkah)

Israel Mattuck, "The Condition of Jewish Survival," Liberal Jewish Synagogue, London. Unpublished

(2:) The point about the power of religious loyalty which emerges from the story of the Maccabaean struggle has an immediate relevance to the present position and problems of the Jews. Several million Jews are suffering from a persecution more vile, cruel and far-reaching than any which our forefathers ever had to endure. The invasions by the German forces have brought several million Jews under the power of Hitler, who pursues against them a policy of extermination that spares none. The sufferings of these Jews lay a heavy and constant burden of pain on the hearts of Jews and all men of good will and human decency. In our pain we cry out for some way to stop this bestial destruction of Jewish lives; and because there seems to be none, the feeling of helplessness is added to the pain. Israel mourns, and there is no consolation.

But the foul purpose which Hitler cherishes in the blackness of his heart will be defeated. Against his power the Jews put the power of the Jewish spirit which will live on though he slay a million Jewish lives and break a million Jewish bodies....

(3:) There is, however, an inescapable condition for the Jews' persistence. It is illustrated in the Maccabaean struggle; it is imposed, as it is evidenced, by the whole of their history. And that is that they cherish the Jewish spirit with its devotion to God. The Jews' loyalty to their religion is the condition of their survival....

The nineteenth century so exalted nationalism that it tended to become a religion. It was perhaps inevitable that Jews should be infected by this general tendency. But for the Jews any substitution for religion as the basis of their collective life would be fatal. It would run counter to our whole history. Moreover, the day of small nations is over. They may continue their existence with more or less independence, but with little or no influence. The future of the Jews is bound up with their religious loyalty.

December 6, 1942 (Sunday during Hanukkah)

Israel Abrahams, "The Maccabean Peace," Broadcast from Great Synagogue, Cape Town, South Africa, Special Hanukkah Military Service. *War and Peace: Selection of Sermons and Addresses*, pp. 17–20

(18:) Chanukah does not commemorate War, it celebrates Peace.... War in itself is not worthy of honour; it is unspeakably horrible at the best of times; it is the negation of all that the soul of man holds precious; it is the polaric opposite of religion, of civilization, of our innate humanity.... Judaism has never celebrated war, even when so righteous and so successful as the Maccabean struggle....

(19:) 2000 years of almost unrelieved suffering!... The Nazi regime came. Ghettos and concentration camps grew up in benighted Europe, like some foul, noisome weed.... War broke out.... Stirred by the old Hasmonean spirit, nine thousand Jewish Springboks flocked to the colors.[69] Myriads more of their brethren in Britain, in the Dominions, in Russia, in all parts of the world, felt an ancient impulse stir within them. Hand in hand with the rest of freedom-loving humanity, they formed an impassible barrier against the onrushing flood of the new barbarism. The brown-black waters of destruction were held. To-day the tide has turned. The liberating forces of the United Nations have taken the offensive. The Lights of Freedom shine more brightly; their illumination is growing; the Maccabean spirit lives again....

(20:) We are fighting a Maccabean War, a Holy War, a war against tyranny and oppression. Will our Victory be a Maccabean Victory? Will it bring a Maccabean Peace? Are we going merely to defeat the Axis aggressors, or is it our aim to banish all forms of persecution, of idolatry, of race and blood, of unfair treatment of minorities, from human life as a whole?

December 13, 1942, (Sunday, Jewish National Day of Fast and Mourning)[70]

Joseph H. Hertz, "England Awake," Bevis Marks Synagogue, London. *Early and Late*, pp. 80–85

---

69 "Springboks" was the nickname of the South African national rugby union team, here apparently used metaphorically to express physical ability and enthusiastic loyalty.

70 The *JC* of December 11 carried the front-page headlines: "TWO MILLION JEWS SLAUGHTERED – Most Terrible Massacre of All Time – APPALLING HORRORS OF NAZI MASS MURDERS." The editorial page (8) of the *JC* included the following: "Week after week, during these many sad and weary months, this paper has striven to awaken the public mind to the facts of the Jew-extermination being carried on by the Nazi monsters in Europe.... No one now doubts – certainly not official circles – the reality of the extermination plan, and its progress towards achievement.... The extermination crime is not only the most colossal human massacre in all history.

(80:) The tragedy that has called us together in this ancient House of Worship is immeasurably greater than that which stirred Jeremiah to the deeps of his being [31:14]. In vastness of extent and diabolic cruelty, the Terror against the Jews in present-day Poland is unsurpassed in the annals of barbarism. In consequence, few fully realize the implications, physical and moral, of that unprecedented Terror....

(81:) Our brethren in the Holy Land paid their tribute of tears to our martyred brethren, as soon as the dread decree of annihilation became known. Their example has been followed by the Jewries of North and South America. And to-day, British Jewry raises its voice in weeping to our Father Who is in Heaven, over the million and more Jewish men, women, and children that have been done to death by the Nazi murderers....

But deeper than the woe over a single calamity, or even a series of calamities, is the continuous anguish of the four or five million Jews upon whom the Nazi rulers have passed a sentence of death, and who are now trembling on the brink of destruction.... Poland has been turned into a vast slaughter-house for all the Jews of Europe. The anguish of these latest victims is too vast for tears; it is the dumb woe of doomed men....

To-day, any man who has a spark of religion in him is dumbfounded at the fact that human beings *plan* the cold-blooded mass-slaughter of millions of fellow-men. Utter (82:) bewilderment seizes him when he further learns that these mass-slaughters are carried out with the maximum of torture and prolongation of agony to the victims.... Hitler and all his fiendish agents love to bathe in mothers' tears, but they also love to wade in human blood....

And now I must add that I for one am also dumbfounded by the amazing indifference displayed in high and low places in this country towards the annihilation of millions of defenceless people.

Unlike its predecessors, it has been cunningly planned in cold blood and is being carried out with the same diabolical and perverted ingenuity that has cheated, deluded, and overcome statesmen in all parts of the world." For the background planning amongst the Jewish leadership that led to the establishment of this Day of Mourning, see Bernard Wasserstein, in "Patterns of Jewish Leadership in Great Britain During the Nazi Era," pp. 38–40; Chanan Tomlin in *Protest and Prayer*, pp. 215–18.

Ignorance of the facts would explain (83:) much; but the ignorance is to a considerable extent artificial ignorance. It is unshaken by pronouncements of the Primate, of Cardinals and Ecclesiastics, who have denounced this most appalling crime that the world has ever seen. Despite it all, a large portion of the Press, as well as some Government circles, for a long time maintained a studied silence....

What practical atonement, we ask, are the Free Peoples willing to make for their share in building up that moral or, more truly, immoral climate? Will they, among other things, open the gates of their countries to those few who, as if by a miracle, escape from the Nazi inferno?...

(84:) Shame covers us, as Jews, as Englishmen, as human beings, that even to such questions we are not sure of an affirmative answer. Public opinion must be roused to the foul and Satanic crime of massacring an entire people, and to the eternal infamy that would be ours, if we were to close our ears to its death-cries.

Alexander Altmann, Higher Broughton and Higher Crumpsall Synagogues, Salford, England. *The Manchester Guardian,* December 14, 1942, p. 3, headline: "Jewish Day of Mourning." University College London, Alexander Altmann Archives

It has become unmistakably clear that there is a plan, a devilish method of extermination, behind it all. Hitler has vowed to wipe out and destroy all Jews under his sway, and the more he realizes that he is not going to win the war and the more clearly he sees the writing on the wall the more fanatical becomes his insane hatred of the Jewish people.

Can we remain composed and calm when this wholesale massacre of our innocent and defenceless brethren is going on day and night? The voice of humanity must be raised in a most solemn protest and warning. Let the German people know that the blood of the Jewish men, women, and children is on the heads of their own people.

But it is not enough to issue a protest and a warning. Practical measures should be taken at once to rescue as many as possible. The Chief Rabbi of Palestine has approached the head of the Roman

Catholic world. Let us hope that the Pope will take this matter in hand. He should be able to organize, with the help of the Red Cross, rescue and relief work on a grand scale and should be able to send a delegation to the ghettoes and camps to take out the tortured prisoners, the remnant of the people that gave the world the Bible and the message of faith in humanity. Let them save, above all, the children. They ought to be transferred to neutral countries and cared for by an international body until the downfall of Hitler is achieved.

Eliezer Berkovits, "Exit Europe?," United Hebrew Congregation, Leeds, England. *Between Yesterday and Tomorrow*, pp. 66–72

(67:) Four million Jews – our kith and kin, our fathers and mothers, our brothers and sisters, our people – are faced with ruthlessly planned systematic extermination. And in their hour of agony they are alone. No one can help them. They are delivered up into the bloody hands of a ruthless foe. To whom can we look for help? We, I say, not they. They, of course, will look for help to their Father in Heaven. But dare *we*, their more fortunate brothers, console ourselves with this thought? … Faith is a great thing if one has it for oneself, for one's own hour of mortal trial. It is not right to have faith for the sufferings of others.

The Jewish tragedy has reached a climax when Jews must find it immoral to look for comfort in their Faith.…

The Day is on its way, the great and terrible day of the Lord. There is no other explanation for the tragedy. We cannot comprehend it otherwise. Inhumanity, barbarism, madness – intensified to a pitch that surpasses every cruelty recorded in history – are words which no longer explain. What is happening to European Jewries to-day cannot be expressed in words for it surpasses human imagination.

(68:) There is but one explanation: the Day of the Lord is on its way. Let the world tremble! (cites Zeph. 1:17–18).… I repeat: this is the End. But not the end of Judaism or the Jewish people – the end of Europe.

(69:) A whole nation of 80 million human beings has turned mass-murderer on six million of their fellow-men. Not in a war in which armies stand face to face. There are no armies, there is no fight or battle; there is mere butchery....

This is the end of Germany as a factor in civilisation and human progress. But, unfortunately, it is also the end of Europe. ... The innocent blood of the massacred European Jewries undermines the very foundations of the whole of Europe. It is spreading a moral pestilence all over Europe from which there can be no recovery.

The doom of European Jewries is the doom of Europe. It is the end of European civilization as we have known it in the past. No new and good generation will ever again be able to breathe and to live happily on European soil, till an entirely new civilization arises that has moral power enough to sweep away the contaminated debris of old Europe.

Exit Europe! The end of the Jew marks always and everywhere (70:) the end of a civilization.... Does the world realise that Germany is drowning herself and Europe in Jewish blood?...

Almighty God, here we are, your people, waiting for you to rise. Rise up to the prey!

(71) We have been spared to rescue Judaism, that through us Judaism may live.... In the presence of this inconceivable catastrophe, let us become one great brotherhood of Jews. A great brotherhood, I say. Let our answer be: Greatness. Nothing less will do from now on, nothing less than greatness. Let us be great Jews....

Kopul Rosen, Higher Crumpsall Synagogue, Salford, England. *JC*, December 18, 1942, p. 10

Apart from the immediate necessity of declaring that every criminal perpetrating these acts shall be punished, apart from the need for assuring that every Jew who is able to escape to a neighbouring state will be granted immediate asylum, there are two main demands. One that Jews may be allowed to fight in a Jewish army *as Jews*; and above all, that the gates of Palestine be opened wide.

Emil Ehrnthal (later Michael Elton), Intercession, 1942: "The Death Camps," Bedford United Hebrew Congregation, Bedford, England. *The Challenge of Destiny*, pp. 29–33; see Complete Sermons

December 19, 1942 (Saturday)

David de Sola Pool, "A Remnant Shall Return," Congregation Shearith Israel, New York. *Rabbi David de Sola Pool: Selections from Six Decades of Sermons, Addresses and Writings*, pp. 91–99.

(97:) As the war drags along its exhausting course, one might fear that Hitler may still make good his evil determination to wipe out several million of the Jews of Europe in addition to the two million whom he has already "liquidated." But if history which we have been surveying has any message for us, it gives us the assurance that though in his maniacal ferocity Hitler may make a holocaust of millions of Jews, he will not, for he cannot, obliterate from the face of the earth the Jew and Judaism. As the rabbis constantly affirm, the Holy One, blessed be He, prepares the healing before the blow falls.[71] While the Jewries of Europe are being made into one vast charnel-house, refugee Josephs taken from the prison-house have been sent before their brethren[72] to new continents to open up new havens of hope and life for new remnants of Israel.

Today remnants of the new dispersion from Europe are establishing communities and dedicating synagogues in such points as Nakuru in Kenya, Lusaka in Northern Rhodesia, in Tanganyika, in Nyassaland and other parts of Africa. Refugees have found their way to various countries of Latin America, there to lay the foundation of new centers of Jewish life, even as they did centuries earlier following the dispersion from Spain. The new diaspora has brought to our own United States rabbis, scholars, pietists, and many Jews whose temper has been steeled in the white hot (98:) flames of persecution. Throughout our land a new breath of life blows with vivifying strength through the Yeshivoth and other institutions of higher learning because of the religious loyalty and learning of men whom the floodtide of European terror has washed up on our shores.

Above all is Palestine serving as the land of refuge for the body and the soul of the driven Jew. The remnant of a cruelly stricken

---

71 b. Megillah 13b.

72 An allusion to the beginning of the sermon describing Joseph, who had been in prison, making himself known to his brothers.

people is thronging to the barely opened doors of the ancient homeland....

December 27, 1942 (Sunday)

Zelig Kalmanovich, Vilna Ghetto, in Dawidowicz, *A Holocaust Reader*, pp. 228–30; Roskies, *Literature of Destruction*, pp. 510–11, translated by Shlomo Noble[73]

(D: 228:) Who mourns the destruction of East European Jewry? The destruction is a hard fact. Undoubtedly also those who predicted it did not envisage it in this form. Three or four years ago the central Zionist organ was writing of a Jewish center in the Diaspora parallel to the center in Palestine. But the catastrophe was nevertheless a definite thing, its contours so visible. Indeed, the innovative horror for our human consciousness is the personal destruction of human lives: old people, children, blossoming youth, weak and old men, but also those in full vigor. There is no doubt, it tears the heart.....

(D: 229:) History will revere your memory, people of the ghetto. Your least utterance will be studied, your struggle for human dignity will inspire poems, your scum and moral degradation will summon and awaken morality. Your murderers will stand in the pillory forever and ever. The human universe will regard them with fear, and fear for itself, and will strive to keep from sin. People will ask, "Why was it done so to this people [i.e., the perpetrators]?" The answer will be, "That is the due of the wicked who destroyed East European Jewry." Thus the holocaust will steal its way into world history....

(D: 230:) If we only had a guarantee of survival! But that does not exist and one cannot always be fearful, for then the feeling of fear is projected into mourning for the fallen, and sorrow over the destruction of Jewry. Spare yourself the sorrow! The Jewish people will not be hurt. It will, it is to be hoped, emerge fortified by the trial. This should fill the heart with joyous gratitude to the sovereign of history.

---

73 See Roskies, p. 620 n. 90. This passage may be just a Diary entry, not a sermon, although the second paragraph is addressed to a contemporary audience, not to future readers.

December 29, 1942 (Tuesday)

Israel Abrahams, "Jewish Day of Mourning," Speech at Citizens' Mass Meeting, City Hall, Cape Town, South Africa. *War and Peace: Selection of Sermons and Addresses*, pp. 21–25

My first impulse was not to speak to-day. I felt that we were mourning an unspeakable tragedy. Where, I asked myself, could we find the words to describe the fiendish atrocities perpetrated by the Nazi hell-hounds: the enslavement, the beating, the torture, the mass executions – by shooting, gassing and electrocution – of non-combatants, even of women and children? Two million lives destroyed – each one a soul fashioned in the image of God! If one ransacked the vocabularies of the world, could they furnish adequate terms in which to condemn the inhuman bestiality, the nauseating sadism of this new barbarism: or language capable of expressing our heart-rending grief for our people's utter helplessness in this latest phase of Israel's endless martyrdom?

A modern Jewish writer did attempt to find the words, and this is what he penned:

> They make the Balabatim dig deep trenches.
> And put a Sepher Torah in each one's arms.
> Now they are through with blows and typhus and alarms.
> Can you see those eyes, as the frail hand clenches
> The Scroll, and they are hurtled into the grave? And now
> Earth is flung down upon them, breast and brow,
> And only the black earth shows, the infamous and brittle.
> The S.S. Men stamp with hard heels. It moved a little.[74]

I saw those eyes, and then I heard the heartless mocking jeer. "Propaganda!" – that sickening abracadabra with which every Jewish cry of agony is met by those who glory in the imperviousness of

74 Ludwig Lewisohn. See Ralph Melnick, *The Life and Work of Ludwig Lewisohn*, vol. 2: *This Dark and Desperate Age*, chap. 26, "Damning Assertions," p. 199. This is the longest poem of the Edna-inspired series. Lewisohn was described as "The most formidable Jewish figure in present-day American literature" (Joseph Leftwich in *Yisroël: The First Jewish Omnibus*, p. 173).

their armour-plated consciences. What shattering proof, what moral dynamite, I wondered, could ever pierce the hardening casings of those well-protected souls? I preferred to mourn in silence, wearing perhaps the yellow badge, like my persecuted brethren, as the only outward sign of (22:) inward suffering, and to lay humbly on the altar of my God, the Father of all mankind, this one unuttered prayer-laden question: "Is it nothing to you, all ye that pass by?" (cf. Lam. 1:12).

But the darkness of my mood passed. New thoughts, like rays of light, pierced the overhanging clouds of sorrow. I realized that there was an answer to my question, that Israel's travail did mean something to some of those who passed by. Not a few paused, and considered, and stretched out a hand of friendship and help. In tortured Europe, fellow citizens – fellow sufferers – sought to aid the Jewish victims, even at the risk of their own lives. Great voices were uplifted in sympathy with Jewry's calamities; statesmen like Mr. Churchill, President Roosevelt and Field Marshall Smuts, spiritual leaders like the Pope and the Archbishop of Canterbury, spoke unforgettable words.[75] The United Nations issued a joint declaration, condemning in horror the appalling Nazi brutalities. To-day, noble utterances of protest and consolation were heard from this platform, expressing the truest feelings of justice- and freedom-loving South Africa. Manifestly, the Jew did not stand alone in this grimmest hour of his tribulation.

75 Today it is rather difficult to understand how Pope Pius XII deserved to be put in the same category with the others regarding "unforgettable words" in "sympathy with Jewry's calamities."

1943

January 2, 1943 (Saturday, *Shemot*)

Emil Ehrnthal (later Michael Elton), "A Future for Israel," Bedford United Hebrew Congregation, Bedford, England. *The Challenge of Destiny*, pp. 150–54

(153:) For all our contributions in the last two thousand years, what have we received from the world? "Where is he? Why is it ye have left the man?" (Exod. 2:20). Where is the Jew today? Half of Jewry is faced with the threat of extinction. The darkest clouds hang over the fate of continental Jewry; imprisoned, tortured, hunted to death, with no means of escape. No land extends an inviting call to them. Silently they look towards us. Our hearts quiver in suspense for our kith and kin. We know that in the fight for liberation the loss of every moment means the loss of another Jewish soul.

We Jews are not unmindful of the sympathy of the world at this time of our greatest crisis in history. It is a source of comfort for us to know that at the request of the Archbishop of Canterbury, prayers will be offered for the Jews in the churches of England. We are grateful for this brotherly feeling. We are also appreciative of the distinction of Companion of Honour conferred on Dr. J.H. Hertz by His Majesty King George VI.[1] Although these rays of light are welcome, yet we must bring to the conscience of the world: "Where is he?" Where is Jewry? Why is it that we have forsaken our people? Why is Jewry denied the hope of a place in the post-war plans of the United Nations? Last week, a tiny people in the Balkans were assured of independence after the war. Why of all nations shall

1 This honor was listed in the *London Gazette* of January 1, 1943, p. 21, https://www.thegazette.co.uk/London/issue/35841/page/21, and highlighted on the first page of the *JC*, January 1, 1943.

Israel wander about aimlessly on the highways of history? "Call him, that he may eat bread" (Exod. 2:20). Are not the islands of the seven seas large enough to receive them? Cannot Palestine become the Mother-country to those of our brethren who choose to live as Jewish nationals in Eretz Yisrael, or, wherever they may be, as groups or individuals? Why is it that the Jew is not included in any of the concrete post-war planning (154:) for reconstruction? The Jewish people must demand the answer to this question. And we, ourselves, must help to provide an adequate reply, worthy of Israel, in this great test of our times.

January 11, 1943 (Monday)

Isaac Herzog, "Address at the Gathering of Representatives of the Yishuv in Support of Voluntary Military Service," "Ohel Shem" (School), Tel Aviv, Palestine. *Masu'ah leYitzḥak*, pp. 133–35, translated by MS

(133) Approximately two thousand five hundred years ago, soon after the first destruction, we sat by the rivers of Babylon as exiles, disdained (cf. Ps. 137:1).... Today, we are the ones who are sitting comfortably in Zion, as we too weep when we remember our brothers by the rivers of Poland and the other Nazified lands. We weep because of the third destruction at the beginning of all our gatherings and festivities. Let us then place the tattered Diaspora at the head of this gathering of ours.

When we look at the terrible destruction that this evil man has brought upon the world in general, and upon the Jewish people in particular, we can understand completely how our sacred Torah... commands us to blot out the memory of Amalek from under the heavens (Deut. 25:19); how the God of Israel, the Father of mercy and forgiveness, sometimes is compelled to be described as "God of vengeance" (Ps. 94:1).

Today there can be no Jew who has a brain in his head and a heart in his chest that does not understand that the qualities of justice and mercy come together in the commandment of blotting out [Amalek], of removing these evil ones from the face of the earth, for in comparison with them all the evil ones who ever lived, all the enemies of Israel who opposed us in every generation, were like quiet doves in their nests, like sheep grazing within their flocks.

Why did these murderous, profane Nazis perform such horrifying murder, such wholesale, sadistic, satanic persecution, with victims rising already to the millions? There is only one answer: because the victims were the descendants of those who stood at Mt. Sinai and heard the word of the living G-d commanding from the midst of the fire, "You shall not murder" (Exod. 20:13)....

(134:) These hundreds of thousands who have been wiped out with such terrifying cruelty, in Poland and the other countries of Hitler, may his name be blotted out, are our brothers, our sisters, our bones, our flesh. Our sacred Torah contains the commandment of the blood avenger (Num. 35:19), and we indeed are their blood avengers. Our own soldiers who have enlisted and volunteered for military service have taken upon themselves the fulfilment of this commandment to be the blood avengers of hundreds of thousands of Jews whose blood has been spilled like water.... Not only this, they are helping to save the entire Jewish people from the total annihilation that would be expected if – Heaven forbid! – the enemy should prevail.... On the other hand, from those who have money, it is expected that they will make financial contributions....

January 24, 1943 (Sunday)

Ferdinand M. Isserman, "The Seventh Cross," Temple Israel, St. Louis, MO. AJA, MS-6, Box 16, Folder 5

(1:) It is very difficult for people in the United States to appreciate the meaning of concentration camps. We have concentration camps here.[2] Although they bear the same title as Dachau and Oranienburg,

2 It is somewhat surprising to see this terminology used for the camps in the geographical center of the United States to which all Japanese Americans living on the West Coast (but not German Americans on the East Coast) were compelled to relocate after Pearl Harbor. The preacher proceeds to emphasize the distinction between the German and the American institutions, and the terminology may have been chosen as a rhetorical means to capture attention. See the final sentence, below.

they fill different functions. After Pearl Harbor, our government established concentration camps for Japanese residents of the United States, even for American citizens of Japanese parentage who lived in the Pacific Coast military areas, and very few of whom were regarded as possible enemies, ready to betray our country. These concentration camps resemble small boom cities where people carry on the normal functions of life, where there is even a modicum of self-government, but where freedom of movement outside the area is restricted. The residents of these camps are not subjected to floggings or other forms of uncivilized cruelty. They have been torn from their homes. They were compelled to dispose of their businesses, and I do not want to minimize their suffering or appear insensitive to it. Throughout this country there are high-minded citizens who are grievously concerned about their plight and are planning relief for them....

The concentration camps in Germany were as different from the ones maintained by our government as night is from day....

Israel Abrahams, "Thanksgiving Service," Great Synagogue, Cape Town, South Africa (auspices of Hebrew Congregations of Cape Town, service marking safe return of First South African Division). *War and Peace: Selection of Sermons and Addresses*, pp. 26–30

(26:) For our boys, too, had crossed the Red Sea – a Sea of Blood, fed by the streams of the war's unending sacrifices. Our sons, too, had faced the desert, and had trodden the very ground familiar to our ancestors in Egypt. They, too, had fought against Pharaoh – Pharaoh in his modern guise – and had triumphed....

(27:) The catastrophe known as the Nazi regime came upon the world in 1933. From the beginning, Hitler sought by all means in his power to crush the Jew to the very dust. The bestial policy of exterminating our people was pursued with ruthless brutality. There were cold pogroms and blood-hot pogroms. But we were helpless; we had no means of defending ourselves. By and large, the world paid little heed to the Jewish cry of distress. We were alone.

But the Nazi menace grew. Gradually but ineluctably, the great nations began to realize that the danger threatened them too. War was declared; and for the first time the opportunity came to us to join issue with the enemy of mankind, the arch-oppressor of our people. The hour had arrived when we could strike a blow for freedom, for humanity, for South Africa, and for Israel. Then a burning question stabbed at our heart: Would our youth respond to the call of duty?... God be praised! The answer was not long in doubt. The Maccabean spirit manifest itself immediately.... You marched to battle not as conscripts but as volunteers....

The Jew was being denigrated as well as persecuted. Outside Nazidom, too, we were being depicted as soulless, cowardly parasites, worshippers of Mammon, mercenary in all our motives. It was an infamous calumny. We knew its vale, source and origin. But how disprove it? You demonstrated the utter falsehood of the (28:) slander....

(29:) So long as the world is in chains, so long as our brothers and sisters live in that vast concentration camp called Nazi-occupied Europe, so long as they are worked to death and slaughtered like cattle, so long can we not give expression to a full "Hallel" of jubilation, or speak of our victories with finality....

And when the day of victory comes, as come, pray God, it will, let us not be content merely with the overthrow of Hitler. כי מחה אמחה את זכר עמל (Exod. 17:14), the Bible tells us. It is the *memory*, the *spirit* of the Amalekite, that has to be obliterated. It is Hitlerism, in all its manifold, abominable aspects, that we must destroy. We must banish racialism and anti-Semitism from every part of the earth.[3] We must rid the world of injustice, of social insecurity, of national homelessness. The world must become free with all the four freedoms so often listed; (30:) and from this total freedom the Jew must not be excluded. He, too, must have a home; he, too, must be allowed to enjoy all human individual and national rights.

Men of the Forces! In peace-time we shall need your help no less than in war-time....

---

3 It is left ambiguous whether the preacher intended to include South Africa in this general statement.

January 30, 1943 (Saturday)

Louis I. Newman, "Jewish Message to a Troubled World," Radio Broadcast, "The Message of Israel." *Sermons and Addresses*, vol. 4, 59–63

(61:) Ten years ago today, Hitler came to power, and one of his very first deeds in an all-inclusive campaign to undermine the world's liberty and safety was to attack the German citizens of Jewish faith.... (62:) Perhaps if the world had been more anxious in 1933 when Hitler launched his barbarities against German Jewry, his conspiracy against the world's security might have been nipped in the bud. But now that the full scope of his nefarious plan has been revealed in the decade which has ended, it is equally true that the fate of the enslaved in France, Czecho-Slovakia, Poland and other lands in pitiful homage to the Nazis is inexorably bound up with the fate of the children of Israel. When all mankind is free, Israel will be free; when Israel is truly free, all humanity will be truly free.

February 21, 1943 (Sunday)

Solomon B. Freehof, "A Just Cause Wins," Rodef Shalom Congregation, Pittsburgh, PA. *Rodef Shalom Pulpit*, vol. 9, no. 5, pp. 3–15, and *Best Sermons: 1944 Selection*, pp. 300–7

(305:) The practical question with us is to what extent we have been crushed by our disappointing experience in the modern world. We know what the doctrine of divine justice means. It is ultimate; it is useful; it would strengthen us. But can we still believe in it? Can we convince the embittered (306:) modern mind that it is really true? We might as well know that it cannot be proved. That justice will triumph and a just cause win cannot be proved until the millennium comes, and you and I will not be here to see it....

I suggest that there has been in recent months enough moral triumph to help us make a choice in our life philosophy. Hitler has been forced back onto his heels.... He had plans for absolute conquest. He knew that you cannot conquer everybody, but that you can win rapid victories and scare the rest of the people into helplessness and terrify them by remorseless brutality. You can break their hearts and thus build up your new Europe. That is why Rotterdam, after the city had surrendered, was systematically wiped out from the air, and fifteen thousand men, women, and children were killed.[4] It was not senseless cruelty; it was purposeful cruelty. It was an assertion of an essential satanism, anti-morality. But what happened? Hitler's very immorality, the very brutality defeated him. It was that systematic cruelty which convinced people that they will never live at peace with Nazi Germany and that they might as well bring their revolt now.... Thus did a moral law work out before our eyes.

March 1, 1943 (Monday)

STEPHEN S. WISE, Excerpts from the Address delivered as chairman of the "Stop Hitler Now" Rally at Madison Square Garden, New York. "Reports of the World Jewish Congress (British Section)," no. 3, March 1943. Cf. AJA MS-49, Box 5, Folder 9[5]

It may bring some understanding of what has happened to the Jewish people in Hitler-conquered Europe, when you are told that more Jews have been slain in every brutal way in Hitler-Europe within this year than will be the number of deaths in the English and the American Armies throughout this war. The number of Jews slain in one way or another stands between two and three million. I pray God we shall have no such list of casualties in the course of the war....

For five or six years, from 1933 to '39, the democracies refused to stop Hitler, in part, alas, because only Jews were being exterminated. Hitler must be stopped and he will be stopped. He has been stopped in Russia by the armies of Stalin. He is being stopped in Tunisia by the armies of Eisenhower and Montgomery. He will be stopped elsewhere. Stop him now, before he can execute his threat to exterminate the Jewish people. He would destroy us solely because we are

4 The Nazi bombardment of Rotterdam occurred on May 14, 1940; the number of victims cited here is significantly exaggerated, but the impact of the bombing led to a revision of British policy that had until this point avoided bombing civilian centers in Germany.

5 Cf. also the coverage in the *NYT*, March 2, 1943, pp. 1, 4; Wyman, *The Abandonment of the Jews*, pp. 87–88.

the oldest of warriors for human freedom and the ideals for which the United Nations today stand.

Stop him now, before he can visit his wrath over defeat upon and against the civilian populations of brave Poland, of heroic Czechoslovakia, of unconquered Greece, of invincible Austria, Belgium, Holland, Denmark, Norway. He would exterminate the Jews. Other evil men before him have been obsessed by the same evil dream of executing the Jewish people. Their evil dreams, from Pharaoh to Pobiedonostzeff, were in vain. We were not destroyed! We will not be destroyed! We cannot be destroyed, for we are an eternal people! Hitler *can* be destroyed! He *will* be destroyed! Stop him! Destroy him NOW!...

What can be done? Children can and must be saved. Havens of refuge must be provided for those who are able to escape within the British Empire and the Western world... The doors of Palestine must be opened, despite all the White Papers in the world. If we tonight are in earnest, and we are, the Jewish people, the great labour organizations here represented, and the strong Church groups, which speak here tonight, may move our country and the United Nations to act NOW, in order that a halt may be called to the direst, the most damnable, crime of history.

Joseph H. Hertz, Message to "Stop Hitler Now" Rally at Madison Square Garden, New York. *NYT*, March 2, 1943, p. 4

It is appalling to think that the whole of mid-European Jewry stands on the brink of annihilation, and that millions of Jewish men, women, and children have already been slaughtered with fiendish cruelties which baffle belief, but equally appalling is the fact that those who proclaim the Four Freedoms have so far done very little to secure the freedom to live for 6,000,000 of their Jewish fellow-men by readiness to rescue those who might still escape Nazi torture and butchery. May God grant that your great demonstration of American Jewry be the means of overcoming the strange and calamitous inertia of those who alone can initiate the sacred work of human salvage.

March 7, 1943 (Sunday)

Abba Hillel Silver, "The Undefeated Optimism of Our Faith," The Temple, Cincinnati, OH. *Therefore Choose Life*, pp. 17–21

(21:) Our people today face another crisis, perhaps their greatest in history – the crisis of mass slaughter, the crisis of extermination. This is the time to draw consciously and deliberately upon the undefeated optimism of our people, based upon confidence in a just God, based upon the conception of the noble ministry of suffering, and based upon faith in the perfectibility of human society. The world is suffering for its sins. It is atoning for its sins. God will accept the atonement. Even as He has smitten, so will he forgive. That is the law implicit in the history of our people. Men and nations are suffering today. Israel is suffering more than anyone. That has been our tragic noble privilege through the ages. We are again the anvils upon which history is being fashioned. Out of this history, out of the evils of our day, out of the bitter conflict of our world, a new and better day will come. "The redeemed will yet sing a new song" [quoted as if a biblical verse, but source unclear, closest is Isa. 42:10].

March 21, 1943 (Sunday, Purim)

Julian B. Feibelman, "The Festival of Discovery," Temple Sinai, New Orleans, LA. Radio Address, WSMB. AJA MS-94, Box 15, Folder 1

(1:) This story [of Purim] is quite apposite today. In fact, the same setting can be duplicated. Again the children of Israel are doomed by false accusation, as if there were to be no end to this repetitious libel. This time it is Hitler, not Haman. The heroine is a composite of modern Esthers who have heroically shared desperation and exile.

I read recently an account of the Warsaw Ghetto, where 600,000 people were jammed into the filth and squalor of that city's worst section.[6] Walls and barbed wire imprisoned them helplessly. The

6 Occasionally accounts of life in the ghetto were smuggled out of Warsaw for the Polish government-in-exile in London, where they were publicized. By March 21,

Gestapo seized them for the slightest provocation. There was scant food, no (2:) medicines, and no decent burial facilities for the hundreds who daily died. Yet these thousands eked out some kind of miserable existence. The agony of fear and the anguish of constant terror ran their cup of desperation over.

Into this overcrowded, filthy and disease-ridden ghetto there were forcefully injected hundreds of uprooted German exiles. A young Jewish girl says, "To share what little we could to help others worse off than ourselves proved to be the first joy and spiritual refreshment we experienced." This girl shared the strain of Esther's heroism. She discovered a new-born faith by sharing valiantly the fate of others.

There is another most pitiful account of 93 young Jewish girls in Poland who were rounded up and sent from their homes to serve the lust of German soldiers. These girls each carried a vial of poison. They wrote a joint letter, which was smuggled out and has been published. Their last testament was a vindication that death is sweeter than disgrace, dishonor, or treachery. These 93 girls discovered a strength within which bequeaths a memory to revivify the weakness of those with little faith....[7]

(3:) There is no more pitiful chapter in all the unrelieved agony of German persecution than the ironic and tragic discovery Hitler made for those who had forgotten, ignored, or concealed their Jewishness. Martyrdom is to die for something; it is but bitter irony to live for nothing....

1943, some eight months after systematic deportation to Treblinka had begun, and a month before the Uprising, there were far fewer than 600,000 Jews remaining.

7 The story of the 93 girls is based on a *NYT* report of a letter describing the incident, published on January 8, 1943, p. 8; the letter was publicized by the New York Rabbi Leo Jung. See the fascinating discussion of this by Baumel and Schacter, "The Ninety-three Bais Yaakov Girls of Cracow." As the title indicates, the letter states that the incident occurred in Cracow, but the accompanying explanation from Rabbi Jung placed it in Warsaw (apparently a clerical error!), which is how it was reported in the newspaper, and in the sermon. For reference to this incident in a sermon delivered on Shabbat haGadol (April 17), 1943 by a rabbi preaching in the Great Synagogue of Ra'anana, Palestine, see Ephraim Sokolover, *Penei Efrayim*, sermon 36, p. 279. Cf. also Walter Wuerzburger, October 8, 1943, below.

March 27, 1943 (Saturday)

Maurice N. Eisendrath, "For Such a Time as This,"[8] Founder's Day Address at Hebrew Union College, Cincinnati. Printed Pamphlet, Center for the Study of the American Jewish Experience, nearprint, Series P. Convocations and Programs, Sub-series 1. Founder's Day, Box P1-1, Folder 11

(1:) But at such a time as this: when the earth is convulsed and the mountains are sunk into the depths of the sea; when peoples have beaten their plowshares and pruning hooks not only into spears and swords, but into Stuka dive-bombers and fire-spitting tanks and death-dealing submarines; when nation not merely lifts up sword against nation but when they pulverize whole populations of defenseless women and children... (2:) who is so presumptuous as to believe that he can speak the word of wisdom, of encouragement, of challenge in such a day as this?

A day of darkness it is for all mankind; but a day of thick, black, well-nigh impenetrable darkness, without seemingly a single glint of light, for the bleeding sons of Israel. From mass meetings of Jews and conclaves of Christians; from houses of Parliaments and halls of Congress; from pulpit and public platform, have come such harrowing descriptions of the plight of Israel today that no words can add a single syllable to this lexicon of Hell that has been able even to approximate the hideous, haunting picture of an entire people being hemorrhaged mercilessly to death. "There are no words, there is no speech" (cf. Ps. 19:3), not alone to portray the tragedy of our people, but to bring hope to so many hopeless souls. What, then, can one say in such a time as this?

That at least so long as Israel stands united no danger need daunt us, no adversary shall finally prevail against us....

Jacob Kaplan, Synagogue de Lyon, France, in Shapira, *Jacob Kaplan*, p. 151. Fonds Kaplan, Box 1517–79, translated by MS

---

8 The title echoes the statement of Mordecai to Esther in Esth. 4:14; the address was delivered six days after the Scroll of Esther had been read in synagogues on Purim. Despite the negative presentation of the contemporary reality, the title implies some element of hope for the future.

Actually, the events that we will commemorate have never been buried in the shroud of the past. This intrusion of suffering throughout the entire span of our history has occurred too frequently for it to be considered as fortuitous. It seems as if it has a purpose.... Why do we suffer in this way?...There is, to be sure, the familiar biblical explanation, which explains suffering as a punishment for those who are blameworthy and a test for those who are just. This explanation has always been valid, for in every age there were sinners to be punished and righteous to be tested. But this explanation – as we look at it more closely – does not respond to the question that preoccupies us. It provides an answer to the problem of human suffering in general, it serves to explain why a particular person suffers, whoever this person may be, whether a Jew or a non-Jew. But it does not provide a solution to the specific problem of Jewish suffering, it does not tell us why the Jew suffers solely because he is a member of the community of Israel.

April 4, 1943 (Sunday)

Barnett Brickner, "The Future of Israel," Address at 38th Council of UAHC, New York. AJA MS-98. Printed pamphlet

(8:) It will not be easy for European Jewry to reconstitute itself. Already 2 million of our people are gone, and Heaven alone only knows how many of the remainder will be left before Hitler is stopped. Nevertheless, Jewish life in Europe will continue after the war. Nobody has a right to say Kaddish for all European Jewry. However, the social and economic pattern of a capitalistic world into which the Jews fitted will have suffered such major dislocation as will prevent Jews from returning to their former economic positions. The seeds of anti-Semitism sown by Hitler in all the occupied countries will not be so readily destroyed.

Any attempt to restore Jewish property now in the hands of others will of itself create terrific friction and lead to more anti-Semitism. This adds up to the observation that, whereas millions of other people who are exiles from their countries will be able to return and reconstruct their lives, that will not be so easy for the Jews. All other peoples will return to countries where they and their kind are in the majority. The Jews will return everywhere as a minority, and thus maintain a status which has bred friction.

Even more shattering and tragic than the loss of Jewish lives and economic position has been the destruction of Jewish religious and educational institutions and their leaders and scholars. That cannot be so easily restored, for when a milieu that has bred scholarship for centuries has once been destroyed, it takes decades and perhaps centuries to restore. This means that reconstituted European Jewry will have lost the role of spiritual leadership which it occupied for centuries. This leadership will have to be taken over by America and by Palestine.

April 14, 1943 (Wednesday)

STEPHEN S. WISE, Address at Protest Meeting, Chicago, IL. AJA, SSW Microfilms of AJHS Papers, Box 23

(1:) I have no wish to bring this great meeting to tears, but I owe it to my fellow Jews – threatened, imperiled, and all but exterminated! – to read to you a message which has come to some of us from the Jewish National Committee of Poland:

> (2:) The remnants of the Jewish community in Poland exist in the conviction that during these most terrible days of our history you have not brought us help. Respond at least now in the last days of our life. This is our final appeal to you.[9]

Within some days after the receipt of this message, underground information has reached the Jewish Agency in Jerusalem that the Nazis are burning alive thousands of Jews in Eastern Galicia. The

9 Compare the following message printed in the *NYT*, March 2, 1944, p. 4, based on a London report read in Parliament "from the Jewish National Committee in Poland" (with no date attached): "In our last moment before death the remnants of Polish Jewry appeal for help to the whole world. May this, perhaps our last voice from the abyss, reach the ears of the whole world" (cited in Laurel Leff, *Buried by The Times*, p. 1, also cited in an article by Leff in Shapiro, ed. *Why Didn't the Press Shout?*, p. 74). The number 250,000 to 300,000 Polish Jews still alive seems totally inappropriate for 1944; the Report read in Parliament by the Jewish MP S.S. Silverman may have been considerably older.

Hitler-conquered lands are being made free of Jews, which is another way of saying that Hitler's purpose to exterminate Jews is being fulfilled to the letter. Hitler breaks every promise, but fulfills every threat....

The threat of immediate extermination cannot be averted by the temporizing process of exploration at Bermuda.[10] This is no time for exploration. Either save those threatened with extermination, or say frankly, as has been said in the House of Lords and the House of Commons, "Nothing can be done."

April 17, 1943 (Shabbat haGadol)

Shlomo Zalman Ehrenreich, Simleul-Silvaniei, Transylvania, in Katz, Riderman, and Greenberg, eds., *Wrestling With God*, pp. 68–72, translated by Gershon Greenberg from *Derashot Leḥem Shelomoh*, pp. 212–16

(68:) Today we see that the hatred of Israel is increasing greatly. When, heaven forbid, some Jew does or says something reckless, the punishment is very great. Immediately there are witnesses who [claim to have] seen or heard that so-and-so spoke against the government. Or because of some insignificant thing, they say that some Jew is a secret agent and wants to hand over the country to the enemy. They call him a "spy." One needs to be very careful not to utter anything at all regarding the war or the government.[11] It is very dangerous. Someone might see or hear something and twist it for evil. One needs to keep one's mouth closed. It was similar in Egypt....

(69:) Furthermore we see today how the enemies of Israel rise against us and torment us with all sorts of persecutions. They remove every source of livelihood from us. Many thousands and tens of thousands of Jews are exiled from their country and land. How many tens of thousands have been killed by the evildoers for no reason? How many have been buried alive: they, their wives, their sons, and their daughters? The reckless among us will open their

---

10 See below Isaac Herzog, May 3, 1943, with accompanying note.

11 At this time the Jews of Transylvania, now part of greater Hungary, were still living in their communities alongside larger non-Jewish populations, some of whom were only too eager to denounce them.

mouths, asking questions and doubting G-d: "Why did G-d do this to pious and good Jews?" They actually ask, "Where is our G-d?" But we remain silent and closed. For we are unable to answer these people at all until G-d has mercy on His people and sends us our redeemer and takes us out of this dark and long exile.

Ephraim Sokolover, Great Synagogue, Ra'anana, Palestine. *Penei Efrayim*, pp. 268–81, translated by MS

(268:) We are in the fourth spring of this savage and horrifying war. But how different the spring of this year is from last year or two years ago. There was a three-year period when the spring time was transformed into an abomination.... When we would say the blessing for the first day of Adar, we said another prayer in a whisper: "would that the winter would last at least another few weeks," for it was when the nights were long that we felt more or less secure....

(269:) The heart throbs continuously in expectation of the day when the leaders of the democratic nations – those who went to war on behalf of justice and righteousness, to save the world from plunder and rupture – will sit together and make important decisions....

Who knows whether they will take us into account, whether they will consider the claims of the Jewish people – broken and despoiled – to give to it some portion of the rights that will be granted to all the other peoples that have suffered?... There are signs that this will not be the case, that they will not encourage or fulfill our hopes in this direction. The most striking fact is that after all the universal shuddering over the destruction of European Jewry, and despite all the governments that have endorsed our cause, some of them claiming to share, as it were, in the agony of the Jewish people, the fact is that they have not yet succeeded in saving the life of even one single Jew!

(271:) When we review this entire horrifying story [of oppression by Pharaoh] and compare it with the story of the Jewish people (272:) in our own time, it turns out that there is no comparison to be made. For we live in a world that is so modern, so cultured! And precisely at the hands of the nation that excels in its etiquette, in courtesy regarding how one person encounters another, as it were, and is considered to be one of the most cultivated, and is famed for its technological inventions, so that it has a distinguished place in the world market: *this* nation has proclaimed the annihilation of the Jewish people, heaven forbid! They don't even try to explain or to justify their malicious behavior!...

Sometimes it is claimed that the Jews have taken over the best businesses and dominate all aspects of commerce. But after they have been consigned to sealed ghettos and denied any kind of interaction with the external world, their spirits broken and their souls crushed to the ground, dying of hunger and frozen in the cold, this still is not enough! They need to announce the goal of total annihilation, Heaven forbid! In what manner? Using what technique? There is nothing like this in the history of the Jewish people that is so saturated with blood and tears....

(273:) Pharaoh did what he did to the Israelite male infants because he foresaw that one child to be born would deliver the Jewish people and take vengeance against him.[12] But now!? There is no difference in age: young and old, man and woman, boy and girl: all of them are killed and slaughtered every day, without end....

(279:) After partaking of the suffering of our tormented and aching Jewish brethren, after the emotional recognition of all these horrifying pictures, we must come to one sole conclusion: to strengthen ourselves through our faith in G-d and His Torah, and to remember our exalted and lofty role: "through your blood you shall live; through your blood you shall live" (Ezek. 16:7).

April 20, 1943 (first day of Pesach)

David de Sola Pool, "The American Passover," Congregation Shearith Israel, New York. *Rabbi David de Sola Pool: Selections from Six Decades of Sermons, Addresses and Writings*, pp. 100–5

(105:) Forces of terror have arisen in the world, spurning liberty, democracy and a humanity that is broader than race. These are termed effete teachings of a civilization that is doomed by ruthless

12 See Rashi on Exod. 1:16.

supermen. In the face of this challenge to the fundamentals of our moral social order, America needs to reconsecrate itself to its historic declaration of faith "that all men are created equal, that they are endowed by their Creator with certain unalienable Rights"....

Zelig Kalmanovich, Vilna Ghetto, in Dawidowicz, *A Holocaust Reader*, pp. 231–33; Roskies, *Literature of Destruction*, pp. 511–13, translated by Shlomo Noble[13]

(D: 231:) Now these diverse people were herded together and imprisoned within the narrow confines of the ghetto. People of diverse languages, diverse cultures, diverse interests and beliefs, of diverse and, at times, conflicting hopes and desires were assembled in one category: Jews. Confined as if being punished for that; that is, they committed a crime and the crime consisted in being Jews.

(D: 232:) The temporary suffering and blows that descend upon the Jew have a meaning, are not merely oppressions, and do not degrade the Jew. For a Jew is part of the sacred triad: Israel, Torah, and the Holy One, blessed be He. That means the Jewish people, the moral law, and the Creator of the universe.... The Jew who does not cling to this triad is to be pitied. He wanders in a world of chaos, he suffers and finds no explanation for his suffering. But the Jew who clings to the sacred triad needs no pity.... To be sure, history rages now, a war is waged against the Jews, but the war is not only against one member of the triad but against the entirety: against the Torah and God, against the moral law and the Creator. Can anyone still doubt which side is the stronger? In a war it happens that one regiment is defeated, taken into captivity. (D: 233:) Let the ghetto Jews consider themselves as such prisoners of war. But then let them also remember that the army as a whole is not defeated and cannot be defeated. The Passover of Egypt is a symbol of an ancient victory of the sacred triad. My wish is that we shall live to see the Passover of the future.

13 See Roskies, p. 620, n. 90. This was a Diary entry dated April 30, written after end of Pesach, beginning with the statement, "At the second seder I spoke briefly."

April 24, 1943 (Shabbat of *Ḥol haMo'ed* Pesach)

Yissachar Shlomo Teichthal, *Ḥevrat Shas Yere'im* Synagogue, Budapest. *Em Habanim Semeḥa: Restoration of Zion as a Response to the Holocaust*, pp. 149–50, translated by Pesach Schindler

Now on this past Sabbath of the intermediate Passover festival, I was invited to preach in the local *Ḥevrat Shas Yere'im* Synagogue, which was crowded on this occasion. I inserted in the sermon the matter of rebuilding our Land, which, considering what has befallen us, is now incumbent on all of us. We have no other option except that we all rebuild our Land upon its (150:) ruins.

I proceeded to preach on this subject with considerable passion. Many were upset with me.[14]

April 26, 1943 (seventh day of Pesach)

Abraham Cohen, "God and Evil," Birmingham Hebrew Congregation, Birmingham, England. Unpublished, David Cohen Private Collection

(5:) The past has its parallel in the present.[15] The doubts of God which harassed the minds of the Israelites in the house of bondage, the criticisms of Him which sprang to their lips, are reproduced in our own tragic age. Innumerable men and women in our time have felt themselves compelled to ask the same question as did the slaves in Egypt in the remote past: מה שמו?, *mah shemo*? (Exod. 3:14). What are we to think of God in these dreadful days? For years evil has been triumphant; innocent human beings, whose colossal num-

14 This passage stretches the usual requirements of the present book, which limits documents to texts of sermons delivered, while this is the preacher's later report. But it provides the specific date, occasion, content, and reaction of listeners to a controversial issue, and I have therefore included it. The passage continues, "This [controversy over the sermon] reached the attention of the *gaon* [R. David Meisels], who reacted as follows: 'In reality, it has turned out we were in error in withdrawing from the movement to build the land (Yiddish).' These were the words of this great *gaon*, a leader of his generation. And he said further, 'A great many of our Jewish brethren would have been saved had we all been involved in the rebuilding of our Land and not feuded among ourselves.' He then burst forth weeping, for some of his children as well who were trapped in Slovakia."

15 This comes after the first half of the sermon, discussing the liberation from Egypt.

ber He alone knows, have been tortured, robbed and murdered by fiendish monsters; right is stamped under foot; whole nations have been overrun and their lands devastated. Is God powerless to save? Or, worse thought still, is He indifferent? How can He be so callous as to allow them to continue? These questions are inescapable; and because no convincing reply is forthcoming, the faith of many has been shattered. The bitterness of their experience has forced them to the conclusion (6:) that there is no God and the world is at the mercy of blind forces without any directive Mind. Is that conclusion justified?

The horrifying facts of life as we now witness them do undoubtedly bring us face to face with this overwhelming problem; but it is a problem which cannot be satisfactorily solved by heated emotions, frustrated hopes and the despair of suffering. It demands cool, dispassionate thinking of which very few are capable....[16]

April 27, 1943 (eighth day of Pesach)

Abraham A. Kellner, "Triumph Over Adversity," Congregation Sons of Abraham, Albany, NY. *A Rabbi's Faith*, pp. 80–85

(80:) This energizing faith ... is certainly the paramount need of our times, and must be brought into play to help abjure the pessimism and banish the hopelessness created by the frightful ravages of global war, and caused by the bestial policy of Horrendous Nazidom.

(83:) In our time, when it seems that the nightmare of the darkest ages stalks menacingly across the stage of our world, we too must be steadied with the defensive weapons of *Emunah* and *Tzedek* that sustained our illustrious forebear [Abraham] when he faced the mounting tribulations of his times.... There are those among us who view with abject resignation the crushing blows dealt to Israel, and discern in the lamentful woe of our martyrs the death-knell of a historic people....

(84:) There are countless numbers of Jews crushed to the ground

16 The preacher then turns to a recent book, *God and Evil*, by C.E.M. Joad; most of the rest of the sermon is devoted to a discussion of this work.

by the sledge hammer blows of adversity, who look upon the stream of blood flowing from the myriads of wounds inflicted upon our people as blood flowing from the body of a dead people.

May 1, 1943 (Saturday)

Irving F. Reichert, "Futile Weapons," Radio Address on "The Message of Israel." *Judaism and the American Jew*, pp. 97–100

(98:) "No weapon that is forged against thee shall prosper; And every tongue that is raised against thee in judgment thou shalt confute" (Isa. 54:17).

I suspect that possibly at no time since [the prophet] spoke those words has Israel more sorely needed the courage they convey than today. To be sure, we have known periods of cruel suffering many times before this tragic age.... But even these dismal chapters of our history pale before the enormity of the terror that has engulfed our people on the European continent today. Two million Jews have been slaughtered. They were not killed on the battle-field, where they might bravely have met a patriot's death. They were not casualties of bombing raids, victims of the terror that knows no race or creed, but falls from the skies indiscriminately upon a whole community. They did not starve to death, sharing on terms of equality with their Greek and Polish fellow-countrymen the famine which the apostles of the New Order in Europe deliberately created. No, these two million Jews were never even given a chance to share the common suffering and the common sacrifice. With cold and precise calculation, with that Teutonic thoroughness which has surely earned the Nazis a special niche in the halls of infamy, these valiant warriors of the Master-Race singled out the Jews of Germany and of every land they conquered as the special beneficiaries of their perfected persecution techniques.

They stripped them of their property. They took away their citizenship. They branded them as outcasts. They made them wear a badge of shame. They burned their synagogues. In community after community they rounded (99:) them up.... They actually loaded them into cattle-trains, or into hermetically sealed freight cars, without food or water – old men and little children, terror-stricken women, and men who had been leaders of culture and enlightenment in their communities, and they sent two million of them off to be butchered in slaughter-houses, to face firing squads in lonely forests, to starve to death or to die of disease in the pestilential ghetto of Warsaw!

This much has already happened. More millions are marked for extermination....

The Federal Council of Churches of Christ in America has proclaimed tomorrow, May 2nd, a Day of Compassion and Intercession for the suffering Jews of Nazi Europe. The announcement describes that suffering as "beyond anything the civilized imagination can picture," and it continues, "it is impossible to dismiss the reports as 'atrocity stories.' When the full story is known, the actual facts may turn out to be worse than the fragmentary reports have indicated."

May 2, 1943 (Sunday)

Abba Hillel Silver, "The Conspiracy of Silence," Address to National Conference on Palestine, Philadelphia, PA. *JC*, May 7, 1943, p. 1; Silver, *Vision and Victory*, pp. 2–12

(2:) Within the last few months, as if by concerted action, there has set in a very definite and noticeable withdrawal on the part of our official family in Washington from anything which might even remotely suggest a recommendation or endorsement of the Jewish homeland. The whole subject has suddenly become taboo in Washington.... (3:) Our former friends in Government circles content themselves with sending us apologetic expressions of sympathy on the Jewish persecution. When pressed to do something about it, to help save a race from annihilation, they regretfully remind us how difficult it is to do anything for these poor unfortunate people under present war conditions. They counsel us to have patience, and the suggestion is even made that anything which may be done for these unfortunate Jews now might, in some way, postpone the day of their ultimate liberation. That they may all be dead when the ultimate day of liberation arrives does not seem to arouse these friends of ours to any extraordinary emergency acts of rescue and deliverance. These are men of many words and few deeds. Whose compassion never goes beyond political expediency....

May 3, 1943 (Monday)

Isaac Herzog, Address at the Special Session of the Assembly of Representatives (*Asefat haNivḥarim*), Jerusalem. *Masu'ah leYitzḥak*, pp. 136–38, translated by MS

(136:) Once again we have gathered the Assembly of Representatives with the authority of the entire Jewish population in the land of our patriarchs and prophets, and once again we turn to the nations of the world and cry out: "To the rescue!" The slaughter continues; you have finally begun to move, but we call to you in the words of our prophet Isaiah, "We hope for justice, but there is none; for deliverance, but it is far from us" (Isa. 59:11). We hear the sound of words, but we do not yet see the actual deeds of rescue. You have not yet elevated yourselves to the necessary level. You have not yet publicly recognized the fact that pierces the eyes: that the Jewish people is the only people for which the anguished enemy has decreed total annihilation.

Once again we announce that if – Heaven forbid! – you will have disappointed the hopes we bound up with the Bermuda Conference, this would be an enormous defeat in the ethical realm.[17]...

(137:) Listen, all you nations! We have an historic account with the nations of the world. For the past two millennia, world history has been stained with the blood and tears of the Jewish people, the sheep scattered among the nations. Now our sacred Torah teaches us to pardon and to forgive. We are prepared to forget the accounts of the past, provided that you will fulfill your sacred obligation. Whatever you accomplish toward the rescue of the remnant of Israel

---

17 The Bermuda Conference, April 19–30, 1943, opened with hope but ended with painful disappointment. On May 4, the day after Herzog's address, the *NYT* published on p. 17 a large advertisement entitled "To 5,000,000 Jews in the Nazi Death-Trap Bermuda Was a 'Cruel Mockery.'" See David S. Wyman and Rafael Medoff, *A Race Against Death,* 11th page of photographs, and Monty Noam Penkower, "The Bermuda Conference and Its Aftermath."

should not be considered to be acts of kindness. It will serve only as a sin offering, which will atone for the substantial historical sin humanity has committed against this people that has bequeathed it so much of its spiritual and ethical possessions, and also of its intellectual capacities....

Open the gates! Open *all* the gates, including the gates to the land of our forefathers, as shelters for our wretched brothers and sisters. You have the capacity to implement a broad and an encompassing program of rescue. The matter depends (138:) only upon your powerful will. The final moment has already arrived. "If not now, when?" Rescue! Save lives! And G-d will protect you.

May 16, 1943 (Sunday)

JOSEPH H. HERTZ, "The Function of Jews' College," Chairman's Address on Speech Day, London. *JC*, May 21, 1943, p. 5; *Early and Late*, pp. 181–86

(185:) The *Churban* [destruction] that has overtaken European Israel is not only physical – ghastly and unparalleled in human history as it is. All the Seats of Jewish Learning in Germany, Poland, and Russia – the Seminaries of Breslau and Vienna, the *Lehranstalt* [academy] and the *Rabbiner-Seminar* of Berlin, the Yeshivahs are no more. Is English-speaking Jewry willing and ready to build hearths for Jewish Learning in England and America, now that its fire has been extinguished on the European Continent? May God give the men and women of Anglo-Jewry the wisdom, by doing their duty to Jews' College, to share in the rekindling of Jewish religious (186:) life on the rebirth of European Jewry that shall follow a victorious and righteous peace.

May 24, 1943 (Monday)

DANIEL ZION, Address to congregants in the Iuch Bunar Synagogue, Sofia, Bulgaria, in Issac Avramov, "Daniel Zion (1883–1976)," *Annual*, 22 (1987): 399–403, translated by Rumyana Marinova-Christidi

Brothers and sisters, don't be afraid, hope to God! God hears our prayers! Bishop Stefan [the Bishop of Sofia] has told me that the Tsar has promised that the Bulgarian Jews will not leave the country. If we die, let us die here, and not in Poland.... Let us go to the Palace to defend our right to remain here, to protest against the decision for our deportation. God is within us, in our deeds, actions and thoughts. In these testing times, I urge you to remain united and help each other and let us not forget our humanity! It has been said that "For in the same way you judge others, you will be judged, and with the measure you use, it will be measured to you" [Matt. 7:1–2]. Don't forget, that God is observing our deeds from the sky.

Asher Hananel, Address to congregants outside the locked gates of the central Sofia Synagogue, in Michael Bar-Zohar, *Beyond Hitler's Grasp*, p. 193

Why do you cry? You are the descendants of the Maccabees.... I know what awaits us. I declare that Sofia's cemetery is more beautiful than any other cemetery. You know what you have to do. Let the trains leave empty, we shall stay here, we shall not go to the slaughter.[18]

June 6, 1943 (Sunday evening)

Abraham Cohen, "The Problem of War and Peace," at Central Hall, Birmingham, England. Unpublished, David Cohen Private Collection[19]

(1b:) I feel that I should not be making the best use of this precious opportunity if I were, as announced, to devote my time to a description of the ghastly harvest which is being reaped as the effect of the past ten years of intensive anti-Semitic campaigning. For a few pence the facts are available in a White Paper recently issued by the Government, and in Doctor [Victor] Gollancz's pamphlet, "Let My People Go."[20] It is impossible to understand the modern phase of

18 Neither of these quotations of rabbinic messages at a critical moment in the history of Bulgarian Jewry is based on documents written at the time of delivery. The first is based on reports of Jews who were present and heard the message, the second is based on a later report by Chief Rabbi Hananel (his testimony before the People's Court in March 1945). It is possible that the words are a later reconstruction, but there is no reason to question the situation and the underlying message.

19 Cohen's hand-written text includes the assertion that he never imagined he would be invited to give an address to a "Christian congregation" (p. 1a).

20 The Government "White Paper" probably refers to the declaration of the United Nations (Allies), based on a British draft, and issued on December 17, 1942, with a two-minute period of silence in the House of Commons. Cf. Sharf, *The British Press*

anti-Semitism when it is isolated and viewed apart from the current of world affairs during the last decade or so....

(2b:) The German Propaganda Ministry knew what it was doing when it spent millions annually in spreading this deadly mental poison [anti-Semitism] throughout the world. The purpose was to disrupt the unity of each country and to undermine its morale. Hitler acknowledged that anti-Semitism was to be the spearpoint of his attack upon his intended victims. It is not accidental that the traitors on the Continent who delivered their respective countries into the hands of the enemy were, without exception, leaders in the anti-Jewish movements before the war.

June 9, 1943 (Shavu'ot)

Eliezer Berkovits, "The Breath of His Lips," United Hebrew Congregation, Leeds, England. *Between Yesterday and Tomorrow*, pp. 93–99

Hosea 2:1: "The number of the children of Israel [...cannot be measured or counted]" – bitterness wells up in the heart of the Jew as he meditates upon the phrase. Which number cannot be counted? That of the multitudes who have lost their number among the living because they were of the seed of Israel, or the dwindling number of the shrinking remnant of Israel? Life seems to have made (94:) mockery of the phrase, "The number of children of Israel that will be as the sand of the sea."...

As it is, our numbers are not like the sand of the sea. Our measure seems to be so negligible that the United Nations deems it policy to ignore the existence of a Jewish nation.

Then there is our own estimation of ourselves, which unfortunately is very similar to that of other nations. Jews (95:) have lost faith in their own strength. They no longer believe that with their own action they can influence their own future.

---

and Jews Under Nazi Rule, p. 87, and Tomlin, *Protest and Prayer*, pp. 89–91 (with House of Commons records, n. 40). Gollancz's thirty-two-page pamphlet, with the subtitle "Some Practical Proposals for Dealing with Hitler's Massacre of the Jews, and an Appeal to the British Public," first appeared in January 1943, and was reissued in several additional editions with an Addendum before the sermon was delivered.

To-day Jews should be seized by a burning desire to save what can be saved, to plan and prepare for the future.... But instead, Jews continue in the old ruts as if nothing had happened; steeped in apathy and given over to fatalism, they wait for a miracle to redeem them....

Even to-day, after the most crushing blows ever suffered by a nation have been inflicted upon us, our barbarous (96:) enemies on the Continent still pretend that their quarrel is only with the Jew. When every sane man is fully aware that the Jewish nation has been utterly broken, they still speak of the Jewish menace, and in every stroke dealt at them by the mighty democracies, they see the hand of the Jew. "Stalingrad," according to them, "was the work of World Jewry, and so was the Allied victory in North Africa, and so is everything else that is battering at the foundations of their evil regime."[21]...

Who is right? The nations that take so little notice of us; we who have lost all faith in our own strength; or our enemies, who so immensely exaggerate the power of Israel?

I believe that though all three are wrong, our enemies have come closest to the truth....

But how strong Israel? Can one find the answer to this question in a figure? Sixteen, to-day it may be only thirteen, million Jews – is that really all? Sixteen million Jews without a State, without a land, without visible power anywhere on earth – does this give the strength of Israel?...(97:) Our enemies forget statistics and exaggerate our number because they feel instinctively that Israel is much stronger and considerably more powerful than figures would suggest. And in this one thing they are right. How strong Israel? – the answer cannot be given in numbers, Israel cannot be explained by statistics....

The Bible has had a more profound influence upon the development of humanity than many a great empire. The Revelation of Sinai and the moral code emanating from it have been among the greatest civilizing factors on earth. Can one express this in numbers?...

21 A good example of this Nazi worldview, blaming World Jewry for everything antithetical to Nazi values (though without the exact quotation), can be seen in the speech delivered by Goebbels in the Berlin Sports Palace on February 18, 1943, entitled: "Nation, Rise Up, and Let the Storm Break Loose," http://research.calvin.edu/german-propaganda-archive/goeb36.htm.

June 25, 1943 (Friday)

Julius Gordon, "A Light to the Nations," Address at 54th Annual Convention of the Central Conference of American Rabbis, New York. *CCAR Yearbook* 53, 1943, pp. 204–16

(215:) We cannot dream of a restored and redeemed humanity without expressing our fervent hope that a sincere effort will be made in the world of tomorrow to put an end to the Great Hatred directed against Israel. I need not tell you what this movement of organized hate has done to our people in the last decade. Words fail to sound the depth of our tragedy. Paraphrasing the rabbis, I would say, "If all the oceans were ink, all the heavens parchment, all the reeds pens, and all men writers, we would still be unable to describe the misery and suffering of our people in the ghetto of Europe." Now this does not mean the end of the Jew and Judaism. Israel will survive. Ruthless tyrants may drive us out of one community and another, of one country and another. They cannot drive us out of the world. What we would ask of humanity is not to drive the world out of us, not to render us cynical and skeptical, not to banish faith and hope from our hearts.

I believe the time has come when Christian leaders the world over should confess with Pastor Niemoeller, and openly declare that the true Christian could never be anti-Semitic. You cannot be a Christian first and an anti-Semite last. You cannot preach a gospel of love and continue to indulge in human hate. You cannot teach children to love their enemies and then allow them to hate their friends. You cannot ask people to extend their other cheek and then proceed to smite that cheek also. The task of Christian leaders is to tell their followers to stop hating altogether, to put an end to the greatest crime in Christendom, which is the crucifixion of the people of Jesus.

June 26, 1943 (Saturday)

Louis I. Newman, "Why Jews Become Skeptics," Congregation Rodeph Sholom, New York. *Biting on Granite*, pp. 162–77

(163:) If there are Jews who refused to give their full-hearted faith and allegiance to a Benevolent God, it is because they remember the long and bloody chronicles of persecution, massacre and expulsion which have been the portion of Jewish communities down to our very day. I take it that you have read this week of the wholesale deportation of the Jews in the Netherlands, and of the new restrictions imposed upon the Jews of France by the infamous Laval.[22] Is it any wonder – some may ask – that there is a negative and insurgent element in the psyche of Israel? It is as if a child had become disillusioned with respect to an adored father who had cruelly betrayed its trust.

July 8, 1943 (Thursday evening)

Stephen S. Wise, Address at Mass Meeting, Polo Grounds, New York, in honor of Soviet Representatives, Colonels [Solomon] Mikhoels and [Itzik] Feffer. AJA, SSW Microfilm of AJHS texts, Box 23

(1:) We who are Americans…have no quarrel with Russia over its Socialist ideology, though we cannot accept it nor any of its Socialist orthodoxies. We would quarrel bitterly with Russia if she refused not a Second Front but a First Front, that First Front which is one of the mightiest military feats of history. That unyielding, unshatterable First Front presages and makes possible the destruction of Hitlerism and challenges as does nothing else England and the United States of America with regard to that Second Front that cannot much longer be delayed.[23]

August 14, 1943 (Saturday, Shabbat Naḥamu)

Louis I. Newman, "Comfort Ye, Comfort Ye, My People," Congregation Rodeph Sholom, New York. *Biting on Granite*, pp. 178–84.

---

22 Newman may have been referring to the following announcement from the JTA on June 23, 1943: "Not a single Jew now remains in occupied Holland outside of concentration camps, after the deportation of the majority of the Dutch Jews to Poland and other Nazi-held territories in the East, it was reported here today by the Netherlands Government-in-Exile." Pierre Laval was a leading French politician, who became vice-premier of the Vichy government under Marshal Pétain in July 1940, and premier in April 1942. JTA reported on June 27, 1943 that Laval signed an order annulling the citizenship of some 100,000 Jews who had been naturalized since 1927. This may have been the item to which Newman was referring, having had access from a somewhat earlier source.

23 It would, of course, take almost eleven more months before that "Second Front" would be opened on D-Day.

(179:) Surely the people of Israel need solace in these troublous days. The leaders of Jewry everywhere, who are preparing for the American Jewish Conference on August 29th,[24] are profoundly concerned with the fate of their brethren in all lands of persecution and war.... (180:) The victories of the arms of the United Nations, especially in Russia, bring increasing liberation to our oppressed brethren who are surviving the pestilence of Nazi fury – but it is now a tragic race between our liberating armies and the Teutonic madness which seeks the extermination of our fellow-Jews abroad.... And we need the comfort at this time that the great program of rebuilding Zion will not be endangered. Ominous reports have come to us of the intention of some of the representatives of the United Nations to freeze the Palestinian enterprise, and to appease the Arab extremists. There is every likelihood that the Jewish people again will be thrown to the wolves....

(183:) Because God looks in His notebook, He gives to posterity this apportionment of recompense and penalty – thereby granting us the comfort of knowing that His is a world of righteousness and of ultimate victory for the men of virtue and fortitude.... And to every enslaved people – the French, the Austrians, the Yugoslavians, all who have felt the lash of the persecutor, let us speak the words that Isaiah addressed to Jerusalem: "Take heart, and proclaim unto her/ That her time of service is accomplished" (Isa. 40:2)....

August 28, 1943 (Saturday, *Re'eh*)

Louis I. Newman, "God's Promise to the Anti-Semites," Congregation Rodeph Sholom, New York. *Biting on Granite*, 185–91

(186:) Can we win continuous triumphs over those who malign and slander us? Surely we know that in every generation, our enemies have risen up to defame and misrepresent us. From the days of Amalek through Haman, Apion, Fettermilch, Ahlwardt[25] and down

24 On this Conference with its powerful endorsement of Palestine as the national Jewish homeland, see below, August 29, 1943, and Monty Noam Penkower, "American Jewry and the Holocaust," reprinted in *American Jewish History*, vol. 7: *America, American Jews, and the Holocaust*, pp. 357–76.

25 Vincenz Fettmilch led an uprising against the Jews of Frankfurt in 1614 which forced

to Goebbels and Hitler, we have been made the target for almost insufferable abuse.[26]

(187:) Another classic example of the promise God makes to the anti-Semites is Spain. Torquemada and his fellows of the Inquisition drove out the Jews of Spain, even as Hitler has driven out the Jews of Germany. And Spain, as a direct consequence of this folly and insanity, having crippled herself, (188:) became a decrepit, fifth-rate nation – today a beggar-ridden nation, in the hands of a despot.[27] And look, too, at the fate of the German people who acquiesced in Hitler's anti-Semitism. Has this weapon, forged against Israel, prospered? The newspapers carry the stories that the Germans are fleeing to Poland, to Lodz and other Polish cities out of fear of bombardment by the British and Americans. And they live in constant terror that the Poles when liberation comes will take revenge upon them.... In the very Poland where so many Jews have been slaughtered, the German culprits themselves are seeking refuge.[28]

Shlomo Zalman Unsdorfer, Weidritz Alley Synagogue, Bratislava, Slovakia, in Katz, Riderman, and Greenberg, eds., *Wrestling With God*, pp. 59–60, translated by Gershon Greenberg from Unsdorfer, *Siftei Shlomoh,* pp. 141–44

(59:) When there is a pouring out of wrath, heaven forbid, when God's wrath goes forth, heaven forbid, and we eat stalks and grains, when the righteous and evil are condemned together and we all have one fate, we do see a great difference with our senses. Every day we see instances of sinful Jews, who did not know God and were estranged from faith and trust, committing suicide, heaven forbid. They have nothing to rely upon. They abandon hope and possibility,

---

the Jewish population to leave the city until the Emperor ordered their restoration. Hermann Ahlwardt, an antisemitic journalist, author and leader of the "Antisemitic People's Party," served in the Reichstag from 1892 until 1902.

26 Newman continues to specify historical examples of spurious anti-Jewish accusations: poisoning of wells, ritual murder, usury, radicalism, slanders of the "Protocols."

27 This is of course a piece of homiletical *léger de main*, apparently assuming that his listeners will not know that the peak period of flourishing Spanish wealth and culture was in the sixteenth century, after the 1492 expulsion of the Jews.

28 I have not been able to find contemporary newspaper reports that would confirm this broad generalization about "the Germans."

having lost everything, including their love of life. Not so with the righteous, who fulfill God's commandments and trust in God with all their heart and soul. They do not get depressed. They strengthen themselves through every attribute that He extends to them. They put themselves under the protection of the Blessed Creator in every respect, to the point that they are prepared to sacrifice their body and soul should that be His will. They have no true anguish, because they have faith about what is prepared for them in the world to come. This is the true blessing....

(60:) Four years ago, on this very holy Sabbath, *parashat Re'eh*, the troubles began in our community. They publicly destroyed the great synagogue here and destroyed and desecrated holy books and Torah scrolls.[29] From then unto now, because of our many sins, we have had no peace or respite from trouble after trouble, decree after decree, heaven forbid, one order rushing after the other. May God have mercy. This is why the verse reads, "Behold, I set before you this day a blessing and a curse" (Deut. 11:26). That is, do not forget that G-d resides in heaven, sees everything, and in the end of time He will repay those who lit the conflagration [echoing Exod. 22:5], measure for measure. "The wicked is snared in the work of his own hands" (Ps. 9:17). Do not despair, heaven forbid! "For My salvation is near to come, and My favor to be revealed" (Isa. 56:1).

August 29, 1943 (Sunday)

Stephen S. Wise, Address at Opening Meeting of the American Jewish Conference, New York. *As I See It*, pp. 67–79

(68:) The Polish Underground relates the unbelievably hideous details of the death camps at Tremblinka [*sic*],[30] for example, in the

29 JTA, August 14, 1939 from London, August 13, 1939: "Windows and doors of the principal synagogue were smashed and the interior was demolished. The basement was flooded from broken water mains. Objects of worship were piled in the street and burned." *JC*, August 18, 1939, referring to a "pogrom" that occurred the previous Saturday, August 12, when the *parashah* was indeed *Re'eh*: "In one Synagogue, reports THE TIMES, the furnishings were broken up, the Scrolls of the Law defiled and torn, and many gold and silver ornaments stolen. Rioters entered another Synagogue and turned on all the water hydrants flooding the entire building."

30 This spelling of the name of the death camp was not unusual at the time.

railway running from Warsaw to Bialystok, the death houses, the special extermination machinery, the liquidating gases piped into death cells, the victims dying daily by thousands. A huge poster greets the newcomers to Tremblinka: "You can be confident of your future." An ironic invitation to death at its cruelest. For the victims, we say to these bestial executioners: "Unlike the death with honor you have brought to your victims, death and shame are swiftly becoming your portion. The United Nations have made us confident of your immediate future, and there is and will hereafter be no future anywhere on earth for such as seek to set race against race and faith against faith."

(77:) A new and more, indeed, most, immediate objective presses itself upon this body of American Jews: solemnly to demand of the United Nations that not another hour be lost in rescuing from the lands in the hands of Hitler the remaining Jews, the less than 3,000,000 survivors of the 8,000,000 Jews who lived in pre-Hitler Europe. Further delay in rescue would doubtless mean that there would be no Jews to save in what was Hitler Europe.[31] Never was it truer that a way, the way, the ways of rescue will be found, provided the United Nations, led by our own, have the will to rescue our harassed, despoiled, tortured brothers. Such rescue of the surviving may in part redeem the world's shame of the years 1933–1939. Throughout these years every manner of nameless crime was committed against our brothers with none, save a handful of Christians such as Cardinals Faulhaber and Mundelein, the Archbishop of Canterbury and Dr. Cadman, to plead angel-tongued for the victims of the devils of extermination.[32]

September 1, 1943 (Wednesday)

Abba Hillel Silver, "Toward American Jewish Unity," Address to Amer-

31 These two sentences were highlighted in the JTA account of the opening session, published on August 30, 1943.

32 George Mundelein was Cardinal of Chicago; he was known especially for a speech to some five hundred Chicago priests delivered on May 18, 1937, in which he caustically derided Hitler and the sixty million intelligent Germans who submitted to him. Wise had spoken about Faulhaber, The Archbishop of Canterbury (Cosmo Gordon Lang in the 1930s), and S. Parkes Cadman (a close friend) in earlier sermons.

ican Zionist Emergency Council," Hotel Waldorf Astoria, New York. *Vision and Victory*, pp. 14–21

(14:) My dear friends, the Jewish people is in danger of coming out of this war the most ravaged of peoples and the least healed and restored.

The stark tragedy of our ravage has been abundantly told here and elsewhere – tragic, ghastly, unredeemed. To rehearse it again is only to flagellate one's self and to gash our souls again and again. But what of the healing? What is beyond the rim of blood and tears? Frankly, to some of us, nothing. We are being comforted at the moment with the hope that the Atlantic Charter and the Four Freedoms and victory will bring the healing of our people.

I am afraid that we are again sacrificing cool, albeit bitter reasoning and logic to beguiling romancing in the voice. We are again turning away from history to dreams and to apocalypses which some of us amazingly enough choose to call realism and statesmanship...

(15:) There is a tragic fact which seems to escape so many students of anti-Semitism. The story of Jewish Emancipation in Europe from the day after the French Revolution to the day before the Nazi revolution is the story of political positions captured in the face of stubborn and sullen opposition which left our emancipated minority in each country encamped within an unbeaten and unreconciled opposition, so that at the slightest provocation, as soon as things got out of order, the opposition returned to the attack and inflicted grievous wounds.

And in our day, stirred by the political and economic struggles which have torn nations apart, this never-failing, never-reconciled opposition swept over the Jewish political and economic positions in Europe and completely demolished them....

(18:) From the infested, typhus-ridden Ghetto of Warsaw, from the death-block of Nazi-occupied lands where myriads of our people are awaiting execution by the slow or the quick method, from a hundred concentration camps which befoul the map of Europe, from the pitiful ranks of our wandering hosts over the entire face of the earth, comes the cry: "Enough; there must be a final end to all this, a sure and certain end!"

How long is the crucifixion of Israel to last? Time and again we have been stretched upon the rack for other peoples' sins. Time and again we have been made the whipping boy for blundering governments, the scapegoat for defeat in war, for misery and depression, for conflict among classes.

How long is it to last? Are we forever to live a homeless people on the world's crumbs of sympathy, forever in need of defenders, forever doomed to thoughts of refugees and relief? Should not, I ask you fellow-Jews, ought not, the incalculable and unspeakable suffering of our people and the oceans of blood which we have shed in this war and in all the wars of the centuries; should not the myriad martyrs of our people, as well as the magnificent heroism and the vast sacrifices of our brave soldier sons who are today fighting on all the battle fronts of the world – should not all this be compensated for finally and at long last with the re-establishment of a free Jewish Commonwealth?

September 3, 1943 (Friday), National Day of Prayer

Emil Ehrnthal (later Michael Elton), "Darkness and Light," Finsbury Park, London. *The Challenge of Destiny*, pp. 34–37

(34:) "A man may be justified in extinguishing the Sabbath light because of the fear of the heathens, because of robbers and because of the evil spirit" (Mishnah Shabbat [2,5]).

It has been said that the lights of peace went out all over Europe, twice in living men's memory. The rulers of Germany, after having destroyed the homes of 600,000 Jews, after having made widows of our women and orphans of our children, after all this diabolical work, extended the trail of bereavement and destruction to every land under their sway. With proud bluster they proclaimed, and many seriously believed: "Germany is ours today. Tomorrow, the whole world."[33]

(35:) We realized that fear, terror and treachery had invaded our shores as forerunners of the Nazi monsters of Germany. Gloomy

33 Reference is to the refrain of the official song of the Hitler Youth, beginning in 1932: "*Denn heute, da gehört uns Deutschland und morgen die ganze Welt.*"

forebodings harassed minds in the free countries of the world. It was then that we extinguished lights of peace and took up the weapons of war in order to restore man's right to live in freedom from fear. We extinguished the lights "because of the heathens," because of the evil of destructive nationalism. We extinguished the lights "because of the robbers," because of that State which, after looting and robbing her own helpless citizens, turned to plundering, ransacking, and exploiting every country on the continent of Europe.

We extinguished the lights because of the "evil spirit," because of the evil spirit of force, brutality and controlled ignorance that was propagated by every means at the disposal of the tyrants of Germany. We extinguished the lights that "the sick may sleep," that even a sick man may live out his days in peace....

(37:) Then we can truly march forward in unity, in confidence and strength, hoping to see soon, new lights in the homes of our dear ones on the continent of Europe, new lights of peace which will never be extinguished again through man's inhumanity to man.

Salis Daiches, Special Synagogue Service, 6:30 p.m., Edinburgh Hebrew Congregation, Scotland. Salis Daiches Archives

(2:) Four years have elapsed since the aggression of those mighty and terrible men began – and many have been waiting ever since to see on which side God was and whether the God of Israel would reveal His hand at all. But today, those that have their ears open – not only among our people – can hear a Divine voice speaking: "And I will contend with him that contended with thee, and I will save My children" (Isa. 49:25). The God of Israel has appeared on the scene of the struggle, and He is fighting against the... powers whom the free nations have been endeavouring to beat down. There can only be one end to such a struggle: the defeat of the ungodly and the victory of those who fight for God....

And this day of National Prayer has been largely instituted for the purpose of making this clear to us and to the whole world. Let us make it clear to ourselves. We have reached the turning point in the gigantic struggle in which the nations are engaged. The armies of the aggressor are going back, fleeing everywhere.... Its ruler, whose name was on everybody's lips only a short while ago, is now almost forgotten. And when he is recalled to memory, it is only with an expression of contempt and a warning to those who followed his example....

(3:) There can be no peace, and there will be no thought of peace in our minds, until the oppressed are liberated and those who have survived the enemy's fiendish cruelty have been saved and restored to freedom and security. However long it may take, this aim must be achieved. Our prayers today are not only to prepare us for a great feat of arms by which final victory is to be achieved, but also for the gigantic task of rescuing the survivors from the ruins which threaten to a[???] them even after the evil power of the adversary has been broken. "Prepare a place of refuge for those about to be rescued from martyrdom and death": this is the cry we must utter today, and utter in such a way that the leaders of the free nations should hear it and answer it.

The time has come to mention by name clearly and unmistakably the captives that are to be released from their captivity, the children of Israel among them. We often hear the names of the conquered peoples and suffering communities mentioned in the pronouncements and speeches of our statesmen and the heads of the free nations. But we ask, as we have a right and a duty to ask, why is the Jew not mentioned clearly and openly in these utterances? Why is the people that has suffered most at the hands of the cruel enemy not referred to distinctively as a victim of the enemy's blood lust?[34] Why are we not told, and why is not the enemy told, that the wrong done to the children of Israel is to be righted, and that their yearning for redemption and restoration will be realized?...The enemy mentions

34 This theme, which has been raised in earlier sermons, may reflect the influence of Vladimir (Ze'ev) Jabotinsky, *The War and the Jew* (written January–February 1940, published 1942): "Despite the deliberate policy of Jewish extermination pursued by the Germans in the occupied territories, the Jewish angle has been almost completely suppressed in the Allied press and radio reports. Allied statesmen, while consistently referring to any and every aspect and phase of the war, with a studiousness that cannot be regarded as accidental, have carefully eschewed references to the Jew.... The general effect of this policy was to render Jews, so to say, non-existent for the duration of the war" (p. 103).

us by name in all his attacks, in all his decrees of extermination and his perpetrating of acts of savagery. Why should our friends hesitate to mention us by name when they condemn the savage deeds of the foe and promise redress to those who have suffered, as well as retribution to those who have inflicted the suffering?...

Let us therefore begin to (4:) make our position clear. We have no desire to give the world the impression that this is a Jews' war, for it is not true.[35] And even our enemies who delight in so describing this world war know that it is false. But to say that this is a Jews' war is one thing, a wrong thing. To say that the Jews are the greatest sufferers in this war and that it is the duty of the free nations to save them from the distressing positions in which they have been placed both before and during this war is another thing, and it is the right thing. We ought to take every opportunity that affords itself to make this clear to our friends and the defenders of our cause against injustice and inhumanity....

We have hesitated long enough in making our aspirations known and our vision for the future clear. Now is the time to make our voice be heard, and the significance of our prayers and yearnings to be understood. This will not hinder us in making common cause with all who fight for justice, equity and liberty, as we have done all along. On the contrary, it will enhance our zeal and it will enable our neighbours to understand and appreciate our devotion to the cause even more fully and more clearly. Above all, it will enhance our self-respect and will strengthen our faith not only in the future of Israel but in the future of humanity as a whole. We do believe that the God of Israel is today fighting our battle, and we need not hesitate to proclaim our faith in the world. We do believe that the God of our fathers will grant victory to the Allied nations because they are defending the cause of justice and righteousness, which is also our cause. And therefore we feel that the coming victory will only become real and final when we are given our share in the fruits of this victory, and that in the new world which is to come, God's will will be known and His Law will be obeyed....

---

35 Cf. Jabotinsky, *The War and the Jew*, p. 37.

September 29, 1943 (Wednesday, Erev Rosh Hashanah)

Marcus Melchior, Great Synagogue, Copenhagen, Denmark, Address delivered at the morning service preceding Erev Rosh Hashanah, in Emmy E. Werner, *A Conspiracy of Decency*, pp. 41–42[36]

(41:) I have very important news to tell you. Last night I received word that the Germans plan to raid Jewish homes throughout Copenhagen to arrest all the Danish Jews for shipment to concentration camps. They know that tomorrow is Rosh Hashanah and our families will be home. (42:) The situation is very serious. We must take action immediately. You must leave the synagogue now and contact all relatives, friends, and neighbors you know are Jewish and tell them what I have told you. You must tell them to pass the word on to everyone they know is Jewish. You must also speak to all your Christian friends and tell them to warn the Jews. You must do this immediately, within the next few minutes, so that two or three hours from now everyone will know what is happening. By nightfall tonight we must all be in hiding.

Irving Reichert, "A Faith to Live By," Temple Emanu-El, San Francisco, CA. *Judaism and the American Jew*, pp. 81–84

(83:) None of us tonight can for a moment forget the tragedy that has overwhelmed our co-religionists in darkest Europe, the torture and degradation, the exile and mass murder that have destroyed entire Jewish communities. Who can or would escape on such a day as this – a day of memorial – from reflecting on the enormity of the pain and suffering that racks this convulsed planet; the incalculable destruction that has blown the creative efforts of the centuries into rubble; the hordes of tyranny that now, at long last, are slowly but irresistibly being driven back to their rendezvous with retribution?…

36 The following text is not based on a contemporary written document; according to Werner, it was "recorded by Rabbi Melchior in the documentary film, "An Act of Faith," broadcast by CBS, December 31, 1961" (p. 187, n. 18). It is unclear to me whether any written text from September 1943 has been preserved, and if so whether it was written in advance of delivery or shortly afterward, or whether the text was reconstructed by Melchior in 1961. Cf. also Marcus Melchior, *A Rabbi Remembers*, pp. 178–79, and Leni Yahil, *The Rescue of Danish Jewry*, p. 207.

(84:) In Europe tonight millions of our brethren know that they must confront torture and death once more, as Hitler's beaten troops limp back to their lair. The line of retreat from Russia leads through the heart of the most densely Jewish-populated area on the continent. Despite our most heroic efforts, and the cost in blood and treasure, many will have to die. Where shall they find the courage and strength to face the frenzy of their foes, save in the secret places of the spirit, where weapons of torture can never reach?

Louis L. Mann, "Where Now Is Thy God?," Chicago Sinai Congregation, Chicago, IL. *Best Sermons: 1944 Selection*, pp. 236–44

(241:) It has now become clear why dictators persecute Jews. Jews stand for everything that dictators defy. The dictators stand for everything that the Jews deny. If you should think that this statement is a bit overdrawn, read [Hermann] Rauschning's *The Revolution of Nihilism*, in which it is made clear that Fascism is destructionism, the destruction of all values: justice, love, mercy, morality, decency, righteousness, and God. It is the destruction of everything except force. It is destruction for destruction's sake.... That will explain the utilization of anti-Semitism as a spearhead to destroy every form of liberalism and co-operation looking to the ultimate brotherhood of man. That will throw light on the false identification of Judaism and Communism, making each of two unpopular philosophies of life doubly unpopular by linking them together. That will explain the hypocrisy of Hitler in shamelessly aligning himself with Russia for a time and then, without rhyme or reason, going forth to crush her. The differences between Judaism and Christianity pale into insignificance when compared to the colossal challenge that now confronts them both. Now they will stand or fall together.

Bertram Korn, "The Prayer for Life," Government Street Temple (Sha'arai Shomayim), Mobile, AL. AJA, MS-99, Box 30, Folder 16; see Complete Sermons

Harry Joshua Stern, "A Rosh Hashanah Creed," Temple Emanu-El, Montreal. *Martyrdom and Miracle*, pp. 28–32 (evening or morning, possibly both)

(31:) On Rosh Hashanah 5704 we shall think especially of the heroes of the European ghettos who, facing sure death at the hands of the Nazis, fought the heroic fight against Fascism and dealt blow after blow, though poorly armed, to the enemies of Israel and mankind.[37] We find courage in the thousands of Jewish heroes who, under allied direction, are giving all to liberate mankind from the pestilence of Nazism and Fascism. We trust the world will ever remember the achievements of Palestine Jewry in helping General Montgomery to drive Rommel and his legions out of Africa and thus to avert the threat to the Suez and the entire Near East.

But Judaism's great preaching has been for moral heroism which in an hour of distress can be more uplifting than mere physical or military heroism. We hear on our holy days the voices of Rabbi Akiba, the victims of the Inquisition, the victims of Nazism who died with the *Shema Yisroel* on their lips assured of the triumph of the Jewish spirit, come what may....

(32:) And finally on the New Year we Jews become especially aware of the sense of the Messianic. On this holy day we look forward in hope for a new day and a better world despite the fact that the world has gone back to ancient prejudices. No matter how dark is the contemporary hour, Judaism urges us to look beyond the hour, beyond the century....

September 30, 1943 (first day of Rosh Hashanah)

Israel Goldstein, "New Year Summons," Congregation B'nai Jeshurun, New York. *Best Sermons: 1944 Selection*, pp. 229–35

(231:) Fortunately for all of us, and especially for those of us who have kin on the war front, the great portion of the war is behind us. The beginning of the end is in sight, though not so near as some of us wish or think it to be. Luckily for us, Russia is bearing the brunt of the ordeal. It is something to think about when we think about Russia. True, Russia is fighting for her own life and had no choice

---

37 A clear reference to the Warsaw Ghetto Uprising, news of which had recently become more public. See below, Reichert, on Yom Kippur, October 8.

but to fight. Yet the fact remains that five million Russian dead and wounded have made it possible for us so far to win our victories at a relatively small cost in human life. Let us not forget our debt to Russia when the time of reckoning comes.

And let us not forget or permit others to forget our Jewish contribution to the war effort....

(232:) The Shofar is also a call to penitence.... The whole world is called to penitence for having permitted this war to come to pass. It is a man-made catastrophe, not like the earthquake or the flood which we call an act of God...

And as always happens, the Jewish problem is a reliable barometer. Where was the conscience of Europe when Hitler proclaimed war against the Jewish people in 1933? The statesmen in the chancelleries of England and France preferred not to see and not to hear. "It was Germany's internal affair," said the meticulous lawyers. "Hitler must not be crossed," said the timid politicians. "He has a great mission to immunize Europe against Bolshevism and must not be disturbed," said the reactionaries. So the Jew was left to his fate. Only an Isaiah could muster the language to (233:) excoriate the misleaders of our generation: "Thy leaders are misleaders who have corrupted the highways.... Woe unto those that draw iniquity with cords of vanity" (Isa. 5:18).

So let no one wring his hands against God's injustice. Let us rather indict our own human stupidity, cowardice, and venality.

Louis Hammer, "Taking Stock," Congregation B'nai Shalom, Brooklyn, NY. *A Word in Season*, pp. 35–42

(36:) We are in a war against an enemy more cunning, more (37:) subtle, more dangerous than Edom of old, whom the prophet Isaiah had in mind when he spoke these words [Isa. 21:11–12]. We, too, are in constant fear of an attack from this ruthless foe, who has declared war against our people and is desirous of exterminating us completely.... "Morning is coming." But *v'gam lailah* – "It is still night."

As we look back over the events of the past year, there are many encouraging happenings to inspire us with faith and hope. Last year at this time thick clouds obscured our horizon. The German hordes were knocking at the gates of Alexandria in Egypt. The fall of the city seemed inevitable. After that the enemy would threaten Palestine. Our hearts were filled with trepidation. The most optimistic among us thought that all was lost....

(38:) But today the scene has changed. The clouds have almost disappeared.... But... the danger remains. The Nazi armies are still powerful. Many battles will still have to be fought....

Aaron David Burack, "What Have We Reduced the Shofar To?," Congregation Ohel Moshe Chevra Thilim, Brooklyn, NY. *Pirchei Aharon* (*Flowers of Aharon*), Part 4, pp. 12–17[38]

(15:) But, my friends, do we understand the greatness of the shofar: Do we elevate ourselves to the lofty ideas and ideals of this holy and inspiring day? Are we ready to listen to the sound of *Tekiah*, that straight and happy sound which reminds us of our great past? Are we not listening instead to the *Shevorim Teruah*, the sounds of weeping and the bitter lamentations of the millions of our victims who are gassed, mutilated, electrocuted and buried alive? Has not the world been transformed into a hell instead of remaining a beautiful paradise as it was intended to be? Are we not listening to the heartbreaking request of children begging for a piece of bread when there is none to give it to them?

The voice of G-d, which Rabbi Jose heard in one of the destroyed sanctuaries in Jerusalem, speaking to us today:

אוי לבנים שבעונותיהם החרבתי את ביתי ושרפתי את היכלי והגליתי את בניי לבין האומות, "Because of their sins I have destroyed My Temple, and have consumed by flames My sanctuary, and have exiled My children among the nations of the world."[39] The entire world is weeping today

38 No date is provided for the sermon text in the published collection. The title and the emphasis on the sounding of the shofar suggest that it was delivered on Rosh Hashanah, the prayer for victory in the final paragraph below shows that it was delivered during the war, and the reference to "millions of our victims who are gassed, mutilated, electrocuted and buried alive" suggests September of 1943 (see above, November 27, 1942, December 9 and 29, 1942, and below March 31, 1944).

39 b. Berakhot 3a.

because of the iniquities and the greed of man. It is because we do not elevate ourselves to the greatness of the shofar that the world has become a vale of tears and sorrow....

(16:) My dear friends: The Books of Life and Death are now open not merely for individuals but for the entire world.[40] How dare we, then, reduce the שופר גדול – the great shofar – and make of it a קול דממה דקה – a still, small voice?[41] How can we go about our own petty lives in silence and in activity when the blood of our brethren cries to us from the ground? We can be the angels of mercy to them. We, who were destined by Providence to preserve the lives of our own flesh and blood....

We pray for our own Book of Life and for our own redemption for our land, for our salvation, and for the reestablishment of our national religious homeland in Eretz Israel. But we also pray for victory for our beloved country and for a just and enduring peace, for all the children of men.

ABRAHAM M. KELLNER, "The Truth that Giveth Life," Congregation Sons of Abraham, Albany, NY. *A Rabbi's Faith*, pp. 16–21

(19:) A still, small Voice was heard after these manifestations of power and immensity [in 1 Kings 19:11–12] – this still small Voice was the implement of God's revelation and it was the still, small Voice that murmured in soothing accents to the weary soul of the sorely tried prophet.

My people, the noisy blasts of the enemies of mankind, the fiery holocaust which consumes so many of our people, the disturbances and dislocations that mark our tragic period, are not the manifestation of the Godly Voice; the soft, still Voice of hope that wells up within every one of us and the hushed and stilled voices of our heroes

40 Based on a well-known rabbinic statement (b. Rosh Hashanah 16b) about three books being opened on Rosh Hashanah, with individuals by the end of Yom Kippur being inscribed either for life or for death in the coming year.

41 1 Kings 19:12, although in its original context, the phrase has a positive resonance – referring to the way in which Elijah heard the divine message (cf. the following sermon by Abraham Kellner) – while here the softness is negative in comparison with the blast of *teru'ah*.

who become martyrs in lands of sorrow and death, God hears them though the world does not and will not....

(20:) The Voice of the Shofar today will be heard all over the world, in myriads of places. The underground caves and the hidden cellars will resound to the call of the Shofar in terror-stricken Europe....

Jacob Kaplan, "Renew Our Days As of Old" (*Renouvelle pour nous les jours d'autrefois*), [Lam. 5:21], Synagogue de Lyon, France. *Les Temps d'épreuve*, pp. 121–27, translated by MS

(123:) Think of the inconsolable grief of those who have had the misfortune of losing in torment beloved people whose presence will be missed forever and even more, upon re-entering the home where they once lived so happily. Is it possible that even one of those among us can imagine himself capable of returning to the "days of old"? We have been too deeply branded by suffering, both physical and emotional, to be able to rediscover the liveliness, the gaiety, the carefreeness, and in one word all that gave evidence of our *joie de vivre*. For all of us, "the days of old" are gone, alas! unquestionably gone....

(127:) Why indeed should it be important to me that people say, that people believe, we are rejected, abandoned by God, when I profoundly feel that it is not so, and that what happens to us bears witness precisely to the opposite, to the knowledge that God has *not* renounced us, that He waits, hoping for our return; when I perceive, without a shadow of a doubt, God's summons to Israel. I prefer persecution that leads us back to God, rather than tranquility in contempt of God.

Armin (Avraham Ada) Frieder, Great Synagogue, Nové Mesto, Slovakia, delivered "before the blowing of the Shofar," in Emanuel Frieder, *To Deliver Their Souls*, pp. 117–18

(117:) Glancing back and recalling the High Holy Days, taking stock of what has befallen us in the past few years, we see a bleak, sad and woeful picture. These have been days of Judgment, marked by deep concern for our fate and our future. Days of Awe, marked by upheaval. During the New Year of 5700 (1939), when I stood in this pulpit on this holiday, the war was just beginning. The youth had been called up for army service. The military draft, at a time when Jews were already being deprived of equal rights, was doubly worrisome for Jewish women and mothers. In the sermon which I delivered then, I tried to calm the women and comfort them.

On the New Year 5701 (1940), during the period when the demoniacal dance against us had already begun, as men and youths were being taken to special labor camps for Jews and the younger generation was no longer present in the synagogue, again I had to find words of comfort and encouragement for the mothers and women worrying for their dear ones.

The third New Year, 5702 (1941), was marked by severe persecution, as the bread was taken out of the mouths of our congregants and the first intimations of deportation began to be heard; my sermon, too, dwelled on the difficult times.

Today we are facing the New Year following our punishment, our affliction, after tens of thousands of our fellow Jews have been exiled to the land of doom,[42] after we have given our (118:) sacrifices, and now we must examine our deeds. We stand with burdened, aching hearts, shaken to the core by the holocaust of our people, unable to express that which is in our hearts. Therefore my afflicted soul would rather sound its prayer in a still, silent voice, for Thou, Lord of Mercy, shalt well understand my thoughts and the ponderings of my heart.

October 1, 1943 (second day of Rosh Hashanah)

Abraham M. Kellner, "So Proudly We Give," Congregation Sons of Abraham, Albany, NY. *A Rabbi's Faith*, pp. 22–27.

(24:) Yes, we have given; we give, and that regardless of cruel injustice, baseless slander, wicked criticism, and ferocious onslaughts. We give our best means, our highest endeavors, our noblest efforts, our deepest sentiments, our most precious possessions, on the altar of patriotism. Now, as on no other occasion, when Israel's great ideal of sacrificial giving is read anew at our Divine Services in every Syn-

42 Referring to Poland, specifically to Auschwitz.

agogue throughout the land, we defiantly proclaim that **so proudly we give** [*sic*] our share and more than our share for our country's defense, and we hurl the challenge to the cowardly forces of evil that seek to undermine the unity of the home front by driving a wedge between the diverse strata of American life....

(26:) That the world is not anxious to register gratitude, worse yet, that it is heaping ignominy and persecution upon the anguished head of Israel, is but the world's treatment of Prophets. Israel, the classic prophet of the nations, will not be dismayed if her recompense is not forthcoming in the ordinary terms of reward and appreciation. Our deepest satisfaction must come from the realization that we always dreamed of kindling the lights of humanity rather than darkening its cloudy horizons.

Louis Hammer, "Your Religion - What Kind?," Congregation B'nai Shalom, Brooklyn, NY. *A Word in Season*, pp. 26–34

(33:) We now stand face to face with the greatest tragedy that has ever confronted mankind. We are going through a deluge of fire, of war, of slaughter, of devastation. It is a war which is found on land and sea and in the air. Cities are burned and countries laid waste. Millions are killed and tens of millions made widows and orphans and homeless refugees. Myriads of our brethren have been killed with the sword, by hunger or by plague, as we shall soon read in our *Unsaneh tokef* prayer. We are mournful over the tragedy that has overtaken mankind, and must lend every effort to see the war to a successful conclusion. We must offer our sons to the army and navy and the other arms of our war machine. We must buy bonds and more bonds and bring every monetary sacrifice we can. We must cooperate with the Civilian Defense and the Red Cross and other agencies. But that is not all. We must also think of the world after the war and "*the shape of things to come*."[43] We dare not close ourselves up in the modern Noah's Ark of isolationism and permit the world outside us to perish from want and deprivation....

43 Echoing the title of a work of fiction by H.G. Wells.

(34:) Like Abraham we must build *hamizbeach* [the altar], the true religion that shall conceive of God as Judge of all the Earth. Now that we have gone through the experience of father Abraham in a national *akedah*, in a sacrifice not of one son but of millions of beloved sons, let us come to a real understanding as to what religion should mean to us. It must be a religion that embraces in its purview all mankind, not even excluding today's sinful Sodom, Nazi Germany. We must insist upon justice to punish the culprits, responsible for this calamity. But we must feed the hungry, clothe the naked and shelter the refugee and exile....

Ephraim Sokolover, Great Synagogue, Ra'anana, Palestine. *Penei Efrayim*, pp. 34–38, translated by MS

(36:) At this time we have ourselves a "binding of Isaac" in a new version on such a grand scale: not just of one or a few individuals, but of entire ancient communities, each one of which consists of tens of thousands of Jews, or even hundreds of thousands as in the capital city of Warsaw. All of them have been entirely devastated and destroyed. All of conquered Europe – home of the cream of the Jewish people – is under the control of the obscene Nazis and has become transformed into one great dreadful "binding," with the descendants of Isaac slaughtered like lambs by the butcher in all kinds of bizarre deaths. If there remains a saving remnant, their decree has already been enacted by the insane annihilators. It is for the victims that we dedicate a special prayer: "Guardian of Israel, Watch over the remnant of Israel against the destruction of Israel, who say, 'Hear, O Israel.'" And it is not only in [organized] prayer that we must remember that we pray for "the *remnant* of Israel," for so very few remain.

But we must remember this also through practical help, about which all the institutions of our Jewish population here have officially declared that during these days of compassion it is permitted to devote some words to inspire public opinion on this supremely important matter, which is close to the hearts of us all. I would like simply to inform this entire congregation of some extremely important and urgent information that, with God's help, there are those who may be saved in various ways that may not be publicly disclosed....

(37:) And if the Sages said, "Whoever has saved a single soul from Israel it is as if he had saved the entire world,"[44] how much merit there is now in this time of horrifying destruction to save a single soul! For each individual or group of individuals who remain in whatever location they may be are representatives of entire congregations of thousands of souls.

October 2, 1943 (Shabbat Shuvah)

Shlomo Zalman Ehrenreich, "What I Preached on *Shabbat Shuvah*, 5704," Simleul-Silvaniei, Transylvania. *Derashot Leḥem Shelomoh*, pp. 73–74, translated by MS

(74b:) We cannot recount or even imagine the enormity of the many strange forms of suffering that we endure at present. Some tens of thousands (75a:) of Jews have been killed, along with their wives and children; tens of thousands more have been impoverished; they suffer from hunger and go without proper clothing in the snow and the bitter cold, almost naked, their garments torn and worn out. Some tens of thousands of orphans and widows remain, our children and brothers working actually like horses and mules, pulling heavily loaded wagons in the snow and the cold, and without proper footwear they become sick with typhus.[45] It is as if they are adjudged to the four kinds of death: stoning, burning, slaying and strangling, for thousands and tens of thousands have buried them alive, they and their wives and children, and they perform acts upon them that seem simply unbelievable to report, forcing them to drag themselves on their bellies and to lick the earth with their tongues.

But we are the cause of all this, through our many great sins. These curses are already explicit in the Torah, in the passages of rebuke in the *parashah BeḤukkotai* [see Lev. 26:14–43] and in the

---

44 Mishnah Sanhedrin 4,9.

45 The Hebrew text reads "Flecktyphus," which, together with "Fleckfieber" is the German term for typhus: http://medical-dictionary.thefreedictionary.com/typhus.

parashah Ki Tavo [see Deut. 28:15–68]. The Creator has warned us that if we do not follow the way of the Torah, all of the curses that are specified there will fall upon us. All of the types of suffering that we currently endure today are to be found in these passages of chastisement. That Jews have been ordered to drag themselves on their bellies and to lick the dust of the earth is hinted at in the rebuke of *Ki Tavo* in the verse, "Cursed are you in the field,... cursed are you in your goings" (Deut. 28:16,19), for the serpent was "cursed from among all the beasts... you shall crawl on your belly" (Gen. 3:14). This is in the category of "cursed are you in the field." And furthermore, their using of Jews to pull wagons, like horses, is hinted there in the verse, "He shall place a yoke of iron upon your neck" (Deut. 28:48). If we look carefully, we will find that every form of our suffering is explicit in the Torah. That is why the Holy One warned us of this suffering, but we did not listen, we did not pay attention. That is why all this suffering has come upon us.

October 8, 1943 (Kol Nidre)

Akiba Predmesky, "The Ark of G-d Has Been Taken" (Kol Nidre), Jewish Center of Williamsburg, Bronx, NY. *Manual of Holiday and Occasional Sermons*, 51–60; see Complete Sermons

Irving F. Reichert, 135 "Where Do You Stand?," Temple Emanu-El, San Francisco, CA. *Judaism and the American Jew*, pp. 135–43[46]

(141:) The savagery and brutality of the Nazi slaughter of Polish Jewry, where probably more than one million people were exterminated, is of all the black pages in the record of this war, the foulest. By the same token, when the history of this struggle is written, one of its noblest paragraphs will be devoted to the gallant resistance of the Warsaw Jewish ghetto against the German troops. William Zukerman, who for twenty years was the Chief European Correspondent of the New York *Jewish Morning Journal*, tells that story in the September

46 The complete text of this sermon was placed online on the 70th anniversary of its delivery, with many responses: http://bit.ly/2wXrM63.

issue of *Harper's Magazine*.[47] By April 19th of this year, the more than six hundred thousand Jews crowded into the unspeakably vile ghetto of Warsaw had been reduced by famine, epidemics and mass murder to 35,000. Those remaining Jews obtained arms secretly through underground channels. At a prearranged signal they offered open resistance to the Nazis. For one long month the struggle raged until nearly every house in the district had been razed to rubble, and from twenty to twenty-five thousand Jews had been slain.

The heroic men and women who died on the barricades of Warsaw belonged to a section of Jews who held that their (142:) home was in the countries where they had been born had worked, and had contributed to wealth and culture.... To them the future of the European Jews, after the war, lay in Europe, in the homes which they had loved and fought for. They always opposed the various plans made by their charitable brothers overseas for their evacuation after the war. There you have it. Nothing could be more completely devastating to the Zionist contention of Jewish homelessness.[48]

October 9, 1943 (Yom Kippur)

Abraham M. Hershman, "The Short Time and the Great Task," Congregation Shaarey Zedek, Detroit, MI. *Israel's Fate and Faith*, pp. 80–84

(81:) This is the zero hour in Israel's life.... The grim reality we now face exceeds in horror the brutal forecast of [Constantin] Pobyedonostseff.[49] About one-third of all the Jews in the world have been ruthlessly massacred. What we have now in Europe is the "remnant

---

47 Zukerman's article was entitled "The Revolt in the Warsaw Ghetto," pp. 352–55 of the September 1943 issue of *Harper's Magazine*; it was one of the first full reports of the uprising made available to general readers.

48 The context of this passage in a Kol Nidre sermon was a powerful critique of the September 1943 convention of the Zionist Organization of America on behalf of the anti-Zionist American Council for Judaism of which Reichert was a leader. I have presented it as evidence of knowledge available of the Warsaw Ghetto communicated in a sermon on the most important preaching occasion following the event.

49 Referring to the Procurator of the Holy Synod of Russia. When asked about the fate of Russian Jewry, he allegedly replied that "one-third will emigrate, one-third will be baptized, and one-third will perish with hunger."

that escaped." When we survey the present condition of our people, we recall the fateful words of Isaiah: "But this is a people robbed and spoiled. They are all of them snared in holes; and they are hid in prison-houses. They are a prey, and none delivereth; for a spoil, and none saith: Restore." (Isa. 42:22).... Here and there we may find individuals, even a nation, such as Sweden, that is ready to do everything possible to rescue Jews who are exposed to death. But these are the exception. By and large, sympathy for the Jews is of a platonic character. It consists of "words, words, mere words."[50]

When all is well with the world at large and only Jews are singled out for suffering, there are many non-Jews who will cry out against the injustice to Jews. But when the whole world suffers, but few non-Jews are affected by the anguish of the Jews and are moved to intervene in their behalf. And the suffering of our people today beggars description. Said General Smuts recently, "The Jewish horror has no parallel in history; a whole race is proscribed and crucified in what surely is the most poignant tragedy of our era."[51]

(82:) The world may be indifferent to the fate of our people. We Jews, however, dare not neglect our duty. We are called upon to save Jews. "Hide not thyself from thine own flesh" (Isa. 58:7), says the Prophet in today's Haftarah. How many Jews can be saved? I do not know. We are not masters of our political destiny. Let us, however, bear in mind the admonition of the sage, whose words form the text of this sermon: "It is not thy duty to complete the work, but neither art thou free to desist from it."[52]

---

50 *Troilus and Cressida* 5,3.

51 I have been unable to find a source for this precise statement, which was repeated by Rabbi Hertz in his address of May 22, 1944 (below). The *JC* reported the following statement by General Smuts to the South African Jewish Board of Deputies, "Jews were the first victims of the barbarous regime which has trampled down the cherished principles of Western Civilization" (August 7, 1942, p. 7). Smuts used similar language in a speech he delivered in Birmingham on May 19, 1944: Jews had been subjected to "sorrow and suffering on a scale unexampled in history." *Bulletin of International News*, 21:11 (May 27, 1944): 438. In a sermon delivered to his Free Synagogue congregation on October 30, 1942 (see above), Stephen S. Wise characterized Smuts as the "greatest human figure south of the equator,.... He is one of the world's great figures,... one of the wisest, truest friends of the Zionist movement."

52 m. Avot 2,16.

But saving Jews is only part of our duty. What we have been doing is good as far as it goes, but it does not go far enough and deep enough to exhaust the obligation which reposes in us.... God demands from us not only our substance but ourselves. He demands that we dedicate our lives to His service...(83:) European Jewry is now bleeding. It pleads with us to take the banner of Judaism and carry on the work. American Jewry must heed the plea. Our *fate* is intimately bound up with the fate of the world, but our *faith* is our own.... America must become the arsenal of Judaism, the arsenal in which should be forged our most effective weapon – the weapon of the spirit.

"And for the cities of our God!" (2 Sam. 10:12). It is our heaven-appointed task to labor to the end that Palestine become the Land of Israel.... We must strain every effort to make "the cities of our God" safe for Israel. How many of those cities will be ours I do not know. Partition is bad. It will keep us in a constant state of dread of attack on the part of our surrounding neighbors, and thus distract our attention from the main work before us...A bi-national state is bad. I am frank enough, however, to say that I am more concerned about the "state of Judaism," which is inextricably bound up with the future of Palestine, than with a *Jewish State.* I know now what the future has in store for us. I know, however, that it is our bounden duty to do all we can for the cities of our God. We must keep alive the age-long hope that Palestine will eventually be ours and labor for the realization of this great hope.

Walter Wuerzburger, "The Individual in Crisis," Congregation Chai Odom, Brighton, MA. *Manual of Holiday and Occasional Sermons*, 1943, pp. 61–70[53]

(61:) The modern preacher has of late assumed the Miltonic task of justifying the ways of G-d to man either because of his anxiety to bring a message of hope to a suffering and toiling humanity, or in order to sell a sugar-coated religion to his congregants....

---

53 For the complete text of the sermon with annotation, see *Jewish Preaching in Times of War*, pp. 471–80.

Many of us, for example, have come today to this place of worship in order to receive an answer to the question, "Where is G-d in this crisis?" We yearn for a message of hope in the face of the tormenting problems that demand a quick solution. A world gone mad with insane ideologies, a universe that is reduced to a vale of tears, the fate of a civilization on its last legs, all these deserve the attention of the pulpiteer, we feel.

Yet let us remember that this is a day of Atonement, when we should be *at one* with our G-d.

(64:) How much time and energy do we waste in condemning the Nazis and Fascists! We witness a conflagration of the world that is unparalleled in history. A civilization goes to pieces, and we seek comfort and consolation in the thought that ידינו לא שפכו את הדם הזה, "our hands did not spill this blood" (Deut. 21:7).

(65:) There comes to my mind the heroism of the 93 girls in the dark ghettos of Warsaw.[54] They were instructed by the Nazis to beautify themselves with cosmetics, to put on their best dresses and to prepare for the ordeal of an encounter with the filthy German officers in their quarters.

A terrible struggle went on in the minds of these girls: "Here we are confronted with a world of brutality, bestiality and tyranny. We witnessed how our fathers were murdered, our mothers violated, our brothers tortured to death, our friends sent to concentration camps. A world has abandoned all that is holy and noble. What is the wrong that is demanded of us in comparison with these crimes, with the blood that cries unto heaven? This is our chance for a life of comfort and security. Why sacrifice ourselves for decency in an already indecent world, for justice in a universe that is full of injustice, for goodness in a criminal social order?[55]

Thus many of us would have thought, had we been in the place of these 93 girls. But every one of them remained steadfast. They real-

54 The story of the ninety-three girls dates the sermon to 1943, as it is based on a *NYT* report of a letter describing the incident, published on January 8, 1943, p. 8. Cf. Julian Feibelman, March 21, 1943, above.

55 This is all the preacher's imaginative reconstruction; nothing like it appeared in the letter or the article.

ized their responsibility towards Israel and the world! They preferred death to a life bought by desecration of their souls and their bodies. They recited the וידוי: they confessed their sins and ended their precious lives.[56] They understood that a human being is not merely a piece of chaff tossed to and fro by the wind, the hail and the rain.

How willing we are to blame the Nazis and Fascists for the chaos that engulfs our civilization! How gladly we accuse England and America for their failure to save the Jews who are being exterminated in war-torn (66:) Europe! We hold protest meetings and demand "action, not pity!"[57]

We are always ready to condemn others. But do we ask ourselves these discomforting questions? Did I send a letter to my Congressman to intervene in behalf of these Jews? Did I join a national Jewish organization that strives to save these doomed people? Did I contribute my money to help those that still can be helped? Did I buy war bonds so that this war may be shortened?...

(67:) Do we have to travel to Europe in order to discover racial persecution? Why not go to Detroit with its race riots? Couldn't we have stopped Hitler back in 1933? Of course, we could have, had we not adopted the policy of isolationism and appeasement! And so we behold a world of agony, misery, cruelty, injustice, brutality and tyranny. We are responsible for it. It is our world. No complaints! No excuses! No defense mechanisms! No passing of the buck! ... Had we abandoned our selfish attitude in the days before Pearl Harbor these brutalities would never have been committed. Each and every one of us is responsible for the debacle of civilization.[58]

---

56 The letter states, "Today we are together and are learning the *vidui* [liturgical confession upon the deathbed] all day."

57 This was the motto of the Zionist Revisionist group led by Peter Bergson, which was often critical of the mainstream leadership of American Jewry.

58 Cf. the sermon delivered by Akiba Predmesky, also a young Orthodox rabbi in New York, on the same Yom Kippur of 1943 ("Complete Sermons" section). Predmesky emphasizes the devastation of loss for European Jewry and ends with the need for Jewish action to strengthen Judaism at home; Wuerzburger emphasizes the responsibility of congregants in the genre of rebuke.

Eliezer Berkovits, "Head and Heart," United Hebrew Congregation, Leeds, England. *Between Yesterday and Tomorrow*, pp. 136–39

(136:) Succot is called "the season of our joy." It used to be a happy time of rejoicing.... But what is the season of our joy to-day? There is little "*Simchah*" left in a world in which Death has become the richest harvester. We have forgotten the meaning of joy. It is, however, important to realize that it is not only this war, with its small and great tragedies, or the overwhelming martyrdom of Israel in its wake, that has caused us to forget the meaning of joy. Long before its outbreak, true joy had left our hearts. Joy, happiness, harmony, contentment and peace left this world long before the present catastrophe. The generation of those born not many years before 1914 has never really known of these blessings of life....

(137:) How was it that joy vanished from the earth long before the present war?....

(139:) A powerful human intellect combined with the stupidity of the heart has become the deadliest weapon of devastation the world has ever seen; it has created the most tragically idiotic caricature of man: the mechanized super-beast.

Abraham M. Kellner, "Beautiful Though Incomplete," Congregation Sons of Abraham, Albany, NY. *A Rabbi's Faith*, pp. 41–45; reprinted from *Rabbinical Council Manual of Holiday and Occasional Sermons*, 1944.

(44:) The brutal bestiality of German banditry crushed the last waning embers of life in Eastern Europe, but the picture of the haunted Ghetto Jew of Warsaw who pitted the ebbing strength of his emaciated body and the inflamed spirit of his scarred and seared soul against the devastating might of his murderers will live enshrined in the hearts of sensitive men long after their tormentors are blotted out from the memory of man....

Those of us who have drunk in our time the brimming cup of sorrow as we watched the wretched slaughter and sacrifice of the millions of our co-religionists ... know that our homes are incomplete, that our Sukkah is lacking in more than just one side. Nevertheless, we are firm in our faith and strong in our hope that this humble Sukkah will bring the eagerly desired warmth of light into our lives...

October 15, 1943 (second day of Sukkot)

Abraham M. Kellner, "Shadows and Sunbeams," Congregation Sons of Abraham, Albany, NY. *A Rabbi's Faith*, pp. 49–54

(49:) [Attack on the American Jewish Committee and the American Council for Judaism, following "the American Jewish Conference"]: The shocking exhibition of that small and sinister force in American Jewish Life which sought to confuse the proceedings with venomous discord has all the more earned our severe condemnation, since its cynical disregard for the woes and laments of a tortured people found no sympathetic response in the hearts of those who perpetrated the schism in the ranks of Israel.

We will gain little by merely denouncing the culprits or by simply dismissing their nefarious schemes as the neurotic convulsions of a small segment of American Jewry that refuses to adjust its thinking to the changing patterns of historical developments. The tragedy of their lives that impels them to repeat parrot-like the time-worn shiboleths and platitudes first heard in the land of Nazidom is especially disheartening, since it indicates that people otherwise responsible choose to bury their obstinate heads in the shifting sands of time without giving heed to the changing winds of circumstance that shake the earth to its very foundations.

(50:) The painful record of the American Jewish Committee reinforced by the more open depredations of the Council for American Judaism [*sic*], may be new in their current manifestations, but the symptoms reveal that their minds merely suffer from chronic ills that plague humanity whenever traitorous individuals cheerfully sacrifice their people for the supposed advantages gained by their class. This tendency is not limited to our own ranks. The appeasers in every country, as recent experience has shown, have acted likewise.

October 21, 1943 (Shemini Atseret)

Shelomo Zalman Ehrenreich, "What I Said on Shemini Atseret,

5704," Simleul-Silvaniei, Transylvania. *Derashot Leḥem Shelomo*, pp. 128–29, translated by Gershon Greenberg[59]

All those troubles which we suffer today by the hands of the evil ones: it is not the evil ones who are hitting us. They are but the staff of God. God is chastising and hitting us. To be sure, the evil ones are evil: Good things come to pass on auspicious days and bad things come to pass on unholy days [b. Ta'anit 29a]. But the nations are not doing the hitting. God alone does that.

October 22, 1943 (Simḥat Torah)

Shlomo Zalman Ehrenreich, "What I Preached on Simḥat Torah, 5704," Simleul-Silvaniei, Transylvania. *Derashot Leḥem Shelomoh*, pp. 151–53, translated by MS

(152b:) I will tell you what I have heard from reliable men, eye witnesses, about what occurred in the city of Mihajlović in Slovakia. Last year there was a massive expulsion: all the Jews, men, women, and children, were expelled, bereft of everything, forced to leave behind all their possessions, including their silver and gold, and they were taken to who knows where. There was there a Jewish advocate, not at all a G-d-fearing man, who was a friend of the local priest. The priest said to him that if he converted to Catholicism, they would allow him to remain in the city rather than going into exile. He liked the idea, and he converted. Later that night, he was unable to sleep at all, due to his deep remorse over what he had done. He thought to himself that he was like a man who had lived with his wife for forty years, but when his wife became ill he divorced her and sent her away from his house. So he went back to the priest and wept before him, pleading with him to remove from the records the entire Protocol, as if he had never converted, promising that he would in return give the priest so many thousands [of the currency]. This the priest did. The man left behind his money and his possessions – he was extremely wealthy – and went into exile with the other Jews. It

59 Greenberg, "Shlomo Zalman Ehrenreich's (1863–1944) Religious Response to the Holocaust," p. 72.

is indeed extremely wondrous that such a man had the strength to endanger his life and leave behind his wealth and go into exile.

We have heard something else from eye witnesses. In a certain place in Poland. A witness saw that the wicked ones took 2,000 Jews, men, women, and children. They dug a huge ditch, and they made all the Jews walk there and pushed them into the ditch, killing them all. But as they were walking there, they lifted their voices to the Holy One, all together in a loud voice, saying *Shema Yisrael… Eḥad*, again and again. They walked as if they were going to a banquet.

This was a one-time event. What shall we say about the behavior of the lovely, pious Jewish boys who were sent to a work detail, where they remained for two or even three years, and disciplined themselves not to eat anything forbidden. They suffered from hunger and thirst rather than eating forbidden foods. They would not even drink black coffee. This was a unique kind of dedication, to endure insults and agonies, exposing themselves to mockery and contempt. Despite it all, they would not eat or drink what is forbidden by the Torah to eat or drink even though if they had asked [a halakhic authority], they would have been given permission.

November 5, 1943 (Friday evening)

Jacob Kaplan, Synagogue de Lyon, France, in Shapira, *Jacob Kaplan*, p. 153. Fonds Kaplan, Box 1517-5, translated by MS[60]

You are not unaware of the painful new ordeals that have recently befallen us. Within a few days, the *Consistoire Central* and the community of Lyon have been harshly affected.… We do not know why God sends us these painful ordeals. Our human mind is too limited to comprehend the divine intentions.… The ordeals are not something new for Israel. To the contrary, one could say that they have been the destiny of Israel.… Israel is God's people.… That is the reason for its indelible glory, but it also provides the opportunity for unparalleled ordeals.…

60 This was delivered a week after the arrest and deportation of Jacques Helbronner, President of the *Consistoire Central Israélite de France* to Drancy, from which he would be deported a few weeks later, with his wife, to Auschwitz, where they were sent to the gas chambers upon arrival.

November 14, 1943 (Sunday)

Judah L. Magnes, "The Source of Prophetic Morality," Opening of the Academic Year 1943/44, Hebrew University, Jerusalem. *In the Perplexity of the Times*, pp. 55–64

(56:) This *Herrenmoral*, this morality of the blond Aryan beast of a superman, being the very antithesis of the Hebrew and Christian morality, can be satisfied with nothing less than the extermination of the prophetic morality and of those peoples, foremost among them the Jews, who cling to this morality more tenaciously than to life itself....

(57:) These loathsome trappings of *Wissenschaft* bedeck the whole structure of this thinking. In an academic *Festausgabe* in honour of Heinrich Himmler, published in 1941, a Gauleiter, the legal adviser of the Gestapo, wrote: "The extermination and removal of foreign peoples does not, according to the historical experience, conflict with the law of life, if carried out totally."[61] ...

Every one of us knows there is a beast within each of us.... (58:) These cruel passions in men, in ourselves, all too often degrade us, overwhelm us, and nations and societies. The mere quantity of evil is terrifying, the weight of numbers, the numbers killed and maimed and tormented: and the smell of blood seems to stimulate the beast's appetite for more blood, while scientific methods of persecution awaken the desire for ever more devilish refinements of torture. A great book on the history of persecution would contain a disproportionately large section concerning the persecution of the Jews. Yet in this vast history there would be nothing to compare in bulk or depravity with the persecution of this hour in the name and under the aegis of this scientific *Herrenmoral*...

Not even the Germans engage upon such massive operations without some higher sanction. Only because of their belief that these actions are somehow ordained for a higher purpose can the modern Germans have the strength and the *Wille zur Macht* to sustain such

---

61 Magnes's book provides a reference to this quotation: Jacob Robinson, *Uprooted Jews in the Immediate Post-War World* (1943), p. 292. The "legal advisor of the Gestapo" who wrote these words was Karl Rudolf Werner Best.

diabolic enterprises. The modern Germans are fighting their holy war inspired by their *Herrenmoral*, and this is derived from some of the ancestral gods still abroad in the dark Teutonic forests.

It is these gods, or gods like them, the Molochs and the others, whom the prophets of Israel rose up against, and it is a choice of gods that is before men to-day, as it was then....

November 27, 1943 (Saturday following Thanksgiving)

Louis I. Newman, "Thanksgiving 1943," Radio Address for WMCA. *Biting on Granite*, pp. 192–94

(193:) It requires a hardy courage to be convinced of the goodness of man and the mercy of God, in days when man is wolf to his fellow, and humanity is so savagely inhuman. Among the people of (194:) Israel, the sight of the mass murder of their helpless co-religionists abroad is a grievous test and challenge to their faith. Like Jesus in his death agony, they can repeat the words of the Psalmist: *Eili Eili lamah azavtani?* "My God, My God, why hast Thou forsaken me?" (Ps. 22:1; Matt. 27:46 and Mark 15:34). We would doubtless have every right to be skeptical of God's providence, as we behold the brutalities inflicted upon our people. But the very grandeur of our tragedy is the spur to a new grandeur of faith. We are repeating the words of Job, the afflicted: "Yea, though He slay me, yet will I trust in Him" (Job 13:5). God has given us this faculty to believe in Him though He torments us, and for this celestial gift, let us be grateful to Him....

If we open our hearts in fervent supplication, it may well be that before Thanksgiving season is at hand once more, God will have sent liberation to the captives, and salvation to those without hope....

December 17, 1943 (Friday evening)

Jacob Kaplan, "The Attack against the Synagogue of Lyon" (*L'Attentat contre la Synagogue de Lyon*), Synagogue de Lyon. *Les Temps d'épreuve*, pp. 129–32,[62] translated by MS

62 Author's note: "The previous Friday, December 10, 1943, grenades were thrown into the synagogue during the Sabbath worship service. A dozen of the worshippers were

Last week, in association with the biblical chapter recounting the struggle of Jacob with the angel [*parashat Vayishlaḥ*, Gen. 32:25–32], I intended to present to you the history of the Jewish people as a super-human struggle sustained from age to age, throughout all the generations that have preceded us, challenging you to display the same fortitude, the same stability as did our ancestors. I intended to add that for this we will need considerable courage, indeed even heroism. It was not possible for me to say this to you; indeed, it was not necessary to say it. You yourselves – in the midst of the abhorrent (130:) attack that bloodied our sanctuary – you showed yourselves worthy of the great tradition of Israel. You revealed an exemplary composure, and the courage of our beloved wounded was indeed admirable. Not a single cry, hardly any complaints.

Happily we have reassuring news about our dear brothers and sisters who were injured by the fragments of the grenades....

Praise God: for given the circumstances in which this sacrilegious and criminal act was performed, we were justified in fearing the worst. Praise God: who, at the moment of greatest danger, extended over us His miraculous protection....

Some of you noticed at the very beginning an irony in the event, for at the very moment when we were poised to welcome Shabbat, at the moment when we turned to face the entrance [to the sanctuary] and were declaring our desire to welcome the Sabbath,[63] it was the devices of death that exploded in the synagogue.

As we think about this, we may discover in this coincidence a providential purpose.... (131:) Think now of the man who moved forward with his grenades.... He knows that he will be able to act unperturbed because no one will be paying attention, as no one would be thinking of any kind of danger. He opens the door. His surprise is immense: the entire congregation is turning toward him,

injured." Cf. Poznanski, *The Jews in France during World War II*, p. 426, reporting the incident in one sentence with no mention of the sermon or the rabbi, and David Shapira, *Jacob Kaplan*, p. 154. A fuller discussion is in Pierre Pierrard, *Le Grand Rabbin Kaplan*, pp. 78–80.

63 Reference is to the final verse of "Lekha Dodi," in which the congregation turns to welcome the Sabbath personified as a bride entering the sanctuary.

looking at him, apparently waiting for him, but without revealing any degree of fear. This unexpected sight troubles him, indeed it frightens him....

It took only one moment. A moment earlier, a moment later, we would have been in the usual mode of prayer, turned toward the Holy Ark, and what losses we would then have had to bewail among us!...

December 25, 1943 (Shabbat during Hanukkah)

Abraham A. Kellner, "In Order of Their Eminence," Congregation Sons of Abraham, Albany, NY. *A Rabbi's Faith*, pp. 60–64

(62:) There are many in our midst today who view our bleeding world with the skeptical distrust of the house of Shammai;[64] gloomily do they assert that humanity is sliding steadily downward because of man's inability and unwillingness to challenge his finest energies, deepest sentiments, and highest aspirations toward the elimination of the iniquities of society and the inequities of our social order. They see in the terrifying holocaust of this war for survival merely another expression of the madness and lust for power that everlastingly divides humanity into the categories of the oppressor and the oppressed....

(64:) When the darkness of the present world-upheaval extinguished one by one the lights that kept our hopes aflame, there remained one light as in ancient times, which was kept undefiled by impure hands and unprofaned by degenerate fingers. It was the light of the Torah which continued to be aglow, though our Yeshivas had to be transplanted from land to land and from continent to continent....

---

64 Expressed near the beginning of the sermon with the quotation, "It had been better for man not to be created at all" (b. Eruvin 13b).

1944

January 15, 1944 (Saturday, *Shemot*)

Abraham M. Hershman, "The Growth of Moses," Congregation Shaarey Zedek, Detroit, MI. *Israel's Fate and Faith*, pp. 176–79

(177:) So too, it is well to bear in mind that the aid which we extend annually to our brethren who are pining in Eastern Europe is no panacea for their ills. Soon large numbers of them will have to be transported to Palestine, where they will have to be given a new start in life. One of our urgent needs today is to create a vast fund, say $200,000,000 or $300,000,000, so that, as soon as conditions permit, we may be able to do something substantial, something on a large scale, to solve the problem of our people in Eastern Europe....[1]

January 16, 1944 (Sunday)

Mordechai (Mottl) Rokeach of Biłgoraj, "Sermon of Departure from Budapest, 1944." "HaDerekh," February 7, 1944, pp. 18–19, and Mendel Piekarz, *Ḥasidut Polin*, pp. 432–33, translated by MS[2]

(18/432:) This is like the situation of Israel now. We have reached a point of crisis and there is no strength to give birth, because of the accusers who denounce us and stand over us, all around us, in order to delay the redemption. That is why the advice is to "tell the people

1 This passage seems extremely strange for a sermon delivered in early 1944, when most of East European Jews (except for those in Hungary), had already been murdered, and "to solve the problem of our people in eastern Europe" was no longer an option.

2 http://bit.ly/2xbeUIU. See also Esther Farbstein, *Hidden in Thunder*, pp. 86–97 and 108–11, noting (p. 108) that "the sermon was written down by listeners, and several versions circulated in Budapest." For strong criticism of this sermon published in Budapest shortly after its delivery, see Isaac Hershkowitz, "'This Enormous Offense to the Torah,'" especially pp. 112–26.

of Israel that they must go forward" (Exod. 14:15): namely that they must divert their minds from the Exile, as if all of the suffering has been completed, and the Redeemer is standing behind the door, and redemption is imminent. Then the accusers will be obliterated, and redemption will truly come.[3]....

I have something else to say, which I hope will awaken your heart and illumine your eyes regarding reports I have heard about negative whispers by many who are deeply afraid and seized with trembling, saying that while our departure is difficult for them, what concerns them the most pertains to the future. (19/433:) They say that "Perhaps – God forbid – this country will come into danger, and my brother – may he live a long and good life! – one of the most righteous in this generation, is able to foresee what will happen, and that is why he is departing, travelling to the land of Israel, for that is where God has commanded the blessing, 'I will give peace in the land' (Lev. 26:6). He is therefore moving to a place of rest and tranquility, and thereby abandoning us (God forbid) to our sorrows. What will happen to us? Who will protect us? Who will save us? Who will supplicate for us, or make any effort on our behalf?"

I therefore feel obliged to inform you, dear friends, scholars of Hungary, "the absolute truth of the matter" (Prov. 22:21).

For whoever is close to my brother, the greatest of rabbis, and spends time in his presence, knows for certainty that he is not going away in flight, not running precipitously, in haste, as if he wants to flee and escape from here. His only desire and yearning is to go up to the Holy Land, sanctified in ten levels of holiness.[4] I know that this is a time of tremendous importance in which he has a powerful desire for the land of Israel; his pure soul longs to go up to the city of the Lord there, in order to arouse mercy and favor toward the entire

3 Piekarz, in analyzing this sermon in comparison with other contemporary Hasidic sermons (pp. 82, 424–34), notes that the interpretation of Exod. 14:15 is antithetical to those who assert that all remaining Jews must literally abandon the exile and move on to the Holy Land. Here the preacher is urging a metaphorical movement of mind: that repudiation of exile while still suffering in it is the way to bring about the redemption, which – despite all apparent realities – is actually imminent.

4 Mishnah Keilim 1:6, quoted by Maimonides, *Hilkhot Beit Habechirah* 7:13–22.

people, so that there will no longer be distress, and that "the camp that remains may yet escape" (Gen. 32:9),[5] and quickly there will be fulfillment of the verse, "All the horns of the wicked I will cut down, but the horns of the righteous I will lift up" (Ps. 75:11).

This is hinted in the verse, "When he [Issachar] saw how good was restfulness, and how pleasant was the country, he bent his shoulder to the burden, and became a toiling servant" (Gen. 49:15). Rashi explains this to mean that he became a toiling servant for all his brothers by teaching them the instructions of Torah. It is indeed marvelous: what did he intend to teach by this interpretation?[6] It would seem that the phrase "*va-yar menuḥah*" [lit.: he saw restfulness] means that the *tsaddik* sees that here, for the inhabitants of this country, there will be rest and tranquility, and *ki tov* [lit.: that it is good] means that the *tsaddik* sees the goodness, all goodness, that "goodness and lovingkindness shall pursue" (Ps. 23:6) and overtake our brothers of the House of Israel living in this country. *Ve'et ha'arets*, and as for the Land: [of Israel], this is the source of his desire to go up to the Land: the reason being *ki na'ama*, that it is so pleasant, because that is where the ultimate loveliness dwells. A "land flowing with milk and honey" is delightful, pleasant, and sweet, both physically and spiritually.

While he was still at home, years ago, he spoke of travelling to the Holy Land; his desire was aroused in his heart to go up to the land of Israel, and many waters could not quench the love and desire he felt for the Land. This is the sign for you that the journey of our Rabbi – may he live a long and good life! – is not in order to live at ease, or to enjoy some rest, or to improve his status or his prestige, for the Sages said "the land of Israel is acquired through painful suffering."[7] His intention is certainly about the holiness of the Land.

5 Referring apparently to Hungarian Jewry, which has not yet been persecuted by the Nazis.

6 Rashi's interpretation was drawn from Genesis Rabbah 99,10; David Kimhi notes that it was probably based on 1 Chron. 12:33: "And the men of Issachar, who knew how to interpret the signs of the times, to determine how Israel should act."

7 b. Berakhot 5a.

January 22, 1944 (Saturday)

Abraham M. Hershman, "A Peacetime Conception of Religion," Congregation Shaarey Zedek, Detroit, MI. *Israel's Fate and Faith*, pp. 180–82.

(180:) There are two ways in which God reveals Himself to us. At times He appears as the God of might, the God Who resorts to catastrophic measures. More often, however, He discloses Himself as the God of law and order, the God who speaks to us in "the still small voice" (1 Kings 19:12). We can see Him in the destructive processes of nature, in its terrifying convulsions, in the tempest of the earthquake, and the fire; and in the tragic aspects of human life, in adversity and suffering, in a world-devastating war.

(181:) The question which disturbs my mind is this: when the war is over, what then? When our boys will be out of the foxholes and resume the even tenor of their ways will they be able to see God as the God of law and order? He is now audible to them in the tumultuous crash of cannons. Will he be audible to them in the "still small voice"?

February 6, 1944 (Sunday)

Solomon B. Freehof, "'Thy Neighbor as Thyself' (Lev. 19:18)," Rodef Shalom Congregation, Pittsburgh, PA. *Rodef Shalom Pulpit*, vol. 9, no. 8, pp. 3–14

(3:) The American people sustained a severe shock two weeks ago. Stephen Early, the Secretary to the President, revealed the accumulated record of torture to which our American and Filipino soldiers were subjected by their captors in the Philippines....[8]

After having said that about the Japanese, it is good to stop and think of a European people which is not yellow of skin: the Nazis. Have they acted better than the so-called "yellow barbarians"? What of the three million Jewish men, women, and children, and the millions of helpless Poles and Czechs who have been butchered? What of the people who did the (4:) butchering – the young, blue-eyed

8 This report was featured in American newspapers on January 28, 1944, often with the word TORTURE as a front page headline.

Nazi boys who touched the trigger on the machine gun and killed the shivering groups of helpless men, women, and children? What of the skilled German doctors who devised the methods of suffocating tens of thousands by gas? They were not yellow barbarians. They were white men, and cultured. How do we explain that? Well, we generally say that these Nazis, like these Japanese, are not human. That is a mistake. What the Nazis did and what the Japanese did is human enough. It is, traditionally, quite human.... Our earth has constantly seen the bloody massacre of millions of helpless non-combatants.

February 19, 1944 (Saturday)

Abraham M. Hershman, "*Shabbat Shekalim*," Congregation Shaarey Zedek, Detroit, MI. *Israel's Fate and Faith*, pp. 204–6.

(205:) In 1938 there were, according to the figures given by Doctor Ruppin, 16,717,000 Jews all over the world.[9] But the plague that had been stayed for a fairly considerable time broke out anew in all its ferocity and worked havoc in Israel. About 6,000,000 Jews perished in the second World War.[10]

A devastating plague has thus carried off more than one-third of our people. The blood of Jews is flowing like water in the lands which are under the heels of Nazi Germany. We too, "the redeemed of the Lord," who have escaped ravages of the plague, are exhorted to take stock of our human resources.... But for the grace of God, His signal mercy, we would have shared the fate of the millions of our brethren across the Atlantic; we too would have been the victims of ruthless Nazism. God says to us, as He said, according to the Midrash, to those who were included in the first census, "You owe me a tax on your life, which I have preserved."[11]

(206:) Every one of us, rich or poor, high or low, is called upon

---

9 See Arthur Ruppin, *The Jewish Fate and Future*, p. 35.

10 This last sentence could not have been said in February 1944. In the Foreword to his book (published in 1952), Hershman wrote that in this case he "deemed it necessary, in the interest of correctness, to revise the figures given in two paragraphs" of this sermon. I have no access to any original text used during the delivery.

11 Author's note: Exodus Rabbah 39:1; Pesiqta Rabbati, 10:15.

to pay a "ransom for his soul," to take the place of those who have fallen in the battle for Judaism. The catastrophe which has overtaken European Jewry should serve as a challenge to him. He should answer to his name, as the roll of those who have been providentially spared the fate of their fellow-Jews is called, by devoting himself to the cause for which those martyrs have died, and thus compensate for our appalling loss in numbers.

March 12, 1944 (Sunday)

Solomon B. Freehof, "Our Mass Bombing: Is It Morally Right?," Rodef Shalom Congregation, Pittsburgh, PA, from Rodef Shalom Archives, Solomon B. Freehof Rabbinic Writings, BA175 FF33

(1:) For the Eighth Army Air Force this has been a solemn week.... We lost almost two hundred machines, some of them containing ten to eleven highly trained men; we lost fifteen hundred American aviators.[12]

It was a week of perilous adventure, of pain over the loss of comrades of unforgettable memory. And in this very week – this solemn, tragic week – twenty-eight American ministers decide to sign a manifesto drawn up by an English pacifist woman, Vera Brittain, denouncing the bombing of Berlin as mass murder....[13]

---

12 The first American bombing of targets in Berlin occurred on March 6, with seven hundred heavy bombers and eight hundred escort fighters of the Eighth Air Force. This was followed by additional raids on March 8 and 9. The *NYT* reported these events from March 7 through March 12, including the number of lost American aircraft, but it does not appear to report the number of Air Force personnel lost, and it seems rather extraordinary that the specific figure of fifteen hundred airmen lost would be accessible to the general public so soon.

13 The protest of twenty-eight American clergy and other leaders including John Haynes Holmes and Harry Emerson Fosdick was reported in newspapers on March 6; see, e.g., *St. Louis Star and Times*, p. 2. Vera Brittain's short book, *Seed of Chaos: What Mass Bombing Really Means*, was published in the United States by the "Bombing Restriction Committee" in April 1944; the Foreword, "Massacre by Bombing," was published separately in early March, as mentioned in the above article. For a recent collection of her pacifist writings, see Vera Brittain, *One Voice: Pacifist Writings from the Second World War*, esp. pp. 91–174, with Berlin discussed on pp. 121–28.

(2:) Let them reflect on the possibility that pacifists, too, need to repent.... The pacifist mood which swept our hearts made us hold in contempt every form of military preparedness; and that was Hitler's chance... If that is so, maybe we pacifists are partly guilty for the hundreds of thousands of innocents that Hitler has killed....

(4:) The Nazis have put to death millions of helpless innocents, cold-bloodedly with wholesale brutality, and we haven't enough tears left for those Aryans in Berlin. That is the fact of it. Among them are many Gestapo and S.S. men; let them go, they deserved it. Among them are many who believed the Nazis are a little crazy but will be good for Germany; let them go. Among them are many who did not have the courage to resist Hitler; we're sorry for them. But as far as tears are concerned, we are wept dry.

(6:) Let Berlin remain a ghost city forever. Let the Germans build another capital. We will help them build it; we will feed them; we will heal them, but let Berlin remain a ghost city... in "perpetual ruins."

Julian B. Feibelman, "The Choice Before Us," Temple Sinai, New Orleans, LA. Radio Address, WSMB. AJA MS-94, Box 14, Folder 4

(1:) It has been said by Dr. [Carl] Hambro, former President of the League of Nations, that more than 35 millions of people were killed, or died, as a result of the First World War.... At first blush we are tempted to say that life, as it is treated in war, with emphasis on expendables of humans and material, is the only cheap thing left in the world. But that is not so. Life, as it is expended today – those killed outright, those who have perished as a result of being uprooted from their homes and homelands, starved in prison and concentration camps, gassed in lethal chambers, poisoned, drowned in the seas, and buried alive for the sake of reclaiming their threadbare clothing – is still not cheap.... No, not even the human life aspect is cheap, as war sucks it into its insatiable maw. We shall never see the end of payment for this colossal war....

(2:) This war must not only be paid for, it must itself pay: in dividends of security, peace, and human welfare for all time to come....

March 21, 1944 (Tuesday)

Abba Hillel Silver, "As the Deadline Approached," Address to American Zionist Emergency Council, Madison Square Garden, New York. *Vision and Victory* pp. 39–46

(41:) We had hoped that in view of the terrible tragedies which have overtaken our people during the war, there would come about a full realization that everything should be done in order to make the position of the Jewish people more secure in the world, and that in order to avert such recurrent tragedies in the future generous measures would immediately be taken to insure the full rehabilitation of the Jewish National Home in Palestine. This was our hope. Unfortunately, nothing of the sort has happened. It is "business as usual" with empires, and it is "business as usual" with oil concessionaires.

(43:) In Palestine, the tragedy of a people given over to centuries of persecution, hate, and exile, met up with the tragedy of a land given over to centuries of plunder and exploitation and neglect, and the result has been an inevitable blessing both to the people and the land. They brought healing one to another....

(45:) As the deadline of March 31, 1944 originally set by the White Paper approaches, we recall with grief and indignation the fate of hundreds of thousands of our fellow-Jews who were consigned to the concentration camps and death chambers of Hitler and who, but for the policy of that White Paper, might have been saved and given sanctuary in Palestine; of those who were drowned on the *Struma* and the *Patria* because they were denied refuge in the Jewish homeland; and of the 1500 Jewish refugees who, having finally reached Palestine, were deported as "illegal" immigrants to the tropical island of Mauritius, where for the past three years they have been rotting away in detention camps....[14]

We greet with satisfaction and gratitude the statement of our own

---

14 These Jewish refugees were interned on Mauritius by the British, after an unsuccessful attempt to enter Palestine. More than one hundred died of disease during their four-year confinement.

President on March 9th, that the Government of the United States has never given its approval to the White Paper, and his assurance that "when future decisions are reached full justice will be done to those who seek a Jewish National Home, for which our Government and the American People have always had the deepest sympathy."[15]

March 31, 1944 (Friday evening)

Maurice N. Eisendrath, "Freedom: For What?," Excerpts from Address to Joint Services at Rockdale Avenue Temple, Cincinnati, OH. Unpublished, AJA Eisendrath Papers, MS-167, Box 2

(1:) Never before has the Jew recalled with such anguish of heart the serfdom which his forebears knew in Egypt, as will the Jews be reminded during the forthcoming Passover season of the present bondage, to which so many of our brethren are subjected today, a bondage more grinding, devastating and death-dealing than any known before. Never in the past have the cries of the enslaved ascended with such terrifying horror as do the cries of our brother-Jews today ascending from a score of valleys of the shadow of death.

What amateurs the ancient Egyptians were in contrast to their contemporary followers. They only used the whip and the scourge – knowing other [instruments of torture], they disdained their barbarity. But today, mass murder in human abattoirs by means of electrocution and poison gas has already annihilated several millions of our co-religionists.

April 1, 1944 (Shabbat haGadol)

Emil Ehrnthal (later Michael Elton), "The Testimony of Ages," London. *The Challenge of Destiny*, pp. 164–68

We, who are about to celebrate the festival of Passover for the fourth time during this ever-growing and desolating war, are becoming

15 In response to significant public pressure, Roosevelt authorized Stephen S. Wise and Abba Hillel Silver to issue a public statement in his name including the formulation quoted by Silver (*Vision and Victory*, p. 38).

more and more conscious of the (165:) bitter meaning and eternal reality of the story of Israel in Egypt.[16]...

The meaning of that last Great Sabbath in slavery in Egypt has a living message for us now. For we also hope that this Great Sabbath will be the last spent in slavery, in darkness, or engaged in the fierce toils of war. On this day, when we think of the many Seder tables which will *never* be filled; when we, while sitting at the Seder table, think of those who are languishing in prison camps, in dungeons, or fighting in the frontline; when thoughts of this kind pass through our minds, we look for a message of encouragement in the meaning of this day....

(167:) But it is undeniable that the position of our people in the world today is the gloomiest in all our history. No one dare minimize the gigantic proportion of the tragedy of our brothers and sisters on the Continent. Nor dare we forget that the poison of anti-Semitism has penetrated every corner of the world. Yet there is reason to lift up our hearts on this Sabbath which signifies our unshakeable trust in God's providence and our unquenchable faith in the certainty of victory and liberation.

Allow your eyes to rove over the vast expanse of history and see if our Jewish past abounds only in suffering and humiliation. True enough, we have paid with oceans of blood for our existence and survival. But so also have the other nations of the world....

See the real outlines of our history, which are hewn in rock and illuminated by a continuous glow of humanity, service to mankind and the improvement of civilization.

(168:) When we recount the glory of the Eighth Army, let us proudly recall that great *first army* that marched out of Egypt. That army sounded the death-knell to Pharaoh and his like for all time.

Ephraim Sokolover, Great Synagogue, Ra'anana, Palestine. *Penei Efrayim* pp. 284–93, translated by MS

(284:) The day preceding Rosh Ḥodesh Nisan this year [Friday, March

16 The statement is confusing, in that this would be the fifth Pesach during the war (1940, 1941, 1942, 1943, and 1944).

24, 1944] was proclaimed by the International Rabbinate[17] as a day of fasting (285:) and prayer. On the preceding day, the terrifying news came to us that the axe was raised over the remnant of Israel: over a million Jews of Hungary, three hundred thousand Jews of Romania and the other Balkan countries. Throughout the year we had still found comfort in the hope that we would succeed in saving them from the claws of the wild beast. After the destruction of Polish Jewry, we said to ourselves what R. Yohanan said after the death of his ten sons, finding comfort in a small bone that remained for him as a memorial, saying "this is the bone of my tenth son" (b. Berakhot 5b): R. Yohanan always kept this small bone in his pocket as a source of comfort following the disaster of the loss of all his sons.

And so we thought, that a small part of European Jewry, the splendor of Judaism, remains to us. And now once again, misery and heartache, wailing and lamentation! Before we found consolation – if indeed it would ever be possible for find consolation – for the horrific catastrophe of the loss of Poland and Lithuania, now comes a new catastrophe facing the surviving remnant of Israel...

(288:) It is extremely difficult to believe, but it is not matter of belief, but rather of [reliable] reports. To our deep sorrow and distress, the facts are accumulating before us; there is no exaggeration or rhetoric in what we have heard; the information has been provided for us by eye-witnesses who were there in the terrifying hell of Treblinka and Auschwitz.[18]

And if there is still any doubt about whether to rely on these reports, we have the statement by the President of the United States, Mr. Roosevelt, with an emotional address to the Nazi hangman

---

17 *Harabbanut ha'olamit*: Proposals to establish this institution began in 1935, and the first meeting was held in the spring 1936. Despite its name, it never became international, but consisted of rabbis from the land of Israel: http://www.hebrewbooks.org/pagefeed/hebrewbooks_org_39157_3.pdf.

18 This is rather problematic, as the only known prisoners who escaped from and reported about the mass gassings in Auschwitz (not Treblinka) were Rudolf Vrba and Alfred Wetzler; they escaped on April 10 and reached Slovakia on April 24, where they began writing their report. Since Sokolover could not have been referring to them on Shabbat haGadol (April 1), his sources are unclear.

and to all his associates "to cease the systematic destruction and to provide refuge in the lands of the Allies."[19]

For two years, the high and mighty of the [free] world have heard and remained silent; we have not heard a single word about saving anything. Now it has reached the point where even the stone heart is bursting, and is listening to the voice of human blood calling out from the earth (cf. Gen. 4:10). And if no practical rescue has yet occurred, we can nevertheless find some small comfort in this proclamation to the free world, in this unique appeal to the murderer to cease the devastation....

Every day we read in the newspapers about the victories of the Red Army. They are amazing victories, and the entire world admires and praises their heroism.... But woe to us if *they* are the ones serving as our physicians, our comforters, our supporters. For they were the first ones who stole millions of our Jewish brethren from us! To be sure, it was not by burning of the body, but the great majority of Russian Jews were lost to us by burning of the soul, which is also a kind of burning.[20] And there are tens of thousands of refugees who were exiled to forced labor in distant Siberia for no justified reason. Where are the tens of thousands who have died there by the sword or by famine? And now, these are the ones who are saving us!

---

19 Roosevelt's statement, issued on March 24, 1944 (a week before the sermon), included the following: "In one of the blackest crimes of all history – begun by the Nazis in the day of peace and multiplied by them a hundred times in time of war – the wholesale systematic murder of the Jews of Europe goes on unabated every hour. As a result of the events of the last few days, hundreds of thousands of Jews, who while living under persecution have at least found a haven from death in Hungary and the Balkans, are now threatened with annihilation as Hitler's forces descend more heavily upon these lands. That these innocent people, who have already survived a decade of Hitler's fury, should perish on the very eve of triumph over the barbarism which their persecution symbolizes would be a major tragedy.... Hitler is committing these crimes against humanity in the name of the German people. I ask every German and every man everywhere under Nazi domination to show the world by his action that in his heart he does not share these insane criminal desires. Let him hide these pursued victims, help them to get over their borders, and do what he can to save them from the Nazi hangman." Sokolover's presentation, including the phrase "the Nazi hangman" (*hatalyan haNatzi*) shows that he had direct access to this statement (probably from the Jewish press in Palestine), and incorporated it accurately into his sermon.

20 Referring of course to the suppression of religion that was an integral component of Communist ideology.

April 8, 1944 (Saturday, first day of Pesach)

Abraham A. Kellner, "The Passover Ideal of Freedom," Congregation Sons of Abraham, Albany, NY. *A Rabbi's Faith*, pp. 65–70

(65:) It is timely and fashionable to speak today of freedom and liberation. The Jew, especially, who has been so sorely oppressed throughout the continent of Europe, awaits most anxiously the call to freedom. Yet, gnawing doubt and depressing uncertainty assail many careful observers as they see the pattern of salvation presented in recent months…

(68:) Humanity was plunged into this war and the world turned it into a shambles because the only consideration of the people was land, and the only concern of Government was territory. A tyrannical dictatorship clamoring for more and more "*Lebensraum*" ran roughshod over peoples and their possessions, caring very little for right, justice, or human decency. Israel, on the other hand, had in times of olden, set the classic example, that in days of spiritual self-sufficiency, earthly considerations rank little if at all….

(70:) Yes, my friends, the task of the world today is to put man together, place hope in his heart, music on his lips, enlarge his vision and extend his spirit, and the world will blossom forth like the Garden of the Lord on the day of Creation.

Ferdinand M. Isserman, "Thumbs Up," Temple Israel, St. Louis, MO. AJA, MS-6, Box 16, Folder 7

(3:) That spirit symbolized by "thumbs up" is to be seen in the heroic struggle of the ghetto of Warsaw whose first anniversary we mark and celebrate today. You know the tragic story of Poland's Jewry. You know of the cattle trains which took our co-religionists to the execution chambers, fouler and more brutal than any hell spawned in the weird imagination of a medieval mind. You have heard of the execution chambers, of the experiments of poison gasses with Jews as guinea pigs. You have heard of the forest of death where machine guns mowed down human beings in the largest slaughters of all the cruel history of mankind. You have heard of the remnants saved to toil and to labor for the "master race" to be slain as soon as their usefulness came to an end. You would imagine that Polish Jewry was crushed, that the pall of death was upon it and the paralysis of a doomed man filled it.

But beginning last Passover, out of the underground of Poland again came the rumors that their thumbs were up, that Polish Jewry had not succumbed, that it had not yielded. On the first Seder night in 1943, German soldiers entered the Warsaw ghetto, arrived with six tanks to continue the mass deportations and the mass slaughter. But fired by the spirit of the festival, a fuselage of bullets greeted the would-be murderers. Ghetto fights opened fire on Nazi tanks. The tanks exploded and their occupants were killed. This was the signal for a heroic revolt which lasted for forty days.... Regiment after regiment of Germans came with tanks and all the equipment of war, only to be slaughtered. Young Jews with hand grenades in their pockets flung themselves beneath advancing German tanks, heedless of (4:) life, preferring to die as free men, striking a blow for freedom, rather than being massacred like pigs in the human abattoir erected by the fiendish Gestapo. For 42 days, they resisted, almost until the Shavuoth festival. Finally the Nazis realized that they could never crush the Warsaw ghetto without planes, and so bombing planes with their incendiary bombs carried on the work of destruction and Jewish defenders died amidst the ruins of their ramparts.... That was the spirit of "thumbs up" as revealed in the magnificent struggle of the Warsaw ghetto, an epic in Jewish history, in universal history.

April 9, 1944 (second day of Pesach)

Abraham A. Kellner, "The Passover Guarantee of Freedom," Congregation Sons of Abraham, Albany, NY. *A Rabbi's Faith*, pp. 71–74.

(71:) If judged by surface indications alone, there will be little to rejoice about at the current Passover Festival; indeed, the Guarantee of Freedom is conspicuous by its absence, throughout most of the world. In a state of darkness, when the sun of Freedom goes down, only a hardy spirit like that of King David can stand firm and stoutly proclaim his faith supreme – "*Vemunoscho balelos*" (Ps. 92:3) – although the shadows of the night envelop man and terrify him with a thousand images of haunting horror. Indeed one poet felt that nothing that the blue coolness of an evening sky decorated by the starry vault above could offer would compensate one for the loss of the brightness of the day when the dazzling radiance of the sun sheds its cheerful rays.

> The Night has a thousand eyes
> And the day but one
> Yet the light of the whole world dies
> With the dying sun.[21]

One can trace this fearsome distrust to the early days of creation when Adam first was confronted with it as the terror of the night settled over his head and the lurking (72:) shadows brought a fear of unknown horrors to his primitive conscience....

It is small wonder then that even profound observers find little to rejoice about, in the shadowy days of Jewish existence....

(73:) Surely in the days of those talmudic giants, as in our own day, one can find more to weep for, than to be jubilant about.... Those happy experiences that we may find in our present generation become subdued and colorless in the light of the indescribable bestiality and horror experienced by our people in the lands of their sorrows. But Jewish History as a whole – the story of the Jew as told in *kol y'mei*, recounting ALL his days – replaces the somber color of desolation with the bright panorama of triumphant achievements. In the Spiritual heavens of our harassed people shine countless luminaries whose (74:) light no human hand can dim, no mortal man can extinguish....

April 15, 1944 (eighth day of Pesach)

Jacob Kaplan, "The Suffering of Israel is not a Curse" (*La souffrance d'Israël n'es pas une malédiction*), Synagogue de Lyon, France. *Les Temps d'épreuve*, pp. 133–40, translated by MS

(133:) "I shall not die but live, and declare the work of the Lord" (Ps. 118:17).

(134:) Pesach tells us that liberation will always follow slavery, not

21 The poet was the Victorian Francis William Bourdillon.

that slavery will always follow liberation. One day the circle will be broken, and it will be not during a period of oppression, but in a time of liberty.

But the Messianic age is still far away; it is always a movement of fluctuation that governs the history of Israel. Now it has plunged our generation into the dark zone, alongside shadows, gloom, suffering, enslavement. We now know what it is to be persecuted; we know the frightful state of mind experienced by our ancestors in the most dismal periods of our past....[22]

April 19, 1944 (Wednesday)

Isaac Herzog, "Address at the Meeting of Solidarity with the Fate of European Jewry," Technion, Haifa, Palestine. *Masu'ah leHerzog*, pp. 145–47, translated by MS

(145:) We do not have the ability to bring to life the millions that have been destroyed, but we do have the ability to sustain life for those still alive. We do have the ability, for example, to sustain the lives of 55,000 who are imprisoned in the valley of the shadow of death called Transnistria, who are disintegrating in the starvation and diseases described in the biblical passages of rebuke [Lev. 26, Deut. 28], walking about like shadows, swollen with hunger, naked without clothing, covering themselves with sheets of newspapers. We have the ability to hasten the deliverance of the living refugees who are terrified day and night. We can indeed bring the refugees to the land of Israel, and as it appears in the information that was published in the newspapers yesterday, this possibility is now developing and expanding, thanks to an easing in the process of transfer that will be given by the government of Turkey, the government which opened its gates widely before the exiles from Spain.[23]

---

22 For another selection from this sermon in the original French, see David Shapira, *Jacob Kaplan*, p. 161.

23 The newspaper report was apparently the announcement by an American official, Ira A. Hirschmann, that arrangements had been made for a Turkish passenger ship to take 1,600 refugees from a Romanian port to Haifa. Herzog himself had been sent by the Yishuv to Turkey, together with Isaac Ben-Zvi, to help arrange for Jewish

April 23, 1944 (Sunday)

Julian B. Feibelman, "Unless the Lord Build the House," Temple Sinai, New Orleans, LA. Radio Address, WSMB. AJA MS-94, Box 18, Folder 4

(4:) Let me revert to the war situation. Here is the case of Poland, for whom we all feel a very decided sympathy. Its nation has been ravaged, its cities destroyed, its people enslaved. Naturally, it claims and deserves, it would seem, a restored nation. It wants to build again its house. But at this very moment in the Free Polish fighting legions scattered within the allied armies, there is so much anti-Semitism, so much discrimination against Jewish soldiers who are actually fighting (5:) side by side with their Polish brothers, that these Jews have requested to be transferred to British fighting units. Poland has never been a nation free of the scourge of unbrotherly as well as outright wicked relationships with other peoples, and yet it is trying today to rebuild its house without the mortar that would cement brotherhood.

Claims of this nature, actual facts of violation of liberty, direct interference with the greater objectives of our war sacrifice, are doing more to perpetuate the seeds of discord and hatred and inequality, and the failure to recognize one's self as his brother's keeper.

May 5, 1944 (Friday evening)

Ferdinand M. Isserman, "Palestine, Zionism and the Jew in the Postwar World," Temple Israel, St. Louis, MO. AJA, MS-6, Box 16, Folder 7

(1:) Newspaper reports from England tell that 30 Polish soldiers serving with their country's army in England were recently charged with desertion, court-martialed, found guilty, and given prison sentences. Considering that the Polish armies in England may now be

---

refugees from the Balkans (*American Jewish Year Book 5705*, vol. 46 [1944–1945], pp. 271–72; Shulamit Eliash, *The Harp and the Shield of David*, pp. 66–67). In March and April 1944, more than one thousand Jewish orphans from Transnistria were permitted by the Turkish authorities to land in Istanbul, and by the British authorities to enter Palestine (Martin Gilbert, *The Holocaust*, p. 637). The rest of Herzog's address was a powerful fundraising appeal for contributions to facilitate this process.

poised for the invasion of Europe, the sentence seems to be light, for a soldier who deserts on the eve of an invasion is liable to the death penalty. All 30 soldiers were of the Jewish faith; they had deserted not because they did not want to do their share in the liberation of Europe, but because they wanted to enlist in the British army where there would be as much danger, as much action. They wanted to leave the flag of the country, under which they were born, to fight under another flag because in the armies of their country they had encountered that anti-semitism, the destruction of which is said to be one of the goals of the allied armies.[24] Because the same anti-semitism with which Hitler debased Germany and then Europe is rampant in the Polish army, even in England.

(3:) In one Romanian city where there were 80,000 Jews, 200 were left when the Russian Army captured it. In Chernowitz, where there were tens of thousands of Jews, less than 1000 were left. Before the Nazis came, Romania was rotten with anti-semitism.

(6:) More than 2,000,000 Jewish civilians have perished, exclusive of Jews who died in the armies of Poland and France and Russia, Greece, Belgium, Holland.

(7:) Wherever possible Jews should be given a chance to return to the country of their origin. But what of those who cannot do so, who will not be admitted to the democratic nations? For them there is Palestine. The gates have been kept open by the enterprise, the energy, the intelligence, the aggressiveness and the sacrificial spirit of the Zionist organization. One can admit this without subscribing to the Zionist philosophy....

(10:) Because of all this the allied nations should make a place for the Jew in Palestine and throw its gates wide open to Jewish immigrants.... (11:) I am convinced that what they will build in Palestine will be a blessing to humanity.

May 22, 1944 (Monday), Service of Mourning and Prayer for the Martyrs of the Warsaw Ghetto

Joseph H. Hertz, "The 'Battle of Warsaw'," Bevis Marks Synagogue,

24 This information was undoubtedly based either directly or indirectly on a front-page article in the *JC* of April 28, 1944, continued on p. 5 and taken up again on p. 6.

London. *JC*, May 26, 1944, pp. 1 and 7; Pamphlet published by the Office of the Chief Rabbi; see Complete Sermons

June 5, 1944 (Monday)

Isaac Herzog, Address at the Communal Gathering on the "Day of Outcry" for the Rescue of the Few Remaining Survivors in Europe (in Hungary and the Balkans), Jerusalem. *Masu'ah leHerzog*, pp. 148–49, translated by MS

(149:) So much for internal matters. Regarding the outside world: Once again we look out from the holy mountain, from Jerusalem, the well-spring of justice and mercy, and we call out to the populations of the Allies: Indeed, you have done something, but you have not fulfilled even a significant component of your obligations. We entreat you to act to save the surviving remnant of Israel in exactly the same manner that you would act to save your own sons and daughters if they were in the same perilous situation. If that were the case, would you not do whatever you possibly could? Would you not open all the gates widely, would you not pressure the neutral countries to open their gates as a refuge for the surviving remnant in the valley of slaughter? And now that Jewish blood, in its innocence, has already been spilt like a flood of water, and the remainder are hovering between life and death, with a sword placed against their throats, what indeed are you doing? You have not even annulled that black decree called "the White Paper," which shuts off the path to the land of our forefathers in the face of their sons and daughters who are being led to their deaths....

And now, our brothers in the *Yishuv* and the Diaspora: Let us commit ourselves to do whatever is possible for us in order to save – even though a sword is pressed against the neck of the remnant of Israel in Hungary and elsewhere.... Though all the [other] gates are locked, the gates of Mercy are never locked. Zion, "the Home of our Life," was in severe danger, and it was saved by the mercy of heaven.[25] Had it not been for divine providence, who knows whether any one of us

25 Reference is undoubtedly to the advances made by Rommel in the summer of 1942, potentially threatening the land of Israel, until the victories by the British forces under Montgomery. Herzog apparently presents divine providence as working to protect the Holy Land, but not to protect Jewish populations elsewhere.

gathered here today would still be alive. We must never despair! Let us do whatever is in our power, and *beyond* what is in our power, and on this day of fasting, mourning, and prayer, let us arouse the mercy of heaven for the remnant of our people.... And may we be worthy of seeing soon the downfall of the wicked, the victory of justice, the salvation of Israel and fullness of its redemption!

June 9, 1944 (Friday)

Israel Zolli, Chief Rabbi of Rome, at Service in Tempio Israelitico/Maggiore, Rome, commemorating the liberation of Rome by American Armed Forces. JTA, June 16; *NYT*, June 17, 1944[26]

JTA: LONDON (Jun. 15): The Vatican radio, describing today the first Sabbath services held by Jews in Rome since their liberation by the Allied armies, said that Rabbi Zolli, the aged rabbi of Rome, expressed from the pulpit the thanks of the Jewish community for the aid extended to Jews in Italy by the Catholic Church and clergy during the months of German persecution....[27]

Rabbi Zolli, who was the only rabbi left alive by the Nazis in Rome, devoted his sermon to prayers for the suffering Jews who have not yet been liberated from the Nazis and for the victory of the Allied Armies. He told all worshippers to pray for the Allies, to whom they owed their freedom.

"Everywhere Abel's blood comes from the earth, the blood of innocent Abel slain by Cain. Nevertheless, we shall rebuild the ruins and reconstruct upon the ruins." It was insufficient to rebuild towns and factories, he declared. An edifice of universal love had to be erected.[28]

Morris Kertzer, an American Chaplain, also delivered a sermon in English, which was summarized in Italian [JTA].[29]

---

26 See Louis I. Newman, *A "Chief Rabbi" of Rome Becomes a Catholic*, pp. 161–62.

27 The question of the extent to which in his sermon Zolli expressed gratitude to the Vatican for its protection of Italian Jews, as reported in the media, became a matter of controversy; see Newman, ad loc.

28 This paragraph is taken not from the JTA report but from a direct quotation in Weisbord and Sillanpoa, *The Chief Rabbi, The Pope, and the Holocaust*, p. 129; the note (9) provides the source as "[Rabbi Jacob] Hochman Papers, 'Message from chief Rabbi I. Zolli, Rome.'"

29 Cf. Morris Kertzer, *With an H on My Dog Tag*, pp. 56–57, providing a one-paragraph

June 11, 1944 (Sunday after D-Day)

Michael Elton (formerly Emil Ehrnthal), "D-Day," (London), in *The Challenge of Destiny*, pp. 43–46

(44:) Nothing could hide the news [about the advance of the liberators] from the suffering men and women of Theresienstadt, no one could keep it from the martyred Jews of Poland. The Jews of Hungary, suffering cruelly under the heavier oppression of foreign (45:) fascism, have heaved a great sigh of relief that, with Russia at the gate of the Carpathians, with Alexander advancing from the South, and Montgomery from the West, the hour of liberation would not be long delayed.[30] Even in the concentration camps and reservations for Jews there will be a rising hope of redemption, that "they that hate Thee shall flee before Thee" (Num. 10:35).

(46:) Almighty Father, we have come to Thee today, to the Well of Salvation and Hope, to offer thanksgiving for Thy great mercies which Thou hast hitherto granted us and for having enabled us to see the beginning of the Liberation of Europe from the shores of this our land....

June 23, 1944 (Friday evening)

Solomon B. Freehof, President's Message to CCAR Convention, Cincinnati, OH. *CCAR Yearbook* 54 (1944), pp. 151–73

(171:) We American Jews, secure and safe, have witnessed perhaps the greatest misfortune in Jewish history. Day after day the newspaper headlines and the radio reports have dinned into our consciousness the ever-repeated story of expulsions and massacres. Whether we read carefully the Jewish news from Europe or whether we look at it

summary of his "brief address": "I told the people of Rome that we knew what burdens they had borne. But for us [American soldiers] too, the road to the synagogue had been a bitter one. Hundreds of our closest friends lay buried in Nettuno, thirty miles from this House of God. They, more than any of us in *Templo Israelitico*, had opened these portals of prayer."

30 The Fifteenth Army commanded by General Harold Alexander conquered Rome in early June, 1944, but – poignantly – none of these military advances would have any impact on the fate of Hungarian Jewry.

hastily and nervously and shift to another item, every one of us has been deeply affected, more deeply than he knows....

What makes our unhappiness dangerous is the awareness of our futility. As we read daily of further massacres, we were forced to admit to ourselves that there was nothing we could do about it. Those immured in Hitler's fortress were beyond our effective help. We who were strong and powerful and were proud of our influence in world affairs as citizens of the mightiest republic in human history, had to confess our futility. Of course, we made protests. We called upon governments. But they were as helpless as we. We knew that millions were going to their death and we were powerless to aid. We have failed our brothers at the time of their greatest need....

June 28, 1944 (Wednesday)

Louis M. Levitsky, "Spiritual Leadership in the Post-War World," President's Message to the Forty-Fourth Annual Convention of the Rabbinical Assembly, Lackawanna, PA. *Proceedings of the Rabbinical Assembly of America,* vol. 8, pp. 281–97

(291:) The Jewish scene offers at the moment very little light and hardly any sweetness.... Some of the problems are so mammoth that we have been stunned by them. For one thing, because of the (292:) enormity of the problem of the new dispersion, we are beginning to hear the voices of some Jews who are ready to give up our claims to our rights in the Diaspora. There are some world powers, notably the Polish Government in exile, that are attempting to intimidate us into accepting such a view. The claim is that there will be no room for Jews in a reconstructed Europe; that Jews in Poland were regarded before the war as the marginal population; and that the hate rooted in Germany against the Jews will make that country an impossible place for them to live in. We are beginning to be told not to expect any further immigration into this country after the war. We have been told to accept these verdicts in silence, that this is not the time for us to reaffirm our rights in the Diaspora, even as we have been told that this is not the time to carry boldly our rightful and righteous demands for Eretz Yisroel. We are being told that as Jews we must do nothing that will create any dissension among the United Nations at the moment, or that will irritate the British Government at present.

We must not yield to such council.... As descendants of the Prophets, we rabbis must not keep silent. We must cry aloud on behalf of our people. We must have our demands impressed clearly upon the world....

August 26, 1944 (Saturday, *Shoftim*)

Louis I. Newman, "The Cup of Fury," Congregation Rodeph Sholom. *Biting on Granite*, pp. 250–57; see Complete Sermons

September 3, 1944 (Sunday, National Day of Prayer)

Samuel Daiches, (no title), Harrowgate Synagogue, printed as eight-page pamphlet by Oxonian Press, Oxford

(3:) We are assembled here, before God, to ponder over what has befallen humanity during the last five years. We scan the horizon of history, and we cannot find such dehumanization of man as has taken place in certain parts of Europe in this short period of time. Wars, devastating wars, have been waged before; cruelties, bestial cruelties have been committed before; lies, deadly lies have been invented before. But never did man resort to such inhuman warfare as we have witnessed in this war. Never have such fiendish cruelties been perpetrated by man against man as during the last five years. Never has man's mind shot out such bestial lies as we have been forced to hear and to read since September 3, 1939. In the morning shame covered our faces, and in the evening the oncoming darkness of the night seemed to be pellucid light compared with the blackness of the soul of the blackest demon of the human race.

Need I recite instances? Need I remind you of the cruel happenings? They have been graven on our minds and our hearts with a pen of iron. It is sufficient to mention one name: Lublin. A city that was made famous by Jewish saints and scholars was made a byword for devilish cruelties by the foul Nazis. Concentration camps, gas chambers, death-dealing furnaces arise before our eyes when we think (4:) of Lublin, and the cries of hundreds of thousands of human beings reach our ears. Whole parts of the Continent of Europe were turned into places of torture and death. Our people, our brothers and sisters, were the greatest sufferers, but there were victims, many victims everywhere. Nearly every country in Europe was blighted by the cruel hands of the creatures of Satan.... [Mentions sufferings of England, especially Coventry]

They began their dehumanization of man long before September 3, 1939. Their first and chief target was Israel, the Jewish people. If the civilized statesmen had read the portents aright, the terrible ordeal that came to humanity might have been avoided....

(5:) But, my Friends, this day is not only a day for expressing indignation. It is also a day for feeling exultation. We have survived five years of destruction....

September 9, 1944 (Saturday, *Ki Tavo*)[31]

Louis I. Newman, "What Liberation Means," Congregation Rodeph Sholom, New York. *Biting on Granite*, pp. 264–70

(264:) [Deut. 26:7–8, Isa 60:1] Both the Sedrah and the Haftarah for this Sabbath are in a mood of exultation, for they tell in certain sections of the deliverance of the people of Israel from the hands of their oppressors....

(265:) Liberation means physical liberty. The concentration camps, the dungeons, and other centers of imprisonment are yielding up their victims....

Liberation means a cessation of horrors in the regions where the Nazis have been in control. We read (*NYT*, Sept. 4) that in a tiny restaurant members of the staff of the Lyon edition of the *Paris-Soir* told of some of the crimes committed by the Germans in the last few days. Ten days ago, they said, fifty Jews and thirty-eight Catholics, including Rabbis and priests, were put into a house near Fort Montluc, the doors locked, and the house blown up....

---

31 The printed text of the Newman sermon (p. 264) states, erroneously, September 10, then states Sabbath morning, which was Sept 9.

(266:) Liberation means the coming of the humane Allies, with the British and the Americans foremost in the ranks of the liberators.... (267:) Soon we shall know – to paraphrase the words of the Prayer: *Unethanneh Tokef* – "How many have passed away, and how many came into existence; who has lived, and who has died; who has accomplished the full number of their days, and who has not accomplished them; who has perished by water, and who by fire; who by the sword and who by hunger; who by earthquake and who by plague." For liberation means an end to the isolation which has cut off the enslaved countries from contact with the rest of the world....

(268:) And liberation means for the peoples of Europe a new opportunity at life. For European Jewries it means more, much more. Their civil and human rights must be restored; they must be welcomed back to the places whence they have been driven forth....

(270:) God is on the side of the strongest battalions to be sure,[32] but we have witnessed in our own day the miracle of strong battalions gathered because of the righteousness of our cause. And with liberation from want, from fear, from hatred, and from tribulation, let us together work, hand in hand, to see to it that "violence shall no more be heard in the earth; desolation nor destruction within its borders, but let us call our walls Salvation, and our gates Praise" (Isa. 60:18).

September 10, 1944 (Sunday)

Louis I. Newman, "Anti-Semitism: A Beloved Frailty," Radio Address on "The Message of Israel." *Biting on Granite*, pp. 271–77

(275:) By the same token, friendly non-Jews have sheltered some Jews in their homes, in the monasteries, and other places of concealment, lest they be deported to the hideous centers of mass-murder at Treblinka, Maidanek, Sobibor, and elsewhere. The Pope likewise gave refuge to numbers of Jews in Vatican City during the Fascist-Nazi pogroms.[33] King Christian of Denmark, when Jews were ordered to

32 Echoing a well-known statement often attributed to Napoleon, but cited by Voltaire as a common witticism (see Saperstein, *Jewish Preaching in Times of War*, p. 292, n. 24).

33 In late 1943, after the October Round-up in Rome, Jews were indeed hidden in

wear the yellow badge, donned it himself, and ordered his family and (276:) retinue to do the same, as a protest against Nazi cruelty.[34] Many are the heroic non-Jews who, by one gesture or another, have defied the war "without moral barriers" as Kurt Dittmar described it, which Hitler has waged against humanity, and against unoffending Jews, in his most fiendish rage.[35] Many are the Christians who have acted upon the rabbinic word: "It is better to be among the persecuted than among the persecutors."[36]

Anti-Semitism is too costly a luxury for any individual, community or nation to cultivate. In the hands of (277:) Hitler and Goebbels, it nearly wrecked Western culture by sowing divisiveness and domestic confusion; let us never forget that anti-Semitism, in the words of Everett Clinchy, is like the bubonic plague against which the whole world must immunize itself.[37] "Woe to the victors" if, after Hitler and his ruffians are gone, and Nazism is crushed, its anti-Semitism lives on, because some people consider it an enjoyable and valuable personal prize and possession.

September 15, 1944 (Friday evening)

Max Nussbaum, "The Crisis of Our Generation," Temple Israel, Hollywood, CA. *From Berlin to Hollywood*, pp. 37–38

(38:) We are accusing the world, and justifiably so, of having developed political systems with complete disregard of the ethical system

---

Vatican institutions such as the Pontificio Seminario Romano Maggiore, as well as in convents and monasteries outside the Vatican, but the role of Pius XII regarding these rescue efforts has been described as "complex and elusive": Susan Zuccotti, *Under His Very Windows*, p. 206, and all of chap. 14.

34 This was reported by the JTA on October 11, 1942, based on a London report two days earlier, with the headline, "Danish King Will Don Mogen David if Nazis Force Jews to Wear Yellow Badges." Though King Christian himself protested any requirement for Danish Jews to wear a Star of David, his own public donning of the Star is apparently an urban legend. See Vilhjálmur Örn Vilhjálmsson, "The King and the Star: Myths Created During the Occupation of Denmark," in *Denmark and the Jews*, pp. 102–17.

35 General Kurt Dittmar was a *Wehrmacht* radio commentator; his critical message using this phrase was widely cited in American newspapers in early September.

36 b. Bava Qamma 93a.

37 Clinchy was Director of the Williamstown Institute of Human Relations and President of the National Conference of Christians and Jews.

of Western Civilization. Only those whose hands are clean have the right to accuse others. Modern Judaism has to be the vanguard in this plan of spiritual reconversion. It seems that destiny has chosen American Israel to fall heir to European Jewry and to take the lead. It is upon us to fulfill the promise given to a generation whose sons and daughters are dying on every battlefield of our global war.

Jacob Kaplan, Synagogue de Lyon, France,[38] in David Shapira, *Jacob Kaplan*, p. 165; Fonds Kaplan, Box 1517–5 and 1517–7, translated by MS

During the darkest of our ordeals, we never had doubts about France. When the racial laws were passed against us, when the Jewish star was imposed upon us, when the criminal deportations delivered to Germany, by the thousands, French Jews as well as aliens, in each case we said to ourselves, "France, the *true* France, is not totally lost."… Why did we retain our unshakable confidence in the Resurrection of France?…

September 17, 1944 (Erev Rosh Hashanah)

Maurice N. Eisendrath, "New Year, New World: For Whom?," Temple Israel, Boston, MA. Unpublished, AJA, Eisendrath Papers MSS-167, Box 1

(1:) Out of the blood and tears of the present agonizing hour, out of the prison cells and death camps,… out of a myriad of worshipping hearts, whether they beat together beneath the towering dome of some great metropolitan synagogue or in a rude hut of some army cantonment in the Aleutians, in the South Seas, in Italy or France, or in some hastily improvised shack in a Nazi concentration camp; wherever there be a Jewishly conscious son of Israel tonight there rises within his soul a single hope, a poignant prayer, a fervent dream: that all the agony of body and anguish of soul that humanity, that Israel especially, has suffered during the year to which we are about to bid a none-too-reluctant farewell will soon be ended, and that the promise wherewith we greet the year even now emerging from the womb of time will be fulfilled. Nor does this hope seem quite

38 The Synagogue of Lyon was liberated by the Resistance on Sunday, September 3; this was the first service since synagogues were closed the previous June.

as quixotic as it has appeared during the past too many years. At long last, it does seem as though there can be a ring of reality and confidence to our traditional greeting of *Le'shono tovo tikosevu*, "May you be inscribed in the Book of Life for a *good* year."...

(14:) Our destroyers make no subtle distinction in their slaughter houses and gas chambers between Jew and Jew. Into their slave battalions they have dragooned Zionists and anti-Zionists, reformers and orthodox, bankers and beggars, nationalists and assimilationists, God-fearing and godless – all of them, in their sight, just Jews. If we cannot feel the blood of our fathers coursing through our veins, if we be not impelled by the tug of a common tradition, if we be not inspired by the tale of heroic martyrdom to preserve so great a heritage for our sake – if all this cannot bind all Israel together this day, then at least let us have sense enough to band together in self-protection against a foe that would extirpate us all, and emulate the fighting Jews of Warsaw who found neither time nor place for ideological disputes, but as a solid phalanx pitted their united bodies, Zionist and Bundist, radical and reactionary, against the steel of their adversaries, and sealed their unity with their martyrs' blood.

Can we do less in the face not alone of an enemy that would destroy us all, but of a new world that we must unite to rebuild? For that world *can* be ours, despite all the darkness which yet enshrouds the earth; that darkness which, though it may be lifting slightly on the military front, still enfolds a large portion of mankind in stygian moral depths....

Louis I. Newman, "God's Good Time," Radio Address for "The Message of Israel." *Biting on Granite*, pp. 278–83

(278:) "I the Lord will hasten it in its time" (Isa. 60:22)...Looking back upon the anxious days and years that have passed, we, the survivors, can truly count our benedictions. It was only yesterday that we were at Dunkerque and the Nazi conqueror was dancing his jig at Compiègne.[39] Do you remember those men and women

---

39 This was the town where the Armistice was signed on November 11, 1918, and where France and Germany signed a very different Armistice on June 22, 1940.

who, at the advent and during the course of the War announced that they had lost their faith in God, and that religion was a (279:) sham? How, they asked, with sophomoric simplification, could a gracious and clement Deity permit such sufferings and tragedies to befall mankind? It is always easy to be negative in judgment, and to indicate the shortcomings, both of our fellow-men and of our Heavenly Father. I wonder whether the doubters are so vehement in their denunciations today, now that God seems to be smiling upon our fortunes.[40]

Stephen S. Wise, "A New Year and a New World," media Excerpts, Free Synagogue at Carnegie Hall, New York. AJA Microfilms of AJHS texts, Box 23

(1:) The day of rejoicing is at hand.... Let Jews rejoice but with a sense of dignity growing out of the self-restraint of those who have suffered the most awful of losses.... Jews as a people have suffered greater losses than any warring people. Nearly one-fourth, or more than one-fourth, of the Jewish population has been destroyed not on the field of battle but at the hands of executioners, in the gas chambers, by the most ruthless and savage methods of destruction that men, if humans they are, could invent. Rejoicing over victory cannot wholly stay our tears over our losses, the death of the young and the old unarmed victims by the millions whom Hitlerism succeeded in exterminating. Years and years will pass before the scars of human suffering and the anguish of human sorrow shall have passed out of the life of shattered though invincible Israel.

Harold I. Saperstein, "The Call of the Shofar," Grenoble, France (as US Army Chaplain). *Witness from the Pulpit*, pp. 106–9

(108:) In the past few years, the Jewish people have had their cup of suffering filled to overflowing. Our people have been the victims of the most inhuman and barbaric program in history – a program designed simply and openly to exterminate the Jewish people, to

---

40 An apparent reference to the victories of Allied armies on the Western and Eastern Fronts, though God "smiling on our fortunes" seems to overlook entirely the tragedy of Hungarian Jewry during the previous months.

solve the "Jewish problem" by destroying every Jew. The program almost succeeded. The soil of Jews in Europe will long remain saturated with the blood of the Jewish people, the very air will long echo with the cries of those who have perished. As the forces of the enemy are being driven back, the story of the tragedy of Jews in lands they had conquered are being revealed. The number of those who have died *Al Kiddush Hashem* [for the sanctification of the Divine Name] can hardly be counted....

(109:) A year ago, the pattern was not so clear. We prayed for victory and hoped for peace – but that prayer and hope were not based on realistic observation but on the yearnings of our heart. Today only the blind cannot see the handwriting on the wall. The struggle is not yet over. But a ring of steel has been forged around the enemy that will relentlessly tighten until he is crushed.

September 18, 1944 (first day of Rosh Hashanah)

Louis I. Newman, "A Kingdom of Priests and a Holy Nation?," Congregation Rodeph Sholom, New York. *Biting on Granite*, pp. 284–95

(293:) The Jews of Europe did not court martyrdom; they enjoyed their security and comfort as much as did we. But there was a Jewish mayor who rather than submit to the Gestapo a list of the Jewish community, knowing they would use it to round up deportees, took his own life.[41] And there was Madame Tamara Schorr, who, when she found that the Nazis had tricked her into misleading her fellow-Jews into the trap they had set, died "*likdushat haShem* [for the sanctification of the Divine Name]."[42] Jews in the days of the Crusades, at the time of the Chmielnicki massacres in 1648, the Kishineff pogroms of 1903, the Petlura atrocities of 1919, were no different from us. Yet

41 The reference is to Adam Czerniakow, Head of the Jewish Council in the Warsaw Ghetto, who took his own life on July 23, 1942, rather than participate in fulfilling Nazi demands for providing a fixed quota of Jews to be "resettled" in the east (actually, to be killed by gas in Treblinka).

42 Madame Tamara Schorr was the wife of the distinguished Polish historian and rabbi Moses Schorr, who died of illness in a concentration camp in July 1941. Tamara and her daughter Felicia took their own lives in the Drancy Internment camp in April 1944. (Reported in *JC*, July 21, 1944; JTA August 2, 1944).

when they were faced by the choice between infamy and the sanctification of God's name by martyrdom, they chose the latter course. Cannot we take pride in the heroic resistance of the Jewish guerrillas in all the captive countries under the Nazis, and in the magnificent battle of the Jewish underground at Warsaw? You may not think that you could perform, under fire, similar feats of bravery. But having seen how your sons comport themselves on the battlefields of freedom, I know that you, being members of the "*Goy Kadosh*" [holy people], despite yourselves (294:) could not do less....

You see, my friends, how our writers and poets still insist upon holding us fast to our mission as the "Suffering Servant of the Lord," the "*Eved Adonoy*."....

Beryl D. Cohon, "A Heap of Witness," Temple Sinai, Brookline, MA. *Shielding the Flame*, pp. 100–9

(103:) All Israelites know one fate. The world about us with its sledgehammer blows fuses us into one, even if we would sever ourselves from our brethren. In the slaughterhouses of the Nazis, in the sealed cattle-cars of Germany, before the firing squads in Hungary, Jews were not asked whether they were Orthodox or Reform, whether they were Zionist or anti-Zionists, whether they were rich or poor. They were Jews, and they shared the same fate.

(104:) We are links in a mighty chain. We of this generation are not the last link. If we are in the depths of a dark night, we must brace ourselves with the conviction that every night gives way to a new morning. "I shall not die but live and declare the glory of the Lord" (Ps. 118:17). As long as we say that in sincerity, we are invincible and immortal.

Past, present and the dawn of tomorrow merge into one reality – a reality that absorbs all our arguments and all our divisions and makes us one. We are Jews. From Ankara, several weeks ago, came a newspaper report which illustrates this truth [of the unity of the Jewish people]:

> ANKARA (JPS) – Many thousands of Hungarian Jews who in recent months were baptized to avoid the Aryan laws, which at

> first seemed to be aimed only at those professing the Jewish faith, are now relinquishing Christianity and returning to the faith of their fathers, according to the official organ of Hungarian Jewry, Magyar Szideklatia.
>
> Within the past two months, 9745 Jews returned to their ancestral religion, the newspaper states.
>
> Partners to mixed marriages, children of mixed marriages and others, entitled to privileged treatment and even exemption from ghetto internment, have refused to avail themselves of these opportunities and declared themselves willing to share the common fate of all Jews in Hungary.
>
> (July 1944, *Jewish Advocate*)[43]

(106:) We are told that hard times are ahead [for American Jews] and that prudence dictates that we prepare another home for ourselves. Let's not pack our bags yet; let's not think in such panicky terms. We proceed on the conviction that we are here forever.

(107:) I know – and you know – that many centers of Jewry that have felt themselves rooted and secure were uprooted and banished, or destroyed. Some there are among us who are constantly pointing to German Jewry as a horrible example [of the inevitable precariousness of Jewish life in Diaspora]....

It is a surrender to fatalism and despair to say that because it happened before it must of necessity happen again, that because it happened in Spain or in Poland or in Germany, it must happen in the United States. We Jews are not fatalists. That is why we have survived....

---

43 This passage was based on an article on the first page of the *Boston Jewish Chronicle*, Thursday, July 20, 1944, under the headline "Baptized Jews Return to Their Ancestral Faith." I have found the same article in the *Wisconsin Jewish Chronicle* and the *Detroit Jewish News* of July 21, and it was undoubtedly printed by other Jewish periodicals as well. I cannot, however, find the "Ankara (JPS)" source for the article, and the content seems so totally distant from the contemporary reality in Hungary that it may well have been a hoax. In July 1944, many Hungarian Jews were converting to Christianity in the hope that this would protect them from deportation; see Moshe Y. Herczl; *Christianity and the Holocaust of Hungarian Jewry*, pp. 224–27. Compare the story in a sermon by Shlomo Ehrenreich about one individual Jewish convert who decided to return (October 22, 1943, above).

Granted that we American Jews are in danger, granted that what has happened to German Jewry is likely to overtake us,[44] our acceptance of this tragic possibility does not mean that we are to build bridges for our retreat. What it should mean is that when that evil hour comes we shall be strong and determined and organized to fight for our heritage as Americans – fight with all we have and are, with no thought of retreat, fight like brave soldiers, and if we go down in defeat, we go down with the conviction that from our blood and our tears America will arise reborn as the land of the free and the home of the brave, and that in (108:) re-born America our children's children will find peace and security, even as our fathers found under the stars and stripes.

Israel Mattuck, "A New Era," Liberal Jewish Synagogue, London, unpublished[45]

(1:) The end of the war will begin a new era.... The Nazis wanted to make the world different, they planned "a new order," but it was all wrong because it meant merely a world dominated by them, with many nations serving Germany's interests and satisfying the boastful delusion that the Germans are the master race....

The victory of the Allies will save mankind from degradation and civilization from destruction. But it will have to do more. Nazism was a horrible symptom of a diseased condition in the state of humanity. And like a parasite, it aggravated the weakness which first gave it the chance to establish itself. When it is extirpated, the weakness on which it fed must be remedied...

44 A rather extraordinary expression of insecurity concerning the fate of the American effort, which seems totally out of place for September 1944, although that is the way it is marked in the published collection of Cohon's sermons, and the date is confirmed by reference to persecution of Hungarian Jews as reported in the July 1944 *Jewish Advocate* (103), and to "our new house of prayer" (101), with confirmation on the website of Temple Sinai that the congregation moved to its new location in 1944.

45 19.9.1944 is written on text, but this could not have been delivered on the second day of Rosh Hashanah (a Tuesday), as British Liberal Jews observed only one day; my assumption is that it should have been Sept. 18, 1944, the first day, although there is no explicit reference to the holiday.

(3:) The persecution of the German Jews by the Nazis was a warning signal. The danger to civilization which it signified has been overcome at a terrible (4:) cost in blood, tears and toil. But what of the future?...It is our hope that in the new era which will begin with the victory of the United Nations all men everywhere will be protected against oppression and persecution....

In Italy, Romania and Bulgaria the oppressive laws decreed against [the Jews] under the direction of the Nazis have been cancelled. Even in Hungary, which remains bound to the shattered Nazi chariot, the doom which hung over its Jews a year ago has been lightened.[46] The Jews in the countries liberated from the Nazi yoke have the promises of their respective governments that they will be restored to their full rights. All that gives solid ground for our hopes for the future. We cannot, and should not forget the past, the millions of Jews who have been slaughtered, and the others whose lives have been broken. But their death and suffering will not have been in vain if they have roused the conscience of humanity to realise the duty to assure all men everywhere their human rights....

Michael Elton (formerly Emil Ehrnthal), "Post-War Plans," London. *The Challenge of Destiny*, pp. 38–42

(40:) Great is the human misery in this vast conflict, but far greater is the *Jewish* misery. Year after year we read with resignation and war-torn apathy about the abominable massacres of our women and children, the ghastly labour camps for our young brothers who still had the strength to work for the Nazi slave-drivers, about "plague, death and famine" daily ravaging the surviving Jewish quarters under the power of the savage oppressor.... The Jewish masses have been on a daily retreat before the Nazi power ever since 1933.

---

46 This is a rather strange statement, as it shows no apparent awareness of the massive deportation of Hungarian Jews to Auschwitz-Birkenau during the preceding months, following the German occupation of Hungary in March 1944, and the death by gassing of hundreds of thousands. This was reported in the *JC* on June 2, p. 7 (preparations for deportation); June 30, p. 1 ("100,000 Hungarian Jews Perish"); July 14, pp. 1 and 7; July 21, pp. 1 and 9; and August 11, pp. 1 and 7. *JC* September 1, p. 8, carried a report that deportations to Auschwitz, which had been halted, were beginning again.

[The heroic Jews of the Warsaw Ghetto] brought reality to the words, "Who shall die by fire, by water, by the sword or by famine."[47] They were the first people who openly, even though hopelessly, (41:) tried to defy the Nazi monster. Theirs was not the way of retreat, theirs was the cry of the men who rode in the Valley of Death.[48]

Jacob Kaplan, "The Rosh Hashanah of Liberation and Justice" (*Le Roch Hachana de la libération et de la justice*), Synagogue de Lyon, France. *Les Temps d'épreuve*, pp. 143–48, translated by MS

(143:) Five years we have passed in anxiety and pain, an ever deepening anxiety and pain. Remember:

- Rosh Hashanah 1939: husbands, fathers, sons, brothers departing for the front, a terrible threat weighing upon every home in France;
- Rosh Hashanah 1940: the first of our defeats, the "Jewish Statute" is enacted,[49] anti-Jewish persecution is organized;
- (144:) Rosh Hashanah 1941: the hunt for Jews has begun, the Drancy camp is open, every day many of our brothers succumb to mistreatment and malnourishment;
- Rosh Hashanah 1942: deportations to Germany, by the thousands, Jews both French and alien, from the northern Zone and the southern Zone, Lyon observing trains filled with the wretched coming from Rivesaltes, from Marseilles and from Nice;
- Rosh Hashanah 1943: French Judaism is on the road to vanishing, without any further kind of security, its only hope, in human terms, remains with the arrival of the liberators, though it is still necessary that they arrive in time;
- Rosh Hashanah 1944: the liberators have arrived, almost all of French territory has been freed, the dark veil has been torn off, we stand alongside life, light, liberty. We are revived....

---

47 Citing a passage from the *Unetaneh Tokef* passage of the High Holy Day Liturgy. The same passage is cited in the following sermon by Jacob Kaplan.

48 Citing a passage from Tennyson's "Charge of the Light Brigade."

49 The "Jewish Statute," addressed in earlier sermons by Kaplan, was passed on the first day of Rosh Hashanah, October 3, 1940.

(145:) Yet... the blessed hour has not yet sounded. There are our dear prisoners, there are our dear deportees. For this last group, we do not know that they are returning. There are more than 100,000, the population of a large French town; will they all come back? How sorrowfully resonant in our hearts are the words which we read in our prayers today: "Who shall live, who shall die; who of natural death, who of accidental death; who by steel [*fer*], who by fire [*feu*]; who by water, who by famine?" At least we have retained a glimmer of hope....

(146:) While the families of those who have been deported are in a state of poignant uncertainty, a prey at times to anguish, at times to hope, there are also the homes among us that have been visited by death. Many of our fellow Jews have fallen on the battlefield, as well as in the front line of the resistance. Many are those who have been savagely massacred by the Hitlerian monsters and their mignons; those who have lost their lives during military operations in which the victims were civilian populations. Brothers and sisters who have disappeared: you have your place – a place of honor – in our thoughts on this Rosh Hashanah when we celebrate our resurrection....

Ephraim Sokolover, Great Synagogue, Ra'anana, Palestine. *Penei Efrayim*, pp. 39–42, translated by MS

(40:) Is there a more appropriate way [than silence] to articulate the distress of the Jewish people at this moment before the sounding of the shofar? Is there amongst us *anyone* who would dare to open his mouth to arouse or inspire, beyond an outpouring of the soul? If we could find the right moment, serious and stirring, in which we could unite ourselves with the millions of "the fallen of my people" (Jer. 8:23), in this moment, in which would be heard the voice of our brothers' blood "crying out to us from the land" (cf. Gen. 4:10), would not this terrifying voice silence our own voice, so that we would not be able to utter a single sound?...

(41:) Recently we have issued an announcement coming from the leaders of the Polish state, calling upon all citizens of the state "to refrain from joyous celebration," because of the distress of the people and the state. Similarly, our own highest institutions have decreed that this should be a year of mourning, after having confirmed with certainty all the reports that have reached us throughout the past year until now. But practically speaking, it is apparently difficult to impose a decree with full force upon the public, when the public is not prepared to accept such a decree....

Zvi Hirsch Meisels, Sermon to children in Auschwitz. *Mekaddeshei HaShem*, *"Sha'ar Maḥmadim,"* pp. 12–13, translated by MS[50]

(12:) I therefore responded to their request,[51] and I thought, "Let come what may" upon me. And so I began to preach: "Regarding the verse, 'Blow the shofar on the new moon, when it is concealed (*bakheseh*) for the day of our rejoicing' (Ps. 81:4): note today, how so much is concealed, and no one among us knows where it all leads: where the evil ones will bring all of our families, and what will become of us, who will emerge from this place in peace, and the great extent of divine self-concealment," and so forth. And I cited for them the rabbinic statement from Berakhot (10a), "Even if there is a sharp sword placed against a man's neck, he should not abandon his hope for compassion," and in the Yerushalmi of Avodah Zarah (1,1), the statement is continued: "Not only this but even when there is a sword against a man's neck, the Holy One, praised be He, may

50 I first learned of Rabbi Meisels through an unpublished article by Daniel Landes entitled "Death, Deconstruction and *Derashot*: The Auschwitz Sermons of Zvi Hirsch Meisels," cited in a long footnote by Gershon Greenberg. Rabbi Landes graciously sent me the article, and responded to several of my questions.

51 The context is explained on the previous page: a group of some four hundred teenagers had been consigned to a special bloc on Rosh Hashanah, with the understanding that they would be sent to the gas chambers at the end of the day. Meisels recognized that some were his own students from his community. He started to cite, "Out of the depths I call to You, O Lord" (Ps. 130:1) as an introduction to the sounding of the shofar, but the youngsters beseeched him to speak to them directly. For the details of the situation as described by Meisels, see Robert Kirschner, *Rabbinic Responsa of the Holocaust Era*, pp. 114–21; for a description of Meisel's speech describing this situation, delivered in London at an Agudas Israel World Conference in December 1945, see *JC*, December 7, 1945, p. 6 (I am grateful to Menachem Butler for this reference). Chana Hendler has discussed this text in a Hebrew article, in *Zikaron baSefer* (2008), pp. 87–91.

save him from it, for Moses said, 'He saved me from the sword of Pharaoh'" (Exod. 18:4).

And I explained the verse from Psalms, "I raise my eyes to the mountains, from where will my help come? My help is from the Lord, creator of heaven and earth" (Ps. 121:1). Now apparently there is a question: why did he have to explain about the Lord, blessed be He, that He created the heaven and earth? And why did he need to raise his eyes to the mountains in order to find help? (see in *B'nai Issachar*, Hanukkah, passage 2, what he says about this.)[52]

It seems to me that we can explain this as follows. Sometimes a person may be surrounded on all sides by high and lofty mountains, to the point where he knows inwardly that there is no natural way of escaping. Even if he knows that eventually a general deliverance will come, and even if the believer knows that those who hate the Jews will reach a downfall, this knowledge is not a source of comfort and strength, for he also knows that his life is hanging on the balance for the next few moments.

That is why David came to strengthen the person who is in an evil situation like this, telling him that he should believe in God, who created the heaven and the earth in a single moment, as it says in Psalms, "By the word of the Lord the heavens were made" (Ps. 33:6), and by a signal from God the entire world was created. If that is true, how much more is it totally clear that God can deliver a person in a single moment, even when there is a sharp sword placed against his neck. That is why the Psalmist said, "I will raise my eyes to the mountains," for I am totally surrounded by cursed people who hate me, enclosing me like the mountains. "From where will *my help* come?" – for my own deliverance depends upon a single moment. That is why the answer comes to strengthen him: "My help comes from the Lord, *Creator of heaven and earth*," which was created in a single moment; therefore I can trust in God that he will send His sacred help.

I also cited the words of my honorable grandfather, the holy

52 This parenthetical statement, referring to a large book of homiletical material by Zvi Elimelech Shapira, was obviously intended for later readers, not for the children he was addressing.

gaon from Uhel [Ujhely], regarding the prayer of Moses in Psalm 62: "Trust in Him at all times, O people; pour out your hearts before Him, God is our refuge, Selah" (Ps. 62:9), based on the Gemara in tractate Rosh Hashanah,[53] that with regard to the Jewish people, even after the evil decree has been issued, when they cry out to God, they are answered. This is the meaning of "Trust in Him at all times" - even after the evil decree has been issued. The meaning of "O people" is that their uniqueness as a people is to "pour out your hearts before Him," and when you pour out your hearts before God, who is the attribute of Mercy, "He will be our refuge, Selah."[54]

September 19, 1944 (second day of Rosh Hashanah)

Abraham E. Halpern, "Labor Looks to Religion," Congregation B'nai Amoona, St. Louis, MO. *A Son of Faith*, pp. 70–74

(71:) This summer I heard the eminent Christian minister, Harry Fosdick, speak in his church at Riverside Drive, in New York. In the course of his address, he too took cognizance of the failure of the church in preventing the horrible war. But, he added, "so did science fail; and so did other institutions outside the Church fail." But while no one denies the truth of the assertion that science and the universities failed to prevent the war, yet it does not mitigate in any way, and doesn't excuse religion for its failure. From religion we expected a courageous voice to condemn not only the apparent sins against God, (72:) but also the real sins of evil committed by men against God's children. It was in this that we find the breach between the realities of life and the abstractions of theology. Very often people asked "Where is God?" I will venture to say it was not done to deny the existence of God, but to challenge the institutions that assumed to speak in the name of God. It was a challenge that struck at all who were the official spokesmen of religion and religious institutions.

---

53 Cf. b. Rosh Hashanah 17b.

54 This is followed by seven paragraphs of smaller type, which is clearly intended for subsequent readers, not as a record of what he said to the children under these harrowing conditions. After the seven paragraphs, there is a new section entitled "Final conversations before they were burned."

The war will soon end, please God, and we are told, as the Germans surrender, millions of our boys will return home; then the real problem of adjustment will have to be made....

(73:) Many a man is broken and becomes desperate when he finds that he is helpless to provide for his dear ones. It was this that gave Hitler his first power. It was this that strengthened the hands of Mussolini. They took advantage of the helplessness in which the great mass of people found themselves. It was when the people lost hope that they became the followers of the false Messiahs who promised (74:) them security in exchange for the priceless possession of man: liberty.... The rabble rousers and raucous voices took advantage of all this, and we have plenty of would be dictators and rabble rousers here in America....

Abraham M. Hershman, "God and Man," Congregation Shaarey Zedek, Detroit, MI. *Israel's Fate and Faith*, pp. 55–58

(56:) The old world is passing; a new one is struggling for emergence. The war is not yet over. We know, however, that final victory is only a matter of time. He who runs may read the writing on the wall announcing the doom of Nazidom, "the dominion of tyranny." But we too are anxious, troubled. In the light of past experience, we ask, What will the New Era look like? Will the war be followed by creation and construction or by chaos and confusion?

(58:) The world was shocked when it learned of the outrages committed in Lidice. We Jews have had hundreds of Lidices.[55]

> The air is full of farewells to the dying,
> And mourning for the dead;
> The heart of Rachel, for her children crying,
> Will not be comforted.[56]

Tens of thousands of our people are pining in concentration camps. Multitudes are either in hiding or on the high seas looking for a

55 See above the phrase used by Stephen S. Wise and Harold I. Saperstein (and undoubtedly others as well) in 1942.

56 Citing Longfellow, "Resignation."

place of refuge. To us too comes the call, "And there is a time to build up." If this call is not to fall on deaf ears, we must present a united front to the world.

We are told that, when King Albert of Belgium addressed Parliament on the eve of Germany's invasion of his country in 1914, he said, "The Assembly has only one party, that of the country."[57] We too must feel in the present emergency that we have only one party, that of Israel.

Abraham A. Kellner, "The Tomorrows That Sing," Congregation Sons of Abraham, Albany, NY. *A Rabbi's Faith*, pp. 9–15

(14:) Life's greatest need, man's most compelling necessity, civilization's most urgent obligation is to interpret properly the impact of our times and to discern in the rhythm of the cosmic forces unloosed about us an inherent promise of faith in the ultimate goodness of humanity that will transform our weeping yesterdays into singing tomorrows. . . .

I ask you, sisters and brethren, to believe with me in the tomorrows that will sing, to believe that out of the chaos and confusion caused by the cruel abominations of a demolished domain, that out of the sorrow and suffering that walk in the wake of global war, that out of the debris of desolation that is the tragic concomitant of the powers of destruction, that out of all these tragic (15:) manifestations and harrowing experiences will emerge the forces of peace and unity that will burst terrestrial bounds, mending the broken fragments of man with the age old and never tarnished assurance, *Shalom, shalom larochok v'la korov omar hashem u'rfosiv* ["'Peace, peace to the far and the near,' says the Lord, 'and I shall heal them'"] (Isa. 57:19).

September 24, 1944 (Sunday)

Louis I. Newman, "Good People and Their Atonement," Radio Address for "The Message of Israel, Station WJZ. *Biting on Granite*, 296–302

57 The preacher here appears to have confused the Belgian king with Kaiser Wilhelm II, whose famous speech to the German Parliament on August 4, 1914 contained the words, "*Ich kenne keine Parteien mehr, kenne nur noch Deutsche.*"

(300:) It behooves us, also, as Americans, to make atonement before the God of the Nations for our sins of omission and commission in days past. It is true that we came to the assistance of free Europe a generation ago and a second time in our own day. But in the intervening years, the historians (301:) agree that we dedicated ourselves to our national self-aggrandizement, careless of the well-being of other countries.... *Noblesse oblige*! Let us not be niggardly with our surplus wealth, we whose cities have been unbombed and whose losses have been fractional compared to the tragedies undergone by our European and Oriental comrades. Let us remember that America must never deviate from her mission to be "a light to the world."

September 26, 1944 (Kol Nidre)

Ferdinand M. Isserman, no title, Temple Israel, St. Louis, MO. AJA, MS-6, Box 16, Folder 8

(4:) Germany...massacred the Jews of Europe, beginning with the massacre of Jews within its own borders. No darker page has ever been written in the whole story of mankind than the record of the mass execution with modern scientific equipment in the murder factories created in Poland by the Nazi regime. Mass production, conceived to elevate the common man, was used to destroy human life. How many Jews there will be left in Europe occupied by the Nazis no one can tell as yet. Five to six million Jews lived in these territories; eight million if we include the Jews in occupied Russia. How many will be left when the roll will be called? Slaughtered like cattle, in Bukarest the Abitour [*sic*] was used.[58] Communities that have existed in Europe since the early days of the Roman Empire have been extirpated, and the murderers have tried to obliterate by scientific chemistry the evidence of their crime so that not even the skeletons of the victims shall remain to testify against the murderer. But why plague your ears with further details. The tragic tale has been with you, alas, too much....

---

58 See above, Ephraim Sokolover, April 18, 1941. It is unclear why Isserman chose to emphasize more than three and a half years later this one event, in which some two hundred Jews were tortured and killed, and whether any of the congregants listening to his sermon would have understood the allusion.

Our time of service is accomplished. We have paid doubly for our sins [cf. Isa. 40:2]. Tonight we see the dawn. With the fall of the Nazi regime will go the repudiation of the Nazi philosophy and anti-semitism, its corner stone....

(6:) No greater calamity can befall the Jewish community than for it to become embittered and to yield to cynicism, to turn its back upon idealism, to sneer at world brotherhood and at good will between men, to become skeptical of the capacities of the human spirit. Such a spiritual calamity would be far more devastating than anything the Nazis have done. They have destroyed the bodies of Jews, but they must not be permitted to destroy the inner citadel, the stronghold of the soul, for then they will have achieved (7:) their goal.

(8:) What shall we Jews demand that the victorious powers do to the Nazis? If we speak with our first emotions we might be tempted to demand that the German peoples be obliterated from the face of the earth, that their cities be destroyed, their fields laid waste, and chemicals that will destroy the fertility be introduced into the soil. I have personally experienced in my own family the cruelty, the brutal insensitivity of the Nazi leaders. My father's brother died in a concentration camp. One of my mother's sisters died in another concentration camp. My brother and sister and my mother and their families in Belgium have disappeared as if they had vanished from the face of the earth.[59]...

(9:) At times in the bitterness of my soul I have cried out "*Germania delenda est*: Germany must be destroyed" as completely as ancient Hebrew tribes destroyed the peoples against whom they fought. If I yielded to these thoughts, I might have temporary emotional satisfaction, but when I think about it, I realize that it is absolutely impossible to achieve that.... (10:) Let us not share in the wholesale condemnation of any group.

Abraham Cohen, "Kol Nidre, 1944," Birmingham Hebrew Congregation, Birmingham, England. Unpublished, David Cohen Private Collection

(1:) It is not customary in this congregation for a sermon to be included in the Kol Nidre service, and if I do so this evening it is

59 Isserman continues describing his own experience with the Nazis during his three visits; see his earlier sermons from 1933, 1935, and 1938, above.

because, for obvious reasons, this is no ordinary occasion. In the long history of this community, extending back nearly two centuries, the holding of this most solemn service of the whole year was interrupted for the first time in 1939 by the stringent black-out regulations which followed the declaration of war. For five years we have been unable to assemble for Kol Nidre, and we must all have keenly felt the deprivation.... [Now] the tide of battle has receded from the shores of this country and is overflowing the enemy's frontiers....

(5:) Throughout our prayers this evening and tomorrow runs the word "sin."...That there is a pronounced lowering of moral standards in our time is admitted by competent observers. It stands to the credit of the Nazis that, unlike other peoples, they had the honesty to make no pretense that they recognized abstract rightness and wrongness. What was advantageous to their cause, that was right. Hitler once unwittingly paid Jewry a high compliment by saying that conscience was a Jewish invention!...

Under the influence of our (6:) religious doctrine, we should see in the doom of the Nazis clear evidence of Divine judgment, the punishment for sin....

Two years ago, in a Yom Kippur sermon, I quoted a passage from a book then recently published by the famous Jewish novelist, Shalom Asch, entitled, *My Personal Faith*. It is worth quoting again...:

> Who, then, can fail to see, in that which has happened to us (he means mankind at large) the finger of God?...Hitler first tried the sword with which he now destroys nations on the throats of Jews; now the nations pay, one by one, for the indifference - or was it (7:) worse than indifference; was there in it a touch of malicious delight? - which they displayed when Nazism acquired by practice on Jews that expertness in savagery which it now visits on all.... We have all sinned. We are all guilty in the calamity which has come upon us. All of us must beat our breasts in confession. A great Day of Atonement must come over the world.

How truly that was said.... When the thoughts and feelings that this day aims at arousing in our hearts are stirred in the hearts of all peoples, then there is hope for a bright future - a future in which the martyrdom of man, and with it the martyrdom of Jewry, will end.

September 27, 1944 (Yom Kippur)

Abraham A. Kellner, "Three Years of Famine" (*Yizkor*), Congregation Sons of Abraham, Albany, NY. *A Rabbi's Faith*, pp. 34–40

(34:) The painful record of wartime losses, augmented so heavily by the destruction wrought upon European Jewry, causes us to mourn this morning more than our own personal sorrows and anguish would warrant....

(39:) This obligation imposed upon us [to safeguard the legacy of freedom of those killed in combat] is rendered all the more difficult because the attainment calls for battling two foes, not only those from without, but also those forces of entrenched social reaction in our midst, those sinister voices of chauvinistic nationalists who are already at work seeking to engulf within their prisoned tentacles the soul of American Public Opinion.

All our sobbing laments and profuse tears will not memorialize our people's martyrs who were the first victims of the present world conflagration. Our Yiskor will be lacking in completeness unless we reinforce it with diligent activities to rescue and rehabilitate those of their kin who are still within the reach of merciful salvation.

Louis I. Newman, "The Message of Jonah," Congregation Rodeph Sholom, New York. *Biting on Granite*, pp. 309–19

(317:) Yes, there is compassion here, and immense pity for human beings and other dumb creatures. But the essential point is that the people of Nineveh underwent genuine penitence. I suppose that many an indignant prophet today speaking of Fascist Italy, Germany and Japan will be disappointed like Jonah, if the Lord and His mortal emissaries do not visit (318:) complete punishment upon the sinful nations. We have yet to be convinced that they will undertake sincere and authentic contrition; that they will make restitution, insofar as it is possible. But if the reliable proofs are brought, and if the people truly reform, then God will enjoin us to show the pity He displayed towards the erring Ninevites.

Edward Klein, "Navigators of the Soul," Stephen S. Wise Free Synagogue, New York. AJA, MS 702, Box 2, Folder 7

(1:) What *are* the sins we would confess? Though they be many, *three* seem central.

We have sinned as Americans, and in this horrible war are reaping the harvest. We failed to understand that peace must be won as war is won, by effort.... (2:) Woodrow Wilson was crucified for his dream of one world, supervised by a League of Nations. American citizens crushed that dream to earth, and trampled it in the mud....

Japan invaded Manchuria, and we supplied the armaments. Italy invaded Ethiopia, and we looked the other way. Hitler declared war on the Jews, thus announcing his intention of war on the world. Some saw the danger. This very pulpit rang with warnings.[60] But we did not heed. Nazis and Fascists warred on liberal Spain, and we withheld the arms that alone make effective resistance possible. But these are sins of the *past*.... Will we lose another opportunity to build a lasting peace?...

"*Al Chet she-Chatanu*," for the sin which we have sinned as Jews. Even (3:) as American foreign policy has been isolationist, so American Jews have been isolationist. We have isolated ourselves from our culture. All too many American Jews are Jews by the grace of Hitler, driven back to their people by the slings and arrows of the anti-Semite. They have no roots in Judaism, they have no burning love for their people; they would salve a troubled conscience by an occasional gift to a Jewish charity, or a casual visit to the Synagogue. Every hour of every day, the breath of life is crushed from our people in the charnel-house of Europe, yet how many American Jews have given their support to programs of rescue? 3,000,000 European Jews will be homeless after this war; how many of their American brothers give their support to Palestine that the homeless may find life instead of lingering death? While Jews are being crucified, we argue about Zionism: is it practical? is it nationalistic? will it endanger our status? Hatred of the Jew is preached on street corners throughout the land, we hesitate to discuss it, to support Jewish defense organizations, lest we set ourselves apart....

"*Al Chet she-Chatanu*," for the sin which we have sinned as individ-

---

60 Obviously referring to sermons and addresses by Rabbi Stephen S. Wise.

uals, as men. Even as America, before the war, isolated itself from the nations of the world, and as some American Jews have isolated themselves from their people, so too many of us have isolated ourselves from God....

Jacob Kaplan, "That Our Test May Not Be in Vain, (*Pour que notre épreuve ne soit pas vaine*)," Lyon Synagogue, France. *Le Temps d'épreuve*, pp. 149–56, translated by MS

(151:) For us as Israelites, the downfall of Hitlerism entails spiritual consequences that we must contemplate. We have to ask ourselves: will we know how to render the horrifying test through which we have passed fully effective? You certainly know that each test must result in our coming closer to God, inspiring in us a religious reawakening. God make it be so for our own experience, for if it were anything else, all these martyrs of Judaism, whose number totals in the millions, would have perished for nothing! All (152:) the blood spread across the earth as it had never before been in any previous time in our history would have been spilt in vain!...

(153:) And the magnificent example of our brothers in the concentration camps who organized religious ceremonies and openly, publically affirmed their commitment to the God of Israel; and that of our fellow Jews in Montluc Fort who, under the guidance of the first minister of our community,[61] celebrated morning and evening worship services; and that of all the young people who were given the task of studying and extending Judaism, who struggled against persecution with courage and self-sacrifice that bears witness to the number of them who were martyred and deported, among whom we sense the throb of the noble ambition to do honor even in the worst circumstances to the name of Israel.[62]

61 Note in the text: "M. Dreyfus, arrested, disappeared in deportation." Montluc Fort was a prison in Lyon that was used by the Nazis from November 1942 until its liberation in late August 1944. Many of the Jews who were interned at Montluc were deported to Auschwitz during the summer of 1944. Dreyfus is said to have held the position of "premier ministre-officiant."

62 For a selection from this sermon in the original French, see David Shapira, *Jacob Kaplan*, pp. 167–68.

October 1, 1944 (Sunday, Erev Sukkot)

David B. Hollander, "The Blessing of Small Beginnings," Mount Eden Jewish Center, Bronx, NY. In Rosenberg and Heuman, eds., *Theological and Halakhic Reflections on the Holocaust*, pp. 29–38

(29:) The festival of harvest brings to our mind this year [1944] not a harvest of crops and of food to gladden the heart of man, but a grim harvest of death. The fields which God intended to produce for man the staff of life have been turned into huge battlefields and graveyards for the flower of youth. Perhaps never before in the history of man's corruption has his capacity for crime reached such terrifying proportions and taken such a heavy toll of human life....

(30:) Wherever we cast our eyes we see nothing but the destruction of thousands of cities, towns, and villages with their inhabitants blown off the face of the earth. Cities formerly inhabited by tens of thousands of Jews became overnight cities without Jews. Our hearts ache as we think of the huge centers of Jewish intellectual and religious endeavor, the great centers of commerce and industry built with weary but determined hands that are today no more than a graveyard of nameless tombs. Vilna, the cradle of Jewish learning in Lithuania, Minsk, the great White Russian center, Warsaw, Kovno, Bialystok, Pressburg, Lemberg, unthinkable but true: cities without Jews!

(31:) The ruthless powers of the world, those that plunged mankind into this great war, have chosen that criminal course primarily because they forgot that once they, too, were not greater than the small nations they now chose to devour. In short, they did not observe and study the character of the sukkah....

(32:) But it is not only the enemy countries that are now reaping the harvest of their failure to recall that the *dirat arai* [temporary abode] preceded their *dirat keva* [permanent abode], and consequently they lost all sense of justice, but also the enlightened nations of the world, those in whose hands has been entrusted the destiny of freedom and democracy, they too are desperately in need of the message of the sukkah.... Today, when America is great and strong and rich, at a time when its vast expanse of fertile land and natural resources could sustain half the world, it would be very beneficial indeed if the immigrant haters, the race mongers, and that whole lunatic fringe of native Fascists would go over to the chest, as it were, and look down upon that curious array of Dutch, French and English immigrants, (33:) yes, not pioneers, but immigrants, refugees. Then perhaps they would not employ the term "foreigner" as the most disgraceful epithet in the American vocabulary....

(33:) But an even more glaring example of the sin of not celebrating Sukkot is presented by Great Britain.... And perhaps its first manifestation of the abandonment of the sukkah and the return to its haughty feeling of empire has been [its attitide] toward the question of the Jewish National Home. The sympathy of this great power for wretched world Jews, for the tattered remnants of Israel, has varied inversely with its successes in this war. If only England could place itself into the *dirat arai* in which the Jew has been living all these centuries; if only England would remember that the Jews have suffered a thousand Dunkirks to its one, without the facilities of naval evacuation at their command, it would no doubt fulfill its obligations toward the people who wrote and lived the sacred writ – the Bible – which the English people cherish.

(38:) Will American Israel remember that he too was pulled out of the holds of ships coming over the Atlantic drawn out of the flood of hatred and pogroms? Will he remember now that he considers himself as living in a *dirat keva*? Will he remember that but for the grace of God his fate today might have been indescribably tragic? Will he remember? Our ancient sukkah answers in the affirmative....

October 8, 1944 (Sunday, Erev Shemini Atseret)

Abraham M. Hershman, "Sowing and Reaping," Congregation Shaarey Zedek, Detroit. *Israel's Fate and Faith*, pp. 120–23.

(120:) Think, for instance, of Palestine as it is today – the hope it holds out for those who languish in concentration camps, or those who live in lands where life is insufferable and in a higher sense for Israel the world over – and Palestine as it was sixty years ago. But for the foundation laid by the early settlers, the spade work done by them, Palestine (121:) would still be a barren wilderness.... The hostile Arabs did their utmost to crush the hope of the pioneers. But the latter, undaunted, proceeded with their task....

(122:) We are all warriors in the battle of life – the battle of humanity. It is true that most of us may be characterized as "unknown" soldiers. It is well to remember, however, that the lion's share of the victory won in any battle belongs to the "unknown" soldier. But for him the fight would have been lost.

Louis I. Newman, "The Pangs of the Messiah," Radio Message on WOR. *Biting on Granite*, pp. 328–34

(328:) The essential theme of this great Hebrew concept is that it is darkest before the dawn; that the very moment we least expect deliverance, it is certain to come.

It may well be that the worst of our tribulations are in the past – that nothing can equal our despair when France fell, when England was under fire, when the first news came to us of the slaughter of more than five millions of the Jewish people in Eastern Europe.... Yet we know that there are days of tribulation and suffering ahead, and it has been correctly said that the march to victory and deliverance will subject us to the most terrible anguish. And when will our heartache end?

(331:) Another assurance that the very depth of our anguish is a harbinger of better days can be found in the fact that the pogroms and massacres inflicted upon European Jewries serve as a goad to the conscience of Israel and mankind.... The American Jewish community has learned anew that a primary task is to rescue before it is too late the remnants of our people who have survived the Nazi horrors of mass extermination in gas-chambers and at graves dug by the hands of those about to be slain. The problem of finding asylum for the survivors in Palestine and other lands was considered in statesmanlike spirit at the recent sessions of the American Jewish Conference in New York City – one of the greatest assemblages in the annals of the ancient people of Israel....[63]

63 This may be referring to the massive Open-Air Demonstration held at and outside Madison Square Garden on July 31, 1944 (with extensive coverage by JTA, August 1).

(332:) And let us believe that the very horrors of the war itself are likewise akin to the "pangs of the Messiah." The pulverizing of European cities by bombardment – the man-made ruins of Pompeii side by side with the nature-made ruins of centuries ago – the wreckage of beautiful Naples, and the increasing destruction of German cities by aerial attack – all of these horrors should impress upon present-day war-makers, and any would-be conspirators of tomorrow, that war is so hateful and horrible, it must be abandoned forever.

(333:) Yes, the advent of the Allied Armies is like a Messianic miracle for the occupied countries. In the days to come let us believe that this marvel will be attained by the millions still in bondage; that step by step as our victorious armies advance – even into Germany itself – liberation from the barbarians (334:) will be granted; those in bondage will emerge from their caves and their cellars, and once again mankind will be free, free from tyranny, from savagery and all the torments which have afflicted us until now.

JACOB KAPLAN, "Spiritual Rebirth and Material Reconstruction (*Renaissance spirituelle et reconstruction matérielle*)," Synagogue de Lyon, France. *Le Temps d'épreuve*, pp. 157–63, translated by MS[64]

(161:) Where our enemies sought to humiliate us, have I sufficiently explained to you the grandeur of the name of Israel? Where they sought to drive us to despair, have I sufficiently communicated the reasons for confidence in the future? Have I sufficiently shown that, despite all appearances, we were NOT abandoned by God, but to the contrary, our trials testified that we were always representing the ideas of the divine, and that these were what was being attacked through [the attacks on] our people?

October 15, 1944 (Sunday)

ABBA HILLEL SILVER, Address to the Zionist Organization of America Conference, Atlantic City, NJ. Selections taken from Ofer Shiff, *The Downfall of Abba Hillel Silver*, p. 57

64 At the beginning of his sermon, Kaplan announced to his congregation that he would be leaving Lyon at the end of the holiday in order to return to his position in Paris, and emphasized the attachment he felt for the community of Lyon in its suffering.

The world was silent at the ruins and outrage of a whole people.... A ten-year cycle of slaughter and assault at the hands of a people and a government...which sacked and ravaged a thousand Jewish communities, slew 3 million men, women, and children in horrible human abattoirs and crematories, and filled the highways of the earth with frightened feeling refugees, evoked from the civilized world, from the democracies, from our own country, a few perfunctory acts of rescue which resulted in little more than nothing.... All our representations to our government to help save our doomed people in any way whatsoever resulted in pitifully little.... With all my supreme admiration for the great personalities who are our friends...I still say unto you, what the Psalmist said long ago, "Put not thy trust in princes" (Ps. 146:3).

November 1, 1944 (Wednesday)

Judah L. Magnes, "For Thy Sake Are We Killed All the Day Long" (Ps. 44:23): Opening of the Academic Year 1944/45, Hebrew University, Jerusalem. *In the Perplexity of the Times*, pp. 65–78

(65:) About four months ago a document was handed me in Istanbul. Forgive me for reading from so harrowing a statement:

> The newly built crematory and gas-chambers were opened in February, 1943. At the present moment 4 crematories are operating at Birkenau.... (66:) The daily capacity of the furnaces is about 2000 bodies. Alongside is a large waiting hall, constructed so as to give the impression of baths.... The victims are led into the hall where they are told that they are to bathe. There they undress, and in order to strengthen them in this belief, they are given a towel and soap. Then they are driven into the gas-chamber. When the doors are shut, S.S. men scatter a powder from metal containers through the opened valves into the room. The containers are marked "*Zyklon zur Schaedlingbekaempfung*" [for use against vermin] and have the trade-mark of a Hamburg firm. This seems to be a preparation of cyanide which becomes gaseous at a given temperature. In three minutes all are dead.[65]

65 The document which Magnes received in late June or early July 1944 was the Report

In all of human history there has never been anything like this, either in extent or in the methods employed. Even now, as proofs continue to pile up, our minds prefer to reject the truth. The hunt for myriads of human (67:) beings created in the Image is organized scientifically, and they are transported to these gates of hell and destroyed scientifically. One of our University chemists said, after reading this document, "As though it had been prepared for a scientific text-book, objectively, calmly." …

Is it possible that this can happen under God's heaven? I must raise this question, even though I have no adequate answer. It gives millions of men no rest. The world to-day faces many fateful problems, but none so momentous as this. Is there a living God for whom all this has meaning? Is there design and purpose? Or, is the universe ruled by a blind, unmoral force, by some *deus absconditus*, who created the world and is no longer interested in its fate – withdrawn, asleep, or gloating over the writhing of his creatures upon the earth? I try to evade this question, and cannot.

December 4, 1944 (Monday)

YEHEZKEL SARNA, "Toward Repentance and Resurgence," Address at mass gathering at Musar Knesset Israel-Slobodka Yeshiva in Jerusalem; Hebrew original in *Daliyot Yehezkel* III, pp. 303–23, translated by MS[66]

(306:) The Terrifying Destruction (*haḤurban haAyom*)

"I will make for it a unique mourning [*ke-evel yaḥid*], the end of it as on a bitter day" (Amos 8:10).

---

by Alfred Weczler and Rudolf Vrba, who had escaped from Auschwitz/Birkenau a few months earlier, reached Slovakia, and compiled a complete description of the camp, which eventually came to the US War Refugee Board and was released to the media. Cf. Dawidowicz, *A Holocaust Reader*, pp. 118 (obviously the same text in a different translation), and Lipstadt, *Beyond Belief*, p. 234, for newspaper reports. The opening of the academic year was apparently the first occasion when Magnes could speak publicly in detail about the reality of Birkenau and its implications.

66 See on this text Gershon Greenberg's article, "A Musar Response to the Holocaust: Yehezkel Sarna's *Le'teshuva U-le'tekuma* of 4 December 1944," and his own full translation in *Wrestling with God*, pp. 134–45. I am grateful to Prof. Greenberg for bringing this text to my attention; his discussion is primarily of theological issues not treated in the passages I have included.

Indeed, unique is our mourning. There is nothing like it in any other nation, nor [previously] within our own nation. The various expressions [*meshalim*] used by our predecessors to express the suffering of Israel during its exile do not fit the reality today. When David said, "For Your sake we are slain all day long; we are regarded as sheep to be slaughtered" (Ps. 44:23), it was not his intention to describe the greatness of the suffering but rather the tranquility of soul of those Jews who were giving their lives as martyrs, as the early commentators have written. "We are regarded as sheep to be brought to the slaughter": but has the world ever seen a flock of sheep brought (307:) to a slaughter like this? Brought in death trains by the tens of thousands for years, as our brothers have been transported by the vicious enemy? Has there been anything like the cruelty of the slaughtering? Woe to us for our calamity! At the time of the destruction [of the first Temple in 586 BCE], our nation was devastated, and from a people of many millions, only some tens of thousands were left, as explained at the end of Jeremiah [cf. 52:28–30]. Yet that was a war with heroism also on our side, and tens of thousands of our enemies fell in battle.

The slaughter and killing [of our ancestors] was not like the killing of flies, without any possibility of resistance: ugly deaths, fathers [falling] upon sons, mothers upon their children, the old together with the young. The humane animals come upon their prey, whether by trampling or tearing, for even they have an established practice – some trample but do not tear, others tear but do not trample. But these evil beasts trample and tear and show no compassion. There were those killed at Betar, a terrible, catastrophic destruction of an entire great city devoted to God, but together with their destruction, were they not worthy of a great act of kindness through a miracle revealed from heaven? Up to this day and forever the whole Jewish people recites a blessing for this favor, the blessing "Who is good and does good" [*hatov u-meitiv*], in that they were allowed to have a proper burial.[67] But millions of our fallen, "the slain of my people" (Jer. 8:23) have not even merited this. Woe to us.

---

67 Cf. Yitzhak Katz, Warsaw Ghetto, January 5, 1942, in "Complete Sermons," presenting a different aspect of the tradition. For rabbinic traditions on the massive

Our Sages tell us that after the destruction [of the first Temple], the prophet Jeremiah went and gathered the bones [of the dead] and hugged them and kissed them.[68] But we have not even been worthy of this merit. For where are the beloved bones [of our dead]? Who will give them to us to hug and kiss them? Are they not dust, turned into ashes in their ovens, where they were burned in their thousands and tens of thousands and then trampled upon in the black road of the enemy?

Yes indeed, our mourning is unique. What else is like it? What can be compared with it? It has nothing comparable.

The extent of the destruction is so terrifying; our calamity is as great as the sea, to the point where we cannot fathom it at all; it is not integrated within our ideas or encompassed within our thinking. We stand before it as if stricken dumb. We are like a baby at a time of grave misfortune in the home: he sees gloomy faces all around him – sorrow and grief – but his mind does not process all of the prevalent sadness and melancholy. What he notices most of all is something practical: that no food is given him at the usual time, and his needs are not attended to as normally. That is our lot today.

Therefore, the advice we receive is like that written in Scripture, "Mourn as an individual" (*evel yaḥid*, Jer. 6:26). That means, it is impossible to comprehend the mourning in its entirety, for it is too great for our minds to encompass, too deep for our accustomed emotions. Therefore each one of us must process this on our own, as an individual, for there is not a single individual Jew who will not have a share in this destruction, his very own share, whether for his father or mother, for his brother or another relative, for his teacher or his student, for his friend or his beloved. Let each one of us take our portion and make for ourselves an "individual mourning."...

---

slaughter and destruction of Betar, see Bialik and Ravnitzky, *The Book of Legends/ Sefer ha-Aggadah*, pp. 184–95, including "By Hadrian's decree, the corpses [of the thousands of Jews slain] remained unburied, until finally another king came to power and ordered their burial." For the addition of the blessing "...who is good and does good" to the *Birkat haMazon* (Grace after meals), see b. Ta'anit 31a.

68 See Louis Ginzberg, *Legends of the Jews* 4: 312 and 6: 403, n. 44, citing Eikha Rabbah, Introduction, 34, and Pesiqta deRav Kahana 13, 113b; also Micha Joseph bin Gorion, *Mimekor Yisrael*, 1:192.

(308:) The Spiritual Destruction

Country after country filled with Torah and fear of God has been lost with their brilliant scholars, their righteous and holy people, their rabbis and their students. Who can provide a replacement for them? Who can give us Lithuania with the depth of its scholarship? Who can give us Poland with the brilliance of its erudition? Who can give us Hungary with the integrity of its study? Who will provide us with the shining lights of Musar and the Rebbes of Hasidism? Our world is dark; who will illumine it?

After the incomparable destruction and mourning of the individual has been confirmed among us, the following biblical verses state, "A time is coming – declares my Lord God – when I will send a famine upon the land: not a hunger for bread or a thirst for water, but for hearing the words of the Lord. Men shall wander from sea to sea and from north to east to seek the word of the Lord, but they shall not find it" (Amos 8:11–12)....

(319:) Deeds of Lovingkindness

(320:) There are two kinds of lovingkindness: physical and spiritual. The physical:... for those who have been worthy of escaping from the inferno and have come [up] to our Holy Land, we must receive them with love and with joy, as a brother receives his brother after years of suffering and yearning, to care for them as a parent cares for his child, to behave toward them in accordance with the quality of hospitality appropriate for descendants of our father Abraham,[69] to remove from ourselves any sense of the terrible shame that these brothers might possibly feel in coming to us – that we have been worthy of divine mercy in living peacefully all these years while they were suffering hellish afflictions, wandering without a roof over their heads, impoverished, lacking everything, without food and shelter: Would it not make our faces red with embarrassment to be thinking of such things?...

(321:) As for spiritual lovingkindness, this is the constant concern that brings about spiritual improvement for our environment, to

69 Abraham as a model of hospitality, based on Gen. 18:1–5.

those near and far,... and especially to strengthen all of our efforts and thoughts concerning the condition of the darling children who have come to us from the Diaspora – the brands saved from the fire (cf. Zech. 3:2), most of whom are orphans, with no father or mother. Care and concern for them is handed over to the Jewish courts, which serve as the parents for orphans. We must fight their battle, lest they be taken away by oppressive individuals who will lead them to sin, worse for them than those who would have killed them.[70] We must bring them into our homes – whether individual or public homes – and we must be to them as fathers and mothers, reviving their souls by meeting all their physical and spiritual needs for a life of Torah and piety, as their holy parents would have wanted...."

December 30, 1944 (Saturday, *VaYeḥi*)

Abraham M. Hershman, "Hardheadedness and Softheartedness," Congregation Shaarey Zedek, Detroit, MI. *Israel's Fate and Faith*, pp. 173–75

[Gen. 50:17] (174:) The story of Joseph's reconciliation with his brothers should give us food for thought for these days. Germany has come to grief. It has sustained a crushing defeat at the hand of the Allies. The question is: "Does Germany grieve over its defeat or over the great crime it has perpetrated upon humanity?" Twice in a comparatively short time, it has plunged the world into the most ruthless wars in history.... No doubt, there are Germans who did not approve (175:) of the unspeakable brutalities of Hitler and his cohorts. But these were bereft of power, and probably constitute a minority. The German people as a whole cannot disclaim responsibility for the atrocities committed by the dominant and predominant element who have shaped the policy of that country. What is there to warrant the naïve belief that this global war will end war? The cessation of hostilities to which we are looking forward may be no more than a truce, an armistice, such as followed the last war.

A "soft peace" advocated by sentimentalists may lead to disastrous consequences. Not until Germany is prepared to admit its

70 Possibly referring to secular *kibbutzim*? Or sexual abuse?

culpability and say, "We are verily guilty concerning our brother nations! We have sown the dragon's teeth and are fully accountable for the welter of ruin into which the world has tumbled"; not until the world is convinced that what has happened twice before will not happen again, can it feel safe and breathe freely. In dealing with Germany, we dare not forget that "eternal vigilance is the price of liberty,"[71] that "the work of righteousness shall be peace, and the effect of righteousness, quietness and assurance forever" (Isa. 32:17).

---

71 A frequently cited quotation, often erroneously attributed to Thomas Jefferson; the original source is probably the American abolitionist Wendell Phillips, speaking to an Anti-Slavery Society in January, 1852.

1945

January 1, 1945 (Monday)

Woolf Hirsch, "Misunderstood Religion," Address at a Military Reception held by Christian Principal Chaplains, Pretoria, South Africa. *Selected Sermons and Addresses*, pp. 126–28

(128:) Jews will not forget the Christian priests in France, Holland, Belgium, Italy, maybe also in other countries, who, forgetting religious difference, at great peril to themselves saved thousands of Jewish children from the Nazi child-killers,[1] and they do not detain them in Christian monasteries, as they might have done a thousand years ago under the influence of misunderstood religion, but many at any rate hand them over to their kin, or to their people to whom they properly belong. Even in Germany, while science remained dumb, religion, in muffled voice, spoke out at times against Nazi inhumanity. And, if Germany is to be redeemed, she will be redeemed by this spirit of religion, if it survives there, and not by her *Kultur*, of which she boasted too loudly, and which a world, easily misled by appearance, appraised too highly.

January 19, 1945 (Friday evening)

Ferdinand M. Isserman, "The Christian Conference on Palestine," Temple Israel, St. Louis, MO. AJA, MS-6, Box 17, Folder 1

(1:) My mother's oldest sister lived in Belgium. When the Germans came, her daughter and granddaughters fled to France. She refused to accompany them, being over 70 years old she believed that she

1 For another contemporary reference, written by a French rabbi, to the role of French clergy in arranging for the concealment of Jewish children in the homes of French Christians or in convents, see Nathan Netter, *La Patrie égarée et la patrie renaissante*, p. 134–35.

could not stand the hazards of flight across the crowded highways of France, nor did she want to be in any way responsible for retarding the escape of her daughter and grandchildren. She decided to remain in Belgium. Not a word came from her after the German occupation. We presumed that she had fallen a victim to Nazi fury.... Several months ago, through the Belgian underground, my aunt's daughter, established in this country, received word that her mother was alive and well, that Belgian Christian families had sheltered her and had saved her from death in the murder camps of Poland. This episode of the rescue of a member of the Household of Israel through the courage and daring and sacrifice of Christians can be multiplied a thousand- and ten-thousand-fold. As the light of publicity is turned on liberated countries, we hear from France, from Italy, from Belgium,[2] from Holland, from Jugoslavia, from Greece, how tens of thousands of Jewish lives have been saved by merciful and compassionate Christians. This should serve to dissipate in the minds of Jews the horrible thought that the whole Christian world has turned against them.

January 30, 1945 (Tuesday)

Isaac Herzog, Address at the Gathering to Elect the (Third) Chief Rabbinic Council for the Land of Israel, at the Orphanage [*Beit haYetomim*], Jerusalem. *Masu'ah leYitzḥak*, pp. 150–54, translated by MS

(152:) Were it not that time is pressing, I would tell you at length about rabbis who devoted and endangered their lives to save their communities; about many rabbis who were given the possibility of escaping while there was still time but refused to leave their homes and abandon their community in its danger and died together with their congregation; about rabbis who [at a later time] could have been saved but refused, and went together with their flock on the path to slaughter, and made only one single request from the officer

2 For an example from Belgium, see Harold Saperstein, *Witness from the Pulpit*, pp. 110–11 and 233–34.

in charge of the execution: to be given time – half an hour – before the train started to move from the station, when he could deliver a sermon to his sacred congregation. What sermons, what inspiration: an echo of the voice of Micah and [Isaiah] the son of Amoz, what a flame they kindled deep in the hearts and souls of the sheep of their flocks during those awesome final moments!

How did that evil man begin (may his name be blotted out!)? He sensed in his satanic way that the Torah is the soul of the Jewish nation; thus before he would burn the Jews alive, he burnt the scrolls of the Torah. And when he began the actual annihilation, he first stretched his murderous hand against the rabbis, the bearers of Torah, the masters and fathers of Israel.

Since this Rabbinate is authorized especially to speak on behalf of the entire Jewish people, a great cry goes forth from here, from the Rabbinate to the nations of the world: "Listen, all you people. We have a grievance against you: that you have not done all that was possible for you to do to save most of the Jewish people from the hands of the cursed murderers.... Instead of opening the gates, there was a locking of the gates, including a locking of the gates to our land, through the black decree known as the "White Paper"... But it is not my intent at this lofty moment only to cast blame. My intent is to rouse you to repentance....

(153:) Almost all of Europe has become for us a gigantic cemetery. The prophet Ezekiel saw in his vision a great valley filled with many desiccated bones (Ezek. 37:1–2). That is what we see today.... Allied nations: you are not able to open the graves and bring the dead back to life, but you *are* able to bring up these dry bones that are still alive – the wretched remnant – from the European cemetery, and bring them to the land of Israel. Hurry, act to remedy your great sin, the sin of all humanity against the Jewish people throughout all the generations, and especially in this present generation! Establish quickly the Jewish State in Zion, "the home of our life," that the survivors in the murderous valley may come to it, returning to live, to work and to labor, to build and to plant together with us, as a source of blessing to all the families of the earth.

February 5, 1945 (Monday)

Woolf Hirsch, "Faith and Fear," spoken at reception for Jewish soldiers in Cape Town, South Africa. *Selected Sermons and Addresses*, pp. 120–25

(120:) Cast your minds back to the dark and dreary days of 1940 and 1941, when defeat and disappointment dogged the Allies, while the enemy passed in boisterous triumph from land to land, conquering new nations and subjecting new states. What stood then between the conquest by the enemy of Europe and ultimately of the world, and what we know now will be his utter defeat? It was just an act of faith. Belief in a good cause and the ultimate triumph of justice enabled (121:) England, when she stood alone, unarmed and unprepared, to challenge the overwhelming might of victorious Germany and thereby saved the world from catastrophe. On the other hand, those who had nothing more to depend upon in a time of crisis than calculating reason, political sagacity, or what they might call foresight, were convinced that Germany was invincible and yielded themselves to an abominable slavery.

The Quislings whom this war brought to the fore are not just soulless traitors....

(124:) With the horrors which Nazi domination perpetrated on defenceless people, with the prospect of perpetual enslavement to a *Herrenvolk* before our eyes, what was there for a people with courage but to fight? Now home comfort is alluring. But what attraction had it five years ago, when the Nazis threatened to come and destroy our homes, ravish the womenfolk, dash the children against the walls, and send the men to be gassed or work in abject slavery? Do not belittle your achievement by thinking of your losses and forgetting your gains....

(125:) And finally have faith in God... In the dark days of the war I urged my hearers not to think that God would abandon the world to the forces of evil. It was difficult to preach such doctrines at a time when faith was severely tested by the visible triumph of wickedness. But many things have happened since then to justify our hope.... The world is in travail now. It is our hope that it will bring forth something better than what we had, a more equitable order of life in which everyone will have a place and an opportunity of sharing the abundance which a beneficent Creator has provided for his children....

February 14, 1945 (Wednesday)[3]

MILTON STEINBERG, "When I Think of Seraye,"[4] Address to the Women's Division of the United Jewish Appeal, Waldorf Astoria, New York (based on a sermon delivered at Park Avenue Synagogue, New York, on September 18, 1944, second night of Rosh Hashanah),[5] in Milton Steinberg, *A Believing Jew*, pp. 181–95.

(181:) I have been thinking about Seraye a great deal of late, and for a compelling reason. I cannot think about all of Europe's Jews; the six million dead, the one and a half millions of walking skeletons.[6] Such numbers are too large for me to embrace, the anguish they represent (182:) too vast for my comprehension. And so I think of Seraye instead.... Let me then speak to you of Seraye, and do, as I speak, translate it into its equivalent in your own lives. So we will make real and concrete for ourselves the largest and most terrible tragedy in all recorded time....

(184:) And now, Seraye, at least the Jewish part of Seraye, is gone, wiped out, expunged by a ruthless hand almost to its last trace. To be sure, I have no specific information about its fate. We do not yet know in detail what befell cities like Vilna or Suwalki. How then shall we have heard concerning villages? And yet it is safe to venture

3 Date confirmed by JTA, Feb. 15, 1945, regarding an event that occurred the previous day. Other speakers were Eleanor Roosevelt and Edith Lehman (spouse of Herbert Lehman).

4 Seraye was a village in the Lithuanian province of Suwałki, characteristic of so many other small communities where Jews were living at the time of the German invasion.

5 Cf. Simon Noveck, *Milton Steinberg*, pp. 157–58 (where erroneously he writes that the UJA address was given "a year and a half later" rather than "five months later"), and 193–94; Jonathan Steinberg, "Milton Steinberg, American Rabbi," pp. 590–91.

6 This sentence does not seem appropriate for an address delivered in February 1945, as the earliest references to "six million" as the number of Jews killed by the Nazis do not appear until several months later. It is likely that the original formulation in the UJA address was modified either when the text was published in *Reconstructionist* (March 8, 1946, pp. 10–17) or, some years later, in *A Believing Jew*.

a guess. After all, when evil men went about destroying a whole world, it is unlikely that they spared one tiny and insignificant corner of it, especially evil men so efficient in their wickedness. Seraye is no more. Of that I am certain....

(185:) Let us, however, be optimists and say that, of two thousand Jews, as many as twenty came through alive.

These twenty Jews haunt me.

In the first place, I cannot figure out why they are they and I am I. Through what merit of mind am I safe, secure, free and light in heart whenever I watch my wife going about her household duties or hear my children laugh as they play? What was their offense that (186:) they are cold, naked, hungry, haunted by horror? I simply cannot puzzle out what sin they committed so terrible as to merit the torments meted out to them; to look on while one's wife disappears into a death train or gas chamber, to see one's children spitted on bayonets, or to ponder their slow starvation, their bellies waxing great with bloatedness, their arms and legs turning match-stick thin, their bodies growing feeble with lassitude until life and death can no longer be told apart.

That is what haunts me: the thought that there, but for the grace of God and a capricious decision made by my father, but in any case through no virtue of mine, there go I, there my wife there my children....

(192:) Let us think, then, on these twenty Jews of Seraye, and on the Jews of your ownSerayes, human beings like yourselves, your own kith and kin. Let us reflect on the unspeakability of their present misery, on what they need to return to Seraye, or to come to America, or to go to Palestine. Can we delay for a moment our work of deliverance?

Sometimes, when I think about Seraye, I am ashamed (193:) to be a human being, ashamed to be a member of a species which could perpetrate the evil done to Seraye, and almost as much ashamed of the supposedly good people of the world who stood by when the evil was being perpetrated, and who stand idle now.

Sometimes, when I think of Seraye, I want to hurl hard words at God, that terrible saying of Abraham, "Shall the Judge of the whole earth not do justly?" (Gen. 18:25), that soul-searing inquiry of the prophet:

"Thou, too pure of eyes to behold evil, Thou that canst not look on oppression, Wherefore hast Thou looked on when men did treachery, and did hold thy peace when the wicked swallowed up the righteous?" (Hab. 1:13).

Sometimes, on the other hand, I want to slip into some synagogue and say Kaddish.... (194:) Such are the mingled emotions that attend my thoughts of Seraye....

February 16, 1945 (Friday evening)

US Army Chaplain Jacob Hochman, Worship Service at Tempio Israelitico, Rome: four thousand worshippers (according to JTA, February 20) present for the first Shabbat following the conversion of Rabbi Zolli.[7] Robert G. Weisbord and Wallace P. Sillanpoa, *The Chief Rabbi, the Pope and the Holocaust*, p. 138, citing Hochman Papers: "Statement by Chaplain J. Hochman, Rome Synagogue, 16 Feb. 1945"

Never had Jewry been more broken or tortured than it is now in Europe and in Italy, as a result of the Nazi-Fascist years.... [But it was a fact,] proven in countless centuries of history, that our people never permitted itself to remain broken because of its sufferings. Rather by a dauntless spirit it ever rose above the conditions that would hold it down, to emerge a purer, stronger, more creative community.

February 17, 1945 (Saturday)

Israel Mattuck, "The Treatment of Germany," Liberal Jewish Synagogue, London. Unpublished

(1:) On one point there can be no doubt. Those who have been guilty of barbaric cruelties which even the laws of war forbid among

7 Louis I. Newman, *A "Chief Rabbi" of Rome Becomes a Catholic*, pp. 181–82, briefly summarizes sermons or speeches delivered by Assistant Rabbi David Panzieri, Chaplains Meyer Berman and Jacob Hochman, and Solomon Umberto Nahon (representative of the Jewish Agency of Palestine), but provides no indication of the source for his information about the speeches.

civilized countries must be punished. The men who tortured and killed, and those who gave the orders to torture and kill, old men, women, and children, cannot morally and in fairness to humanity be absolved from their guilt. To overlook their crimes would itself be a crime against humanity....

(2:) The reasons for punishing those guilty of atrocities apply with a thousand-fold force to those who launched the war against humanity, with all its terrible suffering and destruction, to satisfy their ambition. Their black record begins long before the war. I do not refer only to the treatment which the Nazis inflicted on Jews, but to their whole policy of gangsterism which filled life with a haunting fear, for all decent men, wherever their power or influence reached. If it is ever right to punish wrong-doers then it is right a thousand times in their case....

(4:) Let us not confuse the judgment of justice with hatred, or a policy to defend humanity, righteousness, civilization and peace with mere enmity. The moral issues in the war and the record of Germany make it immoral to adopt the kind-hearted sentimentalists' plea to treat Germany as if there had been no Nazis and no war. But at the same time we must remember our human duty to other human beings.

February 24, 1945 (Shabbat Zakhor)

Abraham M. Hershman, "Raising the Hand Against the Throne," Congregation Shaarey Zedek, Detroit, MI. *Israel's Fate and Faith*, pp. 207–10

(207:) [Deut. 25:19, Exod. 17:14] The cause of the world's hostility toward us is beyond our control. It has its origin in prejudice which dies hard and cannot be removed by mere argument. The prejudice is widespread and deep-seated. It is in the air. It is causeless hatred. It is nurtured in the young. Amalek perished long ago, but his "ungracious progeny" survives....[8]

8 Quotation marks in the original. The source of the phrase is a poem by Robert Burns, "The Cotter's Saturday Night," which contains the lines, "The priest-like father reads the sacred page,/ How Abram was the friend of God on high;/ Or Moses

(208:) Considering the fact that, as a general rule, animosity towards the Jew is unprovoked and gratuitous, the enemies of Israel... are consciously or unconsciously the enemies of God. True religion, the hope of the establishment of God's kingdom on earth is incompatible with causeless hatred.

(209:) The first part of the text exhorts us to grapple with Amalek. "Thou shalt blot out Amalek" (cf. Deut. 25:19). It is beyond our power to put an end to the prevailing prejudice against us. We must, however, be on guard against furnishing our disparagers any ammunition for their hatred. To provide them with any pretext or excuse for their ill-will toward us is to play into their hands.... Whenever the Jew resorts to questionable business methods, contravenes O.P.A. [Office of Price Administration] regulations – regulations intended to check the growing danger of inflation – or is guilty of black market practices, he invites antagonism to his people....

March 10, 1945 (Saturday)

Louis Rabinowitz, "Responsibilities and Rights," United Hebrew Congregation, Johannesburg, South Africa. *Out of the Depths*, pp. 106–9

(107:) Who shall be invited to that Conference – the Conference which is to take place at San Francisco next month? The answer is surely obvious.... (108:) He who has borne the heat of battle, who has suffered and toiled, he shall decide his fate. But a most generous interpretation is placed upon the principle of contribution. Whoever declared war against Germany before March 1st [1945] is to be given a seat at that Conference....

It is not against the inclusions that I raise my voice in indignant protest, but against the exclusions. Of whom can it be said more than of the Jewish people that "all of them contributed to the work of the sanctuary."[9] *All* of them, the whole Jewish people, men, women, and children, offered their all that this sanctuary might become a reality.

---

bade eternal warfare wage/ With Amalek's ungracious progeny." One wonders how many of the American listeners would have picked up this allusion.

9 Quoting Nahmanides on Exod. 35:1, from earlier in the sermon.

We Jews who have been in the forefront of the battle not for six but for twelve years; we Jews whose casualties in this war number over 6,000,000; we Jews who, in the one country where the Jewish effort could be separate from that of the country of which we are citizens, in Eretz Israel, have given an example of free will offering in a cause which might serve as an example and a model to the world. We alone, of all those who have made contributions, we who have made the largest sacrifice, we Jews alone will not be represented, and our voice will not be heard. And that silence (109:) will speak more eloquently than all the multitude of words which will be spoken.

March 11, 1945 (Sunday)

Solomon B. Freehof, "'Vengeance is Mine' (Deut. 32:35)," Rodef Shalom Congregation, Pittsburgh, PA. *Rodef Shalom Pulpit*, vol. 10, no. 7, pp. 25–35

(32:) The most heinous crime in the moral judgment of humanity is murder: willful, premeditated murder. There has never been so much willful, carefully premeditated mass murder in the history of mankind. Not even the Mongols, who massacred the population of whole cities, approached (33:) anywhere near this mass murder, carefully premeditated, organized. You cannot possibly kill three million Jews and two million Poles within a year[10] unless you gather your best scientific brains, your finest minds to do it at the rate of some many thousands a day. There never was such a careful and cold-blooded premeditation.

How are we going to punish them for it? A life for a life? The whole Gestapo, the whole S.S., millions of German soldiers participated in it. Are we to apply retributive justice and get them into slaughter camps and kill them off – a life for a life? Certainly not.... It is clear that here is a situation in which the human process for executing punishments falls helpless. It is beyond us....

10 I do not know of a contemporary source for these figures. Christopher Browning has written that the peak of Nazi murderous efficiency, a "veritable blitzkrieg" against the Jews, occurred between March 1942 and February 1943; during this period at least fifty percent of the ultimate number of Jewish victims were killed (*Ordinary Men*, Preface, p. xv).

March 14, 1945 (Wednesday, Day of Fast and Mourning for Victims of Nazi Mass Murder in Europe)

Isaac Herzog, Radio Appeal to the Nations of the World on the Eve of the Fast. JTA, March 15, 1945

Deploring the serious cleavages within the nation which are weakening the Jewish position just now when the day of decision is rapidly approaching, the Chief Rabbi declared that the present tragedy is far more grievous than the destruction of the Temple.

Speaking of the miracle which saved Palestine from the ravages of war and destruction, Dr. Herzog said: "By the mercy of Providence we have been left with the foundation on which we may rebuild our national life." He appealed to the nations of the world to "repair a two thousand-year-old wrong" by returning to Israel the land of its fathers so that it may establish therein its national life.

The Chief Rabbi then addressed a message of comfort to the Jews in the Diaspora emerging from the crucible of affliction, and called upon the remnants of the people to pray to God and have faith in their redemption, which will come soon when they will be brought to the land of their fathers. He concluded by appealing to Jewry all over the world to "return to our sacred religion, which alone can give us inspiration and strength to march forward to our redemption."

March 21, 1945 (Wednesday)

Abba Hillel Silver, "Nothing to Lose but Illusions," Address at Testimonial Dinner for Silver, Hotel Commodore, New York. *Vision and Victory*, pp. 73–84

(75): It is not for us *at this time* to stress Palestine as a place of refuge for homeless Jews and concentrate in this brief, tense hour of fugitive political opportunities when the great bell of history is tolling for us the final summons, on immigration certificates for refugees – if what we have in mind is national restoration and a Jewish State. The Arabs are not deceived by such a maneuver. The world is not moved to greater exertions in our behalf when we speak of saving refugees instead of building a Jewish State. The world was not greatly moved by our desperate pleas in behalf of our millions of doomed fellow-Jews now lying dead in their nameless graves, many of whom might have been saved. The great democracies heard the tortured cry of a dying people. They wagged their heads in sympathy and then proceeded to speak, in the barren legalism of constricted hearts, of their inability to intervene in the domestic affairs of other nations and of their own inviolate immigration laws.

Those who tell us to forget or forego our national claims at this time so as to reinforce our refugee claims are talking sheer nonsense. Thus far the refusals have stood as adamant against their humanitarian pleas as against our national demands....

March 29, 1945 (first day of Pesach)

Leo Jung, "Passover – Birthday of Freedom," The Jewish Center, New York. *The 1945 Manual of Holiday and Occasional Sermons*, pp. 107–11.

(108:) These days spell the immediate downfall of the world's worst tyrant....

(109:) All over the world the Swastika is being trampled underfoot, chains are bursting, the abominations of modern heathenism are being cast down. The curses of the crushed and chained millions are frightening Hitler's fleeing hordes; Hirohito's bestial henchmen are trembling. Internationally, yesterday's admirers of the Fuehrer are whining their penitence, beating their breasts, professing their new enlightenment. Tank generals, diplomats, leaders of labor and industry are rejoicing over the debacle of the man whose very name made nations quake in terror. In America the would-be Hitlers are now biding their time in their foxholes plotting a new crusade of evil, a new campaign of befogging and misleading the American masses.

So it is essential that we sound the tocsin to warn the American people and the nations of the world that victory will not be achieved before a determination penetrates the mind and heart of every democrat everywhere, bidding him build up the ruins of the second world war, commanding him to destroy the causes, to obliterate the cesspools of wickedness from which had come the devilish vapors that led astray a whole generation, robbing common men of their faith, betraying leaders into cowardice, and swaying parliaments so that they had no power to resist, no eyes to see, and no conscience to direct them.

Israel, the oldest nation on earth, who has seen kingdoms crumble, and powers disintegrate, great names humbled and arrogant dictators smashed (110:)...we have the right and feel the obligation to tell the nations of the world: Far too long has the human family waded through the morass of hatred....

Israel Mattuck, "The Jews' Future," Liberal Jewish Synagogue, London. Unpublished

(1:) There will probably be two or three million Jews left in the countries liberated from the Nazis. They will require help to restore their lives which the Nazis broke, to rebuild the Synagogues the Nazis burned, and to care for the children whose parents the Nazis murdered.

Their immediate material problem must not, however, be allowed to obscure their more permanent need, the need for a sense of security, the need for an assurance that they can look to a future for themselves and their children free from this danger of persecution. Such an assurance can come only from an international authority which will undertake the obligation to enforce on all nations full respect for the rights of man, and which will have the power to fulfil it.[11]...

(2:) Moreover, to obtain for Jews in their homelands a status with the full rights and responsibilities of citizenship is the one aim on which all Jews are agreed. That fact has unfortunately been obscured by the shrill clamour of a section of Jews for a political State.[12] Though they constantly call for Jewish unity, they prevent it by putting their sectional aim above the one aim which all Jews can and will support. Not all Jews want a Jewish State. Far from it. But

11 Mattuck continues here with a prayer for the success of the San Francisco Conference.

12 For example, Abba Hillel Silver, above, March 21, 1945.

all Jews want that Jews everywhere should have, with all other men, their human rights....

April 5, 1945 (eighth day of Pesach)

Abraham M. Hershman, "The Achievement of Peace," Congregation Shaarey Zedek, Detroit, MI. *Israel's Fate and Faith*, pp. 20–22

Isa. 11:9 – (21:) [T]he scene so vividly depicted by Isaiah (10:28–32) has been reenacted on a much larger scale in our own time.

The year was 1942, barely three years ago, when the military fortunes of Great Britain were at their lowest ebb. The world held its breath as the news of Rommel's blitzkrieg victories was flashed. In a few brilliantly conceived and masterly executed strokes, he routed the British Army, drove it out of Libya, and recaptured all the territory won by [Field Marshal Archibald] Wavell after much hard fighting. In an incredibly short time, Rommel, at the head of the famous African Corps, stood at the gates of Cairo, Egypt, "shaking his hand at the mount of the daughter of Zion, the hill of Jerusalem" (Isa. 10:32). All seemed to be lost. England ordered its army to be prepared to flee to Iran. There was dread in our hearts, lest the Jewish population of Palestine be massacred. But a miracle occurred. Behold, the Lord, the Lord of Hosts lopped off the boughs with terror; and the high ones of stature were hewn down, and the lofty were laid low! (cf. Isa. 10:33)

The scene shifts from Cairo and Palestine to Russia, Eastern Europe, which was to be subjugated in the short period of between forty-five to ninety days. Germany's march through Russia was a triumphal one. Fortress after fortress fell like a house of cards. Everything went as planned. Resistance proved futile. Nothing could withstand Germany's steamroller. The goal was in sight. Leningrad, penetrated by the invincible Nazi armies, was practically devastated. But something happened to check the advance of the invader. If the Russians were not so anti-religious, if they could see their own situation with the eyes of Isaiah, they too would read God into their marvelous deliverance.

(22:) Mankind, shot through with the knowledge of the Lord, will transfigure the world, extend the sphere of love, establish justice and peace. We are a long, long way off from this ideal; but there is no short-cut to the golden age, no snapshot process for attaining it. May we all work toward this great objective!

April 12, 1945 (Thursday)

Zvi Hirsch Meisels, "Liberation by the Americans, and the First Sermon," Buchenwald Concentration Camp, Germany. *Mekaddeshei HaShem*, 1, "*Sha'ar Maḥmadim*," pp. 23–24, translated by MS

(23:) On Thursday, around noon, we suddenly became aware that the guards at the camp gate were beginning to flee from their watch posts, leaving us free without any oversight. We immediately realized the significance of this flight of theirs: that the Americans would arrive at the camp any moment. Not an hour passed and the *machines* [tanks] with the Americans reached the camp. There was no end or boundary to the depth of our joy and elation. People threw their arms around their fellow prisoners and embraced and kissed them in their jubilation. They lifted me on their shoulders, saying that I had contributed significantly to their deliverance by infusing within them a spirit of encouragement and spiritual fortitude throughout the times of destruction and spiritual danger. Through my recitation of Psalms, I influenced our redemption from descent to the Pit of annihilation. We said the blessing of thanksgiving to God, our eyes flowing with tears, and I turned to them and spoke:

Rabbotai: We must now say *Shema Yisrael* with total enthusiasm and deep devotion, for now we are able to accept upon ourselves the yoke of the kingdom of heaven with all our hearts. Up to now, while we were standing on the threshold of death day after day, we were simply unable to accept for ourselves the yoke of the kingdom of heaven. But now that through God's mercy upon us we have emerged to freedom, we must accept the yoke of the kingdom of heaven with total eager devotion.[13]

---

13 As in the previous text by Meisels, this is followed by several paragraphs in smaller type that appear to be intended for later readers, not to report what he actually said at that dramatic moment. The text above continues with material in the larger print.

(24:) And I continued to discuss the verse, "All my bones shall say, 'O Lord, who is like You?'" (Ps. 35:10). The *Yalkut* [*Shimoni*] explains this as pertaining to the time after the Resurrection of the Dead, for then all the human bones will sing a song. But perhaps we can say that it also applies to the present time. For if we can examine our bones and see that, with God's help, they are healthy and intact despite the power of the beatings and tortures that have passed over us, then we can see through our senses the power of God who has saved us from the hands of those murderers, may their names be blotted out. This is the meaning of "All my bones": through our ability to see that we have all our bones, "they will say," that is, they themselves indeed say, "Lord, who is like You," for only through the power of God have we reached this point.

April 28, 1945 (Saturday)

Israel Mattuck, "Faith Justified," Liberal Jewish Synagogue, London. Unpublished

(2:) We have lived through a miracle of history. Four years ago, the victories of the German army had covered the prospect for this country and for the world with pitch darkness unrelieved by anything which the eye could see. Only faith could discern a light which shone far above the darkness from the sky of righteousness. And now the Forces that had risen to the zenith of power have been hurled into the lowest depths of defeat. The magnitude of the change overpowers thought. On the one hand, "How are the mighty fallen!" (2 Sam. 1:27); on the other, "They who were bent low have been lifted up" (cf. Ps. 145:14). Surely it is a miracle! It is no less a miracle because we can see how it was produced. . . .

(3:) In the last analysis, the shattering defeat of the Nazis is due to their unrighteousness, and to forces moved by a hatred of it, and by a corresponding pursuit of righteousness. It may be unrealistic to define the issues in the war wholly in moral terms; but it is equally unrealistic not to recognize the working of moral factors on its course.

When things were at their worst, we drew on our faith to maintain our hopes. What was that faith? Did we believe that God would send bolts from the heaven to destroy the enemy or open the earth to swallow them up? Our faith was the belief that the God of righteousness would guide and strengthen unto victory the forces fighting for righteousness....

(4:) It was the kind of faith which Habakkuk says God had bid him have when he was in a similar case, and the kind of justification he was promised when he complained of an enemy "terrible and dreadful," who "march through the breadth of the earth, to possess dwelling places not theirs" (Hab. 1:6), an enemy "puffed up," whose "soul is not upright in him" (Hab. 2:4); he learnt that the time of the enemy's downfall is certain, that because he has "spoiled many nations, all the remnant of the peoples shall spoil" him (Hab. 2:8). But "the just shall live by his faith" (Hab. 2:4). And in our time we have experienced anew the truth in the prophet's vision. The vision has tarried, but it approaches fulfilment.

April 29, 1945 (Sunday)

Abraham E. Halpern, "Slaughter for Sale," Radio Address for KMOX. *A Son of Faith*, pp. 291–93

(291:) It is with mixed emotions that I speak this morning. I realize the tenseness of the hour. It is an hour that should be the deep concern of every man and woman throughout the world because the fate of the world will be decided by the nations' representatives who are gathered in San Francisco....[14]

The light of a new day is beginning to appear. Not so long ago we did not know whether the dim light was the twilight of the day to be followed by deep darkness; or whether it was the dawn of a new day to be followed by a rising sun that would again brighten the hearts of men.

For a short time the outlook was far from hopeful. We saw our men driven back by the renewed effort of the enemy that seemed to have taken on some devilish strength. But thank God our men have

14 Reference of course is to the "United Nations Conference on International Organization," which began on April 25.

taken Berlin, and we are happy at the prospect that will liberate the world from the hands of the bloodiest tyrant of all times....[15]

May 6, 1945 (Sunday)

David Max Eichhorn, Sermon delivered in Dachau, Germany, following the liberation of the camp. *The GI's Rabbi: World War II Letters of David Max Einhorn*, pp. 188–90[16]

In the portion that we read yesterday in our holy Torah we found the words [Hebrew]: "Proclaim freedom through the world to all inhabitants thereof; a day of celebration shall this be for you, a day when every man shall return to his family and to his rightful place in society" (cf. Lev. 25:10).[17]

Today I come to you in a dual capacity: as a soldier in the American Army and as a representative of the Jewish community of America. As an American soldier I say to you we are proud, very proud, to be here, to know that we've had a share in the destruction of the cruelest tyranny of all time. As an American soldier I say to you that we are very, very proud to be with you as comrades in arms to greet you and salute you as the bravest of the brave.

We know your tragedy. We know your sorrows. We know that upon you was centered the venomous hatred of power-crazed madmen, that your annihilation was decreed and planned systematically

15 The radio message proceeds to focus on the needs of soldiers returning from combat with terrible physical and mental wounds, asserting that the needs of similar maimed veterans of the previous World War had been largely overlooked. Only one sentence pertains to the Jewish victims: "Let the delegates see the pictures of the horror camps" (p. 292).

16 Used by permission of the publisher, University Press of Kansas, and Mark Zaid.

17 The last phrase was an addition to the translation of the biblical verse. The sermon had obviously been prepared for Shabbat on the preceding day, when the Torah reading was *BeHar–BeḤuqqotai*, but the Jewish prisoners were prevented from using a large public space until the following day, Sunday, May 6. This service was filmed by George Stevens of the US Army Signal Corps and can be viewed in the US Holocaust Museum; it provides a rare example of a sermon delivered in Europe for which there is a visual and auditory dimension in addition to the written text. I am deeply grateful to David Balto for calling my attention to this important text.

and ruthlessly. We know too that you refused to be destroyed, that you fought back with every weapon at your command, that you fought with your bodies, your minds and your spirit. Your faith and our faith in God and in humanity have been sustained. Our enemies lie prostrate before us. The way of life which together we have defended still lives, and it will still live so all men everywhere may have freedom and happiness and peace.

I speak to you also as a Jew, as a rabbi in Israel, and as a teacher of religious philosophy which is dearer to all of us than life itself. What message of comfort and strength can I bring to you from your fellow Jews? What can I say that will compare in depth or in intensity to that which you have suffered and overcome? Full well do I know and humbly do I confess the emptiness of mere words in this hour of mingled sadness and joy. Words will not bring the dead back to life nor right the wrongs of the past ten years.

This is not the time for words, you will say, and rightfully so. It is the time for deeds of justice, deeds of love. Justice will be done. We have seen with our own eyes and we have heard with our own ears and we shall not forget. As long as there are Jews in the world, "Dachau" will be a term of horror and shame. Those who labor here for their evil master must be hunted down and destroyed as systematically and as ruthlessly as they sought your destruction.

And there will be deeds of love. It is the recognized duty of all religious people to bestir themselves immediately to assist you to regain health, comfort, and some measure of happiness as speedily and as is humanly possible. This must be done. This can be done. This will be done. You are not and you will not be forgotten men, my brothers. In every country where lamps of religion and decency and kindness still burn, Jews and non-Jews alike will expend as much time and energy and money as is needed to make good the pledge which is written in our Holy Torah. "Every man who has been oppressed must be and will be restored to his family and to his rightful place in society" (cf. Lev. 25:10, as above). This is a promise and a pledge which I bring you from your American comrades in arms and your Jewish brethren across the sea.

May 8, 1945 (Tuesday, V-E Day)

Louis Rabinowitz, "V-E Day," United Hebrew Congregation, Johannesburg, South Africa. *Out of the Depths*, pp. 391–96

> This is the day which the Lord has made,
> Let us rejoice and be glad thereon.
> O God save us!
> O God, send success! (Ps. 118: 24–25)

(392:) But can we Jews rejoice and be glad? "It is not given to the Jew to fill his mouth with laughter in this world."[18] Not for us the gay abandon, the light-hearted jubilation the mafficking and the jollification. Our joy is a tempered joy, tempered by the thought of the millions of corpses whose ghosts haunt us, of whole communities wiped (393:) out for the sanctification of God's name; it is a joy tempered by the terrifying thought of Treblinka, of Maidanek, of Osviciem,[19] of Bergen-Belsen and Dachau. It is a joy tempered by the revelation of the bestiality and sadism of man, of the insecurity and peril of our people. Why, O Lord, why? We ask in futile revolt, and we find no answer…

As General Smuts said in his message to the world, "Before this mystery of suffering and sacrifice we bow our heads in awed silence." Yes, we bow our heads in awed silence, but after that silence we raise our heads again and address ourselves to the world. The Jew, hunted, persecuted, despised, stands as the infallible barometer showing the spiritual atmospheric pressure, the sensitive seismograph which unerringly records hidden faraway subterranean disturbances. It is just because of his helplessness, (394:) just because he cannot call upon armies and navies and air forces to attain his just demands,

---

18 b. Berakhot 31a.

19 Rabinowitz uses the Polish name for the city (properly spelled Oswiecim) next to the concentration camp/death camp established by the Germans. The first news of this camp came to the western media through reports from the Polish government-in-exile, which used the Polish name of the city to name the camp; the German name Auschwitz did not appear in the media until later. Thus the *JC* was still using "Oswiecim" through July of 1946, although occasionally (beginning November 17, 1944) it used "Auschwitz (Oswiecim)," or just "Auschwitz" (first on July 7, 1944).

that all protestations of justice, democracy, and liberty will be judged against the measuring rod of the treatment of the suffering servant Israel. The restoration of Palestine to our people, the succor of refugees, their rehabilitation in the lands of their dispersion, the ruthless stamping out of anti-Semitism, it is by them that the victorious Powers will be judged before the Judgment Seat of the Almighty.

May 9, 1945 (Wednesday); French Liberation Day

Nathan Netter, "*Sermon de la Libération*," Metz, France. *La Patrie égarée et la patrie renaissante*, pp. 289–96, translated by MS

(293:) Could one ever spread the veil (294:) of forgetfulness and of pardon over the monstrous crimes committed against us, our meager minority without defense, without protection, which it proposed to exterminate – men, women, and children – in order to satiate its implacable hatred? In its colossal audacity, did it not reach the point of declaring war against God Himself? It ravaged and sullied God's sanctuaries – those that it did not burn down as it did almost everywhere else – and delivered to the flames our holy books.

This is what explains why our ceremony, so unusual in its significance, is celebrated today so modestly, so inadequately, without organ and without choir. Our ancient synagogue, in a pitiful state, pillaged, despoiled, ravaged, is unable to receive you. It bears too clearly the evidence of Teutonic vandalism, and is therefore excluded from such an impressive ceremony, despite having shared so faithfully with and so affectionately with the fatherland its destiny: its joys and its grief. But have confidence in the future: it is as if we can hear in this moment the words of the prophet Haggai which he addressed long ago to those who also returned from an exile: "The glory of this Second Temple will be greater than that of the first" (Hag. 2:9)....

May 13, 1945 (Sunday)

Abraham Cohen, "Peace Celebration," Birmingham Hebrew Congregation, Birmingham, England. Unpublished, David Cohen Private Collection; see Complete Sermons

Israel Mattuck, "The Meaning of Victory," Victory Thanksgiving Service, Liberal Jewish Synagogue, London. Unpublished

(4:) The Jews who have survived again "stand at the grave of their persecutors."[20] But the millions who were killed, with the hundreds of thousands other human beings who refused to accept Nazism and were killed by the most cruel methods that a diabolical ingenuity could conceive, show the evil power from which humanity has been saved by the victory of the United Nations.

In relation to the past, then, the victory means a great salvation. It saved Britain and the British Empire from a great peril, perhaps the gravest in their history; it saved humanity from servitude to a dark power; it saved from destruction the ideals of democracy, freedom and human rights which have given our incomplete civilisation its beauty and its hope. And it saved the Jews from the murderous intention of a mighty foe.[21] All that, and more, the victory means because it brought to an end and complete destruction the power of the Nazis with the blight it has for more than a decade laid on the life of humanity. But what about the future?...

Alexander Altmann, Great Synagogue, Manchester, England. *The Manchester Guardian*, May 14, 1945, p. 3, University College London Altmann Archives

Speaking at the Great Synagogue, Manchester, [Altmann] said that the sense of triumph and victory which Jews felt was somewhat different from that experienced by the rest of mankind. To Jews the triumph and victory marked the end not only of six years of war but of twelve years of Hitlerite tyranny, of which they were the first

20 Mattuck is here citing what was apparently a familiar phrase. It was used in an address by James G. MacDonald, former League of Nations High Commissioner for Refugees, at a dinner held in Chicago on January 5, 1939, which raised more than $1,000,000 for "racial refugees" from Germany and other European countries: "Sooner or later, the persecuted peoples of today will stand at the graves of their persecutors" (*Chicago Daily Tribune*, Jan. 6, 1939, p. 4).

21 Certainly a strange formulation following the preceding paragraph which speaks of "the millions [of Jews] who were killed." Perhaps the intention is "saved the surviving Jews of Europe...."

victims. Their sacrifices in a prolonged agony of death, torture, and humiliation were unparalleled.

ISRAEL ABRAHAMS, "Total Victory," Address Delivered on Goodwill Sunday, Cape Town, South Africa. *Living Waters: Collection of Sermons, Addresses and Prayers*, pp. 310–13.

(311:) There is one aspect of this unbrotherly spirit [racialism] of which I may speak with especial knowledge. I have in mind anti-Semitism. If anti-Semitism were purely a Jewish issue, I should be inclined, being a Jew, not to advert to it today. But I venture to submit that Judophobism [*sic*] is by no means a matter affecting Jews solely. It concerns the well-being of the entire world.... Let us never forget that the war began as a manifestation of anti-Semitism. (312:) The Nuremberg Laws were the prelude to the conflagration that eventually girdled the earth....

Let us be warned for the future. Let us realize that anti-Semitism is a diabolical form of camouflage screening evil designs of far greater magnitude than the hurt of the Jews. Let us understand that all humanity is closely interconnected. The entire world is, so to speak, wired together as a vast circuit of civilization. The Jewish race is weak. In the moment of tension and danger, the Jewish link is the first to fuse. In Germany, as elsewhere, we were the primary sufferers. But ultimately the "short circuit" created by persecution of the Jews inevitably reacts upon the rest of mankind.... Today the supreme question confronting humanity is whether, (313:) despite our differences – racial, national, religious or cultural – we can get together.

July 2, 1945 (Monday)

JACOB KAPLAN, "Remember What Amalek Did to You" (*Souviens-toi de ce que t'a fait Amalek*), Ceremony organized by "Souvenir Francais," Synagogue de la Rue de la Victoire, Paris. *Les Temps d'épreuve*, pp. 173–77, translated by MS

(174:) When we recall those who have suffered, we ask ourselves whether we don't need to beat our own chests. The civilized nations allowed such crimes to be committed! We cannot avoid thinking that if the world's indignation had been what it should have been,

Germany would have been forced to take account of it. At least there will be no obstacle to the protest of the victims (175:) that the earth will not cover their blood. Let us not forget!

To forget would be to spread a shroud of silence over their martyrdom, to their detriment, and to the advantage of the perpetrators of these atrocities unparalleled in previous history. By contrast, to remember is to refuse to wipe the slate clean over the Hitlerian crimes, to remember is to stigmatize forever the Hitlerian doctrine, those who created it, who spread it, who collaborated with it. If a new world is to be born, it is impossible for the swastika not to appear as a cursed sign, the sign of Cain, murderer of his brother.

July 13, 1945 (Friday evening)

Jacob Kaplan, "From Darkness to Light" (*Des tenebres à la lumière*), celebration of July 14, Synagogue de la Rue de la Victoire, Paris. *Les Temps d'épreuve*, pp. 179–85, translated by MS

(182:) We have had our soldiers fallen on the field of honor like the others; we have (183:) had our resistance fighters [*maquisards*] fallen on the field of honor like the others; we have had our hostages executed like the others; we have had our victims of German atrocities massacred on site like the others. But more numerous than the others – much more numerous – have been the Jews who were deported, and less numerous – far less numerous – our fellow Jews who have returned from deportation. No, there has never been a fixed quota for us in this context. A third of the Jewish population of the country has been deported; how many will return?[22] Can we measure what this represents in proportion to the losses sustained by the country as a whole? If it is true that those who have fallen under the blows of the enemy were the ransom for deliverance, let us appreciate how great has been the role of the French Jewish community in this ransom. For the memory of our dead, for the recollection of ours who have disappeared, for our homes that are in mourning, for our families still waiting in anxiety, I have considered it to be an imposing

22 It is estimated that only three percent of the 75,721 French Jews deported from France ever returned: Renée Poznanski, *Jews in France During World War II*, p. 462.

obligation to recall on this July 14 the martyrdom of French Jewry, and I would like so much to have the assurance that this sacrifice will never be forgotten.

Let us set aside this final word, for it is of an impious nature. The government of Vichy which abandoned the Jews and which handed them to Germany did not represent the true France. (184:) The true France does not know racism, does not know antisemitism; it does not make distinctions among her children based on their origins or their religious beliefs....

August 14, 1945 (Tuesday, V-J Day)

Louis Rabinowitz, "V-J Day," United Hebrew Congregation, Johannesburg, South Africa. *Out of the Depths*, pp. 397–401

(400:) Never before in the history of mankind has so much territory been placed at the disposal of conquerors. The very thought of it makes one reel. From the west coast of France, across Germany, Poland, Russia, Siberia, China, Japan, the Aleutian Islands to the vast hemisphere of America and back to England, the Allies circle the globe and have it at their disposal. It is a tremendous and heavy responsibility.

One feels almost ashamed, when viewing these vast vistas, of lodging a claim for the small and insignificant Jewish people, but, as I said on V-E Day, we Jews are the barometer of the ethical and moral standard of world civilisation. And one is constrained to ask, in that vast territory at the disposal of the Allies, will a tiny corner, whose associations with our history are so close, be set aside for the afflicted, storm-tossed, uncomforted children of Israel who not only have suffered immeasurably more than any other of the victims, but whose wounds still bleed from a hundred places?

August 19, 1945 (Sunday, National Day of Prayer and Thanksgiving)

Samuel Daiches, Harrowgate Synagogue, London, printed as eight-page pamphlet by Oxonian Press, Oxford

(3:) The nightmare is ended. Man's self-destruction is halted. The war is over. The world can breathe freely. The tyrants have fallen.

The chief workers of iniquity have met their doom. The forces of wickedness have been overcome, first in Europe, and now in Asia....

My friends, we have come to-day to the House of Prayer to give thanks to God for the great deliverance, for the victory granted to Britain and her allies, for the victory of the forces of light and freedom over those of darkness and slavery.... It is through the lovingkindness of God that we are alive today, that the British Empire is alive to-day, and that a remnant of Jewry is alive today.

(4:) We give thanks unto God. But, my friends, can we rejoice? Can we rejoice with a full heart? As much as we should like to feel the full force of unlimited joy, it does not arise within us. We have lost too much. We have lost too much as human beings and as Jews. Humanity – the part of mankind that deserves that designation – has lost too much. Every war demands sacrifices, in every war lives are lost and shadows darken many homes. But the carnage and destruction in this war are unparalleled in recorded history. Torture, murder and annihilation sent millions of human beings to horrible deaths. Europe is in ruins, Jewry is in ruins. Parts of the world are devastated. And, to make grief still more grievous, there is ruin in the heart of man. In many parts of mankind respect for life has gone, respect for the dignity of man has gone, love of fellow-man has gone, and love of God has gone. The shadow of death is spread over the inhabited earth. The angel of destruction holds unchallenged sway. There must be a return; there must be a return to God, a return of human love, a return of the fear and love of God, a return of the love of life and respect for life. The divine image of man must be restored to its glory.

The King in his speech at the opening of Parliament last Wednesday [August 15] spoke these words: "The devastating new weapon which science has now placed in the hands of (5:) humanity should bring home to all the lesson that the nations of the world must abolish recourse to war or perish by mutual destruction."

Israel Mattuck, "Victory and Peace," Liberal Jewish Synagogue, London. Unpublished

(1:) The democracies had been slow to perceive their danger, the danger to their civilization and the danger to the ideals they cherished for the life of humanity, and when it broke over them with all its fury, they were ill-prepared to meet it. But they were upheld by their spirit, the spirit of Britain in the terribly dark days of 1940, the spirit of the United States after that attack on Pearl Harbour, the spirit of Russia at Stalingrad, the spirit of the peoples in the occupied countries of Europe, (2:) the spirit of China in her long drawn-out agony. It was the spirit that comes from the conviction that freedom and justice are greater than life itself. That spirit shines through the horror of the war to send its rays down the ages....

(3:) The Jews have a special interest in the peace of the world. Because of their unique position, they have suffered most from war and from the evil forces that make war.... The victory of the United Nations in the world war has delivered the Jews from the evil power that destroyed millions of them and sought to exterminate all of them. In the world's peace, will they find peace from the tribulations that have afflicted their history?...

September 7, 1945 (Erev Rosh Hashanah)

Samuel S. Cohon, "The Dawn of a New Era," Temple Emanu-El, Wichita, KS (Visiting Rabbi). AJA, MS-276, Box 7, Folder 3

(1:) [Pleasure in leading worship is] enhanced by the glorious events of the past months, which reached their climax in Tokyo Bay last Saturday night. Though the official termination of the war, in view of the legal technicalities connected with it, is still far off, the actual fighting has come to an end, and we together with the rest of the world can breathe freely again.... With the signing of the terms of the surrender in the Pacific, a whole era of human history died, and a new one is now dawning for suffering humanity.... [The past year] was one of the most devastating in the annals of man, and also was one of the most momentous. The sixth day of May and the fourteenth day of August are red-letter days in the history of the world....

(2:) In the spirit of the Jewish tradition, we and the whole world praise God for having kept us alive and preserved us to this hour....

(3:) Countless millions of Chinese and other Asiatic peoples were enchained by the conscienceless conquerors even as millions of

Europeans groaned in Nazi fetters. The fate of the free world hung in the balance. The sinister shadows of Axis tyranny obscured the hope of the world.

Our first thought in this hour is one of thanksgiving to God.... We are grateful to Him for helping us break the sword of the enemy and granting us the victory for which we labored and prayed so long....

Ferdinand M. Isserman, Erev Rosh Hashanah Sermon: no title, Temple Israel, St. Louis, MO. AJA, MS-6, Box 17, Folder 2

(1:) There was the birth of Naziism with its cruelty to the Jews of Germany and its clever propaganda like an octopus stretching its tentacles to the far corners of the universe to sink its poisonous fangs into the household of Israel everywhere. There was the echo of Nazi philosophies throughout the world, the bloody pogrom of 1938 and the second world war of 1939. It was not easy to stand before you in the days when Nazis were sweeping on to victory and Nazi prestige in the minds of materialistic-minded men rose from mountain peak to mountain peak and cast an ominous shadow over the tents of Israel. Then came the years of the war...; these years brought their anxious hours.... All during these trying years I stood here before you trying to sound the basic faith of our fathers, anxious to be your articulate conscience and secretly beseeching God to wing my words that they might penetrate into your hearts and help you sustain yourselves by the faith which generated hope and courage for centuries. I weighed my words these days and chose my emphases with unusual care and much contemplation.

How much easier is my task tonight when our faith has been vindicated....

September 8, 1945 (first day of Rosh Hashanah)

Stephen S. Wise, "Has the World Tragedy Really Ended?," Free Synagogue at Carnegie Hall, New York. AJA Microfilms from AJHS Papers, Box 23

(1:) The world tragedy is not ended for the bereft, who will, as long as life lasts, bear wounds and scars in their hearts, even though victory has achieved the best for the most. The world tragedy has not ended nor can it end for the Jewish people, whom it has stricken sore, annihilating millions of men, women, and children who fell not on the battlefield.

How can we hold the world tragedy to have ended, seeing that it marked the discovery and utilization of the atomic bomb? The most terrible significance thereof lies not in its visible destructiveness, but as a sign of what war might at its most terrible become, above all of the power of science, unfettered and unleashed by moral imperatives. The world tragedy will not end with the ending of the war or with its victories. It will end only when the causes thereof shall have been ended....

Least of all has the world tragedy ended for the Jewish people. Of every (2:) five Jews on earth that were in 1939 at the war's beginning, two have been slain. I would not speak of the offendings of a bitter past against Israel, but only of an unaltered faith in and hope for its future. The world tragedy will not be ended until justice be done to the Jew.... Once again Jews shall have home and habitation of their own – not a refuge for the homeless, but a State, a free and democratic Commonwealth in the midst of the comity of nations for such Jews as wish to live as Jews, to build as Jews, to create as Jews, and to contribute the loftiest Jewish ideals to the purposes and the program of the free people of a reborn humanity.

Abraham A. Kellner, "The Peace that Builds," Congregation Sons of Abraham, Albany, NY. *A Rabbi's Faith*, pp. 1–8.

(1:) Surely people will want to seek the road that will lead to permanent and universal peace for the sacrifice of blood and treasure that was expended in the prosecution of this horrible holocaust....

(3:) We will gain nothing by ignoring the fact that when this holocaust of fire was first unloosed upon the world, there was a tendency to view aggression in a (4:) detached manner and with an attitude of indifference. Now, when the world is about to constitute itself anew, shall we cover up the crime of the nations who violently deprived minorities within their borders and neighboring peoples of the wells of living water that gave them sustenance and hope?...

(5:) When the barbaric atrocities were first visited upon our suffering co-religionists, the conscience of civilization was not too deeply mortified, and the nations of the earth seemed perfectly content to feed the unprotected Jew to the ravenous beast of Nazidom. Little did they consider that once having disposed of Israel, the monster would seek new victims to devour. Somehow the people imagined that though a terrible fire consumed the homes of their neighbors, the conflagration would stop before it reached their possessions. The people that *could* and *should* have stopped this terrifying octopus before he spread his poisoned tentacles over half the globe somehow believed that our world could continue half dark and half illuminated.

Ernest I. Jacob, "Mobilization for Peace," Temple Israel, Springfield, MO. *Paths of Faithfulness*, pp. 7–10

(7:) For us as Americans the result of victory is an unequaled ascent of our nation over all others; Soviet Russia is the only exception.... For us as Jews the war has brought an unequaled decline in our status. Never before has the Jewish people been weaker; never has it suffered greater losses. Never has it lost so much in resources and influence among the nations of the world. As religious people we realize that the ascent of America and (8:) the decline of the Jewish people leave us with terrible responsibilities. We American Jews feel like victors and vanquished at the same time. We must bear the double load of victory and defeat; no one will take it from our shoulders....

(9:) The moral collapse of which we speak is of course most conspicuous in the German and Japanese people. Even the greatest skeptic must finally believe in the reality of the incredible brutalities of the Nazi concentration camps. We have been shown the pictures of piles of human bodies, of innocent people brought to a cruel death by torture and starvation. We have seen the even more pitiful photographs of the survivors whose bodies and minds have been utterly destroyed.[23] But let us not deceive ourselves, not on this *Yom*

23 Note that this refers to pictures of the German camps (Dachau, Bergen Belsen and others) at liberation. There seems to be no awareness of the mass murder in the

Hadin – this Day of Judgment – which our religion affords us. Such inhumanity, such callousness and brutality is not solely German or Japanese. It is part of the essence of our modern civilization, the cancer which eats into the flesh of men everywhere. There is only one distinction – we pay no attention to it as long as it does not turn against us. Until our age certain minimal ethical standards accepted by all men existed.... Our age has repudiated them shamelessly. Our morality now consists of "every man for himself" – though we dare not admit it. We live in a complete moral vacuum. As nature abhors a vacuum, any new bestiality may rush in, as Nazism in Germany.

We have heard a great deal about the re-education of the German and Japanese people; this is to be a condition of lasting peace. I believe that we cannot limit re-education to the vanquished, for we the victors need it as much....

(10:) Religion is the only power which can bring about a change of heart in man.

Israel Mattuck, "The Problems of Peace," Liberal Jewish Synagogue, London. Unpublished

(1:) This is different from any former Rosh Hashanah in our lives.... We have endured much and survived. We have witnessed the downfall of mighty powers that practice and planned unrighteousness. We have seen many Jews rescued from the hands of a cruel and powerful enemy, though – alas – only after many more had been tortured and killed by him. We behold democracy and its principles of humanity and freedom triumphant over the tyranny that plotted to put its yoke over the world. All that moves in us solemn but boundless thanksgiving.

The peace is, however, disturbed by grave and far-reaching problems.... After the last war we made the mistake of ignoring our critical situation, with the disastrous consequences first of social collapse and then of the most devastating war in history. We mistook peace for ease, when it really called for determined endeavor in hard

extermination camps (Treblinka, Sobibor, Birkenau), which represented more clearly the essence of the Holocaust.

thinking and arduous labour. If we make a similar mistake now, the consequences will be terribly worse....

(3:) It would be idle, and dangerous, not to recognize the fact that the peace of the world may be threatened in the future not as in the past by nations addicted to militarism as the basis of national glory, but by a new kind of nationalism which puts economies above righteousness....

(4:) It is most unfortunate that at such a time many Jews have made it appear that they ignore this larger responsibility [for the future]. The tragic fate of millions of Jews has made them so fearful about the future that they seek physical escape from the dangers that cause their fears. There is only one real solution for the problem of antisemitism, and that is moral decency.... Antisemitism, and it is true of all unreasoning hatreds, is a moral disease. It calls for a moral cure. The search for a cure in any other direction must end in futility and create disaster. And it prevents Jews from realizing fully the responsibility which they share with others to use the solemn opportunity which the present offers to work for a better world.

September 9, 1945 (second day of Rosh Hashanah)

Jacob Kaplan, "Our Father, Our King, We Have No Other King But You" (*Notre Père, notre Roi, nous n'avons pas d'autre Roi que toi*), Synagogue de la rue de la Victoire, Paris. *Les Temps d'épreuve*, pp. 187–93, translated by MS

(188:) A year has passed. If almost all of our prisoners [of war] have returned, only a tiny minority of those [Jews] who were deported have returned. We have no news concerning 115,000 of our deportees. Close to six million Jews are missing. We cannot, we *must* not, think only of ourselves. The Hitlerian crimes are the shame of our era....

(189:) I am not unaware that there were Aryans who were also subjected to atrocities like that of the Jews, but I also know that the slaughter of the Aryans remained in general a surprise for all until the last moment, while the extermination of the Jews was known long ago.[24] I wonder if the world would not, all the same, have found

24 It is not clear to me whether the preacher is referring to the murder by starvation

some way of intervening if it had known that at the same time that millions of Jews were passing through the crematory furnaces, millions of Aryans were passing through as well.

I am trying to represent the tragic state of mind of the wretched person shut tight within the gates of the Nazi hell. He sees himself entirely consigned to the mercy of his tormentors who took pleasure in making him suffer and in killing. He knows that the Allied armies are struggling heroically to demolish Hitlerism, but he also knows that in the interim, there is no one who can help him. What moral torment, not to mention the physical torture...

(190:) O Israel, do you not know the words of your Psalmist, "Put not your trust in the great, in mortal man who cannot save" (Ps. 146:3)? Do you not know through the experience of millennia that your fate depends only upon God?...

September 16–17, 1945 (Yom Kippur)

Abraham J. Feldman, "Why Will Ye Die, O House of Israel," Temple Beth Israel, Hartford, CT. Unpublished, AJA MA-38, Box 44

(6:) You remember that in November, 1938, at a pre-determined hour, all the synagogues in Berlin were set on fire. Firemen were stationed all about the buildings to prevent the flames from spreading to neighboring structures. Crowds of sight-seers gathered about the flaming synagogues, and firemen were on guard, keeping the people from coming too close. Suddenly there appeared a Jew near the synagogue of Fasanenstrasse, who attempted to break through the guard of the firemen. "Where to, Jew?" the firemen shouted. "I want to pray," the Jew replied. "Don't you see that your synagogue is on fire?" the fireman asked, barring his path. And he answered, "*Eine*

---

of Soviet POWs, the gassing of Gypsies in Auschwitz, or other victims. Recent historians have noted that in many reports, various categories of Nazi victims were mentioned without highlighting Jews. For example, the Moscow Declaration of Autumn 1943 spoke of Germans responsible for "the execution of French, Dutch, Belgian, or Norwegian hostages, or Cretan peasants, or who have shared in slaughters inflicted on the people of Poland...," without ever mentioning Jews (Lipstadt, *Beyond Belief*, p. 251).

brennende Synagoge ist auch ein Gotteshaus (A burning synagogue is also a house of God)."[25] He went through the lines. He vanished in the clouds of smoke enveloping the burning building. His identity was never established, and it is not known whether he escaped alive carrying some Sefer Torah (sacred scroll) to safety or whether he perished in the flames.

I would say to you, my people, that unless a synagogue is spiritually on fire, it is not a house of the Lord....

Harry Joshua Stern, "God's Chosen Fast," Temple Emanu-El, Montreal. *Martyrdom and Miracle*, pp. 42–45

[Isaiah 58: "Is this the fast...?"] (43:) There is no doubt that wartime and post-wartime have forced us to comply with the prophet's demands regarding our ethical duties toward our fellow man. We have been engaged in a bitter six years of war to free the oppressed, and now in the great process of liberation we have resolved to feed the hungry of suffering Europe and Asia and to clothe the naked. That is why this very week Canada has again introduced rationing of meat.[26] That is the very reason we are now engaged in Dominion-wide collection of clothing.

We realize that the ethical precept summons us to do all these brotherly acts and more on behalf of those humans of whatever race or creed that have been victimized by the brutality of World War II. In these days we are fulfilling much which the prophet defines in terms of the Ethical as to the understanding of the Kippur Day.

Marcus Ehrenpreis, The Great Synagogue, Stockholm. *Fragetecknet Israel*, p. 307, translated by Göran Rosenberg[27]

---

25 This statement (in German and English) appears in a radio play by Morton Wishengrad entitled "The Scroll on the Doorpost," in the "Eternal Light" series broadcast over NBC by the Jewish Theological Seminary on June 16, 1946: http://bit.ly/2yGbFtF. I have not yet found an earlier source.

26 Jeffrey A. Keshen, *Saints, Sinners and Soldiers: Canada's Second World War*, p. 118. Meat rationing went into effect on September 9 ("this very week"); a September poll showed that sixty-eight percent of the population favored or accepted the government's decision.

27 See Göran Rosenberg, "Philo of Stockholm: The Unrequited Love of Rabbi Marcus

(307:) If there has been a meaning to the unspeakable sufferings and to the extermination of millions of people and the larger part of the Jews on our continent, then it is only this: that we, the survivors, the spared ones, shall be chastened, that we shall reduce our demand for affluence and imagined needs, that we shall become freer in our thoughts, purer in our hearts. Then the sufferings shall not have been in vain.... The people of Israel must learn to find its place in the world right now; we must be determined to fill that task which has befallen on us, to reignite the spiritual light that has gone out, to infuse again the souls of the young with the power of the spirit. Thereby will the words of the prophet come true: "'Not by might, and not by power, but by my Spirit,' says the Lord of Hosts" (Zech. 4:6).[28]

Ehrenpreis," *European Judaism* (Spring, 2017):12–24, with translation of the passage p. 17.

28 See also Erika Larsson, "Hope Through Disaster," with reference to the sermon but no direct quotation: http://www.kulturaihistoria.umcs.lublin.pl/archives/43.

COMPLETE SERMONS

Jacob Xenab Cohen (1889–1955)
"The Menace of Hitlerism to American Jewry"
Free Synagogue, New York
February 14, 1932 (Sunday)
AJA MS-146, Box 2, Folder 3

INTRODUCTION

Jacob Cohen (later known as Rabbi J.X. Cohen) was born in New York City to immigrant parents from Lithuania.[1] His road to the rabbinate was not direct: he was trained as an engineer and worked for almost twenty years in this field. However, like more than a few others (see Saperstein *Witness from the Pulpit*, p. 148 including n. 1), he was deeply moved by hearing Stephen S. Wise speak, and in 1925, at age thirty-six, he entered the rabbinical training program at the newly established Jewish Institute of Religion that Wise had founded. As soon as he completed the program (1929), he became an Associate Rabbi under Wise at the Free Synagogue of New York. A biography written by his wife Sadie and published after his death is entitled "Engineer of the Soul."[2]

The text below is an example of the kind of address delivered by many Reform rabbis in late nineteenth- and early twentieth-century synagogues as part of a weekday religious service on Sunday morning intended primarily for members of large congregations who were unable to take a second day off from work on Saturdays. Because there was no fixed weekly reading from Scripture (Torah *parashah*

1 The text was later published in *The Current Jewish Record: A Digest of International Opinion*, vol. 2, no. 5, May, 1932, and in *Opinion: A Journal of Jewish Life and Letters.*

2 The biographical material is taken in part from the Biographical Note on Cohen in the collection of the American Historical Society.

and *haftarah*) as there had been on the previous Saturday, these addresses are frequently made without reference to biblical or rabbinic material. They often addressed issues of contemporary social justice, as well as delivered messages derived from great works of general literature.

Here, Cohen addresses the theme of antisemitism in a very immediate manner, describing in detail a meeting held in New York by a group of German Americans strongly supportive of the National-Socialist (or Nazi) party in their homeland, and its leader Adolf Hitler. The purpose of the address is to inform listeners that there may be serious challenges to Jewish life not only in Germany and other European countries (it was delivered almost a full year before Hitler came to power) but even in the United States.

The style of capturing an audience's attention with a dramatic incident rather than beginning with background and context reveals a distinctive approach to public speaking, perhaps influenced by the awareness that Kurt Luedecke himself, the self-styled "Amerikaner Hitler," (see the sermon below) – not to mention the Nazi Party leader in Germany – was apparently a captivating public speaker.

Many of the direct quotations cited by Cohen seem to be too long for a listener hearing the Nazi speaker to have remembered; assuming that Cohen himself did not use shorthand, it is possible that he brought someone with him to the meeting who did.

THE CRY, "*ER IST EIN JUDE*" FILLED THE MEETING HALL WITH clamor, as an angry group surged around the stock chap who had declared the speaker in error. "Throw the Jew out," came the command, and with swift shoves the protesting chap was propelled into the street. He was saved from a bad mauling in the street by the lucky presence of a "cop," for the Nazis were holding their propaganda meeting not in Munich or Berlin, but in the Yorkville district of New York City. The *Nationalsozialistische Vereinigung*,[3] New York Branch, was

3 The official title was *Nationalsozialistische Vereinigung Teutonia*, founded in Detroit in 1923 by Friedrich Gissibl (see below, n. 6). It was dissolved in March 1932 (a month after the sermon), and eventually replaced by the "Friends of the New Germany,"

in session that Saturday evening, propagating the Hitler program on fertile soil in the great metropolis. The meeting room, packed with many hundreds of men, was being sprayed with the vilest venom against Jews that has ever publicly received utterance in America, outside the pages of Henry Ford's infamous and unlamented *Dearborn Independent.*[4]

The hall was decorated with a diminutive American flag and nearly a dozen large Nazi banners, with their ominous *Hakenkreuz* emblem. Kurt Luedecke was the speaker.[5] He was introduced as the leader of propaganda for the eastern United States, for Hitlerism in America has already reached the point where it can boast of two travelling propagandists. The other is Fritz Gissibl; his territory is the western part of the country.[6] The propagandist Luedecke is an unprincipled inciter of *Judenhasse*, Jew hatred. Without restraint he spewed forth every manner of falsehood, innuendo and slander, no matter how absurd it might sound to an intelligent person.

Under the steady barrage of accusations and denunciations which the speaker uttered during his address of two and a half hours, such elements of intelligence as his audience possessed were dispersed and shattered. A socio-psychic thermometer (which some day may be invented) would have registered a rapid, even violent, rise of the hate-temperature of the audience as the speaker progressed in his attacks on the Jews. He was not abusing and denouncing the Jews

---

which would in turn be replaced by the German-American Bund. Peter H. Peel, "The Great Brown Scare: The Amerika Deutscher Bund in the Thirties and the Hounding of Fritz Julius Kuhn," http://www.ihr.org/jhr/v07/v07p419_Peel.html.

4 The weekly *Dearborn Independent* was purchased by Henry Ford in 1919, and quickly began a series of attacks on Jews that continued until 1927 under the heading "The International Jew." See Leonard Dinnerstein, *Anti-Semitism in America*, pp. 80–83, and Albert Lee, *Henry Ford and the Jews.*

5 Luedecke would later write *I Knew Hitler: The Story of a Nazi Who Escaped the Blood Purge*, 814 pages; most relevant to the material presented here is chap. 17, "Selling Hitler in America," pp. 284–303. The earliest references to Luedecke appearing in an archival search of the *NYT* are from 1934 and 1935; the earliest in JTA is from February 1933.

6 Luedecke mentioned Gissibl in *I Knew Hitler* only in passing: "[Walter] Kappe and Gissibl, the leaders [of the Teutonia] impressed me as young men who wanted to do things but didn't really know how.... I agreed to interest myself in the Teutonia only if they would break with [Dr. Hans] Nieland, make themselves independent of Germany, and proceed as a truly American organization...." *I Knew Hitler*, p. 295.

of Germany alone. His shafts were aimed at the Jews of America, whom he declared are a menace to our "Nordic Civilization." The Jews are not a race, he continued, but a bastard mongrelization, a second-rate mixture of Assyrians, Egyptians and Babylonians, with one principal branch wholly Mongolian in origin.

Loud cheers and a crescendo of bravos greeted each successive sally of the speaker against the Jews. "The Hitlerites," proceeded this sneering defamer of Jewry, "are not anti-Semitic. Oh, no! They are only against the infiltration of the inferior Jewish strains into the World Nordic stream. Nordics must unite the world over," he added, "to restore and maintain the purity of the Nordic peoples."

"We don't want a people in our land," he said, "who have no land, no culture, no language, nothing to contribute to Nordic civilization except enervating influences. The Jew is a biologic parasite, and if Nordic race purity is to be preserved the parasite must be removed. The Jews," he continued, "were not a nation; they never were. Never possessing Palestine or any other soil, they yet developed a closely built organization that is stronger than any nation's on earth. To weaken the bonds of the peoples in different nations, however, they cunningly preach internationalism to the Christians.

"Throughout Europe and America," he added, "it is a fixed Jewish policy to be represented on all political parties so that the central Jewish organization will know all that is going on on every side."[7] Then came the proud boast that "at least one party, the Nazi, is *Judenrein*" – free of Jews.

[The recent Maccabean Hanukkah rally in Madison Square Garden was described. Louis Lipsky's address that night, in which he described Hitlerism as "the darkest forces of rampant chauvinism,"[8]

---

7 Empirical evidence that Jews are NOT all supporters of the same party or ideology is made part of the sinister conspiracy based on the assumption of absolute uniformity of values among all Jews.

8 The rally was featured in a *NYT* article published on December 13, 1931 under the headline "A Menace to Jews Seen if Hitler Wins," and subheadline "[Louis] Lipsky, Zionist leader, Warns Maccabeans of Peril Looming in Germany." The phrase quoted by Cohen appears in the *NYT* article.

was attacked. The speaker declared that the Jews are afraid Hitler will begin, in Germany, a destruction of Jewish influence the world over.][9]

Almost stunning in its vehemence was the salvo of BRAVOs which greeted the speaker when he shouted, "We must destroy the Jews' power, with wild force if necessary."

Hitler, whose name of course received the wildest applause, is an anti-Semite on the "academic ground that Germany cannot become free other than through breaking down the Jewish control which holds Germans bound for unborn generations. Of course the Nazi is an anti-Semite, but oh, no, he does not want pogroms; he only wants to rid Germany of Jews." Continuing in this strain, Luedecke added, "Hitler is not for war, but the Jews of the world, recognizing that when Hitler comes into power they will suffer, are doing all they can to breed war in order to stop him." Bernard M. Baruch, whom the speaker labelled the Jewish dictator of America and Hoover's financial adviser, is favoring the moratorium to undermine Hitler's power and to save the international bankers.[10] The Jews, he said, are inciting France against Germany to help destroy Hitler.

This led the speaker to a consideration of the German Army. The Germany Army (great applause) was the only organization in Germany before the War free from Jewish control. Unable to control it, the Jews decided to wreck it. To do so they intrigued and brought on the war, but to their dismay the German Army was more powerful than they had reckoned on. To forestall the victory almost in the Army's grasp, the Jews of America, through Jewish leaders' manipulation of Wilson, brought America into the war. Then, having conquered the German Army, they influenced Wilson to write

9 This paragraph from the original typescript was not included in the *Opinion* publication.

10 Bernard Baruch, a Wall Street Banker who was an advisor to President Hoover and would become a key policy advisor to President Roosevelt, played an important role in Nazi propaganda. See Jordan Schwarz, *The Speculator: Bernard Baruch in Washington 1917–1965*. The one-year "moratorium" on the repayment of war debts by Germany was proposed by President Hoover and supported by Baruch in June of 1931 and was currently in place when Luedecke was speaking. But instead of recognizing this as an act that helped the German economy, Luedecke presents it negatively as a way of undermining Hitler's potential influence.

the "Fourteen Points," and later the Versailles Treaty. Thus the Jews chained and enslaved the German people. Discussing the present German economic plight, the Dawes and Young plans were both labelled Jewish devices to enslave Germany for generations to come.[11]

At this point a heckler cried out, "JESUS WAS ALSO A JEW," to which the speaker responded, "Jesus obviously was not a Jew because he was an idealist. He wasn't a Jew, he was a Nordic, as Houston Stewart Chamberlain and other noted authorities have indisputably established.[12] Why, look at any painting in the great galleries of Europe," the speaker went on, "in which Jesus is presented - and not one of them gives Jesus even a Jewish nose!" (Wild applause.) "If you want to know what the Jews think of Christians," went on the speaker, "read the Talmud and the *Shulchan Aruch* and learn the vile things they say there about them."[13]

For a moment I closed my eyes and felt myself drawn back to the Middle Ages, listening to the vilifying harangue of some bloody crusader spewing venom into dull but receptive minds.[14] Only the modern garb of the men, when I again looked around the room, made me feel I was really in the Twentieth Century. I prayed the

---

11 Charles Dawes led a committee established in 1923 to produce a plan that would enable Germany to pay its reparations bill for the War as required by the Treaty of Versailles; cf. the reference by Luedecke, *I Knew Hitler*, pp. 241–42. With Germany unable to meet its large annual payments, another committee was established in 1929 led by Owen D. Young. The obligations of annual payments were to continue for fifty-eight and a half years. Cf. Luedecke, pp. 309–10

12 For this theme, see Susannah Heschel, *The Aryan Jesus: Christian Theologians and the Bible in Nazi Germany*, esp. pp. 41–44 on the influence of Chamberlain.

13 Relevant academic studies of rabbinic sources on Jesus and Christians: Peter Schäfer, *Jesus in the Talmud*; Ruth Langer, *Cursing the Christians: A History of the Birkat Haminim*.

14 This formulation reveals more about popular rhetoric than it does knowledge of the relevant texts. The attacks on Jews by Crusaders - behavior opposed by official Church doctrine - were apparently not produced by "vilifying harangues" (as was the case with the anti-Jewish attacks in Spain, 1391); the only justification preserved in the texts was along the lines: We are preparing to travel a thousand miles to fight the enemies of God (i.e., the Muslims) in the Holy Land; why should we allow even worse enemies of God (the Jews) to remain protected in our own neighborhoods? See Robert Chazan, *European Jewry and the First Crusade*, pp. 225, 244, 248. On the other hand, the Jewish sources reveal extremely insulting language about Christians and Jesus.

poison now being vented would not find the victims it had claimed in those dreaded yesterdays.

The speaker then described the Hitler propaganda machine in Germany, with its seventy newspapers and periodicals, "including a humorous weekly substitute for the Jew-ridden Simplicissimus," its several books and many scores of pamphlets.[15] He closed with an appeal that the audience give encouragement to the Brown Battalions in Germany, through enrollment in the American Branch of the *Nationalsozialistische Vereinigung.*[16]

The iron fist of Hitlerism is thus reaching over from Germany into America in order to help build political bulwarks for its German reign of terror. Hitler hopes to make Berlin a world center of Fascism and anti-Semitism. To this end he has already created "cells," units and groups in Sweden, Norway, Flanders and Holland. A separate division is strenuously at work in the United States rapidly creating "cells" in every receptive environment. Already they have radiated out of Chicago, where the headquarters are located, and have created branches in New York, Albany, Boston, Philadelphia, Detroit, Milwaukee, Memphis and San Francisco. The propagandists Luedicke and Gissibl are touring the United States in an effort to enlist American Nazis, their armory of argument devoid of aught but sneers, gibes, and defamation of Jews.

Hitlerism menaces American Jewry because the Nazi organization is an international anti-Semitic body. Nazis in America will make the Jewish populace here their target, using every form of libel to further their vicious program, utterly unmindful of humanity or truth.

At the propaganda meeting described above, where, incidentally, I too was personally asked to enroll as an American Nazi, a large table

---

15 "Propaganda" here was clearly not a negative term, but a synonym for "information" to be broadly disbursed. *Simplicissimus* was a satirical German weekly magazine founded in 1896. During the Weimar Republic it was critical of the radical left and the radical right. Under the Nazis it continued publishing until 1944, although its Jewish co-founder and leading caricaturist, Thomas Theodor Heine, fled Germany in 1933.

16 The term used for the National Socialist Germany Workers Party (NSDAP) outside of Germany.

carried a heavy sales display of Nazi anti-Semitic literature. The one volume that interested me most was entitled, *Henry Ford: Der Internationale Jude*. To prove that this book – which Ford had published a decade ago in America, and concerning which he had made his famous though fruitless apology – was still being sold publicly in America, I purchased a copy.[17] To further confirm its purchase I took it to Luedecke after the meeting and had him autograph it.[18] (NOTE: The volume purchased was from the 28th edition, 3000 copies, 101st to 104th thousand.)

With the crack of doom reverberating in their ears, and filling their souls with dread of the morrow, the variegated segments of Germany Jewry are now rushing into "an all German Jewish Congress" the better to meet the deadly menace of Hitlerism.[19] American Jewry is not now, nor is ever likely to be, as well established in our social, economic, and political life as was German Jewry in Germany until a decade ago. It therefore behooves American Jewish leadership to recognize promptly and deal adequately with this new menace to American Jewish life, compounded of a Hitler program which battens on the mischievous mess of slanders misbegotten by the tardy Detroit apologist.

We must not overlook the lure the Nazi movement holds out in America to an unscrupulous leadership. To them it will bring position and quick notoriety through unrestrained agitation and unvarnished sophistry. To American Jewry it will bring many heartaches and much misery.

---

17 Ford's "International Jew" was a series of articles originally published in his *The Dearborn Independent*. See Lee, *Henry Ford and the Jews*; Leonard Dinnerstein, "When Henry Ford Apologized to the Jews." For Luedecke's encounter with Ford and his unsuccessful effort to convince Ford to provide funding for the Nazi regime, see Luedecke, *I Knew Hitler*, pp. 183–90.

18 Luedecke may have signed this with a certain ambivalence, as he was appalled by the public apology made by Henry Ford to the Jews in July 1927: "I had never expected one of the richest men in the world to be willing thus to repudiate his editor [of the *Dearborn Independent*] and to make such a humiliating kowtow to Jewry (*I Knew Hitler*, p. 288).

19 Apparently on the model of the American Jewish Congress. Such an institution was proposed immediately after the War in late 1918, but it was not implemented, and I have not found evidence of it in 1932.

The Hitlerites sing many songs of hate. I close with one verse from their

WE ARE THE STORM BRIGADE!

Leave words, which are no use,
Let Adolph Hitler lead!
Come, let us smash the Jews,
And then we shall be freed!

We are the Storm Brigade!
The class-war fighters, we.
In Jewish blood we'll wade
And then we shall be free![20]

Hitlerites always close their meetings with the rousing cry of "*Deutschland, Erwache!*" May I close this presentation of the menace of Hitlerism to American Jewry with "Hear, O Israel," and with the earnest hope that no further watchman's call will be needed to awaken our American Jewish leadership to the new danger, and to their new duties.[21]

20 The JTA of October 14, 1931 printed the same translation of this song with additional stanzas, based on a report from the Central Union of German Citizens of the Jewish Faith: http://www.jta.org/1931/10/14/archive/the-hitlerist-battle-songs.

21 Permission granted by Lorraine Sayers, granddaughter.

Harry Joshua Stern (1897–1984)
"Hitlerism, Germany and Civilization"
Temple Emanu-El, Montreal
April 6, 1933, Mass Rally
Judaism in the War of Ideas, pp. 83–85

INTRODUCTION

Harry Joshua Stern was born in eastern Europe, near Kovno/Kaunas, Lithuania, and grew up in a large, traditional, Yiddish-speaking family. When he was about ten years old the family moved to the United States and settled in Ohio. After finishing his secondary education, he began to study in programs at both the University of Cincinnati and at the nearby Hebrew Union College. Like his role model, Stephen S. Wise, he became a Zionist, even though Zionism was treated with disdain by most HUC faculty – by 1937, in fact, Stern will have visited Palestine three times. Stern earned a Bachelor of Hebrew Literature from HUC in 1919, a BA from the University of Cincinnati in 1920, and was ordained in 1922.

After five years in his first pulpit in Uniontown, Pennsylvania, Stern was invited to a large and prestigious congregation, Temple Emanu-El of Montreal, where he continued to serve until his retirement in 1972. As a leading historian of Canadian Jewry has put it, "Harry Joshua Stern, who took up Merritt's pulpit in 1927, was an ideal rabbi for the Montreal scene. He not only possessed enormous energy, imagination, and courage, but he also had great empathy for the poor downtrodden Jews."[1] Like many other contemporary Reform rabbis, he established a reputation for social justice activism, condemning unfair, exploitative labor practices. He was also committed to inter-

1 Gerald Tulchinsky, "'Justice and Only Justice Thou Shalt Pursue': Considerations on the Social Vice of Canada's Reform Rabbis," p. 317.

faith work, often exchanging pulpits with Protestant pastors; on a visit to Europe he was given an audience with Pope Pius XI.[2]

Most important for our purposes, he established a reputation as a powerful and inspiring pulpit orator. He published five volumes of sermons, two of which are directly relevant to our topic: *Judaism in the War of Ideas: A Collection of Addresses* (1937), from which the following address is taken; *The Jewish Spirit Triumphant: A Collection of Addresses* (1944); *Martyrdom and Miracle: A Collection of Addresses* (1950); *Entrusted With Spiritual Leadership: A Collection of Addresses* (1960); and *One World or No World: A Collection of Sermons, Essays, and Addresses* (1973), all published by Bloch Publishing in New York. These addresses were published without formal dates provided, which excludes many of them from our use, but some of them – including the following – can be dated by internal information. A biographical/autobiographical study of Stern's career is Kenneth Irving Cleator and Harry Joshua Stern's *Harry Joshua Stern: A Rabbi's Journey* (New York: Bloch, 1981).

The address presented below represents a sub-genre of Jewish preaching in response to Nazi persecution: it was delivered at a public rally of protest against Nazi policies. Stern spoke as the rabbi of the largest synagogue in Montreal, but since this was a community rally including Christian speakers as well he quickly turns to rhetoric that is widely inclusive: he speaks not as a rabbi, and not even as a Jew, but as a human being committed to human progress and human freedom.[3] Yet only a few sentences later he is emphasizing the unique situation of German Jewry as the primary victim, using language – e.g., Via Dolorosa, mount of crucifixion, "the Christ people" – intended to appeal to Christian listeners as well as Jews, including the Bishop of Montreal, whom Stern had personally invited to speak.

2 The biographical material is based largely on the *Encyclopedia Judaica* (2008) article on Stern. For both the audience with the Pope and Stern's visits to Palestine, see his sermon "Palestine: The Land of Promise," in *Judaism in the War of Ideas,* p. 50.

3 It was estimated that 10,000 people were present at the Mount Royal Arena in Montreal. See James Walker, "Claiming Equality for Canadian Jewry," in *Nazi Germany, Canadian Responses*, ed. Ruth Klein, p. 224 (and n.12).

"HITLERISM" IS A CULT WHICH HAS FOR ITS DOCTRINE THE ABSOLUTE state. It negates liberalism and democracy and its philosophy is that of fanaticism and racial bias. The result of this cult has been a reign of terror, a horror which the world has not witnessed since the days of Russian pogroms under the rule of the Czar. Hitlerism is a menace to civilization.

I lift my voice in protest tonight not as a Jew but as one interested in human progress and human freedom, for the persecution of Hitlerism is directed not only against the Jew, but against German liberals of all schools, the founders of the German Republic, the supporters of German democratic government, the independent working man of the Social Democratic party. All these are the victims of Hitleristic dictatorship. But primarily the Jew has felt the iron rod of persecution; Jews of all ranks, the rich and the poor, the great and the humble, are thrust beneath the yoke of oppression. Once again my people Israel is made to tread the Via Dolorosa and made to climb the hill of crucifixion. Verily we Jews are "the Christ people"; a thousand times have we been crucified and a thousand times we shall yet be crucified until the truths taught by our faith become the common possession of all mankind.[4]

Yes, the famous Jews are also the targets of persecution! Thus it is that a Bruno Walter dare not lift his baton over an orchestra![5] Theodor Wolff fled from his newspaper office of the "Berliner Tageblatt"

4 This is indeed a powerful rhetorical claim, and one wonders how Christian listeners would have responded to it. The "Christ people" was a term synonymous with the more widely used "Christians," first used by pagans to characterize those for whom Jesus Christ was central to their religious identity. I have not found a precedent for the formulation "We Jews are 'the Christ people.'" Cf. Cleator and Stern, *Harry Joshua Stern*, p. 79. For a later citation of Stern's sentence, see http://bit.ly/2wRkCmr, p. 46.

5 Walter, born (Bruno Schlesinger) in Germany in 1876, had a highly respected international musical career, and was conductor of the Leipzig Gewandhaus Orchestra until March 1933. He was scheduled to conduct the Berlin Philharmonic on March 20, but pressure from Goebbels and indirectly from Hitler led him to move with his family to Austria, and from there to the United States, where he had already conducted for several major orchestras.

and is in hiding;[6] a Lion Feuchtwanger finds refuge in Switzerland,[7] and an Einstein in Belgium![8] What a tragic hour is this in the history of Jewry. Perhaps the greatest tragedy of modern times.[9]

What can we do in this hour of tragedy? What can we do? We can cry aloud in grief and in shame. We can protest, we can mobilize public opinion and perhaps our cry will be heard; heard at least if not by the Nazi then by the millions of Germans who are possessors of the spirit of Goethe, Kant, Schiller, Lessing, Einstein. We can appeal to Christendom that is not Christless.

A few days ago I called on His Lordship, the Bishop of Montreal, and invited him to come to this meeting of protest.[10] I saw tears in his eyes and I read in those tears the shame which this religious leader felt that he should be called upon to protest against the barbarism of the so-called Christian Germany. Only this morning I read that the Nazis are about to make an alliance with the Lutheran Church, that the swastika is to be united with the cross.[11] Think of it! The cross, the symbol of that Jew of Galilee who taught "love ye one another," and the swastika, the symbol of hate and autocracy. I

---

6 Wolff, one of the founders of the German Democratic Party (DDP), was chief editor of the liberal *Berliner Tageblatt* from 1906 until 1933. He fled from Berlin in late February, finding temporary asylum in Switzerland and then in Nice. When Italian forces took Nice, he was handed over to the Gestapo, and, after some time in concentration camps, died in 1943.

7 Feuchtwanger, perhaps best known for his novel *Jud Süss*, had been strongly opposed to the Nazi Party from its beginnings. He was on tour outside Germany in spring 1933, and settled in southern France; after the German invasion, he received political asylum in the United States. Like Wolff, his books were listed among those to be burned on May 10, 1933.

8 Einstein left Germany in 1932 for the United States; he would never again return to Europe.

9 A fine example of a formulation that seems both hyperbolic (a tragedy greater than the "Great War"?) and ironic in light of what was to come, serving as a reminder that even the most sensitive opponents of Nazi Germany had little inkling of the catastrophe that the future would hold.

10 Bishop of Montreal Emmanuel (Abo-Hatab) of Brooklyn was Bishop of the American Orthodox Catholic Church in Montreal.

11 On the German-Christian Church: see Doris Bergen, *Twisted Cross: The German Christian Movement in the Third Reich*. For a picture of a church altar with both swastika and cross, see Susanna Heschel, *The Aryan Jesus*, p. 4, Figure 1.1.

hope and pray to God that such an alliance never takes place. Thrice shame upon Christianity if such a union ever comes to be.

What else can we do? We can turn to the responsible governments of the world and ask these to speak for Israel even as in the past they have spoken in behalf of the Armenians who were persecuted by the Turks.[12]

And if the world fails us, what else can we do? My people Israel, if the world fails us we need not despair. *Al Tiro Avdi Yaakov Ki Itecho Oni* – "Fear not, my servant Jacob, for I am with thee" (Jer. 30:10). We Jews need not fear Hitlerism. We, who have met with the legions of Rome; we, who have battled with the horsemen of Assyria and Babylon; we, who wrestled with the Hellenism and Hellenists of Greece, we, who have seen persecutors come and go; we shall not be intimidated by the bigotry and prejudice of the Nazis. If the world fails us, surely the God of Israel will not fail us in this tragic hour of our history.[13]

12 Another rather ironic statement, as condemnations of Turkish persecution of the Armenians had little capacity to save Armenian lives. Note the absence of any recommendation of concrete measures (such as an economic boycott) that might have been thought to punish the new German government.

13 A poignantly painful expression of faith that could readily be challenged in retrospect. Stern referred back to this "vast meeting at the Mount Royal Arena" in a sermon delivered five years later, published in *The Jewish Spirit Triumphant*, pp. 63–64. Permission granted by Stephanie D. Glayman, daughter.

Israel Levinthal (1888–1982)
"The Old Pharaoh in Modern Garb"
Brooklyn Jewish Center
April 11, 1933 (First day of Pesach)
A New World Is Born, pp. 148–54

INTRODUCTION

Israel Herbert Levinthal was born in Vilna, Lithuania into a family with a long rabbinical tradition. Levinthal's family immigrated to the United States in 1891, where his father, Bernard, became the rabbi of the Orthodox community in Philadelphia, and helped establish the Union of Orthodox Rabbis in the United States and Canada.

Bernard Levinthal's son Israel received his BA from Columbia University in 1909 (having won a silver medal in the university oratorical contest), and was ordained at the Jewish Theological Seminary the following year. He earned a law degree from New York University in 1914, and received the degree of Doctor of Hebrew Letters from the Jewish Theological Seminary in 1920.

Levinthal began his rabbinical career in Brooklyn, first at Temple B'nai Shalom (1910–1915), moving afterwards to Petach Tikvah (1915–1919). In 1919, Levinthal accepted a position as the first rabbi of the incipient Brooklyn Jewish Center. An early realization of Mordecai M. Kaplan's synagogue-center idea, the Brooklyn Jewish Center fostered Levinthal's interests in communal activities and Zionism.

Levinthal served as the rabbi of the Brooklyn Jewish Center during the institution's period of growth between the world wars. The Center's membership, consisting of a thousand families in 1923, doubled by 1946. In order to meet the religious and communal needs of this expanding constituency, the Center offered religious services with thought-provoking sermons, youth and adult educational opportunities, recreational activities, and cultural programs.

Rabbi Levinthal additionally played a prominent leadership role in the Conservative and Zionist movements, including a term as president of the Rabbinical Assembly (1930–1932). He also established a national reputation as one of the outstanding Jewish preachers of his time.[1]

The books of his published sermons and addresses – *Steering or Drifting: Which?: Sermons and Discourses* (1928); *A New World Is Born: Sermons and Addresses* (1943); *Judaism Speaks to the Modern World* (1963); *The Message of Israel: Sermons, Addresses, Memoirs* (1973) – reveal an unusual homiletical artistry. The hand-written texts of his sermons (preserved in the Archives of the Jewish Theological Seminary of America) were not fully written out; some serve as extensive outlines, others are no more than a list of phrases. In some cases, therefore, we have three different versions of the sermons that his congregants heard: handwritten notes, a brief newspaper account with quotations, and the published text, often with footnotes added by the author identifying the sources of traditional texts cited.

The following sermon was delivered on the first day of Pesach, and it therefore fits the model of what is sometimes called "the classic Jewish sermon." The central message of the sermon is that there is a direct connection between the holiday of Pesach, the statements of the Haggadah, the narrative of oppression at the beginning of Exodus, and the dramatic events of the present in Germany. "History repeats itself" is the core premise of the discourse. There is nothing new; it has all been foretold in our sacred texts. And so, there is a constant movement between the familiar account of the past and the current reality, between the Pharaoh of the enslavement and the Exodus and the current dictator of Germany. Even the nuances of Hebrew narrative style can be interpreted as forecasting that the events were not a one-time past occurrence. Since everyone knew

1 The biographical material is taken largely from Saperstein, *Jewish Preaching in Times of War*, pp. 441–42, which itself is indebted to Kimmy Caplan, "The Life and Sermons of Rabbi Israel Levinthal."

how the biblical story of enslavement would eventually end, and listeners had celebrated the happy denouement in their seders the night before, the underlying message was one of reassurance for the listeners and the Jews of Germany.

Absent from this sermon is any suggestion of what listeners – or the American government – might do to alleviate the suffering of the Jews in Germany. Other sermons (such as the following, by Jacob P. Rudin), are quite different in this regard. It is as if Levinthal's message here is that the best policy for American Jews is simply to "keep the faith."

Reading the text today, it is possible to conclude that the fundamental assertion – "It is remarkable how history repeats itself" – is misleading, in that there would be something radically new in the Nazi program, something unprecedented in the biblical narrative: mass murder of the great majority of Jews in continental Europe. Yet the final sentence, referring to a future "When Hitler's name, like Pharaoh's of old, shall have become a mockery," may be read as revealing a powerful and admirable certitude of faith.

NOT FOR MANY YEARS HAS THE STORY WE READ IN THE PASSOVER Haggadah, as we sit at our Seder table, had the reality for us that it has in our day. What new meaning do we find in the words, "For not one alone arose to destroy us, but in every generation some rise up against us to destroy us!"[2]

We thought that now, at least, in this glorious twentieth century, we had passed this stage of history – that Pharaohs were a thing of the past – when, lo and behold, another Pharaoh rises before our very eyes. "In every generation it is incumbent on every Israelite to look upon himself as if he had actually gone forth from Egypt," the Haggadah says. Alas, in this generation, it has become necessary for every Israelite in certain lands of Europe to look upon himself as if he were actually living in Egypt once again.

---

2 A quotation from the Passover Haggadah. Levinthal did not cite here the final phrase of the passage: "and the Holy One, blessed be He, saves us from their hands."

It is remarkable how history repeats itself. Suddenly the clock of civilization was turned backwards, and we are back again in the Egypt of more than three thousand years ago, the old Pharaoh reincarnate before our very eyes. We can read the chapters in the Book of Exodus, and just changing the word Egypt to Germany, and the name Pharaoh to Hitler, then word for word, how truly they describe Jewish life in Nazi-land today!

"These are the names of the children of Israel *Ha-ba-im*, who came to Egypt, with Jacob did every man and his household come" (Exod. 1:1). The Rabbis, in reading this opening verse of the Book of Exodus, were struck by the fact that the Hebrew word *Ha-ba-im* (who came) is in fact in the present tense, and that literally the passage reads, "These are the names of the children of Israel who *come now* to Egypt." *V'ḳi Ha-yom Ba-im*, "Did they just arrive in Egypt?" ask the Sages in dismay. "Is it not many years that have passed since they migrated here? Already with Jacob had they arrived!" Ah, but the answer is quite simple. True they had been living in Egypt almost a century, they had already become Egyptian in their ways and mode of life; but the Egyptians, despite the fact that the Jews had been in Egypt since the days of Jacob, looked upon them as strangers, as *Ha-ba-im*, as newly-arrived immigrants, *K'ilu Oto Yom Niḳnesu L'Mitzraim*, "as if they had just today come to the land of Egypt."[3]

Is it not the same with German Jewry? Think of it: they came to Germany more than a thousand years ago; as early as 916, according to written records, there were Jewish communities in Germany.[4] They came at the very dawn of German history. They helped to build up

---

3 Exodus Rabbah, 1,4 (author's note). Here and throughout the sermon, I have followed the rather idiosyncratic transliteration system, including a capital letter for the beginning of each Hebrew word, that is used consistently throughout the collection of his sermons published in 1943.

4 It is unclear to me which written records cite 916 as the beginning of a Jewish presence in Germany. A Church council in Mainz stipulated in 906 a severe punishment for killing a Jew or a heathen, and it is believed (though without specific textual evidence) that the Kalonymos family migrated from southern Italy to Mainz, arriving around 917. Other Jewish preachers will place the Jewish presence in Germany centuries earlier (cf. Marvin Lowenthal, *The Jews of Germany: A Story of Sixteen Centuries*).

the German land, German culture, German art, German finance. Like Joseph who served Egypt, so did these Jews serve Germany for ten centuries. But now, suddenly they are looked upon as *Ha-ba-im*, as strangers within the gates, as if they had no right whatsoever to live in that land, as if they had arrived just today or yesterday from strange shores.

Let us proceed with that ancient story and see how well it fits in this modern setting. *Vayakam Melek Chadash Asher Lo Yoda Et Yosef*, "And there arose a new king who knew not Joseph!" (Exod. 1:8). Here, too, a new ruler arose, who knew not or did not want to know the role that Joseph – the Jew – played in German life these thousand years. He did not want to know that though the Jew in Germany represented less than one per cent of the total population, twelve per cent of his number died on the field of battle defending the German flag in the last world war.[5]

But here too the Rabbis were quick to note the strange language in the Hebrew text. It does not say "*Va-yimlok*," "And there reigned a new king," but "*Va-yakam*," "And there *arose* a new king." And they wisely point out to us that this word "*Va-Yakam*" implies rising with intent to kill and to murder! They point, by way of illustration, to the phrase, "*Va-Yakam Cain*," – "And Cain arose against Abel his brother" (Gen. 4:8).[6] To Nazi Germany, the same text may be applied. "It is not only that a change in government has taken place, but [that] Hitler arose with hate and murder in his heart, with a fiendish desire to ruin and to destroy the whole people of Israel!

And we hear this new ruler speaking the same language as Pharaoh of old: "Behold the people of the children of Israel *Rav v'otzum Mimenu*, are more numerous and more mighty than we!" (Exod. 1:9).

---

5 This does not quite make sense as written. The population of Jews in Germany during the war was about 550,000, and the number that served in the German military was about 100,000. Twelve percent of the German Jewish population would be 66,000, or sixty-six percent of the Jewish soldiers, which is obviously impossible. The number commonly cited by German Jews was that 12,000 (or twelve percent) *of the Jewish soldiers* were killed, slightly less than one percent of the total number of German soldiers, and about two percent of the German Jewish population. For this figure, see Derek J. Penslar, *Jews and the Military*, p. 185.

6 *Torah Temimah* on Exod. 1:8, note 2; cf. b. Sotah 11a (author's note).

The Egyptians numbered in the millions – the Jews were only a small minority in their midst – and yet the Egyptians cried that the Jews were too numerous and too mighty for them! In Germany today the Jews are less than one per cent of the country's population, and yet we hear the Nazis crying these very words: "The Jews are more numerous and more powerful than we!" Such is the result of a blindness that comes from bigotry and prejudice.

But there is an added significance, a sinister meaning in this complaint. The Hebrew text is far more meaningful. The Hebrew word *Mi-menu* does not only mean "*than we*," but also means "*from us*." What the Egyptians also said was that the children of Israel had become strong and mighty *Mi-menu*, "from us." It is the old anti-Jewish cry: "Whatever the Jews have, whatever they own, whatever they have achieved, is – *mi-menu, from us* – they have robbed us of everything!" How quickly the vilifiers forget the toil, the labors, the hardships, the sacrifices, that enabled these Jews to achieve what they have! And these words of falsehood spread like wild fire, in Germany as well as in Egypt, causing the degradation and the enslavement of an entire people.

For all the ills that come upon the German people, these new rulers offer but one remedy: *Destroy the Jews!* Our Sages, with their keen insight into human history, tell us that the old Pharaoh in Egypt was leprous and was seeking a cure for his deadly disease. When all else failed, his soothsayers said to him, "We have a cure that is certain of its effect. Slay every day a number of Jewish children, *U'rechotz Be'damehem*, and bathe in their blood!"[7] Poor, deluded Pharaoh tried this remedy but, of course, it was to no avail. The new tyrants in Germany have offered the deluded German people this familiar age-old remedy: "Let us bathe in Jewish blood!" And they seized upon that advice and began to bathe in a river of Jewish blood.[8]

But let us continue with our ancient tale. Moses, you recall, inspired by God, came to protest against the Egyptians' inhuman

---

7 Exodus Rabbah, 1,41 (author's note).

8 This is obviously a hyperbolic allusion to incidents of violence that occurred at the very beginning of the Nazi regime, which did *not* yet indicate a cohesive policy of mass murder.

treatment of the Jews. See what happened! Exactly the same thing has happened to-day in Germany. The world began to protest against German atrocities. Very well, they answered, we shall kill no more, we shall cease our butchering; but we shall slay them without shedding their blood. Like Pharaoh who demanded that the Jews make bricks without straw, so, too, this modern Pharaoh decreed that all avenues of livelihood be closed to the German Jews. Let them live, but take away from them every opportunity for the maintenance of life – that was the new Gospel. No more public atrocities, but in Hitler's language: "*Alle Juden blutlos totzuschlagen!*" – that was the new method in dealing with the Jew.[9]

More than that, the Egyptians of old made the same mistake that the people of Germany make – they thought that Pharaoh sought only the enslavement of the Jew. The old Pharaoh, like his modern successor, was a master in the technique of propaganda. The Jew is a useful scapegoat with which to blind the masses to a tyrant's true intent. But it was not only the Jew who suffered – soon the best and finest of the Egyptians also became enslaved. Indeed, other peoples and other nationalities, too, soon found themselves in bondage. That can be seen from the very statements in the Biblical story. When the redeemer Moses appeared and brought hope to the downtrodden and enslaved he was welcomed not only by the Israelites, but by all the oppressed Egyptians as well, "Moreover, the man Moses was very great in the land of Egypt, in the sight of Pharaoh's servants, and in the sight of the people" (Exod. 11:3).[10] And when freedom finally

---

9 R. Elijah, Gaon of Vilna, interprets the words of Haman, "If it shall please the king, let it be decreed *l'obdom*, to destroy them" (Esth. 3:9) as *lo b'dom*, "without blood," an analogy to Hitler's "*blutlos totzuschlagen*." It is to be noted that this was the policy in the early years of the Hitler regime. Soon, this policy, too, was considered too lenient, and the slaughter of Jews continued (author's note).

I have not found this phrase associated with Hitler as applied to the early years of his regime. The phrase was used by Joseph Hertz (applied to Prussian Government law of 1812) in his 1923 address to the Jewish Preachers Conference, though removed from the later 1938 edition), http://bit.ly/2w1tyFW.

10 Cf. the striking passage in Mekhilta to Exod 14,5, that Pharaoh conquered and enslaved the whole world, and also the statement, ibid., "Any nation that begins to rule oppressively over the Jews soon rules oppressively over all, from one end of the earth to the other" (author's note).

came, it came not only to the Jew but also to that great *Erev Rav, mixed multitude* of other people and nationalities that were equally enslaved. The Jew then, as now, was the first to bear this attack of the tyrant upon human freedom and liberty.

And stranger than all these comparisons between the old Pharaoh and his modern reincarnation is the fact that both challenge not only the Jew, but even more so the God of the Jew – the God whom the Jew made known to humanity. When Moses brought his immortal message to Pharaoh, the latter cried out, "Who is this God that I shall hearken unto His voice?" (Exod. 5:2). In like fashion, this modern Pharaoh has cried out, again and again, "We know not this God, who speaks in terms of love and justice and mercy. We know but one god – the god of blood, of brute force, and of hate!"

One thing Pharaoh certainly did not know: "He knew not Joseph!" He did not know the nature of the Jew. Neither he nor his modern reincarnated spirit seems to realize the great truth of history: that persecution can never destroy the Jew. The Bible records the verdict of history: "But the more they afflicted them, the more they multiplied and the more they spread abroad!" (Exod. 1:12). The Rabbis were quick to observe that in this verse the Bible speaks in the future and not in the present tense. R. Simon ben Lakish declared, *Ruach Ha-kodesh Mevasratan Ken Yirbeh ve-ḳen Yifrotz*, "It was the Divine Spirit that then assured them, so *shall* they multiply and so *shall* they spread abroad in the days to come!"[11]

The end of the story is not yet told. We are still here – a vital factor on the world's stage. Pharaoh and his hosts are long forgotten – mummies in museums. The Jew sits today at his *Seder*, and with pride and humility retells the story of countless ages ago. When Hitler's name, like Pharaoh's of old, shall have become a mockery, even then the Jew will sing as he sang in the days of his youth, the song of faith, the song of triumph![12]

---

11 b. Sotah 11a; Exodus Rabbah, 1,14 (author's note).

12 Permission granted by Judith Lyons, granddaughter.

Jacob P. Rudin (1902–1982)

"Dark Horizons – 1933"
Temple Beth-El, Great Neck, NY
September 20, 1933 (Rosh Hashanah Evening)
Very Truly Yours: A Creative Harvest of Forty Years in the Pulpit
pp. 227–32

INTRODUCTION

Jacob Philip Rudin was born in Malden, Massachusetts. He received a bachelor's degree from Harvard College in 1924 and a master's degree and rabbinic ordination from the Jewish Institute of Religion in 1928. He received a Doctor of Divinity degree from the Institute in 1948. He served as president of the Institute's alumni association and of the Hebrew Union College Alumni Association. The influence of the President of the JIR – Rabbi Stephen S. Wise – is obvious from the sermon below.

After his ordination, Rudin served as assistant rabbi at the Stephen Wise Free Synagogue in Manhattan and as assistant to Wise at the JIR. In 1930, he became rabbi of Temple Beth-El in Great Neck, New York, a suburban community on Long Island; he remained in this position until his retirement in 1971, with a period as Chaplain in the Naval Reserve during the war. He later served as president of the Central Conference of American Rabbis, past president and treasurer of the New York Metropolitan Association of Reform Rabbis, and a member of the executive board of the New York Board of Rabbis.

Rudin also served as president of the Synagogue Council of America, during which time he was appointed by President Lyndon B. Johnson to an observer team for the Vietnam elections in 1967. As president of the Council, he represented the Jewish community at the funeral of the Rev. Dr. Martin Luther King Jr. in 1968.

A collection of his sermons, *Very Truly Yours*, was published in 1971 (New York: Bloch Publishing Company); the sermon below is taken from this book.[1]

This sermon is strikingly different in style from the previous sermon by Israel Levinthal, a Conservative Rabbi. Levinthal constantly refers back to biblical themes and rabbinic interpretations as a background for contemporary events. Although Rudin's sermon was delivered on the Jewish New Year, he does not refer to a single Jewish text. Indeed the only direct quotation in the sermon is from an antisemitic broadside. The focus is not on connections between past and present, but entirely on the present.

The issue at stake is at the core of a serious division in policy among major Jewish organizations following Hitler's accession to power. Should the Nazi regime be engaged through a network of contacts that might moderate its extremism, or should it be isolated, treated as a pariah, brought to its knees through an economic stranglehold? Wise and the American Jewish Congress did not originally support the economic boycott of Nazi Germany, but they came aboard in August of 1933. The American Jewish Committee and the B'nai B'rith remained opposed. At the time, strong arguments on both sides were made more complicated by the apparent ambivalence of German Jews on this issue. Rudin, following his mentor Stephen S. Wise, although recognizing and citing the contending arguments, expressed a powerful endorsement of the boycott policy. How could any self-respecting American Jew continue to purchase German products?

SELDOM IN OUR LONG HISTORY HAS THE SUN OF A NEW YEAR RISEN upon so dark and mournful a horizon. Seldom have the Jewish people come together in their synagogues to celebrate the coming of a New Year with hearts so charged with tragedy over the events of a year

1 The biographical material in this Introduction is based on the *NYT* obituary written by Walter H. Waggoner and published on September 11, 1982. Cf. also Saperstein, *Jewish Preaching in Times of War*, pp. 399–405.

just closed and with such bitter forebodings of what the New Year will bring. The wheel of time has made but a single turning, but in that turning it has shaken the Jewish world to its very foundations. Even the most farsighted of our leaders, even the most pessimistic among the bearers of evil tidings of a year ago, did not dream of such a cataclysm as has befallen us. But the sternest warnings were not stern enough and the loudest cries not loud enough. The worst has come to pass and there seems to be no end. We are facing the greatest crisis in our annals.[2] That is the bald truth that we must face unblinkingly at this, the beginning of a New Year. If Jewry, as the German Jews represent it, is defeated in its struggle for life, then I tremble to think of what will happen to the rest of the world over. If we do not beat into submission the vicious hounds that have German Jewry by the throat, their baying will soon be heard in this and in every other country, the deadly padding of their paws will be heard around our doorstep, the snap and click of their bloody jaws will ring in our ears.

For a long time we counseled prudence. We said that Hitler would never come to power. Then when he came into power, we said that responsibility would sober him and teach him moderation. How foolish were our hopes, the past seven months have shown. Fury has been unleashed. Death, destruction and despair are riding wild. Six hundred thousand Jews have been brought to the brink. Three percent of all the Jews in the world are crushed, broken and enslaved.

I will grant that the whole thing sounds like some madhouse nightmare and impossible dream. "It cannot be," we say, "that at least three hundred Jews have been killed by the Nazis. It cannot be that at least three thousand Jews have been cruelly tortured, that thousands are in concentration camps under so-called protective arrest, that at least fifty thousand Jews are homeless refugees abroad, that the great majority of the more than five hundred thousand

2 Rudin's discourse – "The worst has come to pass.... We are facing the greatest crisis in our annals" – seems of course poignantly hyperbolic in light of future events. It is another reminder that we must read this material removing from our minds everything we know about what happened later.

Jews remaining are reduced to the worst kind of poverty. It simply isn't conceivable that the German Jew who dates his ancestry back for so many centuries in Germany has been expelled from citizenship, forced out of economic life, denied the practice of the liberal professions, barred from labor unions, from sports organizations, forbidden an education for his children, his property confiscated, passport withdrawn, free exit abroad cut off, his movements, mail and family the objects of spying and surveillance." It is to become part of a lunacy, but it is one that has been and continues to involve us and to certify to its truth.

This is the situation, just as I have briefly summarized it. German Jewry is finished – through. The best we can hope for is to salvage the sad remnants of what was once their flourishing life. But even to salvage the wreckage demands immediate, united, consistent, unremitting and relentless opposition to the bestiality, the uncleanness, the blasphemy of every decent human instinct that the sadists who now rule Germany exemplify.

We have had protest meetings, we have held parades, we have expressed the indignant sorrow that fills our hearts in a thousand different ways. Germany has been excoriated for its policy in the general press. For its anti-Jewishness and for the menace it represents to the peace of Europe and the peace of the world, Germany finds itself completely isolated by world opinion. It is regarded on all sides with suspicion and open dislike. The very fact that this world antagonism hasn't made the slightest difference to Germany and hasn't caused either a cessation of its assaults upon the Jew or a change in its general attitude proves more convincingly than anything else that we are not dealing with sane and responsible people. There is neither conscience nor normal intelligence to which one can appeal.

Were an individual to run amuck as Germany has, he would be clapped into an insane asylum, as indeed one of the foremost powers of the Nazis was confined some eight years ago.[3] But even with

3 This apparently alludes to Hermann Göring, currently Deputy Führer, who was briefly confined to a Swedish lunatic asylum in 1925, partly because of morphine addiction.

a nation the same principle must be invoked. As long as Germany proves herself by her conduct to be an evil recrudescence of barbarism and a danger to mankind, just so long must it be excommunicated from decent society and excluded from the circle of civilized nations. And because we Jews have thus far been the tragic victims of her fanaticism and have borne the brunt of her madness, upon us devolves the double duty of leading the fight against everything that Hitler and his band stand for.

I am convinced that there is but one and only one language that Hitler understands: Boycott.[4] We have no alternative. We are in a desperate, desperate situation. The repercussions of the German situation are appalling to consider. I repeat in all soberness: if Hitler succeeds in his Jewish policy, the Jews will be safe nowhere in the world. This is a battle for our very life and for the principles of humanity that we as a people have advocated throughout our history.

We still hear arguments against the boycott. It will prove a boomerang and in the long run do us more harm than good. It will bring increased hardship to the very German Jews whom we seek by this method to aid. It will give credence to the old cry that the Jew is truly an international people.

What further misfortune, I would ask, can be visited upon the sorrowful heads of German Jews that has not already come to them? They have nothing left to lose. Starvation is theirs, torture is theirs, death is theirs. There can be no worse.[5]

As for being called an international people, would to God that we were. It would be a badge that we can proudly wear. No greater honor can be ours than to be known as a people that dwells everywhere, and wherever it dwells is consecrated to the loftiest ideals and the noblest

---

4 On the boycott see Moshe Gottlieb, "The Anti-Nazi Boycott Movement in the United States: An Ideological and Sociological Appreciation," pp. 198–227; Richard A. Hawkins, "'Hitler's Bitterest Foe': Samuel Untermyer and the Boycott of Nazi Germany, 1933–1938," pp. 21–50.

5 Needless to say, this last sentence is poignantly ironic in terms of what was to come. The idea of systematic mass murder for all Jews in Nazi-occupied Europe was apparently inconceivable at the time. The immediate response to the announcement of a boycott by Americans in the anti-Nazi rally of March 27, 1933 was a one-day boycott of Jewish businesses, held on April 1.

ends. It is, indeed, my most fervent prayer that we shall soon be able to present to the world, to friend and to foe alike, an unbroken front, that we show that no nation can attack us with impunity and make us the scapegoat for its own weaknesses and crimes. I do hope that a world-Israel will fight and fight to the last ditch by every honorable means to preserve its honor, its self-respect and its dignity. If this German situation did not touch us too closely and were it merely an outrage to the decency of mankind, it would still be our duty to act and to act decisively as a single, indivisible people.

Nor let us deceive ourselves about the first of the arguments that I have mentioned. If, for defending ourselves, we shall be made the object of recriminations, let us at least know now who is with us and who is against us. Let us at least have the honorable satisfaction that we have done our duty to the fullest measure of our power and our resources, for let us remember that if Hitler succeeds, it is only a question of time before we experience the same outbreak of hatred against us somewhere else.

Goebbels, Hitler's minister of enlightenment and propaganda,[6] has admitted that the German government is spending $200,000,000 for propaganda purposes. A not inconsiderable part of that huge sum is being spent here in this country at the present time to defame the Jew and to arouse the non-Jew against him. The country has been flooded with hate-arousing material. The repercussions of the boycott that we fear may come anyway. Let me read you a sample of the kind of thing that is being circulated right here in the metropolitan area of New York. Copies of this letter have been found in Newark subways, in a Sunnyside, Long Island bus, a Boro Park street car, in the New York Public Library and on park benches.

"HIT THE JEWS WHEREVER YOU CAN"

Following are the contents of a chain letter being thoroughly circulated throughout the Metropolitan area.

---

6 The German title was *Reichsminister für Völksaufklärung und Propaganda.* "Propaganda" in this context has the broader meaning of the spread of information in support of a particular cause, not necessarily inaccurate or false information, and would probably better be translated "Minister of Popular Enlightenment and Information."

"American Gentiles:

"Do you realize that we are nothing but *Jewish slaves?*

"Do you realize, the danger which confronts us by the Jews in the United States, is much greater than we all anticipate?

"Do you realize that every nation which accepted the Jews signed its own doom? The Jewish sharks own already New York City. *Who works for* the Jews under most unsanitary conditions, long hours and for slave wages until body and mind is a wreck? *The Gentile.* We *Must* face the fact that hundreds of thousands of us will either on account of the Jewish lowdown racket *starve or be driven to suicide* in the near future. *We ask you:* Will a Jew buy from a Gentile? NO. Why do *you* buy from a Jew? Make it a principle to *boycott every Jewish business* and hit the Jews at their weakest spot - the possibility of *making money through you.* Do not read nor advertise in a Newspaper which is controlled by Jews. The Jews are the lowest international race on earth, prospering through thievery without consciousness [*sic*], they are the biggest enemies and the cause of the destruction of the USA.

"Hit the Jews Wherever You Can"[7]

Clearly the only course left for us is to fight Germany at every turn of the road. We must have no dealings with her in any way. We shall not buy German goods. We shall not buy German books, nor patronize German plays and films. We shall not buy anything which, although not manufactured in Germany, was made of German raw materials. We shall not patronize stores and shops which continue to buy from Germany or patronize German concerns and shipping.

We must not falter. There must be no relenting from this program. When Germany's export trade is strangled, when the falling off of orders increases unemployment, when Germany is thoroughly discredited in the eyes of the world, then and then only will Hitler come

7 The text was published on the first page of the *Ohio Jewish Chronicle* on August 4, 1933 (apparently taken from a New York source), next to an article entitled, "Nazis Open Underground Anti-Jewish Drive: Hitlerites Launch New Offensive in New York with Anti-Semitic Chain Letters," http://bit.ly/2yl9qQe. See also John Louis Spivak, *America Faces the Barricades*, pp. 195–96.

to his senses. There is no other language that he understands. We must speak it, then, so that he will not mistake our meaning. Boycott.

Nor should we attempt to keep the fact of the boycott quiet. It is not the part of brave men and women to make believe that things are other than they are. Hitler is our enemy. He ranks with the devilish few who have brought misery and tragedy to a whole section of our people without cause, without justice. The German people, as long as they tolerate this madman, as long as they support him in his fiendish policy, applauding his course of action and accepting his inhuman leadership, so long are they, too, our enemies. They have martyred our brothers and sisters. We cannot, in common decency and self-respect, have anything whatsoever to do with them until they regain their senses, and we must tell them this without ceasing.

This boycott must succeed. But it will succeed only by the union of all Jews.[8] Let us not lose courage. We are yet the deathless Jew who shall witness the death of Hitler and his message of violence and hate. We must keep the fountainhead of our faith clear and untainted. Justice is on our side. The truth is our defense. These have never failed us in the past; they will not fail us now.

Let us but pause for a moment and reflect that at this very moment, everywhere, Jews are gathered in their synagogues to greet the New Year. This *is* A New Year, and as Jews we will greet it in the truly Jewish fashion: with hope, with courage, with unquenched fire. Germany must go the way of all nations who have lined themselves on the side of oppression, of bigotry and of hatred. It digs its own grave, and the sun of our faith will yet rise above the dark horizons and shine upon its tombstone.[9]

---

8 Such unity was never achieved, as there were many American Jewish leaders who remained opposed to the boycott, not in principle but for tactical reasons.

9 Permission granted by Stephen L. Rudin, son.

Harold I. Saperstein (1910–2001)
"The Call to Battle"
Temple Emanu-El, Lynbrook, NY
September 10, 1934 (Rosh Hashanah Morning)
Witness from the Pulpit, pp. 37–43

INTRODUCTION

Harold I. Saperstein was born in Troy, New York; his grandfather, Chaim Mordecai Lasker, a Lithuanian Orthodox Rabbi, ordained in Kovno, served the Troy congregation. While a student at Cornell, Saperstein was deeply impressed when Stephen S. Wise visited the campus to speak at Sage Chapel, and at the newly formed Hillel House where he spoke about Zionism. A long conversation with Wise on that occasion convinced him to apply to the Jewish Institute of Religion.

On Rosh Hashanah 1934 Harold Saperstein was still a rabbinical student, not yet twenty-four years old, and about to enter his final year at JIR. The previous December he had begun to substitute in a small Reform congregation on Long Island for his uncle, Rabbi Adolph Lasker, an early graduate of JIR, who had become ill. Saperstein would remain at this congregation until his retirement in 1980, with two years leave of absence as Chaplain in the American Army.

The sermon below begins negatively, reviewing the suffering of Jews in Germany and other European countries, especially emphasizing the utterly bleak situation of Polish Jews. Then the sermon shifts to a message intended to galvanize and inspire. The transition is made through an appeal to a statement of the French General Foch in the Great War. When the situation looked bleak, almost hopeless, Foch announced, "I shall attack." Thus, the sound of the shofar becomes, in this sermon, a call to battle – not to military battle, to be sure, but a call for unified support for the boycott of Nazi Germany.

ANOTHER YEAR HAS PASSED INTO HISTORY. A NEW YEAR BEGINS. AND once more in the ears of Jews all over the world rings the blast of the Shofar. The Shofar in ancient times had a deep religious significance. We read, for instance, that the revelation on Mount Sinai was accompanied by the blast of the Shofar (Exod. 19:19). But the Shofar also served another function in ancient Israel. It was used as a call to battle. It was the signal that warned the people in moments of great national danger. It meant that every Israelite must forsake his own activities, forget petty differences, and join the ranks of his brothers ready to fight against the common enemy.

Today once more the blast of the Shofar must be our clarion call to battle. For as we gather on this Rosh Hashanah to usher in the New Year, the shadow of national danger hovers over us. Once more our people must take up arms and fight for their existence. The past year has been one of the most tragic in all Jewish history.[1] A year ago the world stood aghast at the spectacle of the barbaric persecution of German Jews at the hands of the Nazis. Today it is true that the stories of brutal physical torture, which were rife then, are no longer so much in evidence. But this does not mean that the position of the Jew in Germany has been made secure. There has been no let-up in the moral and economic and legal persecution.

The Jew in Germany is still a second- or third-class citizen. He is still denied every opportunity of worthwhile activity. Schools are still closed to him, public service is still closed to him, the professions are still closed to him, the boycott of Jewish business continues. Particularly tragic is the lot of German Jewish youth, who face a future dark and without hope, a future where opportunity is an unknown word. Indeed, every class of German Jewry has been affected. The masses live in abject terror, faced by the prospect of starvation and dangers of which they can only surmise. And the latest authentic

1 A rather poignantly ironic statement in light of what was to come.

report shows that as many as 15,000 families of German Jewish professionals, doctors, lawyers, artists, professors and journalists have been reduced to degrading beggardom. Once the leaders of the intellectual and communal life in Germany, the very cream of German Jewry, but now forbidden to practice their chosen professions by the infamous "Aryan paragraph,"[2] they find themselves dependent for the barest necessities upon help from Jewish charitable organizations.

Thus in Germany a new type of pogrom is being waged: a pogrom that works by killing not the body but the spirit, a pogrom that degrades and humiliates, destroys self-respect and crushes all hope. A type of pogrom that is far more cruel than the bloody ones of former days – for it works quietly, stealthily, but all the more effectively.

And the events of the past few months bode ill for the future. For with the growing opposition to the Hitler regime[3] and the harassing economic problems that the Reich must face this winter, it will be necessary again to divert the interests of the German masses. When we consider the new powers which Hitler wields,[4] and the presence in his cabinet of men like Goering, an inveterate Jew-hater with an arrogant German contempt for world opinion, we do not need the recent speeches in Nuremberg to show us who will be made the scapegoat.[5]

But not only in Germany is Jewish life in a critical position on this Rosh Hashanah. In Austria, caught in the three-cornered struggle for power between Nazis, Reds, and Fascists, oppressed by constant fear of the spread of Hitlerism, the Jews are beaten on every side. It would be difficult to distinguish the view of the leaders of the new regime, Chancellor Schuschnigg and Vice Chancellor Starhemberg,

---

2 A provision of the Civil Service law of April 7, 1933, stating that "civil servants who are not of Aryan descent are to be retired."

3 Some contemporary writers, perhaps with an element of wishful thinking, did cite "evidence that unrest and opposition to the economic policies of the Hitler government are growing." *American Jewish Year Book 5696*, vol. 37 (1935–1936), p. 182.

4 Following the death of President Paul von Hindenburg on August 2, 1934, Hitler combined the offices of Chancellor and President and assumed the title of Führer and Reich Chancellor, including Commander in Chief of the Armed Forces.

5 Referring to the Nazi Party rally beginning September 4, 1934, the subject of Leni Riefenstahl's propaganda documentary "Triumph of the Will."

with regard to Jews, from those of dyed-in-the-wool Nazis. Both are outspoken in their opinion that Jews should be eliminated from all fields of public and economic activity. Already great progress has been made unofficially in this direction. Jewish children have been segregated into special schools. The other day Chancellor Schuschnigg was reported to be negotiating with the Austrian Nazis to include them in the Fatherland Front which now rules Austria. But there is a saying current in Austria that by the time the Nazis get into power, there will be nothing left for them to do. Whatever turn the unstable politics of Austria may take in the near future the prospects look equally bad for the Jews.[6]

In Poland, the situation of the Jew is just as tragic. Inspired by a new wave of Nazi anti-Semitic propaganda, there has been a terrible recrudescence of Jew-hatred. When a delegation of Jews came to Col. Slawek, head of the government party, pleading for protection against the attacks of the anti-Semitic Naras, his only answer was, "The Jews are now hated all over the world. Poland is no exception. I am sorry, I can do nothing for you."[7]

Economic ruin and distress is the common lot. A recent visitor described the situation in terms that seem incredible even to Depression-conscious Americans. A man ordering a pair of shoes would never think of giving the shoemaker money to buy the leather, he said, for the destitute shoemaker would immediately rush off to buy bread for his starving family. Denied all government aid such as is given to non-Jewish citizens, the average Jew in Poland is fortunate to be able to earn a few cents a day to keep body and soul together. In the large Polish cities like Warsaw, so dire is the situation that as many as forty percent of the Jewish population applied last year to charity organizations for Passover aid.[8]

---

6 Schuschnigg became Chancellor of Austria following the assassination of Chancellor Dollfuss on July 25, 1934, heading a "Fascist dictatorship in opposition both to the National Socialists and to the radical parties." *American Jewish Year Book 5696*, vol. 37 (1935–1936), p. 187.

7 "Naras" refers to members of the National Radical Camp. It was outlawed by the government during the summer of 1934, but it remained active illegally. See Emmanuel Melzer, *No Way Out*, pp. 6–7.

8 On the deteriorating economic conditions of Polish Jews in 1932–1934, see Melzer, *No Way Out*, pp. 3–4.

These are but indications of the Jewish situation throughout the world today: everywhere gloom and desolation, nowhere a spark of hope; everywhere the menace of Nazism and rising anti-Semitism, nowhere a vision of Jewish strength and solidarity. Surely, if ever, this Rosh Hashanah ushers in a critical year in Jewish history. What are we to do? How are we to answer the call of the Shofar?

I am reminded of the celebrated report of Marshall [Ferdinand] Foch to General [Joseph] Joffre, at the first battle of the Marne. You will recall how Foch was suddenly thrown into the battle in command of the French troops, to fill a gap in the line of defense. The Allied army was crumbling before the powerful German offensive. The situation seemed almost hopeless. It was under these circumstances that he sent the thrilling message, which was to take its place among the great military documents of all time. "My center is yielding," he said. "My right is retreating. Impossible to maneuver. Excellent situation. I shall attack."[9]

Dear friends, the Jewish people today are in just such a situation – a situation where danger threatens on every side. There is no time for compromise, no use in self-deception. Our only hope is to gather our strength and to fight for our existence. But as always, it is the tragedy of our people that there are those among us who never learn their lesson, who refuse to see the necessity for action, who put their factional interests above the common good. Blind cowards, they fritter away their strength by stupid internal dissension and dicker with the enemy at a time when every bit of strength is necessary to forestall the doom, which hangs over our heads.

In Germany, for instance, we find the League of National German Jews issuing an appeal before the recent plebiscite asking all Jews in Germany to vote for Hitler.[10] Later we find this same organization protesting against the activities of the World Jewish Conference and

---

9 For the details of Foch's statement, see *Witness from the Pulpit*, p. 40, n. 7.

10 The *Verband nationaldeutscher Juden*, founded in 1920 by Max Naumann, supported German nationalism and therefore vehemently opposed the Zionist movement and all links with international Jewish organizations. After Hitler came to power, it attempted to prove its German loyalties by supporting the new regime, until it was finally disbanded by the Nazis. See Steven Ascheim, *Brothers and Strangers*, pp. 220–24.

its advocacy of the anti-Nazi boycott.[11] "Jews who feel themselves Germans," they said, "oppose every foreign intervention in German affairs." Such Jewish cowards – willing to accept shame and disgrace, willing to cringe before their oppressors, willing to kiss the Nazi boots which kicked the Jewish people in Germany – deserve the contempt of every human being with a spark of dignity and self-respect. Fortunately, the League of National German Jews represents only a small minority of the Jews in Germany. Yet the distressing fact remains that in no European country has Jewish unity as yet been achieved.

In America too, we have those Jews who counsel silence rather than outspoken truth, and still condemn democratic action of the masses, favouring diplomatic dickering which avails naught. Thus, while the World Jewish Conference was being held, the American Jewish Committee felt called upon to deliver a statement to the press denying that the Conference represented American Jewish opinion.[12] And in a similar vein, the *American Hebrew* carried in its editorial columns a scathing criticism of the Conference and its leaders.[13] These same groups from the very beginning have refused their support to the boycott of Nazi Germany; thus we find on every side a lack of vital determination, a lack of unified organization, a lack of purposeful effort for self-preservation.

Jews and friends, on this New Year's Day, let us cry, "Enough of such stupidity, enough of such cowardice, enough of such selfishness!" It is high time for the Jew to straighten out his bent spine and to raise his bowed head. For 2000 years the Jew has been a homeless wanderer, everywhere considered an alien, everywhere oppressed

---

11 The "World Jewish Conference" held meetings in Geneva in August 1932, September 1933, and August 1934, to plan for a "World Jewish Congress," which met eventually in August 1936. On the anti-Nazi boycott, see annotation to the Rosh Hashanah 1933 sermon by Jacob Rudin, above.

12 On the American Jewish Committee's public dissociation from the World Jewish Congress movement, see Naomi Cohen, *Not Free to Desist*, pp. 222–25.

13 The *American Hebrew*, a New York Jewish weekly founded in 1879, offered a rather conservative outlook on Jewish affairs; taken over in 1906 by a group of leading New York Jews, it was generally anti-Zionist and held positions on Jewish affairs similar to those taken by the American Jewish Committee.

and persecuted. For 2000 years he has been the scapegoat of every national tragedy, the victim of every hateful backward force. Yes, for 2000 years and more the Jew has been beaten, crushed and twisted. How long will the tragic spectacle continue? How long will the Jew continue to bear his shame in grovelling, cowardly obsequiousness? To turn the other cheek, to kiss the hand that beat one – these are not and never were fundamental Jewish teachings. Rather, to fight for the right, to struggle against tyranny, to combat every wrong and every injustice – this is what prophetic Judaism should and must stand for.

What shall we answer to this new challenge to Jewish dignity and to Jewish existence? At the World Jewish Conference in Geneva, the answer of the Jewish people was given. For one thing, in the words of Dr. Wise, "The boycott of Germany must continue until the Hitler regime cancels every law or practice violating human freedom, political equality, and the ideals of civilization."[14] That must be our answer to Nazi hatred and Nazi persecution. Germany must realize that she shall continue to be isolated economically and otherwise until she comes back into the realm of civilization. The importance of the boycott far transcends narrow Jewish interests. Not only German Jewry, not only world Jewry, but civilization itself is under attack. It is the protest of Humanity against Nazidom's return to barbarism.

The boycott of Germany has thus assumed a world-historical importance. It will prove whether or not the righteous indignation of the civilized world has an instrument by which, without resort to bloodshed, it can oppose the trampling of fundamental human rights. The Jew, as always, is in the vanguard of the battle between paganism and civilization. It is a place of honor. Any Jew who, because of personal gain or lack of interest, does not support the boycott while Germany continues to deny civilization's demands has sacrificed his honor, betrayed his people, and forfeited the respect of humanity; already the boycott has shown its effectiveness and power. Germany today must yield shortly or face inevitable material ruin. No compromise must be accepted. We must not cease until the battle is won.

---

14 Cf. Stephen S. Wise, *Challenging Years*, pp. 256–57.

But even this is not enough. World Jewry has at last come to realize that the problem of one nation's Jews is the problem of all Jews. We must not let this lesson be wasted. Out of the chaos of contemporary conditions, there must arise some permanent representative organ to defend Jews all over the world from the hatred of their enemies and from the infringements upon their rights. The World Jewish Congress, which will convene next August, will give us such a body, able to champion the cause of the Jewish people before the world.[15]

Through the centuries in which Jews have been in *golus* [exile], they have never yet been able to join all forces for the common good. Now at last the opportunity is in their hands. Unless they take it, the Jews will merit the contempt of their Christian neighbors. This is no occasion for hesitancy or timidity. We have nothing to do that demands secrecy. We are merely fighting for equal human rights for our people. Must we sneak into the back door and beg for them? I, for one, would rather demand them from the housetops.

Most of you will recall the intensely moving scene in the motion picture presentation of "The House of Rothschild," wherein the aged Mayer Anschel Rothschild dies. His five sons are grouped about his deathbed listening to the venerable father's last words of advice. Gasping for breath, he tells them how they are to carry on the banking business that he has worked all his life to build up. "Remember," he says. "Unity is strength. All your lives you must stand by one another; no one brother must be allowed to fail while another brother succeeds. The Rothschilds work always together. That will be your power; and when that power comes, remember the Ghetto. Remember this before all: that neither business nor power nor all the gold in Europe will ever bring you happiness until. . . ." He pauses a moment. Gathering together his failing strength he lifts himself out of the restraining hands of his wife and, sitting erect for a moment,

---

15 The first full Convention of the World Jewish Congress occurred in Geneva in August 1936 (see Wise, August 8, 1946, above); the initial expectation to meet in the summer of 1935 did not materialize. For preliminary meetings, see Zohar Segev, *The World Jewish Congress during the Holocaust: Between Activism and Restraint*, pp. 11–13; Melvin I. Urofsky, *A Voice that Speaks for Justice*, pp. 300–2.

his voice rings true and clear as he continues: "until we, our people, have equality...respect...dignity.... To deal with dignity...to live with dignity...to walk the world with dignity."[16]

My friends, as we enter a New Year in Jewish life, there is no message more significant than that embodied in those memorable words: that nothing matters, that no success can ever bring true happiness so long as the blessing of self-respect is lacking, so long as Jews fear to hold their heads erect and face the world like men.

At the peal of the Shofar on this New Year's day every Jew must feel that it is the call of his people who need him. Once more, the battle cry is heard, "Arise, ye sleepers...." Join your brothers to fight for the cause of Israel. No Jew can afford to stand alone. Your strength, your will, your support is needed. Come, gird your loins for the fray, that we may hasten the day when the Jewish people shall truly be able to deal with dignity, to live with dignity, to walk the world with dignity.[17]

---

16 The United Artists movie, based on an unproduced play by George Hembert Westley, opened on March 14, 1934. For Rothschild's will and death-bed charge to his sons, see Amos Elon, *Founder: A Portrait of the First Rothschild and His Time*, p. 174.

17 Permission granted by Rowman & Littlefield on behalf of Lexington Press.

Ferdinand M. Isserman (1898–1972)
"My Second Visit to Nazi Germany"
Temple Israel, St. Louis
October 25, 1935 (Friday evening)
AJA, Manuscript Collection 6, Box 14, Folder 2

INTRODUCTION

Ferdinand M. Isserman was born in Antwerp, Belgium. His family immigrated to the United States in 1906, settling in Newark, New Jersey. Isserman attended schools in both Antwerp and Newark, graduating from Newark's Central High School in June 1914.

That September, Isserman entered Hebrew Union College (HUC) where, in conjunction with the University of Cincinnati, he earned two bachelor's degrees while training for the rabbinate. In June 1922, together with Harry Joshua Stern (above), he was ordained a rabbi.

Upon ordination, Isserman became Assistant Rabbi under Rev. Dr. Harry W. Ettelson at Congregation Rodeph Sholom in Philadelphia, Pennsylvania. He remained in this position for three years, during which he studied at the University of Pennsylvania, receiving a Master of Arts degree in comparative religion in 1924.

In 1925, Isserman assumed the position of Rabbi of the Toronto Hebrew Congregation ("Holy Blossom") in Canada. There he distinguished himself by arranging Canada's first pulpit exchange between a Christian minister and a rabbi. In 1929, Isserman became rabbi of Temple Israel in St. Louis, Missouri, where he remained until his retirement in 1963.[1]

In the summer of 1933, Isserman spent a month in Germany, and

1 The biographical material is largely dependent on the Biographical Sketch in the AJA.

upon returning in the autumn he preached about the situation of German Jews. On October 27 of that year, after reporting extensively on the tragic experiences of individuals he had met, he concluded by warning Americans against being deceived by the disinformation circulated by Nazi propagandists.[2] Two years later, he made a second visit during the summer; following is the text of the sermon he delivered to his congregation after that autumn's holiday season. He would make yet a third visit in the summer of 1937.

Isserman's fierce antipathy toward Nazism continued unabated throughout the Second World War. Yet it is worth noting that in October 1939, like so many other American rabbis, especially those affiliated with Reform Judaism, he insisted in the pulpit that "America should stay out of the war."[3] It was only after Pearl Harbor and the German Declaration of War against the United States that Isserman used his rhetorical skills in support of the American war effort, insisting that "we are not at war with the cultural traditions of Germany and Italy, [and] we are not at war with the peoples of the axis countries. We are at war with their governments."[4]

The sermon below, delivered at the late Friday evening service, is clearly not a model of traditional Jewish homiletical art. It is, however, a fine example of making information, based on personal experience, about Nazi Germany and its persecution of Jews and other groups available in a compelling manner to a large congregation of Jewish worshippers.

IT IS NEVER EASY TO SPEAK IN PUBLIC ABOUT EXPERIENCES IN A dictatorship. Dictators have their ubiquitous spies and thus know what is being said about them and who is saying it. When a colleague of mine visited Soviet Russia at a time when its anti-religious poli-

2 See the selections in the Chronological section.

3 See the passages in the Chronological section, and the discussion in Saperstein, *Jewish Preaching in Times of War*, pp. 451–53.

4 For the complete text of this sermon, delivered on December 12, 1941, see *Jewish Preaching in Times of War*, pp. 454–61.

cies were a sensitive nerve in Russia's foreign relations, and reported about his contacts with Jewish officials in a synagogue, I understood that he was so specific that Russian authorities could trace the men to whom he referred, and thus he exposed them to hardship. Of this difficulty, I am very conscious tonight as I venture to speak from the pulpit of my second visit to Nazi Germany.[5] I shall, therefore, refer to no cities by name nor to any specific individuals, in order not, unnecessarily, to expose innocent people to the reprisals of Nazi leaders.

I was anxious to revisit Nazi Germany, first as a human being interested in the welfare of my fellowmen and in the progress of civilization, and conscious of the threat to man's welfare and to civilization that the Nazi philosophy is [represents?]. Second, I was anxious to revisit Nazi Germany as an American, as a believer in democracy, in free institutions and the liberties of men, who knows that the success of Nazism would jeopardize the status of democracy in all nations. Third, I was anxious to revisit Nazi Germany as a Jew eager to learn what the fate of my co-religionists was, and how the outside world could be of service to them. Having been refused a visa by the local consul, and the German Embassy in Washington, contradicting its own local representative, [having] informed me that it could not go over his head, I applied and received a visa from German officials in Paris in the usual manner sanctioned by international conventions and laws.

The casual tourist in Germany will notice few external changes which indicate that Germany has been subjected to a profound revolution in the past few years. Many of us know revolutions only from having read of them in novels or in history text-books. In our minds they are associated with stirring dramatic events, with barricaded streets, with the explosion of gun-fire, the flowing of blood, the presence of corpses, and demolished buildings. Having such

5 His first visit occurred during the summer of 1933, and a sermon reporting on his experience was delivered to the same congregation on October 27 of that year. A statement similar to the following sentence was made at the beginning of this earlier sermon, and the eight individuals whose stories are recounted by the preacher are not identified by name. This text is also preserved among the Isserman papers in the AJA. See also Isserman's *Sentenced to Death!*, published originally in 1933.

bookish and naïve beliefs about revolutions, we are apt to return from a tour of Germany stating that all is well, that business goes on as usual, and that people live and die in normal fashion as they do in any other European country. Externally, except for a change of flags, except for the Swastika symbol displayed in store windows, which the non-observant tourist may not even notice, there is little to indicate to the uninitiated that Germany has been changed. The sun shines as usual. The seasons come and go regularly. The wheat ripens in the fields. The orchards yield their fruit. The grapevines climb along the banks of the Rhine and produce their annual vintage. The German landscape remains as attractive as ever. Yet the new Germany is but a shadow of the old. The casual tourist who knows no German, or even if he does know German and speaks only to Nazi enthusiasts, may get no inkling of the overwhelming tragedy which now afflicts that country, once in the van of civilization and once the seat of culture and of science.

I shall briefly try to enumerate some noticeable changes in the German scene since my visit two years ago.

1. Change in the Color Scheme

The color scheme in German streets has changed.

Two years ago, the streets of Germany were always filled with storm-troopers in brown shirts.[6] Germany seemed to be an armed camp in which the brown uniform predominated overwhelmingly. Here and there the black shirts of the elite guard were to be seen, but they were in the minority. This year, even in the old strongholds of the Nazi party, the brown shirts have almost disappeared from the scene. A new uniform dominates, and that is the greenish-grey of the regular army. In cafés, in dance halls, in other amusement places, along the popular promenades, young men are seen wearing the garb of Germany's new army. This change in uniform is not merely a change in color. It indicates the change in the source of power of

6 In the 1933 sermon, Isserman referred several times to "a band of brown shirts." This was an informal way to characterize the *Sturmabteiling* (SA) or Storm Troopers, who would become overshadowed by the more elite and disciplined *Schutzstaffel* (SS).

the Nazi regime. In a democracy, the power of the ruler rests upon the consent of the governed. In a dictatorship, the power of the ruler rests upon the physical force that he can rely upon to support him. When Hitler first assumed power, that physical force lay in the brown shirts. They had fought his political battles. They were prepared to crush his political foes. Since the executions of the 30th of June, 1934, the army of brown shirts steadily lost its prestige and its numbers were decreased. Today, Hitler depends for his strength upon the regular army. If that army refused to support him, he is lost. It was reported that Hitler had asked for the resignation of General Fritsch, the head of the German army. Fritsch, it is said, refused to give it to him, and informed Hitler that he will resign only if forced to do so, and then Hitler would have to take the consequences. Fritsch is still in command of the *Reichswehr.* A few weeks after this incident, Hitler sent him a telegram of congratulations on his birthday.[7]

With the new civilian army now being enrolled, Hitler will be as strong as the officers of that army will be loyal to him. Those who predict the downfall of Hitler believe that he will be succeeded by a military dictatorship. The change in the color scheme in the streets of Germany's cities is indicative of a profound political change, of the shift of ultimate power in Germany from the ranks of the storm-troopers to the officers of the *Reichswehr.* Whoever controls the *Reichswehr* controls Germany. Two years ago, when I returned and reported that Germany was rearming and drilling, Nazi spokesmen here challenged my assertion. Today the rearming of Germany is a publicly acknowledged fact. In the Italian-Ethiopian dispute the attention of the League is as much on Germany as it is on Italy. And the severity of the action against Italy may have been meant in part as a warning to Hitler. The Nazis are not yet ready for war. Only in chemicals are they said to be fully prepared. It will take a year or two to drill the civilian army. It will also take some time to perfect its

7 Werner von Fritsch (b. 1880) was involved in the rearmament of Germany already in the 1920s, and was appointed Commander-in-Chief of the Armed Forces in May, 1935. He was later forced to resign in early 1938, but returned to a high position as General when the war began, and was killed in action in Poland several weeks after the invasion.

aviation corps where casualties are said to be very heavy, and where young lives are said to be freely sacrificed.

2. Shortage of Foods

Another difference between Germany two years ago and Germany today is a very apparent shortage of certain foods. In the railroad station of a very large city, I tried in vain to secure some orange juice for breakfast. No oranges were available because oranges have to be imported, and the Nazis being unable to get credits abroad must husband whatever foreign exchange they have to purchase the raw materials essential for war. This shortage of credits is due to no external pressure. It resulted from the fact that the government is buying war materials with all the foreign exchange it can get, and because the Nazis have failed to meet their obligations and have not paid their bills. Bankers are more hesitant today about loaning funds to customers who do not pay their bills than ever before. Besides a shortage of oranges, there were scarcities of other essential food products, such as eggs, butter, pork and onions in certain localities. This shortage was due somewhat to an inability to import, but also to the fact that the German peasant, who has been promised everything by the Hitler regime and has received nothing, has become disgruntled with the administration with its high taxes, with its continuous drive for funds to maintain Nazi officials in luxury, so that not merely the William Randolph Hearsts[8] of Germany pay a large proportion of their earnings either to the government or to the party, but humbler people as well. Some of these German farmers are said to be sabotaging the government because of their discontent with national policies, and are withholding their products from the market.

3. Open Discontent

Two years ago, whereas I found dissatisfaction among the elements specifically crushed, it was always voiced behind closed doors. This

8 The American newspaper publishing magnate, used here as a model of a person with extremely high income who pays extremely high taxes.

time, to my amazement, in the restaurants and cafés I found men and women who freely spoke of their dissatisfaction with the present regime. In one large café, I engaged in a discussion with a number of strangers who sat at my table. They asked where I was journeying. I informed them that I was on the way to Salzburg in Austria. One of them stated that he used to go to Salzburg, but now must pay a thousand marks for a visa to Austria, and if he goes after paying such a large sum, he is regarded as a traitor. Only if you are a Nazi official, he stated, can you get permission to go to Austria. In the course of the discussion, I mentioned the fact that America has no institutions like these large German cafés where men gather with their families and sit and talk the entire evening. To this statement, one German replied that this is the only respect in which Germany is better off than the United States. As I left this particular group, one asked me to bring this message to America. "Tell them that everything is wonderful here." And then he made a grimace of disgust, and vigorously shook his head.

Nor is this a unique experience. In another restaurant, I sat at a table with a German family. Not far from us sat some Nazis in brown uniforms. A newsboy came in and from him I bought *Die Frankfurter Zeitung*. Knowing that this newspaper is not in good standing with the Nazis, that it is the only paper in German which has retained a semblance of independence because it is sponsored by Von Neurath, the Minister of Foreign Affairs, I was anxious to get the reactions of this family to the newspaper. I told them that the University of Missouri, on the occasion of *Die Frankfurter Zeitung*'s hundredth anniversary, had awarded it a medal of honor and designated it the leading newspaper in the entire world.[9] Whereupon the head of the family said to me, "and now look at our papers." His daughter whispered in my ear, "Instead of that once-great newspaper, we now have *Der Völkische Beobachter*, the official Nazi newspaper." The head of the house then asked me how conditions were in America. I replied that

9 The award was bestowed upon this liberal newspaper by the University's School of Journalism in 1932. This was not however its hundredth anniversary, as it began publication in 1956.

they might be better. His answer was, "It is always much worse here." Then the conversation became more guarded for some persons at another table were anxiously trying to overhear our remarks.

While eating at another very popular restaurant at the noon hour, which two years ago had always been crowded and now was empty, I asked the waiter where the patrons were. He replied, without batting an eyelash, "Conditions here are very bad and getting worse. No one has any money and consequently no one can come here." Two years ago, such dissatisfaction was not to be voiced by the masses. Many then believed that the new ruler might accomplish something for them. Today, they are disillusioned. With the exception of a larger army, Germany has gained nothing from the Hitler regime. Prices have risen. Wages have been decreased. Profits have dwindled, and the standard of living of all Germans is continuously falling.

Of course, in America too we can hear plenty of dissatisfaction with the Roosevelt regime. One can voice one's criticisms freely in the press. In Germany, it is dangerous to voice such criticism, for the concentration camps, the Nazi schools for adult education, are still open. That these criticisms were made to a stranger is an index of the undercurrent of hostility to the Nazi regime. Other investigators in Germany, whom I met subsequently in Geneva, had similar experiences.

4. Persecution of Catholics

When I returned from Germany two years ago, I reported that the Nazis were anti-Catholic, and that the Concordat with the Vatican had been broken, that priests had been imprisoned in concentration camps, and even a Cardinal's house had been fired upon.[10] On all sides, there are visible evidences of increasing anti-Catholic hostility and persecutions to which Catholic youth, Catholic lay-leaders, Catholic sport associations and Catholic prelates of all ranks are continuously subjected. The Catholic bishops have accepted the

---

10 This is not in the text of the sermon delivered on October 27, 1933; it may be in the more extensive pamphlet report published by Isserman, called *Sentenced to Death!* (St. Louis, 1933; republished 1961).

Nazi challenge at a conference held at Fulda this summer, declared their opposition to the National Socialist philosophy, and pointed out that the attempt of Nazi leaders to base their opposition to Catholicism on political grounds is false and without foundation.[11]

Caricatures of Catholics and attacks on the Church were paraded on trucks in large German cities. Billboards attacked the work of the Catholic priests. On one occasion, when – with the consent of the government – a Catholic charitable organization was collecting funds in the streets of a German city, the girls in charge of the collection were molested by bands of Nazis, and would-be-donors were frightened away. The evening before this collection was held, Nazi orators had attacked the Catholic religion and the Catholic priesthood. These attacks upon Catholics are found in the publication of Nazi organs. Remembering that the press of Germany is censored, that editors may print only what the government sanctions, these anti-Catholic attacks become almost official. Wherever you went in Germany, there were reports of the ill treatment of nuns, priests, Catholic lay leaders and Catholic youth.

5. Persecution of Protestants

On my return from Germany two years ago, I reported my conversations with Protestant leaders who had been deposed by the Nazi regime, which had interfered with their religious liberties.[12] That interference with the Protestant religion has not ceased. But last week [ca. Oct. 15–22] the Nazi government itself admitted that it released thirty Protestant ministers from concentration camps. Whereas two years ago I had no difficulty making contacts with Protestant clergy, this time I found them unwilling to see me because of the reign of terror, because of the continual surveillance to which they were subjected, and because of the continuous threats of arrest. The Nazis' philosophy does not permit any religious freedom, and consequently Protestants, with strong convictions, had to be crushed. The Nazi

11 For the documents issued at the Fulda conference of August 1935, see Guenter Lewy, *The Catholic Church and Nazi Germany*, pp. 128–30 and 154.

12 Also not in text of the October 27, 1933 sermon; possibly in *Sentenced to Death*.

nationalism conflicts with the Churches' universalism, the Nazis' malice with the Churches' mercy, the Nazi deification of the state with the Churches' worship of God. In one proclamation issued by the Nazi party, the church is attacked in this fashion: "The church asked men to serve God. We Nazis serve the people."[13]

An interesting example of Protestant-Catholic cooperation was reported to me. In one city, a lecturer on the new paganism sponsored by Rosenberg, the philosopher of the Nazi party, was scheduled to speak, and Catholics and Protestants were forced to come to hear him. As this lecturer arrived at the railroad station a large group of Catholics met him and chanted a Catholic hymn, "Te Deum." As he arose to speak in a hall filled with Catholics and Protestants, the Protestants chanted the well-known hymn, "A Mighty Fortress is Our God." When they were through, a group of Catholics arose and sang a Catholic hymn. This was continued until finally the speaker left without having been able to deliver his lecture. The bishop of the city was believed to have been responsible for this humiliation to the Nazi representative. The police determined to arrest him. His followers assembled to prevent the arrest. He asked them to disperse and bade the police officials wait a few moments. Attired in his clerical garb with mitre on his forehead and staff in his hand, he offered himself for arrest. Ashamed, the police withdrew. In opposing Nazism, all branches of Christianity are united.

6. The State of the Jews

Two years ago, I reported that Nazis had informed me that their aim in Germany was to bring about the humane extirpation of the Jews, and that I believed that the Jews of Germany were condemned to death. Today the Jews of Germany are aware of that. In the mountains of Colorado, one can see uprooted evergreen trees, seemingly as fresh as trees whose roots are still in the soil. This freshness lasts for a while, but in time the lack of nourishment begins to tell. The leaves

---

13 This is based on a speech by Goebbels delivered on August 4, 1935, also translated, "Let the Churches serve God; we serve the People." John S. Conway, *The Nazi Persecution of the Churches*, p. 115; also cited in Samuel Solomon Cohon, *Religious Affirmations*, p. 135.

slowly become brown and fall away, and the tree withers and perishes. Two years ago, the Jews of Germany were like an evergreen tree which had just been uprooted. They still possessed the semblance of health and virility. Today the leaves are becoming brown and falling, and the death pallor is evident. The Jews of Germany know that as long as the Nazi regime lasts, there is no future for them. Two years ago they spoke of the migration of their children. Today they speak of the migration of all. The law announced in Nuremberg in September did not alter their status, as everything they made legal had already been in practice by the Nazis. The Jews of Germany are being isolated. In some cases, they can get no service whatsoever, neither street car service, nor light service, nor even the necessities of life. I spoke to one individual who had to bring his mother from a small community because people were afraid to sell her milk and bread.

But worse than the economic strangulation and the social degradation is the continuous suspense. Jews have no rights. They do not know whether they are to be massacred tomorrow. They do not know what fresh blow they may be asked to bear. What amazed me was that despite the Nazi power and prestige, despite the ceaseless propaganda, many Germans still have to be forced to anti-semitic practices. There is even a new resistance evident to anti-semitism on the part of those who previously had believed in it. One Nazi leader voiced his disillusion when he said, "All that Hitler has done in the past two years is to harass Jews and to eliminate them from the national life. With what result? Things in Germany have only become worse and worse. I fought for the revolution, and what have I received? Higher taxes! Lower wages! Higher food costs! I wish Hitler would leave the Jews alone and remedy the conditions truly responsible for our plight."[14] This from a trusted Nazi.

What does it indicate? The putting into practice of anti-semitic policies has proved to some Germans the falsity of the anti-semitic philosophy that Jews were responsible for the ills of Germany. The synagogue is the only religious institution not molested in Germany

14 It is unclear from the formulation whether this reports a private conversation or (unlikely) a public statement. If the former, it will probably be impossible to identify the speaker..

because, if Nazi policies succeed, there will be no Jews left in Germany. But where are these Jews to go? No land will receive them. No country will welcome them. Palestine can accommodate some but not all. What is to be their fate? What are civilized nations going to do about it? Can mankind sit idly by and let this tragedy of tragedies occur without speaking one word, or doing one deed, in behalf of these helpless victims?

7. The Heroic Foreign Journalists

My second visit to Nazi Germany has convinced me again of the heroic work being carried on by the foreign correspondents representing the newspapers of the world, who are writing a great chapter in the history of journalism. They are reporting the truth as well as they can, and every obstacle of a fiendish department of propaganda is thrown in their paths to prevent them from learning the truth. One American newspaperman told me that when the subway tunnel caved in, in which scores of lives of German workers were lost, and from his office he heard the honking of ambulance sirens and the ringing of police bells, he telephoned to the police department, which informed him that nothing of any importance was taking place, only a slight fire. When he continued hearing the commotion, he put on his hat and went out and investigated. Near his office was the scene of a subway cave-in. He presented his press badge and was refused permission to enter the police lines. Finally, by bribing a fireman, he secured the news.

All newspapermen informed me that their work is made impossible because the government tries to prevent them from learning the facts. One journalist told me, as I sat in his office and spoke to him, that in order to get at the truth he must have a larger number of underground contacts with Catholics, Protestants, university men, Jews, and members of all the former political parties, so that he can know what is actually going on in the country. A coal strike took place this summer in which thousands of men participated. Not one word of it was reported in the German press.[15] He said to

---

15 I have found a report attributed to the Berlin correspondent of the London *Daily Herald* stating that "for the first time in two and a half years, strikes have occurred

me that in the chair in which I was sitting, a week ago had been a former German official who wept as he gave him some news, and told him of the constant terror under which he lives.

The German government is doing everything in its power to discredit the foreign press because it alone is giving the world the truth. This summer, there was a radio exhibit in Berlin. A fire broke out in the Exposition hall. The members of the foreign press were not permitted to examine the exhibit to see the damage that had been done. From the government news bureau, foreign newspapermen received the information that the exhibition building had been burned so badly that the radio exhibit had been called off. This news was then called to the press of the world. The following day in the city of Berlin, that same department of propaganda that gave the news to foreign newspapermen issued posters and placards in conspicuous places throughout the city which read: "Note the lies of the foreign press. They said that the radio exhibit was completely burned and called off. Go with your own eyes and see the radio exhibit. Thus is Germany misrepresented by its foes of the foreign press." Thus we have concrete evidence of the heroic work done by a brave group of men who serve only one cause, the cause of truth as they see it, and who serve it at inconvenience and risk to themselves.

Conclusion

Revisiting Germany after two years, I find:

- that the anti-democratic, anti-Christian nationalistic Nazi philosophy is relentlessly being worked out, creating, however, a vast and increasing opposition;
- the army has supplanted the brown shirts as a source of power;
- increased attacks upon the Catholic Church and Catholic priests;
- continued persecution of Protestant clergy and lay Protestants who believe in Christianity;
- the Jews of Germany lost and helpless;

---

among workers who have been disillusioned regarding Nazist promises. The correspondent says that coal miners in the Ruhr are averaging only 16 days a month, and arrangements are being made to distribute food tickets among them." *The Argus* (Melbourne), July 9, 1935, p. 7, http://trove.nla.gov.au/ndp/del/article/11746487.

- the foreign newspapermen continuing their heroic task;
- freedom of the press abolished, the universities degenerating, the students, previously enthusiastic Nazis, now in silent revolt, the populace discontented.

The future of Germany I cannot predict. No one can predict it. Whether the Nazi Party, in an attempt to make up for its failure at home, will seek a foreign war, no one can tell. The army generals might prevent that. What can the world do to arrest this threat to civilized values? It can refuse to give the Nazi regime any moral support. Whoever gives the Nazi regime moral support, whether by participating in the Olympic Games or in any other fashion, is strengthening the hands of the barbarians who are in the process of ruining Germany and who may bring chaos upon all of Europe and destroy western civilization.

The Jewish situation in Germany is but a mere episode. The destiny of half a million Jews is important, but not all-important [not all that is important?]. Their fate, however, is symptomatic of the soulless character of the Nazi regime. The challenge of Nazism is a challenge to humanity, to Christianity, to Judaism, to democracy, to science, to learning. To help Nazism is to work against the representatives of the old Germany, the Germany of song and of poetry, or philosophy and of music, of Goethe and of Kant, of Thomas Mann and of Albert Einstein.

The Olympic Games: A Moral Issue[16]

I would not ask an American Olympic Committee composed of a few individuals to decide whether Americans should participate in the Olympic Games. I would ask the youth of America, the athletes of America, whether they care to give moral encouragement to that group of men whose point of view, if it prevails, will make of Europe a madhouse and of civilization a shambles. I would ask the American athletes whether, in order to have a trip abroad and win some

16 For a sermon delivered a week later devoted entirely to this contentious issue, see Harold Saperstein, "The Great Olympic Idea," November 1, 1935, in *Witness from the Pulpit: Topical Sermons 1933–1980*, pp. 44–49.

transient glory, they are willing to encourage this new barbarianism and this new paganism. I would ask them whether they could dare to discourage these Catholic bishops and priests, these Protestant ministers and laymen, these Jewish rabbis, these university professors, these former statesmen and labor leaders, who today are suffering in concentration camps, and in the terror in which they live are buoyed up by one hope: that they have the good will of the world, the good will of decent men and women who have retained their sanity amidst the confusion of our age.

I feel certain that the answer of America's youth will be, if the facts are fairly presented, that it will choose not to traffic with the Nazi Frankenstein, but that it will refuse to give moral support to an immoral regime. By non-co-operation with the Olympic Committee, American youth can send fresh hope and new inspiration to the German men and women suffering under Nazi rule who pray and long for the time when freedom of conscience, freedom of thought, freedom of the press, and freedom to worship God will once more be their privilege as it is ours. I propose that a group of Catholic, Protestant and Jewish religious leaders, and a few presidents of our representative universities, draw up a statement of facts about the philosophy of Nazis and their achievements in Germany. Then let this statement be given to every prospective Olympic athlete and let that athlete know that by participation in the Olympics he gives moral encouragement to the Nazi regime. Then the soul and conscience of America's athletes will give the answer.

I am opposed to preventing any qualified American athlete who desires [to do so] from participating in the Olympic Games. However, I believe that American athletes should know that their participation in these games will give moral support to the Nazi philosophy and increase the despair of Germans of all walks of life who seek to save Germany for civilization. This final message I bring from Germany to American athletes and to the American public.[17]

17 Permission granted by the American Jewish Archives.

Abba Hillel Silver (1893–1963)

"But Mordecai Bowed Not Down"
The Temple, Cleveland, OH
March 8, 1936 (Sunday, Purim)
Therefore Choose Life, pp. 277–81

INTRODUCTION

Like so many of the American rabbis represented in this book, Abraham (later Abba Hillel) Silver was born in eastern Europe, in his case, in Lithuania.[1] Also like many others, he came from a family of Orthodox rabbis and was the first in his family line to identify with Reform Judaism. Again following the pattern of others, he entered the joint program leading to a BA at the University of Cincinnati and rabbinic ordination from the Hebrew Union College, both received in 1915 at age 22. During his studies in Cincinnati, he changed his name to Abba Hillel, notably not choosing an Americanized name.

Silver's first rabbinical appointment was to a small congregation in Wheeling, West Virginia. But in 1917, with the retirement of Rabbi Moses Gries, spiritual leader of the The Temple-Tifereth Israel in Cleveland, Ohio, he was invited to serve as rabbi of this considerably more important congregation. One of the most attractive features of the young rabbi was his oratorical skills. A younger colleague, Herbert Weiner, who edited the first collection of Silver's sermons, *Therefore Choose Life*, described him in his prime as follows:

> Nature endowed him with a tall, handsome, and impressive presence. He had a magnificent and perfectly-controlled voice....

1 Much of the factual information in this Introduction is based on the Biography in the Abba Hillel Silver Papers at the Western Reserve Historical Society in Cleveland, OH.

> He had a natural flair for the poetic and striking phrase, a sense of the dramatic, and the instinct of the actor who can rivet the audience's attention by a gesture.... He knew how to approach the pulpit, then stand there polishing his glasses until the expectant hush deepened to the point of high drama. But when he spoke, it was the thought, the logic, the carefully worked out phrase that carried the listener along until the desired conclusion appeared inevitable to the mind as well as the heart.

In addition to regular Shabbat and holiday sermons, Silver followed the pattern used by many leading Reform rabbis of large urban congregations and delivered major addresses at the Sunday morning weekday service. Attendance at these services, which included non-Jews as well as members of the congregation, was generally higher than on Shabbat (at its peak, the congregation numbered some two thousand families). Many who attended these Sunday morning services came primarily to hear Silver speak.

The sermon below, delivered on Purim, which fell on Sunday, March 8, 1936, is characteristic of a significant homiletical reaction to Nazi persecution. As noted in the Introduction, there were many rabbis who argued in their sermons that while Nazi Germany represented a major threat to German Jewry and perhaps also to Jews beyond the borders of the Reich, this was not something new in Jewish history. The Hebrew Scriptures and post-biblical Jewish history – the destruction of the Second Temple, the massacres of the Crusades, the expulsion from various European countries, the Spanish Inquisition, the pogroms of eastern Europe – all of these established a pattern that could be summarized in a simple thought: until the coming of the Messiah and the dawning of an age of universal peace – and Silver's interest in this topic is shown in his book *A History of Messianic Speculation in Israel*, first published in 1937 – Jews were destined to suffer from the persecution of the Gentile majorities in the countries where they lived. Many preachers apparently thought it would be comforting to their listeners to be reminded of the persecutions of the past, which ultimately ended in the defeat and destruction of the persecutors, and the continued existence of the Jewish people.

Certain holiday sermons were especially appropriate for this point. We have seen how the New York Conservative Rabbi Israel Levinthal, preaching on Pesach in 1933, draws continuous connections between the behavior of Pharaoh and that of the Nazi oppressor. Here Silver does the same using the Purim story. He insists that there is nothing new about the anti-Semites in Germany. Hitler is the new Haman; the biblical and rabbinic descriptions of Haman's hateful policies are recapitulated in the Nazi regime, which is destined to be humiliated just as Haman was. Reading this, now, knowing what happened to the Jews during the war, it seems as if the parallels are misguided, as Haman was defeated before he was able to put his anti-Jewish policies into effect. But in March 1936, before any policy of mass murder was in effect, the possibility of a humiliating failure of the regime seemed not entirely implausible.

"THE JEWS REJOICED – IN JOY, HAPPINESS, AND HONOR" (ESTH. 8:16). That is the keynote of Purim. Purim is a festival of relaxation for the Jewish people. The Jew, in spite of the strain and tension of his life in the Galuth, in the exile, knew how to relax. He knew how to distill some joy and gladness out of his life's experience, however somber and tragic it ofttimes was. For the Jewish people was always a healthy people, not given to moodiness, moroseness, pathological depression. The Jewish people always believed in a God of whom it could exclaim time and time again, "Thou hast turned my mourning into rejoicing" (Ps. 30:11). A bow which remains constantly strung taut sooner or later breaks. Our people knew how to unbrace, how to relax.

Israel had its Sabbaths, its festivals, its seasons of gladness. And the happiest day of all its seasons of gladness was Purim. Purim was a carnival, a festival of hilarious joy, masquerade, dancing, singing, feasting. On Purim the spirit of revelry was introduced into the most sacred of places, and during the reading of the Megillah, the Scroll of Esther, pandemonium broke loose in the synagogue when the name of Haman was mentioned.

"These days shall be remembered and observed in every generation" (Esth. 9:28), you read in the Megillah. And the days of Purim were observed and remembered in every generation. Why? Because the festival of Purim is so characteristic of Jewish experience in the exile. Purim is the one festival whose locale is in the exile, outside of Palestine, and everything connected with the story is typical of Jewish experience in exile from those days to these.

First of all, the story of Esther is a story of the uncertainty and impermanence characteristic of Jewish life in the Diaspora. For years people had lived at peace in the vast empire of Persia. Suddenly out of the clear sky came this desperate fact into their lives: that a man close to the king had been angered by a Jew, and because of his anger he had persuaded this king to destroy not merely this man and his family, but the entire Jewish people. The tragic insecurity of the Jews in the Diaspora is brought out most dramatically in the Megillah: "And thy life shall hang in doubt before thee" (Deut. 28:66). You will have no assurance in your life. That has been the mark of the exile.

In those days as in these days, there came a recrudescence of anti-Semitism. Haman was not the first nor the last of the anti-Semites. A thousand years before Haman, Pharaoh sought to destroy the Jews of Israel, and twenty-five hundred years later, another anti-Semite in Germany is seeking to annihilate the Jews.[2] In a few weeks we will celebrate Passover and will read in the Haggada this rule of exile life: "Not one man alone arose to destroy us, but in every generation people will arise to seek and destroy."

From a reading of the Book of Esther, we learn how little originality there is to these foes of Israel – how identified are all their motives and their methods in those days as in these days. For example, Haman was not at all of Persia any more than Hitler is of Germany – Haman was an Amalekite, an immigrant.[3] The naturalized must

2 This is a rather surprising formulation for March 1936, when the idea of annihilation as a policy even for the Jews of Germany, let alone the entire Jewish people, was simply not in the public domain. It is not inconceivable that occasionally the original text of the 1936 sermon was later modified for publication.

3 There is nothing in the Book of Esther about Haman being an "immigrant." His connection with the Amalekites – archvillains in traditional Jewish consciousness – comes from his identification in Esth. 3:1 as "the son of Hamadatha the Agagite," which is linked with King Agag the Amalekite, who was spared by Saul and killed by Samuel (1 Sam. 15:8, 20, 32–33). Rabbinic aggadah makes Haman the grandson

prove their loyalty. Because Haman was an Amalekite, and a stranger, he was a super-patriot. Haman started out on his anti-Semitic career with a personal grudge against Mordecai. Mordecai, who sat in the gate of the palace of the king, would not kneel to Haman as did all the other people. The rabbis explained Mordecai's boldness by saying that Haman carried upon his garment the symbol of an idol, and as a Jew Mordecai was forbidden to kneel to any idol.[4] Be that as it may, Haman became angry at Mordecai. Hurt pride led him to turn against Mordecai and his people. Haman was not satisfied to put his hand out toward Mordecai alone; he turned against Mordecai's people. How characteristic this is of Jewish experience in exile! The anti-Semite starts with a personal grudge against some individual Jew and ends up as an enemy of the entire people.

There is no originality among the anti-Semites. Haman, like all anti-Semites preceding and following him, found high-sounding titles and phraseology for his spite and enmity. He masked greed and malice under the cloak of patriotism. Because of his personal grudge against Mordecai, Haman proceeded to incite charges against the Jews on the ground that all Jews are disobedient, traitorous, dangerous to the empire. Today in Germany, economic rivalry, competition, hatred of the competitor, and envy of the Jew cloak themselves in the garb of patriotism, nationalism and pride of race – the blood. Haman resorted to bribery: he offered ten thousand talents of silver to the king in order to win his signature on an edict of annihilation. The anti-Semite either bribes outright or with promises of the great boon which will come to the nation if the Jews are expelled or annihilated. Hitler promises golden days of glory for a Germany *Judenrein*.

Haman appealed to the king on the basis of differences which exist between the Jew and the non-Jew – a favorite device of all enemies of Israel. "There is a scattered people and their religious customs are different from ours" (cf. Esth. 3:8). Suspicion and fear of the unknown can easily be stimulated in the masses. The masses

---

of King Agag (see Bialik and Ravnitzky, *The Book of Legends/Sefer ha-Aggadah*, p. 156a), which of course is chronologically impossible.

4 Targum on Esth. 3:2; Esther Rabbah 7,6; Ibn Ezra on Esth. 3:2.

love conformity, unity. When you arouse them to a sense of fear, a sense of difference, you are on the way to victory – in those days as in these days in Germany.

Haman did not persuade the king at once. The king was unwilling to destroy the Jews. Our Midrash tells us that Haman carried on a protracted campaign of propaganda before he finally persuaded the king,[5] just as the Nazis have carried on fifteen, eighteen, years of propaganda to poison the German mind against the Jews. If you repeat something often enough the people come to accept it as an axiom, something which requires no proof, no investigation: that is the dangerous power of propaganda and its appeal to the anti-Semite.

There is no originality in the anti-Semite even in his ruthlessness. Pharaoh in Egypt was satisfied with the destruction of children. Every male child that was born was to be thrown into the Nile. Nebuchadnezzar destroyed the First Temple and rooted out a nation. Haman, too, tried to uproot, to annihilate. He wanted to uproot the last germ of the house of Israel. Haman then and Hitler now. There is little imagination among our enemies.

And from the Book of Esther, we read how deliverance comes to our people, how our people are saved from hate. Deliverance comes as a result of the loyalty of the Jews. Mordecai was strong, proud, persevering: Mordecai would not bow down, would not court toleration through kneeling. Esther, at the risk of her life, intercedes for her people. Courage, faith, loyalty – these are the factors which will save our people whenever persecution comes. The Jews in these trying times must remember the lesson and not kneel, must not bow down to untoward circumstances, must not become servile or stampeded.

Our strategy must always be to join forces with all the liberal elements in the world and fight this recrudescent barbarism with every power at our disposal, to harass, to undermine, and ultimately to destroy it. The German problem will be solved when the Nazis are destroyed, and in no other way. Any Jew who, because of his

---

5 b. Megillah 13b–14a; Bialik and Ravnitzky, *The Book of Legends/Sefer ha-Aggadah*, pp. 154b–155a.

timidity or complaisance, does not enter the struggle today to save the precious values of civilization, who does not fight for democratic human life, is underwriting his own suicide.

There can be no peace for sixteen million Jews in the world, if the program and the policies of the Nazis spread throughout the world. It is not going to spread if the Nazis are destroyed. Even if we get two or three million Jews out of countries in Europe and settle them in Palestine, that does not solve the problem for the rest of the Jews who are going to remain in the Diaspora. So, our problem is to fight for an order of society which will allow us to live any place, anywhere on the face of the earth.

It is not enough to raise money for relief. It is important to raise money for relief, but it is more important to raise money for war against the enemies of civilization.

Haman prepared the gallows for Mordecai, and on those gallows not Mordecai but Haman was hanged. The Nazis prepare destruction for the Jewish people, but there is a law of history which operates not only in Shushan but in Berlin. And that law of history says that in the long last, bigotry, intolerance, and hate do not win the day. Haman, the symbol of hate, is led by Mordecai, the symbol of faith, in triumph through the capital. In the long last, it is the ideals of freedom, good will, and tolerance that will win in these days.

So Purim comes to us with a reassuring message. When Mordecai heard the decree that the king had issued on the thirteenth day of Adar that all the Jews of Persia were to be destroyed, he was, of course, terribly depressed. He put on sackcloth and ashes and went through the streets wailing and bemoaning the fate which was to overtake his people. He met three little Jewish boys coming from school. He stopped one and asked him, "What did you study in school today?" And the lad recited to him a verse from the Book of Proverbs which he had learned that morning: "Do not be afraid of a sudden terror and the wickedness of thine enemies, for God will be kind and He will keep thy foot from being caught" (Prov. 3:25).

Mordecai turned to the second lad. "What did you study in school this morning?" And the boy quoted a verse from the prophet Isaiah:

"You enemies of Israel, take counsel together but your counsel will be destroyed. Speak the word of destruction but it will not come to pass, for God is with us" (Isa. 8:10).

And he turned to the third little lad and asked, "What did you study in school this morning?" And he also quoted a verse from Isaiah: "Listen to me, O House of Jacob: unto old age I shall be with you. Even to hoary hair I will carry you. I made you and I will carry you. I will bear you up and I will deliver you" (Isa. 46:4).

When Mordecai heard what these three little Jewish lads had learned on that day, on the day of the dire decree, he laughed long, loud, and joyously.[6] Mordecai laughed on that day, and for the twenty-five hundred years since that day, Mordecai's fellow Jews throughout the world, however dark the world around them may be – on the festival of Purim, on this festival of reassurance, on this day which reminds them of recurrent threats and of the deliverance of their people, the brothers of Mordecai laugh joyously and confidently and, laughing, they face the future.[7]

---

6 This section of the sermon is not based on the Book of Esther but rather on a rabbinic expansion in "Aggadat Esther," ed. Buber, 45–46, Esther Rabbah 7:13 and 9:4. Silver may well have taken it from Bialik and Ravnitzky, *Sefer ha-Aggadah*, published in Odessa in 1908 and in Berlin in 1922; see Bialik and Ravnitzky, *The Book of Legends/ Sefer ha-Aggadah*, p. 156b.

7 Permission granted by Adele Silver, daughter-in-law, wife of Daniel Jeremy Silver.

Israel Mattuck (1884–1954)

"The Church Conflict in Germany: Its Significance for the Jews"
Liberal Jewish Synagogue, London
February 28, 1937 (Sunday)
Unpublished, Leo Baeck College Library, London

INTRODUCTION

Israel Mattuck was born in Lithuania and educated at Harvard (where he studied Semitics with Professor George Foot Moore) and the Hebrew Union College, Cincinnati. When Claude G. Montefiore consulted leaders of the American Reform movement for advice on finding a religious leader for the Jewish Religious Union, Mattuck was recommended. He first preached for the Union in June 1911 and was swiftly invited to become Minister by the Council. Mattuck was inducted to his position by Montefiore in January 1912, and soon became a major figure in the Jewish Religious Union, attracting large numbers of people to the London synagogue.[1]

Like Chief Rabbi Joseph Hertz and Abraham Cohen of Birmingham, Mattuck came to his position shortly before the Great War began (1912), and remained actively involved as spiritual leader of a major congregation through the Second World War. The unpublished texts of his sermons are a rich resource for seeing how a respected Liberal Rabbi processed the two world wars with their implications both for Jewish life and for the nature of civilization.

The sermon below was delivered at a Sunday morning weekday

1 On Mattuck, see Lawrence Rigal and Rosita Rosenberg, *Liberal Judaism* (2004), pp. 45–55 *passim* on the early years; Edward Kessler, *A Reader in Early Liberal Judaism* (2004), pp. 16–18; Danny Rich, *Israel Mattuck* (2014); Pam Fox, *Israel Isidor Mattuck* (2014).

service, following the response of many significant American congregations to working conditions which required many Jews to work on Saturdays. It therefore supplemented but did not replace the Shabbat morning worship, at which passages from the Torah and the prophetic literature would be read and discussed by the rabbi. Here there is no connection with traditional readings; only in the final paragraph is there a passing connection made with a biblical theme: Elijah facing the prophets of the false Phoenician god Baal. This is essentially a lecture or address, filled with facts, presented in order to educate (if not inspire) the listeners. There is no evidence in this text of an especially impressive writing skill or rhetorical style.

The most important point made by the speaker, from the very beginning, is that what was occurring in Germany was not exclusively persecution of Jews. Mattuck wanted his listeners to know that believing Christians in Nazi Germany were endangered as well, and were resisting their oppressors. The conclusion in the penultimate paragraph that there was no fundamental difference between the persecution of the two groups – believing Christians and Jews – seems rather misguided in retrospect. But it led to a constructive conclusion: that it was best for Jews to endeavor to forge a broad alliance in protest against the Nazi regime.

THE RESISTANCE OF THE GERMAN EVANGELICAL CHURCH TO THE Nazi rulers in Germany has been the only bright element in that country's moral and spiritual darkness. When the Nazi Party came into power, it sought to get control over the organisation of the Protestant Christian Church by appointing for its head a man who had shown allegiance to the full Nazi idea of the absolute supremacy of the State.[2] While a section of the Church accepted the rule of a Nazi Bishop, another section adopted a course of organised resistance to the appointment. The Nazi Government then tried to put into control over Church affairs a lay political administrator, but he met

2 Ludwig Müller. In 1933 he was imposed by the government as *Reichsbischof* (Bishop) of the Protestant Reich Church (*Deutsche Evangelische Kirche*). See Doris L. Bergen, *Twisted Cross*, pp. 75–78 and Index.

with the same opposition.[3] All the efforts which the Government has made to establish its totalitarian control over the Church have broken down on the opposition of the Evangelical group. No threat has moved them; no danger has cowed them; they seem to be fearless in the face of power that appears both unlimited and ruthless.

The first thought, or lesson, that issues out of these facts is about the evidence it shows of the power which religion gives. There is much significance in the comparison between what happened to the Communists, and Socialists, and Trade Unions, on the one hand, and, on the other, the attitude of the Evangelicals. In the last free election in Germany, which occurred only [less than three] months before Hitler came to power, the Communist Party received six million votes, the various Socialist parties together [7.25 million] votes, yet the loyalties of these millions vanished over night when the Nazis became the rulers.[4] The same thing happened with the Trade Unions. When the Government ordered them to close down, they closed down, and their millions of adherents accepted the Government edict without open opposition.

The Evangelicals behaved differently. When the Government tried to assert its power on the Church, they opposed it openly, showing publicly and emphatically their support of the leaders that resisted the Government edicts. Some of the leaders of the Roman Catholic Church in Germany also deserve to be named with honour in this context. Some of them, Cardinal Faulhaber of Munich, for example, dared to condemn in a series of public addresses the Nazi attitude to the Jewish Bible.[5] In that case, and in other cases recently, large numbers of Roman Catholics have shown openly their support

3 This is apparently a reference to Hanns Kerrl, Vice-President of the *Reichstag*, who was appointed on July 16, 1935, to head a newly created ministry as Minister of Ecclesiastical Affairs. See Bergen, *Twisted Cross*, pp. 18–19 and Index.

4 The "last free election" was held on November 6, 1932. The typescript of the sermon leaves blank spaces for the number of months before Hitler's rise to power on January 30, 1933, and for the number of Socialist (non-Communist) votes. The Nazi Party received 11.7 million or thirty-three percent of votes, down from thirty-eight percent in a previous election five months earlier; Communists received 5.9 million and Social Democrats received 7.25 million votes.

5 See the passages from Faulhaber's sermons of December 3, 10, 17, 24, 1933 and January 1, 1934 cited above.

of their priests in their criticism of the Nazis. Such action must require great courage and a readiness to face grave risks, which only an overpowering loyalty could create. It is significant that the adherents of religion have dared to do what Communists, Socialists, and trade unionists did not dare. Here is impressive evidence that no secular loyalty can be a substitute for religious faith and the loyalty that issues from it. Loyalty to a secular cause cannot have the same strength, it cannot give the same power. In different ways, the Jews and Christians in Germany have shown the dynamic quality in religious faith, and the Communists have shown the weakness of secular idealism when submitted to the final test.

It is possible to find excuses for the Communists. They were bitterly treated by the Nazis, so that there was no influence among the Nazis working to mitigate violence against them. Open resistance from them would have meant death, and torture that was worse than death. The risk was undoubtedly great, but so was the number of Communists. And the ordinary Christians who publicly showed themselves in opposition to the Government must have had grounds to think that they were facing similar risk. Moreover, if the Nazis did not dare treat the Evangelicals in the same way that they would have treated the Communists, that fact only shows again the power which religious loyalty gives.

Whatever the outcome of the present Church conflict in Germany, I think there can be only one – that being the victory of the Church – but even if it should be the reverse, the Evangelicals have added a new and not inglorious chapter to the story of heroism which religion has produced issuing from the staunch loyalty it creates and manifesting the great power it establishes. In that, Jews and Christians alike must find encouragement in their religious adherence and support for the belief that the ultimate value and power of human life lies in the spirit of man related to God.

The point of significance in the Church conflict lies in its context. In the Church's opposition to Nazi control over its affairs is implied opposition to the fundamental doctrine of Nazism. The Church refuses to recognize the supremacy of the State and its materialistic national interests.

Nazism has not officially shown any open opposition to religion. But it wants to use religion for its own political or national ends. Its doctrine is very simply *Deutschland über Alles*, including in *Alles* also God, and meaning by *Deutschland* Germany's military power and national glory. Such a doctrine is obviously opposed to Christianity. The Roman Catholic organization thought for a while it could come to terms with it in practice; but soon found it could not.[6] The children could not at the same time be educated both for Nazism and Christianity. The Evangelicals attempted no compromise, but asked for a division of functions. They were prepared to accept Nazism in politics, but in spiritual matters claimed supremacy for Christianity. But the Nazis recognized the unreality of such a division, and the danger it threatened to them. Totalitarianism cannot allow religion its freedom without jeopardizing its own existence. It must be to endure what its name indicates.

Moreover, there is something in Christianity which must be opposed to all that Nazism stands for. The senior pure exponents of Nazism, from Rosenberg down, have declared open war on Christianity, calling it Jewish, and seeking to put in its place the worship of the German nation symbolized in the gods of Nordic mythology.[7] The worship of the State is an idolatry which violates the worship of God for which Judaism and Christianity alike stand. And the consequences of the two forms of worship in practice are totally divergent. The worship of God leads to a love of humanity, the pursuit of righteousness, and the efforts to establish peace; the worship of the

6 Referring to the Concordat between the Nazi government and the Catholic Church, officially signed in July 1933 by the Vatican Secretary of State Eugenio Cardinal Pacelli (later to become Pope Pius XII), and by German Vice-Chancellor Franz von Papen, after approval by Hitler. See Guenter Lewy, *The Catholic Church and Nazi Germany*, pp. 57–93. A similar Concordat had been signed with Italy in 1929.

7 Alfred Rosenberg (1893–1946), had a significant influence on Hitler and other Nazis, especially through his book *Der Mythus des .20 Jahrhunderts* (1930). See Robert S. Wistrich, *Who's Who in Nazi Germany*, pp. 209–12, including the statement, "The neo-paganism which Rosenberg preached consciously aimed to extirpate the influence of the Old and New Testaments and eradicate the Christian ideals of love, charity, humility and mercy.… In its place, Rosenberg affirmed…Wotan worship, solstice celebration, the old Norse gods and runes" (210b).

state leads to hatred, cruelty and war. The worship of God leads to the recognition of human rights of individuals and nations; Nazism leads to the violation of all rights for the supposed aggrandizement of the State. In the Church's conflict in Germany the ultimate issue is between the worship of God and national idolatry.

This analysis of the conflict reveals that it has at bottom the same significance as the persecution of the Jews. Both issue from the same quality in Nazism: its opposition to God and what follows from the worship of Him; it is an opposition to what Judaism and Christianity have in common. Nazi "philosophers" have poured scorn on Jesus the Jew, and his Jewish teachings.[8] In this attitude their hostility to Judaism and Christianity are identified. It is a mistake to think that the Nazis were anti-Semites first and then scorned Jesus. Their anti-Semitism and scorn of Jesus are co-existent; the two are the same thing. They hate what the Jews stand for, and that has been expressed in what Christianity finds in the life of Jesus: the Kingdom of God with righteousness, brotherly love, and peace.

The conflict in Germany is the old conflict between God and Baal in a new form.[9] On the side of God are Jews and Christians alike, the former bearing silent witness to Him in their suffering, the latter, because of their position, bearing a more active witness to Him. Something of the same conflict exists also elsewhere, but in Germany it has reached its culmination. The fate of humanity is involved in it. And it reveals once again a truth, of which our generation needed to be reminded, that the life and progress of humanity are bound up with the recognition of God's rule.[10]

---

8 There were two distinct positions taken by Nazi "philosophers" regarding Jesus. One was to claim that he was really an Aryan who represented Aryan values and opposed Judaism, but whose teachings as represented in the Gospels were distorted and perverted by Jews: see Susannah Heschel, *The Aryan Jesus*, especially chap, 1. In this approach, Jesus could be accepted as consistent with Nazism. The other, more extreme position, was to repudiate Jesus because of his Jewishness and to substitute the historical pagan gods (see previous note).

9 Known especially from the dramatic confrontation between Elijah and the prophets of Baal in 1 Kings 18.

10 Permission granted by Alexandra Wright on behalf of Liberal Jewish Synagogue, Danny Rich on behalf of Liberal Judaism, and Deborah Kahn-Harris on behalf of Leo Baeck College.

Abraham Mayer Heller (1898–1975)
"A People's Voice Is Silenced"
Flatbush Jewish Center, Brooklyn, NY
March 17, 1938 (Purim)
Jewish Survival: Sermons and Addresses, pp. 217–26

INTRODUCTION

Like many other American rabbis featured in this book, Heller was born in Europe (Lithuania), and came to the United States with his family at age eleven. Family tradition traced his direct ancestors back to a leading sixteenth-century rabbi of Prague. Following undergraduate work at NYU and the University of Minnesota, he earned an MA in Social Science at Columbia, and a Master of Hebrew Literature at the Jewish Theological Seminary, receiving ordination in 1924. This was the year he began his service at the Flatbush Jewish Center in Brooklyn, which had had only visiting rabbis since its establishment in 1921. While serving as rabbi, he studied law and became a member of the New York State Bar in 1931, although he never actually practiced as a lawyer.[1]

In addition to *Jewish Survival*, the collection of sermons in which the following text appears, he wrote *The Vocabulary of Jewish Life* (New York: Hebrew Publishing Co., 1942), focusing on Jewish rituals. He was actively involved in Zionist causes, and served two terms as President of the New York Board of Rabbis. In 1974, he completed fifty years as rabbi of the Brooklyn Congregation.

The sermon entitled "A People's Voice Is Silenced" was delivered

1 This biographical material is based on an article published in the *Brooklyn Eagle* on January 22, 1950, Section 2, p. 23, focusing on the celebration of twenty-five years of Heller's tenure as rabbi of the Flatbush Jewish Center.

on the morning of Purim. It is rooted in biblical material from the Book of Esther, yet it is very much about contemporary issues. Thus what is emphasized is the apparent continuity with the past record of the enemies of Jewish people, as in the sermon delivered by Israel Levinthal on Pesach 1933, and the sermon by Abba Hillel Silver on Purim 1936. Before *Kristallnacht*, there is no reason why any Jewish leader would present the current events as unprecedented.

Occasionally there appears to be some skewing of the biblical material in order to fit it into the contemporary framework. While the biblical idea of murdering all the Jews in the 127 provinces spreading from India to Ethiopia (Esth. 3:6 and 1:1) goes far beyond any recorded German plans at the time, Heller taking Ahasuerus – "the real dictator" – as the model for Hitler, and Haman as the model for Julius Streicher, simply does not seem to fit either the biblical narrative or the rabbinic traditions, where Haman is clearly the villain. In this regard, A.H. Silver's presentation, in which Haman is the prototype for Hitler, seems more plausible. Also, Heller includes far more references to contemporary issues than does Silver.

It is worth noting in this sermon that Heller, a Conservative rabbi, has apparently taken up a pacifist position; this was not at all uncommon among non-Orthodox rabbinic leaders at the time, and can be detected in many of the passages cited above in the Chronological section.[2] The common idea was that American entry into what was then called "the Great War" had been a disastrous mistake; the hopes of a "war to end war," or of "making the world safe for democracy" hadn't been realized despite unprecedented bloodshed. These rabbis believed that they were learning "the lessons of history" by avoiding war at all cost, and this would remain true for quite a while in America even after the European war began.

It is also striking that the sermon presents Nazi Germany and Stalinist Russia on what appears to be equal basis, and is always balanced in its attributions of evil and its accessment of these gov-

2 See also the two strong pacifist sermons from 1936 and 1937 in Saperstein, *Witness from the Pulpit*, pp. 50–61, and Lee Mandel, *Unlikely Warrior*, chaps. 3–14, based largely on the unpublished sermons of Roland Gittelsohn.

ernments' dictatorships. Not surprisingly, this attitude would be strengthened with the startling Molotov-Ribbentrop Pact of late August, 1939, which led to the Russian occupation of eastern Poland. On the other hand, there appears to be an idealization of Democracy as rule by "the people," without any explicit recognition of the problems that were testing democratic nations at the time.

Nevertheless, it seems quite plausible to conclude that a congregation listening to this extremely serious sermon after the raucous reading of the Megillah might well have been impressed with the preacher's exposition of the relevance of the biblical text to the current situation in Europe.

WHAT HAPPENED TO PUBLIC OPINION IN PERSIA WHEN THE FATE OF Israel was in the balance? A country responsible for the return of the remnant of our people to Palestine surely must have included numbers of liberal citizens favorably disposed to the Jewish minority within its gates.

The answer to this puzzling question may be found in the opening verse of the Book of Esther as interpreted in the Midrash: "And it came to pass in the days of Ahasuerus, this is the Ahasuerus who reigned, from India even unto Ethiopia, over seven and twenty and a hundred provinces" (Esth. 1:1). "Why," ask the rabbis, "this seemingly superfluous word '*hamolekh*' – 'who reigned'? All know that the function of a king is to reign." But they reply, "We are to infer from this *shemolakh me'atsmo* – he was a self-appointed ruler."[3] The power that was his did not emanate from the will of the people. He was a dictator. Under his tyrannical rule all liberal public opinion was silenced. "At first he ruled over seven provinces, then he enforced his will upon twenty, and finally he subjugated one hundred states."

Ahasuerus, according to the rabbis, personified autocratic dictatorship in the ancient world, with power of life and death over all. The salient facts in the Book of Esther corroborate this rabbinic

3 b. Megillah 11a. Rashi repeats this interpretation that has no real basis in the biblical text.

version. Haman was only the anti-Semitic German Streicher of the Persian era.[4] With all his influence and power, his life was forfeit at the first displeasure of Ahasuerus, the real dictator.

As I listened in the synagogue to the reading of the tale of woe, recounted in the Purim Scroll, my very being rebelled against dictators of all times, including those of our day. Suddenly a wishful dream took hold of me: I am the inventor of a new airplane with a cruising capacity of a thousand miles per hour and more, sailing silently in the stratosphere undetected by human eye and ear. And within the grasp of hand is a powerful magnet, capable of drawing to itself human beings selected at will. With such power at my command, I cover the habitations of men, and out of the mass of humanity I lift out a Hitler, a Mussolini, a Stalin, a Franco, and a few of the lesser known but equally dangerous breed. I set them down securely in "no man's land" to fight out among themselves their respective ideologic *Kampfs* and theories. But the noise-makers, at the mention of the name Haman, brought me back to earth with the realization that the problem is not dictators but dictatorship, the knowledge of its cause and the method of its elimination. The mere forceful removal of an individual does not change the course of events. To substitute a Goering for a Hitler or the dictatorship of a Trotsky for a Stalin will not bring to the world the relief it so much needs.

What is the cause of this evil thing which silences a people's voice? The answer is found in the wisdom of our sages as applied to the introductory verse of the Book of Esther, "*Vayehi*" – "And it came to pass" (Esth. 1:1). Our rabbis tell us: "*Kol mokom sheneamar vayehi bime zoroh*" – "Wherever the phrase 'And it came to pass' is mentioned, it is to be associated with distressing times."[5] They further remark that this word is repeated five times in early biblical literature, each instance recalling to mind a human calamity.

---

4 Founder and editor of the viciously antisemitic periodical *Der Stürmer*, Julius Streicher was a friend and associate of Hitler from 1934 through the 1930s. It seems rather strange, however, that he would be presented as a contemporary model of Haman, as Streicher never was given direct authority to harm Jews, and certainly not to order mass murder, which was not even under consideration in the spring of 1938.

5 b. Megillah 10b, and see also Genesis Rabbah 42:3.

This is the chronological order given by the rabbis: "And it came to pass in the days of Amraphel, Ahaz, Jehoiakim, during the reign of the Judges, and in the days of Ahasuerus."[6] To these simple facts, our sages add their significant interpretation to throw new light on everlasting human problems. In sum: war leads to dictatorship, which inevitably results in suppression of freedom, confusion of ideologies, and inequitable economic systems which are destructive of human values. How similar are these ancient experiences to those of our day! It would seem as if our sages in their day were gazing into the far-distant future. The truths which they expounded centuries ago are applicable to the problems of our age. In the light of their understanding let us diagnose the human ills which have halted progress in this the twentieth century of so-called civilization.

The first *Vayehi* our sages related to the days of Amraphel (Gen. 14:1). What happened then? "*Osu milhomo*" – "They waged war."[7] The most important kingdoms of the then known world applied their powers and talents to the battlefield just like the moderns, with allies and opposing forces. This has been the basic human tragedy with evil consequences leading to recurrences of the expression, "It came to pass." They "waged war" but settled nothing.

The fruits of war are defeat or triumph but they do not permanently solve any problems. The contempt of victor for the vanquished and the spirit of revenge that moves the defeated are the sordid motives of further catastrophes. After these thousands of years of human strife resulting only in bloodshed, we in our generation wage war, too, learning nothing from the past. This time it was for the high-sounding ideal: "A war to end war." And now twenty years after the Armistice of 1918 international morality has reached a new low. In 1914 Great Britain's political thought was symbolized by the liberal Asquith; in America Woodrow Wilson, a historian and philosopher, was writing a new chapter in the life of democracy. Even in the monarchical governments of Germany and Russia eloquent voices championed the cause of liberalism. The war to end war solved

6 Ibid.

7 Ibid.; cf. Gen. 14:2.

nothing. It served to silence the voice of liberalism everywhere. Its main consequence was the loss of millions of lives and the destruction of material wealth beyond human calculation. But to what avail? Only to produce impractical treaties of peace, economic chaos and political dictatorships.

As a natural outgrowth of the first: "And it came to pass," the tragedy of war, the succeeding generations became the heirs of the second *Vayehi* which relates to the days of Ahaz, king of Judea (Isa. 7:1), "Who seized assembly places and houses of learning" (ibid.). Ahaz, according to the rabbinic interpretation, put an end to free assembly and free speech. In time of war, freedom of expression, like every other freedom, is crushed with an iron hand – a people's voice is muzzled! Faulty though human memory be, we surely can recall how, in our own free America at the declaration of war under the leadership of Wilson, the humanitarian, only one voice was audible, "Down with the Huns!" The slightest difference of opinion expressed in opposition to human bloodshed brought with it ruthless suppression.[8]

And what of the aftermath? Has humanity retained its cherished possessions, the freedom to think, to speak and teach, unmolested by the will of tyranny? No elaborate answer is needed. War, true to its nature, advanced the evil of dictatorship and it, in turn, "seized all assembly places and houses of learning."

Schools and universities in the totalitarian states are no longer concerned with the quest of truth. They are but propaganda instruments in the hands of usurpers. There is no freedom of assembly in those states. Men may read and listen only to that which is permitted by governing authority. In no country has the ideal of free assembly and free speech been more passionately pursued than in America. Thank the Almighty, our government still belongs to the people and not the people to the government – but alas, since the war days even in America, group after group, bent upon the subversion

8 For a contemporary rabbinic critique of the attempts by the US government "to suppress the inalienable liberty of expression of opinion by the people," see the sermon by Stephen S. Wise in *Jewish Preaching in Times of War, 1800–2001*, esp. pp. 357–59 on the "Censorship Bill."

of the inalienable rights of minority opinion, has sprung up. The dismissal of students from universities because of differing views on economics or politics is an un-American tendency now poisoning the free air of our country.[9] This is a direct outcome of the world war which was intended to bring the free play of democratic principles into the affairs of humanity. Thus came to pass the second *Vayehi* in our days as in the days of Ahaz, the tragedy of an imprisoned mind.

"Destruction followeth upon destruction" (Jer. 4:20). Another *Vayehi*, borrowed from the sad experience of ancient Israel, tells another tale of woe, a by-product of the evils of dictatorship. "And it came to pass in the days of Jehoiakim" (Jer. 1:3): *Vehine tohu vobohu*, "And behold [everything] was unformed and void."[10] In the wake of the devastation caused by war the suppression of personal freedom followed; the world was a world of chaos and confusion. What should be done to make people forget their bitter experiences? How shall the populace be diverted from thoughts of bread and oppression? The Babylonians in the days of Jehoiakim had but one reply: Foreign expansion – conquest![11] This resulted in the loss of independence of Palestine; the flower of its youth was taken into captivity and the national wealth was despoiled. Other nations, too, suffered Israel's fate in the Babylonian territorial expansion. But the world remained chaotic and confused.

In our day the results are not dissimilar, though the various ideologies have changed considerably. We, too, have our *Tohu vobohu*, a distortion of human values – the negation of the principle of the sacredness of human life. Conquest by first arousing popular passions under the cloak of patriotism is a direct inheritance of the world conflict. The world is split into "right" and "left" – and between these grindstones civilization is crushed. Weird programs of

---

9 At issue were left-wing (Socialist and Communist) student groups such as the National Student League. See Robert Cohen, "Student Activism in the 1930s," and *idem*, *When the Old Left Was Young: Student Radicals and America's First Mass Student Movement, 1929–1941* (New York: Oxford University Press, 1993).

10 Author's note: b. Megillah 10b (cf. Gen. 1:2).

11 The formulation of the three previous sentences appears clearly to be based on an understanding of the German situation, and not on any evidence from ancient Babylonia.

all sorts, economic, political and social, are running amok. The new ghastly philosophies of dictators lead only to a human holocaust of titanic proportions.[12]

Yet at the height of the international struggle for supremacy, in 1917 a group, believing that all human ills are economic problems created by the inequitable distribution of material wealth, succeeded in overthrowing the "powers that be" for the purpose of bringing greater happiness to man; this Russian dictatorship of the proletariat, with all its relentless force, is the inevitable offspring of the autocracy of the Czarist regime.

State Socialism appeared on the horizon, proclaiming its Messianic panacea to an exhausted humanity impoverished materially and spiritually by a war intended to make the world safe for democracy. According to that doctrine everything belongs to the State, and the State alone has the power and right to distribute the products of nature and man. The radicals on the left, to prove their loyalty to that idea, ruthlessly sacrificed millions of human lives as though they were guinea pigs, for the purpose of experimentation.[13]

To counteract the dictatorship of the proletariat came state capitalism to plague humanity. The voice of the people was silenced here too. More than that. The dictatorship on the right declared the people mere vassals of the State. "Everybody and everything belongs to the Fascist government for the purposes of making the nation 'great.' 'Pull in your belt for the leader's sake; starve yourselves into greatness'" is the propaganda of Nazi Germany to bamboozle its citizenry into doing without those essentials, which are needed for the manufacture of armaments to be used in a planned war of world conquest. The one takes everything on its economic theory; the other worships the idol of national chauvinism; but in both the individual is only the means to an end, the pawn in the political game of life

12 A formulation that seems rather prophetic in retrospect, although the preacher had no clear concept of the nature of who the predominant victim of the "holocaust" would be.

13 This apparently refers to the mass starvation in the Soviet Ukraine as a result of Stalin's first Five-Year Plan; for recent treatment in a broader context, see Timothy Snyder, *Bloodlands: Europe Between Hitler and Stalin*, pp. 21–58.

and death; after twenty years of experimentation with life, liberty and happiness, we are still in a world of *Tohu vobohu*, of chaos and confusion, which may be charged directly to the first *Vayehi, bime Amrophel* – the tragedy of war.

"Pull in the belt" is the fourth "And it came to pass": "in the days when the judges judged" (Ruth 1:1). What calamity befell then? "There was famine in the land" (ibid.), not an infrequent occurrence in Palestinian Jewish history. Drought, locusts and the like brought economic hardship to ancient Israel. But today is this the reason why everywhere in the world millions are undernourished and housing conditions are intolerable? Here in America, the most prosperous country in the history of civilized man, ten millions and more plead for employment.[14] Despite droughts and floods, sufficient is produced to satisfy man's elementary needs. Why this anomalous spectacle of starvation in the midst of plenty?

This *Vayehi* of our generation is often ascribed to the phenomenal technological progress made in the past few decades. We are informed that machinery displaced men; hence the curse of widespread unemployment. It is true that in a mechanized society one can do the work of two, three and more; but this is only a half-truth in the dark side of the economic picture. Invention speeds production but it also creates new opportunities for employment. Consider the vast numbers of people gaining their livelihoods, directly and indirectly, from the automobile industry. The "horse and buggy" age that is displaced could under no stretch of imagination employ such large numbers. To mention but two more: the moving picture and radio industries displaced little or nothing and brought gainful occupation to multitudes.

The present day "And it came to pass," as applied to our economic travail, is the result neither of intractable nature nor of man's inventive genius. It is the consequence of a vicious cycle of war-produced dictators and dictators planning for wars. At the command of bloodthirsty despots the peoples of the world, already armed to

---

14 Unemployment increased significantly in 1938, from some 7,700,000 in 1937 to 10,390,000, almost nineteen percent of the work force: http://bit.ly/2yl9qQe.

the teeth, are investing more and more of their energies and their substance in enterprises of destruction. With back-breaking burdens created by the mad international race of armaments, they cannot afford to buy the surplus products of industrial countries for their sustenance. Free trade is less a reality today than ever. Economic self-sufficiency becomes the program of the militarist dictatorship. Due to the concentration of power in the hands of groups or individuals, boundary lines are emphasized, forbidding interchange of goods as well as ideas. If the people were permitted to consume the natural yield of their labors, there would be abundance for all and no need for "belt-pulling."

"And it came to pass," twenty years ago when the nations chose to solve their problems on the battlefields, that the world again witnessed the tragedy of humanity disillusioned and broken; destruction followed destruction – dictatorship came with its denial of personal liberty, abrogation of the right of freedom of assembly and speech, and distortion of truth, making man only a means to an end. To make the populace of autocracies subservient to political pressure in spite of extreme economic dislocation the "powers that be" resort to the tactics of terror so well described in the fifth and final *Vayehi* and related by the rabbis to the days of Ahasuerus. His was the decree inspired by Haman: "To destroy, to slay, and to cause to perish" (Esth. 3:13). Of course in every calamity the Jew is the first scapegoat. His physical and spiritual life is least safe when reaction, be it right or left, expresses itself in merciless dictatorship. But the blood purges, suicides, and murders by public trials select no race or creed. All who harbor a personal opinion are doomed. The rise of totalitarian power means the death of all liberal voices raised in behalf of man's greater good.

Well, what is the way out of this frightful world mess, this violation of the sacredness of individuality? Must we choose between dictatorship of the right or the left? Our answer is unconditional. A plague on both houses. Dictatorship is the evil fruit of *Vayehi* and is responsible for another "And it came to pass" – human catastrophes of man's own making. Ours is the time-tested doctrine: The ideal of DEMOCRACY. Let the real voice of the people be heard, without rabble-rousing, national chauvinism or aggrandizement, and the world will rid itself of much of its present-day tragedy. Wars are not the way of democracies but of autocracies. If man's right to rule himself had not been surrendered to misguided, impractical fanatics and insincere power-seeking demagogues, the fate of human happiness would not hang in the balance today. Autocracy thrives on war, and war breeds dictatorship with all its attendant evils.

To justify itself, at least one dictatorship claims that the sacrifice of liberty by revolution is a prerequisite to true democracy.[15] It was Chesterton who, paradoxically but effectively, exposed the illogic of that claim: "You can never have a revolution to establish a democracy. You must have a democracy to establish a revolution."[16] Even a people's good cannot be superimposed from above. The people itself must genuinely desire it and its voice must be heard through truly representative government. But the way of democracy implies more than the true collective expressions of group or nation. To put it in the words of Woodrow Wilson, "I believe in democracy because it releases the energy of every human being."[17] In a dictatorship man is the means to an end; in democracy, he is the end and the State is the means.

Democracy must become more vigorous in those lands where dictatorship has not as yet fully raised its ugly head. While evil forces are multiplying, the believers in democracy look idly on. The message of the great ideal of human freedom and liberty must be revitalized if it is not to speak in the past tense of man-made tragedies – "And it came to pass." Noble voices in the days of Persia were silenced because of the dictatorship of Ahasuerus who, as the self-appointed ruler, made foreign conquest and internal oppression the policy of his reign; the policy is no less pursued by the dictators of our day. It therefore becomes our stupendous task to bring democracy back to a stricken world – to return to man his right to self-rule and his

---

15 Apparently referring to the ideology justifying the Stalinist Soviet Union.

16 Author's note: "[G.K.] Chesterton, 'Tremendous Trifles.'"

17 Author's note: "Wilson, Address–1912." (This statement was also quoted by President John F. Kennedy in his State of the Union Address delivered on January 11, 1962.)

confidence in the solution of human problems through arbitration and conciliation instead of combat on the battlefield. Thus will man free himself from the scourge of *Vayehi*. "The voice of the people is the voice of God,"[18] and it is this voice that again must become articulate in the world.[19]

18 Author's note: "Sefer Zemanim, Le Saadyah" [*sic*]. The only connection to a "Saadia" I can find is not to the famous Saadia Gaon but to sixteenth-century poet Saadia Longo, who translated the well-known Latin version of this statement – *vox populi vox dei* – into Hebrew as *kol hamon hu kol Shaddai*. Israel Davidson, *Otsar haMeshalim ve-haPitgamim*, p. 191, no. 3134, attributes it to the sixteenth-century Midrash Shemuel [Uceda] on Avot 1, p. 111. A similar Hebrew formulation, beginning with *kol haRabbim* was used earlier by Abravanel in his commentary on Avot 3,9. I have no idea how the "Sefer Zemanim" (or "Seder Zemanim") is relevant.

19 Permission granted by Rabbi Joshua Heller, grandson.

Tobias (Tuvyah) Geffen (1870–1970)

"Sermon on *Ḥayyei Sarah* 5699, at the Time of the Great Destruction of the Jews in Germany at the Hands of the Evil Oppressor, Hitler, May his Name and his Memory Be Blotted Out"
Congregation Shearith Yisrael, Atlanta, GA
November 19, 1938
Naḥalat Avot, pp. 60–64
Translated by MS

INTRODUCTION

Like Harry Joshua Stern (above), Geffen was born in the Lithuanian city of Kaunas (called Kovno at the time, part of the Russian Empire). Unlike Stern and various foreign-born Reform rabbis, the Orthodox Geffen was educated and began his rabbinic career abroad, immigrating to the United States at age thirty-three in 1903, undoubtedly influenced by the latest series of pogroms. His first rabbinic position in America was at New York's Congregation Ahavat Zedek. In 1907, he became rabbi of a small synagogue in Canton, Ohio; then, in 1910, he moved to Atlanta, Georgia, to serve as rabbi of Congregation Shearith Israel, founded by emigrants from eastern Europe. This was his commitment for the rest of his long and productive life.

Geffen organized the first Hebrew school in Atlanta, and began a daily class in Talmud. He also standardized the regulation of kosher supervision in the Atlanta area under his central authority. He is perhaps best known for his 1935 decision that certified Coca-Cola as kosher. One of the leading Orthodox rabbis in the South, he became the head of the Southern division of the Union of Orthodox Rabbis. Yet he also had a strong friendship and working relationship with a leading Atlanta attorney who was a member of the city's Reform congregation.[1]

Geffen published eight books of talmudic studies, biblical exegesis, and traditional sermon texts wherein there is extremely little engagement with contemporary historical events. That is what makes the current text so noteworthy.

The Hebrew text of the sermon raises an obvious question about the language of delivery. Throughout the history of medieval Jewish preaching, it was standard for sermons to be delivered in the vernacular language, but if the preacher decided to gather his texts and present them in book form, it was almost always in Hebrew. The obvious reason is that this would make the book intelligible to educated Jews throughout the world, and not just in the country of the preacher's congregation.[2]

Although in one case – a sermon delivered soon after the establishment of the State of Israel – Geffen did apparently preach in Hebrew, for most of his career he apparently preached in Yiddish.[3]

Like many traditional sermons, this one begins with a somewhat puzzling quotation from rabbinic literature – making a rather surprising connection between Sarah and Esther, with interpretations that explain the statement in the context of Akiva's encounter with Roman oppression. The second part of the sermon presents a natural shift from the time of Akiva to the present, immediately following *Kristallnacht*. It ends with an expression of the hope – so painfully

---

1 Kimmy Caplan, *BeSod haSiaḥ haḤaredi* [*Internal Popular Discourse in Israeli Haredi Society*], p. 265 n. 36. The biographical material is also partially based on the Wikipedia article on Geffen.

2 On this issue of language for medieval and early modern preaching, see Saperstein, *Jewish Preaching 1200–1800*, pp. 39–44.

3 On the sermon following the establishment of the State of Israel, see Caplan, *Ortodoksiah baOlam haHadash*, p. 133, citing an archival manuscript: "Truly I don't know how to speak and what to say. If I speak in the English language, I am not expert enough to be able to express my ideas and my heartfelt feelings in English; if I were to speak in Yiddish, I am certain that almost all of those gathered would not understand what I said. That is why I have decided to speak in the Hebrew language." In an email I received on January 19, 2016, the preacher's grandson, Rabbi David Geffen, wrote (in response to my query): "My grandfather gave all his sermons in Yiddish – when he wrote them for publication he translated them into Hebrew."

ironic in retrospect – "that this is the beginning of the downfall of the evil ones."[4]

MIDRASH RABBAH ON OUR TORAH READING [*ḤAYYEI SARAH*]: "R. Akiva was sitting and preaching, when he saw that the congregation was dozing. Wanting to arouse them, he asked, 'What made Queen Esther worthy of ruling over 127 principalities? [cf. Esth. 9: 29–30]. Let Esther, the descendant of Sarah, who was 127 years old [Gen. 23:1] come and rule over 127 principalities'" (Gen. Rab. 58:3).

I have seen among the commentators on the Torah (*Tishbi, ve-Ha-Derash ve-ha-Iyyun*) that they explain this midrash as Akiva wanting to arouse the people so that they would not despair of redemption, and not fall spiritually upon an evil day. For the last days of Akiva were when the Roman Emperor Hadrian ruled over Israel, seeking to kill and destroy all of the Jews, from the children to the elderly. Terrible decrees were ordained against the people of Israel, and cruel persecution came upon them. Understandably, the Israelite people were left perplexed, at a loss for any hope in the future. That is the reason why when R. Akiva was preaching to the congregation, he saw that the congregants were dozing off, meaning that he observed around him the signs of despair and spiritual indifference, indications of weakness and laziness, like the behavior of those who are dozing, whose powers weaken and they are no longer alert – that no one was listening to him because their spirits had been crushed and their strength was absent.[5]

---

4 On this sermon, see the brief discussion by Gershon Greenberg, "Kristallnacht," pp. 157–58. I am grateful to Rabbi David Geffen (acting on behalf of the Geffen family) for permission to publish my translation of this text. This is the only sermon text included in *Naḥlat Yosef*, and one of the very few of his printed sermons responding directly to a historical event that can be dated. It is unclear why he did not include it in his *Hadrat Yosef*, published in 1942, which commemorates the fortieth year since his arrival in the United States.

5 This paragraph is largely based on Aaron Levin, *Ha-Derash ve-ha-Iyyun*, vol. 1, (Bilgoria-Piotrkow, 1928), p. 111a, a work mentioned in parentheses near the beginning of the sermon, but the formulation seems especially appropriate for the time of the sermon.

Similarly we have found in the Talmud that the Sages used the word "dozing" for a time when a person was near to death, when his powers had abandoned him. When a certain Amora came to visit his sick friend and saw that he was dozing, he realized that his friend was near to death and the departure of his soul.[6]

This was also the case in the time of R. Akiva, for the congregation was weak, its powers were feeble like one who is sleeping, or close to death. R. Akiva wanted to arouse them so that they would not act like people who have lost all hope, who despair of the redemption, for there is no impediment to God's ability to save. He therefore said to them, "Have you not forgotten what has happened to the Israelite nation in the past? Certainly you know what happened to the Israelite people in the days of the wicked Haman, who sought to destroy all the Jews; their fate was already sealed and it was but a single step between themselves and death, when suddenly God showed that He holds kings in derision and sports with regents [cf. Hab. 1:10], for He set up against the mighty a frail young lady, namely Esther, the Queen, the daughter of Mordecai's uncle [cf. Esth. 2:15], and through this young lady whom He set up He annulled the plan of the enemies of Israel. It was not through human strength that Esther prevailed, but rather through the merit that Sarah exemplified, for she was 127 years old: when 100 she was as if 20 with regard to sin, and when 20 she was as if 7 with regard to beauty,[7] that is to say that there was perfection in the beauty of her body and the purity of her soul. And Esther was compared with Sarah." From both of them [Akiva's congregation] could learn not to be overwhelmed by difficult times and drastic changes, but rather to muster their remaining strength and to make their arms as firm as bronze, and God will send them deliverance.

And so I say now, when sorrows and misfortunes have mounted against the Jews in Germany like a sweeping wind and a tempest [cf. Ps. 55:9], and all of the Jews there are now sinking in a sea of tears and of blood, devoid of hope, for they have no way to escape from

6 I have not been able to find this talmudic reference.

7 Genesis Rabbah 58,1 and Rashi on Gen. 23:1; some textual traditions reverse the terms "sin" and "beauty."

the depths, and the entire community is dozing, indeed the world Jewish congregation is dozing, almost without believing that Jacob will survive [cf. Amos 7:2 and 7:5]. Let us awaken our brothers that they may remember the past persecutions in the history of Israel; remember how in the days of Haman, God overturned the plot of the enemy, who was left hanging on a tree, while the Jews were saved from disaster and experienced deliverance, as is written in the Book of Esther, "The Jews had light and joy, happiness and honor" (Esth. 8:16). So it is our hope that God will deliver us now from our sorrows, that relief and deliverance will come to the Jews (Esth. 4:14), and that the wicked Hitler, may his name and his memory be eternally blotted out, will be destroyed forever together with all his wicked associates, for all the righteous of the world's nations will withdraw from him, and he will remain alone within his camp.

We may mention in this context the words of a midrash on our weekly Torah reading, on the verse, "Abraham paid out to Ephron the money: four hundred shekels of silver at the merchants' rate" (Gen. 23:16). On this the midrash states, "'A greedy man runs after wealth; he does not realize that loss will overtake him' (Prov. 28:22): 'A greedy man [*ish ra ayin*, lit.: a man evil of eye][8] runs after wealth': that is Ephron, for he caused the evil eye [*ayin haRa*] to penetrate the money of the righteous Abraham, 'and he did not know that loss will overtake him,' for Ephron is written here without the letter *vav*."[9]

We need to understand the meaning of this great punishment given to Ephron: that the letter *vav* was removed from his name. Even if Ephron knew that the *vav* was missing from his name it would not have bothered him very much, for it was more important for him that he received the 400 shekels of silver even if this meant the loss of the *vav*. But there is truly a marvelous idea here, for the letter *vav*

8 The Hebrew *ish ra ayin*, "a man evil of eye," understood to mean a greedy man who wants whatever he sees. This is associated in the rabbinic exegesis with the term *ayin haRa*, "the evil eye," a phrase implying very bad luck. On this midrashic passage, see Rivka Ulmer, *Ayin ha-Ra: The Evil Eye in the Bible and in Rabbinic Literature*, pp. 109–10.

9 Shemot Rabbah, 31,17. Throughout the chapter, and even at the beginning of verse 16, Ephron is written in Hebrew אפרון, but in the phrase that states that Abraham paid Ephron (Gen. 23:16), the name is written אפרן, indicating that he has lost something because of his greed or "evil eye."

in the Hebrew language consistently functions as a letter of connection which brings two things together.[10] Therefore, the connecting *vav* is a sign and a symbol of connectedness and unification between one person and another, whereas without the connecting *vav* there is an indication of solitude, suggesting someone who is separated from the rest of the world, and has no interaction with others. That is what the Sages mean to teach us with their homiletical interpretation of the verse: "'A greedy man runs after wealth' (Prov. 28:22): that is Ephron," who was so eager to receive some of the wealth of Abraham, even though at the beginning he said, "A piece of land worth four hundred shekels of silver – what is that between you and me?" (Gen. 23:15).

But in the end, it was not enough that Ephron failed to give Abraham the burial place gratis; more than this, he insisted that he be paid with centenaria shekels, as the Gemara states in tractate Baba Metsia 87a, for they learned from this that the evil say much but they do very little: at first Ephron said that he would give the land to Abraham as a gift, but afterward he accepted from Abraham shekels worth a hundred times the amount of the simple shekels.[11] Yet even though he received this fortune from Abraham, who was compelled to give it because Sarah's body was lying there and he needed a place for burial, Ephron ended up losing his reputation and his stature, for all of the other Hittites withdrew and separated from him and no longer wanted to be his friend, for everyone despised him because he took so much money from Abraham, who was beloved and respected by all, as we see in that they exalted him and addressed him as "the prince of God among us" (Gen. 23:6). This is the meaning of the midrash that interprets the verse "and he did not know that loss will overtake him," to mean that Ephron did not know that as a result of his obnoxious behavior he would lose the letter *vav* from his name, for the connectedness with other people would be disrupted, and all would distance themselves from him, so

10 *Vav haḥibbur* in Hebrew, usually translated "and," does indeed generally connect two items, although this is not its function as a vowel in the middle of a name.

11 On the "centenaria shekels," see Genesis Rabbah 58, 7.

that he would be left in solitary isolation. How wretched is the man who has lost his friends and his comrades, and is left "outside the camp" like a leper. This is truly a great punishment for any man, as it was for the greedy Ephron.

And so I say of the greedy man (*ra ayin*) of our own time, the wicked Hitler, may his name be blotted out, that he turned his evil eye upon the wealth and possessions of the Jews. All of the oppressive regulations that he passed upon them were nothing more than libelous pretexts intended to rob and steal from them their wealth and possessions, leaving them naked and barefoot, dying of hunger. In addition to this, he imposed upon them a punitive fine of 400 million dollars, backed by silver.[12] I have seen that the author of the *Turim* has written that 400 in *gematria* is the numerical equivalent of the phrase *ra ayin*, [meaning stingy, miserly, jealous], and also the name Ephron [in the *parashah*] is equivalent to 400.[13] We can therefore apply to the oppressor Hitler the verse, "A greedy man runs after wealth; he does not realize that loss will overtake him" (Prov. 28:22).

For the evil Hitler, who ran to steal the wealth of the Jews by demanding 400 hundred million, is "a greedy man, who does not realize that loss will overtake him." For he too will be missing the *vav* that binds together, and all the peoples and the nations will separate themselves from him and leave him isolated, outside the camp, like the leper. They will distance themselves from him and abandon all the agreements they have made with him. We have already seen that the President of the United States, that righteous man among the Gentiles, Franklin Delano Roosevelt, peace be upon him, has spoken with a voice that kindles flames of fire (Ps. 29:7), thunderously condemning the Nazi "kingdom of insolence"[14] and its rulers,

---

12 The fine imposed upon German Jewry following *Kristallnacht* was one billion German marks, equivalent to four hundred million US dollars.

13 Taken from Jacob ben Asher's *Perush al ha-Torah*, a work far less known than his legal compendium, *Arba'ah Turim*.

14 *Malkhut zadon*, from *birkat haminim*, from the daily Jewish liturgy, asking for divine punishment of the wicked. This is rather hyperbolic: Roosevelt's statement, issued on November 15, contained no explicit reference either to the Nazi regime or to its Jewish victims. Following is the text: "The news of the past few days from Germany has deeply shocked public opinion in the United States. Such news from any part

and after him other great figures in the United States have spoken, and also well-known English writers have launched public protests, inspiring anger in the hearts of many decent people, casting scorn and contempt upon the cruel Nazi murderers.

There is hope that this is the beginning of the downfall of the evil ones, when all the nations of the world will stand together against them and save the oppressed from their oppressors. Let us hope in God that just as He saved the people of Israel in the days of the wicked Haman, sending His help through Queen Esther, so He will help us now if we too will do what Queen Esther did in her command: "Go, assemble all the Jews" (Esth. 4:16).[15] This is the key to the salvation of Israel: that there be no separate entities and denominations within the Jewish people – Orthodox and Reform, Conservative and Radicals.[16] For the enemies of Israel don't know about different categories of Jews; for them, every Jew, no matter what his denomination, is a Jew whose blood and whose money is fair game. If one young Jew has mortally attacked one of the Nazi officials, all Jews are held responsible for him and obligated to pay the punitive fine because of him, and they may be killed because of the deed of this young man.[17]

Therefore for us too there is an obligation to unite and become as one together. In this evil time we must from the outset share in

---

of the world would inevitably produce a similar profound reaction by the American people in every part of this nation. With a view to gaining a first-hand picture of the situation in Germany, I asked the Secretary of State to order our Ambassador in Berlin to return at once for report and consultation. I myself could scarcely believe that such things could occur in a twentieth-century civilization": http://www.fdrlibrary.marist.edu/archives/pdfs/holocaust.pdf.

15 The continuation of the verse mandates a three-day fast for the entire Jewish community, which is not made explicit in the sermon.

16 The word *Radikalim* appears in Hebrew, as do the other words *Ortodoksim, Reformer, Conservativim*. It is unclear whether "Radicals" refers to secularist Jews, perhaps with Socialist or even Communist sympathies, or to the Reconstructionists led by Mordecai Kaplan, whose theology was indeed radical but in other ways was traditional. In either case, this is a rather impressive call for unity among Jews in the context of the current disaster.

17 This is of course reference to the assassination of Ernst vom Rath, an official in the German Embassy of Paris, by Hirschel Grynszpan on November 7, 1938, twelve days before the sermon was delivered, with *Kristallnacht* following two days later.

the suffering of our Jewish brothers in Germany: to comfort them, to speak with them words of reassurance that we are endeavoring with everything within our power to act on their behalf:

- through prayer to God
- through charitable giving sharing our own financial resources, and also
- by urging the leaders and governors of the American states and the other democratic nations to find a place of rest for the refugees in their misery.[18]

Then all of us together, all of the denominations without exception will unite as a single person. At that time, may God provide safety for us; may He send salvation to us, and may we be worthy of seeing the downfall of the oppressors – Hitler, may his name be blotted out, and all his minions, who will descend to the nethermost pit (Ps. 55:24) – while the people of Israel will receive perpetual salvation, as God restores the captivity of His people to Zion (cf. Ps. 126:1). May it come speedily and in our time!

POSTSCRIPT

I delivered this sermon seven years ago on the *parashah Ḥayyei Sarah* in Congregation Shearith Yisrael in Atlanta, Georgia. On that Sabbath, the wicked Hitler, may his name be blotted out, began to display his harsh hand against the Jews who were living in Germany, and from there the fury spread to all the Jews of Europe.[19] If indeed we find some small comfort in the fulfillment of our prayers – that we have been worthy of seeing the downfall of the cruel and oppressive murderers: Hitler and his cohorts, may their names and their memory

18 The most important fulfillment of this hope was the establishment of the *Kindertransport* program by Great Britain. The United States had nothing comparable.

19 It seems surprising to read the assertion that only with *Kristallnacht* did Hitler "display his harsh hand" against the German Jews. But despite the broad discriminatory legislation that made life miserable, Nazi policy, at least until this point, did not condone acts of violence, and certainly not mass murder, against the Jews.

be blotted out, may they descend to the pit of destruction, for they are now to be found chained in prison in their own country, waiting to hear of the verdict against them, whether they will be shot or hanged, from judges sitting on the judgment seats so that they will receive punishment for all of the murder and destruction they have inflicted upon millions of human beings, and the entire Nazi entity with its kingdom of arrogance has been annihilated from the face of the earth, so that we can cite the biblical verse, "When the wicked perish, there are shouts of joy" (Prov. 11:10) – nevertheless there is devastation in our hearts that because of our many sins, the evil in their cruelty succeeded in destroying and wiping out more than six million Jews in the European countries with strange and cruel deaths which had never before been heard of in this world. O earth, earth, do not cover up their blood (cf. Job 16:18). Let the verse be fulfilled, "Before our eyes let it be known among the nations that You avenge the spilled blood of Your servants" (Ps. 79:10).[20]

20 https://www.lbi.org/digibaeck/results/?qtype=pid&term=1712363. Permission granted by Rabbi David Geffen, grandson.

Julius Cohn (1878–1940)

Farewell Sermon (*Abschiedspredigt*)
Ulm Congregation
April 4, 1939, First Day of Pesach
Unpublished, Leo Baeck Institute, Center for Jewish History, New York
Translated by MS

INTRODUCTION

Julius Cohn was born in a small city near Danzig/Gdansk. His father was a cantor and religion teacher. After a short period of study in Leeds, England, Cohn returned to Germany for the remainder of his primary, secondary, and higher education. Although he initially enrolled in a medical program, he soon shifted to the field of Oriental Philology and Philosophy, eventually (in 1908) receiving a PhD at the University of Heidelberg, based on his translation (from Arabic) and annotation of a work by the fifteenth-century Karaite scholar Samuel al-Mahgribi. He also studied at the *Hochschule für die Wissenschaft des Judentums*, where he received his rabbinic ordination in 1913. During the period of his rabbinical studies he served as teacher and preacher for the Liberal Community in Berlin.

After positions in Karlsruhe and Stuttgart, in 1928 Cohn became *Bezirksrabbiner* (District Rabbi) in Ulm, where he remained for the rest of his rabbinic career. His synagogue was partially destroyed on *Kristallnacht*, though it was apparently intact enough for him to be able to deliver his farewell sermon there four and a half months later; Cohn himself was seriously beaten and injured on *Kristallnacht*, spending several weeks in the hospital until December 5, 1938. When he delivered the sermon presented below, his face still showed the signs of having been badly burned.

Many German rabbis were able to find new homes in Great Britain during the spring of 1939. Cohn went to Edinburgh in May of that year, and his young son joined him from the *Kindertransport* shortly after. His wife remained behind, possibly because of an unwillingness to leave her own family. She eventually perished in Auschwitz. Cohn had died earlier, in 1940; his name never appears in *The Jewish Chronicle*.[1] After his parents' death the Cohn's son was raised by an English family.

For a rabbi preparing to leave Germany, preaching a farewell sermon on this first day of Pesach was indeed a challenge. At every Jewish worship service there was a member of the Gestapo assigned to sit in the front row to ensure that nothing critical of the Nazi regime would be uttered. Virtually everyone in the congregation had experienced the trauma of *Kristallnacht* five months earlier, yet no condemnation of the government or even of the people who burned the synagogues could be articulated. Some of the congregants had relatives who had already left Germany, others were hoping to be able to leave soon, others (especially the older members) had made their peace with remaining. Despite the injuries he had suffered, the preacher himself must have felt considerable ambivalence about abandoning his congregation and leaving his people behind.[2] What advice could he give, and how could he relate it to the exalting mood of the Pesach holiday?

The sermon begins with a recognition of the tension between the spirit of Pesach and the realities of the present. Yet the preacher finds in the biblical verses relating to the Exodus a message that he feels comfortable sharing. The theme of emigration was obviously relevant. The memories of good times in the past overshadowed by recent oppression fit both sets of circumstances. The encouragement not to despair no matter how bleak the present may seem applied to

1 This biographical material is based on Michael Brocke and Julius Carlebach, eds., *Biographisches Handbuch: Teil 2: Die Rabbiner im Deutsche Reich, 1871–1945*, with additions from Michael Simonson of the Leo Baeck Institute Archives.

2 For a fine discussion of the moral struggle of rabbis deciding whether to emigrate and abandon their congregations, see Astrid Zajdband, *German Rabbis in British Exile*, pp. 84–91.

ancient Israelites as well as to contemporary listeners. Particularly striking is Cohn's treatment of the story of the Israelites who were able to take gold and silver with them, but for whom that gold and silver ended up causing significant problems in the wilderness. That one should "forget the fleshpots of Egypt" – the good times in the past – and concentrate on the present is another message that applied to the distant past as well as to the current situation.

And finally, at the end of the sermon, Cohn, in perhaps the most poignant message of all, addresses "the elderly, the sick, those who lack the strength for emigration or for work." There is not much that the preacher can say beyond urging them, in as compassionate a manner as possible, to retain their faith in God and their fellow human beings. There must have been tears in the congregation as they heard these words. But perhaps there was some comforting reassurance as well.

"I LIFT UP MY EYES TO THE LORD [*SIC*]; FROM WHENCE COMES TO ME my help? My help comes from G-d, the Creator of Heaven and Earth. (Ps. 121:1–2)[3]

Reverent Community!

We celebrate today the holiday of Pesach, the holiday of the spring. The spring wields upon the human heart a liberating, redemptive impact. "O new fragrance, O sweet sound," sings the poet of the spring; "Now, poor heart, be not afraid. Now must everything, everything change."[4] But is this really true? Is not the current situ-

3 The error in the first phrase of Psalm 121 (in the German: *zu dem Herrn*) is rather striking: it should of course be "I lift up my eyes to the mountains," or "to the hills." Unless the change was intentional, it certainly would have been corrected if Cohn had published the text that he has typed. I have used "G-d" because Cohn consistently uses "Gtt" throughout the sermon text.

4 The citation is from "*Frühlingsglaube*," written in 1812 by the German Romantic poet Johann Ludwig Uhland. The first line is actually misquoted slightly; it should read "*O frischer Duft, o neuer Klang!*" It is striking that the sermon begins with a citation from German literature following soon after the traditional citation of a biblical verse.

ation really a matter of suffering and pain that the sight of nature's renewal does not at all alleviate, much less heal? Indeed, is it not so that the unfortunate person, when everything around him seems to be surrounded by sublime springtime, when others near and far are ringing the bells of renewed life-happiness, feels his own grief all the more deeply?

We do not want to make a final judgement on the matter, but we cannot deny that the words of jubilant gratitude prescribed for us in the liturgy of the pilgrimage festivals come to our lips only with difficulty. They come from hearts that are depressed, and this is not only the case for the Passover holiday this year, but has been the case for a number of years. But this time, the mood that dominates us as we remember the oppression of our forefathers in Egypt and their exodus from the land of slavery has a unique urgency. Why this is so, I need to explain to you. We see the gaps in our ranks, we see everywhere the signs of decline, we feel the tragic nature of our unique destiny.

What was the message to our ancestors in Egypt, as they sat down for the last time for their Pesach meal? "And thus shall ye eat it: with your loins girded, your shoes on your feet, and your staff in your hand" (Exod. 12:11). They ate the Pesach meal under the sign of new beginnings, of emigration. Many of us today are meeting the same destiny. I too am speaking to you – with humane discretion – for the last time. I will not be delivering a "Farewell Address" in the ordinary sense of the word. I will not be rendering an account of my activities, or speak of how through years of joy and of sorrow – and more of sorrow than in joy – I have been bound together with you in times of severe anxiety and severe distress. I will not speak about how difficult the departure from this precious office, and from you – my friends, my brothers and my sisters – will be for me.

(2:) "Stand fast" (Exod. 14:13). This means surely and above all: "Do not despair." Let's face it: there may indeed be circumstances in which this command seems to go beyond the capacity of our resources. As long as the sunshine of happiness illumines us, as long as we face and must overcome only the ordinary difficulties and challenges of life that weigh upon us, though sometimes rather heavily, we straighten ourselves out; some are of a lighter nature, others are more serious, but we straighten ourselves out, and time brings a healing balm to our wounds. It is very different when we confront events that, with catastrophic power, steal all that had made life lovely and worthwhile, when removed from our comfortable bourgeois existence, from many a garden of pleasure and joy, we must survive in the desert of misery and deprivation.

Yet that was the situation of our ancestors, as they left Egypt behind. It is instructive to bear in mind the development of events at that time. During most of their years in Egypt, our ancestors did not fare so badly. They lived in an especially desirable location, they were able to develop freely, so that they increased in number and power and influence. But they retained their own language, their own moral values, their own religion – and so they suffered the fate that always threatens minorities living in a different kind of environment. They were viewed with suspicion – and from suspicion unjust accusations developed, from which came hate, and from hate came increasingly harsh persecution, until they moved from the land.

Fortunately, they were able to take gold and silver with them, and some may believe that this became a great advantage for them. But the aftermath teaches us something better. For what purpose did the gold serve them? No purpose but to regress to the behavior of the Egyptians! This is how it served them: it allowed them to erect the idol of the "golden calf," the adoration of which does not follow the rigorous mode of Israelite worship; rather, it expressed itself as boisterous pagan ecstasy, and it resulted in new devastation. That was the first blunder to which the gold they had taken led them. A second misstep/blunder followed: that notwithstanding all the abuses they had suffered, the memory of the former good times in the land where they had once lived was such that they could not suppress their longing for the teeming fleshpots of Egypt (cf. Exod. 16:3).

Here there is something important for us to learn, for those of us who are again focusing on the demand and the necessity of emigration. A compound lesson applies here for us to heed. One lesson teaches: do not overestimate the value of external possessions, which are often a source of misfortune. Heed the word of the poet, "Do not hang your heart on goods that adorn life ephemerally; Let those who possess, learn to lose; let those who enjoy prosperity, learn of pain."[5]

Forget the teeming fleshpots of Egypt: that is the second lesson. Forget the carefree merriment and glamor of former days, and look to building a new life through serious work. Work is never shameful, be it even the mundane work of a servant or a maid. Work ennobles; it ennobles more than a gentle idleness that bedecks itself with gold and jewels. Work does not rob you of your dignity, it bestows dignity upon you. Through work you may find rest in your soul, joy in your heart, and peace in your days.

(3:) "Stand firm, and see the salvation of G-d" (Exod. 14:13). Look inside yourself, and look around you. You will recognize the mistakes of the past, mistakes that you or others in your neighborhood have committed; you will transcend these mistakes, and become convinced that the humble, hard-working pursuit of success is even today not rebuffed. Then you may restore your trust in G-d, the trust that these times of testing have often threatened to destroy. Yes, your trust in G-d has wavered, and I do not accuse because of this. All too great has been the suffering that many of us – no, *all* of us, and most of us certainly undeserving of it – have experienced. And when you ask me, "Why has G-d sent all this evil upon us," I can give you no answer, for I have not fathomed His thoughts. I limit myself to the words of the Prophet: "My thoughts are not your thoughts, and your ways are not My ways" (Isa. 55:8). And yet I believe in one G-d in whom we can once again regain confidence, in one G-d who can indeed make us strong again so that we may endure in the battle of life. But we must remain aware of the limits that eternally separate us from Him. We should not ask: if we have done this or that, why this or that is being imposed upon us. Our question should be, "What powers do You want to arouse in us?"

In all of us there remains something G-dly, call it human dignity, call it nobility of soul, call it moral consciousness, call it what you will: it remains, it is there. And is now this G-dly quality, which dwells

5 The quotation is from Schiller, "Der Braut von Messina."

within us in a time of trouble, derived wholly from ourselves? Has it developed entirely due to our own efforts? If so, then, even in the most difficult suffering we have not lost G-d, but rather we have truly found Him; if not, then, although we may have lost Him we must once again seek to find Him. As we strive this way, then we are responding correctly to our destiny, with action and creative work. Then, even in our suffering, we are near to G-d, perhaps even more so than in days of happiness. Then we will have properly grasped and properly fulfilled the words, "Stand firm, and see the salvation of G-d."

But what shall I say to those who can no longer help themselves in this way: the elderly, the sick, those who lack the strength for emigration or for work. Well, I bring to them the words of the prophet: in repenting and returning to G-d, in the peace and serenity of your heart, "you will be comforted" (Isa. 66:13).[6]

Our ideals have been destroyed, but love of our fellow human beings is not yet dead, it will never die; and though all too often we have to witness with deepest horror acts of violence and brutality, so too on the other hand we see beautiful images of human goodness and life-saving help. You will not be forsaken; even if you have no children from whom a new salvation can flourish, the love that every true religion prescribes for its adherents - the Jewish religion along with its daughter religions - the brotherly love of one person for another, will intervene and protect you in your distress and your feeling of abandonment. Only do not let yourself be outraged against God; remain standing, and see His salvation.

(4:) And so in conclusion I pray for you, for myself, for all the oppressed in Israel near and far: May the Eternal, our G-d, be with us, as He was with our ancestors; may He never abandon us or cast us out, may He sustain His protection over us, over us and our children, may He guard our going out and our coming in. Farewell, my beloved community, farewell, my brothers and sisters, farewell, old and young. May G-d bless you with the threefold blessing of Israel:

---

6 The biblical verse in which the German phrase occurs actually speaks about being comforted "in Jerusalem"; it is a very different phrase here.

May G-d bless you and protect you,

May He shine His countenance upon you and be gracious unto you,

May He direct His countenance toward you, and give you peace. (Num. 6:24–26).[7]

AMEN! AMEN!

7 Permission granted by Leo Baeck Institute, NY.

Ignaz Maybaum (1897–1976)
"The Anniversary of November 10"
Brondesbury Synagogue, London
November 11, 1939 (*Toledot*)
Man and Catastrophe, pp. 84–91

INTRODUCTION

Born in Vienna, Ignaz Maybaum served in the Austrian Army during the Great War. He enrolled in the Orthodox rabbinical seminary in Vienna, but soon shifted to the *Hochshule für die Wissenschaft des Judentums* in Berlin, where he lived with his uncle Sigmund Maybaum, a distinguished rabbi and preacher. Ignaz served in German congregations beginning in 1925, with his longest term at Frankfurt-an-der-Oder. He was arrested and temporarily imprisoned by the Gestapo in 1935, after which he became one of three communal rabbis of Berlin, preaching in several different synagogues.

In March 1939, following *Kristallnacht*, Maybaum left Germany for England (through a program sponsored by the Chief Rabbi Joseph Hertz), together with a significant number of rabbinic colleagues. He had no specific pulpit – indeed he knew little if any English when he arrived in England – but he was assigned to lead worship and deliver sermons at special services under the auspices of the United Synagogue for German refugees, mainly at Hampstead and Brondesbury and later at half a dozen other synagogues.[1] At first

1 Hampstead, Brondesbury, Golders Green, and St. John's Wood are identified as the synagogues where the sermons published in *Man and Catastrophe* were delivered (all Orthodox, though he was a Liberal rabbi). For others, see Astrid Zijdband, *German Rabbis in British Exile*, p. 197. For further biographical material, see Alisa Jaffa, "Ignaz Maybaum: Memories of My Father," in *Ignaz Maybaum: A Reader*, ed. Nicholas de Lange, pp. ix–xv.

he delivered sermons in German, but eventually he decided that "One cannot, even when most of the listeners are German-speaking, preach in the German language while German bombers, as on the Day of Atonement, 1940, roar overhead during the service." The texts of sermons he delivered between May 1939 and February 8, 1941 were published in *Man and Catastrophe* in 1942, with a Foreword by the Archbishop of York. Those that had been delivered in German were translated by Joseph Leftwich, who had written extensively on Jewish literature, but there is no indication in the book exactly which sermons were actually delivered in English. He simply writes in the Preface, "Till the war the sermons were preached in German. Then it was gradually replaced by English, until only English was used." Thus the original language of delivery for the sermon delivered in November 1939 is unclear.

In 1949 Maybaum would become rabbi of the Edgware Reform Synagogue, where he remained throughout a stellar career. He continued to publish, as can be seen in the anthology edited by Nicholas de Lange: *Ignaz Maybaum: A Reader*. Perhaps the best known of his works are another collection of sermons entitled *The Face of God After Auschwitz* (1965), and *Trialogue between Jew, Christian and Muslim* (1973).

The following sermon was delivered in London a full year after *Kristallnacht*, to a congregation of refugees, each one of whom had powerful personal memories of that disastrous night. It must be said that this is not a model of homiletical artistry. The *parashah Toledot*, which begins the narrative of the relationship between Jacob and Esau, provided a natural connection with the anniversary of *Kristallnacht* in the sermon's theme verse. Maybaum then follows this theme with a reference to David fleeing from danger, which was apparently selected as a special *haftarah* for the occasion (see note 2 below). But these themes are never picked up after the Introduction. There is no sophisticated theological or political message, there are no polished sentences of literary significance; frequently there are only simple short statements that bring back an aspect of the event. But the memories of the destruction of "one year ago" are powerfully communicated, helping readers today to imagine the experience of the congregants as well as the experience of these congregants' loved ones who were still in Germany.

"AND ESAU HATED JACOB BECAUSE OF THE BLESSING" (GEN. 27:41).

This explains Jewish history as far as it is a history of suffering. "Because of the blessing!" The hatred that turns against a man because of some advantage he possesses descends to the bottomless pit of evil. Such hatred is devilish. And Jacob-Israel must for a part of his life's road be accompanied by this devilish hate.

The picture of David in flight which we meet in our Lesson to-day is one in which the Jew in many periods has recognized his own fate.[2] To be chosen means not only fulfilment and grace. We see from the story of David that it may also mean flight, danger and suffering. All these aspects of what is involved by being chosen are brought home to us by this present commemoration.

"A year ago to-day." For some days past when Jewish refugees have met, their conversation has usually begun with these words, "A year ago to-day."

I must admit that I do not find any one definite attitude that is common to all who have shared this experience with me. The 16th day of Marcheshvan, which was last Sunday, according to the Jewish calendar the anniversary of the day when the synagogues were burned down in Germany, the anniversary of the pogroms, was observed by many of us as a day of fasting. The rest said, "God has nothing to tell me on this day."

We must not be unjust to this second group, people whom suffering has embittered. It is to such embittered ones that the Prophet Malachi speaks, "I have loved you, saith the Lord. Yet ye say, wherein hast Thou loved us?" (Mal. 1:2). The whole sense of our commemo-

2 No section from the biblical narrative of "David in flight" (1 Sam. 19:11–27:4) is part of the traditional *haftarah* for *Toledot*. It may have been chosen as a special reading because of the date and its resonance with German Jews in the congregation who shared the experience of having to flee from potential danger.

ration is this very thing, to make strong our souls against embitterment, against despair, because of all that was done to us on this day, all that began on this day. The whole sense of this commemoration is to promise us hope, the hope that this same Prophet proclaimed, "And your eyes shall see and ye shall say, the Lord is great beyond the borders of Israel" (Mal. 1:5).

The day when the synagogues were burned down is of greater concern than only to the Jews of Germany, Austria and Czechoslovakia. Else people might well say, "Why all this fuss about November 10th? So much suffering has descended upon the world since then. Here was the catastrophe in Poland, which has also overwhelmed Polish Jewry. And now there is the second world war."

But these events are all linked up with November 10th, 1938, the day when the synagogues were burned down in Germany, the day of the pogroms, the day on which thousands of Jews were carried off to the concentration camps. For on that day it became clear that German barbarism not only brings suffering to Jews, but means a complete break with civilization as such. What was done to the Jews showed that it was a European co-operation that was being undermined. Here again the fate of the Jews was only a pattern for the fate of mankind. The betrayal of justice, the betrayal of civilisation, began on November 10th, 1938, against the Jews, but it is not for the sake of the Jews that Germany's betrayal of civilization has impelled Britain and France to go to war. And in the same way as our suffering, hard though it bears upon our own shoulders, is suffering endured for the sake of humanity, so is our hope for mankind. This is a war of good against evil. Many have said so, and solemnly before God I declare that it surely is so. And the good will prevail. It is not only because we are grateful to Britain which has received us refugees, but much more so because of our faith in God that we pray for Britain. It is God's cause that is at stake, and Britain and France are defending it. The good will prevail. Our hope is for all humanity. "And your eyes shall see and ye shall say the Lord is great beyond the borders of Israel" (Mal. 1:5).

Here, my friends, you see the Jewish destiny. I want to comfort you, but you see how I do it; it is the only way I can do it. I can give you hope only by showing you that there is hope for mankind. I cannot say that the suffering inflicted on the Jews will be atoned for, will find reparation as a single injustice might. Your suffering has been suffered and no human power can make reparation for it. But I can say that mankind as a whole will be rehabilitated.

And now I want you to realise the sacredness of this hope. I want you to understand how wonderful it is that we, when we hope for ourselves, hope at the same time for all people. When you realise the sacredness of this hope you have attained the sublime height of Judaism. You will then also understand the words with which Isaac blessed Jacob, the words we have read to-day from the Scriptures, "Cursed be everyone that curseth thee, and blessed be every one that blesseth thee" (Gen. 37:29).

How shall we prosper, how can we live and be happy, we Jews?[3] Only in an atmosphere of justice. At the same time, an atmosphere of justice is the prime requisite for the existence of mankind. Justice was betrayed in Germany against us Jews. And this betrayal against us has as a necessary corollary revealed itself also as a curse to all mankind, which it has again plunged into war. The renewal of justice for which we hope, a hope that concerns ourselves, implies at the same time the renewal of mankind, which can prosper and be happy only in the blessing of justice. "And your eyes shall see and ye shall say, The Lord is great beyond the borders of Israel" (Mal. 1:5).

We recall November 10th as Jews. Which is to say, we are reminded of God as the great comforter. A year ago to-day.... The burning of the synagogues. One who has seen a burning synagogue or the ruins left after the burning of a synagogue will never forget it. It is a part of us now. Children and grown-ups said, "The Scrolls of the Law are being desecrated! They are being burned!" And they wept. A year ago to-day. The pogroms and the mass arrests. Children asked their mothers, "Where is father?" And the mothers bit their lips and did not answer. But the children knew. Jewish children, the children of a martyr epoch. God bless and guard these Jewish children! The Lord

3 A few months later, on March 1, 1940, Maybaum would preach to the same congregation another powerful sermon entitled, "Can We Ever Be Happy Again?" (p. 478).

make His face to shine upon them and be gracious unto them! The Lord turn His face unto them and give them peace (Num. 6:24–26).

A year ago to-day. No White Paper will describe this Jewish agony. Not because its author can never be a Dante, who took it on himself to describe Inferno, hell. But even a Dante can describe horror only as a poet. He must obey the laws of art and must moderate the gruesome in his description. Even a Dante cannot bring horror itself on the stage. Suffering is unutterable. Grossness cannot for shame be spoken of aloud. The sub-human cannot without repugnance be shown by human beings in all its raw nakedness. This is the limit to the writing of history. No description can do justice to the facts. He who has suffered, endured the torments of hell, knows what he has endured. But no one who has not himself been through it can ever have it brought home to him – unless he possesses that great love by which a man can enter into the feelings of others.

The sufferer and that other who can really enter into his feelings must unite in that great love. The sufferer, so that he is not isolated through embitterment and torment, the other that he may grasp the full extent of the reality for which he must exert himself. Thus they both experience God as Comforter. They join together, and so each has his appointed part to play in the actuality of Revelation. On this earth the sacred light of Revelation shines wherever men practice compassion and take hold of it. But where compassion is comprehended there God is manifest. God is our Comforter. This too is our Jewish destiny, that we cannot contemplate retaliation or vengeance. Retaliation has its place in politics, and as political reparation it justifies war and can demonstrate that pacifism is immoral or even folly.

But for us Jews there can be no question of retaliation nor of vengeance. We are left inconsolable or we must find consolation in faith. God is indeed our comforter, and that is true of every aspect of our suffering.

There is a wonderful prophecy that connects the fact of suffering with the fact of humiliation, in other words, with violated human dignity.

Since I have been in a concentration camp myself I have come to feel a special predilection for this prophecy. I love it. This is the passage: "And the Lord God will wipe away the tears from off all faces, and the reproach of His people will He take away from off all the earth. For the Lord hath spoken it" (Isa. 25:8).

Where the honour of Judaism is violated, human dignity too is violated. But both for Judaism and human dignity the same holds true: all humiliation, all insult, must recoil upon the insulter. And from this very obvious consolation in ethics we rise upward to the radical consolation of faith, which consoles us thus: "And the Lord God will wipe away the tears from off all faces, and the reproach of His people will He take away from off all the earth." This is our consolation, consolation for the Jewish people, consolation for all mankind. "And your eyes shall see and ye shall say the Lord is great beyond the borders of Israel."

And one last consolation. When Rabbi Hananya ben Teradion was led to the stake by the Roman henchmen of Hadrian, he was wrapped in Scrolls of the Law which, burning, were to consume his earthly body till he was dead. To those who wept seeing their master and the Holy Scrolls burn, the martyr called out: "The Torah is fire, and fire cannot consume fire." We, who will all our lives never be able to forget the picture of the burning synagogues in our native places, feel strengthened by these words of comfort: "The Torah is fire, and fire cannot consume fire."[4]

4 This rabbinic story is most familiar from the Ten Martyrs passage in the *Musaf* of Yom Kippur. Permission granted by Elisa Jaffa, daughter.

Leo M. Franklin (1870–1948)

"Is This the End?"
Temple Beth El, Detroit, MI
June 7, 1940 (Sabbath Eve)
Unpublished, Beth El Archives, now
at AJA, MS-246, Text 1474

INTRODUCTION

Leo M. Franklin studied at the University of Cincinnati and the Hebrew Union College, where he received rabbinic ordination in 1892. From then until 1899 he served as rabbi of Congregation Temple Israel in Omaha, Nebraska, where he gained a reputation as an eloquent and idealistic preacher. In 1899, he began his career as rabbi of Temple Beth El in Detroit, a post he held until his retirement in 1941. Temple Beth El was Michigan's first Jewish congregation, founded in 1850, but it remained relatively small until Franklin undertook to revitalize it. He instituted the regular Sunday morning service oriented around a major weekly address. He organized the children's choir, the children's Sabbath morning service, Bible classes for young people, a Women's Auxiliary, a Young People's Society, and the publication of a regular Temple Bulletin.

Franklin's activities were not confined to the pulpit. He was the Jewish Ambassador to the community. He oversaw the organization of United Jewish Charities, Detroit's first umbrella philanthropic group. His philosophy was a reflection of the goals of classical Reform Judaism: to integrate Jews into the American Community, so that they might be considered as Americans who believe in and practice the Jewish Faith.

The story of Franklin's relationship with Henry Ford, who – until the publication of antisemitic material in Ford's *Dearborn Independent* and *The International Jew* – had been a friend of Franklin's, is far more relevant to his preaching in the 1920s than during our period. The connection between the two men was re-established when, in 1938, Franklin worked with Ford to formulate a public statement condemning the treatment of Jews in Nazi Germany.[1]

A clear indication of Franklin's absorption with the implications of the new Hitler regime for the welfare of German Jewry is evidenced in four consecutive Sunday morning addresses, delivered on April 2, 9, 16, and 24, 1933 (see "Chronological Selections" above). Despite his recognition of the danger and his clear condemnation of Nazi policies, Franklin differed from other rabbis, such as Stephen S. Wise and Abba Hillel Silver, in opposing public protests filled with eloquent condemnations, and militant economic sanctions to be taken against Germany, fearing – as did some of the German Jewish leaders – that such confrontation might have the effect of increasing anti-Jewish sentiment within the German population and the German government.

On May 31, 1940, the Friday evening before the present sermon, Franklin had preached a Memorial or Decoration Day sermon (the first preaching occasion after the federal holiday, observed on the last Monday in May, commemorating those who had died in the military service of their country). That sermon was filled with strong rhetoric against the "mad dictator of Europe" and a world overrun by "hordes of untamed savages." The situation during the following week leading up to this sermon seemed even more appalling. There had been a succession of German military victories: the Belgian Army had surrendered on May 28; the remainder of the British Expeditionary Force was evacuated by June 4 (the day on which Churchill's "We shall fight on the beaches" speech was delivered in the House of Commons); French troops in the area were surrendering, and German troops were on French territory. On June 7, the day the sermon was delivered, the British abandoned Norway to the Germans. A week later German forces would enter Paris.

---

1 For the statement, including reference to a joint conference with Franklin, see the *NYT*, Dec. 1, 1938, p. 12; JTA, Dec. 2, 1938.

On June 5, Hitler broadcast the following message to the German people: "Our soldiers have emerged victorious from this greatest battle of all time. In a few weeks, we have taken over 1.2 million enemies as prisoners of war. Holland and Belgium have capitulated. The British expeditionary Force has been largely destroyed, the remainder either taken prisoner or driven from the Continent. Three French Armies no longer exist."[2]

It is not surprising, therefore, that the mood of the sermon is extremely negative. Its title, "Is This the End?" represents a question that many must have been asking: not so much the end of the Jewish people, but the end of a democratic Europe. Using powerful rhetoric, Franklin almost sounds like a prophet as he talks about the future. The only hope expressed is in prayer to God for a "miraculous" victory for righteousness. There is one allusion to the possibility of the United States entering the war on the side of Allies, but this is not at all central to the sermon.

ONE QUESTION IS UPPERMOST IN THE MINDS OF ALL THOUGHTFULLY courageous men and women in the world today. It is a question that has already been answered by a dozen countries in the Old World, but one which is still to be frankly faced by the peoples of this Western Hemisphere. Austria was the first to answer it, and then, in rapid succession, came Czechoslovakia and Poland and the Northern countries and all those that in his rapacity for further conquests Adolf Hitler first viewed with greedy eyes and then, when his opportunity came, ruthlessly crushed underfoot. The question is: "Is This the End?"

If "the end" means the absolute subjugation of the conquered peoples to the iron will of the demon madman's power;

- if it means giving up every right of self-expression and freedom of conduct and conscience that should inherently belong to every individual and to every group;

2 Max Domarus, *Hitler: Speeches and Proclamations, 1932–1945*, 3: 2014.

- if it means the perversion of national and racial genius; if it means spiritual slavery and intellectual bondage;
- if it means the reduction of once free peoples to a state of serfdom and peonage;
- if it means the establishment of a system of government in which the state is supreme and the individual is nothing;
- if it means that the ideals of Nazis and Fascism are to prevail in the world and the ideology of democracy and political freedom are to be forgotten; then there can be only one answer to the question, "Is this the end?"

Recent events in the world all point practically in one direction. Europe is temporarily, at least, lost to the cause of democracy. Whatever may have been said about the mistakes of England and France in the past, it remains a fact that since the fighting has begun in earnest they have both shown a spirit of courage and of bravery and of determination that is worthy of their best traditions. Of the heroic struggle made by the little band of Belgians, betrayed by their own king, no word of praise that history shall write will be overmuch.[3] But despite these things, before the onward march of Hitler – who with a determination seldom equaled by any ruler in history has gone forward through the years in his preparation for this bloody struggle for domination – what people in the world could stand?

It is, of course, as yet too early to interpret with absolute certainty what the events of these last two weeks may ultimately spell in the destiny of man. Only this is certain: That the clock of Time has been turned back by at least a thousand years; that a new and different world than that in which we have been living is in the making; and that, at least for a century or more, the peoples of Europe will be dominated by a political philosophy that means the crushing of individualism and the destruction of freedom in every realm of

3 The German invasion of Belgium began on May 10 (despite an earlier agreement of neutrality). King Leopold III ordered the surrender of the vastly outnumbered Belgian army on May 27, to the consternation of the French and the British. Like many others, Franklin apparently considered this to be an act of betrayal, perhaps because of his statement, "The cause of the Allies is lost."

human activity.[4] Doubtless there will be uprisings and protests against the new order of things, but it is likely that for a long, long time they will be utterly unavailing. The triumph of might over right has been so overwhelming and so definite that to close our eyes to its implications would be madness on our part. The end of a cycle is definitely at hand. The Europe of yesterday is a thing of the past. Its glories have departed. Its story will henceforth be read in the ruins of what was once a great civilization. One will visit its cities, once the center of world culture, but they will be as so many valleys of dry bones. One will hear the great songs that free peoples wrote and sung, but they will affect us as so many dirges might affect us. One will look upon those great works of art that the madmen have not destroyed, but they will only serve to recall a culture that is no more. One will read such of the literature of great European writers as have not been fed to the flames, but it will be with a sense of great sorrow that the hands of the writers have been estopped by the sponsors of a recurrent barbarism.

Where once men walked the streets with heads erect and with a consciousness of human dignity, they will slink along, fearful that for some innocent word they spoke or even for some deed they did that they construed as kindly to another, they will be arrested and sent to some loathsome prison or even perhaps, without trial, to the execution block. The victory of Hitler over the Allies, should it be complete, as many fear it will be, will mean nothing less than this: Freedom, justice, humanity, brotherhood will be cast into the lumber room of things that were but are not. Peace will be regarded as an unmanly attribute. Any of the gentler virtues will be looked upon as the mark of femininity or childishness. As in ancient Sparta, the strong body and the mailed fist will be more highly valued than the gentle spirit and the kind heart. For the dreams of the poet, for the searching of the philosopher, for the admonitions of the preacher there will be no place left in the new regime. Teachers will be told to teach only what the state tells them to teach. The Gospel of the

4 A strikingly pessimistic prognosis, underlining the reality that rabbis are no better at forecasting the future than are historians.

Christian Christ and the Jewish Prophets will no longer be told by preachers to their people, but the God of human might shall be exalted. The cross will be twisted into the form of a swastika,[5] and instead of the Torah, the code of Hitler shall be followed.

I do not believe that I paint the picture of a Europe that is to come, should Hitler absolutely prevail, in colors that are too dark, for I believe that his victory is the death blow to civilization as we know it. And therefore, in common with all good persons here and everywhere, I lift my voice in prayer to the God of all, that by some miracle the tide of battle may yet be turned and victory come to righteousness.

I have an unfailing faith that ultimately such will be the case. It cannot be that the God of the world, Whose children, according to the word of the Psalmist, are but little lower than the angels and whom He has crowned with glory and honor (Ps. 8:16), shall always be the victims of such untoward fate as now besets them. It cannot be that He Whom, through the centuries, we have addressed and adored as the God of justice and of truth, and in Whose sight even the lowest living creature is precious, can abandon His handiwork to utter destruction. It cannot be that as in ancient days, the heathens shall cry out, "Where, now, is thy God?" (Ps. 42:11) and we shall have no answer to give to them. It cannot be that all the bloodshed that has soaked the soils of many nations and all the tears that have been shed by women and children for their husbands, their sons, and their fathers shall have been in vain. Great God! Give us the assurance, we beseech Thee, that things shall not be always as they are today and that sometime, somehow, normal conditions of living shall return again to the earth and to Thy children.

In attempting to answer the question, "Is this the end?" there are, I believe, two phases of the subject that should give us who are here assembled special reason for concern. I know it is one thing to think of what may befall the peoples of Europe, and especially those who

---

5 This motif was used as the title for several studies, including Doris L. Bergen, *Twisted Cross: The German Christian Movement in the Third Reich*, and James David Patton, *A Twisted Cross: German Clerical Resistance to National Socialism, 1933–1939*.

are unrelated to us by racial and religious ties, and quite another to ask the same question as it bears upon the fates of the peoples of this Western Hemisphere, and especially of the United States and upon us as Jews. And so we consider tonight the question, "If, as seems probable, the life of all Europe should collapse, how could its destiny react upon us over here, and especially upon those of us who happen to be of the Jewish faith."[6]

Needless to say we must look upon the situation quite objectively. While the question, for the moment, is still hypothetical because, actually, one man's guess as to the outcome of the conflict over there is as good as another's, we cannot blink at the fact that anything is liable to happen, even the things that only a little while ago were unthinkable to us. While I speak to you, the fate of Europe hangs in the balance, for the bombings of great cities during the last few days may actually be the prelude to a blackout of European civilization.[7]

Now, to hold that there can be a complete breakdown of the cultures of the peoples of Europe and a shifting of the ideologies upon which the economic, and the political, and the social life of England and France, for instance, to that upon which the Hitler philosophy is based, or if, as we pray, victory may come to the cause of the Allies and Germany and its allies should be utterly crushed – to hold, I say, that such a change could take place over there and leave us wholly unaffected by it, is illogical and even puerile thinking. Of course, the reaction upon us would not be the same in either instance. Should the cause of democracy prevail in the great conflict, then it is likely that America could exert a tremendously powerful influence in the building of post-war Europe. Indeed, it is not unlikely that in such an event a federation of European states upon the model of the United States could be established. In such case, the genius of each of the peoples of Europe might still assert itself and there would be

6 This indicates that the preacher will address the situation as it obtains to Americans in general, and then turn specifically to the implications for Jews.

7 Germans had bombed the center of Rotterdam in mid-May; the preacher was undoubtedly referring to the German bombing of Paris on June 3, widely covered in newspapers the following day, e.g., http://bit.ly/2fDimIA. The Blitzkrieg against England was still in the future.

complete opportunity for each country, more or less independent of the other, to restore its life upon the basis of its own inherited traditions. The peoples of the various states of Europe would bear exactly the same relationship to some central government and to each other as do our various states to our Federal Government and to each other. Of course, such a federation will not in any event spring up over-night, but whatever shall happen over there in case England and France are victorious in the battle will take its inspiration from this country.

We shall have to be the spiritual backbone of a rebuilt Europe. Of that, it seems to me, there can be no possible doubt, and to this end we must prepare ourselves to bear a huge responsibility. There must not be another Versailles. It must not come to pass that when the day of armistice arrives, it will be only another brief respite in which the hosts of Hitler, conquered for the moment, shall be able to recruit themselves for yet another war in a decade, or a score of years, or after half a century, to repeat the horrors of the time through which we are living. Whatever settlement shall be made must be one based in justice, in reason, in humanity, but yet of such a character as to insure the safeguarding of the democratic principle for all time to come. Anything short of that would be a defeat rather than a triumph even for those who are supposedly the winners of the war.

If, on the other hand, what many believe to be inevitable, victory should go to Hitler's hordes, and peace should be made on his terms, it would mean not only that democracy would be dead in Europe, but it would mean beyond the shadow of a doubt that our own country would be menaced by the poison which issues out of Germany.

I am no crier of calamity, but I cannot forget that Hitler's ambition is not merely the conquest of Europe, but his desire is for world supremacy. That having built up the morale of his people by triumph in this war, even though for it he may have sacrificed millions of lives and uncounted millions of property, there can be little doubt that after a little while he would push his way across the seas and with his eyes perhaps to the South of us in Mexico or South America or to the North toward Canada he would engage in warfare against those countries which would bring him to the very gates of these

United States. We are far beyond the stage of believing that this would be quite impossible. Utterly blind must that person be who, after the events of the past few weeks, can still hold to the belief that in modern warfare anything is impossible. Anyone who can read the mind of the President between the lines of his recent addresses must know that to his thinking, there is more than a little likelihood of an attempt on the part of a victorious Hitler to gain dominance over here as he will have achieved it over there.[8] And the opinion of the President is definitely shared by what I believe is a majority of the men at Washington of both political parties. These men have their ears to the ground and, moreover, they have sources of information that are not available to the average man, here or anywhere else. They do not make their decisions upon the basis of what is printed in the newspapers, for all of us know that such accounts, whether they come from Berlin or London or Paris, are all colored in one way or another and are more or less propagandistic in character. But one could not have listened to Winston Churchill in recent days, with his courageous but pitiful picture of what is happening, without realizing the catastrophe that seems to face the democratic peoples of Europe and, by that token, also threatens us.[9]

I am in no position to speak as an expert upon these matters, but it does seem to me that the time has already come when, unless we are willing to see democracy laid upon the altar as a fire offering,[10] we must be ready to take a more decisive attitude in regard to our own relationship to the affairs of Europe than we have yet

---

8 Franklin was probably referring to FDR's radio address of May 26, "We Must Defend Our Foundations," which began, "My friends, at this moment of sadness throughout most of the world, I want to talk with you about a number of subjects that directly affect the future of the United States. We are shocked at the almost incredible eyewitness stories that come to us; stories of what is happening at this moment to the civilian populations of Norway and Holland and Belgium and Luxembourg and France." The next part of the address is entitled "Isolation is Held Impossible": http://bit.ly/2yl9qQe.

9 John Lukacs, *Five Days in London: May, 1940* (New Haven: Yale, 1999), covering May 24–28. Churchill's speech of June 4, 1940: "We shall fight on the beaches…" seems to anticipate the possibility of a German invasion. The complete text is accessible at http://www.ibiblio.org/pha/policy/1940/1940-06-04a.html.

10 Lev. 2:9 and 11: *isheh*, used here metaphorically.

done because, it seems to me, that whether or not we now enter the war as actual participants, we will be in it to one degree or another whether we want to or not. I am not urging that we send our men over-seas, though the day may come when we may find even that to be necessary for the salvation of our democratic institutions, but I do believe that there ought not be a moment's hesitancy at this time to supply to the Allied cause everything that we possibly can in the way of armament while, at the same time, continuing to build our defenses here at home without abatement. Indeed, I urge the whole program of help to the Allies as a self-defensive measure. We are as much a target for the wrath of Hitler as are the people of England and France. How any sane person can doubt this I do not see. True, with France and England crushed, should Hitler's purpose, announced this week as the complete annihilation of these peoples and all they stand for, be achieved,[11] it might take a year or a decade for him to build his strength sufficiently to warrant his attack upon the Western Hemisphere; but that this attack would come sooner or later is as inevitable as that night should follow day. And therefore, the whole problem, "Is this the end?" affects us as Americans quite as much and with almost the same immediacy as it does the peoples over there.

The second phase of the situation to which I call your attention is that which affects us especially as Jews. What, in the event of Hitler's triumph, would be the fate of the Jew in the world? You think that you are cognizant of what has already happened to the Jew in Europe. You think that because you have read that a few hundred thousand Jews have been driven out of Germany and that Austria has expatriated all Jews who had lived within her boundaries, and because in Poland literally millions have been beaten and starved, and that the story repeats itself in every country, large and small, upon which the poisoned breath of Hitler has breathed – you think,

11 The "complete annihilation of these peoples" is hyperbolic. Reference is probably to Hitler's June 5 messages to the German people and to the German soldiers on the Western Front (see Introduction), in which he speaks about the annihilation of the French and British forces fighting in the Lowlands, including the capture of "over 1.2 million enemies as prisoners of war."

I say, that because you have read these things, you know the whole story. But I assure you, my people, you do not know that story, nor the half of it, nor the tenth of it, nor the hundredth part of it.

The Jews in all these countries have simply been the grist for Hitler's mill of hate. Not only have they been decimated in numbers, but the few of them who have been brave enough to withstand the lure of suicide as their only means of escape are utterly crushed in body and in spirit. They have become the pariahs of the earth. Not Egypt, with its slavery, not Babylon, with its exile, not Spain, with its Inquisition, not Russia, with its pogroms, not Romania, with its persecutions, not Poland, with its starvation, nor all of them together have written in the story of the Jew a chapter of suffering that is remotely comparable with that which has been written in their blood and their tears during these last few years. All history records nothing like it, not only in the history of the Jews, but in the story of any people that has ever lived.[12]

It is true, Palestine has been a haven of refuge to some hundreds of thousands and for this we praise God. But who knows what may happen to Palestine once the war shall be carried, as in all likelihood it will be carried, into the region of the Mediterranean. Britain, France, Holland, and a few other countries opened their doors to other thousands of these Jewish expatriates, but you know what inevitably has been their fate in these last times. America! The one place on the face of the earth to which the Jew may look with any confidence. And therefore, America must be regarded as the key to such survival of our people as we dare to hope for. The center of Jewish life is with greater definiteness every day being transferred from the Old World to the New. And therefore, this whole problem of the war has a particular bearing upon us as Jews.

And if we ask the question, "Is this the end?" then we must answer it in the light of what we are willing to do, of what sacrifices we are ready to make to keep alive upon this soil the spark of Jewish life. If we allow that spark to be quenched through our indifference or

---

12 Note the hyperbole in the period still *before* the beginning of systematic mass deportation and mass murder.

through our carelessness or through our selfishness, then I say that we are answering the question "Is this the end?" and we are answering it in a way for which history will hold the prosperous American Jew responsible. In a sense, then, I believe that the ultimate fate of Israel is in our hands. If the Jew shall survive, it is because we shall have made it possible for him to do so. And if he goes down to death, to destruction, to oblivion, it will be because you and I who have been fortunate enough to live in these blessed United States have failed to do our part. Personally, I do not believe that we will be craven enough to permit this to happen, but, on the contrary, I have the conviction that true to the spirit of our great past, we shall realize that, in a sense, in our determination to save the Jews, we shall be saving all the world, for when the Jew shall perish, civilization itself will inevitably perish.

And so, in this dark and tragic hour of history, I am comforted by the words of the prophet who foresaw what would happen in the end of days. His words are familiar to you all, for do you not hear them read each Sabbath in your synagogue? "And it shall come to pass at the end of days that the mountain of the Lord's House shall be established as the top of the mountains, and it shall be exalted above the hills, and all nations shall flow unto it, and many people shall go and say, 'Come ye, let us go up to the mountain of the Lord, to the House of the God of Jacob; and He will teach us His ways and we will walk in His paths, and out of Zion shall go forth the Law and the word of God'" (Isa. 2:2–3).[13]

In that utterance lies, as I say, the hope of mankind's salvation. At the end of days God's house shall be exalted above all the houses of royalty, and His way above the way of kings and potentates. Whatever may happen to us in our own day and among our own people, ultimately in the end of days these better things shall come. Then tyrants will be despised as they deserve to be despised. Dictators shall have met their doom. Persecution and oppression shall

13 It is striking that at the end of this quotation Franklin omits the final words: "from Jerusalem," probably because he is suggesting that the future of the Jewish people and of human civilization will be not in Palestine but in the United States.

have been banished from the earth. The equality of men shall have been established. Brotherhood shall have become a reality and not a phrase. Justice shall be exalted, and men shall follow the way of righteousness, because that is the way that leads to peace and to security and to enduring human happiness.[14]

14 Permission granted by Judge Walter Shapero, grandson-in-law; and by Barbara and William Fleischaker, grandchildren.

Eliezer Berkovits (1908–1992)
"Because of Our Sins?"
United Hebrew Congregation, Leeds, England
July 26, 1941 (*Mattot-Masei*)
Between Yesterday and Tomorrow, pp. 78–84

INTRODUCTION

Eliezer Berkovits was born in Oradea, Romania. After study at the Pressburg (Bratislava) Yeshiva, he received his rabbinical ordination in 1934 at the Berlin ("Hildesheimer") Rabbinical Seminary, where he studied under Rabbi Jehiel Jacob Weinberg, one of the giants of German "neo-Orthodoxy." In parallel, he earned a doctorate in philosophy at the Friedrich-Wilhelms (now Humboldt) University of Berlin. Following his ordination, he served as rabbi of the Pestalozzistrasse Congregation, Berlin. After escaping from Germany to England in the spring of 1939, Berkovits served as a communal rabbi in Leeds, England (1940–46); he later moved to rabbinical positions in Sydney, Australia (1946–50) and Boston, Massachusetts (1950–56). In 1958 he accepted a position as chair of the philosophy department at the Hebrew Theological Seminary in Skokie, Illinois, which he held until 1975. At that time, at the age of sixty-seven, Berkovits relocated to Jerusalem, where he lived and worked until his death. During his lifetime, Berkovits wrote nineteen books and hundreds of essays and articles, covering every major area of Jewish philosophy.[1]

The most significant theological question for Jewish thinkers (as well as for many ordinary Jews) concerns the problem of evil, especially in the wake of the Holocaust. Berkovits treated this subject

1 This biographical material is based in part on the Jewish Virtual Library using the *Encyclopedia Judaica* (2008).

most extensively in his *Faith After the Holocaust* (1973) and *With God in Hell: Judaism in the Ghettos and Death Camps* (1979). Berkovits' sermons also have theological content, but they are different from academic texts written by a philosopher or theologian, who can take as much time as needed to work out positions and formulations that will be coherent and consistent. Every preacher has a limited amount of time to respond to contemporary, time-bound challenges while facing a congregation of listeners whom he wants to educate, challenge, criticize, or comfort, depending on the circumstances. It is not sufficient for a preacher simply to convince himself; the listeners are an integral part of the sermon's dynamic. This is especially true when the preacher is a new arrival from another country, preaching in a language that is not his native tongue.[2]

What seems clear is that several of Berkovits' sermons articulate some of the most pessimistic presentations of the contemporary Jewish situation in the literature, along with some of the sharpest criticisms of Jewish leadership, including of Zionist leadership.

The heart of the present sermon is a direct challenge to a well-known passage of traditional Jewish liturgy, taken from the holiday *Musaf* service: "Because of our sins we were exiled from our land and removed far away from our country." On one level, this appears to be an appropriate explanation for the exile of the Jewish people. In his commentary on *The Authorized Daily Prayer Book of the United Hebrew Congregations*, Israel Abrahams, who was respected in the world of British Orthodoxy though he was affiliated with Liberal Judaism, wrote, "That the exile was the consequence of Israel's sin is the frequent burden of the prophets from Amos to Jeremiah (cf. also Ezekiel 34:23) and the same connection is expressed in the Pentateuch (Leviticus 26:23, Deut. 28:64)."[3] In addition to the biblical tradition, the assertion seems to follow from the belief that God is in control of the events that occur in the world, and that God is just and good,

2 This was apparently not a significant problem for Berkovits; his son, Professor Avraham Berkovits, has written to me that "His English, in vocabulary, style and accent, were from the start a definitive example of the King's English of a native-born, well-educated Englishman."

3 *The Authorized Daily Prayerbook*, 1924, p. cxcvi.

alongside the recognition that Jews did not always properly fulfil their religious obligations. Conclusion: the exile must have been God's punishment for the sins of the Jewish people, and its continuation the punishment for continued sinfulness and God's way to bring the Jewish people back to proper observance and behavior.

For a Reform or Liberal British rabbi to question this assertion would not be surprising. But for a United Synagogue rabbi in the traditionalist congregation of Leeds to repudiate this theological assertion unambiguously from the pulpit is certainly noteworthy and courageous. His position is clearly and powerfully expressed: "The traditional answer to such questions is: All this has come upon us 'because of our sins.'... No longer is this a satisfactory explanation. No longer is it true to say that we have deserved it. We have not, and God Himself is our witness that we have not deserved it.... No, I do not believe in 'because-of-our-sins.' What I believe is that we have been suffering for two thousand years not because of our sins but because of the sins of the world, because of the sins of the nations in whose midst we have had to live."[4] The next question might be whether he continued to use the passage from the holiday *Musaf* service despite his disbelief in its content.

(78:) ACCORDING TO JEWISH CUSTOM THE THREE WEEKS FROM Tammuz 17th to Av 9th are regarded as days of mourning. Twice in our ancient history a double national catastrophe occurred in this period: the piercing of the walls of Jerusalem and the destruction of the Temple. Remembering these tragedies, the Jewish nation customarily observes certain signs of mourning during the so-called "*Drei Wochen* [Three Weeks]."

Although even the second of those events happened almost two

4 Cf. Berkovits' discussion of this issue in a separate book published not long after this sermon was delivered: "To try to explain anti-Semitism as being caused by Jewish faults...is either naïve or hypocritical. Two thousand years of Jew-hatred because of our sins, because of the evil in us! Such a conception of anti-Semitism credits our civilization with a sustained moral indignation that is contrary to all historic experience." *Towards Historic Judaism*, p. 129.

thousand years ago, they are not only remembered, they are remembered because they are still felt by us.

The Jewish Question is certainly no mere dream of the past; it is the nightmare of the present. It is part of our daily life. Yet the Jewish Question was created 2,000 years ago. Then, when the walls of Jerusalem were broken through and the Temple went up in flames.

True, this is an old story; it happened very very long ago. And yet, millions of Jews feel it as if it had happened yesterday. For the wound is still aching; it could not heal. It has been kept open by the consequences of that one great national tragedy: the fall of the Jewish State. All the subsequent sufferings of the Jews, up to the present destruction of European Jewries which we have witnessed, all our miseries in the various countries of the world, can be traced back in a straight line to that one important event of 2,000 years ago.

People often think that Jews have too good memories. All our Jewish life to-day is built up of mere reminiscences. For us there is always something to remember that happened so long ago that no other nation on earth would ever care to remember it. The destruction of the Temple, the Fall of Jerusalem....[5] Why not forget it? What good can there be in nursing the memories of an unhappy past?

The answer is this: that we Jews have no exceptionally good memories. It is not true that we do not try to forget. On the contrary, whenever a Jew has a chance to forget, he is only too eager to do so. Jews, usually, wish to get rid of all the nightmares of their past, even more than is good for them. Whenever they are left in peace, they will forget. Yes, whenever they have a chance....

But, when are they granted the chance of forgetting? Whenever we are about to forget, something happens to remind us that we are only Jews, homeless and powerless, guests in the world and at the mercy of others; that once upon a time the life of the Jew was different, for there was the Temple, there was Jerusalem, there was a Home for a Jew, a place where he belonged to, there was – there is no more.

We cannot forget because they in the world around us do not do not allow us to forget.

5 The dots here and elsewhere in the text are in the original published version.

There is, of course, the old question which is so often asked by Jews in these days. Why must there always be some kind of Jewish tragedy in order to remind us of the tragedies of the past? Why must there always be some new destruction of Jewish existence to remind us of the "*Churban* [Destruction]." Why should Jewish history be a continuous story of "sticks and wanderings,"[6] of persecution and homelessness?

The traditional answer to such questions is: All this has come upon us "because of our sins." The story of suffering that commenced with the destruction of the Temple is due to the sins of our people.

No longer is this a satisfactory explanation. No longer is it true to say that we have deserved it. We have not, and God Himself is our witness that we have not deserved it.

I have seen Jewish sins, and I have seen Jewish sufferings. What I have not seen is the just relationship between punishment and sin. We still remember the sufferings of Russian Jewry under the Tsarist state, and later the pogroms in the Ukraine at the close of the last war. Let us speak the truth, however contrary it may be to the conception of "Because-of-our-sins": Russian Jewry did not deserve it.

We know of the Jewish persecution in the "gallant" anti-Semitic Poland between the two wars, and we know equally well that Polish Jewry did not deserve it.

With my own eyes I have seen the systematic and ruthless destruction of German Jewry and I do not hesitate to declare that, in spite of its sins, German Jewry did not deserve it.[7]

We know of the mass-slaughtering of Jews in Romania, of the

---

6 Author's note: "Cf. the Hebrew name of a weekly portion of the law, 'Mattot-u-Massey'." This is actually the traditional terminology used when the last two portions of Numbers are combined, as they were on July 26, 1941, when the sermon was delivered. "*Matteh*" in the original context (Num. 30:2) means "tribes," but the word can also mean "stick," and Berkovits is giving a homiletical interpretation which would have been intelligible only to listeners with a sound Jewish education: that the wanderings of the Jews (*Mas'ei Yisrael*, Num. 33:1) are closely connected with the sticks of persecution.

7 Note the distinction between the presentation of Polish and German Jewry: no sins are attributed to the Polish Jews, while sins (undoubtedly referring to the sins of

untold sufferings of millions of our brethren in the whole of that tremendous battle-area in eastern Europe today. Who would dare say that they are passing through such hell because of their sins?

No, I do not believe in "because-of-our-sins." What I believe is that we have been suffering for two thousand years not because of our sins but because of the sins of the world, because of the sins of the nations in whose midst we have had to live.[8]

2

To illustrate the point I have made, let me give one important historic example.

In Talmud and Midrash we find a number of reasons for the fall of Jerusalem. They all follow the line of "because-of-our-sins." I will offer an explanation that is much more in keeping with the teaching of history.

The Jewish State fell because in moral development it was far in advance of the rest of the world, too near to becoming a true Kingdom of God on earth. It fell because the Jewish nation did not sin as much as was needed at that time in order to maintain the existence of an independent State.

This is our argument: For many a century the record of the Jewish State was as bad as that of most of its neighbours. But it never was as good as at the time of its destruction. It was the time at which the religious reforms of Ezra were the everyday law of Jewish life. It was the period in which the greatest teachers of Israel lived and brought up numberless pupils; the epoch in which Sh'mayah and Abtalyon, the great Hillel and Shammai, were the recognised national authorities; the time of Rabbi Jochanan ben Zakkai, who in spite of all his greatness was only the least among his colleagues and friends.[9] If there ever lived a generation worthy of the land it was

---

assimilation) are indeed attributed to the German Jews, but they are not sufficient to justify the persecution.

8 A rather courageous statement by an Orthodox rabbi, placing him theologically much closer to Liberal Jewish thinkers.

9 This would not be recognized as an accurate presentation of Palestinian Jewish society in the first century of the Common era, which was characterized by fierce

this one. But yet, the Temple was destroyed and Jerusalem lost. Why? Because of the sins of the nations around Jerusalem. Because in a world in which barbarous Rome was mistress, in the midst of states ruled by force and crime and intrigue, no state could exist that was striving to become the Kingdom of God on earth, to be governed by the rule of the Torah.

In the midst of a world dominated by the madness of Caesars, there was no place for a state in which men like Rabbi Jochanan ben Zakkai were the great national authorities. Such a state could not exist. It had to disappear, not so much because of its own sins but mainly because the world was not yet ripe for it.

The same thread runs through the whole course of Jewish history since then. The nations have not yet been able to cede equality to the Jew, who is claiming nothing but his right to live. Just as in the past the world was morally not ripe for a Jewish State, so in the present the nations have not yet grown up so far as to recognize and to accept the existence of the Jewish nation. The endless suffering of our people is the measure of the immaturity of the world.

Only one thing could change the plight of the Jew: the betterment of mankind. For this we have been waiting these two thousand years. Unfortunately, the process is a very slow one.

People often ask: Why does God not intervene with some miracle to help us? A miracle would mean changing all the laws of nature. It would mean that the sword should not hurt, the bullet not kill; that a concentration camp should overnight turn into a sort of earthly paradise. Dare we ask for as much as all that? Dare we pray for such a miracle that would change the whole course of world history, only because we are suffering? Are we worthy of such a miracle? Here I do refer to our sins. One of the reasons why the miracle cannot happen is "because-of-our-sins."

We suffer because of the sins of the world; we are not redeemed by some miracle because of our own sins. This is the key to Jewish history since the fall of Jerusalem.

---

internal struggles and many Jewish groups who did not at all consider rabbinic figures such as Hillel and Shammai or Jochanan ben Zakkai to be the "recognized national authorities."

3

Speaking of redemption, we would add a few words on the new Eretz-Israel.

For many a month now, we have felt deep anxiety for the Land.[10] Eretz-Israel is in danger. But this is no surprise. It is the most natural thing on earth that at a critical moment when all the hopes of humanity are in jeopardy, Eretz-Israel – this great symbol of Justice and Truth – should also be menaced. There would be reason for anxiety if Eretz-Israel could be exempted from a peril that threatens to engulf all the moral purposes of man. Eretz-Israel cannot flourish in a corrupt world. It is too holy, too noble for that.

There is a saying in the Talmud which may help us.[11] Referring to Caesarea – which was the headquarters of Rome in Judea – and Jerusalem, it runs: "Do not believe people who tell you that they are happily settled together. Believe those who tell you that Caesarea is destroyed and Jerusalem peacefully established, or that Jerusalem is destroyed and Caesarea is established...."

In other words: Jerusalem and the symbol of evil and wickedness cannot exist side by side. Jerusalem cannot grow in a world in which wickedness is triumphant, as wickedness cannot flourish in a world in which Jerusalem is happy.

The living-space of our nation is freedom, truth, justice, and peace.[12] This is the explanation of the Jewish tragedy. The Jewish State was destroyed, we went into exile because there was no living-space for us; no living-space for justice and reason and humanity. This, however, is also the very root of our hope. For we know that one day the power of evil will be wiped out, and living-space on earth will mean – decency on earth. This is all we need for Jewish happiness.

4

Of course, people might say: All this is very well, but not more than

---

10 Author's note: "In the summer of 1941 victorious Axis armies were advancing towards the Near East."

11 Author's note: "Cf. Talmud Megillah 6a."

12 A play on the word *Lebensraum*, used by the Germans to justify their program of territorial expansion.

a hope for a distant future. What about tomorrow? What about the immediate danger to Eretz-Israel?

There is a reply to this question in terms of what we have called the Strategy of Faith. It was given many centuries ago in the Midrash:[13] "On the day of the destruction of the Temple of Jerusalem the Jewish nation received a perfect guarantee for the future. For it is said in the Bible: 'The punishment of thine iniquity is accomplished, O Daughter of Zion; He will no more carry thee away into captivity'" (Lam. 4:22).

This is the faith upon which we shall build the Jewish future. Whatever the dangers and threats, there will be no new exile from the Land. We are living in the period of the re-building of the Land; once it has started it will not end before the redemption has been completed. Whatever may happen, the New Eretz-Israel will remain, thanks to that great Strategy of Faith by which we Jews lived in the past and by which we shall live to see a better day.[14]

---

13 Author's note: Midrash Rabbah, Genesis 42 and Numbers 13.

14 Permission granted by Prof. Avraham Berkovits, son.

Yitzhak (Icchak) Katz

"Things I Intended to Say..."
Conference of Jewish Social Self-Help
(Zydowska Samapomoc Spolczna, ZSS) Warsaw Ghetto
January 5, 1942
To Live With Honor, to Die With Honor!, pp. 355-57
Translated from the Yiddish (translator unidentified)
Yad Vashem Archives ARG I-423

INTRODUCTION

Very little is known about the author except from the text below. I have found no reference to this rabbi in any of the Indices of Warsaw Ghetto Diaries available in English. The Yad Vashem Central Data Base of Shoah Victims contains about a dozen listings for various spellings of Yitzhak/Icchak Katz in Warsaw, but none is identified as a rabbi. A Hebrew document in the Ringelblum Archive listing the rabbis in the Warsaw Ghetto includes Yitzhak Katz as a *dayan*.[1] In the middle of his discourse below, he refers to his book entitled *Kerem Yavneh*, but there is no record of such a book ever having been published. Yad Vashem Archives include a group of letters written in Hebrew in 1938-1939 by Rabbi Yitzhak Katz of Tuczyn to his uncle Aron Nadel in London; it is possible that this rabbi could have ended up in Warsaw. Essentially we have only the original Yiddish text, with the setting stated in the heading, and translations into English, German, and most recently Polish.[2]

---

1 I am grateful to Eleonora Bergman for this information, and for providing me with a copy of the typed Yiddish text.

2 The German translation is in *Die Verfolgung und Ermordung der europäischen Juden durch das nationalsozialistische Deutschland 1933–1945*, Band 9: *Polen: Generalgouvernement,*

The institution that is cited in the Introduction to the address was one of the most important organizations in the Warsaw Ghetto, perhaps second only to the Jewish Council (*Judenrat*), which was responsible for the implementation of orders from the Nazi government and the internal decisions that were critical to Jewish life. "Jewish Social Self-Aid" (or Self-Help) went into effect soon after the final establishment of the ghetto; its purpose was essentially to provide to the greatest possible extent for those in need, for example by supporting soup-kitchens for those who simply had no money to purchase food. It was an organization that rabbinic leaders, such as Shimon Huberband, could also strongly support; its headquarters were in the impressive building of the Jewish Library on Tlomackie Street, now within the Ghetto.[3]

Chaim Kaplan's Diary includes frequent entries about the Jewish Social Self-Aid program. On October 30, 1940, he wrote, "Today I was invited to a meeting called by the Self-Aid Center to urge greater activity in the aid project. I didn't hear speeches, I heard eulogies. They didn't speak, but wept" (*The Warsaw Diary of Chaim A. Kaplan*, p. 217). But a month later, on November 29, he was recognizing its positive significance: "The Jewish Self-Aid, which no-one believed would succeed at the time of its establishment, has become a far-reaching charitable organization which brings in more than 100,000 zloty a month...At every meeting there is a broad field for politics, rumors, and all manner of gossip and slander. Everyone says whatever enters his mind without fear that his words will be carried to those in power" (*Warsaw Diary*, pp. 227–28).

This atmosphere may well be the basis for the text of the Yiddish address translated below. The author was apparently an official delegate to the conference, and the ambiguity of the title seems to be in the Yiddish original.[4] It could mean that this is the text prepared

---

August 1941–1945, ed. Klaus-Peter Friedrich, Document 32, pp. 173–76 (some of the notes below are taken from this text). The Polish translation, by Magdalena Siek, will be included in volume twenty-seven of the Ringelblum Archive.

3 See the Introduction and documents included in Joseph Kermish, *To Live With Honor and Die With Honor!*, Section 8, pp. 332–69.

4 וואס איך האב געוואלט זאגן, German translation: *Was ich sagen wollte.*

in advance for the speech he delivered at the conference, or it could mean that at the end of the conference he wrote down what he would have liked to have said but did not or could not. In either case, it is a powerful expression of the traditional genre of rebuke regarding the behavior of wealthy Jews in the Ghetto.[5]

ONE OF THE GREAT PHILOSOPHERS, A PROMINENT THINKER, remarks about the Talmudic term *tsedakah*, which pertains to the giving of alms, that its meaning includes both Righteousness and Duty. It is not – he says – just philanthropy. And he is quite right. For, according to the Jewish tradition, the giving of alms for the poor is not dependent on a person's will, but rather an obligation which turns into a law, and becomes a mandatory tax.

Thus the Law of Moses imposed obligations on the people to give offerings and tithes to priests and Levites in terms of produce, prescribed parts of meats and cattle; and to set aside for the poor gleanings, forgotten sheaves, corners of the field, gleanings of grapes from the vineyards, as well as a poor tithe and charity. The Torah specifies the share due to be "sufficient for whatever he needs" (Deut. 15:8). This states that it is a religious obligation to give to the poor as much as is necessary. And an obligation it is, indeed, a law, for the Law of Moses imposes laws and statutes, warnings and rules upon humanity, unlike other religions which built their foundations upon utopias and believe the Law to be superfluous. One of the great thinkers even said that the goal of Law is its dissolution [Yiddish: צעשטערונג, German translation: *Auflösung*], by which he meant that the legal rules should evolve to the point where they penetrate the human heart and human thought.

This idea is not alien to the Talmud either. But it pertains only to the future, perfect world, in which, as the Talmud states, "commandments will be abolished."[6] For in that future world rules will

5 The label for the text actually gives the date as "Monday, January 6, 1942," although Monday came on January 5 that year. I have modified it on the assumption that it would be easier to forget the date than the day of the week.

6 b. Niddah 61b.

not be necessary, since duty felt in the heart will suffice. Not so in the present, when "the generations have not improved in their morals."[7] We need laws, and we need also constraint. Thus the Talmud ordains that "collectors can take a pledge for a charity contribution even on the Sabbath."[8] For alms are a duty imposed.

One sage in the Talmud is known to have compelled a person to get four hundred silver pieces in order to give them as alms.[9] There is no relying on the pious will of man, particularly concerning issues which are the "foundations of the world." No, never. It is not lawful to tolerate one dying of surfeit while the other dies of starvation, one dying of overwork while the other dies of idleness. Each man has the right to live in this world, and therefore he has the right to eat. God, the Lord of the Universe, created the food for the ant just as He did for the elephant, so how could He not create it for man? Who would agree to tolerate crooks to grab all, letting others starve?

You, Jews of Warsaw, stand charged with a heavy guilt that you do not acquit yourself of your elementary duty of commiseration. In the streets we see people dying of hunger, starving, stumbling and falling in the street, without anyone showing compassion for them, the unfortunate who could be saved just with some tea and bread. Woe and pity, Jews! Where did you get this cruelty?

Let's turn again to the Talmud, Tractate Bava Metsia, where this problem is discussed: Two people in a desert are left with one small flask of water between the two of them; if both drink of it, both shall die; if one only, he may survive. Said one sage, both should drink and both should die so one does not witness the death of his companion. But Rabbi Akiva, quoting, "one's life comes first," declared that one should save his own life.[10] To this Rabbi Shneur Zalman of Lyady commented in one of his responsa that such is the case only in extreme necessity of life, never in anything beyond it. Never should one gorge on sweetmeats while another dies like a pariah.

Our legends tell of the time of the destruction of the Temple,

7 Cf. b. Yevamot 39b.
8 b. Bava Batra 8b.
9 Ibid., with Raba said to have compelled R. Nathan b. Ammi.
10 b. Bava Metzi'a 62a.

when Betar fell to the enemy: people were feasting on one side while blood was running on the other side, one side knowing not of the other.[11] Is the same thing being repeated here? Some who are fully satiated, frequenting places of entertainment and absolutely refusing to take notice of those who are starving? Even worse, for this indifference is more blatant now than before the war. Man no longer preserves God's image, rather more like a rat he grabs his crumb and runs into his hole. This is how you look, Jews of Warsaw. The future historian will not extol your memory. The Law prescribes a rite for a single unaccounted death, with all the elders of a town participating in striking the neck of the sacrificial heifer and taking an oath of innocence (Deut. 21:1–9). How many rites like this would be necessary now for so many deaths? How sad to behold all this! Not even little children evoke compassion.

I want to mention a comment to the biblical phrase concerning an idolatrous city, namely, "And He shall show you mercy and have compassion on you" (Deut. 13:18). Rabbi Akiva in Tosefta Sanhedrin (14,3) asks, "How was compassion associated with an Idolatrous City?" His answer is, "Compassion was granted to small children." As I noted in my book, *Kerem Yavne*,[12] there is a difference between compassion and love. Love is a lofty ideal for all mankind and all creation; Compassion, however, is not more than an instinct. If love can be felt only for a sound human being and not for one intellectually defective, pity, compassion, can be felt for all living creatures. It is this which the Law of Moses states: In the Idolatrous City, inhabited by cruel idolaters, pity, but not love, can be shown for such creatures, especially for children.

You, Jews of Warsaw, have no pity for little children, walking naked in the streets, entering stores to beg for a piece of bread only to be cruelly chased out. Those children hear the sated obese asking for fresh buns from Kagan's,[13] and making anxiously sure that they are not yesterday's buns. The same sated people look on, unmoved,

11 See b. Gittin 57a. For a similar usage by an American Orthodox rabbi in the context of the First World War, see Saperstein, *Jewish Preaching in Times of War*, p. 308.

12 Apparently this book was never published.

13 One of the most prestigious bakeries in Warsaw, now within the Ghetto.

when the little ones die of hunger and cold. This is a desecration of the divine name, as viewed by any race and any people.

I therefore believe that at the present moment one must not play with illusions, conferences, and house committees, all this waste of time. Rather, a compulsory tax must be imposed on those who have, for the sake of those who have not. I doubt whether people who did not see their proper way clearly in the light of such thunder and such flames as are overhead will respond to speeches and propaganda. This is just self-deception. The Jewish populace must be forced instead to tax itself for the sake of the hungry and the needy. And this must be done as soon as possible. The men of Sodom were said in our legends to have been moderate and slow in extending help. The responsa of Maimonides contain a verdict prohibiting the raising of questions in the face of emergency.[14] A popular anecdote recalls the rabbi, Reb Yoshe of Brisk who, examining a young candidate asked him "What is the proper thing to do if one cuts his finger on Shabbat?" As the young man stood thinking, the rabbi shouted at him, "Blood is running and you deliberate?"[15]

Well, this is precisely our present situation. With a flood of blood around us we must not deliberate, but do. We must immediately resort to compulsion. The sooner we tackle the emergency and save some lives, the closer we come to salvation and consolation.[16]

---

14 Cf. Maimonides *Code of Jewish Law (Mishneh Torah)*, Laws of Sabbath 2, chap. 2 on saving of life taking precedence over observance of Sabbath laws; law 2 in this chapter states that it is not necessary to get permission from a rabbinic court in these circumstances.

15 The rabbi cited is the father of R. Dov Baer Soloveitchik.

16 From *To Live With Honor and Die With Honor!*, edited and annotated by Joseph Kermish, Section 8, "The Social Self-Help and Its Institutions," pp. 355–57. Permission granted by Ayela Peretz, Yad Va-Shem Publications.

Emil Ehrnthal (later Michael Elton) (1911–1987)
"The Death Camps"
Bedford, England
December 13, 1942
The Challenge of Destiny, pp. 29–33

INTRODUCTION

Ehrnthal was born in Hungary, but moved to England and became a naturalized English subject. After receiving a BA in Semitics from London University and a ministerial diploma from Jews' College in 1937, he became a librarian at Jews' College and began serving as a minister in various United Synagogue congregations, including Bognor Regis (Sussex), Hammersmith, and West Kensington (London), and the Bedford United Hebrew Congregation.[1] In June 1944 he changed his name to Michael Elton, and not long after began to serve as a Chaplain in the British Army. In this capacity he entered Bergen-Belsen with British forces, and stressed the need for liaison with other Jewish officers for the purpose of an interchange of lists between Dachau, Buchenwald, Bergen-Belsen, and other camps (*JC*, June 8, 1945, p. 1). According to his son, Howard, the experience of administering the mass funeral service at Bergen-Belsen had a powerful impact on his father.[2] After the war, in 1952, Elton moved to South Africa, where he served as a Reform rabbi; in 1963 he returned to the UK to serve in Progressive rabbinical congregations in London and Dublin.[3]

The following sermon was delivered on a special occasion, a Sun-

1 Bedford was a relatively small community, established "during the Second World War" (Palgrave Dictionary).
2 Personal communication, March 1, 2017.
3 See the *JC* Obituary, January 16, 1987, p. 30.

day designated as a "Jewish National Day of Fast and Mourning." Two days before, *The Jewish Chronicle* of December 11 carried the front-page headlines: "TWO MILLION JEWS SLAUGHTERED – Most Terrible Massacre of All Time – APPALLING HORRORS OF NAZI MASS MURDERS." Texts of other sermons delivered on this occasion, by Chief Rabbi Joseph Hertz, Communal Rabbi of Manchester Alexander Altmann, and Eliezer Berkovits are included above. For the background planning among the Jewish leadership that led to the establishment of this day, see Bernard Wasserstein, "Patterns of Jewish Leadership in Great Britain During the Nazi Era," in *Jewish Leadership During the Nazi Era*, ed. Randolph Braham, pp. 38–40.

Perhaps because this was a special service with no traditional readings from the Bible, following a single verse from Psalms Ehrnthal begins with a lengthy citation from a poem by the great modern Hebrew poet Bialik. This poem, entitled "In The City of Slaughter," was written in response to the Kishinev pogrom of 1903, in which forty-nine Jews were murdered. The selection must have seemed surprising to at least some of Ehrnthal's listeners, because it focuses not on the crimes of the perpetrators, but rather on the cowardly behavior of the Jewish victims.

That is not the theme of the message, however. The victims are presented as helpless before the mechanisms of murder mobilized by the Nazi forces: "the sealed wagons of death, poison gas, mass executions, mass burials of the living." The main critique is focused not on the victims as in the Bialik passage, or on the perpetrators, but rather on the Allied forces fighting against the Germans: a world that "looked on" for six years while the Nazis developed their murderous plans, a world that "has no rescue plans for the doomed millions of Jewry," a world that refuses to permit a separate brigade of Jewish fighters, leaving the Jewish community he is addressing, together with those in so many other congregations, as "impotent spectators of the total collapse of Continental Jewry."

After this disturbingly pessimistic message, the only resort seems to be a strong assertion that despite the devastating losses, "Israel marches on invincible, indestructible, *linked to eternity*."

The title of the sermon appears in the book published in 1961, but it is likely that this title was added for the sake of publication, as "Death Camps" was not a phrase used by Jews in December 1942. Contrast the introductory label serving as a title for the original text ("On the Tragedy of the Jews in the Concentration Camps").

INTERCESSION ADDRESS DELIVERED IN BEDFORD, ENGLAND, IN 1942, ON THE TRAGEDY OF THE JEWS IN THE CONCENTRATION CAMPS

Behold, the Guardian of Israel will neither slumber nor sleep. (Ps. 121:3)

Here is a vivid and heart-breaking picture of a pogrom by our great poet, Bialik. Many years ago he had been a witness of the incident, and it brings forcibly to our hearts and minds the significance of this day of intercession and prayer, fasting and mourning.

> Of steel and iron, cold and hard and numb,
> Now forge thyself a heart, O man, and come
> And walk the town of slaughter,
> Go half distraught, and scramble to a garret
> And there remain alone in musty gloom.
> Alone? The fear of death is breathing round there!
> Look, here and here, and in between the rafters,
> Are eyes and eyes that gaze at thee in silence,
> The eyes of martyred souls,
> Of hunted, harried, persecuted souls,
> Who've huddled all together in the corner,
> And press each other closer still and quake,
> For here it was the sharpened axes found them, [...]
> And thence they gaze at thee with dumb wild eyes,
> That follow thee and ask the old, old question
> The one that never yet has reached to heaven,
> And never will:
> For what, for what? And once again, for what?
> Yes, crane thy neck... behold, there is no heaven!
> There's nothing but a roof of blackened tiles.

Thence hangs a spider [...] spinning in the garret,
She knows a lot of stories – bid her tell them. [...]
A story of a suckling child asleep,
A dead and cloven breast between its lips,
And of another child they tore in two
Thus cutting short its last and loudest scream,
For 'Ma' was heard, but 'Mama' never finished.[4]

We are gathered in solemn assembly to remember the martyrdom of our brethren in the numberless massacres of the last two years in the lands under the sway of the monstrous enemy, and we are here also to pray to the Almighty God to stay, in His mercy, the savage hands of the oppressor. The ready response of Anglo-Jewry to the call to prayer shows that although we are steeled against the horrors and havoc of war, there is still that chord in the Jewish heart which responds to the cry of our tortured brethren who call from out of the depths of human suffering. Our hearts are filled with anguish and sorrow. We shrink back with horror at the thought of where our brothers and sisters might be at this moment. We are tormented by suspicions and haunting dreams about the fate of our nearest of kin. Many of us shed tears in secret and pray within the walls of our homes. We are weighed down by the overwhelming burden of grief and inward pain.

In these fearful times when the world stands embattled in a mortal grapple with the forces of evil, we can depend only on God's supreme intervention to frustrate the diabolical designs of extermination pronounced against the millions of our brethren.[5] "O Guardian of Israel, guard the remnant of Israel, and let not Israel perish, who say 'Hear O Israel.'"[6]

The catastrophe which has overtaken Polish Jewry in particular is

4 This excerpt from Bialik's long poem was probably taken from *Poems from the Hebrew*, ed. L.V. Snowman (London: Hasefer, 1924), translated by Helena Frank. Frank's translation of the full poem is accessible at http://www.poetrynook.com/poem/city-slaughter.

5 A rather surprising formulation, almost implying that the role of the British, American, and Russian Armies can play no significant role in putting an end to the mass murder.

6 From the daily morning worship service; see *The Authorised Daily Prayer Book of the*

appalling both in its magnitude and in the manner of its unfolding. For six years Nazi Germany prepared for war while we watched with complacent detachment.[7] For six years Nazi Germany experimented in tortures of every kind on its Jewish citizens for later application to all resistance to Nazi rule. The world looked on. Now we see the fruits of those experiments in Norway, in Holland, in Bohemia, and in Poland. At the outbreak of the war the Germans were ready with the blueprints for the destruction of European Jewry. They have proceeded with those plans with Teutonic, or shall we say Satanic thoroughness. But the Jew survived even the concentration camps, the ghettos and the fiendish tortures. Then came the sealed wagons of death, poison gas, mass executions, mass burials of the living, and yet the Jew survived.

The world has no rescue plans for the doomed millions of Jewry.[8] They are not protected by the Geneva Convention. They are not prisoners of war. No. The Jew's status has sunk so low that the recognized humanity, obligatory even to animals, cannot be extended to him. How fitting are the words of our ancient prayer we recited today: "Look from heaven and see how we have become a scorn and a derision among the nations, we are accounted as sheep brought to the slaughter, to be slain and destroyed or to be smitten and reproached."[9]

Our tragic position is our helplessness in the face of this great catastrophe. We cannot take any practical steps to avert the disaster hanging over our surviving brethren. Deeply sensitive as we are of

---

United Hebrew Congregations of the British Empire, 12th ed. (1924), p. 64 bottom, and pp. lxvii–lxviii for Israel Abraham's commentary.

7 A rather strong and not entirely fair general condemnation of total indifference on the part of the Jewish and general population, despite several similar days of mass protest in the 1930s.

8 Implied in the sentence is "except to win the war against Germany." This issue of whether the Allies should undertake a special effort to save Jews independent of the general military strategy would become increasingly controversial during the following two years.

9 This passage is a medieval *piyyut* used on Mondays and Fridays in the conclusion of the *Taḥanun* liturgy following the Amidah of the Morning Worship service. See *The Authorised Daily Prayer Book*, 12th ed. (1924), p. 63, and p. lxvii for Israel Abraham's commentary.

this tragedy, we ponder, hesitate and wait for months before we can deem it expedient to proclaim our indignation and protest to the world. We are a declared enemy of Nazi Germany, but still we cannot fight under the banner of our religion and make it clear to foe and friend alike that Jewry is ready and capable of military resistance and offensive power as any of the United Nations.

There are forty thousand Jews, or thirteen per cent of Jewry, in Great Britain alone fighting under the Union Jack. Yet the existence of a Jewish army would make all Jews feel that they are contributing a mighty and visible share in bringing victory nearer.[10]

The tragedy of being impotent spectators of the total collapse of Continental Jewry spreads additional gloom over millions of Jewish homes. Vainly we seek for comfort. Vainly we grope for a helping hand. But have we given way to despair? Have we wavered in our allegiance to our God and our religion? No!... When we are almost buried by a tottering world around us, we cry out "*Ashamnu*" – it is *we* who have sinned.

This *eternal loyalty and companionship* between God and Israel is expressed in a Midrash of incomparable beauty. Rabbi Simeon ben Lakish related this homily in the name of Rabbi Yannai. "The Holy One, Blessed be He, linked His great name to Israel. This act resembles the story of the King who had a key to a small safe. The King said: 'If I leave this key as it is, I am bound to lose it. Therefore I am going to have a chain made for it. If it should get lost, the chain will prove to whom it belongs.' In similar fashion God said: 'If I leave Israel as they are – they would be swallowed up by other nations. Therefore I am going to link my great name to them and therefore they will never be lost.'"[11] Thus Israel marches on invincible, indestructible, *linked to eternity*. In the confidence of this companionship we pray today: "O Guardian of Israel, guard the remnant of Israel."[12]

We shall not be demoralized or daunted by our enemies. With every means available to us we shall hasten the speedy destruction of

10 Here and at the end of the previous paragraph, Elton is calling for the establishment of a special Jewish Legion.

11 m. Ta'anit 2,6.

12 Repeating the passage quoted above (note 6).

our cornered and despairing enemy.[13] As far as it lies in our power, we shall persist in our endeavour to thwart the evil decrees on our brethren from being fulfilled. We shall not forget the destruction of Jewries in Germany, Slovakia, Poland, Roumania, and elsewhere. As we have not forgotten the Inquisitions of Spain, so we shall not forget Warsaw, Lublin, Auschwitz, Kieff and countless other cities.[14] WE SHALL NOT FORGET, WE DARE NOT FORGET. While they destroy, we will build. For every demolished synagogue a new one will rise, for every burnt school a new one will be erected, for every destroyed Jewish home a new Jewish home will be built to take its place. This is our responsibility and our sacred resolve. This lies within our power. This we can do.

We can and we will build anew the Land of Israel. We can plan for and build a better and fuller Jewish life. We can proclaim with assurance to the world our hope and faith:

Behold, the Guardian of Israel will neither slumber nor sleep (Ps. 121:3).[15]

---

13 This formulation seems rather surprising for December 1942, when Allied forces were nowhere on the continent and Russian forces had not yet begun the recovery of conquered territory.

14 It is striking that he includes Auschwitz in a list of three other major Jewish communities from before the war. Auschwitz was hardly known in December 1942, certainly not in the category of the other Jewish communities, and not even as a major concentration camp. The first appearance of the word "Auschwitz" in the *JC* was in the issue of July 7, 1944, p. 7. See also Martin Gilbert, "What Was Known and When," in *Anatomy of the Auschwitz Death Camp*, ed. Gutman and Berenbaum, pp. 539–52.

15 Permission granted by Howard David Elton, son.

Bertram Korn (1918–1979)

"The Prayer for Life"
Congregation Shaarei Shomayim, Mobile, Alabama
September 29, 1943/5704 (Rosh Hashanah)
AJA, MS-99, Box 30, Folder 16

INTRODUCTION

Bertram Korn was at the very beginning of his rabbinic career when he delivered this sermon.[1] Not quite twenty-five years old, he had been ordained at the Hebrew Union College the previous May. The High Holy Days at the Reform congregation in Mobile, Alabama were the first he led as a rabbi. After one year at the congregation, he entered the United States Navy as a chaplain, serving in California and the Pacific Theatre. But at the time of the sermon below, it was "systematic liquidation" of European Jewry and the stifling of refugee immigration to Palestine that was his central concern, and these themes are addressed with considerable rhetorical power.

After the war, Korn maintained his connection with the Navy, as he went on to have a distinguished career as rabbi of Congregation Keneseth Israel in Elkins Park, Pennsylvania, and published important books on American Jewish history, focusing especially on the Civil War and Jews in the South. He also taught at the New York school of HUC-JIR, and at Dropsie College in Philadelphia.

Several introductory paragraphs about hunger in ancient Egypt and the Islamic conquest, and one sentence following the first below

1 The biographical material is largely dependent upon the AJA Introduction to MS-99. I am grateful to my former student Alan Dodkowitz for having called to my attention this stunning text from the AJA which he discovered while on a research visit there.

referring back to the Introduction, are omitted as distractions from the main point of the sermon.

ON THIS BIRTHDAY OF THE WORLD THE MASSES OF THE PEOPLE OF Israel are gathering by the thousands in their synagogues the world over.... [I]n vague outlines the Jew imagines, stretched across the skies from horizon to horizon, a vast open book, and poised above the book a hand immense and magnificent, and in that hand a pen – and the prayer that is offered to God from the heart of Israel is the prayer for life that we read a few brief moments ago.

זכרנו לחיים, מלך חפץ בחיים, וכתבנו בספר החיים, למענך אלהים חיים.

> "Remember us unto life, O King Who delightest in life, and inscribe us in the Book of Life, for Thy Sake, O God of life."[2]

This is a simple prayer, unpretentious in language and in idea, undemanding in word and in spirit. It is the prayer of plain people and plain-spoken people, who hold nothing so dear as the God-given privilege of every person to live his own life and to be responsible only to God for that gift of life. In every age this prayer has had a deep and abiding significance for the hearts of men who love their God. But in this age and in this very hour, when men young and old all over the world are torn from the arms of their kinfolk and die on pain-swept battlefields, in this hour when death is a byword and violence the tempo of our life, on this Rosh Hashanah, the prayer for life assumes gigantic stature. It speaks in clear, irrefutable terms, terms that cannot be twisted and perverted and explained away by modifying clauses, as the Atlantic Charter has been explained away.[3]

---

2 This sentence is added on the Days of Awe to the first blessing of the Amidah, the central prayer of Jewish liturgy. The image of an open book in the heavens is based on a well-known rabbinic aggadah, actually about three books, in b. Rosh Hashanah 16b.

3 The Atlantic Charter was issued by President Roosevelt and Prime Minister Churchill on August 14, 1941, a little more than two years before the sermon was delivered (and before the United States had entered the war). Its purpose was to define Allied goals for the post-war period, at a particularly bleak period of German military

It expresses clearly and boldly the dreams and the prayers of every Godly man in the world.

And indeed Israel must speak for men today who cannot speak for themselves, men whose prayers are smothered deep in their throats by the violence of the invader, and for them it is not only a prayer we speak, but a shrieking cry – a cry for peace and surcease from anger and hatred and pain and torment. Mere physical relief, or even overwhelming military victory, will not answer that cry. It is life that humanity yearns for: life with all its joys and sorrows, and personal victories and defeats, life with hunger and satiety, with needs and their fulfilment, life with fears and hopes and ecstasy and chagrin – but life where man is not ground up into nothingness by huge impersonal forces mighty and cruel, life where a man's days are his own to mete out and to count, where each man and woman and child in the world may once again take up the individual task of striving to achieve the will of God, the will of God that is continuously frustrated by the forces of no-God that roam the earth. So as we here tonight join the long and honorable line of our forebears who gathered in solemn worship to greet the New Year, we can pray no better prayer and speak no more meaningful words than these words of hope and quiet faith that God may soon grant life and peace to the heart of mankind.

But what of Israel, what of this people that prays tonight for the life of humanity, what of this people that reaffirms its faith in life and in the God of life?

It is with tears and not with joy that Israel greets this New Year, with defeat written unmistakably in its eyes, not the exulting light of victory. We have had to endure suffering and agony and death for so many years that it almost seems as though we can no longer cry for help. So much desolation and destruction and fearful cruelty have been visited upon us that it must seem hopeless for us to say this prayer for life. For Israel has already lost the war, even as the Allied nations shift into high gear to win the war.

---

expansion. While one of its eight principles was that all peoples had a right to self-determination, this was not applied by the British to Jewish rights in Palestine, which may explain the allusion to its terms being "twisted and perverted."

We Jews rejoice with all free men over the world as the tremendous military machine of the United Nations threshes its way towards victory. We thank God with all men of good will for the freeing of Africa and Sicily, for the downfall of Mussolini's Fascist empire, for the surrender of Italy, for every foot closer to Berlin and Tokyo that our armies conquer. And yet we cannot rejoice as Jews. When we remember that our helpless people in Europe are still helpless, that no step has been taken, directly or indirectly, to help our brethren, who have suffered so unmercifully these ten and a half years of Nazi power, who have been beaten and murdered and martyred in all innocence of crime or treachery or evil, we cannot find it in our hearts to rejoice.

They said just last winter [December 1942] that two millions of our brethren had been done to death in Europe since the invasion of Poland in 1939. Last month they revised the estimate. In the six months of battle for Tunisia and Sicily, while the bombers dropped their loads of death all over Germany, and Russia moved slowly but powerfully to the west, while unrest seethed all over Europe to token the loosening of the chains of oppression, during those six months of hope for the world, another million Jewish souls were snuffed out in the darkness of Nazi fanaticism.[4]

And tonight, at this very moment, the systematic liquidation of our people goes on apace; the mass deportations tear more souls away from familiar surroundings, the sealed freight cars ride silently through the stretches of central Europe 'til they reach the mass slaughtering houses in Poland and dump out their merchandise. Tonight while we pray do you think our brethren are able to pray? Who knows where a minyan may gather in safety to intone the words we have spoken tonight? Consider how horrible Nazi hearts can be, how deadly and full of venom, if even while their armies are retreating, even while the bombs rain hot and heavy on their cities and factories and railway centers, if even then they can take time and supplies and men to continue their all too literally-intended policy of Jewish extermination.

And while European Jewry gasps out its last breath, sighs its last

---

4 On these figures, see the sermon for the following Kol Nidre by Akiba Predmesky, note 9.

sigh, can we remain silent? The nations still tell us that Israel must be patient. Israel must wait longer yet before steps of rescue can be taken. Only when the war is won and only through the winning of the war can Israel's wounds be healed – they said at the Bermuda Conference.[5] But by the end of the war there may be no more Jews to save!! Surely there are techniques for saving lives even in the midst of war; surely the Allies could rescue at least the Jews of the Balkans *if they wanted to badly enough*. Three million Jews have already perished because the democracies would not be their brother's keeper, because they would not assume the role of the Good Samaritan. How many more Jews must perish before the nations finally hearken to our cry for life?

Such a spectacle of death and defeat would surely be enough to dampen the spirits of any people, enough to dishearten and disillusion the hopes of any nation. But there is yet more tragedy, more defeat. Palestine has been a beacon of hope to our people to receive and comfort and feed and clothe our fleeing brethren. While the other lands of the world only put stumbling blocks in the way of the exiles, Palestine smoothed their path and opened the gates of refuge. There was no obstacle so great that the Jews of Palestine could not overcome it – if it would enable their fellow Jews to find a haven.

But today Palestine and the hope of the Jews of Europe suffers political defeat, defeat as real as that of the ghetto of Warsaw without even the chance to fight back.[6] The British Government, with the assent of our own State Department it seems, has determined to abandon the Jewish homeland in Palestine. In six months Jewish immigration into Palestine will be stopped. The refuge will be gone. The haven will be closed. The last gate destroyed. Even those few miserable creatures who are able to escape the ever watchful eyes of the Gestapo and make the long torturous trip from Europe to

5 The Bermuda Conference brought together representatives of the US and Britain in late April 1943 to discuss the issue of Jewish refugees who might escape from Nazi-occupied territories. It was viewed by many as a dismal failure. See the critique made before the House of Lords by George Bell, Bishop of Chichester, on July 28, 1943 (in Bell, *The Church and Humanity*, pp. 123–28), and Monty Penkower, "The Bermuda Conference and Its Aftermath," pp. 145–73.

6 Note the reference to the Warsaw Ghetto Uprising, assuming that most listeners will be aware of it as a source of pride.

the Near East will be refused admittance into the ancestral home of their people. This is fact, not pessimistic worry. This is real, not imaginary. According to the terms of the British Colonial Office's infamous White Paper, Britain feels that in the spring of 1944, six months from now, she will have fulfilled her pledge to the world through the League of Nations mandate and her solemn obligation to the Jewish People through the Balfour Declaration.

In 1939 when this White Paper was forced through Parliament as the official policy of the Chamberlain appeasement government, Winston Churchill, then only a mere member of the House of Commons, had this to say:

> I feel bound to vote against the proposals of His Majesty's Government. As one intimately and responsibly concerned in the earlier stages of our Palestine policy, I could not stand by and see solemn engagements into which Britain has entered before the world set aside for reasons of administrative convenience or – and it will be a vain hope – for the sake of a quiet life. I should feel personally embarrassed in the most acute manner if I lent myself, by silence or inaction, to what I must regard as an act of repudiation.... I select the one point upon which there is plainly a breach and repudiation of the Balfour Declaration – the provision that Jewish immigration can be stopped in five years' time by an Arab majority.... What is this but the destruction of the Balfour Declaration? What is that but a breach of faith? Is our condition so parlous and our state so poor, that must, in our weakness, make this sacrifice of our declared purpose?[7]

Churchill recognized that the White Paper was just another link in the chain of appeasement and opportunism which were bringing civilization to the brink of destruction. He realized full well that the stoppage of Jewish immigration into Palestine would be an act of treachery, of bribery, of international immorality. And now as 1944 fast approaches, Winston Churchill, in a position now to rectify the breach of faith he once attacked, is silent.

---

7 Churchill's speech was delivered in Parliament on May 23, 1939. The entire speech is readily accessible online, e.g., http://bit.ly/2w1xgj2.

My friends, this is not a question of Zionism or anti-Zionism. This is not part of the long debate of whether Israel is a religious community or a nation or an ethnic or cultural entity. This question of immigration into Palestine is a question of good faith, testing the sincerity of the publicly proclaimed war aims of the democracies. The solution of this question will demonstrate whether an international obligation assumed by a great power will be kept even when that obligation is to a little people with a little prayer and a little hope, but without power and without influence. And so surely as this fearful war and the attack upon American civilization followed fast upon the heels of the callous disregard by the democracies of the oppression and degradation of German Jewry, so surely will the reaffirmation or the betrayal of Palestine be a sign-post towards the future peace and security of all free peoples all over the world. If appeasement and deception survive this war – this war will not really have ended but will be rekindled in another twenty years.

This is a dark and desolate picture we have viewed tonight, but a true and realistic one. There are critical days that lie still ahead, perhaps more tragedy and death and destruction. And in an age of despair like this it is perhaps inevitable that there should be misgivings in our minds and fear in our hearts. Sometimes we feel like giving in to the nations – and defeat weakens our will to live. And there seem to rise up out of the abyss of desolation, out of the vanished centuries, the ghosts of departed civilizations: Egypt and Rome, Greece and Assyria, Babylonia and Persia, and all the empires and all the alliances and all the mighty kingdoms that have played on the stage of the world during our lifetime. Their eerie voices seem to speak to us on this day of despair and say, "Why do you want to live? Have you not suffered enough defeat and enough horror? Is it not better to die than to keep on struggling, better to disappear than to live on into new ages of doom? Give up, give up your stubborn hold on life and join us in the pit of oblivion."[8]

But we of Israel, even in this hour of the mass crucifixion of our

8 Up until this point, the sermon has been entirely bleak. Because of the nature of the occasion and the genre, there has to be a rhetorical turning point toward hope. This is now introduced with the following word, "But…"

people, reject the counsel of despair. We will not commit national suicide. We will not negate our prayer for life. We have had too sublime a spiritual life in the past and we have yet to live too inspiring a role in the future for us now to give in to the evil of the world. No matter how hopeless and helpless our cause may seem, we will continue to resist evil and struggle against oppression, with the prayer for life on our lips and faith in God in our hearts.

Solomon ibn Verga tells this story in his *Shevet Yehudah*. A shipload of Jewish refugees from Spain was swept by the plague, and the captain of the ship cast them all ashore upon a barren and uninhabited coast. Most of the unfortunate exiles perished from hunger. Some of them pressed on desperately to find some human habitation. Among them was a man, his wife, and his two children. They struggle on through the barren waste, until the wife fainted and died. Then the man carried his children in his arms and upon his shoulders until he too fell down and fainted from hunger and exhaustion. When he revived, he discovered that his two children had died. He then arose and said, "Master of the Universe, Thou art doing much to force me to forsake my faith. Know, for sure, that in spite of these desolate visitations, I am a Jew and shall remain a Jew and that nothing that Thou hast brought upon me or art likely to bring upon me will make any difference." He then covered the bodies of his dead children with earth and scrub and walked on into the wilderness in search of a refuge.[9]

Here, in the bitter cry of challenge wrung from the heart of this tortured Spanish refugee, is the spiritual courage and determination which we of today, in another day of exile, echo in our prayer for life and our fight for life.

So too we of today say our prayer for life with courage and determination, bury our dead, say our Kaddish, and walk on into the wilderness in search of justice and decency and honor and peace.[10]

---

9 Ibn Verga's *Shevet Yehudah* is one of the most important works of Jewish historical writing produced in the generation of the Expulsion from Spain. The latest publication before 1943 was in Hanover, Germany, 1924. This striking passage was not infrequently cited in times of persecution.

10 Permission granted by the American Jewish Archives.

Akiba Predmesky (1914–1998)
"The Ark of G-D Has Been Taken"
Jewish Center of Williamsbridge, Bronx, NY
October 8, 1943 (Kol Nidre)
Manual of Holiday Sermons, 1943, pp. 51–60

INTRODUCTION

Not much is on the public record about our preacher. Yeshiva University Archives reveal that he was born in Kovno/Kaunas, Lithuania, and came with his family to the United States in 1922. His father, Rabbi Louis/Eliezer Predmesky, was Vice President of the Union of Orthodox Rabbis of the United States and Canada. The son graduated from NYU in 1936, and received rabbinic ordination at the Rabbi Isaac Elchanan Theological Seminary of Yeshiva University in 1938 after completing the two-year program. He apparently considered a career in Law, as he completed the program at Harvard Law School in June, 1940 and was admitted to the New York Bar later that year. He was inducted by his father into his first rabbinic position, at Agudath Sholom of Flatbush, on November 17, 1940.[1] During the summer of 1943, he moved to the Jewish Center of Williamsbridge in the Bronx, where he would serve for fifty years.[2] Like those of Harold Saperstein and Bertram Korn, above, the sermon below was delivered near the beginning of a rabbinic career, during his first Yom Kippur in the Bronx Synagogue. It was printed in the first issue of a new journal published by the Rabbinical Council of America,

1 *Brooklyn Daily Eagle*, November 18, 1940, p. 18.
2 A brief mention in the *Brooklyn Eagle*, March 5, 1943, p. 16, shows that he was still rabbi of *Agudath Sholom* on that date.

the *Manual of Holiday and Occasional Sermons*. Predmesky served as Associate Editor of the 1943 *Manual*.

As noted above in the Introduction to the previous sermon, the circumstances for Jews facing the Days of Awe in late September and early October 1943 were terribly bleak. Predmesky decided to base his sermon on a text that is not traditionally connected with Yom Kippur, and is never part of the traditional scriptural readings. It describes one of the greatest disasters of biblical history, a battle with the Philistines that ended with a crushing defeat. The focus is on the elderly priest Eli; the historical background is presented, and then the sermon touches three themes relating to the contemporary realities of the preacher's congregants and the entire Jewish people. All three are based on a single biblical verse, which contains three announcements concerning the war with the Philistines given to Eli by a member of Israel's army (1 Sam. 4:17). Predmesky takes each of these announcements and applies them convincingly to the recent and current experience of Jews in Europe, and by extension in the United States. Unlike some of the earlier sermons on Purim and Pesach where the connections with Nazi Germany are not always fully convincing, here we have an outstanding example of a biblical passage used compellingly as a template for contemporary events. More than a few members of the congregation listening to the message with its application must have been moved to tears.

Yet, although the biblical narrative ends with Eli's sudden death, the sermon could not end with its report of the current disaster for European Jewry. The true challenge of the preacher was both to make listeners aware of the ongoing catastrophe and to communicate the message that, just as in the biblical period the devastating defeat (including the capture of by the enemy of the Ark of the Covenant) was not the end of the people of Israel, so the current nightmare is not the end of our story. There is hope for the future, with a challenge to fulfill that hope. Hitting the proper balance between the two themes was a homiletical challenge that the preacher appears to have handled impressively.

WHEN ISRAEL WAS AN INDEPENDENT NATION, AND MILLIONS OF JEWS gathered at the Temple for the Atonement Service on Yom Kippur, there was no man so important, no personage so great as the כהן גדול, the High Priest, who symbolized the spiritual unity of Israel. It was on him that the people's attention was concentrated, to him all eyes in Israel were raised. It was he who represented the entire nation on this Day of Atonement. It was he who was to atone for the sins and transgressions of his people in the Holy of Holies in the sublime and sanctified Yom Kippur service וכפר בעדו ובעד ביתו ובעד כל קהל ישראל, "And he shall atone for himself, and for his household and for the whole congregation of Israel" (Lev. 16:17).

The High Priest was the direct descendent of the most princely line of Israel, of the noblest of Jacob's children. He was of the lineage of Aaron, who with Moses liberated his people from bondage and slavery. He was of the seed of Pinchas, that courageous and self-sacrificing man who stayed the disintegration of Israel in its long and arduous journey in the wilderness while on the road to the Land of Promise. He was of the progeny of Eli, the first High Priest that Jewry had in Palestine, and who served not only as the spiritual leader of his people, but who also as councillor, advisor and judge led and guided the destinies of Israel for forty years.[3] It is of the life of this great High Priest, Eli, that I want to speak to you tonight, for like ourselves he lived in one of the saddest and most pathetic periods in Jewish history.[4]

Eli lived in the early days of the Jewish Republic in Palestine, when the Jewish government was not yet centralized under powerful kings. The people of Israel had settled in Palestine only a few score years before, and they were still beset with periodic border wars, especially with the neighboring Philistine tribes.

Eli was then the High Priest of the Temple at Shilo. He had served his people loyally and well when a fierce war broke out between the Jews and the Philistines. But to his great sorrow, Eli could not this

---

3 1 Sam. 4:18.

4 The phrase "like ourselves" signals to the congregation that the message will not be limited to the biblical past.

time go out at the head of his troops, for he was too old, having already reached the ripe age of 98.[5]

As the bloody battle rolls through the plains and mountains of Israel's borders, the aged High Priest remains at the Temple-town of Shilo. Dressed in his beautiful vestments, his face expressing pain and agony, he sits nervously at the dusty roadside on the outskirts of the town awaiting word from the battlefield. The flower of the youth of Judea is fighting fiercely in this war against aggression. His two sons Chophni and Pinchos are in command of the hosts of Israel. What is more important, the Ark of the Lord has been taken from the Temple at Shilo and is now in the field with the Jewish armies, to give them courage to fight against the mighty hordes of the Philistines, and to serve as a constant reminder that the very existence of the Jewish homeland and the Jewish religion is at stake.

For many hours this saintly priest sits and waits, his lips muttering a silent prayer for the victory of Jewish arms. As hour after hour passes without news, without even a word from the camp, his old heart begins to tremble; a tear may be seen in his old and weary eyes. But silently he waits on.[6]

Suddenly he hears the clanking of horses' hoofs in the distance. Could it be a messenger from the battlefield? With expectant eyes and with an anxious heart he watches the approaching figure. Yes, he is the long-awaited messenger, the insignia of the Jewish battle-dress is now distinctly discernible. But why does he walk so slowly? Why is his head bowed? With measured steps the messenger comes forth, his eyes full of tears, his garments rent, his face covered with blood. He hesitates. Shall he tell the old High Priest the whole truth? Will he be able to bear the sorrow of this message? Falteringly the words come out of his mouth: אנכי הבא מן המערכה, "I come from the battlefield," he mutters. "Yes, yes, my son, what news do you bring?" breathlessly exclaims Eli. And the messenger continues: נס ישראל לפני

5 1 Sam. 4:15.

6 This paragraph and the following sentences up to the quotation from the messenger are all the preacher's dramatic reconstruction of the circumstances; the biblical text says only, *When [the messenger] arrived, he found Eli sitting on a seat, waiting beside the road, his heart trembling for the Ark of God* (1 Sam 4:13).

פלשתים, וגם מגפה גדולה היתה בעם, וגם שני בניך מתו חפני ופנחס, וארון האלהים נלקחה, "Israel has fled before the Philistines and there hath been also a great slaughter among the people, and thy two sons Chophni and Pinchos are dead, and the Ark of G-d is taken" (1 Sam. 4:17). And the Bible continues describing this scene by relating, ויהי כהזכירו ארון האלקים ויפל...וימת, "And it was when the messenger mentioned the capture of the Ark of G-d, that Eli, the High Priest, fell off his chair and died" (1 Sam. 4:18).

Heart-breaking, indeed, is the grim portrayal of this appalling episode.[7] Very sorrowful tidings are brought to this sage and leader of the Hebrews. Israel has been defeated in its most crucial battle, the flower of Jewish youth lies slaughtered on the bloody arena. But the old High Priest listens silently. Tears are flowing down his pale cheeks, for he, above all, realizes what this defeat means to his land and to his people. But Eli bears the tragic news well. What is more, his two sons, his only children, who together with him served the G-d of Israel in His Temple at Shilo, have fallen on the field of honor; his children who had commanded the Jewish armies are no more; all alone must he carry on at the age of 98. The old father still listens without flinching. But when he hears that the Ark of the Lord has been taken by the enemy, that the Torah of G-d has been captured and is in enemy hands, the great High Priest falls and dies.

The story does not end here. The news spreads quickly in the little town of Shilo, and Eli's daughter-in-law, on the verge of giving birth, hears the calamitous tidings. In her moments of great agony, this princely daughter of Israel thinks not of her unbearable labor pains, nor so much of the tragic death of her great father-in-law, nor even of the heroic death of her husband on the bloody battlefield, but mutters: "The Ark of G-d has been taken! The Ark of G-d has been taken!"[8] And when her midwife tries to comfort her, אל תיראי כי בן ילדת, "Fear not for thou hast given birth to a son" (1 Sam. 4:20), the unhappy woman refuses to be comforted: ולא ענתה ולא שתה לבה.

---

7 Here the preacher takes his time to amplify the pathos of the biblical scene, while the congregation of listeners must know what is coming.

8 The preacher's amplification, not in the biblical text.

And before death overtakes her also, she utters one final wish, one last desire, ותקרא לנער אי כבוד, "Call my child אי כבוד, name my son 'Dishonor,'" ותאמר גלה כבוד מישראל כי נלקח ארון האלקים, "For glory is departed from Israel, for the Ark of G-d has been taken!" (1 Sam. 4:22).

My friends, as I now stand before you on this Kol Nidre night, in the holiest moment of the Jewish year, the message that the old High Priest Eli received, rings: נס ישראל לפני פלשתים, וגם מגפה גדולה היתה בעם, *Israel has fled before its enemies and there has been a great slaughter among the people*. Aye, from the English Channel to the Mediterranean, from the Baltic to the Black Sea, from the marsh-lands of Russia to the yellow earth of China, Israel has been defeated. In the past year, two million Jews have been murdered in cold blood, in Hitler's Europe alone.[9] Five millions more are now imprisoned behind thick Ghetto walls and enslaved in his labor camps, driven out of all phases of normal economic life, forced to wear yellow patches and armbands as a badge of shame. Everywhere millions of Jews have been robbed, despoiled, disfranchised, tortured and degraded.

But no matter how tragic the Jewish scene, no matter how filled we are with pain for the suffering of our brethren, we know that Jewry has, and will in the future, survive persecution. When we read the history of our people and see its many pages written with blood and

---

9 This figure enables us to date the sermon as Yom Kippur 1943 rather than 1942. The figures publicized in late June and early July of 1942 over the radio and in the press in Britain and the United States were 700,000 Jews killed in Poland, one million in total since the beginning of the war (Martin Gilbert, *Auschwitz and the Allies*, pp. 43–44). Thus there was no way a preacher the following September could have claimed two million killed during the past year. The two million figure was highlighted on the first page of the *JC* on December 11, 1942, based on a US Government statement (sub-headline: "Most Terrible Massacre of All Time"). This figure was publicized by Ben Hecht in March and April 1943 in connection with his pageant, "We Will Never Die" (see Harold Saperstein *Witness from the Pulpit*, p. 115). An article in the *NYT* of April 20, 1943, p. 11, states, "Two million Jews have been wiped out since the Nazis began their march through Europe in 1939 and five million more are in immediate danger of execution. These figures were revealed in the sixth report on conditions in occupied territories issued by the Inter-Allied Information Committee." Chief Rabbi Hertz used the figure in this New Year Letter for 5704 (*JC*, September 24, 1943, p. 1). Predmesky uses the two million figure not as the total number killed, but as the number in the "past year," although it turns out that this was not an inaccurate estimate.

tears, we say with our prophet Ezekiel, ואעבור עליך ואראך מבוססת בדמיך ואמר לך בדמיך חיי ואמר לך בדמיך חיי, "I have gone through the pages of your sad and tragic history, O Jew, and I saw thee stained with thine own blood and I said unto thee as thou hast lived in thy blood, so wilt thou continue to live even if it must be in thy blood."[10]

Yes, we are the only people on the face of the earth that has come down intact from the days of antiquity, that can boast of a civilization of thirty-five centuries. We have survived these thousands of years, though we were the object of destruction, the subject of persecution, the target toward which madmen and murderers in every generation have trained their hate as well as their guns. Yet we survived. Aye, we were exiled over the face of the earth, hounded and harassed by crowned heads, preachers of religion and infuriated mobs. Nevertheless we still exist.[11]

Aye! The very words of Kol Nidre we just uttered were written by the Jews of the Middle Ages, hiding in cellars to worship their G-d on Yom Kippur Eve, in mortal fear of their enemies. Yes! That sad melody we now chanted, which symbolizes the song of the Jew, was written by our Jewish composers to the strains of our holy martyrs shouting שמע ישראל, "Hear, O Israel, the Lord our G-d, the Lord is One" (Deut. 6:4), while burning in the hellish fires of the auto-da-fé, and while being broken on the rack and tortured to death by the so-called "Holy Inquisitors."[12] And yet, though the bones of the

10 Ezekiel 16:6 (the preacher's homiletical interpretation and application of the Hebrew verse).

11 The argument from Jewish survival throughout the centuries despite terrible persecution in the past was one of the most common sources of encouragement used by preachers during this period, although it was often in tension with their insistence on the unprecedented nature of the contemporary devastation.

12 This passage is much closer to the popular mythos of the "Marrano" than to history. The "Kol Nidre" text certainly pre-dates the fifteenth-century Spanish Inquisition and auto-da-fé, as it was criticized by Babylonian geonim of the tenth and eleventh centuries, and discussed by the Tosafist Rabbenu Tam in the twelfth. In his *History of the Marranos*, Cecil Roth mentions "one theory" that the Kol Nidre was instituted for the benefit of the forced converts of the Visigothic period in the seventh century who, of course, had nothing to do with the Inquisition, but he does not endorse this theory (p. 379 n. 4). As for the *melody* to which the words are sung, this was composed by an Ashkenazi Jew of southwestern Germany in 1500, at

Inquisitors have turned to dust, Israel lives on to tell his sad but glorious tale.

Yes, we know that we have survived and that we will in the future survive persecution and slaughter by our enemies. נס ישראל לפני פלשתים [Israel has fled before the Philistines] is indeed a painful message, but one that does not threaten our survival and our immortality as a people.

To many of you I bring still another message, וגם שני בניך מתו חפני ופנחס, [and thy two sons Chophni and Pinchos are dead], a message not only of national tragedy but also of personal grief. How many of us who are here tonight had fathers and mothers in Poland, brothers and sisters in Germany, relatives and friends in Russia, of whom we have not heard since the beginning of the war; relatives by blood and marriage whose whereabouts are unknown, whose very life and death is in the balance!

Aye, how many of us men and women of America, who have come to pray to G-d, the giver of life, have tonight sons and brothers on every one of the world's far flung battle-fields, who may at this very moment be engaged in mortal combat with Nazi arms – on land, at sea and in the air! Yes, how many fathers and mothers of Israel throughout our nation weep for the loss of beloved sons and dear brothers who have sacrificed their young lives on the altar of liberty so that we may live as free men! True, we are faced tonight not only with national calamity but also with innumerable personal tragedies.

But there is still a third and more tragic message that I must bring to you on this holy eve – a message which even the heroic High Priest Eli felt to be the most heart-rending and the most threatening of all: וארון האלהים נלקחה, *The Ark of G-d has been taken* by the enemy! In every land that has been conquered, in every country that has

---

the time of the Inquisition, but this melody was not known to the Sephardim (A.Z. Idelsohn, *Jewish Liturgy and Its Development*, p. 228). A recent survey of crypto-Jewish observances of Yom Kippur attested in contemporary records does not even *mention* Kol Nidre: see David M. Gitlitz, *Secrecy and Deceit: The Religion of the Crypto-Jews*, pp. 357–71, indicating that there is no evidence it had any special significance to the "Marranos." And for a general review, see Marc Saperstein, "Sermons and History: The 'Marrano' Connection to *Kol Nidre*," in *All These Vows: Kol Nidre*, ed. Lawrence Hoffman, pp. 31–38.

been vanquished, in every city where the hordes of barbarians have passed, our synagogues have been burned to the ground, the Holy Arks desecrated and the ספרי תורה, the Scrolls of the Law, trodden and spat upon. Our great schools of learning in Lithuania and Poland are closed; our famous Yeshivoth of Slabodka, Telz, Mir, destroyed; and countless numbers of their scholars, rabbis, and leaders, tortured and executed. It is in this last phase of destruction, in this capture of the Ark of G-d, that our greatest danger lies. A danger that threatens the very survival of our people, a danger that imperils the immortality of Israel.[13]

My friends, on this Kol Nidre night it will not do for us to come to our synagogues, chant our prayers and go home. We, the Jews of America, are the only ones who can save Israel today. We alone of the millions of our brethren are now in a position to rescue our people and to recapture the ארון האלהים [ark of G-d]. We must take the place of our brothers and sisters. Our children must now become the upholders of our Torah. For every synagogue destroyed on the other side, we must build another here. For every Yeshiva closed down by the Nazi fiend, we must open another here. For every *Aron Hakodesh* [holy ark] desecrated, we must construct another here. For every Sefer Torah violated, we must write another here.[14]

I am reminded of a little story that I heard after the invasion of Poland, that I wish to relate to you now. You remember, that it was in September, 1939, before Rosh Hashanah, that the invasion of Poland began. The Nazi armies captured one Polish city after another in their sweep onward. On Yom Kippur night they entered the town of Radzilow. All the elderly Jews not mobilized yet had gathered in their synagogues to pray. The Kol Nidre prayer had just been recited, and the old and venerable rabbi of the town had begun his sermon on the meaning of the Holy Day, when a Nazi gang broke into the synagogue shouting that they were looking for secret weapons hidden by

13 The preacher contrasts this loss with his statement at the end of the first section, that the demographic loss of even millions of Jews "does not threaten our survival and our immortality as a people."

14 At this point, the preacher shifts for the first time from lamentation to exhortation, and the rest of the sermon will be upbeat and inspirational.

the Jews. They looked under the benches, they roamed through every room, they searched every nook and corner of the synagogue, but no weapons were to be seen anywhere. Their leader then approached the old rabbi: "Hand over your secret weapons," he shouted, "or we will burn down your synagogue and all your Jews in it." The Rabbi looked down at him from the pulpit, in disgust and pity. Then turning to the Holy Ark, he pulled the string of the *Poroches* [curtain] and opened the *Aron Hakodesh*, so that the beautifully ornamented Sifrei Torah [Torah scrolls] could be seen by all. Pointing his finger at the Scrolls, the wise sage cried out in a heart-rending voice: "*Diese, diese sind unsere waffen!* These, these are our weapons!"[15]

My dear friends, on this holy eve of Yom Kippur when we are all gathered in our synagogues for prayer and supplication, in this holiest moment of the Hebrew calendar, when every nation in the world is spending billions for defense to forge the weapons of victory and freedom, I appeal to you for weapons for the defense of Israel.[16] Now when thousands of our sons and brothers are preserving with their life's blood the American way of life, let us do something concrete for the preservation of Israel's heritage.

As Jews we cannot compete with Hitler's tanks; we have no army to fight for us, no navy to defend us, no air force to protect us, no country even to shelter us. But there are two weapons that we do

---

15 As a historical report, this account is problematic. Radzilow, in the Lomza district of north-eastern Poland, near Bialystok, was in the Soviet-occupied region and did not come under German control until after the June 1941 invasion of the USSR. Thus there were no German forces in this town on Yom Kippur of 1939. On July 7, 1941, with Germans in control, Polish inhabitants of Radzilow were responsible for a massacre by gathering most of the town's Jews into a large barn, which was burned, behavior similar to that which occurred three days later in Jedwabne, as chronicled by Jan Gross in *Neighbors*. If there is any historical basis to this incident, it must have been in a different town. But the behavior of the German soldiers searching under benches for "secret weapons" while the Jewish worshippers were present, and the officer threatening burning the synagogue with the Jews in it, does not seem believable. (For descriptions of German acts against Polish Jews on Yom Kippur 1939, see Martin Gilbert, *The Holocaust*, pp. 89–91, and Shimon Huberband, *Kiddush Hashem*, pp. 49–50: gratuitous humiliation, but no threat of a massacre). One function of the story is to make a connection with the congregation, also listening to a sermon on the evening of Yom Kippur.

16 "Weapons" in the figurative sense of the exemplum just cited.

have at our disposal, two secret weapons with which we can assure victory to ourselves and to our people. These weapons are the Torah, and the synagogue which houses it.

I, therefore, appeal to you now, men and women of Israel, for these weapons of victory, for these weapons of Jewish defense. Become a member of your synagogue, send your child to study in a Talmud Torah, where the knowledge of the Torah and the spiritual values of the Ark of G-d[17] will be taught to him. Will you let your people down now? Is there a man, woman, or child here who will refuse to contribute to the cause of victory? Who will fail to buy Jewish defense bonds[18] for themselves and their children in times like these?

Grasp your chance now! Seize your opportunity tonight! Forge the secret weapons of Israel's defense! Become a soldier in the camp of the Lord! The Ark of G-d must, and will, be retaken![19]

17 Picking up the motif of the climactic disaster of biblical times and of European Jewry.

18 A figure of speech drawn from the US Defense Bonds sold during the war.

19 Permission granted by Shulamith Predmesky Cohn, daughter.

Joseph Hertz (1872–1946)
"The 'Battle of Warsaw'"
Bevis Marks Synagogue, London
May 22, 1944, Service of Mourning and Prayer
for the Martyrs of the Warsaw Ghetto
Published as a pamphlet by the Office of the Chief Rabbi

INTRODUCTION

Born in Slovakia, Joseph Hertz immigrated with his family to the United States when he was twelve years old. He received a BA from the College of the City of New York, and in 1984 he became the first graduate from the Jewish Theological Seminary of America, the flagship institution of American Conservative Judaism. His first congregation was in Syracuse, New York. After two years in Syracuse he accepted a rabbinical position in Johannesburg, South Africa, where he remained through 1911. In January 1912 he was installed as rabbi of Orach Chayim Congregation in New York, but little more than a year later he accepted the position of British Chief Rabbi, succeeding Hermann Adler. The outbreak of the Great War not long after he arrived in London brought unprecedented challenges to produce sermons and addresses responding to reports of massive loss of life, including of Jews fighting on both sides of the conflict.[1]

These challenges near the beginning of his tenure as Chief Rabbi would be exceeded in the 1930s and '40s. From the very beginning of Hitler's rise to power and the beginning of discriminatory legislation imposed by the Nazi regime, Chief Rabbi Hertz spoke powerfully from his pulpit about the fate of German Jewry (see passages from

1 See Saperstein, *Jewish Preaching in Times of War*, pp. 317–23.

April 11, 1933, July 9, 1933, April 6, 1934, etc.). The outbreak of war in September 1939 summoned the aging Chief Rabbi to mobilize his full personal resources to sustain the morale of his people. In addition to his usual holiday sermons and messages, he was frequently expected to speak at special mass gatherings of protest and prayer, when the rhetorical challenge was to balance an articulation of unprecedented and ever-worsening tragedy with an expression of invincible faith and hope.

The sermon below was delivered at a special worship service commemorating the anniversary of the Warsaw Ghetto uprising. Reports of the military resistance of ghetto fighters who challenged German forces committed to eliminating the remaining Jews in the ghetto were published in early May, 1943.[2] A year later, a special service of mourning and prayer was held at the Bevis Marks Synagogue in London, on Monday, May 22; the service was covered by *The Jewish Chronicle* on May 26, pages 1 and 7, including much of the text of the sermon delivered by Rabbi Hertz. Particularly striking in this text is Hertz's condemnation of the "silence" of the world, and of the non-rabbinic Jewish leadership of England with regard to the suffering of Jews, and the desperate hope that some arrangement will be made for the almost one million Hungarian Jews, standing "on the brink of annihilation," to find refuge, including in Palestine.

This is the latest of the many sermons and addresses by Hertz included in the present collection. In his review of *Early and Late*, published in *The Jewish Chronicle* in the same issue (p. 6), Alexander Altmann, who had arrived as a refugee from Germany in October 1938 and was appointed Community Rabbi of Manchester, wrote: "No one has done more to expose, from the very outset, the bestial character of the Nazi regime." And in his Memorial Address following Hertz's death on January 14, 1946, Altmann said, "He was one of the first to expose the diabolical nature of the Nazi ideology to the British people. He gave expression to the outraged feelings of

2 See Deborah Lipstadt, *Beyond Belief*, pp. 216-17; Andrew Sharf, *The British Press and the Jews Under Nazi Rule*, pp. 111–13; Yosef Gorny, *The Jewish Press and the Holocaust, 1939–1945*, pp. 8–11. The information in these articles was based largely on reports from the Polish government-in-exile.

humanity in language of sublime moral pathos; He organised, and helped others to organise, succour and relief on a large scale. He solicited and found support from the heads of the Christian denominations. Though aging and entitled to a more restful life, he gave himself unsparingly (6:) and self-sacrificingly, to the cause of Israel and humanity. The agony of the last few years and their unspeakable Jewish tragedy must have broken his heart. He died before one could discern the contours of a brighter Jewish future."[3]

WE ARE ASSEMBLED IN THIS VENERABLE HOUSE OF WORSHIP TO CALL to mind, with poignant sorrow and sacred pride, the lightning-flashes of deathless glory that a year ago illumined the terrible darkness which enveloped the last days of the Warsaw Jewish community. It is a story that would require the pen of a Prophet, and should be written in letters of fire; and as for Israel's martyrdom of to-day, only a *paytan* – one of those great elegiac poets of the Middle Ages who gave voice to the storm of sighs and torrents of tears that accompanied the massacres of which they were eye witnesses – could depict its horror and woe. One who is neither Prophet nor *paytan* must confine himself to a bald statement of the heart-breaking facts.

Destruction of Polish Jewry

The Nazis had fixed upon Poland as the slaughter-house for the total extermination of European Jews. They were given only one-fifth of the quantity of food required to maintain life. It was a diet for death; so much so that, in 1940, of Warsaw's 500,000 Jews, no less than 60,000 died of starvation; Moreover, tens of thousands were being deported to labour camps. Of these deportees, not one ever returned alive. They either died of exhaustion in the slave battalions, or were consigned to a speedier death in gigantic crematoria, monster lethal chambers, and vast electrocution centres.[4] For a long time the general Jewish population did not suspect what was in store for

3 *Essays and Addresses in Memory of Dr. Joseph Herman Hertz*, ed. Wolf Gottlieb, pp. 5–6.
4 At this time, the reality of the gas chambers, and the fact that "giant crematoria"

those deported, and it was adjusting itself to conditions. Hunger and disease continued to take their terrible toll, but Jewish optimism was uncrushable. We are told:

> One phenomenon was the growth of religious feeling. Jews who had never been to the synagogue before used to go there to pray three times a day. Education went on all the time. Debating societies were a common activity. At first, the Germans were puzzled by the refusal of the Jews to give in. Later, this grew to a kind of fury, which made them increase their efforts to wipe the people out.[5]

Battle of Warsaw

In March, 1942, Himmler decreed that deportations to the death-camps must be at the rate of 100,000 per month. A large portion of this number were Warsaw Jews. In August all the Jewish children were deported from its schools and orphanages; and by spring 1943, the largest Jewish Kehillah in Europe had been reduced to 40,000 souls, who by now knew full well the doom that awaited them. And then the unexpected happened. This remnant of Warsaw Jewry, starved and enfeebled by physical and mental suffering that had passed the limit of human endurance, resolved to fight their fiendish

---

and "vast electrocution centres" were NOT used as part of the mechanism of mass murder, was apparently still not known.

5 This is presented as a direct quotation, but no source is given. It seems as if it was based in some ways on an article printed on pp. 1 and 9 of the *JC*, November 4, 1943, entitled "A Witness from Warsaw," based on the experience of Eduard Warszawski (not his real name), who escaped from the ghetto in September 1942 and reached London in September 1943. Warszawski is quoted as stating (about the early period of the ghetto): "Very good schools for the young and professional courses were established, and theatres, concerts, and lectures were organised; in fact, our cultural life at that time began to prosper." The article continues, "Warszawski spoke of the wonderful revival in religion and said that a large number of small synagogues were established and minyanim held every day." He then proceeded to speak of the atrocities, beginning in 1942. The article ends stating that Warszawski has been invited to give an account of his experiences to members of Parliament, and it may be a report from this that provided Hertz with the direct quotation. It may also be based on an article entitled "Behind the Wall: Life - And Death - in Warsaw's Ghetto," by Tosha Bialer, published by Collier's, February 20, 1943, pp. 17–18, 66–67, and February 27, pp. 29–33; the Introduction says that the author, her husband, and son are the only persons known to have escaped from the Warsaw Ghetto: https://www.unz.org/Pub/Colliers-1943feb20-00017.

murderers to the last drop of blood. The Nazi troopers who came on Passover eve for the usual number of victims for deportation were met by a fusillade on all sides, and died in the flames of their own exploded tanks. Soon the whole Ghetto turned into a fortress. Women fought and young girls operated machine-guns. The Nazi arsenals were seized and blown-up, and the enemy replied by use of artillery, cannon and incendiary bombs. In vain. Jewish suicide squads broke through the German lines and blew up the tanks with hand grenades, at the price of their own lives. The Nazis rained down from the air high explosives upon the Jewish quarter, and later set it all on fire. Hosts of men, women, and children were burnt; and others were murdered *en masse*. But the surviving defenders barricaded themselves in factories, houses and streets; and desperately contested every inch of ground – till food and weapons failed them. They killed one thousand of the enemy during the six weeks that they had held their ground, and they fought and died to the last man.

For staggering courage, this Battle of Warsaw is unsurpassed in the whole history of heroism. It is an epic struggle that recalls the glories of the Maccabees and the amazing self-slaughter at Masada.[6] Like them, the men and women who in our day fearlessly defied the fury of the inhuman oppressor, died for the honour of their people. And they died in the hope that a free world would emerge from this war; a world in which, even for the Jew, there would be freedom from fear, freedom to live. Their dying was a Kiddush Hashem; a sublime proclamation for all time, "magnified and glorified be God's great Name," *Yisgaddal v-yiskaddash shemeh rabbo.*

Israel's Greater Woe

Our tribute of reverence and unbounded admiration to these heroes and martyrs will be mere lip-service, unless we endeavour to comprehend the vaster woe of which their last stand is but an incident; or, if we shut our eyes to the sinister fact that this woe has evoked but

6 One might certainly question this analogy between the mass suicide on Masada as reported by Josephus and the decision in the Warsaw Ghetto to fight to the death while taking the lives of as many German soldiers as possible. The link for the preacher is the concept of martyrdom.

feeble reactions outside, and even within, the House of Israel. "The Jewish horror," General Smuts declares, "has no parallel in history; a whole race is proscribed and crucified in what is surely the most poignant tragedy of our era."[7] The facts in this tragedy stand irrefutable, authenticated, nay, self-confessed in Satanic boast by the ghouls of Berlin. So far, at least three million helpless and inoffensive men, women, and children have been done to death with diabolic tortures and the maximum prolongation of agony that numb the imagination. They have been killed by hunger and cold; by burning and drowning; by poison, gas, and electrocution. They have been machine-gunned by the thousands into graves which they themselves were forced to dig, their little children being thrown into, and buried alive in, those same graves.[8]

And Hitler's satellites faithfully follow his example. The Rumanians have shown themselves his equals in sadism. And in Yugoslavia nearly every Jew has been wiped out. A large portion of French and Belgian Jewry perished in death trains that were despatching them to the human stockyards in Poland. A similar fate seems to have befallen the Holland community, besides having 25,000 of its Jews sterilized.[9] By comparison with the tortures devised by German science, the cruelty of the ancient Romans, or even of the Mongol builders of pyramids of human skulls appears amateur; and episodes like the Black Hole of Calcutta, as tales for the nursery.

World's Reaction

What has been – we wonder – the reaction in Allied lands to this stark Satanism? Well, the Press – with few honourable exceptions – passed it over in silence; and the larger public has thus remained unmoved by this mass crucifixion of a whole people. Only men and women

7 See Hershman, October 9, 1943, above.

8 Alluding to the *Einsatzgruppen* massacres in the east following the invasion of Soviet-held territory in the summer of 1941.

9 The *JC* of December 10, 1943, p. 7, reported "Dutch Jews Sterilised"; this policy applied to Jews married to non-Jews, who could in this manner avoid wearing a yellow star and being deported to Poland. I have not been able to find the basis for the 25,000 number.

of light and leading realized that Nazism was a maniacal assault on all the ethical foundations of society – pity, decency, and respect for life; an attempt to make a clean sweep of the sacred Heritage of Man. Foremost among them were the Heads of the Churches, with their passionate plea that, as the crimes were unheard of, unheard-of measures were called for to stop them. At last there were made, both in Washington and Westminster, grave pronouncements of sympathy with the victims denouncing in the strongest possible terms the policy of bestial murder, and threatening dire retribution on the criminals.

Little was said about opening the gates to those that might still escape Hitler's clutches. Eventually some schemes of rescue were formulated, and these are now being carried into effect – with the result that one-half of one per cent, possibly as much as one per cent, of the victims may yet be saved. Meanwhile, Sweden set a noble example by welcoming to her shores the Jews of Denmark fleeing for their lives. But, alas, nearly a million more Jews now stand on the brink of annihilation through the nazification of Hungary. *Is it – we ask – beyond the might of Britain and her Allies to ensure for surviving Jews of Europe the status of prisoners of war, with facilities for exchange, and the offer of sanctuary somewhere, even in Palestine, to those who escape from the Nazi inferno?*[10]

Anglo-Jewry's Reaction

And what has been *our* reaction to this unparalleled breakdown of all civilisation? What has Anglo-Jewry done to rouse world opinion in regard to a moral cataclysm that threatens to engulf half the Jewish race, together with all those higher values that distinguish human society from the wolf-pack?

When 25 years ago I circulated a brief account of the fiendish slaughter of the Jewish population in the Ukraine by the White Russian forces, one British Archbishop wrote to me that those appalling facts were new to him, and he wondered why the Jewish community

10 Italics in original.

had not made them known.[11] I fear that many people will wonder as much over our recent silence. Thus, although the Nazi killing of thousands daily began in early 1941, it was October 29, 1942, before the lay leaders of Anglo-Jewry arranged a public protest meeting.[12] Some of these leaders were quite distressed even over the Day of Mourning and Prayer I proclaimed in the December following.[13] I need not now comment on such Olympic calm, strange reticence and heathen indifference. Suffice it to say, that they were not calculated to stir the men at the helm of the political universe to speedy action in human salvage; so that dismay seized many a one at the procrastination and inertia of those who alone had the power to save.

What of the Future?

As to the future, the outlook is far from rosy. It seems certain that the Nazis will go down in defeat and everlasting dishonour. But "the evil that men do lives after them."[14] Consider the legacy that Nazism is leaving behind it: torture reduced to a science; hatred as a religion planted in the minds of millions of the young; and the hellish example of extermination of entire peoples. Add to this the knowledge that even in the freest lands there were found groups of quislings, men ready to betray their country and commit every conceivable crime for the spread of totalitarian doctrines, and, I repeat, the outlook is far from rosy. Every possible circumstance exists

---

11 Italics in the original. Cf. *Addresses*, 105–7, part of the Opening Address delivered to the Conference of Anglo-Jewish Preachers on July 10, 1923, with a detailed factual addendum on pp. 121–22.

12 This event at The Royal Albert Hall was announced by the *JC* in its October 23 issue, and reported by the *JC* on November 6, p. 5. The Chairman was the Archbishop of Canterbury, Dr. William Temple, who read a message from Churchill and delivered a major address. The Chief Rabbi's address was similarly summarized in the article (see above under the date). The statement that "the Nazi killing of thousands daily began in early 1941," seems incorrect; systematic mass murder did not begin until after the German invasion of Russian-held territory in the summer of 1941, and this was not known until considerably later. Reports of mass murder of Polish Jewry were widely publicized in June 1942.

13 See the selection from Hertz's sermon "England, Awake" delivered on that occasion, above.

14 Shakespeare, *Julius Caesar,* Act III, Scene 2.

that could contribute to a lasting and righteous peace, yet, political storm and social upheaval may precede the sure establishment of the Four Freedoms; and that storm and upheaval may bring with them much frustration, at any rate defamation, to the Jew, even in democratic lands. What is sorely needed in our spokesmen, Jewish and non-Jewish, is wisdom, courage and *trustworthiness.*

May our solemn remembrance to-day of the immortal heroes and heroines of Warsaw, and our mourning for the millions of our brethren from the Atlantic to the Volga, from Norway to Crete, to whom a cruel death was meted out simply because of their creed and blood, rouse in men of goodwill everywhere a new pity, a new justice, and new humanity. And may the whirlwind of calamity that has passed over the House of Israel fill us with a new loyalty to the ideals of our Sacred Faith, a new submission to God's inscrutable will, a loyalty that shall, in life and in death, enable us to exclaim: *Yisgaddal v-yiskaddash shemeh rabbo.*[15]

15 Permission granted by Jeremy Schonfield on behalf of the Hertz family.

Louis I. Newman (1893-1975)
"The Cup of Fury"
Congregation Rodeph Sholom, New York
August 26, 1944 (Saturday)
Biting on Granite, 250–57

INTRODUCTION

Louis Israel Newman was born in Providence, Rhode Island. He received a BA degree from Brown University in 1913, and an MA from the University of California in 1917. Following this degree, he became an assistant to Rabbi Stephen S. Wise at the Free Synagogue in New York City. A year later, he received private ordination from Wise and a rabbinical colleague in California, after which he began to serve small congregations in New York, while continuing working for a PhD at Columbia University, which he received in 1924. He then served for six years as rabbi of Temple Emanu-El of San Francisco, after which he returned to New York where he served at Congregation Rodeph Sholom until his retirement.

During the 1930s, Newman became identified with the Zionist revisionist movement associated with Vladimir (Ze'ev) Jabotinsky, with whom he had a a friendly relationship. Many Reform rabbis were still anti-Zionist at the time, and few of those committed to Zionism thought of it as essentially a political movement committed to the establishment of a Jewish state in Palestine. In this he went beyond his mentor, Stephen S. Wise.[1]

Newman published several significant academic books, including *Jewish Influence on Christian Reform Movements* (1924), and *Hasidic*

1 The biographical material is taken in part from the AJA MS-320, "Biographical Sketch."

Anthology: Tales and Teachings of the Hasidim (1934); his commitment to making the major texts of Hasidism accessible to American Jewish readers was also unusual for contemporary Reform. For our purposes, the most important works are his collections of sermons. Four volumes of his *Sermons and Addresses* were published by Bloch Publishing Company in mimeograph form, with the text looking as if it was simply reproduced from sheets of typing paper. In 1945 he completed a larger text of 436 pages published in traditional format: *Biting on Granite: Selected Sermons and Addresses* (Bloch, 1946). These collections, with texts clearly dated, are a major source for Jewish preaching in response to Nazi persecution and mass murder between 1933 and 1945.

At the time the sermon below was delivered (late August, 1944), most of the last remaining community of European Jews – those in greater Hungary – had been transported to Auschwitz-Birkenau, where many of them were murdered in gas chambers upon their arrival. While this latest chapter was not yet widely known in the west, the basic outline of the "Final Solution" was indeed known, most recently from reports by the Soviet forces advancing to the west and encountering the remains of the Polish death camps. Newman was therefore justified in saying, "Every century has chronicled the tribulations of Israel, but it has remained for the twentieth century to witness the most savage persecution of Jewry in all the annals of history."

His sermon begins with a verse from the prophetic reading of the week (Isa. 51:12–52:12), focusing on the metaphorical phrase "the cup of My fury," acknowledging that this divine anger had indeed been directed against the Jews, but promising that the time for Jewish suffering has ended, and that the cup of divine fury will now be shifted to the oppressors. The application of this assertion to the recent experience of European Jewry asserts a connection with the past, despite the insistence that the suffering of the most recent years has been unprecedented in previous history. Now "the promise of the Prophet is being fulfilled in our own times," with the Allies routing German forces both in the west and the east, and the shattered remnants of Jewish communities appearing to suggest the possibility of belief in "a rebirth of Israel both in Palestine and in the lands of her most terrible trials."

> "BEHOLD, I HAVE TAKEN OUT OF THY HAND THE CUP OF STAGgering; the beaker, even the cup of My fury; Thou shalt no more drink it again; and I will put it into the hand of them that afflict thee." (Isa. 51:22–23)

The Haftarah for this Sabbath, Isaiah 51:12 to 52:12, contains a graphic portrayal of the sufferings of the people of Israel in the days of the Exile, following the Destruction of the First Temple in the year 586 B.C.E. The Prophet's message is one of comfort and assuagement; in fact, the selection for this Sabbath commences with the words, *Anoki Hu menaḥemkhem*, "I, even I, am He that comforteth you" (Isa. 51:12). God, through the lips of His Seer, reminds the stricken Children of Israel, in the midst of their anguish, that they have forgotten the Lord their Maker, since they fear "continually all the day because of the fury of the oppressor" (Isa. 51:13). It must be remembered that the plight of Israel was dire indeed. The Northern Kingdom had been destroyed, and the tribes scattered. The Southern Kingdom, with its capital, Jerusalem, had fallen before the Babylonian conqueror, and the very existence of the Jewish nation was imperilled. The people had despaired, very much as the peoples of France, Greece, and other countries of our times, under the yoke of the Nazis, lest their future, as a nation, be impossible.

Therefore the Prophet utters words of solace and encouragement, saying, "Awake, awake, stand up Jerusalem, that hast drunk at the hand of the Lord the cup of His fury; Thou hast drunken the beaker, even the cup of staggering, and drained it" (Isa. 51:17). The Prophet uses the image of the woman "drunken, but not with wine: with none to guide her among all the sons whom she hath brought forth; neither is there any that taketh her by the hand of all the sons that she hath brought up" (Isa. 51:18). It is an effective comparison, in direct line with the vivid imagery which characterizes the writings of the Prophets of Israel, and it forcibly brings home to his listeners the picture which the Seer seeks to convey. "The captive daughter of Zion" (Isa. 52:2) is enjoined to "awaken," for the Prophet cries out, "Awake, awake, put on thy strength, O Zion, put on thy beautiful garments, O Jerusalem, the holy city" (Isa. 52:1).

Carrying forward the metaphors, the Prophet says, "Thus saith thy Lord, the Lord and thy God that pleadeth the cause of His people: Behold, I have taken out of thy hand the cup of staggering; the beaker, even the cup of My fury; Thou shalt no more drink it again; And I will put it into the hand of them that afflict thee; that have said to thy soul, 'Bow down, that we may go over': And thou hast laid thy back as the ground, and as the street, to them that go over" (Isa. 51:22–23).

The phrase *Kos Ḥamati*, "the Cup of My fury," has a potent meaning for Israel even today – more than 2500 years after the Second Isaiah utilized it. *Zot Aniyah u-Shekhurat ve-lo miy-yayin*, "Thou afflicted and drunken, but not with wine" (Isa. 51:21) is descriptive of the people of Israel today. For surely it may be said that millions of our brothers have partaken of the dreadful *Kos ha-Tar'eilah*, "the cup of staggering." Every century has chronicled the tribulations of Israel, but it has remained for the twentieth century to witness the most savage persecution of Jewry in all the annals of history. I speak not of the pinpricks and irritations to which American Jews are constantly being subjected; nor do I speak of the sufferings which Jews in lands over-run by the Nazi invaders have undergone as citizens of the vanquished countries. If young Jews die fighting with the Polish patriots in Warsaw, they die as soldiers, with guns in their hands. If Jews of France meet the same unhappy fate that is meted out to Frenchmen of non-Jewish faith when the *patrie* is occupied, no especial word, except one of commiseration, need be said.

But when Jews are singled out for especial hatred and brutality, then it may truly be said that the "Assyrian has oppressed them without cause" (Isa. 52:4). We are encountering now the vestiges of the Nazi frightfulness, as it has been visited upon the Jews of Eastern Europe. Pictures are being found by the advancing Russians of the *Vernichtungslager*, of the "Extermination Camps," where hundreds of thousands of Jews from all parts of Europe have been obliterated.[2]

---

2 See Lipstadt, *Beyond Belief*, pp. 260–62 on Russians NOT emphasizing victims as primarily Jews.

We learn that the shoes and garments of the victims bear trademarks from the leading countries of Europe where the Nazis have entered, indicating that French, Austrian, German, Bulgarian, Jugo-Slavian, Dutch, Belgian, Italian and other communities of Jews have been transported to Treblinka, Lublin and other centers of massacre, and they have been slaughtered there.[3] Not merely the "*Ostjuden*," upon whom German and other Western Jews looked with condescension, and often disdain, have been overwhelmed by Hitler's savagery, but Jews from countries which have known only the "*Bekovedte Rishus*," the "Respectable Prejudice," familiar to us in America, have been deported, and slain. The full story of the "Greuel-taten"[4] may never be known, for we are being told that the Nazis in retreat have eliminated traces of these murder-camps, and have plowed the fields with grain.

To be sure, too, there will be some Americans – and, I am ashamed to say it, some anti-Zionist Reform rabbis, who will declare that the story of the Nazi crimes was exaggerated.[5] In fact, a few years ago, a Reform Rabbi in the South said and wrote publicly that when the curtain is lifted in Eastern Europe, it will be found that the reports of Nazi brutalities have no real foundation in fact. I have written to this rabbi asking him to retract this accusation, and from time to time, I send him clippings and pictures which perhaps, by this time, have caused him to change his mind. Suppose we discover that not five million, but only three million of our fellow-Jews have been massacred! Is this smaller figure sufficient to awaken a sense of horror in the bosom of this comfortable and secure rabbi of the South?

I am reminded of the remark of a young Confirmation candidate who, when informed by the rabbi that the story of the difficulties in the pathway of Zionism must be read in the light of the accounts of the extermination of Jewish communities in the Ukraine and

---

3 Details about Auschwitz-Birkenau, where the largest number of Jews from various countries had been killed, were reported in American newspapers at the beginning of July 1944, but the information did not as yet make a significant impact on the general population: Lipstadt, *Beyond Belief*, pp. 234–35.

4 "Atrocities," more commonly *Gräueltaten*.

5 This was a period of ongoing tension between anti-Zionist Reform rabbis, who were the great majority for the first decades of the Zionist movement, and an increasing number of Reform rabbis committed to Zionism. Newman was strongly in this category, a friend and follower of the Revisionist Zionist Vladimir (Ze'ev) Jabotinsky.

elsewhere, exclaimed, "They don't kill all of them; only some of them." And a boy pupil interjected, "Only the old ones!" Youngsters of fourteen even cannot be forgiven such callous comments; how much less a rabbi who forgets the rabbinic injunction, "Ye Sages, be careful of your words."[6]

Whatever may be the selfish doubts of a few American Jews, who have never known more distressing anti-Semitic experience than being denied accommodations at a summer hotel or a privately endowed college, the authentic evidence assembled by the United Nations proves beyond question that the Jewish communities of Central and Eastern Europe have suffered beyond all comprehension. When the Russian forces entered Lublin recently – Lublin, the home of the great Zaddik in days gone by[7] – Lublin, the center of great Jewish cultural and religious life – they found not a single Jew left in the city! Yes, our people have drained "the cup of fury," the *Kos Ḥamah.*

In the midst of this indescribable agony the prophet chides the people of Israel because they have forgotten Him. This 51st Chapter contains a theophany, namely a portrayal of the glories and triumphs of God, Who has covered Israel in the shadow of His hand (cf. Isa. 51:16). It may well be that many of the martyrs have forgotten the God of Israel *mipneh ḥamath hameitzik*, "because of the fury of the oppressor" (Isa. 51:13). Yet I venture to say that American Jews in their present prosperity have been more inclined to depart from God than their co-religionists in their terrible adversity. Jews have gone to their death with the Psalms on their lips. They may have been unable to understand the ways of the Almighty who "sells them for nought"; but they have not doubted the Power of God, nor His eventual triumph over evil in the universe.

A tale has come to us (by F.C. Weiskopf, courtesy *Reader's Scope*, New York City), which illustrates the faith of the martyrs at the moment of their destruction.

---

6 Quoting Avot 1:11.

7 Newman was extremely interested in Hasidic leaders such as the Zaddik of Lublin, having published *The Hasidic Anthology: Tales and Teachings of the Hasidim*, in 1934. The Majdanek concentration camp was established on the outskirts of Lublin in October 1941; it was discovered by Russian forces virtually intact in late July 1944.

> Among the bands of Jewish partisans, of which there have existed not a few in the so-called Reich-Government of Poland, the following story was told towards the end of the year 1943. When the Warsaw ghetto was stormed and destroyed by the Panzer regiments of the fighting SS, after having been for days heroically defended by its badly armed and exhausted inhabitants, the Storm Troop Leader [*Hauptsturmführer*] Mettemeier distinguished himself by brutalities, which, even among his own kind, were rare. It was his special predilection to pour gasoline over prisoners that had fallen into his hands – wounded women, children, and old men – and to have them burned alive. At one of these executions, one of the victims shouted to Mettemeier that in him the words of the Prophet Ezekiel would be fulfilled: "And though I shall cause it to return into the sheath, I will judge thee in the place where thou wast created and in the land of thy nativity" (Ezek. 21:35). To this the Storm Trooper is said to have replied with gruesome hilarity that that would be rather difficult of accomplishment, since he had come into the world in a drifting lifeboat at an unknown spot in the midst of the ocean. A short time later, a German patrol found him stabbed to death; on his chest was a slip of paper with nothing on it but "Ezekiel 21:30." The body of Storm Troop Leader Mettemeier was discovered in a dung pit.[8]

Yes, abundant information is at hand to indicate the reliance of the persecuted in the Gehinnom of Eastern Europe upon the Promises and Consolations of our Scripture.

The Prophet continues his pledge of God's assistance to the Children of Israel in the words, "And I will put it (the cup of God's fury) into the hand of them that afflict thee; that have said to thy soul, 'Bow down, that we may go over'" (*We-samtihah be-yad Mogayik asher amru le-nafshekh sheḥi we-naavorah*) (Isa. 51:23); "Ye were sold for nought, and ye shall be redeemed without money" (Isa. 52:3). In other

8 Ezek. 21:30 reads, "And to you, O dishonored wicked prince of Israel, whose day has come – the time set for your punishment." The vignette is taken from Weiskopf's *Das Anekdotenbuch*, apparently translated for the journal "Reader's Scope," which began publication only in 1943. I have not found historical confirmation of the incident, which is introduced as a "tale."

words, the cup of fury, the cup of staggering, shall pass from the hands of Israel into the hands of Israel's oppressors. They shall know the very anguish they have visited upon Israel and their other victims.

Behold, how the promise of the Prophet is being fulfilled in our own times. The Nazis are tasting the *Kos Ḥamah*, the "Cup of Wrath," at this very moment. Paris was occupied four years ago by the boastful and savage Nazis; today, the invaders have been driven out, and Paris is liberated. Not so long ago the Nazis were riding roughshod over the inhabitants of Eastern Europe; now they are being pushed back to their own borders. Four years ago this week the Nazis had launched their mass air attacks upon England; today Berlin, Munich, Hamburg, and a multitude of other German cities have felt the heavy metal of desolation descending from the skies upon their own heads.

Of course, the advancing Allies will not envisage for a moment perpetrating the horrors upon the Germans that they have imposed upon the conquered. There is nothing in the psyche of the Allied soldier which impels him to the brutalities which the Germans have invented and brought to pass. Already we are hearing the voices among the Allies which urge a "soft peace" for the defeated. In fact there is the gravest danger that those guilty of the massacres against innocent civilians will never be brought to trial. Every effort will be made to conceal those whose hands are stained with the blood of the unoffending, and, since so many of them were Jews, the likelihood is all the greater that punishment will not be meted out. A few weeks ago I saw an American troop-train filled with Nazi prisoners of war. There they were, the Huns, the Boches, the barbaric Teutons - only a few yards away. I shall never forget the growl of rage which swept through the passages on *our* train. After a moment, however, they were silent, as silent as the throngs in Moscow who saw the parade of tens of thousands of Nazi captives.[9] Civilized people wish the culprits to be given over to the due processes of law, but these move with exceeding slowness.

---

9 The parade occurred on July 17, 1944, with twenty German generals and other officers leading some 57,000 captured Nazi soldiers. *The Times of London* described the people watching the procession through the streets with a "deep and eloquent silence."

Yet we know that Germany, the outlaw of the nations, is destined to drain to the dregs the "cup of fury." When the First Isaiah speaks, *Oy, Asshur Shevet Appi*, "Ho, Assyria, rod of my anger" (Isa. 10:5), he is giving us a symbolic phrase for the Allies of today, who are the "Rod of God's Anger" against the guilty. Let us, therefore, take heart out of the preachment of the Seer. He has commanded Zion to awake and put on her strength: "Shake thyself from the dust, arise, and sit down, O Jerusalem; Loose thyself from the bands of thy neck, O captive daughter of Zion" (Isa. 52:2). And Jerusalem responded to these appeals, maintaining her courage in the days of darkness, until at last restoration came to pass. By the same token, we are witnessing a rebirth of Israel both in Palestine and in the lands of her most terrible trials. Out of the caves, the dungeons, the cellars, the forests, the non-Jewish institutions where courageous Christians have hidden some of them – the survivors are coming at last. How many have been able to live through the tempest, we do not as yet know. But even as a *Shearith Yisrael* remained in the days of the Isaiahs, so, today, in Central and Eastern Europe, the vestiges of the communities are to be found. Let us go to their succor; let us make them the nucleus for the rehabilitation of the shattered Jewries of the continent; let us repeat to them the words of Isaianic renewal: "I, even I, am He that comforteth you" (Isa. 51:12).

It has all happened before.[10] May the God of Mercies so order the future that it may never happen again. And as for the present hour, let us rejoice and be glad; let us be refreshed by the teachings of the Prophet, "Therefore My people shall know My name; therefore they shall know in that day that I, even He that spoke, behold, here I am" (Isa. 52:6). Then in truth will God's pledge to us be brought to fruition, "Behold I have taken out of thy hand the cup of thy staggering; the beaker, even the cup of My fury; Thou shalt no more drink it again" (Isa. 51:22–23).[11]

---

10 A rather surprisingly strong statement negating the radical innovation of Nazi mass murder.

11 Permission granted by Debbie Neuman Fine, Lisa Newman Eckstein, Martha Gay Newman: grandchildren.

Abraham Cohen (1887–1957)
"Peace Celebration"
Birmingham Hebrew Congregation, England
May 13, 1945 (Sunday)
Unpublished, Personal Archive of David Cohen

INTRODUCTION

Abraham Cohen was born in Reading and grew up in London's East End. Educated at Emmanuel College, Cambridge, he continued Jewish studies in Manchester and eventually earned a PhD from the University of London.[1] In 1913 he came to the Birmingham Hebrew Congregation of Singer's Hill, where he would serve for some thirty-six years, becoming highly esteemed in the community and widely known beyond it for his publications on classical Jewish texts, especially *The Soncino Chumash* (London, Soncino Press, 1947), *Everyman's Talmud* (London: J.M. Dent, 1934), and *The Teachings of Maimonides* (London: Routledge, 1927). His Sieff Lectures on Preaching at Jews' College were published as a wonderful handbook for preparing and delivering a sermon.[2]

Cohen's wide reading in what he calls "the by-paths of English literature" is revealed in his illuminating anthology of English travel literature describing actual Jewish communities throughout much of the world: Rev. Dr. A. Cohen, *An Anglo-Jewish Scrapbook, 1600–1940: The Jew Through English Eyes* (London: M.L. Cailingold, 1943).

After his retirement from the synagogue leadership role, he served

1 Following the custom of British Jewry, Cohen did not use the title rabbi; at first it was "Rev." then "Rev. Dr."

2 Rev. A. Cohen, *Jewish Homiletics*; the actual texts of his sermons reveal how he implemented these guidelines over three and a half decades.

as president of the Board of Deputies from 1949–1955, the only religious leader to have held this position.[3]

Like Israel Mattuck, Cohen was spiritual leader of a significant British congregation from before the beginning of the Great War until after the Second World War. The unpublished texts of his sermons through this period, in a neat handwriting with title and date clearly stated, are a rich resource for rabbinical leadership and congregational information pertaining to these catastrophic events of twentieth-century history.

The sermon below was delivered on May 13, 1945, the first Sunday after the official VE-Day, designated as an occasion for special worship services of Thanksgiving for Victory. Many Jewish communities respected this occasion, celebrated in churches throughout the land, by having a special weekday service focused on a sermon. The theme of Thanksgiving implies that gratitude would be expressed not just to those who had given their lives for the cause, but to a greater power as well.

But for all religious people, and especially for Jews, there was an element of ambivalence. If an omnipotent God was ultimately responsible for the final crushing defeat of Nazi Germany, why did it take so long, and why were so many millions of innocent Jews destroyed by the enemy? No rabbi could avoid expressing a position on the role of God not just in the final victory but throughout the nightmare that preceded it. These questions are explicitly acknowledged near the very beginning of the sermon. Perhaps the most surprising response is the assertion that "Many years hence, when the course of the war will be studied as a connected whole, much that seems dark to us will be clear then; and I am confident that the verdict of history will be that victory came at the right moment, that if it had come sooner, the rich harvest of world changes which it actually yielded would not have been reaped." Part of the response is also turning the blame on those on the victorious side who failed to intervene against the Nazi regime at a much earlier date. But would those in the congregation not continue to ask whether God

3 Raphael Langham, *250 Years of Convention and Contention*, p. 180.

was really incapable of ensuring the downfall of Hitler's Germany without the loss of six million innocent Jews, as well as the premature death of so many other civilian victims and soldiers?

I am deeply grateful to Abraham Cohen's grandson, David J. Cohen, Esq., of London, for graciously making these handwritten unpublished texts available to me for my research and publication.

> מאת ה׳ היתה זאת היא נפלאת בעינינו, From the Lord was this; it is marvelous in our eyes" (Ps. 118:23)

This familiar sentence from the Hallel Psalm, spoken probably after deliverance from some grievously threatening peril, gives expression to our innermost and deepest pent-up feeling as we assemble to offer thanksgiving to God for the signal victory that has crowned the long and bitter struggle which was forced upon us. מאת ה׳ היתה זאת, "From the Lord was this." I believe *that* with all my heart; and future generations, who will enjoy the fruits of the success which has been bought at so tragic a cost at home and on far-flung battlefields, will perhaps believe that more earnestly even than we are now able to do.

At the outbreak of the War, people spoke – and if they did not speak they thought – as though God were on trial. Even if they did not raise the unfair question, "Why did God permit the war to happen?" – unfair because the responsibility for the catastrophic clash of nations was entirely men's – the problems: Why does God allow the war to continue? Why does He grant the evil enemy triumph after triumph? Why does He not send us speedy victory, since we are innocent? – did persistently haunt the mind and test our faith. It has been difficult for us – nay, impossible for us – who have been called upon to live through these terrible years of stress and strain, to understand the trend of events and their underlying meaning, just as one cannot understand a picture by examining it inch by inch.

Many years hence, when the course of the war will be studied as a connected whole, much that seems dark to us will be clear then; and I am confident that the verdict of history will be that victory came at the right moment, that if it had come sooner, the rich harvest of world changes which it actually yielded would not have been reaped. Next to defeat, the gravest danger which beset us was a premature, inconclusive peace. And if we rejoice to-day that we have won the European war, our joy must be deeper through the conviction that the victory we have gained is the victory we hoped for and prayed for – complete and decisive.

If, then, we brought the name of God querulously to our lips in the dark days of anxiety and danger, let us not keep the thought of Him away from our hearts when we rejoice in victory. מאת ה' היתה זאת, "From the Lord was this." It will be to the peril of the future if men and women, both in the victorious and the defeated nations, fail to trace His hand in the course of events. If we have eyes to see and hearts to understand, we witness the greatest act of retributive justice in the entire annals of history.

When we consider the conditions at the opening stage of the war, the long-prepared and overwhelming military strength of the enemy as against the tragic unpreparedness of those who had to resist it, the confidence of the Nazis that their bid for world domination could not fail did not seem unreasonable. The boast that the Nazi Reich would endure for a thousand years did not seem far-fetched in the circumstances. But in twelve years from its inception, it has collapsed in irretrievable ruin. Has man ever had a more telling illustration of the adage, "Man proposes, God disposes"?[4] How remarkably does contemporaneous history justify the claim and exhortation made by the Psalmist, "Let all the earth fear the Lord; let all the inhabitants of the world stand in awe of Him. For He spoke, and it was; He commanded, and it stood. The Lord bringeth the counsel of the nations to naught; He makest the thoughts of the peoples to be of no affect. The counsel of the Lord standeth for ever, the thoughts of His heart to all generations" (Ps. 33:11).

Let, then, our hearts be filled with gratitude to Him who controls the destinies of kingdoms, Who has humbled the arrogant to the dust, and vindicated the cause of right. Let us recognize that it is His

---

4 A concise, popular formulation of the idea expressed in biblical verses such as Prov. 16:9 and 19:21.

will which has been accomplished in His own good time. Nay, let our sense of pride and exultation be tempered by the recognition that wonderful as has been the heroism of the armies which defended the liberties of man, praiseworthy as have been the skill and planning of the supreme leaders of the forces, and wise and courageous as has been the direction of the statesmen of the Allied Nations, ימין ה׳ רוממה ימין ה׳ עשה חיל "The right hand of the Lord is high, the right hand of the Lord doeth valiantly." Therefore, in accordance with traditional Jewish practice, I offer on this historic and soul-moving occasion the benediction, ברוך אתה ה׳ אלהינו מלך העולם שהחיינו וקימנו והגיענו לזמן הזה, "Blessed art Thou, O Lord our God, King of the universe, Who has kept us in life, and hast preserved us, and enabled us to reach this season."

מאת ה׳ היתה זאת היא נפלאת בעינינו, "From the Lord was this; it is marvelous in our eyes" (Ps. 118:23). Yes, this is certainly an occasion for full-hearted rejoicing. The menace has been imminent and dreadful, threatening our lives as well as all the values of living. In the event of defeat they who survived would have existed under conditions which make life worthless and intolerable. Enslavement and degradation was the fate in store for this and other countries, had the issue of the war been different. Victory means everything to us and is surely a time for joyful celebration.

בנפל אויבך אל תשמח, "When thine enemy falleth rejoice not" (Prov. 24:17). That exhortation refers to a personal enemy, not the enemies of mankind, the embodiment of all evil and vileness, which the Nazi leaders and their supporters undoubtedly were. It is right to exult over the downfall of these fiendish monstrosities, guilty of sadistic cruelty beyond anything the human race has ever known. Earth will be a cleaner place when the whole brood of heartless torturers and super-gangsters has been swept away. At long last the civilized world has been convinced by irrefutable evidence that the unimaginable depths to which these beasts in human form descended are not merely the invention of war propaganda. The unbelievable has actually happened in a scale far greater than even the bitterest anti-Nazi had alleged.

There is now universal acceptance of the reality of the charges which had for years been laid against the rulers of the Reich, but there should not be surprise. Did they not demonstrate during the six years preceding the war, by the treatment of the Jews, what they were capable of doing, how they scorned all accepted standards of morality and banished the word "pity" from their vocabulary? If only due heed had been paid to those early barbarities and the obvious deduction drawn from them, if the democratic governments and nations had re-acted as they should have done by regarding the perpetrators as moral lepers with whom no decent minded person could have any dealings, the horrors and the holocaust and the bitter anguish of the past 5½ years could have been avoided. Regrets are vain now; the price has had to be paid in full for condoning evil; but it is a fitting subject for meditation on this day. The future will be brighter if there is an awakening to the truth of the warning uttered by the Jewish writer, Shalom Asch, "When you have become indifferent to crimes committed against others, you have dug a pit for yourself."[5]

The joy which spontaneously wells up in our hearts to-day must, however, be tempered with sobering reflections. The enemy who could have been easily suppressed, perhaps without bloodshed, in the early stages of his career, was allowed to grow so strong that it has taken nearly six years to reduce him to impotence. The cost has been heavy in precious lives. Hundreds of thousands of men and women will offer their thanksgiving for victory to-day with stricken hearts and tear-dimmed eyes because of the painful recollection of personal bereavement. Some of them are among this congregation, and we deeply sympathise with them. Happily the casualty list of Birmingham Jewry is but a third in this war of what it was the last war. Nevertheless, we have paid our toll in the sacrifice of young men who have been taken from us prematurely and made our Community the poorer for their loss. A tinge of sadness must therefore colour our rejoicing.[6]

As Jews, we have our own special problems which arouse grave

5 Sholem Asch, *What I Believe*, translated by Maurice Samuel, p. 190.

6 The following paragraph was written after the original text; it replaces a paragraph, set by the preacher in square brackets to indicate that it would not be spoken, which

meditation even in this time of jubilation. Hitler has gone, but will there pass away with him that conspicuous feature of Hitlerism which he spread throughout the world – the singling out of Jewry as the victim of a vicious campaign of lies and an orgy of hatred? What is to become of the small remnant on the Continent which has survived the Nazi war of extermination waged against Jewry? What is to be the fate of the Balfour Declaration and the Palestine Mandate in the post-war changes of policy? These are momentous questions which must occupy our minds and we cannot ignore.[7]

But above all, there should be the awareness of the colossal task that faces mankind when all the fighting is over. We discovered over a quarter of a century ago that the problem of peace-making far exceeds in difficulty and complexity the problem of winning victory. We threw away the opportunities of world reorganization which were presented to us by the triumph of 1918 and drifted into a chaotic international relationship which culminated in a tragedy immeasurably greater than the last. Much of the world is literally in ruins; there is economic disorganization more fundamental and widespread than ever experienced before. The prospect of general scarcity is very real. Hunger and disease will stalk through Europe. These are disturbing facts, but they have to be faced.

I am afraid that there may be widespread reluctance to do this. For long years men and women have been subjected to intense strain. Their enemies are spent and their vitality is sapped. Peace brings them relief, but they must resist the temptations to lapse into apathy. A respite there must be and nature will demand it. But the call to work for the rebuilding of a devastated world will be insistent and it can only be neglected at the peril of the future. If from the hearts of countless millions the cry issues "never again," they have their

---

speaks of "the war in the Pacific" that still needs to be won despite the continued "price in blood."

7 This paragraph concerning the unique situation of Jews on this day appears to have been added to the original text almost as an afterthought. The absence of direct expression of the loss of millions of Jewish lives, and the implications of this catastrophic loss for the insistence that God was fully in control and that victory came at precisely the right time, are not addressed, and one wonders how congregants whose families had been destroyed would have reacted to this.

essential part to play in seeing that it does never again happen. Were I asked to put into one word the cause of the catastrophe which has all but submerged mankind and destroyed civilization, the word I would choose is "complacency." If we did not fiddle while the world was burning, we danced carelessly while the fuel was being piled up for the conflagration. That tragic error must not be repeated, if the cataclysm is never to recur in a still more dreadful form. We know the shape of things to come in a future war. We can foresee from the trying experiences of the Southern Counties during the last months of the European conflict what are the devilish engines of wholesale destruction which will be employed in the next, if there is a next. Men must stand aghast at the prospect and turn their minds and energies away from the preparation of these infernal devices to wholesome and constructive purposes. Human ingenuity has to be concentrated upon, and directed towards, the problems of rebuilding, and of making life secure and happy. It can be done if only the determined will exists among the peoples of the earth.

[Among the most fertile places of the world are areas which had once been made desolate by the eruption of a volcano. A stream of liquid fire poured down the mountain slope and wrought havoc far and wide. After a while, bounteous nature seems to try to make amends for the harm that was done. Gradually the scene of death and desolation becomes covered with rich vegetation, and the traces of the destructive lava are hidden under a cloak of luxuriant fields and orchards. So may it be with the Continent which has been swept by the ravages of war.][8]

On its ruins we can, if we so will, build afresh and turn the desolate scene into a radiant prospect. The bitter pain of the numberless tragedies the war has caused will long persist, but the future can be bright with hope. The night has been long and dreadful, but the dawn of a new day has broken upon a stricken world, bringing promise of happiness. Time has wonderful healing powers. It will assuage grief and allay pain. It will turn eyes toward the future, so

8 This paragraph, marked by the preacher in square brackets, was probably omitted from delivery for reasons of time.

that the tragic past will fade into the memory of a nightmare. The glamour with which warfare used to be surrounded has not been dissipated. We have seen it in all its terrible nakedness and power of destruction. We should have learnt from experience to appreciate the blessings of peace and co-operation. Pray God we plant their seeds deep in the earth, tenderly watch over their early growth until they produce a mighty tree, with branches extending throughout the world, in whose shade mankind will dwell in confidence and safety.[9]

9 Permission granted by David Cohen.

Sources and Bibliography

Texts of Sermons and Studies of Specific Preachers

Unpublished Individual Collections: [names in **bold** indicate complete sermons]

Archival Collections

AMERICAN JEWISH HISTORICAL SOCIETY (CENTER FOR JEWISH HISTORY, NEW YORK)

Tobias Geffen
Stephen S. Wise

ARCHIVES OF THE RATNER CENTER FOR THE STUDY OF CONSERVATIVE JUDAISM

Israel H. Levinthal: Boxes 6 and 7, Sermons and Addresses

CENTRE DE DOCUMENTATION JUIVE CONTEMPORAINE (CDJC)

Jacob Kaplan (David Shapira) - Fonds Kaplan

DAVID M. RUBENSTEIN RARE BOOK AND MANUSCRIPT LIBRARY, DUKE UNIVERSITY

Abraham Joshua Heschel

FORTUNOFF VIDEO ARCHIVE FOR HOLOCAUST TESTIMONIES, YALE UNIVERSITY

Temple Beth-El, Detroit, MI, Archives
Rabbi **Leo Morris Franklin** Papers (now held by AJA, MS-246)

JACOB RADER MARCUS CENTER OF THE AMERICAN JEWISH ARCHIVES

Barnett Brickner MS-98

Jacob X. Cohen, MS-146
Samuel S. Cohon, MS-276
Maurice N. Eisendrath, MS-167
Julian B. Feibelman, MS-94
Abraham H. Feinberg, MS-85
Ephraim Frisch, MS-187
Samuel H. Goldenson, MS-81
Solomon Goldman, MS-203
Ferdinand M. Isserman, MS-6
Bertram Korn, MS-99
Morris S. Lazaron, MS-71
Max Nussbaum, MS-705, Series C, Sermons
Harold I. Saperstein, MS-718
John J. Tepfer MS-586
Stephen S. Wise, MS-49

JEWISH HISTORICAL SOCIETY OF DELAWARE ARCHIVES

Jacob Kraft

LEO BAECK INSTITUTE (CENTER FOR JEWISH HISTORY, NEW YORK)

Max Dienemann, including bound volume of hand-written and typed sermons and lectures, http://bit.ly/2yGQcRt
Julius Kohn, AR-A.420 1233 (559, loc: V2/2 http://bit.ly/2fHwgWW)

NATIONAL LIBRARY OF SCOTLAND, GLASGOW

Salis Daiches

ROBERT D. FARBER ARCHIVES AND SPECIAL COLLECTIONS, BRANDEIS UNIVERSITY

Stephen. S. Wise

RODEF SHALOM CONGREGATION ARCHIVES

Solomon B. Freehof Rabbinic Writings

UNIVERSITY COLLEGE LONDON ARCHIVES

Alexander Altmann

UNIVERSITY OF SOUTHAMPTON, THE PARKES LIBRARY AND ARCHIVES, HADLEY LIBRARY, SOUTHAMPTON

Harold Reinhart

WESTERN RESERVE HISTORICAL SOCIETY, CLEVELAND, OH

Abba Hillel Silver Papers, Series III

YESHIVA UNIVERSITY ARCHIVES

Aaron David Burack
Leo Jung

Private Collections

Abraham Cohen Sermons. David Cohen Private Collection
Israel Mattuck Sermons. Catalogued at Leo Baeck College Library, London (owned jointly by Liberal Judaism Liberal Jewish Synagogue, Leo Baeck College)

PUBLISHED SERMONS AND SECONDARY WORKS ON PREACHERS [NAMES IN BOLD INDICATE COMPLETE SERMONS]

NB: Full indentation (———.) indicates additional collections of sermons by the same preacher. Partial indentation (——.) indicates a study of the preacher by a different author.

COLLECTIONS

Manual of Holiday and Occasional Sermons, ed. Bernard L. Berzon. New York: Rabbinical Council Press, 1943, 1944, 1945. *Manual of Holiday and Occasional Sermons.* New York: Rabbinical Council Press, 1943, ed. Bernard L. Berzon; 1944, ed. David B. Hollander; 1945, ed. Mendel Lewittes.
A Set of Holiday Sermons (SHS). Cincinnati: The Tract Commission of the Union of American Hebrew Congregations and the Central Conference of American Rabbis. 5700/1939, 5701/1940, 5702/1941, 5703/1942, 5704/1943, 5705/1944.
Best Sermons: 1944 Selection, edited by G. Paul Butler. Chicago, New York: Ziff Davis Publishing Company, 1944.
Holy Blossom Pulpit. Holy Blossom Synagogue, 1932–1942.

Rodef Shalom Pulpit, New Series. Pittsburgh, PA: Rodef Shalom Temple, 1935–1945.

INDIVIDUALS

Abrahams, Israel. *Living Waters: Collection of Sermons, Addresses and Prayers*. South Africa: Cape Town Hebrew Congregation, 1968.

———. *War and Peace: Selection of Sermons and Addresses Delivered in the Course of 1942–1943*. Cape Town Hebrew Congregation, s.n., n.d.

———. *War and Peace: Second Series: Sermons Delivered in the Course of 1943–1944*. Cape Town: Mercantile-Atlas Printing Co., 1944.

Altmann, Alexander. "Rosh Haschana 5695," in *Predigten an das Judentum von Heute*. Berlin: Joachim Goldstein Verlag, 1935, pp. 12–17.

Amir, Yehoshua [earlier Hermann Neumark]. *Deraschot: Jüdische Predigten*, edited by Peter von der Osten-Sacken. Berlin: Selbstverlag Institut Kirche und Judentum, 1983.

Bell, George (G.K.A.), Bishop of Chichester. *The Church and Humanity, 1939–1946*. London: Longmans, Green and Co., 1946.

———. Chandler, Andrew, ed. *The Church and Humanity: The Life and Work of George Bell, 1883–1958*. Franham, Surrey: Ashgate, 2012.

Berkovits, Eliezer. *Between Yesterday and Tomorrow*. Oxford: The East and West Library, 1945.

———. *Faith After the Holocaust*. New York: KTAV, 1973.

———. *Towards Historic Judaism*. Oxford: The East and West Library, 1943.

———. *With God in Hell: Judaism in the Ghettos and Death Camps*. New York: Sanhedrin Press, 1979).

Bosniak, Jacob. *Interpreting Jewish Life: Sermons and Addresses*. New York: Bloch Publishing Co., 1944.

Burack, Aaron. *Pirchei Aharon (Flowers of Aharon)*, vol. 2. New York: self-published, 1954.

Calisch, Edith Lindeman. *Three Score and Twenty: A Brief Biography of Edward Nathan Calisch, Selected Sermons and Addresses*. Richmond: Old Dominion Press, 1945.

Chameides, Kalman. *On the Edge of the Abyss: A Polish Rabbi Speaks to His Community on the Eve of the Shoah*, edited, annotated, and translated by Leon Chameides. Wethersfield, CT: Dauphin Design, 2013.

Cohen, Abraham. Unpublished sermon texts in David Cohen Collection

———. *Jewish Homiletics*. London: M.L. Cailingold, 1936.

———. *Sabbath Sermons*, selected by Chaim Pearl and Alex Tobias. London: Soncino Press, 1960.

Cohen, Jacob Xenab (J.X.). "The Menace of Hitlerism to American Jewry," Free Synagogue, New York. AJA MS-146, Box 2, Folder 3.

—. Alta Cohen, Sadie. *Engineer of the Soul: A Biography of Rabbi J.X. Cohen.* New York: Bloch Publishing Co., 1961.

Cohon, Beryl D. *From Generation to Generation*. Boston, MA: B. Humphries, 1951.

———. *Shielding the Flame: A Personal and Spiritual Inventory of a Liberal Rabbi.* New York: Bloch Publishing Co., 1972.

Coughlin, Charles E. *Am I an Anti-Semite? 9 Addresses on Various "ISMS" Answering the Question* (Nov. 6, 1938–Jan. 1, 1939). Detroit: Condon Printing Co., 1939.

Daiches, Samuel. *Essays and Addresses*, edited by Maurice Samuel and Isaac Levy. London: Samuel Daiches Memorial Committee, 1955.

———. "The Present Jewish Tragedy: A Message of Hope." London: B'nai Brith, 1939. [Pamphlets presented in chronological order.]

———. "The Revelation of Hope." Pamphlet printed by Oxonian Press, Oxford, 1944.

———. "Sermon Preached at the Service Held on the National Day of Prayer, Sunday, September 3, 1944." Pamphlet printed by Oxonian Press, Oxford, 1944.

———. "Sermon Preached at the Service Held on the National Day of Prayer and Thanksgiving, Sunday, August 19, 1945." Pamphlet printed by Oxonian Press, Oxford, 1945.

———. "Comfort Ye, Comfort Ye My People." Pamphlet printed by Oxonian Press, Oxford, 1947.

Edgar, Leslie I. *Some Memories of My Ministry*. London: Liberal Jewish Synagogue, 1985.

Ehrenpreis, Marcus. *Fragetecknet Israel: valda essäer fran aren 1923 till 1948.* Stockholm: Bonnier, 1948.

—. Fruitman, Stephen. *Creating a New Heart: Marcus Ehrenpreis on Jewry and Judaism*. Monograph, Umeå: Institutionen för historiska studier, Umeå Universitet, 2001 (based on dissertation), http://bit.ly/2xQ6dF7.

—. Larsson, Erika. "Hope Through Disaster," in *Kultura i Historia*, KiH 1/2001 (December 17, 2006), http://www.kulturaihistoria.umcs.lublin.pl/archives/43.

——. Rosenberg, Göran. "Philo of Stockholm, The Unrequited Love of Rabbi Marcus Ehrenpreis." *European Judaism* 17:1 (Spring, 2017): 8–20.

Ehrenreich, Shlomo Zalman. *Derashot Leḥem Shelomo: Al Mo'adim u-Zemanim Shonim*, edited by Joshua Katz. Brooklyn: Y. Katz, 1976.

——. Greenberg, Gershon. "Shlomo Zalman Ehrenreich's (1863–1944) Religious Response to the Holocaust: February 1939–October 1943, Simleul-Silvaniei (Szilágysomlyó), Transylvania." *Studia Judaica* 9 (2000): 65–93.

Krawcowicz, Barbara. "Paradigmatic Thinking and Holocaust Theology," *Journal of Jewish Thought & Philosophy* 22, 2 (2014) 164–189.

Eisendrath, Maurice N. *Holy Blossom Pulpit*, III–X; AJA, MS-167.

———. *The Never Failing Stream*. Toronto: The Macmillans in Canada, 1939.

——. Schulman, Avi M. *Like a Raging Fire: A Biography of Maurice N. Eisendrath*. New York: UAHC Press, 1993.

Eichhorn, David Max. *The GI's Rabbi: World War II Letters of David Max Eichhorn*, edited by Greg Palmer and Mark S. Zaid. Lawrence, KS: University Press of Kansas, 2004. www.kansaspress.ku.edu

Elton, Michael. *The Challenge of Destiny*. Johannesburg: Exclusive Books, 1961.

Epstein, Harry H. *Judaism and Progress: Sermons and Addresses*. New York: Bloch Publishing Co., 1935.

Faulhaber, Michael. *Judaism, Christianity and Germany*, translated by Rev. George D. Smith. New York: Macmillan, 1934 (Five Advent Sermons, delivered December 3, 1933–January 1, 1934). Translation of *Judentum, Christentum, Germanentum; Adventspredigten, gehalten in St. Michael zu München 1933*. Munich: A. Huber, 1934.

Feinberg, Abraham L. *Storm the Gates of Jericho*. Toronto: McClelland and Stewart, 1964.

Feldman, Abraham J. "Judaism in a Changing World: A Lenten Sermon." Pamphlet published in Hartford, CT, 1937.

———. *Sources of Jewish Inspiration*. Hartford, CT: Beth Israel Pulpit, 1934.

Fosdick, Harry Emerson. *A Great Time to Be Alive: Sermons on Christianity in Wartime*. London: S.C.M. Press, 1945.

Ryan, Halford Ross. *Harry Emerson Fosdick: Persuasive Preacher*. New York: Greenwood Press, 1989.

Freehof, Solomon B. *Spoken and Heard: Sermons and Addresses*. Pittsburgh: Rodef Shalom Congregation, 1972.

———. "Race, Nation, or Religion?: Three Questions Jews Must Answer,"

Rodef Shalom Pulpit, New Series, 1:3–5, 1935. [Pamphlets presented in chronological order.]
———. "When Religion Goes to War: A Call to Jews and Christians." *Rodef Shalom Pulpit, New Series*, 2:2, 1936.
———. "Getting Old or Growing Up: A Series of Three Addresses," *RSP*, 2:4–6, 1937.
———. "A Man and His Friendships," *RSP*, 4:4, 1939.
———. "To the American Jews: A Series of Three Addresses," *RSP*, 4:5–7, 1939.
———. "Living in Crisis: A Series of Three Addresses," *RSP*, 7:1–3, 1941.
———. "The Course We Take: A Series of Three Addresses," *RSP*, 8:2–4, 1942.
———. "The Religion of Our National Anthem: A Series of Three Addresses," *RSP*, 9:5–7 1943.
———. "Bible Words Which Changed the World: A Series of Four Addresses," *RSP*, 9:7–11, 1944.
———. "Bible Words in Wartime, A Series of Three Addresses," *RSP*, 10:5–7, 1945.
Frieder, Abraham-Abba (Armin). Sermon in Emanuel Frieder, *To Deliver Their Souls: The Struggle of a Young Rabbi During the Holocaust*, translated by Rachel Rowen. New York: Holocaust Library, 1990.
Geffen, Tobias. *Karnei ha-Hod.* St. Louis: Zalts-Gelman Publishers, 1935.
———. *Naḥalat Yosef.* New York: Moineshṭer Pob. Ḳomp., 706 (1946).
———. *Fifty Years in the Rabbinate: An Autobiography*. Atlanta: Tobias Geffen, 1951.
——. David Geffen, "The Literary Legacy of Rabbi Tobias Geffen in Atlanta, 1910–1970," *Atlanta Historical Journal* 23:3 (Fall 1979), 85–90.
——. Joel Ziff, ed. *Lev Tuviah: On the Life and Work of Rabbi Tobias Geffen.* Newton, MA: Rabbi Tobias Geffen Memorial Fund, 1988.
——. "Israel's Rivlin Honors Geffen Descendants," *Atlanta Jewish Times,* January 19, 2017, http://bit.ly/2xVErZE.
Gerstein, Israel. *Reveille or Taps? Sermons, Essays and Addresses.* New York: Bloch Publishing Co., 1943.
Gittelsohn, Roland. Sermon text in Mandel Lee, *Unlikely Warrior: A Pacifist Rabbi's Journey from the Pulpit to Iwo Jima*. Gretna, LA: Pelican Publishing Co., 2015.
Goldenson, Samuel H. *World Problems and Personal Religion: Sermons, Addresses, and Selected Writings*. Pittsburgh, PA: Rodef Shalom Congregation, 1975.
Goldstein, Israel. *Toward a Solution*. New York: G.P. Putnam's Sons, 1940.

Halpern, Abraham E. *A Son of Faith*, edited by Bernard S. Raskas. New York: Bloch Publishing Co., 1962.

Hammer, Louis. *A Word in Season*. Brooklyn: Judaica Publishing Co, 1944.

Heller, Abraham Mayer. *Jewish Survival: Sermons and Addresses*. New York: Behrman's Jewish Book House, 1939.

Hershman, Abraham M. *Israel's Fate and Faith*. New York: Bloch Publishing Co., 1952.

———. *Religion of the Age and of the Ages*. New York: Bloch Publishing Co., 1953.

——. Ruth and Eiga Hershman, "Rabbi Abraham M. Hershman," *Michigan Jewish History*, June 1981, pp. 16–32.

Joseph H. Hertz, "The Battle of Warsaw: The Chief Rabbi's Sermon at the Service of Mourning and Prayer for the Martyrs of the Warsaw Ghetto." Pamphlet published by the Office of the Chief Rabbi, London. 1944.

———. *Early and Late: Addresses, Messages, and Papers*. Hendhead, Surrey: Soncino Press, 1943.

———. *Sermons, Addresses, and Studies*, 3 vols. London: Soncino Press, 1938.

——. *Essays and Addresses in Memory of Dr. Joseph Herman Hertz*, edited by Wolf Gottlieb. London: Mizrachi Foundation of Great Britain and Ireland, 1948.

——. Taylor, Derek. *Chief Rabbi Hertz: The Wars of the Lord*. London: Vallentine Mitchell, 2014.

Herzog, Isaac. *Masu'ah leYitzḥak*, 2 vols., edited by Shulamit Eliash, Itamar Verhaftig, and Uri Desberg. Jerusalem: Yad haRav Herzog, 2009.

——. Eliash, Shulamit. *The Harp and the Shield of David: Ireland, Zionism and the State of Israel.* New York: Routledge. 2007.

——. Eliash, Shulamit. "Rabbi Herzog, Chief Rabbi of Palestine During the Struggle for a Jewish Homeland, and the Plight of European Jewry." *Bar-Ilan Studies in History* v, 2007 (*Leadership in Time of Crisis*, edited by Moises Orfali: 71–93).

——. Eliash, Shulamit "The 'Rescue' Policy of the Chief Rabbinate of Palestine Before and During World War II." *Modern Judaism,* 3,3 (1983): 291–308.

Hirsch, Woolf. *Selected Sermons and Addresses*. London: Edward Goldston, 1946.

Hochberg, Raphael Yehezkel. *Mar'eh Yehezkel*, Book 2. Biłgoraj, Poland, 1938.

———. *She'elot u-Teshuvot Mar'eh Yeḥezkel*. Monroe: Yitzhak Brack, 1991.

Israelstam, J. and L. Weiwow, eds. *"Ye Are My Witnesses"*: *Sermons and Studies by Former Students of Rabbi Dr. Samuel Daiches at Jews' College London.* London: M.L. Cailingold, 1936.

Isserman, Ferdinand M. Unpublished sermon texts in American Jewish Archives, MS-6.

———. "Sentenced to Death!: The Jews in Nazi Germany, an Opinion Based on One Month's Study in the Third Reich from June 1 to July 1, 1933." St. Louis: s.n., 1933; republished 1961.

———. "My Second Visit to Nazi Germany." St. Louis: s.n., 1935.

—. Schwartz, Daniel Aaron. "Rabbi Ferdinand M. Isserman: A Critical Study of His Life and Career." MA Thesis, HUC-JIR Cincinnati, 2008.

Italiener, Bruno. *Einziger Gott–einziges Volk. Predigt-Cyklus. Gehalten an den Hohen Feiertagen 5697 (1936) im Hamburger Tempel.* Hamburg: Druck Ackermann & Wulff Nachfig., 1936.

Jacob, Ernest I. *Paths of Faithfulness: A Collection of Sermons*, Pittsburgh: s.n., 1964.

Jacob, Walter, ed. *Pursuing Peace Across the Alleghenies: The Rodef Shalom Congregation, Pittsburgh, Pennsylvania, 1856–2005.* Pittsburgh: Rodef Shalom Press, 2005.

Jung, Leo. *Crumbs and Character: Sermons, Addresses, and Essays.* New York: Night and Day Press, 1942.

———. *Harvest: Sermons, Addresses, Studies.* New York: Philipps Feldheim, Inc., 1956.

—. Penkower, Monty Noam. "Jewish Cataclysm and Jewish Restoration: The Response of Leo Jung," in *The Holocaust and Israel Reborn: From Catastrophe to Sovereignty.* Urbana: University of Illinois Press, 1994, pp. 237–70.

Kahlenberg, Moses. *Darash Moshe*, 2 vols. Biłgoraj, Poland, 1935.

———. *Shalosh Dema'ot shel Semaḥot: Asher Hurdu beEvel biKehillat Metz al Me'ora'ot haDamim beArtsenu haKedoshah.* Biłgoraj: N. Kronenberg, 1937.

———. *Yedei Moshe: Derashot beMaḥaneh Hesder beTsorfat biYmei haShoah*, edited by Esther Farbstein. Jerusalem: Merkaz leḤeker haSho'ah, 2005.

—. Farbstein, Esther. "Sermons Speak History: Rabbinic Dilemmas in Internment between Metz and Auschwitz." *Modern Judaism* 27:2 (May 2007): 146–72.

Kaplan, Jacob (Grand Rabbin de Paris). *Les Temps d'épreuve: Sermons et Allocutions.* Paris: Les Éditions de Minuit, 1952.

—. Korsia, Haïm. *Être Juif et Français: Jacob Kaplan, le rabbin de la République.* Éditions Privé, 2006.

——. Pierrard, Pierre. *Le Grand Rabbin Kaplan*. Paris: Le Centurion, 1977.

——. Shapira, David. *Jacob Kaplan, 1895–1994: Un rabbin témoin du XXe siècle*. Paris: Albin Michel, 2007.

Katz, Yitzhak. "Things I Intended to Say…," in *To Live With Honor, to Die With Honor!*, edited and annotated by Joseph Kermish. Jerusalem: Yad Vashem, Menachem Press, 1986.

Kellner, Abraham A. *A Rabbi's Faith: Sermons of Hope and Courage*. Albany: Earle Printing Corp, 1945.

Kertzer, Morris. *With an H on My Dog Tag*. New York: Behrman House, 1947.

Lev, Aryeh. *What Chaplains Preach*. Thesis for Promotion to Rank of Captain, US Army, 1941.

Levine, Ephraim. *The Faith of a Jewish Preacher: Sermons Spoken and Written*. London: Edward Goldston, Ltd, 1935.

Levinthal, **Israel H.** *Judaism: An Analysis and an Interpretation*. New York: Funk & Wagnalls, 1935.

———. *A New World Is Born: Sermons and Addresses*. New York: Funk & Wagnalls, 1943.

——. Caplan, Kimmy. "The Life and Sermons of Rabbi Israel Herbert Levinthal." *American Jewish History*, 87 (1999):1–27.

Levy, Felix A. *His Own Torah: Felix A. Levy Memorial Volume*, edited by Sefton D. Temkin. New York: Jonathan David Publishers, 1969.

Lookstein, Joseph. "The Sources of Courage: War Time Sermons." Pamphlet, New York: Bloch Publishing Co., 1943.

Magnes, Judah L. *Addresses by the Chancellor of the Hebrew University*. Jerusalem: Hebrew University, 1936.

———. *Dissenter in Zion: From the Writings of Judah L. Magnes*, edited by Arthur Goren. Cambridge, MA: Harvard University Press, 1982.

———. *In the Perplexity of the Times*. Jerusalem: Hebrew University, 1946.

Mattuck, Israel. Unpublished sermon texts at Leo Baeck College, London

——. Fox, Pam. *Israel Isidor Mattuck: Architect of Liberal Judaism*. Edgware: Vallentine Mitchell, 2014.

——. Rich, Danny. *Israel Mattuck: The Inspirational Voice of Liberal Judaism*. London: Liberal Judaism, 2014.

Maybaum, **Ignaz.** *Man and Catastrophe: Sermons Preached at the Refugees Services of the United Synagogue London*, translated from the German by Joseph Leftwich. Foreword by His Grace the Archbishop of York. London: Allenson & Co., 1941.

———. *Ignaz Maybaum: A Reader*, edited by Nicholas de Lange. New York: Berghahn Books, 2001.

———. *The Face of God After Auschwitz*. Amsterdam: Polak and Van Gennep, 1965.

———. *Trialogue between Jew, Christian and Muslim*. London: Routledge, 1973.

—. Hershkowitz, Isaac. "Ignaz Maybaum and the Call for an Anti-Nazi Crusade," http://bit.ly/2xVfygA.

Meisels, Zvi Hirsch. *Mekaddeshei HaShem*, vol. 1. Chicago: s.n., 1955.

—. Landes, Daniel. "Death, Deconstruction, and Derashot: The Auschwitz Sermons of Rabbi Zvi Hirsch Meisels," unpublished.

—. Schmidt, Shira. "Sounding the Shofar in Auschwitz," *Cross-Currents*, September 10, 2007, http://bit.ly/2wvrtyC.

Munk, Kaj. *By the Rivers of Babylon: The Wartime Sermons*. Port Townsand, WA: New Nordic Pres, 2013.

Netter, Nathan, *La Patrie égarée et la patrie renaissante*. Metz: Paul Even, 1947.

Newman, Louis I. *Sermons and Addresses*, vol. 2. New York: Bloch Publishing Co., 1941.

———. Louis I. Newman, *Sermons and Addresses*, vol. 3: "The Modern Clergyman and His Duties." New York: Bloch Publishing Co., 1941.

———. *Sermons and Addresses*, vol. 4: "On the Eve of the War and During the War (1941–1943)." New York: Bloch Publishing Co., 1943.

———. *Biting on Granite: Selected Sermons and Addresses*. New York: Bloch Publishing Co., 1946.

Nussbaum, Max. *From Berlin to Hollywood: A Mid-Century Vision of Jewish Life*, edited by Lewis M. Barth with Ruth Nussbaum. Malibu, CA: Joseph Simon/Pangloss Press, 1994.

Pool, David de Sola. *David de Sola Pool: Selections from Six Decades of Sermons, Addresses and Writings,* edited by Marc D. Angel. New York: Union of Sephardic Congregations, 1980.

———. *Predigten an das Judentum von Heute*. Berlin: Joachim Goldstein Verlag, 1935.

Prinz, Joachim. *Joachim Prinz: Rebellious Rabbi: The German and Early American Years*, edited by Michael A. Meyer. Bloomington, IN: Indiana University Press, 2008.

Rabinowitz, Louis. *Out of the Depths: Sermons for Sabbaths and Festivals*. Johannesburg: Eagle Press, Limited.

—. Mazabow, Gerald. *To Reach for the Moon: The South African Rabbinate of*

Rabbi Dr L.I. Rabinowitz as Reflected in his Public Addresses, Sermons and Writing. Johannesburg: G. Mazabow, 1999.

Rapoport, Shabbetai. *Siftei Kohanim*, Biłgoraj, Poland: N. Ḳronenberg, 1936.

Reichert, Irving Frederick. *Judaism and the American Jew: Selected Sermons and Addresses*. San Francisco: Grabhorn Press, 1953.

Reinhart, Harold. *Harold Reinhart, 1891–1969: A Memorial Volume*, compiled by Lewis and Jacqueline Golden, with a Memoir by Leo Bernard. Westminster Synagogue, London, n.d.

Risikoff, Mnachem. *Palgei Shemen*. Brooklyn: Shulsinger Bros., 1939.

Rokeach, Mordechai (Mottl) of Biłgoraj. "Sermon of Departure from Budapest, 1944," printed in "HaDerekh," February 7, 1944, pp. 18–19, and in Mendel Piekarz, *Ḥasidut Polin*, pp. 432–33.

——. Hershkowitz, Isaac. "'This Enormous Offense to the Torah': New Discoveries about the Controversies over the Escape of the Rabbis from Budapest, 1943–1944." *Yad Vashem Studies* 37,1 (2009): 109–36.

Rosenblatt, Samuel. *Our Heritage*. New York: Bloch Publishing Co., 1940.

Rudin, Jacob Philip. *Very Truly Yours: A Creative Harvest of Forty Years in the Pulpit*. New York: Bloch Publishing Co., 1971.

Saperstein, Harold I. *Witness from the Pulpit: Topical Sermons 1933–1980*. Lanham, MD: Lexington Books, 2001.

Sarna, Yehezkel. "*LeTeshuvah uleTekumah* [Toward Penitent Return and Restoration], in *Daliyot Yeḥezkel*, vol. 3. (Jerusalem, 5738), pp. 303–23. Translation in Katz, Biderman and Greenberg, *Wrestling with God*, pp. 133–45.

——. Greenberg, Gershon. "A Musar Response to the Holocaust: Yeḥezkel Sarna's *Le'teshuva Ule'tekuma* of 4 December 1944." *Journal of Jewish Thought and Philosophy*, 7:101–138.

Schonfeld, Solomon. *Message to Jewry*. London: Jewish Secondary Schools Movement, 1959.

——. Kranzler, David and Gertrude Hirschler, eds. *Solomon Schonfeld: His Page in History*. New York: Judaica Press, 1982.

Taylor, Derek. *Solomon Schonfeld: A Purpose in Life*. London: Vallentine Mitchell, 2009.

Tomlin, Chanan. *Protest and Prayer: Rabbi Dr. Solomon Schonfeld and Orthodox Jewish Responses in Britain to the Nazi Persecution of Europe's Jews, 1942–1945*. Oxford: Peter Lang, 2006.

Shachter, Jacob. *Ingathering: Collected Papers, Essays, and Addresses*. Jerusalem, self-published, 1966.

Shapira, Kalonymus Kalmish. *Esh Kodesh*. Jerusalem: Va'ad Ḥasidei Piaseczno, 1960.

———. *Sacred Fire: Torah from the Years of Fury, 1939–1942*. Translated by J. Hershy Worch, edited by Deborah Miller. Northvale, NJ: Jason Aronson, 2000.

———. *Derashot meShenot haZa'am* (Sermons from the Years of Rage), vol. 1: A Critical Edition; vol. 2: Facsimile Edition with Transcription, by Daniel Reiser. Jerusalem: Herzog Academic College, World Union of Jewish Studies, Yad Vashem, Jerusalem, 2017.

—. Abramson. Henry. "Metaphysical Nationality in the Warsaw Ghetto: Non-Jews in the Wartime Writings of Rabbi Kalonymus Kalmish Shapiro," in *Contested Memories: Poles and Jews during the Holocaust and Its Aftermath*, edited by Joshua D. Zimmerman. New Brunswick: Rutgers University Press, 2003, pp. 258–69.

—. Polen, Nehemia. *The Holy Fire: The Teaching of Rabbi Kalonymus Kalman Shapira, the Rebbe of the Warsaw Ghetto*. Northvale NJ; London: Jason Aronson, 1994.

—. Seeman, Don. "Ritual Efficacy, Hasidic Mysticism, and 'Useless Suffering' in the Warsaw Ghetto." *Harvard Theological Review* 101:3–4 (2008): 465–505.

—. Zur, Avichai. "'The Lord Hides in Inner Chambers:' The Doctrine of Suffering in the Theosophy of Rabbi Kalonymus Kalman Shapira of Piaseczno." *Dapim: Studies on the Shoah* 25 (2011): 183–237.

Shulman, Charles E. "The Jewish Future," and "The Will to Live." Pamphlet: Glencoe, IL: North Shore Congregation Israel, 1940.

Silver, Abba Hillel. *Therefore Choose Life: Selected Sermons, Addresses, and Writings of Abba Hillel Silver*, vol. 1. Cleveland and New York: World Publishing Company, 1967.

———. *A Word in Its Season: Selected Sermons, Addresses, and Writings of Abba Hillel Silver*, vol. 2. New York and Cleveland: World Publishing Company, 1972.

———. *Vision and Victory: A Collection of Addresses by Dr. Abba Hillel Silver, 1942–1948*. New York: Zionist Organization of America, 1949.

—. Ganin, Zvi. "Activism versus Moderation: The Conflict between Abba Hillel Silver and Stephen Wise During the 1940's." *Studies in Zionism* 5 (1984): 171–95.

—. Raider, Mark A., Jonathan Sarna, and Ronald W. Zweig, eds. *Abba Hillel Silver and American Zionism*. London: Frank Cass, 1997.

——. Shiff, Ofer. *The Downfall of Abba Hillel Silver and the Foundation of Israel.* Syracuse: Syracuse University Press, 2014.

Sokolover, Ephraim. *Penei Efraim.* Ra'ananah: s.n., 1966.

Steinberg, Milton. *A Believing Jew: The Selected Writings of Milton Steinberg.* New York: Harcourt, Brace and Company, 1951.

———. *From the Sermons of Rabbi Milton Steinberg: High Holydays and Major Festivals*, edited by Bernard Mandelbaum. New York: Bloch Publishing Co., 1954.

———. *Only Human – The Eternal Alibi: From the Sermons of Rabbi Milton Steinberg: The Weekly Sidrah and General Themes*, edited by Bernard Mandelbaum. New York: Bloch Publishing Co., 1963.

——. Noveck, Simon. *Milton Steinberg: Portrait of a Rabbi.* New York: KTAV, 1978.

——. Steinberg, Jonathan. "Milton Steinberg, American Rabbi: Thoughts on His Centenary." *The Jewish Quarterly Review*, 95:3 (Summer 2005): 579–600.

Stern, Harry Joshua. *The Jewish Spirit Triumphant: A Collection of Addresses.* New York: Bloch Publishing Co., 1944.

———. *Judaism in the War of Ideas: A Collection of Addresses.* NewYork: Bloch Publishing Co., 1937.

———. *Martyrdom and Miracle: A Collection of Addresses.* New York: Bloch Publishing Co., 1950.

——. Cleator, Kenneth Irving and Harry Joshua Stern. *Harry Joshua Stern: A Rabbi's Journey.* New York: Bloch Publishing Co., 1981.

Swift, Harris. *Because I Believe: Sermons, Addresses and Essays.* New York: Bloch Publishing Co., 1954.

Teichthal, Yissachar Shlomo. *Em Habanim Semeḥa: Restoration of Zion as a Response to the Holocaust*, edited and translated by Pesach Schindler. Hoboken, NJ: KTAV, 1999.

Temple, William, Archbishop of Canterbury. *The Church Looks Forward.* London: Macmillan, 1944.

Unsdorfer, Shlomo Zalman. *Siftei Shlomo.* Brooklyn: Bilshon Printing Corporation, 1972.

——. Greenberg, Gershon. "Shlomo Zalman Unsdorfer: With God through the Holocaust." *Yad Vashem Studies* 31 (2003): 61–94.

——. Greenberg, Gershon. "The Suffering of the Righteous According to Shlomo Zalman Unsdorfer, 1939–1944," in *Remembering for the Future,* edited by John K. Roth, 3 vols. Hampshire, UK: Palgrave Publishers, 2001, pp. 422–38.

——. Unsdorfer, S[imha] B[unem]. *The Yellow Star.* New York: T. Yoseloff, 1961.

Wise, Stephen S. Unpublished sermon texts at Robert D. Farber University Archives and Special Collections Department, Brandeis University (BUASC); American Jewish Historical Society (AJHS), P-134; American Jewish Archives (AJA), MS-49.

———. *As I See It.* New York: Jewish Opinion Publishing Corporation, 1944.

———. *Challenging Years.* New York: G.P. Putnam's Sons, 1949.

——. Ganin, Zvi. "Activism versus Moderation: The Conflict between Abba Hillel Silver and Stephen Wise During the 1940s." *Studies in Zionism* 5 (1984): 171–95.

——. Martel, Myles. "A Rhetorical Analysis of the Anti-Nazi Protest Speech of Rabbi Stephen S. Wise, Delivered March 27, 1933, Madison Square Garden." MA thesis, Temple University, 1967.

——. Medoff, Rafael. *The Anguish of a Jewish Leader: Stephen S. Wise and the Holocaust.* Washington DC: David S. Wyman Institute for Holocaust Studies, 2015.

——. Rudin, A. James. *Pillar of Fire: A Biography of Rabbi Stephen S. Wise.* Lubbock, TX: Texas State University Press, 2015.

——. Stern, Harry Joshua. "Stephen S. Wise - in Memoriam." *Canadian Jewish Review,* April 29, 1949, p. 16.

——. Urofsky, Melvin I. *A Voice That Speaks for Justice: The Life and Times of Stephen S. Wise.* Albany: SUNY Press, 1982.

Wolsey, Louis. *Sermons and Addresses.* Philadelphia: Drake Press, 1950.

SECONDARY WORKS ON GENERAL CONTEXT

Abella, Irving and Harold Troper. *None is Too Many: Canada and the Jews of Europe, 1933–1948*, 3rd ed. Toronto: Lester Publishing, 1991.

Adunka, Evelyn. "Oberrabiner David Feuchtwang (1864–1936)," in *DAVID: Jüdischer Kulturzeitshcrift*, Ausgabe 104.

American Jewish Year Book, 5695, vol. 36 (1934–1935); *5696*, vol. 37 (1935–1936); *5699*, vol. 40 (1938–1939); *5705*, vol. 46 (1944–1945). Philadelphia: JPS.

Arad, Yitzhak, Yisrael Gutman, and Abraham Margaliot, eds. *Documents on the Holocaust: Selected Sources on the Destruction of the Jews of Germany and Austria, Poland, and the Soviet Union*. Jerusalem: Yad Vashem, 1981.

Arad, Yitzhak, Shmuel Krakowski, and Shmuel Spector, eds. *The Einsatzgruppen Reports: Selections from the Dispatches of the Nazi Death Squads' Campaign Against the Jews, July 1941–January 1943*. New York: Holocaust Library, 1989.

Asch, Sholem. *My Personal Faith*, translated by Maurice Samuel. London: Routledge, 1942.

———. *What I Believe*, translated by Maurice Samuel. New York: G.P. Putnam's Sons, 1941.

Aschheim, Steven. *Brothers and Strangers: The East European Jew in German and German-Jewish Consciousness*. Madison: University of Wisconsin Press, 1982.

The Authorised Daily Prayer Book of the United Hebrew Congregations of the British Empire, 12th ed., translated by S. Singer; Companion by Israel Abrahams. London: Eyre and Spottiswoode, 1924.

Avramov, Issac. "Daniel Zion (1883–1976)," Organization of the Jews in Bulgaria "Shalom." *Annual*, 22 (1987): 399–403.

Baker, Leonard. *Days of Sorrow and Pain: Leo Baeck and the Berlin Jews*. New York: Macmillan, 1978.

Bauer, Yehuda. *A History of the Holocaust*. New York: Franklin Watts, 1982.

Bar-Zohar, Michael. *Beyond Hitler's Grasp: The Heroic Rescue of Bulgaria's Jews*. Holbrook, MA: Adams Media, 1998.

Baumel, Judith Tydor and Jacob J. Schacter, "The Ninety-three Bais Yaakov Girls of Cracow: History or Typology?," in *Reverence, Righteousness, Rahmanut: Essays in Memory of Rabbi Dr Leo Jung*, edited by Jacob J. Schacter. Northvale, NJ: J. Aronson, 1992, pp. 93–130.

Beaken, Robert and Rowan Williams. *Cosmo Lang: Archbishop in War and Crisis*. London: I.B. Tauris, 2012.

Beer, Max. "The Montreal Jewish Community and the Holocaust." *Current Psychology*, vol. 26, Issues 3 and 4 (December, 2007): 191–205.

Ben-Gurion, David. *My Talks with Arab Leaders*, translated and edited by Misha Louvish. Jerusalem: Keter Books, 1972.

Bentley, James. *Martin Niemöller, 1892–1984*. New York: Free Press, 1984.

Berenbaum, Michael. *Witness to the Holocaust*. New York: HarperCollins, 1997.

Bergen, Doris. *Twisted Cross: The German Christian Movement in the Third Reich*. Chapel Hill: University of North Carolina Press, 1996.

Berger, David. "Torah and the Messianic Age: The Polemical and Exegetical History of a Rabbinic Text," in *Studies in Medieval Jewish Intellectual and Social History: Festschrift in Honor of Robert Chazan*, edited by David Engel, Lawrence H. Schiffman, and Elliot R Wolfson. Leiden: Brill, 2012, pp. 169–88.

Bernstein, Michael André. *Foregone Conclusions: Against Apocalyptic History*. Berkeley, CA: University of California Press, 1994.

Besdin, Abraham. *Reflections of the Rav: Lessons in Jewish Thought*. Hoboken, NJ: KTAV, 1989.

Bialer, Tosha. "Behind the Wall: Life - and Death - in Warsaw's Ghetto." *Collier's Weekly*, February 20, 1943, pp. 17–18, 66–67, and February 27, pp. 29–33, https://www.unz.org/Pub/Colliers-1943feb20-00017.

Bialik, Hayim Nahman. *Poems from the Hebrew*, edited by L.V. Snowman, translated by Helena Frank. London: Hasefer, 1924.

Bialik, Hayim Nahman and Yehoshua Hana Ravnitzky. *The Book of Legends/ Sefer ha-Aggadah*, translated by William G. Braude. New York: Schocken Books, 1992.

Bischoff, Erich. *Das Blut in jüdischem Schrifttum und Brauch*. Leipzig: Beust, 1929.

Braber, Ben. *Jews in Glasgow 1879–1939: Immigration and Integration*. London: Vallentine Mitchell, 1997.

Biélinky, Jacques. *Journal 1940–1942: Un journaliste juif à Paris sous l'Occupation*, edited and annotated by Renée Poznanski. Paris: Éditions du Cerf, 1992.

bin Gorion (Berdyczewski), Micha Joseph. *Mimekor Yisrael: Classical Jewish Folktales*, 3 vols., edited by Emanuel bin Gorion, translated by I.M. Lack. Philadelphia: JPS and Indiana University Press, 1976.

Blatman, Daniel, ed. *Geto Varsha Sippur Itona'i: Mivḥar meItonut haMaḥteret, 1940–1943*. Jerusalem, Yad Vashem, 2002.

———. "Poland and the Polish Nation as Reflected in the Jewish Underground Press," in *Contested Memories: Poles and Jews during the Holocaust and Its Aftermath*. New Brunswick: Rutgers University Press, 2003, pp. 123–33.

Blondheim, Menahem. "Divine Comedy: The Jewish Orthodox Sermon in America, 1881–1939," in *Multilingual America: Transnationalism, Ethnicity, and the Languages of American Literature*, edited by Werner Sollors. New York: NYU Press, 1998, pp. 191–214.

Boismorand, Pierre, ed. *Magda et André Trocmé: figures de résistances, textes choisis et présentés par Pierre Boismorand*. Paris: Éditions du Cerf, 2007.

Braham, Randolph L., ed. *The Destruction of Hungarian Jewry: A Documentary Account*, 2 vols. New York: Pro Arte, 1963.

———. *Jewish Leadership During the Nazi Era: Patterns of Behavior in the Free World*. New York: Social Sciences Monographs, 1985.

———. *The Politics of Genocide: The Holocaust in Hungary*. New York: Columbia University Press, 1981.

Brämer, Andreas. *Judentum und religiöse Reform: Der Hamburger Israelitische Temple 1817–1938*. Hamburg: Dölling und Galitz, 2000.

Brittain, Vera. *One Voice: Pacifist Writings from the Second World War*. London and New York: Continuum, 2005.

Brocke, Michael and Julius Carlebach, eds., *Biographisches Handbuch: Teil 2: Die Rabbiner im Deutsche Reich, 1871–1945*. Berlin: de Gruyter, 2009.

Bronner, Stephen Eric. *A Rumor About the Jews: Antisemitism, Conspiracy, and the Protocols of Zion*. New York: Oxford University Press, 2003.

Browning, Christopher R. *Ordinary Men: Reserve Police Battalion 202 and the Final Solution in Poland*. New York: HarperCollins, 1993.

Bytwerk, Randall L. *Landmark Speeches of National Socialism*. College Station, TX: Texas A&M University Press, 2008.

Caplan, Kimmy. *BeSod haSiaḥ haḤaredi* [*Internal Popular Discourse in Israeli Haredi Society*]. Jerusalem: Merkaz Zalman Shazar, 2007.

———. *Ortodoksiah baOlam haHadash: Rabbanim veDarshanim baAmerika (1881–1924)* [*Orthodoxy in the New World: Immigrant Rabbis and Preaching in America*]. Jerusalem: Merkaz Zalanab Shazar, 2002.

Carpenter, Ronald H. *Father Charles E. Coughlin: Surrogate Spokesman for the Disaffected*. Westport, CT: Greenwood Press, 1998.

CCAR Yearbook, vols. 44 (1934), 46 (1936), 47 (1937), 49 (1939), 50 (1940), 51 (1941), 52 (1942), 53 (1943), 54 (1944). Philadelphia: JPS.

Cesarani, David. *Final Solution; The Fate of Jews 1933–1945*. London: Macmillan, 2016.

———. *The Jewish Chronicle and Anglo-Jewry, 1841–1991*. Cambridge: Cambridge University Press, 1994.

Cesarani, David and Eric J. Sundquist, eds. *After the Holocaust: Challenging the Myth of Silence*. London: Routledge, 2012.

Chadwick, Owen. *Hensley Henson: A Study in the Friction Between Church and State*. Oxford: Clarendon Press, 1983.

Chamberlain, Houston Stewart. *Foundations of the Nineteenth Century*. New York: John Lane, 1914.

Chare, Nicholas and Dominic Williams. *Matters of Testimony: Interpreting the Scrolls of Auschwitz*. New York and Oxford: Berghahn Books, 2015.

Chazan, Robert. *European Jewry and the First Crusade*. Berkeley, CA: University of California Press, 1987.

Cohen, Israel. *The Jews in the War*. London: Frederick Muller Limited, 1942.

———. *Vilna*. Philadelphia: JPS, 1943.

Cohen, Naomi. *Not Free to Desist: The American Jewish Committee, 1906–1966.* Philadelphia: JPS, 1972.

Cohen, Nathan and Dominic Williams. "Diaries of the 'Sonderkommandos' in Auschwitz: Coping with Fate and Humanity." *Yad Vashem Studies* 20 (1990): 273–312.

Cohen, Robert. *When the Old Left Was Young: Student Radicals and America's First Mass Student Movement, 1929–1941.* New York: Oxford University Press, 1993.

Cohn, Norman. *Warrant for Genocide: The Myth of the Jewish World-Conspiracy and the "Protocols of the Elders of Zion."* New York: Harper & Row, 1967.

Cohon, Samuel Solomon. *Religious Affirmations.* Los Angeles, CA: s.n., 1983.

Cole, Wayne S. *America First: The Battle Against Intervention, 1940–1941.* New York: Octagon Books, 1971.

Confino, Alon. *World Without Jews: The Nazi Imagination from Persecution to Genocide.* New Haven, CT: Yale University Press, 2014.

Conway, John S. *The Nazi Persecution of the Churches, 1933–1945.* Toronto: Ryerson Press, 1968.

Czerniakow, Adam. *The Warsaw Diary of Adam Czerniakow,* edited by Raul Hilberg, Stanislaw Staron, and Josef Kermisz. New York: Stein and Day, 1982.

Daiches, David. *Two Worlds: An Edinburgh Jewish Childhood; Promised Lands: A Portrait of My Father.* Edinburgh, Canongate, 1997.

Dan, Joseph. *The Teachings of the Hasidim.* West Orange, NJ: Behrman House, 1983.

Davidson, Israel. *Otsar haMeshalim ve-haPitgamim.* Jerusalem: Mossad HaRav Kook, 1979.

Dawidowicz, Lucy S. *A Holocaust Reader.* New York: Behrman House, 1976.

———. *The War Against the Jews, 1933–1945.* New York: Holt, Rinehart and Winston, 1975.

Dinnerstein, Leonard. *Antisemitism in America.* New York: Oxford University Press, 1994.

———. "When Henry Ford Apologized to the Jews." *Moment* 15 (February, 1990): 20–27, 54–55.

Dodd, William E. *Ambassador Dodd's Diary,* edited by William E. Dodd Jr. and Martha Dodd. New York: Harcourt, Brace and Company, 1941.

Domarus, Max. *Hitler: Reden und Proklamationen, 1932–1945, kommentiert von einem deutschen Zeitgenossen,* 4 vols. Munich: Süddeutscher Verlag, 1965.

———. *Hitler: Speeches and Proclamations: The Chronicle of a Dictatorship,*

1932–1945, translated by Mary Fran Gilbert, 4 vols. Würzburg: Domarus Verlag; London: I.B. Taurus & Co. Ltd., and Wauconda, IL: Bolchazy-Carducci Publishers, Inc., 1990–1997.

Dreyfus, Marianne C. "Remembering My Grandfather, Leo Baeck." *CCAR Journal* 46, no. 1 (Winter 1999): 50–55.

Dubnow, Simon M. *History of the Jews in Russia and Poland, From the Earliest Times Until the Present Day*, translated by I. Friedlander. Philadelphia: JPS, 1916–1920.

Edelheit, Abraham J. *History of the Holocaust: A Handbook and Dictionary*, 2 vols. Boulder, CO: Westview Press, 1994.

———. *The Yishuv in the Shadow of the Holocaust: Zionist Politics and Rescue Aliyah, 1933–1939*. Boulder, CO: Westview Press, 1996.

Eliach, Yaffa. *Hasidic Tales of the Holocaust.* New York: Avon Books, 1982.

Eliash, Shulamit. "The Political Role of the Chief Rabbinate at Palestine During the Mandate: Its Character and Nature." *Jewish Social Studies* 47:1 (1985): 33–50.

Ericksen, Robert P. *Complicity in the Holocaust: Churches and Universities in Nazi Germany*. New York: Cambridge University Press, 2012.

———. *Theologians Under Hitler: Gerhard Kittel, Paul Althaus, and Emanuel Hirsch*. New Haven, CT: Yale University Press, 1985.

Evans, Richard J. *The Coming of the Third Reich*. London: Allen Lane, 2003.

———. *The Third Reich in Power, 1933–1939*. London: Allen Lane, 2005.

———. *The Third Reich at War, 1939–1945*. London: Allen Lane, 2008.

Elon, Amos. *Founder: A Portrait of the First Rothschild and His Time*. New York: Penguin Books, 199.

Farbstein, Esther. *Hidden in the Heights: Orthodox Jewry in Hungary During the Holocaust*, 2 vols., translated by Deborah Stern. Jerusalem: Mossad HaRav Kook, 2014.

———. *Hidden in Thunder: Perspectives on Faith, Halachah and Leadership During the Holocaust*, translated by Deborah Stern. Jerusalem: Mossad HaRav Kook, 2007.

———. *The Forgotten Memoirs: Moving Personal Accounts from Rabbis Who Survived the Holocaust*, compiled and edited by Esther Farbstein. Brooklyn: Shaar Press, 2011.

Feuchtwanger, Lion. *The Oppermanns*. New York: Viking Press, 1934.

Fine, Lawrence. *Physician of the Soul, Healer of the Cosmos: Isaac Luria and His Kabbalistic Fellowship*. Stanford, CA: Stanford University Press, 2003.

Frantz, Douglas and Catherine Collins. *Death on the Black Sea: The Untold Story of the Struma and World War II's Holocaust at Sea*. New York: Ecco, 2003.

Gannon, Franklin Reid. *The British Press and Germany, 1936–1939*. Oxford: Clarendon Press, 1971.

Garber, Zev. "The Ninety-Three Beit Yaakov Martyrs: Toward the Making of a Historiosophy." *Shofar* 12,1 (1993): 69–92, and in Franklin H. Littell, Alan. L Berger, and Herbert G. Locke, eds. *What Have We Learned?: Telling the Story and Teaching the Lessons of the Holocaust: Papers of the 20th Anniversary Scholars' Conference*. Lewiston, NY: Edwin Mellen Press, 1993, pp. 323–49.

Gerlach, Wolfgang. *And the Witnesses Were Silent: The Confessing Church and the Persecution of the Jews*. Lincoln, NE: University of Nebraska Press, 2000.

Gilbert, Martin. *Auschwitz and the Allies*. New York: Holt, Rinehart and Winston, 1981.

———. *The Holocaust: A History of the Jews of Europe During the Second World War*. New York: Holt, Rinehart and Winston, 1985.

———. *Kristallnacht: Prelude to Destruction*. London: Harper, 2006.

———. "What Was Known and When," in *Anatomy of the Auschwitz Death Camp*, edited by Yisrael Gutman and Michael Berenbaum. Bloomington, IN: Indiana University Press, 1994, pp. 539–52.

Ginzberg, Louis. *Legends of the Jews*, 7 vols. Philadelphia: JPS, 1968.

Gitlitz, David M. *Secrecy and Deceit: The Religion of the Crypto-Jews*. Philadelphia: JPS, 1996.

Goda, Norman J.W., ed. *Jewish Histories of the Holocaust: New Transnational Approaches*. New York: Berghahn Pres, 2014.

Gollancz, Victor. "'Let My People Go:' Some Practical Proposals for Dealing with Hitler's Massacre of the Jews, and an Appeal to the British Public." London: V. Gollancz, Ltd., 1943.

Gordon, Julius. *Pity the Persecutor*. New York: Richard R. Smith, 1938.

Gorny, Yosef. *The Jewish Press and the Holocaust, 1939–1945: Palestine, Britain, the United States, and the Soviet Union*. New York: Cambridge University Press, 2012.

Gottlieb, Moshe. *American Anti-Nazi Resistance, 1933–1941: An Historical Analysis*. New York: KTAV, 1982.

———. "The First of April Boycott." *American Jewish Historical Quarterly*, 57 (1967–1968): 516–56.

Gottlieb, Moshe R. *American Anti-Nazi Resistance, 1933–1941: An Historical Analysis*. New York: KTAV, 1982.

——. "The Anti-Nazi Boycott Movement in the United States: An Ideological and Sociological Appreciation," *Jewish Social Studies* 35 (1973): 198–227.

Green, Arthur. *Tormented Master: A Life of Rabbi Nahman of Bratslav*. New York: Schocken Books, 1981.

Greenberg, Gershon. "Between Holocaust and Redemption: Silence, Cognition, and Eclipse," in *The Impact of the Holocaust on Jewish Theology*, edited by Steven T. Katz. New York: NYU Press, 2005, pp. 110–31.

———. "Elhanan Wasserman's Response to the Growing Catastrophe in Europe: The Role of Ha'gra and Hofets Hayim Upon His Thought." *Journal of Jewish Thought and Philosophy*, 10 (2000): 171–204.

———. "Foundations for Orthodox Jewish Theological Response to the Holocaust: 1936–1939," in *Burning Memory: Times of Testing and Reckoning*, edited by Alice L. Eckardt. London: Pergamon, 1993, pp. 71–94.

———. "Jewish Mysticism and Kabbalah Through the Holocaust," in *Back to the Sources: Reexamining Perpetrators, Victims and Bystanders*, edited by Sara Horowitz. Evanston, IL: Northwestern University Press, 2012, pp. 37–67.

———. "Kristallnacht: The American Ultra-Orthodox Theological Response," in *American Religious Responses to Kristallnacht*, edited by Maria Mazzenga. New York: Palgrave Macmillan, 2009, pp. 145–81.

———. "Mahane Israel-Lubavitch 1940–1945: Actively Responding to *Khurbn*," in *Bearing Witness to the Holocaust, 1939–1989*, edited by Alan L. Berger. Lewiston: Edwin Mellen Press, 1991; Symposium Series, vol. 31, pp. 141–63.

———. "Metahistory, Redemption, and the Shofar of Emil Fackenheim," in *The Philosopher as Witness: Fackenheim and Responses to the Holocaust*, edited by Michael L. Morgan and Benjamin Pollock. New York: SUNY Press, 2008, pp. 207–223.

———. "Orthodox Theological Responses to Kristallnacht: Hayim Ozer Grodzensky and Elhanan Wasserman." *Holocaust and Genocide Studies* 3 no. 4 (1988): 341–42 and no. 4 (1989): 519–21.

———. "Wartime Jewish Orthodoxy's Encounter with Holocaust Christianity," in *Antisemitism, Christian Ambivalence, and the Holocaust*, edited by Kevin P. Spicer. Bloomington, IN: Indiana University Press, and Washington, DC. United States Holocaust Memorial Museum, 2007, pp. 237–69.

Grobman, Alex. "What Did They Know? The American Jewish Press and the Holocaust, 1 September 1939–17 December 1942." *American Jewish History*, 68:3 (March 1979): 327–52.

Gross, Jan T. *Neighbours: The Destruction of the Jewish Community in Jedwabne, Poland, 1941*. Princeton, NJ: Princeton University Press, 2001.

Grove, Warren. *Nazis in Newark*. New Brunswick, NJ: Transaction Publishers, 2003.

Grunwald-Spier, Agnes. *Who Betrayed the Jews?: The Realities of Nazi Persecution in the Holocaust*. Strout, Gloucestershire: The History Press, 2016.

Gurock, Jeffrey S., ed. *America, American Jews, and the Holocaust*, vol. 7 of *American Jewish History*. New York and London: Routledge, 1998.

Gutteridge, Richard. *The German Evangelical Church and the Jews*. New York: Barnes and Noble, 1976.

Hamerow, Theodore S. *On the Road to the Wolf's Lair: German Resistance to Hitler*. Cambridge, MA: Harvard University Press, 1997.

Hanyok, Robert J. *Eavesdropping on Hell: Historical Guide to Western Communications Intelligence and the Holocaust, 1939–1945*, 2nd ed. Fort Meade, MD: Center for Cryptologic History, NSA, 2005.

Haussy, Christiane d', ed. *Christian Sermons: Mirrors of Society*. Toulouse: Presses Universitaires du Mirail, 1995.

Hawkins, Richard A. "'Hitler's Bitterest Foe': Samuel Untermyer and the Boycott of Nazi Germany, 1933–1938." *American Jewish History* 93:1 (2007): 21–50.

Heller, James G. *Isaac M. Wise: His Life and Work*. New York: UAHC, 1965.

Hendler, Chana. "HaShimush baDerashah vaSippur haḤasidiyim baMevo'ot laSifrut haRabanit" (The Use of the Sermon and the Hasidic Story in Introductions to Rabbinic Literature), in *Zikaron baSefer*, edited by Asaf Yedidyah, et al. Jerusalem, Reuben Mass Publishers, 2008: 71–99.

Hercz, Moshe Y. *Christianity and the Holocaust of Hungarian Jewry*, translated by Joel Lerner. New York and London: New York University Press, 1993.

Herskowitz, Isaac. "'This Enormous Offense to the Torah': New Discoveries about the Controversies over the Escape of the Rabbis from Budapest, 1943–1944." *Yad Vashem Studies* 37,1 (2009): 109–36.

Heschel, Susannah. *The Aryan Jesus: Christian Theologians and the Bible in Nazi Germany*. Princeton, NJ: Princeton University Press, 2008.

Historical Guide to Western Communications Intelligence and the Holocaust, 1939–1945, 2nd ed. Fort Meade, MD: Center for Cryptologic History, NSA, 2005.

Hochstadt, Steve, ed. *Sources of the Holocaust*. New York: Palgrave Macmillan, 2004.

Hoess, Rudolf. *Commandant of Auschwitz: The Autobiography of Rudolf Hoess*. London: Weidenfeld and Nicholson, 1959.

Hoffman, Lawrence A., ed. *All These Vows: Kol Nidre*. Woodstock, VT: Jewish Lights, 2011.

Horowitz, Elliott. *Reckless Rites: Purim and the Legacy of Jewish Violence*. Princeton, NJ: Princeton University Press, 2006.

Huberband, Shimon. *Kiddush Hashem: Jewish Religious and Cultural Life in Poland During the Holocaust*. Hoboken, NJ: KTAV; New York: Yeshiva University Press, 1987.

Hunterberg, Max. *Tragedy of the Ages: Anti-Semitism: The Root, Cause and Cure*. New York: Association Press, 1937.

Ibn Verga, Solomon. *Shevet Yehudah/Liber Schevet Jehuda*. Hanover: Ḳ. Rimpler, 1924.

Idel, Moshe. *Hasidism Between Ecstasy and Magic*. New York: SUNY Press, 1995.

Idelsohn, A.Z. *Jewish Liturgy and Its Development*. New York: Holt, Rinehart and Winston, 1932.

Imber, Elizabeth E. "Saving Jews: The History of Jewish-Christian Relations in Scotland, 1880–1948." MA thesis, Brandeis University, 2010.

Jabotinsky, Vladimir. *The War and the Jew*. New York: Dial Press, 1942.

The Jews in Nazi Germany: The Factual Record of Their Persecution by the National Socialists. New York: American Jewish Committee, 1933, http://www.ajcarchives.org/AJC_DATA/Files/THR-18.PDF.

Joad, C.E.M. *God and Evil*. New York and London: Harper, 1943.

Jospe, Alfred. "A Profession in Transition: The German Rabbinate 1910–1939." *Leo Baeck Institute Yearbook* 19 (1974): 51–62.

Judd, Robin. *Contested Rituals: Circumcision, Kosher Butchering, and Jewish Political Life in Germany, 1843–1933*. Ithaca, NY: Cornell University Press, 2007.

Kalmanovich, Zelig. *Diary*, in *YIVO Annual of Jewish Social Science* 8 (1953): 9–81. Yiddish original in *Yivo-bleter*, 35 (1951), 18–92.

Kamanec, Ivan. *On the Trail of Tragedy: The Holocaust in Slovakia*, translated by Martin Styan. Bratislava: Hajko & Hajková, 2007.

Kamenetsky, Dovid. "Ha'im Gozrim Ta'anit Tsibbur Kelalit baZeman HaZeh?" [Is it Permissible to Establish a Fast Day Nowadays?] *Tevunot*, 2 (2016): 876–909.

Kaplan, Chaim A. *The Warsaw Diary of Chaim A. Kaplan*, translated and edited by Abraham I. Katsch. Revised Edition. New York: Collier Books, 1973.

Kaplan, Edward K. and Samuel H. Dresner, *Abraham Joshua Heschel: Prophetic Witness*. New Haven, CT: Yale University Press, 1998.

Kassow, Samuel D. *Who Will Write Our History? Emanuel Ringelblum, the Warsaw Ghetto, and the Oyneg Shabbes Archive*. Bloomington, IN: University of Indiana Press, 2007.

Katz, Jacob. "Was the Holocaust Predictable?," in *The Nazi Holocaust*, vol. 1: *Perspectives on the Holocaust*, edited by Michael R. Marrus. Westport, CT: Meckler, 1989, pp. 118–137.

Katz, Steven T. *The Impact of the Holocaust on Jewish Theology*. New York: NYU Press, 2005.

Katz, Steven T., Shlomo Biderman, and Gershon Greenberg, eds. *Wrestling with God: Jewish Theological Responses During and After the Holocaust*. New York: Oxford University Press, 2007.

Kent, Madeleine. *I Married a German*. London: G. Allen & Unwin, Ltd., 1938.

Kermish, Joseph, ed. *To Live with Honor and Die with Honor! Selected Documents of the Warsaw Ghetto Underground Archives*. Jerusalem: Yad Vashem, Menachem Press, 1986.

Keshen, Jeffrey A. *Saints, Sinners, and Soldiers: Canada's Second World War*. Vancouver, UBC Press, 2004.

Kessler, Edward. *A Reader in Early Liberal Judaism*. London: Vallentine Mitchell, 2004.

Kirschner, Robert. *Rabbinic Responsa of the Holocaust*. New York: Schocken, 1985.

Klemperer, Victor. *I Will Bear Witness: A Diary of the Nazi Years, 1933–1941*, translated by Martin Chalmers. New York: Random House, 1998.

———. *I Will Bear Witness: A Diary of the Nazi Years, 1942–1945*, translated by Martin Chalmers. New York: Random House, 1999.

Kook, Abraham Isaac and Chanan Morrison. *Silver From the Land of Israel: A New Light on the Sabbath and Holidays*. Jerusalem: Urim Publications, 2010. Adapted from *Mo'adei haRe'iyah*. Jerusalem: Mishpaḥat Neriyah, 2010.

Korczak, Janusz. *Ghetto Diary*. New York: Holocaust Library, 1978.

Kranzler, David. *Thy Brother's Blood: The Orthodox Jewish Response During the Holocaust*. New York: Masorah Publications, 1987.

Kris, Ernst and Hans Speier. *German Radio Propaganda: Report on Home Broadcasts During the War*. London: Oxford University Press, 1944.

Lachmund, Margarithe and Albert Steen, eds. *Begegnung mit dem Judentum: Ein Gedenkbuch*. Bad Pyrmont: L. Friedrich, 1962.

Langer, Ruth. *Cursing the Christians: A History of the Birkat Haminim*. Oxford University Press, 2012.

Langham, Raphael. *250 Years of Convention and Contention: A History of the Board of Deputies of British Jews*. London: Vallentine Mitchell, 2010.

Lanzmann, Claude. *Shoah: An Oral History of the Holocaust: The Complete Text of the Film*. New York: Pantheon Books, 1985.

Laqueur, Walter. *The Terrible Secret: Suppression of the Truth About Hitler's "Final Solution."* Boston, MA: Little, Brown, 1980.

Lawson, Tom. *The Church of England and the Holocaust*. Woodbridge: Boydell Press, 2006.

Lee, Albert. *Henry Ford and the Jews*. New York: Stein and Day, 1980.

Leff, Laurel. *Buried by the Times: The Holocaust and America's Most Important Newspaper*. New York: Cambridge University Press, 2005.

Leftwich, Joseph. *Yisroël: The First Jewish Omnibus*. London: Heritage, 1934.

Leo Baeck Werke, ed. Albert H. Friedlander et al., 6 vols. Gutterloh: Guttersloher Verlagshaus, 1998–2003.

Levin, Aharon. *HaDerash veha'Iyyun al Ḥamishah Ḥumshei Torah*, vol. 1. Bilgoria-Piotrkow, 1928.

Levin, Nora. *The Holocaust: The Destruction of European Jewry: 1933–1945*. New York: T.Y. Crowell Co., 1968.

Levinthal, Marvin. *The Jews of Germany: A Story of Sixteen Centuries*. Philadelphia: JPS, 1938.

Levitt, Ruth. ed. *Pogrom, November 1938: Testimonies from 'Kristallnacht.'* London: Wiener Library and Souvenir Press, 2015.

Lewin, Abraham. *A Cup of Tears: Diary of the Warsaw Ghetto*, edited by Antony Polonski. Oxford: Basil-Blackwell, 1988.

Lewy, Gunther. *The Catholic Church and Nazi Germany*. New York and Toronto: McGraw-Hill, 1964.

Liepman, Heinz. *Murder – Made in Germany: A True Story of Present-Day Germany*. New York: Harper, 1934.

Lipstadt, Deborah E. *Beyond Belief: The American Press and the Coming of the Holocaust, 1933–1945*. New York: Free Press, 1986.

———. "Witness to the Persecution: The Allies and the Holocaust: A Review Essay." *Modern Judaism* 3,3 (1983): 319–38.

Lookstein, Haskell. *Were We Our Brothers' Keepers? The Public Response of American Jews to the Holocaust, 1938–1944*. New York: Hartmore House, 1985.

Lowenthal, Marvin. *The Jews of Germany: A Story of Sixteen Centuries*. Philadelphia: JPS, 1938.

Luedecke, Kurt. *I Knew Hitler: The Story of a Nazi Who Escaped the Blood Purge*. New York: C. Scribner's Sons, 1937.

Lukacs, John. *Five Days in London: May 1940*. New Haven, CT: Yale University Press, 1999.

Maracin, Paul. *The Night of the Long Knives: 48 Hours that Changed the History of the World*. New York: The Lyons Press, 2004.

Marrus, Michael, ed. *The Nazi Holocaust: Historical Articles on the Destruction of European Jews*, 9 vols. Westport, CT: Meckler, 1989.

Maurer, Trude. "From Everyday Life to a State of Emergency," in *Jewish Daily Life in Germany, 1618–1945*, edited by Marion A. Kaplan. Oxford: Oxford University Press, 2005, pp. 271–85.

Mayse, Ariel Evan and Daniel Reiser. "*Sefer Sefat Emet*, Yiddish Manuscripts and the Oral Homilies of R. Yehudah Aryeh Leib of Ger." *Kabbalah: Journal for the Study of Jewish Mystical Texts*, 33 (2015): 9–43.

Mazzenga, Miriam, ed. *American Religious Responses to Kristallnacht*. New York: Palgrave Macmillan, 2009.

McIntire, Suzanne and William E. Burns. *Speeches in World History*. New York: Facts on File, 2009.

McMillan, Neil R. "Pro-Nazi Sentiment in the United States: March, 1933–March, 1934," in *America, American Jews, and the Holocaust*, edited by Jeffrey S. Gurock. New York and London: Routledge, 1998, pp. 239–61.

Medoff, Rafael. *The Deafening Silence*. New York: Shapolsky Publishers, 1987.

Melchior, Marcus. *A Rabbi Remembers*, translated from the Danish by Werner Melchior. New York: Lyle Stuart, 1968.

Melnick, Ralph. *The Life and Work of Ludwig Lewisohn*, 2 vols. Detroit: Wayne State University Press, 1998.

Melzer, Emanuel. *No Way Out: The Politics of Polish Jewry, 1935–1939*. Cincinnati: Hebrew Union College Press, 1997.

Mendelsohn, Ezra. *The Jews of East Central Europe Between the World Wars*. Bloomington, IN: Indiana University Press, 1983.

Mendes-Flohr, Paul and Yehuda Reinharz. *The Jew in the Modern World: A Documentary History*, 2nd ed. New York and Oxford: Oxford University Press, 1995.

Menkis, Richard and Harold Troper, *More Than Just Games: Canada and the 1936 Olympics*. Toronto: University of Toronto Press, 2015.

Meyer, Michael A. *Response to Modernity: A History of the Reform Movement in Judaism*. New York and Oxford: Oxford University Press, 1988.

Michman, Dan. "Jewish Religious Life under Nazi Domination: Nazi

Attitudes and Jewish Problems." *Studies in Religion/Sciences Religieuses* 22/2 (1993): 147–65.

Mikva, Rachel S. *Midrash va-Yosha: A Medieval Midrash on the Song at the Sea.* Tübingen: Mohr Siebeck, 2012.

Morse, Arthur. *While Six Millions Died.* London: Secker & Warburg, 1968.

Narkiss, Bezalel. "Pharaoh is Dead and Living at the Gates of Hell." *Journal of Jewish Art* 10 (1984): 6–13.

Neumann, Emanuel. *In the Arena: An Autobiographical Memoir.* New York: Herzl Press, 1976.

Newman, Louis I. *A "Chief Rabbi" Becomes a Catholic.* New York: Renaissance Press, 1945.

———.*The Hasidic Anthology: Tales and Teachings of the Hasidim.* New York and London: Scribner, 1934.

Niemoeller, Martin. *Here Stand I*, translated by Jane Lymburn. Chicago, New York: Willett, Clark & Company, 1937.

Oort, Johannes van. "Augustine, His Sermons and Their Significance." *HTS Theological Studies*, 65:1 (2009), Article 300: 363–72.

Oshry, Ephraim. *The Annihilation of Lithuanian Jewry*, translated by Y. Leiman. Brooklyn: Judaica Press, 1995.

Patton, James David. *A Twisted Cross: German Clerical Resistance to National Socialism, 1933–1939.* MA thesis, Hardin Simmons University, 1984.

Peel, Peter H. "The Great Brown Scare: The Amerika Deutscher Bund in the Thirties and the Hounding of Fritz Julius Kuhn." *The Journal of Historical Review*, 7:4 (Winter 1986–87): 419–42, http://www.ihr.org/jhr/v07/v07p419_Peel.html.

Penkower, Monty Noam. "American Jewry and the Holocaust: From Biltmore to the American Jewish Conference [1942–1943]." *Jewish Social Studies* 47, 2 (1985): 95–114, reprinted in *America, American Jews, and the Holocaust,* edited by Jeffrey S. Gurock. New York and London: Routledge, 1998, pp. 357–76.

———. "The Bermuda Conference and Its Aftermath: The Allied Quest for 'Refuge' During the Holocaust." *Prologue* 13 (Fall, 1981): 145–73.

———. *The Swastika's Darkening Shadow: Voices before the Holocaust.* New York: Palgrave Macmillan, 2013.

Penslar, Derek J. *Jews and the Military: A History.* Princeton, NJ: Princeton University Press, 2013.

Piekarz, Mendel. *Ḥasidut Polin: Megamot Ra'ayaniyot bein Shetei haMilḥamot uviGezerot TaSh – TaShHeh ("HaSho'ah")* [Idealogical Trends of Hasidism in Poland During the Interwar Period and the Holocaust]. Jerusalem: Mossad Bialik 1990.

Plaut, W. Gunther. *The Growth of Reform Judaism: American and European Sources Until 1948*. New York: World Union for Progressive Judaism, 1965.

Poland: Ministry of Information. *The Black Book of Poland*. New York: G.P. Putnam's Sons, 1942.

Poliakov, Léon. *L'Étoile jaune*. Paris, Éditions du Centre, 1949.

Polonsky, Antony. *The Jews in Russia and Poland*, vol. 3. Oxford: Littman Library, 2012.

Poznanski, Renée. *Jews in France during World War II*, translated by Nathan Bracher. Hanover and London: University Press of New England, 2001.

Proceedings of the Rabbinical Assembly of America, vol. 5 (1938); vol. 7 (1940), vol. 8 (1944). Philadelphia, JPS.

Rabinbach, Anson and Sander L. Gilman, eds., *The Third Reich: Sourcebook*. Berkeley, CA: University of California Press, 2013.

Rauschning, Hermann. *The Voice of Destruction*. New York: G.P. Putnam's Sons, 1940.

Reitlinger, Gerald. *The Final Solution: The Attempt to Exterminate the Jews of Europe, 1939*–1945. New York: Beechhurst Press, 1953.

Reports of the World Jewish Congress (British Section). London: British Section of the World Jewish Congress, 1942–1946.

Rigal, Lawrence and Rosita Rosenberg, *Liberal Judaism: The First Hundred Years*. London: Liberal Judaism, 2004.

Ringelblum, Emmanuel. *Notes from the Warsaw Ghetto: The Journal of Emmanuel Ringelblum*, edited and translated by Jacob Sloan. New York: McGraw-Hill, 1958.

Robison, Jacob. *Uprooted Jews in the Immediate Post-War World*. New York: Institute of Jewish Affairs of the American Jewish Congress and World Jewish Congress,1943.

Rosenbaum, Irving J. *The Holocaust and Halakhah*. New York: KTAV, 1976.

Rosenberg, Bernhard H. and Fred Heuman, eds. *Theological and Halakhic Reflections on the Holocaust*. Hoboken: KTAV, and New York: Rabbinical Council of America, 1992.

Roskies, David. G., ed. *The Literature of Destruction: Jewish Responses to Catastrophe*. Philadelphia: JPS, 1988.

Ross, Robert. *So It Was True: The American Protestant Press and Nazi Persecution of the Jews*. Minneapolis: University of Minnesota Press, 1980.

Roth, Cecil. *A History of the Marranos*. Philadelphia: JPS, 1932.

Ruppin, Arthur. *The Jewish Fate and Future*, translated by E.W. Dickes. London: Macmillan, 1940.

Saperstein, Marc. *Jewish Preaching in Times of War: 1800–2001*. Oxford: Littman Library, 2008.

———. "Christian Doctrine and the 'Final Solution': The State of the Question," in *Remembering for the Future: The Holocaust in an Age of Genocide*, edited by John K. Roth and Elisabeth Maxwell, 3 vols. New York: Palgrave, 2001, 2:814–41.

———. "'Normative Judaism' in the Crisis of War: Sermons by Abraham Cohen and Israel Mattuck," in *'Normative Judaism?' Jews, Judaism, and Jewish Identity*, edited by Daniel Langton and Philip Alexander. Piscataway, NJ: Gorgias Press, 2012, pp. 52–65.

———. "Sermons and History: The 'Marrano' Connection to *Kol Nidre*," in *All These Vows: Kol Nidre,* edited by Lawrence Hoffman. Woodstock, VT: Jewish Lights, 2011, pp. 31–38.

———. *"Your Voice Like a Ram's Horn": Themes and Texts in Traditional Jewish Preaching*. Cincinnati: Hebrew Union College Press, 1996.

Schäfer, Peter. *Jesus in the Talmud*. Princeton and Oxford: Princeton University Press, 2007.

Schenderlein, Anne Clara. "Making German History in Los Angeles: German Jewish Refugees and West German Diplomats in the 1950s and 1960s." *Jewish Culture and History* 17:1–2 (2016): 133–51.

Schindler, Pesach. *Hasidic Responses to the Holocaust in the Light of Hasidic Thought*. Hoboken, NJ: KTAV, 1990.

Scholder, Klaus. *The Churches and the Third Reich*. Philadelphia: Fortress Press, 1988.

Scholem, Gershom. *Major Trends in Jewish Mysticism*. New York: Schocken Books, 1941.

Schwartz, Yoel and Yitzhak Goldstein. *Shoah: A Jewish Perspective on Tragedy in the Context of the Holocaust*. New York: Mesorah Publications, 1990.

Schwarz, Jordan A. *The Speculator: Bernard Baruch in Washington 1917–1965*. Chapel Hill: University of North Carolina Press, 1981.

Segel, Benjamin W. *Die Protokolle der Weisen von Zion, kritisch beleuchtet*. Berlin: Philo Verlag, 1924.

———. *Welt-Krieg, Welt-Revolution, Welt-Verschwörung, Welt-Oberregierung*. Berlin, 1926; translated as *The Protocols of the Elders of Zion: The Greatest Lie in History*. New York: Bloch Publishing Co., 1934.

Segev, Zohar. *The World Jewish Congress during the Holocaust: Between Activism and Restraint*. Berlin: De Gruyter, 2014.

Seidman, Hillel. *The Warsaw Ghetto Diaries*, translated from Hebrew by Yosef Israel. Southfield, MI and Jerusalem: Targum Press, 1997.

Shapiro, Robert Moses, ed. *Holocaust Chronicles: Individualizing the Holocaust through Diaries and Other Contemporaneous Personal Accounts*. Hoboken, NJ: KTAV, 1999.

———. *Why Didn't the Press Shout?: American and International Journalism During the Holocaust*. New York: Yeshiva University Press, 2003.

Sharf, Andrew. *The British Press and Jews Under Nazi Rule*. London: Oxford University Press, 1964.

Sheean, Vincent. *Not Peace But a Sword*. New York: Doubleday, Doran & Company, 1939.

Shirer, William L. *The Collapse of the Third Republic: An Inquiry into the Fall of France in 1940*. New York: Simon and Schuster, 1969.

Shub, Boris. *Starvation Over Europe (Made in Germany): A Documented Record, 1943*, based on research by Z. Warhaftig. New York: Institute of Jewish Affairs of the American Jewish Congress and the World Jewish Congress, 1943.

Skiles, William S. "Protests from the Pulpit: The Confessing Church and the Sermons of World War II." *Sermon Studies* 1,1 (2017): 1–23, http://mds.marshall.edu/sermonstudies/vol1/iss1/1.

Snyder, Timothy. *Black Earth: The Holocaust as History and Warning*. New York: Tim Duggan Books, 2015.

———. *Bloodlands: Europe Between Hitler and Stalin*. New York: Basic Books, 2010.

Soloveitchik, Joseph Dov. "Kol Dodi Dofek," translated in *Fate and Destiny: From the Holocaust to the State of Israel*. Hoboken, NJ: KTAV, 2000.

Sombart, Werner. *The Jews in Modern Capitalism*. New York: E.P. Dutton, 1914.

Spear, Sheldon. "The United States and the Persecution of the Jews in Germany, 1933–1939." *Jewish Social Studies* (October, 1968): 215–42.

Spivak, John Louis. *America Faces the Barricades*. New York: Covici-Friede, 1935.

Stein, Alexander. *Adolf Hitler. Schüler der "Weisen von Zion."* Karlsbad: Graphia, 1936.

Stewart, Herbert. *Nietzsche and the Ideals of Modern Germany*. London: Edward Arnold, 1915.

Strasser, Otto. *Hitler and I*, translated by Gwenda David and Eric Mosbacher. Boston, MA: Houghton and Mifflin, 1940.

Strauss, Herbert A. and Kurt T. Grossman. *Gegenwart im Rückblick: Festgabe für die Jüdische Gemeinde au Berlin 25 Jahre nach dem Neubeginn*. Heidelberg: Lothar Stiehm Verlag, 1970.

Stroud, Dean G., ed. *Preaching in Hitler's Shadow: Sermons of Resistance in the Third Reich*. Grand Rapids, MI; Cambridge, UK: William B. Eerdman's Publishing Company, 2013.

Thomas, Gordon and Max Morgan-Witts, *The Voyage of the Damned: A Shocking True Story of Hope, Betrayal and Nazi Terror*. New York: Stein and Day, 1974.

Thompson, Mark. *Enough Said: What's Gone Wrong with the Language of Politics*. New York: St. Martin's Press, 2016.

Thurlow, Richard C. *Fascism in Britain: A History, 1918–1985*. Oxford, UK and New York, NY: Blackwell, 1987.

Tomlin, Chanan. *Protest and Prayer: Rabbi Dr. Solomon Schonfeld and Orthodox Jewish Response in Britain to the Nazi Persecution of Europe's Jews*. Oxford: Peter Lang, 2006.

Trunk, Isaiah. *Jewish Responses to Nazi Persecution*. New York: Stein and Day, 1979.

———. *Judenrat: The Jewish Councils in Eastern Europe Under Nazi Occupation*. Introduction by Jacob Robinson. New York: Macmillan, 1972.

Tulchinsky, Gerald. "'Justice and Only Justice Thou Shalt Pursue': Considerations on the Social Voice of Canada's Reform Rabbis," in *Religion and Public Life in Canada*, edited by Marguerite Van Die. Toronto: University of Toronto Press, 2001, pp. 313–28.

UAHC, 1941, Sixty-Seventh Annual Report.

Ulmer, Rivka. *Ayin haRa: The Evil Eye in the Bible and in Rabbinic Literature*. Hoboken, NJ: KTAV, 1994.

van Paassen, Pierre. *The Days of Our Years*. New York: Hillman-Curl, 1939.

van Paassen, Pierre and James Waterman Wise, eds., *Nazism: An Assault on Civilization*. New York: H. Smith and R. Haas, 1934.

Vilhjálmsson, Vilhjálmur Örn. "The King and the Star: Myths Created During the Occupation of Denmark," in *Denmark and the Jews*, edited by Mette Bastholm Jensen and Steven L.B. Jensen. Copenhagen: Institute for International Studies, Department for Holocaust and Genocide Studies, 2003, pp. 102–117.

Waite, Robert G. "'Raise My Voice Against Intolerance': The Anti-Nazi Rally in Madison Square Garden, March 27, 1933, and the American Public's

Outrage over the Nazi Persecution of Jews," *New York History Review* (Blog Archive, October 20, 2013), http://bit.ly/2xPYeld.
Walker, James. "Claiming Equality for Canadian Jewry," in *Nazi Germany, Canadian Responses: Confronting Antisemitism in the Shadow of War,* edited by Ruth Klein. Montreal: McGill-Queen's University Press, 2012, pp. 218–62.
Wallace, Max. *The American Axis: Henry Ford, Charles Lindbergh, and the Rise of the Third Reich.* New York: St. Martin's, 2003.
Wasserman, Jakob. *My Life as German and Jew,* translated by S.N. Brainin. New York: Coward-McCann, 1933.
Wasserstein, Bernard. "Patterns of Jewish Leadership in Great Britain During the Nazi Era," in *Jewish Leadership During the Nazi Era*, edited by Randolph Braham, pp. 29–44.
Weinreich, Max. *Hitler's Professors: The Part of Scholarship in Germany's Crimes Against the Jewish People*, 2nd ed. New Haven, CT: Yale University Press, 1999.
Weisbord, Robert G. and Wallace P. Sillanpoa. *The Chief Rabbi, the Pope, and the Holocaust.* New Brunswick and London: Transaction Publishers, 1992.
Wells, H.G. *The New and Revised Outline of History: Being a Plain History of Life and Mankind.* Garden City, NY: Garden City Publishing Company, 1931.
Werner, Emmy E. *A Conspiracy of Decency: The Rescue of the Danish Jews During World War II.* Boulder, CO and London: Westview Press, 2002.
Wiesel, Elie. *Against Silence: The Voice and Vision of Elie Wiesel*, edited by Irving Abrahamson, 3 vols. New York: Holocaust Library, 1985.
Wilhelm, Cornelia. "German Refugee Rabbis in the United States." *European Judaism* 45:2 (Autumn 2012): 78–89.
Wise, James W. *Swastika: The Nazi Terror.* New York: H. Smith and R. Haas, 1933.
Wistrich, Robert. *Routledge Who's Who in Nazi Germany*. London: Routledge, 1995.
Wolf, Lucien. *The Myth of the Jewish Menace in World Affairs, or The Truth About the Forged Protocols of the Elders of Zion*. New York: Macmillan, 1921.
Wyman, David S. *The Abandonment of the Jews.* New York: Pantheon, 1984.
Wyman, David S. and Rafael Medoff. *A Race Against Death: Peter Bergson, America, and the Holocaust.* New York: The New Press, 2002.
Yahil, Leni. *The Rescue of Danish Jewry*. Philadelphia: JPS, 1969.
———.*The Holocaust: The Fate of European Jewry, 1932–1945*. New York: Oxford University Press, 1990.
Yedidyah, Asaf, Nathan Cohen, and Esther Farbstein, eds. *Zikkaron baSefer: Korot haSho'ah baMevo'ot leSifrut Rabbanit* [Remembrance in the Book:

Holocaust Events in the Introductions to Works of Rabbinic Literature]. Jerusalem: Reuven Mass, 2008.

The Yellow Spot: The Outlawing Half a Million Human Beings, a Collection of Facts and Documents Relating to Three Years Persecution of German Jews, Derived Chiefly from National Socialist Sources, Very Carefully Assembled by a Group of Investigators. Introduction by the Bishop of Durham. London, 1936. London: v. Gollancz, Ltd., and New York: Knight, 1936.

Zajdband, Astrid. *German Rabbis in British Exile: From 'Heimat' into the Unknown.* Berlin: De Gruyter Oldenbourg, 2016.

Zelkowicz, Josef. *In diesen albtraumhaften Tagen: Tagebuchaufzeichnungen aus dem Getto Lodz/Litzmanstadt, September 1942*, edited by Angela Genger et al., translated from the Yiddish by Susan Hiep. Göttingen: Wallstein Verlag, 2015.

Zimmels, H.J. *The Echo of the Nazi Holocaust in Rabbinic Literature.* s.l.: s.n., 1975.

Zuccotti, Susan. *Under His Very Windows: The Vatican and the Holocaust in Italy.* New Haven, CT: Yale University Press, 2002.

Zylberberg, Michael. *A Warsaw Diary, 1939–1945.* London: Vallentine Mitchell, 1969.

RABBIS CITED (BY COUNTRY) (SOME DUPLICATE LISTINGS)

Austria

David Feuchtwang, Vienna, Austria (Orthodox)

Bulgaria

Asher Hananel, Sophia, Bulgaria (Orthodox)
Daniel Zion, Sofia, Bulgaria (Orthodox)

Canada

Maurice N. Eisendrath, Toronto, Canada (Reform)
Harry Joshua Stern, Montreal, Canada (Reform)

Denmark

Marcus Melchior, Copenhagen, Denmark (Orthodox)

England

Israel Abrahams, Manchester, England (Orthodox)
Alexander Altmann, Manchester, England (Orthodox)
Eliezer Berkovits, Leeds, England (Orthodox)
Abraham Cohen, Birmingham, England (Orthodox)
Samuel Daiches, London (Orthodox)

Leslie Edgar, London (Liberal)
Emil Ehrnthal (later Michael Elton), Bognor Regis, England; London (Orthodox)
Solomon Fisch, Sheffield, England (Orthodox)
Joseph H. Hertz, London (Orthodox)
Gatchell Isaacs, London (Orthodox)
Ephraim Levine, London (Orthodox)
Raphael H. Levine, London (Liberal)
Israel Mattuck, London (Liberal)
Ignaz Maybaum, London (Reform)
D[avid] Bueno de Mesquita, London (Orthodox)
M.L. Perlzweig, London (Orthodox)
Harold Reinhart, London (Reform)
Kopul Rosen, Manchester, England (Orthodox)
A.S. Super, Leeds, England (Orthodox)
Harris Swift, London (Orthodox)

France

Moses Kahlenberg, Metz – La Lande Internment Camp, France (Orthodox)
Jacob Kaplan, Paris – Vichy – Lyon, France (Orthodox)
Nathan Netter, Metz – Vichy – Avignon, France (Orthodox)

Galicia

Raphael Yehezkel Hochberg, Gliniani, Eastern Galicia (Orthodox)

Germany

Leo Baeck, Berlin, Germany (Reform)
Julius Cohn, Ulm, Germany (Reform)
Max Dienemann, Offenbach, Germany (Reform)
Abraham Joshua Heschel, Frankfurt-am-Main, Germany (Orthodox/Conservative)
Bruno Italiener, Hamburg, Germany (Reform)
Ignaz Maybaum, Frankfurt-an-der-Oder, Germany (Reform)
Hermann Neumark [later Yehoshua Amir], Wuppertal, Germany (Reform)
Werner van der Zyl, Berlin, Germany (Reform)

Hungary

Mordechai (Mottl) Rokeach of Biłgoraj, Budapest, Hungary (Orthodox)
Gavriel Gestetner, Szombathely, Hungary (Orthodox)

Yissachar Shlomo Teichthal, Budapest, Hungary (Orthodox)

Ireland

Isaac Herzog, Dublin, Ireland (Orthodox)

Italy

Israel Zolli, Rome, Italy (Orthodox?)

Palestine

Isaac Herzog, Jerusalem (Orthodox)
Abraham Isaac Kook, Jerusalem (Orthodox)
Judah L. Magnes, Jerusalem (Reform)
Ben-Zion Meir Ouziel/Uzziel, Jerusalem (Orthodox)
Yehezkel Sarna, Jerusalem (Orthodox)
Ephraim Sokolover, Ra'anana, Palestine (Orthodox)

Poland

Kalman Chameides, Katowice, Poland (Orthodox)
Zelig Kalmanovich, Vilna, Poland/Lithuania (Orthodox)
Yitzhak Katz, Warsaw, Poland (Orthodox)
Shabbetai Rapoport, Pinczów, Poland (Orthodox)
Kalonymus Kalman Shapira, Warsaw, Poland (Orthodox)

Scotland

Salis Daiches, Edinburgh, Scotland (Orthodox)

Slovakia

Armin (Avraham Ada) Frieder, Nové Mesto, Bratislava, Slovakia (Orthodox)
Shelomoh Zalman Unsdorfer, Bratislava, Slovakia (Orthodox)

South Africa

Louis Rabinowitz, Johannesburg, South Africa (Orthodox)
Israel Abrahams; Cape Town, South Africa
Hirsch Woolf, Pretoria, South Africa (Orthodox)

Sweden

Marcus Ehrenpreis, Stockholm, Sweden (Orthodox)

Transylvania

Shlomo Zalman Ehrenreich, Simleul-Silvaniei, Transylvania (Orthodox)

United States (23 states)

Bertram Korn, Mobile, AL (Reform)

Samuel Teitelbaum, Fort Smith, AR (Reform)

Max Nussbaum, Hollywood, CA (Reform)
Irving F. Reichert, San Francisco, CA (Reform)

Abraham L. Feinberg, Denver, CO (Reform)here

Abraham J. Feldman, Hartford, CT (Reform)

David Polish, Waterbury, CT (Reform)

Jacob Kraft, Wilmington, DE (Conservative)

Abraham A. Kellner, Miami, FL (Orthodox)

Harry H. Epstein, Atlanta, GA (Conservative)
Tobias Geffen, Atlanta, GA (Orthodox)

Abraham H. Feinberg, Rockford, IL (Reform)
Solomon Goldman, Chicago, IL (Conservative)
Felix A. Levy, Chicago, IL (Reform)
Louis L. Mann, Chicago, IL (Reform)
Charles E. Shulman, Glencoe, IL (Reform)

Solomon N. Bazell, Louisville, KY (Reform)
Milton L. Grafman, Lexington, KY (Reform)

Julian B. Feibelman, New Orleans, LA (Reform)

Beryl D. Cohon, Brookline, MA (Reform)
Joshua Loth Liebman, Boston, MA (Reform)
Mendell Lewittes, Dorchester, MA (Orthodox)
Walter Wuerzburger, Brighton, MA (Orthodox)
Morris S. Lazaron, Baltimore, MD (Reform)

Solomon Rosenblatt, Baltimore, MD (Orthodox)

Leo M. Franklin, Detroit, MI (Reform)
Abraham M. Hershman, Detroit, MI (Conservative)

Julius Gordon, St. Louis, MO (Reform)
Abraham E. Halpern, St. Louis, MO (Conservative)
Ferdinand M. Isserman, St. Louis, MO (Reform)
Ernest I. Jacob, Springfield, MO (Reform)
Julian Miller, St. Louis, MO (Reform)
Phineas Smoller, Joplin, MO (Reform)

Solomon Foster, Newark, NJ (Reform)
Leon S. Lang, Newark, NJ (Conservative)

Louis M. Levitsky, Newark, NJ (Conservative)
Joachim Prinz, Livingston, NJ (Reform)

Charles J. Abeles, New York, NY (Conservative?)
Jacob Bosniak, Brooklyn, NY (Conservative)
Aaron David Burack, Brooklyn, NY (Orthodox)
Jacob X. Cohen, New York, NY (Reform)
Ira Eisenstein, New York, NY (Reconstructionist)
Roland B Gittelsohn, Rockville Center, NY (Reform)
Samuel H. Goldenson, New York, NY (Reform)
Israel Goldstein, New York, NY (Conservative)
Louis Hammer, Brooklyn, NY (Conservative)
Abraham Mayer Heller, Brooklyn, NY (Conservative)
Jacob Hoffman, New York, NY (Orthodox)
David B. Hollander, Bronx, NY (Orthodox)
Leo Jung, New York, NY (Orthodox)
Abraham A. Kellner, Albany, NY (Orthodox)
Edward Klein, New York, NY (Reform)
Israel Levinthal, Brooklyn, NY (Conservative)
Joseph H. Lookstein, New York, NY (Orthodox)
Alexander Lyons, Brooklyn, NY (Reform)
Elias Margolis, Mount Vernon, NY (Conservative)
Louis I. Newman, New York, NY (Reform)
David de Sola Pool, New York, NY (Orthodox)
Akiba Predmesky, Bronx, NY (Orthodox)
Mnachem Risikoff, Brooklyn, NY (Orthodox)
Jacob P. Rudin, Great Neck, NY (Reform)
Harold I. Saperstein, Lynbrook, NY (Reform)
Sidney S. Tedesche, Brooklyn, NY (Reform)
James Waterman Wise, New York, NY (Reform)
Jonah B. Wise, New York, NY (Reform)
Stephen S. Wise, New York, NY (Reform)

Barnett Brickner, Cleveland, OH (Reform)
Samuel S. Cohon, Cincinnati, OH; Wichita, KA (Reform)
James G. Heller, Cincinnati, OH (Reform)
David Philipson, Cincinnati, OH (Reform)
Abba Hillel Silver, Cleveland, OH (Reform)

Max Nussbaum, Muskogee, OK (Reform)

Max Arzt, Scranton, PA (Conservative)
Max C. Currick, Erie, PA (Reform)
Solomon B. Freehof, Pittsburgh, PA (Reform)
Simon Greenberg, Philadelphia, PA (Conservative)
Louis Wolsey, Philadelphia, PA (Reform)

Israel Gerstein, Chattanooga, TN (Orthodox)

Ephraim Frisch, San Antonio, TX (Reform)

Edward N. Calisch, Richmond, VA (Reform)

Wales

H. Jerevitch, Cardiff, Wales (Orthodox)

Index to Rabbis and Dates of Included Sermons

Dates with Bold Type Indicate Complete Sermons

Charles J. Abeles, New York, NY (Conservative)
Sept. 14, 1939

Israel Abrahams, Manchester, England; Cape Town, South Africa (Orthodox)
July 3, 1937
May 17, 1942
Aug. 23, 1942
Oct. 25, 1942
Dec. 6 and 29, 1942
Jan. 24, 1943

Alexander Altmann, Manchester, England (Orthodox)
Sept. 10, 1934
Nov. 20, 1938
Dec. 4 and 18, 1938
Oct. 15, 1939
May 26, 1940
March 23, 1941
Sept. 3, 1942
Dec. 14, 1942
May 14, 1945

Max Arzt, Scranton, PA (Conservative)
June 25, 1940

Leo Baeck, Berlin, Germany (Reform)
Oct. 6–7, 1935

Solomon N. Bazell, Louisville, KY (Reform)
June 28, 1941

Eliezer Berkovits, Leeds, England (Orthodox)
June 15, 1940
Dec. 14, 1940
March 8, 1941
April 12, 1941
May 17(?), 1941
July 26, 1941
Aug. 16, 1941
Sept. 7 and 22, 1941
Nov. 8, 1941
Dec. 13, 1941
April 2, 1942
May 22, 1942
Aug. 29, 1942
Sept. 12 and 26, 1942
Dec. 13, 1942
June 9, 1943
Oct. 9, 1943

Jacob Bosniak, Brooklyn, NY (Conservative)
Sept. 5, 1936
Sept. 13, 14 and 22 1939
May 10, 1940

Sept. 30, 1941
Jan. 2, 1942

Barnett Brickner, Cleveland, OH (Reform)
March 13, 1937
April 4, 1943

Aaron David Burack, Brooklyn, NY (Orthodox)
Sept. 21, 1933
Sept. 30, 1943

Edward N. Calisch, Richmond, VA (Reform)
Nov. 24, 1938

Kalman Chameides, Katowice, Poland (Orthodox)
Nov. 11, 1933
July 19(?), 1935
Aug. 8, 1935

Abraham Cohen, Birmingham, England (Orthodox)
Jan. 3, 1937
Nov. 20, 1938
Aug. 26, 1939
Sept. 14, 1939
Sept. 8, 1940
Oct. 3, 1940
Aug. 23, 1941
Oct. 1, 1941
March 29, 1942
Sept. 3, 1942
April 26, 1943
June 6, 1943
Sept. 26, 1944
May 13, 1945

Jacob X. Cohen, New York, NY (Reform)
Feb. 14, 1932

Julius Cohn, Ulm, Germany (Reform)
April 4, 1939

Beryl D. Cohon, Brookline, MA (Reform)
Sept. 18, 1944

Samuel S. Cohon, Cincinnati, OH; Wichita, KA (Reform)
May, 1934
Sept. 21, 1941
Sept. 7, 1945

Max C. Currick, Erie, PA (Reform)
Oct. 3, 1940

Salis Daiches, Edinburgh, Scotland (Orthodox)
July 29, 1933
Nov. 6, 1933
Feb. 16, 1935
Sept. 10, 1938
Nov. 20, 1938
March 4, 1939
May 25, 1939
Sept. 9, 1939
Sept. 3, 1943

Samuel Daiches, London (Orthodox)
March 2, 1934
March 18, 1938
Nov. 27, 1938
Sept. 3, 1944
Aug. 19, 1945
Aug. 2, 1947

Max Dienemann, Offenbach, Germany (Reform)
March 1, 1934

Leslie Edgar, London (Liberal)
Nov. 20, 1938

Marcus Ehrenpreis, Stockholm, Sweden (Orthodox)
April 11, 1933
Sept. 16–17, 1945

Shlomo Zalman Ehrenreich, Simleul-Silvaniei, Transylvania (Orthodox)
April 9, 1938
Feb. 26, 1939
April 17, 1943
Oct. 2, 21 and 22, 1943

Emil Ehrnthal (later Michael Elton), Bognor Regis, England; London (Orthodox)
May 26, 1940
June 9, 1940
March 23, 1941
Dec. 13, 1942
Jan. 2, 1943
Sept. 3, 1943
April 1, 1944
June 11, 1944
Sept. 18, 1944

Maurice N. Eisendrath, Toronto, Canada (Reform)
Feb. 14, 1932
Sept. 30, 1933
Nov. 19, 1933
Dec. 10, 24 and 31, 1933
Dec. 23, 1934
Feb. 24, 1935
Nov. 10, 17 and 24, 1935
Sept. 26, 1936
Feb. 14. 1937
April 4(?), 1937
May 29, 1937
Oct. 4, 1938
Nov. 20, 1938
May 26, 1940
Nov. 3, 1940
Dec. 8 and 29, 1940
Jan. 12, 1941
Feb. 23, 1941
April 27, 1941
Sept. 21, 1941
Dec. 7, 1941
Nov. 1 and 8, 1942
March 27, 1943
March 31, 1944
Sept. 17, 1944

Ira Eisenstein, New York, NY (Reconstructionist)
Sept. 15, 1939

Harry H. Epstein, Atlanta, GA (Conservative)
Sept. 21 and 22, 1933

Julian B. Feibelman, New Orleans, LA (Reform)
March 5, 1939
April 2, 1939
March 21, 1943
March 12, 1944
April 23, 1944

Abraham H. Feinberg, Rockford, IL (Reform)
April 7, 1933
April 18, 1934
Nov. 10, 1934
Sept. 27, 1935
Oct. 4, 1938
Sept. 13, 1939

Abraham L. Feinberg, Denver, CO (Reform)
Sept. 12, 1942

Abraham J. Feldman, Hartford, CT (Reform)
Oct. 1, 1932
Sept. 20, 1933
March 18, 1934
March 14, 1937
Sept. 16, 1945

David Feuchtwang, Vienna, Austria (Orthodox)
Sept. 27, 1935

Solomon Fisch, Sheffield, England (Orthodox)
Jan. 23, 1938

Solomon Foster, Newark, NJ (Reform)
September 13, 1939

Ephraim Frisch, San Antonio, TX (Reform)
Sept. 13, 1939

Leo M. Franklin, Detroit, MI (Reform)
April 2, 9, 16, and 24, 1933
Sept. 20 and 21, 1933
Nov. 26, 1933
Sept. 25, 1938
Nov. 25, 1938
Sept. 13, 1939
May 3 and 31, 1940
June 7, 1940
Oct. 3, 1940
Sept. 21, 1941
Dec. 14, 1941

Solomon B. Freehof, Pittsburgh, PA (Reform)
Feb. 24, 1935
Dec. 13, 1936
April 4, 1937
Dec. 18, 1938
Jan. 22 and 29, 1939
April 23, 1939
April 6, 13 and 27, 1941
April 5 and 26, 1942
Feb. 21, 1943
Feb. 6, 1944
March 12, 1944
June 23, 1944
March 11, 1945

Armin (Avraham Ada) Frieder, Nové Mesto, Slovakia (Orthodox)
March 14, 1942
Sept. 30, 1943

Gatchell Isaacs, London (Orthodox)
April 7, 1933

Tobias Geffen, Atlanta, GA (Orthodox)
Dec. 12, 1933
April 18, 1935
Nov. 19, 1938

Israel Gerstein, Chattanooga, TN (Orthodox)
Jan. 12, 1935
Oct. 4, 1940
Dec. 20, 1940
Jan. 17, 1941
Feb. 14, 1941
March 25, 1941
Oct. 1 and 17, 1941
Jan. 23, 1942
March 3 and 13, 1942
Sept. 13, 1942

Gavriel Gestetner, Szombathely, Hungary (Orthodox)
Oct. 2, 1940
Sept. 14, 1941

Roland B Gittelsohn, Rockville Center, NY (Reform)
Oct. 21, 1938

Samuel H. Goldenson, New York, NY (Reform)
March 1, 1934
June 14, 1934
Feb. 7, 1937
April 3, 1937
Jan. 23, 1938
May 28, 1938
Nov. 27, 1938
Feb. 26, 1939
March 5, 1939
Feb. 4, 1940

Solomon Goldman, Chicago, IL (Conservative)
Jan. 12, 1936
April 24, 1938
Dec. 16, 1938

April 7 and 20, 1939

Israel Goldstein, New York, NY (Conservative)
Jan. 20, 1935
Oct. 1 and 4, 1938
Jan. 19, 1939
May 14, 1939
April 23, 1940
May 20, 1940
June 1, 1940
Sept. 30, 1943

Julius Gordon, St. Louis, MO (Reform)
Nov. 18, 1938
April 29, 1941
June 25, 1943

Milton L. Grafman, Lexington, KY (Reform)
March 2–3, 1942

Simon Greenberg, Philadelphia, PA (Conservative)
June 27, 1938

Abraham E. Halpern, St. Louis, MO (Conservative)
April 6, 1934
Oct. 3, 1940
Sept. 19, 1944
April 29, 1945

Louis Hammer, Brooklyn, NY (Conservative)
Sept. 12, 1942
Sept. 30, 1943
Oct. 1, 1943

Asher Hananel, Sophia, Bulgaria (Orthodox)
May 24, 1943

Abraham Mayer Heller, Brooklyn, NY (Conservative)
May 20, 1934
Sept. 17, 1936
March 17, 1938
April 16, 1938
July 4, 1939

James G. Heller, Cincinnati, OH (Reform)
Feb. 24, 1942

Abraham M. Hershman, Detroit, MI (Conservative)
Nov. 2, 1940
Sept. 22, 1941
Dec. 19, 1941
April 2 and 9, 1942
Sept 19, 1942
Oct. 9, 1943
Jan. 15 and 22, 1944
Feb. 19, 1944
Sept. 19, 1944
Oct. 8, 1944
Dec. 30, 1944
Feb. 24, 1945
April 5, 1945

Joseph H. Hertz, London (Orthodox)
April 11, 1933
July 9, 1933
April 6, 1934
July 2, 1934
May 28, 1935
June 5, 1938
July 17, 1938
Nov. 20, 1938
Dec. 1, 1938
Sept. 3, 1940
March 23, 1941
Sept. 7, 1941
April 2 and 6, 1942
May 22, 1942
Sept. 20, 1942
Dec. 13, 1942
March 1, 1943
May 16, 1943
May 22, 1944

Abraham Joshua Heschel, Frankfurt-am-Main, Germany (Orthodox/Conservative)
Feb. 27, 1938

Isaac Herzog, Dublin, Ireland (Orthodox)
May 18 and 31, 1933
April 1, 1934
Sept. 17, 25 and 26 , 1936
Jan. 1, 1939
Feb. 15, 1939
June 27, 1942
Nov. 30, 1942
Jan. 11, 1943
May 3, 1943
April 19, 1944
June 5, 1944
Jan. 30, 1945
March 14, 1945

Woolf Hirsch, Pretoria, SA (Orthodox)
Feb. 1, 1934
March (?), 1937
March 10, 1938
Jan. 1, 1945
Feb. 5, 1945

Jacob Hoffman, New York, NY (Orthodox)
Jan 1, 1942

Raphael Yehezkel Hochberg, Gliniani, Eastern Galicia (Orthodox)
March 27, 1933

David. B. Hollander, Bronx, NY (Orthodox)
Oct. 1, 1944

Ferdinand M. Isserman, St. Louis, MO (Reform)
Feb. 28, 1933
March 24, 27 and 31, 1933
April 7, 11 and 28, 1933
Sept. 20 and 29, 1933
Oct. 20 and 27, 1933
Dec. 29, 1933
Feb. 16, 1934
March 2, 1934
May 16, 1934
Sept. 18 and 19, 1934
Dec. 28, 1934
March 22, 1935
Oct. 6 and **25, 1935**
Dec. 6 and 20, 1935
Jan. 10, 1936
March 20, 1936
May 1, 1936
Aug. 9, 1936
Sept. 25, 1936
Dec. 11, 1936
Jan. 1, 1937
April 2, 1937
Sept. 5, 1937
Oct. 29, 1937
Feb. 4 and 25, 1938
March 11, 18 and 25, 1938
May 26, 1938
Sept. 25, 1938
Oct. 4, 21 and 28, 1938
Nov. 18 and 25, 1938
Dec. 2, 16 and 30, 1938
Feb. 3, 1939
March 17, 1939
April 28, 1939
May 12, 1939
Sept. 13, 1939
Oct. 20, 1939
Dec. 1, 1939
Jan. 5, 1940
April 5, 12 and 26, 1940
June 21, 1940
Oct. 12, 1940
Nov. 29, 1940
Dec. 13, 1940
March 14, 1941
April 4, 1941
May 23, 1941
Sept. 21, 1941

Dec. 12, 1941
Sept. 11 and 21, 1942
Jan. 24, 1943
April 8, 1944
May 5, 1944
Sept. 26, 1944
Jan. 19, 1945
Sept. 7, 1945

Bruno Italiener, Hamburg, Germany (Reform)
Sept. 18 and 26, 1936

Ernest I. Jacob, Springfield, MO (Reform)
Feb. 21, 1942
Sept. 8, 1945

H. Jerevitch, Cardiff, Wales (Orthodox)
Sept. 14, 1939

Leo Jung, New York, NY (Orthodox)
Sept. 23, 1933
June 5, 1938
Dec. 17, 1938
Sept. 28, 1940
Oct. 3, 1940
March 29, 1945

Moses Kahlenberg, Metz, France; La Lande Internment Camp (Orthodox)
March 11, 1933
Sept. 23, 1933
March 23, 1936
Sept. 14 and 27, 1941
Oct. 1, 1941
Jan. 10, 1942
June 13, 1942

Zelig Kalmanovich, Vilna, Poland/Lithuania (Orthodox)
Oct. 11, 1942
Dec. 27, 1942
April 20, 1943

Jacob Kaplan, Paris – Vichy – Lyon, France (Orthodox)
April 11, 1933
Sept. 21 and 30, 1933
June 17, 1935
April 2, 1937
Jan. 22, 1938
Nov. 21, 1938
Nov 15 and 29, 1940
Dec. 13 and 27, 1940
April 19, 1941
Sept. 4, 1942
Oct. 23, 1942
March 27, 1943
Sept. 30, 1943
Nov. 5, 1943
Dec. 17, 1943
April 15, 1944
Sept. 15, 18 and 27, 1944
Oct. 8, 1944
July 2 and 13, 1945
Sept. 9, 1945

Yitzhak Katz, Warsaw, Poland (Orthodox)
Jan. 5, 1942

Abraham A. Kellner, Miami, FL; Albany, NY (Orthodox)
Oct. 5, 1939
April 27, 1943
Sept. 30, 1943
Oct. 1, 9 and 15, 1943
Dec. 25, 1943
April 8 and 9, 1944
Sept. 19 and 27, 1944
Sept. 8, 1945

Edward Klein, New York, NY (Reform)
Sept. 27, 1944

Abraham Isaac Kook, Jerusalem (Orthodox)
Sept. 21, 1933

Bertram Korn, Mobile AL (Reform)
Sept. 29, 1943

Jacob Kraft, Wilmington, DE (Conservative)
Sept. 15, 1939

Leon S. Lang, Newark, NJ (Conservative)
September 13, 1939

Morris S. Lazaron, Baltimore, MD (Reform)
June 25, 1936
July 3, 1938
Nov. 20, 1938

Ephraim Levine, London (Orthodox)
May 31, 1933
June 9, 1934

Raphael H. Levine, London (Liberal)
Sept. 13, 1939

Israel H. Levinthal, Brooklyn, NY (Conservative)
April 11, 1933
Sept. 22, 1933
Sept. 11, 1934
Dec. 22, 1934
Sept. 28, 1935
Oct. 6, 1935
Sept. 18, 1936
Oct. 8, 1936
Jan. 17, 1937
Sept. 15 and 20, 1937
Oct. 9, 1937
March 18, 1938
May 9, 1938
June 6, 1938
Sept. 27, 1938
Dec. 23, 1938
March 30, 1939
Sept. 14 and 15, 1939
Oct. 4 and 10, 1940
June 28, 1941
Sept. 22, 1941
Oct. 1, 1941
April 2, 3 and 11, 1942

Louis M. Levitsky, Newark, NJ (Conservative)
June 28, 1944

Felix A. Levy, Chicago, IL (Reform)
June 24, 1936
May 25, 1937

Mendell Lewittes, Dorchester MA (Orthodox)
Sept. 13, 1942

Joshua Loth Liebman, Boston, MA (Reform)
June 25, 1941

Joseph H. Lookstein, New York, NY (Orthodox)
January 3, 10 and 17, 1942

Alexander Lyons, Brooklyn, NY (Reform)
October 29, 1933

Judah L. Magnes, Jerusalem (Reform)
Nov. 5, 1933
Nov. 10, 1938
April 11, 1939
Oct. 29, 1939
Nov. 5, 1941
Nov. 24, 1942
Nov. 14, 1943
Nov. 1, 1944

Louis L. Mann, Chicago, IL (Reform)
Sept. 21, 1941
Sept. 29, 1943

Elias Margolis, Mount Vernon, NY (Conservative)
July 3, 1934

Israel Mattuck, London (Liberal)
Feb. 12, 1933
March 19 and 30, 1933

Sept. 21 and 30, 1933
Oct 8, 1933
Feb. 18, 1934
March 18, 1934
April 8, 1934
Sept. 8, 1934
Feb. 17, 1935
Oct. 20, 1935
March 15, 1936
April 7, 1936
Sept. 26, 1936
Feb. 28, 1937
July 17, 1938
Oct. 4 and 30, 1938
Sept. 14 and 28, 1939
Nov. 19, 1939
Oct. 11, 1940
Dec. 5, 1942
Sept. 18, 1944
Feb. 17, 1945
March 29, 1945
April 28, 1945
May 13, 1945
Aug. 19, 1945
Sept. 8, 1945

Ignaz Maybaum, Frankfurt-an-der-Oder, Germany; London (Reform)
Jan. 13, 1934
May 12 and 19, 1939
June 16 and 30, 1939
July 8, 14 and 21, 1939
Nov. 11, 1939
March 1, 1940
April 12,1940
July 27, 1940
Oct. 3 and 12, 1940
Nov. 16, 1940

Marcus Melchior, Copenhagen, Denmark (Orthodox)
Sept. 29, 1943

Zvi Hirsch Meisels, Auschwitz, Buchenwald (Orthodox)
Sept. 18, 1944
April 12, 1945

D[avid] Bueno de Mesquita, London (Orthodox)
July 17, 1938
March 23, 1941

Julian Miller, St. Louis, MO
Nov. 18, 1938

Nathan Netter, Metz – Vichy – Avignon, France (Orthodox)
Sept. 30, 1941
Sept. 21, 1942
May 9, 1945

Hermann Neumark [later Yehoshua Amir], Wuppertal, Germany (Reform)
Sept. 7, 1937

Morris Newfield, Birmingham, AL (Reform)
June 22, 1933

Louis I. Newman, New York, NY (Reform)
Nov. 12, 1933
Sept. 17, 1936
Feb. 25, 1939
July 13, 20 and 28, 1940
Oct. 3, 5 and 11, 1940
April 12, 19 and 26, 1941
Sept. 13, 21, 22 and 30, 1941
Oct. 1 and 4, 1941
Sept. 12, 20 and 26, 1942
Oct. 31, 1942
Jan. 30, 1943
June 26, 1943
Aug. 14 and 28, 1943
Nov. 27, 1943
Aug. 26, 1944
Sept. 9, 10, 17, 18, 24 and 27, 1944
Oct. 8, 1944

Max Nussbaum, Berlin, Germany; Muskogee, OK; Hollywood, CA (Reform)
- March 11, 1938
- Nov. 4, 1938
- April 5, 1939
- Oct. 21, 1939
- Nov. 11, 1939
- June 13, 1940
- Sept. 27, 1940
- Oct. 25, 1940
- April 29, 1941
- May 24, 1942
- Sept. 11, 1942
- Nov. 27, 1942
- Sept. 15, 1944

Ben-Zion Meir Ouziel/Uziel, Jerusalem (Orthodox)
- Nov. 11, 1942

M.L. Perlzweig, London (Orthodox)
- Nov. 20, 1932

David Philipson, Cincinnati, OH (Reform)
- March 12, 1933

David de Sola Pool, New York, NY (Orthodox)
- Nov. 30, 1934
- Sept. 14, 1939
- May 4, 1940
- Feb. 14, 1942
- Dec. 19, 1942
- April 20, 1943

David Polish, Waterbury, CT (Reform)
- Sept. 19, 1942

Akiba Predmesky, Bronx, NY (Orthodox)
- **Oct. 8, 1943**

Joachim Prinz, Livingston, NJ (Reform)
- Early–mid April, 1935
- Sept. 14, 1939

Louis Rabinowitz, Johannesburg, South Africa (Orthodox)
- March 10, 1945
- May 8, 1945
- Aug. 14, 1945

Shabbetai Rapoport, Pinczów, Poland (Orthodox)
- Feb. 23, 1936

Irving F. Reichert, San Francisco, CA (Reform)
- Sept. 20, 1933
- April 6, 13, 20 and 27, 1940
- Oct. 3 and 11. 1940
- May 1, 1943
- Sept. 29, 1943
- Oct. 8, 1943

Harold Reinhart, London (Reform)
- Sept. 29, 1933
- Nov. 11, 1933
- June 1, 1941

Mnachem Risikoff, Brooklyn, NY (Orthodox)
- March 5, 1939

Mordechai (Mottl) Rokeach of Biłgoraj, Budapest, Hungary (Orthodox)
- Jan. 16, 1944

Kopul Rosen, Manchester, England (Orthodox)
- Dec. 13, 1942

Samuel Rosenblatt, Baltimore, MD (Othodox)
- Sept. 27, 1938
- April 4, 1939
- Sept. 23, 1939
- Nov. 11, 1939

Jacob P. Rudin, Great Neck, NY (Reform)
Sept. 20, 1933
Oct. 3, 1940

Harold I. Saperstein, Lynbrook, NY (Reform)
April 28, 1933
Nov. 27, 1933
Sept. 10, 1934
Sept. 14, 1939
Oct. 2 and 3, 1940
Sept. 22, 1941
Sept. 11, 1942
Nov. 27, 1942
Sept. 17, 1944

Yehezkel Sarna, Jerusalem (Orthodox)
Dec. 4, 1944

Jacob Shachter, Belfast, North Ireland (Orthodox)
Sept. 10, 1934
Nov. 11, 1938

Kalonymus Kalmish Shapira, Warsaw, Poland (Orthodox)
Nov. 11, 1939
Jan. 20, 1940
March 23, 1940
April 13, 1940
Oct. 18, 1940
Dec. 14 and 21, 1940
July 26, 1941
Aug. 16, 1941
Sept. 13, 22 and 27, 1941
Dec. 15, 1941
Feb. 28, 1942
March 14, 1942
June 27, 1942
July 11, 1942

Charles E. Shulman, Glencoe, IL (Reform)
Oct. 3, 1940

Abba Hillel Silver, Cleveland, OH (Reform)
Oct. 21, 1935
March 8, 1936
April 11, 1936
May 23, 1936
March 7, 1937
Jan. 14 and 17, 1939
Feb. 19, 1939
March 18, 1939
June 14, 1939
Dec. 10, 1939
Jan. 21, 1940
Oct. 3, 1940
Dec. 22, 1940
Dec. 21, 1941
March 7, 1943
May 2, 1943
Sept. 1, 1943
March 21, 1944
Oct. 15, 1944
March 21, 1945

Phineas Smoller, Joplin, MO (Reform)
December 4, 1942

Ephraim Sokolover, Ra'anana, Palestine (Orthodox)
Sept. 14 and 15, 1939
April 20 and 29, 1940
Oct. 3, 1940
April 5 and 18, 1941
Sept. 22, 1941
March 28, 1942
Sept. 13, 1942
April 17, 1943
Oct. 1, 1943
April 1, 1944
Sept. 18, 1944

Milton Steinberg, New York, NY (Conservative)
Feb. 14, 1945

Harry Joshua Stern, Montreal, Canada (Reform)
- **April 6, 1933**
- Late August, 1934
- Nov. 20, 1938
- Sept. 13, 1939
- Jan. 12, 1940
- Aug. 9 (?), 1941
- Sept. 21, 1941
- Sept. 29, 1943
- Sept. 17, 1945

Harris Swift, London (Orthodox)
- Nov. 10, 1934
- April 24, 1935
- Nov. 23, 1935
- July 18, 1936
- Nov. 28, 1936
- May 8, 1937

A.S. Super, Leeds, England (Orthodox)
- Nov. 16 and 20, 1938

Sidney S. Tedesche, Brooklyn, NY (Reform)
- Oct. 11, 1940

Yissachar Shlomo Teichthal, Budapest, Hungary (Orthodox)
- April 24, 1943

Samuel Teitelbaum, Fort Smith, AR (Reform)
- Dec. 27, 1940

Shelomoh Zalman Unsdorfer, Slovakia (Orthodox)
- Jan. 3, 1942
- March 12, 1942
- Aug. 28, 1943

Werner Van der Zyl, Berlin, Germany, London (Reform)
- Feb. 17, 1938

James Waterman Wise, New York, NY (Reform)
- June 25, 1933

Jonah B. Wise, New York, NY (Reform)
- Dec. 20, 1941

Stephen S. Wise, New York, NY (Reform)
- Feb. 12 and 26, 1933
- March 19, 26 and 27, 1933
- April 16, 1933
- June 4, 1933
- Sept. 14 and 21, 1933
- March 4, 1934
- April 1, 1934
- Aug. 21, 1934
- Sept. 9 and 10, 1934
- Dec. 16, 1934
- April 7, 1935
- Aug. 26, 1935
- Oct. 6 and 27, 1935
- Feb. 2 and 16, 1936
- Aug. 8, 1936
- Sept. 16 and 17, 1936
- Sept. 6, 1937
- March 22 and 27, 1938
- May 1, 1938
- Oct. 10, 1938
- Dec. 18, 1938
- Jan. 8, 1939
- March 12 and 19, 1939
- Sept. 13 and 14, 1939
- Oct. 8, 10 and 15, 1939
- Feb. 25, 1940
- April 21, 1940
- Oct. 2, 1940
- Jan. 7, 1941
- Sept. 30, 1941
- Nov. 23, 1941
- Dec. 14, 1941
- March 8, 1942
- May 9, 1942
- July 21, 1942
- Sept. 11, 1942
- Oct. 30, 1942

March 1, 1943
April 14, 1943
July 8, 1943
August 29, 1943
Sept. 17, 1944
Sept. 8, 1945

Louis Wolsey, Philadelphia, PA (Reform)
March 25, 1935
Sept. 17, 1936
Dec. 6, 1936
June 21, 1940
Feb. 25, 1942
Oct. 17, 1942

Walter Wuerzburger, Brighton, MA (Orthodox)
Oct. 9, 1943

Daniel Zion, Bulgaria (Orthodox)
May 24, 1943

Israel Zolli, Rome, Italy (Orthodox?)
June 9, 1944

General Index*

The names of rabbis whose sermons appear in the index to rabbis and dates of included sermons, above, will not be included in the General Index, unless they are mentioned elsewhere (in the Preface, Introduction, or in a sermon by a different preacher).

A

Aaron, High Priest, 993
Abraham, 345, 579, 593, 695, 723, 923–24
  challenging God, 521, 802–3
  finding burial place, 924
  as model of hospitality, 794
  and sacrifice of Isaac, 146, 443–44, 518–19
  and Sodom, Gomorrah,158
  testing of, as with America, 443
  as wanderer, 453
Abrahams, Israel, 960
Abtalyon, 964
Achad HaAm, 152
Acropolis, 563
Adam, confronted with terror of night, 753
Adler, Frances, 614
Adler, Hermann, 1003
Affidavits, 320, 370
Africa, 543
  liberation of, 702, 716, 986
African Corps, 810
Agudath Sholom, Flatbush, NY, 991
Ahasuerus, 65–66, 391, 909, 911, 916
  as dictator, 908, 909–10, 917
  as model for Hitler, 908
Ahaz, 911–13
Ahlwardt, Hermann, 705
Akedah, 69, 146, 335, 444, 519
  ours is sacrifice of millions of sons, 723
Akiba/Akiva, 146, 561, 624, 716, 920–22, 972–73
Albert I, King of Belgium, 779
Aleutians, 765
  controlled by Allied armies, 821
Alexandria, 144, 244
  German hordes at gates of, 718
Alexander, Harold, 759
Algiers, 267
Alienism, 217
Allied armies,
  circle the globe and control huge territories, 821
  like a Messianic miracle, 789
  no rescue plan for Jews by, 976

Allies, some urging a "soft peace," 1020
Almosnino, Moses, 56–57
Altmann, Alexander, xxiii, 42–43, 199, 352, 367, 372, 451, 482, 542, 638, 669, 818, 976
  Memorial Address for Joseph Hertz, 1004–5
Amalek, 61–63, 259, 389, 400, 415, 538, 566–67, 678, 705, 917
  among other biblical foes, 24, 68, 72
  archetypal enemy of Jews, 24, 61–62
  continuous enemy, 63, 178
  represents secular wisdom, 63, 466
  modern: "enemy of the Jews, enemy of the world," 538–39
  "ungracious progeny" survives, 804
Amateur Athletic Union, 235, 241
America
  anti-Jewish uprisings in, 267
  battle for, 573
  conscience of, 359
  fighting for "spiritual Americas," 601
  hope it will remain out of war, 443
  hope for refugee acceptance in, 370
  Jews not allowed to enter, 387–88
  Jews safe in, 405
  keep out of war by helping Britain, 545
  "Keep Safe for World Peace," 427
  as key to Jewish survival, 955
  may need to enter the war, 479
  mental depression in, 554
  must avoid new war, 408, 425, 450, 468
  must become arsenal of Judaism, 728
  needs to demonstrate its moral invincibility, 553, 693
  neutrality of action imperative, 425, 452
  pall of gloom over Jewish life in, 366
  purpose of Jews in, 393
  will ultimately go to war, 444
  See also: United States
"America First Committee," 573
American Association for the Advancement of Science, 171
American Council for Judaism, 726, 732
American Embassy, Germany, 108
American Federation of Labour, 191
American Hebrew, 872
American Jewish Archives, xix, xxi–xxii, 28, 57
American Jewish Committee, 13, 318, 732
  opposition to anti-German boycott, 860, 872
American Jewish Conference, 705, 707, 732, 788
American Jewish Congress, 13, 92–93, 102, 318, 842
  1933 protest rally of, 102, 166
  support of anti-German boycott, 860
American Jewry/Jews, 573
  and boycott of Germany, 191, 872–73

becoming mainstay of Diaspora Jewish life, 378
in danger, must be organized to fight, 771
donations for European victims, 575
failure to understand significance of the current war, 489
feel both like victors *and* vanquished, 826
flood of sympathy for, 422–23
as heir to European Jewry, 765
implications of European tragedy for, 133
must not sound like war-mongers, 424, 450
need to save people of Israel, 999
response to decree of annihilation, 668
should present solid front to the world, 134
spiritually depressed, 399
American Press, relative silence of, 140
American public opinion, respected by Hitler, 461
American Zionist Emergency Council, 709
Americans, liberation of Buchenwald by, 811
Amir, Yehoyada, 296
Amos, 345, 598
Amraphel, 911,
Angel of Death, 511, 626
Anglo-Saxon race, 492
Ankara, Turkey, 769
Annihilation,
of all civilization, 431
of human good, 470
of human race, 206, 511
mid-European Jewry on brink of, 684
See also: Jews, annihilation of
Anschluss [Invasion of Austria], 64, 227, 312, 320
Antiochus Epiphanes, 24–25, 67–68, 72, 144, 154, 241, 278, 369, 460, 517, 531
came to enslave Jews, 601
as model for Hitler, 241, 531
and modern Neo-paganism, 68, 460
Anti-humanism, 126
Antisemitism/anti-Semitism, xiii, 60, 115, 181, 221, 256, 261, 293, 306, 366, 387
antisemitic legislation, 625
in Austria, 196, 311
chain letter circulated in New York, 864–65
condemnation of, 104, 153
in Eastern and Central Europe, 89, 190
in England, 267, 270, 280
as exotic poisonous plant, 195
in France, 251
in free nations, 220
in Germany, 96–97, 101, 112, 125–26, 133, 139–40, 161, 170, 176, 184, 196, 323, 331
here to stay, 647
Hitler's, 195, 701
like the bubonic plague, 764
matter of political action, 412
as moral disease requiring a moral cure, 828
new resistance to in Germany, 887

no originality in, 897–98
ominous rising of, 429
penetrated throughout the world, 748
in Poland, 196
in Polish Army in England, 755–56
Reich's Fifth Column, 412
resurgence of, 316, 896
in Romania, 330
roots of, 402
ruthless stamping out of, 817
seeds of sown by Hitler not readily destroyed, 688
in US, 235, 258
widely discredited, 294
and world's well-being, 819
Anti-Slavery Society, 796
Anti-war pacifist vow, 586
Anti-Zionist Reform rabbis, 1013
Antwerp, Belgium, 522–23, 877
Apion, 705
Appeal for German Jews, 213
Appel, Ernst, 39
Appel, Martha, 39
Arctic Circle, 203
Arabs, 50–51
hostility of, 393
slaughter by, 263, 321
Archbishop of Canterbury, *see:* Lang, Cosmo Gordon
Argentina, protest in, xiii
Ark of the Covenant/of G-d, 992, 994–96, 998–1001
in Radzilow, 1000
Armageddon, 198, 255, 398
Armenia/Armenians, 212, 563, 626, 849
Armistice of 1918, 911
Aryan paragraph, 869
Aryan supremacy, 329, 338, 637
Aryan "*Uebermensch,*" 334
Aryans, also subjected to atrocities, 828
Asch, Shalom (Sholem), 782, 1028
Asquith, Herbert Henry, 911
Assassination, 15, 27, 143, 197, 210
of Ernst vom Rath, 358–59, 926
of Wilhelm Gustloff, 246–47, 275, 350–51
Assembly of Representatives, 661, 664, 698
Assyria, Assyrians, 332, 346, 838, 849, 989
Atlantic Charter, 564, 566, 624, 647, 709, 984–85
Atomic bomb, 825
Atrocities, 61, 74, 83, 110, 128, 155–57
"Atrocity propaganda," 469
Attila, 312
Attlee, Clement, 629
Auschwitz (Oswiecim), 4–7, 9, 53, 81, 617, 721, 734, 749, 772, 775, 785, 791, 816, 829, 930, 981, 1014, 1017
as "death camp," 53–54
escape from, 9, 749, 791
gassing of Gypsies in, 829
Sonderkommandos in, 7
Austria, 13, 64, 66, 97, 179, 261, 267, 285, 304, 342, 431, 440, 684
anti-Semitism in, 196
expulsion of Jews from, 378, 387
German annexation of 344, 420, 489
Hitler as outsider from, 94–95
Jewish history in, 327
Nazi invasion of, 66, 309, 376
Nazification of, 310
no intention to annex, 489
in shambles, 573

spiritual murder of, 515
unkept promises to, 392
Zionist office closed in, 310
See also: Anschluss
Austrian Jewry, 608
Churban [destruction] of, 318–19
helpless and timorous, 300
forced to clean streets, 310
leaders of arrested, 310
must leave within four years, 315
persecution of, 316, 330
profound suffering of, 474
suicides of, 310
Austrians,
knew what was happening in Germany, 488501
Axis, 412, 567, 573, 596, 598
aim of to enslave mankind, 615–16
mortal danger of its victory, 626
wages war of annihilation against Palestine, 631
at war with its governments not its people, 596, 878

B

Babylon, Babylonia, 346, 849, 955, 989
waters of, 554, 678
Babylonian Exile, 502, 694, 977
Babylonians,
conquest of Judea by, 1015
territorial expansion of, 913
Bach, Johann Sebastian, 108, 214
"Back to Judaism" movement, 469
"Backshadowing," 55
Baeck, Leo, 44, 50, 229
Baghdad, 395
Balaam, 415
Balak, 414, 415
Balfour Declaration, 378–79, 393, 436, 481, 492, 988, 1029
Balkans, Jews of, 749, 750, 755
could be saved, but Allies indifferent, 987
Baltic Sea, 996
Basel, 146, 193
Bastille Day, 491
Bataan, 627
Battlefields, sons and brothers of congregants on, 998
Bauer, Yehuda, 2
Beck, Ludwig, 295
"Bed of Procrustes," 658
Bedford United Hebrew Congregation, 975
Beethoven, Ludwig van, 346
Belgian peasant, blind, 484
Belgians, 488
Belgium, 77, 142–43, 157, 249, 309, 454, 684, 756, 797–98
Christian priests in, 797
Christian residents of wear six-pointed star, 522–23
Christians shelter Jews in, 798
Einstein returns to, 142–43
heroic struggle of, 948
Jews of perish in death trains, 1008
King Leopold III of, 948
Rabbi Isserman's aunt in, 797–98
in shambles, 572–73
surrender of to Germany, 494, 505, 947–48
violation of treaty with, 489
Bell, George, 987
Belzec, 4
Benet, Stephen Vincent, 640

Ben-Zvi, Isaac, 384, 754
Berchtesgaden, 310
Bergen-Belsen, 816, 975
Bergman, Eleonora, 969
Bergson, Peter, xv, 730
Berkovits, Avraham, 967
Berkovits, Eliezer, 40, 63, 487, 526, 538–39, 547, 557, 562, 564, 567, 581, 583, 593, 596, 622, 630, 637, 643, 654, 670, 701, 731, 959–67, 976
courage of to challenge "because of our sins," 959
critique of Jewish leadership by, 960
pessimism of on Jewish situation, 960
Berlin, 64, 105, 123, 136, 189, 190, 234, 241, 280, 324, 394–95, 397, 417, 625, 630, 889, 899
American ambassador in recalled, 926
bombing of by Allies, 744, 1020
burning of synagogues in, 357, 829
captured by Allies, 814
correspondents in, 12, 888–89
Einsatzgruppen reports to, 10, 14
Jewish sermons in, 25, 42, 46–47, 182, 486
Jews dying in alleys of, 214
Lehranstalt and *Rabbiner-Seminar* of, 699
let it remain a ghost city forever, 745
munition factory in, 525
Olympic Games in, 236, 241, 245
Orthodox Rabbi attacked in, 99
Peace Conference (1878) in, 340
Sports Palace in, 40, 516, 702
synagogues in, 937
as world center of Fascism, 841
Berlin Philharmonic, 847
Berliner Tageblatt, 847–48
Bermuda Conference, 690, 698
as dismal failure, 987
Bernhardi, Friedrich von, 227
Bernstein, Michael Andre, 55
Bessarabia, 299, 576
Best, Karl Rudolf Werner, 735
Betar, 599, 792–93, 973
Bevis Marks Synagogue, 1003–4
Bialer, Tosha, 1006
Bialik, Chaim Nahman, 223
"City of Slaughter," 976–78
Bialystok, 8, 708
as city without Jews, 786
Bible, 62, 131, 153, 178, 345, 400, 542
attempt to revise, 124, 254, 480–81, 609
as book of the Jews, 254–55
burning of, 122, 641
of the Church, 93, 122, 254
complex teachings of on war and peace, 479
demands the utmost, 402
imposed conscience of righteousness, 334
love of justice in, 254
moral teachings in, 263
most precious gift, 193
punishments of being fulfilled, 608
See also: Old Testament
Birkenau, four crematories operating at, 790
Birmingham Hebrew Congregation, 1023
Biro-Bidjan, 448
Bischoff, Erich, 221

Black Book of Poland, 652
Black Market, 591, 622
Blackout, 77, 459, 474, 503, 577
of civilization, 578, 951
of humanity, 77, 503
physical and spiritual, 578, 646
regulations, 507, 591, 782
Black Sea, 996
Black Shirts, 265, 371, 880
"Black Thursday," *see: Kristallnacht*
Blitzkrieg and *Blitz-Freiheit*, 492
Bloch Publishing Company, xix, 846, 860, 1014
Blondheim, Menahem, 30, 49
Blood and soil, 609
Blum, Leon, 294, 520
in a lonely dungeon, 558
B'nai B'rith, and anti-German boycott, 318, 860
Bohemia-Moravia, 13
Jews of sent to Poland, 459
plains of, 341
Bolivia, 264
Bologna, University of, 346
Bolsheviks, 480, 546
Bolshevism, 324, 560–61, 717
Jews and, 280, 302–3, 383, 440, 537
See also: "Communism"
Books, burning of,
in 1933 Germany, 121, 124
in Paris, 124
Boston Jewish Chronicle, 770
Boston, MA, 841, 959
Bourdillon, Francis William, 753
Boycotts,
of German businesses, 111–13, 120, 133–34, 147, 191–92, 203, 554, 595, 860, 863–64, 866, 868, 872–73
of Jewish businesses, xiii–iv, 42, 97, 108, 112–13, 118, 121, 123, 257, 347, 469, 632, 865
of little avail, 330
of Olympic Games, 235, 237
only language Hitler understands, 863
Braham, Randolph L., 3–4, 18
Brahms, Johannes, 346
Bratislava, 8, 36, 49, 604–7
Great Synagogue of destroyed, 706
Breaking of the vessels, 582
Breslau, 699
British authorities,
allow refugee ship to land in Haifa, 754
British Commonwealth of Nations, 451, 542
British Empire, 58, 335, 341, 353, 446, 616, 630, 684, 818, 822
dominates subject races everywhere, 549
British Expeditionary Force, evacuated, 946
Brittain, Vera, 744
Brondesbury Synagogue, London, 937
Brooklyn Jewish Center, 851
Brotherhood Day (1934), 183
"Brown Battalions," 841
"Brown Bolshevism" of Berlin, 324
Brown, Francis (Bishop of Jerusalem), 394
Brown University, 1013
Browning, Christopher, 806
Bruening/Brüning, Heinrich, 515
Bucharest, 630
massacre of Jews in ritual slaughterhouse, 550, 780

Buckingham [Palace], 310
Bucovina, 299, 576
Budapest, 739
Bueno de Mesquita, D., 74
Bulgaria, 267, 772
  in grip of terror, 573
  Jews prefer to die in, 699–700
  protest in, xiii
Burns, Robert, 804–5
Bytwerk, Randall L., 40

C

Cadman, S. Parkes, 166, 192, 708
Caesar, 257, 328, 965
Caesarea, Palestine, 966
Cain, 413
  and Abel, 264
  mark of, 304
  murderer of his brother, 758, 820
Cairo, Rommel at gates of, 810
Calcutta, black hole of, 1008
Caleb, 188
Canada, antisemitism rising in, 519–20
  internment camps in, 539
  involved in war, 425
  and Olympic Games, 238
  protest in, xiii
  rationing of meat in, 830
  resistance of toward Jewish immigrants, 537
  S.S. Wise 1933 speech in, 132
Canadian Jewish Congress, 354
Canadian Nationalist, The, 282
Cantor, 535
Cape Town, SA, 203, 292
Caplan, Kimmy, xxiv–xxv, 41, 852, 920
Carnegie Hall, S.S. Wise sermons in, xiii, 19, 22, 101, 207
Carpathian Mountains, Russian army at gate of, 759
Catalina bombers, Jewish crewmen on, 660
Catholics,
  oppressed in Mexico, 212
  persecution of in Germany, 884–85, 889
  victims of religious bigotry, 477–78
Catholic Church,
  aid extended to Jews by, 758
  growing strength of in America, 371
  importance of liturgy to, 524
Central Conference of American Rabbis (CCAR), 25, 859
Central Consistory (*Consistoire Central*), 657, 734
Cesarani, David, 2, 17
Chamberlain, Austen, 196
Chamberlain, Houston Stewart, 209, 360, 840
Chamberlain, Neville, 329, 333, 339–42, 425–26, 437, 448, 988
  appeasement policy of, 395
  brought dishonor without peace, 340
Chameides, Kalman, 50
Chernowitz/Czernowitz, Romania, 589, 756
Chesterton, G.K., 917
Chicago, 78, 314, 404, 708, 818
  as headquarters of American Fascism, 841
Children, 6, 14, 69, 77, 687
  as chief victims of war, 206

cruelty toward, 214, 245, 260, 633–34
denial of proper schooling to, 108, 123, 184, 214, 471
donning gas masks, 421
German: poisoned by new paganism, 324, 365
German and Italian: carry guns, 227
hidden to escape deportation, 587
humiliation of, 359
kidnapping of, 211
murdered because they are Jews, 633–34
need to remove from danger, 665
parents of murdered by Nazis, 809
priority to save, 669
protection of, 98
refugee, 354, 370, 375, 394
seeking food for, 148
special names for, 433
suffering of German after war, 321
surviving as orphans, 795
China, 71, 264, 394, 616, 1020
admiration for, 659
controlled by Allied Armies, 821
long drawn-out agony of, 823
Cholera, Jews blamed for, 302
Chophni, 994
Chopin, Frédéric, 346
Christian Century, 279
Christian X, King of Denmark and Yellow Badge, 763–64
Christian leaders,
current task of, 703
passionate pleas from, 1009
Christianity,
failure of to bring end of war, 372
as great civilizing power, 372
hated with Judaism by tyrants, 654
Hitler's war against, 469
Nazi movement's fight against, 202, 305–6, 515, 905
oppressed along with Judaism, 601–2
reviled along with Judaism, 400
to be superseded by Nazi state, 610
versus Hitlerism, 157
Christians
American resolution of protest by, 225
fate of intertwined with that of Jews, 329
German pastors defy Nazism, 225
need to speak out, 122
protesting Nazi persecution, 112, 207
united with Jews in Canada, 462
voice of Christian America, 407
Churban [destruction], 131, 318, 699, 963
Church of Scotland,
condemnation of antisemitism by, 411
General Assembly of, 411
Churchill, Winston, 186, 598, 675, 984
"Fight on the Beaches" speech, 946, 953
refusal of to surrender, 494

signing Atlantic Charter, 578, 647
White Paper speech in Commons, 988
Cicero, 30, 328, 399
Cincinnati, University of, 845, 877, 893, 945
Civilian Defense, 722
Cleator, Kenneth Irving, 846
Clinchy, Everett, 764
Codreanu, Corneliu Zelei, 300
Cohen, Abraham, xxii, 21, 26, 47, 74, 80, 700, 901, 1023–31
Jewish Homiletics by, 18, 29–31, 1023
president, Board of Deputies, 1024
Cohen, David J., 1025
Cohen, Israel, 12
Cohen, Jacob/J.X., 168, 648, 835–36
Cohen, Sadie, 835
Cohen, Thelma, 47
Cohn, Julius, 929–36
farewell sermon delivered by, 931
Cohon, Beryl D., 769
College of the City of New York (CCNY), 1003
Columbia University, NY, 38, 851, 907, 1013
Commercy, la Meuse, 551
Communism, 275, 284, 289, 417, 446, 525, 661
as the cholera of our age, 302
evil of, 371
Fascism and, 275, 279, 284, 289-90, 371
Hitler actually promoting it, 279
as Jewish movement, 107, 161, 181, 214, 263, 290, 302, 312–13, 368, 715
Nazism as defense against, 386, 440, 443
Communists, 903–4
allies of Nazis, 464
blamed for Reichstag fire, 648
enemies of antisemitism, 661
in ghettos, 8
German: denounced, 91, 96, 98, 105, 904
Jewish, 181
Jews accused of being, 313, 368, 446
Jews as brains of, 101
Jews in League with, 573
Russian and Lithuanian: murdered, 10
Compiègne, 81, 766
Compromise, 340, 488, 494, 905
no time for, 127, 636, 871, 873
on Palestine, 393–94
Concentration camps, 211, 525, 667, 745, 781,
affidavits and, 370
after *Kristallnacht*, 611, 940
anti-Fascists in, 537
as threat to Christians, 192, 278
Christians imprisoned in, 164, 304, 891
Danish Jews in, 714
divine intervention and, 965
French Jewish children in, 638
Germany as one large, 457
in Holland, 704
hope in, 759, 765, 787, 891
incredible brutalities of, 826
Jews imprisoned in, 110, 344, 397, 426, 558, 559–60, 861
in Lublin, 761

martyrs in, 204
Nazi-occupied Europe as, 681
no new invention, 187
Niemöller confined to, 227, 327, 574
at Osthofen, 168
Passover prayer for, 474
pastors and priests in, 355, 464, 884
in Poland, 593, 625
Protestant ministers released from, 885
rabbis and teachers in 428, 465, 891
refugees of, 628
release from, 364, 535
religious ceremonies in, 785
replacing Sinai, 609
savage butchery of, 359
savagery of, 214, 363–64, 541
survivors of, 631, 979
tens of thousands of Jews in, 386, 626, 662, 746, 778
throughout Europe, 709
in United States, 679–80
women and, 729
yielding up their victims, 762
Concordat with Vatican, 884, 905
Conference on Refugees [1938], 329
Confessional Church, 357
"Confessions of a Nazi Spy," 407–8
Congregation Keneseth Israel, Elkins Park, PA, 983
Congregation Rodeph Sholom, NY, 1013
Copenhagen,
threat to Jews in, 714
Cornell University, NY, 34, 867
Corsica, 374
Cossacks, 183, 499
Coughlin, Charles E., 360, 376, 386, 396, 505, 648
Coventry, 762
Cracow, 434, 686
Crete, 1011
Cross of Christ, 179
Crowther, Bosley, 568
Crucifixion,
of God, 303
of the Jews, 97, 118, 703, 710, 727, 784, 846–47, 989–90, 1008
of Jews in Palestine, 341
submission to, 337
universal, 79, 571
Crusades, 69, 72–73, 256, 271, 334, 768, 840, 894
Cuza, Alexandrer, 295, 300, 310
Cyrus, 517
Britain as, 518
Czar,
autocracy of, 96, 914
imprisonment of Rebbe by, 94
pogroms under rule of, 847
ruthlessness of, 147
saint compared with Bolsheviks and Nazis, 480
Czechoslovakia, Czecho-Slovakia, 157, 416–21, 431, 684
allowing itself to be dismembered, 336–37
annexation of, 336, 342, 376, 394, 440
annihilation of Jews in, 421
as Jewish homeland, 427
as refuge for Jews, 397
betrayal of, 340, 391, 393, 443, 530
burning of synagogues in, 662
courage of, 333–34, 337
crisis of, 330, 342

crushed, 341, 393, 572
dismemberment of, 515
exile of Jews from, 608
fate of the enslaved Jews in, 469, 682
German treatment of, 390
gratitude to for treatment of Jews, 333–34
harassment of, 460
martyrdom of for sake of peace, 337
must be freed, 449
Nazi soldiers in control of, 652
no longer exists, 395–96, 421
preparing its Army, 287
profound suffering of Jews in, 474, 580
pulverization of, 398
rape of, 382, 431
sacrifice of, 341, 445
universities in, 416
unkept promises to, 391
See also: Sudentenland
Czechs, 333–34, 337, 417, 433, 476, 488, 490, 508, 535, 742
Czerniakow, Adam, 7, 607, 768

D

Dachau, concentration camp, xxv-vi, 662, 679, 815–16, 826, 975
eighty rabbis imprisoned in [1938], 465
US rabbi delivers sermon in, 814–16
Daiches, Salis, xxii-xxiii, 47, 58–59, 131, 159–60, 212–13, 307, 327, 353–54, 388, 411, 419, 711,
Daiches, Samuel, 26, 47, 178, 363, 761, 821
Daily Herald, London, 99, 888
Daily Mail, UK, 195, 439
Daladier, Édouard, 333, 340, 425
Damocles, sword of, 156, 558
Danish Jews,
arrest and deportation of all, 714
Dante Alighieri,
cannot bring actual horror onto the stage, 942
Danzig/Gdansk, 662, 929
David,
as despotic dictator, 261
facing Goliath, 223
in flight from Saul, 939
as "sweet singer of Israel," 261–62
David's Shield, 593
See also: Six-pointed star, Jewish/ Yellow badge
Dawes, Charles, 646, 840
Dawidowicz, Lucy, 3–5, 7–8, 618
Day of Atonement, 23, 51, 272, 339, 651, 729, 938, 993
must come over the world, 782
Day of Compassion and Intercession (May 2, 1943), 697
Day of Fast and Mourning (Dec. 13, 1942), 667, 807, 976
Day of Mourning and Prayer (May 22, 1944), 756, 1003–4, 1010
Dearborn Independent, 837, 842, 946
Death camps, 4, 9, 53, 360, 467, 544–57, 599, 639, 671–72, 707, 746, 765, 816, 975, 1006, 1014
See also: Extermination camps
Death trains, 802, 1008
Decoration Day, 946
De Lange, Nicholas, 938
Delft, Holland, 522
Democracies, 291, 312, 361, 384, 403,

424, 445, 449, 450, 660–61, 702, 790
fascism's assault on, 311
failure of to act against Nazism in 1933, 424
faith in victory of, 597
have not asked US to fight, 465
Hitler on Jews and, 525
may save themselves at last, 425
no further contact of with Germany, Italy, 399
refusal of to stop Hitler, 1933–39, 683
surrender of, 986
tragic and bitter path of, 553
unwillingness to intervene for Jews, 808, 822–23, 987, 989
wars not the way of, 916–17
Democracy, 65, 94, 229, 266, 283, 298, 345, 355, 359, 362, 425, 435–37, 443, 503, 575, 661, 786, 817, 847, 879, 916–17, 951, 954
American, 383, 396, 408, 450, 452, 468, 543, 548–49, 557, 598, 911
and anti-Semitism, 384, 537
attack against since 1933, 311, 334, 359, 376, 379, 598
close to Judaism, 598
Czecho-Slovak Republic as outpost of, 382, 396
destroyed before Nazism could triumph, 596, 616
enemies of, 376
fading from Germany, 96
failures of, 500
Hitler's view of, 170, 175, 334
idealization of, 909
in place of dictatorships of right or left, 916–17
interpreting events in light of, 533
Jewish stake in, 318, 339, 345, 379, 402, 434, 505, 522
"making the world safe for," xvi, 908, 914
many lost faith in, 627
provides safety for Jews, 331
"putrescent corpse of," 537
senility and weakness of, 542, 546
solidly entrenched in France and England, 294
sympathetic but evasive, 597
ultimate triumph of, 447, 561, 579, 827
vindicating itself, 337, 549
war has weakened in England and France, 452, 491
Demosthenes, 399
Denenberg, Noach, 5
Denikin, Anton, 404
Denmark, 625, 684
catastrophe has overwhelmed, 471
Jews fleeing from, 1009
King Christian of, 763
violation of pledge to, 490
Depression, 171, 483
economic and financial, 150, 267, 870
misery of, 426
psychological, 189, 373, 407, 554–55, 710, 895
Derasha, Derashot. See: Sermon
Detention camps, 746
See also: Concentration camps
Detroit, MI, 47, 51, 74, 841–42, 945
Father Coughlin in, 376

Nazi organization founded in, 866–37
race riots in, 730
Detroit Jewish News, 770
Deus absconditus, 791
"Deutschland, Erwache," 843
"Deutschland über Alles"
"*Alles*" includes God, 905
De Vries, David, xxiii–xxiv
Diaries, 6–7, 29, 33, 535, 595, 618, 655, 673, 693, 969–70
Diaspora, 199–200, 378, 418, 478, 672–73, 678, 757, 899
Chief Rabbi's message to, 807
children arriving from, 795
future rights of Jews in, 760
uncertainties of, 770, 896
worry about brethren in, 620, 664
Dibelius, Otto, 118
Dictatorship of the proletariat, 914
Dienemann, Max, 168–69
Dieppe, France, blood flowing in, 660
Diplomacy, 132, 161
of blackmail vindicated, 336
British and French, 435
Rabbi charged with lack of, 355
Disarmament Conference (1933), 171
"Dishonor" [Ichabod], 996
Disraeli, Benjamin, 340
Dittmar, Kurt, 764
Dodd, William E., 595
Dodkowitz, Alan, xxii, 983
Dollfus, Engelbert, 210, 365–66, 870
Domarus, Max, 9–10, 29, 32
Donat, Alexander, 4
Drancy Internment Camp, 734, 768, 773
Dresden,
burning of synagogue in, 534–35
Dropsie College, Philadelphia, PA, 983
Dunelm, Herbert (Bishop of Durham), 11
Dunkirk/Dunkerque, 77, 81, 486, 766, 787
Dutch, 476, 488, 535
hostages, 829
immigrants, 787
Jews, 53, 704, 1008, 1017

E

Economic Conference [1933], 119, 171
Edelheit, Abraham J., 2
Eden, Anthony, 302–3
Edgware Synagogue, London, 938
Edinburgh, Scotland, xxii, 47, 59, 353, 930
Edison, Thomas, 553
Edom, 390–91, 413, 415, 717
Egypt, 60–61, 115–16, 120, 183, 204, 220, 286–87, 313–14, 322, 338, 346, 455, 473–75, 552, 621, 624–25, 955, 989
compared with Nazi Germany, 61, 115, 853–57
fleshpots of, 931, 933–34
many oppressed peoples in, 244
modern state, 636, 649
punishment of, 297
slaves and overseer's whip in, 625
Egyptians, xxx, 24, 115, 178, 220, 313–14, 332, 838, 854, 856–57, 933
amateurs in comparison with Nazis, 747

drowning in the sea, 479
Ehrenpreis, Marcus, 61, 115, 830
Ehrenreich, Shlomo Zalman, 49, 79, 312, 387, 770
Ehrnthal, Emil, *see:* Elton, Michael
Eighth Army (UK), 748
Eighth Army Air Force (US), 744
Einsatzgruppen, 1008
Jews as victims of, 14, 78, 563
reports of, 10, 563
Einstein, Albert, 108, 189, 209, 211, 245, 848, 890
banishment of, 121
as man without a country, 142
renunciation of citizenship by, 111
as Zionist, 152
Eisendrath, Maurice N., 18, 22, 34, 39, 52, 169, 239–40, 272, 520, 537
Eisenhower, Dwight D., 683
Eisenmenger, Johann, 221
Elazar, R., 624
Eli, 992–96, 998
Elijah, 331, 503, 719
and prophets of Baal, 902, 906
Elijah, Gaon of Vilna, 857
Elisha, 331
Elton, Howard, 975
Elton, Michael (Emil Ehrnthal), 52–53, 975–81
conducted Bergen-Belsen mass funeral service, 975
critique of world indifference to Jews, 976
as Progressive rabbi, 975
Emancipation, 13, 190, 200, 203, 220, 319, 709
Emergency Committee to Save the Jewish People of Europe, 38
Emerson, Ralph Waldo, 628
Emmanuel (Abo-Hatab), Bishop, 848
Emmanuel College, Cambridge, 1023
Endeks/Endecja (National Democratic Party), 248, 265
England, 398, 404
calm dignity of in time of crisis, 290
challenge to for "Second Front," 704
churches bombed in, 509, 522
courage displayed by, 485
defeat after defeat for, 555
delusion of peace in, 336
determined to destroy Hitlerism, 447
failures of, 578
Fascist movements in, 267, 294
fear of offending, 245
fights with back to the wall, 505
glory of, 497
hospitality to Jews in, 352
ignoring Arab attacks in Palestine, 321
Jewish delinquents in, 591, 621
many admirers of Hitler in, 439
and Munich Conference, 339
Nazi ambassador as guests of King, 310
opened doors to Jewish refugees, 441
optimism of, 493
Polish government-in-exile in, 8–9
prayers offered for Jews in churches of, 677
protest rallies in, xv
rearming and becoming bolder, 287

remaining European Jews in, 630
safety of?, 395
silence of regarding Austria, 312
stood alone against victorious Germany, 800
tide of antisemitism in, 267, 270, 276, 280
victory of only hope for Jews, 517
warned by Hitler: "I'm coming," 516
See also: Great Britain

English Channel, 71, 996
Ephron, 923–25
Epsom Brotherhood, 213
Eretz Yisrael/Yisroel, Eretz Israel, 168, 199, 413, 403, 481, 579, 617, 622, 678, 760, 806
cannot flourish in corrupt world, 966
currently in danger, 966
pray for re-establishment of homeland in, 719
See also: Palestine

Erfurt "World Service," 414
Esau, 70, 316, 335, 523, 938–39
Esperanto, 160
Esther, 177, 249, 392, 477, 686, 895–98, 926
Book/Scroll of, 24, 65, 687, 895–98, 900, 908–10, 923
Fast of, 251
a modern, 67, 614–15, 685–86
Sarah and, 920–22

Estonia, 449
Ethiopia, Ethiopians, 227, 264, 394, 515, 578, 784, 881, 908–9
Europe,
as armed camp, 249, 263, 290
Central, 82, 89, 164–65, 190, 213, 222, 315, 336, 342, 395, 412, 451, 474–75, 485, 531, 635, 651, 659, 986, 1018, 1021
chain of tyranny in, 321
conscience of in 1933, 717
Eastern, 10, 20, 82, 89, 164, 183, 213, 215, 378, 395, 412, 448, 451, 475, 635, 650–51, 659–60, 674, 731, 739, 788, 810, 845, 893–94, 919, 964, 1016–21
future of hanging in balance, 421
German claims in, 419
"Jewish problem" of, 448–60
medieval, 143, 154, 233, 607
Nazi and Fascist forces in, 327
now a thing of the past, 949
refugees from, 400, 456–57, 535–36
so-called democracies of, 445
as vast prison camp, 542
Western, 124, 128, 294, 364, 420, 440

European Jewry/Jews, xi, 16, 69, 125, 334, 396, 548, 558, 562
annihilation of, 160
bottomless pit of horror, 648
catastrophe of, 378, 397
destitute masses of, 451
destruction of, 12, 690, 783
devastating impact of new war upon, 40
difficult to reconstitute itself, 688
doom of is doom of Europe, 671
driven to verge of extermination, 474
fate of, 23, 36, 94, 594, 677, 744

fine record and drab fate of, 558
living in ghettos, concentration camps, dungeons, 631
loss of educational institutions and scholars, 689, 699
now bleeding, 728
systematic mass murder of, 556
tragic story of, 260
trapped in no-man's land, 580
as vast martyr community, 469
will probably never recover, 564
Évian Conference, 329, 386, 470
Exile, 79, 110, 256, 304, 328, 377, 393, 413, 427, 463, 531, 535, 554, 585, 619, 628, 639, 644, 685, 704, 690–91, 714, 721, 740, 792, 817, 895–97, 960–61, 966–67, 987, 997
all going into exile, 304
as consequence of Israel's sin, 248, 718, 960
as way of Satan's Torah, 187
avoidance of, 733–34
of Czech Jews, 608
diaspora and, 200
Europe as land of, 168
exile after exile, 608, 619, 630
from cradle-land of the Jewish race, 270
of German Jews, 135, 209, 267, 366, 522, 686
of German rulers, 119
God with Israel in, 304
great minds of Germany driven into, 371
help for those in, 203
of Italian Jews, 330
Netherlands government-in-, 704
Polish government-in-, 8, 53, 630, 685, 760, 816, 1004
reception of, 151
from Spain, 754, 990
to Siberia, 750
of thinkers, writers, and students, 209
unending, 642
See also: Babylonian Exile, *Galut, Golus*
"Extermination camps" (*Vernichtungslager*), 53, 827, 1016–17
See also: Death camps
Eybeschuetz, Jonathan, 57
Ezekiel, 626, 799
Ezra,
religious reforms of, 964

F

Farbstein, Esther, xxiv, 3, 5, 18, 608, 631, 739
Fascism, 275, 290, 484, 500, 522, 537, 948
and antisemitism, 176–77
as assault against democracy, 311
Berlin as world center of, 841
and Communism, 275, 279, 284, 289–90, 371
destroys freedom of the individual, 610
as destructionism, 715
in Europe, 329
evil becomes world power through, 547
heroic fight against in ghettos, 716
inherent evil of, 298
of Italy, 328
method is race war, 371

misguided encouragement of, 661
opposed by American Protestant leaders, 279
our job to outlive it, 289
three Great Powers of, 255
use of antisemitism, 311
Vatican allied with?, 279
Fasanenstrasse Synagogue, ruins of, 357
Fast and Mourning, Day of,
December 13, 1942, 667, 975
March 14, 1945, 807
Faulhaber, Michael von, 175–76, 192–94, 197, 355, 357, 708, 903
1933 Advent sermons of, 175, 180, 548
fabricated sermon by, 193, 197
opened gates of palace to Jews, 519
Federal Council of Churches of Christ in America, 489, 697
Feibelman, Julian B., 43, 729
Feinberg, Abraham H., xxii, 28, 111, 183, 225
Feinberg, Abraham L., 34
Fettmilch, Vincenz, 705
Feuchtwanger, Lion, 183, 212, 848
Finland, 449, 481
in grip of terror, 573
maimed and impoverished, 505
First Temple,
destruction of, 78, 530, 625, 792–93, 898, 1015
Flanders, 250, 841
Flatbush Jewish Center, 907
Foch, Ferdinand, Marshall, 867, 871
Food, 354, 496, 570, 621, 640, 656, 793–94
children suffering from hunger, 148, 241, 321
from public kitchens, 534
help Britain with, 545
little for Polish Jews, 461, 540, 686, 970, 1005
none in sealed freight cars, 696
problems with *kashrut*, 528, 564, 606, 734
shortage of in Nazi Germany, 882
Ford, Henry, 837
Dearborn Independent, 837, 946
Der Internationale Jude, 842
The International Jew, 946
relationship with Leo Franklin, 945–46
Fortunoff Archive of Survivors' Testimonies, xxii, 5, 37, 42
Fosdick, Harry Emerson, 192, 225, 503, 588, 744, 777
Foster, Solomon, 18, 55
Four Freedoms, 623–24, 649, 681, 684, 709, 1011
Fourteen Points, 840
Fraenkel, Jonas, 99
France, xiii, xv, xxv, 77–78, 80, 88, 139, 142, 157, 216, 218, 249–51, 267, 329, 340, 361, 398, 423, 445–46, 449, 451–52, 454, 485, 537, 544, 591, 625, 682, 756
annexed, 490
antisemitic leader of, 251
armed to the teeth, 287
belief that "*true* France is not totally lost," 765
Christian priests in, 797
Christians save Jewish lives in, 798

clergy of take marvelous position, 587
contemplating surrender, 488
courage displayed by, 485
defeatism of, 588
delusion of peace, 336
democracy entrenched in, 294
desolation and humiliation of, 486, 491, 551
determined to destroy Hitlerism, 447
failures of, 578
fate of as warning to Britain and US, 491
fate of Jews in occupied, 1015
future crushing of, 342
government of allows children sent to concentration camps, 638
"Jewish Statute" passed in, 520–21, 773
Jews blamed for collapse of, 520
Jews of forced to wear Yellow Badge, 551
Jews of perish in death trains, 1008
Louis IX of, 124
and Munich Conference, 340
opened doors to refugees, 955
Petain on reason for failure, 512
protest in, xiv, 253, 310
safety of?, 395
share of responsibility for current disaster, 431
special laws for Jews announced, 505
surrender of to Germany, 494, 505
temporary breathing spell in, 506
threats from Mussolini against, 374
Zionism compatible with loyalty to, 286
Franco, Francisco, 295, 910
Franco-Russian Alliance, 250
Frank, Anne, 6
Frank, Hans, 130
Frankfurt-am-Main, 141, 168, 414, 417, 705
Frankfurt-an-der-Oder, 937
Frankfurter, David, 246–47, 350
Frankfurter, Salomon, 310
Frankfurter Zeitung, Die, 176, 883
Franklin, Leo M., xxii, 22, 47, 74, 134, 360, 945–48
opposes economic sanctions and public protests, 946
Free Synagogue, New York, 19, 235, 727, 835, 859, 1013
Free Synagogue Weekly Bulletin, 118
Freeden, Herbert, 15
Freehof, Solomon B., 22, 41, 46, 67
Freemasonry, 160
French Assembly, 139, 233
French Christians, reaction to Yellow badge, 632
French Revolution, 170, 294, 709
French troops,
and Marshall Foch, 871
surrendering to Germans, 946
Freud, Sigmund, 528
Friedlander, Saul, 2
Friedrich-Wilhelms University, 959
Fritsch, Werner von, 881
Fuehrer, Führer, see: Hitler
Fulda Bishops Conference, 885

G

Galicia, 299

Jews burned alive in Eastern, 689
Galut/Galuth, 314, 453–54, 895
See also: Exile, *Golus*
Gamaliel, Rabban, 220
Gannon, Franklin, 15
Gas chambers, 360, 647, 708, 734, 745, 762, 766–68, 790, 800, 802, 829, 1005
for 400 teenagers, 775
Hungarian Jews murdered in, 772, 1014
mass extermination in, 788
Sonderkommandos in, 7
Gas mask, 421
Gas, poison, 53, 206, 443, 496, 663, 708, 743, 747, 751, 790, 976, 979, 1008
of hate, 426
of propaganda, 342
Gassing, 544, 639, 674, 718, 743, 749, 772, 800, 829
Gdansk. *See* Danzig.
Geffen, David, 443, 920–21
Geffen, Tobias (Tuviah), 49, 167, 220, 919–21
certified Coca-Cola as kosher, 919
hopes for end of denominations within Jewry, 926–27
Geneva Convention, 88
no protection for Jews in, 979
Gentile, Giovanni, 276
George VI, King, 677
speech at opening of Parliament (1945), 822
German American Bund, 217, 371, 837
German Army, 148, 150, 812, 839
Fritsch as head of, 881
Jews in, 408
in Poland, 461
size of, 137
Soviet forces pushing out, 80
German Bund, 396
German-Christian Church, 848
German Communists, 98, 903–4
German culture,
fine expression of, 124
Jewish contribution to, 414, 855
nail in the coffin of, 110
German Embassy,
in Paris, 926
in Washington DC, 101, 879
German Evangelical Church, 118, 902–5
"German Jewish Congress," 842
German Jewry, 334, 379–80, 416–17, 922–23
absent from World Jewish Congress (1936), 259
appeal to Hindenburg, 111
assimilationists among, 138–39, 146
between Eastern and Western Jewry, 417–18
blamed for *Kristallnacht*, 15
borne itself with honor, 257
branded as "traitors," 114–15
as builders of Germany, 108
cavernous pit of, 608
"cold" boycott of, 121
condemned to death, 886
crushed into Nazi mire, 503
desolation of, 294
excluded from professions, 194, 213–18, 523, 862, 868–69
expulsion of the best of, 245
"finished – through," 862

in Germany for 1000 years, 91, 284, 424
hopelessness of its lot, 133, 246
huge financial penalty imposed, 348–49
humiliation of, 88, 99, 129, 135
impotent and defenceless, 326
kaddish for (1933), 417
leaders warn against criticism of Germany, 109
limited emigration of, 195
literature of, 174
living in a Ghetto, 218–19
lost and helpless, 889
love of country by, 347
loyal citizens in Germany, 517
most must remain in Germany, 253
multitudes of seeking synagogues, 151
no longer exists (1939), 417, 630
opposed boycott of German goods, xiv, 608
oppression and degradation of, 989
practically destroyed, 344
in process of liquidation, 293, 356
repudiated the God of Israel, 249
as saints treated as sinners, 380
as scapegoat, 129, 150, 520, 573, 857
second- or third-class citizens, 868
sentenced to death, 298
sermons on situation of, 18, 55
should be allowed into Western Europe, 364
speaking German in England, 410
stricken, shattered, and crushed, 295
suicide within, 135, 141
their martyrdom is their glory, 270
in the World War, 408
would be annihilated in new war, 408
Zionist section of, 418
German people, 110, 250
Allies guilty of wrongs against, 102, 426
cannot disclaim responsibility for atrocities, 795
honored and cherished, 102
fate of, following Hitler, 706
fleeing to Polish cities, 706
impact of the Treaty of Versailles on, 159, 541
Lebensraum and, 549
many sane and sound, 97
not the real enemy, 155, 438
re-education of required, 827
revival of sadism among, 136
spirit of, 110
suffering of, 100–101, 150, 596
surrendered its soul, 490
German propaganda machine, 67, 555, 614–15
German Socialists, 91, 303, 903
German Trade Unions, 164, 903–4
German universities, 121
Germany, 281, 284, 329, 511, 652
anti-Christian movement in, 245
battlefield in, 336
bestial hatred of Jews in, 263
betrayal of civilization by, 940

better spirit of, 92, 108, 159, 254
broken and thwarted, 189
catastrophe in, 194
censorship of press in, 128, 263
children of carrying guns, 227
cholera in medieval, 302
Christian suffering in, 326, 418
Church alone found courage to resist, 278, 283
criminal character of, 299
culture in, 136, 371
demands complete domination of Europe, 419
embraced by anti-Fascist Russia, 443
expulsion of Jews from, 37, 387–88, 412
as focal point of Jewish danger, 291
government of requires distinctly Jewish names, 433
gravity of Jewish position in, 92
has driven out 100,000 Jews, 284
Hitlerized, 624
humiliation of, 88, 119
inner decay of, 287
Jew-hatred in, 380, 410
Jewish graves plundered in medieval, 506
as menace to World Peace, 165
Ministry of Propaganda in, 281, 414, 636, 701
must admit its culpability, 795–96
new paganism in, 227
no further contact with, 399
one large concentration camp for Jews, 457
pact of with Russia, 446
pre-1933 Hitlerist policies in, 89
relatives of congregants in, 998
religious figures of and Nazism, 797
right of Jews to remain in, 185
seats of learning in, 297, 699
silent suffering of Jews in, 273
synagogues burned in, 351, 353, 357, 358, 365, 386, 428, 444, 455, 502, 509, 519, 522, 566, 943, 939–41
tortures inflicted on Jews in, 325
tradition of antisemitism in, 323
venomous propaganda in, 164
Gerstein, Israel, 66
Gerstein, Kurt, 4, 5
Gestapo, 5, 315, 369, 519, 534, 640, 745, 752, 768, 806, 848, 937, 987
banned reading of sermon/prayer by Leo Baeck, 229
concentration camps and dungeons of, 631
brutal deeds of, 640
legal adviser of, 735
member of assigned to each synagogue service, 18, 24, 39, 42, 302, 307, 930
seized Jews, 369, 686
Gettysburg Address, 29
Ghetto/Ghettos, 271, 523, 540, 642, 648, 667, 670, 692–93
of Europe, 667, 703, 716
Germany's return to, 232–34, 361
of Lublin, Bialystok, and Lodz, 8
of "Middle Ages," 218–19, 361, 607, 874
newspapers of, 8

not established in Germany, 240
of Poland, 6–7, 474, 477, 653, 652–53
re-establishment of, 581, 631, 639
of Rome, 74, 543
tenuous security of, 377
of twentieth century, 558
See also: Warsaw Ghetto
Gilbert, Martin, 2, 246, 362, 535
Gissibl, Fritz/Friedrich, 836–37, 841
Gladstone, William, 365
Gleichschaltung (imposed uniformity) 68, 320, 460
God, G-d, 204
abandoned us?, 78, 530, 720
allowing Hitler to triumph?, 311
all who believe in must unite, 420
calling out Hitlerian crimes to, 116
can turn to in sorrow, 405
chastening and hitting us, 733
continued faith in, 349
controls destinies of nations, 1026
critics of, 508
ending Torah study and prayer, 471
enormous anguish of, 590
every human being a child of, 428
faith in severely tested, 800
fighting the battle of, 543
and flourishing of evil, 447
gave superabundance to New World, 537
gives insight through sorrow, 612
giving power to crushed German Jews, 232
gratitude to for dawn of victory, 664
as the great comforter, 941
great message of, 644
hard to believe in mercy of, 736
has smitten, and will forgive, 685
haunting questions on role of, 1025
helped Jews bear their pains, 501
of history, 200, 203, 287, 294
Hitler fights against, 490
Hitler's god, 303
imperative that He act, 493
in control, just and good, 960
in the hearts of wanderers, 271
in the blackout, 503
is being forgotten, 394
and Jewish suffering, 75–83
judgment of upon the world, 656
light of seems disappeared, 429
lovingkindness of, 607, 822
making war with, 298
may wish us to suffer, 613–14
miraculous protection of, 737
must rush to deliver Jews, 527–28
Nazi war aimed at God of Israel, 489
negation of as a system, 365
omnipotence of, 483
as only salvation for Israel, 217
and Orthodox rabbis, 83
our sins against as cause of suffering, 313
personal providence of, 560

powers seeking to dethrone, 125, 298
prayer to for miraculous victory, 947, 950
prayers to are not answered, 584
punishing the German people, 294
punishing for sins of assimilation, 388
putting an end to remnant of Israel?, 664
questions about, 694–95
quoting biblical verses to, 802–3
reliance on supreme intervention of, 978
role of preceding victory, 1024
sanctifying name of, 576, 634, 655
saved survivors from the murderers, 812
silence of, 117, 653
smiling upon our fortunes, 767
source of succor and salvation, 272
speaks through historic events, 581
spirit of triumphs in human hearts, 567
step down from your high throne, 583
strange workings of providence of, 429
suffering brings us nearer to, 935
suffering for the sake of, 417
suffers along with us, 83, 367, 527
teaches us to be happy, 414
thanksgiving to, 811, 824, 1025
trust in has wavered, 934
as if on trial, 1025
trust in power of, 239
voice of, 178, 203, 304, 581, 718
war against, 385, 400, 693, 817
ways of mysterious, 97, 294
weeping in His inner chamber, 618
where is?, 75, 77–80, 286, 496, 503–4, 515–16, 577, 590, 691, 729, 777
who can know His will and purpose?, 432
why does He not interfere?, 317
will grant victory to the Allied Nations, 713
will have compassion, 463
will not fail us, 849
will work miracles for us, 249
worshipped by Christians and Jews, 208
and Zionistic program, 165
See also: Deus absconditus
Goebbels, Paul Joseph, 114, 118, 161, 168, 233, 276, 280, 356, 380, 414, 706, 847, 886
American imitators of, 514
justifying Nazi government, 364
propaganda purposes of, 864
says Jews must be annihilated to save Germany, 636
speech of at Berlin Sports Palace, 40, 702
speech of copied by Father Coughlin, 376
use of antisemitism by, 764
Goering/Göring, Hermann, 118, 161, 245, 315, 862, 869, 910
Goethe, Johann Wolfgang von, 92, 321

as model of good German, 93, 108, 214, 848, 890
Gog and Magog, 490
Goga, Octavian, 310
Golders Green Synagogue, London, 487, 937
Goldstein, Israel, 61, 68, 73, 475
Golem, 333–34
Golgotha, 377
Gollancz, Victor, 700–1
Golus, 200–1, 874
See also: Exile, *Galut*
Gordon, Julius, 11, 155, 349
Gorny, Yosef, 15, 1004
Goshen, Land of, 338
Gospel/Gospels, 906
preaching the, 327, 703
a new/old devilish, 268, 857
will no longer be preached, 949–50
Göttingen, 297
Gottschalk, Albert, 33–34
Grobman, Alex, 15
Great Britain, Britain, xv–xvi, 237, 240, 250, 361
fighting a "holy war," 522
fleet of sinks Nazi ships, 471
gratitude for accepting refugees, 940, 955
help for Jewish refugees, 410
House of Commons debate, 364
and Jewish National Home, 787
little short of a dictatorship, 485
moral strength of, 364
must have no war [1936], 250
pledge full support of, 430
proposal of to settle Jews in Tanganyika, 360
responsibility of for Holy Land, 375
saved from great peril, 818
share of responsibility for current disaster, 431
spirit of in 1940, 823
virtually closes doors to Palestine, 531
See also: England
"Great Hatred, The," 531, 703
"Great War," *see:* World War I
Greece, 346, 453, 553, 557, 576, 639, 684, 756, 849, 989, 1015
Christians save Jewish lives in, 798
Nazi soldiers in control of, 652
in shambles, 572–73
Greenberg, Gershon, xxiv, 3, 49, 81, 83, 387, 392, 733, 775, 791, 921
Grey, Edward, 338
Gries, Moses, 893
Gross, Jan T., 1000
Grosswardein [Oradea], 388
Grynszpan, Hirschel, 926
Gustloff, Wilhelm, 246, 275, 350–51
Gypsies, gassing of in Auschwitz, 829

H

Habakkuk, 562, 813
Haber, Fritz, 204
Haber, Sylvia, 46
Hadrian, 793, 921, 943
Hadrianic persecution, 582
Haggadah, 60, 95, 220, 313
reality for present, 60, 852–53
special relevance of, 551
Haggai, 817
The Hague, 461

Hale, Everett, "The Man Without a Country," 433
Hallel, 681, 1025
Halpern, Abraham, 76
Haman, 64–68, 72, 74, 78, 117–18, 248, 282, 296, 358, 442, 543, 685, 705, 857, 898–99, 916, 922–23, 926
as Amalekite immigrant, 897
as classical anti-Semite, 24, 222, 897
as code for Hitler, 177, 217, 307–8, 390–91, 614, 895–98, 908
differences from Hitler, 614
as equivalent of Streicher, 908, 910
regime of, 258
stranger and super-patriot, 897
Hambro, Carl, 745
Hamburg, 454, 790
bombed by Allies, 1020
Hampstead Synagogue, London, 406, 937
Hananel, Chief Rabbi of Bulgaria, 700
Hananya ben Teradion, 943
Hanukkah, 24, 67, 75, 167, 207, 241, 277, 370–71, 373, 776
for all mankind, 600
rally on in Madison Square Garden, 838
Harper's Magazine, 726
Harvard University, MA, xii, 1, 135, 859, 901
Law School, 991
Stephen S. Wise speaking at, 33
Hasidism, xii, 387
Hasidic preaching, 21, 48, 740
major texts of, 1014
Piekarz on, xxiv, 740
Polish, xxiv, 18
rebbes of, 94, 388, 794, 1018
Hauptmann, Bruno, 211–12
Hazkarat Neshamot (commemoration of the departed), 550
See also: Yizkor
Headlam, A.C., 327
Hearst, William Randolph, 882
Hebrew Immigrant Aid Society (HIAS), 369
Hebrew Prophets, 411
Hebrew Theological Seminary, Skokie, IL, 959
Hebrew Union College, 34, 845, 877, 893, 901, 945, 983
Alumni Association, 859
Hebrew University, Jerusalem, 26
Hecht, Ben, xv, 996
Heidelberg, 297
University of, 929
Heilbronn, Isaak (Ernst), 465
Heimler, Eugene, 4
Helbronner, Jacques, 734
Hell, 364, 751, 964, 1010
anvil of, 336
Central Europe as a human, 531
concentration camp as, 465
Dante's description, 942
darkness of, 70, 560
Diaspora Jews living in, 575, 620
of Eastern Europe, 215
of Europe, 603
four years of, 162
fury greater than, 468
gates of, 60, 114, 791, 829
of Germany, 133, 135
Hitler's, 320
jaws of will open, 561
Jewish communities plunged into, 3765
lexicon of, 687

Nazi, 466, 674, 829
of Treblinka and Auschwitz, 749
world transformed into, 718
Hellenism, 174, 849
Heller, Abraham Mayer, 54, 65, 907–8
pacifist position of, 908
Zionist causes, 907
Henson, H. Hensley, 247, 327
Herod, King, 168
Herrenmoral (Master Morality), 735–36
Herrenvolk (Master Race), 65, 308, 493, 626, 661, 800
Hershkowitz, Isaac, 739
Hershman, Abraham M., 41, 51, 53–54, 659, 743, 1008
Hertz, Joseph, xiv–xv, xxiii, 42, 47, 114, 120, 183, 365, 591, 629, 727, 857, 901, 976, 996, 1003–6
address to Jewish Preachers by, 72–73, 1010
agony of his last few years, 1005
circular of limiting holy day rituals, 507
"Companion of Honour" conferred by the King, 677
condemns "silence" of the world, 1004
conducts services in ruins of Great Synagogue, 566–67, 572
establishes services for German Jewish refugees, 406
on history of Austrian Jewry, 319
holiday messages of, 58
on Jewish profiteers, 621
leads Induction Ceremony for Altmann, 367
leads Service of Mourning and Prayer (May 22, 1944), 1004, 1010
memorial address for, 42
organizes Shabbat services for refugees, 406, 937
Pesach sermon by, 60–61, 114
rhetorical challenges of preaching, 1004
sermon passages printed by *JC*, 56
sermons of responding to two World Wars, 901
Hertzberg, Arthur, 37–38
Hertzberg, Zvi Elimelech, 37–38
Herzl, Theodor, 146, 190, 223
Herzog, Isaac, xxiv, 50, 181, 375, 384, 690, 698, 757, 807
and Jewish refugees from Balkans, 754–54
meets with Pius XII, 669–70
"no third destruction," 634, 649
Heschel, Abraham Joshua, 303, 451
Heschel, Susannah, 255, 303, 609, 840, 848, 906
Heydrich, Reinhard, 618, 635
High Priest/*Cohen Gadol*, 71–72, 248, 993–96, 998
Hilberg, Raul, 2
Hildesheimer Rabbinical Seminary, 959
Hillel, 964–65
injunction of the Hillelites, 373
Hillel House, Cornell, 867
Himmler, Heinrich, 356, 636
Festausgabe in honor of, 735

new decree on deportations by, 1006
Hindenburg, Paul von, 111, 869
Hirohito, 625, 808
Hirschmann, Ira A., 754
History, 72–74, 82, 89, 111, 114, 117, 135, 139, 142, 151, 154, 167, 193, 196, 389
biblical, 71
contemporary relevance of, 269
crisis in, 208, 336
cruel irony of, 120
darkest page in, 133, 144, 157, 198, 225, 349
diaries as sources for, 6–7
divine directing of, 177
dusty pages of revitalized, 542
forces of are inexorable, 490
German, 100, 159
God of, 177, 193, 200, 203, 230, 287, 294
greatest massacre of innocent people in, 13
Hitler's most monstrous lie in, 247
inexorable law of, 335
Jewish consciousness of, 234
Jewish suffering throughout, 70, 143, 177, 261, 269, 939
Jews take up heaviest responsibility in, 198
knows nothing as fiendish as Nazi persecution, 663
law of, 64
learning nothing from the past, 911
lessons of, xvi, 251, 280, 672, 908
most ruthless Jew-haters in modern, 220
of Nazi mass murder, 10
new insight into, 188
no precedent in, 75, 276, 277, 310, 325, 327, 341, 348
obligation of Jews to preserve, 469
one of the great sins in all of, 340
pattern of, 59–61
repeating itself, 95, 150, 182, 220, 291, 316, 369, 419, 614, 645, 852–54
sermons as source for, 17–19
shatters despair of defeatism, 114
shows Jewish contribution to civilization, 234
of spiritual greatness and dignity, 326
stained with blood of Jews, 698
strength of Jews in, 68
suffering not a new phenomenon in, 261
teaches Jews to be patient, 285
teaches what persecution means, 122
three most agonizing years in world [1940–1942], 656
travesty of, 188
voice of, 207, 581
with the forces of freedom, democracy, 229
History, Jewish, 73, 95, 117, 177, 230, 251, 665–66, 696
antisemitism in, 280
continual process of renewal in, 305
darkness and light of hope in, 285
epic hour of in Palestine, 263
extraordinary stage in, 198

fate of in balance, 271
great event in, 167
greatest catastrophe/crisis in, 143–44, 183, 350, 431, 653
in Germany, 109
as history of suffering, 70, 939
Kristallnacht surpassed blackest pages of, 662
loneliness in, 643
most critical period in, 654
most tragic hour in [1940], 497
most tragic year in [1933, 1942], 137, 641
nothing in like current persecution, 276, 692
not only suffering and humiliation, 748
persecution in, 122
protest rally a great event in, 166–67
proud page in, 155, 260, 263
religious heroism in, 552
remains sacred, 517
sermons in, 20
suffering in, 70, 142, 268, 291, 688
thousands of years of, 183, 284, 305, 335, 428, 574, 644
tragic moment of our, 384
as vibrant flowing stream, 269
in Vilna, 12
as a whole, 753
Yishuv as gleaming page in, 260
See also: Jews

Hitler, Adolf, 189, 238, 284, 295, 310, 321, 394, 398–99, 625, 636, 756, 910
actually promoting Communism, 279
allergic to Judaism and Christianity, 335
ambition of for world supremacy, 952
and annihilation of Christianity, 484
and Haman, 67, 14–15, 895
and "Jewish State" in Poland, 448
and Old Testament, 93
appeal of to German youth, 288–89
arousing many to oppose him, 435–36
as anti-Messiah, 492
as apotheosis of present world, 429
as arch antisemite, 397
attack of against Poland, 424
attacked by Pope Pius XI, 279
attacks Jews as war-mongering and pacifist, 544
audio-visual records of speeches by, 29, 32
barbaric Reich of, 282
breaks every promise, fulfills every threat, 690
broadcast, June 5, 1940, 947
as chief slaughterer of our time, 510
claims Bolshevism is 90 percent Jewish, 280
claims no intention to invade America, 489
coming to fate of all liars, 547
considers converts as Jews, 106, 158
crimes against humanity by, 750
"death to the Jews" policy of, 161

declared war on the Jews, 784
as demagogue of genius, 541
as demon of barbarism and savagery, 624
exploitation of the Church by, 290
extermination policy of, 666
as false/anti-messiah, 100, 492
as fanatical maniac, 157
fleeing hordes of, 808
forced back onto his heels, 682
funeral address by, 246
goal of to destroy Jews of Germany, 305
as the great hater, 529
has uprooted five million Jews (May, 1941), 558, 563
hates the Jews, 406
his hold on some Americans, 422
his name almost forgotten, 711–12
how can he be defeated?, 558
as incarnation of the devil, 454
as instrument of God, 82
invited to Economic Conference, 119
January 30, 1939 Address, 125, 383
like Antiochus Epiphanes, 241, 460, 531
like Shabbatai Zevi, 100
Machiavellian desire of, 303
as mad dictator, 485
may last for many years, 592
may kill millions of Jews, 672
Mein Kampf of, 32, 160, 258, 262, 341–52, 376, 426, 625
as menacing madman of Europe, 171
messiah complex of, 204, 561, 77
as modern, crueler Pharaoh, 491, 548
as modern Korah, 70–71, 560–61
name written as "H-r," 390
"not for war," 839
as orator, 9–10, 32, 33, 160
out-bluffs the world, 356
policies of beginning 1933, 334
prestige and power of, 340
promises a Germany *Judenrein*, 838, 897
propaganda machine of, 841
purge by henchmen of, 209
Reichstag Address of (January 1939), 432
rejection of democracy by, 170
as representative of German nationalism, 159
as Satan, 490, 525, 579, 592, 646
six-year reign of, 376
sought all means to crush the Jew, 680
speaks of "Jewish Problem," 448
speeches of, 9–10, 29, 262, 302, 621, 947
states intention to exterminate Jewry, 621
struck hands with Stalin, 449
as substitution for God, 609
as Teutonic madman who would be God, 265
unspeakable brutalities of, 795
use of antisemitism by, 764
utters most monstrous lie in history, 247
vainglorious madness of, 339
victory of over the Allies, 949

vow to burn every Jewish book, 641
vulture rather than buzzard, 349
whole world menaced by, 320
will not stop with Czechoslovakia, 42
world-wide movement led by, 198
as world's most dangerous criminal, 425
"would-be"s in America, 808
Hitlerism, 157, 180, 189, 449, 500
as activated anti-Jewish policy, 91
bound to provoke a world war, 246
boycotts against, 111
eternal warfare of with Prophetism, 94
Germany greater than, 93
Jews as crushed victims of, 197
Jews as historic enemy of, 266
means rule of hatred, 93
means war, 218
as menace to civilization, 846
must be crushed, 641, 681
as new philosophy of government, 175
nightmare of, 500
no need for Jews to fear, 849
now to be extirpated by war, 441–42
succeeded in exterminating millions, 7867
three years of, 244
will be forgotten, 113
world's growing protest against, 435
Hitler Youth, 202, 710
Hlond, August, Cardinal, 464
Hochschule für die Wissenschaft des Judentums, 296, 929
Holland, 157, 309, 351–52, 395, 494, 522, 572, 591 , 625, 684, 756, , 841, 953, 979
Christian priests in, 797
Christian residents of wear Shield of David, 586
Christians save Jewish lives in, 798
lost independence in battle, 505–6
no Jews left in, 704
opened doors to refugees, 955
sterilization of Jews in, 1008
surrender of to Germany, 494, 947
See also: Netherlands
Hollywood, 660
Holmes, John Haynes, 140, 192, 235, 744
holocaust [pre-1946 usage], 158, 205, 315, 624, 825, 914, 1028
consumes so many Jews, 719
horrible and unique in Jewish history [April 1941], 545
of millions of Jews, 672
of remorse, 514
shaken to the core by, 721
terrifying of current war, 738
that has consumed Europe [Sept 1941], 575
will enter world history, 673
Holocaust [post-1945 usage], xi, xxiv, 1–3, 5, 14, 19–20, 37, 55, 81, 83, 370, 827, 959
Holy Blossom Temple, Toronto, 34, 877
Holy of Holies, 208, 324, 531, 993

Holy Land, 149, 375, 410, 576, 668, 740–41, 794
another Munich in the, 393
assault by Arabs in, 321
Nazis standing at gates of, 649
no third destruction of, 634, 649
protected by divine providence, 757
See also: Eretz Yisrael, Land of Israel, Palestine
Horsemen of the Apocalypse, 504
Hosea, 149, 175
House of Commons, 196, 321, 364, 629, 690, 700, 988
House of Lords, 690, 987
"House of Rothschild," 874
Huberband, Shimon, 19, 970, 1000
Huguenots, 478
Humanism, 548
Hungarian Jews, 741, 767
at brink of annihilation, 1004
backs to the wall, 293
catastrophe of, 81, 749
deportation of to Auschwitz, 772, 1014
doom over has lightened, 772
hope of for liberation by Russians, 759
lengthening shadow over, 330
mass murder of, 54
report of converts returning to Judaism, 769–70
rights of partly abolished, 344
sword against the neck of, 757
Hungary, 13, 36, 97, 179, 344, 367, 376, 393–95, 585, 690, 739–40, 975
absorption of Ruthenia by, 397
anti-Jewish legislation in, 397
anti-Semitism encouraged in, 505
economic *numerus clausus* in, 412
firing squads in, 769
haven from death in, 750
in grip of terror, 573
integrity of study in, 794
Nazification of endangers a million Jews, 1009
pogroms in, 165
remnant of Israel in, 757
al-Husseini, Amin (Mufti of Jerusalem), 403

I

Ibn Verga, Solomon, 990
Iceland, 203
Ickes, Harold, 645
Idel, Moshe, 48
India, 108, 239, 395, 549, 616, 908–9
Inge, William Ralph, 166, 174
Innitzer, Theodor, 227, 355, 357
Inquisition (of the Gestapo), 369
Inquisition (Spanish), 53, 69, 72–73, 114, 182–83, 189, 221, 271, 334, 501, 607, 706, 716, 894, 955, 981, 997–98
International Conference of Baptists, 234
International News Service, 535
International Rabbinate, 749
Isaac, 69, 228–29, 335, 345, 518–19, 521, 552, 723, 941.
See also: Akedah.
Isaac Elchanan Theological Seminary, 991
Isaiah, 148, 161, 175, 263, 345, 430, 574, 698, 705, 717, 727, 799, 810, 899–900, 1015
First Isaiah, 1021

Second Isaiah, 1016
suffering servant of, 221, 644
Isolationism, Isolationists, 464, 730
of America and American Jews, 588, 648, 784
repudiates modern Noah's Ark of, 722
Ishmael, 226, 228–29
Israel,
ancient, 140, 192, 200, 324, 868, 913, 915, 931
antisemitism forged against, 706
appeal for "weapons" for defense of, 1000–1
appeal to return to the land, 807
archival material in, 19
army of, 992, 994
battles of, 486
belief in rebirth of, 1015
borders of, 940–41, 943, 994
camp of, 199
catastrophes that have befallen, 498
Chief Rabbi of, 649
children/sons (and daughters) of, 62, 115, 183, 259, 271, 295, 330, 476, 488, 502, 548, 559, 605, 612, 641, 648, 682, 685, 687, 701, 712, 821, 854–56, 1015, 1019;
See also: Children
committed massive, serious sins, 590
community of and its suffering, 688
conscience of, 788
courage needed by, 696
critical period for, 511, 559
crucifixion of, 710
"cup of My fury" for, 1016
current plight/situation of, 687, 739
danger imperils immortality of, 999
darkness for, 222, 363, 378, 503
daughter of, 995
declaration of war against, 432
descendants of will be blessed, 526
desire to destroy the whole people of, 855
devastating defeat not the end of, 992
down in the dust, 583
in Egypt, 748
end to the agony/misery of, 392, 493
endless martyrdom of, 674
enemies of, 678–79, 690, 716, 805, 897, 900, 922, 926
evil beast pounced upon, 577
exemplary composure as tradition of, 737
faith of, 313, 391, 540
fate of in the balance, 271, 909, 913, 955–56
fathers and mothers of, 998, 1001
fled from the Philistines, 995
fight for the cause of, 875
foes of, 331, 896
friends of, 375
future of, 688, 713
German, 258
glory of, 517, 996
God and/God of, 193, 217, 229–30, 249, 269, 272, 286, 304, 455, 489, 527, 552, 562,

590–91, 664, 678, 693, 711, 713, 720, 785, 849, 926, 980, 995, 1018
governments asked to speak for, 849
grandeur of the name of, 789
greater woe of, 1007–8
greatest teachers of, 964
greets New Year with tears, 985
guardian of, 455, 493, 723, 977–78, 980
Hadrian ruled over, 921
has been defeated, 71, 995–96
haters/hatred of, 414, 500, 629, 690, 703
having disposed of, 826
heavens of beclouded and befogged, 585
Hertz gave himself unsparingly to the cause of, 1005
historical role of, 645
history of, 134, 177–78, 182, 198, 268, 291, 346, 422, 644, 754, 923
[Hitler] has vowed destruction of, 646
holidays of, 895
hope of, 375
house/household of, 125, 138, 149, 152, 249, 271, 292, 318, 337–38, 421, 502, 582, 633, 655, 664–65, 741, 798, 824, 898, 1008, 1011
as independent nation, 993
is indestructible, 530
land of, 149, 267, 275, 332, 387, 389, 620, 649, 728, 740–41, 754, 799, 981; *See also: Eretz Yisrael*
lives on to tell sad but glorious tale, 998
is made to tread the Via Dolorosa, 847
marches on invincible, 976, 980
martyrdom of, 731, 1005
masters and fathers of, 799
meaning of travail of, 675
message of peace from, 515
mission of, 409
millions of harassed and homeless, 426
mourns with no consolation, 666
must speak for those who cannot, 985
need of for rebirth, regeneration, 627
new defamation of, 231
offendings of a bitter past against, 825
the oldest nation on earth, 809
ominous shadow over the tents of, 824
one fellowship for all of, 588
oppressed in, near and far, 935
oppressors of, 1020
ordeals as destiny of, 734
Palestine contrasted with, 787
people of, 145, 253, 268, 346, 385, 418, 492, 590, 633, 659, 705, 736, 762, 788, 831, 855, 921, 926–27, 984, 992–93, 1015–16, 1018
persecution being heaped upon, 722
plague (of war) worked havoc in, 743
power of exaggerated by enemies, 702
prayer from the heart of, 984
as prophet of the nations, 722

prophet chides, 1018
prophets of, 161, 230, 436, 736, 1015
psyche of, 704
race of, 255
redemption of, 392
rebirth of, 1015, 1021
rejects counsel of despair, 990
religion of, 560
a religious community or nation?, 989
remnant/s of, 411, 455, 574, 664, 672, 672, 698–99, 701, 723, 749, 757, 787, 978, 980
response of to Arab savagery, 263
responsibility of 93 girls towards, 729
Rock of, 664
sacrificial giving ideal of, 721
the saintly of being slaughtered, 633
salvation of, 758, 926
saving single soul from, 724
schism in the ranks of, 732
shattered though invincible, 767
sin of leads to exile, 960
son of, 765
soul of, 339
speaking as a rabbi in, 815
spirit of, 254, 268, 434
as spiritless, hopeless, 556
spiritual self-sufficiency of, 751
spiritual weapons of, 558
stands divided, 322
stands together with Christendom, 208
State of, 920
strength of, 95
as "Suffering Servant," 221, 817
sufferings of, 367, 416, 562, 599, 656, 685, 792, 1015
survival of?, 577
"Sweet Singer" of, 261
there will always be an, 589
threefold blessing of, 935–36
told it must be patient, 987
tragedy of, 385
tribulations of, 1014, 1016
unheard-of troubles for, 388
ultimate victory for, 463
ultra-Orthodox communities in, 41
uniqueness of, 215
as victim of appeasement politics, 531
voice of, 504
wanders aimlessly on highways of history?, 678
will not be destroyed, 203
World, 127, 864
year [5702] of violence and slaughter for, 644
zero hour in life of, 726
See also: Jews
Israel, American, 765, 787
Israel, European,
calamity/destruction has overwhelmed, 623, 699
Isserman, Ferdinand M., xxi–xxii, 10–11, 23, 27, 47, 155, 187, 215, 243, 251, 260, 286, 298, 305, 357, 450, 525, 576, 641, 780–81, 781, 877–78
aunt of sheltered by Belgian Christians, 798
fierce antipathy toward Nazism of, 878
preliminary text of the sermon, 383

visits to Germany by, 156, 877–78
wants America to stay out of war, 878
Istanbul, 616, 755, 790
Italian-Ethiopian dispute, 881
Italian Jews, 330, 344, 758
Italy, 13, 73, 142, 218, 227, 249, 255, 327, 395, 412, 431, 547, 596, 624, 765, 772, 798, 803, 854
antisemitism introduced to, 344, 505
Catholic church extends aid to Jews in, 758
Christian priests in saved Jewish children in, 797
compassionate Christians saved Jewish lives in, 798
copying Nazi Germany, 327
diplomacy of blackmail, 336
exile of thousands of Jews from, 328–29, 330
foreign students in, but no Jews, 346
incarceration of Jewish refugees, in, 315
in grip of terror, 573
invasion of Ethiopia by, 784
Jewish graves plundered in, 506
no further contact by democracies with, 399
racial poison accepted in, 331
slaughtered unarmed Abyssinians, 508
struggle against racism in, 386

J

Jabotinsky, Vladimir (Ze'ev), 11, 712
influence of on Louis I. Newman, 1013, 1017
The War and the Jew by, 16
Jacob, 70, 148, 316, 325, 335, 399, 456, 521, 526, 854, 923, 939, 941
house of, 379, 900
struggle with angel, 737
soul of, 95
Jacob, Walter, 41, 46
Japan, 255, 393, 624, 648–49
antisemitism in, 409, 505
bombed civilians in Manchuria, 508
controlled by Allied Armies, 821
Fascist, 409
no further contact with, 399
Japanese, 82
declaration of war against US, 595
invaded Manchuria, 264, 784
residents of United States, 679–80
superior to Chinese?, 637
Jedwabne, 1000
Jehoiakim, 911, 913
Jeremiah, 355, 387, 486, 533, 571, 668, 792–93, 960
a new must arise, 352
the godly elegist, 473
Jerusalem, 107, 155, 341, 634, 689, 705, 757, 810, 935, 956, 959, 1016, 1021
as city of God, 248
Bishop of, 394
contrast with Caesarea, 966
fall of, 964–67, 1015
fear of Nazi desecration of, 563
Grand Mufti of, 403
piercing the walls of, 961–62
ruins of, 468, 718
siege and fall of, 74, 543

Jesus, 175, 305, 345, 430, 641, 736, 847
as "first antisemite," 208–9
contrast with Hitler of, 94
crucifixion of the people of, 703
Jew or Aryan?, 906
Jewishness of, 255
Nordic, not Jewish, 840
rebuke to fellow Jews by, 208
Talmud on, 840
Jewish Agency, 616, 631, 689, 803
Jewish/Yellow badge, 257, 281, 551, 586, 606, 631–33, 675, 764
as "badge of shame," 257, 593, 696, 996
See also: Six-pointed star, David's Shield
Jewish Center of Williamsbridge, Bronx, 991
Jewish children, 184, 214, 223–24, 856, 870, 941, 1006
saved by Christian priests, 797
See also: Children
Jewish Chronicle (JC), xxiii, 16–17, 42, 53, 56, 58–59, 89, 99, 114, 130–31, 193, 229, 240, 247, 251, 279, 292, 354, 361, 363, 406, 438, 438, 457, 487, 539, 550, 591, 622, 629, 640, 649, 667, 677, 707, 727, 772, 775, 816, 930, 975–76, 981, 996, 1004, 1006, 1008, 1010
Jewish Commonwealth,
re-establishment of, 710
Jewish Community, 132, 154, 181, 274, 331, 475, 571, 576, 768, 780–81, 976
in America, xii, 407, 501, 788, 814, 859, 923
in Austria, 310
in France, 36, 820
in Germany, 6, 136, 226, 254, 363, 535
in Palestine, 305, 341, 649
in Poland, 442, 689, 1005
in Romania, 301
Jew-hating, 223
See also: anti-Semitism
Jewish Historical Society of Offenbach, 168
Jewish Institute of Religion/JIR, 19, 33, 835, 859, 867
Jewish Legion,
call for rejected, 980
Jewish Morning Journal, 725
Jewish National Committee of Poland, 689
Jewish National Day of Fast and Mourning, 668, 807, 976
Jewish (National) Homeland, 124, 622, 746–47, 787
may pass to fascist rule, 492
Palestine as, 285
Washington avoiding endorsement of, 697
See also: Eretz Yisrael, Palestine
Jewish Preachers Conference, 857
Jewish Question, 224, 312, 439, 442, 510, 595
as fundamental in Germany, 164
Institute for Research into the, 414
as nightmare of the present, 962
Jewish Religious Union (London), 901
Jewish State,
fall of the ancient, 962, 964, 966
national restoration and, 807
not all Jews want, 809

in Poland?, 448–49
as potential Switzerland of Asia, 341
and "state of Judaism," 728
world not morally ripe for, 965
in Zion/Palestine, 799, 1013
Jewish Telegraphic Agency (JTA), xiii, xxiii, 4, 11, 16, 53, 96, 99, 131, 137, 151, 187, 193, 205, 207, 251, 260, 293, 295, 310, 315, 361, 393, 461, 464, 486, 522, 586, 593, 636, 640–41, 704, 707–8, 758, 764, 768, 788, 801, 803, 837, 843, 946
Jewish Theological Seminary of America (JTSA), 830, 851–52, 907, 1003
Jewry, 115, 133, 147, 151, 198, 200, 213, 265, 306, 458, 512, 568, 591, 646, 659, 663, 782, 838, 1029
Anglo/British/English, 115, 131, 270, 280, 319, 572, 629, 668, 699, 978, 1009–10, 1023
Belgian, 1008
Birmingham, casualty list of, 1028
Bulgarian, 700
centers of banished or destroyed, 770
Canadian, 845
of Central Europe, 475
continental, 677, 976, 980
Czech, exile of, 608
dark and critical hour for, 403
dire troubles of, 239
East-European, 418, 667, 673
English speaking, 699
enmeshed in an inescapable web, 293
extirpation of in Europe, 353, 562
French, 581, 821, 1008
gratitude of for friends, 375
greatest calamity of since destruction of Temple, 182
history of, 461, 848
Hitler aim to exterminate, 621, 638
Hungarian, 81, 293, 330, 741, 759, 767, 770
incitement and hatred against, 386
international, 432
leaders of, 705
martyrdom of, 782
modern, 597
most savage persecution of, 1014, 1016
never more broken or tortured than now, 803
no rescue plans for doomed, 976, 979
Palestinian, 173–74, 716, 993
prayers of, 482
ready for military resistance, 980
remnant of remains alive, 822
responsible voices of, 126
in ruins, 822
Russian, 417, 630, 726, 963
as a separate race, 214
Slovakian, deportation of, 617
Spanish, 462
sympathy for calamities of, 675
threat of extinction for half of, 677
tragic disintegration of, 199
Western, 418
will always survive, 574, 996
world/universal, 126, 143, 165, 173, 191, 246, 260, 277, 291,

294, 322, 404, 422, 577, 702, 807, 873–74
See also: American Jewry, Austrian Jewry, European Jewry, German Jewry, Polish Jewry

Jews,
accused of wanting war against Germany, 184, 437
annihilation of, 74, 125, 127, 129, 160, 206, 218, 325, 432, 477, 491, 511, 544, 619, 636, 641, 668, 679, 684, 692, 697–98, 750, 799
as arch-enemy of the world, 267
barbaric plan of extermination against, 554, 663, 670, 767
as barometers of civilization, 488, 717, 816, 821
as bastard mongrelization, 838
as biological parasite, 838
by the grace of Hitler, 784
choices of behavior in age of oppression, 475
as "the Christ people," 846
cities without, 786
condemned to slow death by starvation, 461, 576, 583
as conscience of the world, 339
cowardice and apathy of, 315
crushed to the ground, 692, 695
deprived of their homes, 495
driven into state of despair, 556
dying of hunger, 444, 468, 478, 571, 583; *See also:* Starvation
as eternal strangers, 527
extermination of, 11, 13, 40, 53, 130, 134, 142, 156, 161, 177, 359, 404, 413, 446, 464, 474, 554, 592, 596, 631, 652, 639, 663, 666, 667, 669–70, 685, 690, 697, 705, 708, 712–13, 735, 788, 827–28, 831, 978, 986, 1005, 1016–17, 1029
as first appeasers of Nazism, 553–54
as first scapegoat, 916
as first victims of Nazi bestiality, 154, 324, 439, 476, 482, 485, 541, 563, 615, 645, 727, 783, 818
five million imprisoned, 996
gargantuan conflict for preservation of, 342
as greatest sufferers in the war, 713
as grist for Hitler's hate, 955
harrowing descriptions of their plight, 687
have become pariahs of the earth, 955
have sixth sense of calamity, 611
helplessness of, 130, 169, 265, 271, 293, 293, 324, 348, 356, 365, 420, 431–32, 439, 474–75, 505–6, 555, 593, 652, 666, 674, 680, 736, 816, 990, 1008
homeland of, 145, 185, 285–86, 306–7, 393, 397, 453, 492, 557, 673, 697, 705, 719, 744–46, 809, 987, 994
as impotent spectators, 976
international character of, 301
libels concocted against, 570
losing sense of identity, 446
loyalty of to their country, 195, 313
martyrdom of, 83, 138, 154, 204, 223–24, 257, 270, 306, 355, 428, 438, 445, 469, 477, 501, 519,

576, 582, 589, 635, 639, 653, 665, 668, 674, 710, 731, 719–20, 744, 766, 768–69, 782–83, 785, 792, 820–21, 866, 978, 986, 997, 1005, 1007, 1018
mass crucifixion of, 989
mass electrocutions of, 663, 674, 718, 747, 1005–6, 1008
mass shooting of in Poland, 593
must be allowed a Jewish Army, 631, 671, 980
must not irritate British government, 761
nationalists and assimilationists, 766
need rebirth of ancestors' courage, 330
no longer safe anywhere, 268, 332
no precedents to suffering of, 955
not fatalists, 770
not included in post-war planning, 678
one million additional killed by September 1943, 986
as organic body, 286
persecution of unprecedented, 343, 955
Reformers and Orthodox, 766, 769
shall not forget destruction of, 981
sinfulness of, 590
some indulging in self-hate, 513
suffered even more in the past, 644
suffering of, 104, 129, 251, 253, 272–74, 373, 392, 663, 724–25, 853, 962; *see also:* Suffering
suicides of, *see:* Suicide
survival of, 41, 530, 666, 757, 955, 1021
two million killed (by December 1942), 71, 631, 667, 672, 674, 696–97, 976, 986, 996
uniqueness of present crisis for, 72–75, 434, 545, 639, 644, 792–93
used for testing poison gasses, 663
utter defeatism of, 292
volunteered for military service, 679
war of extermination against, 404, 554, 631, 1029
war has brought decline in status, 826
weaklings who flee to South America, 456
will have a free and democratic Commonwealth, 825
will live on, 487
as worshippers of Mammon, 681
Zionists and anti-Zionists, 766, 769
See also: Israel; History, Jewish
Jews' College, London, 26, 699, 975, 1023
Job, 406, 418, 492–93, 612, 654, 736
every refugee is a, 76
story of as parable of the present, 651
Jochanan ben Zakkai, 304, 964–65
Johannesburg, SA, 1003
Johnson, Lyndon B., 859
Joffre, Joseph, 871

Joint Distribution Committee, 379, 534, 653
Jonah, 337, 783
Joseph, 94, 379, 672, 795, 855, 858
Joseph, Morris, 27, 43
Joshua, 188, 492
Joshua ben Hananiah, 150
Jospe, Alfred, 39, 406
Journalists, 9, 12–13, 32, 369, 446, 461, 622, 706
  foreign, in Germany, 888
  Jewish, 213, 869
Judah Maccabee, 68, 154, 460
Judaism, 273, 291
  answer to Nazi lies, 204
  assassination not the way of, 350
  and Bolshevism, 280, 302, 440
  cannot escape from, 147
  and Christianity, 180, 303, 324, 326, 334, 355, 398, 400, 402, 480, 502, 601–2, 654, 715, 905–6
  and Communism, 290, 715
  defeat Hitlerism by strengthening, 558
  Eisenmenger as vilifier of, 221
  extermination/extirpation/ obliteration of, 119, 134, 562, 566
  French, 773
  gate of remains open, 272
  may disappear from the earth, 597
  martyrs of, 785
  modern, 765
  Nazism fighting against, 204, 269, 420, 592, 890
  never celebrated war, 666
  part-way return to, 650
  of Poland being destroyed, 454
  propaganda for needed, 204
  prophetic, 873
  return to, 188, 200, 650
  sublime height of, 941
  suffering in Soviet Russia, 104, 181, 462
  systematic obliteration of, 566
  target of enemies of civilization, 154
  teaches hopeful overcoming of suffering, 466
  war against Jews and, 469,
  will live on, 113, 217, 556, 666
Judas, 118
Jude/Juda Verrecke ("Jew/Jewry Perish"), 412, 514–15
Jüdische Rundschau, 231–32, 257, 259
Jugo-Slavia/Jugoslavia, 476, 573, 1017
  Christians save Jewish lives in, 798
  Nazi soldiers in control of, 652
  See also: Yugoslavia
Jung, Carl, 528
Jung, Leo, 28, 46, 78
  account of 93 Polish girls, 686
  promoting affidavits for refugees, 320, 370

K

Kaddish, 204–5, 298, 417, 688, 803, 990
Kahlenberg, Moses, 49, 422, 589
Kalmanovich, Zelig, 7, 655
Kalonymos family, 854
Kamanets-Podolski, 36
Kant, Immanuel,
  as model of good German, 92, 214, 346, 848, 890

Kaplan, Chaim, 7
Diary of, 970
Kaplan, Jacob, 36, 78, 286, 521, 530, 551–52, 657, 773, 788
Kaplan, Mordecai, 851, 926
Katten, Max, 228
Katz, Yitzhak, 792, 969
Kellner, Abraham, 30, 719
Kellogg, Frank B., 512
Kennedy, John F., 27, 917
Kennedy-Nixon Debates, 31
Kent, Madeleine, 438
Kertzer, Morris, 758
"Khaki Shirts," 136
Kiev, mass murder of Jews in, 6, 53, 630
Kindertransport, 364, 927, 930
King, Martin Luther, 859
Kishinev, 240, 301
pogrom in, 976
Kittel, Gerhard, 221
Klemperer, Eva, 6
Klemperer, Victor, 6, 535
Koheleth, 447
Kol Nidre, 23, 72, 514, 618, 996–99
medieval context of, 997–98
sermons delivered on, 36, 43, 68, 71, 73, 77, 342, 726, 986, 997
services prohibited in UK for 5 years, 591, 781–82
Korah, 70–71, 490,
Hitler as a modern, 560–61
Korczak, Janusz, 7
Korn, Bertram, 983, 991
Kosak-Szczucka, Zofia, 8
Kovno/Kaunas, Lithuania, 61, 845, 867, 919, 991
as city without Jews, 786
"*Kraftanschauung*" (power outlook), 334
Kristallnacht, xv, 42, 67, 70, 76, 320, 326, 343, 349, 465, 469, 534, 611, 908, 920, 925–27, 929–30, 937–38
eyewitness reports of, 4, 15–16
as greatest crisis of Jewish history, 350
Nazi explanation of, 363
"November pogrom/s," 407, 422, 470, 522
memory of, 662
Kurfurstendamm, Berlin, 357

L

La Lande Internment Camp, conditions in, 569, 608–9
Landes, Daniel, 9, 775
Lamentations/*Eicha*, 355, 481, 571
Land of Israel, 267, 332, 389, 620, 649, 740–41
general fear encompassing in, 620
immigration to, 149
Jews not allowed to enter, 387
must bring the wretched remnant to, 799
obstacles and difficulties in, 384
Palestine must become the, 678, 728
Rommel's forces threatening, 757
we will build anew the, 981
See also: Eretz Yisrael, Holy Land, Palestine
Lang, Cosmo Gordon (Archbishop of Canterbury), 166, 186, 195, 240, 372, 458, 675, 677, 708
Lang, Leon S., 18, 55
Lanzmann, Claude, 5
La Rocque, François de, 251
Lashon hara (evil tongue), 627

Lasker, Adolph, 867
Lasker, Chaim Mordecai, 867
Laski, Harold, 533
Latvia, 449, 576
Laval, Pierre, 515, 657, 662
  new restrictions imposed by, 704
Laziness of heart, 483
League of National German Jews, 185, 871–72
League of Nations, 163, 195, 234, 492, 563, 745, 784, 818, 901, 988
  abandoned by United States, 563, 648, 784
  can we return to?, 512
  German withdrawal from, 213
  must take political action, 243–44
Lebensraum (living space), 609, 966
  German people lack, 549
  dictatorship clamored for more, 751
Leeds, England, 40, 63, 929, 959, 961
Leff, Laurel, 15, 689
Leftwich, Joseph, 51, 674, 938
Lehman, Edith, 801
Leipzig Gewandhaus Orchestra, 847
Leipziger Tageszeitung, 130
"*Lekha Dodi*," 737
Lemberg, as city without Jews, 786
Lenin, Vladimir, warned against antisemitism, 660–61
Leningrad, 480, 810
Lev, Aryeh, 57
Levi, Primo, 4
Levi, Solomon ben Isaac, 57
Levin, Aaron, 921
Levin, Moritz, 182
Levin, Nora, 2
Levine, Ephraim, 56
Levine, Ralph, 429
Levitt, Ruth, 4, 15
Levinthal, Bernard, 851
Levinthal, Israel, xxii, xxiv, 20–21, 28, 44, 55, 74, 202, 227–28, 298, 560, 579, 851–53, 860, 895, 908
  four books of sermons by, 852
  interest of in Zionism, 851
  Nazism as equivalent evil to Communism, 275
  on Hamans of all ages, 64–65
  on Korah risen to do devilish work again, 70–71
  on modern successors to Amaleks, 62
  on Pharaoh in modern garb, 60
Levinthal, Marvin, 121
Levy, J. Leonard, 46, 76
Levy, Yosef Yehuda, 36
Lewin, Abraham, 7
Lewis, Sinclair, 485, 629
Lewisohn, Ludwig, 674
Liberal Judaism, 901, 906, 960
Liberation, 621, 716, 785, 789, 826, 830
  America supporting the forces of, 543
  of Dachau, xxv–xxvi
  day of, 594, 59
  embraces Four Freedoms, 624
  of Europe, 756, 759
  fight for, 677
  freedom and,751
  from Egypt, 694
  God will send, 736
  meaning of, 762
  not long delayed, 759
  in Pesach seder, 621, 753

of Poles, 706
of Rome, 758
victory and, 659, 705, 748
Lidice, Czechoslovakia, 635, 637, 642, 647, 778
Liebermann, *see:* Liepmann, Heinz
Liepmann, Heinz, 208–9
Lincoln, Abraham, 29–30, 208, 228–29, 536, 652
Lincoln-Douglas Debates, 31
Lincoln Memorial, 652
Lindbergh, Charles, 211–12, 544, 573
Lipsky, Louis, 314, 838
Lipstadt, Deborah, 15, 16, 140, 791, 829, 1004, 1016–17
Lisbon, 535–36
Lithuania, 10, 309, 449, 550, 576, 801, 835, 867
depth of scholarship in, 72, 786, 794
Jews of drowning in sea of persecution, 478
loss of, 749
rabbinic preachers born in, 845, 851, 893, 901, 907, 919, 991
Lloyd George, David, 321
Locarno, Pact/Treaty of, 249, 489
Lodz, 8, 11, 426, 480, 706
London, 11–12, 14, 22, 26, 28, 43–44, 47, 56, 73–74, 76, 250
bombs falling on (1940), 497
Jewish refugees in, 70, 417
Maybaum arrives in, 50
in midst of battlefield, 509, 572
Mosely in East End of, 280
newspapers of, 96, 99, 439
Polish gvernment-in-exile in, 685
Protocols launched in, 629
Round Table Conference in, 393, 397
London University, 975
Longfellow, Henry Wadsworth, 778
Lookstein, Haskel, 20
Lookstein, Joseph H., 20
Lorraine, France, 525
Louis IX of France, 124
Lublin, 8, 53, 426, 457, 761–62, 981
Majdanek camp on outskirts of, 1018
Russian forces find no Jews in, 1018
slaughter of Jews there, 1017
"Lublin Reservation," 457, 514
Luedecke, Kurt, 836–37, 839–40, 842
as "Amerikaner Hitler," 836
Luftwaffe, 531
Luria, Isaac, and Lurianic Kabbalah, 582
Lusaka, Northern Rhodesia, synagogue dedicated in, 672
Lyon, France, 762, 785
attack on synagogue of, 737
consistory, 657, 734
harshly affected by painful new ordeals, 734
police enter synagogue to make arrests, 657
synagogue of liberated, 765
trains observed in with deported Jews, 773
Kaplan leaving to return to Paris, 789

M

Maccabees/Maccabeans, 67–68, 74, 78, 241, 369, 371, 373, 530, 543, 602, 636, 667, 700

ghetto uprising recalls glories of, 1007
Maccabean courage and Akiba-martyr-spirit, 146
Maccabean spirit lives again, 667, 681
resistance against totalitarianism, 459
these days demand new, 531
valor on military and spiritual battlefields, 600
wanted emancipation, 601
willingness to martyrdom of, 665
Maccabean Hanukkah rally, 838
MacDonald, James G., 818
MacDonald, Malcolm, 403
Machiavellian,
desire, 303
goals, 269
heresies, 557
purpose, 108
MacMichael, Harold, 616
Madison Square Garden, 788
dramatic pageant at (1943), xv
German Bund Rally in, 396
Hanukkah Rally in (1932), 838
Protest Rally at (1933), xiii, 25, 101, 104, 140, 166, 177
S.S. Wise speeches in, 19, 642
Maginot Line, 486, 629
Magnes, Judah L., 26, 152, 455, 593, 735, 790–1
Magyar Szideklatia, 770
Mahoney, Jeremiah, 235
Maidanek, 763, 816
Maimonides, Moses, 740, 974
Mainz, Germany, 854
Malan, D.F., 283
Malino, Jerome, 43
Manchester Guardian, 12, 348, 352, 367, 372, 482, 669, 818
Manchuria, 264, 508, 515, 578, 784
Mandelbaum, Bernard, 43
Mann, Louis L., 78
Mann, Thomas, 168, 189, 890
Mannheim synagogue, 131
Manning, William T./J., xiii, 166–67, 186, 192, 372
Manual of Holiday and Occasional Sermons, 991–92
Marranos, 997–98
Mars, 206, 646
Marseilles, France, Jews deported from, 773
Martyr/s, 154, 169, 204–5, 212, 223, 290, 477, 501, 576, 589, 653, 668, 759, 783, 785, 792
Akiba as, 146
blood of, 766
burnt alive in public, 552
cause of, 744
children as, 223, 941
epoch of, 941
faith of the, 1043
of Germany, 438
Hananya ben Teradion as, 943
lamentful woe of our, 695
myriad, 710
Niemoeller as Christian, 305–6, 568
of the past, 544
our holy, 997
period of, 665
scroll of, 138
some may have forgotten God, 1018
Ten, in rabbinic literature and Kabbalah, 582, 633, 943
tribute to mere lip-service, 1007

vast community of, 469
voices of, 721–22
of the Warsaw ghetto, 1003
willingness to die as, 83
Martyrdom, 13, 68–69, 154, 460, 639, 686, 1007
Akiba-martyr-spirit, 146
call for, 665
of children, 223–24
of Czecho-Slovakia, 337
desire for in *Akedah*, 518–19
epoch of, 941
European Jews did not court, 768
of French Jewry, 821
Israel's endless, 674, 731
of the Jew/s, 355, 428, 438, 445, 477, 668, 866, 1005
of Jews from Poland, 759
must never forget, 820
of our brethren, 978
rescue from, 728
"sanctifying the name," 257, 769
sin and, 635
spared from, 653
will some day end, 782
Marxism, 197
Masada, ghetto uprising recalls suicidal martyrdom at, 1007
Mass execution/s, 629, 674, 780, 976, 979
Mass murder, xiv–xvi, xxi, xxvi, 1, 6–7, 10–17, 20, 27, 53–54, 66, 68–69, 73, 75, 78, 80, 125, 144, 227, 326, 343, 412, 506, 544, 556, 563, 630, 640, 667, 670, 714, 726, 736, 744, 747, 763, 806–7, 826, 853, 856, 863, 895, 910, 927, 955, 976, 978, 1006, 1010, 1014, 1021
Mattathias, 531
Mattuck, Israel, xxii–xxiii, 22, 47, 58, 75, 100, 233, 274, 514, 809, 818, 901–2
sermons of responding to two World Wars, 901, 1024
Sunday morning services of, 901
Mauritius, 746
Mauthausen, 53
Maybaum, Ignaz, 50–51, 70, 76, 406, 409–10, 937–38, 941
as disciple of Rosenzweig, 409
was in concentration camp, 942–43
Man and Catastrophe, 937–38
Maybaum, Sigmund, 937
McConnell, Francis J., xiii, 167, 192
McDonald, James, 243–44
Mediterranean Sea, 71, 453, 659, 955, 996
Medoff, Rafael, 19–20, 102, 394, 698
Meisels, David, 694
Meisels, Tzvi Hirsch, 9, 775, 811
Melchior, Marcus, 714
Memphis, Egypt, 244
Mendes-Flohr, Paul, 146, 432
Mesha, king of Moab, 565
"The Message of Israel" (radio broadcasts), 25
Messiah,
anti- success of, 492
birth pangs of, 82–83, 562, 789
coming of, 894
false, 100, 182, 189, 778
Hitler combines m.-complex with cruelty, 204
Hitler not a, 157
imminent coming of, 392
a modern m. fighting against Bolsheviks, 561

trumpet/Shofar Call of, 147, 333
Messianic age, 83, 297, 716
still far way, 754
Messianic enthusiasm, 384
Messianic ideals, 147
Messianic miracle, 789
Messianic patience, 518
Messianic redemption, 66
Messianism, 518
Nazism and, 914
Mettemeier, Storm Troop Leader, 1019
Metz, France,
ancient synagogue of totally ravaged, 817
Polish Jewish refugees in, 49
Mexico, 212, 952
Meyer, Dr. Ernst Wilhelm, 323
Micah, 799
Middle Ages, 74, 105, 124, 126, 154, 163, 169, 218–19, 240, 284, 349, 361, 368, 840, 1005
ghetto of the, 218, 240
Jews in, 600, 997
tortures and cruelties of, 542
Mihajlović, Slovakia, 733
Miltonic task of modern preacher, 728
Minute books, 8
Minsk,
as city without Jews, 786
massacre of 60,000 Jews in, 641
Missouri, University of, 576, 883
Molech/Moloch, 158, 403, 565, 593–94, 646, 736
Molotov-Ribbentrop Pact, 909
Mongols, 806, 838, 1008
Montgomery, Bernard Law, 649, 683, 716, 757, 759
Montluc Fort, Lyon, 762, 785
Montreal, Canada, 28, 57, 79, 187, 520, 845
Bishop of, 846, 848
protest rally in, 132, 354, 846
Moore, George Foot, 901
Mordecai, xi, 64, 177, 249, 392, 477, 687, 897–99, 922
and three Jewish boys studying, 899–900
Moriah (Mount), 69, 335, 444
Morning Post, London, 99
Morteira, Saul Levi, 50, 57
Moscow, 324
Declaration of Autumn, 1943, 829
Hitler at the gates of, 592
more tolerant of Negros than US, 660
Nazi POWs paraded through, 1020
Moses, 24, 62, 244, 345, 472, 492, 856–58, 993
Hitler as substitute for, 609
last words of, 147, 268
Law of, 971, 973
leadership of, 70, 187
lesson of, 221
like, 314
obliterate the name of, 641
prayer of, 777
spirit of, 528
uplifted hands of, 62, 259
Mosley, Oswald, 184, 195, 261, 280, 440
campaign of, 629
Mothers, 205, 292, 343, 594, 651, 668, 721, 729, 792, 795, 941, 998
Mount Royal Arena, Montreal, 355, 846, 849
Mount Vernon, VA, 652

Mourning, 455, 611, 664, 673, 778, 783, 820, 895, 1011
  days of, xv, 25, 354, 668–69, 758, 807, 961, 976–77, 1010
  individual, 793–94
  special services of, 316, 664, 775, 1004
  uniqueness of, 791–92
  year of, 775
Mueller/Müller, Ludwig, 176, 207, 209, 902
Mundelein, George, Cardinal, 708
Muni, Paul, xv
Munich, Germany, 146, 356, 393, 421, 519
  bombed by Allies, 1020
  "Brown House" in, 146, 609
  Cardinal Faulhaber sermons in, 175, 180, 192, 195, 548, 903
  Hitler's speech in, 262
  Institute on "Jewish Question," 414
"Munich Conference/Agreement/ Pact," 336, 337, 339–40, 344, 361, 395, 484
  effect on Jews of, 336
Munition makers, profiting from war, 499
Musar, 590, 791, 794
Mussolini, Benito, 33, 227, 237, 778, 910
  backed down from threats against France, 374
  Fascist empire of defeated, 986
  Hitler and, 341, 394, 399, 402
  name written as "inilossuM," 390
Mysticism, among Polish Jews, 458
  See also: Kabbalah.

N

Nakuru, Kenya, new synagogue dedicated, 672
Namur, Belgium, xxvi
Naples, Italy, 789
Napoleon, 312
National Conference of Christians and Jews, 764
National Conference of Jews and Christians, 183, 225
Nationalism, 112, 180, 189, 285, 293, 337, 666, 828, 897
  false, 326
  German, 159, 184–85, 871
  Jewish, 122, 152, 184–85, 297, 301
  Nazi, 122–23, 885–86
  negative, 258, 261, 433, 526, 711
  prophet of, 446
National Radical Camp (Naras), Poland, 870
National Refugee Service, 662
National Socialist (Nazi) Party, 11, 96, 103, 446, 597, 836, 870, 885
National Student League, 913
Naumann, Max, 185, 871
Nazi Germany, 10, 41, 65, 164, 175, 191–92, 232, 263, 305, 298, 316, 371, 536, 575, 683, 743, 848, 855, 878–79, 888, 894, 914, 946, 979–80
  America destined to go the way of?, 536
  barbarism and savagery in, 624
  biblical links with, 66, 70, 282, 287, 723, 992
  books banned in, 209
  Canada's business with, 132
  chaos of paganism in, 372
  Czechoslovakia and, 395
  Christians endangered in, 902
  covert extenuation of, 450

defeat of, 1024
economic boycott of, 860, 868, 872
on equal basis with Stalinist Russia, 908
as Esau, 70
as fierce giant sharpening its dagger, 362
as ghetto, 240
Great Brittain opposed to, 394
hatred of, xvi
Hitler's rule of, 187
Jews as untouchables in, 495
most highly-cultured state of, 545
murder and massacre in, 660
not a unique challenge to Jews, 264, 275
pact with "Red Russia," 446
persecution of Jews in, 131
"Positive Christianity" in, 305
propaganda directed against, 382
refugees from, 429, 441
as sinful Sodom, 723
Spanish Inquisition and, 73
support of, 217
as torture chamber, 246
Vienna compared with, 310
wants hegemony of Europe, 258
ways of copied by Fascist Italy, 327

Nazis,
antisemitic policies of, 277, 366
"Brown House" of, 146, 156, 609
cautious and conservative, 356
and Communists, 464
cruel, brutal gangsters, 364
economic death sentence by, 155
experimentation in tortures by, 979
exterminationist policies of, 11, 53, 154, 413, 986
feared the Jewish spirit, 430
give Germans 600,000 Jewish scapegoats, 129
hope to be world masters, 546
make cruelty a fine art, 578
as Molech-worshippers, 565
opposed to pogroms, 839
persecution of Christians by, 273, 324
persecution of Jews by, 11, 44, 154, 166, 169, 182–83, 397, 430, 440, 520, 633, 651, 846, 868, 873, 878, 894, 1014
plan to annihilate, 14, 209, 270, 511, 636, 723
policy of gangsterism, 804
power of completely destroyed, 818
propose releasing 450,000 refugees to US, 535
radicals of, 356
ravings of against Jews, 96, 153
reducing German Jews to level of gypsies, 183,
relapse to barbarism of, 153
song of, 183
special niche in halls of infamy for, 696
staging tragic opera, 395
tasting "Cup of Wrath," 1020
teach to hate Jews, 516, 529
use of antisemitism by, 516
victorious armies of, 395, 555
want elimination of Jews from Europe, 642

warred against liberal Spain, 784
written as "sizaN," 390–91
Nazism/Naziism/Nazidom
alarming strides in nine years of power, 626
as "anti-Christ," 324
catastrophe brought on Jews by, 441
conflict with Christianity, 306, 355
declared war against the Bible, 647
declares all Jews inferior, 224
degradation of a noble people, 157
destroyed economic basis of Jewish life, 594
as "dominion of arrogance," 432, 646
fighting Judaism with poisoned weapons, 420
its "humane extirpation "of the Jews, 187, 353, 356, 886
lure of in America, 842
menace of threatens the world, 534
nihilistic terror of, 425
as a persecuting paganism, 365
propaganda for in US, 166, 217, 244, 382, 549
a ravenous beast, 826
turned Jewish citizens into outcasts, 420
victims of dying with *Shema*, 716
Nebuchadnezzar, 497, 517, 898
Nebuzaradan, 510
Negroes,
can be a hero in Moscow (Robeson), 660
as oppressed minority in America, 119, 212
Nero, 358
Netherlands, 77, 454
deportation of Jews from, 704
violation of pledge to, 490
See also: Holland
Netter, Nathan, 36, 797
Neurath, Konstantin von, 310, 883
Neutrality, 37, 162, 670, 757, 948
questions about, 443, 479, 548
US should commit to, 255, 425–26, 450–52
"Never again," must work to ensure this, 1029–30
Newark, NJ, 55, 864, 877
Newark Evening News, 18, 42, 55, 436
Newman, Louis I. 20, 30, 81, 101, 386, 501, 566, 574, 652, 704, 706, 758, 803, 1013–14
for Jewish State in Palestine, 1013
on Anti-Zionist Reform Rabbi, 1017
published "Sermons and Addresses" (4 volumes) and *Biting on Granite*, 1014
as Revisionist Zionist, 1013, 1017
Newspapers, xiv, xv, 15–18, 20, 55, 58, 156, 158, 168, 314, 428, 524, 549, 555, 5762 686, 706, 750, 759, 770, 791, 888–90, 951, 953
American/US, 202, 300, 534–35, 544, 742, 744, 764, 852, 882, 1017
Ankara, 769
British, 11, 99, 439, 660, 755

German/Nazi, 13, 15, 112, 176, 194, 214, 362, 841, 847, 883
ghetto, 8
Jewish, 16, 17, 59, 310, 360, 865
London, 17, 99, 439
used as covering, 754
Prague, 193
Scottish, 131, 353
See also: New York Times
New Friends of Germany, 217
New York Board of Rabbis, 859, 907
New York Times, xii–xiv, xxiii, 18, 20, 33, 43, 101, 105, 175, 229, 243, 300, 310, 316, 386, 464, 501, 568, 636, 663, 683, 689, 698, 744, 762, 837–38, 860, 996
account of 93 Jewish girls in Poland, 686, 729
New York University (NYU), 851, 907, 991
Nice, Italy, 374, 848
Jews deported from, 773
Niebuhr, Reinhold, 112
Niemöller/Niemoeller, Martin, 227, 305–6, 327, 355, 357
message as Protestant martyr, 568–69, 574
teaches true Christian cannot be antisemitic, 703
Nietzsche, Friederich, 338, 346, 480
Nineveh, 337, 783
Nissenbaum, Isaac, 475
Nordic peoples, 338, 637, 838, 840
mythology of, 905
Norway, 514, 625, 684, 841, 946, 953, 979, 1011
catastrophe has overwhelmed, 471
in shambles, 572–73
violation of pledge to, 490
Norwegians, 476, 488
North Africa,
Allied victory in due to World Jewry, 702
blood flowing in, 660
Nuremberg, 263, 869
great synagogue of, 465
laws, 13, 226, 233, 239–40, 347, 397, 412, 609, 646, 819, 887
rally, 224, 226
trials, 14
Nussbaum, Max, 24, 46–47, 457, 486
Nyassaland (British Central Africa), Jewish refugees settling, 672

O

Offenbach, 168–69, 177
Office of Price Administration (O.P.A.), 805
Ogpu, Russian, 369
Old Testament, 334
defended by Faulhaber, 175, 180, 192
to be eliminated, 93–94, 113, 121, 124, 609
Olympic Games [1936], 252
decision to participate in, 235–37
opposition to participate in, 240–41, 245, 890–91
Opinion, 424
Orach Chayim Congregation, NY, 1003
Oranienburg, concentration camp, 662, 679
Ormsby-Gore, William, 195
Oshry, Ephraim, 61, 550

P

Pacelli, Eugenio, 905
See also: Pius XII
Pacifism, Pacifists, xvi, 164, 178, 197, 206, 239, 464, 504, 526, 586, 600
Abraham Heller as, 908
as immoral folly, 942
French pacifists, 45
Jews stigmatized as, 543
may need to repent, 745
non-pacifist peace-lover, 258
S.S. Wise as, 180, 312, 450
Vera Brittain as, 744
Paganism, 179, 208, 285, 398, 429, 469, 503, 873
chaos of has beat Christendom, 372
Christian revolt against, 192
hatred of those with faith, 406
Nazi, 225, 241, 365, 462
neo/new, 68, 227, 257, 303, 324, 460, 601, 886, 891, 905
poisoning life of the world, 403
world returning to, 416
Palestine, 204, 261, 296, 352,
ancient, 332, 369, 913
antisemitism in British administration of, 280
assurance to Great Britain by Jews of, 436
asylum for survivors in, 788
beacon of hope, 138, 987
beginning of Jewish military force in, 11, 631, 640, 671
British administration in, 280, 431, 531
British Governor of, 616
British plan for, 393, 397
can become a Switzerland of Asia, 341
cannot accommodate all German Jews, 186, 195, 887–88, 899
certificates needed for, 266
as challenge to philosophy of brute force, 402
Chief Rabbi in, xxiv, 50, 375, 634, 649, 669, 807
cruel and bloody warfare in, 266
demand for Great Britain to sacrifice, 341
deportation of refugees from, 539, 746
dream of, 281
Eli as High Priest of Jewish republic in, 993
end of Jewish hope for, 393
establishment of Jewish State in, 1013
fate of Mandate, 393, 1029
as focal point of Jewish danger, 291
future role of for Jewish people, 451
gates of must be opened, xv, 50, 165, 375, 557, 612, 671, 684, 699, 756
German Jews homesick in, 219
growth of Jewish settlement in, 379
haven of refuge in, 135, 186, 190, 739, 955
as indictment of totalitarian states, 402
Jewish claim to indestructible, 410
Jewish Commonwealth in, 35, 631, 710

Jewish homeland in, 285, 393, 697, 705, 987, 994
Jewish immigration to, 394
Jewish National Home in, 492, 622, 705, 746, 747, 787
Jewish Republic in, 993
Jewry of, 17374, 404, 563, 636, 987
Jews of and Arab uprising, 267, 270–71, 442
Jews of not armed by British, 563
Jews of help Montgomery, 716
Jews of must not be left defenseless, 636
Jews of respond to decree of annihilation, 668
Jews of saved by a miracle, 807, 810
as "land of Israel," 728
as land of refuge, 672
looming danger now over, 664
Maccabean spirit resurrected in, 373
Magnes moves to, 26
massacre of Jews in feared, 810
as mother-country for Jews, 678
must labor to realize hope it will be ours, 728
need to expand borders of, 628
no danger of Germans occupying, 634
no safety even in, 332
offers no adequate escape, 344
only place where Jews are assured of welcome, 623, 631
and post-War Peace Conference, 481, 597
protest in, xiv
rebirth of Israel in, 1015, 1021
rebuilding of, 126, 173, 285, 305
wisdom of in question, 506
reign of terror in, 321
representatives of at World Jewish Congress, 260
restoration of to the Jewish people, 817
savage slaughter of Jews in, 263
saved from war and destruction, 807
sixty years ago and today, 787
stifling of refugees to, 983, 987–88
suffers political defeat, 987
survivors will seek new life in, 659, 784
threatened by German forces, 649, 718
three visits by H.J. Stern to, 845
transporting surviving Jews to, 739
and White Paper, 11, 410–11, 415, 436, 457, 684, 746–47, 757, 799, 988,
Winston Churchill on, 988
See also: Eretz Yisrael, Holy Land, Jewish National Homeland, Land of Israel
Palestine Conference, *see:* Round Table Conference
Papen, Franz von, 905
Paris, 190, 222, 251, 404, 446, 515, 632, 879
assassination of German official in, 365, 926–49
burning of Talmud in, 124
German bombing of, 951
German forces enter, 946
Kaplan leaves for Vichy, 78; returning to, 789

liberation of, 1020
Paris-Soir, 762
Parliament,
British Houses of, 16, 130, 247, 361, 438, 658, 689, 822, 988
German, 779
Hungarian, 344
"Pastor Hall," 568
Patria (refugee ship), 746
Peace,
achievement of, 810
Allies won war but lost the, 623
Americans enjoy blessings of, 507
book-burning as threat to, 124
boycott leads to, 192
celebration of, 817
choice of war or, 206
circumstances could contribute to, 1010–11
Conference,
in past, 321, 340, 481
in future, 481, 597
Cross of, 179
danger of premature, inconclusive, 1026
dawning of universal, 894
difficulty of making, 1029
disastrous consequences of a "soft," 795, 1020
dishonor without, 340–41
doubts and confusion about, 464
in Empire of Persia, 896
England and France: delusion of, 336
Fascist defiance of, 177
fifth-columnists cry, 483
and future of Palestine, 989
Germany as menace to, 143, 862
God as source of, 230
grave problems of current, 827
Great Britain holds key to, 250
great nations sacrificed the weak for, 564
high price for, 339, 419
Hitler looked upon as prince of, 340
Hitler's profession of, 157, 165, 215, 263, 449, 489
Hitler's scorn for, 170
on Hitler's terms, 952
hope for, 87, 171, 241, 333, 342, 438, 441
hope that Germany will choose, 93
impractical treaties of, 912
incompatible with Hitlerism, 420, 648
Jews last to enjoy fruits of, 505
Jews' special interest in, 823
"keep America safe for," 427
lesson of last war concerning, 468
lights of extinguished twice in Europe, 710
lovers of, 77, 197, 259, 345, 436, 505, 515, 544, 572
Maccabees and, 602, 667
martyrdom of Czecho-Slovakia for, 337
meaning of, 495–96
in Messianic age, 297
as "Mirage of Civilization," 426
muddle-headed advocates of, 449
Nazi policies threaten, 899
new day of for mankind, 431
no hope for until tyranny crushed, 642

none without liberation of oppressed, 712
only for the dead, 589, 601
"piping days of," 512
prayed for victory and hoped for, 768
". . . proposal" from Hitler is mockery, 449
and Protestant Christian leaders, 279
and rebirth of European Jewry, 699
re-education as condition of lasting, 827
regarded as unmanly, 949
as result of economic justice, 268
road to permanent and universal, 825
sacrifice of Palestine for, 341
and Shavu'ot holiday, 487
shrieking cry for, 985
to suffer, to die for, 317
terms of eventual, 480
threats to world, 264
and Tower of Babel, 298
war against evil by instruments of, 278
"Winning the," 657
"with honor," 333
worship of God and efforts to establish, 905
Pearl Harbor, 27, 627, 679–80, 730, 823, 878
Pelley, William Dudley, 136, 648
Penkower, Monty, 3, 4, 16, 370, 698, 705, 987
Pennsylvania, University of, 877
Persecution, 128, 131, 151, 232, 239, 252, 267, 272, 294, 325, 416, 437, 500, 551, 722, 785, 933
aims to exterminate Jews from Germany, 154
American isolation from, 359
anti-Jewish organized in France, 773
as antagonistic to Divine Laws, 120
in Austria, 316
as badge of honor, 270
as bankruptcy of humanity, 418
based on race, 129, 205, 730
biblical precedents of, 60, 64, 66–69
books about, 10–12, 652
can never destroy the Jew, 858
of Catholics and/or Protestants, 218, 283, 349, 358, 418, 586, 884–86, 889–90, 902
contemporary Jewish victims of, 106, 652
of defenseless minorities, 359
economic, practiced relentlessly 474
five million Jews suffering from, 106
forms of past brought together, 523
French government afraid of protest against, 662
future children free from danger of?, 809
German Christian periodicals denounce, 166
of German Communists, 98–99
Germany, Poland, Romania as lands of, 284
growth and spread of, 440
Hadrianic, 582, 921, 943

Herzl's forecasts of, 190
and Hitlerism, 167, 847
how/why does God allow, 9, 76–77, 79, 165, 516, 704, 720
of Hungarian Jews, 771
Irish free from anti-Jewish, 126
of Italian Jews by Germany, 758
Jewish history a continuous story of, 963
Jewish steadfastness in face of, 230
Jewry has and will survive, 996–98
of Jews, Christian protests against, 166, 192–93, 240, 411
Jews destined to suffer from, 894
Jews endured it for 2000 years, 644
Jews fleeing from to England, 441
Jews singled out for, 430, 502
Julius Gordon book on, 349
lands of, 284
loss of identity by victims of, 456
and mass murder, xxi, xxvi
medieval, 73–74, 143, 256, 506
mere expressions of sympathy for, 697
and messianic birth pangs, 82
never has entirely ceased, 529
new scientific methods of, 735
Niemoeller response to, 305
no one interfered with, 446
no religious protest to philosophy of, 112
not abating but intensifying, 243
novelty of current, 362
perfected techniques of, 696
persecutors have no justification for, 517
of Polish Jews, 478, 503, 586, 963
present darkness of Nazi, 651
prohibition of ritual slaughter as, 117
protests against, xii–xv, 186, 213, 364–65, 373
rabbinic responses to, xxiv
reasons given for, 253
reduction of for Olympic Games, 252
of Romanian Jews, 261, 955
sermon texts responding to, 27, 43–44, 58, 846, 894, 1014
suffering in Soviet Russia, 181
S.S. Wise on German, 20
as storm signal for humanity, 488
temporary or permanent?, 125
threatens annihilation of German Jewry, 129
torments by all forms of, 690
uniqueness of current, 75, 183, 641, 665, 735, 1014, 1016
unrelieved agony of German, 686
unthinkable in 1932, 343
victims of want Palestine, 186
as wake-up call, warning signal, 145, 772
what was known about, 13–16
wholesale, sadistic, satanic, 679
will be banished from the earth, 956–57
world stood aghast at spectacle of, 868
Zionism as reaction to, 122, 165

Persia, 65–67, 282, 308, 346, 391, 477, 614, 909–10, 899, 917, 989
Persian Empire, 24, 117, 222, 896
Pesach, Passover, 18, 24, 220, 753
how possible to observe?, 472, 478, 620–21
of Egypt and of the future, 693
sermons on, 21, 60–61, 63–64, 76, 79–80, 286, 851–58, 929–36
Pestalozzistrasse Synagogue, 959
Pétain, Philippe, 486, 512, 704
Petliura, Symon, 404
Pharaoh, 24, 69, 72, 74, 114, 244, 543, 625, 684, 851–58
continuity with current, 60–61, 117–18, 180–83, 254, 286, 474, 548, 603
current atrocities worse than Pharaoh's, 147, 622, 691–92
death knell for ancient and his like, 748
in modern guise, 680
a new and modern, 473, 491
old Pharaoh reincarnated, 854
Philanthropy, 142, 243, 315, 343, 945, 971
Philistines, 71, 94, 332, 992–94, 998
still walk the earth, 472
Phillips, Wendel, 796
Piekarz, Mendel, xxiv, 18, 740
Piłsudski, Jozef, 162
Pinchas, High Priest, 993
Pinchos, son of Eli, 71, 994–95, 998
Pius XI, Pope, 846
Christmas message of, 279
critique of Communism by, 289
support of Jews by, 385–86, 640
Pius XII, Pope, 640, 675
provided refuge in Vatican City, 763–64
Pobdonostieff/Pobiedonostzeff/Pobyedonostseff, Constantin, 118, 684, 726
Pogroms, 72, 271, 337, 361, 501, 787–88, 839, 894
of 1881, 604
cold and blood-hot, 680
Bialik poem, 977
bloodless/economic, 103–4, 128
in Germany, 366, 386, 407, 412, 422, 470, 522, 824, 869, 939, 940–41
in Hungary, 165
Nazi, 203, 353, 763
new type of spiritual, 869
in Poland, 251, 265–66, 626
in Romania, 616
in Russia, 220, 768, 847, 919, 955, 976
in Ukraine, 182, 404, 493, 963
Poland, 284–85, 319, 367, 376, 394–95, 419, 511, 591, 682, 684
American consular officials expelled from, 467–68
atrocities of Cossacks in, 499
belief in that Jews are superfluous, 382
Black Book of, 652
brilliance of erudition in, 794
catastrophe in, 749, 940
as center of all Jewish life, 442, 455
continuous pogrom throughout, 626
a corpse picked clean, 506
dangers to Jews in new war, 408
day of fasting and prayer in (1939), 442
day of Fasting and Repentance in (1940), 499

died an agonizing death, 505
divided between two mighty tyrants, 448
eastern part given to Soviet Union, 449
economic strangulation of Jews in, 263, 368
as focal point of Jewish danger, 291
Germans fleeing to for safety, 706
Government favors mass exodus of Jews, 284
Hitler's attack against, 425
Jewish life well organized in, 368
Jewish university students in, 299, 368
Jews in Army of, 756, 1016
as land of oppressive bigotry, 425
loss of, 749
medieval, 282
no more seats of Jewish learning in, 699
preparing its Army, 287
prohibition of ritual slaughter in, 149, 247–48, 251–52
protecting rights of Jews, 196
relatives of congregants in, 998
reports of revolt in, 294
resurrection of, 162
rich reservoir of Jewish life in, 462
in shambles, 572–73
slaughter-house for European Jewry, 668, 986, 1005
suffering of Jews in, 97, 222, 240–41, 294, 474
uncertain status of, 412
unsurpassed terror against Jews in, 668
utter hopelessness of Jews in, 260
year-long anti-Jewish pogrom in, 493
Polen, Nehemia, xxiv, 3, 455, 569, 599
Poles, 488
being killed by pneumonia, 625
forced Jews out of industry, 368
Nazis incited hatred of, 529
throw flowers over ghetto walls, 586
two million killed within a year, 806
Polish Bund, 623
Polish government-in-exile, 8, 53, 630, 685, 760, 816, 1004
Polish Jewry, 13, 16, 266, 270, 334, 424, 461, 469, 499, 689, 963
and American Jews, 393
anti-Jewish legislation and, 412
appalling plight of, 270, 472–73, 867
catastrophe of, 462, 940, 978, 1005–6
consigned to massacre and spoliation, 481
declared day of fasting and prayer, 442
deportation to death camps, 360
deported back to Poland, 409, 663
deprived of their synagogues, 444
destruction of, 550, 608, 749
drowning in sea of suffering, 478

economic conditions, 870
emigration of, 11, 388
German actions against, 1000
ghastly carnage passing over, 622
had come to Germany from, 388
literature of, 369
mass murder of, 1010
no help for, 473
no longer exists, 630
paralyzed, baffled, helpless, 293
persecution of continues, 503
relevance to world Jewry, 458
resettlement of, 457–58
sins of, 388, 963
slaughter of, 623, 725
suffering more than German Jews, 252
survival of, 752
terrible situation of, 222
too many deaths for burial, 583
utter hopelessness of, 260
Polish Ministry of Information, 652
Pompeii, 789
Pontius Pilate, 180
Portugal, 264
Prague, 99, 193, 421, 446, 490, 907
Preacher, preachers,
unprecedented responsibility of, 524
Predmesky, Akiba, 71, 730, 986, 991–1001
Predmesky, Louis/Eliezer, 991
Press, xiii, 16, 22, 25, 51, 98, 130, 146, 202, 221, 314, 360, 433, 471, 484, 595, 627, 669, 689, 862, 872, 889
Allied, 12, 712
American, 15, 140, 359, 396, 525, 884, 889
British, 15, 114, 457–58, 700–1, 996, 1004
censorship of, 128
Christian religious, 15, 166
freedom of the, 278, 359, 382, 495, 884, 890–91
French, 251
German/Nazi, 114, 128, 175, 278, 885, 888
Irish, 170
Jewish, xxiii, 8, 15, 25, 750, 1004
largely silent on mass murder of Jews, 1008
oppression of German Jews reported in, 98, 109
Pressburg/Bratislava, as city without Jews, 786
yeshiva in, 959
Prinz, Joachim, 18, 39, 41–42, 55, 436
Prns, Jacob, 614
Propaganda, xiv, 103–4, 136, 210, 256, 371, 401, 421, 479, 501, 514, 529, 552, 559, 596, 648, 654, 857, 898, 912, 974, 1027
"atrocity," 469
anti-German, 156, 243, 317, 382
anti-Jewish, 103, 161, 164, 258, 280, 414
antisemitic, 102–3, 331, 380–81, 384, 547, 555, 870
false must be met with truth, 408
German/Nazi, 67, 102, 104, 115, 166, 217, 281, 293, 363, 382–84, 395–97, 432, 438–0, 528, 549, 555, 614, 841, 887–89, 914
for Judaism, 204

Jewish cries of agony dismissed as, 674
on *Kristallnacht*, 363
like an octopus stretching its tentacles, 824
Minister/Ministry of, 265, 281, 364, 409, 414, 636, 701, 864
people constantly subject to, 401
poisonous gases of, 342
Riefenstahl documentary, 869
totalitarian, 78, 496
in United States, 166, 217, 244, 382, 452, 836–37, 839, 841
venomous, 164
Prophets,
in times of national crisis, 524
world's treatment of, 722
Protestant ministers, 891
most in Germany Hitlerites, 112
protest by 6000, 175
released from concentration camps, 885
Protestants, persecution of, 176, 218, 304, 323–24, 326, 329, 349–50, 568, 586, 885–86, 889, 891
Protestrabbiner, 146
Protest Rallies, xiii, 60, 100, 102–4, 122, 140, 189, 220, 790, 862
in St. Louis Cathedral, 104
in Galicia, 104–7
limitations of, 222, 330
Protests, 355
against persecution of Jews, 373
by Christians, 112, 245, 372
by Jews, 203, 220, 222
voice of America's, 359
"Protocols of the Elders of Zion," 160, 282, 381, 629, 706
Providence, 149, 375, 379, 429, 482, 560, 719, 736, 748, 757, 807
Providence, RI, 1013
Prussian Government: Law of 1812, 857
Purim, 18, 24, 64–66, 177, 282, 307, 373, 389–90, 538, 614–15, 685, 687, 893–900, 899–90
comfort from the story?, 614
festival of relaxation, 895
locale of in the Exile, 896
Puritans, 478

Q

Quakers, 303, 478
Queen Mary, 312
Queens Hall, London, xiv–v, 196
Quislings, 622, 625, 800, 1010
American quislings, 581

R

Rabbenu Tam, 997
Rabbinical Assembly, 25, 852
sermons delivered at Convention of, 191, 322, 415, 490, 760
Rabbinical Council of America, 991–92
Rabbis,
behavior of under persecution, 798
impossible to preach when spirit is crushed, 634
inspirational sermons of, 799
preaching sermons, but unable to help, 473
refused to leave congregations, 798
Rabinovich, Baruch, 36
Rabinowitz, Louis, 28, 120, 816

Racial hatred, 193, 197, 276, 482, 629
Radzilow, 999–1000
Polish inhabitants of massacre Jews, 1000
Rallies, xiii, xv, 8, 60, 100, 126, 167, 283, 355, 373, 636
by American German Bund, 396
by Christians, 245, 354
critique of, 101, 396
by Germans at Nuremberg, 224, 226, 233, 869
at Madison Square Garden, xv, 19, 101–2, 140, 166, 177, 396, 642, 683–840, 788, 838–39
voice of America's, 359
Rashi, 71, 106, 560, 692, 741, 909, 922
Rassenblut [foreign/racial blood), 148
Rath, Ernst vom, 926
Rathenau, Walther, 365
Ratibor (Polish Silesia), 168
Rauschning, Hermann, 484
The Voice of Destruction, 484, 529
The Revolution of Nihilism, 715
Reading, England, 1023
Reconstructionist, 801
Reconstructionist Judaism, 926
"Red Bolshevism" of Moscow, 324, 560
Red Cross, 670, 722
Red Heifer, 560
Redemption, 105, 201, 246, 249, 272, 307, 433, 550, 712, 719, 758–59, 807, 811, 921–22, 966–67
imminent, 392, 739–40
messianic, 66
shofars of, 145
Rees, Lawrence, 2
Reform Judaism, 21, 23, 286, 878, 893
classical, 945
mistaken optimism of, 291
Refugees, 456–57, 535–36, 628
America unable to help most, 555
homeless, 539, 722, 861
influx of into America, 603
Jewish, 106, 151, 181, 243, 312, 330, 406, 410, 469, 506, 539, 639, 746, 987, 990
material support of, xv, 126, 182, 320, 354, 385, 536, 723, 818
obligation to face problem of, 557
sermons delivered to, 417
settlement of, 457
situation of, 400, 466
Reich, Das, 636
Reichstag, 233, 262, 706, 903
burning of, 357, 648
elections to, 96, 114
Hitler addresses to, 302, 383, 432, 516
special meeting of, 226
Reichswehr (German Army), 881
Reinhardt, Max, 121
Reinhart, Harold, 43–44, 58, 151
Reinharz, Jehuda, 146, 432
Reitlinger, Gerald, 2
Religion,
arsenal of persecution against, 468
calumnies about Jewish, 230
deliberate destruction of, 432
enemy of all dictatorship, 485, 905
failures of, 777
freedom of, 175, 253, 495, 663

of Hitler versus of prophets, 94
in Germany, 283, 797
Jews' loyalty to their, 666
Jews returning to, 770, 807, 1006
Jews suffering for their, 144, 265, 417, 517, 583
Jews who have forsaken, 36
light of refuses to be extinguished, 225
nationalism as foremost rival to, 112
Reich as enemy of all, 574
sorely needed now, 552, 646
will never be permanently controlled, 67, 278
Religious bigotry, 477
Rephidim, 61–62, 259
Rescue of survivors , 712
"Respectable Prejudice" (*Bekovedte Rishus*), 1017
Responsa, rabbinic, 9, 775, 972, 974
Responsibility,
of Allies, 821, 952
of congregants, 730
of contemporary preachers, 524
of England regarding German Jews, 195, 250, 431
for evil, 77, 504, 508, 1025
of German Christians and churches, 100, 234
of German people, 795
of Germany for World War I, 118
of Jews, 198, 280, 345, 378, 828, 981
and League of Nations, 563
meaning of, 274
of ninety-three girls, 730
of political office, 96, 861
of religious leaders, 217
Revere, Paul, 646
Rhineland,
German troops sent into, 249–50, 255, 257, 489
Rhodes, Cecil, 658
Ribbentrop, Joachim von, 310, 356
Riegner, Gerhart, 14
Ringelblum, Emanuel,
Archive, 969–70
Diary of, 7,
Risikoff, Mnachem, 66, 390, 392
Ritual murder accusation, 115, 706
Rivesaltes, France,
Jews deported from, 773
Robeson, Paul, 660
Robinson, Edward G., xv, 408
Robinson, Joseph T., 186
Rolland, Romain, 376
Roman Catholic Church, 112, 386, 903
Roman Catholic/s, 91, 167, 279, 669–70, 903, 905
Roman Empire, 565, 780
Roman legions, 69, 73, 334
Romania/Rumania/Roumania, 13, 97, 164–65, 179, 218, 244, 261, 267, 282, 284–85, 294, 328, 376, 386, 403–5, 981
antisemitic wave from government, not masses, 301–10, 339
belief in that Jews are superfluous, 382
broken promises to Jews of, 299–300
cruel slaughter of Jews in Bucharest, 550
dangers to Jews in new war, 408
equal to Hitler in sadism, 1008

exclusion of Jews from, 299
in grip of terror, 573
Jews of and America, 393
Jews of facing new catastrophe, 749
mass-slaughtering of Jews in, 963–64
oil wells of, 341
pall of gloom engulfs Jews of, 293
refugees fleeing from, 616, 622, 754
revision of Citizenship decree, 299–300
rotten with antisemitism, 756
stands helplessly by, 505
suddenly went Fascist, 310
suffering of Jews in, 294, 301
territorial expansion of, 299
torture and abuse of Jews in, 88
Rome,
ancient, 150, 183, 244, 328, 346, 390, 578, 849, 965–66, 989, 1008
first ghetto in, 74, 543
modern, 245, 264, 289, 315, 328, 390–91, 402
October round-up, 763
services held in after liberation, 758, 803, 823
Rommel, Erwin, 636, 649, 716, 757
Blitzkrieg victories of, 810
Roosevelt, Eleanor, 801
Roosevelt, Franklin Delano, 170, 189, 455, 595, 598, 615, 690, 859
at invasion of Austria, 309
calling of Economic Conference, 119
calling of Evian Conference, 329
cited by S.S. Wise, 19, 635
condemns Nazi "kingdom of insolence," 925–26
dissatisfaction with regime of, 884
fireside Chat on National Defense, 581
humanitarian president, 359
inauguration of, 95–96
no condemnation of Germany by, 129
policies of endorsed (1934), 210
rebuke in inaugural address by, 208
recall of US Ambassador to Germany by, 350, 422, 926
recent addresses of [May 1940], 953
and re-opening of Red Sea, 548
and risk of new World War, 340
signing Atlantic Charter, 566, 624
speech of on July 19, 1940, 494
statement of March 9, 1944, 746–47
statement of March 24, 1944, 750
vilification of, 648
Roosevelt, Theodore, 309
Rosenberg, Alfred, 202, 245, 356, 414, 609, 905
humiliation of by Protestants and Catholics, 886
Rosenzweig, Franz, 409
Rosh Hashanah/New Year, 9, 18, 21, 23–24, 28, 36, 42, 44, 52, 55, 68, 71, 73–74, 77–79, 81, 132, 147, 225, 260, 332, 440, 443, 446, 576, 578, 582, 584, 586, 605, 646, 714, 716, 718, 773–75, 827, 867–75, 983–990, 999

arousal of Jewish consciousness and, 199
dark day, 430
greeted by Jews with tears of defeat, 1007
three books of, 719
three shofars of, 145
tractate, 608, 719, 777, 984
Ross, Robert, 15
Roth, Cecil, 997
Rothschild, Mayer Anschel, 874–75
Rotterdam, Holland,
German bombing of, 683, 951
Round Table Conference (1939), 384, 393
breakdown of, 397
Royal Albert Hall, London, xiv–xv, 129, 1010
Ruppin, Arthur, 53–54, 743
Rudin, Jacob P., 33–34, 77, 118, 503–4, 853, 859–60
Russia, 6, 10–11, 71, 92, 299, 497, 506, 630, 715, 786, 821, 919, 996
admiration for as fighting nation, 659
afflicted by "Jewish bolshevism," 302
alliance with France, 254
atrocities against Jews by Czarist, 309
bearing brunt of the ordeal, 716
challenge to mankind by Germany and, 436
conflict with Germany, 580, 636, 663, 683
Czarist, 73, 96, 111, 221, 329, 847, 911
dangers to Jews in new war, 408
embraces anti-Communist Germany, 443
forces of moving westward, 442, 759, 986, 1016
German attack against, 561
German triumphant march through, 810
Germany preparing for war against, 216, 218
invaded portions of, 78, 580, 1010
Jews coming to Germany from, 388
Jews died in Army of, 756
millions of Jews in greater, 583
Nazis control territories of, 652
Nazis heading eastward to, 395
occupation of Poland, 909
Ogpu, 369
Orthodox Church of, 118, 726
pact with Nazi Germany, 446
pogrom-ridden, 220, 955
possible settlement for Jews, 190
preparing its Army, 287
relatives of congregants in, 998
remaining European Jews in, 417, 630
retreat of German soldiers from, 715
is robbing three million Jews of God, 97
seats of Jewish Learning in are gone, 699
Stalinist, 908
socialist ideology of, 704
Soviet, 104, 181–82, 210, 249, 616, 826, 878–79
spirit of at Stalingrad, 823
spiritual sterilization of Jews in, 88

State Socialism of as messianic panacea, 914
suffering of Jews in, 61, 104, 106, 181–83, 404, 417, 622
strangulation of Judaism in, 182, 281, 462
triumph of at "First Front," 704–5
wholesale executions frequent in, 264
See also: Soviet Union
Russian army, 454, 756, 978, 981, 1018
Russian Jewry, 417, 630, 667, 780
lost by the burning of the soul, 750
on fate of, 726
no longer exists, 417, 630
suffering of under Tsars, 963
wave of carnage over Polish and, 61, 622

S

Saar, plebiscite of, 489
Sachsenhausen, concentration camp, 227, 662
St. Bartholomew's Eve, 240
St. Patrick's Cathedral, 652
St. Paul's Cathedral, London, 174, 50–2
Saliège, Jules-Géraud, 662
Salonika, 37
Salzburg, Austria, 883
San Domingo,
offers asylum, 623
San Francisco, 77, 841, 1013
Conference, 805, 809, 813
Saperstein, Harold I., xxv–vii, 34, 235, 778, 867
Witness from the Pulpit, 27, 34, 48, 102, 134, 475, 640, 798, 835, 871, 890, 908, 991
Sarah, 228, 920–22, 924
Sarajevo, 205
Satan,
battle against, 579
creatures of, 762
cruelty invented only by, 545
the Destroyer, 490, 525
Hitler as, 311, 454, 646, 799
the Nazi, 592
still dancing among us, 107
Torah of, 187
winning the wager with God, 406
Satanic,
boast by the ghouls of Berlin, 1008
crime of mass massacre, 130, 669
leadership, rule, 187
lie of Jewish ritual murder, 115
persecution, 679
plan to make Jews like "untouchables," 109
refrain, 515
revolt against the Power above, 647
or Teutonic thoroughness, 979
treatment of Jews as, 458
Satanism, 683, 1008
Savoy, 374
Schiller, Friedrich, 92, 214, 321, 848, 934
Schindler, Pesach, 19
Schocken Verlag, 258
Schoengold, Joseph, 614
Schopenhauer, Arthur, 306
Schorr, Felicia, 768
Schorr, Moses, 768

Schorr, Tamara, 768
Schrecklichkeit [Awfulness], 133, 397, 493
Schulte, Karl Josef, 118
Schuschnigg, Kurt, 310, 869–70
Das Schwarze Korps, 362
Scotland, 58
  Church of, 411
  Jewish citizens of, 411
Scylla and Charybdis, 260–61
Sealed freight cars, 8, 535–36, 652, 696–97, 769, 979, 986
Second Temple, 817
  destruction of, 78, 530, 894
Seidman, Hillel, 7
Semper, Gottfried, 534
Sennacherib, 517
Seraye, Lithuania, 801–3
  no longer exists, 802
Sermon, Sermons
  biblical themes in, 59–73
  by Christians, 59
  date of delivery, 26–28, 52, 56, 58, 183
  delivered before trains would leave, 799
  delivered by refugee to refugees, 417
  delivery an integral part of, 29–30, 33–34, 39–40
  difficulty of preparing (RH, 1939), 421
  as historical source, 17–59
  importance of to congregants, 17–18, 31, 524
  language of delivery and texts, 48–51
  length of, 31
  occasions for delivering, 21–26
  oratorical component of, 30, 32
  overlooked as historical source, 18–19
  preacher's 1943 review of his, 720–21
  publication of, 52–54
  radio broadcasts of, 25, 81
  recorded stenographically, 45–47, 361, 368
  tape-recordings of, 40–41, 45–47
  timeless vs. topical, 26–27
Service of Intercession and Prayer (1938), 74, 324, 326
Shammai, School of, 373, 738, 964–65
Shanghai, 612
Shangri-La, 413
Shapira, David, 144, 286, 552, 638, 657, 737, 754, 785
Shapira, Kalonymus Kalman , xxiv, 49, 62, 69, 79, 455, 518, 599
Shapira, Zvi Elimelekh, 69, 518, 794
Shapiro, Robert, 7, 15, 689
Sharf, Andrew, 15, 458, 700, 1004
Shavu'ot, Shavuoth, Shavuos, Shevuoth, 56, 125, 319, 487, 752
Shearith Yisrael, Atlanta, 919, 927
Sheean, Vincent, 445
Shema Yisroel/Yisrael, 319, 716, 734, 811
Sherrill, Charles H., 235–37
Shield of David, 586, 631
Shilo, 71, 993–59
Sh'mayah, 964
Shneur Zalman of Lyady, 972
Shofar, ram's horn, 198–200, 333, 507, 580, 581, 648, 718–20, 774–75, 867–68, 871, 875
  call to repentance, 717
  heard in underground caves and hidden cellars, 720

three types of, 145
Shub, Boris,
Starvation Over Europe (Made in Germany), 13
Shulman, Charles E., 73
Shushan, 64, 177, 307, 899
Siberia, controlled by Allied Armies, 821
refugees exiled to forced labor in, 750
Sicily, liberation of, 986
Silence, 121, 226, 230, 307, 340, 354, 515, 653, 675, 719, 760, 774, 806, 816, 820
accusation of, xi, xiv
of American Jews, 872
of American press, 140
before God, 230, 906
of British press and government, 16, 312, 669, 700, 1008
of Churchill, 988
conspiracy of, 697,
The Deafening (Medoff), 19
of F.D. Roosevelt, 129
of free nations, 66
of general media, 16
of German churches, 140, 323
of German government, 12
of German Jews, 103, 273
of God, 117, 591
Jewish religious leaders not guilty of, xvii
of non-rabbinic UK Jewish leadership, 1004, 1009–10
"A People's Voice is Silenced," 907–18
of a somnolent humanity, 587
world silent at ruins of a whole people, 790, 987, 1004, 1010
Silver, Abba Hillel, 20, 22, 48, 504, 529, 809, 893–900, 908, 946
authorized for public statement from FDR, 747
changes name to Abba Hillel, 893
on Haman, 64, 895–900
on Maccabees, 68
power of as preacher, 34–35, 893–94
on Rosh Hashanah, 77
Silverman, S. S., 689
"Silver Shirts," 136, 265, 648
Simplicissimus, 841
Sinai, Mount, 868
commanded at: "You shall not murder," 679
every Jew carries spark from, 528
Jews equipped at, 221
Judaic ethic from, 202
opposed to mountain of hate, 322
replaced by concentration camp, 609
revelation at emanating a moral code, 702
voice will sound on, 487
Six-pointed star, yellow, 523, 593
See also: Jewish/Yellow badge, Shield of David
Slawek, Walery, 870
Slovakia, (German Protectorate), 10, 13, 396, 604, 1003
birthplace of Joseph Hertz, 1003
children trapped in, 694
government deporting Jews to Poland, 617–18, 733

persecution of Jews in, 605–6, 981
Vrba and Wetzler reach, 9, 749, 791
Wiessmandel in, 8
See also: Czecho-Slovakia
Smith, Alfred E., 138, 167, 186
Smuts, Jan, 658–59, 675, 727, 816, 1008
Sobibor, 4, 763, 827
Sodom, Gomorrah, 158, 521, 658, 974
Nazi Germany as, 723
Sofer, Moses, 57
Solidarity, 521, 657
of American citizens, 350
claimed by Hitler, 190
not among Jews, 138, 189, 871
Solomon Islands, blood flowing in, 660
Solomon, King, 261
Soloveitchik, Dov Baer, 974
Soloveitchik, Joseph Dov, xi–xii
Sombart, Werner, 360
South Africa, 283, 292, 304, 602, 667, 681, 975,
Joseph Hertz in, 1003
justice- and freedom-loving, 675
Louis Rabinowitz in, 28
"native problem" in, 629
South African Jewish Board of Deputies, 727
South America, 456–57, 668, 952
South Seas, 765
Soviet Army, advancing westward, 1014
Soviet POWS, murder of by starvation, 829
Soviet Russia, 104, 181–82, 210, 249, 616, 826, 878–79
Soviet Union, 497, 616
alliance of with Hitler, 449
enters war against Germany, 575
German invasion of, 14, 78, 561, 630
given eastern Poland, 449
ideology of Stalinist, 917
Jews of, 259–60
temporarily conquered territories of, 597
tolerance of Jews in, 660–61
See also: Russia
Spain, 279, 309, 443, 706, 784, 955
betrayed by Western powers, 530
civil war in, 264
democracy remains in, 294
devastation of, 515
dictator of (Franco), 393
exiles from, 754
expulsion from, 322, 412, 543, 672, 770, 894
Inquisition in, 53, 114, 981
Jewish graves desecrated and plundered in, 73, 506
medieval, 74, 92, 138, 237, 443, 462, 506, 706, 840
refugees from, 990
See also: Inquisition
Sparta, 949
Spira, Chaim Elazar, 37
Springboks, South Africa, 667
Stalin, Josef, 237, 321, 496, 932
armies of, 683
empire of, 451
pact of with Hitler, 449
proclaims Communists sworn

enemies of antisemitism, 661
Stalingrad, 661, 823
Jews blamed for German defeat at, 702
Starhemberg, Ernst, 869–70
Starvation, 123, 125, 265, 320, 366, 444, 46173, 468, 470, 537, 564, 607, 636–37, 652–54, 660, 826, 972
in America, 915
of children, 648, 802
death by in alleys of Berlin, 214
death of Jews through, 356, 359, 576
among German Jews, 361, 863, 868
in midst of plenty, 915
among Polish Jews, 222, 653, 954, 1005
of post-WWI German children, 321
of relatives, 650
and slavery for tens of millions in Europe, 555
of Soviet POWs, 828
in Soviet Ukraine, 914
in Transnistria, 754
in *Unesaneh Tokef* liturgy, 583
as weapon of war, 625
Starvation Over Europe, 13
State Capitalism (Germany), 914
State Socialism (Russia), 914
Statue of Liberty, 362, 652
Stefan, Metropolitan of Sofia, 699
Stein, Leo, 569
Steinberg, Milton, 42–44
Steinthal, Heymann, 182
Stern, Harry Joshua, 28, 57, 79, 193, 197, 520, 562, 845–47
five volumes of sermons by, 846
on S. S. Wise's Address, 132
as Zionist, 845
Stettin, Germany, 175
Stevens, George, 814
St. Louis (steamship), 19, 422–23, 454
St. Louis Post-Dispatch, 29–30, 315
Stockholm, Sweden, 61, 115
Straits of Magellan, 203
Strasser, Otto, 529
"Strategy of Extermination," 13
"Strategy of Faith," 553, 557–58, 967
Streicher, Julius, 65–66, 233, 356, 380
equivalent to Haman, 65, 908, 910
would kill every Jew in Germany, 408
Struma (Refugee ship), 616, 622, 746
Stuka dive-bombers, 687
Stuttgart, Germany, 382, 929
Sudetenland, 66, 228,
German occupation/annexation of, 329, 336, 339
Germans of, 382, 489–90
Suffering, 68, 78, 79, 81–83, 98–99, 104–6, 116, 186, 201, 203, 210, 214–15, 261, 269, 285–86, 291, 315
in ancient Egypt, 313
because of our sins?, 248, 634, 960–61, 963–64
as birth pangs of Messiah, 82
causes devastation of divine service, 528
of children, 211, 224
of German Communists, 98
of Germans after Treaty of Versailles, 100, 150–52, 321
as holy, 651

in Jewish history, 70, 143–44, 268
of Jews in general, 12, 72–73, 128, 138, 193–94, 197, 253, 272–74, 688
of Jews in Germany, 75, 99, 129, 132, 142, 165, 183, 212, 220, 237–38, 254, 274–75, 317
of Jews in Soviet Russia, 104, 106, 181
in Middle Ages, 163
of a Niemöller, 227
no reparation for, 941
in Poland, 251, 294
power of God to relieve, 239, 248
unutterable, 941
Zionism as solution to Jewish, 201
"Suffering Servant," 221, 769, 817
Suicide/s, 237, 263, 314, 320, 348, 356, 438, 447, 475, 514, 865, 899
of Austrian Jews, 310
of German Jews, 135, 141, 204, 213–14, 232, 955
on refugee ships, 423, 428
safeguard against, 131
sinful Jews committing, 706
Sukkoth, Sukkah, 297, 631, 731
contemporary message of, 654, 786–87
See also: Tabernacles, Festival of
Sunderland bombers,
Jewish crewmen on, 660
Suwalki, Lithuania, 801
Swastika/*Hakenkreuz*, 131, 154, 161, 228, 388, 425, 493, 566, 602, 837, 880
cross twisted into, 848, 950
a cursed sign, 820
trampled underfoot, 808
written as "akitsaws," 390
Sweet, Sidney, 93
Sweden, 61, 449, 631, 727, 841
rescue of Danish Jews by, 1009
Swift, Harris, 61
"Swiss Assassination," 246
See also: Assassination
Switzerland, 14, 19, 142, 146, 246, 341, 350–51, 395, 631, 848
Sydney, Australia, 458, 959
Synagogues, 122, 459
in Austria, 327
burning and destruction of, 16, 72, 351–52, 362, 357–58, 365, 375, 386, 407, 422, 428, 444, 455, 502, 509, 519, 522, 564, 566, 569, 572, 662, 696, 809, 817, 829, 939–43, 999
celebration in Polish (1933), 162
denied the right to exist, 501
desecration of in Mannheim, 131
destruction of in many countries, 652–53
filled in Germany (1933), 151
Friday evening services in, 23
German not disturbed (1934), 187
Gestapo assigned to, 18, 24, 302, 307,
Jews reunited in, 116
must not be destroyed, 329
new synagogues being dedicated, 672
newspaper reporters coming to, 18
peak attendance in, 23, 151–52
possible closing of, 117

provinces abstaining from services in, 141
sense of foreboding accompanies into, 419
service of Intercession in (1938), 324
Synagogue Council of America, 662, 859
Syracuse, NY, 1003
Syria/Syrians (Greek), 144, 665

T

Tabernacles, Festival of, 297, 446
See also: Sukkoth, Sukkah
Tanganyika, 360–61, 672
Target
American Catholic Church as, of slanders, 371
Jews as, 126, 154, 328, 335, 706, 841, 847, 954, 997
Jews as first, 202, 573, 762
Tempio Israelitico, Rome, 758, 803
Temple, destruction of, 72, 78, 182, 322, 355, 463, 530, 599, 625, 718, 792–93, 807, 894, 898, 961–65, 967, 972–73, 1015
Temple, William (Archbishop of York and Canterbury), 166, 938
speech by on Day of Mourning and Prayer, 1010
Temple Beth El, Detroit, 945
Temple Beth-El, Great Neck, NY, 859
Temple Emanu-El, Lynbrook, NY, 867
Temple Emanu-El, Montreal, 28, 57, 132, 845
Temple Emanu-El, San Francisco, 1013
Temple Israel, Omaha, 945
Temple Israel, St. Louis, 877
The Temple–Tifereth Israel, Cleveland, 893
Sunday morning services at, 894
Ten Martyrs, 582, 633, 943
Thanksgiving for Victory Service (May 13, 1945), 1024
thanksgiving with stricken hearts, 1028
Théas, Pierre-Marie, 662
Theresienstadt, 53, 759
Third Reich, 11, 32, 188, 287, 358, 386
condemnation of Caesarism in, 355
decision of to impose economic strangulation on Jews, 123, 412, 887
denunciation of by S.S. Wise, 132
ethnic Germans brought into, 412
Jews being destroyed in, 462
Christian revolt against paganism in, 192
status of Jews in, 224
warfare against civilization by, 224–25
Thom, Karl, 176
Thor's hammer, 154
"Thousand Year Reich," 490, 1026
The Times of London, 12, 327, 381, 457, 502, 1020
Tiso, Josef, 617
Tokhecha(h)/Tochechah [rebuke, chastisement], 138, 201
biblical passages of, 754
ours is age of the, 510–11
Tokyo, 264, 986
Tokyo Bay, Japanese surrender, 823

Toledo, 244
Toller, Ernst, 568
Torah scrolls, 657
burning, defiling of, 455, 653, 657, 707, 799, 830, 941, 943, 999
destroyed, 79
"these are our weapons," 1000
Toronto, Canada, 22, 34, 39, 282, 877
Torquemada, Thomas de, 92, 118, 138, 706
Totalitarianism, 68, 261, 290, 292, 345, 402, 905
and brutalitarianism, 603–4
Maccabean resistance to, 459–60
Totalitarian, 39, 215, 315, 626, 1010
countries, 324, 508, 598, 661
power, 505, 916
propaganda, 78, 496
rule established by Antiochus, 369
state/s, 241, 261, 284, 318, 359, 402, 462, 530, 662, 912
war, 509
Tower of Babel, 298
Tragedy, 77, 306, 322, 366, 405, 437, 458, 488, 489, 514–15, 569, 623, 662, 674, 703, 709, 736, 750, 814, 860, 1029
for American Jews, 133
to balance ever-worsening with invincible faith and hope, 1004
of being impotent spectators, 980
chain of through history, 69, 73, 334
more grievous than destruction of the Temple, 807
of Denmark and Norway, 471, 489
of Europe, 594
of European Jewry, 425, 469, 495, 670, 714, 748, 768
fall of Jewish State as great national, 962, 966
of France, 520, 638
of German Jewry, 72–73, 127, 132, 136, 352, 375, 422, 888
of German people, 100
greatest of modern times, 848
of Hungarian Jewry, 81, 767
of (people of) Israel/Jews, 385, 431, 434, 440, 583, 597, 687
Jews as perennial scapegoat of every national, 873
in Palestine, 746, 987–89
of Polish Jews, 467, 668
uniqueness of contemporary, 74, 511, 566, 574, 664, 722, 727, 801, 1008
of Vienna, 318
of war, 643, 912, 915
of the world, 502, 554, 588, 824
Transnistria, 754–55
Transylvania, 49, 79, 299, 388, 690
Treaty/Pact of Locarno, 249, 489
Treaty of Versailles, 87, 100–102, 118, 137, 157, 159–60, 321, 484, 541, 840
German re-armament despite, 213, 216
must never be another, 952
paved road for Hitler, 515
Treblinka/Tremblinka, 4, 53, 686, 749, 763, 768, 816, 827
details of death camp, 707
slaughter of Jews there, 1017

Trinity Church, New York, 652
Trocmé, André, 45
Trotsky, Leon, 910
Troy (ancient), 514
Troy, NY, 867
Trunk, Isaiah, 5, 6, 8
Tsedakah: obligation to give to poor, 971
Tunisia, 374, 683, 986
Turkey, 212
  annexing of Hatay by, 453
  authorities allow ship to proceed to Haifa, 754
  government orders *Struma* to leave harbor, 616
Twersky, Isadore, xii
Tydings, Millard, 186
Tyrer, Chaim ben Solomon, parable of, 589

U

Uebermensch (Superhuman), 334, 493
Ukraine, 448, 576, 1009
  dangers to Jews in new war, 408
  extermination of Jewish communities in, 1017
  mass starvation in, 914
  pogroms in, 182, 404, 963
  rich grain fields of, 342
Uhland, Johann Ludwig, 931
Ulm, Germany, 931
Unetaneh/Unesaneh Tokef, 478, 583, 722, 763, 773–74
Union Jack, 40,000 Jews fighting under, 980
Union of Orthodox Rabbis, 38, 851, 919, 991
United Jewish Charities, 945
United Kingdom, xxii, 249, 507, 591
  See also: Great Britain, England, Scotland
United Nations, 53, 630, 635–36, 647, 667, 675, 677, 684, 684, 700, 708, 761, 772, 813, 980
  assembled evidence of incomprehensible Jewish suffering, 1018
  ignores existence of Jewish nation, 701
  moving toward victory, 986
  must help rescue Jewish survivors, 708
  reportedly planning to freeze Jewish enterprise in Palestine, 705
  victory of, 705, 818, 823
United States, 57, 118, 142, 201, 404
  affidavits for entry to, 320, 370
  alienism must be destroyed in, 217
  anti-Semitism in, 258
  archival material in, 19
  challenge to open "Second Front," 704
  concentration camps in, 679–80
  Einstein in, 143
  fate of France is warning to, 491
  German government proposal to send refugees to, 535–36
  government of denounces barbarities suffered by European Jews, 323, 364
  government of never gave approval to "White Paper," 747
  government's efforts to preserve integrity of, 573
  Jews accused of dragging into war, 424

Jews safer in the, 331
and League of Nations, 563
learned, pious Jews have come to, 672
Leo Baeck's speaking tour in, 50
may enter war with Allies, 947
military budget of, 250
moral strength of, 364
must keep clear of European nations' intrigues, 443
Nazi propaganda in, 382, 841
only haven of liberty and democracy, 557
President of [FDR], 129, 329, 494, 566, 749, 925
program of help to Allies, 954
protest rallies in, 60, 104, 251
rabbinic refugees from Germany to, 42 (Prinz), 416 (Jospe), 465 (Heilbronn), 487 (Nussbaum)
Reform Judaism in, 21, 46
will become center of Jewish life, 576
See also: America
United Synagogue, 51, 937, 961, 975
Universal right to life, 972
University of California, 1013
Unsdorfer, Shlomo Zalman, 36, 49
Unsdorfer, Simha Bunem, 36–37
Uzinsky, Jacob, 640

V

Vago, Bela, 19
Valley of Tophet, 664–65
Van Paassen, Pierre, 401–2, 515
Via Dolorosa, 355, 846–47
Vichy, France, 36, 78, 520, 551, 640, 704
authorities in, 625
government of abandoned Jews, 821
Victims, of revolt against Jewish values, 476
Victory, at the right moment, 1024
VE-Day (Victory in Europe), 1024
Vienna, 78, 310, 459, 937
frightful scenes in, 385
Jewish intelligentsia of, 190
Jewish population of, 309
Jewish problem in, 312
Jews of sent to Poland, 458
mass hooliganism in, 347
Nazi conquest of, 310
plans to expel Jews from, 315, 318
seminary of, 699
sins of Jewish women in, 388
staggering tragedy of, 318
Villard, Oswald, 461
Vilna, Lithuania, 801, 851
cradle of Jewish learning in Lithuania, 786
history of Jews of, 12–13
Jews of sent to Poland, 458
slaughter of Jews in, 12
"Voice of Religion, The," 166
Volga, 1011
Völkischer Beobachter, 32, 262, 489, 883
Vrba, Rudolf, 9, 749, 791

W

Wagner, Richard, 108, 346
Walter, Bruno, 847
"Wandering Jew," 63, 201, 271, 538
War,
breeds Hitlerism, 180

demands dictatorship for efficient waging, 470
devastating dangers of another, 206, 408
drifting toward another, 206
of extermination against Jews, 404, 554, 596, 631, 669–70, 1029
has weakened democracy in England and France, 452
Jewish hatred of, 450
Holy War against tyranny and oppression, 667
never celebrated by Judaism, 666
not righteous but necessary, 403
preacher's support of, 642
See also: World War [1]
Warhaftig, Zerach, 13
War Refugee Board, US, 791
Warsaw, 5, 53, 241, 266, 723
as city without Jews, 786
bombing of, 69, 459, 518
crushed and terrorized Jews of, 426
dire situation for Jews in, 870
gallows in the streets of, 467–68
Heschel escaped from, 451
Jewish "ghettos" in (1938), 366
large number of dying in, 583
railway from, 708
Warsaw Ghetto, xxiv, 4, 7, 49, 455, 540, 639, 697, 969–74
Bund in, 8
compulsory tax urged to feed the starving in, 974
conditions in, 685–86
establishment of: a vast dungeon, 540
gallant resistance of against German troops, 725
Jewish Council (*Judenrat*) in, 970
Jewish Self-Help/Aid in, 970
Kagan's Bakery in, 973
many dying of starvation in, 583, 653, 972–73
play performed in, 614
Polish Christians throw flowers over walls of, 586
sermons delivered in, 3, 49, 62, 69, 79
typhus ridden, 709
wealthy Jews in unmoved by starving Jews, 971–72
Warsaw Ghetto Uprising, 716, 726, 748, 751–52, 766, 769, 773, 987, 1004
decision to fight, 1006
Jewish suicide squads in, 1007
one thousand German soldiers killed in, 1007
recalls Maccabees and Masada, 1007
Warszawski, Eduard, 1006
Washington, DC, 37, 404, 535, 697, 879, 953
pronouncement of sympathy for victims, 1009
Washington, George, 208, 396, 536
Wasserman, Jakob, 204, 212
Wasserstein, Bernard, 17, 19, 668, 976
Wavell, Archibald, 810
Weczler/Wetzler, Alfred, 9, 749, 791
Weimar Republic, 117, 366, 414, 841
Weinberg, Jehiel Jacob, 959
Weiner, Herbert, 48, 893
Weinryb, Bernard Dov, 13
Weiskopf, F.C., 1018

Weissmandel, Michael Dov, 8
Weizmann, Chaim, 384, 393
Wells, H.G., 216, 722
Wells, Leon W., 4
Weltsch, Robert, 257, 632
Werfel, Franz, 333
Westley, George Hembert, 875
Westminster, pronouncement of sympathy for victims, 1009
Wheeling, WV, 34, 893
White House, picketing of, 37
"White Paper" (1939), 11, 403, 410–11, 415, 436, 457, 468, 684, 700, 942, 988
 black decree known as the, 799
 deadline of approaches, 746–47
 still not annulled, 757
 US Government never approved, 746–47
Wiesel, Elie, xi–xii, 4
Wilde, Gerhart, 175
Wilhelm I, Kaiser, 182
Wilhelm II, Kaiser, 779
Wilson, Woodrow, 512, 784, 839, 911–12, 917
Wise, James W., 139, 140
Wise, Jonah B., 129
Wise, Stephen S., xiii, xxi, 93, 129, 140, 247, 535, 635, 835, 845, 859–60, 867, 912, 948, 1013
 approach of, 109
 attacks Reichsbishop's assertion, 207
 audio-recordings of sermons/speeches by, 41
 authorized for public statement from FDR, 747
 and boycott of German goods, 134, 873
 and boycott of German Olympics, 235
 call to from German Embassy regarding rally, 101
 on Christian leaders speaking out for Jews, 708
 on Hitler and the "Jewish Problem," 449
 impact of speeches by, 33–34, 167, 867
 and Jews of Germany, 233, 295
 meets Max Nussbaum, 487
 on *Mein Kampf*, 376
 Montreal speech, 132
 as pacifist, 180, 312, 450
 on Palestine (St. James) Conference, 394
 praise of Jan Smuts by, 724
 radio addresses of, 533
 on re-establishment of the ghetto, 639
 and Riegner Cable, 14–15
 sermons of from 1933–1945, 19–20, 22, 47, 132, 784
on sinking of the *Struma*, 616
 unpublished sermons of, 92
 as Zionist rabbi, 233
Wishengrad, Morton, 830
Wolff, Theodor, "Berliner Tageblatt," 847–48
Wolsey, Louis, 34
"Working Group," Slovakia, 618
World Jewish Conference, 871
World Jewish Congress, 13–14, 198, 259–60, 872, 874
World tragedy, 502, 824
World War I/Great War, 76, 182, 206, 299, 309, 336, 562, 603
 thirty-five million deaths a result of, 745

Allies won the war but lost the peace, 623
cruel indifference of victors made Hitler possible, 320
"ended" September 29, 1938, 336
exchange of populations (Greece and Turkey) after, 453
Hertz sermons responding to, 1003
as Golgotha for Jewish people, 377
impact of, 911–12
Jews responsible for, 150, 214
Maybaum in Austrian army during, 937
memory of bitterly emblazoned, 162, 206, 427
no victor during, 216
sermon from, 565–66
vital mistakes that followed, 484
world went mad with hate, 206
World War II, 180, 447, 559, 830, 878, 901, 1024
carnage and destruction unparalleled in, 822
as "second world war," 464, 808, 824, 940
Jews who perished in, 53–54, 743
visible and spiritual weapons for, 559
as war of good against evil, 940
will destroy European civilization, 287, 437, 671, 951
World Zionist Congress, 233
Worship, of God or Nazism, 906
Wotan, 193, 262, 905
Wrangel , Petr/Pyotr, 404
Wright, Orville and Wilbur, 553
Wuerzburger, Walter, 686, 730
Wyman, David, xv, 19, 635, 683, 698

Y

Yahil, Leni, 2, 618, 714
Year of Mourning, 775
The Yellow Spot, 11, 218, 234
Yelsk, Belarus, 640
Yeshiva University, Archives, 991
Yeshivas, 369, 471, 738
all destroyed, 498, 699
of Lithuania, Poland closed, 999
of Slabodka, Telz, Mir destroyed, 999
Yishuv, Yishub, 19, 50, 199, 260, 436, 481, 649, 754, 757
Yizkor (Remembrance of the Dead), 36, 204, 232, 447, 518, 589, 638, 652, 783,
See also: Hazkarat Neshamot
Yohanan, 304, 749
Yorkville, Manhattan, NY, 836
Yoshe Ber of Brisk, 974
Young, Owen D., 840
Yugoslavia/Yugo-Slavia, 350, 376, 576, 625,
nearly all Jews wiped out, 1008
See also: Jugo-Slavia
Yugoslavs/vians, 547, 705

Z

Zangwill, Israel, 322, 540
Zevi, Shabbatai, 100
Zionism,
and German Jewish youth, 122
German persecution and Zionist program, 165
as indispensable ideal, 378
Jews arguing about, 784

Jews connecting with, 650
as only great achievement of modern Jewry, 597
organization and philosophy of, 756
shows Jewish wandering as civilizing, 416
Smuts a friend of, 658
unethical for any Jew to oppose, 623
whole movement a reaction to persecution, 122
and Zionistic program, 165
Zionist Organization of America, 726, 789
Zionist/s
all [Jews] must be, 152
and/or anti-Zionists, 766, 769
and Bundists, 766
Zitik, Poland, 266
Zolli, Israel, 758, 803
Zukerman, William, 13, 725–26
Zylberberg, Michael , 7